Italy

From the Italy Experts

Touring Club of Italy

Touring Club of Italy
President and Chairman: *Roberto Ruozi*
Chief Executive Officer: *Guido Venturini*

Touring Editore
Chief Executive Officer: *Guido Venturini*
Managing Director: *Alfieri Lorenzon*

Editorial Director: *Michele D'Innella*
Series Editor and Editorial Co-ordinator: *Anna Ferrari-Bravo*

Translation: *Antony Shugaar*
Editing and layout: *Voltapagina Associati*
Copy Editor: *Richard Pierce*
Jacket layout: *Federica Neeff*, with *Mara Rold*
Map design: *Cartographic Division - Touring Club of Italy*
Drawings: *Antonello* and *Chiara Vincenti*
Production: *Vittorio Sironi*

Picture credits:
Cover: *Michelangelo's David* by Bullaty Lomeo/Image Bank
Foreword: *photos* by Tony Nicolini/Archivio T.C.I.; Grant Faint/Image Bank

Colour separation: *Centro Grafico Linate, San Donato Milanese*
Printed by: *New Litho, Milano*

Touring Club of Italy
Corso Italia 10
20122 Milano
www.touringclub.it

© 2002 Touring Editore s.r.l., Milano
Code L2AAA
ISBN 88365 27469
Printed in October 2002

Florence: Duomo

ITALY is a guide to the treasures of Italy, its monuments and scenery, its natural and artistic heritage. This book provides a thorough description of places and sights, and offers everything you need to travel well in Italy: 80 excursions, with related maps, through the loveliest and best-known areas; 110 entries in alphabetical order of cities, villages, resorts and archeological sites, with a large number of maps, plans and illustrations; a wealth of practical suggestions, in the opening section, to gain a better understanding of local customs and lifestyle; and, in the final section, a listing of hotels and restaurants. Each entry begins with a brief introduction, followed in most cases by a historical note. Then one or more itineraries are suggested, with detailed descriptions of sights, monuments and places of interest. Useful addresses are listed in the final section. TCI's criteria in ranking and classifying monuments and artworks have been recognized by the Italian government, and TCI is the only institution to compile a complete catalog of Italian treasures. It is our hope that foreign tourists visiting the many sights and attractions described here will grasp the complex intertwining of past and present, the history, art and lifestyle that are so much a part of the Italian experience.

Reggio di Calabria: Bronze of Riace

CONTENTS

INDEX OF MAPS AND PLANS

CITY MAPS

PLANS OF MUSEUMS AND ARCHEOLOGICAL SITES

We have attempted to use the original Italian names of all places, monuments, buildings, and other references where possible. The traveller is thus made to feel more at home with the names he or she is likely to encounter in Italy on signs and printed matter. Note also that maps in this book for the most part carry the Italian version of all names. Thus, we refer to Siracusa and S. Pietro, rather than to Syracuse and the cathedral of St. Peter's. On first mention, we have tried to indicate both the Italian and its English equivalent; this is done again when the name is first mentioned in a specific section. With regard to Italian names, one of the most common abbreviations is "S." for saint. Note that in Italian the "S." may be "San", "Sant'", "Santo", or "Santa"; "Ss." means saints. Other terms are: "cattedrale" or "duomo" for cathedral, "museo" for museum, "biblioteca" for library, "cappella" for chapel, "chiostro" for cloister, "oratorio" for oratory, "torre" for tower, "giardino" for garden, "pinacoteca" for art gallery, "ponte" for bridge, "porta" for city gate, "sala" or "salone" for hall or room, "monte" for mount...

ITALY: INSTRUCTIONS FOR USE

This section contains all the information needed to organize a tour through Italy, in order to see all the most interesting sights and to avoid snags: from tips on how to use public transportation and drive to the type of hotels, how to use telephones and cell phones and how to cope with daily problems; from suggestions for shopping to others concerning local cuisine; and from a description of the peculiar character of the Italians to useful addresses of embassies, consulates and tourist offices.

EXCURSIONS

The 80 excursions proposed in this section extend from the Alps to the islands. Carefully selected and laid out by experts, each one covers an area in Italy which is noteworthy either for its artistic heritage or for its natural scenery.
Each itinerary is presented in the following manner: there is an introduction that fully illustrates its features, followed by a detailed description of the route with indications of the streets to take, and then a thorough presentation of the sites, localities and natural highlights you should visit and see.

ITALY A TO Z

The section of individual geographic entries is arranged in alphabetical order, and comprises towns and villages (such as Mantua or Lucera), landmarks and monuments (such as the Charterhouse of Pavia and the Abbey of Fossanova), and archeological sites (such as the Excavations of Pompeii). There is also a succinct description of each place, and most are given a short historical profile as well. Differences in typography (names shown in **bold** or *italics*), and one or two asterisks (*

(**) indicate the importance of each monument, museum, site or attraction. The texts are accompanied by drawings to help the reader to visualize works of art and architecture that should not be missed. Opening hours are indicated in italics immediately after the name of the monument or museum they refer to. Such information is updated to the publication date of this guidebook; however, changes many occur at any moment after this date. The main city entries include maps indicating the attractions to visit.

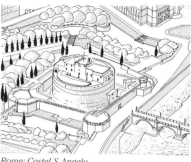

Rome: Castel S. Angelo

HOTELS, RESTAURANTS, AND TOURIST SERVICES

This section is a compendium of useful addresses, hotels and restaurants which suggests – town by town, site by site – a selection of the finest tourist facilities, including the tourist offices, railway stations, ship passenger terminals, airports and the nearest accessways. Hotels and restaurants are classified in conformity with the Italian laws on tourism. Related symbols and criteria are described on page 446.

MAPS AND PLANS

The maps of tours illustrate the 80 introductory itineraries, which are numbered progressively. Three key maps of Northern, Central and Southern Italy open this section, in which each route is indicated by a numbered inset. The city plans indicate monuments, railway stations and other useful places. In the text proper with a description of the city, each place of interest shown on the map is followed by a map coordinate consisting of a letter and number, e.g. Palazzo Vecchio (*D-E4-5*). In those cities with more than one such map (Rome and Venice), the coordinates are preceded by the Roman numeral indicating the specific map, e.g. Piazza San Pietro (I, *D-E2*). A key to signs and symbols is on page 8. The guide also has three plans of the sites of Herculaneum, Pompeii and the Vatican Museums.

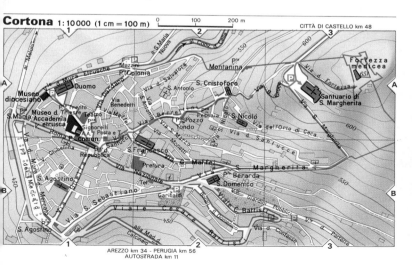

CONVENTIONAL SYMBOLS USED IN THE MAPS

CITY PLANS

Lines of communications

≡≡≡	Highways
━━━	Highways and throughfares
═╤═	Main roads
═╤═	Other roads
═▥═	Pedestrian ramps
═ ═ ═	Secondary roads
─·─·─·	Trails
═ ═ ═ ═	Roads under construction
▬■▬	Railroad lines and stations
PORTO DI MARE Ⓜ	Subway lines stations
─×─×─×─	Cableways
─•─•─•	Chairlifts
─+─+─+─	Cable cars

Monuments and buildings

▰	of exceptional interest
▬	quite interesting
▬	interesting

Other indications

▨	Public offices
⊞	Churches
✚	Hospitals
i	Tourist information offices
P	Principal parking areas
▨	Gardens and parks
◯₅₀	Contour map showing elevation and grade
▨	Arcades

EXCURSIONS PLANS

Lines of communications

═▷═	Excursion, with direction followed
═▷	Detour from the route
═(A1)═	Highway, with route number
═══	Main roads
═══	Other roads
─+++++++++─	Cableways and chairlifts
─ ─ ─ ─ ─	Shipping lines

Towns and cities

○	Places to see along the excursion
◪	Urban area
○	Other places

Symbols

♦	Churches
♜	Castles
🏛	Villas, monumental palaces
▮	Monuments
∷ ⸪	Ruins
❋	Prehistoric remains (Nuraghi, etc.)
◔	Caves
✳	Waterfalls, natural curiosities
◭	Mountain huts
≍	Mountain passes
·	Mountain peaks
347	Elevations
✈	Airports
⊕	Geographic directions
─·─·─·─·	Borders of countries

8

taly is known throughout the world for the quantity and quality of its art treasures and for its natural beauty, but it is also famous for its inimitable lifestyle and fabulous cuisine and wines. Although it is a relatively small country, Italy boasts an extremely varied culture and multifarious traditions and customs. The information and suggestions in this brief section will help foreign tourists not only to understand certain aspects of Italian life, but also to solve the everyday difficulties and the problems of a practical nature that inevitably crop up during any trip.

This practical information is included in brief descriptions of various topics: public transport and how to purchase tickets; suggestions on how to drive in this country; the different types of rooms and accomodations in hotels; hints on how to use mobile phones and communication in general. This is followed by useful advice on how to meet your everyday needs and on shopping, as well as information concerning the cultural differences in the various regions. Lastly, there is a section describing the vast range of restaurants, bars, wine bars and pizza parlors.

TRANSPORTATION

From the airport to the city
Public transportation in major cities is easily accessible and simple to use. Both Malpensa Airport in Milan and Leonardo da Vinci Airport in Rome have trains and buses linking them to the city centers. At Malpensa, you can take a bus to the main train station or a train to the Cadorna train station and subway stop.

Subways, buses, and trams
Access to the subways, buses, and trams requires a ticket (tickets are not sold on board but can be purchased at most newsstands and tobacco shops). The ticket is good for one ride and sometimes has a time limit (in the case of buses and trams). When you board a bus or tram, you are required to stamp your previously-acquired ticket in the time-stamping machine. Occasionally, a conductor will board the bus or tram and check everyone's ticket. If you haven't got one, or if it has not been time-stamped, you will have to pay a steep fine.

Trains
The Ferrovia dello Stato (Italian Railways) is among the best and most modern railway systems in Europe. Timetables and routes can be consulted and reservations can be made online at www.fs-on-line.com. Many travel agents can also dispense tickets and help you plan your journey. Hard-copy schedules can be purchased at all newsstands and most bookstores.
Automated ticket machines, which include easy-to-use instructions in English, are available in nearly all stations. They can be used to check schedules, makes reservations, and purchase tickets.
Many of the express trains need to be reserved in advance. When you reserve a ticket on a Eurostar express train, for example, or the Pendolino, Italy's high-speed train, you will be assigned a seat number. Note that reservations must be made at least one day in advance and that you will not be allowed to board a train where a reservation is required if you haven't got one.
Local trains (classified as "Espresso", "Diretto" or "Locale") require a simple ticket, but express Eurocity and Intercity trains require a supplementary ticket ("supplemento"). Almost all of them carry both first- and second-class cars. Only a few ("Locale") usually are second-class only.
All tickets must be time-stamped before boarding: there are numerous time-stamping machines in every station (failure to do so will result in a moderate fine).
On those trains that do not require a reservation, tickets can also be purchased on board from the conductor (a surcharge is included).

Taxis

Taxis are a convenient but expensive way to travel in Italian cities. There are taxi stands scattered throughout major cities.

You cannot hail taxis on the street in Italy, but you can reserve taxis, in advance or immediately, by phone: consult the yellow pages for the number or ask your hotel reception desk or maitre d'hotel to call for you.

Taxi drivers have the right to charge you a supplementary fee for every piece of luggage they transport, as well as evening surcharges.

DRIVING

Especially when staying in the countryside, driving is a safe and convenient way to travel through Italy and its major cities. And while it is best avoided for obvious reasons, driving in the cities is not as difficult as it may seem or may have been reported to be. It is important to be aware of street signs and speed limits, and many cities have zones where only limited traffic is allowed in order to accommodate pedestrians.

The town streets are patrolled by the Polizia Municipale (municipal police). The roads outside cities are patrolled by the Carabinieri (the Italian State Police): they may set up road blocks where they may ask you to stop by holding out a small red sign. Steep fines are given for not wearing your seatbelt (which is obligatory), for overcrowding a car (most vehicles are allowed to accommodate 4-5 persons maximum), or for using a cellular phone (which is prohibited). Although an international driver's license is not required in Italy, it is advisable. ACI and similar associations provide this service to members.

The fuel distribution network is reasonably distributed all over the territory. All service stations have unleaded gasoline ("benzina verde") and diesel fuel ("gasolio"). Opening time is 7-12:30 and 3-7:30; on motorways the service is 24 hours a day.

HOTELS

In Italy it is common practice for the reception desk to register your passport, and only registered guests are allowed to use the rooms. This is mere routine, done for security reasons, and there is no need for concern.

Room rates are based on whether they are for single ("camera singola") or double ("camera doppia") occupancy. In every room you will find a list of the hotel rates (generally on the back of the door). While 4- and 5-star hotels have double beds, most hotels have only single beds. Should you want a double bed, you have to ask for a "letto matrimoniale". All hotels have rooms with bathrooms; only 1-star establishments usually have only shared bathrooms.

Most hotel rates include breakfast ("prima colazione"), but you can request to do without it, thus reducing the rate. Breakfast is generally served in a communal room and comprises a buffet with pastries, bread with butter and jam, cold cereals, fruit, yoghurt coffee, and fruit juice. Some hotels regularly frequented by foreign tourists will also serve other items such as eggs for their American and British guests.

The hotels for families and in tourist localities also offer "mezza pensione", or half board, in which breakfast and dinner are included in the price.

AGRITURISMO

Located only in the countryside, and generally on a farm, "agriturismo" – a network of farm holiday establishments – is part of a growing trend in Italy to honor local gastronomic and wine traditions, as well as countryside traditions. These farms offer meals prepared with ingredients cultivated exclusively on site: garden-grown vegetables homemade cheese and local recipes. Many of these places also provide lodging, one of the best ways to experience the "genuine" Italian lifestyle.

Cellular phones and pre-paid phone cards

Nearly everyone in Italy owns a cellular phone. Although public phones are still available, they seem to be ever fewer and farther between. If you wish to use public phones, you will find them in subway stops, bars, along the street, and phone centers generally located in the city center. Pre-paid phone cards can be purchased at most newsstands and tobacco shops, and can also be acquired at automated tellers.

For European travelers, activating personal cellular coverage is relatively simple, as it is in most cases for American and Australian travelers as well. Contact your mobile service provider for details.

Cellular phones can also be rented in Italy from TIM, the Italian national phone company. For information, visit its website at www.tim.it. When traveling by car through the countryside, a cellular phone can really come in handy.

Note that when dialing in Italy, you must always dial the prefix (e.g., 02 for Milan, 06 for Rome) even when making a local call. For cellular phones, however, the initial zero is always dropped.

Internet access

Cyber cafés have sprung up all over Italy and today you can find one on nearly every city block. The Italian national phone company, TIM, has also begun providing internet access at many of its public phone centers.

The bar

The Italian "bar" is a multi-faceted, all-purpose establishment for drinking, eating and socializing, where you can order an espresso, have breakfast, and enjoy a quick sandwich or lunch or even a hot meal. You can often buy various items here (sometimes even stamps, cigarettes, phone cards, etc.). Bear in mind that table service ("servizio a tavola") includes a surcharge. At most bars, if you choose to sit, a waiter will take your order. Every bar should have a list of prices posted behind or near the counter; if the bar offers table service, the price list should also include the extra fee for this.

Lunch at bars will include, but is not limited to, "panini," sandwiches with crusty bread, usually with cured meats such as "prosciutto" (salt-cured ham), "prosciutto cotto" (cooked ham), and cheeses such as mozzarella topped with tomato and basil. Then there are "tramezzini" (finger sandwiches) with tuna, cheese, or vegetables, etc. Often the "panini" and other savory sandwiches (like stuffed flatbread or "focaccia") are heated before being served. Naturally, the menu at bars varies according to the region: in Bologna you will find "piadine" (flatbread similar to pita) with Swiss chard; in Palermo there are "arancini" (fried rice balls stuffed with ground meat); in Genoa you will find that even the most unassuming bar serves some of the best "focaccia" in all Italy. Some bars also include a "tavola calda". If you see this sign in a bar window, it means that hot dishes like pasta and even entrées are served.

A brief comment on coffee and cappuccino: Italians never serve coffee with savory dishes or sandwiches, and they seldom drink cappuccino outside of breakfast (although they are happy to serve it at any time).

While English- and Irish-type pubs are frequented by beer lovers and young people in Italy, there are also American bars where long drinks and American cocktails are served.

Breakfast at the bar

Breakfast in Italy generally consists of some type of pastry, most commonly a "brioche" – a croissant either filled with cream or jam, or plain – and a cappuccino or espresso. Although most bars do not offer American coffee, you can ask for a "caffè lungo" or "caffè americano", both of which resemble the American coffee preferred by the British and Americans. Most bars have a juicer to make a "spremuta", freshly squeezed orange or grapefruit juice.

Lunch and Dinner

As with all daily rituals in Italy, food is prepared and meals are served according to local customs (e.g., in the North they prefer rice and butter, in South and Central Italy they favor pasta and olive oil).

Wine is generally served at mealtime, and while finer restaurants have excellent wine lists (some including vintage wines), ordering the house table wine generally brings good results (a house Chianti to accompany your Florentine steak in Tuscany, a sparkling Prosecco paired with your creamed stockfish and polenta in Venice, a dry white wine with pasta dressed with sardines and wild fennel fronds in Sicily).

Mineral water is also commonly served at meals and can be "gassata" (sparkling) or "naturale" (still).

The most sublime culinary experience in Italy is achieved by matching the local foods with the appropriate local wines: wisdom dictates that a friendly waiter will be flattered by your request for his recommendation on what to eat and drink.

Whether at an "osteria" (a tavern), a "trattoria" (a home-style restaurant), or a "ristorante" (a proper restaurant), the service of lunch and dinner generally consists of - but is not limited to - the following: "antipasti" or appetizers; "primo piatto" or first course, i.e., pasta, rice, or soup; "secondo piatto" or main course, i.e., meat or seafood, "contorno" or side-dish, served with the main course, i.e., vegetables or salad; "formaggi", "frutta", and "dolci", i.e., cheeses, fruit, and dessert; caffè or espresso coffee, perhaps spiked with a shot of grappa.

The pizzeria

The pizzeria is in general one of the most economical, democratic, and satisfying culinary experiences in Italy. Everyone eats at the pizzeria: young people, families, couples, locals and tourists alike. Generally, each person orders her/his own pizza, and while the styles of crust and toppings will vary from region to region (some of the best pizzas are served in Naples and Rome), the acid test of any pizzeria is the Margherita topped simply with cheese and tomato sauce.

Beer, sparkling or still water, and Coca Cola are the beverages commonly served with pizza. Some restaurants include a pizza menu, but most establishments do not serve pizza at lunchtime.

The wine bar (enoteca)

More than one English-speaking tourist in Italy has wondered why the wine bar is called an enoteca in other countries and the English term is used in Italy: the answer lies somewhere in the mutual fondness that Italians and English speakers have for one another. Wine bars have become popular in recent years in the major cities (especially in Rome, where you can find some of the best). The wine bar is a great place to sample different local wines and eat a light, tapas-style dinner.

CULTURAL DIVERSITY

Whenever you travel, not only are you a guest of your host country, but you are also a representative of your home country. As a general rule, courtesy, consideration, and respect are always appreciated by guests and their hosts alike.

Italians are famous for their hospitality and experience will verify this felicitous stereotype: perhaps nowhere else in Europe are tourists and visitors received more warmly. Italy is a relatively "new" country. Its borders, as we know them today, were established only in 1861 when it became a monarchy under the House of Savoy. After WWII, Italy became a Republic and now it is one of the member states of the European Union.

One of the most fascinating aspects of Italian culture is that, even as a unified country, local tradition still prevails over a universally Italian national identity. Some jokingly say that the only time that Venetians, Milanese, Florentines, Neapolitans, and Sicilians feel like Italians is when the national football team plays in international competitions. From their highly localized dialects to the foods they eat, from their religious celebration to their politics, Italians proudly maintain their local heritage.

This is one of the reasons why the Piedmontese continue to prefer their beloved Baro o wine and their white truffles, the Umbrians their rich Sagrantino wine and black truffles, the Milanese their risotto and panettone, the Venetians their stockfish and polenta, the Bolognese their lasagne and pumpkin ravioli, the Florentines their bread soups and steaks cooked rare, the Abruzzese their excellent fish broth and seafood, the Neapolitans their mozzarella, basil, pizza, and pasta. As a result of its rich cultural diversity, the country's population also varies greatly in its customs from region to region, city to city, town to town. As you visit different cities and regions throughout Italy, you will see how the local personality and character of the Italians change as rapidly as the landscape does. Having lived for millennia with their great diversity and rich, highly heterogeneous culture, the Italians have taught us many things, foremost among them the age-old expression, "When in Rome, do as the Romans do."

state tobacco shops and pharmacies

Tobacco is available in Italy only at state licensed tobacco shops. These vendors ("tabaccheria), often incorporated in a bar, also sell stamps.
Medicines can be purchased only in pharmacies ("farmacia") in Italy. Pharmacists are very knowledgeable about common ailments and can generally prescribe a treatment for you on the spot. Opening time is 8:30-12:30 and 3:30-7:30 p.m. but in any case there is always a pharmacy open 24 hours and during holidays.

shopping

Every locality in Italy offers tourists characteristic shops, markets with good bargains, and even boutiques featuring leading Italian fashion designers. Opening hours vary from region to region and from season to season. In general, shops are open from 9 to 1 and from 3/4 to 7/8 p.m., but in large cities they usually have no lunchtime break.

banks and post offices

Italian banks are open from Monday to Friday, from 8:30 to 1:30 and then from 3 to 4. However, the afternoon business hours may vary.
Post offices are open from Monday to Saturday, from 8:30 to 1:30 (12:30 on Saturday). In the larger towns there are also some offices open in the afternoon.

currency

Effective 1 January 2002, the currency used in all European Union countries is the euro. Coins are in denominations of 1, 2 and 5 cents and 1 and 2 euros; banknotes are in denominations of 5, 10, 20, 50, 100 and 200 euros, each with a different color.

time

All Italy is in the same time zone, which is six hours ahead of Eastern Standard Time in the USA. Daylight saving time is used from March to September, when watches and clocks are set an hour ahead of standard time.

passports and vaccinations

Citizens of EU countries can enter Italy without frontier checks. Citizens of Australia, Canada, New Zealand, and the United States can enter Italy with a valid passport and need not have a visa for a stay of less than 90 days. No vaccinations are necessary.

payment and tipping

When you sit down at a restaurant you are generally charged a "coperto" or cover charge ranging from 1.5 to 3 euros, for service and the bread. Tipping is not customary in Italy. Beware of unscrupulous restaurateurs who add a space on their clients' credit card receipt for a tip, while it has already been included in the cover charge.

Foreign Embassies in Italy

Australia:
Corso Trieste 25, Rome, tel. 06852721

Canada:
Via G.B. de Rossi 27, Rome, tel. 06445981

New Zealand:
Via Zara 28, Rome, tel. 064402928

United States of America:
Via Vittorio Veneto 119/A, Palazzo Margherita, Rome, tel. 0646741

Great Britain:
Via XX Settembre 80/A, Rome, tel. 0642200001

Ireland:
Piazza Campitelli 3, Rome, tel. 066979121

Foreign Consulates in Italy

Australia:
Via Borgogna 2, Milan, tel. 0277704217

Canada:
Via Vittor Pisani 19, Milan, tel. 0267583420/22

New Zealand:
Via Francesco Sforza 48, Milan, tel. 0258314443

United States of America:
Lungarno A.Vespucci 38, Florence, tel. 0552398276
Via Principe Amedeo 2/10, Milan, tel. 02290351
Piazza Repubblica, Naples, tel. 0815838111
Via Vaccarini 1, Palermo tel. 091305857

Great Britain:
Lungarno Corsini 2, Florence, tel. 055284133
Via S. Paolo 7, Milan, tel. 02723001
Via dei Mille 40, Naples, tel. 0814238911

Ireland:
Piazza San Pietro in Gessate 2, Milan, tel. 0255187641

Italian Embassies and Consulates Around the World

Australia:
12 Grey Street - Deakin, Canberra, tel. (06) 273-4223
Consulates at: Adelaide, Brisbane, Melbourne, Perth, Sydney

Canada:
275 Slater Street, 21st floor, Ottawa (Ontario), tel. (613) 2322401
Consulates at: Edmonton, Montreal, Toronto, Vancouver

New Zealand:
34-38 Grant Road, Wellington, tel. (4) 4735339
Consulates at: Auckland, Christchurch, Dunedin

United States of America:
3000 Whitehaven Street, NW, Washington DC, tel. (202) 612-4400
Consulates at: Boston, Chicago, Detroit, Houston, Los Angeles, Miami, New York, Newark, Philadelphia, San Francisco

Great Britain:
14, Three Kings' Yard, London, tel. (020) 73122200
Consulates at: London, Bedford, Edinburgh, Manchester

Ireland:
63, Northumberland Road, Dublin, tel. (01) 6601744

ENIT (Italian Tourist Board)

Canada:
Office National Italien du Tourisme/Italian Government Tourist Board, Toronto, Ontario M4W 3R8, 175 Bloor Street, Suite 907 - South Tower, tel. 001416-9254882, fax 001416-9254799

United States of America:
Italian Government Tourist Board, New York, N.Y. 10111, 630 Fifth Avenue, Suite 1565, tel. (212) 2454822-2455618, fax (212) 5869249
Italian Government Tourist Board, Chicago 1, Illinois 60611, North Michigan Avenue, Suite 2240, tel. (312) 644-0996, fax (312) 644-3019
Italian Government Tourist Board, Los Angeles, CA 90025, 12400, Wilshire Blvd., Suite 550, tel. (310) 820-9807, fax (310) 820-6357

Great Britain:
Italian State Tourist Board, London W1P 2AY, 1 Princes Street, tel. (020) 73993562

Emergency numbers

112 Carabinieri
113 Police
115 Fire Department
116 Road Assistance
118 Medical Emergencies

Excursions

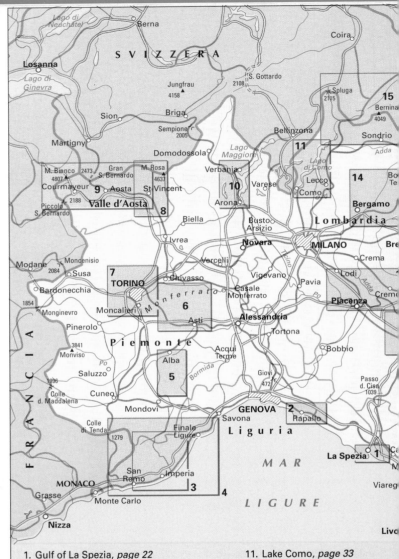

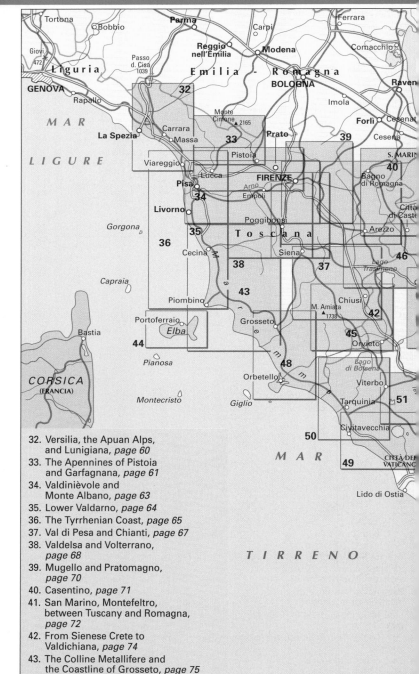

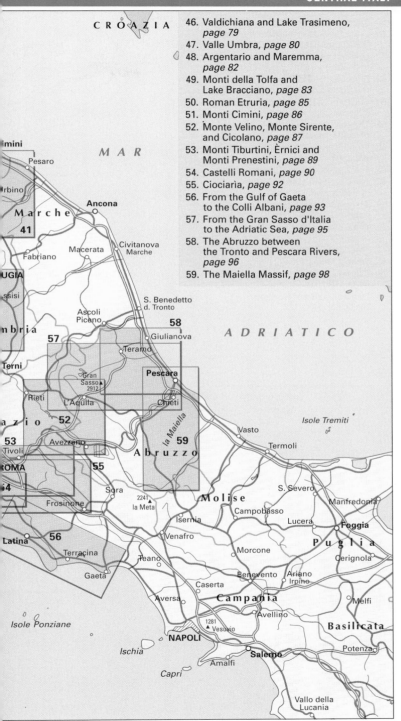

CROAZIA

Pesaro

MAR

rbino

Ancona

Marche

41

Fabriano   Macerata   Civitanova Marche

UGIA

ssisi

S. Benedetto d. Tronto

mbria

Ascoli Piceno

58

Giulianova

ADRIATICO

57

Teramo

Terni

Gran Sasso▲ 2912

Pescara

Rieti   L'Aquila

Chieti

azio   52

Isole Tremiti

53

Avezzano

la Maiella   59

Vasto

Tivoli

ROMA

55

Abruzzo

Termoli

54

Sora

S. Severo

Frosinone

2241 ▲ la Meta

Molise

Manfredonia

Isernia   Campobasso   Lucera   Foggia

Latina   56

Venafro

Puglia

Terracina

Teano

Morcone

Cerignola

Gaeta

Benevento   Ariano Irpino

Caserta

Isole Ponziane

Aversa

Campania

Melfi

Avellino

Basilicata

1281 ▲ Vesuvio

NAPOLI

Ischia

Salerno

Potenza

Amalfi

Capri

Vallo della Lucania

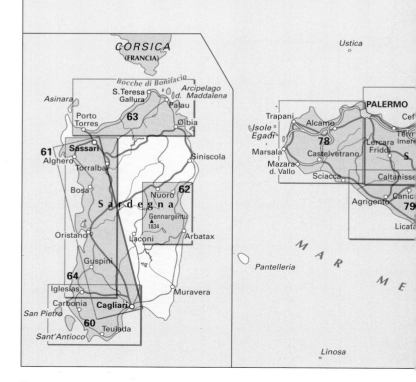

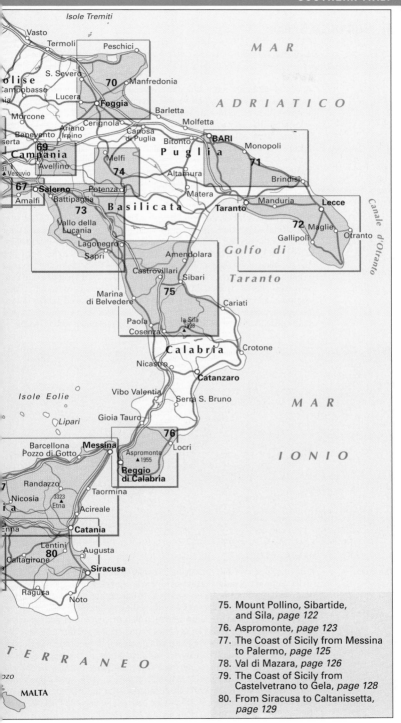

Isole Tremiti
Vasto
Termoli
Peschici
S. Severo
70 Manfredonia
lise
Campobasso
Lucera
Morcone
Foggia
Barletta
MAR
ADRIATICO
Cerignola
Molfetta
Benevento
Ariano
Irpino
Carosa
di Puglia
Bitonto
BARI
Monopoli
serta
69
Campania
Avellino
Melfi
Puglia
71
Vesuvio
74
Altamura
Brindisi
67 Salerno
Potenza
Matera
Amalfi
Battipaglia
73
Basilicata
Taranto
Manduria
Lecce
Vallo della
Lucania
Sersa
72 Maglie
Lagonegro
Gallipoli
Otranto
Sapri
Amendolara
Golfo di
Castrovillari
Marina
di Belvedere
Sibari
75
Taranto
Cariati
Paola
Cosenza
la Sila
1928
Calabria
Crotone
Nicastro
Catanzaro
Isole Eolie
Vibo Valentia
Seria S. Bruno
MAR
Lipari
Gioia Tauro
76
IONIO
Barcellona
Pozzo di Gotto
Messina
Locri
Aspromonte
1955
Randazzo
Reggio
di Calabria
Nicosia
3323
Etna
Taormina
a
Acireale
Catania
nna
Lentini
80
Augusta
Caltagirone
Siracusa
Ragusa
Noto
TERRANEO
MALTA

1 | Gulf of La Spezia

La Spezia - Portovènere - Lérici - Ameglia - Luni - Sarzana - La Spezia (107 km)

A mix of nature's bounty and strategic planning, with olive groves, jutting cliffs, and a historic naval base: in this distant corner of eastern Liguria the interaction between man and earth, sea, and plants has always smacked of the presence of the navy, a navy that has left visible marks in its wake, so to speak. In terms of the geography of the Ligurian littoral, the deep cleft of the Gulf of Spezia is unique along the entire arc of that coastline: it flows inland for better than 13 km, stretching nearly 9 km across at the mouth, lying open to southern breezes. Like extended pincers of the Apennine range, the two mountainous arms that stretch out on either side of La Spezia to enfold and shelter the waters of the gulf – one running southeast as far as the promontory of Montemarcello, the other southwest to the promontory of Portovènere, with the islands of Palmaria and Tino extending the pincer's grasp out into the waters of the Ligurian Sea – remained under uninterrupted Ligurian rule until the fall of the Genoan Republic. The living forms of this world – grapevines, olive groves, farmers and fishermen – are at the heart of this route. North lies the coastline of the Cinque Terre, south is the Valle della Magra and the Luni littoral; they meet at the foot of the promontory of Montemarcello, where Punta Bianca joins two worlds. To the west, the jagged Ligurian coast, with crashing waves and drifting spray; to the east, the crescent-shaped Tuscan dunes, the sea lapping gently at the sandy beaches, the black line of pine forests, and in the distance, the white line of the Apuan Alps, mountains rich in marble.

The route. Leave La Spezia via the SS 530 road, following the gulf; at a distance of 13.5 km to the SW, you will reach Portovènere. As you head back to La Spezia, the road that climbs up from the Arsenale leads on to Riomaggiore and Manarola, in the Cinque Terre, with magnificent views along the coastline of the Mar Ligure, or Ligurian Sea, as far as the Punta del Mesco. Return to La Spezia, and follow the eastern shore of the gulf as far as Lérici. From here it is another 4.5 km to Tellaro. From Lérici the route continues along a road with panoramic views, midway up the slope, amidst pine woods and olive groves, to Montemarcello. The scenery changes as you descend from Montemarcello to Ameglia: before you stretches the green countryside of Versilia, at the foot of the Apuan Alps. Cross the river Magra to reach Marinella di Sarzana, Luni, and Sarzana; from here, you will drive up the narrow little valley between Romito and Pùgliola, to return to the gulf of La Spezia, along a panoramic route.

Places of interest. Portovènere*. With its compact colorful rows of tall houses perched over the waves, the ancient fortified coast town is one of Liguria's most charming spots; note the enchanting church of S. Pietro. Riomaggiore, easternmost of the Cinque Terre, boasts lovely and cleverly built houses, high on the steep slopes of the valley of a covered mountain stream; you can reach Manarola by following a walkway carved into the rock high over the waves (Via dell'Amore). San Terenzo: Villa Magni was the last residence of the poet Shelley. Lérici, with its looming castle, was built in the 13th c. by Pisa as a military counterweight to the fortress of Portovènere; the coast route through Fiascherino leads to the almost intact coastal village of Tellaro (you can also go by boat), perched on a rocky spur. Montemarcello towers 266 m over the sea. Walk to Punta Corvo, with its vast panoramic view. Ameglia is a hill town of high narrow houses, topped by a castle. Luni: archeological excavations and a museum of the ancient Roman town, which once thrived on shipping marble and was later stranded by a receding sea. Sarzana is a city with a long and complex history, studded with monuments, including a Romanesque-Gothic cathedral which dates back to the 13th century.

2 | Monte di Portofino and Gulf of Tigullio

Nervi - Camogli - Santa Margherita - Portofino - Rapallo - Chiàvari Sestri Levante (63 km)

When you think of the word "riviera," this elegant section of the Riviera di Levante is probably what comes to mind: once a watering hole of high society, now a popular resort area, made lovely by nature and tirelessly improved upon by man. They've been seen a thousand times, yet they never grow old – sun, sea, palm trees, colorful houses, jagged rocks, dishes laden with seafood. Generations of the leisured class have planted exotic plants here. The olive tree is a symbol of the Mediterranean landscape, but it was introduced to these dizzying terraced slopes 300 years ago; just 150 years ago, odd to say, the farmers here planted "grapevines beneath the olive trees, and between the rows of vines wheat and rye..." (D. Bertolotti, 1838). In the sweeping views you must visualize the sweat and back-breaking fatigue of generations of farmers; in the glittering waves, danger to sailors, even death. Only then can you appreciate the votive offerings in the local churches. Seaside villas are girt with medieval towers and a vast array of eclectic styles; a few are authentic mansions of Genoan nobles. There are also turn-of-the-century hotels and many noteworthy monuments, such as the 13th-c. basilica, S. Salvatore dei Fieschi. Portofino, Camogli, and Chiàvari are jewels of Ligurian history; the Monte di Portofino is a splendid piece of Ligurian/Mediterranean nature.

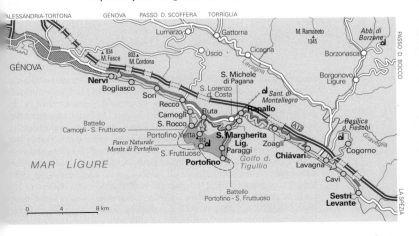

The route.

The stretch of the Riviera di Levante along which runs the route recommended here and shown on the map, has heavy traffic in summer and on weekends. Beginning from Genoa, take the Via Aurelia (SS 1 road), which offers many spectacular vistas. The name of this road (from Caius Aurelius Cotta, consul in 241 B.C.) originally described the ancient Roman road, which however only went as far north as Vada Volterrana or Pisa; the Ligurian coastal road was first completed around 1830. You will leave the Via Aurelia for the first time at Recco, to reach Camogli, and then you will return to the Via Aurelia at Ruta (from here, you can take detours to the viewpoint of San Rocco and, along a private toll road, to Portofino Vetta); you will leave the Via Aurelia a second time just past the tunnel of Ruta to drive down to Santa Margherita Ligure, Portofino, and Rapallo. Follow the SS 227 road, a splendid coast road, from Santa Margherita Ligure to Portofino (built in 1878); however, especially in summer you may encounter long delays (better to take a motorcoach or a boat). The route then proceeds back along the Via Aurelia, from Rapallo as far as Sestri Levante.

Places of interest.

Nervi* is a famed resort town with an enchanting marina, waterfront promenade, and the Serra-Gropallo park. Camogli*: this ancient fishing village has tall, colorful houses, facing the sunny waterfront; on the second Sunday in May, the chararteristic annual Fish Festival takes place here. Portofino Vetta, a fine panoramic viewpoint (416 m), is the starting point of many paths that pass through the Monte di Portofino nature reserve. San Lorenzo della Costa: in the parish church, an exquisite late-15th-c. Flemish triptych. Santa Margherita Ligure*: straddling two inlets, this little seaside resort town still has the dignified elegance of the 19th c., when it was developed; it is surrounded by villas with parks. Paraggi, a small cluster of houses once inhabited by fishermen and millers, who ran its 20 mills; note the landscape around the inlet. Portofino**: the tall houses overlooking the little marina are no longer inhabited by sailors and fishermen, but by celebrities and society folk; by boat or via a footpath, you can reach San Fruttuoso di Capodimonte*, a remarkable little village. Monte di Portofino*, a unique promontory on the Ligurian coast, is crisscrossed by trails through the Mediterranean maquis, or underbrush, with fine views of jagged coastline. San Michele di Pagana has colorful houses lining the beach; in the parish church is a canvas by A. Van Dyck. Rapallo is an elegant resort town which has expanded in recent years, though the waterfront is still intact. Chiàvari is a historical little town with a lively center lined with low porticoes and dignified 19th-c. architecture; at a distance of 4.5 km, across the river Entella is the 13th c. Basilica dei Fieschi*, one of the most important Romanesque-Gothic buildings in Liguria. Sestri Levante: the promontory shelters the delightful hidden inlet to the south known as the Baia del Silenzio, an important holiday resort.

3 | Ligurian Alps

Albenga - Garessio - Ponte di Nava - Viozene - Mònesi - Colle di Nava - Imperia (147 km)

Coastline and countryside, followed by Alpine sweep, the realm of generations of mountain shepherds. Though it does not appear to the eye, the Sella d'Altare, west and high above Savona, separates Apennines from Alps, as the ancient Roman historian Strabo first noted. The route recommended here goes through the hinterland of the Riviera di Ponente, and then cuts across a patch of Piedmont; it is a course from the sea to a remarkable sort of Alpine universe, and then back down to the sea, up high valleys and over passes where salt caravans once jolted along the mountain trade routes. The landscape changes as you approach the mountains: kitchen gardens, olive groves, the greenhouses of the great "flower industry" of the Riviera di Ponente; the tortuous course of the Valle del Neva and its "borghi" lost in time; the wild high valley of the river Tànaro; larch trees and green pastures in the Ùpega basin; beech trees and stands of pine, with spectacular panoramic

views from the ridge separating Mònesi and Nava; fields of lavender bloom from May to June on the Colle di Nava and outlying slopes; chestnut woods in the Valle dell'Arroscia. We end with the endless olive trees that dot the hills of Imperia, their leaves rustling at the sight of the glittering sea below. As you pass from the high valley of the Tànaro to the river Arroscia, you may note borrowed styles, distinctly non-Ligurian: Alpine houses, with more wood than is common in Liguria and roofs of overlapping slabs of stone, known here as "ciappe."

The route. Beginning in Albenga, take the SS 582 road, following the Val Neva, driving over the Colle S. Bernardo (957 m), and then driving down to Garessio, in the Tànaro valley, in Piedmont. Turning on to the SS 28 road, which runs up the Tànaro, you will pass through Ormea, and then Ponte di Nava; from here, a local road runs through the wild Valle del Negrone, and on to Mònesi, a Ligurian summer resort and center for winter sports. Crossing over the crest between the rivers Tanarello and Arroscia, at Nava you return to the SS 28 road; this road, after passing the Colle di Nava (941 m), leads to Pieve di Teco. On your way back to the coast, we recommend the detour that runs up to the Colle S. Bartolomeo (620 m), along the watershed between the Arroscia and Impero rivers. Following the valley of the Impero, again along the SS 28 road, you will arrive at Imperia.

Places of interest. Albenga*, an ancient village with an inland main square, is noteworthy in general for its numerous monuments. Zuccarello is a walled village, with a street lined with medieval porticoes. Castelvecchio di Rocca Barbena is another walled village with narrow streets, typically Ligurian houses, and, in its midst, a castle perched on a gigantic rock; from the Colle S. Bernardo is a fine view of the sea and the Isola Gallinara. Garessio is a spa, while Ormea is a resort town with a medieval center. Ùpega has rustic mountain houses, each fronted by a broad balcony. From Mònesi, take a chairlift up to Monte Saccarello (2070 m) to gaze out over the Alpi Marittime. Colle di Nava: a wide hollow of meadows, a pass linking the valleys of Tànaro and Arroscia. Pieve di Teco is a nearly intact 14th-c. Ligurian village; there are 15th-c. frescoes in the church of S. Maria della Ripa. Colle S. Bartolomeo has a splendid view of the Alpi Liguri (Ligurian Alps). Pontedassio has a Museo Storico degli Spaghetti featuring the history of pasta.

4 | Riviera di Ponente

**Spotorno - Albenga - Imperia - Taggia - San Remo - Ventimiglia
Ponte San Luigi (112 km)**

Landscape and climate shift considerably as you follow this stretch of the Ligurian Riviera; Bordighera is considerably south of Genoa. Contrary to common belief, the "tall palm trees" were introduced much earlier than the 19th c., when the English first discovered this part of Italy; Leandro Alberti wrote about them in 1550, describing the vegetation as "lovely to behold and fragrant as well," adding that there are "delightful gardens, in which to rest and banish all melancholy." And the description holds true. If you expect this coast road to offer a continual view of the sea, "as it murmurs and whitens the length of the shore" (Tasso), bear in mind that the sight, smell, and sound of the sea can be had only on beaches and waterfront prome-

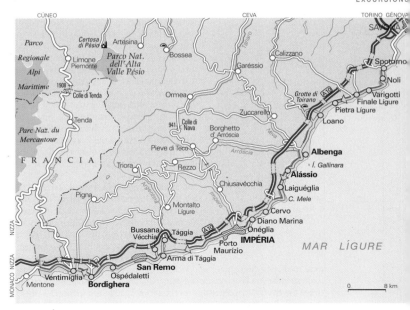

nades. This road offers only a few fine views, mainly from the capes and points (Noli, Mele, Cervo, Berta, for example). Along the so-called "Riviera dei Fiori," or Riviera of Flowers, in the westernmost section of the route there is a profusion of greenhouses. There are many places to stop and enjoy the sights and works of art, but they must be sought out with patience and skill.

The route.

The route to be followed is quite simple: it corresponds to the SS 1 road, the Via Aurelia (which you can take from Spotorno, after exiting the Autostrada A10), all the way to the French border. The road follows the coast the whole way; only in the last stretch, after Mòrtola, does it split into a high and low road. As the road winds through the many beach resorts, traffic slows down and is often routed through less interesting outskirts. Handsome beachfronts, old streets of unmistakably Ligurian flavor, and excellent architecture can be found all over this coastline: park your car and seek them out.

Places of interest.

Noli*: an ancient village beneath the fortified Castello Ursino. Varigotti, with singular terrace-roof Ligurian houses. Finale Ligure: don't miss the 15th-c. town walls at Finalborgo, the historical section of town. Loano, with the renowned caverns of Toirano*. Albenga* is the centerpiece of this route, in terms of atmosphere and monuments; note the Museo Navale Romano. Alassio*: an extensive and elegant beachside resort; take a boat to the Isola Gallinara. Laiguéglia, with the nearby Colla Micheri (162 m; 3 km away), a perfect little village with olive groves. Cervo*, an intact Ligurian fishing village. Imperia: Oneglia and Porto Maurizio, two towns with two ports, flank the city. Taggia*, a well preserved ancient village, dotted with lovely sights; there are paintings by L. Brea in S. Domenico church. Bussana Vecchia, partly destroyed in 1887, is now an art "colony." San Remo*: the Pigna, the medieval center of town with steep narrow streets overlooks the 19th-c. resort town. Bordighera* is an elegant sunny town shaded by palm trees; the petroglyphs in the Museo Bicknell are worth seeing. Ventimiglia still has a medieval air; to the east are Roman archeological excavations. Mòrtola Inferiore boasts the celebrated Giardini Hanbury, a botanical garden on the steep slopes. The Balzi Rossi*, or red cliffs, tower over the sea; the caverns inhabited by humans in the Paleolithic epoch and the museum are noteworthy.

5 | Langhe

**Bra - Cherasco - La Morra - Monforte - Dogliani - Murazzano
Bossolasco - Alba (101 km)**

Two etymologies provide hints regarding the nature of this area. "Langa," the singular of Langhe, means, in local dialect, the narrow ridge of a chain of hills. Following the "langa" means staying in the highlands, avoiding the valleys, and in fact this route offers fine views of vineyards and castles, perched on the higher hills. The other etymology is for truffle, or "tartufo." It originally derived from Latin; Petronius Arbiter speaks of "territubera," while in rural dialect the term was "territufer." In any case, its meaning is "tuber of the earth." Alba, where the route comes to an end, has a famed annual truffle fair; there are also excellent mushrooms ("porcini", or boletus mushrooms, and "ovoli", or royal agaric), vegetables, fruit, rabbits, pheasants, and partridges. Hilly landscapes and excellent food and wine, therefore, can be derived from these two etymologies. The wines are classic Piedmontese varietals; the grape harvest, gathering mushrooms, and tours of the autumn colors are popular pastimes here.

The route.

Beginning in Bra, head south along a regional road that crosses the Stura di Demonte River, passing through Cherasco, and then reaching Narzole. Here, you will drive down to cross the river Tànaro and then back up to La Morra. Then continue along hilltop ridges, "per langa," as the local expression goes, southward, passing through Monforte d'Alba, Dogliani, Belvedere Langhe (literally, "fine view of the Langhe"), and Murazzano. From this last town, the general direction of the route changes, heading north. With a fine view of the Valle del Belbo, you will head over the Passo della Bòssola and through the towns of Bossolasco (known as the "pearl of the Langhe") and Serravalle Langhe. A bit further on, at the fork in the road at Pedaggera, take a left onto the road that leads to Serralunga d'Alba. After following this road as far as Gallo d'Alba, turn right and drive to Grinzane Cavour; then, from Diano d'Alba, drive down toward the Tànaro River and the city of Alba.

CORTEMILIA

Places of interest. Bra is a handsome town full of Baroque architecture, and was once known as "Brayda." Cherasco boasts an improbable Visconti castle, dowry for the Visconti bride of Louis d'Orléans (1387), and used as a pretext a century later when Louis XII of France laid claim to the duchy of Milan. La Morra, a medieval hilltop village, offers a fine view. Along the road to Grinzane Cavour, note the former Abbey of the Annunziata, with private wine cellar and museum. Barolo: in the Castello Falletti is the Museo della Civiltà Contadina, featuring exhibits of rural life. Dogliani is a wine-making town with a high medieval section; take a detour down to the river Tànaro, and then to Carrù, with a Baroque parish church by F. Gallo, and then to Bastìa Mondovì, where you can see late Gothic frescoes in the church of S. Fiorenzo. Murazzano is a resort with excellent views. Bossolasco (see Dogliani), is another resort with a view from the central square. Serralunga d'Alba is a hilltop town, with the elegant Castello Falletti di Barolo. Grinzane Cavour: fine wines, a regional wine-cellar in the Castello Cavour, residence of Camillo Cavour, the 19th-c. statesman who united Italy. Alba is a little town with medieval architecture, towers and tower-houses; sections are strongly redolent of the 19th c. It is renowned for its white truffles and its wines.

6 | Northern Monferrato

Asti - Moncalvo - Santuario di Crea - S. Maria di Vezzolano - Cortazzone - Asti (119 km)

In the heart of the Middle Ages, a "Codex Astensis" praises the excellence of the local wines; in the 13th c. another manuscript praises the wines of Monferrato, a highland over the Po, at the foot of the Ligurian Apennines, north of the Langhe, and mingling with it. This is the northern Monferrato, high in elevation, stretching north from Asti and the Turin-Piacenza freeway running through it to the Po, arching between Moncalieri and Valenza. These highlands are dotted with vineyards facing the sun, towns perched on ridges and peaks, and views that change with each curve in the road. And then there are the castles...

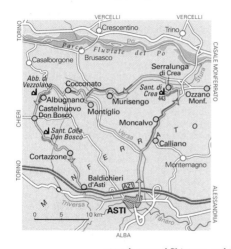

The route. The route recommended here is circular, beginning from and returning to Asti. You will follow the SS 457 road as it climbs over the ridge separating the rivers Tànaro and Po, following the course of the river Versa for a stretch, passing through Calliano and Moncalvo. Further along, just before you reach the banks of the river Stura, at La Madonnina, take a left along a road that leads to the Santuario di Crea; then, through Serralunga di Crea, you will reach the SS 590 road (which runs up the Stura valley), turning off to enter Murisengo. Further along, a detour to the left will take you to Montiglio, once again in the valley of the Versa River. As you continue NW, you will reach Cocconato, a village with a splendid vantage point; from here, you will drive down to the SS 458 road, following it for a short stretch, toward Chivasso, and then turn left, passing through Albugnano until you reach the Abbey of Vezzolano. The next segment of the route leads from Albugnano south to Castelnuovo Don Bosco and the village of Colle Don Bosco (8 km further south). As you take secondary roads over small rises, heading SE, you will reach first Cortazzone, then Baldichieri d'Asti, not far from the SS 10 road, the Padana Inferiore; you can take this road back into Asti.

Places of interest. Moncalvo: home of 17th-c. painter G. Caccia; from the tower in Piazza Carlo Alberto, a fine 360-degree view of Monferrato, the Po, and the Alps. Santuario di Crea, a 16th-c. sanctuary, with 23 chapels scattered in the woods. Murisengo, with a fine 17th-c. castle and a Piedmontese-Rococo parish church. Montiglio, with a noted series of 14th-c. frescoes, in the park of the castle. Cocconato, a hilltop town with a 15th-c. Gothic town hall and noted for its fine food. S. Maria di Vezzolano** (open daily, closed Mon.), noteworthy Romanesque-Gothic abbey, said to have been founded by Charlemagne but in fact built in the 13th c. Castelnuovo Don Bosco: birthplace of a noted Italian man of the cloth, Don Bosco. Cortazzone boasts a handsome Romanesque church, S. Secondo, perched on a hilltop outside of town. Asti*: a town of red brick and yellow tufa, medieval architecture, farmers and vintners.

7 | Amphitheater of Avigliana

Turin - Giaveno - Sacra di S. Michele - Avigliana - Viù - Lanzo Torinese - Turin (151 km)

Leaving aside Turin's "collina," which overlooks the town from across the Po, there are mountains close to Turin to the west as well. The route recommended here explores, along unusual routes, the landscape of the Alpine ridges, in a farflung range of mountains, valleys, and hills, from the Chisola to the Stura. There are views of placid foothills; the hills in the three concentric belts of the morainic amphitheater of Rìvoli, where glaciers once carved out vast hollows, now blue with the lakes of Avigliana; the harsh, stern mountains of the narrow pass of the Valle di Susa; occasionally, a forested wilderness. This itinerary will allow you to reach panoramic overlooks that show the geography of this area. Monuments and architectural flavors are as interesting as the nature here: Avigliana, the Sacra di S. Michele, and S. Antonio di Ranverso are three notable examples of medieval Piedmontese architecture. These are lands with old legends, preserved and perhaps engendered by Alpine isolation: the devil cheated out of a soul by the astute stratagem of a peasant of Lanzo, and the lovely Alda, who hurled herself from high atop a crag to defend her virtue from lusting soldiers, and was held up by angels (Alda jumped a second time, to show off to her friends, and this time the angels let her fall).

The route. Drive out of Turin and head SW, toward Orbassano and Piossasco. A modern detour allows you to avoid the two small towns, converging with the SS 589 road near the fork that leads to Cumiana. From here, continue north along a scenic road that runs over a mountain ridge – Colletta (621 m) – passing from the Valle della Chisola to the Valle del Sangone, entering the plain of Giaveno. A steep and winding road will then take you on to the Colle Braida (1007 m), and to the Sacra di S. Michele (962 m), overlooking the Valle di Susa. You can then drive down another stretch of scenic road to the two lakes and the town of Avigliana. Follow the road to Rìvoli for a while, running over morainic hills on the right side of the lower Susa valley, as far as Buttigliera Alta; there, a left turn will take you to S. Antonio di Ranverso. A short stretch of the SS 25 road in the Valle di Susa, heading west, will take you to the fork in the road, near Avigliana, that goes over the river Dora Riparia and climbs up to Almese. Continue north from Almese, and you will climb over the Colle del Lis (1311 m), between the valleys of the Susa and the Stura di Viù (one of the Valli di Lanzo). Follow the wooded lower valley of Viù down to Lanzo Torinese. You can drive back to Turin on either the right or left bank of the river Stura di Lanzo; on the right bank, you will drive past the Parco Regionale La Mandria, a regional park, and pass by Venarìa, while on the left bank you will go past Cirié and Caselle Torinese.

Places of interest. Piossasco: the quarter of San Vito boasts a Romanesque parish church and three hilltop castles. Giaveno is a resort and a manufacturing town; from the Alpe Colombino (1240 m, 10 km west), enjoy the view of the morainic arena of Rìvoli. Sacra di S. Michele*: this renowned abbey, also known as the Abbazia della Chiusa, is one of the masterpieces of medieval architecture in Piedmont, the high point of the route. Avigliana has a handsome medieval center; in the morainic hollow are two lovely little lakes, now part of a national park. S. Antonio di Ranverso*, a fine example of medieval architecture in Piedmont of

French-Gothic influence. Lanzo Torinese is a thriving little manufacturing town, with a medieval center of narrow lanes and arches. Around the 14th-c. Ponte del Diavolo hovers a legend that it was built in one night by Satan, who was cheated of the soul promised in exchange. Ciriè, an industrial town at the mouth of the Lanzo valleys, has a notable Duomo. Venarìa Reale, once a Savoy hunting lodge, is now an industrial town in the orbit of Turin.

8 | From the Valle d'Aosta Castles to Mt. Cervino (Matterhorn)

Pont-Saint-Martin - Issogne - Verrès - Saint-Vincent - Châtillon - Breuil-Cervinia (66 km)

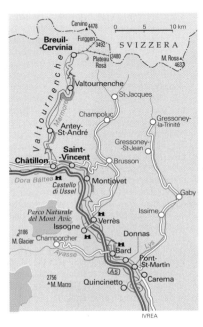

IVREA

Around 1750, a physician from Bern, Johannes Georg Zimmermann, wrote that when standing before mountains, "the imagination soars to greater heights." In the face of the "grandeur of nature, amid vast masses of ice, when dangling over bottomless chasms or wandering past thundering torrents and through deep forests," the mind "begins to ponder the nullity of human strength." It is hard to say whether any of us today would be able to summon such a pre-Romantic lyric vision, but this may be as close as we get: the sight of the Matterhorn (called the Cervino in Italy). This is the destination of the route. The Cervino was first climbed, up the Swiss side, on 14 July 1865, by the English mountaineer Edward Whymper with a party of six (four died on the way down). On the Valle d'Aosta side, on the same day, the abbot Aimé Gorret, Jean Antoine Carrel, and Jean Baptiste Bich were just beneath the peak, which they attained, a close second on the 17th. Along this route, for a number of reasons, getting there is as enthralling as actually arriving due to the stark Alpine landscape of the lower Valle d'Aosta and the feudal, late-Gothic atmosphere of the castles; then, as if you were climbing a staircase, you go from lake to lake, through meadows, past villages, through the lovely Valtournenche

The route.

The beginning of this route is the Quincinetto exit of the Autostrada to Aosta. You thus turn from the right bank of the Dora Baltea River and take the SS 26 road toward Pont-Saint-Martin, Bard, Verrès – from here, there is a short detour to Issogne, on the far side of the valley – and Saint-Vincent. Once you have reached Châtillon, you will take the SS 406 road through the Valtournenche, a tributary valley on the left of the Valle d'Aosta, following it for 27 km, climbing all the way up to the hollow of Breuil-Cervinia.

Places of interest.

Carema: last town of the Canavese, surrounded by steep slopes dotted with vineyards (fine red Nebbiolo). Pont-Saint-Martin: the bridge over the Lys is Roman (1st c. B.C.), as is the stretch of road just beyond Donnas, with an arch cut into the rock. Bard, locked in a narrow gorge, over which towers a spectacular fortress, was rebuilt in the 19th c. Verrès, with the square 14th-c. Castello degli Challand, atop a lofty crag. Issogne (see Verrès): the 15th-c. castle may be the loveliest in the entire Valle d'Aosta. Montjovet: looming over the town are the ruins of the town's castle. Saint-Vincent, an elegant spa resort which hosts one of Italy's four municipal casinos; its popularity dates back to 1770, when an abbot discovered the curative properties of the springs. Châtillon is a market and manufacturing town at the mouth of the Valtournenche. On a rocky crag overlooking the river Dora stands the 14th-c. Castello di U sel. Valtournenche is perched high in the valley of the same name; you can descend to the Gouffre des Busserailles, an "orrido" or gorge of the Marmore River. Breuil-Cervinia*, renowned mountain resort, surrounded by high rocky peaks sheathed in ice; fine view of the Matterhorn (in Italian: Cervino). Take a cableway up to the Plateau Rosà* (3480 m) and to the Cresta del Furggen** (3488 m), on the Swiss-Italian border.

9 | Aosta and Monte Bianco (Mont Blanc)

Châtillon - Fénis - Nus - Aosta - Pré-Saint-Didier - Courmayeur - Entrèves (71 km)

In the Valle d'Aosta region the landscape, both natural and human, varies widely. Let us leave for another visit to the 14 tributary valleys that lead up to the ridges of the Pennine and Graian Alps and the Gran Paradiso massif. The main valley, fed by the Dora Baltea, ranges from a valley floor, at Pont-Saint-Martin, just over 300 m, to the 1000 m of Pré-Saint-Didier. On either side, ranks of mountains are dotted with fields, vineyards, and warehouses; then there are tiny villages, perched high on mountain slopes, with no apparent means of reaching them. There are patches of high mountain meadows, set amidst forests, naked boulders, little waterfalls that freeze solid in winter, and ice raking the sky. Castles and once-mighty ruins line the valley and rise on dizzying ridges, guardians of an ancient and violent history. Trade between France and Italy continues to flow through this valley, along with hikers, mountaineers, and skiers. Mont Blanc, or Monte Bianco, towers at the end of this route; scaled for the first time on 8 August 1786, it can be reached by a cableway.

The route. This route hooks up with the preceding one. The route follows the SS 26 road from Châtillon, up the Valle d'Aosta; except for one short detour – just before Nus, to Fénis – you will stay on this route as far as Pré-Saint-Didier. From there you will be following the SS 26 *dir* road, which runs through Courmayeur and Entrèves. Just past this latter town, you will find the entrance of the Mont Blanc (Monte Bianco) tunnel. The road runs parallel to the Autostrada A5, with the intense traffic from the Mont Blanc tunnel.

Places of interest. Chambave is a small town surrounded by vineyards. Just north, on the road to Saint-Denis, are the ruins of the Castello di Cly, atop a panoramic crag. The 14th-c. Castello di Fénis is certainly the most intact of Valle d'Aosta's castles. Further on, at Nus, the 13th-c. Castello di Pilato; another 14th-c. castle stands at Quart (2 km along the road that runs off to the right of the quarter of Villair). Aosta*, with its walls virtually intact, the Collegiata di S. Orso with its Ro-

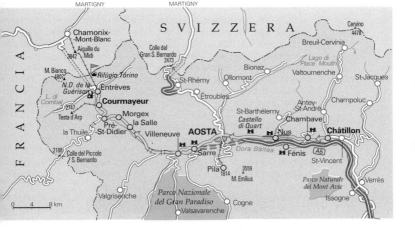

manesque cloister, and its odd mountain-urban air, is a city of remarkable artistic, architectural, and historical value. Sarre: the castle, rebuilt in the 18th c., has remarkable interiors; another castle, at Saint-Pierre, has a museum of natural science. La Salle houses vineyards that climb up to 1000 m, and produces fine white wines. Pré-Saint-Didier: from the hot springs, renowned among the ancient Romans, you can walk down to the "orrido," or dramatic steep gorge, of the Dora di Verney. Courmayeur*: the oldest and best known ski resort in the Italian Alps, is also a capital of mountaineering; the peak of Mont Blanc is 9 km from town as the crow flies; excursions first took place in the 19th c. Entrèves: from La Palud take a cableway up to the Punta Helbronner (3642 m), and then up over the dizzying rock spires of Mont Blanc, to Chamonix (France).

10 | Lake Maggiore and Lake Orta

Arona - Mottarone - Orta San Giulio - Omegna - Baveno - Stresa - Arona (104 km)

One somewhat excitable geographer wrote of these lakes that they are "isolated depressions and valleys, in which the rushing waters of land and sky finally find peace, unable to thunder off elsewhere." These lakes are of glacial origin. The Lago d'Orta comes from the glacier of Ossola or the Toce River. The little lake of Mergozzo was separated from Lago Maggiore a thousand or more years ago. The remarkable views should be understood in the context of a climate that allowed the introduction of exotic species, of mountains rearing straight up from the lake shore, and distant snow-capped peaks, of a history of churches, castles, and sanctuaries, surrounded by compact little villages. In recent centuries, noble villas and imposing middle-class hotels have been built up along the lakefront. Literary travellers have provided descriptions; the Isole Borromee – perhaps the jewel of this route – are called "art playing with nature" (J. Cambry, 1788); while E. Quinet (1832) said that they "resemble a creation of Ariosto. They have the same inventive grace as the Orlando Furioso, with an added pinch of the savage...."

The route. The hilly and mountainous area overlooking the western shore of the Lago Maggiore, from Arona to the Toce River, is called the Vergante. From Arona you climb up to the S. Carlone plaza and, driving through the Vergante, you will pass through Dagnente, Ghevio, Massino Visconti, and Gignese, and then you will drive up to the Mottarone (private road). This is the watershed between lakes Maggiore and Orta; drive down to Lago d'Orta, passing through Armeno until you reach the eastern shore at Orta San Giulio. Along the SS 229 road, follow this shore of the lake as far as Omegna, and then drive down the valley of the Toce River, to Gravellona. Go around Monte Orfano and, after passing through the town of Mergozzo, you will drive around the little lake of Mergozzo; after crossing the river Toce, you will find yourself on the shores of Lago Maggiore at Feriolo. Then you can drive back to Arona, on the state road 33, enjoying the varied landscapes of Baveno, Stresa, Belgirate, and Mèina. Bear in mind that during the fine season, this road is often plagued by heavy traffic.

Places of interest. In the old part of Arona there is still a flavor of the ancient lake-front marketplace; note the nearby gigantic 17th-c. statue of St. Charles Borromeo, the "S. Carlone." Massino Visconti has a castle that was the origin of the Visconti, lords of Lombardy until the mid-15th c. Carpugnino has a handsome Romanesque-Gothic parish church, S. Donato. Gignese (see Stresa): this town produced many master umbrella-makers, who emigrated throughout Europe; now there is a Museo dell'Ombrello e del Parasole (Museum of Umbrellas and Parasols). Alpino: 1 500 species and varieties of Alpine plants and medicinal herbs, in the Giardino Alpinia. Mottarone, with the 1491-m peak looming above the road; when the sky is clear, the view is spectacular: Monte Rosa and all the western Alps, seven lakes, and the Po valley. Orta San Giulio has ancient houses, loggias, Baroque facades, and lovely narrow lanes. Behind it is the Sacro Monte d'Orta, a series of spectacular hilltop chapels; take a boat to the Isola di S. Giulio*, with its fine Romanesque basilica. Omegna, at the northern tip of the Lago d'Orta, is a manufacturing town with medieval and Renaissance structures. Mergozzo: a high road above the isolated little lake leads to Montòrfano, with the Romanesque church of S. Giovanni. Baveno: aristocratic homes and gardens overlook Lake Maggiore from the southern shore of the Golfo Borromeo. Stresa*, an exclusive lake-side resort, with a strong Belle Epoque flavor; from here you can take a boat to the renowned Isole Borromee*, three small islands called Isola Bella, Isola dei Pescatori and Isola Madre. Belgirate: distinctive houses, with porticoes and loggias, in the upper, older part of town.

11 | Lake Como

Lecco - Onno - Asso - Bellagio - Como - Gravedona - Còlico - Varenna - Lecco (183 km)

The magnolia tree, with its dense shadow of glistening leaves, the delicate wisteria, clinging to a gazebo, dark cypresses standing against the bright sky or the soft light colors of the mountain slopes, azaleas, rhododendrons, and, in the words of Stendhal, "groves of stunningly green chestnuts, bathing their branches in the lapping waves"; 16th-c. villas, late-Baroque and Neo-Classic estates, parks built and defended over the centuries; venerable lakefront towns, their houses clustered together, with the whisper of the lapping wavelets; Romanesque parish churches made of grey stone. The blend of natural beauty, art and history is perfectly balanced here. Merged with the gentle climate, the "manmade" landscape attains something close to perfection. From the shore roads and the lakefront promenades, shaded by ancient trees, you can always see the opposite banks; thus, each place you visit will first be seen from across

a silvery sheet of lakewater. And this preliminary view is linked with the preconceptions provided by literature and fame. Indeed, sometimes the view is even superfluous. For example, one morning in 1865, H.A. Taine, the French critic and historian, boarded a steamboat in Como. The white boat with black smokestack and thundering wheels took him for a tour of the lake, and the French writer spent the entire day amidst the red velvet of the salon, reading, researching, and writing about Venice. He emerged on deck only in the evening, but later wrote of the trip: "All day long, thoughtlessly, effortlessly, we sailed across a goblet of light...."

The route. Starting out from Lecco, you will cross the Adda River and then take the SS 583 road, which runs along the western shore of the branch of the lake identified with the great Italian author Alessandro Manzoni, until you reach the village of Onno. This is where you start on a road that enters the Valbrona – with a steep climb and fine views of the Grigne mountains beyond the lake and, high above, the Corni di Canzo – and then descends to Asso. From Asso, you will take a scenic road that goes up the Valassina – or upper valley of the Lambro River – as far as the Passo del Ghisallo, (754 m), a name that is tinged with heroism for fans of mountain bike racing; then you drive down to Bellagio. From this central point of the three branches of Lake Como, you will take the SS 583 road, following the eastern or "inland" shore of the Como branch of the lake. From Como, the route continues up the western shore, following the Via Regina (SS 340 road), which is splendidly scenic (after Cernobbio and as far as Torriggia, the new road rides high above the lakeshore villages; elsewhere, the road hugs the shore, sometimes passing through the villages), back to the central basin of the lake and then up to the northern branch. When you reach the northern tip of the lake, you will cross the Mera River, drive across the so-called Piano di Spagna and cross the Adda River. On your way back to Lecco along the eastern shore of the lake, you can choose – at least as far as Abbadia Lariana – between the old and scenic road, which skirts the lake, and the new, faster road, the SS 36 road, which runs through many long tunnels. This entire route has heavy traffic on weekends.

Places of interest. Lasnigo: along the climb from Asso to the Ghisallo, note the Romanesque church of S. Alessandro, with its handsome 12th-c. campanile and late-15th-c. Lombard frescoes. Passo del Ghisallo, with the little church of the Madonna del Ghisallo, patron saint of bicyclists; splendid views of Lake Como during the descent to Civenna. Civenna offers another spectacular view from the tree-lined plaza of the Belvedere Grigne. Bellagio* is well located, at the juncture of the three basins of Lake Como; it has an old center with narrow lanes, hotel parks, and noble villas. Torno has two centers: one down near the marina, and another up toward the church of S. Giovanni; the 16th-c. Villa Pliniana graces the view from the far bank. Como*: in this "city of silk," exquisite relics of the age of the medieval communes and of the Lombard Renaissance stand side-by-side with notable buildings from the early 20th c. Cernobbio, practically a residential suburb of Como, has grand villas and a fine lakefront promenade; from the sanctuary atop Monte Bisbino is a panoramic view of the lake, the plains, and the Alps. Sala Comacina: take a boat to the Isola Comacina, the only island in the lake. Ossuccio: the church of S. Maria Maddalena has an impressive late-Gothic bell tower. Tremezzo: visit the early 18th-c Villa Carlotta*, with its azaleas and rhododendrons blooming in April and May. Gravedona: fine views of this lovely town, and the church of S. Maria del Tiglio, a major Lombard Romanesque work. Còlico: follow the shore of the lacustrine gulf called the Lago di Piona; a short detour takes you to the Abbazia di Piona, an ancient monastery (a fine 13th-c. cloister). Corenno Plinio: this village is clustered and perched on a lakefront crag. Bellano, a pleasant health resort which boasts the renowned gorge of the Pioverna stream. Varenna boasts the lakefront promenade and the stairs leading up between houses, with fine views of the old center. Fiumelatte, named after the river that tumbles down, from spring to fall, white with foam; it is only 250 m in length.

12 | The Lodigiano and Cremonese Areas

Lodi - Sant'Angelo Lodigiano - Casalpusterlengo - Pizzighettone - Cremona (89 km)

The 15th-c. Bolognese architect A. Fieravanti (who later went to Moscow to build cathedrals in the Kremlin) worked on the irrigation and reclamation of southern Lombardy for the duke F. Sforza (1460). He noted that this area is not blessed by nature, and that hard work and organization were needed to make it the rich agricultural region that it has since become. This route invites you to perceive how humans have changed this landscape, sunny in summer, foggy in winter, vast, flat, and abundant. The subtly varied riverside views of the last part of the route are dotted with distinctive Lombard features: farmland, churches, town squares, castles, and cities – such as Lodi and Cremona – that form part of this agrarian world with its long and venerable history.

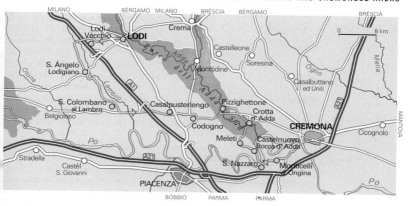

The route.   Starting from Lodi, you head west to Lodi Vecchio. From here, the general direction of this route is south at first, and then east. After crossing over the superhighway (autostrada) and the river Lambro, you will reach Sant'Angelo Lodigiano. You will then follow the river Lambro through the hills of San Colombano al Lambro, to the south of town, then take a left turn onto the SS 234 road, which leads through Casalpusterlengo and Codogno, to the river Adda and to Pizzighettone. Just beyond this town, you will leave the SS road, taking the road to the right through the territory of the Parco dell'Adda Sud, and on to Crotta d'Adda. You will then cross back over the river, passing through Meleti and Castelnuovo Bocca d'Adda, before reaching the Po River, at the S. Nazzaro Bridge. Take the SS 10 road – Padana Inferiore – past Monticelli d'Ongina and back over the Po; you will finally reach Cremona, where the itinerary ends.

Places of interest.   Lodi* is a distinctly medieval Po valley town, picturesque and monumental; in the Renaissance Santuario dell'Incoronata are four exquisite panels by Bergognone; in the Romanesque Duomo, note the relief from the wealthy old town of "Laus Pompeia," attacked and leveled by Milan in 1158. Lodi Vecchio has an isolated Romanesque-Gothic basilica (S. Bassiano), with notable frescoes. Sant'Angelo Lodigiano: the restored castle has fine art collections. San Colombano al Lambro is an ancient farming village at the foot of a hill studded with grapevines. Casalpusterlengo still has a few traces of its rural origins and a large town tower, a relic of the feudal castle. Codogno, now a modern manufacturing town, has fine paintings in the 16th-c. parish church. Pizzighettone is surrounded by the bastions of its venerable fortifications, defending the bridges across the river Adda. Cremona*, a modern bustling city, has a splendid monumental center, with much surviving intact from the Middle Ages.

13 | The Po River and Oltrepò Mantovano

Mantua - Sabbioneta - Guastalla - Suzzara - San Benedetto Po - Mantua (135 km)

Stands of tall poplars, irrigation canals, and embankments bordering the fields, a landscape of carefully tended, low-lying farmland: Sabbioneta is just 25 m above sea level; San Benedetto Po, 19. The immense volume of silt borne by the river continually raises its waters; near Pavìa the Po is already higher than the surrounding farmland. Reclamation, drainage, and construction of earthen banks along the Po began in the early Middle Ages and continue to this day. The embankments tower as high as 10 m (villages lie at their base); climb the banks, or cross a bridge, and you will note that vast expanses of land lie within the embankments, sometimes dry in the hot Po Valley summers, sometimes wreathed in heavy fog or blanketed with snow, and sometimes lying under by a flooded river (high-water season in May-June and October-November; low-water in January-February and August-September). The two art

35

centers along this route – aside from the point of departure and terminus, Mantua – are San Benedetto Po and Sabbioneta, representing two different phases in the construction of this riverine realm. Benedictine monks undertook the first drainage and reclamation, beginning in 1007, while Sabbioneta was one of the "little capitals" of the Gonzaga during the Renaissance, with a sophisticated princely court and remarkable architectural treasures.

The route. You leave Mantua via the SS 420 road, which runs straight SW. After crossing the Oglio River near Gazzuolo, you will run through a number of small towns before reaching Sabbioneta. From there, the route continues south, heading toward the Po; once you reach the SS 358 road, turn toward Viadana. Remaining on the left bank of the river Po, you will pass through Pomponesco, Correggio Verde, and over the bridge to Guastalla, in Emilia. Take the SS 62 road toward Mantua, cross through Luzzara and, as you return to Lombardy, you will pass through Suzzara, in the Oltrepò Mantovano. From here you will continue east, over the Autostrada A 22 (Mòdena-Brenner Pass), and through Pegognaga and then San Benedetto Po. In the last stretch of this route you will first turn west, up the course of the Po River, through Portiolo and Motteggiana, and then onto the SS 62 road, to cross the Po a second time, on the Borgoforte bridge, to return to Mantua.

Places of interest. Mantua**: this city's superb architecture is matched by the charm of its silent streets. It was the birthplace of Vergil. It is surrounded by three lakes, formed by the Mincio River as it flows past the city. Villa Pasquali is a small town whose spectacular parish church is one of the most significant creations of the late Baroque in the Mantua region, both in terms of size and inventiveness. Sabbioneta* is a fortified, complete, unchanging "ideal city" of the 16th c., the dream of a Gonzaga prince, splendid and perfectly useless. Viadana: the ruins of extensive settlements of stilt-dwellings, dating from the Bronze Age, discovered in 1885, are on display in an 18th-c. palazzo. Pomponesco has a large late-Renaissance porticoed square. Guastalla still has a few relics of its past as a "minor Gonzaga capital"; the monument to Ferrante I Gonzaga (Leone Leoni 1564), the Palazzo Ducale, and the Cattedrale, both 16th-c., are noteworthy. Nearby, Gualtieri has a handsome porticoed square and the 16th-c. Palazzo Bentivoglio. Luzzara has Palazzo della Macina, a Gonzaga residence. Outside town, toward Suzzara, a former convent now houses a museum of primitive art. Suzzara: the Galleria d'Arte Contemporanea features the artworks awarded the "Premio Suzzara" (1948 to the early 1970s). Pegognaga has a handsome Romanesque church, S. Lorenzo. San Benedetto Po dates back to the foundation of the Benedictine abbey of Polirone: church, re-built by G. Romano in 1539-47, refectory, and three cloisters, all 15th-c. Motteggiana: the Corte Ghirardina*, a 15th-c. country home, possibly by L. Fancelli, is an interesting blend of palazzo-court-villa-castle.

14 | Lake Iseo, Valcamònica, and Valle Seriana

Sàrnico - Lóvere - Pisogne - Darfo - Breno - Capo di Ponte - Boario Terme
Passo della Presolana - Clusone - Albino - Bèrgamo (166 km)

The lake, the petroglyphic "stories" carved into rocks, the hardworking people of the foothills, and fine paintings: there are numerous attractions in the course of this route. The traveller is free to choose those found most appealing. Writing about the Lago d'Iseo in the early 19th c., one author cited the "beaches crowded with olive groves" and the "theatrical savagery of certain points, which contrast so well with the glittering shoreline" ... This region wa also the birthplace of Italian industry: the low and middle Valcamònica, traversed by the Oglio River, are forbidding pre-Alpine valleys; the slopes are dotted with vineyards and chestnut groves, while the valley floors feature farmland and factories. All around are iron mines; in this region, the highest point, physically, is the Passo della Presolana, with a fine distant view. The artistic high points are Capo di Ponte, with prehistoric petroglyphs, and the gallery of Lóvere, with Venetian paintings.

he route.

The route recommended and shown on the map begins at Sàrnico, where the Oglio River flows out of the Lago d'Iseo; for the first stretch it follows the western – or Bergamasque – shore of the lake, along the SS 469 road. You should stop at Tavèrnola Bergamasca for a tour of Monte Isola. From Lóvere, at the northernmost tip of the Lago d'Iseo, you will cross the Oglio to the far bank, at Pisogne. The lower stretch of the Valcamònica, which opens out here, is traversed by two roads, on opposite sides of the river: from Pisogne you can get to the easternmost of the two and drive up the valley, through Darfo and Breno, as far as Capo di Ponte (SS 42 road). You then double back to Breno, following the road on the right bank of the Oglio River as far as Boario Terme, where you will enter the Valle di Scalve (SS 294 road); after reaching Dezzo di Scalve you take the road that – after crossing over the Passo della Presolana (1297 m) – drops down to Clusone (648 m). The last segment of the route runs down through the Valle Seriana, through Ponte Nossa and Albino, to Bèrgamo.

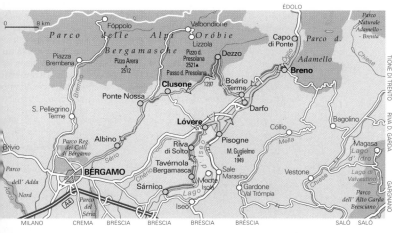

laces of interest.

Sàrnico is a summer resort, with some medieval architecture in the town center. Tavèrnola Bergamasca is an old harbor, from the days when there were no coast roads. There are houses with loggias and fine frescoes, including a youthful effort by Romanino, in the church of S. Pietro. Steamers will take you out to Sensole, on Monte Isola; walking tours of the island. Lóvere, overlooking the lakefront, has noteworthy medieval architecture. Do not miss the Galleria dell'Accademia Tadini. Pisogne: note the frescoes by Romanino in the 15th-c. church of the Madonna della Neve. Breno: again, go see the frescoes by Romanino in the former church of S. Antonio and in the town parish church. Capo di Ponte boasts over 100 boulders with rock-carvings, in the Parco Nazionale delle Incisioni Rupestri di Naquane*; do not miss the Romanesque church of S. Salvatore and, in the village of Cemmo, the 11th-c. parish church of S. Siro. Boario Terme, an important spa since the 19th c; as you drive up the Val di Scalve, beyond Àngolo Terme, the "Via Mala" – an old mountain road, which you can take, though you may prefer the more modern detour – penetrates into the Dezzo deep gorge. Clusone has a handsome old town center, in a tranquil setting. A Triumph of Death and a Danse Macabre are frescoed (1485) on the walls of the Oratorio dei Disciplini. Albino: this was an early manufacturing center; don't miss the paintings by G.B. Moroni, who was born here, in the church of S. Giuliano and the Santuario della Madonna del Pianto.

15 | Engadina and the Upper Valtellina

Còlico - Chiavenna - Sankt Moritz - Passo del Bernina - Livigno - Bormio (160 km)

In the heart of the mountain fastness, the Alpine range extends endlessly. A impressive as the length of this great mountain range – running from the Co di Cadibona all the way to Augsburg and Vienna, sloping down to the Danu – is, so to speak, its "breadth": about 150 km, on a line with Mont Blanc, an more than 330 km, on a line between Verona and Augsburg. Since Italy's nor ern border, as is well known, runs nearly entirely along the high crest of t Alps, save for in the Canton Ticino, the steeper and short slopes, facing sou are part of the Italian landscape; every stream runs down to the river Po an to the Adige. The route suggested here, which runs across the Swiss bord allows you to enjoy views of the far side of the watershed, to the other ed of the Rhaetian Alps, and, in particular, to the north slope of one of the mo notable Alpine mountain groups, the Bernina, a mighty colossus of rock an ice, with the highest summit (4049 m, therefore constituting the last 4000 the east of the Simplon Pass), and watered by torrents and rivers which w flow all the way through Europe, to the Black Sea. The names of the valle through which you will travel or which you will cross are evocative of so ma different faces of the Alpine world: Val di Chiavenna, Val Bregaglia, Engadin (the first syllable is merely the Romanche version of the name of the Inn Ri er, the tributary of the Danube that runs through the Engadina), Val Bernin Val Poschiavina, Val di Livigno (a little patch of Italy just jutting over the w tershed), Val Viola, and Valtellina. Along the way, there are a few artistic lan marks, but the enjoyment of this route lies chiefly in the variations of lan scape through which you will travel, as you head over passes and drive dov into valleys. Note another feature of this route: cableways take you quickly t to high altitudes and spectacular views.

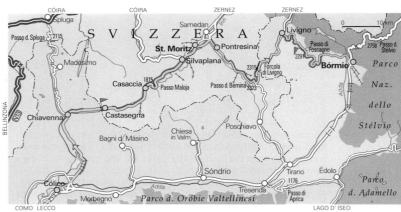

The route.

The recommended route winds along mountain roads and crosses passes th should not be attempted during the winter months. Beginning in Còlico, the northern end of Lake Como, you cross the river Adda and, following th SS 36 road, you will reach Chiavenna. From here, climbing the Val Bregag along the SS 37 road and entering Switzerland on the n. 3 road, you will rea the Passo Maloja, which takes you into the Alta Engadina, along which you c go as far as St. Moritz. Just outside of town, near Celerina, is the fork fro which the n. 29 road runs to Pontresina and then on to the Passo del Berni (2323 m). Just 3 km beyond the pass, as you descend into the Val Poschiavi (basin of the river Adda), you take a left turn onto the road that runs into Ita at the Forcola di Livigno (2315 m), passing through the town of the same nan (Valle dello Spöl, a tributary of the Inn River). At Livigno the route continu along the SS 301 road, which runs up the east slope of the valley, and over the Passo d'Eira (2208 m), and then the Passo di Foscagno (2291 m; customs checkpoint; Livigno is a free-trade zone) and finally, through the wooded Val Viola, down to Bormio, in the Alta Valtellina.

Places of interest. Còlico, overlooking the water, with a 19th-c. landing embarcadero, offers a last glimpse of Lake Como. Chiavenna is well located, with fine views, excellent scenery, historic heritage, and much art (church of S. Lorenzo, Baptistery, and treasury). Casaccia: at the first ramps of the steep climb up to the Passo Maloja, note the path to the gorge and waterfall of Orlegna. Passo Maloja, with a fine view of the Val Bregaglia; in the small town, visit the house of the artist Segantini and a castle dating from 1885. Silvaplana: from nearby Surlej you can take a cableway up to Piz Corvatsch (3303 m), amidst glaciers; there is a spectacular view of the Engadine Alps. St. Moritz*: note the spectacular scenery at this world-famous ski resort; also, visit the Museo Engadinese and the Museo Segantini, with works by the Tridentine artist who painted in the Engadina late in life. Pontresina lies surrounded by a great Alpine arc. On your way up to the Passo del Bernina you will pass by the base-stations of two high cableways: one leads to the Diavolezza (2973 m), a remarkable high-elevation viewpoint overlooking the glacier of Morteratsch, the Bernina, and the Piz Palù; the other runs up to the Piz Lagalb (2959 m), with an equally fine view of the Bernina group. Livigno lies on the broad valley floor; its houses were all once made of wood, widely separated for fear of fires. The old part of Bormio is still a typical Alpine village; in the Torre degli Alberti, in 1496, Ludovico Sforza "the Moor" and Beatrice d'Este lived here for a while.

16 | Lake Garda

Salò - Tremòsine - Riva del Garda - Malcésine - Peschiera del Garda Sirmione (134 km)

To quote a 17th-c. author: "delightful gardens, full of lemon trees, orange trees, and cedars, lush and flowering throughout the year, offer an exceedingly agreeable view, amidst laurel and myrtle, in a temperate and fragrant climate." He was describing the microclimate of Italy's largest lake, a slice of the Mediterranean amidst the Alps: the cypress became common here under Venetian administration, the grapevine dates back to remotest times, the olive tree may have been introduced by the Etruscans, but the Austrians developed it as a business. The mulberry has long vanished. Citrus trees were first grown by Franciscan brothers under Venetian rule; there are ruins of ancient winter greenhouses on the terraced slopes. Under Austrian rule, many towns without roads were served by a steamer called the "Archduke Ranieri"; on the Lombard side, a coastal road was not built until 1931. This route runs through a varied succession of landscapes: steep slopes and villas below, then even steeper rocks; the breathtaking view from the highlands of Tremòsine, overlooking Monte Baldo; the colors of Venetian architecture, venerable little ports along the east shore; vast views, more like an arm of the sea than a lake, lie beyond Punta di S. Vigilio. Last comes Sirmione, frequented and described by Catullus: "Paene insularum, Sirmio, insularumque ocelle," the "delight of peninsulas and islands."

The route. From Salò you follow the Lombard shore of Lake Garda, on the SS 45 bis road, or Gardesana Occidentale. Once you have passed through Gargnano, you will take the road that climbs up to the highland of Tremòsine, and then drops back down to Limone sul Garda. From here, again along the shore, you proceed to Riva del Garda and Tórbole, at the lake's northern tip. The route then runs the length of the eastern, Venetian shore on the SS 249 road, as far as Peschiera del Garda. Then you take the SS 11 road west, turning right at the fork for Sirmione and its peninsula, the final point along the route. Throughout this route traffic will be heavy, especially during the summer months.

Places of interest. Salò*, with a handsom historical center, lies in an inlet, amidst gre hills: the beauty of the site is the reason f its renown. Gardone Riviera*: a lovely lak front promenade embellishes this exclusi resort; also worthy of attention is the markable Vittoriale, home of the early-20th poet Gabriele D'Annunzio. Maderno lies the delta of the river Toscolano, with the F manesque church of S. Andrea. Pieve, cent of the township of Tremòsine, has a rema able overlook; to reach it you must take a c tour up a twisting mountain road, into t gorge of the Brasa River. Limone sul Garc set amidst abandoned olive, cedar, ar lemon groves, has lovely homes in the o center, at the end of the lakefront prom nade. Riva del Garda: this little town is a p fect combination of Alpine, Tridentine, ar Venetian flavors (for a few brief decades, the 15th c., it was ruled by Venice). Tórbc has an enchanting lakefront. "Marmitte c Giganti," notable geological formations, li the road to Nago and from Nago to Arco. M césine: the most remarkable features of this old town are the Palazzo dei Ca itani del Lago and the Castello; you can also take a cableway up to Tratto Spi (1780 m), on the crest of Monte Baldo, with a twofold vista of Lake Garda ar the Adige valley. Torri del Benaco: a Scaliger castle dominates this lovely lit village. Punta di S. Vigilio*, among olive and cypress trees, deserves its rep tation as the most romantic place on the lake. Garda: again, an enchanting lak front, lined with fine old houses. Bardolino lies amidst vineyards whose grap are used to produce the wine of the same name; in the town, visit the F manesque church of S. Severo and the little church of S. Zeno, surrounded small quaint houses. Lazise has a nearly intact ring of medieval walls. In t lovely panorama of the broad basin of the southern lake, note the enchanti – though often overcrowded – setting of the marina. Peschiera del Garda wa Venetian outpost fortress, the stronghold of the Austrian Quadrilateral: t town's military function can be seen in the fortifications that surround t markedly Venetian center, where the Mincio River flows into Lake Garc Sirmione*: the spectacular medieval walls of the Rocca Scaligera, the rema ably twisting streets of the "borgo," and the fine views of the lake are all w known, printed on too many postcards, perhaps, but still eminently enjoyab The celebrated, so-called Grottoes of Catullus are actually the ruins of t largest existing ancient Roman villa from imperial times in northern Italy.

17 | Dolomiti del Brenta and Palade

Riva del Garda - Ponte Arche - Stènico - Tione di Trento - Madonna di Campiglio Malè - Fondo - Passo delle Palade - Merano (162 km)

There is an odd similarity in the history of the two towns on either end of tl route, Riva del Garda and Merano; both were "patches of southern sun" for t Austro-Hungarian Empire and its client states. There, however, the similariti end. Riva del Garda is dotted with olive trees, lemon groves and cypresse and overlooks a glittering blue lake; Merano blooms with apple trees again a backdrop of snowcaps and crags. Moreover, these two extremes are just t beginning and end of a startling array of mountain landscapes, following route that links Trentino with Alto Adige: chestnut groves and stands of bee trees line the turquoise waters of the Lago di Tenno; in the Val Rendena, b neath slopes dark with conifer forests, are delicate green fields of good ear

– one etymology holds that the name "Rendena" means "land of generous yields." Then there is the broad and sunny Anaunia, or Val di Non, where hidden torrents rush through deep gorges. The high notes of this symphony of landscapes, at any rate, come from the two mountain groups on either side of the Val Rendena. They differ even in their component rock: the Adamello-Presanella, crystalline, to the west, the limestone Dolomiti di Brenta (Brenta Dolomites), to the east. The latter can be seen from Madonna di Campiglio, while the former can be viewed from a detour to Val Genova. These are exquisitely Alpine mountains, with high ridges looming well above tortuous glaciers, jagged rock arenas, titanic stairways of seracs, little lakes, unexpected waterfalls thundering in the silence. The Adamello (3539 m; the highest peak) stands to the left of the valley; the Presanella (3558 m) is at the right. The valley itself forms part of the Parco Naturale Adamello-Brenta: this is a haven for ermines, marmots, martens, and grouse. Overhead soars the golden eagle, and moving timidly through the forests are the last brown bears in the Alps. Here, we have spoken almost exclusively of nature; in the Val Rendena you can admire a number of paintings by the Baschenis family, a 15th-c. dynasty of artists from Averara near Bèrgamo.

The route. From Riva del Garda, the SS 421 road leads north through Tenno, Vigo Lomaso, and Ponte Arche in the Sarca valley; from here, a 5-km detour leads to Stènico. Follow the SS 237 road along the river, pushing into the Giudicarie; from Tione di Trento, you will take the SS 239 road up the Val Rendena. At Carisolo, you can turn off from the main road along an alternative road into the verdant Val Genova, as far as Pian di Bédole (19.5 km). Then, after returning to the SS 239 road, you follow the Valle di Campiglio as far as Madonna di Campiglio and the high pass of Campo Carlo Magno (1681 m). Follow the Val Meledrio down into the Val di Sole, at Dimaro. Then you will follow that valley, and its continuation, the Val Anaunia, through Malè, Ponte Mostizzolo, and – to the north of the Lago di S. Giustina – Revò. You will then reach Fondo, at the beginning of the SS 238 road; this proceeds up the valley of the river Novella, reaching the Passo delle Palade/Gampenpass (1512 m), and then drops down the Adige valley to Lana and then to Merano.

Places of interest. Riva del Garda*: this little town is a blend of Alpine, Tridentine and Venetian qualities; at the start of the road to Tenno you can admire the waterfall of Varone, where the water plunges 80 m into a narrow gorge. Tenno: the old village lies in the shadow of a castle; from the church of S. Lorenzo (with 14th-/16th-c. frescoes) is a fine view of the plain between Riva and Arco. Lago di Tenno: a small tree-lined island lies amidst calm waters. Fiavè, a panoramic resort; during the Bronze Age, a large settlement of lake-dwellings was built here. Stènico: the castle is one of the oldest in the Trentino, with sections from the 13th c. Pelugo: the church of S. Antonio has exterior frescoes by D. Baschenis (1493). Pinzolo has a "Danza Macabra," or 'dance of death,' by S. Baschenis (1539) on the side of S. Vigilio, a small cemetery church; inside is another fresco by the same artist. Val Genova*, mantled with woods, is a majestic landscape that leads up to the Adamello and the Presanella: 4.5 km from Carisolo is the waterfall of Nardis* with a sheer drop of over 100 m, 19.5 km away is Pian di Bédole (1578 m) in an amphitheater of rock and ice. Madonna di Campiglio* is an elegant mountain resort, with skiing and mountain climbing;

41

take a cableway up to the Monte Spinale (2104 m), with a breathtaking view of the Brenta group; another fine view from the Grostè (2348 m), accessible by cableway from Campo Carlo Magno, a mile or so further along. Malè, main centre of the Val di Sole, boasts much old architecture; go see the remarkable Cappella di S. Valentino, next to the parish church. Senale (see Fondo): situated in a lonely valley, this village is called Unsere Liebe Frau im Walde in German, after the ancient hospice of S. Maria in Silva; you reach it by leaving the Palade road just before the pass. Lana: the houses are scattered among the vineyards and apple orchards; don't miss the carved gilt 16th-c. altar in the parish church of Lana di Sotto, or Niederlana; a fine view of the Valle dell'Adige, as far as the Dolomites, can be had by taking a cableway up to the Monte S. Vigilio/Vigiljoch (1486 m). Merano/Meran**: the ancient center is typical of the Alto Adige; hotels, parks, and promenades, all with a flavor of Central Europe.

18 | Passo dello Stelvio and the Upper Val Venosta

**Spondigna - Solda - Trafoi - Passo dello Stelvio - Giogo di S. Maria
Santa Maria in Val Monastero - Màlles Venosta - Resia (110 km)**

The first person to reach the peak of the Ortles (3905 m) was Joseph Pichler, known as Passeyer Josele, a hunter of chamois from Sluderno, in Val Venosta, in September 1804; the local peasants said that he couldn't have made the climb without the help of the devil. As you drive up the 48 hairpin turns of the Stelvio road, at each turn a little higher with respect to the glaciers on the Ortles, you can lazily imagine the sensations of that first climb. The road climbs to an elevation of 2758 m – at Rocca Bianca, one of the finest view-points, you pass an obelisk commemorating the climber – and was built for military reasons, with no help from the devil, between 1820 and 1825, at the behest of the emperor Francis I, father of Marie Louise, the second wife of Napoleon. The road was meant to link the Val Venosta in South Tyrol with the Valtellina and Lombardy, which had just been recovered from the wreckage of Francis's son-in-law's enormous empire. Stagecoaches passed here in the summer; the rocks and ice echoed with bells and snapping whips. In winter sleighs whisked past on the snow. After 1859 the pass marked the border between Austria and Italy for 60 years. Aside from the Stelvio, the rest of this route has all the allure of high mountain landscapes: the Val di Solda, with its glittering icy peaks, high above the meadows of the valley floor; the Val Monastero, eastern corner of the Grisons; the vast green expanses and lakes on the way up to the Passo di Resia and the source of the river Adige (in Val di Solda and Val di Trafoi you are in the Parco Nazionale dello Stelvio). All this is expected, given the location of the tour; perhaps more surprising is the art, especially the Carolingian paintings at Màlles and Müstair and the medieval frescoes at Tubre and Monte Maria.

The route. Beginning in Spondigna, in the Val Venosta, this route goes along a stretch of the road through the Stelvio Pass, and then winds up the Val di Solda as far as Solda. After returning to Gomagoi, keep driving up the challenging series of hairpin turns to the Passo dello Stelvio (2758 m). On the way down the Lombard slopes, you will go along the road that turns right onto Swiss territory, over the Col di S. Maria (2498 m), dropping down into the Val Monastero/Münstertal. This valley, which is a collateral to the Val Venosta, leads you back onto Italian soil just a little way before Tubre. Further along, past Glorenza, and at Sluderno, you will join up with the SS 40 road, which runs upstream along the river Adige. Just beyond Màlles Venosta, at Burgusio, there is a short detour (1.5 km) up to the Abbey of Monte Maria. Then, as you follow the SS 40 road, along the shores of the two manmade lakes of Muta and Resia, you reach Resia, not very far from the Austrian border, where this route finally comes to an end. As is the case with other roads leading through high mountain passes in the Alps, a trip along the Stelvio is really advisable only during the summer.

Places of interest. Solda/Sulden: resort famed for skiing and mountain climbing; take a cableway up to the Rifugio Città di Milano (2573 m), an Alpine hut with a fine view of the glaciers of the Ortles-Cevedale group. Trafoi: take a cableway up to the Rifugio Forcola (2153 m, an Alpine hut), with another view of the Ortles; from the town, walk (2 km) to the Santuario della Madonna delle Tre Fontane (1605 m), with many votive offerings. Passo dello Stelvio/Stilfser Joch (2758 m): the surrounding National Park extends into the Ortles-Cevedale group and along the Valtellina and Val Venosta; take a cableway up to the Nuovo Albergo Pirovano, and another up to the Rifugio Livrio (3174 m), an Alpine hut in a high mountain setting surrounded by glaciers. Müstair (Monastero), in the Val Monastero, Switzerland, descends from an abbey founded in Carolingian times, the Abbazia di S. Giovanni Battista: the museum and fine frescoes in the church are well worth a visit. Tubre/Taufers im Münstertal, on the Swiss border, has frescoes from the early 13th c. and others dating from 1370, in the church of S. Giovanni. Glorenza/Glurns*, enclosed by sober, intact 16th-c. walls. Sluderno/Schluderns: armory, art, and furnishings in the towering Castel Coira, 13th-16th c. Màlles Venosta/Mals im Vinschgau: the village is studded with towers, campaniles, and structures of great antiquity; note the exceedingly rare Carolingian frescoes in the little church of S. Benedetto. Abbazia di Monte Maria/Kloster Marienberg founded in the 13th c., a luminous white building with Gothic cloister dating back to the 16th c., set in the spruce forest on the mountainside, with 12th-c. frescoes in the crypt. Curòn Venosta/Graun in Vinschgau: the 14th-c. campanile of the old town rises from the waters of the manmade lake of Resia, which flooded the village in 1950; in the new church are altarpieces from the old one.

9 | Grande Strada delle Dolomiti

Bolzano - Passo di Costalunga - Vigo di Fassa - Canazei - Passo Pordoi
Passo di Falzàrego - Cortina d'Ampezzo (109 km)

The road here was built between 1895 and 1909, during the reign of the Austro-Hungarian emperor Francis Joseph; note the Belle-Epoque hotels along the road. Back then, people traveled these mountain roads in open coaches called "torpedoni"; as protection against the great clouds of white dust they wore dusters, helmets with earflaps, and goggles, cheerfully turning in every direction to see the spectacular Dolomites. This route has few rivals on earth, and is spectacular for the skyline and the steep climbs. Consider these vertical distances: 1745 m from Bolzano to the Passo di Costalunga, 904 m from the Val di Fassa to the Pordoi, 691 m from the Val Cordévole to the Passo di Falzàrego, for a total of 3074 m. The descents are considerable as well: from Pordoi to Arabba, 638 m in less than 10 km. And you can see, or take pictures of many peaks in the Dolomites along the road: the Catinaccio, Latemar, Sassolungo, Sella, Marmolada, Sorapiss, Antelao, Pelmo, Civetta, Nuvolau, Tofane, and Cristallo. If you take the cableway up to the Sass Pordoi (2950 m), the entire vast mountainscape lies before you, beneath the bright sky, as if in a geographic model, all the way to the Alps.

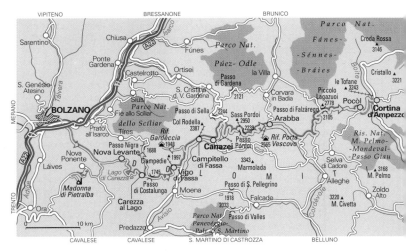

The route.

Just east of Bolzano you leave the road over the Brènnero, or Brenner Pas entering the gorge of the Val d'Ega and climbing up to the Passo di Costalu ga (1745 m). A first 18-km detour leads from Ponte Nova, via Rionero, to tl Santuario della Madonna di Pietralba. From the Passo di Costalunga you driv down into the Val di Fassa, through which the river Avisio flows, driving u this valley as far as Canazei, where a road runs 12 km up to the Lago di Fed ia, a lake at the base of the Marmolada. From Canazei you will make your wa up to the Passo Pordoi (2239 m), the highest pass on this road, the watershe between the basins of the Adige and Piave rivers. During the ensuing descer you cross the Livinallongo, the high course of the mountain stream Cordévol as far as Cernadoi, where you begin to climb up again, toward the thir Dolomite pass, the Falzàrego (2105 m). The final stretch of this route is dow hill, alongside the slopes of the Tofane, into the hollow of Cortina d'Ampezz

Places of interest.

Santuario della Madonna di Pietralba/Maria Weissenstein: a traditional p grimage site in the Alto Adige, this sanctuary dates back to the 17th c., and set among spruce trees and Alpine views. Nova Levante/Welschnofen: a ski r sort amidst the craggy Dolomites. Lago di Carezza/Karersee*: the bright blu water, with hints of cobalt, reflects the dense, dark stands of fir trees, whi slides of gravel, and ridges of the Latemar; this is the first "picture-perfect" se ting in the Dolomites along this route, heartbreakingly lovely. At the Passo N gra/Nigersattel (1690 m) between Carezza al Lago and the Passo di Costalu ga, a road runs off to the left, beneath the Catinaccio; the pass at the end the detour is 6 km away; on the way back there are fine views of the Latem Passo di Costalunga/Karerpass, 1745 m: this marks the boundary between A to Adige and Trentino. Vigo di Fassa is a mountain resort town, with winte sports; in the San Giovanni quarter, go see note the 15th-c. Gothic church San Giovanni, with fine frescoes; take the cableway up to the Ciampedìe mea ows (1997 m), with panoramic views of the Catinaccio, the Pale di S. Martin the Latemar, and the Marmolada group. Rifugio Gardeccia (1948 m), in th high valley of Vaiolét, with a view of the jagged rocks of Larsec; you can wal or take the summer minibus from Pozza di Fassa or from the fork in the roa between Pera di Fassa and Mazzin; continue on foot for an hour to reach th Rifugio Vaiolét (2243 m), an Alpine hut situated in the heart of the Catinacc beneath the celebrated Torri del Vaiolét. Campitello di Fassa, a renowned wir ter sports center; take the cableway up to the Col Rodella* (see Canazei) (238 m), an astonishing overlook with a far-reaching view of the Dolomite Canazei, a resort with skiing and mountain climbing; follow the high Valle de l'Avisio to the lake of Fedaia, and from there take a cableway up to the Ma molada glacier. Passo Pordoi (2239 m) is the highest point along the Grand Strada delle Dolomiti; this marks the shift of the watershed from the Adige the Piave; take a cableway up to the Sass Pordoi* (2950 m), where the 360-degree view is one of the most breathtaking in all the Dolomites. Arabba (see Pieve di Livinallongo), in the Val Cordévole, is the first location in the Cadore in the route; take a cableway up to the Porta Vescovo (2550 m), a balcony overlooking the icy slopes of the Marmolada. Passo di Falzàrego (2477 m): the Swiss stone pine dots the high meadows; take a cableway up to the Piccolo Lagazuoi (2746 m), with another panoramic view of the Dolomites. Pocòl: the nearby viewpoint offers a fine view of the fabulous hollow of Cortina d'Ampezzo; at sunset, before stretching shadows swallow them in darkness, the mountains glow in nuanced shades from pink to violet. Cortina d'Ampezzo**: set in a spectacular location, this world-renowned resort is justly famous.

20 | Val Gardena and the Circuit around the Sella

Bolzano - Siusi - Castelrotto - Ortisei - Passo di Sella - Passo Pordoi - La Villa San Cassiano - Corvara in Badia - Passo di Gardena (119 km)

The Sella group (3152 m) is a magnet for mountaineers, and its architecture is described in terms more typical of military architecture: bastions, curtain walls, towers... Straight and sheer, the mountain appears at the head of four valleys (Fassa, Gardena, Badia, Livinallongo). The color of the rock changes by the hour, as clouds hide the sun or reflections reverberate from the snow that drifts onto the "cenge," or high ledges, that dot the cliff face – this is the classic image of the Dolomites. It is ringed by roads that, from valley to valley, go over four famous passes: Pordoi, Campolongo, Gardena, and Sella; the "Giro del Sella," along these passes, is as classic a climb in the Dolomites as the Grande Strada (and coincides with that route, briefly, over the Pordoi Pass). In these passes, each year, you will see young men in colorful tops, pedalling furiously: on walls and bare rock you will see painted messages of encouragement. In the "magic ring" of the passes you begin with the Val Gardena, taking it from Bolzano along a route that soon leaves the Val d'Isarco and runs up to the Alpe di Siusi. When Montaigne passed through here, he had his secretary note: "Beyond the first mountains, we could see other, taller mountains, cultivated and inhabited, and we learned that still further up there were vast lovely meadowlands that provide wheat to the towns below..." Between the Passo di Campolongo and the Passo Gardena, the route wanders through meadows and forests, in the upper Val Badia and the Valle di S. Cassiano.

The route.

After leaving Bolzano and taking the SS road toward the Brenner via Bressanone, at Prato all'Isarco you turn off toward the Alpe di Siusi, along a road that runs through the towns of Fiè allo Sciliar/Völs am Schlern, Siusi, and Castelrotto; you will then drive down into the Val Gardena/Grödner Tal, to Ortisei or to Sankt Ulrich. The road then climbs up along the loveliest part of this

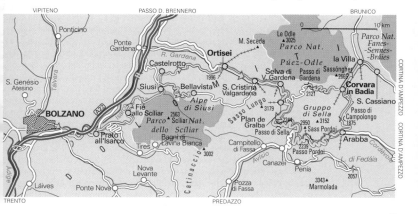

valley, then more steeply up to the Passo di Sella (2214 m), the first of the four Dolomite passes that ring the mountain group, or massif, of the Sella. On the drive down from the high pass, you will come to the fork leading off to the Passo Pordoi (2239 m), after which, at the highest elevation in the whole trip, you drop down into the Livinallongo, i.e., the high valley of the river Cordévole, at Arabba. From here, you return to the climb up over the Passo di Campolongo (1875 m) and enter the Val Badia; after you pass Corvara, you follow this valley as far as La Villa. At this point, you take the road up to the Passo di Valparola, which runs into the Valle di S. Cassiano, a valley that we recommend exploring as far as the town of San Cassiano (beginning in Corvara, this detour is 8 km long). After returning to Corvara in Badia, you begin the climb up to the last pass on this route, the Passo di Gardena (2121 m). At Plan de Gralba, there is a fork for either Selva di Val Gardena or the Passo di Sella and the Val di Fassa; this joins the last link to the first in this chain around the group of the Sella, which is called the "Sella Ronda," or Round Saddle, literally, in Ladin, the Rhaeto-Romanic dialect of the South Tyrol.

Places of interest. Siusi/Seis, a resort surrounded by pine forests; about 10 km to the east is the Alpe di Siusi/Seiser Alm*, rolling and serene. Castelrotto/Kastelruth is another highland resort. Ortisei/Sankt Ulrich*, a famed ski resort, is the capital of the Val Gardena; the Museo della Valle in Cësa di Ladins is noteworthy in terms of the history of local wood-carving. Plan de Gralba/Kreuzboden: a cableway runs up to the Rifugio Piz Sella (2240 m), below the Sassolungo, with a fine view of the upper Val Gardena, the Sella, and the Odle. Passo di Sella: a rather tortuous yet spectacular pass which links the Val Gardena and the Val di Fassa; it is certainly one of the most celebrated passes in the Dolomites. Passo Pordoi: in a harsh and grandiose setting, you cross the watershed between the Adige and Piave. Corvara in Badia/Corvara is a winter sports resort; in the Gothic parish church, note the 15th-c. frescoes. La Villa/Stern, another ski resort, lies in a broad hollow at the foot of the Sassongher. San Cassiano/Sankt Kassian is the chief town of the idyllic valley of S. Cassiano, which runs into the Val Badia. Passo di Gardena/Grödnerjoch: like the other high passes on the "Sella Ronda," it offers remarkable variations on the landscapes and panoramas of the Dolomites.

21 | Pale di San Martino and Val di Fiemme

Fiera di Primiero - San Martino di Castrozza - Passo di Vàlles - Falcade
Passo di S. Pellegrino - Moena - Cavalese (87 km)

The taste for exploring mountains, of course, is historically a fairly recent development. It is part and parcel of a mentality and attitude that date from the late 18th c., when the Enlightenment was in the throes of yielding to early Romanticism, the age in which men and women first began to climb mountains for pleasure and inspiration rather than personal profit. Of this route through the Dolomites, an ancient traveler would undoubtedly have noted the importance of the mines (long since abandoned) of Fiera di Primiero, the amount of fine wood to be cut in the spruce forest of Paneveggio, in the upper Val Travignolo, the hay in the Val di Fiemme, and the annual tribute that the high valleys paid to the bishop-prince in the plains below. Certainly, it is possible our ancient traveler might not even have mentioned the Pale; the Camaldolites, who made their way up to San Martino di Castrozza centuries ago, were interested only in finding solitude and something resembling a certain closeness to God. These historical "interferences" certainly add an extra dimension to this rapid mountain foray from the upper Cismon to the middle Avisio, two Tridentine valleys that are tributaries, respectively, of the Piave and the Adige, through the three passes of Rolle (1970 m), Vàlles (2033 m), and S. Pellegrino (1918 m). Nowadays, most people would seem to agree, however, that the objective and chief place of interest certainly remains the group of the Pale di S. Martino – the highest point being the Cima di Vezzana (3192 m),

while the sharp triangular pinnacle of the Cimon della Pala (3185 m) dominates the landscape of San Martino – with sheer unbroken walls, perpendicular bastions, deep fissures and crannies, and the broad hidden uplands, inconceivable when viewed from the valley below, entirely made of rock, blanketed in snow, pocked with pools of fresh water that springs from the rock, and with patches of glacier in the rough rolling surface. The alternatives among which you are forced choose, between the Passo di Rolle and the Passo di Vàlles, feature a descent into a forest of towering Norway spruce trees, as far as Paneveggio, and Alpine silence amidst the rock arena of the Pale, from the Baita Segantini (an Alpine hut).

The route.

From Fiera di Primiero you climb up through the Val Cismon to the hollow of San Martino di Castrozza and then on to the Passo di Rolle (1970 m). After descending for a certain distance through the Val Travignolo, you will take a right along the road over the Passo di Vàlles (2033 m). Between these two passes, however, there is an alternate route: just prior to reaching the Passo di Rolle you can take a right onto a secondary road that climbs up to the Baita Segantini, an Alpine hut, at the foot of the Cimon della Pala; you will then drive down into the Val Venegia; in time, you will reach the road through the Passo di Vàlles, mentioned above. From the Passo di Vàlles you can descend to Falcade, in the river basin of the Cordévole, and then go back up to the Passo di S. Pellegrino (1918 m), which opens into the Valle di S. Pellegrino, a tributary of the Val di Fiemme. And it is precisely through the Val di Fiemme that the last stretch of this route runs, down from Moena to Predazzo and Cavalese.

Places of interest.

Fiera di Primiero: resort, with skiing and mountain-climbing, once a mining town; in the Gothic church of S. Maria Assunta is the old altar of the miners. San Martino di Castrozza*: a famed mountain resort; take the chairlift up to the Col Verde (1965 m), then a cableway to the Cima Rosetta (2609 m), at the edge of the rock upland of the Pale di S. Martino. Paneveggio Forest: this is the largest forest in the Italian Alps; you pass through it on the route from the Passo di Rolle to the Passo di Vàlles. Falcade is a widespread town in the Valle del Biois; the first little community you reach, as you descend from the Passo di Vàlles*, just beyond the fork for the Passo di S. Pellegrino, is Falcade Alto, within sight of the Civetta. Passo di S. Pellegrino (1918 m), between the Valle del Biois and the Val di Fassa: take a cableway up to the Col Margherita (2511 m), fine view; just beyond the pass, a detour takes you through the larch forest to the lake of S. Pellegrino. Moena is a noted ski resort with the little ancient church of S. Volfango. Predazzo is another ski resort that has a museum of geology and paleontology. Tésero (see Cavalese), with frescoes on houses and churches; go see the frescoes on the little church of S. Rocco, including one that deplores working on Sunday. Cavalese is the chief town of the Valle di Fiemme: art collection in the Palazzo della Magnifica Comunità; medieval in origin, the Palazzo retains a marked 16th-c appearance; take a cableway up to the Alpe Cermìs (2000 m), in the Lagorai chain; fine view.

22 | Lake Misurina and Upper Pusterìa

Cortina d'Ampezzo - Passo Tre Croci - Lago di Misurina - Dobbiaco
Lago di Bràies - Lago di Anterselva - Brùnico (79 km)

A lake, a sheer rock face, idyllic nature, and a fearful challenge. Every mountain has a personality all its own; these are features of the Dolomites. A little, brilliant lake, a flat narrow lakeshore, fragrant with the aroma of spruce trees,

the gaze hemmed in by a round arena of ridges high above the treetops – an overall sense of tranquil serenity. When faced with a bare rock face, a climber coolly calculates the grip, the route, the ledges, the transits, balancing difficulty against strength (anyone else simply gazes in astonishment, admiration, and perhaps a little fear). Lakes and rock faces are the protagonists of a number of the episodes of this route through the inexhaustible Dolomites, which runs from Cortina d'Ampezzo to Brùnico, from the hollow of Cadore, in the shadows of the Tofane and the Cristallo to the broad, open, green Pusterìa, over the Passo Tre Croci and the Valle di Landro. Among the lakes of the Dolomites, it seems that the smaller they are, the greater their fame, aside from the really small ones – the lake of Landro, almost dry now; Dobbiaco, surrounded by a sparse woods; Anterselva/ Antholzersee, with green waters. A good example, however, is the Lake of Misurina, surrounded by such peaks as the Sorapiss, the Cadini, the Marmarole; another is the Lake of Bràies/Pragser Wildsee, reflecting the Croda del Becco in solitary splendor. As for the rock face, the Rifugio Auronzo, an Alpine hut, faces the Tre Cime di Lavaredo, one of the greatest challenges in climbing in the Dolomites: even if you are not about to climb it, with rope, pitons, and crampons, and are only gazing up from below, it is a daunting sight.

The route.

From Cortina d'Ampezzo, the road to the Passo Tre Croci (1805 m) leads into the upper Ansiei valley and to Misurina lake. A bit further along, note a detour onto a private toll road, which takes you 7.5 km to the Rifugio Auronzo, an Alpine hut (2320 m), at the base of the Tre Cime di Lavaredo. On your way back from this side-trip, you will enter Alto Adige; following the SS 51 road through the Val di Landro, you will descend to the hollow of Dobbiaco, in Pusterìa. The second part of the route follows this mountain valley, with the course of the Rienza River. Still, the route splits off from the river twice; once, after Villabassa, up to the lake of Bràies, and once, about 6 km past Monguelfo, to detour into the side valley of Anterselva, toward the Alpine watershed, all the way up to the lake of Anterselva (17.5 km). The route then continues into Pusterìa, ending at Brùnico.

Places of interest.

Rifugio Lorenzi (2948 m): from the road to the Passo Tre Croci via the Cristallo chairlift at Som Forca (2230 m), then take a long-distance cableway to the Forcella Staunies (2989 m); the Alpine hut is nearby; spectacular view of the Dolomites and the Alps. Lago di Misurina*, 1745 m: the peaks surrounding the hollow in which the lake lies form one of the classic settings in the Dolomites; a walk around the lake takes 40 minutes. Rifugio Auronzo (2320 m): it is surrounded by the legendary, mighty Tre Cime di Lavaredo; you can proceed to the Rifugio Lavaredo and then, on foot, to the Forcella Lavaredo (45 minutes), with a notable view of the Tre Cime. Lago di Landro/Dürrensee (1403 m); just beyond, on the right, a view of the Tre Cime di Lavaredo. Dobbiaco/Toblach: the ancient center of this renowned mountain resort has a strong flavor of the Alto Adige; note the Baroque parish church and the castle. Lago di Bràies/Pragserwildsee* (1493 m): this is another of the motionless lakes of the Dolomites; it reflects the dark green fir trees and luminous rocks of the Croda del Becco and the Sasso del Signore; in one hour you can walk around it. Lago di Anterselva/Antholzersee (1642 m): the dark green waters of this lake, surrounded by woods, is the destination of the detour from Valdàora to the Alpine watershed, along the tranquil valley of Anterselva, with a fine view of the Vedrette di Ries. Brùnico/Bruneck: an old road, typical of the Alto-Adige, lies at the heart of the little town; the 13th-c. castle and the nearby war cemetery are noteworthy; in the quarter of Teodone/Dietenheim, visit the Museo degli Usi e Costumi della Provincia Bolzanina, focusing on local folkways.

23 | The Highlands of Trentino and Asiago

**Rovereto - Folgarìa - Serrada - Tonezza del Cimone - Arsiero - Caltrano
Asiago - Passo di Vézzena - Lavarone - Trent (158 km)**

A little museum in Roana, in Val d'Assa, just a few km from Asiago, on the highland of the Sette Comuni, is devoted to "Cimbrian traditions." The Cimbrians, as you may remember from your schooldays, were a tribe swept away by complex migratory patterns in the ancient world. They lived in what is now Schleswig, between the Baltic and the North Sea; they moved with the neighboring Teutons of Holstein into Gaul, and then broke off, in an attempt to settle in the Alps. They entered Italy over the Norico pass, defeating the Romans in the Valle dell'Adige, and then pouring into ancient "Venetia," until Marius defeated them at "Campi Raudii," near *Vercellae* (Vercelli), in 102 B.C. Northern tribes did settle on the highland of the Sette Comuni and other nearby highlands (M.R. Stern speaks of "strange and ancient languages"), but only the scholars of the Renaissance truly thought they were the Cimbri; in fact, Germans colonized this area in the high Middle Ages. In this mountain region, between the Adige, the plains, and the large oxbow curve of the Brenta as it runs through the Valsugana, the highlands of Folgarìa, Tonezza, Sette Comuni, and Lavarone, to name them in the order of this itinerary, wandering from Veneto to Trentino. All share the same lovely landscape, with rolling pasturage, immense forests, high terraces, hills, dales, silhouettes of nearby mountains, spruce trees and beech groves, dizzying views from the ridges overlooking broad valleys, and the clear signs of centuries of back-breaking labor (before resorts and ski slopes came into being). Then came WWI, and the violence here was unthinkable: Austrian offensives were met by Italian counterattacks; ancient Asiago was wiped away, and shells and bombs were so scattered through the valleys that some mountain folk made a precarious, risky living for decades, picking them up carefully and selling them to other people to be utilized as scrap metal.

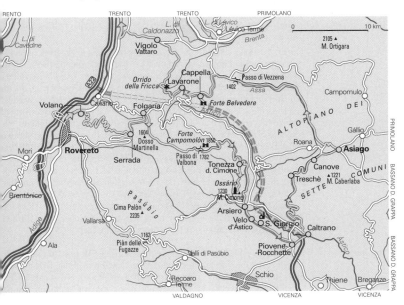

The route.   Climbing from Rovereto through the Val Lagarina toward Trento, you wi
soon leave the SS 12 road, at Calliano, and turn onto the SS 350 road, whic
runs up to the upland of Folgarìa, where a 5-km detour will take you to Serr
da. From Folgarìa you will be following a route through the mountains, alon
secondary roads; after you cross the Passo della Vena (1546 m), you will d
scend to the upland of Tonezza del Cimone (side trip to the Ossuary on th
peak of Monte Cimone) and to the Val d'Àstico, a valley over Vicenza. In th
Val d'Àstico you will pass through Arsiero, Velo d'Àstico, Piovene and, on th
opposite slope, Caltrano. From here, you will be driving uphill again, reachin
the upland of the Sette Comuni and Asiago. From Asiago, the SS 349 roa
along the mountain river Assa, runs up to the Passo di Vézzena (1402 m), an
then on to the upland of Lavarone. To the west, at the crossroads of Ca
bonare, you will be taking the road toward the high Fricca Pass, which ove
looks the Valsugana and then continues, via Vìgolo Vattaro, on to Trento.

Places of interest.   Rovereto: the city, typically Tridentine, with patches of Venetian flavor,
dominated by the great castle erected by the Castelbarco family in the 14t
c., which houses the Museo Storico Italiano della Guerra, or war history m
seum; another museum boasts works by the Futurist Fortunato Depero, wh
was born here. Volano: this village has the small church of S. Rocco, with fre
coes by local, 15th-c. artists. Serrada; take a long-distance cableway to th
Dosso della Martinella (1604 m), with a fine view of the lower Trentino and P
subio. Tonezza del Cimone, winter sport resort; detour of 4.5 km to the Pia
zale degli Alpini (1109 m), then a 15-min. walk takes you to the Ossario (O
suary) atop Monte Cimone (1230 m). Velo d'Àstico: in the village of San Gio
gio, a Romanesque-Gothic parish church with 12th-c. frescoes. Asiago, cent
of the uplands of the Sette Comuni, resort town; you can tour the astr
physics observatory; a 360-degree view of the upland can be had by takin
the chairlift up to Monte Caberlaba (1221 m). Forte Belvedere, an inta
stronghold of the Austrian defenses during WWI (known in Italy as "The Wa
of 1915-18"); to get there, you take a walk from the village of Cappella, on th
Lavarone upland. Orrido della Fricca*: this gorge offers a spectacular view
jagged rocks, worn by water, along the route, after Carbonare.

24 | Colli Euganei

**Padua - Teòlo - Montagnana - Este - Monsélice - Arquà Petrarca - Battaglia Terme
Valsanzibio - Àbano Terme (118 km)**

The Euganei hills rise up from the flat Venetian plain in the form of regula
green cones; the Monte Venda (601 m) is the tallest among them. On th
southern slopes there are many Mediterranean details; elsewhere, you wi
be able to find a wide variety of trees such as chestnut, hornbeam, manna
ash, and durmast; here and there you will come across orchards and veg
etable gardens, vineyards and olive groves. The region had volcanic origins
History has scattered the landscape with jewels: 12th-c. hermitages cun
ningly arranged with spectacular views, medieval castles, villas, gardens
and parks of the Venetian nobility. The waters here have curative propertie
as the Romans already knew many centuries beforehand; over time, it wa
forgotten, but by the 13th c., the city of Padua was passing new laws reg
lating the use of these waters. The route begins just entering the norther
foothills, up to Teòlo, then it runs west and south around them, passin
through the historic cities of the Paduan area – Montagnana, Este, Monsélic
– and returns to the starting point, entering the famous locations of the high
lands: Arquà, Valsanzibio, the hermitages of Monte Rua.

The route.   Beginning in Padua, you will take a road heading SW, past the turnoff fo
Àbano Terme, and up into the Colli Euganei and on to Teòlo. Driving dow
from the hills onto the plains, you will then continue through Vò an
Agugliaro, to Noventa Vicentina; from here, you will continue throug

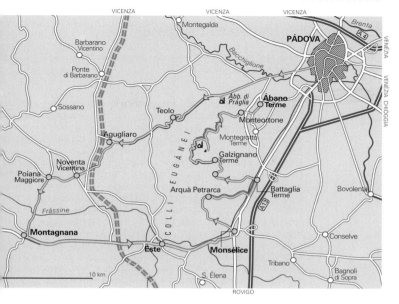

Poiana Maggiore and on to Montagnana. Turning east here, on the SS 10 road, you pass first through Este and then Monsélice. From there, following secondary roads, you drive back up into the Colli Euganei to see Arquà Petrarca. Once you are back in the lowlands, you will drive for a short stretch along the state road Monsélice-Padova, as far as Battaglia Terme. At this point, you will take one last drive through the hills, up through Valsanzibio and Galzignano Terme, to the Hermitage of Monte Rua. On your way down from here, you will pass through Torreglia and Monteortone, ending the route at Àbano Terme.

Places of interest. Abbazia di Praglia**: a boulevard lined with plane trees leads to the solemn Benedictine monastery founded in the 12th c. and almost totally re-built in the 15th-16th c., with a church and four cloisters. Teòlo is believed to be the birthplace of the Roman historian Livy; fine view from the 13th-c. parish church of S. Giustina at the highest point in town; from the square in front of the church, a road enters the Parco Lieta Carraresi, a nature reserve with excellent scenery and views. Noventa Vicentina: Villa Barbarigo, at the center of a small town that grew up around it, is now the town hall; in the parish church is a canvas by Tiepolo. Poiana Maggiore: of the three villas that belonged to the Pojana family, one was designed and built by A. Palladio. Montagnana*: girt with intact medieval walls, among the finest in Europe; in the Duomo are good paintings, one by Veronese; Palazzo Pisani, just outside town, was built by Palladio. Este*: still intact are the walls of the Castello Carrarese around the holiday home of the Mocenigo family (visit the museum on Venetia prior to the Romans); canvas by Tiepolo, among others, in the Duomo. Monsélice*: along the walk on this hill are the Castello, the Duomo Vecchio, the Santuario delle Sette Chiese, the Villa Duodo, and fascinating views of the plains. Arquà Petrarca: here the great 14th-c. poet Petrarch lived in his old age and died; his tomb is in the church courtyard. Battaglia Terme: Stendhal frequented this spa; around it are the Villa Selvatico Capodilista high on the Colle di S. Elena and, along the road to Padua, the Villa Cataio. Valsanzibio (see Arquà Petrarca), with the Italian-style garden of the Villa Barbarigo. Eremo di Rua: this hermitage is inhabited by Camaldolite monks, who live in cloistered seclusion; the setting is green and silent, the view extends to the hills, the plain, the Alps, and Venice. Monteortone*: this 15th-c. sanctuary is supposedly the site of a miracle. Àbano Terme*: the large Venetian "ville d'eaux" is typical of the turn of the 20th c.

51

25 | Brenta Plain and Marca Trevigiana

Padua - Stra - Mira - Mestre - Treviso - Castelfranco Veneto - Cittadella
Piazzola sul Brenta - Vicenza (130 km)

"Beyond the handsome fields that extended on either side, we would pass through merry little villages, and at every hour we saw noble houses, many of them quite splendid, belonging to the powerful of Venice, who come to spend the summer and part of the fall here...." This is the Riviera del Brenta, the first part of this route that Spanish traveler Leandro Fernandez de Moratin described in his "El Viaje de Italia," 1793-96. Even if you leave aside the cities, with their universal culture of art, architectural style, and atmosphere – Padua, Vicenza and Treviso are exquisite – a great deal can be learned from the Venetian countryside: from the fragments of combative medieval culture and the 16th-/18th-c. "villa culture" – the nobility was moving inland, farming, living in the pleasant countryside, studying, socializing, or simply whiling away the newly civilized rustic day. This route links the two eras: the former can be found in the Castello di Castelfranco Veneto and the menacing walls of Cittadella, the latter along the Riviera del Brenta and on the Terraglio (the road from Mestre and Treviso), in Villa Foscari alla Malcontenta, Villa Emo a Fanzolo, or Villa Contarini a Piazzola. As Andrea Palladio put it: "The true gentleman will draw great benefit and consolation from the country home..."; today those gifts can be had by the unassuming tourist as well.

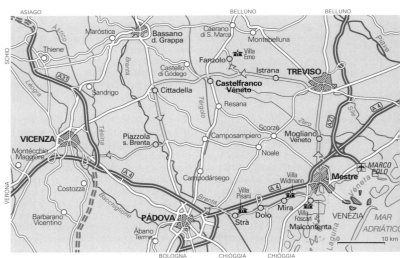

The route.

Starting out from Padua, Stra marks the point at which, on the SS 11 road, you reach the Riviera del Brenta, following it as far as Villa Foscari, the Malcontenta. A stretch of the SS 309 road toward Mestre will take you to the Padua-Trieste Autostrada; a quick jog along this highway ring-road, around Mestre, will avoid the crowded trek through the city of Mestre. You leave the Autostrada at the Mestre Est exit, on line with the SS 13 road, known as the Terraglio, which you will follow to Treviso. You then continue west along the SS 53 Treviso-Vicenza road as far as Castelfranco Veneto and Cittadella, except for the detour to Villa Emo (5 km from Vedelago). At Cittadella you will take the SS 47 road to Padua, following it until you reach the turnoff for Piazzola sul Brenta. Lastly, head for Vicenza, via Piazzola sul Brenta, Camisano Vicentino, and Torri di Quartesolo.

Places of interest.

Stra: Villa Pisani, with its palatial interiors, fresco by Tiepolo, park, and labyrinth, is the sumptuous introduction to this trip along the Riviera del

Brenta. Dolo, main centre of the Riviera in the 18th c.: near the surviving fragments of the 16th-c. locks, note the old plaque with inscribed boat tolls. Mira: go see Villa Widmann, a fine piece of Venetian rococo dating back to 1719. Malcontenta is the name of the place, as well as of the Villa Foscari, both built by Palladio, at the end of the Riviera del Brenta, near the lagoon. Treviso* is an alluring city with fine art and architecture; here the setting counts as much as monuments, canvases, and collections. Istrana (see Treviso) boasts the 18th-c. Villa Lattes with noteworthy artwork. Villa Emo di Fanzolo (see Castelfranco Veneto): you will pass through Vedelago to reach this Palladian villa. Castelfranco Veneto: this dignified little Venetian town is the birthplace of Giorgione; you can tour his home and, in the Duomo, can admire a celebrated altarpiece of his. Cittadella still has its elliptical ring of walls intact. Piazzola sul Brenta: visit the spectacular Villa Contarini and its vast grounds.

26 | Monte Grappa, Asolo Hills, and Strada del Vino Bianco

**Maròstica - Bassano del Grappa - Monte Grappa - Possagno - Asolo - Masèr
Valdobbiàdene - San Pietro di Feletto - Conegliano (132 km)**

It is difficult to weigh the places you will see along this tour, where the Veneto rises up into hill country: Asolo della Regina; the creation of Paolo Veronese and Andrea Palladio in Villa Barbaro at Masèr; Possagno, where the birthplace of Antonio Canova and the museum of his remarkable sculpture

give you a sense of his creative process; the lovely medieval atmosphere of Maròstica; or the river Brenta rushing past the piers of the covered wooden bridge of Bassano. Asolo is certainly the most renowned. Caterina Cornaro, queen of Cyprus, held court here after her abdication in 1489, with twelve handmaidens, eighty servants, a dwarf named Zavir, and as guests, her cousin the Venetian scholar and prelate Pietro Bembo – who as a young man courted Lucrezia Borgia, and at 69 was made cardinal by Pope Paul III – and the three ladies and gentlemen who for three days discussed love in Bembo's "Asolani." In truth, Asolo is one of those places that fame, descriptions, and visitors are unable to wear out: there is always a detail, a color, a lingering summer sunset over a valley in which lights twinkle on one after another in 16th-c. villas, the shiver of the unexpected. And yet it may be bested, in the final analysis, by the hillside villages with taverns and trattorias, with tables set out of doors under the spreading branches of the plane trees, along the Strada del Vino Bianco, or Road of White Wine, toward Conegliano – the specific places to stop are up to the driver, his mood, and the temptation of Cartizze, a fine Venetian white wine. In the end, it is the landscape as a whole, the intertwining confusion and the mingling of art and nature, its flow, varied and constant, rustic and refined, or, to quote a verse by Pietro Bembo, with "... the aroma from far away, the cool air, and the hour / of the green fields..."

The route.

From Maròstica, the starting point of this route, less than 30 km north of Vicenza, you will soon reach Bassano del Grappa. You then drive up to Monte Grappa (1775 m) along the "Strada Cadorna," or SS 141 road, and then you go down along the "Strada Giardino," through Campo Croce and Semonzo. The road running along at the base of the hills, which you will join soon thereafter, goes to Possagno. Take another secondary road to Asolo. After going down from the hill of Asolo, at the crossroads of Casella you continue NE along the route via Masèr, Cornuda, Ponte sul Piave di Vidòr, and Valdobbiàdene; from the last-mentioned, you can take a 12-km detour along a scenic road up to Pianezze (1095 m). After you return to Valdobbiàdene you can take the Strada del Vino Bianco (Road of White Wine; marked as such), which runs through a countryside of hilltop vineyards, through Soligo, Solighetto, Refrontole, and San Pietro di Feletto, ending at Conegliano.

Places of interest. Maròstica: the fortified "borgo," with two castles, and walls running up the hill, offers a rare, dreamy image of the Middle Ages. Bassano del Grappa*: in this compact old city, with fascinating architecture, you can admire the renowned wooden covered bridge which was built to plans drawn up by Andrea Palladio in 1569; the town holds other attractions as well. Cima Grappa* (1775 m) is a site of broad vistas and grim memories of the months of 1917-18, the end of WWI, when the mountain was a bitterly defended anchor of the Italian line. Possagno is the birthplace of the 18th-c. sculptor Antonio Canova; go see his home and the Neo-Classic Temple that he built, and in which he is buried. Asolo*: landscape, architecture, and the legacy of illustrious visitors all form part of the charm of this intact old town. Masèr: Andrea Palladio built a villa here for the Barbaro brothers; it is considered one of the Renaissance architect's finest works, and is frescoed by Paolo Veronese. Pianezze: go through Valdobbiàdene to get up here; take a chairlift to the crest of Monte Barbaria (1464 m), with a panoramic vista. Solighetto: in the 18th-c. Villa Brandolin there is a small museum devoted to the great soprano, Toti Dal Monte. San Pietro di Feletto: note the millennium-old parish church of S. Pietro, on a hill with a view. Conegliano: the old, high part of town is distinctly Venetian; Cima da Conegliano lived here, and there is an altarpiece by him in the Duomo.

27 | The Friùli-Venezia Giulia Coastline

Portogruaro - Cervignano del Friùli - Palmanova - Grado - Monfalcone Trieste (131 km)

"Joyous view, cheerful, and lovely appearance / Such is the sea when, tranquil and calm / It murmurs, whitening, up to the shore." These words are from Torquato Tasso's "Il Mondo Creato." The "lieta vista" appears roughly midway through the route and especially in the last stretch, along the luminous shore of the Gulf of Trieste. The route, which goes from Portogruaro along the littoral, may seem distant from the sea (in atmosphere, culture, and history, if not in actual miles), when it passes through the vineyards and intensive farming of the Friulian plain or past the grassy bastions of the Venetian citadel of Palmanova. In reality, the ties to the sea are close and fertile: observe the landscape of the lagoon of Grado – silent motionless sheets of water, reflecting the flight of aquatic birds and a fringe of pinasters on the horizon – and the all-encompassing relationship between sea, people, and history. Beginning with Portogruaro itself, an ancient market town, greeting

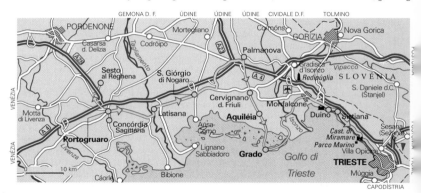

boats and goods; then Aquileia, where the cypress adorns the ruins of the Roman city, another fine river harbor; not to mention cosmopolitan Trieste.

The route.

The starting point is Portogruaro in the province of Venice; from here, we would recommend two interesting excursions: the first, 2 km to the south, is to Concordia Sagittaria; the second, 10 km to the north, leads to Sesto al Règhena, where you can tour the abbey of S. Maria in Sylvis. From Portogruaro you can then take the SS 14 road to Venezia Giulia and Trieste, as far as Cervignano del Friùli. Here you turn onto the SS 352 road, for a northward detour, as far as Palmanova. On your way back, you continue past Cervignano, still on the SS 352 road, toward Aquileia and, across the lagoon, to Grado. Following this road across the island of Grado and through the reclaimed land on either side of the mouth of the river Isonzo, you will reach Monfalcone. Last comes Trieste, along the SS 14 road, which here hugs the coast of the Gulf of Trieste.

Places of interest.

Portogruaro, a small town on the river Lemene, with a marked 15th-/16th-c. Venetian influence, is largely intact; at Concordia Sagittaria, go see the solitary ruins of the late-Roman/high-medieval settlement (cathedral, baptistery, excavations); at Sesto al Règhena is the Romanesque-Byzantine abbey of S. Maria in Sylvis, with frescoes dating from the 12th-13th c. above the entrance and in the vestibule. Latisana: in the Duomo of this little town on the river Tagliamento is an altarpiece by P. Veronese. Palmanova, with a radial plan, is a star-shaped fortress with bastions, ramparts, and embankments, truly a city-cum-citadel; the Venetians built it (1593) to protect their open eastern frontier; take an 8-km detour from Cervignano del Friùli. Aquileia*: Roman ruins, museums, and the basilica with its Early Christian mosaics are all eloquent commemorations of the centuries of late antiquity and the High Middle Ages when this was a prosperous and powerful center of a vast region. Grado*, with its medieval center of narrow lanes and "campielli" and its Early Christian churches. San Giovanni di Duino, with the Bocche del Timavo, where the waters of this river return to the light of day, after their long passage underneath the Carso, or Karst. Duino: in this former fishing village are two castles of local siegneurs, with the legend of the ill-fated Dama Bianca, who was turned to stone; also, literary history tells us that Dante Alighieri spent much time pondering, seated on the rocks overlooking the sea, and that Rainer Maria Rilke took inspiration here for his "Duino Elegies." Sistiana: beach resort, in a small rocky inlet, surrounded by woods. Castello di Miramare: this castle stands between the waters of the Gulf of Trieste and the dark holm-oaks, fir trees, and cypresses inland, a Romantic and princely Hapsburg residence.

28 | The Strada Romea

Ravenna - Comacchio - Abbazia di Pomposa - Mésola - Chioggia - Mestre (158 km)

The SS 309 road, or Strada Romea, between Mestre and Ravenna follows one of the routes used by "Romei," or pilgrims headed for Rome. Our route is not haunted by these phantoms, however; rather it wanders among images of reclaimed farmland and untouched wetlands. In the late 17th c., one traveler was moved by the fertility of the newly drained Ravenna territory, "once so sterile and waterlogged" (Misson); modern sensibilities are different, and the terms "marsh" or "wetlands" have lost their negative connotations. There are rivers (Reno, Po, Adige, Brenta) and branches of the sea as well, and everywhere signs of the impetuous modifications made by man: dry land where water once was. The changes in the littoral can be seen on the map: Ravenna once sat between lagoons and the harbor of the Roman fleet; where ships once rode at anchor, fields now sprout green. In Etruscan times, for instance, the waves of the Adriatic broke against sandy dunes at a point midway between Pomposa and Codigoro (now Taglio di Po). Today, the light-

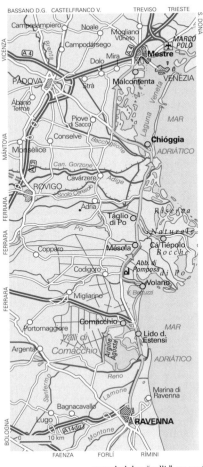

house of Bocca del Po di Pila is 25 km eastward, while the estuaries of Comacchio stretched some 20 km inland. The Valli di Comacchio and the Po Delta are joined, of course, by the Laguna Veneta, or Venetian Lagoon, another realm of water and land, "nature" preserved by the wisdom of the Serenissima, a world of colors that change with the sky. The architecture of Comacchio, Pomposa, Mésola, Chioggia, or La Malcontenta is all worth seeing, whether monumental or minute, all part of the landscape in which it is immersed.

The route. Head north out of Ravenna along the SS 309 road, or Strada Romea, which passes through the pine forest of S. Vitale. At Porto Garibaldi you will turn left, heading inland, for a tour of Comacchio; from here, an 18-km detour along the road to Alfonsine goes over the embankment, or Argine Agosta. Then you will head back toward the coast, and back onto the Strada Romea for a short stretch; then, at the turnoff for San Giuseppe, you will follow secondary roads, to Borgo Manara, Valle Bertuzzi, Lido di Volano, Volano, and then to the Abbey of Pomposa. Here, you are back on the Strada Romea, heading north, leaving it only for two short detours: the first leads to the nature reserve of the Gran Bosco della Mésola (from a crossroads 7 km from Pomposa); the second runs to Ca' Tiepolo from Taglio di Po, with a 12-km drive along the course of the Po di Venezia. After touring Chioggia, get back onto the Strada Romea, including the stretch that runs around the Venetian Lagoon, as far as Mestre.

Places of interest. Comacchio was once surrounded by "valli," or water barriers, and has now been thoroughly reclaimed, crisscrossed by canals, unassuming yet charming; the remarkable landscape can be seen by following the embankment, or Argine Agosta, along the road to Alfonsine. Volano is a village on the banks of the Po di Volano, a branch of the Po, whose delta is a nature reserve. Abbazia di Pomposa**: the bell tower dates from the year 1000; it rears up to mark the site of the abbey, solitary on the vast plain, a notable achievement of Romanesque architecture and art; don't miss the precious series of frescoes in the refectory of the monastery. Riserva Naturale Bosco della Mésola, a nature reserve, was once part of a vast Este hunting park; you can tour it now only on foot or by bicycle. Mésola is a 16th-c. Este hunting lodge. Ca' Tiepolo: on the island of the Donzella, this is the seat of the township of Porto Tolle; you get there by following the Po di Venezia, a branch of the Po, with privileged views of the endless universe of nuances of water textures of the Po Delta. Chioggia* is a town wedged into the southern edge of the Laguna Veneta, or Venetian Lagoon, with the houses, "calli," or lanes, canals, colors, and sounds of a working-class Venice, as Carlo Goldoni must have known it in the 18th c. La Malcontenta or Villa Foscari, built around 1555 for the Foscari brothers by Andrea Palladio, lies just a few hundred meters from the Strada Romea (right at the fork for Fusina). Mestre: Piazza Ferretto, the Duomo, the Torre dell'Orologio, and a few other fragments of ancient architecture show that this town is more than just a manufacturing outpost of Venice and a bedroom community for those who have moved away from the Serenissima.

29 | Eastern Romagna

**Rìmini - Santarcàngelo di Romagna - San Leo - San Marino - Montefiore Conca
Saludecio - San Giovanni in Marignano - Cattolica (128 km)**

The remarkable Sigismondo Malatesta, an accomplished soldier and ruler of
Rìmini, summoned Leon Battista Alberti to transform a Gothic church into a
classical "temple," a mausoleum for himself and his third wife, Isotta degli Atti ("O lovely sweet light, proud soul," as he described her in his poetry; but he
murdered his previous two wives, poisoning one, strangling the other); we see
him depicted by Piero della Francesca, kneeling between two greyhounds.
This route passes almost entirely through lands of his family, in a distant corner of Romagna, bordering the Marche, here and there venturing into that region (Valle della Marecchia, and then up into the lovely green hills of the Valle
del Conca). Amidst the lands and forts of the Malatesta family, however, the
route passes through two other major landmarks. One is San Leo, high overlooking a tributary of the Marecchia; Federico da Montefeltro ordered the fort
built by F. di Giorgio Martini in the 15th c. The other is San Marino, with its
rocky ridge of Monte Titano, crowned with fortifications. Why this little medieval town, no different from many others, should have survived as a sovereign state, is a strange twist of history.

The route.

You leave Rìmini along the SS 9 road, a part of the Via Emilia, and arrive fairly quickly at Santarcàngelo di Romagna; you will then continue south along
the road that hugs the north bank of the Marecchia; at Ponte Verucchio you
cross the river; then drive up to Verucchio (296 m). After that little side trip,
take the SS 258 road toward Novafeltria, turning off at the fork, just after
Pietracuta, where the scenic route leads up to the peak upon which San Leo
is nestled (583 m). Returning along the same route for a stretch, after Pietracuta, take the road that runs via Torello up to San Marino (381 m). Drive back

down from San Marino, leaving this diminu-
tive republic, heading south; you will reach
the valley floor at Mercatino Conca. Now,
staying on secondary roads, follow the
course of the Conca River toward the sea;
then you will come to the fork where a road
splits off toward the hills along the valley's
southern slopes, leading to Montefiore Conca
(385 m). Passing through San Felice, you return along a lengthy stretch of panoramic
road, down toward the Conca Valley floor,
reaching it at Morciano di Romagna. A last
climb takes you up through more hill country
to Saludecio. The return to the coast follows
another scenic route, at first, via Santa Maria
del Monte, and via San Giovanni in Marignano. The route comes to an end at Cattolica.

Places of interest.

Rìmini* is a city of manifold attractions, of which the beach is only the best
known. Santarcàngelo di Romagna: this little farming town has an old section,
perched on a hill, with twisting streets; the fortress dates from the 15th c.; the
"grottoes" are remarkable underground warehouses whose remote origins are
subject to debate; and there is a museum devoted to the folkways of Romagna.
Verucchio: the hills that form bookends for the "borgo" were once topped by
menacing forts, of which one survives; the Museo Archeologico is notable for
its collections of artifacts from the Villanovan culture, centered here in the early Iron Age. San Leo*: this town is inaccessible, or practically so, on its limestone crag; the rustic parish church and the Duomo are Romanesque, while
the renowned fort has the severe 15th-c. perspective and volume given it by F.
di Giorgio Martini; after Rìmini, this is the artistic focus of the route. San Mari-

no*: leave the capital town of the tiny republic, a lofty village straddling the crown of the Monte Titano, and follow the ridge for a pleasant stroll to the Guaita, the Cesta, and the Montale, three impressive towers. Montefiore Conca surveys the valley from atop a hill, with a ring of walls enclosing the old section, in the shadow of a 14th-c. fortress built by the Malatesta (with detached frescoes of figures from the past, and battles). Saludecio is a medieval hamlet enclosed by walls and tapering in plan along the hill road, with terracotta buildings; note the Neo-Classic parish church of S. Biagio. San Giovanni in Marignano: you can still see the 14th-c. layout; in the Biblioteca are archeological finds from imperial Rome. Cattolica is a fishing town and a beach resort; the old part sits on a terrace, 1 km inland, on what was the shoreline.

30 | The Hill Country between Parma and Reggio

Parma - Sala Baganza - Torrechiara - Traversétolo - Ciano d'Enza - Canossa
Quattro Castella - Reggio nell'Emilia (87 km)

The Via Emilia is a single straight road, centuries old, linking Parma and Reggio nell'Emilia (cities located in different states until 1859). The land this road runs through is relatively homogeneous, in terms of dialect, accent, and cordial hospitality. Outside of the cities – with their many relics of long and illustrious histories, with perfect settings and remarkable monuments – everything is farmland, the pride of the plains of northern Italy. The broad sweeping landscape is sealed off to the south, however, by broad rolling verdant hills, climbing up to the Apennines, flanking the long river valleys. This route passes among these hills. The scenery varies widely; it rolls by peacefully, at times solitary and even harsh, invariably abounding in harmonies of color, ranging from tender greens and electric greens in the springtime, sere burnt yellows in the full heat of summer, under a dizzying blue sky, or the majestic array of autumn, with the red and antique-gold leaves of chestnut trees withering, preparing for winter. This place is overflowing with history, which tangles and catches at the castle towers, just as valley-bound fog wraiths and snags at the wizened branches of brier bushes and leafless trees on winter mornings. There are stout castles: Torrechiara, Rocca dei Rossi, Montechiarùgolo dei Sanvitale, Rossena, Canossa (stronghold of the powerful countess of Tuscany, Matilda, the "gran contessa"), a castle built a thousand years earlier by a certain Azzo of Longobard descent. Quattro Castella owes its name to four fortresses that once surrounded it, overlooking the forests beneath from atop four different peaks: Monte Vetro, Monte Bianello, Monte Lucio, and Monte Zane (one survives; the three others lie in ruins). Many local place names seem like a list from the counter of an Italian delicatessen: Felino, synonymous with exquisite salami; Langhirano (on the river Parma, which is slightly neglected in this route) is known for the excellence of its prosciutto, rivalled perhaps only by that of Parma. Mentioning them, however, may help to transport all these castles and the ruins and memories of such castles out of their romantic haze, and present them as genuine military instruments, designed to rule – and defend – this land, made fruitful by backbreaking labor.

The route.

When you leave Parma, head SW along the SS 62 road via Fornovo di Taro, Berceto, and the Passo della Cisa, leaving that road just prior to reaching Collecchio (8 km), at the turnoff for Sala Baganza; stay on this route, along secondary roads, through Sala Baganza, Felino, Pilastro, and Torrechiara. You will return to the crossroads of Pilastro after touring Torrechiara, and from there continue eastward, crossing the Parma River, and then the Enza River, just past Traversétolo, where a 7.5-km detour north leads you to Montechiarùgolo. Before you enter San Polo d'Enza you will cross the SS 513 road, where you will turn right toward Ciano d'Enza. From here, you stay on the scenic route through the hills, on to the castles of Rossena and Canossa; then, via the church of Grassano, you will return to San Polo d'Enza. In the last part of this route, heading toward Reggio nell'Emilia, the scenic road runs via San Polo d'Enza, Quattro Castella, and Scandiano, at the base of the hills and the edge of the plains; you will turn into the plains when you reach the turnoff for SS 63 road, which will take you into Reggio nell'Emilia.

Places of interest. S. Biagio di Talignano is a Romanesque parish church which can be reached from Sala Baganza along a detour of 3 km through the Parco Regionale dei Boschi di Carrega, a regional park. Castello di Torrechiara* is a 15th-c. castle, one of the largest and best preserved in the region; make sure to see the renowned Camera d'Oro, or Room of Gold, with its rare fresco cycle dealing with profane subjects, attributed to Benedetto Bembo (1463). Villa Magnani is located in Corte di Traversétolo, and boasts a notable collection of paintings. From Traversétolo, you will then continue on to Montechiarùgolo with its Rocca, or fortress, with notable frescoes in the interior. Castello di Rossena is a 13th-c. fortress perched on a high crag, with fine views. Castello di Canossa stands on a white rock base in a barren panorama of badlands: note its remarkable history, the view, the ruins, and a small museum. Quattro Castella: these four fortresses were an outpost of Canossa, though only the Bianello survives (privately owned); in town, there is a 16th-c. palazzo and a parish church of Romanesque origin.

31 | Through Verdi's Homeland and along the Po River

Fidenza - Fontanellato - Soragna - Busseto - Roccabianca - Colorno - Parma (97 km)

Perhaps the true sites of Verdi's past are the boards and the backdrops of the stages, the "mystic gulf" of the orchestra pit, the seats, the boxes of the theaters, or La Scala where the composer's first work, "Oberto," was presented when he was 26; the Queen's Theater of London, where "I Masnadieri" was acclaimed; the theater of the Khedive in Cairo, where "Aïda" was produced; the Teatro La Fenice of Venice, the S. Carlo of Naples, the Argentina or the Apollo in Rome; Florence's La Pergola or the Opéra in Paris. Or perhaps we should travel, in our imagination, to other lands, historical times, and settings: those evoked by the props, the Babylon of "Nabucco," Paris of "La Traviata," the grim Hapsburg Spain of "Don Carlos," the bittersweet England of "Falstaff," which the maestro composed at the age of 80 ("I am just writing for my own enjoyment," he commented). But if we are going to tour the land of his youth, where he returned as a grown man, then we will visit the plains between Parma and the Po, farmland, a handsome countryside with distinct seasons, silence and snow, trees like shadows in the fall mists, as the swifts dart back and forth in the sunset, cities, towns, and villages with rich aromatic cooking and a tradition of "bel canto." Those towns are three, to be exact: Verdi's birthplace, Róncole; Busseto, the dignified little town where he learned music and forged his destiny; and Sant'Agata: the maestro, already successful, bought a house and land there, encouraged by his second wife, Giuseppina Strepponi, an

opera singer. In the route that we recommend, these places are parentheses along the way: do not miss the three portals of the facade of Fidenza's Duomo, a masterpiece of Po Valley Romanesque architecture. Then there is the blend of the Middle Ages and Renaissance in the castles of Fontanellato and Soragna. Lastly, the magic landscape of the Po, glimpsed through the trees, or from secluded roads along the banks.

The route.

From Fidenza, head east for 12.5 km along the Via Emilia, as far as Castelguelfo; then turn NW along secondary roads, passing through Fontanellato, Soragna, and Róncole Verdi. From here, along SS 588 road to Cremona, you will reach Villa Verdi, which requires a slight detour, just past the bridge over the Ongina. Just north of Villa Verdi, you will get back on to road 588, heading for Zibello and, with a route that follows the course of the river Po, you will drive through Roccabianca and on to Colorno. The straight SS 343 road leads to Parma, which marks the end of this route.

Places of interest.

Fidenza: the Duomo is one of the finest Romanesque monuments in the Po Valley. Fontanellato boasts the Rocca, or fort, with frescoes by Parmigianino; it stands, pale red and battlemented, facing the broad square of a farming village. Soragna: another farming village, another Rocca, the sumptuous princely home of the Meli Lupi family. Róncole Verdi has the birthplace of Giuseppe Verdi, a modest enough place, and, in the church of S. Michele, the organ on which Verdi first practiced music. Busseto: the cult of Verdi does not interfere with the history and dignity of what was once the capital of the little state of the House of Pallavicino; there is a museum in the Villa Pallavicino; in the church of S. Maria degli Angeli is the Lament for the Death of Christ terracotta group by G. Mazzoni (1476-77). Villa Verdi a Sant'Agata: the maestro spent his summers here, composing opera; you can tour his living quarters. Roccabianca: the Po flows by, slow and majestic, just a few hundred meters away; the 15th-c. Rocca, or fort, was built by P.M. Rossi for his beloved, Bianca Pellegrini, hence the name Rocca-Bianca. Colorno: restoration has helped to recover some of the charm and allure of the ducal palazzo and estate, hunting grounds and holiday spot of the dukes of Parma, upon which many architects worked for long years.

32 | Versilia, the Apuan Alps, and Lunigiana

Viareggio - Camaiore - Pietrasanta - Castelnuovo di Garfagnana - Forte dei Marmi Massa - Carrara - Fosdinovo - Sarzana - Pontrèmoli (180 km)

The glittering blue sea spreading out below the jagged Apuan mountains, studded with white fragments of marble amidst high-elevation forests: this is the setting of a small but ancient principality that once lay along the boundary between Tuscany and Liguria. Between the Magra and Serchio rivers, low sand dunes roll up to stands of pinasters and holm-oaks. Versilia ranges from the lake of Massaciùccoli to the mouth of the Cinquale, stretching inland to the Apuan crest. In the mid-19th c., the first bathing establishments were built, precursors to today's resorts. The swimsuits were far more ample and clumsy then, but the light, the air, and the sparkling water were the same as today. Rising sharply behind green hills, the high Apuans are riven with "canali," as the locals call the narrow and jagged high valleys. They are also a treasure trove of fine marble. Once this was the principality of Massa and Carrara, named for its two capital towns. From the 15th c. until the unification of Italy (1861), these two cities feuded, proud of their marble, mountains, and seacoast. The route ends with the Lunigiana, a land of subtle and melancholy charm. Watered by the Magra River, Lunigiana is a blend of Tuscany, Liguria, and Emilia. This farmland set among terraced mountain slopes and chestnut groves was once so poor that there was only one alternative to eating chestnuts and the occasional bowl of polenta: to emigrate, sailing toward distant shores.

The route. Starting from Viareggio, drive directly to Camaiore; returning along the same road, turn at Pianore toward Pietrasanta. Here, get on to the Via Aurelia (running inland, instead of along the coast, as is usual). At Querceta you turn off – this is part of the route – and drive over the Apuans, passing through Seravezza and the Cipollaio tunnel to Castelnuovo di Garfagnana. Take the same route back to Querceta, and continue to the coast, at Forte dei Marmi. Then follow the coast north, to Marina di Massa. The route then heads inland, passing through Massa and over the hills to Carrara; the panoramic route of the Spolverina (road 446 *d*) goes over the pass of the Foce, at an elevation of 560 m, and from Fosdinovo drops down into Liguria just outside of Sarzana. Lastly, the SS 62 right on of the Cisa Pass takes you through the Magra (or Lunigiana) Valley, to the town of Pontrèmoli.

Places of interest. Viareggio*, with its broad beaches, pine groves, and maritime air, has been a prominent beach resort for the past century-and-a-half, as well as a social and cultural watering spot. Camaiore boasts a Romanesque collegiate church and a backdrop of lovely hills. Pietrasanta is a town of marble carvers and sculptors, with handsome monuments lining the Piazza del Duomo. Castelnuovo di Garfagnana proudly surveys a green expanse of mountains; here two great Italian poets ruled as governors for the Este family: Ludovico Ariosto and Fulvio Testi. Forte dei Marmi*, set amidst the Mediterranean maquis and pine groves, is the most elegantly exclusive beach in Versilia. Massa: the medieval village clusters around the old fortress; beneath it, the 15th-c. town features the palace of the Cybo-Malaspina family, facing a square dotted with orange trees. Carrara is a venerable capital of the marble trade (spectacular quarries at Colonnata, 8.5 km to the east), renowned as well for its rebellious history. Fosdinovo: Dante is said to have looked out from the castle of the Malaspina over the Gulf of La Spezia. Sarzana is a town with an intricate history, its buildings a blend of Ligurian and Tuscan style, especially its 13th-c. cathedral. Santo Stefano di Magra, a Ligurian village, still boasts earmarks of a fortified medieval "borgo." Villafranca in Lunigiana features an Ethnographic Museum which documents local culture. Pontrèmoli is a town with an ancient flavor; on the Piagnaro hill, the castle houses the remarkable museum with a collection of local stelae-statues and other items of archeological interest.

33 | The Apennines of Pistoia and Garfagnana

Pistoia - Abetone - Foce delle Radici - Castelnuovo di Garfagnana - Pistoia (190 km)

"... while the Apuan peaks / are shrouded with a sunlit vermilion mist, / and the rays glitter against the distant / glass panes of Tiglio; / come to this new fountain, with / ewers balanced on your heads, shining like a mirror, / delicately balanced, o maidens / of Castelvecchio..." (Pascoli, "La Fonte di Castelvecchio"). While he was teaching Latin and Greek in the towns of Matera, Massa, and Livorno, Professor Giovanni Pascoli often submitted Latin poetry to competitions held in Amsterdam, and more than once he was awarded first place; with his winnings, the great poet was able to purchase a home in this land on the far side of the Apennines, in the Garfagnana, at Castelvecchio di Barga. The tour of Pascoli's home is a literary parenthesis in this route, which is chiefly focused on mountain landscape, hill country and valleys. High elevations, forests, endless vistas: the many and steep climbs and descents

only contribute to the excitement of th
route. In the first leg, on the Pistoia slopes
the Apennines, for example, you begin clo
to sea level, then you cross the Passo di C
pio at 821 m, at La Lima you are at 454 m,
Abetone at 1388 m. During all these clim
you have passed from one valley to anoth
and though you have never left Tuscany, y
have driven some distance alongside t
course of the Reno River, which then flo
down to the Adriatic through the plains of F
magna. The Reno and its valley are adjace
to other tributaries bound for the Tyrrheni
Sea, in the intricate mountain topograp
over Pistoia. The eye wanders over craggy
houettes, amidst the green of alders, bee
white and red deal trees. After Abetone you head down the Mòdena slopes
far as Pievepèlago, and the climbs and descents continue: after going over tv
high passes, the mouths of the Radici and the Terrarossa, you enter the Va
del Serchio – Garfagnana, part of Tuscany but for three centuries ruled by t
Este family, dukes of Ferrara, later reduced only to Mòdena and Reggio En
ia. You can make out the rolling crests of the Apennine watershed and t
sere, jagged peaks of the Apuans. The circle is closed as you follow the val
of the Lima River, a tributary of the Serchio, running through steep gorges.

The route.

Leaving Pistoia along the Via di Porta al Borgo and heading north along the
66 road, you will drive through Le Piastre and Pontepetri, and over the Opp
pass, and then on to San Marcello Pistoiese and the small town of La Lim
Here you turn right on the SS 12 road toward the Abetone Pass, and from the
down to Pievepèlago, onto the SS 324 road, and past the Foce delle Rad
(1529 m), Foce di Terrarossa (1441 m), and Castiglione di Garfagnana, fina
dropping down to Castelnuovo di Garfagnana. You will drive along the Serch
valley and after Ponte di Campia, then on through Castelvecchio Pascoli, Por
di Catagnana and Barga. From there you return to the road along the river's l
bank, and, at Ponte a Serraglio, rejoin the SS 12 road heading back to Abeto
This will take you to the fork in the road at La Lima. For a short distance, y
will be back on the same road you took earlier, though heading for San M
cello Pistoiese, but you will soon turn right onto the SS 633 road, throu
Prunetta (958 m) and on to Le Piastre. You return to Pistoia the way you left

Places of interest.

Maresca is a resort at the edge of the Teso Forest, and can be reached vi
detour just after the Passo di Oppio. Gavinana: in a small museum, you c
see documents regarding the battle of 1530 between the Florentines und
Francesco Ferrucci and the imperial troops of the Prince of Orange; the F
rentine defeat marked the end of the republic and the return of the Medici
Florence. Cutigliano can be reached via a 1.5-km detour from Casotti, on t
road to Abetone, after La Lima; a cableway takes you up to the 1715-m cre
of the Apennines, between Libro Aperto and the Corno alle Scale, with
panoramic view. Abetone (1388 m), is a noted ski resort near a large fore
fine views from the Rifugio Selletta, a mountain hut at an elevation of 1711
(take a chairlift up) and from Monte Gòmito at 1892 m (another cableway u
Pievepèlago is a resort town in the Modenese valley of the Scoltenna; take
11.5-km road up to the little Lago Santo (1 501 m) at the foot of Monte Giov
Foce delle Radici (1529 m) is a pass between Emilia and Tuscany with a fi
view. At San Pellegrino in Alpe, via a 2.5-km detour, you have a vista th
reaches the sea, as well as an ethnographic museum. Castiglione di Garfagna
lies within the walls of a 14th-c. Lucchese fortress, in the 15th-c. church of
Michele with a Madonna by Giuliano di Simone (1389) and a 15th-c. wooo
crucifix. Castelnuovo di Garfagnana: from 1522-25 the great epic poet Ludo
co Ariosto lived, as governor, in the 12th-c. fortress here. Castelvecchio Pa
coli: the house that belonged to Giovanni Pascoli, a great 19th-c. Italian po
is outside the town, among the houses of Carpona. Barga: the Romanesqu

Duomo stands on the high meadow of the Arringo, towering over the ancient village, with a panoramic view over valley and mountains. Bagni di Lucca is a spa with a venerable reputation, founded by Elisa Baciocchi, sister of Napoleon and princess of Lucca; as the 19th c. wore on, an elect international clientele would come here, including celebrated authors and in 1840 the first casino to be built in Europe was established here. Vico Pancellorum is a secluded village high in the valley of the Lima, at the end of a 2.5-km detour, a few km past Fabbriche and just before Popiglio. Popiglio: note the ancient towers in the village's skyline, and the medieval parish church of the Assunta.

4 | Valdinièvole and Monte Albano

Lucca - Montecatini Terme - Pistoia - Vinci - Prato - Florence (134 km)

The Nièvole is a short mountain stream that flows down from the Apennines to sink into the Padule di Fucecchio, but the Valdinièvole (or Nièvole Valley) is a world to itself: a high hilltop meadowland, fading into hillocks topped by cypresses, chestnut trees, grapevines, light-colored expanses of olive trees, and, in the valleys, fields dense with flowers. The Valdinièvole includes the valleys of the Pescia and the Pescia di Collodi, as well as Montecatini Terme and the town of Pescia. The route runs from west to east. The Florentine author of "Pinocchio," Carlo Lorenzini, took his pen name from the town of Collodi, where he spent part of his childhood. We may suppose that this was the landscape in which Pinocchio "rolled his eyes around to see, amidst the dark green of the trees, a white speck in the distance: a little house as white as snow," the house of the "little girl with light-blue hair." At any rate, the town of Collodi perennially celebrates the little boy carved of wood. Monte Albano is a forest-covered chain of hills, running NW to SE, between Montecatini Terme and the Arno, sealing off the plain of Pistoia and Prato to the south. And these two cities, with their remarkable ancient quarters, certainly offer the artistic highlights of this route: in Pistoia, the silver altar frontal of S. Jacopo (mentioned by Dante); in Prato, Donatello's dancing cherubs on the pulpit of the Sacro Cingolo, to mention only two.

he route.

From Lucca, you head east toward Pescia, along the SS 435 road. From Pescia, you drive north along the river Pescia, then east through Vellano and Marliana, in a wide arc over the hills (this area is known as the "Switzerland of Pescia") that ends at Montecatini Terme. Continuing east, you will first reach Serravalle Pistoiese, then Pistoia itself. Exiting the city southward, along the road to Émpoli, you climb over Monte Albano and reach Vinci. The next leg of the trip runs NE over secondary roads: through Vitolini and Carmignano to Poggio a Caiano. Finally, you will reach Prato. From here, after a detour to the church of S. Giovanni Battista at the motorway interchange of North Florence, or Firenze Nord, you will return to Florence through Sesto Fiorentino.

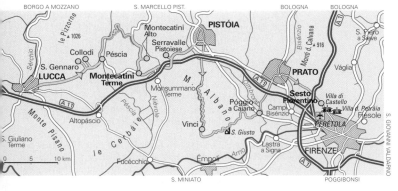

Places of interest. San Gennaro can be reached by taking a detour from the SS 435 road, about ? km from Lucca; it boasts a remarkable Romanesque church. Collodi require another detour, soon after, from the SS 435 road; it is notable for the Parco Pinocchio and the garden of Villa Garzoni. Pescia: in the church of Francesco is a panel by Bonaventura Berlinghieri (1235); flowers are grown i tensively. Montecatini Alto has medieval quarters; to get here, you must d tour 2 km from the road; noteworthy view. Montecatini Terme*: parks, Ar Nouveau (or "liberty," in Italian) architecture and the high-society elegance a spa town. Serravalle Pistoiese has ruins of medieval fortifications; in th former Romanesque church of S. Michele are 14th-c. Florentine frescoes. P toia*: this city rivals Lucca and Florence, both in the history of art and of po itics; you can spend more than one intensely interesting day examining ar collections, monuments, and the old city itself. Vinci has a 13th-c. castle, wit a museum devoted to Leonardo da Vinci; continue along till you come to th Romanesque parish church of San Giusto, on the ridge of Monte Albano. Po gio a Caiano features a Medici villa by Giuliano da Sangallo. Prato*: it is be known as a thriving wool-manufacturing town, but the old area, enclosed b 14th-c. hexagonal walls, has a venerable air and great monuments of Itali art. The Chiesa di S. Giovanni Battista, near a major highway interchange, th Firenze Nord, is a masterpiece of modern architecture by Giovanni Michelu ci (1960-64). Sesto Fiorentino has the Museo delle Porcellane di Doccia, or m seum of shower tiles, and, in the outlying neighborhood of Quinto, the Et uscan tomb of Montagnola. Continue along through the outskirts of Florenc and stop by the Medici villas of Castello and Petraia.

35 | Lower Valdarno

Pisa - Vicopisano - San Miniato - Fucecchio - Vinci - Signa - Florence (128 km)

Although the course of the Arno from Florence to Pisa and on to the sea is an thing but straightforward, it does tend westward. This route runs through th Arno Valley, upstream from Pisa and Florence, and almost entirely forsakes th two more common roads on either bank of the river, in favor of less we known routes, overlooking the winding Arno from the high roads. This rou heads north over Monte Pisano, then south through the Valdera and over th hills between Palaia and San Miniato, and lastly north, through Cerreto Gui and Vinci, over Monte Albano. The thriving and prosperous valley shows th hand of man nearly everywhere. This route offers remarkable vistas, exquisi art and architecture, and lovely stretches of scenery. Let us mention tw which formed subjects for two lost masterpieces of Tuscan art. At Càscin the Florentines, who had pushed thus far in their war against Pisa, risked it on a toss of dice (and won) on 28 July 1364, battling fiercely against the 8(men-at-arms under the Pisan commander-general, Giovanni Acuto (the Itali version of the name of the English soldier John Hawkwood, who fought for Fl rence as well; see the funerary monument painted by Paolo Uccello in S. Mar del Fiore). When commemorating this past glory of Florence, at one point, th Gonfaloniere Pier Soderini commissioned Michelangelo to paint a fresco of th event. Michelangelo "filled the painting with nude men, who were cooling from the summer heat in the river Arno, at the very moment that the batt began in the field" (Vasari): that work is now lost, as is its companion piec the Battle of Anghiari, by Leonardo da Vinci – once they both could be seen Palazzo Vecchio. Drive on through olive groves and vineyards to the town Vinci, where the great artist was born, an "illegitimate son" (according to th town records) of a notary and property owner in Anchiano, and a certain Cat rina, who later married Attaccabriga di Pietro del Vacca.

The route. Heading east out of Pisa (from Via Garibaldi, along the Arno's right bank) y will drive directly to Calci, and then south. At Caprona, north of the Arno, tu left along the road to Florence, until you come to the turnoff to Vicopisano. Y will cross the Arno and drive through the Era valley, past Ponsacco. At Capa

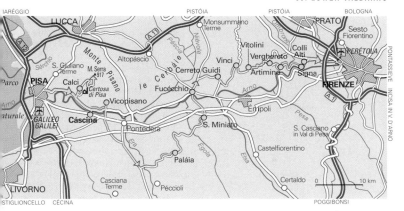

noli, you will turn, cross the Era, and take secondary roads to San Miniato, past Villa Saletta, Palàia, Chiecinella, and La Serra. Driving down from the hilltop town of San Miniato, you will head north, crossing the Arno again, past Fucecchio. You will take the SS 436 road for a short way, and then turn right at Le Corti. Secondary roads, some of them panoramic, take you through Cerreto Guidi, Vinci, Vitolini, Verghereto, and Artimino; you will rejoin the Arno at Signa. You finally reach Florence, on the right bank of the Arno, through Colli Alti, along the SS 66 road from Pistoia. This route follows some very small roads; keep an eye out for roadsigns and use your map.

Places of interest. Calci: the Certosa, or Charterhouse, of Pisa is here, as is an 11th-c. parish church; take a 12-km detour over Monte Serra to the highest peak on Monte Pisano (917 m): there is an immense vista, with the sea, the Apuans, Valdarno, and the Apennines. Càscina: you take a 3-km detour from Lugnano to get here; go see the 14th-c. frescoes in the Oratorio di S. Giovanni and the Romanesque parish church of S. Maria. Vicopisano: a maze of medieval lanes, a Pisan Romanesque parish church, and the ruins of the fortifications restored by Brunelleschi, following the Florentine conquest of 1407. Palaia boasts the parish church in the old town and the church of S. Martino just outside of town, both dating from the 13th c. San Miniato has very fine monuments and collections of art; the views and medieval quarters are noteworthy. A theater festival takes places in the piazza at the end of July, and there is a national market exhibition of white truffles in November. Fucecchio stands on the outlying ridges of the Monte Albano; the Collegiata di S. Giovanni Battista is at the top of a stairway (a fine view from a square to the left). Cerreto Guidi: a splendid stairway by Bernardo Buontalenti leads up to the Medici villa (1576), where Paolo Giordano Orsini strangled his wife Isabella. Vinci: Leonardo da Vinci took his name from this village, although he was probably born in Anchiano; visit the Museo Vinciano in the Castello. Artimino: amid olive groves and vineyards; facing the town is the Medici villa, La Ferdinanda. Signa is a town in which straw and terracotta objects are manufactured; in the upper part of town are a 15th-c. baptismal font and frescoes depicting the life of S. Giovanna in the parish church of S. Giovanni Battista.

36 | The Tyrrhenian Coast

Viareggio - Pisa - Tirrenia - Livorno - Bòlgheri - Suvereto - Populonia
Piombino (146 km)

"...si dice in galea o nave o altra fusta, quando fussino stati alcuno giorno sanza vedere terra..." This is an old chantey from the second half of the 15th c., and it translates roughly: "They say in ships or galleys, or any other vessel, when they have gone several days without sighting land..." At the end of each

verse, the chantey returns to call on the help of the Lord and the saints, naming a patron saint or a sanctuary, with specific reference to stretches of shoreline or points on the coast. This "pilot's log" of the Catholic faith describes – for the short stretch that corresponds to the beginning of this route along the coastline of northern Tuscany, between Viareggio and Livorno – the Volto Santo Lucchese, San Ranieri, Santa Maria del Ponte Nuovo, and San Piero a Grado (Pisan), Santa Giulia and Montenero (Livornese). Here is a typical verse: "Die' n'aì (meaning "God help us") Santa Maria delle Grazie di Monte Nero di Livorno..." The chantey clearly refers to the route that we are suggesting here: the lovely thing about driving along the coastline, for that matter, is the endless series of glimpses it offers of the sea, parallel to the glimpses of land that so comforted the terrified ancient sailors. Leaving aside the marvels of Pisa, there are attractions in this route: the alternating distance and approach to the sea, long beaches and a jagged coastline, little coves with crashing waves and gurgling undertow, and, far above, the Mediterranean maquis, pine trees, holm-oaks, ash trees, elms, the northwest wind or "maestrale" redolent of resins and sap, clouds scudding across the windy sky, the "flocks of black birds" that flap their way "through the vespertine sky" (there are many verses by Nobel laureate G. Carducci that seem to describe this region). In this exchange between earth and sea along the coast, the most beautiful section lies between Antignano and Cècina. And if you look inland instead of out to sea, what draws nearer and further away is the outline of hills and blue hazy mountains; you will see grapevines and olive groves, cypresses, Etruscan ruins, hilltop towns. Lastly, as you move south, the climate becomes slightly milder in winter. The last stretch of road, where you begin to see Elba, is the coast of the Maremma, specifically the so-called Pisan Maremma: from here you can take a lovely inland detour.

The route.

Leaving Viareggio along the Viale dei Tigli, you will drive through the Pineta di Levante, a great pine forest. After Torre del Lago Puccini, take the Via Aurelia (SS 1 road) to Pisa. Leaving Pisa along the Lungarni, or riverfront boulevards of the river's left bank, you will reach Marina di Pisa; from here, follow the coast road (SS 224 road) to Livorno. Take the Viale Italia out of Livorno, along the coast as far as Antignano, where you will rejoin the Aurelia, and take it to San Vincenzo. Here, the Aurelia goes inland; continue along the coast road, which then cuts across the promontory and runs to Piombino. There is a detour through the Maremma, which cuts off from the Aurelia at the fork for Castagneto Carducci. Climbing and descending along secondary roads, you drive past Castagneto Carducci, Sassetta, Suvereto, Cafaggio, Campiglia Marittima, and Venturina. Here, after a brief jog to the right along the Aurelia, at Caldana, take the road to La Torraccia, on the coast south of San Vincenzo, back on the main route. You will then reach Piombino, after a short detour to Baratti and Populonia. This entire detour, which requires you to keep a sharp eye on roadsigns and map, lengthens the drive by 44 km.

Places of interest.

Torre del Lago Puccini, near the Lago di Massaciùccoli, with the stately home and the tomb of Giacomo Puccini. Pisa**: with its Baptistery, Cathedral, Cemetery, and famous leaning bell tower, the Campo dei Miracoli, or Piazza del Duomo mo, a broad meadow, is certainly one of the most famous places on earth; this is the greatest glory of this ancient Tuscan city on the banks of the river Arno, a powerful maritime republic of bygone centuries. Still, Pisa has much more to offer; every visit results in many new discoveries. San Piero a Grado*: this 11th-c. Pisan church with early 14th-c. frescoes can be reached by taking a detour from the road linking Pisa with Marina di Pisa. Livorno: this harbor city is a thriving port with venerable old quarters. It was the first outlet to the sea of the Tuscan grand-duchy; from Antignano you will drive up to the Santuario di Montenero (collection of votive offerings from those who survived perils of land and sea). Castiglioncello: this quietly elegant beach resort stands on a promontory, dense with pine trees and holm-oaks; nearby are inlets and little beaches. Rosignano Marittimo: detour from Rosignano Solvay, 2 km inland; the old town stands on a scenic rise. Marina di Cècina: take a 2.5-km detour; the beach is on the other side of the pine forest. Bòlgheri: in order to get here, you must leave the Via Aurelia at the 18th-c. octagonal chapel of San Guido, driving a little less than 5 km along cypress-lined boulevards described by 1906 Nobel laureate and poet Giosuè Carducci, truly a lovely sight (as a child, Carducci lived in a house in town here). In the variant that we recommend for the last part of this route: Castagneto Carducci, a hillside resort area; the poet lived here as a youth. Suvereto (see Campiglia Marittima) may take its name from the groves of cork-trees that once surrounded it; the Romanesque church of S. Giusto, and the 13th-c. Palazzo Comunale are worth seeing. Campiglia Marittima, for the most part, still has a medieval appearance; on the Venturina road is the cemetery, with the parish church of S. Giovanni (note the late-12th-c. carving on the architrave over the portal). Baratti: on the bayshore, note the Etruscan necropolis. Populonia still has its 14th-c. "borgo," unchanged by time, perched on the promontory; this was the powerful Etruscan town of "Pupluna" and has the small Muses Collezione Gasparri, which contains finds from the Etruscan necropolis.

37 | Val di Pesa and Chianti

Florence - Poggibonsi - Siena - Castelnuovo Berardenga - Greve in Chianti Florence (184 km)

In 1838, Baron Bettino Ricasoli, 29, later the absolute ruler of Tuscany and prime minister of the Kingdom of Italy, took up residence in his castle at Brolio, in Chianti, to devote himself to farming. He wrote that "agriculture in Tuscany takes heart and it takes brains, it is almost a calling." One of the results of that "calling" was Chianti, a wine that had existed since 1716 – along with the now less famous Pomino, Carmignano, and Valdarno – but which Ricasoli made both great and renowned. In the route recommended here, Chianti comes in the latter part, though all of the landscape is enchanting. From Florence you continue on to the Val di Pesa, with its venerable tradition as an aristocratic holiday spot; after driving through this valley for a stretch, you climb through hills in the Valdelsa (the Pesa and the Elsa flow into the lower Arno, from the left bank). After Siena, you return to Florence, with a pause in the land of Chianti. Experts distinguish an aroma of violet in this wine; it is made with Sangiovese grapes, from 75 to 90 percent, while the rest is a blend of black Canaiolo grapes, Tuscan Trebbiano grapes, and Malvasia del Chianti. In the landscape, which varies from grim to lovely, with an endless combination of villas, holm-oaks, farm houses, scrub brush, villages, towers, steep hills, winding roads, parish churches, venerable oak trees, cypresses, and olive trees, you will often see vineyards as well, occupying only the sites that receive plenty of sun and with the finest soil. Save for the secluded Certosa del Galluzzo, with paintings by Pontormo, the turreted skyline of Monteriggioni and, of course, Siena, this tour is of lesser sites, with domesticated nature, and the brilliant clear light, the clear distilled magic essence of Tuscany.

he route.

Leaving Florence from the Porta Romana (left bank of the Arno) along the Via

67

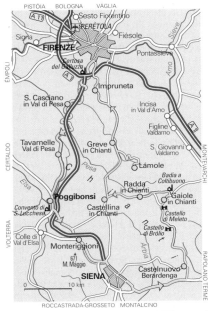

Senese, and taking the Cassia (SS 2 road) through San Casciano in Val di Pesa and Poggibonsi, you will reach Siena. From there, leaving by the Porta Pispini along the road to Arezzo, you will drive about 15 km and then turn left to climb up to Castelnuovo Berardenga. This is the beginning of Chianti, where, partly along SS 484 roads and then 408, you will drive through Castello di Brolio, Gaiole in Chianti, and Badia a Coltibuono. From here, proceed west to Radda in Chianti and, on the SS 429 road, to Castellina in Chianti. The next leg, heading north, runs along the SS 222 road, to Greve in Chianti (midway, detour to the right to Làmole). Beyond is the fork for Impruneta, after Strada. From Impruneta you return to Florence, driving down from the hills south of the city.

Places of interest. Certosa del Galluzzo: church, cloisters, monks' cells, and paintings by Pontormo. To get here, turn off the Via Cassia at Galluzzo and drive for 1 km past cypresses and olive trees. San Casciano in Val di Pesa: a fine Crucifix by Simone Martini in the Misericordia church. Poggibonsi is a thriving modern town; 1.5 km south is the convent of S. Lucchese amid the olive groves. Monteriggioni* was a Sienese outpost; Dante's description – "di torri si corona," or "crowned with towers" – still applies. Siena**: in the history of Italy, this is Florence's great rival. In terms of painting, sculpture, and town planning, Siena expresses a second, world-class Tuscan culture. It is said that the Sienese speak the best Italian. Castello di Brolio: built in the 12th c. by the Ricasoli family, it was later restored in 1860. Gaiole in Chianti lies amid hills covered with vineyards; you can admire the Romanesque parish church of S. Maria a Spaltenna, the Castello di Meleto, a fortified medieval farm, just 2 km away, and the Romanesque church, the remaining part of the nearby Badia a Coltibuono (5 km north). Radda in Chianti has an elongated elliptical layout, a relic of the Middle Ages. Castellina in Chianti has stood on its hilltop since the Renaissance; it lies between the valleys of Arbia, Elsa, and Pesa and has retained much of its Renaissance atmosphere, with a 14th-c. fortress. Greve in Chianti (see Impruneta) has a porticoed asymmetrical plaza; note the terraces. From here, a 6-km detour takes you to Làmole; here is the Villa di Vignamaggio, birthplace of the woman who sat for Leonardo's Mona Lisa (La Gioconda). Impruneta, on the Florentine hills, is known for its venerable October fair, its pottery kilns (here, Brunelleschi fired the bricks used to build the cupola of S. Maria del Fiore), and the basilica of S. Maria.

38 | Valdelsa and Volterrano

Florence - Émpoli - Certaldo - Volterra - San Gimignano - Colle di Val d'Elsa (147 km)

The literary references here are of the highest quality: Certaldo was the birthplace of the 14th-c. author Boccaccio, and here he returned as a bitter old man, to die and be buried. When he returned, he said: "Comincianmi già i grossi panni a piacere e le contadine vivande" – "I am happy to wear rough clothing and eat peasant food." Certaldo lies in the Valdelsa. The Elsa River, which runs through it flows down from the Montagnola, a small mountain west of Siena; it then flows into the Arno near Émpoli. This valley road, which once ran high on the hillcrests before the malarial riverside plain was reclaimed, was the route of the "Romei," pilgrims bound for Rome; it was a main leg of the

Via Francigena, a much-used route in medieval Europe. That may explain the ferocity with which Florentines and Sienese fought over it (the Florentines triumphed in the late-14th c.). The route runs from Florence and enters and goes up the Valdelsa after descending the Arno; it is perhaps at its most intensely Tuscan when it leaves that valley, at Certaldo, and then twists west into valleys and over hills, before ending once again near the Elsa. Along this route, you pass through two exquisitely Tuscan places, different in surroundings and atmosphere. Volterra, with Etruscan and medieval heritages, austere, a clear light silhouetting surrealistic hills, with clayey slopes torn away in desolate washes, and the chasms of the Balze; and San Gimignano, immersed in a landscape with all the gentle lines and delicate colors of Siena's finest painters.

The route. You leave Florence from Piazza Gaddi, along the Via Bronzino (left bank of the Arno), and follow the road to Pisa (SS 67 road), along the Arno, through Émpoli, to Ponte a Elsa. Here, you take the SS 429 road toward Siena, which goes along the Elsa to Certaldo. Turning right, you will follow a road west to Gambassi Terme, Il Castagno, Vicarello, and lastly Volterra. Heading east from Volterra on the SS 68 road, you reach Castel San Gimignano, where you will turn left to then take a twisting but panoramic road all the way to San Gimignano. You will continue east, hitting the Valdelsa (Elsa Valley) at Poggibonsi. After a short drive along the Cassia toward Siena, turn right at the fork for Colle di Val d'Elsa, and this will take you to the end of the route.

Places of interest. Badia di S. Salvatore a Sèttimo: restored following damage inflicted during WWII, this abbey is enclosed by crenelated walls: you must turn off, just outside of Florence, right after the Autostrada. Lastra a Signa (see Signa) still has part of its old walls; nearby, at Gangalandi, is the 11th-c. parish church of S. Martino, with 13th-c. paintings and frescoes. Montelupo Fiorentino has the Museo Archeologico e della Ceramica, in Palazzo del Podestà. Émpoli: Palazzo Ghibellino hosted a council that met to decide the fate of Florence after its disastrous defeat in the 13th-c. Battle of Montaperti; there are frescoes by Masolino da Panicale in the Museo della Collegiata and in the church of S. Stefano; also local glass-making industry. Oratorio della Madonna della Tosse: 2-km detour from Granaiolo, with chapel that once contained frescoes by Benozzo Gozzoli (1484), now in Castelfiorentino. Castelfiorentino: in the old town center are lavish Baroque churches with 14th-/15th-c. artwork. The Raccolta Comunale d'Arte has the two series of frescoes by B. Gozzoli. Certaldo: strongly medieval in flavor; visit Boccaccio's house, rebuilt, set high on the hill. Montaione is an old village with a view; it can be reached by a 3-km detour, at a fork just past Gambassi Terme; another 4.5 km (from a crossroads just before Montaione) takes you to the convent of S. Vivaldo (404 m), with 20 chapels containing Della Robbia terracottas; it is in the forest of Boscolazzeroni, a nature reserve. Volterra* is a windswept hilltop town, austerely alluring; the atmosphere is medieval, with towers and grey buildings. Relics of its Etruscan origins can be seen at the Museo Guarnacci. San Gimignano** is a perfectly intact town of medieval Tuscany: city gates, houses, squares, and roads, as well as the 14 surviving towers, and works by great artists in the churches and the Pinacoteca. In particular, the Collegiata has major works by Giuliano and Benedetto da Maiano, Bartolo di Fredi, and Jacopo della Quercia. Colle di Val d'Elsa: you may reach the old "borgo" by taking the Via del Castello, up high. Don't miss the birthplace of Arnolfo di Cambio, born here in 1232; an exhibit on his work is in the Palazzo Pretorio.

39 | Mugello and Pratomagno

Florence - Pratolino - Borgo San Lorenzo - Vallombrosa - San Giovanni Valdarno Florence (195 km)

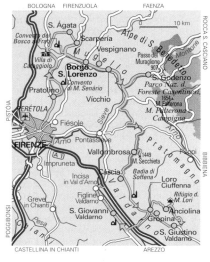

The Mugello, north of Florence, is an exceedingly green hollow, an ancient lakebed, traversed by the river Sieve, a tributary of the upper Arno (this provides much of the Arno's water; in Florence a rhyming proverb goes: "Arno non cresce se Sieve non mesce," that is, "the Arno won't grow if the Sieve doesn't flow"; when the Sieve does flow excessively, flooding ensues, sometimes with disastrous results, as in 1966). The Pratomagno is a long mountain ridge, running crosswise between Florence and Arezzo; around it, the Arno flows in a great oxbow curve. The highest elevation – the Croce di Pratomagno – stands 1592 m above sea level; one slope overlooks the Casentino, the other faces Valdarno di Sopra. The two slopes are linked by the Passo della Consuma. The ridges are expanses of meadow, as one might expect from the name (Pratomagno means "great meadow"). On the side facing Florence is the dense forest of Vallombrosa; the lower slopes are covered with olive trees, vineyards, and fields, especially toward the Valdarno – this is the slope along which our route runs – while in the Casentino chestnut trees grow at elevations of close to a thousand meters. Along the road, you will see sites associated with great Tuscan artists. In Vespignano, a section of Vicchio, in Mugello, a certain Bondone, "a man who worked the land," had a son named Ambrogiotto, or Giotto, for short; near here, the great 13th-c. artist Cimabue discovered him, as a young boy, while on a "flat clean slab or rock, with a slightly pointed stone," he was sketching one of the sheep he was guarding, "without having been in any way taught, save by the instincts of nature" (Vasari). Fra' Angelico was born in nearby Vicchio. Tommaso di Ser Giovanni di Mone, better known as Masaccio, son of a notary, came into the world in San Giovanni Valdarno; during Vasari's lifetime, it was said that one could still see "a number of drawings done by him in his youth" in the area.

The route.

You will leave Florence heading north, through the Porta S. Gallo; take the SS 65 Della Futa road, climbing to Pratolino. Take a right off this road, toward the Convent of Monte Senario, and then rejoin the road at Vaglia; follow it past Cafaggiolo, and then take the road through the hills that goes past Galliano, Sant'Agata (341 m), and Scarperìa. Drive down to San Piero a Sieve, where you take the SS 551 road, which runs down along the left bank of the Sieve. Follow this road through Mugello, past Vicchio, to Dicomano, and continue along the SS 67 road along the Sieve to an intersection just past Scopeti. Here you can turn off on a panoramic road that passes through Pomino. At Borselli, you will rejoin the road that runs from Pontassieve to the Consuma pass (1060 m). Just before Consuma, take a right turn along a local road through the forest to Vallombrosa (958 m). Dropping down into the upper Arno Valley, the road skirts the slopes of the Pratomagno, through Reggello (390 m), Pian di Scó, and Loro Ciuffenna (330 m). After a loop through Anciolina, San Giustino Valdarno, and Gròpina – a recommended detour (37 km, see below) – you will drive down to cross the Arno between Terranuova Bracciolini and Montevarchi. You will return to Florence along the SS 69 road, through San Giovanni Valdarno; at Incisa, take the highway for the last dozen km.

Places of interest. Pratolino: Villa Demidoff with its immense grounds was one of the homes that Francesco I de' Medici gave to the lovely and restless Venetian noblewoman Bianca Capello, his lover and later his wife. Monte Senario: from the 12th-c. convent at 815 m, a notable view; a liqueur is made here called "Gemma di Abete." Cafaggiolo: the Renaissance architect Michelozzo transformed an old fortress into a villa for Cosimo de' Medici; nearby is the Castello di Trebbio, built by Michelozzo for Cosimo il Vecchio. Sant'Agata has a Romanesque parish church. Scarperìa: the craft of fashioning fine knives and cutting implements has been practiced here for generations. Convento del Bosco ai Frati: in the church is the wooden Crucifix believed to be by Donatello; you get here by taking a 3-km detour from a fork just before San Piero a Sieve. Borgo San Lorenzo is the main town of the Mugello, with a Romanesque church, S. Lorenzo, dating back to 1263; its facade was re-built using original materials in 1922. Vespignano: you can visit what is believed to be the birthplace of Giotto. Vicchio has a small Museo dell'Angelico, devoted to Fra' Angelico, who was born here. San Godenzo, an ancient Benedictine abbey, is at the end of a 10-km detour from Dicomano on the road up to the Passo del Muraglione. Vallombrosa: the landscape, with famed woods of fir trees, is stupendous. The abbey was founded in 1051; a detour takes you through the forest and on up to Monte Secchieta (1449 m), 10 km away; vista. Cascia, with the Romanesque parish church of S. Pietro, can be reached from Reggello, with a short detour along the road to Figline Valdarno. The former Badia di Soffena, a 14th-c. abbey, has notable frescoes; nearby is the town of Castelfranco di Sopra. Loro Ciuffenna: you can extend the route from here by taking a panoramic detour of 37 km up to the village of Anciolina (933 m), at the foot of Monte Lori, one of the peaks of the Pratomagno. You then descend to San Giustino Valdarno and return to Loro Ciuffenna via Gròpina, with the Romanesque church of S. Pietro. San Giovanni Valdarno: it is said that the old town was designed by Arnolfo di Cambio; in the Museo della Basilica are noteworthy artworks, including an altarpiece by Fra' Angelico, formerly in the convent of Montecarlo.

40 | Casentino

Florence - Consuma - Camàldoli - La Verna - Arezzo (180 km)

Mastro Adamo Guidi was a counterfeiter of Florentine coins. Burned at the stake for this crime, he later appeared in Dante's "Divine Comedy", punished in the "Inferno" by a burning unslakable thirst, and tormented by visions of the sparkling streams of his homeland. Mountain streams and brooks indeed water these slopes (Pratomagno to the west, Alpi di Serra and Alpi di Catenaia to the east), running down eventually to the Arno. The landscape of the Casentino is framed by mountains of sandstone and limestone, with squat ridges and low peaks (Falterona, 1654 m), snowcapped for much of the year. Their slopes are covered with emerald meadows, dark dense stands of fir trees, and forests of ash, holm-oaks, oak trees, and chestnut trees. In the valleys are fields of wheat, orchards, tobacco, hemp, and – dotting the land – mulberries, olive groves, and vineyards. Woodcutters and shepherds once predominated here, following their flocks down to the Maremma in winter. This is a land of ancient churches, castles, and silent hermitages: Vallombrosa, Camàldoli, and La Verna.

The route. From Florence, you will drive along the Arno to Pontassieve (SS 69 road toward Arezzo). You then turn on to the SS 70 road, which, after crossing the Consuma Pass (1060 m), descends along another stretch of the Arno Valley (the Casentino, through which the river runs before doubling back in an oxbow around Pratomagno). You then arrive at Poppi. Here, you turn on to a secondary road that twists up to the Hermitage (1104 m) and the monastery of Camàldoli. From there, you drive down to the Arno via Serravalle and the SS 71 road, until you reach Bibbiena. Here, the SS 208 road takes you back up to La Verna (1128 m). Then drive back down the road to Chitignano, which will take you once again to the Arno at Ràssina. From here, the SS 71 road continues to Arezzo.

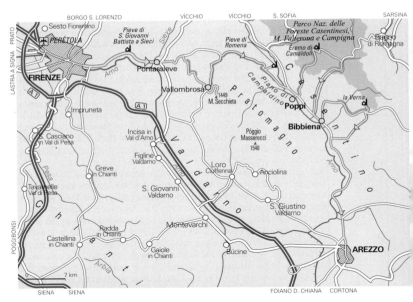

Places of interest. Le Sieci boasts the Romanesque parish church of S. Giovanni Battista a Rèmole, some 12 km outside Florence, on the road to Pontassieve. Vallombrosa: the landscape of the fir forest and the more-than-900-year old convent are remarkable. Take a 10-km detour through the forest, up to the Monte Secchieta (1449 m); fine view. Pieve di Romena* is the most interesting parish church in the Casentino (10th-12th c.); take a short detour past the ruins of the Castello di Romena, descending from Consuma to Poppi. Piano di Campaldino: where the road from Stia intersects with this route, there is a column commemorating the great Battle of Campaldino (11 June 1289), in which the 24-year-old Dante Alighieri fought. Poppi: turn off at Ponte a Poppi; in the 13th-/14th-c. Castello (good artwork) you can sense the power of the Conti Guidi, a noble ruling family. Hermitage and Monastery of Camàldoli: the hermitage is at an elevation of 1104 m, the monastery at 816 m; both stand in a dense fir grove. The monastery was founded by Saint Romualdo and is nearly 1000 years old. Bibbiena is the largest town in the Casentino, with an old center, high on the hill: the panel by Arcangelo di Cola in the church of Ss. Ippolito e Donato and the intense Tuscan vista from the terrace of Piazza Tarlati are noteworthy. Palazzo Dovizi belonged to a cardinal, known as Il Bibbiena, a friend of Raphael and a noted playwright. La Verna*: a limestone peak, a forest, and a convent founded by St. Francis of Assisi.

41 | San Marino, Montefeltro, between Tuscany and Romagna

Pesaro - Cattolica - San Marino - San Leo - Carpegna - Sansepolcro - La Verna (225 km)

Around the yellow and green hills, with red towers adorning their crowns, a network of history weaves the pattern of two family names, Malatesta and Montefeltro. They were both strivers after power and, in the Renaissance, exceptional art patrons. Both are believed to have originated in Montefeltro, the land of mountains, forests, and castles between Romagna and the Marches. The Malatesta possessed the Billi and the Penna, two ranges that combine in the name Pennabilli, (the "mala testa," or evil head, belonged to the founder of the dynasty, Verucchio); in time they ruled Fano, Pesaro, Rìmini, and other parts of Romagna. The Montefeltro were descendants of the Conti di Carpegna, and by the end of the 12th c. they had occupied San Leo. The name Montefeltro came from that place's Latin name, Mons Feretri. The final destiny of this family was to rule Urbino, however. Verucchio, Pennabilli, Carpegna (and you can add the enduring republic of San Marino): the route runs through this region, climbing from Pesaro to high Apennine passes. From there, the Tiber Valley (Val Tiberina) opens out: landscape, color, and light such as in the Baptism of Christ, which Piero della Francesca painted for the priory of S. Giovanni Battista in Sansepolcro (the painting is now in London). As you reach the end of the route, you will see other remarkable places: Anghiari, where a great battle took place in 1440 (Machiavelli says that there was only one death in this battle, and that by accident; the mercenaries were far too professional to hurt each other); Caprese, birthplace of Michelangelo Buonarroti; La Verna, an early Franciscan site, "in the harsh rock between Tiber and Arno" (Dante).

The route.

Starting in Pesaro, you follow the Adriatic coast to Cattolica. Cutting inland along the valley of the Conca, you pass through San Giovanni in Marignano, Morciano di Romagna, and Montescudo. Drive up the eastern slope of San Marino. You will then drive northward down to Verucchio. From here, follow the SS 258 road toward Novafeltria, following the Marécchia Valley for some distance. At Villanova, turn off for San Leo (589 m). You will continue southward, across the Montefeltro, through Madonna di Pugliano, Villagrande (915 m), and Caturchio, to Carpegna; from there, NW to Pennabilli (629 m). Driving downhill, just past Pennabilli, you will reach the SS 258 road. This road will take you back up the Marécchia Valley and over the Apennine crest through the Viamaggio Pass (983 m). From here, drive down through the Tiberina Valley to Sansepolcro. The Ruga road will take you directly across the valley to Anghiari. From here, you will climb to Caprese Michelangelo (469 m). Continue north, along a road that intersects with the route from Pieve Santo Stefano up to La Verna, the end of the route.

Places of interest.

Pesaro: behind the Marina, with its fanciful Art Nouveau Villetta Ruggeri, the historic center features an exquisite art gallery with works by Giovanni Bellini, among others. Gradara: take a 5-km detour from Casteldimezzo inland; the fortress of the medieval "borgo" witnessed the love (and tragic murders) of Paolo and Francesca, real-life characters described in Dante's Inferno. Gabicce Monte (144 m) has a remarkable view of the sea and the endless series of beaches of the Romagna. San Marino*, cheerful and crowded in the summer, is the oldest republic in Europe; of the three fortresses, the Cesta boasts the finest vista. Verucchio, original home of the powerful Malatesta family, has an

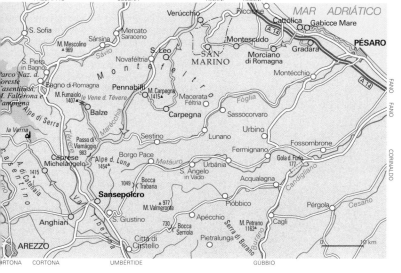

impressive Rocca, or fortress, and an archeological museum in the former convent of S. Agostino. San Leo*: the fort atop the steep crag was the creation of the great Renaissance architect, Francesco di Giorgio Martini. Carpegna: the impressive Palazzo Carpegna stands in the center of town, a resort with fine views; a 3-km side trip takes you up to the Cippo, in the forest of Monte Carpegna. Pennabilli: from the two rocky crags, the two castles of the Penna and the Billi once glared at one another; on one now stand the ruins of a Malatesta fortress, on the other is the medieval heart of the town. Vene de Tevere: (these are the two sources of the Tiber River, at an elevation of less than 1300 m, under the peak of Monte Fumaiolo (1407 m); to get here, take a 17-km detour, making a right turn from a fork in the road 8 km past Badia Tedalda, via the resort area of Balze (1090 m), along the road to the Passo del l'Incisa. Sansepolcro: note the fragments of medieval construction and a predominantly Renaissance architecture; there are celebrated paintings by Piero della Francesca, who was born here, in the Museo Civico. Anghiari: medieval roads, squares, and homes lie within the ring of old city walls; in the Renaissance Palazzo Taglieschi is the Museo delle Arti e Tradizioni Popolari dell'Alta Valle del Tevere, devoted to the folkways and crafts of the upper Tiber Valley. Caprese Michelangelo: the great Renaissance artist was born here, in the Casa del Podestà, now the Museo Michelangiolesco. La Verna* (1129 m): this mountain is sheer on three sides, crowded round with a fir and beech forest, the renowned Franciscan convent stands just beneath the peak.

42 | From Sienese Crete to Valdichiana

Siena - Monte Oliveto Maggiore - Montalcino - Pienza - Chiusi
Città della Pieve (147 km)

In the springtime, the landscape to the SE of Siena becomes green with clover and early wheat; in other seasons, the sere bareness of this land is dramatically evident, amidst an almost treeless landscape. These are the Sienese "Crete," easily eroded hillocks with deceptively gentle silhouettes rutted by washouts of clay. Other colors appear between the Ombrone and Orcia rivers and the Valdichiana, later along the route. The Ombrone rises in Chianti and flows down to the Tyrrhenian across the plain of Grosseto; the Orcia pours down from Monte Cetona, south of Chiusi, and into the Ombrone some distance west, where the rivers flow erratically among gentle peaceful hills. Cypresses stand around the secluded monastery of Monte Oliveto Maggiore, olive trees alternate with vineyards on hilltops. Downhill little towns stand as they have for centuries, stranded by long-vanished ebb tides of history. Montalcino still remembers how the white-spotted banner of the Sienese Republic fluttered high over the town for four years, after the surrender in 1555 following a siege, starvation, and disease: 650 families survived the siege. Pienza, solitary and silent, stands as a visible dream of

Humanistic perfection. Montepulciano is an alternation of Renaissance spaces and palazzi with far more ancient and venerable roots. As you reach the former Etruscan town of Chiusi, you are venturing into the Valdichiana: there is a topographic map drawn by Leonardo da Vinci (1502-1503) with shaded mountains, the round, grey-blue lake of Trasimeno, and even larger and elongated the ancient marsh of the Chiana plain. Chiusi marks the southern edge of this expanse. This route comes to an end with a jog into Umbria: Città della Pieve is your first taste of this region, a cluster of red brick between the green slopes, distant mountain outlines and the blue sky.

The route.

Take Porta Pìspini out of Siena, toward Arezzo and Perugia. At Taverne d'Arbia take the SS 438 road, toward Asciano, via Le Crete. A small road leads up to the abbey of Monte Oliveto Maggiore, and then down to Buonconvento. Continue for a very brief jog along the Cassia (SS 2 road), then cut off to the right along a small road that leads to S. Montalcino (from here, detour to S. Àntimo; km 10) and back to the Cassia at Torrenieri. Take the Cassia to San Quìrico d'Orcia, and then take the SS 146 road east to Pienza, Montepulciano, Chianciano Terme, and Chiusi, until you reach the intersection with the SS 71 road, which you take toward Orvieto, winding up at Città della Pieve.

Places of interest.

Asciano is a medieval "borgo"; adjacent to the Romanesque Collegiata is the Museo d'Arte Sacra; less than a km from the hill of Monteapertaccio, the Guelphs of Florence were defeated by the Ghibellines of Siena, led by Provenzano Salvani and Farinata degli Uberti (this was the Battle of Montaperti, 4 September 1260, described by Dante in his Inferno). Monte Oliveto Maggiore*: this noted Benedictine abbey, secluded amidst cypresses on a hilltop, was founded in 1313 by Bernardo Tolomei; in the cloister are fine frescoes by Signorelli and Sodoma. Buonconvento: girt by a ring of medieval walls, this town has noteworthy artworks in its Museo d'Arte Sacra. Montalcino: the fine red Brunello produced here is considered by many to be Italy's best wine; the fortress was the last bastion of Sienese independence. At a distance of 8 km is the solitary Romanesque abbey of S. Àntimo, said to have been founded by Charlemagne at the end of the 8th c. San Quìrico d'Orcia: a lovely Romanesque Collegiata. Pienza**: here the Renaissance architect Bernardo Rossellino interpreted the scholarly concepts of Enea Silvio (or Aeneus Silvius) Piccolomini, Pope Pius II, in renovating the village in which the pope was born; no other place in Europe came so close to attaining the status of "ideal city" dreamed of by the 15th-c. Humanists. Montepulciano**: the architecture of the Renaissance, which is set amidst the medieval buildings of this ridge-top village between Chiana and Orcia, is by Michelozzo, Vignola, and Antonio da Sangallo the Elder (who also built the lovely, solitary, classical church of S. Biagio). Chianciano Terme*: this renowned spa stands on foothills; the old town is secluded. Chiusi: originally an Etruscan town with artworks and finds in the Museo and an Etruscan necropolis in the nearby countryside. Città della Pieve: the Renaissance artist Perugino was born here, and the countryside reappears in much of his work (paintings by him are in the Cattedrale, in S. Maria dei Bianchi, and other churches).

43 | The Colline Metallifere and the Coastline of Grosseto

Volterra - Massa Marittima - Grosseto - Castiglione della Pescaia - Piombino (189 km)

You can see the Cima delle Cornate on your left as you drive from Larderello to Massa Marittima; it stands on the border between the provinces of Siena and Grosseto, rising to an altitude of 1060 m, high above the smaller hills; geographers consider it to be the nucleus of the "anti-Apennines," also known as the Colline Metallifere ("metal-bearing hills"). Minerals, mining, the "bowels of the earth": these are the main characteristics of this route, which heads south from Volterra, first of all through the Colline Metallifere. In Volterra you will see workshops, walls, and sometimes entire streets covered with the white dust of alabaster (in ancient Latin and Greek, "alabastros" meant a small ointment jar; there has been much discussion as to whether the jar gave the name to the stone, or vice versa; in any case, there are two varieties of alabaster, the calcareous variety, and the dusty, gypsum variety, such as is found in the Volterra region). The Saline, after which the industrial part of Volterra is named, are mines with alternating strata of salt, clay, and gypsum; the boric acid of the "lagoni" of Montecèrboli and the hot "soffioni" bubbling through those bodies of mineral water made the fortune of François de Larderel, a French aristocratic ruined by the Revolution, once a travelling vendor of ribbons and fabrics from Livorno, who established a hot-springs spa here. The

prosperity of Massa Marittima during the Middle Ages, apparent from the many monuments, was produced by veins of copper and silver; also in the region are various pyrites, blende, galena, lignite, quartzite, and alumite. Mineral collectors crowd the annual mineral fair; Gavorrano, surrounded by iron mines, is known for its yellow pyrite crystals. The mineral-rich region borders on the Maremma, dominated by Massa Marittima. There is a bitter old saying: "Va a Massa, guardala e passa," or "Go to Massa, have a look, but don't stay"; the proverb refers to the centuries of abandonment and neglect, the lethal marsh air of the Maremma, where malaria reigned until the Tuscan archdukes began to enact projects of reclamation in the 18th c. This is now a popular vacation spot, though some people still remember how school teachers used to administer a dose of quinine to each pupil every morning, to ward off malaria. Pineta marks the end of this trip, with fragrant aromas of the maquis and the broad gulf of Follonica (midway between Grosseto and Piombino), coming after a visit to the Etruscan ruins of Vetulonia, harkening back to Etruscan Volterra, where this trip started.

The route. From Volterra you will drive down to Saline di Volterra. There, you turn left on to the SS 439 road, to Pomarance (just beyond, at Croce Bulera, you can turn off along a secondary road to San Dalmazio and the Rocca di Sillano, a fortress). At Montecèrboli, a turnoff on the left takes you to Larderello, and then runs back to the road further south. After reaching Massa Marittima, drive back along the same route briefly, then take a secondary road through Bellavista and Perolla, to intersect with the Aurelia (SS 1 road) at Stazione di Gavorrano. Take the Aurelia to Grosseto. The second half of this route takes you from Grosseto along the SS 322 road, which, running mostly along the coast, goes from Castiglione della Pescaia to Follònica. Here, take the Aurelia; turn off at Vignale and you will soon be at Piombino.

Places of interest. Volterra*: the charm of this town lies in the vast landscape that can be seen from the hills between the rivers Cècina and Era, and the stern medieval urban layout; the notable urns of the Museo Guarnacci will take you through the "Etruscan underworld." Many alabaster craftsmen here. Rocca di Sillano: the ruins of this fortress (530 m) dominates the view along the road after Pomarance: you will climb up from San Dalmazio, with the last stretch on foot over mule tracks. Larderello: jets of stream rise here, with cooling towers breaking the horizon; the commercial exploitation of these "soffioni," first undertaken by the above-mentioned Larderel (hence the name), has been going on since 1818; the parish church of the residential area is by the 20th-c. architect Giovanni Michelucci. Massa Marittima*: medieval transformations made the city structure even more complex; and the square, with its Romanesque-Gothic cathedral, is certainly the finest feature of the town; in the landscape of the surrounding Maremma, there is a history of mining; the sea is far off. Vetulonia (5 km from the Aurelia: turn off at I Grilli): this medieval town occupies the acropolis of the Etruscan town; the necropolis is scattered over the countryside. Montepescali (see Grosseto), with a castle on a hill covered with olive groves, is known as the "balcony of the Maremma" for its fine views; a 3.3-km detour will take you here from Braccagni. Grosseto is the prime marketplace of the reclaimed Maremma and is renowned as an agricultural center; the modern city surrounds the small historic nucleus, and the hexagonal enclosure of bastions and walls has been transformed into boulevards and gardens. Castiglione della Pescaia: near the beach is a pine forest, while the town is marked by walls and towers; in the canal-harbor there are more pleasure boats than fishing boats nowadays. Punta Ala*, at the end of a 9-km detour from Pian d'Alma, is an exclusive beachfront residential area, amidst Mediterranean vegetation. Follònica is a beach resort and manufacturing town, with beaches and a pine forest overlooking the gulf. Piombino is a city of iron mills and a port; from a terrace over the sea you can glimpse Elba, the Tuscan Archipelago, and the marina.

4 | Island of Elba

Portoferraio - Marciana - Marina di Campo - Porto Azzurro - Cavo Portoferraio (130 km)

It is said that Elba is a precious stone that fell into the sea, when one of Aphrodite's necklaces broke. Elba is an island with coves, bays, promontories, reefs, and crescent-shaped beaches – the 118 km of coastline is four times the extent one would expect of an island this size – steep slopes dotted with olive and almond trees, silent lofty villages, holm-oaks, and sunny vineyards, producing sweet wines, palm trees, agave plants, eucalyptus trees, and cork-oaks. On the eastern beaches, the sand is mixed with pyrite, and a rusty iron-red dominates in the rocks. The Greek name was "Aethalia," or "place of soot," because of the smoke from the ironworks here; "Ilva," the Roman name, refers to the early lords of the island, the Ligurian Ilvates. Porto Argoo (so-called because Jason, sailing the Argo, landed here during one of his quests), now called Portoferraio, was many centuries ago the main town of Elba. Another name it once bore is Cosmopoli, for the following reason: Cosimo I de' Medici had defended the entire Piombino territory against the wrath of the Barbary pirate and admiral Khair-ed-Din, known also as Barbarossa, or Redbeard. Cosimo then persuaded the Holy Roman Emperor Charles V to let him protect, and rule, the mainland and islands of this patch of what he considered maritime Tuscany, sweetening the pot with a loan of 200,000 ducats. Later, Charles's only son and heir Philip II bestowed Piombino and most of Elba to the Appiani family, leaving Cosimo with Portoferraio. Here, on the site of a modest village, the architect Giovambattista Bellucci had built a city and fortress for the Medici (1548-59): an efficacious piece of military architecture, but also the translation into concrete form of the last tattered dreams of the Renaissance "ideal city." This relic of utopian ambitions, epitomized in the name Cosmopoli, can still be seen.

The route. Thorough exploration of the island starts from Portoferraio, where the car ferry docks. First, take a quick drive to Capo d'Ènfola, then double back almost all the way to Portoferraio before taking the northern coast road, along the water or over hills, around the western half of Elba: Procchio, Marciana Marina, Poggio, and Marciana. After rounding Punta Nera you will follow the southern coast to Fetovaia, Càvoli, Lacona (one detour takes you to the peninsula of Lacona, further on another one leads to Capolìveri and Morcone), and Porto Azzurro. The tour of the eastern half of the island is completed by driving from Porto Azzurro to Rio nell'Elba, Rio Marina, and Cavo – near the northernmost point. Returning along the same road, after Rio Marina but before Rio nell'Elba, take a right on to a secondary road which takes you back to Portoferraio.

Places of interest. Portoferraio: note the strategic position guarding the little bay, the dignified architecture, and the late-Renaissance city layout, the creation of Cosimo I de' Medici; the town also contains the Foresiana art gallery boasting works from the 16th- 19th-c., and an archeological museum with local finds. Capo d'Ènfola: here are the clear waters, abounding in fish, around the promontory. Villa di Napoleone: take a detour from the fork of Bivio Boni; this was Napoleon's summer home. Marciana is a village on the slopes of Monte Capanne, 1018 m (you can reach the peak by cableway and footpaths); on Monte Giove (a bit of a hike is required) is the Santuario della Madonna del Monte. San Piero in Campo: take a detour just before Marina di Campo; this village dating back to Roman times lies at the foot of an old fort. Penisola di Lacona: this peninsula can be reached by a detour from a fork near the Golfo della Stella; forest landscape and beaches of exceedingly fine sand. Capolìveri: there is a spectacular view from the "borgo," which can be reached from a turnoff just before Porto Azzurro; lovely secluded beaches at Morcone. Porto Azzurro: the Spanish built the fortress (now a prison) which looms over the town and the little gulf; from the road to Rio, you can detour to the Santuario di Monserrato (also founded by the Spanish, and dedicated to the Virgin of Monserrat, near Barcelona). Rio nell'Elba is a mining town in iron country. Rio Marina has a small mining museum in the town hall. Cavo: there are ruins of a Roman villa on the promontory of Capo Castello.

45 | Monte Amiata and Valle del Paglia

Chiusi - Radicòfani - Monte Amiata - Acquapendente - Orvieto (150 km)

Here, on the Monte Amiata, they call it "latte di luna," or "moon milk": it is fossil dust, or organic silica, formed by the deposit of countless myriads of diatom algae; it is found in the area around Santa Fiora and is used in the manufacture of dynamite, filters, and insulation. Among the resources of the mountain, it is less well-known than cinnabar, from which mercury is obtained; the Etruscans used it as a dye. As for Monte Amiata itself, the tallest peak in Tuscany south

of the Arno River and the star of this route is an isolated cone, mantled on its upper slopes by beech and chestnut forests. On the north slope, a patch of snow endures through spring; in May the mountain explodes in blooming snowdrops (*Galanthus nivalis*), violets (*Viola odorata*), and broom (*Cytisus scoparia*); the crystal-clear springs that run off this mountain provide the drinking water for the area around Siena, Grosseto, Viterbo, and in the Maremma. Midway up the slopes, where grain, grapes, and olives are grown, the towns ring the mountain like a wreath: you will be exploring them, their dark clustered houses, their narrow steep lanes, the castles, the walls, the abbeys, and the medieval atmosphere. Before you reach Monte Amiata, from Chiusi in Valdichiana, you will join the Via Cassia beneath Radicòfani on its basalt crag. After the circuit around Monte Amiata, you will enter the Valle del Paglia (a tributary of the Tiber that flows down from the mountain); the route, which thus far has remained in Tuscany, proceeds downriver, jogging into Lazio for a short distance, passing through Acquapendente, and then enters Umbria. From crag to crag: the second major crag in this tour is the flat and isolated plateau of tufa upon which stands Orvieto; at its base you will find the Paglia River again.

The route. Drive west from Chiusi along the SS 146 road, and at Querce al Pino you will turn left on to SS 478 road for Sarteano and Radicòfani. From here, take a small road that goes to Abbadia San Salvatore via Le Chiavi and Zaccaria. Here you will turn off to drive counterclockwise around Monte Amiata, via Seggiano, Castel del Piano, Arcidosso, Santa Fiora, and Piancastagnaio. Then drive south along the Paglia Valley, until you come to the Cassia (SS 2 road). Take this, still south, to Acquapendente. Take a left just beyond Acquapendente onto a secondary road that leads to Orvieto, via Castel Viscardo.

Places of interest. Chiusi: the Etruscan origins and heritage (see the museum) are not the only attractions. Sarteano lies in the shadow of a 15th-c. castle, and is renowned as a holiday and spa resort. Radicòfani: medieval houses with rustication, along narrow lanes; Montaigne and Chateaubriand stayed at La Posta, an old hotel here. Abbadia San Salvatore: the medieval village is virtually intact; all around are dense chestnut groves. A road runs nearly to the peak of Monte Amiata (stopping at 1651 m), and you can walk on up to enjoy the immense vista from the peak (1738 m); nearby is the largest mercury mine on earth. Arcidosso is a resort with a well-preserved medieval center. Santa Fiora: the town has a medieval air; the remains of the castle and the Romanesque parish church are interesting. Acquapendente: notable relics in the mortuary chapel of the cathedral. Castel Viscardo is a hill resort with great views; the castle dates from the 15th c. Orvieto**: perched atop a tufa plateau, this town is deserving of its renown; the Duomo, by Lorenzo Maitani, is one of the most exquisite examples of Gothic architecture in Italy.

46 | Valdichiana and Lake Trasimeno

Arezzo - Lucignano - Cortona - Castiglione del Lago - Perugia (168 km)

Every village and town is perched on a hill, overlooking the plain, like a broad green sea, and across that plain to the opposite shore of hills and highlands. The Valdichiana, indeed, is a great rift running north-south across Tuscany, between Arezzo and Chiusi and, following the collapse of the Roman reclamation project in the Middle Ages, was immersed in swamps, marshes, and shallow lakes until the beginning of the 19th c. All around, the background color is provided by the leaves of the olive trees that shade houses, villages, walls, towers, and castles. This route is simple: from Arezzo it runs south, first along the western hills, with Monte San Savino and Lucignano, then on the other side of the valley, with fine views of Cortona, proud on its high perch, with medieval keeps, Etruscan artifacts, and remarkable art (note the 15th-c. clarity of the church of the Madonna del Calcinaio, by Francesco di Giorgio Martini). Once away from the Chiana, you enter Umbria. Gentle slopes, bedecked with olive groves and vineyards, surround the silence and reeds of Lake Trasimeno; the three islands, Polvese, Maggiore, Minore, stand quietly enveloped in turquoise light. You travel almost all the way around the lake, then other hilltop roads take you to lovely Perugia, star-shaped, with long arms of walls and houses reaching out across the ridges. Throughout this trip, history lies at every stop, on every hillside. History is present, in sinister garb, at the Magione, on a rise between Lake Trasimeno and Perugia: in the Magione, or Castle of the Knights of Malta, then held by Cardinal Giambattista Orsini, in September of 1502 a number of local lords angry at and fearful of Cesare Borgia,

son of Pope Alexander VI and brother of Lucrezia, met to conspire against him. Within three months, Borgia had foiled the conspiracy, and four plotters – Vitellozzo Vitelli, Oliverotto da Fermo, Paolo and Francesco Orsini – were killed in Senigallia with what Machiavelli enthusiastically described as a "rare and wondrous deed" (they were poisoned after being invited to dinner). Cardinal Orsini, meanwhile, was dying – or being killed – in Rome's Castel Sant'Angelo.

The route. Leave Arezzo and head for Siena; cross the Valdichiana (SS 73 road) and, at its western edge, climb up to Monte San Savino. A small road takes you to Lucignano and Foiano della Chiana. From here, you will drive back up the Valdichiana along road 327, turning right, after 4 km, on to the road that crosses the valley and intersects the SS 71 road at Castiglion Fiorentino. Take this road toward Rome beyond Castiglione del Lago (on Lake Trasimeno), turning off to the left to skirt the southern and eastern shores of the lake, as far as Passignano sul Trasimeno. Doubling back, via Magione, you will arrive in Perugia. A number of sidetrips, beginning with the climb up to Cortona, are indicated at the respective halts.

Places of interest. Monte San Savino: the feudal holding of the Dal Monte family (Pope Julius II was a Dal Monte), a medieval town now rich in Renaissance art. Lucignano is a medieval village with a remarkable layout; nearby is the Renaissance sanctuary of the Madonna delle Querce. Foiano della Chiana: this thriving hilltop town has old churches and small 16th-c. palazzi; a fine panel by Luca Signorelli in the Collegiata di S. Martino. Castiglion Fiorentino: amid the walls of this medieval town, you can still see the keep of the castle, now the Pinacoteca Comunale, with a notable collection of fine art; further along, to the left of the Valdichiana road, is the large castle of Montecchio Vesponi. Cortona*: you take a fork at Camucìa; landscape, history, and Etruscan relics, medieval townscape, and artworks (by Pietro Lorenzetti, Luca Signorelli, and Fra' Angelico) make this the jewel of the route, one of Italy's artistic capitals. Make a small detour to Madonna del Calcinaio, and visit the Etruscan hypogeum of Tanella di Pitagora; a detour from the road to Città di Castello takes you to the Convento delle Celle. Castiglione del Lago: the old town sits amidst olive trees on a promontory overlooking Lake Trasimeno. Castel Rigone: take a 6-km detour from a fork at San Vito; the Santuario della Madonna dei Miracoli is one of the masterpieces of the Umbrian Renaissance. Passignano sul Trasimeno: also perched on a lakefront promontory, this town has an old center of steep little lanes; on the nearby Isola Maggiore is the 14th-c. Gothic church of S. Michele Arcangelo with a crucifix by Bartolomeo Caporali. Corciano is a turreted medieval village, the last detour on the road from Magione to Perugia.

47 | Valle Umbra

Perugia - Assisi - Spello - Foligno - Spoleto - Montefalco - Perugia (153 km)

When Marco Boschini used the Italian term for "picturesque" in the title of his book "Carta del Navegar Pitoresco," it simply meant "of or about painting." In time, it came to indicate a wealth of nuance, and then to describe a style of painting devote to secluded and evocative landscapes. Nowadays it means "visually charming," "quaint," "graphic," or "vivid." However commonplace the term has become, it may fairly be applied to the Valle Umbra, or Umbrian Valley, watered by the rivers Ose, Topino, Chiona, Clitunno, and Teverone, ringed by hills, farmland, maple trees, vineyards, silvery olive groves, and towns such as Perugia, Assisi, Spello, Trevi, Spoleto, Montefalco, and Bevagna. The "visu ally charming" and "quaint" are unquestionable; as for the "graphic" and "vivid," they apply to the overall panorama, made up of such elements as lovely patches of scenery; remarkable art, ancient and modern; poplars and willows reflected in the clear rippling chilly waters of the Fonti del Clitunno; the wooded Monteluco behind grey Spoleto with its ancient stones; the dreamy medieval air of Bevagna; the glittering color of paintings by Pinturicchio, at Spello, or in the Collegio del Cambio in Perugia; the frescoes by Giotto at Assisi; the pink stones of Assisi, seen from Monte Subasio; the reliefs and statuettes by the Pisano family around the Fontana Maggiore of Perugia, with the white-and-red marble flanks of the cathedral, the Etruscan and Roman fragments, part of an architecture that blends perfectly with the landscape, with masterpieces of fine art side-by-side with jewels of the applied arts. Everywhere is power and restraint. It is not often that Italy, as rich as she is, showers so lavish and enchanting a treasure on so small a space.

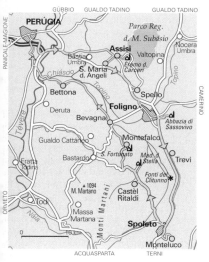

The route. The first part is notably straightforward: take the SS 147 road from Perugia to Assisi; then, heading south, you pass through Spello and Foligno, following the SS 3 road (Via Flaminia) as far as Spoleto. The drive back will follow the other, western side of the Valle Umbra. On secondary roads, through Bruna and Madonna della Stella, you will reach Montefalco, proceed to Bevagna via Pietrauta, and then, remaining on secondary roads, you will reach Bettona; from there, you return to Perugia via Torgiano and the Osteria dei Cipressi. It is advisable to pay close attention to the road signs and your road map, especially in the second part of the route, from Spoleto to Perugia.

Places of interest. Assisi** overlooks much of the Valle Umbra: it has relics of its Roman past and of its medieval existence, but it is quintessentially a Franciscan town; in the basilica of St. Francis, one of Christendom's holy places, are the splendid frescoes by Giotto; plan on spending an intense and fascinating day here. Four km away is the Eremo delle Carceri, a hermitage in which Francis and his brothers "incarcerated" themselves in prayer. S. Maria degli Angeli: this 16th-c. church was built on the site where St. Francis lived and died, and is one of the most important sanctuaries in Italy. Spello*: a medieval town with twisting lanes, churches, old houses and palazzi, luminous orchards and gardens; frescoes by Pinturicchio in the Baglioni Chapel in S. Maria Maggiore. Foligno: the old center of the town lies in the plazas near the Duomo; a little less central is the Romanesque church of S. Maria Infraportas; six km away is the secluded abbey of Sassovivo. Trevi: take a 3-km detour from the Via Flaminia; the town has an ancient air and excellent views: medieval churches and an art gallery in the former convent; the Renaissance Madonna delle Lacrime, 1 km away. Fonti del Clitunno: these freshwater springs feed a small lake surrounded by poplars and willows. Spoleto**, grey on a hill topped by a strong fortress; the Duomo and other monuments stand in medieval surroundings. Monteluco: 8-km detour from Spoleto; a hilltop town, surrounded by holm-oaks and once the home of hermits and anchorites, high up is a convent, with fine view. Castel Ritaldi is a village with a 13th-c. castle, at the end of a short detour from Bruna. Madonna della Stella is a large sanctuary by a grove of holm-oaks and cypresses; take a 2-km detour from Mercatello. Chiesa di S. Fortunato: this church has frescoes by Benozzo Gozzoli; to get here, turn right at crossroads 1 km before Montefalco. Montefalco*: the nickname "ringhiera dell'Umbria," or "balcony of Umbria," describes its location and views. Bevagna: the square is the epitome of an intact medieval scene. Bettona is a village atop an olive-clad hill, with a banner by Perugino set in the 13th-c. church of S. Maria Maggiore.

48 | Argentario and Maremma

Grosseto - Argentario - Capalbio - Magliano in Toscana - Grosseto (172 km)

This is an exploration of the Maremma, along the coast, or inland, beginning in Grosseto and returning to Grosseto. You immediately sense the sea. Stretching from the mouth of the Ombrone and extending to Talamone, the coastline of the Monti dell'Uccellina comprises the Parco Naturale della Maremma. The shore is jagged and wild, the hills are covered with dense Mediterranean underbrush, the solitary towers are old watch posts, built to warn the inhabitants of pirate raids. You must apply to visit the park; further along, however, the so-called Via Aurelia Etrusca runs along the shore of a gulf, with the promontory of the Argentario in the background. In the lagoons of Orbetello, sheets of water separate the necks that link the Argentario to the mainland; this was once an island. More than 150 bird species have been sighted here. Travel around the promontory via a road which gives views both of rocks, inlets, and little harbors, and views of the islands of Giglio and Giannutri. Claudius Rutilius Namatianus sailed these waters, on his way home to Gaul, from Rome, a few years after the sack of Alaric, in 417. His little poem ("De Reditu Suo") tells of his homeward journey; a few verses seem like snapshots. About the promontory, he wrote: "the Argentario plunges down into the midst of the waves, laying a two-fold yoke around bright-blue bays" ("Tenditur in medias mons Argentarius undas / ancipitique iugo caerula curva premit"); of Porto Ercole at sunset: "the light breeze follows gently upon the declining day" ("vergentem sequitur mollior aura diem"); and at Cosa, "the shadow of the pines wavers at the edge of the waves" ("pineaque extremis fluctuat umbra fretis"). The coastal route ends at the fork for Capalbio. Heading inland, on the way back, you go past Capalbio, Magliano in Toscana, and Istia d'Ombrone; it is hard to imagine these lands when they were malarial swamps, before their reclamation. Now they are farmland, forests, or wild grass, with colors ranging from green to reddish brown and ocher; along the embankments, amidst the old red farmhouses, there is a reigning silence and brightness of light that make this land unique.

The route. Except for the detours mentioned at each point in the various stops, you will be following the Via Aurelia, from Grosseto toward Rome, as far as Albinia, where you will turn onto the road that leads to Porto Santo Stefano via the Tómbolo della Giannella. You will drive around the Monte Argentario, going through Porto Ercole, Orbetello, and lastly Orbetello Scalo, where you will rejoin the Via Aurelia. You continue along that road until you reach the turnoff for Capalbio, to the left. After reaching Capalbio you will head north on secondary roads until you hook up with the SS 74 road (Magliano in Toscana-Impostino-Cantoniera dell'Aurelia). Two km north you will leave the Via Aurelia at a turnoff to the right, which will take you to Istia d'Ombrone and then to Roselle. After reaching the ruins of Roselle a little further NE, you will return to Grosseto along the SS 223 road.

Places of interest. Marina di Alberese: take a 14-km detour from Rispèscia and you have fine view of the Uccellina coast. Monti dell'Uccellina: these are within the Parco

Naturale della Maremma, a great nature reserve; the visitor center is at Alberese, not far from the Via Aurelia. Talamone: the old part is a port-side village, overlooking the bay; take a 5-km detour from Fonteblanda. Porto Santo Stefano is an ancient town, elegant and popular, on an inlet of the Argentario. Porto Ercole is a harbor town with a large citadel and three old Spanish forts. Orbetello occupies a remarkable site between the two lagoons. Ansedonia overlooks the sea from atop a promontory; high up are the Roman ruins of Cosa. Take a 3-km detour from the Via Aurelia; nearby is the Tagliata Etrusca, a piece of ancient Roman engineering designed to keep the port free of sand. Capalbio: this medieval hilltop village is now an exclusive resort of Italy's rich and powerful personages; the parish church of S. Nicola contains Roman relics and frescoes from the 15th-16th c. Magliano in Toscana: medieval in appearance, it stands on an olive-bedecked hill in the Maremma landscape. Istia d'Ombrone is an old village on a riverside rise. Rovine di Roselle: these are the remains of what was long ago one of the main towns of northern Etruria; notable Etruscan and Roman ruins have been found here.

49 | Monti della Tolfa and Lake Bracciano

Rome - Cervèteri - Civitavecchia - Tolfa - Bracciano - Rome (194 km)

In the Roman "campagna," or countryside, the days of shepherds wearing fleecy vests and leaning on knobby sticks are long gone; also long vanished are the skittish, unshod ponies of the "butteri," the mounted cowherds of this region, wearing leather chaps and a rifle slung around their neck; no longer do the "seasonal" workers sleep in a circle in the fields. Still, you may glimpse fragments of that lost world now and again: the gritty farmhouse, perhaps, or a stand of pinasters, an ancient clump of ruins, or the gentle curve of the meadowland. Starting from and returning to Rome, this route runs through four different landscapes, redolent with nature and history. The first follows the crescent-shaped Tyrrhenian coastline as far as Capo Linaro and Civitavecchia. You will follow the Via Aurelia, as you head toward the first encounter with the ancient Etruscans: Cervèteri, withdrawn from the shore, with its burial grounds of rounded hillocks, tufted with grass, humping across the countryside around the medieval "borgo," and the ancient ports along the seacoast. After Civitavecchia and its harbor ("interior medias sinus invitatus in aedes / instabilem fixis aera nescit aquis"; as an ancient poet, Rutilius Namatianus, described it, when the port

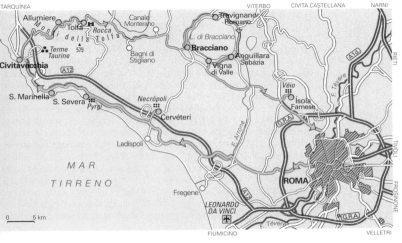

was known as "Centumcellae": "the inner gulf, invited amongst the houses, ignores the skittish winds with its steady waters"), the route turns inland, and the second landscape is that of the Monti della Tolfa. In the seaside maquis, or among the inland forests, you may still chance upon a wolf, lone descendant of the wolves that were forced down out of the Apennines by the icy winter of 1956. Geologists will find ores such as blende, galena, pyrite, alumite, kaolin, and cinnabar, all of which prompted ancient mining operations here. The third landscape surrounds Lake Bracciano: looking down from the high ridge, you will see the lake at the bottom of its funnel-shaped depression, houses crowded along the banks amidst clumps of alders, willows, and poplars; perched on poles, improbable seagulls watch as coots dive into the tranquil waters. Sometimes a sharp-taloned kite will soar overhead. Last comes the solitary landscape of long-lost Veio, and the rustic promenade across fields to the ruins of the Temple of the Vulcan Apollo (the god's statue is now in Rome, in the Museo Etrusco di Villa Giulia).

The route.

You start out from Rome, heading west along the Via Aurelia (SS 1 road), all the way to Civitavecchia; on your right, after Borgo Vaccina, note the short detour (3.5 km) that takes you to Cervèteri, one of the prime destinations on this route. Once you have passed through Civitavecchia, exit through Porta Tarquinia and take the scenic route to Bracciano; this road first goes up the western slopes of Monti della Tolfa, passing through Allumiere and Tolfa, and then begins the long descent toward Lago di Bracciano, passing through Manziana on the way. From the town of Bracciano, the route turns north, making a nearly complete clockwise circuit around the lake, and passing through Trevignano Romano, Anguillara Sabazia, and Vigna di Valle. Then, moving away from the lakeshore drive, you will take the SS 493 road (Via Claudia Braccianese), heading toward Rome until you hit the SS 2 road (Via Cassia). From that crossroads, a detour to the north climbs for 2 km up to the town of Isola Farnese, overlooking the ruins of Veio. Again, take the SS 2 road and then the SS 3 road or Via Flaminia back into Rome, crossing the Tiber on the Ponte Flaminio, or Flaminian Bridge.

Places of interest.

Cervèteri*: the stern medieval center of town, high on a tufa spur, stands on the site of the Etruscan town of Kysry, a wealthy trading port and sea power; in the Castello, don't miss the Museo Nazionale Cerite. Nearby, in the empty landscape of pinasters and cypresses, is a necropolis, with circular barrow tombs. Santa Severa: south of the distinctive castle here, archeologists have excavated Pyrgi, the largest port-of-call of ancient Caere (antiquarium). Santa Marinella: beach resort; the Castello Odescalchi, set amidst pine trees near the little marina of "Punicum," another port-of-call of ancient Caere. Civitavecchia: Michelangelo built the eight-sided keep of the high fort that bears his name; this city is now Latium's most important port. In the Museo Nazionale Archeologico are finds from earliest times to the Roman Empire; the nearby Terme Taurine are the baths of a huge Roman villa, owned by the emperor. Allumiere lies on the slopes of the Monte Le Grazie; as the town's name indicates, this was once a quarry for rock alum, used in dyeing wool. Tolfa gave its name to the surrounding mountain group; the papal state mined iron ore here for three centuries. The shafts are now abandoned. Bracciano: vast view of the Lago di Bracciano from the stern 15th c. Castello Orsini-Odescalchi, with fine furnishings. Trevignano Romano is a village founded in the remote past on the northern lakeshore; the Museo Archeologico houses material from the necropolises of an Etruscan-Roman center. Anguillara Sabazia stands on a point of the shore of Lake Bracciano; it is one of the 13 castles that Pope Paul II seized in the 15th c. from the Anguillara family during a 12-day war. Vigna di Valle: alongside airplanes of every era, this Italian Air Force museum, the Museo Storico dell'Aeronautica Militare, has exhibits on the history of flight and the polar expeditions of the dirigibles Norge and Italia. Isola Farnese: this hamlet stands high on a crag over two gorges; around it are scattered the ruins of Etruscan Veio in a lovely setting.

0 | Roman Etruria

Viterbo - Vetralla - Tuscania - Ischia di Castro - Vulci - Tarquinia (111 km)

Roman Etruria coincided with what is now northern Latium, or southern Etruria, amongst the Monti Volsini, the Monti Cimini, the Monti Sabatini, and the Tyrrhenian coastline. This route runs through the NW section, at the edge of the Maremma along the seaside. There are four noteworthy Etruscan sites, illustrious and timeworn: Norchia, Tuscania, Vulci, and Tarquinia. At Norchia, which may have been called Orcla by the Etruscans, the atmosphere is remote, surreal, among the architectural facades of the cliffside tombs, plundered long ago, and the medieval ruins of the town. At Tuscania, rather than the much faded Etruscan memories, it is the two early Romanesque churches that attract the eye: these are prototypes of the glorious Italian architecture that blends the Mediterranean style with northern European rigor, creating something uniquely independent, complete unto itself. The beautiful landscape of Vulci, not far from the sea – on a tufa highland on the right bank of

the river Fiora – was the site of a heartbreaking act of plunder. In 1828, Luciano Bonaparte, the grasping younger brother of Napoleon, and the papal prince of nearby Canino, excavated in the Etruscan necropolis here, and in four months carried off 2,000 vases. Others followed in the treasure hunt, opening 6,000 tombs, and destroying everything which was not immediately salable, including countless priceless terracottas. Of Tarquinia, and its tomb-paintings, little needs to be said, so great are their fame. Perhaps the native Tarquinian V. Cardarelli said it best: "Here laughed the Etruscan, one day, reclining with his eyes leveled at the harbor. His pupils took in the infinite silent splendor of the lush young land, of which he had so gaily drunk the mysteries...."

he route. From Viterbo you will follow the Via Cassia (SS 2 road) toward Rome as far as Vetralla; from here, a 14-km detour takes you to Norchia. Just prior to entering Vetralla, another road leads north, through rolling countryside, to Tuscania and, still further north, to Piansano and Valentano. Once here, head SW toward the Tyrrhenian coastline, passing through Ischia di Castro – and from here you can venture into the forest of Lamone as far as the ruins of Castro (10 km) – Pianiano, and the archeological site of Vulci, in a countryside frequented for the most part by agricultural machinery and little else, and mantled in long expanses of wheat and other grains. Near Montalto di Castro you can join up with the Via Aurelia (SS 1 road), following it back toward Rome until you reach the intersection for Tarquinia.

laces of interest. Vetralla: this village, partly medieval in appearance, is a point of departure for visiting Norchia*, whose Etruscan necropolis features tombs carved out of the tufa, with architectural facades. Tuscania*: within the medieval walls of this town is a secluded atmosphere; the town was rebuilt after the earthquake of 1971. On a hillside outside of town are the churches of S. Pietro and S. Maria Maggiore, masterpieces of Italian architecture of the High Middle Ages. Valentano, on the lip of the crater hollow of Làtera, with hues of emerald in spring, sere and yellow in summer; note the vista, which extends beyond the great round hollow of Làtera, Lake Bolsena and, in the distance, Monte Amiata. Ischia di Castro is a medieval "borgo" on a tufa-stone crag, with the Palazzo Ducale by Sangallo and Etruscan artifacts from Castro in the Museo Civico. Farnese, where medieval buildings and Renaissance palazzi stand side-by-

side; a fine gilded wooden tabenacle in the parish church of S. Salvato
Rovine di Castro: "Qui fu Castro" – Here stood Castro – is inscribed upon a so
tary column on a great mass of tufa-stone; the city, once capital of the Farne
duchy of Castro and Ronciglione, was leveled in 1649. Vulci: architecture a
landscape are very old friends here, as you may note from the bridge, whic
re-uses fragments of earlier Etruscan and Roman structures; also visit the A
badia, which houses the Museo Nazionale di Vulci, originally a medieval ca
tle, the ruins of the long-vanished Etrusco-Roman town, and the vast Etrusc
necropolises in the surrounding territory. Montalto di Castro, a "borgo" on t
edge of the Maremma, a site noted for the as yet to be completed power st
tion. Tarquinia*: this ancient hilltop city boasts the 14th-c. Palazzo Vitellesc
with the Museo Nazionale Tarquiniense, the Romanseque church of S. Mar
di Castello, and, east of town, the Necropolis of Monterozzi, with outstandir
Etruscan tomb paintings.

51 | Monti Cimini

Viterbo - Bomarzo - Civita Castellana - Caprarola - Viterbo (111 km)

The ambiguous term "Mannerism" was first used by L. Lanzi in the late 18th
to designate a 16th-c. style in the fine arts, "characterized by a complex sy
tem of perspective, elongation of forms, strained gestures or poses of figure
and intense, often strident color." It tended to include the bizarre, the cap
cious, the fantastic, and a tormented restlessness. Anticlassical art, if you wi
self-referential rather than an "imitation of nature," and popular with arist
cratic patrons, who were learned, jaded, and obsessed with a dream of "arti
cial" beauty. This style is found in this route in three exemplary sites: Bagnai
Bomarzo, and Caprarola. At Bagnaia, Cardinal Gambara had the architect Vi
nola create, for what is now Villa Lante, an Italian-style garden replete with o
nate fountains (it appears that work was halted by a visit from St. Charles Bo

romeo, who was auditing for Pope Pius V th
lavish spending of cardinals). Bomarzo, mor
than the other two places, is disquietin
causing intellectual shivers with its Parco d
Mostri, or Park of Monsters, dreamed up b
Vicino Orsini and recently rediscovered wit
the advent of a new attitude toward Manner
ism. At Caprarola, it was again Vignola wh
transformed an old fort, built by Sangallo, in
to the Palazzo Farnese, with a round centra
courtyard and a profusion of virtuoso decora
tions, inside and out. And the surroundin
countryside, dominated by the Monti Cimin
through which the route runs, SE of Viterbo, i
gently rolling, with extinct volcanoes, ser
landscapes, steep bluffs, high tufa cliffs, an
dense forests of oak and chestnut, beneat
the beech groves atop the Monte Cimino
overlooking the solitary Lago di Vico, ancier
boundary of the Roman realm.

The route.

Viale Trieste, which takes you east out of Viterbo, turns into the SS 204 road
passes through Bagnaia, and then turns toward Orte. After the detour (3 km
toward Vitorchiano, at the intersection with the road to Bomarzo (3-km de
tour), you will turn right toward Soriano nel Cimino; from there, along sec
ondary roads, you will head SE, going past Monte Cimino and throug
Canepina, Vallerano, Vignanello, and Corchiano. From Civita Castellana a 6-kr
detour will allow you to tour "Falerii Novi," while the main route runs west, be
yond Castel Sant'Elia, to Nepi and, with a short jog along the Via Cassia (SS 2
road), to Sutri. Then you will head north, and, after Ronciglione, you will fol

low the Via Cimina along the eastern rim of the crater which forms Lake Vico, with fine views of the lake and of the conical Monte Venere, with a steep descent down to Caprarola on the right (3.5 km). Through the Monti Cimini you will reach San Martino al Cimino; from here, you can quickly return to Viterbo.

aces of interest. S. Maria della Quercia*: the sanctuary, a lovely piece of Renaissance architecture, appears at the end of a long avenue, with a Della Robbia terracotta portal; the nearby museum houses a collection of ex-voto offerings dating from 1490-1730. Bagnaia: the medieval section lies on a rocky promontory between two rushing streams; the 16th-c. addition lies uphill and culminates in the Villa Lante, designed by Vignola, with the fountains and streams in the garden. Vitorchiano: this largely intact medieval village has houses overlooking a precipice; the 14th-c church of S. Maria has been largely rebuilt. Bomarzo: dominating the old village is the 16th-c. Palazzo Orsini; in the surrounding area, the Parco dei Mostri, the enigmatic creation of Vicino Orsini, a soldier and man of letters of the late 16th c. Soriano nel Cimino: there are two major attractions in this medieval town – the Castello Orsini and the Mannerist Papacqua Fountain in the Palazzo Chigi-Albani. Monte Cimino: among the beeches that cover the mountain, there is a 250-ton trachyte boulder that will rock back and forth if you pull on a lever; it is called the Sasso Menicante, "naturae miraculum" according to Pliny the Elder. Canepina lies among groves of chestnut and hazelnut trees, with the parish church of S. Maria Assunta by Sangallo. Vallerano has a 17th-c. sanctuary dedicated to a miracle of the Virgin Mary. Vignanello, a town that produces flavorful wines, with a view of the Tiber Valley, lies beneath Palazzo Ruspoli rebuilt in the 16th c. Corchiano: 15th-c. frescoes in S. Biagio church. Cìvita Castellana: the Cosmatesque portico of the Duomo is the most renowned monument of the town, but hardly the only one: in the fortress by Sangallo is a notable archeological museum, and nearby are the ruins of the Roman "Falerii Novi"*. Castel Sant'Elia (see Nepi): pilgrimages are made to the nearby sanctuary of S. Maria ad Rupes, carved out of the rock; tourists instead visit the Romanesque basilica di S. Elia. Nepi: 16th-c. walls enclose the village, extending along a tufa ridge, dating back to the Middle Ages and the Renaissance. Sutri: here too the village is built on tufa stone, along with the Etruscan, Roman and medieval monuments; dark holm-oaks stand around the amphitheater; the shrine to the Madonna del Parto dates back into the mists of time. Ronciglione: the streets and aristocratic 16th-/18th-c. palazzi of this town overlook the Lake Vico; visit the compact medieval "borgo." Caprarola: the Renaissance village lies at the base of the five-sided Palazzo Farnese (with a circular courtyard), built by Vignola for the nephew of Pope Paul III; late-16th-c. frescoes recall the splendor of this powerful family. San Martino al Cimino: medieval walls enclose the 17th-c. town and the 13th-c. abbey of S. Martino, built by the Cistercians of Pontigny.

52 | Monte Velino, Monte Sirente, and Cicolano

Rieti - L'Àquila - Avezzano - Lago del Salto - Rieti (212 km)

From Rieti to the Piana del Fùcino and back again: varied mountainous landscapes, contrasting between narrow passes – the gorges of the Velino on the Via Salaria, the cliffs of the Valle del Salto – and vast horizons – the basin of Aquila, the "plain" of Rocca di Mezzo, the meadows of the Fùcino. Midway through this route, the city of L'Àquila, with its art treasures (though elsewhere in the route you will find castles and Romanesque churches). The names in the title of this route refer to three different worlds, as it were. The Velino River rises in a corner of Latium wedged between Umbria, Marche, and Abruzzo. Velino is also the name of a mountain in Abruzzo (2487 m tall; on clear winter days, you can see both seas, Tyrrhenian and Adriatic, from the peak); like Monte Sirente (2349 m), it is located between L'Àquila and the Piana del Fùcino. As you pass through the "plain" of Rocca di Mezzo, Velino is to the west, Sirente is to the east (the plain is a major feature, a large karstic hol-

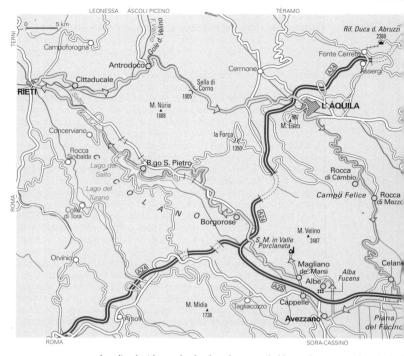

low, lined with meadowland, and surrounded by peaks towering hundreds of meters overhead). Lastly, the Cicolano is an area of Latium, SE of Rieti, that comprises the middle and upper valley of the Salto River, which flows down to Rieti. This route then runs through Latium and Abruzzo; the regional border lies between Antrodoco and the Sella di Corno, as you climb into Abruzzo, and after Magliano de' Marsi, as you leave it. In the division of Italy into north, central, and south, Abruzzo is technically part of central Italy, extending as it does NE of Latium. Historically, however, it has been part of the "southern realm" since the 12th c. The regional boundary is therefore a major one.

The route. The road from Rieti, in Latium, to L'Àquila, in Abruzzo, is the Via Salaria (SS 4 road), running first through Cittaducale and Antrodoco, and then, just past the gorges of the Velino River, on the left, it shifts to the Via Sabina (SS 17 road) which runs over the Sella di Corno (1005 m). From L'Àquila you will continue along the SS road 5 *bis* over the upland of Rocca di Cambio (1433 m). The descent runs through Celano, the Piana del Fùcino, and Avezzano; from here, a 10-km detour will take you to the archeological excavations of Alba Fucens. For the return to Rieti, you will leave Avezzano and head for Cappelle (at the intersection, turn right onto the SS 578 road), Magliano de' Marsi, with a segment of road 7 km long, to the church of S. Maria in Valle Porclaneta, Borgorose, and the Lago del Salto (you will leave the SS 578 road, hugging the north coast of the lake). You will then return to Rieti by way of the Valle del Salto.

Places of interest. Rieti, along the Velino River and at the edge of a broad green valley, within sight of Monte Terminillo, preserves intact the structure and monuments of its medieval town center. Cittaducale, founded in the 14th c. under Angevin rule, has a regular layout; note original towers and intact sections of the walls. S. Maria Extra Moenia, a Romanesque church with, adjacent, the hexagonal Baptistery of S. Giovanni with frescoes from the 15th-16th c. Antrodoco: "Interocrium," or amidst the mountains, is its ancient name, which is certainly still applicable. Gole del Velino*: these jagged wild gorges still have, midway along, the boulder of the Orso, carved out vertically by the Romans for some 30 m. L'Àquila* is a mountain town that savors of ancient history, crowded with monuments, art work, and startling mountain vistas. It is the largest city in Abruzzo. Celano: the old village lies in the shadow of the stern Castello Piccolomini; narrow, jagged, and deep are the nearby Gole, or Gorges, of Celano. Rocca di Cambio is the highest town in Abruzzo, beloved by skiers. Rocca di Mezzo: this resort has a fine little religious museum, with sacred objects and wooden statues. Avezzano: rebuilt after the earthquake of 1915 and again after WWII, this city lies on the western edge of the Piana del Fùcino; near the "borgo" of Albe are the little Romanesque church of S. Pietro and the archeological digs of ancient Roman Alba Fucens. S. Maria in Valle Porclaneta* has a secluded 11th-c Romanesque church on the mountain slope, with an exquisitely detailed interior. Lago del Salto: this man-made hydroelectric basin was built in 1938, submerging Borgo San Pietro; the new town looks down on the lake from above the road.

53 | Monti Tiburtini, Èrnici, and Monti Prenestini

Rome - Tìvoli - Subiaco - Fiuggi - Palestrina - Rome (202 km)

Over mountains and through valleys to the east of Rome: the Monti Tiburtini line the left bank of the Aniene River, from the point where the river turns sharply from NW to SW, down to where they sink into hills on the plain; the highest point is the Monte dell'Ara Salere (795 m). As you head back up the Aniene, you will see them on the right. Beyond that sharp turn, the river borders the Monti Simbruini: this is Subiaco. The Monti Èrnici, which you will cross as you leave the Valle dell'Aniene, crossing the uplands of Arcinazzo and then heading down to Fiuggi, are much taller (Pizzo Deta, 2041 m). They stretch from west to east as far as Sora in the Valle del Liri, north of the broad cut of the Sacco River. The Monti Prenestini, lastly, stretch from north to south, between the basins of the Aniene and Sacco rivers, behind Palestrina; with Monte Guadagnolo, they reach an altitude of 1218 m. The landscape is still that of the Apennines: sere hills, clustered villages, stretches of woods. You begin with the Villa Adriana, or Hadrian's Villa, then Tìvoli with the sound of water amidst the crags. On the way back, at Palestrina, you can see the terraces of the Roman sanctuary, where the oracles foretold destinies; at the halfway point, Subiaco, where the Benedictines founded a world of medieval monasteries. The composer Hector Berlioz came up here in 1832, when he was staying in Villa Medici after winning the "Prix de Rome"; he wrote about "the cavern where St. Benedict lived, where the rosebush he planted still flourishes" and "the cell of Blessed Lorenzo, sheltered by a rock wall which is made golden by the sun," and lastly, the "great groves of dark-leaved chestnut trees, with ruins where, in the evening, every so often a human shadow will appear for a moment and then disappear without a sound... shepherds, or brigands...."

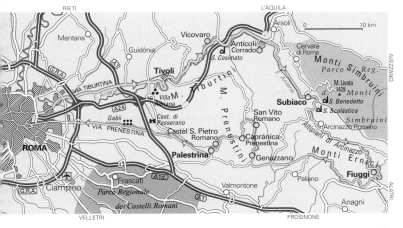

The route.

The Via Tiburtina (SS 5 road; in the city of Rome it begins at the arches of Viviana) goes along the Aniene River to Tivoli and to Vicovaro. You will tu off it after the intersection of Antìcoli Corrado, the destination of a short ∘ tour (3 km, to the right), on a road that continues along the Aniene Riv climbing up to Subiaco and then over the uplands of Arcinazzo (841 m), to t spa of Fiuggi on the southern slopes of Monti Èrnici. On the return to Rom the route follows a circuit through the Monti Prenestini, along seconda roads with scenic stretches, through Genazzano, then to San Vito Roman Capranica Prenestina, and Palestrina. From here the Via Prenestina ru through Santa Maria di Cavamonte and the ruins of Gabii back to Rome.

Places of interest.

Villa Adriana**: a mirror of ancient style, physical catalogue of culture, repo itory of souvenirs from the travels of the Emperor Hadrian, who devoted lo years to its construction; they are now some of the most significant and v ied ruins of antiquity. Tivoli*, overlooking the Roman countryside ("ca pagna"), was an aristocratic watering hole, surrounded by jagged rocks, lu greenery, a circular Temple of Vesta, villas, gardens, parks, waterfalls, ar fountains. Vicovaro, atop a hill on the Aniene's right bank, features ruin walls and a 15th-c. eight-sided church, S. Giacomo. S. Cosimato is a Francisca hermitage set among cypresses and pines; it stands high on a crag overlooc ing the Aniene, over the ruins of a Roman villa. Antìcoli Corrado (see Vic varo): this village, with medieval relics scattered here and there, is renown for the beauty of its women and its 120 years of popularity with artists; t fountain in the medieval quarter is noteworthy. Subiaco*: this small, intens ly medieval town, set amidst mountains dense with woods, is redolent wi the heritage and memory of St. Benedict of Norcia (or Nursia), his broth monks, and the monastic world they created; the monasteries of S. Scolasti and the Sacro Speco stand in seclusion in the narrow Aniene Valley. NE Subiaco you can climb Monte Livata (1324 m), a popular resort both for skii and summering. Fiuggi* was already famous for its mineral waters in ancie times, one of the finest spas in Italy; the greenery of Fiuggi Fonte (or, sprin of Fiuggi) contrasts with the medieval flavor of Fiuggi Città (the town of Fiu gi). Genazzano, on the slope of an isolated hill, boasts the Santuario de Madonna del Buon Consiglio, Gothic houses, and the Castello Colonna, stron hold of the famed family. In the ruins of the nymphaeum, strewn across t fields, it is said that Ovid was smitten with the love that ultimately caused A gustus to exile him to the Black Sea, where he died; in reality they are the r ins of a Renaissance building. San Vito Romano: this "borgo," or village, li snug at the foot of the castle known as Palazzo Tresoldi. Castel San Pietro R mano is a country village lodged on the site of the ancient acropolis "Præneste" ; crowning the hill are the ruins of the Rocca dei Colonna, t Colonna family stronghold, and the immense vista of the Colli Albani and t Valle del Sacco. Palestrina*: the medieval city merges, in the most remarkab way, with the Roman sanctuary of Fortuna Primigenia; in the 17th-c. Palaz: Barberini is the Museo Archeologico Prenestino. The medieval Castello Passerano stands in an inspired setting (go through Santa Maria di Cav monte, turning off for 4 km along the road to Tìvoli). Gabii: the ruins of t Latin city stand on the right side of the Via Prenestina; the cella of the temp of Juno Gabina, dating from the time of the Republic, is impressive.

54 | Castelli Romani

Rome - Frascati - Velletri - Albano Laziale - Marino - Rome (117 km)

"In the morning and evening," wrote Goethe, "a little fog descends up∘ Rome. On the hills outside of town, however, at Albano, Castel Gandolfo, ar Frascati, where I spent three days last week, the air is always clear and pure He visited the hills more than once. Of one stay, with a marvelous Decemb∘ sunshine, he wrote: "Aside from the evergreens, a number of oak trees ai still dense with leaves; likewise the young chestnut trees, though their leave have yellowed. The landscape has hues of remarkable beauty..." The geography of the Colli Albani can best be glimpsed from an airplane, or else from a topographical map, perhaps an old-fashioned, patiently sketched one. In origin, they are a large volcanic system, with a clearly defined crater area, some 30 km across, broken only to the SW, ripped apart by the eruptions that tore open the lesser craters that are now the lakes of Albano, Nemi, and Ariccia – though the latter is now a dry bed. In the center are Monte Cavo (949 m) and Monte Faete (956 m). The chestnuts and oaks mentioned by Goethe are largely found in the central region, while on the gentle outer slopes are olive groves and vineyards, famed for the "vini dei castelli," or "castle wines." About these wines, Leo XIII (pope from 1878 to 1903) wrote: "exilarant animos, curasque resolvunt," i.e., "they cheer the soul and wipe away cares."

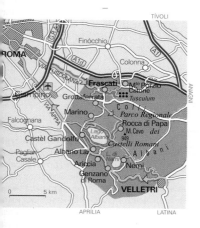

The villages and small towns on the slopes are the Castelli Romani, or Roman Castles, properly speaking, 13 in number (Frascati, Grottaferrata, Marino, Castel Gandolfo, Albano, Ariccia, Genzano, Nemi, Rocca di Papa, Rocca Priora, Monte Còmpatri, Monte Porzio Catone, and Colonna), and called "castles" because noble Roman families and popes owned fortified country houses there. As times became easier, the fortified manors made way for open villas; popes and nobles spent their holidays here, just as the ancient Romans had done (Cicero had a villa at Tusculum, Domitian built one at Castel Gandolfo, the site of ancient Alba Longa). "In the evening" – wrote Goethe, from Frascati, in late September – "by moonlight, we walk around admiring the villas, sketching the most interesting features, even in the dark..."

The route. The Via Tuscolana – which you can reach from central Rome by exiting through the Porta S. Giovanni and following a short stretch of the Via Appia Nuova – leads to Frascati (there are also a number of other routes to Frascati). From Frascati, the first section of the painstaking exploration of the Castelli Romani suggested here involves, in order: a drive to Monte Porzio Catone; a tour of the ruins of Tusculum (with a detour from the main route between Monte Porzio Catone and Grottaferrata); a tour of Grottaferrata; a lovely scenic road from Grottaferrata to Rocca di Papa and a drive up Monte Cavo (949 m; 5.5 km from Rocca di Papa). After descending from Monte Cavo you will take the Via dei Laghi (literally, "lake route"; SS 217 road), following it – except for a detour to Nemi – as far as Velletri. From Velletri, on your way back to Rome along the Via Appia (SS 7 road), you will pass through Genzano, Ariccia, and Albano Laziale. You climb from here up to Castel Gandolfo, and then on the way back down, you will take a drive around the Lago Albano, counterclockwise, with a detour up to Marino. Then back downhill from Marino to the Lago Albano and, once you have completed the drive around the lake, you will see a tunnel on your right; this takes you onto the Via Appia (SS 7 road), which leads back into Rome.

Places of interest. Frascati: this is the most popular of the Castelli Romani; sumptuous villas have been built here since ancient Roman times. Monte Porzio Catone is a 16th-c. village built on a hill blanketed with olive groves. "Tusculum"*: the ruins of this Latin city can be reached by making a 2-km detour from the route to Grottaferrata; there are the remains of the ampitheater, the theater, the forum and the so called Villa di Tiberio. Grottaferrata: the venerable abbey, fortified with walls and moats, is a monastery founded in 1004 by S. Nilo, or St. Niles. Rocca di Papa has a medieval uphill quarter and a modern, prosperous quarter with gardens; continue along your route, through the woods, and above Lago Albano you will find the Santuario della Madonna del Tufo, built around a boulder frescoed by A. Romano. Monte Cavo*: with good weather,

you can see forever across the Colli Albani, glimpsing Rome, the Tyrrheni
Sea, the Circeo, Monte Terminillo, and the Gran Sasso d'Italia. Nemi: the tov
overlooks the lake, deep blue at the bottom of the crater. Velletri lies perch
on a spur of the southern slopes of the Colli Albani, amidst expanses
grapevines. Genzano di Roma fans out across the outer slope of the crater
Lake Nemi; a road along the north bank of the lake takes you to the Mus
Nemorense, or Museum of Nemi. All that survives of the famous late-impe
al Roman ships of Nemi are models and fragments. Ariccia: the cent
square, with fountain and the round church of S. Maria dell'Assunzione, w
designed by G. L. Bernini. Albano Laziale: it is said that the tombs of the H
ratii, early Roman heroes, and their Curiatii opponents, are here; in reality
is an anonymous late-Republic Roman tomb. Castel Gandolfo looks out fro
the rim of the crater of the Lago Albano; the 17th-c. summer residence of t
pope is in Piazza Plebiscito. Marino: "Mole stat sua" is the motto inscribed
the heraldic column of Palazzo Colonna, in the center of this village hi
above the lake, on a peperino spur.

55 | Ciociarìa

Rome - Palestrina - Segni - Anagni - Alatri - Frosinone (136 km)

The Ciociarìa area extends along the Sacco River between the Monti Èrn
and the Monti Lepini. The towns through which this route passes – Seg
Anagni, Ferentino, and Alatri – will surprise you with their intense charact
all of them are pre-Roman, and seem like a rustic symphony. There are t
sharp high notes of cathedrals, town walls, and palazzi, the basso continuo
the lesser architecture, all harmonizing fluently with the surrounding cou
tryside. The land takes its name from Cicero – though the name Ciociarìa o
ly appears in the 18th c. – who described it as "aspera et montuosa et fide
et simplex et fautrix suorum" (harsh, mountainous, faithful, simple, caring f
its own). No traveller can hope to verify all those qualities in a single quick v
it, but one can make comparisons with the land described by A. Baldini in t
1920s: "harsh lands" – again, the adjective used first by Cicero – "perched
steep mountain slopes, black with storms"; "where the stone of the palaz
and the plaster of the more rustic walls easily turn dark as pitch with tim
along with the "burnt autumnal color of dead leaves, spread across the ro
by wandering lichens." Amidst all this darkness, one has luminous views "l
tween one wall and another, or beneath the arches of these steep streets,
distant valleys and mountains," "of bright red geraniums," "of green pergol
behind the houses." Baldini found the men "sun-darkened, hirsute, and grin
while the women he hailed as having "the faces of madonnas, framed by rav
hair," and "a most particularly graceful way of walking" caused by the custo
of "carrying heavy, sometimes immensely heavy objects balanced on the
heads, climbing and descending constantly along these steep stone wa
ways…": yellowed photographs of an Italy long lost.

The route.

Aside from the Autostrada, the route from Rome to Frosinone runs along the Via Casilina (SS 6 road), which begins in the city in Piazza di Porta Maggiore. The route turns off from this route three times, all the same. In fact, just after Stazione di Palestrina, you will take a left onto the detour that runs to Palestrina itself; from this town, you will return to the Via Casilina along the secondary road that rejoins it at Valmontone. You then branch off from the Via Casilina a second time at the turnoff for Colleferro: take secondary roads along the route that leads first south to Colleferro and Segni, and then north across the Sacco River, the Sacco Valley, and the Via Casilina, to climb up to Anagni. From Anagni you will drive right back onto the Via Casilina, leaving it one last time at the fork for Ferentino. From Ferentino you will take a scenic road to Alatri; from here a detour will take you 13.5 km north to Collepardo and to the Certosa di Trisulti. Lastly, you will reach Frosinone from the north, along the SS 155 road.

Places of interest.

Palestrina*: the Roman sanctuary of Fortuna Primigenia, perched high on the slope, constitutes the backdrop of the medieval town; even higher, in Palazzo Barberini, is the Museo Archeologico Prenestino. Valmontone is partly medieval and sits high on a tufa rise at the confluence of two valleys; the 17th-c. Palazzo Doria and the nearby Collegiata dell'Assunta, rebuilt in 1685-89, are worth a visit. Segni lies dark amidst the chestnut groves, staggered down the slope of a spur of the Monti Lepini, with stretches of complex walls, and the renowned Porta Saracena, or Saracen Gate. In the lofty acropolis is a 13th-c. church occupying the cella of an ancient temple. Anagni* sits high atop a spur overlooking the Valle del Sacco; one part of the town has a markedly medieval atmosphere, particularly intense in the "Quartiere dei Caetani," with the palazzo of Boniface VIII (Caetani) – supposedly the site of a slap in the pope's face, inflicted by soldiers of Philip IV, the Fair, of France. Also, visit the Romanesque cathedral, with 13th-c. frescoes in the crypt. Ferentino*: pre-Roman walls hold up the old acropolis and the Duomo that occupies its "platea," or plaza; the town is a trove of ancient and medieval structures, including S. Maria Maggiore, a Cistercian Gothic church. Alatri*: this little medieval city stands on a hill blanketed with olive groves; note the Duomo in the silent tree-lined "piazzale" atop the hill, as well as 2 km of intact polygonal walls. Continue on to Collepardo, with the nearby Grotta dei Bambocci, full of stalactites and stalagmites; there is also the Certosa di Trisulti, an old charterhouse, founded in the 13th c. and restored in the 18th c., with an ancient apothecary shop and a building in which the zealot pope, Innocent III, may have written his manifesto, "De comtemptu mundi," or "Misery of the Condition of Man." Frosinone, chief town of the Ciociarìa, is mostly modern; the old quarter high on the hill overlooks the Piana del Sacco.

56 | From the Gulf of Gaeta to the Colli Albani

Gaeta - Terracina - Circeo - Fossanova - Sezze - Cori - Velletri (183 km)

Gaeta overlooks the blue crescent of the gulf as far as the Circeo, the Agro Pontino, olive groves, limestone landscapes, and the "borghi" of the Monti Lepini. "Gaeta is a fortress, not unlike Gibraltar: an exceedingly well fortified peninsula, capable of becoming more so," wrote Montesquieu, a clear-eyed travel writer. In 1848 the pope, the grand-duke of Tuscany, and the king of Naples took refuge in Gaeta from the rising tide of European revolt. The Circeo takes its name from the Latin "circus," for the shape of the promontory. Though some, including Dante, have linked the name to Homer's Circe, all reference to the Odyssey is spurious. Midway along the coast, however, in the Grotta di Tiberio, near Sperlonga, in the late 1950s fragments of statuary were found that in time proved to be part of four Hellenistic groups: Ulysses and Diomedes plundering the Palladium of Troy; Ulysses with the corpse of Achilles; the blinding of Polyphemus, or Cyclops; and the snakelike Scylla plucking sailors from the vessel of Ulysses (these statues now occupy a museum of their own). The Agro Pontino was once a miserable swamp where, as

Horace wrote: "mali culices ranaeque palustres avertunt somnos" (savag
mosquitoes and marsh frogs drive away sleep); it has since been drained an
entirely reclaimed. The Monti Lepini – Monte Semprevisa is 1536 m tall – form
a backdrop for the plain, distant from the sea; it is in this mountain range tha
the true surprises of this route may be found: the little towns perched on th
slopes were fortresses of the ancient Volsci, before Roman supremacy; cycle
pean stones and stern medieval walls clash in surprising contrast.

The route.

The first part of this route is primarily a coastal road: from Gaeta you follo
a lovely shore road till just past Sperlonga; there you will turn inland, at a for
in the road near the lake of San Puoto, and on to Fondi. From Fondi, you hea
back to the sea, at Terracina, following the Via Appia (SS 7 road); here you re
turn to the coast road. This road, including a scenic stretch with spectacula
views, runs behind the Circeo promontory; a brief turnoff allows you to vis
San Felice al Circeo. At the fork leading to Sabaudia, you will verge off fro
the Tyrrhenian coastline, and, with a road that runs through the Circeo par
and the reclaimed Pontine plain, you will reach the Abbey of Fossanova an
a bit further on, Priverno. This marks the beginning of a different part of th
route, which follows the edge of the Monti Lepini, frequently climbing up t
pass through old villages that look down on what was once a marshy an
malarial plain. As you follow small roads, turnoffs, and detours, you will pas
through Sezze, the abbey of Valvisciolo, Sermoneta, Norma, and the ruins
Ninfa and Cori. As you pass through the village of Giulianello, the route ap
proaches the Colli Albani, ending in Velletri, at the base of these hills.

Places of interest.

Gaeta: of particular note is the older quarter of town, on a peninsula, sepa
rated from the mainland by Monte Orlando (171 m); atop the hill are a Roma
mausoleum and a remarkable view. Grotta di Tiberio*: the Grotto of Tiberius
once part of the emperor's villa, lies just past Torre Capovento and just be
fore Sperlonga, with its white medieval houses huddled on the promontory
note the Hellenistic marble carvings with the myths of Ulysses, found her
but now in the nearby Museo Archeologico Nazionale. Fondi, near the lake
amidst citrus trees, has Roman walls and layout, as well as the Gothic cathe
dral of S. Pietro, a castle, and the Palazzo del Principe, a mix of Angevin an
Catalonian styles. Terracina, on the Golfo di Gaeta: the center was original
the Roman Forum; the Duomo, rich in art treasures, stands on the site of th
chief temple; you can climb up through olive groves to see the ruins of th
Temple of Jove Anxur. San Felice Circeo: an elegant beach, caverns, spectac
ular views, and the road high over the sea, out to the Faro di Torre Cervia,
lighthouse; on your way to Sabaudia, you will pass through the 16th-c. Torr
Paola, near the Roman emissary of the Lago di Sabaudia. Sabaudia, set amids
lagoons, is one of the better-designed building complexes of the great recla
mation project of the Agro Pontino. Abbazia di Fossanova**: this was the ea
liest abbey built in Italy in the Cistercian Gothic style; St. Thomas Aquina
died here. Priverno is the first village along the route to date its origins bac

to ancient times; it looks purely medieval now, and is secluded in the hills, aloof from what was once a malarial plain. Sezze is clustered at the base of a hill; climb up to see the megalithic walls and the Duomo that took so long to build. On Good Friday is the procession of the Passion of Christ. Abbazia di Valvisciolo: this abbey stands among olive and eucalyptus groves; it was built in the 8th c. by Greek monks; the church and cloister date from the 13th c. Sermoneta: another medieval village proudly surveying the plain: powerful and grim, the Castello dei Caetani, built in the first half of the 13th c., in turn surveys it. Norma, firmly saddling a ridge of the Monti Lepini, is strongly medieval, but is best known for the nearby ruins of ancient Norba (see Norma). The medieval ruins of Ninfa* are reflected in an evocative little lake; in the surrounding nature preserve nest a remarkable array of birds. Cori is profoundly medieval, and is surrounded by fragments by a ring of three walls; from its perch on the slope of the Lepini, it overlooks the Pontine plain and the Circeo. The remarkably ancient Velletri stands on a ridge of Monte Artemisio, on the vine-bedecked southern slopes of the Colli Albani; Octavian lived here as a child, before becoming Augustus, the first Roman emperor.

57 | From the Gran Sasso d'Italia to the Adriatic Sea

L'Àquila - Campotosto - Isola del Gran Sasso d'Italia - Atri - Pineto (132 km)

At the Passo delle Capannelle (1299 m) you are on the watershed between Aterno and Vomano, two rivers that "envelop" the massif of the Gran Sasso d'Italia, both flowing down to the Adriatic. All around is quiet seclusion. You make your way up here, on the way from L'Àquila to the Adriatic Sea, winding amidst white badlands, along jagged, forest-covered slopes. You also pass by the ruins of "Amiternum," city of the Sabines; Vergil depicted the Amiternini fighting at Turnus's side against Aeneas. The line of descent is along the Valle del Vomano, but it makes detours and circles so that you have spectacular views of the Gran Sasso d'Italia: at Campotosto, alongside the great manmade lake with jagged shores, you see the Gran Sasso to the NW, at an angle; at Prati di Tivo, the two peaks of the Corno Grande and the Corno Piccolo stand out clear, harsh, and naked, looking like the peaks in the Dolomites, above rolling meadows and steep pastures gouged with gulleys; at Isola del Gran Sasso d'Italia, in the Mavone Valley, near the Vomano, you can see the peaks glow again just after sunset when the weather is good. As you get closer to the Adriatic, amid the gently rolling hills, you head up to Atri, a two-fold balcony: on the one side you bid farewell to the distant mountain, high over the rows of hills; on the other you greet the approaching sea, vast and fresh, with a long coastline. In the city of Atri, you can see the work of the leading Abruzzese painter,

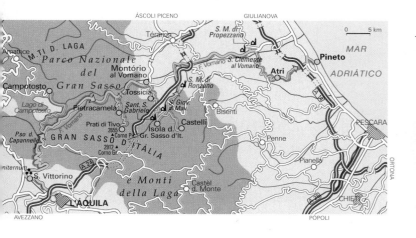

Andrea De Litio. Almost nothing is known of his life, and his work is found al most exclusively here; he is believed to have been active around 1450, and i thought to have been influenced by Piero della Francesca. His painting can b seen in the choir of the cathedral.

The route.

You leave L'Àquila heading NW along the SS 80 road, which goes over the Pa so delle Capannelle (1299 m) and down into the Valle del Vomano. On you way down, at a roadside house (or "cantoniera"), you will see a road runnin off to the left; this road is largely scenic, and leads (18 km) to Campotosto, o the shore of the manmade lake of the same name. Continue back along the S 80 road, passing by an optional detour on the right (16 km) to Pietracame and Prati di Tivo. Near Montorio al Vomano, you can turn south onto the S 491 road, which leads – after Tossicìa and a short jaunt to the Santuario di Gabriele dell'Addolorata – to the Isola del Gran Sasso d'Italia, in Valle d Mavone. Driving downhill from here along the valley, you pass an optional km detour on your right to Castelli, and you then reach the junction with th SS 150 road, which you will then take down toward the Adriatic Sea. We rec ommend two short detours on the left: the first, toward Guardia Voman where you can see the church of S. Clemente al Vomano, and a second detou to the church of S. Maria di Propezzano. From the crossroads for the latter d tour, the SS 553 road leads in the opposite direction through the hills to Atr from here, you drive on down to Pineto, on the Adriatic coast.

Places of interest.

San Vittorino: beneath the Romanesque church of S. Michele, at the center town, is a catacomb with the supposed remains of a Christian martyr, Vitto no; at the foot of the hill are the ruins of ancient Sabine and Roman Amite num, birthplace of Sallust. Campotosto is a summer resort near a manmac lake formed by damming the Rio Fùcino; the lake reflects the peaks of the Gra Sasso d'Italia. Pietracameia, another resort town on the slopes of the Gran Sa so d'Italia, is downhill from Prati di Tivo. From there, you can take a chairl up to the Madonnina del Gran Sasso (remarkable view of the peaks of the Gra Sasso d'Italia and of the Monti della Laga). Montorio al Vomano: the mode district lies on the main road, while the medieval one is high on a hill; note t large 18th-c. wooden altars in the parish church. Tossicìa: venerable hous and a portal by A. Lombardo (1471) at the church of S. Antonio Abate. Sant ario di S. Gabriele dell'Addolorata: the remains of a 19th-c. saint – the patr saint of Abruzzo – are buried here. Isola del Gran Sasso d'Italia stands on ridge of the north slope of the great massif; the windows of the old hous bear sententious Latin mottos. Castelli: the production of fine ceramics he dates from the 13th c.; the local museum has a ceramics collection and a production of a 16th-c. artisan's workshop. S. Giovanni al Mavone is a R manesque church frescoed in the apse and crypt. S. Maria di Ronzano is 12th-c. church with original frescoes. S. Clemente al Vomano* is partly R manesque, with a noteworthy ciborium by a certain Maestro Ruggero and son Roberto. S. Maria di Propezzano* is another Romanesque church, built b tween the 12th-14 c., which commemorates an ancient apparition of the Virg Mary; note the 15th-c. frescoes inside the church. Atri looks out from atop lush spur, to the blue of the Adriatic in the distance; in the celebrated 13th Cattedrale are the frescoes by A. De Litio (15th c.); situated in the piazza is t Teatro Comunale, a reduced version of the Scala opera house in Milan; t Museo Diocesano lies past the adjacent cloister. Pineto (see Atri): a pine gro adorns this beach resort near the mouth of the Vomano River.

58 | The Abruzzo between the Tronto and Pescara Rivers

Giulianova - Civitella del Tronto - Teramo - Penne - Pescara (168 km)

"Behind the Gran Sasso the setting sun filled the whole springtime sky wit brilliant pinkish light: and, since the moist fields and the river waters and t waters of the sea and the ponds during the day had emitted much vapor, ho es and sails and poles and trees and every single thing appeared tinged with pink; as the shapes acquired a sort of transparency, the sharpness of outline began to waver, almost fluttering in that bath of rosy light". This is a glimpse of the Abruzzo coast from "Le Novelle della Pescara" by Gabriele D'Annunzio. The Gran Sasso invariably dominates the horizon throughout this route: through valleys and over hills, along winding secluded roads, down the rolling ridges that drop away to the sea from the high mountains of the Monti della Laga and the Gran Sasso d'Italia: this is seaside Abruzzo, east of the Apennine ridges. The rows of hills are divided by rivers that run, more-or-less parallel, down to the Adriatic, like tines raking the length of the beach. The north-south stretch that you will cover is crossed by the rivers Tronto (bordering the Marche), Vibrata, Salinello, Tordino (the valley of Teramo), Vomano (pouring into the sea between Roseto degli Abruzzi and Pineto), Piomba (this river, with the Fino and the Tavo, empties 8 km from the sea into an exceedingly short river, the Saline), and – last stop on this route – Pescara. You head inland just south of the first river, and you will

cross the valleys of all the others. Crests, isolated hills, clayey badlands, gravel washes, rows of tremulous poplars, olive groves, the evergreen holm-oaks high on the crags: this road goes through ever-new landscapes, surprising at every turn; the clouds are swept inland by the offshore breeze and even the sky and the light are different. Skirting Pescara, you return to the sea coast, described by the native Pescarese D'Annunzio as extending "in an almost virginal serenity, along the shore that arcs slightly toward the south, in its splendor displaying the bright color of a Persian turquoise. Here and there, where currents surge, there are twisting patches of darker hue...."

he route. From Giulianova you head north on the SS 16 road along the Adriatic coastline, and, after crossing the Salinello River, you cut away from the coastline, to the left. Should you choose to drive along the coast a little further, on the other hand, in just 3 km you will be in Tortoreto Lido, the coastal offshoot of the inland town of Tortoreto. First you drive up the left bank of the Salinello River, then you continue along secondary roads as far as Civitella del Tronto. From here you drive down to reach the SS 81 road, which you will take southward. After you pass Campovalano (there is a 1-km detour here to the church of S. Pietro) and the fork where another, 3-km detour leads off to the left to Campli, the road reaches Teramo, crossing the Tordino River and then runs up over the hills that divide this valley from the Vomano River Valley. Continuing over ridges and hilltops, the road crosses the rivers Piomba, Fino, and Baricello, and then heads uphill to Penne. Here, you will leave the SS 81 road, and continue downhill SE to Loreto Aprutino and the floor of the Tavo Valley. Then you drive up a stretch of the left bank of the Tavo River, until you arrive at the SS 81 road again. This road, running SE, past spectacular views, runs along the hill on which Pianella stands; here you leave the main road, just outside of Pianella, for a secondary road that goes 7 km up to Moscufo. Back on the main road, you cross over the Bologna-Tàranto highway and then take the SS 602 road to Pescara.

laces of interest. Giulianova sits atop a low hill to the north of the Tordino River: there is a 15th-c. octagonal Duomo and a gallery, chiefly devoted to 19th-c. Neapolitan painting; downhill, on the Adriatic coast, extends Giulianova Lido, a fishing town and resort. Tortoreto Lido: you can swim among abundant verdant nature, at the foot of gently rolling hills. Tortoreto is a secluded hilltop village; note the 16th-c. frescoes in the church of S. Maria della Misericordia. Civitella del Tronto is a small town straddling a slope, with a slight late-Renaissance flavor; from the high Fortezza, or fortress, which endured four sieges, you have a vista ranging from the mountains to the sea. S. Pietro: take a short detour immediately after Campovalano, and visit the 13th-c. church next to the ruins of 12th-c. Benedictine convent. Campli: extending across a natural terrace, the little city has medieval and Renaissance architecture and an archeological museum located on the site of a former convent, with artifacts from the necropolis of Campovalano. Teramo: most of the city is modern, except for some Roman and medieval parts; in the Cattedrale note the frontal by Nicola di Guardiagrele and a polyptych by Jacobello del Fiore, both dating from the 15 c. Penne stands on two hills with medieval views and ancient churches; outside of town, on a wooded hill, S. Maria in Colleromano still harbors relics of its 14th-c. foundation. Loreto Aprutino: the ceramics of Castelli and other towns of the territory are found in the Galleria Acerbo; south of town is the church of S. Maria in Piano, with remarkable 14th-c. frescoes. Pianella: on a hill outside of town is the Romanesque church of S. Maria Maggiore, with 12th-c. pulpit and 12th-/15th-c. frescoes. Moscufo: near the town, on an olive-clad hill with spectacular views, the 12th-c. church of S. Maria del Lago has an exquisite pulpit (1159) and 12th-/14th-c. frescoes. Pescara: the canal-port, crowded with fishing boats – actually the mouth of the Pescara River – divides the thriving Adriatic town in two, with the pine forest made famous by D'Annunzio to the south, and the long seafront promenade to the north. The Museo delle Genti d'Abruzzo, opened in 1991, is devoted to the folkways and history of the region, and occupies a former Bourbon dynasty prison. In the birthplace of Gabriele D'Annunzio you will see memorabilia of Italy's so-called "vate," or bard. A renowned international jazz festival takes place in town during the month of July.

59 | The Maiella Massif

Pescara - Chieti - Guardiagrele - Pescocostanzo - Sulmona - Caramànico Terme Pescara (237 km)

When the town of L'Àquila dared to raise its head in rebellion, in 1528, Philbert de Châlons, Prince of Orange and Viceroy of Naples (French-born but, to repay a slight offered him by Francis I, a turncoat and renegade, in the service of the Holy Roman Emperor, Charles V), sallied furiously forth with his Lansquenet troops. He sacked the town, fined it 100,000 ducats, and set an additional annual tribute toward the construction of a grim castle. He then turned his troops back to Naples; on the way back he lost 500 of his precious German mercenaries in a sudden March blizzard in the Piano delle Cinquemiglia, which stretches south from Sulmona to Isernia. Given the circumstances, the loss of seasoned troops meant more than the usual chance passerby swept away by a flurry of snow. The emperor ordered five strong towers to be built as shelter for lost wayfarers; they are long gone. Stark, deserted, and with only the 19th-c. road as a mark of man, this mountainous highland is now highly valued for its vast ski slopes and lush lonely meadows in summer. You will pass through it as you begin to return northward on the circuit of the Maiella. The slopes of this mountain bristle with beech trees and holm-oaks and, higher up, with pine trees; the meadows blossom with flowers in spring and the mountainside yawns with deep, wild gulleys, eroding away into the limestone. Second only to the Gran Sasso d'Italia, this is the most notable mountain group in the central Apennines, running roughly north-south, from Chieti to Sulmona. The valleys of the Pescara River and its tributary, the Orta, bound it to the north and west; then come a series of karstic plains. To the south and SE is the valley of the Aventino, which flows into the Sangro; to the east it is lined by low foothills that level away down to the Adriatic Sea. The highest peak, Monte Amaro, stands 2793 m tall. After the thrills and views of the mountain, you will pass by the two cities of Chieti and Sulmona, the Cistercian church of S. Maria Arabona (incomplete) and the lovely town of Guardiagrele, home of the most celebrated goldsmith of Abruzzo, Ghiberti's student Nicola di Andrea Gallucci, known as Nicola da Guardiagrele.

The route. This tour of the Maiella massif goes first along the base of the eastern slope, overlooking the Adriatic, and then over the western slope. Beginning in Pescara, you take the SS 5 road for a short stretch up the valley of the river Pescara, as far as the fork, marked for Chieti. After you pass through Chieti, you will take the SS 81 road, which runs through valleys and over highlands. At the fork of Ponte di Alento keep to left, following the old road, which runs up to Bucchiànico and over the Colle Spaccato until it intersects with the state road 263; turn right onto this road, to take the longest detour in this route (this 32-km detour runs, just after the bridge over the SS 81 road, along the road to Pretoro and the Passo Lanciano, 1306 m) all the way up to the Blockhaus (2142 m) on the high slopes of the Maiella). Just past the fork where the old road joins the modern SS 81 road, take a right onto the road to Guardiagrele, and once past that town, you will be back on the SS 263 road. In succession, you will pass through Pennapiedimonte and Fara San Martino, and then the road runs into the SS 84 road, which runs SW up to the pass of the Forchetta (1270 m). Further along, off to the right, there are two short detours to Pescocostanzo and Rivisóndoli, while if you turn left at the crossroads of the SS 17 road, you will reach Roccaraso in just 2 km. The route then proceeds in the opposite direction on the SS 17 road, crossing the Piano delle Cinquemiglia, and running through Pettorano sul Gizio and on to Sulmona. Now you must take the SS 487 road, which runs over the western slopes of the Maiella, over the Passo San Leonardo (1282 m). Then you will follow the river Orta down to Caramànico Terme and to the valley of the river Pescara. Here the SS 487 road comes to an end, intersecting the SS 5 road; this road will take you back to Pescara, on the Adriatic coast, where you started out; on the right, a short jaunt up to Manoppello Scalo will take you to the church of S. Maria Arabona.

Places of interest. Pescara: modern, active, lively, this city extends along the Pescara River and the canal-port that forms its outlet into the sea: to the south are the Museo delle Genti d'Abruzzo, the birthplace of G. D'Annunzio, and a lovely pine grove; to the north is the Museo Ittico (Museum of Ichthyology) and a long beachfront boulevard. Chieti closely follows the contours of the hillside, high over the Pescara River Valley; the town's backbone is Corso Marrucino. The archaic severity of the Warrior of Capestrano (6th c. B.C.) can be admired in the excellent Museo Archeologico Nazionale, the 15th-c. octagonal church of S. Maria Tricalle stands outside of town, along the road from Pescara. Bucchiànico: spread out on an upland, with fine churches, this town has a notable piece of folk tradition, the "Sagra dei Banderesi" honoring St. Urban (22-25 May). Blockhaus has a spectacular view from the ridge between the Maielletta and Monte Acquaviva (2737 m). Guardiagrele has a venerable crafts tradition of goldwork and wrought iron; adjacent to the 11th-c. Romanesque church of S. Maria Maggiore, the Museo d'Arte Sacra has a processional cross by Nicola da Guardiagrele. Pennapiedimonte is a little town with steep stairways and an 18th-c. white parish church. Fara San Martino, on a terrace on the east slope of the Maiella, was founded in Lombard times; interesting painting in the parish church by T. da Varallo. Lama dei Peligni: take a cableway up to the Grotta del Cavallone. Palena is an old village with lovely bits of architec-

99

ture, rebuilt after being devastated by heavy fighting in 1943; go see the 16th c. wooden statue of the Madonna in the Chiesa del Rosario. Pescocostanzo* this ancient village, with a notable 11th-c. basilica, rebuilt in the 15th c. and enlarged in 1558, overlooks the highland of Quarto Grande; for centuries, it has produced fine lace and is also a renowned winter skiing resort. Rivisóndoli is a resort on a spur overlooking the highland. Roccaraso: people come here to summer and to ski (highland of Aremogna). Pettorano sul Gizio: fine old rustic architecture. Sulmona: set against the mountains girding the Valle Peligna, this town with its ancient atmosphere demands a leisurely tour to admire individual monuments (especially the Cattedrale and the Annunziata) and the surprising elegance of the town itself. Pacentro is a village on the slopes of the mountains of Morrone; note the 14th-c. towers of the Castello dei Cantelmo. Caramànico Terme is a spa; the old town has medieval walls and gates, a castle, and notable churches. San Valentino in Abruzzo Citeriore has a parish church by L. Vanvitelli. S. Maria Arabona is a Cistercian Gothic abbey church (13th c.) with frescoes by A. da Atri.

60 | Iglesiente

Cagliari - Santa Margherita - Sant'Antìoco - Iglesias - Cagliari (192 km)

In 1832, at the beginning of a tour of the East, Lamartine landed in the Gulf of Palmas (between the island of S. Antìoco and the coast of the Sulcis) and described a beach "at the far end of the gulf," in all likelihood, the littoral strip of the Stagno di S. Caterina: white sand, large thistles, little clumps of aloe vera, and, in his words, "little herds of wild horses roaming free through the heath, galloping up to investigate us, sniffing the air and then, with a wild neighing, tearing off again like flocks of crows; a mile away are grey, bare mountains, with patches of dried-out plants on their slopes; a sky you might expect to see in Africa arches over the limestone peaks; an immense silence hangs over the countryside...." This handsome description may serve as an introduction to this first Sardinian route, more than half of it coastline, and a of it encompasses vast landscapes, sweeping horizons, with the colors of the sea, cliffs, shoals, and rocks of every mineral family. Let the sea not distract the traveller from the history that came from that sea: Cagliari, originally Kàralis, which is now a large town, like Nora and Bithia, along the coast of th

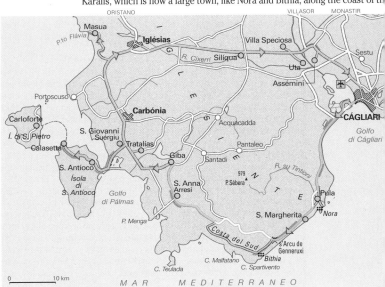

great southern gulf of Sardinia, were all cities founded by Phoenicians. Nora, on a spit of land jutting out into the sea, was the first city on Sardinia, according to classical lore, and was founded by Phoenicians from the Iberian Peninsula; like the other Phoenician colonies, it was absorbed by Carthage, itself a Phoenician colony. Bithia was first discovered in 1835 by A. La Marmora, and as late as the reign of Marcus Aurelius was administered by "sufeti," or Punic magistrates. On the western coast of the Iglesiente, Sant'Antìoco stands on the island of the same name; it occupies the site of one of the earliest Phoenician cities on Sardinia, Sulcis. During Carthaginian times, it was a major mining center in the Sulcis-Iglesiente area.

The route. You will leave Cagliari heading west and will drive along the western coast of the Gulf of Cagliari, at first along the SS 195 road – at Pula there is a turn-off for a 3-km detour to Nora – then, after s'Arcu de Genneruxi, where this road runs inland, along a rough road that offers fine views as it rolls across the Costa del Sud (Southern Coast), past the detour to the left toward Bithia. After rejoining the SS 195 road to the SW of Teulada, you will drive through Sant'Anna Arresi and Giba past the detour toward Tratalìas (4 km) and then on to San Giovanni Suergiu, a town from which the SS 126 road moves toward the island of S. Antìoco (11 km) and the nearby island of S. Pietro. From San Giovanni Suergiu you will again follow the SS 126 road north, as far as Iglesias (a pleasant side trip of 12 km leads to the sea near Masùa), while the SS 130 road, built for fast driving, will take you back to Cagliari by way of Siliqua, Villa Speciosa – from here it is just a 2.5-km detour to Uta – and Assèmini.

Places of interest. Cagliari*, clustered around the Pisan-Spanish castle, Su Casteddu, is the chief town in Sardinia. Nora* was a Phoenician city that later became Roman; it is still being excavated, and certain parts are now under the waves. Bithia is another city of Phoenician origin, extending out along a small promontory. Tratalìas: this village on the edge of the reclaimed marshes of Sulcis has a 13th-c. Romanesque church, S. Maria di Monserrato. Sant'Antìoco is the chief town of the island of the same name, which was known as "Sulcis" in Phoenician times; note the Museo Archeologico and relics of sacrifices. Carloforte is the chief town of the nearby island of S. Pietro; settled by exiled Ligurians, from Tunisia, in the 18th c. Carbonia was a mining town built in the 1930s; most mining has stopped among the bare mountains. Masùa, with a handsome and dramatic port, lies between crags and grottoes. Iglesias, in the heart of the mining region, still has medieval details; note the Museo Mineralogico, which boasts a vast collection of minerals. Siliqua has traditional houses in the old center; to the south are the ruins of the Castello di Acquafredda. Villa Speciosa has a Romanesque church, S. Platano (12th c.). Uta also has a 12th-c. Romanesque church. Assèmini is known for the cross-shaped Oratory of S. Giovanni, in Byzantine style.

61 | From Cagliari to Alghero through the Campidani

Cagliari - Sanluri - Oristano - Bosa - Alghero (202 km)

Sparse trees, prickly-pear bushes, vast horizons: the hill of Monastir, some twenty km north of Cagliari, offers a vantage point from which to appreciate the size of the Campidani, a broad plain in southern Sardinia. One historian wrote that the view helped him understand the seeds of war between Rome and Carthage, when the fault lines of history and geography became evident before his eyes: it was over the harvests of this vast fertile plain that two great ancient powers of the hungry Mediterranean fought to the death. The Campidani was a historic breadbasket of the region. It was created by the ancient Carthaginians, who chopped down dense forests; as late as the 18th c., by the records of the port of Marseilles, this made Sardinia the fifth-largest producer and exporter of wheat and other crops. After crossing the Campidani – note the reclaimed land around Arborèa – you reach the sea, replete with history

and bordered by fragmentary relics of ancien[t] peoples from distant lands. In the Gulf of Oris[tano, set on the slender peninsula of Capo [S] Marco, is Tharros, founded by the Phoenician[s] around 800 B.C. and later used by th[e] Carthaginians as a stopover base on the rout[e] to Massalia (Marseilles). The sea becomes [a] succession of little "calette," or coves, an[d] rocks at Santa Caterina di Pittinuri; nearby a[re] the insubstantial ruins of Cornus, probably [a] Carthaginian settlement. From Bosa, a town o[n] an estuary, you can sail down to the sea alon[g] the Temo River: coral-diving and fine goldwor[k] are pursued here. Then you drive along [a] seashore with vivid pink sunsets, a jagge[d] coastline, attractive little beaches, and, at las[t] Alghero, standing out sharply against th[e] bright waters of the roadstead behin[d] perched on its small promontory: a fortres[s] with the population and facilities of a town [.] "Bonita, por mi fé y bien assentada" (Lovely, i[n] faith, and well built) was the imperial opinio[n] of Charles V, according to local lore – and th[e] Catalonian architecture and language left b[y] mid-13th-c. Iberian colonists.

The route. You will leave Cagliari and hea[d] north; the first leg of the route then run[s] through the Campidani, largely coinciding wit[h] the route of the SS 131 road (the Strada Carl[o] Felice), from which short detours will take yo[u] to Dolianova (13.5 km) and Samassi (6 km[).] Once you have driven through Sanluri and Sà[r]dara, you will be on the plain of Oristano, dri[v]ing along the shores of the vast pond of S. Giu[s]ta, where the church of the same name is lo[o]cated. While an enjoyable detour (21 km) alon[g] the NW coast of the Gulf of Oristano leads t[o] Tharros, from Oristano the route follows the S[S] 292 road north, as far as Santa Caterina di Pi[t]tinuri along the coast, then cuts inland towar[d] Cùglieri (a detour to San Leonardo de Siet[e] Fuentes is 15 km long), splitting off from roa[d] 292 at Suni, toward Bosa. From Bosa, last of al[l] the coast road runs through Sa Mesa de s'A[t]tentu, leading to Alghero.

Places of interest. Dolianova has a Roma[n]esque church, S. Pantaleo, with remains o[f] 12th-13th-c. frescoes in the apse. Samass[i] has another Romanesque church, S. Gem[i]iano. Sanluri: in the middle of this farming vi[l]lage is a 13th-c. castle which also houses th[e] Museo "Duca d'Aosta" with relics datin[g] back to the Risorgimento and the two Worl[d] Wars. Sàrdara boasts the 14th-c. church of [S.] Gregorio and, to the north, the "nuraghi[c] well-temple of S. Anastasia. S. Giusta* is [a] large Romanesque church near the va[st] pond of the same name. Oristano is a thri[v]ing modern town, with few traces of its me[](-) dieval past. Tharros* was a Phoenician cit[y] later Carthaginian and then Roman, now partly underwater and partly on a peninsula near Capo S. Marco. Santa Caterina di Pittinuri is a beach resort with limestone rocks and, nearby, the archeological sites of Columbaris and Cornus. Cùglieri, at the base of the Montiferru, is where you turn off for the detour to San Leonardo de Siete Fuentes, a rustic village with 7 therapeutic springs, amidst holm-oaks, oaks, and elms. Bosa is a little town on the north bank of the estuary of the Temo River, beneath the walls of the Castello di Serravalle; on the other bank is the church of S. Pietro Extra Muros (11th c.). To the west, the port and beach of Bosa Marina. Alghero*: 16th-c. bastions gird the old town, Catalonian in style, set on a promontory overlooking the brilliant roadstead; across the gulf is Capo Caccia*.

62 | Gulf of Orosei, Ogliastra, and Gennargentu

Nùoro - Dorgali - Lanusei - Fonni - Orgòsolo - Nùoro (206 km)

The area overlooking the northern section of the Gulf of Orosei, around Dorgali, and all the way north along the coast to Siniscola and Posada, constitutes the Baronia, a name that dates from the 14th c. The author S. Satta describes spring there: "What sweet aromas amid the reed beds, in the scrub alive with wild hares and partridges, when the bright sunlight revived the dead and abandoned wood of the low-lying vineyards." As you think back on this route, you will certainly remember the coastline, the blue sea, the rosemary growing against the blinding white limestone of Cala Gonone, the Grotta del Bue Marino. Perhaps you will also think of the low circular stone walls of the prehistoric huts, or "nuraghi" (large, tower-shaped prehistoric stone structures peculiar to Sardinia), of the village of Serra Òrrios, with the sound of wind tossing the olive branches; or the Grotta di Ispinigoli, a great cavern with a deep shaft called the Abisso delle Vergini. Carthaginian jewelry found

at the bottom of the shaft, now in the Museo di Dorgali, lends some credibility to the legend of bloodcurdling virgin sacrifices. The Ogliastra is another broad plain of eastern Sardinia. A landscape of rocks, harsh but varied, and dotted with pasturage, vineyards, ancient olive groves; you cross the Ogliastra between Tortolì and Lanusei, after fine panoramic views from the high ridge road over the hills. The region may take its name from the little island off S. Maria Navarrese: Isola dell'Ogliastra, or Agugliastra, with reddish boulders of porphyry in the turquoise sea. A timeless scene, with a sense of how it must have looked to the ancient inhabitants. The last leg of this route, on the way back to Nùoro, runs through mountains: you climb to the slopes of the Gennargentu "where amidst white granite the oaks and the dark ilex toss their leaves" (Cardarelli); then you run through the Barbàgia di Ollolai, a stern archaic landscape peopled by shepherds.

The route. Beginning from Nùoro, this route heads predominantly SE toward Oliena, and then east – note the brief detour on the right (2 km) to the springs of Su Gologone and the other, on the left, to Serra Òrrios. Once you reach Dorgali – detours along the way will take you to the cave of Ispinigoli and to Cala Gonone – you will head south along the SS 125 road, which climbs over the pass of Genna Silana (1017 m) and over five other lower passes before reaching Baunei. A short distance further along, you will head down to the sea at Santa Maria Navarrese. After returning to the main road further south, you will reach Tortolì; from here, you may choose to drive to the seacoast again at Àrbatax (4.5 km), or you may head inland, crossing the Ogliastra on the SS 198 road as far as Lanusei. The route back to Nùoro (SS 389 road) crosses the plain of the Alto Flumendosa and goes over the Arcu Correboi (1246 m) and the Caravai Pass (1118 m), reaching Fonni on the northern slopes of Mt. Gennargentu, and finally descending to Mamoiada. Here you will head east toward Orgòsolo and from there will drive back to your starting point at Nùoro along a road through the valley of the Rio de Locoe, or Cedrino River.

Places of interest. Nùoro: a typical inland Sardinian town, birthplace of 1926 Nobel laureate Grazia Deledda. Oliena is an old town with traditional houses lining long, narrow, twisting lanes, at the base of the limestone mountain, the Sopramonte costumes are worn for the feast of S. Lussorio, on 21 August. Su Gologone is a karstic stream, the most important in Sardinia, in an idyllic patch of landscape. Serra Òrrios* is a village of "nuraghe," amidst olive and mastic trees. Grotta di Ispinigoli: this cave runs for 10 km, one of Italy's largest; one of the stalagmites is 38 meters high. Dorgali is a village sheltered by Monte Bàrdia from the nearby fishing village of Cala Gonone, on the Gulf of Orosei, you can take a boat to the Grotta del Bue Marino (or Grotto of the Monk Seal, an animal which perhaps was once found here). Santa Maria Navarrese: sand shoals, islets, and a venerable old wild olive tree by the church, which may have been built in the 11th c., supposedly in thanks for the survival of a shipwrecked princess; note the 17th-c. Spanish tower situated on the coast. Àrbatax has red porphyry cliffs. Lanusei is the capital of Ogliastra. Fonni is the highest village in Sardinia (1000 m), with skiing in winter. Mamoiada lies secluded in an oak and chestnut forest. Orgòsolo is a harsh town of shepherds by the Sopramonte, with fine views. To celebrate Assumption Day on 15 August, a procession is held with knights in costume.

63 | From the Gulf of Asinara to the Costa Smeralda

Porto Torres - Santa Teresa Gallura - La Maddalena - Olbia (193 km)

Isola di S. Stefano is one of the seven main islands – the other six being La Maddalena, Caprera, Spargi, Budelli, Razzoli, and S. Maria – in the archipelago that lies just off the NE coast of the Gallura region. It is wedged between Pala on the coast and the island of La Maddalena; the channels that separate it from the two shores are only a few hundred meters across. On February 1793 the 500 soldiers of the Kingdom of Sardinia who were garrisoning the island of La Maddalena saw 23 vessels emerge from the sound of Bonifacio, beyond the Strait of Bonifacio, landing cannon and soldiers on S. Stefano. The purpose and consequences of this expedition are still matters for historical study; it was commanded by a Corsican, C. Cesari, while the artillery – two cannon and a mortar – was commanded by a 23-year-old Corsican captain, Napoleon Bonaparte. Bonaparte began to bombard La Maddalena (a shell is still on display in the mayor's office), but his Provençal marines mutinied when ordered to land. A disgusted Bonaparte hastily departed for Toulon. The remarkable archipelago where this minor chapter of history unfolded, overlooking steep jagged rocks, tufts of maquis, inlets, narrow beaches, and sheer rock walls and shoals churning white amidst the cobalt water and the strong winds of the Strait of Bonifacio, lies halfway along this route on the northern coast of Sardinia. Before you get here, you will have seen the broad gulf of the Asinara, the fortifications of Castelsardo, the red cliffs of the Costa Paradiso, the cluster pines and granite of Capo Testa. It ends with exclusive resort areas among the promontories and inlets of the Costa Smeralda, with their "Neo-Mediterranean" architecture, wild nature, and rich guests.

The route. From Porto Torres you will drive along the SS 200 road, following the arc of the Golfo dell'Asinara all the way to Castelsardo; on the right a short but scenic detour (7 km) leads up to the church of Nostra Signora de Tergu. Further along, you will drive across the coastal plain of the Coghinas River, remaining

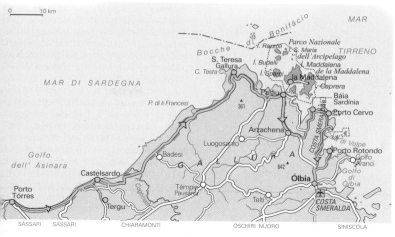

a certain distance from the shore, amidst highlands, maquis, and rocks, until you come even with Vignola Mare. The next stretch of road offers a succession of spectacular sea views, with coastal overlooks from the Punta di li Francesi all the way to Capo Testa; then, along the SS 133 bis and 133 roads, you will continue from Santa Teresa Gallura to Palau, where you can take boats to the islands of La Maddalena and Caprera. From Palau the route runs inland through Arzachena; just past Arzachena and Mulino di Arzachena, you will turn off from the road that goes directly to Olbia and head toward Baia Sardinia, completing the tour of the promontory that extends northward. To the west is the Gulf of Arzachena, to the east is the Costa Smeralda (short detours lead to exclusive beach resorts). At the end of the inlet of Porto di Cugnana, the road turns inland once again, to Olbia.

Places of interest. Porto Torres is a port and industrial town on the Golfo dell'Asinara, with the 11th-c. Basilica di S. Gavino and Roman ruins. Nostra Signora de Tergu is a 13th-c. Romanesque church which originally belonged to a Benedictine monastery. Castelsardo: set on a promontory, surrounded by old walls, this village is crisscrossed with narrow lanes and steep stairs; the castle houses a museum which displays examples of local crafts. Santa Teresa Gallura is a fishing village and a resort town on a deep inlet facing the windy Strait of Bonifacio; to the west is the granite promontory of Capo Testa. Palau is a beach town and landing point for ships heading for La Maddalena: the handsome town is the only one on the island. You can set out for boat trips through the sunny archipelago; Caprera island is where Garibaldi died. Baia Sardinia is a fine beach area. Porto Cervo: the luxurious village and marina are the best-known resort on the Costa Smeralda. Cala di Volpe is an inlet in a glorious setting. Porto Rotondo has a famed beach in a cozy little bay. Olbia is a port at the end of the Gulf of Olbia, with a Romanesque church, S. Simplicio.

64 | Western Sardinia, from Sàssari to Iglesias

Sàssari - Macomèr - Abbasanta - Oristano - Gùspini - Iglesias (224 km)

Many varied images will come to mind after this long tour of the island from north to south: the rolling plain of the Logudoro with Pisan-Romanesque churches, the bare basaltic upland of the Campeda, the broad valley of the Tirso River, with endless vistas, the tree-shaded Campidani, with ponds and the waves of the Gulf of Oristano, the farms and eucalyptus trees of the reclaimed plain of Arborèa, the sere highlands of the Iglesiente – mining country dotted with the dense foliage of cork-oaks and the skeletal remains of a

vanishing industry. The "nuraghe" (a large, tower-shaped prehistoric stone structure) is a leit-motif throughout much of the trip: there are about 7,500 of them on the island, which comes out to one every 4 sq. km (though in places like the meadows of Màrghine, NE of Macomèr, or in the Trexenta, east of Sanluri, the density is twice that). The best-known, the Nuraghe Santu Antine, lies near the beginning of this route. The word "nuraghe" comes from the proto-Sardinian term "nur," meaning both concave and convex. The nuraghe is, indeed, both. A tapered tower of stones stacked without mortar, topped by a terrace with parapet, it has a circular inner chamber – or more than one, stacked – covered by a false vault (the Greek "thòlos"), with a spiral stairway inside the thick wall. Nuraghes range in height from 10 to 20 m, in diameter from 8 to 12 m. The nuraghic culture dates from 1800 B.C. until the end of the 6th c. B.C.; areas of it survived inland until well after the Roman conquest. Over time, multiple nuraghes were built, complex structures with secondary towers, keeps, and curtain walls, built to withstand assault. Castles, in other words, comparable with those of the Middle Ages, with the same social functions.

The route. Running from north to south, this route basically follows main roads: the SS 131 Carlo Felice road, one of the island's most important arteries, from Sàssari to Oristano, and the SS 126 road, from Oristano to Iglesias. You leave Sàssari, heading south and pass, on your left, the SS 597 road to Olbia – you may take a detour here, to see the Romanesque churches of SS. Trinità di Saccargia, S. Michele di Salvènero, and S. Antonio di Salvènero – which takes you through Torralba; near here, you should visit the church of S. Pietro di Sorres and the Nuraghe Santu Antine (there are two detours leading to them, respectively 10 and 4 km long). After Bonorva, where you can take a detour to the necropolis of S. Andrea Priu (9.5 km), the SS131 Carlo Felice road curves around past Macomèr and heads down toward Abbasanta, with the renowned Nuraghe Losa and the Lago Omodeo, at a distance of 11 km from the town. From Oristano you may choose to take the detour to Tharros (21 km) or else, just past Santa Giusta, you may take the SS 126 road, which runs through Arborèa, Terralba, and Gùspini, climbing up to the Arcu Genna Bogai (549 m). There are two other detours here: one to the right to Buggerru (15.5 km) and the other to the left to the temple of Antas (2 km). At the bottom of the descent is Iglesias.

Places of interest. SS. Trinità di Saccargia* is one of the most outstanding Romanesque monuments on the island, with a fine bell tower and the series of 13th-c frescoes in the apse. S. Michele di Salvènero is another 12th-c. church, while S. Antonio di Salvènero is a 13th-c. one. S. Pietro di Sorres* is an isolated Romanesque basilica on a rise. Nuraghe Santu Antine*: the central tower is the largest of all of Sardinia's nuraghes. Necropoli di S. Andrea Priu a hypgaeum of 20 cliff-side tombs. Nuraghe Santa Barbara has a four-tower bastion around the central structure. Nuraghe Losa* has a central tower that once stood three stories high. Lago Omodeo is a manmade basin formed by the Tirso River, which submerged the village of Zuri (the new village, on the west shore, has a Gothic-Romanesque church, S. Pietro). Tharros*: near the rocky Capo S. Marco and partly under the waves, is a city founded by the Phoenicians and later occupied by Carthaginians and then Romans. Oristano: note the medieval architecture in this provincial capital; go see the Duomo, whose 18th-c. appearance belies its 13th-c origins. S. Giusta*: overlooking the immense pond is a 12th-c. Romanesque church. Gùspini is a mining village with many olive groves; to the NW is the mine of Montevecchio (lead and zinc). Buggerru (see Iglesias) is a mining village high over the sea, in a deep inlet. Tempio di Antas: an interesting Roman temple dedicated to a syncretic god, Sardus Pater Babi. Iglesias is the center of the mining region; pay a visit to the Castello di Salvaterra and the 14th-c. Cattedrale.

65 | The Campi Flegrei and Island of Ischia

Naples - Cuma - Baia - Pozzuoli - Pròcida - Ischia (71 km)

"The purity and clarity of that water," wrote the 16th-c. Neapolitan historian, Camillo Porzio, about the Gulf of Naples, "seems to those who see it to be like quicksilver." The western shores of the gulf in question are the subject of this route, along with the incredible "sideshow" of the Phlegraean Fields, in which the phenomena of volcanic activity do some of their less spectacular "numbers." There is the enchanting landscape and there are geological oddities; alongside them, the third attraction for curious sightseers is the aura of classical antiquity, which is so much more intense and evident to the senses here than anywhere else in southern Italy. Here is a brief and far from exhaustive listing of classical sites along this route: at Nìsida, Marcus Brutus, assassin of Julius Caesar, before venturing off to the fatal battle of Philippi, where he was defeated by Augustus and Mark Antony, bade a last farewell to his wife Portia, daughter of Cato; St. Paul debarked in the harbor of Pozzuoli,; Virgil set the entrance to the Underworld at Lake Averno; Liternum was the site of the country estate to which Publius Cornelius Scipio, Africanus Major, the greatest Roman general before Caesar, retired,

disgusted with politics; in Cumae the Sibyl made her prophecies; Lake Miseno was said to be the Stygian swamp across which Charon ferried lost souls; Capo Miseno, according to the ancient historian Strabo, was the land of the Lestrigons, giants who hurled great boulders at the ships of Ulysses; the Gulf of Baiae was without equal on earth in the opinion of the poet Horace (an opinion shared by those who had villas here, among them Marius, Crassus, Caesar, Nero, Pompey, and Varro); in the Lago Lucrino a certain Sergius Orata harvested oysters, while on the banks the architect Cyrus built for Cicero the Cumanum, with a portico extending out into the lake waters; the island of Ischia was also known as Ænaria, and was renowned for its climate and salubrious, curative waters, as much in Roman times as it is today: in Forìo, back then, it was customary to try to see the "green ray" created by the steam at sunset.

The route.

There are two "classic" routes to Pozzuoli: one is the coast road that goes around the Posìllipo promontory (following the Via Caracciolo and then Via Mergellina); the other follows the Via Domiziana (SS 7 *quater* road), inland (from Piazza Sannazaro through the tunnel). From Pozzuoli you continue along the Via Domiziana until you reach a fork 5 km after the junction between Via Domiziana and the Autostrada; here you take a right onto a road that runs near the Lago di Patria. Another road leads to the ruins of Liternum and then back to the Via Domiziana, which you will follow south to the turnoff to Cuma. Then you will follow secondary roads around the peninsula that encloses, to the west, the Golfo di Napoli, or Gulf of Naples, passing through Cuma, past the Lago di Fusaro, Torregàveta, Monte di Pròcida, Bàcoli, Bàia, and finally returning to Pozzuoli. Ferryboats, which will take cars, leave for Pròcida and Ischia from the harbor of Pozzuoli (similar ferries sail from Naples harbor as well). The circuit of the Isola d'Ischia covers a total of 31 km.

Places of interest.

Naples**: the capital of the south welcomes the tourist with open arms in Piazza del Plebiscito. Marechiaro: a village of fishermen and famous trattorias, with the "fenesta" from a classic song by Salvatore Di Giacomo; it lies at the end of a detour from the crossroads of the Capo. Nìsida: you reach the little island, originally an ancient volcanic crater of almost circular shape, by driving along the embankment, turning off from the coast road just past the promontory of Posìllipo. Pozzuoli: set adjacent to the luminous waters of the gulf are the Roman monuments of the Serapaeum and the amphitheater, while the Rione Terra is perched high on a promontory; nearby, note the surprising volcanic phenomena of the Solfatara** (you pass by here if you take the Via Domiziana) and the dark waters of the Lago d'Averno* (a great crater with woods on its steep slopes (fine view). Liternum: the ruins of the little Roman town lie at the edge of the Lago di Patria. Cuma*: classical ruins and memories are to be found in this great archeological field, where a Greek colony was founded, conveying the alphabet in due time to the rest of the Italian peninsula; go visit the cave of the Sibylla Cumana, or Sybil of Cumae, a sanctuary venerated in ancient times. Bàcoli: fishing village, with the Roman ruins of the Cento Camerelle and the Piscina Mirabile. Miseno: this small village is located on the cape of the same name; a short detour from Bàcoli passes over the dam between the coastal lagoon and the ancient port of Miseno; these two features together made this a major Roman naval base. Bàia*: in the archeological park there are the spectacular Roman ruins, probably part of the palace of the emperors. Pròcida presents a brightly colored composition of Mediterranean architecture. Ischia*: you will land at Ischia Porto (the fishing village of Ischia Ponte, with a bridge linking it to the islet of the Castello, is a couple of km east); the tour of the island, involving steep climbs, seascapes with craggy coastlines, green vineyards, citrus groves, and pine woods, takes you, among other places, to: Casamìcciola Terme, destroyed by a earthquake at the end of the 19th c.; Lacco Ameno, a hot springs, with the reef of the Fungo just off the little beach; Forìo, a dazzling white town on a promontory, and renowned for its wines; Sant'Angelo*, a fishing village, at the base of a small peninsula; Barano d'Ischia, located in a pleasant site, from which you may venture down to the long beach of Lido dei Maronti.

66 | From Naples to Sorrento and Capri

Naples - Ercolano (Herculaneum) - Vesuvius - Pompeii - Sorrento - Capri (54 km)

It all began with "a cloud, remarkable in size and appearance," as Pliny the Younger was to write to Tacitus, describing the eruption of 24 August of A.D. 79, and the death of his uncle, Pliny the Elder, who sailed from Capo Miseno to assist the fleeing population. Its shape "most closely resembled that of a pine tree. It rose straight up as if borne upon a high trunk, and then opened out into numerous branches… here it was bright white, there it was mottled and dirty, where earth and ashes had been carried aloft." For many of the residents of Herculaneum, Stàbia, and Pompeii, that was the last thing they ever saw. At the end of this route through another half of the coastline of the Gulf of Naples, a traveller may be tempted to try to rank the remarkable impressions and sights. What ranks first? The dead cities, slain by a volcano, the inimitable island of Capri, the relaxed beauty of Sorrento amid its citrus groves, or the lunar landscape of the crater of Vesuvius? Certainly, there are plenty of powerful impressions here.

The route. The first leg of this route, to Ercolano, or Herculaneum, will follow the SS 18 road (from Piazza del Municipio along Via Nuova della Marina along the port); expect heavy traffic. From Ercolano a scenic road climbs up the slopes of Vesuvio, or Vesuvius; on the way down, you will head directly for the toll booth and on-ramp at Torre del Greco for the Autostrada to Salerno, which will take you along a ring road to Castellammare di Stàbia. You will then continue on to Sorrento via Vico Equense and Meta. At Sorrento you can take a ferry to Capri. Only from November to February can you take your car to the island with you. In the other months, only residents, along with a few other special categories, are allowed to drive on the island.

laces of interest. Naples**: Palazzo S. Giacomo and the Maschio Angioino overlook the bustling port; Portici, and its Railway Museum of Pietrarsa remind visitors that one of the first railway lines linking this town to Naples was built here. Ercolano, or Herculaneum**: all that you see of this small ancient town, with its charming location, once the exclusive holiday resort of the wealthy and powerful of Imperial Rome, was excavated from a dense, compact slab of lava and mud, from 12 to 25 m high. Vesuvio*, or Vesuvius, seen from the west: if you turn off from the main route, following the slopes of Mt. Vesuvius, you will climb up to the lower station of the chair lift, passing by the observatory on your way (the upper station lies at an elevation of 1158 m; from there you can walk up to the great tear in the earth, the now deceptively tranquil crater), or else to the 1017 m of the northern slope of the terminal cone. Torre del Greco: here, craftsmen fashion exquisite work from coral and mother-of-pearl; you can see their creations in the Museo del Corallo. Torre Annunziata: one of the Neapolitan pasta capitals. Pompei, or Pompeii: the excavations** have unearthed at least three-fifths of the city that was buried by the eruption of Vesuvius in A.D. 79 (the town probably had a population of about 30,000); nowhere is the voyage backwards in time so entrancing. Castellammare di Stàbia: note the excavations of the Roman villas of long-vanished Stabiae and the antiquarium. Monte Faìto (1131 m): beech trees, conifers, chestnuts, and cedars crowd its slopes; the view of the Sorrento peninsula and of the gulf is particularly fine from the "belvedere*," or viewpoint; you drive up from Castellammare di Stàbia and then down to Vico Equense with its 14th-c. Cathedral, the total detour is 30 km. Sorrento* lies on a tufa terrace high over the sea, amid gardens and the dark shiny green leaves of the citrus groves; the exuberant style of the applied art of the 17th and 18th c. can be enjoyed in the Museo Correale di Terranova. Isola di (Island of) Capri**: the colors of the sea, sky, rocks and vegetation, the craggy Faraglioni, vineyards, gardens, and breezes: you could easily stay here a lifetime or thereabouts. The Emperor Tiberius was neither the first nor the last to be captivated by the place. You land at Marina Grande; to reach the celestially blue transparency of the Grotta Azzurra**, or Blue Grotto, a marine cave half-filled with sea water, you take a boat. You can take a cableway up to the main town, also called Capri, with its little Mediterranean piazzetta, at once simple and sophisticated: from here, you can walk to see a number of fine sites: the Certosa di S. Giacomo; the Belvedere Cannone, with its view; the ruins of Tiberius's Villa Iovis; the Arco Naturale, a natural arch; the Belvedere di Tragara; and Marina Piccola. The town of Anacapri* is white, suspended in the lush greenery; it is located on the western side of the island: you should tour the Villa S. Michele, once owned by a Swedish author, Axel Munthe. The best view is to be had by taking a chairlift to the peak of Monte Solaro (589 m).

67 | The Amalfi Coastline

Sorrento - Positano - Amalfi - Ravello - Vietri sul Mare - Salerno (90 km)

The coastline faces south here, overlooking sea and bright sunshine. The Monti Lattari plunge sharply down, a rocky bastion broken only by harsh deep valleys, with citrus and olive groves and vegetable gardens on rocky terraces held up by small, rocky walls created by the back-breaking labor of generations; elsewhere, all you can see is Mediterranean underbrush and stones. The houses all cluster around the mouths of the deep valleys: the steep slopes determine the architectural style, which stacks volume, stairways, and roofs crisscrossed by intricate lanes, refreshingly shady after the inexorable sunlight that is reflected by the sea and the whitewashed walls. For the entire 10th c. and much of the 11th c., Amalfi grew quickly and extensively, taking Pisa's place in Mediterranean trade – later ceding its primacy to Genoa. Amalfi had trading colonies in Naples, Messina, Palermo, in the ports of Puglia, and, outside of Italy, in Durazzo, Tunis, Tripoli, Alexandria, Acre, Antioch, and of course, in the great metropolis of this time, Consantinople. Along with wealth, Amalfi took from the Byzantines and the Muslims a cultural influence that can be seen in the art. The little state of Amalfi, the first of Italy's "maritime republics," included the stretch of coastline from Positano to Cetara, with the islands of Li Galli and Capri; inland, it stretched to Tramonti and, over the crest of the Monti Lattari, it included Gragnano and Lettere. The end came late in the 11th c., as the Normans pushed north, allying themselves with the Pisan fleet in order to rid themselves of the pushy maritime merchants of Amalfi. The sun still shines down on the coastline, the sea breezes still brush the aromatic maquis, and in the little cloister bedecked with intertwined arches the palm trees still cast their shade over the "Paradiso."

The route. This route runs from Sorrento west along the Via Capo; soon, you will take a turn onto Via Nastro Verde, cutting across the promontory, passing Sant'Agata sui Due Golfi, and hugging the southern coast of the peninsula as far as Salerno. Aside from the various detours indicated in the next leg of this route, there are two main side trips that will enrich your enjoyment. First, just after you set out, you will follow secondary scenic roads along the tip of the peninsula, passing through Massa Lubrense and Tèrmini, and joining up with the main route again just past Sant'Agata sui due Golfi. The second side-trip turns off at Atrani, climbing up to Ravello, and then on over the high pass, the Valco di Chiunzi (656 m) in the Monti Lattari, and then back down to Maiori along the Valle di Tramonti.

Places of interest. Sorrento*: the sea of the Sirens, the tufa crags and cliffs, the orange orchards and olive groves that so enchanted the 16th-c. poet Torquato Tasso; collections of objects and the applied arts in the aristocratic palazzo of the collectors at the Museo Correale di Terranova; an initial variant on the route offers spectacular views from 18 km of secondary roads; you will pass through Massa Lubrense (120 m), a lovely vacation spot on a rolling verdant plateau (you can make your way down to the village, the marina, and the beach of Marina della Lobra) and Tèrmini (330 m), a secluded village (by mule-track, 45 minutes to the Punta della Campanella, facing Capri). Sant'Agata sui Due Golfi (394 m): the name of this little holiday town refers to the two gulfs of Naples and Salerno. Positano*: the mountain spurs, covered by terraced white houses, run down to the harbor of the old fishing village, long since become an elegant resort. Grotta di Smeraldo*: the Emerald Grotto, with its surreal green light, is located between Praiano and Conca dei Marini. Agèrola (630 m), this highland of the Monti Lattari features resort spots amidst meadows and chestnut groves; fine views of the Amalfi coast, Capri, and the Gulf of Salerno can be enjoyed from the vantage point of San Lazzaro; 18-km detour from Vèttica Minore. Amalfi*: white, stacked in terraces on the steep slopes over the sea; touches of exotic architecture in the Duomo, with its bronze doors from Constantinople (1066), the intertwined arches in the cloister of the Paradiso – all these things are relics of ancient maritime trade with the east, the commerce and glory of the Republic of Amalfi of the 10th and 11th c. Atrani is magnificently situated in an inlet, between high rock walls; the church of S. Salvatore di Bireto, where the doges of Amalfi were elected, has bronze doors from Constantinople (1087). Ravello* (350 m): the site is perched on cliffs and crags, the roads are rustic at best, the landscape is colorful, and there are simple treasures to be found here; to mention the finest aspects, note the Arab-style architecture and the exotic plants of the garden of Villa Rufolo, the bronze doors by Barisano da Trani in the Duomo, the vista of sea, mountains, and coastline from the high terraced land between the valleys of the Dragone and the Reginna in the Cimbrone overlook. Minori, a beachfront town, formerly an arsenal of the Republic of Amalfi, with the ruins of a Roman villa. Maiori: spreading out like an amphitheater in its inlet, at the foot of the majolica dome of the church of S. Maria a Mare; museum. Cava de' Tirreni, with a beautiful ancient village. Abbazia della Trinità di Cava: a 7-km detour from Vietri sul Mare, famed for its majolica, will take you to this abbey, founded in the year 1101 and almost completely rebuilt in the 18th c.; the church dates from the 18th c., the Benedictine monastery includes a little 13th-c. cloister and a museum. Salerno*: two rare and exquisite artworks are in the Museo del Duomo: a 12th-c. ivory frontal and a 13th-c. illuminated "Exultet". The Salerno Duomo itself is one of the most notable monuments in southern Italy, in terms of architecture, history, and artwork; the seafront is lined with palm trees, and is bathed in the light of the gulf.

111

68 | Terra di Lavoro and the Highlands of Roccamonfina

Caserta - Santa Maria Capua Vètere - Capua - Sessa Aurunca - Teàno (72 km)

The name in Italian – Terra di Lavoro – and the appearance of the landscape would seem to suggest, as the origin of the term, "Land of Labor," the great and fruitful work of a people of tireless farmers. Not so: the original Terra Leboria refers to the Leborini, the original inhabitants of this area. Nowadays, the term Terra di Lavoro describes the territory of the province of Caserta between the elevations of Monte Massico and the northern rim of the Phlegraean Fields; in bygone times, the name described a larger portion of Campania. What the 16th-c. Neapolitan historian Camillo Porzio once wrote is still true: this territory is "superior to all other lands on earth in fertility and quality and any other thing that can delight or help the human race, rich and abundant." The cities that you will see there – Caserta, Santa Maria Capua Vètere, and Capua – cast

bright lights on the history of the region from ancient times, as well as on the history of the entire south of Italy, while the artwork in this area (to mention only a few items, the archaic "mothers" of the Museo Campano in Capua; frescoes, with their Byzantine iconography, painted by local artists in the second half of the 11th c., on the walls of the Benedictine basilica of Sant'Angelo in Formis; and the 18th-c. palace, or Reggia, of Caserta) stands out in the body of Italian art. As for the mountain of Roccamonfina, it is a volcano, extinct since antiquity; upon its slopes, softened by the passage of thousands of years, olive trees and vineyards yield to thick dark chestnut groves as you climb: amid the branches and shadows, you will find a classic literary idyll, as is so often the case in southern Italy.

The route. You leave Caserta along Viale Douhet, with the Reggia, or palace, on your right and then continue along to Santa Maria Capua Vètere; from here, you will head north to Sant'Angelo in Formis, cross the Volturno River, and, via Triflisco, arrive at Capua, entering town from the west along the Via Appia (SS 7 road) and the bridge over the Volturno. You leave Capua as you entered it, but immediately afterward you turn off the Via Appia onto the road that runs toward the Piana di Carinola, via Brezza, and Sant'Andrea. From Carinola you will continue on, reaching the Via Appia and following it for a short distance until you come to the turnoff for nearby Sessa Aurunca. Continuing along this road, you will then climb up to Roccamonfina (612 m) and then head down, east, via Filorsi, Preta, and Tuoro, until you get to Teàno.

Places of interest. Caserta*: the Reggia, or palace, and its grounds are the masterpiece of the Neapolitan architect Luigi Vanvitelli, who expressed in stone and brick the ambitions of the first Bourbon king of Naples, probably inspired in turn by his great-grandfather, Louis XIV, the Sun King: the facade of the building extends for nearly 250 m, the grounds cover 120 hectares. The city grew up around the Royal Palace here. Casertavecchia*: the crowning jewel of this still-intact medieval town, overlooking the plain from high atop a hill, is the 12th-c. cathedral, a rich composite of styles ranging from Romanesque to Sicilian Arabic and Benedictine; 10-km detour before leaving Caserta. Santa Maria Capua Vètere is the town known as Capua to classical antiquity, with Roman ruins: the Campanian amphitheater and the Mithraeum. Sant'Angelo in Formis: this basilica from the year 1000 is adorned with remarkable frescoes of the same period. Capua: in ancient times, this was Casilinum; it stands in a curve of the Volturno River, enclosed in 16th-c. bastions; in the Museo Campano note the 200 "madri," archaic votive statues; a Roman bridge stretches over the river. Carìnola: ruined castle, Romanesque cathedral, and 15th-c. Catalonian-Gothic houses. Sessa Aurunca: before you enter this small town, take the country road to see the Roman bridge of the Aurunci*, rearing high against the surrounding landscape, with 21 arches; the village occupies the site of the ancient town of Suessa, of which ruins can still be seen; go see the pulpit supported by carved lions and the paschal candelabrum* in the Romanesque Duomo. Roccamonfina: this resort town lies amidst chestnut groves on the slopes of an extinct volcano; at a distance of 2.5 km is S. Maria dei Làttani, a 15th-c. sanctuary. Teàno: 12th-c. Duomo and the ruins of a Roman theater.

69 | Among the Mountains of Irpinia

Avellino - Bagnoli Irpino - Mirabella Eclano - Avellino (148 km)

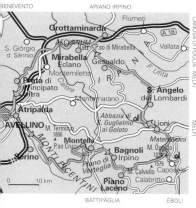

This is a land with scars, where the wounds have healed slowly, where the terrible srents in the architectural and artistic heritage are unmistakable, in some cases irreparable. The earthquake that struck here, in the darkness of an early autumn evening – 23 November 1980 at 7:35 pm – lasted for one long, seemingly endless minute. When seen on a map, the area hit by the earthquake stretches parallel with the overall orientation of the Italian peninsula, elongated, including Naples, Benevento, the Vùlture, Potenza, and the Vallo di Diano. The epicenter, the area of the most violent lurches and jolts, straddles the high valleys of the rivers Òfanto and Sele, bounded by Sant'Angelo dei Lombardi and Laviano. There were 3,000 dead, 10,000 injured, some 70 towns and villages wholly destroyed or badly damaged. The enormous quantity of energy that was unleashed in the space of a minute was measured as a 6.4 quake on the Richter scale. The route through the Irpino Mountains recommended here runs entirely through the greenery of mighty and solitary forests, gently rolling landscapes, mountains, hills, the high valleys of gathering streams, the Apennine courses of the rivers Sàbato, Calore, Òfanto, and Sele. The earthquake has not damaged the patterns of nature, only the rich landscape wrought by man. Among the areas hardest hit is a diffuse "agrarian" architectural heritage, a body of venerable structures and an artistic fabric – not masterpieces perhaps, but eminently worthy – that had long been neglected and ignored, until the earthquake came, swept much of it away, and finally revealed its true worth.

The route.

Leave Avellino on the Autostrada toward Salerno, exiting at Serino. A scenic road, the SS 574 road, leads up through the Piano di Verteglia (1230 m) and the Passo Cruci (980 m) to Montella in the high valley of the river Calore. The SS 368 road then takes you to Bagnoli Irpino. You then climb up to the Lago di Laceno and to Piano Laceno (1053 m) and, along the scenic route running over the northern slopes of Monte Calvello and Monte Oppido, you will reach the turnoff for Caposele. The ensuing landmarks will be Caposele, Materdòmini, and Lioni in the upper valley of the Òfanto. Now you are on the SS 7 Appia road, but you will soon leave that road to drive up to Sant'Angelo dei Lombardi. From here, the SS 425 road will take you in turn to the SS 303 road, which runs over the ridge separating the valleys of the Frédane and Ufita rivers. From the Passo di Mirabella you will continue to Grottaminarda; from there you will return to Avellino on the Autostrada from Puglia. This route is fairly intricate; we recommend studying a road map carefully before setting out.

Places of interest. Avellino is a modern city located in a verdant hollow of the Valle del Sàbato, in a mountainous setting, with the Museo Diocesano and the Museo Irpino. Atripalda: remains of the Sarnites and Roman Abellinum. Serino: summer excursions and winter skiing. Monte Terminio (1783 m) is a nature reserve amidst spectacular forests; it extends on the left of the route, and is accessible from Serino. Bagnoli Irpino is a resort at the head of the Valle del Calore. Caposele: above the town are the intake and pumping stations for the great Pugliese aqueduct. Materdòmini is a resort town, set amid oak groves, with the Santuario di S. Gerardo at Maiella, a pilgrimage site. S. Guglielmo al Goleto is a ruined abbey containing the remains of the large and small church founded in the 12th c. by Saint Guglielmo di Vercelli; this requires a short detour from the SS 7 road, after Lioni. Sant'Angelo dei Lombardi: take a short detour; at the head of the Valle dell'Ófanto, this town was devastated by the earthquake of 1980; the 16th-c. Cattedrale with its late Renaissance portal was only partly destroyed; the "Lombardi" were, of course, the Longobards, who founded the town. Aeclanum was originally a Samnite town, and later a Roman one: the archeological excavations are just a short way west of the Passo di Mirabella. Mirabella Eclano: take a 2.5 km detour from the Passo di Mirabella, a carved and painted wooden 12th-c. Crucifix can be seen in the church of Matrice; on a Saturday in September, during the "Festa del Carro," a 25-m-tall obelisk is transported into town from a hill, with a statue of Our Lady of Sorrows. Grottaminarda is a hilltop farming town, with the 18th-c. church of S. Maria Maggiore designed by Vanvitelli. Basilica dell'Annunciata: founded in early times, the oldest medieval church in Irpinia was partly carved out of the tufa, near a catacomb, and may have been the headquarters of the earliest bishops of Avellino. Make a 7-km detour, exiting the Autostrada at Avellino Est, then along the SS road toward Grottaminarda until you reach Prata di Principato Ultra, noted for its Basilica dell'Annunziata, where a further journey on secondary roads is necessary.

70 | The Gargano and Tavoliere

Foggia - Manfredonia - Monte Sant'Angelo - Vieste - Pèschici - Rodi Gargànico
San Giovanni Rotondo - San Severo - Lucera - Troia - Foggia (309 km)

The Tavoliere is the broadest plain in the entire Italian peninsula, occupying 3000 sq km, one percent of the nation's surface. In ancient times, this was seabed; in centuries gone by it was winter pasturage, where nomadic sheep herders would lead their flocks. At Foggia there was a "dogana della mena delle pecore," or shepherds' customs station (established in 1447 by Alphonse of Aragon, it provided the royal coffers with an endless stream of cash; it was abolished after Italian unification). Today this is farmland, where grain, forage, vineyards, and fruit orchards grow. It is true that the eye sees only an endless tableland here, but that is not the origin of the name, which refers to the *Tabulae Censuariae*, the register in which the immense landholdings of the government in this territory were recorded. At a distance, it is surrounded by the outcroppings and spurs of the Samnite Apennines, the rim of the Murgia highlands, and the Gargano. It is from the last elevations of the Apennines as they sink into the plain that Lucera and Troia look out over the Tavoliere from the west: Lucera, where Frederick II gathered the troublesome Saracens of Sicily, a reserve for recruits to his loyal and much feared royal guard; Troia, with its Romanesque cathedral, an outstanding example of the architectural style of the Apulian Middle Ages, veined with Byzantine and Muslim styles. The Gargano, on the other hand, is the other landscape of this route, which virtually follows the entire Gargano coastline before crossing it. This great karstic limestone massif with rounded mountaintops rises from the plain in two successive terraces; extending out into the Adriatic, it plunges into the sea with high, steep coasts, broken here and there by small beaches. At the base of this massif on the southern side are the churches of the Siponto, a region strangled by malarial swamps and earthquakes; on high is the Santu-

ario dell'Arcangelo Michele in Monte Sant'Angelo, dedicated to the Archangel Michael, perched on a high ridge. The coastline has been a relatively recent discovery here. For many years the peninsula was secluded, trapped between the sea and the marshlands of the Tavoliere; today people are drawn here by the shoals and the sands, the olive groves and pine forests, the bright southern light, inland near the scattered remains of the forest that once extended where now only underbrush and pasturage are seen, where white rocks jut out of the arid soil.

The route. You will leave Foggia on the Via San Lazaro and the SS 89 road, heading for Manfredonia. Continuing along the same road, you will begin the circuit around the Gargano, but at Mattinata you will turn off onto a twisting, scenic coastal route that runs around the promontory, via Vieste, Pèschici, and Rodi Garganico. About 5 km further on, turn left onto the road that runs via Ischitella to Vico del Gargano, where you can turn off onto the scenic road that cuts across the peninsula, from north to south, through the Foresta Umbra, to Monte Sant'Angelo. Retracing your route for a short distance, you then head west on the SS 272 road, which will take you to San Giovanni Rotondo and San Marco in Lamis. From here, secondary roads will take you to Rignano Garganico, and then on down to the Tavoliere, north of Foggia, to Lucera (the landmarks along this route are Ponte Villanova, Masseria Monaco Cappelli, Stazione di Rignano Garganico, and Pàlmori). From Lucera to Troia you will follow the SS 160 road; from Troia you will return to Foggia along the SS 546 road.

Places of interest. Foggia, at the heart of the Tavoliere, is a thoroughly modern town: the Romanesque cathedral was heavily restored in the 18th c.; in the Museo Comunale and the Pinacoteca Comunale there are also exhibits concerning the Foggia-born composer, Umberto Giordano. S. Leonardo di Siponto*: a 12th-c. church, formerly an abbey of the Knights Templar, with a splendid portal decorated with 13th-c reliefs. S. Maria di Siponto**: a lovely 11th-c. Romanesque cathedral, once part of the long-vanished town. Manfredonia: the castle (like the city, founded and built by Manfredi, or Manfred, the natural son of the emperor Frederick II), facing the waterfront, is the site of the Museo Nazionale Archeologico del Gargano. Monte Sant'Angelo*: in the grotto here, the Archangel Michael was purportedly seen in an apparition in the late 5th c. At that time, the Longobards were particularly devoted to Michael, as a national saint; the sanctuary and town grew together, through the faith of the pilgrims. The so-called tomb of the Longobard king Rotari is actually a later baptistery, in all likelihood; the Museo Tancredi features the arts and folkways of the Gargano. Vieste: visit the old town, with stepped lanes amid white houses joined by arches; fine view of the coastline and sea from the castle. Pèschici: high on the coast of the Gargano, perched upon a crag, overlooking the beach below. Rodi Gargànico: set on a promontory on the north coast of the Gargano; twenty nautical miles away are the Tremiti Islands, with their clear waters, rocky coasts, and aromatic vegetation, the maquis. Vico del Gargano: the Trappeto Maratea is an old mill used for producing oil. Foresta Umbra* is a vast forest of beech trees, pines, maples, and hornbeams, in the recently established Parco Nazionale del Gargano. San Giovanni Rotondo: site of pilgrimages commemorating the Christian virtues of Padre Pio da Pietrelcina. San Marco in Lamis, dominated by the like-named convent founded by the Lombards. San Severo: site of medieval churches and widely renowned for the production of white wine. Lucera*: this little town is dense with history, from Roman times, up through the remarkable reigns of Frederick II and of the House of Anjou: the castle that overlooks the plain was enlarged by Charles I d'Anjou with a vast ring of towers and walls; the 14th-c. Duomo is also Angevin; the Museo Civico Giuseppe Fiorelli has exhibits chiefly of archeology. Troia: the rose window and bronze doors by Oderisio da Benevento embellish the cathedral, a sterling example of Apulian Romanesque; Museo Diocesano and Museo Civico; proto-Romanesque church of S. Basilio.

71 | Trulli and Grottoes

Bari - Castellana Grotte - Alberobello - Fasano - Brindisi (146 km)

The Adriatic coast, which you will be following in part along this route, often forms a last little rocky cliffline, in the succession of terraces of "rocky Apulia," as the Murge hills are often called. The "trullo," a remarkable type of dwelling found here (more about "i trulli" below, in due time), gives its name to another part of the Murge, the SE sector (Murgia dei Trulli). This rolling highland, dark green with crops, drops away toward the Adriatic coastline like a steep rampart, between Mola di Bari and Ostuni, covered with white houses; toward the Gulf of Tàranto, on the other hand, it slopes gently in a succession of terraces. The two sections of the Murge differ in terms of agriculture and in terms of population, which is scattered throughout the countryside further south. And there are three notable grottoes or caverns. At Polignano a Mare, the Grotta Palazzese encloses waters of an intense blue-green; it yawns open, with many other marine grottoes, in the steep cliff face, which has been burrowed out by the tireless sea waves. The Grotta di Putignano is a karstic cavity, a treasure chest of alabaster some 20 m tall, covered with pink mineral encrustations. The most notable grottoes, or caves, however, are the Grotte di Castellana, first explored by a group of local youths in the 18th c. They extend for a good 2 km, some 50 m under the surface of the earth; stalactites and stalagmites dangle and jut, stirring the imagination of cave explorers, and prompting fanciful names such as: Ciclopi (Cyclops), Angelo (Angel), Civetta (Owl), Presepe (Crèche), Serpente (Serpent), Altare (Altar), Duomo di Milano (Cathedral of Milan), and Torre di Pisa (Leaning Tower of Pisa). At the end of this succession of caverns you encounter the crystalline whiteness of the Grotta Bianca, which has been described as the world's most beautiful cave. Along the road, there are olive and almond groves everywhere, and more than half of the route runs along the seashore. Toward the end of the route, you will be retracing the steps of Horace, in the voyage he describes in his fifth Satire. Egnazia was the final stage of this trip: "The construction of Gnatia having angered the waters," he wrote, with reference to the aridity of the region. Lastly, Horace described "Brundisium longae finis chartaeque viaeque," calling Brindisi the "end of the journey and of the paper," meaning that his poem ended with the great historic port town, terminus of the Appian Way

The route.

After leaving Bari along the Lungomare Nazario Sauro, you will drive along the Adriatic coast on the SS 16 road as far as Polignano a Mare. A scenic road then leads inland to Castellana Grotte. Soon after, at Putignano, the SS 172 road will take you on to Alberobello and Locorotondo. Then you will head back to the sea along the Fasano Torre Canne route. You will continue on to Brindisi on the beach road (SS 379 road), turning off from it in the stretch between Villanova and Torresabina, to head inland to Ostuni and Carovigno.

Places of interest.

Bari: the historical center of this regional capital contains two Romanesque churches, S. Sabino and S. Nicola. Mola di Bari: set on a promontory, with a 13th-c. cathedral renovated in the Renaissance style by architects from Dalmatia; note the fishing harbor and the Angevin castle, erected in 1278. Polignano a Mare overlook the Adriatic Sea from its jagged cliffs; the light and colors in the Grotta Palazzese are a pale blue: it is the best known grotto in this stretch of coastline, and you can tour it by boat. Conversano: on a detour from the main route between Castellana Grotte and Polignano a Mare, with its Duomo, other old churches, and a vista of the coastline from the square in front of the castle. Grotte di Castellana**: carved by an ancient underground river, this is the largest complex of caves in Italy. Putignano, a resort in the Murgia range; in town is the church of Madre di S. Pietro; 1 km away is the grotto, with pink alabastrine encrustations. Alberobello*: the "trulli," round whitewashed houses with conical grey limestone roofs, line the long steep twisting streets, creating a remarkable townscape. Martina Franca*: take a 6-km detour from Locorotondo*, which offers fine views of the valley of Itria, scattered with "trulli"; the city stands on the highest elevation of the southern Murgia range, and has vigorous architecture and a fine Baroque flavor. Fasano: resort on a spur of the Murgia range; all around, amidst the Mediterranean vegetation are bright white "trulli" and exotic animals. Egnazia: the necropolis, the musem, and the ruins of ancient Gnatia can all be reached via an 11-km detour climbing north along the coast, from Torre Canne. Ostuni glitters white among the olive trees on the hills of the Murgia; note the medieval quarters, illuminated at night. Carovigno, with a 15th-c. castle and the walls of the Messapic town Carbina. Brindisi: two Roman columns mark the end of the Via Appia, or Appian Way, on the shore of the peninsula where the modern city stands between two inlets that constitute an excellent natural harbor; the Museo Archeologico Francesco Ribezza and, at a distance of 2 km, the 13th-c. church of S. Maria del Casale, the most outstanding monument in the city.

72 | Salento

Lecce - Ótranto - Marina di Leuca - Gallìpoli - Tàranto (240 km)

The castle of Ótranto is pentagonal, with three round towers. This menacing military construction was erected by Ferdinand of Aragon at the end of the 15th c. This is the extreme tip of the easternmost cape of the Italian peninsula, surrounded by the waters of the Adriatic, which begins at the channel of Ótranto and the waters of the enveloping Ionian sea. The coast is jagged, in places lined with pine groves; it drops away sheer into the crashing waves, the limestone cliffs studded with marine caves in which humans once lived, in the Paleolithic era. The gently rolling reddish land supports olive groves and vineyards, amid the jutting white rocks. This route runs from Lecce to Tàranto, around the cape of Santa Maria di Leuca – *Iapygium promontorium* – almost invariably hugging the coast. But we have mentioned Ótranto first of all because, in the past, when Apulia was divided into three parts, the Salento peninsula was part of what was then called the Terra d'Ótranto. This comprised the modern-day provinces of Tàranto, Lecce, and Brindisi, but the peninsula nowadays corresponds to the province of Lecce alone. The capital of this province is Lecce, alluring for its remarkable architecture. Paul Bourget saw it in 1890, and wrote about it in his "Sensations d'Italie," admitting that in Lecce he had discovered new meanings for the terms Baroque and Rococo:

"Lecce showed me that these words could also be synonymous with a light fingered fancy, mad elegance, felicitous grace." The city proved to be a "single furor of caprice," even more so in that "its chiseled brightness emanates an almost Eastern light," while "the air is slightly stirred by the breeze that swells the sails of the ships in the Embarquement pour Cythère, reminiscent of the great and melancholy Watteau."

The route. Leave Lecce along the Via del Mare, reaching the coast at San Cataldo. Here you will take the coast route south, along the SS 611 road (as far as Ótranto) and the SS 173 road, as far as Capo Santa Maria di Leuca. A bit further on, at Leuca, you will turn inland to Patù, and from there will drive back down to the sea at Torre San Gregorio on the Golfo di Tàranto. You will then continue along the coast road as far as Santa Maria al Bagno. There is a stretch inland along secondary roads, with the landmarks of Nardò, Galatone, Galatina, and Lever ano; then you return to the coast at Porto Cesàreo. Take the Via Salentina (SS 174 road), directly behind Porto Cesàreo, and you will reach Manduria on the range of the Murge Tarantine. Then, you will reach the coast at Campomarino continuing along the coast road as far as Tàranto.

Places of interest. Lecce**: this town, capital of the Salento area, should be toured carefully, un-hurriedly, and patiently, and not only for the celebrated, flamboyant Baroque architecture of the churches, palazzi, piazzas, and streets. San Cataldo: main beach of the province's capital. Roca Vecchia: the ruins of the castle on the cliffs were once a Messapic city. Ótranto: an enormous and famous 12th-c. mo-saic covers the floor of the cathedral*; in the town, mostly enclosed within walls, also go see the Aragonese castle and the Byzantine-style church of S. Pietro. Santa Cesàrea Terme; the springs pour forth out of caverns in the cliffs and then drop away into the sea. Poggiardo: a 20-km detour from Santa Cesàrea Terme; in a museum you can see the medieval frescoes detached from the crypt of S. Maria; at a distance of 1.5 km is the crypt of S. Stefano, with remains of frescoes dating back to the 12th-/15th-c. Grotta Zinzulusa*: this cavern is outstanding among the caves in the cliffs around Ótranto, in terms of encrus-tations, underground fauna, and prehistoric finds. Castro stands high among the olive groves, with its ancient cathedral, 16th-c. walls, and vast view of sea and coast; beneath it is the little port of Castro Marina. Marina di Leuca: the lighthouse, the Santuario di Finibus Terrae, the caverns in the cliffs, and the waves of the Ionian sea: this is the far tip of the Salento peninsula. Patù (see Marina di Leuca): the Centopietre is a great Messapic or medieval megalithic construction at the edge of town, facing the little Romanesque church of S. Giovanni. Usentum: scanty ruins of the Roman port can be seen in the inlet of Marina San Giovanni; a little further along is the islet of Pazzi, inhabited in pre historic times. Gallìpoli*: the medieval "borgo" with white terraced houses stands on an islet, linked by a bridge to the modern part of town, on a peninsula, jutting into the sea. Galàtone (see Galatina), interesting examples of Lecce style Baroque. Galatina: Stories of the Virgin Mary, painted according to an apocryphal Gospel, and other 15th-c. frescoes, cover the interior of the church of S. Caterina. Nardò rivalled Lecce as the most important cultural and artistic city in the Salento province during the 17th c. Porto Cesàreo, situated along the part of the coast which is to become a marine park. Manduria: in the this little town in the range of the Murge Tarantine, note the ancient Duomo, the medieval ghetto, the Baroque Palazzo Imperiali, the Messapic walls, and the remarkable Fonte Pliniano. Tàranto*, whose splendid past is hinted at in the golden jewels contained in the Museo Archeologico Nazionale.

73 | Cilento and Vallo di Diano

Salerno - Paestum - Palinuro - Maratea - Sala Consilina - Potenza (330 km)

"The air was delicately scented by the remarkably large and lovely violet. At last, we glimpsed the sublime and powerful rows of columns hemming in the horizon, in the midst of a desolate wasteland." These are the words in a letter to a friend by the English poet Percy Bysshe Shelley, who saw Paestum in February 1819. "Between one column and the next in this temple – it is called the Temple of Ceres – you can see in one direction the sea, toward which the gentle slope of the hill on which it stands runs down, and in the other direction you can see the vast amphitheatre of the Apennines, dark-colored, purplish mountains with diadems of snow, over which sail thick and leaden cloud banks." The Greeks of Sybaris sailed across the Mediterranean to found this city, calling it Poseidonia, after their sea god; the Lucanians who later descended from the Apennines to take the city for themselves gave it its modern name. Here Shelley was unable to enjoy the excitement of the sacred dances performed by girls depicted on the metopes of the Heraion of the Sele River; he did not see the diver portrayed on a tomb slab, for neither of these artworks, now in the museum, had yet been unearthed. Beyond Paestum, along the route, one is astonished by the nature of the coast of the Cilento, the crags, the cliffs, the inlets, and the glittering light that flashes off the sea, losing itself among the fluttering leaves of the olive groves. Watchtowers are relics of the centuries of Saracen pirate raids, little harbors are reminiscent of the trade in grain, wine, and olive oil once carried on by the sailor-monks from the abbey of Cava de' Tirreni. Midway up the Cilento coast is another Greek city, Elea (or *Velia* as it was written by Pliny), renowned for the school of philosophy that was begun here by the Ionian Xenophanes of Colophon and continued by Parmenides and Zeno (the latter known for his elegant logical paradoxes, such as that of Achilles being unable to outrun the tortoise; less well known for his participation in an unsuccessful conspiracy against the tyrant Nearchus. When Nearchus interrogated the philosopher, Zeno bit his own tongue off, so as not to betray his fellow-conspirators, and spit it in the tyrant's face. As a result, the tyrant had him crushed to death under a mill stone). Velia, like Paestum, was attacked by the Lucanians, but it withstood the siege. After completing this tour, you will return north along the Vallo di Diano, the highland that separates the Apennine ridge of the Maddalena from the mountains of the Cilento, and then you will head east to Potenza, where you can admire the artifacts of the Lucanians, Italic descendants of the ancient Samnites, in the Museo Archeologico.

The route.

Leaving Salerno along the Lungomare Marconi, you will follow the Tyrrheni
coastline all the way to the southermost point on this route, Praia a Mare (
be precise, the littoral of the Piana del Sele as far as Paestum; from Paestu
is a secondary road to Agròpoli; from there, the SS 267 road along the coa
line of the Cilento continues on through Ascea, Pisciotta, and Palinuro; ta
the SS 562 road from Palinuro all the way to the junction, on the Golfo di P
castro, and the SS 18 road, along which you will continue). From Praia a Ma
heading back north again, you will retrace the same route for a short stint, a
after the bridge over the Castrocucco River, you will turn off onto the road f
Lagonero, taking the Autostrada north at the Lagonegro-Maratea int
change. Then you will leave the Autostrada at the Padula-Buonabitàcolo
terchange, following the SS road through the Vallo di Diano, as far as Sala Co
silina; from here, secondary roads will take you to Teggiano on the weste
side of the Vallo, or great end moraine, then on to Polla and into the Valle c
Tanagro, to Pertosa and Auletta. Finally, at the interchange of Buccino, you w
reach the Autostrada that goes to Potenza (the stretch not on the Autostrad
between the interchanges of Padula-Buonabitàcolo and Buccino allows you
tour the Certosa di Padula and the Grotte di Pertosa, as well as make oth
stops mentioned below).

Places of interest.

Salerno*: set between the hills and the coastline of the gulf, its seafront de
ted with palm trees, this town boasts the medieval Duomo built by Robe
Guiscard, one of the most important monuments in southern Italy; there are
few precious works of art in the Museo del Duomo, and archeological colle
tions in the Museo Provinciale. Santuario di Hera Argiva: take a 2-km deto
from Torre Kernoi, after the Sele River; it is said to have been founded by J
son; among the ruins, not particularly impressive to see nowadays, were th
archaic Greek sculptures (metopes) now in Paestum. Paestum**, with the a
cient Doric columns of the three temples of Greek Poseidonia, the pentagon
walls that mark the perimeter of the vanished city, the excavations, the Muse
with the metopes from the Santuario di Hera Argiva, and painted Greek ar
Lucanian slabs, is one of Italy's leading archeological sites, justly famou
Agròpoli: from the ruins of the Byzantine castle in the old town, perched hig
over the sea, you can enjoy the vista of the Gulf of Salerno, as far as Capri. Sa
ta Maria di Castellabate, whose waters are protected by an underwater par
Scavi di Velia: this town, founded as a Phocaean Greek colony, was the tow
of Elea of the subtle philosophers Xenophanes, Parmenides, and Zeno; the r
ins are scattered across the plain and the acropolis. Palinuro: located in an i
let at the foot of the promontory; by boat, you can go to the Grotta Azzurr
or Blue Grotto, in 10 minutes, to enjoy the amazingly blue light and water. M
rina di Camerota, at the beginning of the Golfo di Policastro, with the Calab
an coast in the background. Sapri, with its annual commemoration of the lan
ing of the 300 soldiers fighting for a united Italy. Maratea, medieval "borgo
perched on a rock, and bathing spots lining the coast; among the numerou
grottoes, note the one of Marina di Maratea with its stalactites and stala,
mites. Praia a Mare: uphill from the beach resort is the Santuario della Mado
na della Grotta; you can take a boat to the island of Dino, about 1.5 km of
shore. Lagonegro: this village stands on a slope of Monte Sirino, set in a rir
of mountains. It is said that the woman who inspired Leonardo da Vinci
Mona Lisa was laid to rest in the ancient parish church. Padula: downhill fron
the town is the immense Baroque charterhouse, or Certosa di S. Lorenzo, sit
of the Museo Archeologico della Lucania Occidentale. Teggiano: the layout c
this medieval town stands high on a secluded hilltop; note the Roman an
medieval marble carvings in the former church of S. Pietro. Sala Consilin
whose historical center overlooks the ramparts of Diano. Polla: 16th-/17th-
paintings and the carved choir chancel in the convent church of S. Antonio, i
the high part of town; from the square in front of the church, fine view of th
entire Vallo di Diano. Grotta di Pertosa*: once the channel of an undergroun
river, this cavern extends its heavily encrusted walls, with galleries, lakelets
and halls, for more than 2 km. Potenza: a modern city stands around the me
dieval center, high atop a ridge, at an elevation of 816 m; go visit the Muse
Archeologico Nazionale.

74 | The Mountains of Northern Basilicata

Potenza - Monticchio - Melfi - Venosa - Potenza (186 km)

As a child, the Latin poet Horace is said to have escaped from his nurse and wandered through the mountain forests until, exhausted, he fell asleep. The tale goes that he was protected by mysterious doves, who covered him with branches of laurel and myrtle, "ut tuto ab atris corpore viperis / dormirem et ursis" (so that he could sleep, his little body safe from black vipers and bears); this remarkable event astounded the woodsmen who later found him. The mountain upon which the infant Horace had his adventure was the Vùlture, an ancient volcano with harsh landscapes, covered with forests of beech trees, oaks, chesnuts, lindens, maples, hornbeams, elms, ashes, poplars, and alders – the high point in terms of views of this route over the Ófanto and the Bràdano. The birthplace of Horace, of course, is nearby Venosa, or Venusia, once a Roman military colony, and now part of the Basilicata region on the border with Apulia. The poet was born here and completed his early studies

under a tutor named Flavius, who taught "magni pueri magnis e centurionibus orti," or "big boys, the sons of big centurions" (later his father took Horace to study with the best masters in Rome). In the other cities and sites along this route – including Melfi, the Castello di Lagopésole, Venosa with the Abbazia della Trinità, Acerenza with its large cathedral with a French-style ambulatory around the presbytery – what prevails is the air of medieval history, of the Normans, Swabians, and Angevins, with the great shadow of Frederick II looming over all. Lagopésole, made of reddish limestone, is the largest and the last of this emperor's castles; from another, Norman castle in Melfi – Frederick had restored Melfi's walls – he decreed his "Constitutiones Augustales," which his jurists, including the renowned Pier delle Vigne, had developed to regulate feudal law.

The route. You will leave Potenza, heading north along the SS 93 road as far as Rionero in Vùlture. This marks the beginnning of the circuit around Monte Vùlture (on the SS 167, 401, and 303 roads), heading for Monticchio, Melfi, and Rapolla. At Rapolla you will rejoin the SS 93 road, taking it toward Lavello, but turning off shortly at a crossroads and taking the road to Venosa. From Venosa, you will head south along twisting, scenic secondary roads, to Maschito, Forenza, and Acerenza, and then onto the SS 169 road. Along this road, through Pietragalla, you will reach the crossroads of San Nicola, where once again you will turn onto the SS 93 road, which will take you back along your tracks to Potenza.

Places of interest. Potenza occupies the crest of a hill in the high valley of the Basento River; the Museo Archeologico Nazionale is devoted to the ancient inhabitants of Lucania, as Basilicata was once called. Castello di Lagopésole* is a monumental residence and stronghold, begun by the emperor Frederick II eight years before his death. Atella: this village was founded in the 14th c. and still has some remains from that period; it is said that Giovanna I, queen of Naples, was held prisoner in the Benedictine monastery. Monte Vùlture is an extinct volcano: you can drive up to an altitude of 1245 m with a scenic road, 5.5 km from Rionero in Vùlture, a town alive with history, situated between two hills, or you can take a cableway from the lakes of Monticchio to an altitude of 1214 m. Laghi di Monticchio*: the larger of these lakes is on the left of the road, the smaller is to the right; their green waters lie in the crater of a volcano. Melfi:

this town lies at the foot of the large old castle and is enclosed by ancient wa[l]
relics of the time when this was the residence of Norman kings and, later, of t[h]
emperor Frederick Hohenstaufen; go see the renowned sarcophagus of Rap[o]
la in the Museo Nazionale Archeologico. Rapolla lies on mountain slopes, wi[th]
a 13th-c. Gothic cathedral whose magnificent portal dates back to 1253 and t[he]
Norman church of S. Lucia, with a clear Byzantine influence. At a distance o[f]
km is Barile, a village of Albanian traditions (settlers from Scùtari and Cro[ja]
fleeing the Turks, arrived here around 1460). Venosa*: in the image of this ci[ty]
birthplace of Horace (the so-called Casa del Poeta, or House of the Poet, is a[c]
tually a tepidarium from Roman baths), the monuments of the Middle Ag[es]
and the Renaisssance, especially the abbey of the Trinità, predominate ov[er]
the Roman ruins. Maschito: beginning in 1467, this town was repopulated [by]
Albanian refugees. Some still speak the dialect. In the Palazzo Comunale is a [re]
markable collection of paintings by the local artist Mario Cangianelli. Foren[za]
is a delightfully situated holiday resort. Acerenza, overlooking the high vall[ey]
of the river Bràdano, has a magnificent large Romanesque cathedral with b[ell]
tower, whose origins go back to the 11th c.; rebuilt in the 16th c., the cry[pt]
contains restored frescoes. Pietragalla, with old dungeons dug out of the tu[fa]

75 | Mount Pollino, Sibaritide, and Sila

Lagonegro - Sìbari - Rossano - Camigliatello Silano - Cosenza (261 km)

This Calabrian symphony develops in thr[ee]
movements, as it were. The first is the va[st]
Pollino massif, the southern terminus of t[he]
Lucanian Apennines, largely stretching east[-]
west, as if it were a barrier warning aw[ay]
would-be visitors to the region. Geograph[ers]
tell us that this is the southernmost Apenni[ne]
group to show the marks of glacial activi[ty]
and for those who love nature, this is a hars[h]
powerful, solitary mountain, dotted with s[e]
cluded and intact settings. This route ru[ns]
across its southern slopes; it would be wise [to]
use Morano Calabro and Castrovìllari as yo[ur]
base for excursions. From the geodetic be[a]
con of the highest peak – Monte Pollino, als[o]
known as the Telegrafo (2248 m) – you can s[ee]
the regions of Calabria and Basilicata and t[he]
Tyrrhenian and the Ionian seas. The secon[d]
leg takes us back to classical antiquity. Sybar[is]
was an Achaean colony, wealthy from its s[il]
ver mines (in what is now San Marco Argentano), a city of refined living, wi[th]
perhaps the worst reputation in all of Magna Grecia, probably because it wa[s]
defeated in war. The army of Crotone, in a campaign lasting 70 days, storme[d]
the city, sacked it, and then destroyed it entirely (510 B.C.). According to tr[a]
dition, they then shifted the course of the Crati River to submerge the ruin[s]
The search for the actual site of the city impassioned scholars and put arch[a]
ologists to stern task for many years: now you can see and explore it. It wa[s]
only discovered several decades ago, in a landscape altered by reclamatio[n]
500 hectares of rolling plains, straddling the modern course of the river Cra[ti]
about 4 km from its mouth, where it empties into the Gulf of Tàranto. The thi[rd]
movement in the symphony involves a drive across the Sila. This area ha[s]
been compared countless times to Switzerland, and with good reason! Th[e]
first mention we are able to find was in the travel journal of the Marqu[is]
Adolphe de Custine, who ventured off the beaten track in Italy. Writing in 181[8]
he said that the Sila forest "occupies a great expanse of mountainous terrai[n]
its chestnut groves shade meadows and brooks, and the villages all show [a]
freshness that makes it hard to believe that these Swiss scenes are located [in]

nearly the same latitude as Sicily. This lovely forest is now a haven for the wealthy invalids of Cosenza and the poor brigands of all the Calabrias... I crossed it without incident, charmed by the pureness of the air and the beauty of the vegetation." Evocative words indeed.

The route. The first stretch of this route follows the Salerno-Reggio Calabria Autostrada, which you will leave at the Morano-Castrovillari exit. Take the ring road, and then the SS 19 road to Morano and Castrovillari. From here you will proceed to Sìbari in the Piana del Crati, in part along secondary roads, driving down from Cassano to the Ionian Sea. Take the recently built coastal road, which runs some distance from the sea (SS 106 *r* road); at Sìbari take the turnoff for Corigliano Calabro, which is an uphill drive, then take the old SS 106 road as far as the Rossano turnoff. This little city marks the beginning of the last mountain route, running along the SS 177 road through the Sila Greca, and reaching the highland of the Sila Grande at Camigliatello Silano (1272 m). You will then continue along the western edge of the highland, finally taking the highway down to Cosenza.

Places of interest. Lagonegro, in a ring of mountains, on a slope of Monte Sirino; at a distance of 2 km in the Valle del Noce is a zoological park. Morano Calabro is scattered over a morainic hill, with lovely geometric buildings. Castrovillari, at the base of Monte Pollino (Parco Nazionale), with a 15th-c. castle in the old section, the church of S. Maria di Castello on a hill, and, on the Corso, or main boulevard, the Museo Civico. Cassano allo Ionio dominates the plain of the river Crati; visit the Museo Diocesano. Sìbari: the Museo della Sibaritide is found in the reclaimed village that bears the name of the ancient Greek colony; the archeological digs of Sybaris, Thurii, and Copia are further along, on the right of the road. S. Maria del Patire* is the solitary church of a long-vanished Basilian monastery founded in 1101-05; in the interior is a precious mosaic floor with animal relief carvings of the 12th-c. Take a 7.5-km detour through the woods after Corigliano Calabro, with a fine view. Rossano overlooks the Ionian Sea from the furthest spur of the Sila Greca: the Byzantine church of S. Marco dates from the 11th c.; in the Museo Diocesano is the exquisite and rare Codex Purpureus. Longobucco is a village overlooking the wild gorges of the Trionto; artworks and fine furnishings are on display in the churches and in the Museo Parrocchiale; wool, silk, and linen are hand-woven here. Camigliatello Silano is a resort area amid the woods of the Sila; you can take a cableway up to Monte Curcio (1760 m); fine view. Cosenza: at the confluence of the Busento and Crati rivers, amid the highlands, with the dense old quarter at the base of the Colle Pancrazio and a Norman castle; in the Gothic Duomo is the 13th-c. tomb of Isabella of Aragon, queen of France.

76 | Aspromonte

Reggio di Calabria - Gambàrie - Locri - Palmi - Reggio di Calabria (285 km)

Although in Italian "aspro," might seem to mean "harsh," the name actually comes from the Greek word *asprós*, or "white." A cluster of gently rounded dome shapes (Montalto, 1955 m) stands at the center of a starburst-shaped plateau, whose spurs run down to the three coasts along the extremity of the peninsula. Even at considerable elevations you can sense the cool air of the Tyrrhenian or Ionian sea. Oaks and holm-oaks blanket the slopes of the mountain; higher up are pine trees and beeches. Always, through the straight trunks of the trees, you can glimpse the sparking blue of the sea. The expanse of the Aspromonte area is crossed by this route from south to north in the high sections, and from north to south along the coastline. The non mountainous landscape: vineyard-bedecked hills with chestnut forests, huge hundred-year-old olive trees looking down on little harbors, the arid river beds, flowering with oleanders – all are surprising, "exotic". Here, for instance, are the impressions of the Parisian author Paul-Louis Courier who, as a soldier with a copy of

Homer in his rucksack, marched through C.
abria with Napoleon Bonaparte's expediti
of 1805, which put Joseph Bonaparte on th
throne of the Two Sicilies. From Reggio
Calabria Courier wrote: "We are triumpha
and on the move constantly, and we ha
stopped only here, where the land came to a
end, " and: "The cities are in no way notab
at least to my eyes; but the countryside is r
markable. It resembles nothing I have seen
far. Let us not even consider the oran
groves and stands of lemon trees; there are
many other trees and exotic plants, whi
spring up in great profusion under the brig
sunlight; you may find the same speci
found in France, but growing larger and lus
er here, giving the landscape an entirely c
ferent appearance. And when you see the crags, crowned everywhere wi
myrtle and aloe and palm trees in great ravines, you might think you were
the banks of the Ganges or Nile, except that there are no pyramids, nor e
phants; instead there are water buffaloes, looking quite at home amidst t
African plants; likewise the color of the inhabitants is not of our world...."

The route.

You leave Reggio di Calabria, heading south along Via Galilei, following t
coast road (SS 106 road) as far as Mèlito di Porto Salvo. You will continue nor
along the SS 183, road which climbs up the Aspromonte, and then you v
cross over the Sella Entrata Pass (1408 m), go through Gambàrie, and reach t
Brandano turnoff. Here you will take the road that runs through Delianuov
Scido, and Santa Cristina d'Aspromonte, running over the watershed at Pia
Zillastro (1057 m), and then descending to Platì and on to the Ionian coa
along the Careri River valley. You will pass through Bovalino Marina, huggi
the coast as far as Locri. Now you will begin climbing again, crossing the pen
sula from the Ionian Sea to the Tyrrhenian Sea, first of all on the SS 111 road
the route through Gerace, over the Passo di Ropolà (465 m) and the Passo
Mercante (952 m), and Taurianova; just past this last town, you will take t
road for Palmi. From Palmi you will return to Reggio di Calabria along the C
ta Viola, on the SS 18 road, and after Villa San Giovanni, via the Autostrada.

Places of interest.

Reggio di Calabria: there is a fine view of both the strait and the Sicilian coa
from the seafront promenade, along the elongated checkerboard of the city;
remarkable bronze statues of Riace, rare Greek originals from the 5th c. B.
are in the Museo Nazionale. Pentedàttilo*: this village is perched atop a sar
stone crag with five pinnacles (named after the Greeek *pentedàktylos*, or five f
gers); an 11-km detour starts 5 km past Saline Ioniche. Mèlito di Porto Sal
where Garibaldi twice disembarked, renowned for its production of bergam
and hand-made pipes. Montalto: a 13-km detour starts about 4 km past the S
la Entrata; this is the highest peak in the Aspromonte. Gambàrie: mountain h
iday resort in the midst of green forests. Cippo Garibaldi: this stele marks t
site on which the general who united Italy was wounded during a battle
tween his troops and the royalist soldiers commanded by General Pallavici
on 29 August 1862; take a 1.5-km detour from the village of De Leo. Delianuo
a resort amidst the olive groves; note the fine old artwork in the parish chur
Locri: the museum and the excavations of the Greek colony of Locri Epize
can be found at Torre di Gerace, just outside of modern Locri. Gerace is a n
dieval town high on a crag overlooking the Ionian Sea, with a grand Byzanti
Norman-Swabian cathedral, the largest sacred monument in Calabria. Pa
overlooks the Marina and the Costa Viola from its high terrace; a remarka
view all the way to Mt. Etna and the Aeolian Islands from Monte Sant'Elia (s
Palmi), which you can reach via a 1.5-km detour, from the highway to Regg
Bagnara Calabra: a fine sandy beach, and a town set between two rocky spu
Scilla: a crag overlooking the sea, a castle, a lighthouse, and the Homeric ref
ence to Scylla, the sea monster foiled by cunning Ulysses.

77 | The Coast of Sicily from Messina to Palermo

Messina - Milazzo - Cefalù - Palermo (371 km)

The Tyrrhenian shoreline is the entrance to Sicily. Here the island gives a first taste, a sampling, of many, if not all, its delights, evoking the counterpoint of literary accounts and recollections. Let's consider the plants: the ubiquitous prickly pear, or Indian fig, a harsh and bizarre piece of vegetal architecture, comes from Mexico, and has been here only since the 17th c.: in origin, the Mediterranean landscape of this ancient, timeless island is that of grains, olive trees, and vineyards. The orange tree, on the other hand, enclosed with its dark-green foliage in secluded seafront gardens, dates from the Arab occupation: "Rejoice in the oranges that you have plucked," advises a poem of those centuries, "to have them is to have happiness. / All hail the pretty cheeks of the branch; all hail the glittering stars of the tree! / You might think that the heavens had rained down pure gold, and that the earth had then moulded that gold into glowing spheres." One of the first places you will encounter is Tìndari, profoundly Greek in nature: the features of the island immediately remind the traveller of that other Mediterranean people, who sailed forth from their cramped archipelago in search of boundless horizons. A few lines by the poet Salvatore Quasimodo (Nobel laureate, 1959), were not long ago more famous than the place itself: "Tìndari, mite ti so / fra larghi colli pensile sull'acque / dell'isole dolci del dio..." which translates as "Tìndari, I know you are mild, among broad hills, above the waters of the gods' soft islands..." Cefalù adds two more pieces to the game-board: the composite culture – Romanesque-Byzantine-Arab-Norman – of the cathedral, with its hieratic mosaics, and the meticulous 15th-c. art of Antonello da Messina, painter of a portrait of a man with a distracting smile ("The interplay of resemblance is a delicate and exceedingly sensitive matter in Sicily, a form of research... Who does the unknown man in the Museo Mandralisca resemble?" – Leonardo Sciascia). Lastly, as you approach Palermo, you can explore the villas of Bagherìa, the images of an aristocratic life of the past, "Gattopardi," or Leopards, as in the novel by Tomasi di Lampedusa, and viceroys; the surrealistic sculptures of Villa Palagonia, then as much as today a must for sightseers. Goethe, a traveller who was also a contemporary of the man who ordered the creation of this villa, vents a page of spleen to it: to stroll amongst those "aberrations" gives one the "unpleasant sensation" of receiving "painful blows of madness."

The route. The coastal SS 113 road runs parallel with the Autostrada. Take the Autostrada for the first leg of the route, until you reach the Milazzo-Isole Eolie exit; then you will continue to Milazzo. On your way back, take the SS 113 road, following it all the way to Cefalù. Here you leave the coast to take a broad circuit through the Madonie, partly on secondary roads, on a route that passes

through Cefalù, Castelbuono, Portella del Bafurco, the fork of Geraci, Petralìa Soprana and Petralìa Sottana, Polìzzi Generosa, and Collesano. You will return to the coast at Campofelice di Roccella, and a bit further along get on the Autostrada (Buonfornello interchange) that leads to Palermo. You will have to leave the Autostrada again, however, first to visit Tèrmini Imerese (exit of the same name) and again to take the scenic route to Capo Zafferano and Capo Mongerbino, and to tour Solunto and Bagherìa (Casteldaccia exit; get back on at the Bagherìa exit).

Places of interest. Messina*: this town overlooking the strait has a modern appearance, the result of bombing and earthquakes; the famed astronomical clock of the Duomo, the Museo Regionale (with among other things the polyptych by Antonello da Messina and canvases by Caravaggio), and the church of the SS. Annunziata dei Catalani are of interest. Milazzo: the walls of the old section of this strategically important town enclose the Renaissance style 17th-c. Duomo and the castle; at a distance of 6 km from the lighthouse at the tip of the narrow peninsula, there is a fine view from Mt. Etna to the Isole Eolie, or Aeolian Islands. Villa Romana di San Biagio: the ruins of this Roman villa, with mosaic floors, are uphill from San Biagio, an outlying quarter of Castroreale Terme. Tìndari: you will turn off the SS road briefly at Locanda; alongside the ruins of Tyndaris, with the 2nd-3rd-c. B.C. Greek theater and a basilica, there is a sanctuary on the site of the acropolis and a fine view of the coast. Sant'Agata Militello: beautiful beaches aside, the Museo Etno-Antropologico dedicated to the farming civilization of the Nèbrodi is worthy of attention. S. Stefano di Camastra: one of the most famous centers of ceramics production in Sicily. Mistretta: you will take a 17-km detour after Santo Stefano di Camastra, on the Monti Nèbrodi; a fine altarpiece by Antonello Gagini in the Chiesa Madre; also other important churches, buildings, and artworks. Cefalù*, at the foot of a massive hill-sized boulder, has a superb Norman cathedral with renowned mosaics, and fine works in the Museo Mandralisca; at a distance of 15 km, near the Santuario di Gibilmanna. Castelbuono is a small resort town in the Madonie; the Matrice Vecchia is a 14th-c. church; in the 14th-c. castle, are the Museo Civico and the Cappella di S. Anna with stuccoes by Giuseppe and Giacomo Serpotta. Petralìa Sottana is a little resort town in the Madonie; here and uphill from here, in Petralìa Soprana, there are noteworthy artworks and architectural details in the churches; fine view of the Madonie, Monti Nèbrodi, and Mt. Etna from the Baroque church of S. Maria di Loreto. Polìzzi Generosa is yet another little resort town in the Madonie: a Flemish triptych in the style of Memling is in the church known as the Chiesa Madre. Collesano lies at the base of the Madonie, with the 16th-c. Matrice church and fine artwork. Ruins of Imera, a Greek colony of Zancle (Messina) with an antiquarium; you will take a detour, continuing along the SS 113 road beyond the interchange of the Autostrada at Buonfornello. Tèrmini Imerese has Roman ruins in the Villa Palmeri, the public gardens; at a distance of 10 km is Càccamo (a name taken either from the Greek *kakkabe*, "partridge," or from the Punic *cacca*, "horse's head," or from the Latin *cacabus*, "boiler"), with a large bastioned castle. Solunto: the Hellenistic-Roman ruins of this city founded by the Phoenicians stand on a spur of Monte Catalfano, within sight of the sea. Bagherìa among the aristocratic villas of this seaside town surrounded by citrus groves and vineyards, of particular architectural note are the Villa Valguarnera and the Villa Palagonia, with its odd statuettes.

78 | Val di Mazara

Palermo - Álcamo - Trapani - Castelvetrano (194 km)

The Arabs first set foot in Sicily in A.D. 827 at Mazara del Vallo, 205 years after the Hegira, and 116 years after Muslim troops invaded Europe across the Strait of Gibraltar; the conquest of the Byzantine-ruled island took some years (the Norman warrior, Count Roger I of Altavilla, began his attack

years after the Saracens first landed, and finally expelled them from Sicily after thirty years of fighting, in 1091). Under Arab rule, the great island was divided into the three "valli" of Mazara, Demone, and Noto. The Val di Mazara comprised the western end of the island; its boundary was a line drawn from a point on the north coast between Tèrmini Imerese and Cefalù and Licata, on the south coast. This route explores the westernmost section of the "vallo." There are three locations in the early part of this route that provide splendid instances of Sicily's originality: Monreale, Segesta, and Érice. In the first of the three, Arab-style stalactites hang down from the cross-vault of the Duomo amidst the glittering gold of the Byzantine style mosaics executed by Sicilian and Venetian master craftsmen. In Segesta the Doric enclosure of the temple of the Elimi features odd, unfluted columns, without any sign of the traditional cella, while in upper Érice you are surrounded by a medieval atmosphere. This route passes through areas that figured in the saga of Garibaldi's unification of Italy: Marsala, where his army of Red Shirts landed; Calatafimi, where they fought their first battle; Álcamo and Partinico, through which the tiny liberation army passed on its way to Palermo to face the 20,000 soldiers under Generale Lanza ("Álcamo: the evocative palm fronds spread over the walls of the gardens here; every house has the appearance of a monastery; a pair of dark eyes flashes down from a high balcony; you stop, you look up, and the lovely apparition has vanished...," writes Giuseppe Cesare Abba, a soldier under Garibaldi). At Mazara, in the narrow lanes of the old town, there is still a flavor of the Arab city; you can hear Arabic spoken by the Algerian and Moroccan sailors who work on the huge fishing fleet.

The route.

In order to drive up to Monreale you will leave Palermo along Corso Calatafimi. From Monreale you continue toward Partinico (SS 186 road), and from there you head down to the Golfo di Castellammare, following the coast until you reach the turnoff for the road up to Álcamo. From here, the SS 113 road will take you to Calatafimi. You retrace your route to tour Segesta, and then you take the entrance to the Autostrada toward Trapani. From the Trapani exit you will climb up to Érice, continuing on into the town of Trapani, and following the coast road to Marsala. Via the SS 115 road you will reach Mazara del Vallo. Lastly, take the Autostrada to Castelvetrano.

Places of interest.

Monreale*: the Norman Duomo, covered with spectacular mosaics, and with a 12th-c. cloister with slender twin columns, is one of the finest medieval monuments in all Italy; at a distance of 10 km is San Martino alle Scale (see Monreale), a resort set amidst pine groves, near a Benedictine abbey. Álcamo: this town features classic 14th-c. architecture and layout, with remarkable artworks in the old churches (S. Oliva by Antonello Gagini in the 18th-c. church of S. Oliva). Calatafimi, set on a ridge amongst hills, at the foot of the ruins of a castle; an Ossuary commemorating a battle in Garibaldi's Sicilian campaign (15 May 1860) stands on a rise at a distance of 4.5 km Segesta*: take a short detour off the road between Calatafimi and the highway entrance; secluded on a high crag is the Doric temple of the ancient city of the Elimi; higher up is a Hellenistic theater overlooking the distant sea; fine view. Érice* stands, medieval and silent in the triangle of walls that enclose it, atop a crag: of particular note in the charming setting are the 14th-c. church of Matrice and its campanile; also note the Annunciation by Antonello Gagini in the Museo Comunale, views of the sea and of the Isole Égadi from the outer roads; detour of 8 km, on the way to Trapani. Trapani, extending over a promontory, boasts the 18th-c. Santuario dell'Annunziata and the impressive Museo Regionale Pepoli (among the items on display are a painting by Titian and a beautiful statue of S. Giacomo by Gagini). Mozia*: you can take a boat out to the excavations and

the museum of the ancient Phoenician city, on the island of San Pantaleo; d
tour for boat slip after San Leonardo. Marsala: the main square has Baroqu
monuments (the Museo degli Arazzi Fiamminghi adjacent to the cathedral ha
Flemish tapestries bestowed by Philip II of Spain); to the west of town, nea
the sea, are the Roman *insula* and the Punic *liburna* (in the Museo di Cap
Lilibeo). Mazara del Vallo: this is an exceedingly active fishing port; in the i
tricate, old Arab town, note the cathedral (with Transfiguration by Antonin
Gagini), the little Norman church of S. Nicolò Regale, and the Museo Civic
Rocche di Cusa: take a 13-km detour after Mazara del Vallo, passing throug
Campobello di Mazara; there are tufa quarries, and through the vegetatio
you can see the cuts where the stones of the temples of Selinunte were e
tracted. Castelvetrano, on a terrace over the coast, with a John the Baptist b
Antonello Gagini in the church of S. Giovanni, along with other artworks an
examples of sacred architecture; at a distance of 3.5 km to the west, is th
12th-c. Norman church of SS. Trinità di Delia.

79 | The Coast of Sicily from Castelvetrano to Gela

Castelvetrano - Sciacca - Agrigento - Gela (208 km)

In 1875 Ernest Renan, professor of Hebrew a
the Collège de France, was invited to Palerm
to attend a scientific conference; among thos
present were Prince Umberto di Savoia, o
Humbert of Savoy, the heir apparent to th
Italian crown, and Ruggero Bonghi, Minister o
Public Education. Bonghi asked Renan to joi
the national commission on antiquities in
tour of "all the major ruins of Sicily," a tour t
decide where archeological excavation
should be concentrated. Renan accepted, an
the scholars and scientists boarded th
"Archimede," a steamer that carried the
from Trapani to Syracuse. Along the way, R
nan and the others landed at Selinunte and travelled inland to Agrigento, th
two most important stops on this route along the southern coast of Sicil
from Castelvetrano to Gela. We can only give you an impression of the Sicil
that greeted their eyes in that distant year. At Selinunte "a fierce harsh su
(even though it was September), a land dried out by five months of hea
pierced only by a delightful little double white lily." Of the temples and the
Doric capitals, he ventured: "In no other place can you so clearly see, step b
step, the progress of these divine curves that so nearly reach perfection
Here is the miracle that only the Greeks managed to achieve: to find an ide
and, having found it, stick to it." Concerning a trip inland toward the sulfu
mining area, he wrote: "We saw Africa stretching before us on that day, in
range of hills burnt by sulfureous fumes, without trees, without greenery, with
out water." At Porto Empedocle Renan landed "under a portico decorate
with statues of King Victor Emmanuel and Empedocles"; the name of Emp
docles "is scattered through the public places as widely as is that of Gariba
di". The "rude journée" of tours also included a "cordial banquet offered b
the people of Agrigento in the very midst of the ruins."

The route. Between Castelvetrano and Sciacca there are two roads, the SS 115 and 18
bis: you will be taking the second one, built more recently, faster and furthe
inland (on your way back from the detour to Selinunte you will find the inte
change for SS 188 bis road on your right, just past the junction with the SS 11
road). From Sciacca you will continue along a scenic secondary road to Calt
bellotta, inland, then returning south to the sea, until you hit the SS 115 roa
which, with the occasional detour, you will follow along the coast, though no
actually near the water, through Porto Empedocle and Licata as far as Gela.

Places of interest. Castelvetrano: amidst olive groves and vineyards, this little town on a natural terrace boasts fine artworks set in its venerable old churches, and a noteworthy Museo Civico; at a distance of 3.5 km, is the Norman church of SS. Trinità di Delia. Selinunte*: you will take a 14-km detour just after Castelvetrano; the columns of the Doric temples and the ruins of the acropolis, overlooking the sea stand in an alluring coastal setting; the Greek colony of Megara Hyblaea was the westernmost of Sicily. Menfi is a village founded in the 17th c., with an orderly checkerboard layout; its blind alleys and courtyards, however, still breathe the air of the long-ago Arab domination. Sciacca: the Steripinto, a remarkable 15th-c. construction, was the "testa della corsa," or finish line, for the races run with riderless Berber horses; high atop Monte San Calogero (388 m), at a distance of 7 km, note the pine grove, the sanctuary, and the "stufe vaporose" (caves with steam vapors), and the fine view. Caltabellotta, with its intense island atmosphere, extends over three rocky hills: venerable old churches with artworks, excellent view from the ruins of the castle. Eraclea Minoa: the ruins of this Greek city founded by the inhabitants of Selinunte and by Spartan settlers stands on the bare upland of Capobianco, overlooking the sea. You will take a 4-km detour just after the bridge over the Plàtani River. Agrigento**: the city extends over a spur dominating the Valle dei Templi, or Valley of the Temples, where an archeological walking tour leads you in succession to the Hellenistic-Roman quarter, to the church of S. Nicola, the Museo Archeologico Regionale, and lastly, the renowned Doric temples of Olympian Zeus (Giove Olimpico), Heracles (Ercole), Concord (Concordia), and Hera (Giunone), exquisite relics of the Greek colony, scattered over a beautiful landscape. Licata: archeological finds from the entire territory in the Museo Civico, fine view from the Castel S. Angelo. Gela*: the city is modern in appearance although its origins can be traced back to a flourishing Greek colony founded in 689 B.C.; the relics of classical times are concentrated in the Museo Regionale Archeologico and the fortifications of Capo Soprano.

80 | From Siracusa to Caltanissetta

Siracusa - Palazzolo Acrèide - Caltagirone - Enna - Caltanissetta (203 km)

Myths chase each other through the landscape of Trinacria, the ancient name for Sicily. The site where Pluto abducted the young Persephone, daughter of Zeus and Demetra, lies in the heart of the island. Vincent Vivant, the Baron Denon, secretary of the French embassy to Naples, travelling through Sicily in 1788, expected in vain to see, in the area around Castro Giovanni (now Enna), "the plentiful waters form placid lakes, whose cool shores were always enameled with the delicate blooms of the plains," the "delightful" countryside where, for six months of every year, Artemis and Athena were said to have come to live. This route, which begins in Siracusa, leads to Enna, continues on to Caltanissetta, and then goes up over the ridges of the Monti Iblei, limestone plateaus broken only by the "cave," or gorges, narrow, deep, with sheer rock walls, dug out by rushing streams and mountain rivers. The road then passes over the terraces and rounded peaks of the Monti Erei, the watershed between the Mar d'Africa, to the south, and the Ionian Sea, to the east. In various spots, you may explore specific sites or themes: at Pantàlica, the cliffside necropolis; the ruins of Akrai near Palazzolo Acreide; the 18th-c. architectural inventions at Caltagirone. Lastly, at the Casale di Piazza Armerina, you will see other myths depicted in the mosaic floors of the Roman villa: the struggle between Eros and Pan, Hercules, Ulysses and the Cyclops, Daphne, Endymion awaiting Selene, Arion riding a dolphin and playing a lyre.

The route. To reach the SS 124 road that leads to Palazzolo Acreide via Floridia, you will leave Siracusa along Viale Paolo Orsi. Continue along this same road through Buccheri, Vizzini, Grammichele, Caltagirone, and San Michele di Ganzarìa. A little further along, at the Gigliotto crossroads, you will join the road from Gela

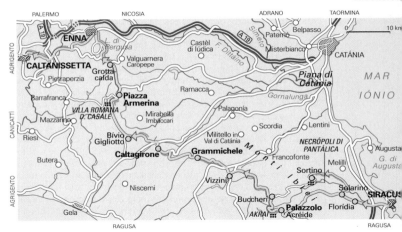

(SS 117 bis road), which will take you to Piazza Armerina and then on to Enna
About 12 km past Piazza Armerina you will take a left through the Portel
Grottacalda and then right at the Ramata crossroads, reaching Enna past th
Lago di Pergusa. From Enna you will take the Autostrada to Caltanissetta.

Places of interest. Siracusa**: in a hard-bitten defense of the town against a besieging forc
Archimedes used an ingenious array of mirrors to focus the bright sunlight c
the Roman ships commanded by Marcellus, setting fire to the fleet, suppo
edly in the port between the island of Ortigia and the immense Greek coloni
city on the coast. The ancient sites range from the Fonte Aretusa to the Cast
lo Euriaio, alongside the well known monuments, the Galleria Regionale
Palazzo Bellomo (with the renowned Annunciation by Antonello da Messina
the archeological finds in the Museo Regionale, and the sun-bathed landscap
– all offer material for patient, unforgettable explorations. Necropolis of Pa
tàlica*: you will take a 26-km detour, turning off at a "cantoniera," or roa
man's house, about 14 km past Solarino, passing through Ferla; there are 5,0
tombs from the long-vanished, indigenous town of Hybla, carved into the roc
walls rising sheer over the Anapo and Calcinara rivers. Palazzolo Acreide
the archeological area of the Greek town of Akrai, founded by Siracusa in 6
B.C., lies on the Acremonte, a hill alongside the little 18th-c. town located
the Monti Iblei. Grammichele: the orderly late-17th-c. layout of this town e
tends from the perfect hexagon of the central square. Caltagirone: the "quee
of the mountains," as the town is known, has an 18th-c. appearance and e
tends over three hilltops; the Palazzetto della Corte Capitaniale was built
Antonuzzo and Gian Domenico Gagini, while the Gesù and S. Giacomo a
Baroque churches. You can reach S. Maria del Monte by climbing up a stai
way decorated with majolica tiles. There is a centuries-old local crafts trac
tion of ceramics: the Museo Regionale della Ceramica documents the histor
of Sicilian ceramics in general, dating back to prehistoric times. Piazza Arm
rina*: picturesque town located in the heart of Sicily; in the Baroque Duom
is an exquisite 15th-c. panel Crucifix. Villa Romana del Casale**: at a distanc
of 5.5 km from Piazza Armerina; the ruins give some indication of the manifo
and vast complexity and luxury of a late-imperial country residence; the m
saic floors are astonishing, both in their expanse and in the variety of depi
tions. The Lago di Pergusa summons up images of the myth of Persephone
Prosperina abducted by Hades; today a motor racing track encircles the lak
Enna*: the "belvedere," or vantage point, of Sicily, this town overlooks th
Valle del Dittàimo from a lofty natural terrace; note the Museo Alessi and th
Byzantine-Norman-Swabian Castello di Lombardia. Caltanissetta, a mode
city set amidst the hills of Sicily's mining region; the Museo Civico, with arch
ological finds, and the Museo Minerario, or mining museum.

Italy A to Z

Aeolian Islands / Isole Eolie

Pop. 12,909; Sicilia (Sicily), province of Messina. This **archipelago** comprises 7 islands: the three largest islands – *Vulcano*, *Lìpari*, and *Salina* – are quite close, while *Filicudi* and *Alicudi* lie to the west and *Panarea* and *Stròmboli* to the north.

Lìpari, with its steep coastline, is surrounded by stacks (columns of rock isolated from shore by wave action) and shoals; it is the largest island in the archipelago; the steep island culminates in Monte Chirica (602 m) and Monte Sant'Angelo (594 m). The lovely little town of **Lìpari** lies at the center of the archipelago, with the port and beach of *Marina Lunga* to the north, and the hydrofoil landing and *Marina Corta* to the south.

The 16th-c. Spanish bastions of the **Castello*** include medieval towers and curtain walls (13th c.), as well as an older Greek tower (4th-3rd c. B.C.); these walls stand on the site of the old acropolis. Until the 18th c., the entire town lay within their perimeter.

In the *archeological zone* the digs have uncovered layers of buildings that range from the oval huts of the early (17th-15th c. B.C.) to the mid- (14th-13th c. B.C.) Bronze Age, ruins of early-Iron Age huts (11th-9th c. B.C.), up to ruins of Hellenistic constructions. The **Museo Archeologico Eoliano*** (*open 9-1:30 and 3-6*) is an archeological museum which offers a remarkable picture of the unbroken human presence on these islands through the Neolithic.

Surrounding areas. From **Canneto**, a little village on an inlet on the eastern coast, 3.5 km to the north, you can reach the enormous obsidian lava flow (30 min.) of the **Forgia Vecchia***, the *pumice quarries** and another obsidian lava flow of the *Rocche Rosse**.

Vulcano. The two picturesque inlets of *Porto di Ponente* and *Porto di Levante* open out onto the short isthmus linking Vulcano and Vulcanello. At Porto di Levante, natural hot sulphur springs boil into the clear waters of the sea.

There is a fine view* from the **Vulcanello** (123 m), the little volcanic cone that comprises the northernmost tip of the island; we know it was formed in 183 B.C.

South of the isthmus you climb up (45 min.) to the **main crater** of Vulcano (391 m), an enormous funnel 500 m wide; there is a spectacular *view*** of the archipelago, the Sicilian coast, and Mt. Etna.

Salina. This is the second-largest island, as well as the tallest (Fossa delle Felci, 962 m).

Santa Marina Salina is at an elevation of 25 m, midway along the eastern coast, on the beach; at a distance of 2.5 km., at *Lingua* is the saline lagoon that gave the island its modern name; in ancient times it was called Didyme (twin) for its two peaks.

Panarea. A *prehistoric village** (*custodian*), wi oval huts (18th-13th c. B.C.) on the promontory Milazzo is the most interesting point on the islar which has three small villages – *Ditella*, *San Pietr* and *Draùto* – among the olive groves on the ea ern slopes of the Timpone del Corvo (420 m).

Stròmboli. The white Mediterranean houses, amidst green palm trees, olive groves, and citrus chards, of the three quarters of Piscità, Ficogran San Vincenzo, which make up the town of **Stròn boli** (43 m), lie on the island's NE coast; Stròmb is a single, huge volcanic cone, harsh and allurii secluded in its stretch of sea.

The **crater of the volcano*** (*3 hours; you sho be accompanied by an authorized guide*) opens at an elevation of 700 m, with a flared basin tl spews forth the products of eruptions on the ste slope of the Sciara del Fuoco. The best vantage pc is from the observation platform of *Punta Labron* You can get a fine view of the *Sciara del Fuoc* from below (*by boat, 20 min.*): lava, blocks of sto and lapilli drop down to the sea from the crater c ing eruptions, whistling as they plunge and spout up columns of steam and water as they hit.

Filicudi. The steep cone of the mountain of I cudi (774 m) is covered with bare rocks; in anci times, it was called Phenicusa, for the many fe (*Filicineae*) that grew here.

At *Capo Graziano* is a Bronze Age *prehistoric vill* (*custodian*), with oval huts (18th-13th c. B.C.).

Alicudi. In ancient times this island was called cusa for the heather (*erica*) that covered it. houses are scattered between the beach and slopes of the Timpone della Montagnola (675 Lobsters are trapped and sold here.

Agrigento**

Elev. 230 m, pop. 55,521; Sicilia (Sicily), pro cial capital. The main reason for going to A gento is certainly to see the amazing array ancient Greek ruins in the old city; nowh else on earth, not even in Greece, will you so many sacred buildings in one place. Greek colony here was founded around B.C. by settlers from nearby Gela and by er settlers from Rhodes. In the century followed, the philosopher Empedocles li and worked here.

Historical note. Modern-day Agrigento is c posed of a city with a strong medieval flavor; it cupies the western hill which, until a century was separated by a depression from the Rupe nea to the east. The depression was filled in now Piazza Vittorio Emanuele and Piazza Aldo ro stand on the site; the 19th-c. town grew here the plain that runs down from the Rupe Ater where the acropolis probably stood, toward the

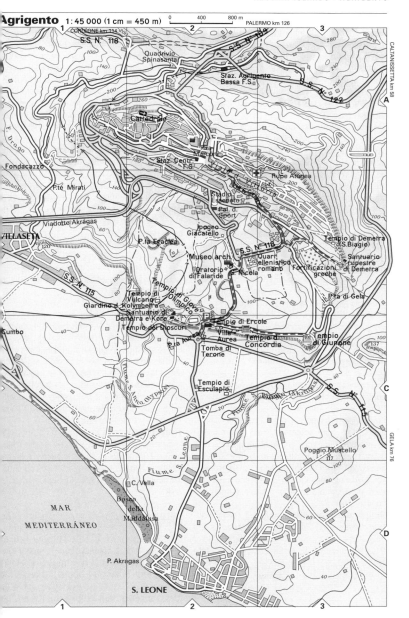

Agrigento 1 : 45 000 (1 cm = 450 m)

0   400   800 m

CONFEONE km 114
S.S. N° 118
PALERMO km 126

Quadrivio
Spinasanta

Staz. Agrigento
Bassa F.S.

CALTANISSETTA km 58

Cattedrale

Marconi
Staz. Centr.
F.S.

Fondacazzo

Rupe Atenea

P.te Mirati

Viadotto Akragas

Stadio
Esseneto
Pal. d.
Sport

VILLASETA

Ipogeo
Giacatello

P.ta Eraclea

Museo arch.

Tempio di Demetra
(S.Biagio)

Quart.
ellenistico
romano

Santuario
rupestre
di Demetra

S.S. N° 118

Oratorio
di Falaride

Fortificazioni
greche

S. Nicola

Tempio di
Vulcano

Tempio di Giove
Olimpico

P.ta di Gela

Giardino d. Kolymbetra
Santuario di
Demetra e Kore

Sumbo

Tempio dei Dioscuri

Tempio di Ercole

Villa
Aurea

Tempio di
Giunone

Tempio di
Concordia

Tomba di
Terone

Tempio di
Esculapio

MAR.
MEDITERRÁNEO

C. Vella

Bosco
della
Maddalusa

Poggio Muscello

P. Akragas

S. LEONE

GELA km 76

---

he ancient city once stood; it is now suffering from
ncroaching and uncontrolled development.

Places of interest. Via Atenea. The crowded and
ovely medieval section of Agrigento is crossed by
he winding Via Atenea, the main thoroughfare, go-
ng from Piazza Aldo Moro, at the boundary of the
ew addition (near *Piazza Marconi, A2*), to Piazza
Pirandello.

. Spirito* is a late-13th-c. abbey, heavily rebuilt;

the stuccoes in the interior (*custodian at n. 2, opposite*) are attributed to Serpotta; in the former
monastery, note the cloister and various remarkable
pieces of medieval architecture.

Cattedrale* (*A2*). The cathedral has a complex
history, ranging from the 11th to the 17th c., and has
interesting architectural details and artworks. Also
note the acoustic phenomenon whereby, from the
cornice of the apse, it is possible to hear a person
whisper at the entrance of the church.

Città Antica. You can reach the ancient city from *Piazza Marconi* (A2), following the first stretch of the SS 118 road (*Via Crispi*) and then driving down into the *Valle dei Templi* (Valley of the Temples), up to the large square (parking area) facing the enclosure of the Temple of Olympian Zeus. You should then continue east, passing the three main temples and returning to road 118: this route is the **archeological tour****.

Quartiere Ellenistico-Romano* (B2-3; open 9-one hour before sunset). More than any other, this site offers a sense of just what the ancient city looked like at its Hellenistic foundation (4th-2nd c. B.C.) and on until the fall of the Roman Empire; the area was crossed by 4 parallel roads (*cardines*) which connected with the *decumanus* (now the SS 118 road at this juncture); the road is lined with homes and shops.

S. Nicola.* The 13th-c. Gothic-Romanesque church is of Cistercian construction; the site it occupies has hosted a Greek, a Hellenistic, and a Roman sanctuary, monasteries, and a Norman church. Note the famous **sarcophagus*** engraved with the myth of Phaedra (2nd-3rd c. A.D.). Fine view* of the temples from the square in front of the church.

Oratorio di Falaride* (B2). This little temple/oratory represents the Hellenistic phase of the sanctuary, on the site now occupied by the church of S. Nicola.

Museo Archeologico Regionale** (B2; open Sun.-Tue., 9-1:30; Wed.-Sat., 9-1 and 2-5:30). This fine archeological museum is located behind the church. It has collections from the city of Agrigento itself, as well as from the various ancient sites in the provinces of Agrigento and Caltanissetta. Of particular note is the **telamon*** (male figure used as a column) from the Temple of Olympian Zeus, *artifacts** from the excavations of the Roman-Hellenistic quarter, a marble *Ephebe** (a beardless youth), dating from about 470 B.C., and a red-figured krater* with a scene of Amazon warriors in combat (5th c. B.C.).

Tempio di Giove Olimpico* (B-C2; open 9-one hour before sunset). This Temple of Olympian Zeus, built after a victory over Carthage at Himera (480 B.C.), was destroyed by earthquakes; you can still

Agrigento: Tempio della Concordia

see the vast perimeter, heaped with rubble. It (not have the normal circuit of columns; rather, outer wall was punctuated by half-columns al nating with telamons (male figures used columns), making it a pseudo-peripteral temple The area to the west of the temple (B-C2) is de with ruins of sacred buildings: the numerous alta the bases of the temples, sacred enclosures, a "favissae" (dedicatory ditches), all dating from 6th to the 5th c. B.C., were part of a *sanctuary the chthonic deities** (or Temple of Demetra a Kore, or Persephone). At the center of this a stand four columns with a fragmentary trabeati from the *Temple of Castor and Pollux** (Tempio Dioscuri, 5th c. B.C.; the trabeation dates from l lenistic-Roman times). This notable group columns is one of the best-known sights in A gento; the other temples are arrayed further along the rocky ridge.

Tempio di Ercole* (C2). Eight columns stand in a heap of rubble belong to the Temple of He cles, a six-column peripteral sanctuary from late-6th c. B.C., perhaps the earliest Doric build in Agrigento.

Tempio della Concordia** (C2-3). The 6th-c. transformation of the ancient Temple of Concord to a Christian church probably helped to ensure survival. It may have been dedicated to Castor a Pollux, sons of Zeus and Leda, and brothers of len. The six-column peripteros, built around the m dle of the 5th c. B.C., is intact in its majestic portions. This is considered to be one of the m perfect works of Greek architecture (the arcac cut into the side walls of the cella date from adaptation of the temple as church).

Tempio di Giunone Lacinia** (C3). Now a tinctive feature of this lovely landscape, the Tem of Hera (C3) stands alone at the edge of the ro terrace; it had a six-column peripteros, much l the Temple of Concord, from the same period.

Alberobello

Elev. 428 m, pop. 10,862; Puglia (Apuli province of Bari. A forest of grey conical ro top the massive round buildings of this tov called "trulli." There are about a thousand these strange round homes in Alberobello; town's architecture is as unique as it is ancie

Places of interest. The **monumental area*** cc prises the *quarters of Monti* and *Aia Piccola*, w the "trulli" aligned along steep and winding lar Looking in through the front doors, you can see interior structure of these remarkable homes (y *should have little difficulty in visiting one*): a cen chamber communicates through archways with kitchen and the other rooms. The most compl and the tallest "trullo" is the *Trullo sovrano*, 2 sto tall. In 1996, Alberobello was inscribed in UNESC World Heritage List.

berobello: "trulli"

ghero

p. 40,574; Sardegna (Sardinia), province of ssari. Charles V landed here in October 1541 hile sailing with 40 galleys to take Algiers; re- ewing the crowd from the balcony of Palaz- ▸ De Ferrera – it is said – he declared, "Es- de todos caballeros," or let all of you be ights. The city (whose name means "place much algae") was at that time securely for- ied; it stands on the promontory that seals f the enchanting bay, extending from the is- nd's western coast. In the 14th c., the House Aragon settled a colony of Catalonians here ne language is still spoken, and the archi- cture shows Catalonian influence), after de- orting the entire native population on ac- usation of treason. The city has been grow- g throughout this century, only in part be- use of its popularity as a resort.

aces of interest. **Mura Catalane**. The Catalon- n walls still enclose the entire historic city cen- ; they are dotted with towers and offer pleasant aces to stroll. Overlooking the harbor is the *Forte* lla Maddalena, a fortress rebuilt in the 18th c. Be- nd it is the *Porta a Mare*, a gate leading into the town. At the NW point of the walls is a tower lled the *Torre de la Polveriera*, at the SW point is e octagonal and slightly Gothic *Torre di S. Giaco-* , and at the SE point is the **Torre di Sulis**, which tes from 1364. Overlooking the new town are the th-c. *Torre de Sant Joan* and the 14th-c. *Torre del* rtal.

ttedrale.* The Catalonian late-Gothic style of e original 16th-c. Cathedral of *S. Maria* can be seen the apse, campanile, aisles, cupola, and in some apels.

Francesco. First built in the 14th c. and rebuilt in e 16th c., this church has a number of impressive tues of Christ.

Amalfi*

Elev. 6 m, pop. 5561, Campania, province of Salerno. As a Maritime Republic the city wrote a major chapter in the history of Europe, to- gether with Pisa, Genoa, and Venice. Today it stretches along the splendid coastline with its blindingly white houses and intricate narrow lanes, some of them roofed over.

Places of interest. By the seaside is the **Piazza Flavio Gioia** (named after the man said to have invented the compass). Nearby, with two aisles crowned with Gothic arches, are the remains of the *Arsenale della Repubblica*.

The **Duomo***, high atop a stairway, dates from the 9th c. and was rebuilt in Sicilian Arab-Norman style in 1203, and again in the 18th c. The polychrome fa- cade was redone in the 19th c.; the handsome cam- panile*, with little towers and interwoven Arab-style arches high atop it, dates from 1180-1276; beneath the Gothic atrium, the central portal features an ex- quisite bronze door*, cast in Constantinople (1065). In the presbytery are two candelabra and two mo- saic ambos (12th-13th c.); in the crypt, with the sup- posed relics of the apostle Andrew, are statues by M. Naccherino and P. Bernini; alongside the left aisle is the Cappella del Crocifisso (Chapel of the Cru- cifix), with fragments of the 13th-c. church.

You can enter the renowned **Chiostro del Pa- radiso*** (*open 9-7*) from the far left end of the atri- um of the Duomo: it served as the burial place of the noble and illustrious citizens of Amalfi.

Anagni

Elev. 424 m, pop. 20,144; Lazio (Latium), province of Frosinone. Tradition has it that the god Saturn founded this ancient city perched

Amalfi: Duomo

atop a ridge overlooking the valley of the river Sacco. Later, it became a sort of papal capital. Here a supporter of the French king Philip IV slapped Boniface VIII, who later died of mortification, and another pope, Alexander III, excommunicated the Holy Roman Emperor, Frederick I Barbarossa.

Places of interest. Casa Barnekow. Best known of the many medieval-style houses of Anagni, it actually dates from the 16th c. The name was given by a Swedish nobleman who bought it in the mid-19th c., decorating it with frescoes and plaques. Facing it is the Romanesque campanile of the church of **S. Andrea**; inside, note the fine 14th-c. triptych in the second chapel to the right.

Piazza Cavour. Created around 1560, this handsome square overlooks, like a broad balcony, the city center and the distant valley of the Sacco and has the elegant church of *S. Maria di Loreto* (1750).

Palazzo Comunale. This 12th-c. building has a Lombard-Romanesque appearance. On the ground floor, a majestic vault leads to the square behind, where markets were held and justice was once meted out.

Cattedrale.** One of the most important and influential pieces of Romanesque architecture in Latium, built in 1072-1104 and renovated in the 13th c. with Gothic accents, this cathedral stands alone high above the town. The magnificent and lively left side features a loggia topped by a statue of Boniface VIII Caetani, and the outer walls of the Cappella Caetani, or Caetani Chapel. Note also the baptistery and apses, and the 12th-c. campanile.

Inside is a Cosmatesque floor (1231). In the *presbytery*, a handsome ciborium* above the altar, a tortile paschal candelabrum*, and the bishop's seat at the end of the apse, are all by P.Vassalletto (1267). In the left nave is the Gothic *Cappella Caetani*. The **crypt**** is decorated with fine frescoes* executed between 1231 and 1255 by Benedictine painters. The *Cappella di S. Tommaso Becket* (Chapel of St. Thomas Becket) was perhaps originally a Roman Mithreum.

Adjacent to the Cathedral is the **Museo del Tesoro** (*open summer, 9-3 and 4-7; winter 9-1 and 3-6*), with a rich treasury, partly comprising objects donated by Pope Boniface VIII (13th c.); one section features ancient and medieval marble carvings.

Palazzo di Bonifacio VIII. Built by Pope Gregory IX, it passed into the hands of the Caetani family in 1295. Note the loggia and mullioned windows on the front, and the high arched buttresses in the back. **Inside** (*open summer, 9-1 and 3-7; winter, 9-1 and 3-6*) are numerous halls, some frescoed; in one of these, the famed "Slap of Anagni" took place, when Sciarra Colonna, a supporter of the French king Philip the Fair, struck the pope, Boniface VIII, so roundly despised by Dante. The palazzo also houses a *Museum* with archeological exhibits and documentation on the history and monuments of Anagni. Not far away is **Palazzo Traietto**, once the home of Boniface VIII.

Ancona

Pop. 99,453; Marche, regional and provinc capital. This active and courageous town (ba ly damaged by bombs in WWII and an ear quake in the 1970s) extends like an a phitheater at the foot of Monte Cònero b yond which, as Goethe wrote, you can see t "loveliest sunsets on earth." It is divided i two parts: the old section, beneath the Bas ca di S. Ciriaco, a landmark for sailors; and t modern area, spilling over to the easte shore. Its importance as a maritime cen dates back to Trajan's time, when the emp or sent his architect Apollodorus of Dam cus to build a mole and a new port after Co Guasco had eroded.

Historical note. Ancona is now a city with t separate parts: the old historical and monumer center, with its medieval lanes, ramps, and sta perched on the Colle Guasco, atop which the Gre acropolis once stood (now the Romanesque cat dral of S. Ciriaco); and the modern grid of the a built since the late-18th c. The chief relics of the man city are the amphitheater and Trajan's ar overlooking the port. After the Western Roman E pire fell, Ancona became part of Byzantium's m itime Pentapolis; Charlemagne made a gift of A cona to the Church. Rebuilt after the ravages of Saracens in A.D. 848, the city traded with Dalma and the Levant from the 10th to the 15th c., c stantly warring with Venetian fleets and impe German armies, and with the local rival towns Òsimo, Macerata and Jesi, and the Malatesta fan Wealth from trading allowed Ancona to build new sets of walls in the 13th and 14th c., comp ing the church of S. Ciriaco and building the chu es of S. Maria della Piazza, S. Francesco delle Sca and S. Agostino, as well as the Palazzo del Gover Palazzo degli Anziani, and Palazzo del Senato. A cona might have become a great maritime pov had it not stood in the shadows of Venice and papacy. In 1532 it fell to Pope Clement VII, who b the Cittadella on the Colle Astagno. Ancona gr over the next few centuries of papal rule, along coast, to Porta Pia and the Mole Vanvitelliana. O after Italian unification in 1861 did the town gr west and east, to the train station and Piazza Cave

Places of interest. Mole Vanvitelliana. Pen onal in shape, this fortress-hospital was begun 1733 by L. Vanvitelli. Nearby, in Via XXIX Settemb is the late-Baroque *Porta Pia* (1789).

S. Agostino. This former church still has a f Venetian Gothic portal*, begun by G. da Seben (1460-75), and completed by M. di Giovanni (149 **Piazza della Repubblica**. In the heart of Anco it opens out over the port between the 16t church of the *Santissimo. Sacramento* and the *Tec delle Muse* (1826). Corso Garibaldi, Ancona's m street, leads to the vast Piazza Cavour.

ale della Vittoria. From Largo XXIV Maggio, this oulevard crosses Ancona, almost reaching the sea, d ending at the **Monumento ai Caduti**, commemorating the WWI dead, by G. Cirilli (1927-33), here steps descend to the sea.

a della Loggia. At the beginning of this road are e *Palazzo Giovannelli Benincasa* (ca. 1450) and e **Loggia dei Mercanti***, with a lovely Venetian othic facade, by G. da Sebenico (1451-59), restored P. Tibaldi; the huge interior hall is also by Tibal-as are most of the statues. Further along is the th-c. Romanesque church of **S. Maria della Piaz-a***; note the facade*, with several orders of blind cades (1210-25), and a large portal. Under the urch (*visible through slabs of glass in the floor*) e remains of the 5th- and 6th-c. churches that ce stood here, with mosaic fragments.

azza del Plebiscito. This elongated square, with 18th-c. statue of Pope Clement XII, is flanked on e side by a 16th-c. tower, the handsome **Palazzo l Governo**, now the Prefettura, or Prefecture, de-gned by F. di Giorgio Martini (1484); a late-15th-c. naissance arch leads into its fine courtyard. At e end of the square, a spectacular stairway leads to the church of **S. Domenico** (1761-83), built the site of a 13th-c. church and damaged by rthquake in 1930, by bombs in 1944, and again by rthquake in 1972. Inside are statues and medal-ns by G. Varlè, and fine paintings by artists such Titian (1558) and Guercino (1656). Nearby, at the outh of Via Matteotti, the *Arco Ferretti*, a city gate ilt in 1221 on the old 9th-c. walls. In Corso Maz-ni is the **Fontana del Calamo**, a fountain de-gned by P. Tibaldi (1560), and in Piazza Roma, the *ntana dei Cavalli* (1758), designed by L. Daretti, th sculpture by G. Varlè.

nacoteca Civica Francesco Podesti and Gal-ria d'Arte Moderna. *Open 10-7, Sun. and Mon., 1*. Located at n. 17 in Via Pizzecolli, in the 16th-c. *lazzo Bosdari*, the two art galleries include works C. Crivelli, Titian, L. Lotto, A. del Sarto, S. del Piom-

bo, N. di Bicci, Pomarancio, Guercino and, among the modern artists, M. Campigli, B. Cassinari, C. Levi, F. Menzio, V. Guidi, and L. Veronesi.

S. Francesco delle Scale. Set high atop a stairway, this church overlooks Piazza S. Francesco d'Assisi. Rebuilt in the 18th c., it has a huge Venetian Gothic portal* by G. da Sebenico (1454); inside, works by L. Lotto, A. Lilli, and P. Tibaldi.

Piazza Stracca. With a panoramic view of the port, this square is flanked by the Neo-Classic church of *Gesù* (1743) designed by L. Vanvitelli, and by the 13th-c. **Palazzo degli Anziani**: in the rear are Gothic-Romanesque elements and 15th-c. windows. Next is Palazzo Ferretti, which houses the Museo Archeologico (see below).

Museo Archeologico Nazionale delle Marche.* *Open 9-7:30*. Located in the 16th-c. *Palazzo Ferretti*, in Via Ferretti 1 and 6, the archeological museum features tomb furnishings; magnificent red-and-black Attic vases*; a 5th-c. B.C. "dinos" on a bronze tripod from Amàndola*; splendid Etruscan bronzes*; Hellenistic and Roman items that range from fine gold and silver to household implements; a group of gold-plated bronzes (two women and two men on horseback), found at Cartoceto di Pèrgola in 1946.

Piazza del Senato. The 13th-c. two-storey **Palazzo del Senato** stands here, facing the 18th-c. church of *Ss. Pellegrino e Teresa*, with a fine 13th-c. Byzantine wood Crucifix.

Anfiteatro Romano. This Roman amphitheater seated 7000-8000. Now only the main entrance and, in the square, stretches of Roman walls and a vault are still visible.

Colle Guasco. At the end of Via Giovanni XXIII, or by stairway, you reach this hilltop overlooking the port; here stands the cathedral of S. Ciriaco; a fine view in all directions*.

S. Ciriaco.** The church is the pride of Ancona, and certainly one of the most interesting medieval buildings in the Marche. It was erected from the 11th to the 13th c. in Romanesque style with some Byzantine influence and a few Gothic features. The 13th-c. dome, the white-and-pink *facade*, and impressive Gothic portal* with reliefs are remarkable.

Museo Diocesano. *Open Sat. and Sun. aft. for guided tours*. To the left of S. Ciriaco, this museum of the diocese features fragments of architecture and sculpture from old and ancient churches in the local area; note the 4th-c. sarcophagus of Flavius Gorgonius*.

Arco di Traiano.* Trajan's Arch overlooks the port, at the foot of the Colle Guasco; the architect was Apollodorus of Damascus (A.D. 115), and the arch was built to commemorate the construction of the wharf. Not far off is the *Arco Clementino*, another arch honoring Pope Clement XII, designed by L. Vanvitelli (1738).

Aosta / Aoste*

Elev. 583 m, pop. 34,741; Valle d'Aosta, regional and provincial capital. All around rises a majestic mountain landscape. In the outskirts of

ncona: San Ciriaco

137

town are signs of recent development, the product of the tourist industry linked to the mountain resorts of the upper valley. International traffic with France and Switzerland has grown greatly since the completion of the Monte Bianco (Mont Blanc) and the Gran San Bernardo (Great St. Bernard) tunnels. Further growth has come about through the city's status as capital of this autonomous region. From the outskirts, we proceed to the city's ancient heart, amid the timeworn stones of the "Rome of the Alps," ancient "Augusta Praetoria." Here we also find remarkable relics of the Middle Ages, a "borderland" artistic culture, and the stern, tranquil atmosphere of a mountain town.

Historical note. Aosta was founded during the reign of Augustus, in 25 B.C. The city's layout still basically reflects the original Roman grid, rectangular, enclosed by walls, with a checkerboard pattern of cross-streets. The main street of the Roman "camp" – the "decumanus maximus" – followed the route of the Little Saint Bernard pass (Piccolo San Bernardo), as can still be clearly seen. In the twilight of the Carolingian Empire, Aosta fell to the kingdom of Burgundy (A.D. 888); in 1025 the Burgundian king ceded Aosta to his chief adviser, Umberto Biancamano, founder of the Savoy dynasty. A few years later (1033), the great bishop of the city, Anselmo d'Aosta (St. Anselm), was born there; Aosta had converted to Christianity in the 5th c. Anselm later became Archbishop of Canterbury, a saint, and a Doctor of the Church. The materials of the Roman walls – a good portion of which has survived, and can be easily seen – and of some of Aosta's 18 proud towers were re-used to build castles; an excellent example is the Torre Bramafam. This tower belonged to the family of the Challant, viscounts of Aosta (and representatives of the counts of Savoy: the bonds between Savoy and Aosta, both city and valley, were always strong). In 1295 the Challant renounced their title of viscounts of the city, allowing Aosta a certain degree of self-government, and a council. Roman monuments aside, history has given the urban grid three distinct focal points, in terms of both art and setting. They are Piazza Chanoux, the very core of Aosta; the Cathedral, which stands near the site of the Roman forum; and outside the walls, toward the Buthier River, and perhaps on the site of Aosta's first cathedral, the collegiate church, or Collegiata, of S. Orso. The latter is an exquisite medieval complex, with a late-15th c. priory facing it across a small square. The priory was built at the behest of the prior, Giorgio di Challant, who also built the castle of Issogne. The original Roman grid has even influenced the most recent additions to the city.

Getting around. The historic center of Aosta, especially the central area from the Arco di Augusto to the Piazza della Repubblica, is closed to private automobile traffic. The route suggested here and marked on the map is a walking tour.

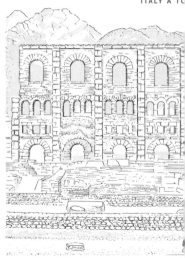

Aosta: Teatro Romano

Places of interest. Arco di Augusto.** Locate outside the walls, this Roman arch was built at t time of the founding of the city (25 B.C.), and w dedicated to Augustus Caesar. It has a single vau ed passageway framed by Corinthian pilasters. T Crucifix under the arch is a copy of a 14th-c. ori nal set there in the 15th c. and now in the Treasu of the cathedral. The square has a fine panorar view of the surrounding mountains. Not far off, t yond the Buthier River, is a single-span *Rom bridge* that once crossed a mountain torrent, whi shifted its course in the 13th c.

S. Orso.* The largest medieval complex in Aos in a secluded corner of town, is dominated by Romanesque *campanile** (1131), with a centu old linden tree. Note the Collegiata (collegia church) and the Priorato (Priory). The *Collegia* founded in early times (994-1025), was rebuilt mo than once, most recently in the 15th c. The faca has a pointed-arch portal. The interior is Gothi with handsome cross-vaults and frescoes from t late-15th c.; fragments of older frescoes (11th c.) the high areas of the nave can be seen in the att (*enquire in sacristy*). In the presbytery is a carv wooden choir* from the late 15th c. Note the 11 c. crypt, with five little aisles. The Tesoro, or Treasu (*closed to the public*) has a rich collection of pr cious medieval objects. From the right aisle (or fro a passageway to the right of the church) you ca enter the Romanesque **cloister**** (12th c.): arch and vaults dating from the 15th c., set on slend columns with intricate carved capitals.

Priorato di S. Orso. This picturesque priory w built between 1494 and 1506. It has elegant crosse terracotta windows and an octagonal tower.

S. Lorenzo. A passageway behind the church S. Lorenzo, facing S. Orso, leads to the remains of a Early Christian complex from the 5th c., which hav been roofed over.

Porta Pretoria.* This gate formed part of the a

ient city walls (1st c.B.C.). It is made of enormous quare-hewn blocks, forming a double curtain wall with three openings (buried about 2.5 m deep by ne rising level of the streets). To the left, note the nassive Torre dei Signori di Quart.

Parco Archeologico del Teatro Romano. * Open ummer, 9-8; winter, 9-6:30. The ruins of this Roman neater include a stretch of the tall facade wall (22 n) with several rows of windows, and the lower ection of the tiers and the skene. To the north of ne theater, in the courtyard of the convent of S. Caterina, dating from the 13th c., you can see ruins of the Roman Amphitheater.

Terme Pubbliche Romane. Situated in an area ehind the Municipio, or town hall, these Roman Baths include apsidal rooms, a calidarium, and a epidarium.

Piazza della Cattedrale. This square occupies in art the old site of the Roman Forum, remains of which can be seen (open same hours as the Teatro Romano) in the enclosure alongside the Cathedral: eneath the level of the street you can see the left de of the podium of a temple; you can descend in- o the cryptoporticus, which runs around three sides f the Forum, part of which is under the church.

Cattedrale. * Surviving from the original Ro- nanesque version of this cathedral (11th-12th c.) re two apsidal bell towers; the rest of the church vas rebuilt repeatedly from the 15th c. on. The fa- ade dates from 1526. The interior is Gothic: note the 5th-c. stained glass windows, the mosaic floor of the resbytery (12th-13th c.), the Gothic wooden choir* ca. 1469), and the funerary monument to Count ommaso II of Savoy (14th-15th c.), in the apse. Beneath the arches of the apse – where, under a lass floor, you can also see the remains of one of ne five Romanesque apses – is the **Museo del Tesoro** (open Apr.-Sep., Tue.-Sat., 8-11:30 and 3-5:30; Oct.-Mar., also Sun. and holidays, 8-11:30 and 3- :30), or Treasury Museum, with collections of ar- hitectural fragments and works of art from the Cathedral and other structures, including an ivory iptych depicting the Emperor Honorius (406), reli- uaries (silver reliquary of S. Grato, 15th c.), a 15th- . wooden altar frontal with 20 carved panels, a 4th-c. Crucifix that once stood beneath the Arco di Augusto, sculptures in stone and wood, goldwork, lass, enamel, and so on. From the aisle you can en- er the cloister* (1460).

Museo Archeologico Regionale. Open Sep.-Jun., -7; Jul.-Aug., 9-8. In Piazza Roncas, near the former Convento della Visitazione, this regional archeo- ogical museum houses a collection ranging from ne Neolithic to Roman times, from digs in sur- ounding areas.

Mura. These Roman city walls date from the reign of Augustus and form a rectangle (727.5 x 574 m). They were punctuated with 20 towers, which are articularly well preserved on the west side (Torre el Lebbroso and the Tour Fromage, or Cheese Tow- r, near the Teatro Romano, both used for tempo- ary exhibitions), and on the south side, with the

medieval Torre Bramafam (13th c.) and, near the railway station, the Roman Torre del Pailleron.

Area Megalitica. In the quarter of Saint-Martin-de-Corléan, to the east of the center, near the church of S. Martino, there stretches an archeological site with megalithic tombs, lines of anthropomorphic steles, and altars from the 3rd millennium B.C.

Villa Suburbana Romana. Recently discovered to the north of town, in the area called Consolata, this Roman villa from the last republican period features remains of mosaic floors and walls.

Aquileia*

Elev. 5 m, pop. 3350; Friùli-Venezia Giulia, province of Udine. Along the road to Grado, just before the last patch of plain gives way to the lagoon, is the Romanesque basilica of Aquileia. The 73-meter-tall campanile no longer towers over the solitary lands that were once so dear to Italy's Nobel laureate, the po- et Giosuè Carducci. Aquileia is now a thriving small town in prosperous farmland; it also boasts one of Italy's most interesting archeo- logical sites. In the shade of tall cypresses, the ruins of a Roman river port evoke ancient trade in exotic merchandise, brought from all over the Mediteranean, and in precious am- ber, gathered on distant Baltic beaches and transported across the European continent.

Historical note. The ruins of what in Roman times was Italy's fourth largest city lie on either side of the SS 352 road, which runs along what was once the "cardo maximus." Founded in 181 B.C., a military base in the war against the Histri, Aquileia's dis- tinctive square plan tells of its beginnings as a Ro- man camp. From camp to trading town and bazaar was a brief step, given its strategic location: to the north lay roads over the Alps, as well as the river traffic of the Danube, where amber was brought from far-off Baltic beaches; to the south lay the broad Adriatic, and the rest of the Mediterranean. Aquileia grew quickly, as can be seen by the pro- gressively larger series of town walls, built up until the late-4th c. A.D. Behind these walls, Aquileia with- stood the attacks of Alaric's Goths (401 and 408); it fell, however, to Attila's Huns in 452, never to regain its standing and wealth. It did survive as a respect- ed bishopric, governing thirty dioceses; its bishop was called "patriarch" (the term reveals Eastern in- fluence) until 1451. One of Aquileia's great patri- archs, Poppone, was elected in 1019; he built new walls, enlarged the harbor, and built the "new" cathe- dral, the Basilica. If the 13th c. was the height of Aquileia's medieval glory, by 1420 it had fallen un- der Venetian rule. In the centuries that followed, it became a desolate village; in 1509 Venice ceded it to Austria; Austria gave it up in 1918.

Places of interest. Basilica. ** Open summer, 8:30- 7; winter, 8:30-12:30 and 2:30-5:30, Sun. 8:30-6.

Among Italy's proudest Romanesque monuments, the Basilica looks much the same as it was when the patriarch Poppone built it in the 11th c.

The first religious structure to stand here dates from A.D. 313, following the Edict of Milan. In 1031, the new Basilica was completed after ten years of construction. An earthquake caused extensive damage in 1348, and restoration gave it a more Gothic appearance. Later, the Venetians added elements of Renaissance style.

The simple facade is joined by a portico, which links the building to the 9th-c. church of the Pagani and the ruins of the 5th-c. baptistery. To the left, the massive 11th-c. bell tower stands alone. The solemn interior features 14th-c. Gothic arcades, raised on columns, and a spectacular 4th-c. **mosaic floor★★** from the original church, discovered in 1909-12. Split into nine large panels, this is the largest surviving sample of Early Christian mosaics in the West. In the right-hand apse, there are frescoes, also from the 4th-c. church. At the center of the stairway leading into the presbytery is an elegant Renaissance tribune★ by Bernardino da Bissone (1491). To the right of the central altar, part of a late-5th-c. mosaic, discovered in 1970, is visible. Beneath the presbytery is the *crypt*, with walls and vaults decorated with frescoes★, perhaps from the late 12th c. At the end of the left aisle is the entrance to the **Cripta degli Scavi★**, or crypt of the excavations (*open same hours as the Basilica*), where fragments of the 4th-c. early Christian basilica are visible, as well as fragments of 1st-c. Roman homes with mosaic floors★.

Cimitero dei Caduti. This small cemetery behind the Basilica contains the remains of some of the first Italian soldiers to die in 1915, and the *tomb of ten Unknown Soldiers*, from WWI battlefields.

Museo Civico del Patriarcato. *Open only for temporary exhibitions.* This museum of the municipality, in Viale Patriarca Popone, casts light on the religious history of Aquileia, mainly through slabs and sacred furnishings.

Case Romane and Oratori Paleocristiani. The site near Viale Patriarca Popone includes a complex of Roman houses, some dating from the late Republic, with mosaic floors, pipes, wells, and two small Early Christian oratories. Another archeological area lies to the left of the Basilica, and can be entered from Piazza del Capitolo.

Museo Archeologico Nazionale.★ *Open Mon., 8:30-2; Tue.-Sun., 8:30-7:30.* It is located in the Villa Cassis, Via Roma 1. One of Italy's leading museums of Roman antiquities, it boasts impressive collections from archeological digs in and around Aquileia. Inaugurated in 1807, it has been enlarged and renovated several times in the past two centuries. Among the items on display are inscriptions and reliefs concerning the foundation of Aquileia; statues and busts; a Venus; a superb collection of glassware, amber, and carved stones; and many remarkable mosaics.

Porto Fluviale. Discovered in the late 19th c., this river port dates from the 1st c. It can be reached from Via Gemina, but we recommend walking alo[ng] the *Via degli Scavi del Porto Fluviale*, a handsom[e] cypress-lined boulevard with altars, architectur[al] fragments, and plaques from local excavations.

Museo Paleocristiano. *Open Mon., 8:30-1:45; Tu[e.]-Sun., 8:30-7:30.* North of the center, a vast form[er] Benedictine convent stands on the remains of a 4[th] /5th-c. *Christian basilica*, with extensive remains [of] 5th-c. mosaic floors★. In the former convent a m[u]seum has been set up, with extensive artifacts of E[ar]ly Christian Aquileia: mosaics, sarcophagi, and [an] early depiction of the Baptism of Jesus.

Foro Romano. The area of the digs is crossed [by] the modern state road, not far from the spectac[u]lar 1st-c. mausoleum, 17 m tall, rebuilt in 1955. [Of] the late 2nd-c. Forum and Basilica, fluted colum[ns] and fragments of the mosaic pavement have be[en] uncovered.

Sepolcreto Romano. *Open 8:30-one hour befo[re] sunset.* This necropolis, 1st-4th c., contains five fa[m]ily tombs.

Arezzo★

Elev. 296 m, pop. 91,729; Toscana (Tuscan[y]) provincial capital. Florence actually pu[r]chased this town twice (the second time, [in] 1384, for 40,000 gold scudi). From the we[st]ernmost slopes of the Alpe di Poti, Arez[zo] looks out over the narrow plain where the va[l]leys of Valdarno, Casentino, and Valdichia[na] converge. The center of Arezzo still has a m[e]dieval appearance, which overlies its earl[ier] incarnations (Etruscan and Roman). In th[is] setting, Arezzo runs the Giostra del Saracin[o,] with Aretinians in medieval dress riding ho[rs]es, pounding through Piazza Grande, past [a] menacing, whip-wielding eastern monarc[h,] Buratto, King of the Indies.

Historical note. High on the hill, S. Francesco, th[e] Romanesque Pieve di S. Maria, the Gothic-R[o]manesque Palazzo della Fraternita dei Laici, a[nd] the Gothic Duomo recall the great centuries [of] Arezzo's history. They range from the 11th c., wh[en] Arezzo rose against the count-bishops, to the e[nd] of the 14th c., when the town was swallowed [by] the burgeoning state of Florence (1384). Betwe[en] these dates stretches a glorious history of warfa[re] with Florence and Siena, dotted with victori[es] (Pieve al Toppo) and defeats (Campaldino; Dan[te] was among the opposing Florentine troop[s]. Around the year 1200, Arezzo built new wal[ls] which ran along what is now the Via Garibaldi; [to] the NE they joined the Etruscan and Roman wa[lls.] Indeed, "Arretium" had once been a major Etrusc[an] town, and an even larger Roman city. Arezzo, [in] its long existence, has produced many notab[le] citizens, from Gaius Cilnius Maecenas, the Rom[an] patron of Horace and Virgil, up to the poet Petr[ar]ch, the artist and historian Giorgio Vasa[ri,] Francesco Redi, and a great figure of the Rena[is-]

Arezzo: Pieve di Santa Maria

sance, Pietro Aretino, satirist and dramatist. Arezzo began its modern growth when the railway from Florence to Rome joined it to the outside world in the 1860s, but since WWII its chaotic expansion has tumbled forth into the plain.

Getting around. Much of the area inside Arezzo's walls is closed to traffic; visitors heading for hotels may pass through. This route may be considered a walking tour.

Places of interest. Piazza S. Francesco. At the edge of the oldest part of town, this square was enlarged in the late 19th-c., at the expense of a wing of the Franciscan convent.

S. Francesco.** This 13th-c. Gothic church, with an unfinished facade, was heavily restored at the turn of the 20th c.; the bell tower dates from the 16th c. The *interior* has a nave and a beam roof. The overall impression, amidst frescoes and austere Franciscan Gothic architecture, is one of grandeur. In the rose window, note the stained glass by G. de Marcillat (1524). Along the right wall are Gothic and Renaissance aediculas and frescoes, some badly damaged. Note the frescoes by L. d'Arezzo, inspired by P. della Francesca; the Crucifix attributed to the Maestro di S. Francesco; and work by S. Aretino, Niccolò di Pietro Gerini, and B. di Lorenzo. Along the walls of the choir is the **Legend of the True Cross**,** the marvelous cycle frescoed by Piero della Francesca probably between 1453 and 1466: in their stylistic discipline and exquisite color, these are towering masterpieces of the Italian Renaissance. In the chapel to the left of the choir are works by S. Aretino, N. di Bicci, and L. Signorelli (attributed).

Chiesa di Badia. On the elegant *Via Cavour*, the 13th-c. *Badia di Ss. Flora e Lucilla* was enlarged around 1550 by G. Vasari (campanile, 1650); the Neo-Gothic facade dates from 1914. Inside, paintings and frescoes by B. della Gatta (1476) and S. di Bonaventura and a ciborium by B. da Maiano. The trompe-l'oeil ceiling simulating a vault is by A. Pozzo (1703). In the nearby *former monastery* are glazed terracotta by the Della Robbia and an elegant 15th-c. cloister (*open by request, contact the custodian*) attributed to G. da Maiano.

Corso Italia. The historic backbone of medieval Arezzo (then called Borgo Maestro), it has been the main street for centuries, with old buildings and fine shops. Toward the center, on the right, is the 13th-c. church of **S. Michele**, with a Neo-Gothic facade but 14th-c. bell tower. Inside, a 16th-c. wooden Crucifix and a panel by N. di Bicci (1466).

At the corner of Via Cavour, note the 15th-c. *Palazzo Bacci* (n. 78-72), and on the right, the 13th-c. *Palazzo Altucci*. Across from the Pieve (see below) are the 13th-c. *tower-house* (n. 24-26), the 14th-c. *Palazzo Camaiani-Albergotti* (n. 4), and the *Torre della Bigazza*, 1351.

Pieve di S. Maria.** One of the most impressive pieces of Tuscan Romanesque, this great sandstone church was begun around 1140, as a renovation of a century-old church. Construction continued into the early 14th c., and G. Vasari turned his hand to it in the next century. It was heavily restored in the late 19th c. The Romanesque facade* is noteworthy, as is the central portal, with reliefs of the Months* (1216). The bell tower* dates from 1330.

The *interior* is vast, and features fine bas-reliefs of the Epiphany (11th-12th c.) and a carved baptismal font by G. di Agostino. On the main altar is the large **polyptych**** by P. Lorenzetti (1320-24). Also noteworthy are the gilt-silver reliquary of S. Donato, the polychrome terracotta Madonna by M. da Firenze, and the 13th-c. marble bas-relief of the Crib.

Piazza Grande.* One of Italy's most spectacular and charming squares, this is the site of the Giostra del Saracino (end of June and early September), and, monthly, of a renowned antiques fair. In the square are the Romanesque *apse* of the Pieve S. Maria, the 16th-c. *public fountain*, the 17th-c. Palazzo del Tribunale and the elegant **Palazzo della Fraternita dei Laici.*** This latter has a Gothic ground floor, portal (1377) and a Renaissance upper floor, by B. Rossellino (1434) – the facade was completed in 1460 by G. and A. da Settignano with balustrade and loggia. Lastly, note the enormous *Palazzo delle Logge*, with its shop-lined portico, designed by Vasari in 1573. On the other sides of the square are old houses, some with walkways and towers.

Via dei Pileati. This uphill extension of Corso Italia overlooks on the left the 14th-c. *Palazzo Pretorio*; at n. 28 in Via dell'Orto is the *Casa di Petrarca* (Petrarch's birthplace; *open 10-12 and 3-5; closed Sat. aft. and Sun.*), rebuilt in 1948 and now the headquarters of the Accademia Petrarca.

Passeggio del Prato. In the huge expanse of public gardens, note the *monument* to Petrarch of 1928; behind it is what is left of the *Fortezza Medicea*, or Medici fortress, by A. da Sangallo the Younger, with a fine view from the battlements.

Duomo. * Set above a flight of 16th-c. steps, this impressive Gothic structure was built between the late 13th and the early 15th c. A Neo-Gothic facade (1901-14) replaced the unfinished original; along the right side is the Romanesque-Gothic portal (1319-37), with a group of terracotta sculptures in the lunette; the bell tower dates from 1859. The *interior*, with a broad nave and two aisles, gives an impression of great soaring height. The large stained glass windows are largely the work of G. de Marcillat (16th c.). The two marble pulpits in the nave date from the same period. In the presbytery, on the main altar, note the 14th-c. Tuscan Arca di S. Donato*, a handsome Gothic marble urn. In the left aisle, fresco* by P. della Francesca; near it is the cenotaph* of the bishop G. Tarlati (1330).

Museo Diocesano. *Open Thu.-Sat., 10-12*. On exhibit in this museum of the diocese are pieces from the Duomo and other churches. Of note are the 13th-c. polychrome wooden Crucifix; three frescoes by S. Aretino; 15th-c. terracotta bas-relief by Rossellino; panel by A. di Nerio; fresco by B. della Gatta; paintings by L. Signorelli and G. Vasari.

Palazzo del Comune. Built in 1333 as the Palazzo dei Priori, the present-day town hall has been heavily rebuilt over the years; tower (1337), courtyard, and, inside, paintings by local artists. If you take Via Ricasoli toward the church of S. Domenico, at n. 1 you will see the Neo-Classic *Palazzo delle Statue* (1793).

S. Domenico. * Isolated in a small tree-lined square, this Gothic church has been heavily modified; it has a Romanesque portal and small bell tower, with 14th-c. bells. *Inside*, badly damaged frescoes, by 14th-/15th-c. painters from Arezzo and Siena; note the Gothic Dragondelli altar (1350). In the middle of the apse is the huge Crucifix**, youthful masterpiece by Cimabue (1260-65).

Casa Vasari. * *Open 9-7; holidays, 9-12:30; closed Tue.* At n. 55 in Via XX Settembre, a handsome piece of Mannerist domestic architecture, the home that G. Vasari built, furnished, and frescoed for himself (1540-48). Now it is the *Museo e Archivio Vasariano*, and features numerous panels and frescoes by the great Renaissance artist and critic; also paintings and other objects dating from the same period.

S. Maria in Gradi. Rebuilt in the Mannerist style (1592) by B. Ammannati, the church dates from the 11th c. Inside, two wooden choirs and a terracotta Madonna del Soccorso by A. della Robbia.

Museo d'Arte Medievale e Moderna. * *Open 9-7; holidays, 9-12:30*. The museum of medieval and modern art is located at n. 8 in Via S. Lorentino, in the 15th-c. Renaissance *Palazzo Bruni-Ciocchi*, at the *Canto alla Croce*, a monumental crossroads lined with lovely and venerable buildings. Note the courtyard, attributed to B. Rossellino.

Arranged in about 20 halls on three floors (some feature Renaissance portals and fireplaces), the collections offer a thorough view of the art of Arezzo and Tuscany, from the 14th to the 19th c.

On the *ground floor*: sculpture from the high Middle Ages to the early Renaissance. *First floor*, overlooking the Renaissance garden, works by G. Vasari, Margarito d'Arezzo, the Maestro della Maddalena, A. di Giovanni, S. Aretino, P. di Spinello, B. della Gatta, and the splendid **collection of majolica and porcelain** (14th-18th c.) from the main Italian workshops. On the second floor are paintings by L. Signorelli and by modern Tuscan painters: G. Fattori, T. Signorini, A. Cecioni.

Santissima Annunziata. Overlooking Via Garibaldi, a long curving road around the old part of Arezzo, this Renaissance church was begun in 1490-91, possibly by B. della Gatta, and continued by A. da Sangallo the Elder (1517). The facade is unfinished, with a 14th-c. fresco by S. Aretino. *Inside*, stained glass windows by G. de Marcillat; painting by P. da Cortona; terracotta sculpture by M. da Firenze (ca. 1430).

Museo Archeologico Mecenate. * *Open 9-2; holidays, 9-1.* Located at n. 10 in Via Margaritone, it is set in a semi-elliptical 16th-c. monastery, partly standing upon and partly overlooking the southern portion of the **Roman amphitheater** (built under Hadrian, A.D. 117-138).

With more than 20 rooms, it comprises private archeological collections and many finds from digs in Arezzo, its region and elsewhere in Italy.

In the *Etruscan section* are Aretinian pieces from archaic and Hellenistic (note the krater* with Hercules and the Amazons by Euphronius) periods; also note the *quincussis**, one of the best preserved Etruscan coins. In the *Roman section*, a considerable collection of the so-called **coral vases** ** (ancient ceramic tableware, varnished red with reliefs). On the *first floor* are the special sections and collections, especially those of ceramics (amphora with black figures and goblet* with red figures), glass and jewel, as well as the *Gamurrini Collection*, with finds from the Agro Falisco, the territories of Chiusi and Orvieto, and Lake Bolsena.

S. Maria delle Grazie. * Out of the city grid, this church stands at the southern tip of Viale Mecenate, where the ancient "Fons Tecta" once flowed. Built in 1435-44, it is a solemn Gothic church, with an elegant portico* by B. da Maiano (15th c.). Inside, the main altar is a marble work by A. della Robbia; fresco by P. di Spinello.

Àscoli Piceno

Elev. 154 m, pop. 51,827; Marche, provincial capital. Located at the confluence of the Castellano and the Tronto, in a steep hollow, 25 km from the Adriatic, this town is a sort of peninsula, protected on the land side by the Colle dell'Annunziata. Àscoli is stern, noble, and compact: a medieval cloth thrown over Roman bones, with the warm glow of the travertine of which its houses, churches, towers, and bridges are built. All that is Renaissance is the work or inspiration of the architect Cola dell'Amatrice. The paintings of the Venetian C. Crivelli are noteworthy.

Historical note. Built by the ancient Piceni in an excellent strategic location, "Asculum" fell to the Romans for the first time in 286 B.C., and again in 89 B.C., after the civil wars. The Roman city straddled the Via Salaria, which entered through the Porta Gemina, still intact, and went out across the Ponte di Cecco over the Castellano; equally important Roman relics are the Ponte di Solestà, the theater, the ruins of the Capitolium on the Colle dell'Annunziata, and the name of "rua" for many streets. The medieval town features such Romanesque monuments as the Battistero, the Palazzetto Longobardo, and the church of Ss. Vincenzo e Anastasio, all from the 12th c. Àscoli enjoyed self-rule from 1185, fought against Frederick II (who sacked the town in 1242), and competed with Fermo for access to the sea. In 1502, the town submitted to papal rule. Renaissance art and architecture prevailed in the following century, encouraged by the artist C. dell'Amatrice, who built the facade of the Duomo and the Palazzo Vescovile, rebuilt the Palazzo dei Capitani del Popolo, and probably designed the Loggia dei Mercanti. There are a few Baroque buildings such as Palazzo Panichi and the rebuilt Palazzo del Comune and probably the Loggia del Mercanti; no further changes occurred in the town's appearance until 1860. The town has tripled in population since then, extending north and east beyond the rivers.

Places of interest. Piazza Arringo.* Rectangular, vast, and monumental, this is the oldest square in Àscoli Piceno; in the shadow of the Duomo (see below), and flanked by the Palazzo Vescovile and the nearby Palazzo Comunale (which houses the Pinacoteca Civica), a complex of medieval buildings, joined by a subsequent, Baroque facade.

Pinacoteca Civica. *Open 9-1 and 3-7:30; Sun. 9-12:30 and 3-7.* Occupying 14 rooms, the art gallery's best known piece is the 13th-c. cope of Pope Nicholas IV*. In the other halls are paintings by: Crivelli, P. Alemanno, C. dell'Amatrice, Titian, Guercino, C. Maratta, O. De Ferrari, S. De Magistris, C. Allegretti, L. Giordano, S. Conca and others. Italian artists of the 19th and 20th c. include D. Morelli, F. Palizzi, A. Mancini, E. Ximenes, Pellizza da Volpedo, and D. Induno.

Palazzo Vescovile. Standing alongside the Palazzo Comunale, this is an 18th-c. renovation of existing buildings. On its first floor is the **Museo Diocesano** (*open Tue., Thu. and Sat., 9-12*), or Museum of the Diocese. In six halls, paintings (by C. dell'Amatrice, P. Alemanno, and L. Trasi; detached frescoes), sculptures in stone, wood, ivory, and silver, and various sacred artworks are all on display. In the nearby 16th-c. *Palazzo Roverella*, note the frescoes by M. Fogolino (1547).

Duomo. Standing on the remains of a Roman basilica, the cathedral preserves its 15th-c. sides, with Gothic mullioned windows set between tall pilaster strips. The facade is unfinished. *Inside*, the 15th-c. wooden stalls, the 14th-c. altarpiece, and the large **polyptych*** by C. Crivelli (1473) are noteworthy.

Museo Archeologico Statale. *Open 9-7; closed Mon.* Set in *Palazzo Panichi*, in Piazza Arringo, facing the Palazzo Vescovile, this archeological museum comprises prehistoric, Italic, and Roman finds from Àscoli and the surrounding territory.

Battistero.* This 12th-c. octagonal baptistery stands near the left side of the Duomo; note the blind loggia and fine dome. In the Via dei Bonaparte, at n. 24, is the 16th-c. *Palazzetto Bonaparte*, with interesting friezes.

S. Vittore. Late-12th-c. church, with pentagonal apse; inside, 13th-/14th-c. frescoes.

Piazza Matteotti. This square lies at the eastern tip of Àscoli, at the head of the rebuilt *Ponte Maggiore*. From here, to the south, you can see the 14th-c. *Forte Malatesta* and the piers of the Roman bridge, the *Ponte di Cecco*, destroyed during WWII.

Palazzo Malaspina. At n. 224 in Corso Mazzini, which crosses Àscoli from west to east, is this stern 16th-c. palazzo, with rustication and a high loggia.

Piazza del Popolo.* Monumental heart of the city, it is lined by low, simple Renaissance palazzi, battlemented and porticoed. Looming over the square is the Palazzo dei Capitani del Popolo and one of the sides of the church of S. Francesco (see below). A lively evening strolling ground, especially for the young, this may have been the Forum in Roman times.

Palazzo dei Capitani del Popolo.* Built with its tower in the 13th c., the palazzo has a statue over the portal of Pope Paul III (by S. Cioli, 1549); noteworthy courtyard with portico and loggia. Inside, in 1982, archeologists uncovered Roman and medieval ruins.

S. Francesco.** Construction on this Gothic church continued from 1258 into the 16th c. Two slender bell towers rise between its lively polygonal apses; along its right side runs the elegant five-arched *Loggia dei Mercanti** (1513). The facade features three Venetian-Gothic portals, the central one particularly rich in ornament. In the majestic and spare *interior*, the complex apse is particularly noteworthy. On the left side of the church is the **Chiostro Maggiore**, built between 1565 and 1623; this cloister is now used as a marketplace; nearby (entrance from Via Ceci) is the 14th-c. **Chiostro Minore**.

S. Maria inter Vineas. In a small square overlooking the Tronto River is a 13th-c. church, partly rebuilt in 1954, with a massive campanile; inside, 13th-/14th-c. frescoes and a handsome Gothic-style funerary monument (1482). Nearby, adjacent to the Ponte Nuovo, is *Porta Tufilla* (1553).

Piazza Ventidio Basso. This square is enclosed by the side of the church of S. Pietro Martire (see below); also, the 11th-c. Romanesque church of **Ss. Vincenzo e Anastasio,*** whose facade is divided into 64 panels. Note the rich Gothic portal and low campanile; inside, the 6th-c. crypt features columns and side apses.

S. Pietro Martire. This monumental Gothic church was begun around 1280 and completed in the early 14th c. On the left side are the portal designed by C. dell'Amatrice (1523) and the three apses. Inside, fragments of 15th-/16th-c. frescoes.

Piazzetta di S. Pietro Martire. This little square is

set at the junction of lanes that run into a notable quarter: Via delle Torri, Via dei Soderini, and Via di Solestà*. This latter street, lined by medieval towers and houses, much rebuilt in the 16th c., leads to the single-arched Roman bridge, or **Ponte di Solestà***, from the early Imperial Age, with a medieval gate (1230) and tower.

Via dei Soderini. This fine street still has a medieval feel to it; at n. 26 stands the tall 11th-c. *Torre Ercolani*, the most notable of Àscoli's aristocratic towers; next to it is the 11th-c. **Palazzetto Longobardo**. Facing it, at n. 11, is another tower-house; further along, in Largo della Fortuna, is the 13th-c. church of **S. Giacomo**, in travertine; interesting campanile and decorated portal on the left side.

Piazza Cecco d'Àscoli. At the western tip of the city is the small Roman 1st-c. **Porta Gemina**, where the ancient Via Salaria entered Àscoli. Beyond the gate is a stretch of *Roman wall*, and at the mouth of Via Angelini are the ruins of the *Roman theater*.

Piazza S. Agostino. At the western end of Corso Mazzini, this square is lined by two tall medieval towers and the 15th-c. facade of the church of **S. Agostino** (portal from 1547); inside, the 14th-c. panel of the Madonna dell'Umiltà. On Corso Mazzini, at n. 90, is the **Galleria d'Arte Contemporanea** (*open 9-1; closed Mon.*), with 20th-c. art works and an interesting section devoted to graphic art. At n. 39 is the Museo di Storia Naturale Antonio Orsini (Museum of Natural History, *open 9-1; Tue. and Thu. also 3-6; closed Sun.*).

Colle dell'Annunziata. This hill is partly occupied by the shaded Parco della Rimembranza, with fine views of Àscoli and the valley of the Castellano. Note the 15th-c. former *convent*, with *church* and two *cloisters*; in the refectory is a fresco by C. dell'Amatrice (1519). Just beneath the square of the church (view) are Roman ruins, commonly called the *Grotte dell'Annunziata*. Climb the hill to the *Fortezza Pia*, a fort built by Pius IV in 1560.

S. Angelo Magno. Take the quaint Via Pretoriana uphill to this church, founded in 1292, on Roman ruins. Note the bell tower and Renaissance interior; the cloister has poligonal pilasters.

S. Gregorio. Romanesque 13th-c. church 17.5 km south of the city that incorporates fragments of a 1st-c. B.C. Roman temple (Corinthian columns on the facade, walls).

Assisi**

Elev. 424 m, pop. 25,464; Umbria, province of Perugia. The Roman city of Assisi – Asisium – was built on a series of terraces which "climbed the mountainside like a great stairway," as it was described in the words of its native son Propertius. The ancient Roman poet would still recognize the landscape, if not the architecture. And Assisi still stands, wrapped in the silence and solitude of the centuries, on a ridge of Monte Subasio, overlooking the plains of the Chiascio and the Topino.

Historical note. Of the rich Roman settlement some notable monuments survive; little or nothing remains from the barbarian era, before Assisi was subjugated by the dukes of Spoleto. Assisi grew considerably after the year 1000, and in 1184 it gained political self-rule, amid a series of wars against nearby Perugia. In this period, St. Francis was born and grew up here. As a young man, he abandoned his knighthood and wealth and devoted himself to helping the poor. From 1206 until his death in 1226, St. Francis preached, meditated, built, and organized his Order in this region. He is buried in the Basilica of his name. St. Francis may have brought Assisi a reputation of saintliness, but war continued – first with Perugia, then the Visconti, the Montefeltro, the Fortebraccio, Francesco Sforza, and even Machiavelli's Valentino (Cesare Borgia); finally, at the turn of the 16th c., Pope Paul III Farnese put the region and the town under papal rule. Assisi was described in reports of those years as "the remains of a town, rather than a real, complete town." Pilgrimages and tourism restored Assisi to prosperity in the 20th c.

Getting around. The first two routes that we recommend are walking tours; therefore, we suggest parking your car outside the town. In any case, traffic regulations and the steepness and narrowness of Assisi's streets should discourage the use of private vehicles. You should plan on driving or taking public transportation to visit the outlying monuments described in the third route.

The Basilica of S. Francesco and the Piazza del Comune

The basilica is the most important monument in Assisi and one of the best known artistic and religious landmarks in Italy; its counterpoint is the medieval Piazza del Comune, center of the earliest Assisi, at the far end of Via S. Francesco.

Porta S. Francesco (*A1*). This 14th-c. crenelated gate is the main western entrance to Assisi; it affords a fine view* of the Convento di S. Francesco, with the massive arched buttresses that make it look like a great grim fortress.

Piazza Inferiore di S. Francesco* (*A1*). Entirely surrounded by low 15th-c. porticoes, this lower square lies in the shadow of the basilica, with its mighty bell tower* (1239). On the left, note the *Oratorio di S. Bernardino*, the main entrance to the Sacro Convento, and, facing it, the entrance to the lower basilica.

S. Francesco* (*A1*). *Open Easter-Nov., 6:30-7; holidays, 6:30-7:30; other months, 6:30-6; closed Sun. morn.* The basilica, begun in 1228, two years after St. Francis's death, was consecrated in 1253. It is a monument that was designed to perpetuate Francis's message throughout Christendom.

The greatest advocate, and perhaps the mastermind behind this complex was Frate Elia, vicar general and architect of the Franciscan Order; apart from a ew 14th-c. additions, the church is as he built it. It comprises two churches, one atop the other. In the lower one the saint was buried in 1230 and still rests. Both basilicas house cycles of frescoes that are virtually unrivalled in 13th- and 14th c. Italian art.

Basilica Inferiore. You enter the Lower Basilica through a late-13th-c. twin portal. The interior, on a Greek cross plan, has a single nave. Low arches divide it into five bays, with side chapels added at the end of the 13th c. In the *first bay*, 17th-c. frescoes, two huge Gothic tombs, and a pulpit. On the left, chapel of St. Sebastian; beyond it, chapel of St. Catherine, with frescoes by A. de' Bartoli (1368) and stained glass windows. From here you can enter an attractive *little cloister** (1492-93), on the right side of the church. On the walls of the *nave*, frescoes – partly destroyed by alterations – with scenes of the Passion (right) and stories from the life of St. Francis* (left), works by the Maestro di S. Francesco (c. 1253). Various frescoes by the workshop of Giotto surround the entrance to the *crypt*, with the stone urn containing the remains of the saint. In the first chapel on the left is an exceedingly fine series of frescoes of the **Life of St. Martin****, by Simone Martini (1321-26). In the *vault* are the renowned frescoes* by the Maestro delle Vele, follower of Giotto (1315-20). In the apse is a carved wooden choir*.

In the *right transept*, frescoes by Giotto's workshop, and a majestic fresco of the **Virgin Enthroned with Angels and St. Francis**** by Cimabue (1280); a fresco* by S. Martini. In the *left transept*, an astonishing cycle of frescoes with the **Passion of Christ**** by P. Lorenzetti and his workshop (ca. 1320).

From the transepts, two stairways lead up to the *great cloister* (1476), with portico and loggia, in the shadow of the tall apsidal section of the basilica. From the terrace of the cloister, you can enter the Treasury; a stairway leads on to the upper church.

Museo-Tesoro e Collezione Perkins.* *Open Apr.-Oct., 9-12 and 2-5:30.* The Treasury museum contains precious reliquaries, manuscripts, and liturgical garb, as well as a fine Flemish tapestry.* The collection includes 14th-/15th-c. paintings on panel with subjects relating to St. Francis; among the artists are Beato Angelico, N. Alunno, A. Romano.

Basilica Superiore. Gothic in style, with French influence, the Upper Basilica has a single nave with four bays. The visit starts from the *transept*, entirely decorated by a vast cycle of **frescoes by Cimabue***, begun in 1277, and sadly deteriorated. In the *apse*, note the wooden choir*, carved by D. Indivini (1491-1501); in the vault above the main altar and on the walls are various frescoes by Cimabue. The upper part of the *walls* of the nave are covered with frescoes* considered to be by Roman painters and by followers of Cimabue and, perhaps, by the young Giotto. In the lower part, beneath the gallery that runs all the way around the nave, is the renowned cycle of **frescoes by Giotto****, depicting 28 panels episodes from the life of St. Francis. Giotto began working on these frescoes probably in 1296. Also worthy of note are the medieval stained glass windows. Despite restoration, they constitute one of the most complete sets to be found in Italy. The oldest, in the apse, may date from before 1253.

Piazza Superiore di S. Francesco (*A1-2*). You exit the church onto the upper square, which is dominated by the simple 13th-c. facade*. Adorned with a French-style twin portal, the facade features an enormous rose window, with the symbols of the four Evangelists.

Sacro Convento (*A1*). Built with the basilica, the massive buttressing pylons were added later; inside, noteworthy are the Sala Capitolare, or Chapter House, with a fresco by P. Capanna; the enormous portico along the SW side of the convent; and the monumental Refettorio, or Refectory (53 x 13 m), with a Last Supper by Solimena (1717).

Via S. Francesco (*A2*). This long medieval road climbs straight from the basilica to the center of Assisi, and is lined by medieval houses and 17th-c. patrician palazzi.

At n. 14 is the 15th-c. *Loggia dei Maestri Comacini*; at n. 12, the 17th-c. Palazzo Giacobetti, and the 15th-c. former hospital, the *Oratorio dei Pellegrini*, with frescoes. At n. 10 is Palazzo Vallemani, which houses the **Pinacoteca Comunale** (*B3*; *open 16 Mar.-15 Oct., 10-1 and 3-7; 16 Oct.-15 Mar., 10-1 and 2-5*), including a fine array of frescoes and paintings, with works by followers of Giotto, Puccio Capanna, Ottaviano Nelli, Niccolò Alunno, Andrea d'Assisi, Tiberio d'Assisi, Dono Doni. At n. 3 is the 13th-c. *Portico del Monte Frumentario* (*B3*), and the *Oliviera fountain* (1570). Past an arch and up the Via del Seminario, you see the 12th-/15th-c. *Seminario Diocesano*; the Via Portica leads past the entrance of the Museo Civico to the Piazza del Comune.

Museo Civico (*B3*). *Open 16 Mar.-15 Oct., 10-1 and 3-7; 16 Oct.-15 Mar., 10-1 and 2-5.* Located in the Romanesque *crypt of S. Nicolò* (11th c.; entrance at n. 2 in Via Portica), this is all that now survives of an old church. The municipal museum features ancient Umbrian and Roman items and art works from the

Assisi: San Francesco

145

local area. A corridor leads to what is thought to have been the Roman forum, with original paving.
Piazza del Comune* (*B3-4*). At the center of Assisi, on the site of the ancient Roman forum, this is a typical medieval square, with a 16th-c. fountain, with three stone lions. Note **Palazzo dei Priori** (1337); this heavily rebuilt complex of buildings features a handsome 16th-c. painted passageway, the *Volta Picta*. The opposite side of the square, marked by the tall crenelated *Torre del Popolo*, features the 13th-c. *Palazzo del Capitano del Popolo* (*B3*), victim of a 20th-c. architectural travesty. Next to it is the **Tempio di Minerva**, or Temple of Minerva, a handsome building from the 1st c. B.C., now a Baroque church inside.
Chiesa Nuova (*B4*). This Baroque church (1615) stands on the remains of a medieval building traditionally said to have been the home of St. Francis's father, Pietro Bernardone. To the left of the presbytery is the entrance to the supposed *house of the Saint*, which has been restored.

The Duomo and the Roman section; S. Chiara and Borgo S. Pietro

From the Duomo, you continue into an area with clearer signs of Roman influence, until you reach the Basilica of S. Chiara, with its fine art works. Borgo S. Pietro is a handsome late medieval district.
Via S. Rufino (*B4*). Steep and twisting, it has a strong medieval appearance. From Piazza del Comune it goes past old houses to *Piazza S. Rufino*; note the 13th-c. fountain and the Duomo facade.
Duomo* (*B4*). Dedicated to S. Rufino, its construction began in 1140; the Romanesque facade is majestic and austere, with three richly carved portals and three rose windows ringed by reliefs. The mighty bell tower belonged to the basilica that previously stood here; it stands on a Roman cistern.
Inside, note the 17th-c. stuccoes, the ancient baptismal font where Sts. Francis and Claire were baptized, and the three 16th-c. paintings by D. Doni. In the apse, a noteworthy wooden choir* (1520).
Museo della Cattedrale (*B4*). *Open Apr.-Oct., 10-1 and 2-5*. You enter the cathedral museum by way of a corridor next to the right aisle. The collections include illuminated codices and detached frescoes. Among the paintings, work by P. Capanna and N. Alunno. From outside the Duomo you can also visit the ancient **crypt***, with fragments of 11th-c. frescoes and a 3rd-c. Roman sarcophagus.
Via S. Maria delle Rose (*B4*). Along this road, from the Duomo, you will see the Romanesque *Palazzo dei Consoli* (1225), and, in a linden-shaded square, the ancient former church of *S. Maria delle Rose*.
Porta Perlici (*B5*). This 12th-c. gate in the medieval walls, at the end of the twisting Via Perlici, which runs from Piazza S. Rufino, has a double arch. The surrounding district has a Roman layout; note the old houses along Via del Comune Vecchio, the *amphitheater* (*B5*; in Via Anfiteatro, terrace with overall view) and *theater* (*B4*; three arches in Via del Tor-

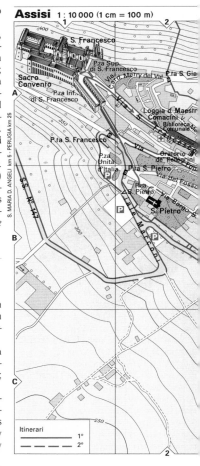

Assisi 1 : 10 000 (1 cm = 100 m)

rione), both from the late Roman Imperial Age.
Rocca Maggiore* (*A3-4*). *Open 10-sunset*. This m dieval fortress, built in 1356, stands on a peak ove looking Assisi and the valley; a road winds up fro Porta Perlici. The fort is a trapezoidal wall with tov ers and a keep with a tall square tower (view* of th Valle Umbra).
Basilica di S. Chiara** (*B-C4*). Just outside th *medieval gate of S. Giorgio*, this church overlooks a immense square, with a fine view of the Valle Un bra (to the right you can see the apse and can panile of S. Maria Maggiore). Built in pure Goth style (1257-65), it has a sober pink-and-white stripe facade, with a single portal and a rose window; o the left are three large flying buttresses (late 14 c.). Alongside, overlooking the valley is the ancien *monastery* of the Clarissan nuns (*C4*).
In the severe **interior** are late-13th-c. frescoes an paintings, as well as a 12th-c. Crucifix which, a cording to tradition, spoke to St. Francis in th church of S. Damiano.
Piazza del Vescovado (*B3*). In this square stand

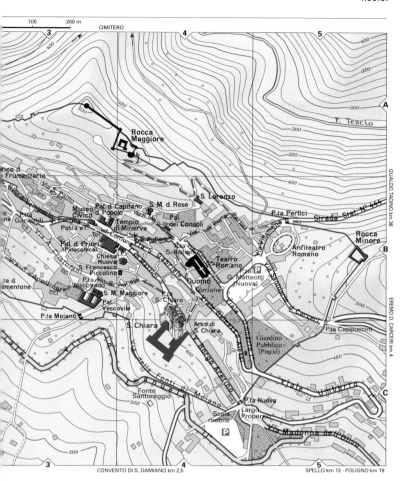

100   200 m

CIMITERO

3   4   5

F. Tescio

Rocca
Maggiore

rico d.
Frumentario

S. Lorenzo

Via S. Paolo

P.ta Perlici   Strada Stat. N° 444

S. M. d. Rose

GUALDO TADINO km 36

Museo
Civico
d. Popolo
Pal. d. Capitano
Pal. A. Cristofani
Posta e T.
Tempio
di Minerva
Pal.
dei Consoli
Rocca
Minore
Via A. Cristofani
Porziano
S. Rufino
Anfiteatro
Romano
Pal. d. Priori
(Pinacoteca)
Chiesa
Nuova
P.za d.
Comune
S. Francesco
Piccolino
Via S. Agnese
Via S. Gabriele
P.za S.
Rufino
Teatro
Romano
G. Matteotti
(Nuova)
Duomo
Torrione
ta d.
ementone
S. Agnese
Vescovado
S. M. Maggiore
Via Fonti di Moiano
P.za
S. Chiara
Pal.
Vescovile
Via Borgo d. Aretino
P.ta Moiano
S. Chiara
Arco di
S. Chiara
Giardino
Pubblico
(Pincio)
P.ta Cappuccini
EREMO D. CARCERI km 4
Viale Umberto
Via Fonti di Moiano
Fonte
Santureggio
Scala
mobile
P.ta Nuova
Largo
Properzio
Via Madonna dell'Ulivo
SPELLO km 12 - FOLIGNO km 19

CONVENTO DI S. DAMIANO km 2,5

3   4   5

A   B   C

e church of S. Maria Maggiore (see below); from
e garden, you can see ruins of the Roman walls.
ear here, in the since-rebuilt *Palazzo Vescovile*,
. Francis renounced his father's wealth.

. Maria Maggiore (*B3*). Assisi's early cathedral
as founded in the 10th c., and has a simple Roanesque facade and a notable semicircular apse.
side, fragments of 14th-c. frescoes.

Pietro* (*B2*). The church was rebuilt in the 13th
and consecrated in 1253. It stands on the edge of
e district of S. Pietro. The facade has three portals
nd three rose windows; *inside*, note the funerary
onuments and fragments of frescoes, all dating
om the 14th c. From the square, a fine view of the
ssisi valley; note nearby *Porta S. Pietro*, a city gate.

**he places associated with St. Francis
utside Assisi**

utside the town walls are a number of sites of ear-
 Franciscan history: Convento di S. Damiano, Ere-
o delle Carceri, Monte Subasio, the ruins of the

Abbazia di S. Benedetto, and the Basilica di S. Maria
degli Angeli.

S. Damiano** (*C4, off map*). *Open summer, 10-
12:30 and 2-6; winter, 10-12:30 and 2-4.* Outside of
Porta Nuova (*C4-5*), some 2.5 km south of the historic town, this simple convent was built around a
country *chapel* where, according to tradition, in the
summer of 1205, a Crucifix (now in S. Chiara) spoke
to St. Francis. In 1212 St. Claire and her sisters took
up residence here. There are various frescoes, by
T. d'Assisi, P.A. Mezzastris, E. da S. Giorgio and D. Doni.
In the *convent* is the garden where St. Francis wrote
his "Cantico delle Creature" and the dormitory where
St. Claire died.

S. Maria di Rivotorto (*C5, off map*). 3.5 km SE on
the SS road to Foligno, this church was rebuilt in Neo-
Gothic style in 1853; it stands on the site where Francis and his companions first lived in 1208-11.

Eremo delle Carceri* (*B5, off map*). *Open Easter-
Nov., 6:30-7:15; other months, 6:30-5:30.* In a thick
oak forest, at an elevation of 791 m on the slopes of
Monte Subasio, 4 km east of *Porta dei Cappuccini*

(B-C5), along a panoramic road that climbs through olive groves, is this Franciscan hermitage. The convent was built by St. Bernardino of Siena in 1426. Note the "Grotta di S. Francesco," the saint's little cell cut into living rock; stroll through the forest.

Abbazia di S. Benedetto (*B5, off map*). Further along on the same road is this 10th-c. abbey (729 m). The original structure was largely destroyed in 1399. Continue another 11.5 km, to the peak of **Monte Subasio** (1290 m), with a fine view* of Lake Trasimeno, Monte Amiata, and the Apennines.

S. Maria degli Angeli* (*A2, off map*). At a distance of 5 km from Assisi, in the plain (218 m) at the foot of the city; leaving the historical center, the view of this church is notable. One of Italy's greatest sanctuaries, this basilica stands on the site where St. Francis founded his Order in 1208, and later died. This monumental Mannerist building, designed by G. Alessi, was built between 1569 and 1679. A Neo-Baroque facade was added in 1928. The large, solemn *interior* has a nave and two aisles, side chapels, and a deep choir. Beneath the dome is the chapel of the **Porziuncola***, a simple 10th-c. oratory. The exterior is frescoed. Inside, amidst the lamp-

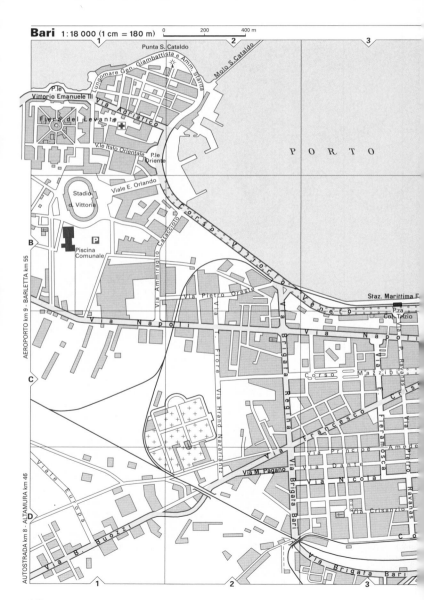

Bari 1:18 000 (1 cm = 180 m)

lack stains, painting by I. da Viterbo (1393). In the presbytery, on the right, is the **Cappella del Transito***, the cell in which St. Francis died, the evening of 3 October 1226; inside, frescoes by Spagna, a statue of the saint by A. della Robbia, and, in a case over the altar, the cord that the saint wore at his waist. To the right of the basilica is the renowned *rose garden*, with thornless rose bushes. In the rectory of the ancient *little convent* is a **Museum** (*open 9-12 and 3:30-6:30; closed Nov.-Mar.*) with a portrait of St. Francis by the Maestro di S. Francesco and a Crucifix* by Giunta Pisano (ca. 1236).

Bari*

Elev. 5 m, pop. 331,848; Puglia (Apulia), regional and provincial capital. The old section of Bari is one of the two parts – one might say three parts – that make up what is now the second largest city in continental southern Italy. Bari lies on the Adriatic Sea, midway up the coast of Apulia. While the old section lies serried and compact in a labyrinth of twisting lanes, where the entire history of Bari has had its long course, the new section developed during the

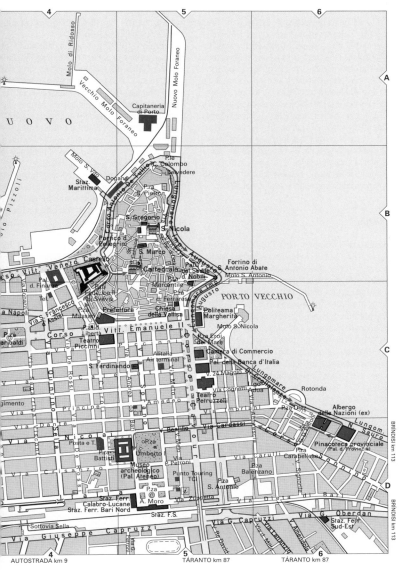

19th c. on a regular plan made up of broad straight streets. Nowadays, one might mention a third Bari, "Bari Nuovissima", which straddled the railroad line throughout the 20th c., expanding into the industrial section and the Fiera del Levante, the site of a major trade fair.

Historical note. A quick perusal of the city map provides a graphic reading of Bari's history and a clear indication of the city's character. Built out onto the jutting protuberance separating the Castello and the Porto Vecchio, or old port, is the Città Vecchia, or old town. The earliest known human settlement, in the Bronze Age, lay on the very farthest tip of the little peninsula. From the 3rd c. B.C. Bari was part of the Roman Empire; subsequently, from 875 to 1071, it fell under Byzantine rule. Its importance as a maritime port grew under the Normans (1071), and later, in the 13th c., under the Swabian emperors. The layout of the Città Vecchia dates back to this period. And the entire history of the city up to the end of the 18th c. took place within this cluttered and close little area. At the turn of the 19th c., Bari had a population of just 18,000; today it is the second largest city in mainland southern Italy. Joachim Murat ruled as king of the Two Sicilies for less than 17 years, but we must give him credit for undertaking the expansion of Bari (1813) with the construction of the Borgo Nuovo or Città Murattiana (a new section that bore his name, lying roughly between what is now Corso Vittorio Emanuele II and the railway station).

Old town

Basilica di S. Nicola** (B5). This basilica, one of the archetypes of the Romanesque style of Apulia, was built to hold the body of St. Nicholas of Lycia, bishop of Myra in Asia Minor, who died in 326 with a reputation for working miracles. In 1087, 62 seafaring men from Bari made off with the saint's 700-year-old relics. A Benedictine abbot named Elia decided to build a new church to contain them, and St. Nicholas became the patron saint of the town. Construction lasted from 1087 until 1197. All the features in the Apulian Romanesque style are here: a tripartite façade (here flanked by two truncated towers) with hanging arches under the eaves, two-light windows, three portals, and large blind arches along the sides with little six-light loggias, an immense transept, a single wall enclosing all three apses. *Inside*, note the nave and aisles lined with columns and pillars. On the main altar is the 12th-c. ciborium*; in the apse is a remarkable marble bishop's throne* and a late-16th-c. monument to Bona Sforza; the altar of St. Nicholas, in embossed silver foil (1684), can be seen in the right apse; in the left apse, note the panel* by B. Vivarini (1476); beneath the altar of the handsome crypt is the body of St. Nicholas. The Treasury (in the Museo della Basilica; *open Wed., 10-12; Fri., 10-12 and 5-7*) is exquisite; note, among other things, the 12th-c. candelabra donated by Charles of Anjou.

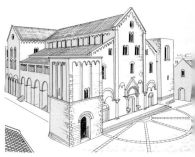

Bari: Basilica di S. Nicola

Facing S. Nicola is the *Portico dei Pellegrini*, rebuilt; to the right, under the 14th-c. *Arco di S. Nicola*, is the little 11th-c. church of *S. Gregorio*.

Cattedrale** (B5). The cathedral, dedicated to St. Sabino, was built after the Norman king William I, known as "Guglielmo il Malo," practically razed Bari to the ground (1156). It is Romanesque, and was built on the site of the old Byzantine cathedral. This is another notable monument of Apulian Romanesque; note the splendid enormous window* in the apse; the large cylindrical structure along the left side, known as the "*trulla*," is an old baptistery, made into a sacristy in the 17th c. Of particular interest in the interior: the pulpit, the ciborium, and the bishop's throne, rebuilt from original fragments; also note the crypt, rebuilt in the 18th c. In the Archivi are priceless codices and the renowned scroll of the *Exultet I**. Beside the cathedral is the **Museo Diocesano**, or Museum of the Diocese (*open Mon., Thu. and Sat. 9:30-12:30*).

Castello* (B4; *open 8:30-7:30; closed Mon.*). The enormous bulk of the castle comprises a keep, or donjon, built on a trapezoidal plan, with two towers left of the original four. Frederick II erected this version, working on the earlier Norman-Byzantine structure. It also comprises the scarps of the ramparts, and the corner towers looming over the moat, added under Spanish rule in the 16th c. to the three landward sides; the fourth side, once bathed by sea waves, still has the handsome twin-light mullioned windows of Frederick's project.

The *interior* is well worth seeing, and features a square Renaissance *courtyard*, an interesting *plaster gallery* (Gipsoteca Provinciale), with a collection of casts of the finest and loveliest monuments of the Apulian Romanesque style.

Lungomare Imperatore Augusto (B5). This handsome seafront promenade runs along the old walls on the east side of the Città Vecchia.

The museums

Pinacoteca Provinciale (D6; *open 9-1 and 4-7; holidays, 9-1; closed Mon.*). Located in the Palazzo della Provincia, on the SE of the Città Vecchia, this art gallery houses a collection touching various aspects of the art of the region, including local medieval statues and paintings. Also noteworthy are the works by the later school of Venetian painters (Bordone, Tintoretto, and Veronese, among others); works by Apulian and Neapolitan painters of the 17th and 18th c. (C. Giaquinto, O. Tiso); the Neapolitan crèches; 18th-c. Apulian ceramics; and a number of 19th-c. paintings (Signorini, Induno, and De Nittis).

Museo Archeologico (*D4-5; closed for restoration*). This archeological museum – located in Palazzo Ateneo on Piazza Umberto I – has the most complete collection of Apulian archeological finds, and is fundamental to understand the 7th-/3rd-c. B.C. cultures of Dàunia (now the Tavoliere), Peucézia (now called Terra di Bari), and Messàpia (the Salento). Note the two fine-columned Attic ceramic kraters*; a hydra*, made of proto-Italic ceramics from Canosa, by the Painter of Àmykos; a scroll-handled krater*; an Apulian red-figure krater* from Ceglie; tomb furnishings** from Noicàttaro and from the Tomba Varrese**; a group of sculpted vases**; bronze armor*, part of the tomb furnishings of Conversano; a bust* and a clay group* from Egnazia.

Acquario Provinciale (*B4*). This aquarium stands at the foot of the Molo Pizzoli, a large wharf running out into the Gran Porto.

Orto Botanico (Via G. Amendola 175). This botanical garden is particularly interesting for its array of wild plants from the Apulia region.

S. Felice. In the suburbs of Bari, near Balsignano, this Romanesque church (12th c.) is made of stone tiles fit one into the other without any linking cement. It testifies to the past richness of this countryside area.

Bèrgamo**

Elev. 249 m, pop. 117,837; Lombardia (Lombardy), provincial capital. The distinctive silhouette that can be seen from the surrounding lowlands, etched out against the mountainous background, is that of Bèrgamo Alta, or upper Bèrgamo, aloof, hushed, and ancient. This is one of the most perfect stratified assemblies of urban construction and historical memory in Lombardy, and perhaps in all of Italy. Roughly one hundred meters below, at the edge of the plain, near the mouth of the Valle Brembana and Valle Seriana, lies the thriving town of Bèrgamo Bassa, or lower Bèrgamo, the modern section, even though it has centuries of prosperous trading, banking, and manufacture behind it. In Bèrgamo you are going to meet the forbidding gaze of the equestrian monument to Bartolomeo Colleoni, great condottiere, but even greater self-aggrandizer; the 16th-c. merchants who look out from portraits by G.B. Moroni; the baleful, disapproving eye that the artist Fra' Galgario cast upon the aristocrats of the 16th-c. provinces; the airy, "musical" still-lifes by E. Baschenis; mellifluous romantic airs by Gaetano Donizetti, or the rough jokes and rapid banter of Arlecchino – Harlequin – both native sons of Bèrgamo.

Historical note. The dichotomy between the two cities – Bèrgamo Alta and Bèrgamo Bassa – can be seen, perhaps, as far back as the first Roman settlement, in the 2nd c. B.C. The "civitas" stood high on the hill, while the "suburbia" lay in the surrounding plains. We do know for certain that under Longobard rule, in the 6th and 7th c., as the dukedom of Bèrgamo was being organized into the manorial system, the city territory was divided into two jurisdictions of two "royal courts". We have documentation of the fair in the field of Prato di S. Alessandro (now the heart of Bèrgamo Bassa) dating back to the 10th c. Bèrgamo Alta during this same period continued to hold the reins of power, at first under a bishop and later under Communal government (from the 12th c. on). The Visconti seized Bèrgamo in 1332 and, in 1428, Venice snatched the city away from them, after the Count of Carmagnola trounced the troops of Filippo Maria Visconti at Maclodio. Bartolomeo Colleoni, a Bergamasque condottiere fighting for the Venetians, staved off a new Visconti offensive a few years later, and the city remained under Venetian rule until 1796. In Bèrgamo Alta, an early seigneur, John of Bohemia, built the town fortress, or Rocca, to the east; on the far side of the high town, the Visconti later built the citadel: with these great works, the medieval setting of the "città alta" was complete, with its twisting streets, now so hushed and still. Further great construction came during the Renaissance, under Venetian administration. The first major project of the Venetians was the construction of the "muraine," an enclosure wall that protected both the hilltop town and the low-lying villages, or "borghi" (on the plains, the wall's one-time location is still marked by the name of Porta Nuova). The most remarkable project, however, with the farthest-reaching consequences, was the construction of bastions around Bèrgamo Alta (1560-1623): the two cities were split apart, with the high town held by the agrarian nobility, while the low town, more commercial, was destined to grow greatly. And in the village of Borgo Pignolo, midway between the two, were rows of the palazzi of the trading aristocracy. Bèrgamo remained essentially Lombard in character and in atmosphere but, like all of the hinterland holdings of Venice, the town acquired a Venetian flavor and in turn enriched Venetian civilization. In 1857, under Austrian rule, Bèrgamo was linked to Milan by railroad; the Via Ferdinandea was extended to the train station, establishing the modern-day thoroughfare of the low town (now the Viale Giovanni XXIII and Viale Vittorio Emanuele II). Two years later, on 8 June 1859, Garibaldi, the "libertador" of Italy, entered Bèrgamo with his troops, the Cacciatori delle Alpi. Following the Unification of Italy, it was decided to tear down Bèrgamo's "muraine," or old walls (1900); by that time, urban growth had spread far beyond the enclosure walls.

Bergamo

1:12 000 (1 cm = 120 m)

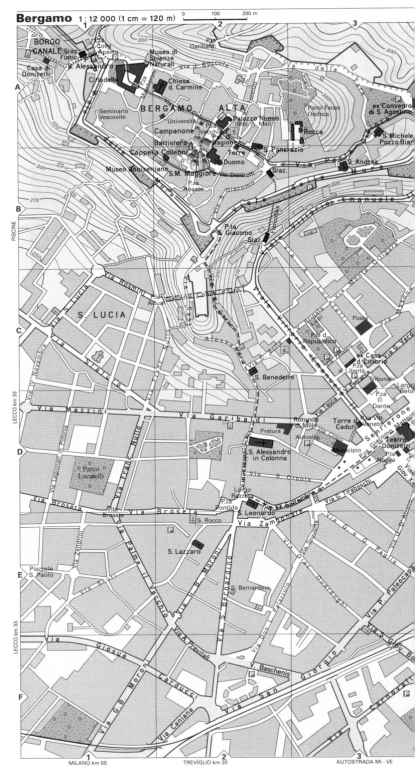

0   100   200 m

1 **2** **3**

BORGO CANALE
Pta Colle Aperto
P
Staz. Funic.
Casa di Donizetti
S. Alessandro
Citadella
Pta Garibaldi
Museo di Scienze Naturali
Via d. Boccola
Via d. della F
300

A
Seminario Vescovile
BERGAMO ALTA
Chiesa d. Carmine
Università
Campanone
P.zza Vecchia
Palazzo Nuovo (Bibl. A. Mai)
Parco Faunà Onobica
ex Convento di S. Agostino
P
Rocca
Battistero
P.zo d. Ragione
Torre
S. Pancrazio
S. Michele Pozzo Bianco
Cappella Colleoni
Duomo
Museo Donizettiano
S.M. Maggiore
Via Donizetti
Staz.
S. Andrea
Mura
Via delle
350
300
275

B
PISCINE
P.zza Rosate
Via Giacomo
300
300
Vittorio
Emanuele
P.ta S. Giacomo
Staz.
Funicolare
250

C
S. LUCIA
Via Rosmini
P.le Alcide
Galleria Conca d'Oro
300
275
Via Alessan
Via d. Botta
Via
Rotonda d. Uff.
Posta
Via G. Verdi
P.le d. Repubblica
ex Casa d. Littorio
P.za d. Libertà
Via
Tribunale
LECCO km 33
Via XX Novembre
Via Statu
Via Garibaldi
Via Mazzini
S. Benedetto
Via Tasca
Largo Belo
P.za Dante

D
Parco Locatelli
Via Tiraquello
Via Nullo
Rotonda d. Mille
Pretura
Autosilo
P
S. Alessandro in Colonna
Torre d. Caduti
P.za Vitt. Veneto
Municipio
Via Crispi
S. Orsola
Sentierone
Via Giacomo Matteotti
Teatro Donizetti
P.ta Nuova
Via Gi

LECCO km 33
Via Broseta
Via Palma il Vecchio
Pta Broseta
Via Broseta
Largo Rezzara
P.za Pontida
S. Leonardo
S. Rocco
Via Zambonate
Via XX Settembre
Via G. Tiraboschi
Via

E
Piazzale S. Paolo
Via Legionari
Via Palma il Vecchio
P
S. Lazzaro
Via B. Moroni
Via Bernardino
S. Bernardino
Via A. Maj
Via Paleocapa
Via P. Paleocapa

F
Via Giosuè
Via G. B. Moroni
Via Carducci
Via Caniana
V. Baschenis
P
Via San Giorgio
Via G. Carnovali
P

1 **2** **3**
MILANO km 50   TREVÍGLIO km 20   AUTOSTRADA MI - VE

152

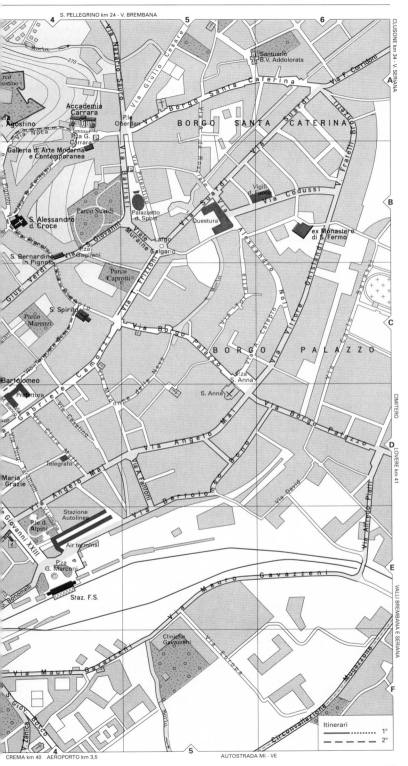

4   5   6

Santuario
B.V. Addolorata

Via T. Corridoni

BORGO   SANTA   CATERINA

Via Giulio Cesare

Via Nazario Sauro

P.le
Oberdan

Accademia
Carrara

Pza G.
Carrara

Galleria d'Arte Moderna
e Contemporanea

S. Agostino

S. Agostino

Via Noca

Via Suardi

Via Fratelli Bronzetti

Vigili
d. Fuoco

Via Codussi

Via Pignolo

Parco Suardi

Palazzetto
d. Sport

Questura

ex Monastero
di S. Fermo

S. Alessandro
d. Croce

Viale Muraine Galgario

Largo

Via Alessandro Noli

S. Bernardino
in Pignolo

Pza
Gagliani

Via Gagliani

Parco
Caprotti

Via Tirizzoni

Via Camozzi

Gtus. Verdi

Via Borgo Palazzo

BORGO   PALAZZO

S. Spirito

Parco
Marenzi

Pza
S. Anna

Via Catebio Noli

Via Libera Tiraboschi

Via Serassi

S. Bartolomeo

Prefettura

Via Gabriele Camozzi

Via Ponte della Neve

Via Borgo Palazzo

S. Anna

Via Bartolomeo Bono

Maria
Grazie

Via Angelo Mai

Via Angelo Mai

Via Alfonso Casatino

Via David

Via Alfredo Piatti

Telegrafo

Via Tasson

Stazione
Autolinee

Via Giovanni XXIII

P.le d.
Alpini

Air terminal

Pza
G. Marconi

Via S. Bonomelli

Staz. F.S.

Via Mauro Gavazzeni

Via Filippo

Cliniche
Gavazzeni

Via Mauro Gavazzeni

S. Giov. Bosco

Via Zanica

Via Magazzeno

Circonvallazione

Itinerari

··········· 1°

--------- 2°

Getting around. For a tour of the city we recommend two routes. You can walk the entire route, or you can use city buses and funicular to cover short stretches of the route. Bèrgamo Alta is closed to motor traffic during holidays.

Bèrgamo Alta

From the modern center of town you climb up to the heart of old Bèrgamo, with its famous monuments and exquisite architecture. After an excursion to the panoramic Colle S. Vigilio and a tour of the secluded and silent Borgo Canale, this route runs along a stretch of the old Venetian walls, with remarkable views.

Piazza Vittorio Veneto (*D3*). This square, with the adjoining Piazza Matteotti, Piazza Dante, and Piazza della Libertà, forms the heart of Bèrgamo Bassa, the lower town. This orderly system of squares, built in the area of the demolished Fiera di S. Alessandro, is a modern piece of urban planning, laid out in the early 20th c. to designs by Marcello Piacentini (1914-34).

Viale Vittorio Emanuele II (*B-C2-4*). This road forms part of the long straight avenue built between 1837 and 1857 with the name of Strada Ferdinandea, linking Bèrgamo Bassa with Bèrgamo Alta, now the chief thoroughfare in the city. Midway, where the road turns beneath the walls, is the lower station of the *funicular* (*B2*) running up to Bèrgamo Alta, built in 1886-87.

Porta S. Agostino (*A4*). Comprising a double curtain wall, this gate dates back to the time when the walled perimeter itself was built (16th c.). The gate takes its name from the nearby former **convent of S. Agostino**, founded at the end of the 13th c. and suppressed in 1797; the *church* of this convent has a late-Gothic sandstone facade and, inside (*closed to the public*), fragments of frescoes, especially from the 14th and 15th c.

Via Porta Dipinta (*A-B2-3*). This street runs steep and winding among palazzi and old houses, going past the 12th-c. Romanesque church of **S. Michele al Pozzo Bianco** (*A3*) (*open by request, tel. 035247651*), renewed in the 15th c. and again later; in the nave and crypt, note the fine frescoes (12th-14th c.): those in the chapel to the left of the presbytery are by Lorenzo Lotto (1525). Further along is the Neo-Classic church of **S. Andrea** (*B3*) with a notable altarpiece* by Moretto in the right-hand chapel. Across the street is the 17th-c. *Palazzo Moroni*, with frescoed interiors and a garden on the hill.

Rocca (*A3*). *Open May-15 Sep., Sat., Sun. and holidays, 10-10; 16 Sep.-Oct., 10-6; Nov.-Feb., 10:30-12:30 and 2-4; Mar.-Apr., 10:30-12:30 and 2-6.* From *Piazza Mercato delle Scarpe* (the upper terminus of the funicular) a narrow lane runs up and off to the right to the 14th-c. fort, with a glacis now used as a park (Parco della Rimembranza); from atop the donjon, a fine view of Bèrgamo, the surrounding plain, and the Alpine foothills (Prealpi).

Via Gòmbito (*A-B2*). Narrow and winding, this road runs up from the Piazza Mercato delle Scarpe to the heart of Bèrgamo Alta. Along this distinctive road you will see a 16th-c. fountain, medieval ruins, old houses, and the 12th-c. *Torre di Gòmbito*. In the nearby Piazza Mercato del Fieno, at the former convent of San Francesco, is the *Museo Storico della Città* (*open Oct.-Mar., Tue.-Sun., 9:30-1 and 2-4; Apr. Sep., Tue.-Fri., 9:30-1 and 2-5:30; Sat. and holidays, 9 7; closed Mon.*), a historical museum which houses finds and mementoes of Bèrgamo from the period of the Cisalpine Republic to the 20th c.

Piazza Vecchia* (*A2*). With the adjoining Piazza del Duomo, this square forms the monumental center of Bèrgamo Alta. Built in 1440-93, it is adorned with an 18th-c. fountain. It is bounded by the late 12th-c. **Palazzo della Ragione***, a venerable town hall with a large ground-floor loggia and three-light Gothic windows; above the 16th-c. balcony stands a lion of St. Mark, a relic of former Venetian rule; adorning the upper hall (*open for exhibits*) are 14th-/15th c. frescoes from churches and palazzi in Bèrgamo. In particular, note the *Three Philosophers*, by Bramante. To the right is the 12th-c. *Torre del Comune* a tower with much-rebuilt crowns. Facing the Palazzo della Ragione is the *Palazzo Nuovo*, designed in 1593 but built in stages; the facade was not completed until 1927-28. This buildings houses the *Biblioteca Civica* (town library), with major collections of manuscripts and antique printed material.

Piazza del Duomo. The square contains, in picturesque asymmetry, the most noted religious monuments of Bèrgamo: from left to right, the Duomo, S. Maria Maggiore, the Cappella Colleoni, and the Battistero, or Baptistery. The **Duomo** (*B2*), with its 19th-c. facade, features paintings by A. Previtali, G.B. Tiepolo, and G.B. Moroni; behind the main altar is an inlaid 18th-c. choir.

S. Maria Maggiore** (*B2*). *Open Oct.-Apr., weekdays, 9-12:30 and 2:30-17; May-Sep., until 6; holidays, 9-1 and 3-6.* This complex Romanesque construction, with no facade, dates from the second half of the 12th c. In the left transept, note the portal with the superb porch by G. da Campione (1353), with columns set on carved lions. Walk around the church toward the left to appreciate its intricate and lively architecture. You should also note another portal by G. da Campione (1367); the Renaissance structure of the Sagrestia Nuova (or New Sacristy, 1491); the apse with archwork and loggia above the stairway; the campanile (14th-16th c.); the right transept with two apsidioles and portal with porch, by G. da Campione (1360); an ancient fountain; and, isolated above the rest, the little 11th-c. church of *S. Croce*.

The **interior,** with gilding and stuccoes, was renovated in the late 16th and 17th c. Along the walls, note the exquisite tapestries, made in Tuscany (16th c.) and Flanders (17th c.). In the right transept, Tree of Life, fresco by followers of Giotto (1347); in the presbytery, six bronze candelabra from 1597, inlaid benches and choir*, in part to designs by Lotto

Bèrgamo: Piazza Vecchia

1522-55). Across from the presbytery: Baroque confessional, carved by A. Fantoni (1704); tomb of the composer Gaetano Donizetti, by V. Vela (1855); 14th-c. monument to Cardinal Longhi, by U. da Campione; tapestry of the Crucifixion (1698), and an immense painting by L. Giordano.

Cappella Colleoni** (*B2*). *Open Mar.-Oct., 9-12:30 and 2-6:30; Nov.-Feb., 9-12 and 2:30-5:30*. Built by Bartolomeo Colleoni, a condottiere who served the Venetian Republic, as his own funerary chapel, the space is a jewel of architecture and decoration, a masterpiece by Amadeo (1476), and a crowning creation of the Lombard Renaissance. All the features that make up the exquisite facade – pilaster strips, portal, windows, rose window, and loggias – blend in the chromatic interplay of the pink-and-white marble facing. *Inside*, amidst the 18th-c. decoration, note the Tomb of Colleoni* (in the facing wall) and the tomb of his daughter Medea*, adorned with statues and reliefs; both are by Amadeo. In the lunettes and the spandrels beneath the cupola and in the votive chapel, are frescoes* by G.B. Tiepolo (1733).

Battistero* (*A-B2*). This small octagonal baptistery, enclosed by a wrought-iron fence and crowned by a gallery with slender columns in red Verona marble, is a 19th-c. reconstruction of the original building by G da Campione (1340). The 14th-c. statues are by the Maestri Campionesi.

Museo Donizettiano (*B2*). *Open Oct.-Mar., Tue.-Fri., 10-1; Sat. and holidays, 10-1 and 2:30-5; Apr.-Sep., Tue.-Sun., 10-1 and 2:30-5*. This museum is located in the *Palazzo della Misericordia* (15th-16th c.), headquarters of the Civico Istituto Musicale, in Via Arena 9. It houses a collection of memorabilia and documents of the Bèrgamo-born composer Gaetano Donizetti. Not far off, in Piazzetta Terzi, is the 16th-c. *Palazzo Terzi* (*B2*), one of the most important private homes in the historical center; the terraced courtyard has a fine view of the plain below. At n. 3 in Via Donizetti is the Renaissance structure of the *Casa dell'Arciprete* by the Bergamasque architect P. Isabello (1520); note the marble facade* with the lovely central window on the ground floor; elegant courtyard, with loggia opening out onto a vast view.

Via Colleoni (*A2*). Setting off from the Piazza Vecchia along the Via Colleoni, you will find at n. 9-11 the *Casa Colleoni* (*open by request, tel. 035244416*), home of the great condottiere, and headquarters of the charitable institution he founded; 15th-c. frescoes. A bit further along is the church of the *Carmine* (*A2*), rebuilt in the 18th c., with canvases from the 16th and 17th c.

Piazza Mascheroni (*A1*). This square features the **Cittadella**, originally built in the 14th c. (note the surviving large tower), which was taken by the Venetian commanders of the occupying forces as their residence. On the eastern side of the square is the entrance to the **Museo di Scienze Naturali Enrico Caffi** (Museum of Natural Science, *open Apr.-Sep., Tue.-Fri., 9-12:30 and 2:30-5:30; Sat., Sun. and holidays, 9-7; Oct.-Mar., closed Sat., Sun. and holidays*), while under the northern portico is the entrance to the **Museo Archeologico Civico** (*open same hours as the Museo Caffi, but Oct.-Mar. it closes at 6*), with archeological material ranging from prehistoric times to the Longobard period. From here, walk under an arch onto the esplanade known as the *Colle Aperto*, with the 16th-c. **Porta S. Alessandro** (*A1*), a gate through which you can walk out to S. Vigilio and the surrounding hills.

Giardino Botanico (*A1, off map*). *Open Apr.-Oct., 9-12; Sat.-Sun., 9-12 and 2-6; closed Tue.* You enter this botanical garden along a stairway that runs from Viale Beltrami, beyond Colle Aperto; it is especially rich in Alpine plants.

Colle S. Vigilio (*A1, off map*). A *funicular* (restored in 1991) runs up to to the top of this hill (elev. 461 m) from the Porta S. Alessandro; from the terminus at the top, you can walk to the summit, with the **Castello** (elev. 497 m), a simple fortress with remains of walls and four round towers. The esplanade, now a public park, affords a fine panoramic view* of Bèrgamo and the surrounding plain. Not far from the Porta S. Alessandro, on the slopes of the hill, extends the distinctive **Borgo Canale**, still rural in flavor. At n. 14 in Via Borgo Canale is the *birthplace of Gaetano Donizetti* (*A1; open Sat.-Sun., 11-6:30; weekdays by request, tel. 035244483*).

Viale delle Mura (*A-B1-3*) runs down from the Colle Aperto along the 16th-c. walls built by the Venetians, ending at the Porta S. Agostino. The **walls*** and the four **gates** that open into each side of the old town offer a vivid image of a 16th-c. citadel; inside the walls and gates is a series of rooms, with internal access roads, garrison halls, and gunports. You can tour them with a guide (*groups of 15 persons, by request, tel. 035251233*). Along this ring of stone, which forms a sort of terrace overlooking Bèrgamo Bassa and the surrounding plains, is a panoramic promenade.

Bèrgamo Bassa

This circuit runs through ancient streets, exploring the part of Bèrgamo that, ever since Roman times, stood here on the plain. Setting out from the Porta S. Agostino for a tour of the nearby Accademia Carrara, the route then reaches the modern heart of Bèrgamo and runs through its most elegant streets; it then ventures into the western sections of Bèrgamo, with small shops and the workshops of fine craftsmen; going up to Bèrgamo Alta, it ends at the Porta S. Giacomo.

Pinacoteca dell'Accademia Carrara ** (*A4*). *Open Apr.-Set., Tue.-Sun., 10-1 and 3-6:45; Oct.-Mar., Tue.-Sun., 9:30-1 and 2:30-5:45.* This art gallery is housed in a Neo-Classic palazzo (1810) which is the headquarters of the Accademia Carrara, founded at the end of the 18th c. by Giacomo Carrara. Currently the gallery, one of Italy's finest in terms of both quality and cultural depth, possesses about 1900 paintings (especially from the Venetian and Lombard schools), as well as major collections of prints and drawings and lesser, but notable, collections of medals, bronzes, sculpture, porcelain, and miniatures. The most outstanding works are on permanent public display in 15 halls on the second floor, arranged by date and historical consequence, from International Gothic to late-18th c. Venetian painting. There are celebrated masterpieces by such painters as B. Bembo, Botticelli, Pisanello, G. Bellini, Mantegna, Carpaccio, Raphael, Bergognone, Lotto, Cariani, Titian, Tintoretto, El Greco, Moroni, Dürer, Clouet, P. Brueghel the Elder, E. Baschenis, Fra' Galgario, Ceruti, Pitocchetto, Longhi, Piazzetta, F. Guardi, Canaletto, Bellotto, and G.B. Tiepolo. On the first floor, in 8 halls that can be toured on request (enquire in the museum offices) are works from the Venetian, Lombard, and Piedmontese areas, between the 15th and 17th c., as well as Baroque works from elsewhere in Europe, and Italian paintings from the 18th to 20th c.

The Galleria d'Arte Moderna e Contemporanea (*B4; open Tue.-Sat., 10-1 and 3-7; Sun., 10-7*) is housed in the buildings overlooking the Accademia Carrara, once part of a 15th-c. convent. On permanent exhibit are the Spajani and Manzù Collections, while several temporary exhibitions offer the visitors insights into 20th-c. Italian art.

Via Pignolo * (*B-C4*). This street descends steeply down from Bèrgamo Alta, and is lined with 16th-/18th-c. palazzi. A short distance from the corner of Via S. Tommaso, near the lovely Piazzetta del Delfino (note the 16th-c. fountain that gives this square its name) is the church of **S. Alessandro della Croce** (*B4*): inside, note the 18th-c. altar* by A. Fantoni and the paintings by Bassano, Lotto, Costa, and A. Previtali. At n. 75 is the *Museo di Arte Sacra Adriano Bernareggi*, a museum of sacred art which includes archaeological finds, paintings, and church furnishings formerly in the Museo Diocesano. At n. 80 is the 15th-c. *Palazzo dei Tasso*. At the corner of Via S. Giovanni stands the church of *S. Bernardino*

in Pignolo, founded in the 16th c. (*B4*); in the apse is an altarpiece by Lotto (1521). At the corner Via T. Tasso is the church of **S. Spirito** (*C4; open weekdays, 7-11:30 and 2-6:30; holidays, 8-12 and 7*), with a rusticated facade; note the bronze sculptures on the facade (1972). Inside, paintings by Lotto, Previtali, and Bergognone.

The **Sentierone** (*D3*), in Piazza Matteotti (see route 1), is a handsome tree-lined avenue, with porticoes on one side, built by the merchants of Bèrgamo 1620 and today a popular promenade and meeting spot. Note the *Teatro Donizetti*, with its late-19th c. facade, and the church of *S. Bartolomeo* (*D4*), the apse of which is an altarpiece* by Lotto (1516) also known as the "Pala Martinengo"; also note the choir with 16th-c. inlay work.

Via S. Alessandro (*B-C-D2*). This road runs down from Bèrgamo Alta, forming the central thoroughfare of one of the old "borghi" that radiate out from the old center; you reach it by following the shopping street, *Via XX Settembre*. Just before the intersection with Via Garibaldi is the church of **S. Alessandro in Colonna** (*D2*), rebuilt in the 18th c., with paintings by Bassano, Romanino, Lotto and Moretto. At the corner of Via Botta is the 16th-c. church of *S. Benedetto* (*C2*), with a terracotta facade and small Renaissance cloister with frescoed lunettes. The last stretch of Via S. Alessandro is like a viaduct, running over large stone arches; this too ends with the monumental *Porta S. Giacomo* (*B2*) the southern gate of Bèrgamo Alta.

Bologna *

Elev. 54 m, pop. 381,161; Emilia-Romagna, regional and provincial capital. When Italy was unified and Luigi Carlo Farini became provisional dictator of the newly joined region (Emilia and Romagna), the political landscape consisted of papal legations and duchies. Parma and Mòdena had been capitals of states until the day before; Ferrara, which had not been an independent state for 350 years, still had the appearance of one (even Ravenna had once – briefly – been the capital of the Roman Empire). The future capital of Emilia-Romagna was nothing more than the headquarters of one of the papal legations. All the same, it did boast a central location, a position that eventually made it one of the crucial centers of communication in Italy. Although it was perhaps then too early to see this clearly, it also had the raw material of its later, startling economic growth. Bologna lies along the Via Emilia, at the base of the Apennines, between the rivers Reno and Sàvena, looking out over an immense fertile plain. The center of Bologna, an elongated polygon stretching along the course of the Via Emilia – an ancient Roman road, once called the Via Æmilia – is medieval in layout. Its architecture dates primarily from the 17th and 18th c., brick-red in color, abounding in porticoes that are exceedingly welcome in the cold winters. This historical center was enclosed within the 14th-c. walled perimeter (the expansion beyond those walls, which now constitutes the bulk of the city, took place at the end of the last century). In the geography of Italian urban attributes, Bologna ranks as "La Dotta" and "La Grassa," literally, "the learned one" and "the fat one." The first adjective refers to the Studio, the university, more than 9 centuries old; the second refers to the rich crops, and the lavish cuisine (swine herding, it is said, dates from Celtic and Longobard times). Together, they describe, in a mysterious synthesis, the cheerfulness, cordiality and human warmth of the people of Bologna.

Historical note. Roman Bononia was founded in 189 B.C. with the settlement of 3000 Latins, in accordance with a plan that called for colonies at regular intervals along the Via Æmilia. But the site had already been inhabited in prehistoric times, and was subsequently settled by Etruscans and by the Boii Gauls. Outside of the perimeter of the Roman city, of which very little survives, Bologna expanded mainly east and west in the Middle Ages. In the preceding centuries, however, Bologna had other, intermediate rings of walls. In ancient times and the high Middle Ages, the city shrank to half its previous size, and the so-called "selenite walls" (named after the variety of gypsum used in their construction) enclosed, in the SE corner of town, the remaining population. Shortly after the year 1000, Bologna was developing one of the first Communal governments in northern Italy. The city began to expand again, occupying again the ancient section outside of the selenite walls; at the end of the 11th c., the Studio was already operating. It is conventially agreed that this nucleus of Bologna's great and venerable university was founded in 1088; in 1116 the privileges conceded by the Holy Roman Emperor Henry V also marked the formal foundation of the Commune; and in the second half of the 12th c. it became necessary to build a new walled perimeter that doubled the surface area of Bologna. When these new walls – called the Mura dei Torresotti – were completed in 1192, Bologna was about to enter the most glorious century of its history, the 13th c. While Bologna came to dominate all of Emilia and Romagna, and after Bolognese soldiers captured the son of the Holy Roman Emperor Frederick II – Enzo, king of Sardinia – at the battle of Fossalta in 1249, construction was proceeding apace. Towers were built, streets were widened, a square was built around the two great Asinelli and Garisenda towers, the church of S. Francesco was built, Nicola Pisano was commissioned to create the Arca di S. Domenico, and Piazza Maggiore was expanded, with the construction of, first, the Vecchio Palazzo Comunale (literally, old town hall), on the site of the earlier Palazzo del Podestà, and then

of the new town hall, known as the Palazzo di Re Enzo. These were great years for the Commune, the first government in Italy to free the serfs, with a law passed in 1256. By 1300, Bologna had a population of 50,000, and was one of the ten largest cities in Europe. In order to bring the "borghi," or districts, that had sprung up outside the walls, into the city, a new walled perimeter was begun – the last – giving the city a six-sided plan, broader than long. These walls were barely finished in 1374, a clear sign of the economic stagnation and political weakness that were afflicting Bologna by this time: the conflict between Guelphs and Ghibellines, in fact, led to the fall of Republican government and the establishment of seigneurial rule, first under the Pepoli. It later led to papal governments, headed by pontifical legates such as Bertrando del Poggetto and Gil Albornoz. Certainly, in the 14th c., Bologna built some new palazzi – Palazzo d'Accursio, Palazzo Pepoli in Via Castiglione, and in Piazza Maggiore the church of S. Petronio was built, the last expression of the power of the Commune, opposing that of the Cathedral – but the enormous energy of the 13th c. was gone. The city was unable to make the leap to become a regional capital, and it was increasingly hobbled by the custodianship of Rome. In the 15th c. following religious conflict of all sorts (there were even two antipopes reigning in Bologna at one point), the city fell under the rule of the House of Bentivoglio, a dynasty that collapsed at the beginning of the 16th c., along with the palazzo of the same name, under the blows of popular revolt. In 1506 the army of Pope Julius II entered Bologna, and from 1513 on the city was a permanent part of the Papal State. From then on the city was no longer a major player on the stage of history, and until the French Revolution the Bolognese did little more than feast, entertain, create art, stage performances, and hold carnivals. Bologna under the pontiff, smaller though it may have been, witnessed considerable changes in its layout and structure during the 17th c.: the development of Strada Maggiore, the construction of the Archiginnasio with the Portico del Pavaglione and the opening of the new Piazza del Nettuno. In the centuries that followed, there were fewer significant changes: at the end of the 17th c. the rubble of the oft-destroyed Castello di Galliera, known as the Montagnola, was transformed into a public garden; in 1763, the new Teatro Comunale was built by Giovanni Bibbiena, upon another pile of historical rubble, that of Palazzo Bentivoglio. A considerable stimulus was given to higher studies during the Napoleonic era: the campus of the University was moved (1803) from the Archiginnasio to Palazzo Poggi, which formerly housed the Istituto delle Scienze, or institute of sciences; this encouraged the formation in NE Bologna of a university neighborhood, which also saw the establishment of the Accademia di Belle Arti, or Academy of Fine Arts, and the Orto Botanico and Orto Agrario, botanical and agrarian gardens. It was not until the 19th c., however, after Bologna was annexed by the King-

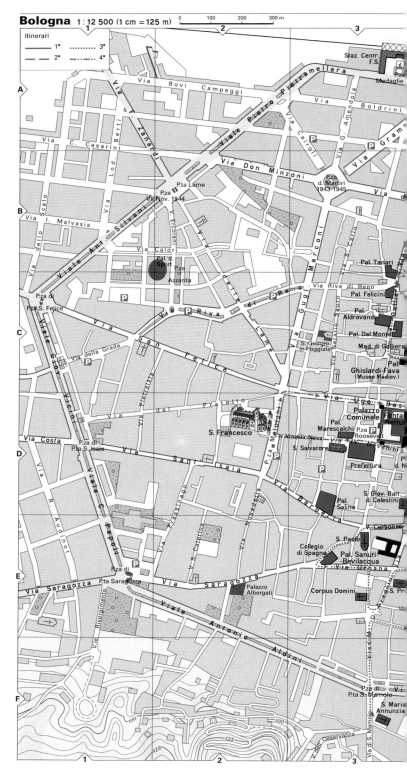

Bologna

1 : 12 500 (1 cm = 125 m)

0   100   200   300 m

Itinerari

——— 1°   ·········· 3°

– – – 2°   –··–··– 4°

Staz. Centr. F.S.

P.za Medaglie

Via Bovi Campeggi

Viale Pietro Pietramellara

Via G. Amendola

Via Boldrini

Via Gram

Via C. Casarini

Via G. Cairoli

P

Via Don Minzoni

Via T. Zanardi

Via Lod. Berti

Via dello Scalo

Via I. Malvasia

P.ta Lame

P.za VII Nov. 1944

P.za d. Martiri 1943-1945

Via

Viale Ant. Silvani

Via Ercolani

Via Calori

Pal. d. Sport

P.za Azzarita

Via Marconi

Pal. Tanari

Via Riva di Reno

Pal. Felicini

P.za di P.ta S. Felice

P

Via Guglia

Pal. Aldrovandi

Via Riva

Via del Pratello

P

Via San Felice

Via della Grada

Via dello Scalo

Via delle Lame

S. Giorgio in Poggiale

Pal. Dal Monte

Mad. di Galliera

Pal. Ghislardi-Fava (Museo Mediev.)

Via Gray.

P

Via Vicini

Via del Pratello

Via Ugo Bassi

Palazzo Comunale

Fontana Nettuno

Via Costa

Via dal Pratello

S. Francesco

Pal. Marescalchi

P

Via Rio Nova

P.za di P.ta S. Isaia

Via San Isaia

Via Marchi

Via IV Novembre

P.za P

Via Roosevelt

S. Salvatore

Prefettura

Via di N

Via R. Audinot

Via Barberia

Pal. Salina

S. Giov. Batt. d. Celestini

Via Pepoli

Via del Pratello

Via Porta Nova

V. Carbonesi

S. Paolo

Collegio di Spagne

Pal. Sanuti-Bevilacqua

Via Urbana

P.za di P.ta Saragozza

Via Saragozza

Via Saragozza

Palazzo Albergati

Corpus Domini

S. Pro

Via Risorgimento

Viale C. Pepoli

Viale Antonio Aldini

Via di S. Mamolo

P.za di P.ta S. Mamolo

S. Maria Annunzia

Osservanza

100

125

125

100

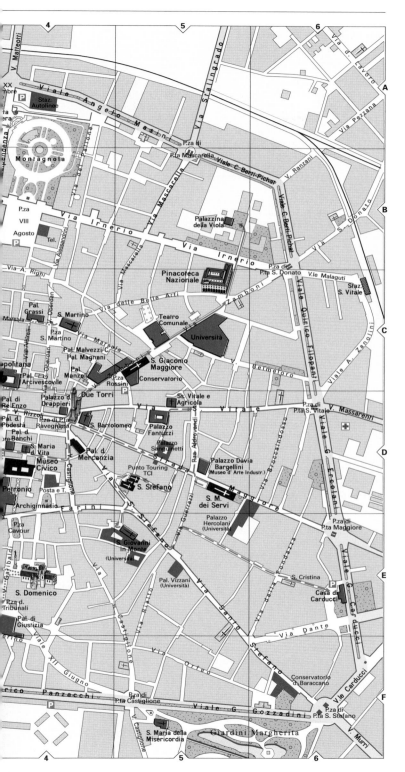

dom of Italy, that the plan of the city again underwent modifications of considerable importance: Piazza Cavour and Via Garibaldi were opened out to the south of S. Petronio, and Via dell'Indipendenza was built to link the center with the train station; at the foot of the hill the Giardini Margherita were built. Later, toward the end of the century, Via Irnerio and Via Dante were laid out; in the center, Via Rizzoli was completed. In 1902 the city walls were demolished, and between WWI and WWII Via Ugo Bassi was widened, and Via Marconi opened. In the 1960s and 1970s, when the population of Bologna nearly tripled in comparison with the early decades of the century (172,806 in 1911, 493,933 in 1973, the highest population to date), the development of the suburbs and outskirts was sufficiently great to outstrip the historic city itself in size and population, and the so-called "Fiera District," with office buildings and conference and trade fair facilities, was built near the ring road.

Piazza Maggiore, the Towers, the University

Three fundamental "images" of Bologna are found along this first tour, which goes NE: the Piazza Maggiore, long-time heart of the town; the remarkable pair of red leaning towers; and Palazzo Poggi, nucleus of the Studio, or university, which dates from the mid-11th c., with Paris, one of the two oldest in Europe and the world.

Piazza Maggiore* (*D3-4*). This square has been the monumental center of Bologna since the early-13th c., with the church of S. Petronio, facing the Palazzo del Podestà, and the Palazzo Comunale. To the right of S. Petronio, on the southern edge of the square, is the 14th-c. *Palazzo dei Notai* (III, *B1*); to the east is the porticoed *Palazzo dei Banchi* (III, *B2*), built by Vignola (1565-68), where bankers once did business.

S. Petronio** (*D4*). Begun in 1390 but finished only in 1659, this church is a splendid example of Italian Gothic. Of the three portals, the central one (Porta Magna) is decorated with **statues**** by the sculptor Jacopo della Quercia (1425-38), masterpieces of the early Renaissance. Along the right side stands the campanile, built in 1481-92.

The Gothic **interior**, with a nave and two aisles, features remarkable artwork. Among the artists worthiest of note: Garelli, Aspertini, Costa, Vignola, Calvaert, Parmigianino, Francia, G. da Modena, and Torreggiani. Also worthy of note are the various frescoes, stained glass windows, marble fretwork screens, terracotta statues, inlaid choir, majolica floors, wrought-iron gates, and vast floor sundial. One of the organs date from 1470-75, one of the oldest in Italy. To the left of the *presbytery* is the entrance to the *Museo di S. Petronio* (*open Mon.-Sat., 9:30-12*). Among the museum collections are plans for the church's facade, liturgical furnishing, jewelry (13th-18th c.), ivory, semiprecious stones, and illuminated choir-books from the 15th-16th c.

Palazzo del Podestà (*D4*). *Open only for exhibi-*

tions. Built from 1485 on, possibly after a model A. Fieravanti, on the ancient site of city governmer this building has a ground-floor portico where tw roads intersect beneath a vault; at the four corner are terracotta statues by A. Lombardi (1525) c picting the town's patron saints. Atop the palazzo the *Torre dell'Arengo* (1212).

Palazzo Comunale* (*D3*). Also known as *Palaz d'Accursio*, it comprises two separate buildings: th one on the left, porticoed with Gothic arches ar with a tower, dates from the 13th c.; the one on th right, with terracotta mullioned windows, dates fro 1428. In the middle, portal by G. Alessi (1555); on th balcony above it, a bronze statue of Pope Grego XIII (1580). Still higher, on the left, a terracotta st ue of the Virgin and Child*, by N. dell'Arca (147 From the porticoed courtyard (1425-1508), alon great staircase attributed to Bramante (1507), ye climb to the first floor, where you can tour the gre *Sala d'Ercole*, or Hall of Hercules (note the ter cotta statue of Hercules by A. Lombardi and th fresco* by Francia); on the second floor are th *Sala Farnese* (noteworthy frescoes) and the *Salo* (marble portal and stucco frieze by Alessi). On th floor are the **Collezioni Comunali d'Arte** (*op Tue.-Sat., 9-6:30; Sun., 10-6:30*) with paintings of th Bolognese school, from the 13th to the 19th Among the noteworthy artists are Vitale da Bologr Francia, and L. Carracci. Also, miniatures, majolic glassware. The *Museo "Giorgio Morandi"* (*open Tu Sun., 10-6*) has many works by the noted Bolognes modern painter.

Piazza del Nettuno (*D3*). This square was built 1564 between the right wing of the Palazzo C munale and the 13th-c. *Palazzo di Re Enzo*, restor in the early 20th c. This latter building was th "palatium novum" of the city magistrates, name after the son of Frederick II, who was taken pr

Bologna: Fontana del Nettuno

...er in the Battle of Fossalta (1249) and who fi-
...lly died here in 1272; inside, note the Salone del
...ecento, a majestic hall by A. di Vincenzo (1386).

...ntana del Nettuno** (*D3*). This fountain is
...the finest of the 16th c.; set on a base by T. Lau-
...ti, with bronze statues by Giambologna: Neptune,
...ith his trident, is calming the waves, on which put-
...dolphins, and four mermaids are seen (1563-66).

...a Rizzoli (*D4*). One of the main streets of Bolo-
...na, a place to promenade and to meet in the var-
...us café's (in the passage between Piazza del Net-
...no and this street, note the few surviving fragments
... ancient Roman "Bononia"). This street ends in
...azza di Porta Ravegnana* (III, *A-B3*), with the two
...aning towers and the porticoed side of the church
... S. Bartolomeo (see below); n. 1 is the *Casa dei
...rappieri*, an elegant Renaissance building (1496).

...rri Pendenti* (*D4*). These leaning towers are
...hat survive of a medieval center that once bristled
...ith towers; they are one of Bologna's hallmarks.
...he taller of the two (97.2 m) is the **Torre degli
...sinelli** (*open winter, 9-5; summer, 9-6*), built in ear-
...12th c., and leaning west. A staircase of 498 steps
...ads to the top, which offers a fine view*. The
...rre Garisenda (*closed to the public*), probably
...ilt at the same time, is 48.16 m tall, and leans even
...ore sharply; on a plaque are lines by Dante de-
...ribing it.

...a Zamboni (II, *C4-6*). This porticoed street is lined
...ith magnificent 16th/18th-c. palazzi. *Palazzo Man-
...li* (*C4*; facade dating from 1760); at n. 13, a palaz-
... dating from 1560; at n. 20, *Palazzo Magnani* (*C4*
... by D. Tibaldi (1587), with the main hall (*open
...t., 9-12; for groups, by request, tel. 0516408220*)
...ecorated with frescoes by the Carracci (1590-92);
...n. 22, the 16th-c. *Palazzo Malvezzi Campeggi*, now
...art of the university. At n. 30 is the 18th-c. *Teatro
...omunale* (*C5*), designed by A. Bibiena and later
...novated.

... Giacomo Maggiore* (*C5*). Founded in 1267.
...he facade, portal flanked by burial niches, and
...ose are part of the Gothic structure (13th-14th-c.).
...long the left side is a 15th-c. portico* with a no-
...ble terracotta frieze. In the huge *interior*, the Re-
...aissance style prevails. Artwork by I. da Imola, L.
...arracci, P.Tibaldi, P.Veneziano, J. di Paolo, S. dei Cro-
...fissi, and J. della Quercia. Note the *Cappella Ben-
...voglio***, a chapel consecrated in 1486, with fres-
...oes by Costa and a paintings* by Francia (1494
...a.). Beneath the portico on the left side of the
...hurch, at n. 15, is the entrance to the **Oratorio di
...Cecilia** (*open by request, enquire at the sacristy
... S. Giacomo*), an oratory with a remarkable series
... frescoes* by Francia, Costa, and others (1506).

...onservatorio di Musica G.B. Martini (*C5*). Lo-
...ated in a former convent, this conservatory stands
... Piazza Rossini, to the right of the church of S.
...iacomo; among its students and professors were
...ossini, Donizetti, Martucci, and Busoni (note stair-
...ase by A.Torreggiani, 1752). One wing of the build-
...g houses the *Civico Museo Bibliografico Musicale
...pen 9-1; closed Sun., Aug., Christmas and Easter

holidays), one of the most important musical collections in existence.

Università (*C5*). Bologna's famous university is
largely clustered around a "campus" running along
Via Zamboni, though it is also scattered throughout
the city and region. **Palazzo Poggi**, at n. 31 and 33
in Via Zamboni, was built in 1549, in part by P.Tibal-
di, renovated in the 18th c., and made part of the
Studio, or University, in 1803; it now houses museums, administrative offices, and university depart-
ments. At n. 31 is the entrance to the *Accademia
delle Scienze* (16th-c. frescoes by P.Tibaldi in the
two ground-floor halls), or Academy of Science. At
n. 33 you will find the main entrance, leading to a
handsome courtyard, in Roman Mannerist style; the
Aula Carducci, a hall named after Giosuè Carducci,
poet and 1906 Nobel laureate, who lectured here;
the *Specola** (one of 18th-c. Europe's leading ob-
servatories); and various museums (*all the museums are open Mon.-Fri., 8:30-5:30; Sat.-Sun., 9-6:30*):
Museo di Astronomia, devoted to astronomy; *Museo
delle Navi*, with a collection of 17th- and 18th-c.
model ships; *Museo Ostetrico G.A. Galli*, on the history of obstetrics; *Museo d'Architettura Militare*, per-
taining to military architecture; *Museo Indiano*, with
collections of Indian history. At n. 35 in Via Zamboni is the entrance to the *Biblioteca Universitaria*,
a splendid library with collections of old books, illuminated manuscripts, autograph manuscripts, and
ancient papyri; the reading room has walnut book-
cases; many halls are decorated with painted
friezes. At n. 63 is the *Museo di Geologia e Paleontologia G. Cappellini* (*open Mon.-Sat., 9-12:30; closed
holidays, 15-30 June, Aug.*), one of the largest Italian
museums of geology and paleontology.

Pinacoteca Nazionale** (*C5*). *Open Tue.-Sat., 10-
6; closed Sun.-Mon. and holidays.* Set in the 17th-c.
Palazzo di S. Ignazio, formerly the art gallery of the
Accademia di Belle Arti – which merged with the
18th-c. donations of F. Zambeccari and the marchese G. Zambeccari with the artworks taken from religious institutions following their suppression from
1794 on – this collection mirrors the artistic history of Bologna (the masterpieces by painters from
other parts of Italy were executed for local churches). It documents the high points of the Bolognese
school, including works by Vitale da Bologna, influenced by Giotto, the eclectic Carracci, the
Baroque Guido Reni and Guercino. Among the earliest artists are a follower of Giunta Pisano, the Pseu-
do Jacopino di Francesco, Giotto, Vitale da Bologna,
Simone dei Crocifissi, L. di Dalmasio, J. di Paolo,
G. da Modena. The *Renaissance section* includes:
A. and B. Vivarini, F. del Cossa, L. Costa, Perugino,
Cima da Conegliano, Francia, Aspertini, Raphael,
Parmigianino, N. dell'Abate, L. Carracci, Agostino Carracci, Annibale Carracci. In the *Baroque section* are
works by Reni, Albani, Domenichino, Guercino, L.
Pasinelli, and Crespi. In the same building is the *Ac-
cademia di Belle Arti*, with several different schools
teaching the visual arts from many standpoints.

Palazzina della Viola (*B5*). In Via Filippo Re, this

"pleasure house" was built by A. Bentivoglio in 1497, and has frescoes by I. da Imola on the walls of the exterior loggias.

Strada Maggiore, S. Maria dei Servi, S. Stefano

The monuments you will discover in this second walk – the church of Ss. Vitale e Agricola, Bologna's first martyrs, possibly located on the site of their execution; a compact group of ancient religious buildings, named after the early martyr St. Stephen, believed to be on the site of the Roman temple of Isis; the secluded church of S. Giovanni in Monte; the Gothic S. Maria dei Servi with Cimabue's Maestà, to mention only the ancient churches – all line the Strada Maggiore, which, in Bologna under papal rule, was the start of the long road to the cathedral of S. Pietro, and corresponded to the Via Æmilia, to the east of Roman "Bononia."

S. Maria della Vita (*D4*). This Baroque sanctuary (1687-90), at n. 10 in Via Clavature, has a superb terracotta group* by N. dell'Arca (1463). In the adjacent *oratory*, another such group by A. Lombardi (1522).

Piazza della Mercanzia (*D4*). This was once a major intersection outside Bologna's earliest walls; it is overlooked by the Palazzo della Mercanzia, and has old houses on the eastern side (n. 1 dates from the 16th c., n. 2 and 3 are Gothic).

Palazzo della Mercanzia* (*D4*). This building, with a late Gothic facade in brick and Istrian stone, was once a customs office where merchandise was unloaded; it was begun in 1384 and has been repeatedly renovated.

Strada Maggiore (*D-E4-6*). Originally part of the ancient Roman Via Æmilia, this porticoed street runs from Piazza di Porta Ravegnana to Porta Maggiore. At the beginning, note the 17th-c. church of **S. Bartolomeo** (*D4*) with paintings by Albani (1632) and Reni (1632).

Ss. Vitale e Agricola (*D5*). At n. 44 in Via S. Vitale, this church was built in the 11th c. (original crypt), and restored more than once; inside are the painted wax group by A. Piò, and paintings by G. Francia and Bagnacavallo. Facing the church, at n. 23, note the facade of *Palazzo Fantuzzi* by A. da Formigine (1517-33).

Palazzo Bargellini (*D5*). This impressive 17th-c. building, at n. 44 in Strada Maggiore, houses the *Museo Civico d'Arte Industriale e Galleria Civica Davia Bargellini* (*open 9-2; Sun. 9-1; closed Mon.*). The collections – of industrial art and fine paintings – occupy seven halls, and include fine furniture, sacred objects, ceramics, leather objects, miniatures, embroideries, crèches, an 18th-c. Venetian marionette theater, and paintings by V. da Bologna, S. dei Crocifissi, Aspertini, Magnasco, and Crespi.

S. Maria dei Servi* (*D5*). This Gothic church, begun in 1346, enlarged in the same century, and completed in the early 16th c., features an elegant quadriporticum*; the lively apse and the campanile form

a lovely composition. The late-Gothic *interior* h
Baroque furnishings. Among the noteworthy artwo
seen here, a fragment of a fresco attributed to L.
Dalmasio, a 16th-c. altar by G. A. Montorsoli, a woo
en inlaid choir from 1450, works by G. M. Crespi, V.
Bologna, L. di Dalmasio, V. Onofri, G.G. and A. Gra
A. Tiarini, I. da Imola, the Bagnacavallo, F. Albani, an
A. Piò. The most outstanding work is the **Maestà**
by Cimabue, to be seen in the third chapel.

Piazzola di S. Stefano (*D4-5*). Aside from t
buildings that make up S. Stefano (see below),
this square are the 16th-c. *Palazzo Bolognini* (n.
11), by Formigine, the *Case Tacconi*, with 15th/16
c. facades (n. 15-21), and another *Palazzo Bolog
ni* (n. 18), built (1451-55) by P. di Lapo Portigia
blending classicism with local Gothic.

S. Stefano* (*D5*). S. Stefano is the name of a co
plex of medieval churches which, from the right, a
the 10th-c. church of the *Crocifisso*; the church of t
S. Sepolcro (possibly dating from the 5th c., but
built in the 11th and 12th c., it contains the tomb
St. Petronius, the 5th-c. bishop of Bologna, with 13
/14th-c. reliefs); and the church of *Ss. Vitale e Ag
cola*, Romanesque in style. From the church of t
S. Sepolcro you enter the 12th-c. *courtyard of the
lato*, with an 8th-c. basin in the center. From he
you continue to the 13th-c. *Trinità* church, with a 14
c. wooden Adoration of the Magi, and, to the right,
into the 11th/12th-c. *Benedictine cloister**. From t
loggia of the cloister you enter a small *Muse
(*open 9-12 and 3:30-6*), including paintings of t
14th c. Bolognese school (A. de' Bartoli, S. dei Cro
fissi, and L. di Dalmasio) and 17th c. sculptures
G. di Balduccio (14th c.), and gold reliquaries.

Via S. Stefano (*D-E4-5*). Lined by 16th- to 18th
houses, this is a fascinating street of old Bologna
runs from Piazza di Porta Ravegnana to Porta S. S
fano; at its start is the 30-m.-tall 12th-c. *Torre Albe
ci* (n. 4). This route goes only from the church of
Stefano to the intersection with Via Guerrazzi.

S. Giovanni in Monte (*E5*). A ramp leads up
this church from Via S. Stefano. The church da
back to 1045, but has been extensively renovate
and has a Venetian-style facade dating from 14
note the terracotta eagle by N. dell'Arca (148
above the lunette. The *interior* has a Gothic a
pearance. Frescoes by G. Francia, on pillars. On t
facade, two stained glass windows*, built to desig
by F. del Cossa. Note several works by L. Costa a
Guercino, and, in the apse, the inlaid choir (152
The small parish *museum* includes reliquaries a
liturgical furnishings.

Casa di Giosuè Carducci (*E6*). At n. 5 on Piaz
Carducci is the house where the Nobel-prize w
ning poet lived from 1890 until his death in 19
(rooms and library are closed for restoration). T
ground floor houses the *Museo Civico del Risor
mento* (*open Tue.-Sun., 9-1; Thu. until 5; closed Mo
6-26 Aug.*), focusing on the role of Emilia-Romag
in the period when Italy fought for its unity. To t
right of the house, the intricate monument to C
ducci by Leonardo Bistolfi (1924-28).

The Archiginnasio, S. Domenico

The Spanish saint, Domingo de Guzmán, founder of the Dominican Order, died in Bologna in 1221. His church, S. Domenico, dominates the district to the south of Piazza Maggiore, through which this route runs. The saint's tomb is a masterpiece of Italian sculpture: N. Pisano began it, and in the 15th c. the great sculptor N. dell'Arca completed it. A few small statues are by the young Michelangelo.

Via Archiginnasio (*D4*). From Piazza Maggiore this street runs along the east side of S. Petronio; on the opposite side is the Portico del Pavaglione, a popular Bolognese promenade.

Museo Civico Archeologico* (*D4*). *Open Tue.-Sat., 9:30-6:30; Sun., 10-6:30.* This major archeological museum has remarkable collections, especially of prehistoric, Villanovan, and Etruscan origin. Many items are famous: prehistoric material from the cave of Farneto; the Villanovan Benacci askos*; the furnishings of the Tomba degli Ori*; tomb furnishings from the late 7th c.; a bronze situla from the 6th c., with fine reliefs; two Villanovan tomb furnishings from Verucchio, with a throne* with scenes of ceremonies and daily life; the Zannoni stone,* with the oldest known depiction of a trip to the Underworld; Etruscan bronzes from the votive centers of Monteguragazza and Monte Capra. Also noteworthy are the many Greek vases found in Etruscan tombs: the Aureli krater* with a scene of Amazons battling; a krater with scenes of the destruction of Troy*; another krater with the myth of Atalanta and Hippomenes*. In the Greek section: the bust of Palagi*, a copy from Augustan times of the long-lost original by Phidias; 5th-c. B.C. Attic bas-relief*. Lastly are the Roman finds and lapidary section (in the atrium and courtyard) and Egyptian antiquities, with the tomb of Horemheb (1332-1323 B.C.).

Archiginnasio (*D4*). This building, erected in 1563 by A. Morandi, houses the *Biblioteca Comunale*, or town library. In the porticoed courtyard, are heraldic crests of the university, which was located here until 1803; it also houses the former church of *S. Maria dei Bulgari* with frescoes by B. Cesi and D. Calvaert. Upstairs is the 17th-c. *Teatro Anatomico* (*open 9-1; closed Sun.*), damaged by bombs in 1944, and the *Sala dello Stabat Mater* (*open by request to the custodian*), a hall where law was once taught.

Corte de' Galluzzi (*D3*). A passageway from Piazza Galvani, facing the Archiginnasio, leads to this profoundly medieval courtyard, with a tower (1257). Another passageway leads to Via D'Azeglio and the 16th-c. church of *S. Giovanni Battista dei Celestini* (*D3*), with works by G. Mazza and M. Franceschini.

S. Paolo (*C1*). This 17th-c. church, with sandstone and brick facade, stands in Via Carbonesi. Inside, paintings by L. Carracci (1616) and Guercino, and a marble group by A. Algardi.

Collegio di Spagna (*E3*). Built in the 14th c. by Gattapone for the Spanish students of the university, the college was restored in 1904. A portico leads to the square courtyard, with frescoes by the young Annibale Carracci; note the Gothic church of *S. Clemente*, with a polyptych* by M. Zoppo.

Corpus Domini (*E3*). This former convent stands in Via Tagliapietre; the church was built in the 15th c. and has a terracotta portal by S. di Bartolomeo. Inside are fragments of 17th-c. decoration by M. Franceschini, paintings by L. Carracci and M. Franceschini, statues by G. Mazza. The Bolognese physiologist L. Galvani is buried here.

S. Procolo (*E3*). This church has three fine 16th-c. cloisters; across the street is the 16th-c. *Portico dei Bastardini*, part of an ancient orphanage.

Palazzo Sanuti-Bevilacqua* (*E3*). Built between 1474 and 1482, in sandstone, with rustication, this is said to be the finest piece of early-Renaissance architecture in Bologna. Note the elegant porticoed courtyard.

Piazza S. Domenico (*E4*). Oddly shaped, this square features two 17th-c. votive columns and the tombs of two noted jurists – E. Foscherari, d. 1289, and R. de' Passeggeri, d. 1300; the latter is celebrated for having held his own, by correspondence, with Frederick II, who was threatening to raze Bologna.

S. Domenico** (*E4*). This church was built in 1228-38 and was renovated, attaining its present appearance, in 1728-32 (C.F. Dotti). To the left of the restored 13th-c. facade juts the Cappella Ghisilardi, a chapel designed by B. Peruzzi (1530-35). **Inside**, in the *right aisle*, is the *Cappella di S. Domenico** (1597-1605), with frescoes by G. Reni, the **Arca di S. Domenico****, or tomb of St. Dominic, by N. Pisano, A. di Cambio, P. di Lapo, and Fra' Gugliemo (1265-67); the frieze* is by N. dell'Arca (1473); the statues of angel* and saints* are by Michelangelo (1494). Elsewhere in the church are works by J. Roseto (1383), Guercino (1662), F. Lippi (1501), B. Cesi (1595), G. Pisano (1250), Pepoli, Terribilia (1551), D. Calvaert, L. Carracci, Reni, Albani, and Ferrucci. You can reach the **Museo di S. Domenico** through the sacristy at the end of the right aisle (*open Mon.-Fri., 10-12*): terracotta sculpture* by N. dell'Arca (1474) and paintings by L. di Dalmasio and L. Carracci, and other precious objects. From here, you can also enter the 14th-c. *Chiostro dei Morti*, or Cloister of the Dead; also note the campanile (1336).

Piazza dei Tribunali (*E4*). This square is bounded by the Palazzo di Giustizia, or hall of justice, thought to have been designed by Palladio (1582). From the courtyard, the late-17th-c. staircase leads up to halls, with decorations by M. Franceschini.

S. Maria Annunziata (*F3*). This church, located in Via di S. Mamolo, was built in the late-15th c., and has a handsome portico; fresco by B. Pupini (1524).

S. Francesco, the Metropolitana, the Montagnola

Near the apse of the church of S. Francesco stand the tombs of Accursio, Odofredo and Rolandino de' Romanzi, illustrious medieval jurists of the University. The powerful French Gothic of the immense church strongly flavors the neighborhood west of Piazza Maggiore. From this first leg of the route, you cross the 19th-c. porticoed avenue of Via Indipendenza, and then venture northward to explore a part of Bologna that mingles austere medieval architecture with opulent homes of Bologna's "senatorial" class. This tour ends with the Montagnola, the hilltop public park formed by the ruins of the Castello di Galliera, repeatedly razed and rebuilt.

Via IV Novembre (*D3*). Beginning from Piazza Maggiore along the left side of the Palazzo Comunale, this street goes past the *Prefettura* (*D3*; 1603), *Palazzo Marescalchi* (n. 5; 1613), and along the side of the 17th-c. church of **S. Salvatore** (*D3*), with the tomb of the artist Guercino and paintings by the Mastelletta, S. dei Crocifissi, V. da Bologna, C. Bononi, and I. da Imola. You then continue along *Via Porta Nuova*, through the 12th-c. gate of the medieval walls.

Piazza Malpighi (*D2*). This square features the apse with radial chapels and flying buttresses and the two bell towers of S. Francesco, the three *tombs of the Glossatori* (13th-c. scholars of jurisprudence), and the Colonna dell'Immacolata, a column with a copper statue by G. Reni (1638).

S. Francesco★★ (*D2*). This church was built between 1236 and 1263, restored in the late-19th c., and rebuilt after WWII. The lower campanile dates from 1260; the other one, by A. di Vincenzo, from 1402. The *interior* shows clear French Gothic influence: on the main altar, note the elegant Gothic marble altarpiece★ by P.P. dalle Masegne (1392). Along the walls, note the Renaissance Albergati tombs, one by F. Ferrucci (15th c.), and the tomb of Pope Alexander V, by N. Lamberti (1424) and S. di Bartolomeo (1482). The late-14th-c. *sacristy* is by A. di Vincenzo. In the convent is the late-14th-c. *Chiostro dei Morti*, or Cloister of the Dead (view of the two bell towers), with tombs of the chancellors of the University; also, the *Chiostro Grande* (*entrance in Piazza Malpighi; 1460-1571*), with a double loggia.

Via Ugo Bassi (*D3*). This lively road leads from Piazza Malpighi to the center of Bologna, running alongside the Palazzo Comunale (fountain by T. Laureti; 1565). In the distance, you see the two towers; on your right, the Piazza del Nettuno.

Via dell'Indipendenza (*C3-A4*). This long porticoed street was created in the late 19th c. to link the center of Bologna with the railway station. The suggested route runs along it for brief stretches. Note the 16th-c. *Palazzo Scappi* (n. 3-5), with 13th-c. tower (39 m tall); on the left, the beflowered *Casa Majani* (n. 4; 1908).

Metropolitana★ (*C4*). Bologna's Cathedral, dedicated to St. Peter, was given its present appearance by reconstruction begun in 1605. The exceedingly tall 18th-c. facade, adorned with marble, is by A. Torreggiani; note the Romanesque campanile, with a 15th-c. pinnacle. *Inside* are two holy-water stoups set on carved Romanesque lions, prior to the renovation, and four little tribunes by A. Torreggiani, above the lesser arches of the nave. The presbytery was rebuilt by D. Tibaldi (1575) on the ancient crypt; in

the lunette is a painting★ by L. Carracci (1618-19). In the Romanesque *crypt*, are a 14th-c. wooden group and 16th-c. terracotta group by A. Lombardi.

Via Altabella (*C4*). Beginning along the right side of the Cathedral (note the bell tower) this road goes past the *Torre Altabella* (a 12th-c. tower, on the right, 60 m tall) and the *Palazzo Arcivescovile* by D. Tibaldi (1575; view of the apse of the Metropolitana). If you then follow Via S. Alò, Via Albiroli, and Via Marsala, you will pass through an old and fascinating **district★**, between the Metropolitana and S. Martino, with medieval houses and towers. In Via S. Alò note the *Torre Prendiparte* (a 12th-c. tower, 59 m tall); in Via Albiroli are the medieval *tower-house of the Guidozagni* (at n. 3) and the 16th-c. *Palazzo Bocchi* (at n. 16, corner of Via Bocchi); at n. 12 in Via Marsala *Palazzo Grassi*, with 13th-c. wooden structures.

S. Martino (*C4*). This church was built in 1227 and renovated in later centuries; 19th-c. facade and Gothic interior, where you will see paintings from the 14th to the 19th c., Baroque chapel by A. Torreggiani and frescoes and paintings by G. da Carpi, L. di Dalmasio, V. da Bologna, A. Aspertini, S. dei Crocifissi, L. Costa, L. Carracci, B. Cesi, F. Francia, and P. Uccello.

Madonna di Galliera (*C3*). This church is just north of the Metropolitana, and has an interesting sandstone facade (1491); inside, painting by F. Albani.

Museo Civico Medievale★ (*C3*). *Open Tue.-Sat., 96:30; Sun., 10-6:30.* This museum of the Middle Ages is located at n. 4 in Via Manzoni in the *Palazzo Fava Ghisilardi★*, a late-15th-c. aristocratic residence. More than 20 halls (some frescoed by the Carracci, 1584) display an odd assortment of works of art and applied arts, not strictly limited to the Middle Ages. Among the most outstanding pieces are the tomb of University doctors; a copper statue of Boniface VII (1301), the pope so greatly reviled by Dante; a Virgin by J. della Quercia; Renaissance bronzes, ivories, Murano glass, ceramics, and musical instruments; a huge collection of weapons and armor. Note also the collections of naturalistic and exotic objects, which testify to the collecting tastes of bygone centuries.

Via Galliera★ (*B-C3*). This street is lined with venerable palazzi: among them, the 18th-c. *Palazzo Tofanini* (n. 4) and *Palazzo Aldrovandi* (*C3*; n. 8); the late-15th-c. *Palazzo Felicini* (n. 14); and the 17th-c. *Palazzo Tanari* (*B-C3*; n. 18). On the other side of the street, note *Palazzo Dal Monte* (n. 3-5, now part of the university), by A. da Formigine (1529).

Montagnola (*A-B4*). You reach the top of the hillock, used as a public park since the late-17th c. by climbing a handsome late-19th-c. stairway, lined by statues and reliefs depicting scenes from the history of Bologna. At the foot of the hill is *Porta Galliera* (*A4*), dating from 1661.

Beyond the gates, on the hills

The church of the Madonna di S. Luca is a symbol of Bologna, marking the skyline where the plain climbs gently toward the distant Apennines. Other landmarks on the hills mentioned here (Villa Aldini, the convent of Ronzano, the monastery of S. Michele in Bosco, and the church of S. Vittore) can be toured in a succession of exquisite views, beginning at the Porta di S. Mamolo and following the Via dell'Osservanza (follow markings). On Bologna's western outskirts, the Certosa, or charterhouse, stands on the site of an ancient necropolis. The congress center (Fiera) to the north is the last stop, and attracts visitors throughout the year for its numerous events.

Museo Storico Didattico della Tappezzeria. *Open Sep.-Jul., Tue.-Sun., 9-1; Thu., also 3-6.* Located in the Neo-Classic Villa Spada, at n. 3 Via di Casaglia, on the way up to the church of the Madonna di S. Luca, this tapestry museum has a collection ranging from antique Oriental fabrics to Bolognese brocades and damasks, from silk prints to rare Fortuny creations, as well as looms dating as far back as 1380. A bit further along, Via Saragozza runs under the Baroque *arch of the Meloncello* (1732), and then more steeply up to the sanctuary of the Madonna di S. Luca.

Madonna di S. Luca.* This is the most important sanctuary in Bologna's religious and civic history, perched atop the Colle della Guardia (289 m), outside of *Porta Saragozza (E1)*. You can drive up (Via di Casaglia, 10 km), off Via Saragozza; or walk (90 minutes) following Via Saragozza, and then *Via di S. Luca*, with its 3.5-km-long portico, built in 1674-1715. The elliptical sanctuary was built in its current form by C.F. Dotti (1723-57). Inside is a 12th-c. Byzantine icon of the Virgin; also paintings by Reni and Guercino. Fine view* of the city.

Villa Aldini. Take Via dell'Osservanza from *Porta S. Mamolo (F3)* to reach this Neo-Classic villa, built by a minister of Napoleon, A. Aldini. Nearby is the 15th-c. **Convento dell'Osservanza** (230 m).

Convento di Ronzano (286 m). *Open by request, tel. 051570435.* Take Via dell'Osservanza and Via Gaibola from *Porta S. Mamolo (F3)* to this former convent of the Order of S. Maria (Dante meets two of these monks in the Inferno, in the Malebolge: "We both were Jovial Friars, and Bolognese," or, in the Italian, "Frati godenti fummo, e bolognesi"). Inside, early-16th-c. frescoes.

Monastero di S. Michele in Bosco* (124 m) *Open 9-12 and 4-19:30.* From *Porta Castiglione (F5)* along Via Castiglione and Via Putti. Now partly an orthopedic institute (fine view of Bologna), it includes a 15th-c. *church*, rebuilt in 1517-23 by B. Rossetti, with a portal designed by B. Peruzzi (1523); inside are Renaissance sculptures and frescoes by G. da Carpi. In the *monastery*, frescoes by I. da Imola, L. Carracci, G. Reni, and other Bolognese painters.

S. Vittore (250 m). You reach this little Romanesque church from *Porta Castiglione (F5)* along Via Castiglione and Via S. Vittore; built in the 11th c. and rebuilt in the 19th c., it has an elegant late-16th-c. *cloister*.

Certosa. *Open Mar.-2 Nov., 7-6; 3 Nov.-28 Feb., 8-5.* This ancient Carthusian monastery, or charterhouse,

stands in Via Certosa, outside *Porta S. Isaia*. Built in the 14th c., it was converted into a city cemetery in 1801. With many cloisters, corridors, and galleries, and the 14th-c. church of *S. Girolamo*, it is the final resting place of Nobel laureate G. Carducci and composer O. Respighi. Note funerary monuments by L. Bartolini, V. Vela, and L. Bistolfi.

Fiera. NE of Bologna's center, this congress center hosts a number of events every year; the main entrance is at n. 6 in Piazza Costituzione. Also here is the *Galleria d'Arte Moderna* (1970-75; temporary art exhibits; *open Tue.-Sun., 10-6; to be moved in Via Riva di Reno at the premises of the former Manifattura Tabacchi*) and the *Palazzo dei Congressi* (1975), for conferences.

Bolzano / Bozen

Elev. 262 m, pop. 97,232; Trentino-Alto Adige, capital of the autonomous region of Alto Adige, and provincial capital. On his way south, Goethe noted the vineyards where "light-blue bunches of grapes dangle on high, ripening in the heat of the earth below," the fruit vendors in the main square, peddling peaches and pears, thriving trade, and the "bright cheerful sunshine." From the south, you are more likely to notice the Gothic appearance of the old town, at the confluence of the rivers Tàlvera and Isarco, and the sense of a mixture of two worlds, Latin and Germanic, beneath the distant skyline of the Dolomites.

Historical note. Not much is known about the ancient city, or where its center once stood. Drusus founded an outpost here in 15 B.C., as an inscription tells us, and some finds suggest Roman settlement, but not until the 12th c. is there any reliable history of Bolzano's development as a city. Amid the wars between the bishops of Trent and the counts of Tyrol, many Gothic churches were built – notably the Duomo and the Chiesa dei Domenicani – in the area around modern-day Via dei Por-

Bolzano: Duomo

tici. Piazza Walther, named for its monument to the great German medieval poet, Walther von der Vogelweide, is still Bolzano's center. The town was a major trading center in the Middle Ages, with four fairs a year, each lasting two weeks. In 1635, a Mercantile Magistracy was established. The headquarters of this magistracy, until 1851, was the Baroque Palazzo Mercantile, built by the Veronese architect Perotti. Despite the existence of this and a few other Baroque buildings, the city remained largely German Gothic, until the 1500s. Meanwhile, Bolzano fell first to the counts of the Tyrol, then to the dukes of Carinthia, and from 1363, to the dukes of Austria. The Hapsburgs held the town until 1918, save for a period under Napoleon, when it was made first part of Bavaria, then part of the Kingdom of Italy. At the end of the 19th c., the elegant suburb of Gries sprang up; in the 1930s Bolzano developed as a manufacturing center, expanding west and south.

Getting around. Part of the historic center is closed to traffic, so we recommend following this route as a walking tour, using cars or buses only to reach the quarter of Gries, across the river Tàlvera.

Places of interest. Piazza Walther. The center of Bolzano is bounded on one side by palazzi now serving as hotels, and on the other by the impressive Gothic cathedral. In the middle is a monument to the great German medieval poet, Walther von der Vogelweide. Beneath the square is a parking lot.
Duomo. * This 14th-c. Gothic cathedral has a fine apse and colorful steep-pitch roof, with a 16th-c. campanile. Outside, 14th-c. portals and reliefs; inside, frescoes and a notable pulpit (1514).
Chiesa dei Domenicani. This Gothic church, once the place of worship for Italians in Bolzano, was rebuilt after heavy bomb damage in WWII. Inside, note 14th-/15th-c. frescoes, an altarpiece by Guercino (1655), and the **Cappella di S. Giovanni** *, a chapel with remarkable frescoes by the Giotto Paduan school (note the Triumph of Death; ca. 1340). In the adjacent Gothic *cloister* (entrance through n. 19 A), frescoes by F. Pacher and paintings by local 16th-c. artist S. Müller; also 14th-c. frescoes in the *Sala Capitolare*, or chapter house, and the *Cappella di S. Caterina*.
Via dei Portici. * This straight road has been the heart of Bolzano for many centuries and is still lined with elegant shops. Note the porticoed houses, esp. n. 39 (main facade in Via Argentieri), and the Baroque *Palazzo Mercantile* (1708).
Piazza delle Erbe. This square is lined with handsome homes and is the site of the fruit market; on one side is the 18th-c. *Fountain of Neptune*, with bronze statue by G. Mayr.
Chiesa dei Francescani. This Gothic Franciscan church has a noteworthy main altar, carved by H. Klocker (1500), and a lovely 14th-c. cloister, as well as good frescoes.
Museo Provinciale di Scienze Naturali. *Open Tue.-Sun., 10-6.* At the corner of Via Bottai and Via Hofer,

this museum of natural science features an exhibitio on the landscape and ecosystems of Alto Adige.
S. Giovanni in Villa. *Open Easter-Oct., by request the APT, t. 0471307000.* Confined to a narrow litt square is a 12th-c. church, with an immense bell tow er. Inside are two series of 14th-c. frescoes.
Museo Civico. * *Open Tue.-Sat., 9-18; Thu,. 9-8.* Th town museum is located in the former Casa Hurlac at n. 14 in Via Cassa di Risparmio. It features arch ological material dating from the Mesolithic (no the menhir of Lungostagno, or Renon; the mi Bronze Age sword of Hauenstein; and a milestor from the reign of the emperor Claudius, A.D. 46); collection of folk costumes and domestic objec and a gallery of local art, dating from the 15th c. o
Ponte Tàlvera. Uphill, along the left bank of the r er, runs the Lungotàlvera Bolzano, a handsome rive side promenade, which passes the *Castel Marecc* (13th to 16th c.), with four massive round towers wi conical roofs, now a conference center; the prom nade then joins the *Passeggiata S. Osvaldo*, whic runs up the slopes of Monte Renon; fine views.
Monumento della Vittoria. Majestic triumph. arch built in 1928 by M. Piacentini; sculptures b L. Andreotti, A. Dazzi, P. Canonica, and A. Wildt. Th monument has been bombed by German-speakir terrorist groups, and is entirely cordoned off.
Abbazia dei Benedettini di Gries. This *Bened tine abbey* lies on the main square of this subu which is popular as a spa, and is amidst garde and vineyards. On the square is also the Baroqu church of *S. Agostino*, built in 1771; note fresco and the altarpiece by Tyrolean painter M. Knolle Nearby, *Gothic parish church* (Parrocchiale: 15th-16 c.; *open Apr.-Oct., Mon.-Fri., 10:30-12 and 2:30-4* with a noteworthy altarpiece by M. Pacher (1475)

Brescia*

Elev. 149 m, pop. 191,317; Lombardia (Lor bardy), provincial capital. After Milan, Bresci is the largest city in Lombardy, both in terms population and economic consequence. "The dig iron from its tall mountains," wrote the Mar tuan chronicler Teofilo Folengo in the 16th c once a Benedictine friar in the convent of : Eufemia: the metal-working tradition date back to the earliest times here. From mining was a short step to the manufacture c weapons, in the lower Val Trompia, still a majc local industry. Located between the Po Valle and the Alpine foothills, Brescia is a large an modern city, with renowned and noteworth monuments and considerable art collection

Historical note. Though this ancient city with thoroughly modern appearance has been ravage by pickaxe and steamshovel during the 20th cent ry, shreds and tatters – but remarkable shreds an tatters – of the ancient city still survive. In the ce tral section of a map of Brescia you can easily sp a roughly rectangular perimeter of avenues, whe the names of city gates (Porta Milano, Porta Trento, Porta Venezia) attest to the former existence of a walled perimeter; within that perimeter, the layout of the streets still adheres to a largely regular grid. In the NE corner there is a hill with castle; in the SW corner is a surprising off-kilter road (Corso Martiri della Libertà), running straight into the center, where it encounters three squares. The Castello, or castle, occupies the site of the earliest settlement, in the 6th c. B.C.; those settlers may have belonged to a Ligurian tribe. Certainly the name of the hill – Colle Cidnéo – was a learned conceit of the 16th c., a name invented to refer to a Ligurian king – Cicno – legendary founder of Brescia. Gallic tribesmen may have been the first to settle on the plain, below the castle. The layout of the streets harks back to Roman times, and to the original Roman layout. The city fell under Roman sway in the 3rd c. B.C., when the city was called Brixia, though it was much smaller then, extending just west of what is now Piazza Paolo VI, with Piazza del Foro as its center. Expansion west and south followed; the first expansion was under Longobard rule, and included the area of what is now Piazza della Loggia (Brescia was the capital of a duchy; the "curia ducis," court of the duke, or Cordusio, was located on the site of the Piazza della Loggia and Piazza della Vittoria; the important convent of S. Salvatore stood where the basilica of that name now stands). Further expansion occurred when the walled perimeter was built in the 12th c. (long since demolished), extending to the west just past the church of S. Giovanni Evangelista (this was headquarters of the Communal government, first mentioned in a document dated 1120; Brescia was part of the Lombard League, which stood up against the emperor Frederick I Barbarossa; in order to be a citizen, you had to build a house of stone). The perimeter of avenues, or "viali," dates from the second set of walls, under the Communal government, 1237-54. The city did not really expand beyond that perimeter until the 19th c., and with the construction of the new walls and the Broletto, Brescia seems to have exerted its last great effort for many centuries. Later, Brescia was ruled by lords from outside: Ezzelino da Romano; the House of Della Scala, from Verona; the Visconti from Milan (and one local seigneury, between 1270 and 1308, under the bishop Berardo Maggi). In 1428 Venice took Brescia from the Visconti, ruling it until 1796 (with a short French interval, 1509-1513, during the war of the League of Cambrai, with insurrection, siege, and plunder by the French nobleman and soldier Gaston de Foix, known as the "Thunderbolt of Italy"). Under Venetian rule, Brescia grew: by 1505, the population had increased from 6000 to 65,000, the same as the population the city had at the turn of the 20th c. (the plague of 1630, however, drove the population back down to 13,000). The ancient tradition of metal-working led Brescia to become a manufacturer of weapons ("Brescia has almost always been the armory of all Italy," wrote the military engineer G. Maggi in the late-16th c.). In terms of art, in the 15th c.,

the Brescian painter Vincenzo Foppa was the greatest artist in Lombardy, but the "Brescian school" of the 16th c., with Savoldo, Romanino, and Moretto, was equally tied to Lombardy and Veneto. The city walls were rebuilt and reinforced with bastions after 1516, along the 13th-c. perimeter; Brescia remained a citadel until Napoleonic times, when the ramparts were converted into promenades. The diagonal line of the embankment, or glacis, of Porta S. Nazaro (Piazza Repubblica) running toward the center, became the access road from the railway station (1852-54). The city walls were torn down beginning in 1875. Industrialization followed the local tradition of "ferrarezza," or metal-working. The three squares at the heart of Brescia almost recapitulate its history. On Piazza Paolo VI, formerly Piazza del Duomo, note the monuments to religious fervor (the Rotonda, or Duomo Vecchio, and the Duomo Nuovo) and the relics of the medieval Communal government, in the Broletto; Piazza della Loggia was the center of Brescia under Venetian rule; the ambitious 20th-c. Piazza della Vittoria, which resulted in the regrettable destruction of an ancient quarter, is the center of modern Brescia.

Getting around. The route indicated runs in a ring, starting from Piazza Vittoria and ending in nearby Piazza della Loggia, and is a walking tour.

Places of interest. Piazza della Vittoria (*C3*) is the center of modern-day Brescia, and was designed in 1932 by M. Piacentini. Among the buildings surrounding this square is the classical *Palazzo delle Poste*, or post office, alongside which stands the *Arengario*, a sort of pulpit in pink Tolmezzo stone, with reliefs by A. Maraini (episodes from the history of Brescia). Nearby is the ancient church of **S. Agata** (B3), rebuilt in the 15th c., with 14th-c. frescoes.

Piazza della Loggia* (*B3*). Largely surrounded by Venetian-style buildings, this square is a vast and harmonious architectural complex. The dominant structure is the Loggia, facing a porticoed 16th-c. palazzo, and the *Torre dell'Orologio* (1540-50), or clock tower. A plaque at the foot of the tower commemorates a terrible terrorist bombing here on 28 May 1974. Bounded to the south by the *Palazzo del Monte di Pietà**, two similar buildings joined by an arch: the right wing (1484-89) has Roman inscriptions and a Venetian-style loggia; the left wing was added in 1597.

Loggia* (*B3*). Now Palazzo del Comune, or city hall, this building was erected between 1492 and 1574 as a meeting hall. The ground floor (1492-1508) is partly porticoed; the upper floor (1554-74) was designed by many illustrious architects of the time, including Sansovino, Alessi, and Palladio, but probably chiefly by L. Beretta. A stairway climbs to the upstairs halls, partly decorated with 16th-c. paintings.

Piazza Paolo VI (*B-C4*). With two 18th-c. fountains, this square is lined by the Rotonda, or Duomo Vecchio (old cathedral), the Duomo Nuovo (new cathedral), and the Broletto.

Rotonda* (*C4*). *Open Tue.-Sun., 8-12 and 3-7; Nov.-Mar., Sat.-Sun., only until 6.* Brescia's premiere Romanesque monument, it sits at the square's 11th-c. level, and is circular, topped by a dome surrounded by small pilastered arches. The interior* comprises a central space covered by a hemispherical dome, ringed by an ambulatory. A presbytery and two chapels were added in the 15th c.; the left-hand chapel holds a rich, rarely shown array of treasures; the right chapel has paintings* by Moretto. Note the mosaic floor, dating from the 1st c. B.C., and two 14th-c. sarcophagi*.

Duomo Nuovo (*B-C4*). *Open Mon.-Sat., 7:30-12 and 4-7:30; Sun., 8-1 and 4-7:30.* Begun in 1604 and no[t] completed until three centuries later (dome by L[.] Cagnola, 1825), this cathedral's classical interior ha[s] various art works, by Moretto, R. Scorzelli (1984) and Romanino.

Broletto* (*B4*). One of the most notable town hall[s] in Lombardy, built between 1223 and 1298, and ex[-]tensively enlarged and rebuilt in later centuries, this building is flanked by the *Torre del Popolo*, a towe[r] dating from the 11th c. Note the courtyard, a mixture of medieval, Renaissance, and Baroque.

Castello (*B4*). This immense fortress, which crown[s] the Colle Cidnéo, dates from the time of the Com[-]

munal government, though its current appearance dates from the 16th c. In the Grande Miglio is the **Museo del Risorgimento** (*open Tue.-Sun.; Jun.-Sep., 10-5; Oct.-May, 9:30-1 and 2:30-5*), devoted to Italy's movement for independence and unification, covering the period from the 18th c. to Italian unity in 1870. In a number of 14th-c. rooms of the Visconti keep is the **Museo delle Armi Luigi Marzoli** (*open Tue.-Sun.; Jun.-Sep., 10-5; Oct.-May, 9:30-1 and 2:30-5*), with collections of weapons. Also in the castle is an observatory (**Specola Cidnea**; *open by request, Fri., 9-11 p.m., tel. 0302978672*). The surrounding area is a park.

Via dei Musei (*B4-5*). Lined by 16th-/18th-c. aristocratic *palazzi* (note n. 45 and 32), this was the old main street of Roman Brescia. Note the entrance to the Galleria Tito Speri (1951), a tunnel which runs under the Colle Cidnéo to the modern section to the north.

Piazza del Foro (*B4*). Covering the ancient Roman Forum only in part, this square is surrounded by the Tempio Capitolino, a number of sections of the eastern portico, the Teatro, and the Basilica. These ruins, which harmonize perfectly with the square's medieval and Renaissance architecture, are Lombardy's most important Roman complex.

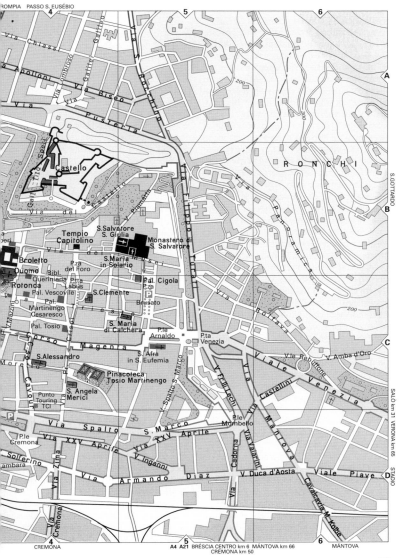

Tempio Capitolino* (*B4*).This ancient temple was built in A.D.73 under the emperor Vespasian; part of the steps, a partly rebuilt Corinthian colonnade, and the pediment, likewise reassembled, survive. Under the pronaos are the ruins of a sanctuary from the Republican period (1st c. B.C.); of the two porticoed wings, only the base of the eastern one remains, from which a passage leads down to a space known as *Aula dei Pilastrini*. On one of its ends are the portals which go into the three cellae. A fourth cella gives access to the impressive ruins of the **Teatro Romano**, an ancient theater partly covered by Renaissance and modern buildings.

Monastero di S. Salvatore (*B5*) *Open Tue.-Sun.; summer, 10-8; Wed. until 10 p.m.; winter, 9:30-5:30; closed Mon. Opening times may differ when exhibitions are held; tel. 0302977834.*This monastery was founded in A.D.753 and suppressed in 1797, when it became a barracks; it contains the churches of S. Giulia, S. Salvatore, and S. Maria in Solario (see below).Since July 1998 it has housed the **Museo della Città***, with documentation on archaelogical, historical, artistic, architectural aspects of Brescia. Among the Roman finds, noteworthy is the **Vittoria Alata***, or winged victory, a huge 1st-c. A.D. bronze statue from the Hellenistic world.

S. Salvatore* (*B5*). This exquisite piece of architecture from the high Middle Ages was built in the 11th c. on the site of an 8th-c. church and Roman ruins.It has capitals from the 6th c. and a crypt, as well as 8th-c. frescoes and stuccoes; in the chapel at the base of the campanile, frescoes by Romanino.

S. Giulia (*B5*).This church was begun in 1466 and enlarged in 1599, with 16th-c. frescoes by F. Ferramola. It once housed the *Museo dell'Età Cristiana*, or museum of the Christian age, the most interesting works of which are now at the Pinacoteca Tosio Martinengo (see below).**S. Maria in Solario***, the former oratory of the monastery, is a Romanesque structure containing 16th-c. frescoes by local artists.

Palazzo Cigola (*C5*).This 16th-c. aristocratic home was enlarged in the 18th c., and overlooks the broad, tree-lined Piazza Tebaldo Brusato. Nearby is the ancient church of *S.Maria di Calchera* (*C5; open 5:30-9:45 and 5:30-7:30*), with a 17th-c. facade; inside, works by Romanino, Moretto, and C. Piazza.

Via A. Gallo (*B-C4*). This road begins on the site of the Roman Forum, running past Piazza Labus (*C4*), where the house at n. 3 includes ruins of the Curia, likely the municipal basilica of Roman Brixia. From this square, a narrow lane runs to the 14th-c. church of *S. Clemente* (*C4; open 4-7 p.m.*), with paintings* by Moretto and Romanino.

Pinacoteca Tosio Martinengo** (*C4*). *Open Tue.-Sun.; Jun.-Sep., 10-5; Oct.-May, 9:30-1 and 2:30-5; closed Mon.*A nobleman from Brescia, Paolo Tosio, donated his picture gallery to the city; another one, Leopardo Martinengo da Barco, used his 16th-c. building to house one of Lombardy's largest collection of paintings.Among the artists whose work on display in this gallery are Veneziano, Civerchio, Foppa, Solario, Raphael, Moretto, Romanino, Lotto,

Brescia: Tempio Capitolino

Savoldo, Piazza, G.B. Moroni, Tintoretto, Ceruti, Zuccarelli, and Hayez.

S. Angela Merici (*C4; open Mon.-Sat., 7:30-9:30 and 3-5:30*).This 16th-c. church, rebuilt after WWII, features paintings by Bassano the Younger, Tintoretto, P. da Cailina the Younger, Procaccini, Palma the Younger, and others.

Via Moretto (*C3-4*).This street is lined by numerous Baroque palazzi; notable among them, *Palazzo Martinengo Colleoni* (n. 78) and the church of **S. Alessandro** (*C4; open 6:30-11 and 5:30-7:30*), with paintings by J. Bellini and V. Civerchio. Turn right in Corso Cavour to Corso Magenta, and then left along Corso Zanardelli, with porticoes, a main shopping street.

S. Maria dei Miracoli (*C3*).Built between the 15th and 16th c., this church has a luminous marble facade* (1488-1500) with bas-relief decorations and marble bas-reliefs inside.

Ss. Nazaro e Celso* (*C2-3*). *Open by request, tel. 0303754387.* This church, with an 18th-c. facade, contains fine paintings by Moretto (1541), Pittoni (1740), and Romanino, and a masterpiece by the young Titian, the **Averoldi polyptych** (1522).

S. Francesco (*C3*). This Romanesque-Gothic church (1265) has a marble portal and rose window; inside, 13th-/15th-c. frescoes and paintings by Moretto and Romanino. In the sacristy, wooden intarsias by F.Morari, 1511; also, note the cloister (*open 8-12 and 2:30-6:30; closed Sun.*).

Torre della Pallata (*B3*).This tower was built in 1248 along the medieval walls, and raised in the 18th c. At its base, a fountain dating from 1596. Continue along Corso Mameli, one of medieval Brescia's main streets.

S. Giovanni Evangelista (*B3*).Rebuilt in the 15th c., this church was further renovated in the interior in the 17th c. Inside are notable paintings by Moretto, B. Zenale, Romanino, and Francia.

. Maria del Carmine (B3). Open Tue.-Sun., 10-12 nd 4-7. A 15th-c. church with a stone-and-brick fa̧ade; the Baroque interior has 15th-c. frescoes (some y Foppa).

. Giuseppe (B3). This church dates from the 16th ., and houses the **Museo Diocesano d'Arte Sacra** open Tue.-Sun., 10-12 and 3-6) with sculptures, paintgs, illuminated codices, votive offerings, and sared objects.

Bressanone / Brixen

lev. 559 m, pop. 18,379; Trentino-Alto Adige, rovince of Bolzano. Two major Alpine rivers onverge here, the Isarco and the Rienza; morever, the Strada della Pusterìa, a road that starts eastern Tyrol and crosses the road of the renner pass (Brennero) not far off. The landcape is broad and open, dotted with cultivatd hills set amidst looming mountains, green orests, and rolling meadows. In the ancient enter, the city still preserves the stern flavor of s centuries of history as the capital of a large cclesiastical principality (the power of its bishp-princes lasted eight centuries, 1027-1803). here is a Germanic flavor to the architecture, onuments, and art, stretching from Romanesque to Baroque – this is the largest art enter in the Alto Adige – but beneath it all are he unique features of a cultural borderland.

laces of interest. **Via dei Portici Maggiori.*** his distinctive road through the old center of town, ned with shops, is still medieval in flavor, lined with 6th-/17th-c. houses, with crenelation and overanging windows. At n. 14 is the old *Municipio*, or own Hall. Note, in the courtyard, the painting of olomon's Judgement; the street ends in the small nd intimate Piazza della Parrocchia.

iazza della Parrocchia. This square is dominatd by the Gothic parish church of *S. Michele*, with its oteworthy campanile, known as *Torre Bianca*. Inde, frescoes by J. Hautzinger. To the left of the hurch, note the Renaissance *Casa Pfaundler* (1581), fine example of the mingling of Northern and Italn styles.

uomo. Founded in the 10th c. and rebuilt in the 8th c., this Romanesque church was converted to aroque in 1745-90; with its tall bell towers it domates the tree-lined Piazza del Duomo. Inside, fresoes by P.Troger and main altar by T. Benedetti, and 5th-/19th-c. tombstones of bishops. On the right, the enowned Romanesque-Gothic **cloister***, with noble frescoes (14th-16th c.); then you enter the *Capella di S. Giovanni* or *Baptistery* (*closed for restoraon*), with more frescoes*.

alazzo dei Principi Vescovi. This palace of the ishop-princes was fortified, with a moat, and stands ear Piazza del Palazzo, before the Colonna del Milnnio, erected in 1909 to commemorate Bresnone's first thousand years.

he palace was built in the early 14th c. and rebuilt,

from 1595 on, by the Austrians; used by the Church as residence or offices until 1964. It has an elegant facade and courtyard; on the 2nd floor are 24 terracotta statues of members of the House of Hapsburg, by H. Reichle (1599).

Inside is the **Museo Diocesano**. *Open 15 Mar.-Oct., Tue.-Sun., 10-5; Dec.-Jan., Mon.-Sun., 2-5, only the crèche section; closed Nov., Feb. and 14 March.* The art collections of this diocesan museum occupy 70 halls, and range from medieval craftsmanship to the original furnishings of the bishops' residence, Romanesque and Gothic wooden statues, Baroque and Renaissance sculpture, and Baroque paintings by S. Kessler, J.G.D. Grasmair, F. (Sebald) Unterpergher, and P.Troger. Also, manuscripts, incunabula, fabrics, embroideries, and sacred garments. Noteworthy collection of crèches.

Excursion. The Città di Bressanone/Plosehütte Alpine hut (2447 m), via cableway or by 23-km panoramic road, through the Valle d'Eores, to *Valcroce/Kreuztal* (2050 m), then on foot, 1.5 hours, or by chairlift; the hut is on the south ridge of the Cima della Plose (2504 m), popular for winter sports (panorama*).

Cagliari

Pop. 165,926, Sardegna (Sardinia), regional and provincial capital. Situated among salt marshes and fish-filled ponds at the center of the broad southern gulf that extends from Cape Spartivento to Cape Carbonara, Cagliari is the main harbor and one of the "gateways" to Sardinia. The French author Auguste Bouillier, who visited it in 1864, wrote movingly of the view, with the "cupolas glittering in the setting sun," the "castle with its belt of grey walls," and the "spectral towers." Dotted with Pisan towers and a Spanish castle, Cagliari has other Spanish touches, such as its flower-lined "patios," decorated with ceramics not unlike Portugal's famed "azulejos."

Historical note. Of the three cities that thrived on the gulf in Phoenician times – Bithia, Nora, and Kàralis – only the last one survived to become present-day Cagliari. Nothing remains from those days, though graves, homes and an amphitheater bear witness to the Roman occupation, which began in 238 B.C. The Romans were succeeded by the Vandals, and then the Byzantines (note the central structure of the basilica of S. Saturno), and, in the 12th c., by Pisans, who built the hilltop Castello, or castle. Three gates, with three towers (S. Pancrazio, dell'Elefante, and dei Leoni) shaped the growth of the city. Pope Boniface VIII gave the city to the Kingdom of Aragon as a feudal holding, and in 1326 the Aragonese took the Castello, marking the onset of four centuries of Spanish dominion. Alongside the medieval quarters of Castello and Marina grew, to west and east, the quarters of Villanova and Stampace. Then the Pied-

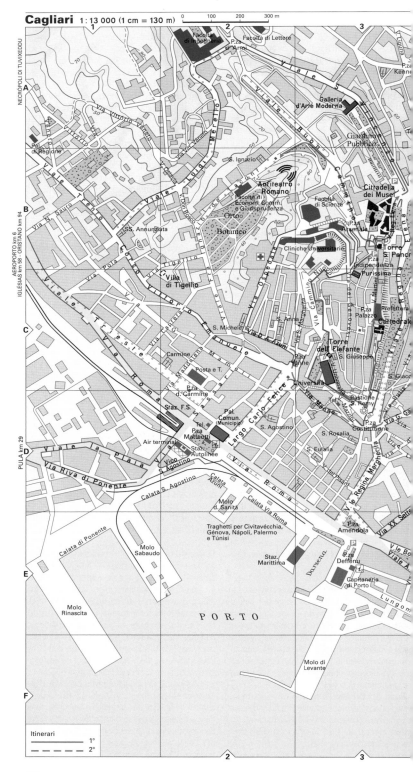

Cagliari 1:13 000 (1 cm = 130 m)

0   100   200   300 m

NECROPOLI DI TUVIXEDDU

AEROPORTO km 6
IGLÉSIAS km 58 - ORISTANO km 94

PULA km 29

Facoltà di Ingegneria
Facoltà di Lettere
P.za d'Armi

Viale Sant'Ignazio

Viale Buon Cammino

Via Vittorio Véneto

Via Luigi Mereto

Via Vittorio Véneto

P.za Kennedy

Galleria d'Arte Moderna

Giardino Pubblico

Pal. di Regione

Viale Trento

Via N. Sauro

S. Ignazio

Anfiteatro Romano

Facoltà di Econom. Comm. e Giurisprudenza

Facoltà di Scienze

Cittadella dei Musei

Viale Luigi Mereto

SS. Annunziata

Via Pola

Orto Botanico

Cliniche Universitarie

P.za Arsenale

Torre S. Pancr.

P.za Indipendenza

Purissima

Corso Vittorio Emanuele

Via Tigellio

Villa di Tigellio

Via Ospedale

Via Cammino Nuovo

S. Anna

P.za Palazzo

Prefettura

Cattedrale

Viale Trieste

Via Roma

Via Trieste

Via Maddalena

Via G. Mameli

S. Michele

Via Azuni

Torre dell'Elefante

S. Giuseppe

S. Giac.

Carmine

Posta e T.

P.za d. Carmine

P.za Yenne

Largo Carlo Felice

Università

Via Manno

Tel.

Bastione S. Remy

P.za Costituzione

Staz. F.S.

Pal. Comun. Municipio

S. Agostino

S. Rosalia

Via Regina Margherita

Air terminal

Tel.

P.za Matteotti

Staz. Autolinee

Vico S. Agostino

Via Roma

S. Eulalia

Via Sardegna

Via XX Settembre

Viale La Plaia

Via Riva di Ponente

Calata S. Agostino

Calata Azuni

Calata Via Roma

Molo d. Sanità

P.za Amendola

Vle Bo
Viale A

Calata di Ponente

Molo Sabaudo

Traghetti per Civitavécchia, Génova, Nápoli, Palermo e Túnisi

Darsena

Staz. Marittima

P.za Deffenu

Capitaneria di Porto

Lungom

Molo Rinascita

PORTO

Molo di Levante

Itinerari
1°
2°

172

montese took over in 1720, leaving little trace of their rule. The walls were torn down in 1858, opening the three main boulevards: Via Roma, Largo Carlo Felice, and Viale Regina Margherita. Since WWII, Cagliari has grown chaotically, endangering some of its finest environmental qualities and features.

Getting around. Two routes are suggested. The first starts at the bastion of Saint Remy, southernmost tip of the Castello, and is walkable (a further excursion to the Necropolis of Tuvixeddu and the Grotta della Vipera requires a vehicle). The other route, from Piazza Costituzione to the base of the bastion of Saint Remy, extends to the west and east in the lower town, or "città bassa," but you may want to drive to S. Saturno and Nostra Signora di Bonaria.

The Castello

"Su Casteddu" stands on a high ground, fortified in the Middle Ages by the Pisans, a symbol of Cagliari. Alongside the Cattedrale, the city museums occupy the former Arsenale Militare (arsenal).

Bastione di Saint Remy (*D3*). At the southern edge of the quarter, this late 19th-c. overlook was built on the Spanish bastions.

Torre dell'Elefante (*C3*). At the end of Via Università, this tower was built by the Pisans in 1307; its name comes from a relief placed some 10 m off the ground.

Cattedrale* (*C3*). Dedicated to Santa Maria, built in the Pisan style and later enlarged (late 13th c.), the Cathedral was reshaped in Baroque style, and then restored to its original style in 1933. The handsome portals in the transept (above right portal, note the front of a Roman sarcophagus) are still original. **Inside**, note the pulpits*, originally built in 1159-62 for the Cathedral of Pisa and donated to Cagliari in 1312. Note the statue of the 14th-c. Black Madonna. In the *right-hand transept*, Aragonese period Gothic chapel. From the presbytery you can descend to the *sanctuary*, with its three chapels; the central one is decorated with a number of Baroque rose windows. In the *left transept*, note the tomb of Martin II of Aragon (1676). Adjacent to the right transept is the **Museo Diocesano** (*open by request, tel. 070663837*), the diocesan museum featuring antiques and precious sacred decorations.

Chiesa della Purissima (*C3*). Built in 1554, with the adjacent former convent. Note the triptych by A. Casula (1593).

Torre di S. Pancrazio (*B3*). This tower was built in 1305 as part of the Pisan fortifications.

Cittadella dei Musei* (*B3*). This modern and panoramic complex stands on the site of the former Arsenale Militare (till 1825); Pisan, Aragonese, Spanish, and Savoy fortifications. The fortress houses the Museo Archeologico Nazionale, the Pinacoteca Nazionale, the Museo Siamese Cardu, and the Raccolta delle Cere Anatomiche.

Museo Archeologico Nazionale.* *Open summer,*

Tue.-Fri. and Sun., 9-1:30 and 3-7:30; winter, Tue.-Sun., 9-7:15; closed Mon. except Easter Mon.; tel. 070655911. With material from digs in Sardinia, this archeological museum provides a lively picture of the civilizations that have occupied this island, from prehistory (6000 B.C.) to the High Middle Ages (7th-8th c.). Ranging from the highly decorated earthenware and statuettes of mother-goddesses made of bone and rock, the collection includes small **bronzes**** from the Iron Age (900-750 B.C.) to Phoenician times, as well as jewelry, ivory, Greek vases and Roman glass.

Pinacoteca Nazionale (*open summer, Mon.-Sun., 9-10; winter, Tue.-Sun., 8:30-7:30; tel. 070674054*). In the collection of retables, canvases, crests, and furnishings, dating from the 15th to 18th c., note the altarpiece "della Porziuncola," as well as art by Spanish and Sardinian painters, and busts by G. Sartorio and V. Vela.

Museo Siamese Stefano Cardu. *Open Tue.-Sun., 9-1 and 4-8; by request, tel. 070651888.* This museum boasts an impressive collection of Far Eastern arms, ceramics, and objects. The original **Raccolta delle Cere Anatomiche** (*open Tue.-Sat., 9-1 and 4-7; Sun., 9-1; tel. 0706754082*) comprises astonishing anatomical wax models executed in 1803-05.

Galleria Comunale d'Arte Moderna (*A3*). *Open Wed.-Mon; summer, 9-1 and 5-9; winter, 9-1 and 3:30-7:30.* This museum has a collection of works by Italian artists of the 1960s and 1970s, and 20th-c. Sardinian art.

Anfiteatro Romano* (*B2*). *Open summer, 9-1 and 3:30-7:30; winter, 9-5; tel. 07041108.* Visible from the Viale Fra' Ignazio da Laconi, this 2nd-c. A.D. amphitheater is one of the finest Roman buildings in Sardinia. Note the ditch in which the wild animals were kept. Nearby, the *Villa di Tigellio* (*C2; only guided tours by request; tel. 070668501*) comprises three city dwellings from the 1st c. A.D.

Necropoli di Tuvixeddu (*A1, off map*). *Only guided tours by request; tel. 0706518841.* This necropolis was first Phoenician and Punic, and was later used by the Romans. Comprising roughly a hundred tombs dating from the 6th-1st c. B.C., it has the *Tomb of the Ureo* (or Uraeus) with fine Phoenician tomb paintings, and at the start of Via S. Avendrace, the *Grotta della Vipera* (*open summer, 9-1 and 3:30-7:30; winter, 9-5; closed Mon.*), a 1st c. A.D tomb.

The "Città Bassa"

At the base of the Castello, the Rione Marina follows the grid of a Roman "castrum," while to the west is the Rione Stampace and to the east, the Rione Villanova. Of particular interest here are the churches.

Piazza Yenne (*C2-3*). This is the heart of Stampace, in the shadow of the S. Croce bastion.

S. Agostino (*D2*). This church is one of Sardinia's few works of Renaissance architecture. The finds discovered here seem to indicate it was once occupied by baths.

. Anna (C2). Set atop a high stairway, this church as bombed heavily in 1943; since rebuilt.

. Michele (C2) One of the finest pieces of Spanish Baroque on the island, it was built in the 17th c.

Piazza S. Giacomo (C3). This is the setting of the rites of Easter Week; in the adjacent *Oratorio del Crocifisso* are the wooden statues of the Misteri della Passione (Mysteries of the Passion; G.A. Lonis, 1758), carried in Easter processions.

. Domenico (C4). Rebuilt in 1954 after damage from WWII; note the handsome late Gothic *cloister*.

. Saturno* (D4). *Open 9-1; closed Sun. and holidays.* This church is one of the most important monuments of Sardinian Christianity.

Santuario and Basilica di Bonaria (F5). Dedicated to the Virgin Mary, protector of sailors, this Basilica is the destination of pilgrims from all over the island. The statue has been venerated here since the 15th c. In the sacristy, note the collection of model ships and votive offerings offered by mariners over the centuries.

Capri (Isola di / Island of)

Pop. 7264; Campania, province of Naples. The astonishing prodigies of nature, the enchantment of the landscapes, the ineffably lovely light of the sky over this massive block of limestone – only 6.5 km in length, rising high (589 m) over the deep blue sea – will always be a siren's lure to travelers.

Places of interest. You land at Marina Grande; at the far end of the beach are the ruins of the *Palazzo a Mare*, possibly inhabited by Augustus; beyond are the enormous ruins of the so-called *Bagni di Tiberio*, or Baths of Tiberius.

The world-renowned **Grotta Azzurra****, or **Blue Grotto** (*open 9-one hour before sunset; by motorboat 25 min.; by rowboat, an hour and a half*) takes its name from the color the sunlight acquires as it filters through the water.

Capri (elev. 142 m), the main town on the island, is of course quite a haven for jet-setters. The **piazzetta**, a central square that lends itself admirably to effortless, enjoyable lounging, is enclosed like a courtyard, and is surrounded by an enchanting medieval district. Alongside the square are the Eastern-style domes of the church of *S. Stefano*.

In the **Certosa di S. Giacomo*** (*open 9-2; Sun. 9-1; closed Mon.*), a 14th-c. charterhouse, the little cloister dates from the 15th c. while the larger one dates from the 16th c. In the halls of the complex there is the *Museo Diefenbach*.

In just 45 min. you are at the excavations of the **Villa Iovis***, also known as the Villa of Tiberius. In 30 min., you can reach the *Arco Naturale**, a natural arch in a landscape of savage beauty, and the *Grotta di Matromània*. In 20 min. you can reach the **Belvedere di Tragara***, (elev. 130 m), and from there you can descend to the beach of the *port of Tragara*, to the right of which are the immense

Capri: Piazzetta

shoals and cliffs of the **Faraglioni***; note the rare blue lizard that lives on the isolated cliff (the third one) of Scopolo.

Caserta

Elev. 68 m, pop. 74,459; Campania, provincial capital. The town is world-famous for the Reggia, or royal palace (1752) that Charles of Bourbon built here to house his newly won throne. The exterior was completed in 1774, the interior a century later – after the Bourbons had been expelled. The modern city, which developed around the "Versailles" of the Bourbon dynasty of the Two Sicilies, is in a certain sense a by-product of the royal palace.

Places of interest. The **Reggia**** (*open 8:30-2*), a royal palace built by the architect Luigi Vanvitelli, has a rectangular plan, arranged around four inner courtyards. The lower vestibule*, the great stairway (or *scalone d'onore**), and the upper vestibule* constitute the most remarkable architectural sections of the palazzo; the charm of the apartments is given by the Neo-Classic decoration and the memories of court life of the Bourbon dynasty and under Joaquim Murat. The tour includes the Royal Apartments, the new apartment, the apartment of the king, the old apartment, an 18th-c. crèche with 1200 figurines, an art gallery, and a vast hall with the Museo dell'Opera (with exhibits on Vanvitelli) and the delightful little court theater (1769).

The splendid **park**** (*open 8:30-one hour before sunset*) has an array of fountains and waterfalls that extend all the way up to the hill and to the **grande cascata***, or great waterfall, with the sculptural group of **Diana and Actaeon**; the **English garden** is one of the most noteworthy aspects of this complex.

Surrounding areas. Three km NW, at **San Léucio**, Ferdinand IV established a famous silk factory (18th c.) with the idea of creating a model city, an example of enlightened industrialization.

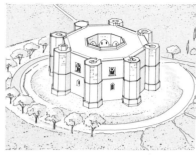

Castel del Monte

Castel del Monte

Elev. 540 m; Puglia (Apulia), province of Bari, township of Andria (pop. 94,443). This castle can be considered the monument that is most expressive and representative of the personality of emperor Frederick II Hohenstaufen (1194-1250), the son of Constance of Altavilla, heiress of Sicily and Henry VI, the German emperor who preferred southern Italy – and Sicily in particular, where he established his court – to his northern homeland.

Tour. *Open Apr.-Sep., 10-1 and 2:30-6:30; Oct.- Mar., 9-1 and 2:30-5:30.* The octogonal-plan **Castle****, built with large ashlars, is punctuated at the corners on the exterior by eight towers, also octogonal. Roughly halfway up the exterior wall there is a horizontal cornice, indicating the separation between the two interior floors. The entrance portal, on the east side, shows an interesting mixture of Gothic style (pointed arches, columns surmounted by lions) and echoes of classical Rome (cusped pediment). **Inside**, after you enter from the second hall through a pointed-arch portal of Muslim derivation, the central courtyard reiterates the octagonal plan of the building. Overlooking the courtyard are three French doors on the first floor, with slender columns supporting archivolts decorated with plant motifs. There are eight trapezoidal rooms surrounding the courtyard. There is a spiral staircase in one tower (the ceiling is attributed to Nicolò Pisano), which allows you to climb to the upper floor. Light comes from the exterior through twin-light and three-light mullioned windows (panoramic view of the Murge and the Tavoliere, the Apulian plains).

Catania

Elev. 7 m, pop. 337,862; Sicilia (Sicily), provincial capital. The second largest city in Sicily is also the birthplace of illustrious men of literature (Giovanni Verga) and music (Vincenzo Bellini). It stands on the shores of the Ionian Sea, amid the citrus groves, in the clear Mediterranean light. Mt. Etna, with its solemn silhouette, its peak brushed by clouds and snow, forms part of the cityscape and part of Catania's destiny. The volcano made the surrounding land fertile, attracting the original founders; it is also the source of the black lava-stone of which the Roman amphitheater was built, as were the medieval cathedral and the Baroque palazzi.

Historical note. Of ancient origins (this was one of the Greek colonies of the 8th c. B.C.), Catania now has the noble, sumptuous 18th-c. Baroque appearance (at least, in the historic center) it was given thanks to the brilliant reconstruction effected by the Palermitan architect Giovan Battista Vaccarini, when the city was rebuilt following the catastrophic earthquake of 1693.

Places of interest. Piazza del Duomo* (*D3*). The 18th-c. atmosphere of the city strikes the visitor immediately in the central cathedral square, with the remarkable *Fontana dell'Elefante* (G.B. Vaccarini, 1736), a fountain inspired by Bernini's Fontana della Minerva in Rome. The elephant, carved of lava stone, is called "u liotru" by the inhabitants and is the symbol of the town.

Duomo* (*D3*). The facade of the cathedral is also by Vaccarini; of the original 11th-c. construction, all that survives are the apses and the transept. In the immense *interior*, note the Norman structure. In the right apse is the *Cappella di S. Agata**, the chapel dedicated to the patron saint of Catania; from here you enter the rich *Tesoro*, or Treasury.

Porta Uzeda (*D-E3*; 1696). From this gate, which opens out onto the harbor area, and from the Piazza del Duomo, runs the *Via Etnea* (*A-D3*), the main road in the reconstruction done after the earthquake. This lively city promenade climbs gently up toward the foothill of Monte Etna.

Piazza dell'Università (*D3*). The street is interrupted by this university square, a harmonious assembly of buildings by Vaccarini, as well as by Piazza Stesicoro (*C3*), to the left of which you can see the ruins of the 2nd-c. **Anfiteatro Romano**, or Roman Amphitheater.

Casa-Museo di Giovanni Verga. To the west of

Catania: Duomo

the Duomo runs Via Garibaldi, where, in an 18th-c. building, the birthplace of Verga is located (*open 9-1; Tue. and Thu. also 3-6:30; closed Sun.*), with books, furniture and objects belonging to the great 19th-c. writer.

Castello Ursino* (*E3; closed for restoration*). The vast solemn square bulk of this castle, built by Frederick II (1239-50) and rebuilt in the 16th c., houses the **Museo Civico*** (*open Tue.-Sat., 9-1 and 3-6; Sun., 9-1*). This city museum comprises varied collections of archeology, ancient and modern art, ivory, terracotta, bronze, weapons, and memorabilia of local history.

Museo Belliniano. Not far off is the museum dedicated to Bellini (*open 9-1:30; Tue. and Thu. also 3-6:30; Sun. 9-12:30*) and the **Teatro Romano** (*D2-3*), or Roman Theater, with an adjacent, semicircular **Odeon** (*open 9-one hour before sunset*).

Via dei Crociferi* (*D3*). It is one of the monumental arteries of the city, lined with Baroque churches and 18th-c. palazzi. Among the former, the sumptuous church of *S. Benedetto* (1771-77), with a carved wooden portal, and the church of *S. Giuliano*, a noteworthy example of Catania Baroque attributed to Vaccarini (1739-51).

S. Nicolò (*D2*). Further west, the church of S. Nicolò, with an unfinished facade, is the largest one in Sicily. On the pavement of the transept, note the marble sundial with inlaid symbols of the Zodiac. The carved wooden choir in the presbytery, elegant armoirs and rich ecclesiastical garb and ornaments in the Rococo sacristy are noteworthy.

Certosa di Pavìa* / Pavìa Charterhouse

Elev. 90 m; Lombardia (Lombardy), province of Pavìa. Anyone who visits the Certosa is inevitably impressed by the contrast between the opulence of the house of worship and the balanced magnificence of the complex as a whole. From the time the cornerstone was laid in August 1396, construction of the imposing complex continued for over two centuries, with the contribution of the newest and most original artists of the Lombard Renaissance.

Tour. *Open Oct.-Mar., 9-11:30 and 2:30-4:30; April, until 5:30 p.m.; May-Sept., until 6:30 p.m.; closed Mon. that are not holidays; guided tours led by a monk.* In the entrance courtyard, note the Baroque structure of the **Foresteria***, or guest quarters, by F.M. Richini (1625), which intersects with the exceedingly rich marble **facade**** of the church, built between the end of the 15th and the middle of the 16th c., chiefly by G.A. Amadeo and C. Lombardo. The church is in the transitional style between Gothic and Renaissance. The interior has a two-aisle nave, is closed at the transept by a sumptuous 17th-c. chancel, and is flanked by a succession of chapels. There are exquisite **paintings*** and **frescoes*** by Perugino and Bergognone (15th c.). Also worthy of note are two bronze *candelabra** by A.

Certosa di Pavìa

Fontana (1580); the **funerary statues of Beatrice d'Este and Ludovico il Moro***, by C. Solari (1487); a 15th-c. ivory *polyptych** from the Embriachi workshop; the wooden stalls of the choir* (1498); the **sepulcher of Gian Galeazzo Visconti*** by G. Romano and assistants (1487). Take a door carved by the Mantegazza (inside) and G.A. Amadeo (outside) to enter the delightful *small cloister** (1462-72), with porticoes adorned with terracotta decoration. There is a magnificent view here of the right side and the transept of the church. The large cloister is lined with the cells of the monks.

Cividale del Friùli

Elev. 135 m, pop. 11,292; Friùli-Venezia Giulia, province of Udine. Standing on the banks of the Natisone, where the river flows out of the foothills of the Julian Alps, this town has layers of history and art, dating from early Roman occupation, through the aristocratic Middle Ages, when it was the headquarters of a Patriarch, and through a period of Venetian rule. Above all it is a town with a heritage of Longobard occupation. These peoples entered Italy in A.D. 568 over the nearby Passo del Predil, ruled here for two centuries, and then vanished.

Places of interest. **Piazza del Duomo**. The monumental center of Cividale, on the site of the Roman Forum, this square is bounded by the Duomo, the *Palazzo dei Provveditori Veneti*, designed by Palladio (1581-96), and the *Palazzo Comunale*, rebuilt in 15th-c. style in 1936.
Duomo.* Built from 1457 on after a design by B. delle Cisterne, it was reconstructed in the following century by P. and T. Lombardo. The simple stone facade has three portals; the middle one is by J. Veneziano (1465). Alongside, note the Baroque campanile. *Inside* (designed by P. Lombardo), beneath

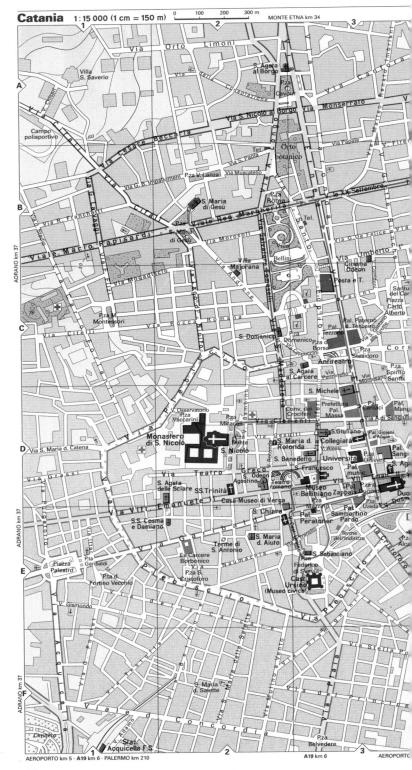

Catania

1:15 000 (1 cm = 150 m)

0   100   200   300 m

MONTE ETNA km 34

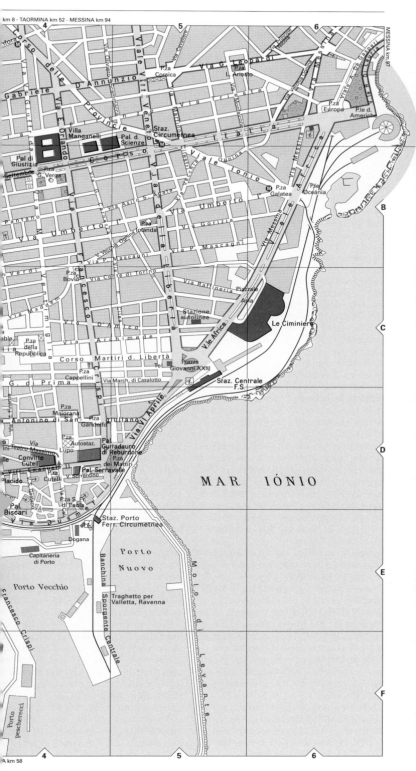

the organ on the right is a fragment of a standard (1536) by G. da Udine. The altarpiece, or Pala di Pellegrino II*, made of gilt silver (1195-1204), and frescoes by Palma the Younger are fascinating.

On the right aisle is the entrance to the **Museo Cristiano e Tesoro del Duomo** (*open summer, 9:30-12 and 3-7; holidays, 3-7; winter, until 6 p.m.*), the museum of the Treasury with remarkable 8th-/9th-c. altars and thrones, and frescoes from the Tempietto Longobardo (see below).

Museo Archeologico Nazionale. * *Open summer, Mon., 9-2; Tue.-Fri., 9:30-7; Sat., until 11 p.m.; Sun. and holidays, 8:30-8; winter, Mon., 9-7; Tue.-Fri., 8:30-7:30; Sat.-Sun. and holidays, 8:30-8.* Located in the 16th-c. Palazzo dei Provveditori Veneti, this archeological museum has some 20 rooms with major collections ranging from Roman times to the high Middle Ages, with special focus on the Longobards and the Friùli in general. Of particular note, on the *ground floor*, is the section of epigraphs, inscriptions, reliefs, and fragments of architecture, from Roman, early Byzantine, high medieval, and Romanesque times; also mosaics. *Upstairs* is the Longobard section, with arms and jewelry, and the psaltery of St. Elizabeth, with 13th-c. Saxon miniatures, and a 13th-c. veil.

From the portico of the Palazzo dei Provveditori, a passage to the right leads to the *Via Monastero Maggiore*, and then on to the medieval district of Borgo Brossana and the Tempietto Longobardo, through two gates, the *Roman arch-gate* and the *Porta Patriarcale*.

Tempietto Longobardo. * *Open Apr.-Oct., 10-1 and 3-6:30; Nov.-Mar., until 5:30.* This remarkable example of the architecture of the high Middle Ages (8th-9th c.) looms over the river Natisone, and can be reached by a short passage overlooking that river. The large square central hall is covered by a tall cross vault; the apse is split into three by columns, supporting low barrel vaults. Note the detached frescoes (12th-14th c.) and the sarcophagus of Piltrude (stone from the 8th c.). The hall has wooden stalls and Byzantine-style frescoes (in poor condition), as well as a rich array of 8th-c. **figured stuccoes** * * and a remarkable frieze.

S. Biagio. Across from the entrance to the Tempietto Longobardo, this little church dates from the 15th c. Returning to Piazza del Duomo you will pass the *Monastero Maggiore*, with the church of **S. Giovanni**, with an altarpiece by Palma the Younger. Also, at n. 6 in Via del Monastero Maggiore is the access to the so-called **Ipogeo Celtico** (*open by request, tel. 0432701211*), a Celtic necropolis formed by a series of narrow tunnels cut into the rock.

Ponte del Diavolo. Built in the mid-15th c. to unite the two rocky banks of the Natisone, this bridge was demolished and rebuilt in WWI; it offers a fine view of central Cividale.

S. Francesco (*open only for exhibitions*). This 14th-c. church has 14th-/16th-c. frescoes. Nearby is the *Palazzo Pontotti-Brosadola*, with a simple facade; also noteworthy is the church of *S. Pietro ai Volti*, with a fine altarpiece by Palma the Younger.

Como*

Elev. 201 m, pop. 82,989; Lombardia (Lombardy), provincial capital. The city is cuppe in a small hollow, surrounded by an arc hills, at the base of the Monte di Brunat overlooking the southernmost tongue of lake, the Lario or Lake Como. This is the c of the Maestri Comacini, or Romanesque master artisans of Como, and of both Pliny Elder and Younger, who are immortalized the statuary on the facade of the Duomo. is also the home of the silk industry, ancie but still thriving, and of the Italian Ration ist architecture of the early 20th c. More tha for the city itself, Como is beloved and f quented for "the enchanting loveliness, th light, and the expressive mobility of the lak (Maurice Barrès). By noticing only the lak however, one is deprived of the pleasure many discoveries, of noteworthy monumer and remarkable atmospheres.

Historical note. There was a large Celtic forti cation here originally, built between the 6th a 5th c. B.C., but the modern city was founded, in certain sense, in 196 B.C., nearly 2200 years ag Marcus Claudius Marcellus defeated the Celts a founded a "castrum," the square Roman camp "Comum Oppidum." Although little survives of t ancient walled perimeters, the inhabitants of C mo still speak of the "città murata" when they fer to the center of the city. In the "città murat about a third of the buildings date back befo 1600, but the "borghi," or districts, outside the w are also ancient. In the history of art the adjecti "Comacini" is used with the substantive "Maest – the first mention of these Como artisans is in t Edict of the Longobard king Rotari (A.D. 643). T new style that these builders, carpenters, mason stonecarvers, and plasterers practiced in Con and throughout Italy developed into what v know as Romanesque. In Como the tradition tak form in the great Romanesque churches: S. Fede within the walls; S. Abbondio and S. Carpoforo surrounding districts. The town government gaine strength in the early 12th c., and the crucial m ment in its history was its decade-long battle wi Milan (1118-27), after which Como was subjug ed; the new walls and the ruins of the castle on t Colle del Baradello date from the reconstructi undertaken with the assistance of the Holy Rom Emperor Frederick I Barbarosssa. From the tim the Visconti took Como (1335) until 27 May 185 when the city welcomed Garibaldi, who had d feated the Austrian troops on the Colle di S. Fern in the fight for Italian unity, Como's political h tory was basically the history of Milan. The Visco built their citadel in the NW corner of Como (b tween the Duomo and the lake); in 1447, when F ippo Maria Visconti died, Como proclaimed t short-lived Repubblica di S. Abbondio, and th

itadel was demolished. Work resumed on the
Duomo, from its beginnings in 1396: this was Como's great architectural project (the Broletto was
avaged, and part of the church of S. Giacomo de-
troyed to make room), and work continued until
he 18th c. to complete the cupola, designed by
uvara. The Neo-Classic period gave the city the
ppearance that Stendhal so loved, and which can
till be seen in the patrician villas on the western
hore of the lake and in the facades along Via Vol-
a. From the lakefront promenade and drive of the
ungolario you can look out over the clear cold
vaters, standing in Piazza Cavour, which was once
he port of Como (filled in with earth in 1871).

Getting around. Much of the historic center is
losed to automobile traffic, especially along the
horoughfare of Via Vittorio Emanuele II; the route
marked on the map can be considered a walking
our, though you may choose to take public trans-
ortation to reach the church of S. Abbondio.

Places of interest. Lungolario, a lakefront drive
and promenade. (A2). The northern part of the city
curves around the little gulf at the base of the lake.

Adjoining *Piazza Cavour*, the heart of Como, and
a harbor that was filled in in 1871, are the docks
of the boats and hydrofoils that carry passengers
across the lake.
Piazza del Duomo (*B2*). The monumental center
of the city lies in this square, along which stand the
Torre del Comune, the Broletto, and the Duomo.
Broletto* (*A-B2*). Once the center of Communal
government, this Romanesque-Gothic town hall
was built in 1215; note the marble facing, with
white, grey and pink stripes, the portico, the mullioned windows and 15th-c. balcony. The tower, or
Torre del Comune, was built in 1215, and rebuilt in
1927.

Duomo** (*B2*). This monument traces its origins
to the architectural culture of the Maestri Comacini. Begun in 1396, work continued until the
17th c., when the dome was added, designed by F.
Juvarra (1740). The Gothic-Renaissance facade,
split in three by slender pilaster strips, features portals, high windows, and a large rose window, and
is enlivened by sculptures, mostly by G. and T. Rodari (15th-16th c.). On either side of the central
portal are two aediculas with statues of Pliny the
Elder (who died in the eruption of Mt. Vesuvius in

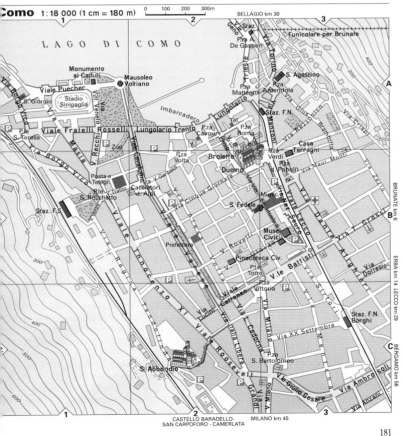

181

Como: Duomo

A.D. 79) and Pliny the Younger, his nephew. Also note the two portals, one on the right side and the other on the left (called the Porta della Rana), by Rodari, and the apse (1513).

The *interior* is a mix of Gothic (nave and aisles) and Renaissance (transept) styles, with a 75-m dome. Along the nave hang 16th-c. tapestries. The side altars have reliefs by Rodari and canvases by Ferrari and Luini.

Casa del Terragni (*A-B3*). Once the *Casa del Fascio*, a building used by the Fascist party, this building stands in the *Piazza del Popolo*, facing the apse of the Duomo; built by G. Terragni in 1932-36, this is one of the most notable pieces of Rationalist architecture in Italy.

S. Fedele (*B2-3*). This basilica was originally Como's cathedral, and dates from the early 12th c. The polygonal apse is crowned with a small loggia; note the portal with reliefs, in Via Vittorio Emanuele. In the little square are two interesting 15th-c. buildings, with terracotta and wood sections, now being restored.

Musei Civici (*B3*). *Open Tue.-Sat., 9:30-12:30 and 2-5; Sun., 10-1.* The town museums are the *Museo Archeologico*, located in Palazzo Giovio, and the *Museo Storico del Risorgimento* (*temporarily closed*), located in Palazzo Olginati; both museums, linked by a gallery, overlook Piazza Medaglie d'Oro. The former contains collections of archeological finds (from prehistoric times to Roman times); the latter, exhibits of local history, from the Renaissance to the present. Now being installed are halls that will exhibit Greek, Etruscan, Phoenician-Punic, Assyro-Babylonian, and Egyptian artifacts, as well as a portrait gallery (Galleria dei Ritratti).

Pinacoteca Civica (*B2*). *Open Tue.-Sat., 9:30-12:30 and 2-5; Sun., 10-1.* This art gallery is housed in the 17th-c. Palazzo Volpi; it has a collection of 17th-c. Lombard canvases, frescoes and bas-reliefs from the 14th c., and work by abstract artists living in Como.

Piazza Vittoria (*B-C2-3*). Note the monument to

Garibaldi, by V. Vela. On one side of this squar stands the **Porta Torre**, also known as the *Torr di Porta Vittoria* (1192), a gate with two passage ways and large windows on the interior, once par of the city walls, rebuilt by the emperor Bar barossa; at the corners, note the two five-sided tow ers. In the cellar of a nearby school are ruins of th *Torre Pretoria*, a tower dating from the Roman Em pire (3rd c.); in the cellars of another school i Via Carducci are ruins from the walled perimete that dates from the Roman Republic. Yet other Ro man ruins (baths and library of Pliny the Younge 2nd c.) are found along Viale Lecco; recently, ru ins of a Roman villa were uncovered at the corne of Via Tommaso Grossi and Via Zezio (*B3; privat property*).

S. Abbondio* (*C2*). This basilica, built in the 11th c., is one of the masterpieces of Lombard Ro manesque architecture. Note the facade, adorne with pilaster strips and cornices in relief, and th two bell towers. The interior features a four-aisle nave divided by columns and tall piers, with deep presbytery. In the loggia over the entrance and in the apse, there is a vast frescoed Life c Christ by Lombard painters of the mid-14th c. T the left of the altar is a marble statue of S. Abbon dio (1490) attributed to C. Solari.

On the western shore of the port is the *Giardin Pubblico*, a public park; at the water's edge is th **Tempio Voltiano** (*A1*); *open Apr.-Oct., 10-12 an 3-6; Nov.-Mar., 10-12 and 2-4; closed Mon.* This clas sical-style building (1927) contains memorabilia and documents concerning Alessandro Volta, Co mo's most illustrious son, inventor of the electri battery (1745-1827). Continuing along past the Mo numento ai Caduti (Monument to the War Dead 1933), there is a tower designed by Futurist ar chitect Antonio Sant'Elia. On the left is the *Stadi Sinigaglia*.

Other monuments. Villa Olmo (*off map, towar Cernobbio*). This large Neo-Classic villa was buil by S. Cantoni in 1782-97; it now belongs to the city of Como, and the handsome grounds are a public park. The halls are used for exhibits, conferences and concerts (*open 9:30-12 and 3-6, closed holi days; park: summer, 8-11 p.m.; winter, 9-7*).

S. Agostino (*A3*). This Gothic church dates from the early 14th c. and has a Romanesque portal decorated with reliefs. Inside, note the 15th- /17th c. frescoes, and canvases by Morazzone (1612). Adjacent are two cloisters.

Villa Geno. Along the eastern shore of the lake runs Viale Geno (*A2*), a handsome drive or strol leading to the *Villa Geno* (1850), on a spit of land with a lakefront and enormous grounds, open to the public.

Museo della Seta (*C3, off map*). *Open Tue.-Fri., 9 12 and 3-6; Sat., by request, tel. 031303180.* This mu seum in the Via Valleggio has a collection of ob jects and documents detailing the history of the silk industry in Como.

Carpoforo (*C2-3, off map*). This church stands the SE outskirts of Como; from Via Milano you ⎵ss under the railroad tracks, with a short detour. ⎵ilt in the 11th c., the basilica is one of the earli-⎵ pieces of Romanesque architecture in Como *⎵en by request, enquire at the adjoining religious ⎵titute, 9-12*). From here, you can proceed for about ⎵other 1.5 km, and then walk about 15 minutes, to ⎵e the ruins of the **Castello Baradello** (*open Thu., ⎵.-Sun., and holidays, 2:30-6; other days, by request, ⎵ 031592805*) built by Frederick Barbarossa in ⎵58 and dismantled by the Spanish in 1527 (view ⎵ the city, the Brianza countryside, and the lakes). ⎵ the Lungolario there is the station of the funicu-⎵ which goes to **Brunate** (716 m), a little village fa-⎵ous for the marvellous views of the lake and as a ⎵rting point for a series of excursions.

⎵ortina d'Ampezzo*

⎵ev. 1211 m, pop. 6467; Veneto, province of Bel-⎵no. The green valley in which this town lies ⎵the Valle del Boite, in that part of the Cadore ⎵ea which is called Ampezzano. The valley is ⎵rounded by a marvellous Dolomitic setting, ⎵ith the peaks of the Tofane Pomagagnon, ⎵istallo, Dorapìss, Cinque Torri, and Croda da ⎵go. The first Grand Hotels were built here ⎵ound 1860, just after the bell tower of the ⎵rish church was rebuilt, a classic image for ⎵e promotion of this little town (it was under ⎵ustrian rule until the end of WWI); in 1909 it ⎵as linked to the Falzàrego pass by a new road, ⎵e Grande Strada delle Dolomiti, which had ⎵en under construction for years, for the use ⎵ the Austro-Hungarian military; the first ski ⎵mpetitions were held here in 1902; in 1874 ⎵ woman climbed the Cristallo. The town is a ⎵gendary holiday resort, a place of elegance, ⎵nown, and luxury, where the social whirl and ⎵inter sports have long come together.

⎵laces of interest. **Corso Italia.** This central thor-⎵ughfare (largely closed to traffic; pedestrians only) ⎵lined with hotels, cafes, and elegant shops; it runs ⎵to the two central squares, Piazza Roma and Piaz-⎵ Venezia, separated by the 18th-c. parish church ⎵ the **Ss. Filippo e Giacomo**. Inside, note the ⎵ooden tabernacle by A. Brustolon (1724) and the ⎵tarpiece by A. Zanchi (1679); from atop the bell ⎵wer, fine panoramic view.

⎵iasa de ra Regloles. *Open Jun.-Sep. and Dec., 10-⎵2:30 and 4-7:30; Mar.-Apr., 4-7.30 p.m.; closed Mon.* ⎵enter of the family communities of Ampezzo, this ⎵uilding is located at n. 17 in Corso Italia. It houses ⎵ rich mineralogic and paleontological collection ⎵ote the fossil collections of Rinaldo Zardini), and ⎵e **Pinacoteca Mario Rimoldi d'Arte Moderna**, ⎵ gallery with paintings by such modern artists as ⎵.Campigli, C. Carrà, G. De Chirico, F. De Pisis, R. Gut-⎵so, G. Morandi, O. Rosai, A. Sassu, A. Tosi, and others.

⎵tadio Olimpico del Ghiaccio. This now historic

Olympic ice-skating structure, on the northern out-skirts of town, has a skating surface of 4230 sq. m, and was built for the winter Olympic Games of 1956. Facing it, on a boulder, a bronze plaque com-memorates the French geologist Dolomieu who was the first, at the end of the 18th c., to describe Dolomitic rock.

Cortona*

Elev. 494 m, pop. 22,436; Toscana (Tuscany), province of Arezzo. Clean air whispering through the olive trees, and a city the color of the sandstone from which it is largely carved, clustered on the steep slopes once enclosed by the vast Etruscan walls, at the edge of the plain of Valdichiana. The medieval past sur-vives here, in the air and the buildings; for two centuries archeologists have been delving in-to the more distant Etruscan past thanks to the foundation of the Accademia Etrusca.

Getting around. Much of the historic center is closed to traffic; therefore, we recommend a walk-ing tour, though you must have a car to reach many of the monuments outside the walls.

The historic center
In the 15th c. Fra' Angelico came here to paint; a generation later, Luca Signorelli, great Cortonese painter, began his career here. This Tuscan hill town is unforgettable in the melting light, when seen from high above, from the Medici fortress.
Piazza della Repubblica (*B1*). Heart of Cortona, the square is lined by the 13th-c. **Palazzo Comu-nale**, and the 12th-c. *Palazzo del Capitano del Popo-lo*; nearby is *Piazza Signorelli*, with the **Palazzo Casali**, the site of the Museo dell'Accademia Etrusca. **Museo dell'Accademia Etrusca*** (*A1*). *Open 10-1 and 3-5; closed Mon.* Founded in 1727, with library (*open by request*), as a branch of the Etruscan Acad-

Cortona: Palazzo Comunale

183

emy, this museum has remarkable collections of Etruscan artifacts. Note the great **bronze lamp**** with satyrs and sirens (5th-4th c. B.C.); it also exhibits Egyptian and Roman objects, a 12th-c. mosaic, medieval and modern pieces of the applied arts (note the little porcelain temple by the Manifattura Ginori at Doccia; 1750-51), coins*, gems, medallions, seals, miniatures and costumes. Among the paintings, work by N. di Pietro Gerini, B. di Lorenzo, F. Signorelli, Pinturicchio, and L. Signorelli; a hall is dedicated to the work by the modern painter Severini, who was born in Cortona.

On the upper floors, three rooms display finds from the Tumulo II of the digs in the so-called Etruscan "meloni" from Il Sodo (see below), including late-Archaic jewelry*.

Duomo (*A1*). Rebuilt in the 15th c., some Romanesque features survive in the facade of this cathedral; note the 16th-c. portal of Cristofanello, under the portico.

Museo Diocesano* (*A1*). *Open Apr.-Sep., 9:30-1 and 3:30-7; Oct.-Mar., 10-1 and 3-5; closed Mon.* The Diocesan museum is located in the former *Gesù* church (1498-1505) and adjacent buildings, facing the Duomo. In one section, works by P. Lorenzetti, L. Signorelli, and a 2nd-c. A.D. Roman sarcophagus*. In the *former church*, works by Sassetta, P. Lorenzetti, Fra' Angelico, B. della Gatta; in the *former sacristy*, more Lorenzetti and the celebrated Vagnucci reliquary*, by G. da Firenze (1457), and other 13th-c. paintings.

Downstairs, in the *lower church*, 16th-c. frescoes, partly attributed to G. Vasari.

S. Francesco (*A-B2*). This 13th-c. church was rebuilt in the 17th c.; inside is a fine 10th-c. Byzantine ivory reliquary*.

Via Berrettini (*A2*). This steep street goes up to the 16th-c. church of *S. Cristoforo*, while Via S. Croce leads further up to S. Margherita, with fine views. Along the way is the little church of S. Nicolò.

S. Nicolò (*A2*). This 15th-c. church stands amidst the cypresses; note the standard* of the Compagn di S. Nicolò painted on both sides by L. Signorell

Santuario di S. Margherita (*A3*). This Neo-Got ic sanctuary (1856-97) is renowned for the spe tacular view from the square before it.

Just uphill is the **Medici fortress**, 651 m (*A3*), bu in 1556 (view*); take **Via S. Margherita** (*A-B2-* back to town; note the mosaic *Via Crucis** by (Severini.

Monuments outside the city walls

The geometric architecture by F. di Giorgio Marti in the church of the Madonna del Calcinaio co trasts pleasingly with the gentle views of Tusca countryside, dotted with cypresses and olive tree

S. Domenico (*B2*). Just outside the Porta Berard is this late Gothic church with a triptych by L. Niccolò Gerini (1402). Take Viale Giardini Pubblic (B2-3) for a walk with splendid views*.

Madonna del Calcinaio** (*B2; off map*). Op summer, 4-7; winter, 3-5; holidays, 10-12:30. Standi some 3 km downhill from the town, near the loc road from Camucia, this elegant Renaissanc church was an archetype for the sanctuaries bu between the 15th and 16th c. Built in 1485-1513 a plan by F. di Giorgio Martini, it has a luminous i terior, in the style of Brunelleschi, with stained gla windows by G. de Marcillat (16th c.); the main a tar, from the same period, is by B. Covatti.

Tanella di Pitagora (*B2; off map*). *Open by* quest, contact the custodian on the site. Some 3 k SW of town, near the Madonna del Calcinaio, is th Etruscan hypogeum, perhaps dating from the 4th B.C., set among the cypresses.

S. Maria Nuova (*A2; off map*). Outside the wal north of town, this mid-16th-c. church is reached exiting the *Porta Colonia*. It was drastically rebuilt G. Vasari.

Convento delle Celle or *Convento dei Cappuc*

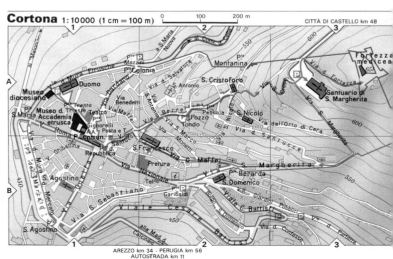

(A2; off map). This convent stands 3.5 km NE, out
Porta Colonia, in a handsome hillside setting, and
as founded by St. Francis between 1211 and 1221.
Meloni" (A1; off map). *Open by request, contact
e custodian on the site.* At Il Sodo, 2 km NW of
wn, near the SS 71 road, are 4th- to 3rd-c. B.C. Etr-
scan hypogea, or underground burial chambers,
rved or dug out of sandstone. Some of the finds
ere are now on display in the Museo dell'Acca-
emia Etrusca (see above).

osenza

ev. 238 m, pop. 74,185; Calabria, provincial
pital. Set in a lovely hilly setting, the town
as an ancient quarter, clinging to the Colle
ncrazio, and a modern quarter, in the plain
elow. The humanistic cultural tradition –
hich lent such renown to the Accademia
osentina, founded in the 16th c. by the great
umanist Aulo Giano Parrasio and still in ex-
tence – was recently rejuvenated with the
stablishment of the Università della Calabria,
the nearby town of Arcavacata di Rende.

laces of interest. Piazza Campanella lies in the
ea where the old town meets the modern town.
verlooking the piazza is the church of **S. Domeni-
**, a Baroque reconstruction of an earlier 15th-c.
uilding, of which the entrance and a handsome
se window survive. In the *interior*, note the rich
ucco ornamentation, the precious canvases, and
e 17th-c. choir. Adjecent to the church is the sump-
ous Oratorio del Rosario, or Oratory of the Rosary.
t the center of the old town, with its intriguing me-
ieval network of alleys and lanes, the **Duomo***
verlooks the square, with a powerful solemn Goth-
facade, made of tufa, with three portals and three
se windows. A Cistercian Gothic building (12th-
3th c.), it was transformed in the 18th c. and re-
ently restored. In the *inside* are a Roman sar-
ophagus and the funerary monument* to Isabel of
ragon, a French creation from the late 13th c.
he *Museo Interdiocesano* is part of the **Treasury**
f the Duomo and includes paintings dating from
e 15th-18th c., goldsmithery, vestments and fur-
ishings, and parchments. One of the most out-
anding pieces is the Stauroteca*, an enameled
eliquary in the form of a cross, a 13th-c. creation of
e Sicilian school, donated by Frederick II for the
onsecration of the cathedral, and ivories by the
chool of Cellini. Overlooking **Piazza XV Marzo**,
t the heart of the old town, are the Prefettura, or
olice courts building, with the extensive gardens
f the *Villa Comunale*, the *Teatro Comunale* and the
alazzo dell'Accademia Cosentina, also the site of
e **Museo Civico Archeologico** (*open 9-1; Mon.
nd Thu. also 3-6:30 p.m.; closed Sat.-Sun.*), the mu-
icipal archeological museum.
. Francesco d'Assisi. This church was founded in
e Gothic period but heavily renovated during the
enaissance and in the Baroque period.

High atop the hill stands the mighty square structure of the **Castello**, a stronghold built in various
phases (Norman and Swabian era – especially the
octagonal tower – and the 16th and 17th c.).
Inside the 18th-c. church of **S. Francesco di Paola** there are a handsome marble sepulcher (1593),
a Baroque wooden choir, and a triptych dating from
the early 16th c.

Cremona*

Elev. 45 m, pop. 71,611; Lombardia (Lombardy),
provincial capital. The Po River, flowing within
the massive earth embankments, runs past the
edge of Cremona, while the Adda is just a short
way upstream. The surrounding countryside is
well watered and fertile. A considerable portion of the city's industry and trade is linked
to agriculture. The Gothic crown of the Torrazzo tower, visible from the surrounding fields
for quite a distance, amid the low-lying Lombard plain, stands in one of the loveliest medieval squares in Italy.

Historical note. We can only speculate about
Celtic and pre-Roman settlement here; the Roman
colony was founded in 218 B.C. The Communal
government was founded in 1098 and the cathedral in 1107: this marked the beginning of three
centuries that shaped the monumental center of
Cremona, which expanded with the growing
monastic settlement and projects of reclamation.
The Communal government brought Cremona into the Lombard League in 1167, prior to the great
Battle of Legnano, but it had long been an imperial ally (the Cremonese fought alongside Barbarossa in the siege of Milan), and had fought repeatedly against the Milanese (whom it defeated
in 1213 at Castelleone), and again alongside the
imperial troops during the reign of Frederick II. In
the meantime, in 1169-87 a walled perimeter had
been built, which included, to the south of the ancient Roman area, the site of reclamation projects,
with a network of roads radiating out from the Duomo, and the Cittanova, to the north. From 1334 on,
when Azzone Visconti took Cremona, the city
linked its fate with that of Milan and of the duchy
of Lombardy, until the unification of Italy. Bianca
Maria Visconti brought the city as part of her dowry
when she married Francesco Sforza in 1441. The
Renaissance created handsome new buildings in
Lombard brickwork, with terracotta decorations,
and witnessed the flourishing of local painting. Perhaps even more illustrious than the artists of Cremona, however, are its violin makers, the pride of
the city's tradition and heritage; the names of the
great masters, who drew exquisite music from fine
wood, are well known: Andrea and Niccolò Amati
(16th-17th c.), Antonio Stradivari (d. 1737), and
Giuseppe Antonio Guarneri (d. 1745). In 1567 the
great composer Claudio Monteverdi was born in
Cremona, and in 1834 another composer, Amilcare

Cremona: Battistero

Ponchielli, was born about a dozen km away. The walls that surrounded the city were modernized; the Castello di S. Croce was demolished, the northern bastions became a public promenade in 1787, and the rest of the walls were demolished at the turn of the 20th c., to make room for a growing town. An iron bridge over the Po, built in 1892, replaced the old bridge laid over a series of boats. The port/canal was built after WWII.

Getting around. A number of the main roads in the historic center are closed to private cars.

Places of interest. Piazza del Comune.** This is the artistic center of Cremona and one of the loveliest medieval squares in Italy. Note the array of monuments lining the square: the Torrazzo, the Duomo, the Battistero, the Loggia dei Militi, and the Palazzo del Comune.

Torrazzo.* *Open Apr.-Oct., 10:30-1 and 2:30-6; holidays, until 7 p.m.; Nov.-Mar., holidays, 10:30-1 and 2-7; weekdays, by request, tel. 330715935.* This exceedingly tall bell tower (111 m), a symbol of Cremona, was built around 1267; the massive brick shaft has an octagonal marble top, added between 1284 and the early 14th c. A stairway (487 steps) leads to the top, with a fine panoramic view*. The Renaissance *Loggia della Bertazzola* (1525; under the arcades, medieval marble carvings and 14th-c. sarcophagus, by B. da Campione) links the Torrazzo with the facade of the Duomo.

Duomo.** This is one of the most notable pieces of Lombard Romanesque architecture, built during the 12th c. and enlarged (transept) in the 13th and 14th c. The marble facade has two orders of loggias, a handsome rose window (1274), and a 15th-c. crown, as well as a 13th-c. arched entranceway (in the front, note the strip of reliefs, depicting work in the fields*, sculpted by the school of Antelami), surmounted by an aedicula with three statues by M. Romano (1310). Overlooking Via Boccaccino is the

northern end of the late 13th-c. transept, with arched entranceway, mullioned windows, rose w dows, and terracotta ornamentation. As you c tinue to walk around the church, you will note complex of three apses, and the southern end the transept (1342).

The **interior*** has a nave and two aisles and is vided by pillars. The rich decoration softens somewhat stern architecture. Along the walls of nave and the central apse is a series of frescoes picting the lives of Mary and Jesus*, by a numl of Lombard-Venetian painters (1506-73), includi Boccaccino, Romanino, and Pordenone. Note Renaissance sculpture in the two pulpits* in fr of the presbytery, with reliefs attributed, in part Amadeo. In the crypt is the Arca dei Ss. Marcelli e Pietro, once attributed to B. Briosco (1506), a reassembled here in 1609.

Battistero.* This octagonal Romanesque bap tery, crowned by a small loggia, dates from 1167

Loggia dei Militi. Built in 1292 as a meeting h for the captains of the city's militia. Notable port and high mullioned windows.

Palazzo del Comune.* The headquarters of g ernment in early Cremona, it was rebuilt in 12 46, and has been greatly renovated since. The c tral pillar of the ground-floor portico bears an "*are gario*," or external pulpit, built in 1507. Upstairs, the are a Renaissance portal; a marble fireplace (15 in the Sala della Giunta, where the city authorit meet; and, in the smaller *Saletta dei Violini* (*op Tue.-Sat., 8:30-6; Sun., 10-6*), five of Cremona's fin violins – by Stradivarius, Amati (two), Pie Guarneri, and Giuseppe Guarneri del Gesù.

S. Agostino.* Church built in 1345, with a mol mental Gothic facade; interesting frescoes in 3rd and 5th chapels at right.

Museo Civico Ala Ponzone.* *Open Tue.-Sat., 8: 6; Sun., 10-6.* Housed in the 16th-c. *Palazzo Affai* (entrance at n. 4 in Via Ugolani Dati), this museu features an *art gallery, collections of fine craftwo* the *collection of Cremona history and iconograp* and the *archeological section.* The noteworthy **Pi coteca**, or art gallery, features many halls decol ed with medieval frescoes and paintings of the C monese school, dating from the 15th to 18th c., well as other Italian and foreign artists, and a c lection of modern Italian art.

The same building contains the **Museo Stra variano** (entrance from n. 17 in Via Palestro; *op same hours as the Museo Civico*), with collectic of documents and objects linked to great musicia and instrument makers of Cremonese history. particular, original drawings, models, and toc made or used by Stradivarius; manuscripts Ponchielli.

Corso Garibaldi. This avenue is lined by notewo thy buildings, especially **Palazzo Raimondi** (178), built in 1496, now housing associations study of ancient music and violin making. On t right, midway along the Corso, **Palazzo di C tanova**, built in 1256 (heavily restored in the 1920

Other monuments. Palazzo Fodri (n. 17 Corso Matteotti) is an early 16th-c. aristocratic mansion.

S. Michele. This 12th-c. Romanesque church was rebuilt in the 19th c.

Palazzo dell'Arte. This modern building overlooking Piazza Marconi contains the school for violin-makers (Istituto Professionale Liutario e del Legno) and the *Museo Civico di Storia Naturale* (*open Tue.-Sun., 9-1; tel. 037223766*), dedicated to natural history.

S. Pietro al Po. Rebuilt in 1575, this church boasts Cremonese Renaissance works of art.

Museo della Civiltà Contadina (*off map*). *Open Tue.-Sat., 8:30-6; Sun., 10-6*. On the Via Castelleone 51 (SS road to Milan), set in the Cascina Cambonino, this museum contains documents on the lives of Cremonese farmers over two centuries, as well as many traditional farming implements.

Cuma

Elev. 80 m; Campania, province of Naples, townships of Pozzuoli and Bàcoli. The **Parco Archeologico***, or archeological site (*open 9-one hour before sunset*), is one of the most important in Italy.

Historical note. A colony of the Chalcidians of Euboea in Greece (8th c. B.C.), Cuma (orig. Cumae) has a historic importance that is not limited to the reputation of the Sibyl: in its waters, the ships of Siracusa, under the tyrant, came to the city's defense against Etruscan raiders (474), who thus lost forever their dominion over the Tyrrhenian Sea. And Cumae was the cradle of reading and writing in Italy; the alphabet spread out from here. At the foot of and spreading up over a hill of lava, isolated close to the sea, the site is one of the classical birthplaces of Italian culture.

Places of interest. The **Arco Felice*** is the vault of a brick viaduct; the acropolis can be seen in the distance, stark against the sea*.

You can see the arched perimeter of the **amphitheater**, of the Campanian type, built in the early Imperial Age.

On the slopes directly above the **acropolis**, note the ruins of the Greek walls, from the 5th c. B.C.

The **Antro della Sibilla Cumana**,* or Cave of the Cumaean Sibyl, is a straight gallery extending for 131 m, a structure built by the Greeks in the 6th-5th c. B.C.; the room at the end of the gallery was believed to be the home of the Sibyl.

Walking along the **Via Sacra** you will find the **Cripta Romana**, a tunnel dating from the reign of Augustus that runs through the hill, or Colle di Cuma; the **Tempio di Apollo**, or Temple of Apollo, which still has the square from Greek and Samnite times and fragments of Augustan columns; the **Tempio di Giove**, or Temple of Zeus, founded by the Greeks and rebuilt by Augustus, later transformed into a Christian basilica (5th-6th c.).

Èrice

Elev. 751 m, pop. 31,026; Sicilia (Sicily), province of Trapani. On the summit of Monte Èrice, this lovely, perfectly triangular town has been a favorite stopping place for many centuries, given its perfect climate and astounding views.

Places of interest. Mura. The walls (well preserved, especially on the NE side) are made of megalithic blocks (5th c. B.C.) in the lower section, and are of Norman material (12th c.) in the upper section and in the three gates.

Chiesa Matrice.* This 14th-c. church features an isolated bell tower* with mullioned windows (1312); *inside*, note the 15th-/16th-c. chapels, and a Virgin, painted by F. Laurana (1469).

Museo Civico Antonio Cordici (*open Mon.-Thu., 2:30-5:30; Fri.-Sun., 8:30-1:30*). The town museum consists of notable collections of ancient artifacts and art (prehistoric, Punic, Hellenistic, and Roman archeological finds), paintings from the 17th-19th c., local handicrafts and silver, and a marble Annunciation* by A. Gagini (1525).

To the right of the *Castello Pepoli*, at the end of a little road, stands the 12th-/13th-c. *Castello di Venere* (12th-13th c.), on the round crag of the acropolis; inside are the ruins of a Temple of Venus, with a sacred well; fine view*.

Faenza

Elev. 35 m, pop. 53,452; Emilia-Romagna, province of Ravenna. At the edge of the plain of Romagna, where the Lamone River crosses the Via Emilia, this city was built by the House of Manfredi (seigneurs here before the town came under the rule of the Church, 1509), and was endowed with a remarkably rich culture, in a happy conjunction with the Florentine artistic world during the Humanist age. The production of ceramics attained a spectacular level in the 15th and 16th c.; there are records of this craft as far back as 1142: the name of the town has survived in the term "faïence," indicating what the Italians call "majolica," a glazed earthenware or pottery, decorated at high heat.

Places of interest. Piazza del Popolo. Lined on both sides by porticoes and loggias, with the adjacent Piazza della Libertà this is the heart of Faenza, with the **Palazzo del Podestà**, the *Torre dell'Orologio*, and the *Palazzo del Municipio*, in the courtyard of which is the *Teatro Comunale Masini*. Overlooking Piazza della Libertà, with the Baroque *Fontana di Piazza*, is the cathedral (see below).

Cattedrale.* One of the most notable works of the early Renaissance in Romagna, this cathedral was begun in 1474 to plans by G. da Maiano and was completed in the early-16th c. The facade is unfinished; the *interior* is clearly Tuscan in style, with the various 15th-/16th-c. works of sculpture, including tombs of saints, and reliefs by B. da Maiano (1476). Among the paintings, a work by I. da Imola.

Corso Mazzini. One of Faenza's chief arteries, it features, at n. 21, a house built by G. Pistocchi for himself in 1788, with others at n. 47, 54, and 60. N. 93 is the 17th-c. *Palazzo Mazzolani*.

S. Maria Vecchia. Rebuilt in the 17th c., it preserves traces of the original medieval building, especially the 9th-c. octagonal **campanile***.

Palazzo Milzetti. *Open 8:45-1; Thu. also 2:15-4:30; closed Sun. and holidays*. In Via Tonducci 15, this is a fine piece of Neo-Classic architecture by G. Pistocchi, with stucco decoration by F. Giani; notable for their stuccoes are the Galleria di Achille and the Gabinetto d'Amore.

Pinacoteca Comunale.* *Closed for restoration.* The municipal art gallery is located at n. 1 in Via S. Maria dell'Angelo, and features works by local artists, 14th-19th c. (G. da Rimini, Leonardo and Luca Scaletti, M. Palmezzano, G.B. Bertucci, Bagnacavallo, S. Foschi, I. da Imola, and F. Fenzoni), and of the Bolognese school, 16th-18th c. (G. Francia, F. Albani, A. Tiarini, Domenichino, and C. Cignani). Also, note a wooden statue* by Donatello; a 16th-c. Virgin and Child*; a marble bust by A. Rossellino; two 15th-c. trousseaux chests*; a fine collection of still life paintings, and works by A. Lombardi and F. Guardi.

Museo Internazionale delle Ceramiche.* *Open Apr.-Oct., Tue.-Sat., 9-7; Sun. and holidays, 9:30-1 and 3-7; Nov.-Mar., 9:30-2; Sun., 9:30-1; Tue.-Fri., 9-1:30; Sat., Sun. and holidays, 9:30-1 and 3-6; Nov.-Mar., 9:30-2; Sun., 9:30-1; closed Mon., 1 Jan., 15 Ago, 25 Dec.* At n. 2 in Via Campidori, at the corner of Viale Baccarini, this museum and research center is devoted to the history and art of ceramics, from every region and era. The 38 halls include Italian Renaissance majolica, Turkish faience, and Chinese porcelain; a wide array of Italian ceramics from the 13th to the early-20th c.; pre-Columbian and prehistoric ceramics; and a wide-ranging section devoted to contemporary international ceramics.

Chiesa della Commenda. In Borgo Durbecco (at the end of Corso Europa), this 12th-c. church has frescoes by G. da Treviso the Younger (1533), restored in 1980.

Fano

Elev. 12 m, pop. 56,175; Marche, province of Pesaro Urbino. The "Fanum Fortunae" or Temple of Fortune, which gave the town its name, lacks in documentary sources, and has eluded archeologists' efforts to identify it. The town is located on the Adriatic, left of the mouth of the Metauro River, where the Via Flaminia reaches the sea. Of the Roman colony, all that remains is the Arco di Augusto, or Arch of Augustus, the regular layout of the center, and a literary mention of a "basilica" built here by the famous Roman architect Vitruvius. The town was shaped by the rule of the House of Malatesta, from the end of the 13th c. unt 1463, when fine art and architecture were th order of the day. Now it is an active tradin town, prospering from its fishing industry, a well as a seaside resort.

Places of interest. Rocca Malatestiana. This mi 15th-c. fortress of the Malatesta family was once prison, and is now an art gallery. Follow a stretch the *Augustan walls*, with cylindrical towers, the take Viale Buozzi and Viale della Rimembranza the Arco di Augusto.

Arco di Augusto.** This arch, made of sandston faced with travertine, was built in A.D. 2 as a mo umental ornament on the Via Flaminia, in honor Augustus, near where the main road reached th sea. Adjacent to the arch are the **loggias** of the 15t c. church of **S. Michele***, with a Renaissance po tal by B. da Carona (1512).

Via Arco d'Augusto. The main street of Fano ru from the arch to the center of town, and down the sea. Immediately on the right is the **Cattedral** or cathedral, by Maestro Rainerio, with an origin 12th-c. facade; inside, note the Cappella Nolfi, chapel decorated by Domenichino (1623), wit paintings by L. Carracci and S. Ceccarini. Furth along, past Corso Matteotti and the tree-lined Pia za Amiani, is the the monumental 18th-c. **Palazz Montevecchio**.

Piazza XX Settembre. Set in the heart of Fano, an adorned with the 16th-c. *Fontana della Fortuna*, th square is bounded by the stern **Palazzo della R gione*** (1299), with portico, mullioned window and a modern tower (inside, the 19th-c. Neo-Class Teatro della Fortuna). On the right side of the buil ing, through the Arco Borgia-Cybo (1491), you e ter the courtyard of *Palazzo Malatesta*, in two par one 15th-c., with portico and crenelation, the oth 16th-c., by Sansovino. Here are the Museo Civic and the Pinacoteca.

Museo Civico and Pinacoteca. *Open 9:30-12.3 and 4-7; summer also 9-11 p.m.; closed Mon.; te 0721828362.* The *archeological section*, on th ground floor, comprises finds ranging from the N olithic to the Roman Empire. On the mezzanine a modern paintings by such artists as G. Induno, Mancini, E. Tito, F. Modesti, and G. Pierpaoli; also collection of coins and medallions (note meda lions by M. de' Pasti) and a collection of theater-r lated graphics (note work by G. Torelli). On the u per floor, the huge *Sala Malatestiana* houses th **Pinacoteca**, with paintings by artists including and P. Morganti, Guercino, Reni, Domenichino, G Guerrieri, S. Cantarini, M. Preti, A. Lilli, C. Giaquinto; a small side room are a polyptych* by M. Giambon (1420 ca.) and altarpiece by G. Santi (1487 ca There is also a section of local 18th-c. painte (A. Amorosi, S. Ceccarini, G. Donnini, F. Mancin P. Tedeschi) and a collection of 18th-c. ceramics.

S. Pietro ad Vallum. This 17th-c. church has Baroque interior decorated with stuccoes, frescoe and paintings (note dome).

rche **Malatestiane**. These are two monumental
mbs* of members of the Malatesta family; the one
the right is by L.B.Alberti (1460), the other, Goth-
in style, by F. di Domenico (1416-21). They are
oth placed beneath the portico of the former
urch of *S. Francesco.*

Maria Nuova. This church is located in Via Gio-
nni de Tonsis. Of the original structure, only the
ortico and the rich Renaissance portal, by B. da
rona, survive. Inside, note 18th-c. stuccoes and
anels by Perugino, some painted in collaboration
ith the young Raphael.

Paterniano. Dedicated to Fano's patron saint,
e church was built in the 16th c. by J. Sansovino
ote the fine Renaissance cloister).

errara**

ev. 9 m, pop. 132,127; Emilia-Romagna, provin-
al capital. The city lies partly concealed be-
nd its walls and rows of trees. The river Po
ow flows at some distance, but its ancient
ed once ran along a road in early Ferrara.
he city lies on the northeast edge of Emilia-
omagna, for three centuries home to the
ourt of the Este family. The Este were patrons
f the arts. Thus, Ferrara attracted artists and
usicians who became skilled in the courtly
ays of cultivating power. Aside from the mas-
rs of the "Ferrarese school," we should men-
on outsiders such as Piero della Francesca,
eon Battista Alberti, and Rogier van der Wey-
en. The poets include Boiardo, Ariosto, and
asso. Frescobaldi, whom Bach so admired, left
errara at the decline of the Este. And the great
wiss historian Jacob Burckhardt called it Eu-
ope's first "modern" city, referring to the "Ad-
izione Erculea" (a new quarter, the third ex-
ansion phase of the city), the town plan of
e architect Biagio Rossetti, and the contrast
etween the Renaissance style and the nar-
ow close-set streets of the medieval districts.

istorical note. Ferrara was founded in the 7th c.
y the hexarchs of Ravenna; it was at one point a
yzantine military camp, stretching along the left
ank of the main course of the river Po, which ran
here Via Ripagrande now lies; the Longobards
led here a century or so later. By the end of the
eventh century, Ferrara was fighting for its inde-
endence from the rule of Matilda, countess of
anossa, to whose family the pope had bestowed
e city a century earlier. Ferrara's prosperous river
ade died out after 1152, when the breach of the
mbankment of Ficarolo, upstream of the city, shift-
d the Po's main course northward. The city finally
on its freedom with the death of Matilda, only to
e caught up in internecine strife between Guelfs
nd Ghibellines. A new and powerful leadership
merged with the Este family during the 13th c., and
as officially recognized by Rome in 1322. The Este
ukes dominated Ferrara's history for centuries

thereafter, bringing it prosperity and magnificence.
Two Este dukes, Niccolò II and Borso, worked
throughout the 14th and 15th c., building the first
two "additions," new walls, and the University. Late in
this period, the Este court boasted such illustrious
guests as Leon Battista Alberti and Piero della
Francesca, along with the artists of the "Officina Ferrarese" (Cosmè Tura, Ercole de' Roberti, and
Francesco del Cossa). Among their masterpieces are
the frescoes in Palazzo Schifanoia. The apex of Este
grandeur, however, came under Ercole I d'Este, who
entrusted his architect Biagio Rossetti with the conception and construction of the third addition, in
1492. This was to be a true Renaissance city, dotted
with parks and gardens. The center lies at the crossroads of Palazzo dei Diamanti, where Corso Ercole
d'Este, running north-south, intersects with Corso
Rossetti and Corso Porta Mare. Ferrara thus doubled
in size, was girt with new walls (partly still standing), and boasted the new Palazzo dei Diamanti and
the Palazzo of Ludovico il Moro. In the 16th c., Ferrara boasted poets such as Ariosto and Tasso and
painters like Dosso Dossi. Musical academies flourished here; when Ferrara's greatest composer, Girolamo Frescobaldi, moved to Rome in the early 17th
c., however, the rule of the Este had already ended.
Pope Clement VIII laid claim to Ferrara, and cardinals ruled here for two centuries, governing a declining city. Napoleonic rule did little to bring new
vigor, nor did the return of papal rule in 1814, or the
Austrian military garrison that followed. The first expansion beyond the 15th-c. walls came at the end
of the 19th c. Ferrara in the 20th c. industrialized to
a considerable degree, but the city is now focusing
on its university and the field of applied research.

Getting around. The center is closed to private
cars; these two routes are walking tours, though you
may choose to use public transportation for some
of the longer stretches.

The medieval city and the first expansion

A long straight roadway, comprising Viale Cavour
and Corso della Giovecca, divides the walled city
in two. Beginning from the cathedral, studded with
little loggias, this first tour captures the ancient atmosphere and hidden nooks of the southern half,
the city in its early phase, and the palazzi of Schifanoia and of Ludovico Sforza, known as "il Moro"
(or the Moor, 14th-15th c.). It ends with a view of the
eastern face of the city walls. Corso della Giovecca,
once the Canale della Zudeca, takes you back to
the city center.

Piazza Cattedrale. Overlooking this piazza in the
heart of Ferrara are the Cattedrale, or cathedral, the
Palazzo Comunale, or town hall, and the *Torre del-
l'Orologio*, or clock tower (1603). At the corner of Via
S. Romano stands the ancient church of *S. Romano*,
rebuilt in the 15th c.

Cattedrale** (*D4*). Medieval Ferrara's chief mon-

Ferrara

1 : 15 000 (1 cm = 150 m)

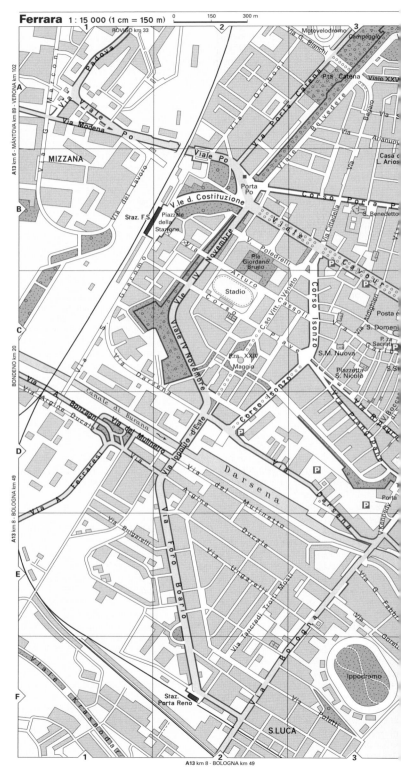

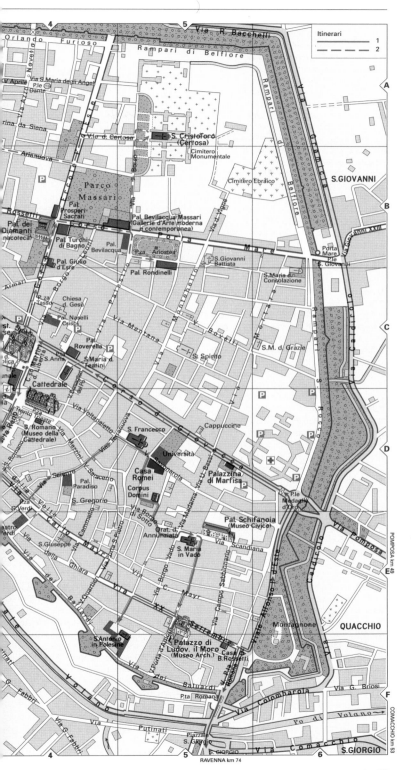

ument, the cathedral was originally Romanesque (1135). The 13th-c. facade* is made of marble; sculptures adorn the 12th-c. portals and the 13th-c. pediment over the porch, topped by a small Gothic mullioned loggia. On the right side, concealed at its base by a 15th-c. portico lined with shops, is the marble campanile* (1441-1596); classical in design, it is attributed to Leon Battista Alberti, and the late 15th-c. apse* is by Biagio Rossetti. An atrium (with a 5th-c. sarcophagus) leads to the *interior*, renovated in the 18th c. and decorated in the late 19th c. On the interior of the facade, frescoes by Garofalo (1530). In the 1st altar, right, is a greatly venerated 15th-c. fresco; in the 3rd altar, right, work by Bastianino; in the right arm of the transept is a painting by Guercino (1629); on the left are bronze statues, including two 15th-c. statues by D. Paris. The main altar dates from 1728; in the choir are inlaid stalls by Bernardino Canozzi (1501-25); in the vault of the apse is a fresco of the Last Judgement*, by Bastianino (1580). In the 6th and 3rd altars to the left are paintings by F. Francia and Garofalo (1524), respectively.

Museo della Cattedrale* (*D4*). *Open Tue.-Sun., 9:30-2.* The cathedral museum is located at the beginning of Via S. Romano, in the ancient former church of S. Romano and its nearby cloister. It features artworks that once hung in the cathedral, by such artists as C. Tura and G.B. Benvenuti, known as Ortolano; six 12th-c. marble panels* from the pulpit; two sculptures by J. della Quercia; eight 16th-c. tapestries*; 12 late 12th-c. marble panels*, with depictions of the months; 24 illuminated* choir-books (15th-16th c.).

Palazzo Comunale (*C4*). Built in the 13th c., this was the Este ducal residence. The facade was rebuilt in 1924. There is a small arch attributed to L.B. Alberti, topped by an equestrian statue of Niccolò III d'Este, and a column with a statue of Borso d'Este (the statues are modern) on either side of the *Volto del Cavallo*, which leads into the courtyard (now Piazza Municipio), which features a number of 15th-c. windows and an external vaulted stairway (1481). Inside, at the top of the main stairway, is the *Sala dell'Arengo* (*open by request*), a hall frescoed by A. Funi (1934-37), a Ferrarese painter, with a series devoted to the myth of Ferrara, while the *Sala del Plebiscito* features the large canvas of The Horrors of War, by G. Previati (1894), another Ferrarese painter.

Corso Porta Reno (*D4*). Beginning at Piazza della Cattedrale at the foot of the *Torre dell'Orologio*, or clock tower; on the right is the 16th-c. church of **S. Paolo**; inside are paintings by Scarsellino, Bastianino, D. Mona, and G. da Carpi.

Via delle Volte* (*D-E4*). Named after the covered arches between the buildings on the Via Carlo Mayr, once the left bank of the Po, and buildings further inland; it is a nearly intact medieval street.

Via Savonarola (*D5*). Backbone of the expansion commissioned by Niccolò II, this is a noble road of the early Renaissance. On the left, note the church of **S. Francesco** (*D5*), built in the 13th c. but renovated in 1494 by B. Rossetti; inside, fresco by Garofalo, paintings by I. Scarsellino, and 5th-c. sarcopha-

Ferrara: Castello Estense

gus. Further along is the main office of the Unive sity, with Renaissance portal and courtyard; it wa once *Palazzo Pareschi*, and the religious reform Calvin once stayed here. Opposite is the 15th-c. **Cas Romei*** (*open Tue.-Sun., 8:30-7*); around the tw courtyards, note the *Sala delle Sibille* and the *Sale ta dei Profeti* (with 15th-c. frescoes) and the d tached frescoes and sculptures.

Corpus Domini (*D5*). The convent was founde in 1406; in the church, painting by G. Cignaroli. the *Coro delle Clarisse**, or Clarissan choir (*open request, inquire with the Clarissan nuns in Via P golato, at n. 4; closed Sat.-Sun.*), with the Crucifixi by I. Scarsellino; also, tombs of various members the House of Este (Alfonso I, Lucrezia Borgia, A fonso II, and Lucrezia de' Medici).

Via Scandiana (*E5-6*). Of note is the church **S. Maria in Vado** (*E5*), rebuilt from 1495 to 151 by B. Rossetti; inside, see paintings by C. Bononi ar D. Mona.

Palazzo Schifanoia** (*E5*). The most famous the Este pleasure palaces, it was begun at the er of the 14th c., enlarged by P. Benvenuti degli Ordi (1464-69), and later by B. Rossetti. The marble po tal* stands out in the brickwork facade, once fre coed. Inside, the **Museo Civico** (*open Tue.-Sun., 7; closed Easter, 1 May, 15 Aug., 25 Dec.*) featurir the Sala dei Mesi, or Hall of Months, decorated wi a renowned series of **frescoes**** by F. del Cossa, de' Roberti, and other Ferrarese artists of the la 15th c. (the overall plan is by C. Tura). In the oth halls are collections of bronzes, ceramics, coins, je els, and paintings. Opposite is the **Civico Lapidar** (*open 9:30-7*), a collection of Roman marble car ings from the surrounding territory.

Palazzo di Ludovico il Moro** (*E-F5*). Built b B. Rossetti between 1495 and 1504, this palazzo h a fine porticoed courtyard.* It now houses th **Museo Archeologico Nazionale,*** (*open Tue.-Su 9-7:30*) featuring archeological finds – especially c ramics* – from the Graeco-Etruscan necropolis Spina (over 4000 tombs; late 6th-3rd c. B.C.), ne Comacchio.

S. Antonio in Polesine (*E-F5*). This monaste

ce stood on an island on the Po, and is now in
e of the loveliest settings in Old Ferrara (Vicolo
ambono n. 17). In the church, note the *Coro delle
onache**, with inlaid wooden choir stalls and three
apels with 14th-c. frescoes.

a XX Settembre (*E-F4-5*). In this street is the
lazzo di Ludovico il Moro. Straight and broad, this
tery was the backbone of the expansion com-
ssioned by Borso d'Este; at n. 152, decorated with
rracotta, is the *home of Biagio Rossetti* (F5), which
e architect built for himself in 1490.

Giorgio (*F5; off map*). Beyond the bridge over
e Po at Volano, this 16th-c. church belongs to a
mplex that existed in the 7th c. The terracotta bell
wer* dates from 1485; inside, paintings by the lo-
l 17th-c. artist F. Naselli.

ale Alfonso I d'Este (*E-F6*). A public promenade
the city walls, and particularly on a huge heap
earth, the *Montagnone*, created during the con-
uction of those same walls.

rso della Giovecca* (*C-D4-6*). This popular
eet dates from the so-called "Addizione Erculea",
Herculean addition, and runs on the course of the
rmer Canale della Zudeca (named after an an-
nt Jewish burial ground). At n. 174 is the **Palaz-
a di Marfisa*** (*D5; open Tue.-Sun., 9:30-1:30 and
*), once the home of an Este gentlewoman; note
e grotesque paintings by C. Filippi and fine fur-
hings; in the garden is the *Loggia degli Aranci*. At
e far end of the Corso, at n. 476, is **Palazzo
verella**, by B. Rossetti (1508), with an exquisite
ade*, and the 17th-c. church of the *Teatini* (*C4*),
h a painting* by Guercino.

---

e "Addizione Erculea"

1492, work began on the new quarter of the city
at more than doubled the area of Ferrara, spread-
north of Viale Cavour and Corso della Giovec-
This project was the brainchild of Ercole I, the
t Este duke.

stello Estense* (*C4*). *Open Tue.-Fri., 8:30-2; Sat.-
n., 8:30-7; closed Mon*. Surrounded by a moat, the
stle was built in 1385 and completed in the 16th
Noteworthy are the 15th-c. courtyard, the various
scoed halls, the Loggia degli Aranci with its hang-
garden surveying the city, the corridor of the
ccanali, the chapel of Ercole II's Calvinist wife,
d the dungeon, with its tragic history (Parisina,
de of Niccolò III, died as a prisoner here, after
ing in love with her stepson Ugo).

rso Ercole I d'Este* (*A-C4*). This was the chief
ery of the new Erculea quarter. At n. 16 is the ma-
tic **Palazzo di Giulio d'Este** (late-15th c.; re-
red in 1932). Interesting sights are the **Quadri-
degli Angeli,*** the crossroads with Corso Ros-
ti and Corso Porta Mare; on the left, is the Palaz-
dei Diamanti (see below), and on the right, at n.
the *Palazzo Turchi-Di Bagno* (1493), now part of
university; at n. 23 is the *Palazzo Prosperi-Sacrati*
93-96), also by B. Rossetti, with a 16th-c. portal*.

Palazzo dei Diamanti** (*B4*). The most important monument in the Erculea quarter takes its
name from its diamond-shaped rustication. Built
largely by Biagio Rossetti (1493-1503), it was completed only after 1567. Note the candelabra at the
corners of the crossroads. This building houses the
Pinacoteca Nazionale, or picture gallery.

Pinacoteca Nazionale* (*open Tue., Wed. and Sat.,
9-2; Thu.-Fri., 9-7; Sun., 9-1*). Occupying a number of
halls of the palazzo (note the Ceremonial Hall, or *Salone d'Onore*) on the piano nobile, this gallery provides some idea of Ferrara's artistic heritage, especially that of the 16th c., with works by C. Tura, E. de'
Roberti, Garofalo, D. Dossi, V. Carpaccio, G. da Fabriano, and A. Mantegna. Also noteworthy are the very
fine 13th-c. frescoes by a Byzantine master, from the
abbey of S. Bartolo, and many 14th-c. frescoes. The
palazzo houses also the *Galleria Civica d'Arte Moderna*, devoted to modern art, the *Museo del Risorgimento e della Resistenza* (*open 9-2 and 3-7; Su., 9-
12 and 3:30-6:30*), dedicated to the history of Italy
from the 19th c. to WWII, and the *Museo Michelangelo Antonioni* (*open 9-1 and 3-6*), with exhibits related to the great film director from Ferrara.

Civici Musei d'Arte Moderna (*B5*). *Open 9-1 and
3:30-7*. Located in two *palazzi* in Corso Porta Mare
(n. 7 and n. 9), they include the **Museo d'Arte Moderna e Contemporanea** (with works by many
Ferrarese artists like G. Previati, A. Funi, F. De Pisis);
the *Museo Monografico Giovanni Boldini* (the famous modern painter from Ferrara); the *Padiglione
d'Arte Contemporanea*, and the *Parco Sculture* (sculpture garden), both devoted to contemporary art.

Piazza Ariostea (*B5*). This broad tree-lined square
was designed by Rossetti. The 17th-c. column at its
center now holds a statue of Ariosto (1833), last in
a succession that included a pope, the figure of Liberty, and Napoleon. At n. 10 and n. 11 stand two
palazzi also designed by Rossetti.

Certosa (*A5*). Founded in the 15th c., the former
charterhouse is now the Monumental Cemetery,
where Previati, Boldini, De Pisis and other artists are
buried.

Casa di Ludovico Ariosto (*B3*). *Open Tue.-Sun., 9-
2; Wed. and Sat. also 3-6 p.m*. Via Ariosto, 67. The poet purchased this late 15th-c. house and lived here.
The Latin inscription reads: "Small, but suited to me,
beholden to no one, not miserable yet built with my
own money."

Surrounding areas. At **Bondeno**, 19.5 km NW, is
a 12th-c. *parish church*. Km 9 N, near the bridge over
the Po at Ficarolo, is Stellata, with an impressive 17th-
c. **Rocca**, or fortress (*open Sat.-Sun. and holidays,
9:30-12:30 and 3-6*).
At **San Vito**, 26 km SE, near Comacchio (you can
take the Rovereto-Portomaggiore exit on the Super-
strada Ferrara-Mare, the highway from Ferrara to the
sea) is an 11th-c. Romanesque parish church.
At **Voghenza**, 15 km SE, is a Roman necropolis; the
local *antiquarium* (*open Sun. and holidays; winter,
3-6; summer, 4-7*) is worth a tour.

At **Argenta**, 33.5 km along the Adriatica highway to Ravenna, is the small but noteworthy *Museo Civico* (*open Sat.-Sun., 3:30-6:30; weekdays, by request, tel. 0532852706*), with works by A. Aleotti, Garofalo, F. Longhi, and others.

The **Parco-Oasi Naturalistica delle Valli Argenta e Marmorta**, 5.5 km SW, is a protected area established in 1977, which extends over 1600 hectares of wetlands; the local museum can be toured (*open 9:30-1 and 3:30-6; Mar.-May and Sep., 9:30-6;, closed Mon.*). One km from the Reno River is the small 6th-c. Byzantine church of **S. Giorgio**, worth seeing.

Fièsole*

Elev. 295 m, pop. 14,876; Toscana (Tuscany), province of Firenze. The inhabitants of Fièsole were Etruscans; from on high they watched the growth of the Italic village of huts that later became Florence, where the Mugnone River flowed into the Arno. The Roman town of Faesulae was the regional capital; then Florence, the "filia", or daughter, conquered (1125) Fièsole the "mater", or mother. Set on a hill amongst other hills, this lofty balcony – with its delicate landscapes, thrilling views, archeological ruins, and art treasures – is the best known side trip from Florence. Fra' Giovanni da Fièsole, better known as Beato Angelico, was born in Vicchio di Mugello; in Fièsole he was prior in the convent of S. Domenico. The sculptor Mino da Fièsole was actually born in Papiano, a section of Montemignano in Casentino, near Poppi. For the best panoramic view of Florence, which spreads out below, you should come up here early in the morning or wait until late afternoon.

Places of interest. Piazza Mino da Fièsole. This square is the heart of the small town; it was the ancient Forum, and is now bounded by the *Seminary*, the *bishop's palace* (Palazzo Vescovile), the cathedral (Duomo), and, at the far end, the handsome and large 14th-c. *Palazzo Pretorio*. This latter is the town hall, and is flanked by the ancient *Oratorio di S. Maria Primerana* (restored), an oratory with a Crucifix on panel attributed to Bonaccorso di Cino, and fragments of 14th-c. frescoes.

Duomo.* Dedicated to S. Romolo (St. Romulus), this cathedral is a Romanesque construction dating from the 11th c. and enlarged in the 13th and 14th c. The facade was rebuilt in the 19th c., and the distinctive campanile dates from 1213, though it was rebuilt in the 19th c. The austere basilican interior has a nave and two aisles with columns (some Roman capitals).

Area Archeologica.* *Open summer, 9:30-7; winter, 9:30-5; tel. 05559477.* The entrance to the archeological site is from Via Portigiani; it includes remains of public buildings from Roman times and a small museum. The **Roman theater** dates from the early Empire; it still has its "cavea," capable of seating 3000 persons, hewn out of the side of the hill and divid-

ed into four sectors. The complex includes the ins of the *Baths*, dating from the 1st c. B.C., a *Rom temple* rebuilt in the 1st c. B.C., and a stretch of *uscan walls**, built with colossal parallelepip blocks of stone. The **Museo Civico**, housed in building made to resemble an Ionic temple, featu material from the excavations of Fièsole and s rounding territory, arranged in eight halls.

Antiquarium Costantini. *Open same days o hours as the archeological area.* At n. 9 in Via Po giani, in the Palazzina Mangani, this antiquari boasts 157 vases of Attic, Etruscan, Italic, and Gr origin, donated by Alfiero Costantini in 1985 to township of Fièsole.

Museo Bandini. *Open summer, 9:30-7; winter, 9. 5; closed Tue.* This museum in n. 1 Via Duprè has lections of della Robbia terracottas and painti from the 13th-/14th-c. Tuscan school and some 1 c. works, too.

S. Francesco. On the top of a hill, where the cient acropolis once stood, this church was buil the 14th c. and was rebuilt several times in ensu centuries.

Florence / Firenze**

Elev. 50 m, pop. 376,662; Toscana (Tuscany) gional and provincial capital. The inhabita of Florence have always been justly prouc their city's remarkable qualities. Dino Cc pagni, a contemporary of Dante Alighier merchant and a chronicler, speaks of "the air, the well-dressed citizens, the exceedir handsome and well groomed women, the v impressive buildings..." And one can reas ably say that, at the time he was writing, best was yet to come. Located on the pl that the river Arno creates between the Inc gorge and that of the Gondolina, about n way between the Alpine passes and the p of Naples, all considerations that have pla major roles in the city's history – a particu ly remarkable history. The city lies on b banks of the river, split into unequal parts. larger section lies on the right bank, a spreads out across the plain, touching the b of the hills of Fièsole; the other half climbs the gentle slopes that adorn the Arno. An for the remarkable trove of art and architecture, Alfred de Musset, lover of George Sand the author of "Contes d'Espagne et d' ie" (1830), noted that, after Rome, Florence the city with the richest array of paintings sculpture." If we wish to sum up Italy's – the world's – debt toward Florence, we ten mention Dante, the perfection of the Italian guage, artists from Giotto to Michelangele so doing we are correct, and, at the same ti guilty of a terrible simplification. Stend wrote of the subtle pleasure of being in rence: the pleasure of watching the shifts in Arno's colors, the age-old stones, the views f

e little lanes, known as "chiassi," from the taut
nes of the dome of the cathedral, designed
nd built by Filippo Brunelleschi. Perhaps
ose who can best describe the measure,
rce, and elegance of Tuscan architecture, the
ne trees and olive groves, the gardens and vil-
s on the hills across the Arno, are the English,
ho made this part of Italy their home away
om home, beginning in the 18th c.

istorical note. This was the site of an ancient Ital-
settlement in the 10th c. B.C.; in later, Etruscan
nes it was a modest offshoot of the larger, more
nportant Fièsole. As a city, "Florentia" originated in
oman times. From the high Middle Ages, nothing
rvives but legendary accounts; we can say with
me certainty that the importance of Florence was
ll minimal, since the capital of the March of Tu-
ia (as the marquisate of Tuscany was called in that
a) was Lucca. It was not until the year 1000 that the
archese Ugo began to prefer Florence to Lucca. In
e second half of the 11th c. the city, having repop-
ated after a long decline, was given a new walled
erimeter, the first in the Middle Ages; it corre-
onded to the route of the Roman walls, save for
e southern stretch. A bridge over the Arno, across
hich ran the Via Cassia, existed as early as A.D. 996;
herefore predated the 14th-c. Ponte Vecchio. It was
the 10th c., as well, that Romanesque architecture
st flourished here, in the Baptistery and in the
urches of S. Miniato and Ss. Apostoli. After the
eath in 1115 of the "Great Countess" Matilda, also
own as the Empress Maud, there was only an in-
rmittent presence of a powerful central authority.
e townspeople managed to establish the first au-
nomous government under the leadership of
elve consuls; Florence began to expand outside of
first walled perimeter. And the first city to suffer
om Florence's growing ambition was Fièsole. In
ne, an aggressive Florence spread war in what is
ow Tuscany, in the form of coalitions of cities (Flo-
nce and Lucca against Pisa, Siena, Arezzo, and Pi-
oia), although the overriding conflict remained that
etween Florence and Pisa, a conflict that centered
 the matter of access to the Tyrrhenian Sea. At the
eginning of the 13th c. these wars took on the
dded tension of the struggle between the factions
 Guelphs and Ghibellines. The Guelphs supported
e papacy and the House of Anjou, the Ghibellines
pported the Holy Roman Empire and the Swabi-
s. In the meanwhile, in 1193, in the hope that en-
usting power to an outsider might settle the grow-
g conflict between aristocrats and commoners,
orence established the rule of the "Podestà." A few
ars earlier, in 1172, the decision had been made to
uild a second circle of walls, to enclose the new dis-
cts built to house the burgeoning trade and man-
acturing of Florence. The succession of Frederick
as Holy Roman Emperor then tilted the delicate
orentine political equilibrium in favor of the Ghi-
ellines, but only briefly. The "commoners" of Flo-
nce ousted the nobility, establishing their own rul-

ing magistracy, called the Capitano del Popolo. These
were the years of glory of the "primo popolo," when
Florence first obtained a clear chance at leadership
among the cities of Tuscany. The disastrous defeat in
1260 at the Battle of Montaperti was only a passing
incident, and marked no permanent military set-
back. The decision of Florence's Guelph government
to support the House of Anjou (Charles d'Anjou was
"Podestà" of Florence for ten years) was a canny
one. Internally, the government was increasingly controlled by merchants and craftsmen, organized into
"Arti," or guilds; the Ordinamenti di Giustizia of 1293
established the hierarchic structure of Florentine
government, under the leadership of the "Arti Maggiori," or leading guilds. In the same period, Florence
thrashed Siena once and for all at Colle di Val d'Elsa in 1269, and in 1289 roundly defeated Arezzo at
Campaldino. Pisa, instead, was defeated by an encroaching Genoa in 1284 at Meloria. These victories
outside the city walls corresponded to the construction, between 1350 and 1450, of those great
works of Gothic architecture that speak so clearly of
Florence's wealth and power in this period: Palazzo
del Podestà (known as Palazzo del Bargello), S.
Maria Novella, S. Croce, S. Maria del Fiore, Palazzo
Vecchio, the bell tower (by Giotto), and Orsanmichele. The decoration of the interiors was entrusted to painters such as Cimabue and Giotto, and
such sculptors as Arnolfo di Cambio and Andrea
Pisano. By this time, the second walled perimeter
was proving insufficient, and between 1284 and 1333
a third, exceedingly extensive ring of walls was completed; this followed the circuit of the "viali," or outer boulevards, and it still stands in part, in Oltrarno.
During the course of the 14th c., Florence consoli-
dated its conquests and its political stability, although during the first few decades of the 14th c. it
became necessary to subdue the Ghibelline uprisings led by Uguccione della Faggiuola, Castruccio
Castracani, the Holy Roman Emperor Henry VII, and
the attempted takeover by the Duke of Athens. In
1343 Gualtiero di Brienne was ejected by a furious
popular uprising, and Florence almost seemed to
return to the golden age of the "primo popolo." Despite the massive bank failures of 1342-45, the Black
Death of 1348, and the growing political strife between wealthy and poor ("popolo grasso" and
"popolo minuto") which led to the revolt of the
Ciompi in 1378, Florence by this time ruled over
most of the rest of Tuscany. In the 15th c., the Florentine republic, based on an oligarchy of leading
citizens, was transformed into a seignory, de facto, if
not yet by law. In 1434, Cosimo de' Medici (Cosimo
the Elder), who had been exiled the year previous
as a citizen, returned to Florence as seigneur, or absolute ruler. As lord, Cosimo maintained intact the
institutions of the republic, though he emptied them
of meaning. His grandson Lorenzo, known as "the
Magnificent," ruled Florence from 1469 to 1492, and
carried on Cosimo's work. His name is often linked
to that great artistic and cultural rebirth usually described as the Italian Renaissance. Great architects

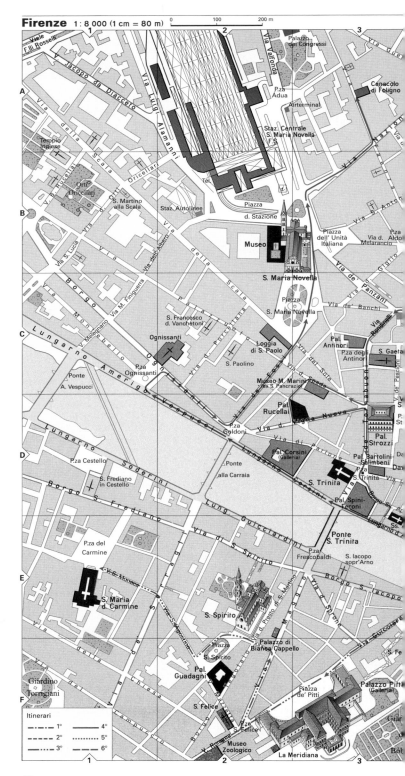

Firenze

1 : 8 000 (1 cm = 80 m)

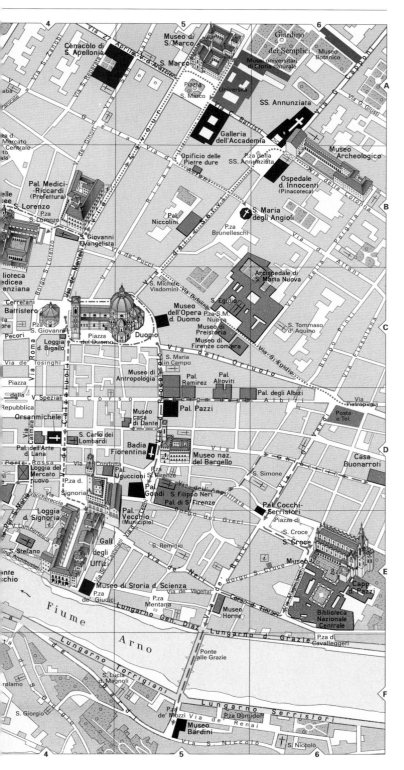

197

interpreted his spirit: Brunelleschi, Leon Battista Alberti, Michelozzo, Benedetto da Maiano, Giuliano da Sangallo. Masterpieces were created by such painters as Masaccio, Fra' Angelico, Andrea del Castagno, Paolo Uccello, Botticelli, Ghirlandaio and Benozzo Gozzoli, and sculptors including Donatello, Verrocchio, Pollaiolo, Luca della Robbia and Ghiberti. When Lorenzo died in 1492, the splendid Medici realm was unable to withstand the brutal assault of Charles VIII of France. The exile of the Medici allowed for two episodes of restoration of the Republic (1494-1512 and 1527-30), which, however, proved to be its swan song. In 1531, in the wake of the imperial army, Alessandro de' Medici entered the city to become the first duke of Florence. In 1569 the duchy of Florence became the grand duchy of Tuscany, under Cosimo I de' Medici, known as Cosimo the Great, who in 1555 annexed the republic of Siena. And it was under this ruler that the "great history" of Florence can be said to have come to an end. Its ancient wealth and power were never seen again. Although 16th-c. Florence was embellished with new works by Ammannati and Vasari, its true geniuses were forced to work elsewhere: Leonardo da Vinci in Milan and France; Michelangelo in 1534 left Florence permanently for Rome. The 17th and 18th c. witnessed the economic and cultural decline of both city and state, as well as the end of the Medici dynasty (1737). Some small revivals of the economy, though largely agrarian in nature, marked the rule of the House of Lorraine, and especially the reign of Pietro Leopoldo, as he was known, later to become Holy Roman Emperor as Leopold II. Napoleon Bonaparte, following the hasty departure of the rulers of the House of Lorraine, placed upon the throne of Florence, in 1801, as King of Etruria, none other than Ludovico di Borbone Parma. This shortlived kingdom was annexed to the French empire in 1807, even though Elisa Baciocchi, Napoleon's sister, was made grand duchess of Tuscany. From 1815 till 1860, the House of Lorraine ruled again in Florence; with the annexation of the duchy of Lucca in 1847, they attained the outdated dream of unifying Tuscany. Following a plebiscite in 1860, Florence, with all of Tuscany, became part of the new Kingdom of Italy; from 1865 to 1870, Florence was this new kingdom's second capital. It was in those years that the 14th-c. walls were razed and the outer boulevards, or "circonvallazione" (ring roads), were built, the riverfront boulevards ("lungarni") were opened up, and Viale dei Colli was linked with Piazzale Michelangiolo. A number of downtown streets were enlarged (Via Panzani, Via Cerretani, Via Tornabuoni, and Via Martelli), and thoughtless demolition opened the perhaps excessively large Piazza Vittorio Emanuele, now Piazza della Repubblica. In the 20th c., with renewed economic growth and an increase in population, Florence expanded, incorporating new districts. After WWII, during which Florence suffered extensive damage, and following the terrible flood of 1966, the city began once again to expand in all directions, but primarily NW, toward the plains and

the highways. Population doubled, from the 200,0 of the turn of the century.

Getting around. Traffic jams and regulations mal driving in town problematic at best; five maj zones in the center of Florence are off limits to p vate vehicles from 7:30 until 6:30 (extending to p.m.-12:30 a.m. on Fri. and Sat. in the summe Tourists with hotel reservations, or those in seare of a room, are allowed to drive in; in the pedest an zones in the more central parts of town, on tl other hand, cars are forbidden entirely. You ca leave your car in one of the many parking garag and areas between the main ring roads arou Florence and the limited access areas. Of the se en routes suggested, the first six can be considere walking tours entirely; for the seventh – as well the outer sections of town – you may choose use public transportation.

The religious center

Between S. Maria del Fiore, which Arnolfo di Camb began to build under the name of the older catl dral that stood on the same site (S. Reparata), and Lorenzo, the church of the Medici, in this small ar you will encounter the work of some of Italy's gre est artists: Giotto, Brunelleschi, Ghiberti, Donate and A. della Robbia, Gozzoli, and Michelangelo.
Piazza del Duomo* (C4-5). Along with Piazza Giovanni, this constitutes the heart of Florence a features its most important religious monumer the Battistero (Baptistery), the Basilica di S. Ma del Fiore (Cathedral, or Duomo), and the campan of Giotto, unified by their vivid polychrome marl facings, in white, green, and pink marble, with ge metric patterns. On Easter Sunday, the remarkal tradition of the "Scoppio del Carro," or "explodi carriage," should not be missed.
Battistero di S. Giovanni** (C4). Open weekda 12-6:30; Sun. and holidays, 8:30-1:30. In the religio heart of Florence, the Baptistery of St. John is one the oldest and most majestic buildings in the c mentioned by Dante as the "bel S. Giovanni." Sor date it back to the 4th c., others call it an 11th-c. F manesque structure. It has an octagonal plan and surrounded by a double order of pillars supporti a trabeation and, higher up, arches; a 13th-c. at topped by an octagonal pyramid conceals t domed roof. The most distinctive aspect is the 11 c. white-and-green marble facing. In the three port are the renowned bronze **doors**** arranged as sort of giant visual Bible. The south (entrance) p tal* is the oldest, and is by A. Pisano (1330); the p tal frames are by V. Ghiberti (Lorenzo's son, 146 while the three statues over the portal are by V. Da ti (1571). The north portal* is by L. Ghiberti (1403-2 who applied a late-Gothic style, ornate and flue to both doors and jambs. Above the portal, statu by G.F. Rustici (1511). The east door**, facing t Duomo, is justly famous – Michelangelo called it t

Florence: Duomo

Porta del Paradiso. This is only a copy of L. Ghiberti's masterpiece (1425-52): some of the restored original panels are now on display at the Museo dell'Opera del Duomo. Over the portal is a marble group by A. Sansovino (1502). The **interior**, to a central plan, is covered by a dome with gores and has an inlaid marble floor*; along the marble-covered walls run, lower down, an architectural composition of pillars and architraved columns, and, up high, a loggia with mullions. The cupola glitters with 13th-c. Byzantine-style mosaics* by Venetian and Florentine artists, Cimabue possibly among them. In the apse, other mosaics by J. da Torrita (1225). Also, note the tomb of the antipope John XXIII*, attributed to Donatello and Michelozzo (1427), and the relief baptismal font (1371), by the Pisan school.

Loggia del Bigallo (*C4*). Set near the south door of the Battistero, at the corner of Via de' Calzaiuoli, this loggia was built in 1352-58 to offer abandoned children and orphans to public charity. It features two lovely corner arcades, and a course of mullioned windows. Inside (*open by request, tel. 0552302885*), in the Sala dei Capitani, a remarkable fresco from 1342 includes the earliest known depiction of the city of Florence. Note the tabernacle by N. d'Antonio (1515), marble statues of angels by A. Arnoldi (1364), the altar predella by R. del Ghirlandaio (1515), and a Crucifix on panel by the Maestro del Bigallo (1260).

Giotto's Campanile * * (*C4*). It stands alone, to the right of the cathedral, rising for 84.7 m. This bell tower is renowned for its slender, soaring Gothic architecture, its elegant polychrome marble facing, and its lavish sculptural ornamentation. It was begun in 1334 by Giotto and A. Pisano, and completed by F. Talenti (1350-59). The base has two areas of 14th-c. bas-reliefs (copies; the originals are in the Museo dell'Opera del Duomo) by A. Pisano and L. della Robbia (first zone) and A. Pisano and A. Arnoldi (second zone). Above these areas, in the niches, are statues by A. Pisano, Donatello, and N. di Bartolo (copies; the originals are in the Museo dell'Opera del Duomo). A staircase, with 414 steps, leads up to the terrace, with a fine view* of the city.

Duomo * * or **Basilica di S. Maria del Fiore** (*C4-5*). This outstanding religious monument, the Florence Cathedral, faces the Baptistery and shows clearly the Gothic influence of broad and simple lines that was so typical of Florence.

Work began on this church in 1296 under A. di Cambio and was halted upon his death (ca. 1310); the project grew in size when it started back up in 1331, and was enlarged even more in 1357, under F. Talenti. In 1378, the vault of the nave was completed; in 1380 the side aisles were covered; and by 1421 the octagonal tambour was finished. Upon it, from 1420 until 1436, F. Brunelleschi built the spectacular dome. It was crowned with a lantern, built by A. del Verrocchio in 1468.

The original, half-finished **facade**, by A. di Cambio, was demolished in 1587; the present facade, less than a masterpiece, is by E. De Fabris (1871-87), who copied the motif on the sides. The bronze doors of the three portals are all less than a hundred years old. On the sides, the polychrome marble face, for all its liveliness, does nothing to diminish the sheer mass of the church; note the doors, especially the late-14th-c. *Porta dei Canonici* *. Then comes the vast bulk of the *tambour* *, with three huge apses and several smaller ones. Above them all stands the tall octagonal tambour (note the unfinished gallery, by B. d'Agnolo, upon which work ceased after Michelangelo's withering dismissal of it as a "cricket cage"), supporting the enormous ribbed dome by Brunelleschi. Along the *left side* is the early 15th-c. Gothic-Renaissance *Porta della Mandorla* *: in the front and the lunette, reliefs and mosaics by N. di Banco (1421), and Domenico and Davide Ghirlandaio (1491).

The **interior** has a broad nave with two aisles, divided by high pointed arches upon tall pillars, and flowing into the immense octagonal space of the tambour. The vast size and simple purity of the composition give an impression of majestic severity. Note the three stained-glass windows by L. Ghiberti; the clock face by P. Uccello (1443); the 15th-c. tomb of Bishop A. Orso by T. di Camaino (14th c.); the bust of F. Brunelleschi by A. Cavalcanti (1446); the tondo of Giotto by B. da Maiano (1490); and the bust of Marsilio Ficino by A. Ferrucci (1521). From the second bay in the *right aisle*, a stairway leads down to the remains of the church of S. Reparata.

S. Reparata. Wrongly described as the "crypt" of the church, this is what remains of the ancient cathedral of Florence, demolished in 1375 and unearthed from 1966 on. Among other things, you can see remains of houses dating back to Roman times, and the tombstone of Brunelleschi.

The cross vault is dominated by Brunelleschi's immense **Cupola*** (91 m), decorated with the fresco of the Last Judgment by G. Vasari and F. Zuccari (1579); in the oculi of the tambour, stained glass windows* done to cartoons by Donatello, Ghiberti, P. Uccello, and A. del Castagno. At the center of the octagon is a marble chancel by B. Bandinelli and G. Bandini (1547-72); on the main altar is a wooden Crucifix* by B. da Maiano (1497). Note, in the *Sagrestia Vecchia*, the glazed earthenware Ascension* by L. della Robbia, and numerous 15th-/16th-c. paintings, and the sarcophagus* with the relics of St. Zanobi, a masterpiece by Ghiberti (1432-42). Next, you will see the entrance to the *Sagrestia delle Messe**, or Sagrestia dei Servi, where Lorenzo il Magnifico took refuge from the attack known as the Congiura dei Pazzi, or conspiracy of the Pazzi family; Lorenzo's brother, Giuliano de' Medici was killed in the attack (26 April 1478). Worthy of note are the bronze door* and the lunette (Resurrection*) by L. della Robbia (1444) and, on the walls and armoires, wooden intarsias* (1465). In the *left aisle*: 14th-c. stained glass panel by D. di Michelino (1465); painted equestrian **monument to Giovanni Acuto (John Hawkwood)****, by P. Uccello (1436); bust by B. da Maiano; and painted equestrian monument to N. da Tolentino* by A. del Castagno (1456). From the head of the aisle, you can climb up to the dome (*open 8:30-6:20; Sat., 8:30-5; 463 steps*), of considerable interest both because of the double-shell structure, and because of the magnificent view* from the external walkway that runs around the lantern (107 m).

Museo dell'Opera del Duomo* (*C5*). *Open Mon.-Sat., 9-7:30; Sun., 8:30-1:30.* Established in 1891, at n. 9 in Piazza del Duomo, this museum features major pieces of 14th-/15th-c. Florentine sculpture, including many originals from the Baptistery, the Duomo, and Giotto's bell tower. In the vestibule, two terracotta lunettes by A. della Robbia and Etruscan and Roman statuary and architectural elements. In the *Sala dell'Antica Facciata*, sculpture, mostly by A. di Cambio, from the earlier facade of the Duomo; on the right, as you enter, a 16th-c. drawing shows how that facade looked. Note some figures by N. di Banco. In two rooms devoted to Brunelleschi: funeral mask of the architect; wooden model of the cupola and lantern; tools and machinery used in building the cupola. In the other halls: illuminated codices, goldsmithery, and a painting by B. Daddi (1334). On the mezzanine is the dramatic and unfinished **Pietà****, by Michelangelo (1550-53), formerly in the Duomo. On the upper floor, in the *Sala delle Cantorie*: **choir**** by Donatello (1433-39), with a line of dancing putti; beneath it, Penitent Magdalene*, a wooden statue by Donatello, once in the

Baptistery; **choir**** by L. della Robbia (1431-3? with reliefs of boys singing and playing; 16 **st**. **ues**** formerly in the niches of the Campanile, A. Pisano, Donatello, and N. di Bartolo. In the ad cent *Sala delle Formelle* are displayed the relief **pa els*** from the Campanile: those in the lower reg ter are by A. Pisano, probably partly based on c signs by Giotto, save for the last five, by L. della Ro bia (1439); the panels in the upper register are A. Pisano and A. Arnoldi. In the *Sala dell'Altare* is silver and enamel **altar frontal**** upon whi Michelozzo, Verrocchio, and A. Pollaiolo worked; so worthy of mention, the silver Crucifix; statues T. di Camaino, A. Pisano, and P. di Lapo and the lit gical array embroidered with silk and gold to c signs by A. Pollaiolo.

Via de' Martelli (*B-C4*). This is one of the livelie streets in Florence; note the former convent of th Jesuits and the church of *S. Giovannino degli Scolo* with facade by B. Ammannati (16th c.).

Palazzo Medici-Riccardi** (*B4*). *Open 9-7; clos Wed.; reservation advisable, tel. 0552491708.* Tl proud square mass of this building was the moc for Florentine aristocratic mansions in the Rena sance; note the three floors of graduated rustic tion, the centered mullioned windows with Medi heraldic devices, and the elaborate cornice. Tl ground-floor windows near the corner may be l Michelangelo (1517).

Construction began in 1444, under Michelozzo, c behalf of Cosimo the Elder; it was the Medici re dence until the grand duchy of Cosimo I. The bui ing then became property of the Riccardi (165! and then the House of Lorraine, and during F rence's short stint as the capital of united Italy, housed the Ministry of the Interior. Today, it is tl building of the Prefecture.

Inside, note the handsome courtyard*, which d plays much of the *Riccardi Collection* of archeolc ical material. Take the first stairway on the right the **Cappella dei Magi***, a masterpiece of the e ly Florentine Renaissance, by Michelozzo. Note tl fresco cycle of the Magi*, by B. Gozzoli (1459-6C many of the figures in the cavalcade are portraits members of the Medici family. Back in the cou yard, a second stair climbs to the *Galleria*, a lor 17th-c. Baroque loggia, in the ceiling of which L. Gic dano painted the Allegory of the Medici (1682-85

Piazza S. Lorenzo (*B4*). Dominated by the facac of the church of S. Lorenzo, with the mighty cupc of the Cappella dei Principi. A charming market held here, surrounded by 15th-/16th-c. aristocrat palazzi, and a marble monument to Giovanni da Bande Nere, by B. Bandinelli (1540).

S. Lorenzo** (*B4*). *Open 7-12 and 3:30-6:30.* O of the great masterpieces of early-Renaissance Fl rentine religious architecture, this basilica is als bound up with the memory of the Medici family. Built by Brunelleschi in 1442-46 and completed 1461 by A. Manetti, it stands on the site of an ancie cathedral consecrated by St. Ambrose in A.D. 3 and rebuilt in Romanesque style in the 11th c. Tl

orence: Palazzo Medici-Riccardi

cade has remained unfinished, though Michelan-
lo, among others, submitted a design for it.

e **interior**, with a nave with two aisles and
lumns, has remained remarkably intact and per-
ctly composed. The mastery of Brunelleschi ap-
ars everywhere; the interior facade is by Michelan-
lo. In the right aisle painting by Rosso Fiorentino*
523); marble altar* by D. da Settignano (1460); and
e of the two bronze pulpits* (a matching pulpit
in the left aisle), by Donatello (ca. 1460) and oth-
s. In the left arm of the transept, among the fine
th-c. statues and altarpieces, are the altarpiece* by
ippo Lippi and a large fresco by A. Bronzino (1565-
). From the left transept, you enter the 15th-c.

agrestia Vecchia. A Renaissance jewel de-
gned by Brunelleschi (1421-26) and decorated by
onatello (1435-43), the Old Sacristy has a square
an and is topped by a hemispherical cupola;
ainst the white walls, the statues stand out sharply,
do the medallions in colored stucco in the pen-
ntives and lunettes and the frieze of cherubs by
onatello. Donatello also executed the bronze
ors* on the sides of the little chapel, and the two
rracotta reliefs* above it. Although the bust* of S.
renzo (St. Lawrence) is attributed to Donatello, it
ay well be by D. da Settignano. To the left of the
cristy entrance, note the funerary monument to
and P. de' Medici*, in porphyry and bronze, a mas-
piece by Verrocchio (1472).

bliotecca Medicea Laurenziana** (B-C4). Open
; closed Sun. and holidays; access to the Library is
* scholars only, tel. 055214443. You enter this re-
arkable library through the *first cloister** (entrance
the left of the facade of the basilica), in the style
Brunelleschi. Founded by Cosimo the Elder, the li-
ary is located in a building designed by Michelan-
lo (1524). The architecture of the *vestibule* and
e *monumental stairway* is daring, a forerunner of
roque architecture; that of the *reading room* is
nple and magnificent. The ceiling, lecterns, and
airs were also designed by Michelangelo.

appelle Medicee** (B4). Open 8:15-4:30; closed
1st, 3rd, 5th Mon. and 2nd, 4th Sun. of the month.
With the entrance at n. 6 in Piazza di Madonna degli
Aldobrandini, the Cappelle Medicee, or Medici
Chapels, comprise the complex of the funerary
chapel of the princes and the Sagrestia Nuova, or
New Sacristy, by Michelangelo, set in the apse of the
basilica of S. Lorenzo. From an immense crypt, you
climb up to the Baroque **Cappella dei Principi***
(Chapel of the Princes), a splendid octagonal
domed construction, lined with marble and semiprecious stones, built by M. Nigetti to plans by Giovanni de' Medici (17th c.). It holds monumental sarcophagi of the grand dukes of Tuscany (above two
of them, colossal bronze statues by P. and F. Tacca).
Sagrestia Nuova** (or burial chapel of the
Medici). This renowned prototype of Mannerist architecture was designed by Michelangelo, who began construction in 1521-24; it was completed some
years later by G. Vasari and B. Ammannati. Recently
restored, it has a square plan. Note in particular the
architectural elements in "pietra serena" that stand
out against the white walls, in accordance with an
approach borrowed from Brunelleschi's Sagrestia
Vecchia; here, they take on a daring new quality that
breaks with the classicistic tradition. In the sacristy
are the two famous **funerary monuments**** to
the Medici by Michelangelo (1524-33), one with the
figures of Dawn, Dusk, Day, and Night, and the other with the Virgin and Child** (1521). In a small underground room to the left of the altar are drawings
by Michelangelo, discovered in 1971.

Piazza della Signoria and the Uffizi

Art and power: this difficult "marriage" can be clearly deciphered in its Florentine version in the short
walk from Orsanmichele to the Lungarno. To decorate the tabernacles on the outer walls of the gra-
nary-cum-church of Orsanmichele, the "Arti," or
Guilds, summoned Donatello and Verrocchio. For
the statue of David, a symbol of the Florentine Republic to be placed before Palazzo Vecchio, the job
was given to Michelangelo. And when Duke Cosimo I ordered the construction of a building to
house his burgeoning bureaucracy, the Uffizi, he also decided to build an area for his art collections.
Via dei Calzaiuoli (C-D4). One of the main thoroughfares in Florence, it links Piazza del Duomo
with Piazza della Signoria. Like much of the center,
it was subjected, in 1841-44, to a "cleaning job" that
aroused much debate. The street is lined with elegant
shops; note Orsanmichele and the Gothic church of
S. Carlo dei Lombardi (D4), by S. Talenti (1404).
Orsanmichele* (D4). This imposing building is one
of the most interesting pieces of 14th-c. architecture
in Florence. Built in 1337 as a loggia for trading ex-
changes, it was given fine three-light windows on the
ground floor, and raised two floors higher, with two-
light windows. At the end of the 14th c., it was made
into a church (*S. Michele in Orto*) for the guilds of Florence. On the outer walls*, in the piers between the

arcades, are aediculas or **tabernacles*** with statues of the patron saints of the various Guilds, executed by the leading artists of Florence in the 15th and 16th c. In the facade on Via dei Calzaiuoli, from left to right: St. John the Baptist, by L. Ghiberti; Incredulity of St. Thomas*, by A. del Verrocchio (1483); St. Luke, by Giambologna. In Via Orsanmichele: St. Peter, attributed to Brunelleschi (1413); St. Philip and the Four Crowned Saints*, by N. di Banco; St. George, by Donatello (copies; originals are in the Museo del Bargello). In Via dell'Arte della Lana: St. Matthew and St. Stephen*, by Ghiberti; St. Eligio, by N. di Banco. In Via de' Lamberti: St. Mark, by Donatello (copy); St. James, by N. di Piero Lamberti; Madonna della Rosa, marble group by P. di Giovanni Tedesco; St. John the Evangelist, by B. da Montelupo (1515).

In the two-aisled rectangular **interior** (*entrance on Via dell'Arte della Lana; open 9-12 and 4-6; Sat. and holidays, 9-1 and 4-6; closed 1st and last Mon. of the month*), note the remains of late-14th-c. frescoes and stained glass windows. Also, the statues by F. da Sangallo; the renowned tabernacle* by A. Orcagna, one of the loveliest creations of Florentine Gothic; and the panel painted by B. Daddi (1347).

Palazzo dell'Arte della Lana (*D4; closed to the public*). In the Via dell'Arte della Lana, this building was, from 1308 on, the headquarters of one of the wealthiest of the Arti Maggiori, or leading guilds of the city. It consisted of a tower-house and a lower building, and on the exterior it incorporates the Gothic *tabernacle of S. Maria della Tromba* (14th c., rebuilt at the turn of the 20th c.), with a panel by J. del Casentino and a painting by N. di Pietro Gerini. In 1905 the restoration of this building was completed, and it became the headquarters of the Società Dantesca. From the interior you can enter the two upper halls* of Orsanmichele; in the hall on the second floor there are detached 14th-c. frescoes.

Piazza della Signoria** (*D4*). The heart of political power and city life of Florence ever since the communal period, this square was laid out in the 13th c. Vast and majestic, it is dominated by the structure of Palazzo Vecchio and lightened by the three spacious arches of the **Loggia della Signoria***, or Loggia dei Lanzi. Built in Gothic style between 1376 and 1382 by B. di Cione and S. Talenti, this loggia in time became a workshop for sculptors, and then an open-air art gallery.

Note from the left, at n. 10, the 14th-c. *Tribunale di Mercatanzia*, at n. 7, *Palazzo Uguccioni*, with the bronze equestrian monument to Cosimo I by Giambologna (1594-98), and the enormous *Fontana del Nettuno*, a fountain by B. Ammannati (1563-75) featuring Neptune surrounded by lively and elegant bronze figures of marine deities and satyrs. On the stairs of Palazzo Vecchio: the lion that symbolizes Florence by Donatello (copy; the original is in the Museo del Bargello); Judith and Holofernes, a bronze by Donatello (copy; the original is in Palazzo Vecchio); and Michelangelo's David (copy; the original is in the Galleria dell'Accademia); and the much-discussed group of Hercules and Cacus, by

B. Bandinelli (1534). In the Loggia della Signor **Perseus***, masterpiece by B. Cellini (1554), **Ra of the Sabines***, by Giambologna (1583), and o er fine sculptures by P. Fedi and Giambologna well as ancient Roman statues.

Palazzo Vecchio** (*D-E4-5*). *Open weekdays, 9 Thu. and holidays, 9-2; 15 Jun.-15 Sep., Mon.-Fri. u til 11 p.m.; tel. 0552768325.* This is the most i portant monument of civil architecture in Florenc and certainly one of the most noteworthy mediev public palazzi in Italy.

Built, from 1299 on, to plans by A. di Cambio as t *Palazzo dei Priori*, it became the *Palazzo della gnoria* in the 15th-c., and from 1540 to 1565 w the residence of the Medici. It became the "Pala zo Vecchio", or old palace, when the Medici move to Palazzo Pitti. From 1865 until 1871, when F rence was briefly the capital of Italy, it became t Parliament; since 1872, it has been city hall. It h been modified to suit its various functions over t centuries; in particular, in the 16th c., G. Vasari re ovated it drastically. A few decades later, it was e larged by G.B. del Tasso and B. Buontalenti.

The original building is a compact parallelepiped rough ashlar, three storeys tall, with two orders of egant Gothic mullioned windows. It is crowned tall jutting crenelation. Above that is the **towe** (1310), 94 m tall, with double jutting crenelation **Inside***, the first, porticoed *courtyard* was reno ed by Michelozzo (1453), and later decorated w stuccoes and frescoes in 1565. In the middle is 16th-c. fountain, atop which is a copy of Verrocchi Putto with Dolphin (the original is now in the T razzo di Giunone). Between this courtyard and t Cortile della Dogana, a monumental *staircase* signed by Vasari leads to the upper floors.

On the *first floor* is the **Salone dei Cinquecento** an enormous hall built by A. da Sangallo (1495-9 for the meetings of the Consiglio Generale del Pop lo, later transformed under Cosimo I into a rece tion hall (Sala delle Udienze). At the left end of t room, note the raised tribunal by B. Bandinelli; so, paintings by Vasari and others; a plaster group Giambologna; and a **marble group*** by Michela gelo (1533-34). Adjacent rooms include: the *Stu lo di Francesco I **, lavishly decorated; the *Tesore (closed to the public)*, decorated by Vasari; and t *Quartiere di Leone X*, with the *Hall of Leo X* (t first Medici pope), also decorated by Vasari, no city government offices.

Second floor: the *Quartiere degli Elementi* was d orated by G. Vasari (on the Terrazzo di Giunone, o inally open to the elements, with a the statue* by Verrocchio). A balcony overlooking the Salone Cinquecento takes you into the *Quartiere di Eleo ra*, decorated by G. Vasari and adorned with Flore tine tapestries; note the *Cappella di Eleonora**, pai ed by Bronzino (1545). Continue through the Ca pella dei Priori, built by B. d'Agnolo (1511-14) a decorated by R. del Ghirlandaio, until you reach t *Sala dell'Udienza**, with gilded coffered ceiling by da Maiano and frescoes by F. Salviati (1560). A irable works are the elegant marble portals, by B. ıd G. da Maiano, in the *Sala dei Gigli**, with a magficent carved and gilded ceiling and a vast fresco D. Ghirlandaio (1485). Also, note the well restored onzes of **Judith and Holofernes*** by Donatello. the adjacent rooms are the Cancelleria della Reıbblica Fiorentina and the Sala delle Carte Geoafiche, with a huge globe (1567).

accolta d'Arte Contemporanea Alberto della agione. *Entrance allowed at 9, 10:30 and 12; osed Thu.* This collection of contemporary Italian t, temporarily installed in the *Palazzo della Cassa Risparmio*, at n. 5 in Piazza della Signoria, includes orks by such painters as Carrà, De Chirico, Moran-, De Pisis, Casorati, Rosai, Scipione, Mafai, Campigli, cini, Cantatore, Sassu, Birolli, Guttuso, Morlotti, Cassiıri, Severini, Maccari, Menzio, Vedova, Tosi, Guidi, ıd Sironi; and such sculptors as Martini, Marini, anzù, Mirko, Fontana, and Broggini.

iazzale degli Uffizi* (*E4*). This square extends ke a majestic courtyard from Piazza della Signoı to the banks of the Arno, enclosed by the **Palaz-) degli Uffizi**, a remarkable construction with ɔrtico and loggia, by G. Vasari (1560-80), who built as the new office building for the ducal bureauacy. Now the building houses the famous art allery of the Uffizi. At the end of the square, overoking the Arno, is a fine view* of the Ponte Vecıio and the hill of S. Miniato.

alleria degli Uffizi** (*E4*). *Open Tue.-Sun., 8:15-50; tickets can be reserved by telephone at 55294883, and must be paid for at least 5 days bere the visit.* Possibly the leading art gallery in Italy, ıd certainly the oldest collection in modern Eupe, the museum possesses masterpieces of Italian ainting from every period, and a select collection work by non-Italian painters and schools. The enance is under the portico of the Palazzo degli Ufzi, at n. 6; the collections are displayed in the halls ı the third floor.

uilt at the end of the 16th c. to house the collecɔn of sculpture and painting of Grand Duke ancesco I (the first architect was Buontalenti), e gallery was enlarged over time, largely due to e interest of the Medici family, incorporating sciıtific and technical areas of interest as well. The ɔllection of paintings, originally limited to 16th-c. orentine artists, was expanded to include Venetn and Flemish painters. In the 18th c. the dukes Lorraine made considerable donations, the sciıtific section was placed elsewhere, and the focus arrowed to painting and sculpture. By the late)th c. new acquisitions of 14th-/15th-c. paintings ade the Uffizi the single most complete collecɔn of great Italian art. As of this writing, about 2000 orks are on display, and a major renovation is anned which will make accessible to the public e other 1800 paintings now in storage. This proct was delayed, however, by the bomb blast of 27 ay 1993, which endangered the safety of the halls n the third floor and in Vasari's corridors.

n the **ground floor** you can see a **fresco cycle**** of illustrious men and women by A. del Castagno (ca. 1450), and a fresco by Botticelli (1481). The stairway, by Vasari, passes the floor of offices and takes you up to the *first floor* (**Gabinetto dei Disegni e delle Stampe**, or Cabinet of Prints and Drawings, *open only to scholars*); on the *second floor*, two vestibules lead into the gallery, with its three corridors.

Florence: Palazzo degli Uffizi

First corridor. The heart of the original gallery, this hallway has ceilings decorated with grotesques; along the walls, Roman statues and busts. The first main section features Tuscan paintings, in chronological order, from the 13th to the 15th c.: D. di Buoninsegna, Cimabue, Giotto, S. Martini and L. Memmi, A. and P. Lorenzetti, B. Daddi, T. Gaddi, Giottino, L. Monaco, G. da Fabriano, Masaccio and Masolino, Fra' Angelico, P. Uccello, D. Veneziano, P. della Francesca, A. Baldovinetti, Filippo Lippi, Filippino Lippi, A. and P. Pollaiolo, H. van der Goes (**Portinari Triptych***), Botticelli (**Birth of Venus*, Spring***), Leonardo da Vinci (**Adoration of the Magi***), Verrocchio, Perugino, Signorelli, and P. di Cosimo. The successive halls (16 to 24) are the oldest in the Uffizi. In hall 18, you can see the 1st-c. Medici Venus*, copy of an original by Praxiteles, and portraits by Bronzino. In the other halls are 15th-/16th-c. paintings from other schools (Venetian, Lombard, Emilian, German, Flemish) and sculpture: Signorelli and Perugino, Dürer, Brueghel the Elder, Cranach the Younger, B. Vivarini, G. Bellini, C. da Conegliano, Giorgione, Carpaccio, Altdorfer, H. Holbein the Younger, Mantegna, Foppa, and Correggio.

Second and third corridors. Cross the second corridor (the small hall 24 can be viewed but not entered) and continue along the third. Here, the halls are devoted to Florentine painting during the early 16th c., with works by: Michelangelo (**Tondo Doni***), Raphael (**Madonna del Cardellino***), A. del Sarto, Pontormo, Rosso Fiorentino, and Bronzino. Then you continue to halls given over to the schools of Venice, Emilia and Ferrara, and Central Italy: Titian, whose work occupies an entire hall, Palma the Elder, Parmigianino, D. Dossi, Mazzolino, S. del Piombo, Lotto, Veronese, Bassano, El Greco, Tintoretto, and F. Barocci. Here, work by 17th- and 18th-c. artists (Rubens and Van Dyck, J. Sustermans) surrounds a group of fine Roman statues, copies of Greek originals; then come other halls with works by Caravaggio (**Bacchus***), F. Albani, Annibale Carracci, Rembrandt, Brueghel the Elder, Crespi, Canaletto, and F. Guardi. You leave the gallery through what was once the entrance, between halls 35 and 41; as you leave, you will pass 17th-c paintings and a few notable ancient and modern sculptures.

Corridoio Vasariano. *Open only for guided tours with compulsory reservation; tel. 0552654321.* You enter from the third corridor of the Uffizi (hall 25); this corridor was built in 1565 by Vasari, to link the Uffizi to Palazzo Pitti across the Ponte Vecchio. On display are major 17th-/18th-c. works, and part of the renowned *collection of self-portraits**, with work by painters from the 16th c. to modern times (Vasari, Bernini, Rubens, Rembrandt, Velázquez, Canova, Delacroix).

Museo di Storia della Scienza* *(E4). Open Oct.-Mar., 9:30-5; Tue., 9:30-1; 2nd Sun. of the month, 10-1; Jun.-Sep., Mon.-Fri., 9:30-5; Tue. and Sat., 9:30-1.* This museum of the history of science is arranged on two storeys of *Palazzo Castellani,* in Piazza dei Giudici; it features a collection of scientific apparatus and instruments begun by Cosimo the Elder, on display until the mid-18th c. in the Uffizi, and the Lorraine collection of instruments and equipment for teaching and experimentation (18th c.). Of particular interest are mathematical instruments, Florentine and from elsewhere (astrolabes, mechanical calculators, measuring systems of all kinds), memorabilia of G. Galilei, optical instruments, instruments for cosmography and astronomy (an armillary sphere* built by A. Santucci delle Pomarance), clocks, magnetic and electrical instruments, pneumatic and hydrostatic apparatuses, mechanical tools, surgical tools and instruments (Brambilla Collection) and teaching models, pharmacists' equipment, and chemical instruments.

The Oltrarno

The second walled perimeter of Florence (1172) crossed over to the left bank of the Arno, when what is now called the Ponte Vecchio, or old bridge, was the only bridge over that river. Starting in Piazza della Repubblica, you cross the Arno over the Ponte Vecchio, stopping at the Pitti Palace, and continue on to the architectural splendor of Brunelleschi's masterpiece, the church of S. Spirito; you can also admire the newly restored frescoes by Masaccio at the Carmine church.

Piazza della Repubblica *(C-D4).* This late-19th-c. eclectic construction entailed the lamentable de-molition of the old medieval market; on the western side, busy porticoes with popular cafes.

Palazzo Davanzati* *(D3).* This building in the Piazza Davanzati is a stern aristocratic home of the 14th c., a tall narrow three-storey building with centered windows and a large 16th-c. loggia. It houses the **Museo della Casa Fiorentina Antica** (*closed for restoration; tel. 0552388610*), which offers an intriguing glimpse of domestic life and culture in Florence during the 14th-18th c. through furniture, paintings, sculpture, majolica, tapestries, fabrics, and lace from all over Europe, as well as an assortment of everyday objects from the past. Note, in particular, the Gothic courtyard, two halls – Sala dei Pappagalli and the Sala dei Pavoni – on the first floor, and the master bedroom on the second floor.

Via Calimala *(D4).* This street runs along the **Loggia del Mercato Nuovo,** built in 1551 by G.B. del Tasso, as a marketplace for fine cloth; now Florentine handicrafts are sold here. On the side facing the Borsa Merci is the fountain known as the *Fontana del Porcellino* (literally, piglet; in reality, a wild boar), a bronze copy by P. Tacca (1612; from a Hellenistic original, now in the Uffizi).

Palazzo dei Capitani di Parte Guelfa *(D4).* Behind the Loggia del Mercato Nuovo, this building dates from the early 14th c. and was enlarged in later periods by Brunelleschi and by Vasari, and restored around 1920. Inside, note the magnificent hall by Brunelleschi, with a lunette in glazed terracotta by L. della Robbia and a wooden ceiling by Vasari, who also did the elegant little exterior loggia.

Museo Diocesano di S. Stefano al Ponte *(E4). Open only for guided tours, Fri., 3:30; tel. 0552710732.* The museum is housed in the church of the same name, and features precious works by Giotto and Uccello.

Ponte Vecchio* *(E3-4).* This is the oldest and best known bridge in Florence and the world, and was built in 1345 by N. di Fioravante on previous structures dating from at least 996. It was the only bridge in Florence to escape destruction, in August 1944 during the German retreat. Its span covers three arches, and it is lined by a double row of shops once belonging to wool merchants and greengrocers, now run by jewelers. Above the shops on the upstream side runs the Corridoio Vasariano, linking the Uffizi with Palazzo Pitti (see above). From the terraces in the center, fine view of the river, Ponte S. Trinita, and the Lungarni, or riverfront avenues.

Via de' Guicciardini *(E-F3).* Rebuilt after WWII, this road opens out into a little square dominated by the church of **S. Felicita,** heavily renovated in the 18th c.; inside, fine frescoes by Pontormo.

Palazzo Pitti** *(F2-3).* The most monumental of Florence's many palazzi, it was built by the Pitti, a family of merchants and bankers, around 1458, and was probably designed by Brunelleschi.

Simple grandeur is everywhere, in the three storeys with graduated rustication, punctuated by arcades. The building was enlarged by B. Ammannati and C. Parigi (1558); it attained its current appearance, with

e two jutting wings, between 1764 and 1839. From
49 on, it was the residence of the grand dukes
Medici first, then Hapsburg-Lorraine), and for a short
ne (1865-71) the residence of Italy's first king, Vic-
r Emmanuel II. Today, the halls of the beautiful
uilding, along with other structures in the adjacent
ardens of Bòboli, house several major Florentine
useums: the Galleria Palatina, the Appartamenti
eali, the Galleria d'Arte Moderna, the Museo degli
genti, the Museo delle Carrozze, the Galleria del
ostume, and the Museo delle Porcellane.

om the central portal, you emerge into the mastic *courtyard* * by B. Ammannati (1570): note the
th-c. Grotto of Moses; on the terrace above is the
vely late 16th-c. fountain known as *Fontana del
rciofo*. From the courtyard, a stairway on the right
ads to the Galleria Palatina, the Appartamenti Rea-
and the Galleria d'Arte Moderna.

alleria Palatina. * * *Open Tue.-Sun., 8:15-6:50.* This
llection, arranged in spectacular halls frescoed
P. da Cortona and C. Ferri, still has the appearce of a princely gallery; in particular, it boasts ex-
llent 16th-/17th-c. art. You enter through the Gal-
ria delle Statue, and, to the left, the Sala delle Nic-
ie, both featuring ancient statues. You thus reach
e Sala di Venere, which takes its name from a mar-
e **Italic Venus** * * by A. Canova. This hall has **four
asterpieces** * * by Titian, and paintings by Rubens
d S. Rosa. In the following halls, which are named
er Greek and Roman deities, are masterpieces by
osso Fiorentino, A. del Sarto, Titian (**Young Eng-
shman** * *), Tintoretto, D. Dossi, Veronese, Rubens,
n Dyck, Murillo, Giorgione, Raphael (**Velata** * *),
a' Bartolomeo, A. del Sarto, Bronzino, and Perugino.
the Sala dell'Iliade, works by Raphael, R. del
hirlandaio, A. del Sarto, and J. Sustermans. The oth-
halls feature frescoes by P. da Cortona and paintgs by Caravaggio, C. Allori. C. Dolci, Raphael, Filip-
o Lippi, Botticelli, Signorelli, B. Peruzzi, Pontormo,
eccafumi, Titian, Veronese, A. del Sarto, Vasari,
ubens, and S. Rosa.

ppartamenti Reali. *Open same days and hours
the Galleria Palatina.* The lavish rooms of the Roy-
Apartments were home to the Medici and then
e Lorraine, and reception areas for the Savoy. Re-
ntly restored to the way they looked in 1911, when
ey were donated to the state.

alleria d'Arte Moderna. *Open Tue.-Sat., 2nd, 4th
on., and 1st, 3rd, 5th Sun. of the month, 8:15-1:50.*
is gallery of modern art offers a complete view
Italian painting from Neo-Classicism to the 20th c.
thirty halls; more halls will open in time, on the top
por. Notable works by: Hayez, Fattori, Previati, Lega,
osso, Signorini, Puccinelli, and Zandomeneghi.

useo degli Argenti. * *Open Tue.-Sat., 2nd, 4th
on., and 1st, 3rd, 5th Sun. of the month, 8:15-1:50.*
the left of the central courtyard, this museum of
verware occupies the summer grand-ducal apart-
ents and the mezzanine; it features remarkable
ojects made of precious metals, semi-precious
ones, crystals, and ivory, as well as amazing array
luxury items and bizarre jewelry.

Museo delle Carrozze. *Temporarily closed.* This
museum features carriages from the courts of Lorraine and Savoy; it is on the ground floor, overlooking the roundabout to the left of the palazzo.

Giardino di Bòboli * * (F3). *Open Jun.-Aug, 8:15-
7:30; Apr.-May and Sep.-Oct., 8:15-6:30; Nov.-Feb., 8:15-
4:30; Tue., 8:15-5:30; closed 1st and last Mon. of the
month.* From the Ammannati courtyard of Palazzo
Pitti you enter one of the largest and most elegant of
all Italian-style gardens. Extending over 45,000 sq m
of the Bòboli hill, between Palazzo Pitti, the fortress
of Belvedere, and the Porta Romana, it was designed
in 1550 by N. Tribolo and others. Its current appearance developed over the centuries. It features wide
lanes with wide-ranging views, fountains, and statues.
Among the best-known features: the great 17th-c. *amphitheater*; the 17th-c. *Fontana del Carciofo*, the *Buontalenti grotto* (1588), with its Venus by Giambologna;
the *fishpond of Neptune* (1565); the high *Garden of
the Cavaliere*, with its magnificent view, and the nearby little lodge (*Casino del Cavaliere*), which houses
the Museo delle Porcellane (see below), and the *Viot-
tolone*, the long straight avenue that runs between
statues and walls of laurels, cypresses, and pine trees
to the *Piazzale dell'Isolotto* *, where Giambologna's
handsome Fountain of the Ocean stands (1576).

Museo delle Porcellane. * *Open 9-1:30; closed 1st
and last Mon., and 2nd, 4th Sun. of the month.* This museum has a collection of porcelain from the Royal
Manufactory of Naples, from the Ginori Manufactory
of Doccia, from Sèvres and other manufactories in
Paris, Chantilly, Vienna, Berlin, Meissen, and Worcester.

Palazzina della Meridiana (F2). This Neo-Classic
pavilion was begun after 1776 by G.M. Paoletti and
completed in 1840 by P. Poccianti, at the SW wing of
the building overlooking the Bòboli gardens. Inside,
note the sumptuous Neo-Classic decoration, partly
touched up around 1860. Restored in 1971, it became the site of the Galleria del Costume and, temporarily, of the Donazione Contini-Bonacossi.

Galleria del Costume. *Open 8:15-1:50; closed 2nd,
4th Sun. and 1st, 3rd, 5th Mon. of the month.* This museum of fashion and costumes displays, with a two-
year rotating exhibit, historical clothing from the ear-
ly-18th to the early-20th c.

S. Felice in Piazza (F2). This church, originally Romanesque, has a handsome Renaissance facade attributed to Michelozzo (1452-60); inside note the
Crucifix painted on a wooden panel by Giotto pri-
or to 1307.

Museo Zoologico La Specola (F2). *Open 9-1,
closed Wed.* In the venerable old Palazzo Torrigiani,
at n. 17 in Via Romana, this section of the Museo di
Storia Naturale of the University has remarkably vast
collections of zoology and wax anatomical models*, housed in 600 display cases from the 18th and
19th c. Upstairs is the *Tribuna di Galileo*, an amphitheater (1841) with lavish marble, mosaics, and
fresco decorations exalting the history of science
and the scientists of Florence.

Via Maggio (E-F2-3). In the old days known as "Via
Maggiore," this is the loveliest street in the Oltrarno

district. Straight and lined with 14th-/16th-c. palazzi, it has an aristocratic appearance. At n. 26, *Palazzo di Bianca Cappello* (the lover and then the wife of Francesco de' Medici), by B. Buontalenti, a fine example of a 16th-c. patrician residence whose facade is decorated with grotesque art.

Piazza S. Spirito (*F2*). This square, with its greenery and simple fountain, is lined by 15th-c. homes; in particular, note the palazzo at n. 10, **Palazzo Guadagni***, a fine Florentine Renaissance building, possibly by Cronaca (1503-06). At the far end of the square is the church of S. Spirito.

S. Spirito** (*E2*). *Open 8-12 and 4-6; closed Wed.* With S. Lorenzo, this church is one of the pre-eminent creations of the architecture of the early Renaissance. Begun in 1444 by Brunelleschi, it was continued after 1446 in conformity with his plans by A. Manetti, and completed in 1488. The facade is austere; the right side, with its simple lines, is particularly handsome. The slender campanile* on the left side is by B. d'Agnolo (1503). The *interior*, refined in its elegance and almost musical in its balanced composition, features a nave with two aisles divided by columns topped with arches, extending into the transept as well. Note the handsome niches, used as chapels. The stained glass windows in the facade were designed by Perugino. On the altars of the side chapels there are copies of statues by Michelangelo; sculptures attributed to Rossellino and Sansovino; numerous panels by 15th- and 16th-c. artists, including Filippino Lippi, C. Rosselli, and A. Allori; polyptych by M. di Banco (14th c.). From the left aisle, through a vestibule* with a coffered barrel vault on columns (by Cronaca, after a design by G. da Sangallo), you enter the octagonal sacristy*, with two orders of pillars and a ribbed cupola, also designed by Sangallo. To the left of the church is the entrance to the **Cenacolo di S. Spirito** (*open 9-1:30; closed Mon.*), a refectory with an impressive fresco (Crucifixion*), by A. Orcagna, covering a whole wall, and various sculptures from the high Middle Ages to the Renaissance.

S. Maria del Carmine* (*E1*). In the Piazza di S. Maria del Carmine, this medieval church, rebuilt in 1771, is renowned for the frescoes by Masaccio and Masolino that adorn the Cappella Brancacci. (*open 10-4:30; Sun. and holidays, 1-4:30; closed Tue.*) Located at the end of the right transept, the chapel can be reached by a door to the right of the facade, by passing through the 17th-c. cloister. The **frescoes**** were begun by Masolino and Masaccio in 1424, and finished by Filippino Lippi after 1480. Recently restored, they include Masaccio's masterpieces, the Expulsion from Eden, and The Tribute Money. The nearby Gothic *sacristy* has various 14th- and 15th-c. paintings and frescoes by L. d'Andrea (1400).

From S. Trìnita to S. Maria Novella

Via de' Tornabuoni, an understated, refined, elegant street, lay at the western extremity of both the Roman city and of the city enclosed within the first medieval circuit of walls. This route runs throu the western districts of the center of Florence, to t Dominican church of S. Maria Novella, still outsi of the walls when construction began, before Dar Alighieri was born.

S. Maria Maggiore (*C3-4*). In Via de' Cerretani, o of the busiest thoroughfares in Florence, note th 13th-c. Gothic church, much renovated over the ce turies. The austere interior features fragments of la 14th-c. frescoes.

Piazza degli Antinori (*C3*). This square takes name from **Palazzo Antinori**, built (1461-69) Giuliano da Maiano; facing it is the Baroque chur of *S. Gaetano*, designed by B. Buontalenti and bu during the 17th c. by M. Nigetti and Gherardo S vani and son.

Via de' Tornabuoni* (*C-D3*). One of the most egant streets in Florence, it is lined by exclusi shops and major palazzi of the 15th-19th c. Note t rear of Palazzo Strozzi.

Palazzo Strozzi** (*D3*). Rivalled only by Palaz Medici-Riccardi as the finest example of Florenti Renaissance palazzo, this building was begun 1489 by B. da Maiano and continued by Crona (1497-1504); one side and part of the cornice, ho ever, remained unfinished. It is simple yet elegant appearance. It has graduated rustication, with tv registers of centered mullioned windows, and a j ting cornice*; at the corners, note the banner land and the wrought-iron torch-holders, also by B. Maiano (1491-98). Inside, a porticoed courtyard ar two orders of loggias, of exquisite elegance, designe and built by Cronaca. Currently, the building hou es cultural institutes and major exhibitions.

Museo Marino Marini (*C-D3*). *Open 10-1 and 4* (*winter, until 6*); *closed Tue.* Established in 1988, th museum stands in Via della Spada, in the form church of *S. Pancrazio*. It features a major collecti of works by this artist, from nearby Pistoia (190 80), including paintings from the 1920s, sculptures various materials, and canvases dating from th 1950s and 1960s.

Cappella Rucellai (*C-D3*). *Open only on Sat. a during the masses.* Adjacent to the former church S. Pancrazio (now a museum), also in Via della Sp da, this 14th-c. structure encloses the *Tempietto d S. Sepolcro**, an elegant creation of L.B. Albe (1467), who was trying to reproduce, to scale, th Holy Sepulcher of Jerusalem.

Palazzo Rucellai* (*D3*). At n. 18 in Via della Vigr Nuova, this palazzo overlooks a piazzetta with t handsome *Loggia Rucellai* (1466). A masterpiece the architecture of the early Renaissance, it was bu in various stages during the second half of the 15 c., by B. Rossellino to plans by L.B. Alberti. Note t cornices, pilaster strips, and mullioned windows. L cated here are the Archivi Photografici Alinari, wit the collection of a great historical photo house, an on the ground floor, the *Museo della Fotografia A nari* (*open 10-7:30; closed Wed.*).

Piazza S. Trìnita (*D3*). In the center of this odd shaped piazza is the *Colonna della Giustizia*, take m the Baths of Caracalla in Rome. At n. 1 stands *lazzo Bartolini-Salimbeni*, with windows with oss-bars and the handsome courtyard by Baccio Agnolo (1523). At the far end, along Via de' rnabuoni, is the crenelated *Palazzo Spini-Feroni* 3th c., rebuilt more than once), with its appearce of a massive medieval fortress-palazzo.

Trìnita* (*D3*). One of the earliest churches in rence, it was built in the late 11th c. and then reilt in the Gothic style in the 14th c., possibly by N. Fioravanti; the stone Baroque facade is by B. ontalenti (1594). The austere *interior*, with a nave th two aisles separated by piers with pointed archand cross-vaults, is one of the earliest examples of othic art in Florence. In the 3rd chapel on the right, the altar, Enthroned Virgin and Four Saints by N. Bicci; on the wall, fresco and preparatory drawing S. Aretino. On the altar of the 4th chapel on the ht, Annunciation* by L. Monaco; on the walls, fresies, also by L. Monaco. In the sacristy, detached 14th-frescoes and the tomb of O. Strozzi, by P. Lamberti 421). In the 2nd chapel to the right of the main alr (Cappella Sassetti), frescoes by D. Ghirlandaio 483-86): on the altar, Adoration of the Shepherds*; the walls, six Scenes from the Life of St. Francis*. the 2nd chapel to the left of the main altar, mare tomb* of B. Federighi, bishop of Fièsole, with a ndsome strip of polychrome majolica by L. della obbia (1454). In the 5th chapel on the left, woodsculpture* (Magdalene), by D. da Settignano, posbly completed by B. da Maiano (c. 1455).

orgo Ss. Apostoli (*D-E3*). This distinctive street the medieval center of Florence is lined by housand towers from the 13th and 14th c. On the all and charming *Piazza del Limbo* is the church the **Ss. Apostoli***, a Romanesque building from e 11th c., renovated in the 15th-18th c., but reored to its original form in the 1930s. Note the 5th-c. central portal. Inside, sculpture by B. da vezzano (tomb of O. Altoviti, 1507) and tabernae by G. della Robbia. Other works, damaged by e flood of 1966, are still being restored. Nearby is e majestic *Palazzo Rosselli del Turco* (n. 19), by B. Agnolo (1507).

onte S. Trìnita* (*E3*). This majestic bridge spans e Arno with three polycentric arches. It is the masrpiece of B. Ammannati (1608), who rebuilt the ve-arch bridge erected by T. Gaddi, which had collpsed in 1557. Destroyed by the retreating Germans Aug. 1944), it was rebuilt in its original form. It ofrs fine views* along the riverbanks as far as the arco delle Cascine, downstream, and of the Ponte ecchio and the hill of S. Miniato, upstream.

alazzo Corsini (*D2-3*). At n. 10 Lungarno Corsini, is building dates from 1648-56, and is one of the nest examples of Florentine Baroque, with terraces ecked with statues. Inside, the **Galleria Corsini** pen by request, tel. 055218994; entrance from n. 1 in Via del Parione) is one of the most notable prite collections in Italy, with spectacular rooms lined ith paintings from 15th-/16th-c. Florence (Filippino ippi, Signorelli, Pontormo, and others) and Italian

and foreign artists from the 17th-18th c.

Chiesa di Ognissanti (*C1-2*). This church, set in the Piazza di Ognissanti, was founded in 1251; it was later renovated, and has a Baroque facade (1637) by M. Nigetti, with a Della Robbia terracotta; only the slender bell tower survives from the original structure. Inside: frescoes by D. Ghirlandaio; a detached fresco by Botticelli; in the sacristy, a panel from the school of Giotto and a detached fresco by T. Gaddi. From the Renaissance *cloister* (17th-c. frescoes) adjacent to the church you enter (*entrance at n. 42 in Borgo Ognissanti*) the ancient refectory of the convent (*open Mon., Tue. and Sat., 9-12*), with a fresco (The Last Supper*) by D. Ghirlandaio.

Piazza S. Maria Novella (*C2-3*). Bounded by the facade of the church of S. Maria Novella, a lovely backdrop, this square is one of Florence's most charming spots. In the middle are the two marble obelisks (1608) which marked the finish lines in the horse race of the Palio dei Cocchi. On the side opposite the church, note the handsome **Loggia di S. Paolo** (*C2*; 15th c.), with ten elegant arches on Corinthian columns; set between the arches, nine glazed terracotta medallions by A. della Robbia, who also did the lunette under the portico.

S. Maria Novella** (*B2-3*). One of Florence's most renowned churches, this is a masterpiece of Gothic architecture, built between 1278 and about 1350. The 14th-c. *facade**, entirely covered with marble, was rebuilt in 1458 to the design of L.B. Alberti; note his classical portal and the section above the central cornice, with volutes on either side. To the right of the facade, an enclosure made up of arcades with the tombs of Florence's leading families surrounds the ancient cemetery.

The **interior** is a harmonious, soaring piece of Gothic architecture, and it abounds with masterpieces of architecture, sculpture, and painting. In particular, note the work of Rossellino and D. da Settignano, L. Ghiberti, N. Pisano, B. da Maiano, Giambologna, B. d'Agnolo, G. da Sangallo, and Brunelleschi. Among the fine **frescoes** and paintings that adorn the interior of the church, is the work by Filippino Lippi, D. Ghirlandaio, Masaccio, N. di Cione, and A. Orcagna. In the *sacristy*, the terracotta lavabo by G. della Robbia, the **Crucifix**** by Giotto, and the extraordinary **fresco**** by Masaccio.

Florence: S. Maria Novella

Museo di S. Maria Novella* (*B2*). *Open 9-1:30; closed Fri.* With an entrance to the left of the church, this museum includes part of the cloisters of the old convent and a number of other rooms. The *Chiostro Verde* (or Green Cloister) was built after 1350 and takes its name from the frescoes in "terra verde" on the walls (Stories from the Genesis*) by various early 15th-c. artists, including Paolo Uccello; by the latter, note in particular the Deluge* and the Drunkenness of Noah*. The *Cappellone degli Spagnoli**, once the Chapter House, is a spacious hall built by J.Talenti (14th c.). It is entirely frescoed by A. di Buonaiuto (1367-69), with a polyptych on the altar by B. Daddi. In the *Sala del Refettorio* (Refectory Hall), 14th-c. fresco.

Piazza della Stazione (*B2-3*). This square overlooks the handsome apse of S. Maria Novella, with its slender and elegant *campanile* (1332-33). In the distance, you can see the train station, or *Stazione Centrale di S. Maria Novella* (*A-B2*), a fine example of Rationalist architecture (1932-35), built by the Gruppo Toscano, under G. Michelucci. On the side facing Piazza Adua, note the marble *Palazzina Reale* (*A2*), where the king of Italy boarded his train, also by Michelucci (1934).

Ex Convento delle Monache di Foligno (*A3*). *Open only for guided tours, 9-12 (ring the bell).* At n. 40 in Via Faenza, this former nunnery features, in the refectory, a fresco of the Last Supper by assistants of Perugino and other detached frescoes by B. di Lorenzo, once thought to be by Raphael.

The areas around S. Marco and the Santissima Annunziata

The focal points of this route lie in Piazza S. Marco and neighboring Piazza Santissima Annunziata, both to the north of the Duomo, just outside the second medieval walled perimeter. Around Piazza S. Marco is the Galleria dell'Accademia and the Dominican convent where Fra' Angelico lived and painted. On one side of Piazza Santissima Annunziata, note the exquisite arches of the portico of the Spedale degli Innocenti by Brunelleschi, and the Museo Archeologico.

Via Cavour (*A-B4-5*). This road is a continuation of Via de' Martelli, known as Via Larga until the 19th c. for its broad and airy appearance. It boasts Palazzo Medici-Riccardi and other aristocratic palazzi of the 17th and 18th c.

Cenacolo di S. Apollonia* (*A4-5*). *Open 8:30-1:30; closed 1st, 3rd, 5th Sun. and 2nd, 4th Mon. of the month.* This is the refectory of the former Benedictine nunnery of S. Apollonia (entrance from n. 1 in Via XXVII Aprile), which Andrea del Castagno decorated around 1450 with major frescoes (**Last Supper****, Crucifixion, Deposition, Resurrection); also, other works by the same artist. You may wish to visit the elegant 15th-c. *Chiostro Grande**, or main cloister (entrance from n. 1 in Via S. Gallo), property of the University.

Piazza S. Marco (*A5*). Spacious and tree-lined, t square is bounded by the church of S. Marco, adjoining convent, site of the museum (see belov and various other buildings, including the *Univers degli Studi* and the *Accademia delle Belle Arti*, w the early Renaissance portico of the former *Hos tal di S. Matteo*; note the three handsome lunet by the Della Robbia.

S. Marco (*A5*). This church, with a Baroque façac dates from the 14th c., but was rebuilt by Mich lozzo (1437-43) and renovated in the 16th and 1 c. Inside are various 14th-c. artworks, painting Fra' Bartolomeo (1509), and a Crucifix by Fra' A gelico (1428) on the main altar.

Museo di S. Marco** (*A5*). *Open Tue-Fri. and M 3rd Mon. of the month, 8:15-1:50; 2nd, 4th Sun. of month, 8:15-7; Sat., 8:15-6:50.* To the right of t church, this museum occupies the handsome a well restored rooms of the Dominican Convent S. Marco, extensively rebuilt by Michelozzo (14 44), which was a major cultural center in the 15 c. Among those who lived here were Fra' Angelic Savonarola, and Fra' Bartolomeo. Of particular terest are the paintings by Fra' Angelico. *Chiostro S. Antonino**: in the lunettes of the cloister portic is a series of frescoes by Fra' Angelico. *Sala d l'Ospizio*: this hall holds a number of masterpiec by Fra' Angelico; note the marble frame around or by L. Ghiberti. Sala del Capitolo: the chapter ha houses the large **Crucifixion**** by Fra' Angelic and a Virgin by P. Uccello. *Refettorio grande*: in the fectory are frescoes and paintings by Sogliani, R. c Ghirlandaio, L. Lippi, and others. In the Sala di Aless Baldovinetti, paintings by the same, by B. Gozzc and A. Romano. In the Sala di Fra' Bartolomeo, large altarpiece and various paintings by the sam The *Chiostro di S. Domenico* (*cloistered area, clos to the public*), built by Michelozzo, can just l glimpsed through a number of windows; at the fo of the stairs is the *Sala del Cenacolo*, named after frescoed Last Supper* by D. Ghirlandaio.

The **first floor** is occupied by the cells of th monks, decorated by renowned *frescoes* by Fra' A gelico. At the end of the second corridor is th *Quartiere del Priore*, where Savonarola once live (note the portrait by Fra' Bartolomeo). In the thir corridor, note the painting by B. Gozzoli, and the *l brary**, an elegant Renaissance room with a nav with two aisles, by Michelozzo.

Chiostro dello Scalzo. *Open Mon., Thu. and Sa 8:15-2.* In Via Cavour n. 69, this small rectangula porticoed courtyard dating from the early 16th has a monochrome fresco by Andrea del Sarto an Franciabigio (1526).

Musei Universitari di Storia Naturale. (*A5-6* These museums of natural history are located i Via Giorgio La Pira n. 4; they are run by the Un versity and comprise three sections. The *Museo Mineralogia e Litologia* (*open Mon.-Fri. and 2nd Sui of the month, 9-1, except Jun.-Sep.; tel. 0552757537* has collections of minerals from all over the worlc of note, the Brazilian topaz weighing 151 kg. (2n largest on earth) and a collection of beryls. The *Museo di Geologia e Paleontologia* (*open Tue.-Sat. and 2nd Sun. of the month, 9-1, except Jun.-Sep.; tel. 0552757536*) is one of Italy's finest geological and paleontological museums, with about 300,000 samples. The *Museo Botanico* (*closed for restoration; tel. 0552757452*) has numerous herbariums (about 4 million specimens), and the most complete tropical herbarium in Italy. Adjacent to the latter herbarium, with entrance from n. 3 in Via Micheli, is the *Orto Botanico Giardino dei Semplici* (*open Mon.-Fri., 9-1; tel. 0552757402*), an ancient garden of medicinal herbs, once called "semplici", founded in 1550, with about 6000 plants.

Galleria dell'Accademia* (*A5*). *Open Tue.-Sun., 8:15-6:50.* At n. 60 in Via Ricasoli, this gallery is renowned for a group of sculptures by Michelangelo, but it also has a notable collection of paintings of the Florentine school (13th-16th c.). In the Galleria dei Prigioni: four enormous unfinished sculptures, known as the *Prigioni**, or Captives, executed around 1530 by Michelangelo for the tomb of Pope Julius II; also, an unfinished S. Matteo (St. Matthew; 1505-06), and the world-renowned **David****, carved in 1501-04, and formerly located in Piazza della Signoria. In the so-called *Sale Fiorentine*, or Florentine Halls, canvases by painters of the Florentine Renaissance: A. di Giusto; G. di Ser Giovanni, known as Scheggia; D. di Michelino; C. Rosselli; Perugino; A. Baldovinetti; Botticelli; Filippino Lippi; and R. del Garbo. The large hall of the *Gipsoteca Bartolini* contains many plaster casts. In the so-called *Sale Bizantine*, or Byzantine Halls, work by Florentine painters of the 13th and 14th c.: panels and Crucifixes of the Tuscan school, P. di Bonaguida, Maestro della Maddalena, B. Daddi, T. Gaddi, G. da Milano, Maestro di S. Gaggio, and others. On the *first floor* are new halls devoted to L. Monaco and Florentine art between the 14th and 15th c.

Museo dell'Opificio delle Pietre Dure (*B5; open Mon.-Sat., 8:15-2; Tue. until 7 p.m.*). This museum of semiprecious stones, with entrance in Via degli Alfani n. 78, is adjacent to the Opificio delle Pietre Dure (literally, workshop of semiprecious stones), established in 1588.

Piazza Santissima Annunziata* (*B6*). This square is lined with handsome Renaissance porticoes; in the middle are an equestrian statue of Ferdinando I, by Giambologna, and two elegant Baroque fountains* by P. Tacca (1629). To the right of the basilica, note the portico of the Ospedale degli Innocenti; to the left, the *Loggia dei Serviti*, by A. da Sangallo the Elder and B. d'Agnolo.

Ospedale degli Innocenti* (*B6*). One of the most significant emblems of Florence's Humanist culture, this foundling hospital is one of the loveliest creations of the Italian Renaissance; designed by F. Brunelleschi (1419), it was completed by F. della Luna (1445). Overlooking the square is an elegant *portico** with arches on slender columns; in the spandrels of the arches, eight glazed terracotta tondos by A. della Robbia. The interior encloses a first court-

yard (*Chiostro degli Uomini*); from here, two stairways lead up to the hall of the **Pinacoteca** (*open 8:30-2; closed Wed.*), with a small number of exquisite works by great artists including: Maestro della Madonna Strauss, Botticelli, L. della Robbia, P. di Cosimo, and D. Ghirlandaio.

Basilica della Santissima Annunziata* (*A6*). *Open 7-12:30 and 4-6:30.* This renowned Florentine sanctuary contains the venerated image of the Madonna Annunziata (Virgin Annunciate): it was built in 1250, rebuilt in the 15th c. by Michelozzo, and subsequently renovated extensively. In front of the church is a 17th-c. portico, and from there you enter a little atrium or cloister called the *Chiostrino dei Voti* (1447). On the walls, detached and restored *frescoes** by Rosso Fiorentino (1517), Pontormo (1516), Franciabigio, and Andrea del Sarto; also a marble bas-relief by Michelozzo.

The *interior* of the church is notably Baroque, and features numerous 17th- and 18th-c. works of art. In the 5th chapel at right, monument to O. de' Medici, by B. Rossellino (1456). In the presbytery, enormous circular apse by Michelozzo and L.B. Alberti, surrounded by nine chapels, with 16th-c. paintings and statues. In the left transept, terracotta statue by Michelozzo. Adjoining it is the 15th-c. *Chiostro dei Morti* (Cloister of the Dead; *open by request, ask for the sacristan*), with fresco by A. del Sarto. In the left aisle: two frescoes by A. del Castagno, in the 2nd and 3rd chapels. At the beginning of the aisle, note the *Cappella dell'Annunziata*, a chapel in the form of a little marble temple*; on the altar is a 14th-c. fresco of the Annunciation.

Museo Archeologico* (*A-B6*). *Open Mon., 2-7; Tue. and Thu., 8:30-7; Wed. and Fri.-Sun., 8:30-2.* In the *Palazzo della Crocetta*, in Via della Colonna n. 36-38. Founded in 1824-28, this is one of the most important and fascinating archeological museums in Italy, especially noteworthy in terms of the Etruscan and Egyptian civilizations. As far as the latter is concerned, it ranks second in Italy only behind the Museo Egizio of Turin.

The 11 halls of the **Museo Egizio** include steles, sculpture, sarcophagi, mummies, wall fragments, jewelry, papyri, ointment vases, tools, and so forth. In particular: granite group with Hathor Suckling the Pharaoh Horemhab* (14th c. B.C.), and other remarkable statues and bas-reliefs. Among **Etruscan stone sculpture**, the most noteworthy pieces are those of funerary statuary. Equally extraordinary are the **Etruscan bronzes** and the collection of **Attic ceramics** and **Greek sculptures**. In a separate section of the museum is the **Collezione Glittica** (*open weekdays, 9:30-12:30; holidays until 11:30*), which exhibits the gems collected by the Medici and Hapsburg-Lorraine, with pieces dating back to the 4th c. B.C.

Via de' Servi (*B-C5*). Formerly known as "Borgo di Balla," this street ran from Piazza del Duomo toward Fièsole, and is lined with interesting palazzi. As you cross Via degli Alfani, on the left, between that street and Via del Castellaccio, note the *Rotonda di S.*

Maria degli Angioli (*B5*), designed by Brunelleschi (1433), the nucleus of an unfinished octagonal church. Back on Via de' Servi n. 15 is the 16th-c. *Palazzo Niccolini*, formerly Palazzo Montalto.

Arcispedale di S. Maria Nuova (*C5-6*). Overlooking Piazza di S. Maria Nuova, with a tripartite loggia, this is the oldest hospital in Florence, founded in 1288 by Folco Portinari. Its modern-day appearance is a result of the renovation done in the late 16th c. by B. Buontalenti. At the center of the portico is the portal of the 15th-c. church of *S. Egidio*; to the right of the church is the *Chiostro delle Medicherie*, a notable cloister with glazed terracotta by G. della Robbia.

Museo e Istituto Fiorentino di Preistoria (*C5*). *Open Mon.-Sat., 9:30-12:30.* Facing the Arcispedale, in Via S. Egidio n. 21, this museum of prehistory is housed in a former convent. It possesses various collections concerning local and world prehistory. In the same building, but with an entrance in Via dell'Oriuolo n. 24, is the **Museo Storico-Topografico Firenze Com'Era** (*open 9-2, closed Thu.*), featuring the development and history of the city from the 15th c. to the present, with woodcuts, etchings, prints, paintings, and photographs. Note the series of twelve Views of the Medici Villas by the Flemish painter, Justus, or Giusto Utens (1599).

S. Ambrogio. This church of ancient origin (the earliest documentation is from the 10th c.), rebuilt repeatedly over the centuries, has an 18th-c. interior; on the exquisite Renaissance altars are paintings from the 14th and 15th c. To the left of the presbytery, in the Cappella del Miracolo, marble tabernacle by M. da Fièsole (1481-83), fresco by C. Rosselli (ca. 1486) and panel of Saints and Angels by A. Baldovinetti.

S. Maria Maddalena de' Pazzi.* *Open 10-12 and 5-5:30.* At n. 58 in Borgo Pinti, this church rebuilt after 1479 to the design by Giuliano da Sangallo; note the handsome cloister. In the former Sala Capitolare (*access from the sacristy*) is a Crucifixion* fresco by Perugino.

The district of S. Croce

This route, which begins among the sculpture of Donatello and Michelangelo at the Bargello, leads to the Basilica di S. Croce, where Giotto painted, and where great Italians are buried, including the poet Ugo Foscolo. The route ends across the Arno River, at the Museo Bardini.

Via del Proconsolo (*C-D5*). One of the oldest streets in Florence runs along the eastern edge of the first walled perimeter. At n. 12, the *Palazzo Nonfinito*, begun in 1593, perhaps to plans by B. Buontalenti, was left unfinished (hence the name); it now houses the **Museo Nazionale di Antropologia ed Etnologia** (*open Wed.-Mon., 9-1*), founded by P. Mantegazza in 1869, with anthropological and ethnological collections. To the left, in *Borgo degli Albizi**, still a clearly medieval street, note *Palazzo Ramirez de Montalvo* (n. 26), built by B. Ammannati (1568), and at n. 18, *Palazzo Altoviti* and at n. 12-14 the *Casa* and the

Palazzo degli Albizi, rebuilt in the early-16th c.

Palazzo Pazzi* (*D5*). At n. 10 Via del Proconsolo, this Renaissance palazzo, known as the "Palazzo della Congiura," after the great conspiracy against the Medici which was the ruin of the House of Pazzi, was built for the family by Giuliano da Maiano (1458-69). It has splendid mullioned windows and an elegant porticoed courtyard.

Casa-Museo di Dante (*D5; open Mar.-Oct., Mon. and Wed.-Sat., 10-6; Sun., 10-2; Nov.-Feb., Mon. and Wed.-Sat., 10 4; Sun. 10-2*). In Via Dante Alighieri (*entrance at n. 1 in Via S. Margherita*), this building was reconstructed in 1910. It houses a museum of memorabilia of the great poet.

Badia Fiorentina* (*D5*). *Open Mon., 3-6; tel. 05523445545.* This ancient Benedictine church was enlarged in the 13th c. (the apse dates from this period) by A. di Cambio, and then further rebuilt in the 15th and 17th c. The elaborate portal, with a terracotta lunette by B. Buglioni, is a 19th-c. copy of the original, which was done in 1494 by B. da Rovezzano, who also did the interior portico. Also note the 14th-c. six-sided campanile*. In the Baroque *interior* are a panel* by Filippino Lippi (1485) and various sculptures by M. da Fièsole: altar frontal with Virgin and Two Saints*; tomb of B. Giugni*; tomb of the Marchese Ugo di Toscana*. A door to the right of the presbytery leads to the *Chiostro degli Aranci*, a cloister with portico and loggia, by B. Rossellino (1432-38); in the loggia, detached frescoes and preparatory drawings, executed in the 15th c.

Museo Nazionale del Bargello** (*D5*). *Open Tue.-Sat., 1st, 3rd, 5th Mon. and 2nd, 4th Sun. of the month, 8:15-1:50.* This museum is located in the rather austere *Palazzo del Podestà*, also known as the *Palazzo del Bargello**, built over the years, in several stages, from 1255 to 1345, with a tower (known as the Volognana), and handsome mullioned windows along the side. It was originally the headquarters of the Podestà and later, after 1574, of the Capitano di Giustizia, also known as the Bargello.

Opened in 1865, with a collection consisting of contributions from the Uffizi, the Zecca (Mint) and the Archivio di Stato (State Archives), as well as considerable private bequests, this is now one of the world's leading museums in terms of its collection of sculpture and various objects; in particular, it has an outstanding collection of Tuscan Renaissance sculpture and French medieval ivory pieces.

Ground floor. You enter the medieval *courtyard**, surrounded by porticoes on three sides, through the Torre Volognana; in the middle of the courtyard is an octagonal well. On the walls are heraldic devices of the various Podestà; notable marble statues from the 15th-17th c., including six statues by Ammannati, the Ocean by Giambologna, and the Little Fisherman by V. Gemito (1877). *Sala del Trecento*: works originally from the Orsanmichele, as well as a Virgin with Child by T. da Camaino and a group by A. di Cambio. *Sala del Cinquecento*, works by Michelangelo: the Tondo Pitti* (ca. 1504), Bacchus* (1496-97); **David-Apollo**** (1530-32), bust of **Brutus***

(1539). There is other major sculpture from 16th-c. Tuscany: Bacchus* by J. Sansovino; bust of Cosimo I*, Narcissus, Apollo and Hyacinth, Ganymede*, by B. Cellini; Winged Mercury* by Giambologna.

First floor. In the loggia at the top of the exterior staircase, statues of animals by Giambologna; in the *Salone del Consiglio Generale**, by N. di Fioravante (1340-45), an array of works by Donatello: bust of N. da Uzzano*, in polychrome terracotta; the Marzocco (1418-20), a lion upholding the lily of Florence; Atys-Amor*, a lovely bronze depicting a winged Cupid; a marble David* (1408-09) and a bronze **David**** (ca. 1440); **San Giorgio**** (St. George; 1416) and a bas-relief of St. George and the Princess, both from the tabernacle of the Orsanmichele; Crucifixion (ca. 1450). Also, work by Brunelleschi and Ghiberti (the 2 panels of the Sacrifice of Isaac** done for the competition in 1402 for the North Door of the Battistero, or Baptistery), Michelozzo, Bertoldo, L. della Robbia, D. da Settignano, and A. di Duccio. Next come the *Sala Islamica* (Islamic Hall), with carpets, fabrics, and other items of Arab culture; the *Sala Carrand*, with items from the Carrand Donation of 1888 (paintings, sculpture, and, above all, objects of the applied arts, such as seals, goldwork, enamels, and glass); the *Cappella di S. Maria Maddalena*, a chapel frescoed by Giotto's workshop, with carved and inlaid stalls (late-15th c.); the *Sala degli Avori* (Hall of Ivory), with 265 items, ranging from the 5th to the 17th c.; the *Sala Bruzzichelli*, with 16th-c. furniture and a Virgin and Child* by J. Sansovino; and the *Sala delle Maioliche* (Hall of Majolica), with a wide range of 15th-c. Italian production.

Second floor. *Sale dei Della Robbia*: glazed terracotta by Giovanni and Andrea; *Sala dei Bronzi* (Hall of the Bronzes): Ganymede* and Greyhound, by Benvenuto Cellini; Hercules and Antaeus, by Antonio Pollaiuolo; *Sala del Verrocchio*, with the renowned bronze David* and the marble Dama col Mazzolino* (Woman with Flowers) by Verrocchio, as well as busts and other works by A. Pollaiuolo, Verrocchio, F. Laurana, A. Rossellino, B. da Maiano, and M. da Fièsole. Last is the *Medagliere* (collection of medals) with work by Pisanello, M. de' Pasti, Michelozzo, Cellini, and L. Leoni.

Palazzo di S. Firenze (*D5*). On the Piazza di S. Firenze, facing Palazzo Gondi (see below), the complex of the Filippini dedicated to S. Fiorenzo is an interesting piece of Florentine late-Baroque architecture. Now in part occupied by offices of the judiciary, it was built in 1645 as a large church, to plans by P. da Cortona; when money became scarce, only the church of *S. Filippo Neri* was built (left; inside, 18th-c. canvases and bas-reliefs), with a 1715 facade. Next to the church, Z. Del Rosso built an *oratory* in 1772-75, repeating the facade, symmetrically, and joining it with the facade of the convent.

Palazzo Gondi* (*D5*). Overlooking Piazza S. Firenze, and built by G. da Sangallo, this is an exemplary aristocratic home of 15th-c. Florence, with graduated rustication and a handsome cornice. Left unfinished, and completed in 1874 on the side facing Palazzo

Vecchio, it encloses an exquisite porticoed courtyard. **Casa Buonarroti** (*D6*). *Open 9:30-2; closed Tue.* At n. 70 in Via Ghibellina, on the site of three houses where Michelangelo lived between 1516 and 1525, is the palazzo built by his great-grandson, the man of letters Michelangelo the Younger. Visit the gallery* and the studiolo*, or study – remarkable relics of 17th-c. Florence. Left by bequest to the city by Michelangelo's last descendant, Cosimo (1858), it contains the collections of art and archeology of the Buonarroti family, and, of course, work by Michelangelo: two reliefs done in his youth (Madonna della Scala*; Battle of the Centaurs*), a wooden Crucifix* (attribution), a model for a river god*, a model for the facade of S. Lorenzo, various sketches, and a numerous array of designs and drawings (attributed).

Piazza di S. Croce (*E6*). This vast and rectangular piazza was, in the 14th c. and in the Renaissance, the site of popular assemblies, jousts, and the playing field for "calcio fiorentino," a rough-and-ready medieval ball game that is still sometimes played in the city. Note the Basilica di S. Croce as well as the handsome palazzi, surmounted by loggias: at n. 1, **Palazzo Cocchi Serristori** (*D-E6*), from the late-15th c., attributed to G. da Sangallo; at n. 20-22, *Palazzo dell'Antella*, with a jutting polychrome facade (frescoed in 1619-20) on notable corbels.

Basilica di S. Croce** (*E6*). *Open weekdays, 9:30-6; holidays, 3-5:30.* One of the most notable churches in Florence and one of the masterpieces of Florentine Gothic, renowned as the Pantheon of "illustrious Italians." It was built from 1295 on after a design by A. di Cambio; it was completed about 1385, although the consecration only took place in 1443. The marble facade is Neo-Gothic (1863), as is the campanile (1847).

The **interior**, impressive and simple, has a broad and luminous nave with aisles divided by large pointed arches on massive octagonal pillars, while the ceiling is open beam; along the walls are tombs, funerary monuments, and plaques commemorating illustrious personages. *Right aisle*: between the 1st and the 2nd altar, the tomb of Michelangelo Buonarroti; on the facing pillar, Madonna del Latte by B. Rossellino (1478); next is the monument to Vittorio Alfieri by A. Canova (1810); on the 3rd pier, a magnificent marble pulpit*, by B. da Maiano. Next are the tomb of Niccolò Machiavelli (1787); Annunciation*, relief by Donatello (ca. 1435) in a Renaissance aedicula in "pietra serena"; the **tomb of Leonardo Bruni**** by Rossellino (1444-45), prototype for all Florentine tombs in the Renaissance; the sepulcher of Gioachino Rossini (1900); the tomb of Ugo Foscolo (1939). In the *right arm of the transept*, the immense Cappella Castellani is adorned with a series of frescoes from the 14th c., by A. Gaddi and assistants; note the marble tabernacle* by M. da Fièsole and a Cross painted on wooden panel by N. Gerini. At the end of the transept is the Cappella Baroncelli, frescoed by T. Gaddi with Stories of the Virgin*, a masterpiece of this artist (1338). A portal, by Michelozzo, leads into the corridor of the 14th-c. sac-

risty, decorated with frescoes by T. Gaddi (Crucifixion), N. Gerini, and S. Aretino, with glazed terracotta by G. della Robbia and inlaid 15th-c. cabinets. This opens into the Cappella Rinuccini, with frescoes (Stories of the Virgin and the Magdalene*) by Giovanni da Milano and assistants (1363-66). In the nearby Cappella Medici, by Michelozzo, altarpiece in glazed terracotta (Virgin, Angels, and Saints*) by A. della Robbia (c. 1480). *Apsidal chapels*: on the sides of the main chapel, the Cappella Peruzzi contains a series of frescoes by Giotto (Stories of John the Baptist* on the left; Stories of St. John the Evangelist* on the right), done in his later years (ca. 1320-25), whitewashed in the 18th c. and uncovered again about 1850. Also by Giotto, **Stories of St. Francis**** in the nearby Cappella Bardi. The *main chapel* is frescoed by A. Gaddi (Legend of the Cross; 1380); the polyptych on the altar is an assembly: Virgin Mary (in the center) by N. Gerini, and Doctors of the Church by G. del Biondo; Cross* painted by the Maestro di Figline (14th c.). In the Cappella Capponi dedicated to the Mothers of Fallen Soldiers, sculptures by L. Andreotti (1926); in the Cappella Pulci-Berardi, frescoes by B. Daddi (1330) and a glazed terracotta altarpiece by G. della Robbia; in the Cappella Bardi di Vernio, frescoes (Stories of St. Sylvester*) by Maso di Banco (ca. 1340). At the head of the church is wrought-iron gate, from 1335 and, above the altar, the renowned wooden Crucifix* by Donatello, criticized by Brunelleschi for its excessive realism. *Left aisle*: monuments to the composer and musician Luigi Cherubini, to the engraver Raffaello Morghen, and to L.B. Alberti; Pentecoste by G. Vasari and monument to Carlo Marsuppini*, by D. da Settignano, one of the most remarkable sepulchers sculpted in the 15th c.; 18th-c. tombs of Galileo and Vincenzo Viviani.
Museo dell'Opera di S. Croce* (*E6*). *Open 10-7; closed Wed; tel. 055244619.* Located in the building adjacent to the church, this museum houses the fa-

mous Cappella Pazzi; the entire complex was horribly damaged by the flood of 4 November 1966, when the water of the Arno rose to a level of 4.92 m. The *first cloister* remains 14th-c. in flavor; in the center are statues by H. Moore and B. Bandinelli. At the far end, note the **Cappella Pazzi,**** one of the most original and harmonious creations of the early Renaissance, a masterpiece by Brunelleschi, who began work on it in 1429-30. Outside the chapel is a handsome portico; note the frieze by D. da Settignano. The barrel vault ceiling of the portico opens in the middle into a small cupola* decorated with terracotta tondos and roses by L. della Robbia; note the wooden door by G. da Maiano (1472). The **interior****, quite similar to the Old Sacristy of S. Lorenzo, is rectangular, with an apsidiole, surmounted by cupolas. On the white walls, traced by light architectural ribbing in "pietra serena," are twelve tondos by L. della Robbia. From the first cloister, you enter the 14th-c. *refectory*, with the justly renowned great **Crucifix**** by Cimabue, badly damaged by the flooding in 1966, and the gilt bronze statue of S. Ludovico*, by Donatello (1424), formerly in Orsanmichele; on the walls, frescoes by T. Gaddi, A. Orcagna, and D. Veneziano. You then enter a series of rooms with 14th-c. frescoes and statuary; an impressive portal, by B. da Maiano, takes you to the elegant *second cloister**, designed and built in 1453, perhaps by B. Rossellino.
Via Magliabechi (*E6*). Veering off from *Borgo S. Croce*, this distinctive Florentine street is lined with palazzi and houses from the 15th and 16th c. (at n. 10, *Palazzo Spinelli*); it goes by the building (1911-35) of the **Biblioteca Nazionale Centrale**, the largest and richest library in Italy.
Museo della Fondazione Horne (*E5*). *Open weekdays, 9-1.* This museum, located at n. 6 in Via de' Benci, in the 15th-c. Palazzo de' Benci, believed to have been built by Cronaca, features a notable collection of paintings, sculpture, majolica, glass, and 14th-/16th-c. coins. The collection was assembled by the English scholar and collector Herbert Percy Horne, who lived in Florence around the turn of the 20th c. The collection includes works by such artists as: Masaccio, B. Daddi, P. Lorenzetti, Giotto, S. Martini, Beccafumi, Michelozzo, Filippino Lippi, and A. Rossellino.
Ponte alle Grazie (*F5*). Built in the 13th c., it was rebuilt in 1957 after being destroyed in 1944. It offers a fine view: downstream, as far as the Ponte Vecchio; straight ahead, of the hill of S. Miniato; upstream, of the 14th-c. tower-gate of S. Niccolò and the stairs that lead up to Piazzale Michelangiolo, the bridge of S. Niccolò, and the Poggio dell'Incontro.
Museo Bardini* (*F5; closed for rearrangement; tel. 0552342427*). At n. 1 in Piazza de' Mozzi, in the Palazzo de' Mozzi, this museum comprises the enormous collection of sculpture, paintings, furniture, and ceramics donated to the city of Florence in 1922 by the collector and antiquary Stefano Bardini. Among the most notable items: Imperial Age Roman sculpture; a capital with Nativity and Adoration of the Magi, by a Maestro Campionese (12th c.); marble group

Florence: Cappella Pazzi

by T. di Camaino; polychrome terracotta by B. da Maiano; group of statues in polychrome and gilt stucco by Donatello and workshop; collections of wooden chests dating from the 15th c.; painted terracotta relief by the workshop of J. della Quercia; St. John the Baptist by M. Giambono; statue of the Annunciation, painted terracotta from the Sienese school of the mid-15th c.; canvas by A. Pollaiolo.

The hills

These verdant hills overlook the Arno from the left bank. Up here you will find the church of S. Miniato, with its Romanesque geometry marked out in white and green marble, and the Forte di Belvedere, a fortress that Buontalenti built for Grand Duke Ferdinando I. There is no end to the beauty here, and you can choose which view of Florence you prefer: the one from the church, from the fort, or from the celebrated Piazzale Michelangiolo.

Viale dei Colli.* This scenic and picturesque continuation of the Viali di Circonvallazione across the Arno, is the most beautiful stroll in all Florence, going for 6 km over the slopes immediately south of town. The route begins in *Piazza F. Ferrucci*, where *Viale Michelangiolo* runs up to Piazzale Michelangiolo.

Piazzale Michelangiolo.* Considered the most magnificent point along the Viale dei Colli, this square offers a renowned view** of Florence; built around 1875, it balances landscape with architecture, and features a *monument to Michelangelo* (1871), a somewhat over-solemn composition on a marble pedestal.

S. Salvatore al Monte. Atop a staircase behind Piazzale Michelangiolo, surrounded by cypresses, this church was built by S. del Pollaiolo, known as Il Cronaca (1499), and has a simple unadorned facade. *Inside*, little survives of the Renaissance decoration. Note the Deposition in terracotta by Giovanni della Robbia.

S. Miniato al Monte.** *Open summer, 8-12 and 2:30-7; winter, until 6 p.m.; tel. 0552342731.* High atop a hill, this church has a broad square with a fine view* of the city below. This is the masterpiece of Florentine Romanesque architecture, along with the Battistero di S. Giovanni, or Baptistery, and was built between 1018 and 1207. The *facade*, with geometric patterns in green and white marble, has five blind round arches, set on Corinthian pilaster strips; above that is an aedicule window surmounted by a 13th-c. mosaic. *Inside*, on the right wall, note 13th-/15th-c. frescoes; in the nave, a remarkable intarsiate marble floor*; at the end of the nave stands the Cappella del Crocifisso* (Chapel of the Crucifix), by Michelozzo (1448), with a majolica vault by L. della Robbia and panels by A. Gaddi (1394-96) on the altar. In the presbytery, enclosed by a marble screen*, is the pulpit* that dates from 1207; inlaid wooden chancel from 1470; 11th-c. high altar with a Crucifix by A. della Robbia. To the right of the presbytery, altar with panel by J. del Casentino (ca. 1320); to the left, panel dating from 1354. In the apse, girded with low hand-

some arches, is the enormous 13th-c. mosaic of Christ Offering Benediction between Mary and St. Miniato. The crypt has seven small aisles, divided by slender 11th-c. columns; in the vault, note the frescoes* by T. Gaddi (1341). In the *sacristy* (entrance to the right of the presbytery) are frescoes by S. Aretino. In the left aisle, the *Cappella del Cardinale del Portogallo**: designed by A. di Manetto (1466), a perfect Renaissance composition; remarkable tondos* by L. della Robbia; in the large niches, a sepulcher of the Cardinal of Portugal* by A. Rossellino (right), a fresco of Two Angels in Flight (far wall), and Annunciation* by A. Baldovinetti (left), above the bishop's throne, also by Rossellino.

Palazzo dei Vescovi. To the right of the church is the main building of the monastic complex, crenelated, built in the 14th c. Restored in the early-20th c., it encloses a cloister with fragments of frescoes by P. Uccello and preparatory sketches by A. del Castagno. To the left of the church you can enter the *Cimitero Monumentale* di Firenze, a monumental cemetery also known as the *Porte Sante*, built in the late-19th c.

Viale Galileo Galilei. This stretch of the Viale dei Colli after Piazzale Michelangiolo runs nearly level, with fine views of slopes dotted with olive groves, as far as *Piazzale Galileo*.

Via di S. Leonardo. This lovely country road runs between walls with overhanging olive branches, and past villas, finally reaching the little Romanesque church of *S. Leonardo in Arcetri* (*open Sun., 8 and 11, Sat., 5 and 6*), with a 13th-c. pulpit and 14th-c. Tuscan paintings. The road ends at the medieval **Porta S. Giorgio** (1224), near the Forte di Belvedere.

Forte di Belvedere.* *Closed for restoration; tel. 055244577.* Also known as the *Forte di S. Giorgio*, this fortress was built by B. Buontalenti and G. de' Medici in 1590-95, linking up with the city walls and serving as both a stronghold and a suburban residence. Connected to Palazzo Vecchio via Palazzo Pitti and the Corridoio Vasariano, it consists of a platform with bastions and a star-shaped plan, dominated by the elegant three-floor *Palazzina di Belvedere*, possibly designed by B. Ammannati; it is now used for temporary exhibitions.

Viale Machiavelli. The last stretch of the Viale dei Colli runs down from Piazzale Galileo, wending its way among villas, with fine views. It ends near **Porta Romana**, a massive lopped-off tower (1328-31) which still has its original wooden doors.

Parco delle Cascine.* This vast park has a surface area of about 118 hectares, and is a popular spot for strolling and relaxing among the Florentines; it runs over 3 km west of the city, between the right bank of the Arno, the Canale Macinante, and the Mugnone. Opened to the public at the turn of the 19th c. (from the 16th c. on it belonged to the Medici), it has broad paths and avenues, dense woods, green clearings, and many sports facilities. At the far end of the park, in the Piazzaletto dell'Indiano, is the *Monumento Funebre dell'Indiano*, dedicated to Rajaram Cuttraputti, Maharajah of Kolepoor, who died in Florence in 1870 and was cremated here.

The outer sections of town

Sixteenth-century knights in armor in the hall of a villa on the Colle di Montughi, a fresco by the "perfect painter" (Andrea del Sarto) in an ancient monastic refectory, codices in Hebrew: other Florentine discoveries, to the north and the east of the center, outside of the avenues of the ring road.

Museo Stibbert. * *Open summer, 10-1; winter, 10-2; Fri., Sun. and holidays, 10-6 all year; closed Thu..* At n. 26 Via Stibbert is one of the world's largest and richest collections of antique arms and costumes, donated to Florence by the British government in 1908, following the death of F. Stibbert (1838-1906). In this home-cum-museum, which occupies more than 60 rooms, there is a vast array of paintings and objects of the applied arts, from every era and every land: sculpture, furniture, porcelain, tapestries, embroidery, and costumes. Of special note is the collection of ancient arms and armor*, from Italy, Spain, North Africa, India, and the Far East ; note the procession of Italian and German knights* (16th-17th c.) and Ottoman horsemen (16th c.).

Museo del Cenacolo di Andrea del Sarto. *Open 8:15-1:15; closed Mon.* In the district of S. Salvi, near the Via Aretina, stands the church of **S. Michele a S. Salvi**, once a Vallombrosan monastery. Inside is the museum (entrance at n. 16 in Via S. Salvi), with early 16th-c. Florentine paintings and the funerary monument of S. Giovanni Gualberto, carved by B. da Rovezzano (1507-13); in the refectory is the famous **Cenacolo***, or Last Supper, frescoed by A. del Sarto in 1526-27, a masterpiece of 16th-c. painting.

Tempio Israelitico. In Via Farini 4, the Jewish synagogue is a Byzantine-Moorish building dating from 1874-82; it includes the **Museo di Arte e Storia Ebraica** (*open Oct.-Mar., Sun.-Thu., 10-1 and 2-4; Fri., 10-1; Apr.-Sep., Sun.-Thu., 10-1 and 2-5; Fri., 10-1*) with ancient Jewish codices, parchments, documents, and religious objects.

Fossanova* (Abbazia di / Abbey of)

Elev. 17 m; Lazio (Latium), province of Latina, township of Priverno (pop. 13,784). At the mouth of the valley of the Amaseno, this abbey lies among the steep slopes of the Monti Lepini. Founded by the Benedictines, it was turned over to the Cistercians (1134-35). In order to reclaim the marshland, the Cistercians dug a canal, the "Fossa Nova." The church is an architectural masterpiece; it was a Cistercian spearhead in Italy of French Gothic architecture.

Tour. *Open summer, 8-12 and 4-7:30; winter, 8-12 and 3-5:30; for groups, by request, tel. 0773939061.* The **church*** was consecrated in 1208. The facade has a portal with Cosmatesque decoration and a huge rose window; above the tall transept is the octagonal tower, with mullioned windows. The *interior* is an exquisite example of early Cistercian architecture; it has a nave with two aisles, lined with pillars. There is a transept and a rectangular choir. To the right of the church is the **abbey** complex through the right aisle, you can enter the *cloister* with little twin columns, built between 1280 and 1300. It is Romanesque on three sides, Gothic on the fourth side, and features an aedicula with a pyramidal roof. Around the cloister are: the *chapter house*, dating from 1250, with two aisles lit by two large, mullioned windows; the "*calefactorium*," a hall for gatherings and meetings in the winter, around a large fireplace; a *refectory*, with a lectern for the reading of the Holy Scriptures. On the upper floor of the guest quarters is a room – since transformed into a *chapel* – in which St. Thomas Aquinas (1274) is said to have died. Separate from the monastery are the *infirmary* and other buildings.

Genoa / Genova**

Elev. 19 m, pop. 636,104; Liguria, regional and provincial capital. One of the leading ports in southern Europe, and certainly the most important port in Italy as well as the nation's fifth largest city, Genoa is the product of events that were played out on a larger stage than the peninsula, events, at the very least, of Mediterranean scope. One of Italy's two largest "maritime republics," as early as the Middle Ages its ships and trade were interacting and intertwining with the world of the East, extending from the Crimea to the ports of Flanders and England, and the Genoan state survived and prospered for at least seven centuries. Situated in the heart of the two Rivieras, at the northernmost point of the Tyrrhenian Sea, it extends really, without a break for 30 km from Voltri to Sant'Ilario ("Grande Genova," as it is called). overlooking the sea, lifted high by the sharp downward plunge of the Apennine slopes. The center of Genoa, set around the narrow arch of the Porto Vecchio, or old harbor, is partly medieval, a splendid mixture of Mannerism and Baroque, with a thoroughly modern, variegated, many-faceted allure. The economic life of this city is undergoing constant transformation, and it remains intensely active. Nearly half the population of Liguria lives in Genoa. It is traditionally called "La Superba," or the Proud One. The 14th-c. poet Petrarch made mention of it: "a regal city, blanketing an Alpine mount, whose men and whose walls are both full of pride, her mere appearance bespeaking her as mistress of the sea."

Historical note. A small group of Ligurians first settled here in the 6th c. During Roman times, the settlement extended slightly downhill; in the high Middle Ages, the first walled perimeter (9th c.), erected to discourage Saracen raids, included the "castrum" or castle. In 1097 ten Genoan galleys took the port of Antiochia. The unbounded energy of Genoa in the fields of navigation, trade and war had already emerged on the Mediterranean stage, and the First Crusade appeared to heighten and focus that energy. Indeed, during the same period, the "compagna communis" (the Commune, or city government), was first founded, an association of associations, as it were, or a consortium, devoted to trade, and including the bishop, nobles, and the emerging artisan and merchant classes, a sort of coalition government. It was at this moment, as well, that the history of Genoa became the history of a state, a victorious sea power that ruled the Mediterranean through the 15th c., building a network of emporiums, colonies, and trading ports, a "colonial empire" embracing Palestine, the islands of the Aegean, the Black Sea, Corsica, and North Africa. Various motifs intertwine through these centuries. First of all, the need to discourage Arab aggression in the upper Tyrrhenian, then the creation of a trading network, the growing control over the Rivieras, the great rivalry and conflict with Pisa (it was first triggered over rights to Corsica and ended with the destruction of the Pisan fleet in the Battle of Meloria, 1284), the seemingly endless duel with Venice (four wars in 120 years: from an early victory for Genoa in the battle of the Curzolari, 1298, when Marco Polo, by the way, was taken prisoner, all the way up to Genoan defeat in the war of Chioggia, 1378-1381). As for early Genoa, the story of the walled perimeter pretty much sums up the development of the city itself. The walls of Barbarossa, so called because they were built (1155-63) as a defense against the incursions of that emperor, enclosed a space extending from Porta Soprana, to the east, to Porta dei Vacca, to the west, and stretching up the hills to the spot now occupied by the Villetta Di Negro. Along the arc of the "ripa maris," or seafront, stand the "contrade," or districts, of the aristocratic consortia, little plazas with porticoed houses, at first only two storeys high and later raised, clustered around the crenelated palazzo on the cape, with its well head, oven, baths, and – for the more powerful – church. What is now the historic center of Genoa, the district of the "carruggi," or lanes, has this urban structure. In 1260 Guglielmo Boccanegra, the first "Capitano del Popolo" (leader of the popular government) had a palazzo built on the "ripa" for his city government (when he was exiled two years later, the building was converted into the customs building, and later the Casa di S. Giorgio, 1405, headquarters of Genoa's state banking system); work began in 1291 on the Palazzo del Comune, later the Palazzo Ducale. There was a lighthouse where the Lanterna now stands, as far back as the 12th c., serving as backup for the lighthouse that stood on the breakwater that extended out from the little spit of land of the Mandraccio. The city continued to grow; and so, two quarters were created and then walled in: the stretch of coastline to the west, as far as what is now the Ponte dei Mille with the hills behind it (1320-27) and, to the east, the Collina di Carignano, a hill rising over the Valle del Bisagno (1345-47). This is the Genoa of

Genoa: Piazza S. Matteo

Christopher Columbus's youth, a city on the brink of decline, a city that had failed to transform itself into a regional state, due to the competition of Venice and to the menacing proximity of Milan and France, but above all, because of two great historical events: the fall of Constantinople, 1453 (Caffa, the Black Sea emporium, remained isolated, and fell to the Turks in 1475), and the decline in importance of the Mediterranean Sea, as a result of the exploits of Columbus, who first learned to sail here. Andrea Doria, "pater patriae," built galleys on behalf of the emperor Charles V; the alliance with Spain that this statesman brought about preserved for some time the independence of the Genoan republic, while his powerful rule emphasized its oligarchic nature – with it came the Genoa ruled by bankers – as well as triggering a remarkable process of transformation of the city itself. Doria built himself a home (1529) to the west of the walls, on the hill of Fassolo, a truly splendid structure (it is the Palazzo del Principe, decorated by Gerolamo da Treviso, Perin del Vaga, Il Pordenone, and Beccafumi). The nobility that ruled the state followed him in his taste for luxury: the Strada Nuova (1551; Via Garibaldi) was its neighborhood; Galeazzo Alessi (who also built the church of S. Maria Assunta in Carignano, one of the few churches erected in the 16th c.) designed the homes of the wealthy, while Rubens painted them as models for the well-to-do of the Netherlands. At the same time, villas were built "from Nervi all the way to Sesto and throughout the Valle di Polcévera as far as Pontedècimo, and throughout the Valle del Bisagno, everywhere you looked were wonderful buildings, gardens and villas, to the great delight of the eye" (Agostino Giustiniani, 1537) – a chapter of Italian architecture that has never been given adequate consideration. The presence of Rubens at the beginning of the 17th c. is a clear indicator of the artistic climate. Van Dyck also came through town to portray the wealthy and the powerful, as well as decorate the Via Balbi (1626); the school of Genoan painters decorated the interiors of noble homes and equally sumptuous churches (L. Cambiaso, V. Castello, the Fiasella, the Piola, the De Ferrari, the Carlone

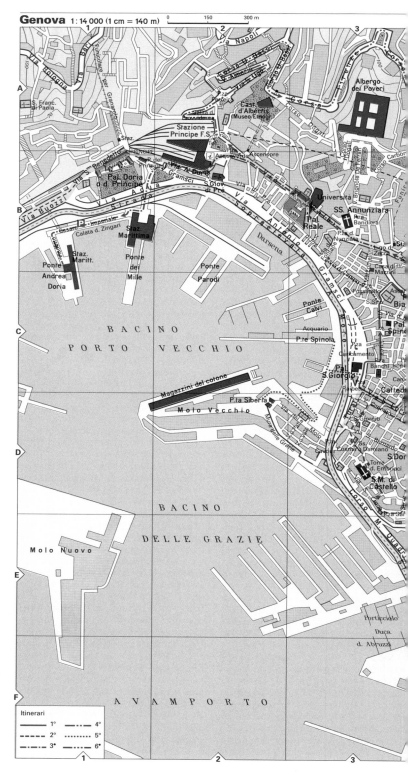

Genova

1:14 000 (1 cm = 140 m)

0   150   300 m

S. Franc.
di Paola

Via Bari
Via Bologna
Funicolare per Granarolo

Via Napoli
Corso di Casa
Via Ugo
Via Almeria
Perretti
Corso Firenze
Corso

Albergo
dei Poveri

Cast.
d'Albertis
(Museo Etnogr.)

Corso Dogali
Corso Carbon

Staz.
PRINCIPE
Stazione
Principe F.S.

Salita d.
Provvidenza

Acquaverde
Ascensore

Corso Dogali
Brignole di Fer...

P. del
Principe
Via A. Dur
Via Gramsci
Via Giov.
di Pré

Via Soprana...
Via Balbi

Università
SS. Annunziata

Pal.
Reale

P.za
Bandiera

Pal. Doria
o d. Principe

Via Buozzi
Via S. Benedetto
Via Adua
Via Sturla

P.za
Nunziata
Largo d.
Zecca

Casa di
Mazzini

P. Cesare - Imperiale
Calata d. Zingari

Staz.
Marittima

Darsena

Via Gramsci
Via Balbi
Canneto

Fossatello

Staz.
Maritt.

Ponte
dei
Mille

Ponte
Parodi

Ponte
Calvi

Via d.
Bia

Ponte
Andrea
Doria

Acquario
P.re Spinola

P.za
Pal.
Spino

BACINO

PORTO   VECCHIO

Caricamento

Banchi, ...

Pal.
S. Giorgio
Cano

Magazzini del cotone

P.ta Siberia

Ripaberto

Caffed

S. Giorgio

Molo Vecchio

Via del Molo
S. Bernardo
Via Canova
SS.
Cosma e Damiano

S. Dor

BACINO

DELLE   GRAZIE

Molo Nuovo

Torre
d. Embriaci
S. M. di
Castello

Corso M. Qua...

P.za Sar

Portacciolo

Duca
d. Abruzzi

AVAMPORTO

Itinerari

———— 1°	—·—· 4°
------ 2°	·········· 5°
—·—· 3°	——·· 6°

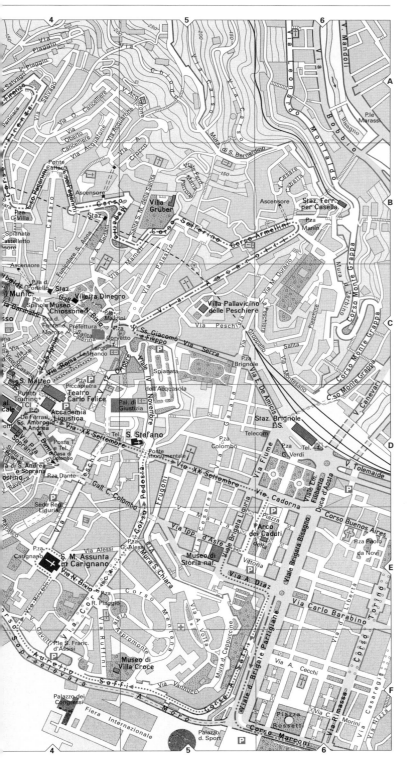

217

family, and the Assereto; the last great artist of Genoa, Alessandro Magnasco, worked mainly outside of Liguria). The construction of the last walled perimeter (Mura Nuove, 1626-32), a result of the growing threat of the House of Savoy, cost a total of 410,000 gold "scudi." The Republic, under aristocratic rule, dragged on amidst the reclusive wealth of its nobility; Louis XIV humiliated Genoa by bombarding it (1684); the history of Italy records the rebellion of Balilla (1746, War of Austrian Succession); 50 years later, the revolutionary "Armée d'Italie" arrived in Genoa; in 1805 the former Republic of Liguria became part of the Napoleonic Empire; in 1814 the duchy of Genoa was annexed to the House of Savoy, with the approval of the Congress of Vienna. Giuseppe Mazzini was a Genoan and an ardent Republican revolutionary, during the Risorgimento; from Quarto, not yet part of Genoa proper, the Ligurian-born Italian patriot Giuseppe Garibaldi sailed with his Thousand to create Italy. And once Italy had been created, Genoa became its leading port and a major industrial center. The 100,000 inhabitants of 1800 had become 200,000 by 1900. The construction of the new harbor (beginning in 1874, through the bequest of 20 million lire by Raffaele De Ferrari, Duke of Galliera), the development of the modern center, uphill from the historic center (Via XX Settembre and Via Dante, which run from Piazza De Ferrari, designating the center of Genoa in the plans of the early-19th-c. urbanist C. Barabino, were built by levelling the S. Andrea hill), and the expansion of far-flung residential suburbs – all these were phases in the growth of the city, along with the absorption of surrounding towns.

Getting around. Of the six routes suggested here, the first three are walking tours, while the others involve travelling considerable stretches by car or public transportation. Keep in mind that in Genoa it is particularly complicated to drive, because of the limited space and heavy city traffic.

The historic center, the Cathedral, and the harbor

Between the modern heart of the city and the waters of its port, this stroll will take you through many settings and districts, differing in origin and style, offering a thorough summary of the history of Genoa, from the Middle Ages to modern times.
Piazza De Ferrari (D4). This vast square, surrounded by impressive buildings, lies in the heart of Genoa. Overlooking the square is the *Palazzo della Borsa* (1907-12), with porticoes and a large bronze fountain (1936). Tucked away is the Neo-Classic facade of the Teatro Carlo Felice (D4, 1828), damaged in WWII and recently restored. To the right is the 19th-c. building of the *Accademia Ligustica di Belle Arti*, which houses the **museum** of the same name (*open weekdays, 9-1*), and whose collections include paintings of the 16th/17th-c. Genoan school.
Piazza Matteotti (D4). In this square stand the

church of S. Ambrogio and the proud Neo-Classic facade of Palazzo Ducale. The 16th-c. church of **S. Ambrogio** (D2-3) is decorated inside with marble, gilt plaster, and frescoes, as well as paintings by Reni and Rubens. **Palazzo Ducale** (D4) was built in the Middle Ages (the 13th-c. section is now part of the palazzo's left wing) and expanded from the late-16th c. on; it has been recently restored and is one of Genoa's cultural centers.
Piazza S. Matteo** (C-D4). This square's distinct medieval flavor makes it one of the old city's loveliest places. Facing it are the black-and-white striped **Case dei Doria*** (n. 15-16-17), the residences of one of the most important families of Genoa, and the 12th-c. church of **S. Matteo*** (C-D4), with its black-and-white bands and Byzantine style mosaic. Inside is the 16th-c. tomb of Andrea Doria.
Campetto (C3). This elongated square in the heart of old Genoa features (at n. 8) the 16th-c. *Palazzo Imperiale*, with noteworthy stucco decoration, and nearby, the 10th-c. church of **S. Maria delle Vigne**, extensively rebuilt. Note the 12th-c. campanile, or top of part of a carved Roman sarcophagus.
Cattedrale** (D3). *Open 8-12 and 3-7; Sun. and holidays, 8-12:15 and 4-7:15*. Dedicated to S. Lorenzo (St. Lawrence), and consecrated in 1118, this is the most important monument of medieval Genoa. Work continued on it for centuries after its consecration. The black-and-white striped facade, clamped between two bell towers, features three impressive 13th-c. portals with handsome sculptures. The stern *interior* is enlivened by the two-toned marble of the nave and the 14th-c. frescoes over the central door. In the right aisle, note a British shell that hit the church in 1941 but failed to explode. In the left aisle stands the **Cappella di S. Giovanni Battista** (1450-65), a chapel with a noteworthy marble facade and, inside, in niches, statues by M. Civitali and A. Sansovino, a 16th-c. baldachin, and the 12th-c. marble Arca del Battista, or Tomb of the Baptist. To the right of the chapel is the entrance to the **Museo del Tesoro di S. Lorenzo*** (*open 9-12 and 3-6; closed Sun. and holidays*), the Museum of the Treasury, features precious objects (sacred basin supposedly used at the Last Supper, 1st-c. Roman glass); jewelry (Byzantine cross; 12th-c. Arca del Barbarossa; silver Arca di S. Giovanni*, 1438-45; casket of the Corpus Domini*, mid-16th c.); liturgical garb.
Via S. Lorenzo (D3). Laid out in the 19th c., this street goes directly down to the harbor, cutting the old city in two. On either side run the alleys of Genoa, called "carruggi."
Palazzo S. Giorgio* (C3). Ancient site of the famed Banco di San Giorgio, this building comprises a Gothic wing (1260) with three- and four-light mullioned windows, and a Renaissance section (1570) with a frescoed facade overlooking the port. Standing alone on one side of the *Piazza Caricamento* (C3), the palace (*open Sat., 10-6*) is lined by the low, busy *porticoes of Sottoripa*, once a lively market street. Between this square and the water of the Old Port runs the *elevated throughway* (1964

Porto* (*B-F1-3*). Italy's largest harbor, Genoa is rivalled in the Mediterranean only by Marseilles. It boasts 19 km of breakwaters and 28 km of wharfs. Passenger docks (for ferries and liners) are the Ponte dei Mille and Ponte Andrea Doria. For a motorboat tour of the harbor, see "Western quarter" route (*tel. 0102657127*); the best points for a view of the harbor are the square of S. Francesco di Paola (*A1*), the Righi and the Castello de Albertis (*A2*). From an elevated vantage point, you can see the outer port, the Porticciolo (marina) of the Duca degli Abruzzi, the basin of the Grazie, the Porto Vecchio, and the basins of the Lanterna and of Sampierdarena. Far to the west, on a 140,000 square meter manmade island just off Cornigliano and Sestri Ponente, is *Cristoforo Colombo Airport*; in front of it are the huge structures of the Porto Petroli di Multedo and, westernward, the Voltri terminal.

Porto Vecchio* (*B-C1-3*). This old harbor is enclosed by the curve of land between the Molo Vecchio (Old Wharf) and the *Torre della Lanterna*, a venerable, 76-m lighthouse, and a symbol of Genoa (last rebuilt in 1543). Major renovations were done on this port, in the area off Piazza Caricamento, between the Molo Vecchio and Ponte Spinola, for the international Expo commemorating the 500th anniversary of the discovery of America (May-Aug. 1992). The famed architect Renzo Piano renovated old harbor structures to create the so-called **Expo district**, a single pedestrian zone that runs from Piazza Caricamento into the port area and is meant to re-establish links between the old port and the historic city center. The Expo facilities have become a permanent part of Genoa. Renovation involved the turn-of-the-century *Magazzini del Cotone* (or Cotton Warehouses, *C-D1-2*), which now house the *Padiglione del Mare e della Navigazione* (*open 10:30-6; Sat. and holidays, 10:30-7; Oct.-Feb., 10:30-5:30; Sat. and holidays, 10:30-6; closed Mon.*) a permanent exhibition on the history of Liguria sea forces, and the **Città dei Bambini*** (*open 10-6; closed Mon.*), a museum offering a series of workshops and didactic aids for children. Also involved were the Molo Vecchio, the buildings of the 17th-c. *Deposito Franco* (*C3*), and the *Ponte Spinola* (*C3*), where Europe's largest **Aquarium*** has been built (*open 9:30-7; Sat. and holidays, 9:30-8; Oct.-Feb., closed Mon.*). On the waters of the Port stands the *"Bigo,"* a structure with a maritime flavor, and a panoramic cabin that rises to an altitude of 45 m. Near the 16th-c. fortification of **Porta del Molo** (also *Siberia, D2*), a new water basin has changed the seaward shape of the wharf. Near the Porto Vecchio is also the *Museo dell'Antartide* (*open Jun.-Sep., Tue.-Sun., 10-7; Fri.-Sat., until 10:30 p.m.; Oct.-May, Tue.-Sat., 9:45-18:15; Sun. 10-7*) a museum devoted to children where the life of the Antarctic continent is explained.

Via S. Luca (*C3*). One of Genoa's oldest streets, lined with 14th-/16th-c. aristocratic palazzi, starts from Piazza Banchi, which boasts both the late 16th-c. *Loggia dei Mercanti* and the 16th-c. church of *S. Pietro in Banchi*. Midway down the street is the church of *S.*

Luca, founded in 1188 and rebuilt in 1650.

Galleria Nazionale di Palazzo Spinola* *Open 9-7; Sun. and holidays, 2-7; closed Mon.* Set in the heart of old Genoa, at n. 1, Piazza Pellicceria, this art gallery occupies a 16th-/18th-c. aristocratic home, with original furnishings, and fine stucco and fresco decoration. The gallery features works by A. da Messina, J. van Cleve, Van Dyck, L. Giordano, Reni, Strozzi, Castiglione, V. Castello, Mignard, G.C. Procaccini, G.B. Gaulli, and G. Pisano.

Porta dei Vacca (*B3*). This oval-arched gate situated between two towers was part of the walls built in 1155-60, and requires a slight detour along *Via Fossatello* (IV, *B1*) and *Via del Campo* (VI, *A1*); along the way, note the portals and reliefs

Casa di Mazzini (*B-C3*). At n. 11 Via Lomellini stands the birthplace of the great Italian statesman, now the site of the *Istituto Mazziniano*, with *Library* and *Archive*, and the **Museo del Risorgimento** (*open 9-1; closed Mon., Wed. and Sun.*).

S. Siro (*C3*). Genoa's first cathedral, extensively rebuilt, features a Neo-Classic facade. Inside are 17th-c. frescoes, paintings and reliefs, a fine example of Baroque; note the high altar in black marble and bronze, a masterpiece by P. Puget (1670).

Via Garibaldi** (*C4*). One of Italy's most monumental streets, lined with 16th-c. buildings; hidden behind the handsome facades are lovely courtyards, porticoes, and frescoed halls. It starts from *Piazza della Meridiana* (*C3-4*), named for the sundial on a building facing it.

Palazzo Bianco (*C4*). At n. 11 Via Garibaldi, this mid-16th-c. building has been redone in Genoan Baroque. It houses the **Galleria di Palazzo Bianco*** (*open 9-1; Wed. and Sat., 9-7; Sun., 10-6; closed Mon. and holidays*), one of the city's finest art collections. It has a beautifully hung collection of Genoan painters, including Brea, Sacchi, Cambiaso, Assereto, V. Castello, Fiasella, and, especially, Strozzi and Grechetto. Among the painters of other schools: F. Lippi, Pontormo, Palma the Younger, Veronese, Moretto, G. David, Provost, Metsys, Aertsen, Rubens, Van Dyck, Zurbáran, and Murillo.

Palazzo Rosso (*C4*). At n. 18 stands this Baroque palazzo, named for its distinctive red color; which houses the **Galleria di Palazzo Rosso*** (*open same hours as Palazzo Bianco*). The halls still have the feel of a princely residence; the upstairs rooms are lavishly furnished and frescoed. Among the works on display are paintings by Pisanello, Veronese, Lotto, Moretto, Bordone, Titian, Tintoretto, Licinio, Palma the Younger, Caravaggio and his followers, Genovesino, Preti, S. Rosa, Guercino, Reni, and various 17th-c. Genoans, including Cambiaso, Fiasella, Strozzi, Grechetto, Guidobono, and De Ferrari. Upstairs are portraits of Genoan noblemen, painted by Van Dyck during his stay here, and works by Dürer, Teniers, Ribera, Murillo, and Rigaud. Various other collections are on display, including coins, antique crèches, and ceramics.

Palazzo del Municipio** (*C4*). This magnificent late 16th-c. building, Genoa's town hall and once

Palazzo Doria Tursi, stands at n. 9 in Via Garibaldi. Among the noteworthy objects here are Paganini's violin and letters by Christopher Columbus, and the document of privileges bestowed upon him by the monarchs of Spain. The rest of Via Garibaldi is lined with splendid 16th-c. *buildings*.

Piazza Fontane Marose (*C4*). One of the loveliest squares in the monumental section of Genoa; note the 15th-c. Gothic *Palazzo Spinola* (*C4*), at n. 6, in white-and-black stripes, mullioned windows, and statues of the family, set in niches.

The Castello Hill

All that remains of the old bishop's castle is the name, but this walk takes you to the spot where the earliest Ligurian tribes first settled. The inlet below, the Mandraccio, since filled in, was the harbor for their trade with the Greeks of Marseilles and the Etruscans.

Piazza Dante (*D4*). The setting of this square is pleasantly paradoxical: two tall buildings (1940) loom over two small structures. One of them is known as the *Casa di Cristoforo Colombo* (*open Sat.-Sun., 9-12 and 3-6; by request, tel. 0102465346*) and is an 18th-c. reconstruction of the birthplace of the great navigator; the other is the 12th-c. Romanesque *cloister of S. Andrea*. Behind this, set between two battlemented towers, is the 12th-c. **Porta di S. Andrea***, or **Porta Soprana**, a city gate leading to the ancient "acropolis," or Castello.

S. Donato* (*D3*). This Romanesque church was built in the 12th and 13th c. with an octagonal bell tower. Inside is a fine triptych* by J. van Cleve (ca. 1515).

Museo di S. Agostino (*D3-4*). *Open 9-7; Sun., 9-12:30; closed Mon and holidays; entrance from Piazza Sarzano*. This museum is located in the square cloister of the church which was built in the 13th c. and later rebuilt extensively, only to be heavily damaged by bombs in 1943, and once again reconstructed. The black-and-white striped facade has a fine portal and two twin-light mullioned windows; the interior consists of a nave with two aisles, with chapels that belonged to the city's various craft guilds. The museum (*being renovated*) features architectural fragments, sculptures, detached frescoes, and other items from Genoan churches and other buildings, dating from the 6th to the 18th c. Of particular note, relics of the **funerary monument to Margherita di Brabante*** by G. Pisano. Also, a Mary Magdalene by Canova.

The Stradone S. Agostino takes you to *Piazza Sarzano*; from the so-called *Kiosk of Janus*, a public fountain set in an elegant 17th-c. six-sided aedicula, you can see the campanile of S. Agostino, with its polychrome roof.

S. Maria di Castello* (*D3*). Originally Early Christian, it was rebuilt in the 12th c. and embellished during the 15th c., when the adjacent convent was built. The facade (restored) is Romanesque. *Inside*, a fine 15th-c. Lombard polyptych and 8th-c. Roman sarcophagus. Noteworthy for the many works of art

they contain are the **Sale dei Ragusei** (*entrance from the sacristy; by request, tel. 0102549511*). Around the apse and along the right side of the church are the various rooms known as the Dominican convent (*open for the tour of the cloisters and loggias, 9-12 and 3:30-6*). In the *Loggia dell'Annunciazione*, above one of the two 15th-c. cloisters, a fresco* by G. d'Alemagna (1451). The gallery gives access to the *Cappella Grimaldi* with a large polyptych of the Annunciation by G. Mazone (1409).

The **Torre degli Embriaci** (*D3*), which rises high atop the Salita degli Embriaci, is a tower built in the 12th c., with stone ashlars and parapets. When all the towers in Genoa were lopped short in 1296, only this one escaped.

Ss. Cosma e Damiano (*D3*). This church is a fine piece of Genoan Romanesque architecture, built in the late 11th c.

Via di Canneto il Lungo (*D3*). One of the loveliest little streets in the neighborhood, it was once the main street of the district, dotted with taverns and workshops. Note the medieval construction (at n. 23, 14, 16) and fine Renaissance portals with reliefs (at n. 13, 15, 21, 27, 29, 31).

The 14th-c. Addizione di Ponente (new western quarter)

This part of Genoa, running along the curve of the port between Porta dei Vacca and Porta Pré, was enclosed by walls in the 14th c. The palazzi of the Balbi family date from the 17th c.; Andrea Doria renovated his own, just outside the old city walls, to the west, around this time.

Santissima Annunziata del Vastato* (*B3*). This, the largest and most exquisite church in Genoa, built in the 16th c., was given its current facade in 1867; it was badly damaged in WWII. The interior is a fine piece of late Genoan Mannerism, with inlaid marble, stuccoes, and frescoes. The paintings on the altar form a gallery of Genoan art of the 17th c., with works by L. Cambiaso, the Carlone, B. Strozzi, G. Assereto, G.A. Ansaldo, and D. Piola. Fine wooden statues by Maragliano. Note the Last Supper* by G.C. Procaccini.

Via Balbi* (*B2-3*). Like Via Garibaldi, this street is lined with monumental aristocratic homes. The Balbi family built the street in the 17th c., and built their own homes here. Note n. 1, *Palazzo Durazzo Pallavicini*, 1618, and n. 5, *Palazzo dell'Università*, 1634-50.

Palazzo Reale* (*B2-3*). At n. 10 Via Balbi, this great building dates from the 17th c.; Carlo Fontana built the double staircase and hanging garden overlooking the port. The halls upstairs, which contain the *Galleria Nazionale di Palazzo Reale* (*open Wed.-Sat. 9-7; Sun.-Tue., 9-1:45*), give an idea of an aristocratic residence in 18th-c. Genoa, with refined furnishings (visit the Sala di Veronese and the Galleria degli Specchi, or Hall of Mirrors). The art works include: Baroque sculptures; paintings by Tintoretto, Bassano, Van Dyck, Giordano, Roos, the Bolognese school,

(Reni, Guercino) and the Genoan school (Strozzi, Grechetto); tapestries and Oriental ceramics.

Piazza Acquaverde (*A-B2*). This square features the railway station of *Stazione di Principe* (1854) and a *monument to Christopher Columbus* (1846-62). Toward the water is the church of **S. Giovanni di Pré** (*B2*), Romanesque and Gothic, 12th-14th c. To its left, note the *Loggia dei Cavalieri Gerosolimitani* (12th-16th c.), or *Commenda di Pré*.

Piazza del Principe (*B1*). The square overlooks the port, facing the *Stazione Marittima* and the *Ponte dei Mille* (1926-30).

Palazzo Doria Pamphilij* (*B1*) *Open Sat., 3-6 p.m.; Sun., 10-1; by request, tel. 010255509*. This is one of the most remarkable and luxurious of Genoa's 15th-c. palazzi, renovated by Andrea Doria from 1529 to 1547. Noteworthy are the arcaded loggias which adorn the long front facing Via S. Benedetto. Inside, frescoes and decorations by Perin del Vaga (1530); sumptuous stuccoes on the portico, Loggia degli Eroi, and the Sala dei Giganti, or Hall of Giants. In the garden (view from Via Adua), note the two 16th-c. fountains.

The Circonvallazione a Monte (hillside ring road)

This route twists and turns over the hills, high above the gulf of the Porto Vecchio, along the late 19th-c. road from Piazza Acquaverde to Piazza Manin. This high section of the city – sunny and panoramic – was enclosed within new city walls, or Mura Nuove, as early as the 17th c. The walls ran along the highest ridge of the astonishing natural arena above Genoa, reaching the mountain slopes to Punta Sperone (512 m), and closing the seafront from San Benigno to the mouth of the river Bisagno.

Circonvallazione a Monte.* A series of roads following the spectacular slopes, in a district of modern houses.

Castello D'Albertis (*A2*). This building, erected in 1886 in Neo-Romanesque style, stands at the end of Corso Ugo Bassi in a garden. It houses the *Museo Etnografico* (*entrance from Corso Dogali n. 18; soon to be open*), which focuses on American ethnography and pre-Columbian civilizations.

Part of the Circonvallazione a Monte, Corso Firenze continues on around the huge 17th-c. *Albergo dei Poveri* (*A3*) and ends in Piazza G. Villa, beneath which lies the **Spianata di Castelletto** (*B4*), a panoramic terrace with a fine view* of city and sea. Further on, Corso Solferino skirts the large park of the Neo-Classic *Villa Grüber* (*B5*); the park is open to the public. The villa housed the interesting *Museo Americanistico "Federico Lunardi"* (*B5*), whose collections of pre-Columbian artifacts are waiting to be placed in a new building.

Righi.* Genoans often take outings to this lovely spot, starting from Piazza Manin and climbing Via Cabella and Via Carso, or by funicular (15 minutes) from Largo della Zecca. The Righi belvedere (302

m) offers a spectacular view* of the city, gulf, valley of Bisagno with the cemetery of Staglieno, and the district of Marassi, as well as the fortresses that dot the surrounding bluffs (the best view is from the terraces over the funicular station). An even broader view can be seen from the *Peralto park*, slightly north and 60 m higher, at the foot of the medieval bulk of *Forte Castellaccio*.

Forti. These are the fortresses which were added in the *Mura Nuove* in the 18th and 19th c. They are *Forte Sperone*, *Forte Puin* (502 m), *Fratello Minore* (622 m) and *Diamante* (667 m).

Parco Urbano delle Mura is a nature reserve with many plants and foxes, squirrels, dormice badgers.

Villa Pallavicino delle Peschiere (*C5*). Possibly built by G. Alessi (1556), this is one of Genoa's finest and most intact set of villas, with a terraced garden. It is east of Via Assarotti, which runs down from Piazza Manin, at the end of the hillside ring road, to Piazza Corvetto.

Piazza Corvetto (*C4-5*). Set among the greenery of the Spianata dell'Acquasola (see below) and the Villetta Di Negro, this is a major traffic artery of the city. Note the equestrian statue of the Italian king Victor Emmanuel II (1886). West of the piazza is the entrance to the hillside *park of the Villetta Di Negro* (*C4*), with waterfalls, grottoes, and aviaries, as well as a monument to Giuseppe Mazzini (1882). The villa itself was destroyed by bombing in 1942, and the modern building that replaced it houses the city's **Museo d'Arte Orientale E. Chiossone*** (*open 9-1; closed Mon. and Wed.*), with its remarkable collections of Oriental art assembled by the painter Edoardo Chiossone during the 30 years he lived in Tokyo (over 15,000 items), with later acquisitions as well. It offers a panorama of Far Eastern art and culture, from 3000 B.C. to the late 19th c. In the *section of large sculptures* of Japan, China, and Siam, note the Kamakura Buddha, the early Ming Buddha, and two 14th-c. Siamese busts of Buddha. The oldest painting here dates from the 11th c. There are 17th-/19th-c. prints, antique weapons (armor, swords, spears, daggers, and "tsubas," or saber sheaths), and

Genoa: Palazzo Reale

masks, musical instruments, fabrics, enamels, ceramics, and lacquers. From the terrace, fine view* of city and harbor.

Spianata dell'Acquasola (*C-D5*). This public park, east of Piazza Corvetto, was built on the burial site for those who died of the plague of 1657; view of the Bisagno valley and eastern forts.

Via Roma (*C4*). This street runs straight down from Piazza Corvetto to Piazza De Ferrari. At the first building (n. 1), note the sumptuous 16th-c. portal, with courtyard; along the street runs the *Galleria Mazzini* (1880).

The Valle del Bisagno and Carignano Hill

The tour, which offers fine views of the newer section of Genoa, includes the city's most luxurious street and the neighborhoods built in the 1930s to cover the last section of the valley of Bisagno and the hill of Carignano.

Via XX Settembre (*D4-5*). This is the always crowded main avenue of modern Genoa, where the locals like to stroll, linking Piazza De Ferrari to Piazza della Vittoria; it runs beneath the 25-m-high *Ponte Monumentale* (1893-99). Lined with porticoes, it is flanked by the church of S. Stefano.

S. Stefano* (*D5*). A combination of Romanesque and Gothic, this church was founded around 960, but the building we see today – damaged during WWII and restored – probably dates from the 13th c. The facade has white-and-black stripes, with a Gothic portal and a rose window.

Piazza della Vittoria (*E5-6*). Set in the modern heart of eastern Genoa, this square is lined with symmetrical porticoed buildings. In the middle stands the **Arco dei Caduti**, a military monument by M. Piacentini (1931), decorated with reliefs and statues. Nearby is Piazza Verdi, with gardens, and the *Brignole railway station* (*D6*), built in 1907; in the distance, the hills of the valley of Bisagno, topped by ancient fortifications.

Museo di Storia Naturale G. Doria (*E5*). *Open 9-12:30 and* (*except on Fri.*) *3-5:30; closed Mon. and holidays.* At n. 9 in Via Brigata Liguria, this museum of natural history features mainly zoological collections. A hall of paleontology, on the ground floor, features a huge skeleton of *Elephas antiquus italicus* and 11 halls of mammals; upstairs, 12 halls of birds, reptiles, fish, invertebrates, and minerals.

Circonvallazione a Mare. A seafront promenade offering a stroll along Corso Saffi (over the buildings of the *Fiera Internazionale*) and on along Corso Quadrio (beneath the medieval *walls of the Grazie*), then runs high over the rocky coast, offering fine views of the small Duca degli Abruzzi port, over the great dry docks, and the western section of Genoa (by bus, you can continue as far as Piazza Caricamento). In the gardens over the Fiera Internazionale is the **Museo d'Arte contemporanea di Villa Croce** (*F4, open 9-7; Sun., 9-12:30; closed*

Mon.; entrance from Via J. Ruffini, 3), with international collections of abstract art, 1930-80, and contemporary local artists.

Fiera Internazionale (*F4-5*). This international trade fair complex covers a huge landfill created between the small port Duca degli Abruzzi and the mouth of the Bisagno. Note the circular *sports hall* and the *conference center*.

S. Maria Assunta in Carignano* (*E4*). This handsome church looms over the hillside square. Built in the 16th c. by G. Alessi, it is one of Genoa's largest churches.

The Levante, or Eastern Section, from Foce to Boccadasse

In 1874, six towns of the valley of Bisagno, to the east of the Mura Nuove, were added to Genoa, in a forerunner of the 1926 annexation of 19 towns which created modern-day "Greater Genoa," extending from Voltri to Sant'Ilario. This route crosses the seaward section of the six towns of 1874 (Foce, San Francesco d'Albaro), with their ancient network of gardens, villages, beaches, convents, and magnificent villas.

Passeggiata a Mare.* Comprising Corso Guglielmo Marconi and Corso Italia, this seafront promenade follows the winding and sometimes rocky coast, looking down onto the sea. The view ranges from the promontory of Portofino to Capo Mele. On the hillside of Corso Italia, note the Neo-Gothic *Villa Canali*, by Gino Coppedè.

S. Giuliano d'Albaro. A small Gothic church situated amidst cypress trees on a little promontory. Founded in 1240, enlarged in the 15th c., it features fine old paintings and reliefs.

Lido d'Albaro. This popular meeting spot features bathing facilities, cafés, a seaside terrace, pools, tennis courts, and the "sferisterio," where a sort of local pelota is played. At the end of Corso Italia is the charming marina of **Boccadasse***, lined with the fishermen's houses.

Via Albaro. Winding along the hill, it is lined with gardens, villas, and homes. Along the way, note the **Villa Cambiaso Giustiniani**** (on the right, now Department of Engineering of the University of Genoa), a masterpiece by Alessi (1548). Further on on the left, in Piazza Leopardi, is the 12th-c. church of **S. Maria del Prato** (*open by request, ask the nuns at n. 4*); and nearby, the 14th-c. church of **S. Francesco d'Albaro**. The interior boasts fine frescoes (*open by request, tel. 0103628624*).

Via Pozzo. At the beginning of this street, on the right, is the huge 16th-c. **Villa Bombrini** or Villa Paradiso, by Andrea Vannone, set in a garden, with two grand loggias. Via Pozzo doubles back on itself, offering fine views of Corso Buenos Aires and Via XX Settembre and the high section of Genoa.

Cimitero di Staglieno.* You reach this cemetery by first taking Via Canevari and later Via Bobbio from Piazza Verdi through an industrial area along the banks of the Bisagno. Built from 1840 on, it is famed for its lavish monuments and floral decorations; high on the hillside is the simple and austere *tomb of Giuseppe Mazzini*.

Gubbio*

Elev. 522 m, pop. 31,483; Umbria, province of Perugia. This town is grey with ancient stone, wedged into its high slope, from which it surveys the plain and hills around it. Little lanes and stairways among the stern limestone houses link the main roads, running parallel one above the other along the slope of Monte Ingino. This intact fragment of the distant past lies in NE Umbria; the waters of the river Carmignano run into the Chiascio and then into the Tiber.

Gubbio: Palazzo dei Consoli

Historical note. The "Tavole Eugubine," displayed in the Palazzo dei Consoli and written in an ancient Umbrian language with a mixture of Etruscan and Latin letters, are relics of pre-Roman "Iguvium." A huge Roman theater at the foot of the city dates from the reign of Augustus. Little history survives from the High Middle Ages: ravaged by the Goths and recaptured by the Byzantines, Gubbio hosted Charlemagne on his return from his imperial coronation in Rome. Gubbio ruled itself from the 11th c. on, maneuvering amongst Guelphs and Ghibellines, often warring with Perugia, and attaining its height of wealth and power in the 14th c. It finally fell to the counts of Urbino (1384). Art flourished all the same, and around 1450, O. Nelli brought the style of international Gothic here; in the 16th c. Mastro Giorgio produced masterpieces in ceramics. From 1631 to 1860, Gubbio was ruled by the Papal States.

Places of interest. **Piazza Quaranta Martiri**. Dedicated to 40 townspeople killed in Nazi reprisals in 1944, this square opens out into the plain at the foot of town; now a parking area, originally a market place. Overlooked by the church of *S. Francesco* (see below), it is dominated from on high by the Palazzo dei Consoli, the long facade of the *Ospedale della Misericordia* (1326), and the *Loggia dei Tiratori* (1603), where cloth was once shaped and ironed.
S. Maria dei Laici. This small church, built in 1313, is next to the Ospedale della Misericordia, and features paintings by F. Barocci, from Gubbio.
S. Francesco.* Part of a vast convent built in the mid-13th c., this church has a simple, unfinished facade, adorned with a Romanesque portal, the twin portal and rose window on the left side, the 15th-c. campanile, and the three original polygonal apses. In the majestic *interior*, note the 15th-c. frescoes by O. Nelli and the anonymous 14th-c. frescoes. In the convent, a notable *collection of art (open Sat.-Sun., 9-1 and 3-6)*, with jewelry, paintings, and archeological finds.
Teatro Romano. Still used for performances, this ancient Roman theater (1st c. A.D.) stands just outside *Porta degli Ortacci*, a gate in the medieval walls.

The theater, one of the largest of its time, indicates Gubbio's rank under Augustus; not far off is the **Mausoleo**, a Roman tomb with a barrel-vaulted ceiling.
S. Giovanni Battista. This 13th-c. church, with a large Gothic portal and campanile, has a single-nave interior, with diagonal arches, a model common in Gubbio. Noteworthy are the panel by Perugino and 15th-c. majolica baptismal font.
Piazza Grande o della Signoria.* The ancient Piazza Grande, a vast man-made platform set on massive underpinnings, opens out like a terrace overlooking the rest of the town below, with a fine view. On either side of the square are the impressive Palazzo dei Consoli and the unfinished 14th-c. **Palazzo Pretorio**, now Gubbio's Town Hall.
Palazzo dei Consoli. ** *Open Oct.-Mar, Mon.-Sun., 10-1 and 2-5; Apr.-Sep., Mon.-Sun., 10-1 and 3-6; closed 12-16 May.* This is a noteworthy example of medieval public architecture, an elegant structure made of hewn blocks of local stone, surmounted by parapets and an elegant turret. It was built between 1332 and 1349 by A. da Orvieto, whose name appears above the main portal.
The **Museo Civico** and the **Pinacoteca Comunale** can be reached by climbing a lovely staircase and passing through a Gothic portal. You will enter the *Sala Maggiore*, an enormous hall with a barrel-vaulted ceiling, used in public assemblies. Along the walls are numerous Roman and early medieval archeological finds. To the left is a small *chapel*, with exhibits of ancient local coins and the renowned "Tavole Eugubine*," seven bronze slabs (3rd-1st c. B.C.) with inscriptions in the ancient Umbrian language, partly in Etruscan and partly in Latin characters. *Upstairs*, paintings by local artists including G. Palmerucci, O. Nelli, V. Nucci and F. Damiani, and other notable items.
Via Federico da Montefeltro. Climbing steeply among old buildings, this road runs past the 14th-c. *Palazzo dei Canonici*, with mullioned windows; note the enormous 16th-c. barrel preserved here. The building houses the **Museo Diocesano** (*open summer, Tue.-Fri., 10-1 and 3-7; Sat.-Sun., 10-7; winter, until 6 p.m.*), the diocesan museum. Intersecting this street, just before Palazzo Ducale, is the **Via Galeotti***, one of medieval Gubbio's most distinctive streets; note the

second facade of *Palazzo Ranghiasci-Brancaleoni*.
Duomo.* Set on the highest point in the city, this cathedral was rebuilt in Gothic style on the site of the original Romanesque cathedral (of which a number of statues survive, surrounding the rose window) in the early 14th c. *Inside*, mention should be made of the 16th-c. Pietà by D. Doni, a crèche by the school of Pinturicchio, a painting by S. Ibi (1507), the stalls of the choir, painted by B. Nucci, and the bishop's throne, carved by G. Maffei. From the portal in the fifth bay on the right, you can enter the refectory of the Palazzo dei Canonici, with a small *art collection*.
Palazzo Ducale.* *Open Tue.-Fri., 8:30-7; Sat.-Sun., 8:30-11 p.m.* Built, possibly by F.di Giorgio Martini, for Federico da Montefeltro, sometime after 1476-77. The great porticoed courtyard*, heart of the palazzo, was conceived in a noble Renaissance style, with a two-toned composition based on "pietra serena" and red brick and extremely elegant windows on the top storey. The complex has become the **Museo di Palazzo Ducale**, including detached frescoes and paintings by local artists from the 14th-15th c. Under the palace is an interesting archeological site.
Via dei Consoli.* This road is lined with late medieval buildings; many have the "porta del morto," or "door of the dead," a narrow pointed door leading directly upstairs. In a square on the left, note the 16th-c. stone basin, called *Fontana dei Matti*; **Palazzo del Bargello** dates from 1302, and in the elegant stone front, note the window with a carved casement.
S. Domenico. Located in Piazza Giordano Bruno, at the end of Via dei Consoli, and after crossing the Carmignano on the Ponte S. Martino (note view of medieval row houses along the mountain stream), this 14th-c. church has a simple, unfinished facade; inside, paintings by local 14th-/15th-c. painters, including O. Nelli; in the apse, wooden choir (1593).
Palazzo del Capitano del Popolo. Take the handsome Via Vantaggi and Via Gabrielli, through a nearly intact medieval neighborhood, to this late 13th-c. building; upstairs is the large Salone del Consiglio, with a 16th-c. fireplace. Just outside the *Porta Metauro* is the church of *S. Croce della Foce*, with Passion Play during Holy Week (note statues of Christ and the Virgin in the main altar); inlaid gilt 16th-c. ceiling.
Via Baldassini.* Also lined by 13th-/14th-c. houses, the Palazzo dei Consoli, Piazza della Signoria – surrounded by four colossal arches – and the Palazzo Comunale loom over this street, with astonishing effect. Continuing along **Via Savelli della Porta**, you will see, at n. 16, *Palazzo della Porta*, with an elegant Renaissance portal. At the end of the street is the little 14th-c. church of *S. Maria Nuova*.
S. Agostino. This 13th-c. church, with a brick facade dating from 1790, stands just outside *Porta Romana*, which cuts through the medieval town walls and houses the *Museo della Ceramica a lustro* (*open 9-1 and 3-7:30*), dedicated to this technique of polishing ceramics. In the church, frescoes by O. Nelli.
S. Pietro. This massive monastic complex was built before the year 1000 and rebuilt in the 13th and 16th c. The much rebuilt 13th-c. facade boasts a Romanesque portal; inside, note the monumental inlaid organ (1598), a wooden 13th-c. Crucifix, and a panel by R. del Colle (1510).
S. Maria della Piaggiola. This 17th-c. church, built to honor a painting by O. Nelli, can be reached by leaving Gubbio through *Porta Vittoria*.

Herculaneum (excavations of) / Ercolano** (scavi di)

Elev. 18 m; Campania, province of Naples, township of Ercolano. Also located on the Gulf of Naples, though less universally renowned than the neighboring Pompeii, Herculaneum was overwhelmed by the same great eruption of Mt. Vesuvius in A.D. 79. Unlike Pompeii, however, it was buried not by a shower of ashes and lapilli, but by a flowing wall of mud and lava which submerged the town and then solidified, binding it in a dense blanket as hard as tufa-stone and from 12 to 25 meters in depth. Herculaneum is only a third the size of Pompeii; it is now an archeological site of equal importance, but it has somewhat different characteristics. Herculaneum was more of a residential town; Pompeii more of a market town. The modern town has preserved, in its 18th-c. villas, the heritage of the town's first rebirth as a holiday spot.

Historical note. This renowned vacation resort for wealthy Romans and Campanians, with its charming location high over a promontory, was founded by the ancient Greeks. As punishment for its participation in the last uprising of the Italic tribes against Rome, Herculaneum was taken by storm in 89 B.C. by an army under Sulla. Damaged by the great earthquake in A.D. 62, the now-Roman Herculaneum was overwhelmed by the eruption of A.D. 79 before reconstruction could be completed. The recent discovery of over 150 skeletons and a charred boat proves that some of the people of Herculaneum had headed down to the seashore in hope of escaping by sea. Here, because of the tidal wave caused by the eruption, they were trapped and engulfed by the wall of lava and mud. The city thus vanished forever, and the land over the blanket of tufa-like stone was partly settled by the present-day town of Resina; in 1969 Resina itself took the name of Ercolano (Herculaneum). All the same, folk tradition still mentioned the town that lay buried beneath, and in 1709 General D'Elboeuf, an Austrian prince, uncovered part of a wall of a skene of the ancient theater, while sinking a well on land he owned there. He carried on excavations and removed statues and marble facings which finally were scattered among the museums of Europe, especially the one in Dresden. Regular excavations were undertaken in 1738 by order of Carlo III of Bourbon, and continued until 1780 with the system of the "cunicoli," narrow tunnels dug to extract objects of interest, and then filled in again. It was not until 1828-1837 and 1850-55 that a system of completely uncovering the excavation finally allowed scholars to

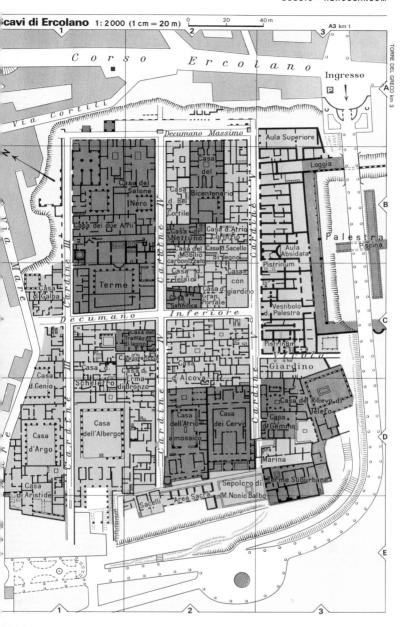

in some idea of the urban layout of Herculaneum; ≈ginning in 1927, a systematic project of excava-∘n and restoration was pursued.

laces of interest. The **excavations**** (*open: ≈0-one hour prior to sunset; closed, 1 Jan., 25 Dec.*). ≈e excavations cover only a minor section of the ≈cient city, because most of it is under modern ≈uses.

≈he large public works that have been uncovered tend to follow a traditional layout, the types of res-idential structures vary widely. For example, villas of the upper classes, built on a single level with the usual succession of atrium-tablinum-triclinium, and inhabited by a single family, were adjoined – par-ticularly during the latter period of the settlement – by smaller apartments that occupied a number of storeys, built to take best advantage of the land avail-able for construction and to maximize the interior space in much the same way as has been documented in Òstia. Like at Pompeii, in this archeological area as well the ongoing efforts to restore the surviving houses and the work of consolidating the trenches surrounding the ancient city in some cases prevent the public from being able to view all of the houses and complexes.

The most important monuments are: on the Cardine III, *Casa d'Argo* (*D1*), *Casa dell'Albergo* (*D-E1-2*); on the Cardine IV, *Casa dell'Atrio a Mosaico** (*D2*), *Casa a Graticcio** (*C1-2*), *Casa Sannitica** (*C2*) from pre-Roman times, *Terme*** (Baths, *B-C1-2*), *Casa di Nettuno e Anfitrite** (*B2*); alongside it stands a well-preserved shop, the *Casa del Bicentenario*** (*B2*). On the Cardine V: *Palestra*** (Gymnasium, *B3*) with a remarkable bronze fountain*; *Casa dei Cervi*** (*D2*), one of the richest and most sumptuous houses; *Casa del Rilievo di Telefo** (*D3*); *Casa della Gemma** (*D3*); *Terme Suburbane*** (Suburban Baths, *D3*).

Ischia (Isola di / Island of)

Pop. 52,981; Campania, province of Naples. "The history of Italy comes from the sea," wrote Sabatino Moscati. Ischia (Pithekoussai, as the Greeks called it) was a key site in this history. Archeologists confirm the traditional date of Greek colonization (775 B.C.), the earliest in Italy; also present were the Phoenicians.

Places of interest. Ischia, the main town on the island, lies at the NE extremity, and has two sections: *Ischia Porto* and *Ischia Ponte*. In the former, the inner harbor – where most of the ferries dock – is formed by an ancient volcanic crater, linked to the sea by a channel dug in 1854.

Follow Via Roma – with cafés, resaurants, and shops – and the successive Corso V. Colonna to reach the fishing village of Ischia Ponte. Here is the **Cattedrale dell'Assunta**, or cathedral, and, beyond the Aragonese bridge, the **Castello** (*open Mar.-Oct., 9- one hour before sunset*).

In the small village of **Lacco Ameno**, the sanctuary of S. Restituta comprises two churches: the smaller one dates from the 11th century and stands on the site of an Early Christian basilica whose remains lie under the church; under the sacristy there is a **Museum** (*open Mar.-mid Nov., 9:30-12:30 and 4-6; Sun., 9:30-12:30*) containing finds from the Bronze Age to Byzantine times, Greek kilns and ceramics laboratories (7th-2nd c. B.C.).

In the town of **Forìo**, the church of *S. Maria di Loreto*, built in the 14th c. but converted to the Baroque style, has marble decoration; the cylindrical *tower* (15th c.) formed of a system of defense against pirates. There are numerous springs yielding mineral water, and beaches, such as Spiaggia di Chiaia and Spiaggia di Citarra.

Sant'Angelo is an enchanting little fishing village, with many-colored houses arranged along stepped walkways (*cars not allowed*). Taxi boats will take you to the Spiaggia dei Maronti, a pleasant beach, or to the Fumarole (hot springs).

L'Àquila*

Elev. 714 m, pop. 69,839; Abruzzo, regional a. provincial capital. This ancient city, set hi. against the Gran Sasso d'Italia, abounds in lo. ly images: the corners and angles of the 16. c. castle built by the Spanish Viceroy, Don l. dro de Toledo; the white-and-red blocks th. checker the Romanesque facade of the chur. of S. Maria di Collemaggio, bound up with t.

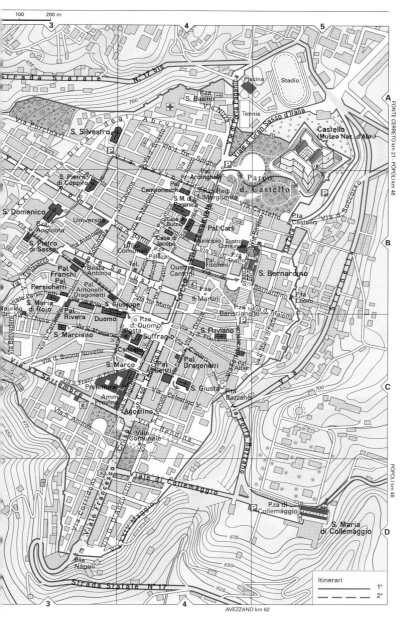

fe of the hermit, Pietro da Morrone, later Pope 'elestine V, who lies in eternal rest in the clas- c 15th-c. church of S. Bernardino, built by Co- a dell'Amatrice; lastly, the Fontana delle 99 'annelle, or Fountain of 99 Spouts, which hon- red the city's original abundance (99 castles, 9 neighborhoods, 99 churches, 99 squares...). ich in monuments, survivor of many earth- uakes, L'Àquila is the greatest – if not the irgest – city in the region of Abruzzo.

Historical note. At the base of the hill on which the city now lies are numerous fresh springs, which at- tracted the first settlement, called "Acculae." But what we now know as L'Àquila dates back only to the 13th c., after Pope Gregory IX called on the local population, in rebellion against the feudal power of the Pope's enemy, Holy Roman Emperor Frederick II, to unite their scattered castles into a single town. In 1254 the city was founded; destroyed by Freder- ick's successor, Manfred, it was rebuilt after 1266, with the arrival in Italy of Charles of Anjou. L'Àquila was said to boast 99 districts, or "rioni," for each of the 99 surrounding castles. The number belongs to the realm of legend, but it was probably not unrealistically excessive. Laid out along the steep hilly grid of the 13th-c. city, and running along the modern Corso Vittorio Emanuele, L'Àquila had been completely enclosed in walls by 1316, and just a few decades later its population of nearly 60,000 made it second only to Naples in southern mainland Italy. The city prospered (its trades included saffron, wool, silk, leather, and lace) and coined its own money until 1556, when it fell under Spanish dominion. Periodic rebellions, terrible epidemics, and ruinous earthquakes (a particularly violent one in 1703) laid the city low. Only in recent decades has L'Àquila again begun to grow in population; its magnificent walls have suffered from this recent growth.

Getting around. In the historic center, partly closed to cars, we recommend two routes, both starting from Piazza del Duomo. The first one returns here, after a circular walk. The second one can be walked as shown on the map, but extends outside the city walls in two different directions, for considerable distances. We recommend driving, first west, to the Fontana delle 99 Cannelle, then east, to the church of S. Maria di Collemaggio.

Piazza del Duomo and the northern districts

This route runs through the old part of town, with fine views of the surrounding mountains. Aside from the main sights, including the church of S. Bernardino and the Museo Nazionale d'Abruzzo, the stroll is lined with lesser architectural jewels.
Piazza del Duomo (*C4*). This is the heart of the city, adorned by two fountains and the site of a daily market. Overlooking it is the **Duomo** (*B-C3-4*), rebuilt after 1703, with a Neo-Classic facade. Inside, note the Agnifili Tomb, by S. dell'Aquila, an early Christian sarcophagus, bas-reliefs by G. de' Rettori, a painting by F. da Montereale, and a handsome "veduta" painting by V. Mascitelli.
Chiesa del Suffragio (*C4*). *Open by request, tel. 086223165.* On the south side of the square, the church's proudest treasure is in the apse: a 17th-c. polyptych by F. and G.C. Bedeschini. To the right, alongside the church, runs Via dei Ramieri, ending at a row of 15th-c. warehouses, called the *Cancelle*.
Corso Vittorio Emanuele (*B4*). The city's main street is a partly porticoed pedestrian mall. Midway along it is the intersection of the *Quattro Cantoni*; of interest are the 15th-c. *Palazzo Fibbioni* and a 14th-c. *tower*, whose bells chime 99 times, two hours after sunset, to honor the 99 castles that helped build L'Àquila.
S. Bernardino** (*B4-5*). Towering high above the city, this church was built in 1454-72, and largely rebuilt following the earthquake of 1703. The majestic facade, built by C. dell'Amatrice in 1540, is still in-

tact. *Inside*, note the handsome gilt carved Baroqu ceiling*; the spectacular Baroque organ, by B. Mosc the terracotta altar-piece* by A. della Robbia; an the tombs of St. Bernardino* and Maria Pereira both by S. dell'Aquila.
Porta Leoni (*B5*). At the end of Via di S. Bernard no, this city gate dates from the late 13th c. and the city's oldest.
Castello* (*A-B5*). Surrounded by a large park, an offering a splendid view of the Gran Sasso d'Ital (the highest mountain in the Apennines), this pov erful square fort, with stout bastions, is surrounde by a deep moat. It was built by the Spanish fron 1530 until 1635, and constituted cutting-edge tec nology in the use of, and defense against, firearm A monumental portal on the SE side leads into th **Museo Nazionale d'Abruzzo** (*open Tue.-Sun. 9- closed Mon.; guided tours only on weekdays; for rese vation, Mon.-Fri., tel. 0862633239; Sat.-Sun., t 0862633220*), which includes archeological, pal ontological, and artistic collections. The *archeolog cal collection* features Italic and Roman artifact noteworthy calendar, from the site of "Amiternun (after A.D. 25). The *collections of art* include work mostly by local artists, ranging from the 12th to th 18th c. Among these artists are: S. dell'Aquila, N. Buonaccorso, I. del Fiore, A. De Litio, P. Cesura, F c Montereale, G.C. Bedeschini, L. Finson, L. Lombar A. Mytens, C. Ruther, M. Preti, S. Conca, F. Solimena De Mura. Note the processional cross* by N. c Guardiagrele (1434). Modern artists include R. Gu tuso, G. Capogrossi, and D. Cantatore. There is a str ing reconstruction of an ancestor of modern el phants, the *Archidiskodon meridionalis vestinus* (1 million years old), unearthed near the city in 195
S. Maria di Paganica (*B4*). Completed in 13(and repeatedly ravaged by earthquakes, this churc boasts a handsome carved Gothic portal (18th-c. i terior). A stroll around the church includes thre *palazzi* (Ardinghelli, Camponeschi, and Carli) ar two medieval houses (*Casa di Buccio and Casa Jacopo di Notar Nanni*).
S. Silvestro (*A3-4*). This 14th-c. church has a simp facade with a handsome portal and rose windo Inside, the central apse boasts remarkable 15th frescoes, as well as paintings by F. da Monterea and G.C. Bedeschini (copy; original now in the Pr do, Madrid).
S. Pietro di Coppito (*B3*). This medieval churc was built around 1300-1350 and often restored, co sequently the carved architrave over the portal one of the few original features. Inside, note the 14 c. frescoes and the badly damaged frescoes of S George (right and left apses).
S. Domenico (*B3*). Situated in a steep, largely inta part of the medieval city, this church was rebuilt a ter the terrible earthquake of 1703; all that survive were the base of the facade, the right wall, and pa of the apse.
Follow **Via Sassa** (*B3*), now Via Buccio di Rana lo, to see a cluster of medieval, 14th-c. and Baroqu buildings.

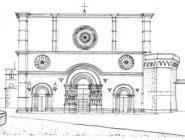

Àquila: S. Maria di Collemaggio

he southern districts and S. Maria
i Collemaggio

his route includes two of L'Àquila's best known
onuments, the Fontana delle 99 Cannelle and the
nurch of S. Maria di Collemaggio, but also passes
rough areas such as the medieval district between
a Fortebraccio and Porta Bazzano, with its stepped
nes.

Maria di Roio (*B3*). First built in the 15th c.,
nd rebuilt after 1703, this church is surrounded by
otable *palazzi* (*Antonelli-Dragonetti, Persichetti,* and
vera).

ontana delle 99 Cannelle* (*B2*). A symbol of
e city, this fountain has a spout and mascaron for
ach of the castles that reputedly helped found the
ty seven centuries ago. Dating from 1272, the foun-
in has been extensively rebuilt over the years.

Marciano (*C3*). The lower section of the facade,
ith the elegant carved portal, is all that survives of
e 14th-c. church.

Marco (*C4*). Built in the 14th c. and rebuilt ex-
nsively in 1750, S. Marco has original portals on
e facade and right side; also note the Virgin and
ild high in the facade, and another version, in
ood, inside.

Giusta (*C4*). Begun in 1257, its solemn facade
ates from 1349, with a handsome portal and Goth-
rose window. Inside, interesting works are the gilt-
ood main altar, inlaid Gothic choir and 15th-c. fres-
o of the Virgin and Child. Around it are *Palazzo
enti* and *Palazzo Dragonetti*.

llow **Via Fortebraccio** (*C4*), which goes through
charming district, once inhabited by the city Jews.

Maria di Collemaggio** (*D5*). This outstand-
g monument of Abruzzo architecture stands just
tside the Porta Bazzano, in a lovely setting. The
urch was begun in 1287, on the site of a mirac-
ous vision of the Virgin Mary, at the behest of
etro da Morrone, the hermit who became Pope
elestine V, and was immortalized by Dante as the
pe "of the great refusal;" crowned pontiff in this
urch in 1294, he abdicated, making way for
nte's enemy, Boniface VIII. The magnificent, early
th-c. facade is adorned with white and pink
ocks of stone, arranged in geometric patterns; of
e three rose windows and portals, note the cen-
al one and the Porta Santa*, on the left side. The
ge *interior* was restored in 1972-74. On the walls,

15th-c. votive frescoes, a polychrome terracotta Virgin and Child, and paintings by C. Ruther; note also the tomb of S. Pietro Celestino* (1517).

Lecce*

Elev. 49 m, pop. 98,208; Puglia (Apulia), provincial capital. As Mannerist art and architecture
gave way to the Baroque style, Lecce developed its own variant, virtually an original creation due to the city's isolation: the so-called
"Barocco Leccese," a welter of spectacular
decor, especially on the exterior of buildings:
spiral columns, outsized cornices, curving
pediments, festoons, swags, vases full of flowers or fruit, ribbons bedecked with putti, mas-
carons, and caryatids. In any case, a world of
spectacular architecture, making the historic
center of the city entirely unique. Lecce lies in
the Salento plain. It should be visited on foot
to appreciate its fame as the "Florence of the
Baroque style."

Places of interest. The **Piazza del Duomo*** (*D2*)
is a harmonious and spectacular Baroque setting.
The magnificent palazzo of the **Seminario***
(Giuseppe Cino, 1709) encloses an interior courtyard with a lovely Baroque puteal. To the left of the
Palazzo Vescovile (1632), with a light loggia along
the front, is the **Duomo***, rebuilt (1659-70) by
Giuseppe Zimbalo (known as Zingarello), with a
spectacular facade along the side and a slender
campanile* (1682); inside are spiral columns and
excellent paintings.

S. Croce** (*C3*). Further along is the Basilica di S.
Croce (1548-1646), considered the most exquisite
creation of Lecce Baroque; the facade was the creation of G. Riccardi (lower part), A. Zimbalo (central
part) and G. Zimbalo (upper part); the pure and understated *interior** is by Riccardi. Here, Baroque decoration triumphs with the wooden ceiling, the rich
capitals and the spiralling columns. To the left of the
church is the **Palazzo del Governo.*** It is the former Celestine convent, the facade is by G. Zimbalo
and G. Cino, while the enormous courtyard was begun by Riccardi and completed by G. Zimbalo.

To the east of the Duomo, the Baroque church of
S. Chiara. The church is attributed to Cino (1694).
Not far off is the Roman theater (*D2*), possibly dating from the reign of Hadrian. Two other typical creations of Lecce Baroque are the church of **S. Matteo**, by A. Carducci (1667-1700), and the church of
the **Rosario** (*D1*), the last creation of G. Zimbalo,
with odd inventions dotting the elaborate facade
and spectacular altars in the interior.

Piazza S. Oronzo.* The center of the Città Vecchia (old town) is in this square, where the *Column
of S. Oronzo* stands. It is considered to be one of
the two columns that once marked the terminus of
the Via Appia (Appian Way) in Brindisi, and was
erected here in 1666. The square is partly filled with
the excavations of the Roman *Anfiteatro**, or am-

Lecce 1 : 12 500 (1 cm = 125 m)

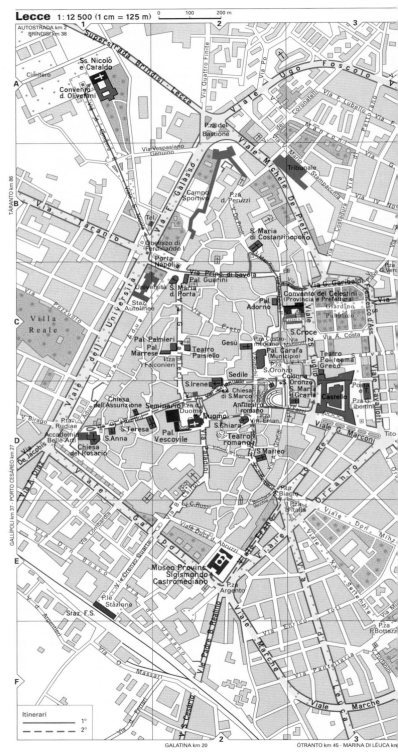

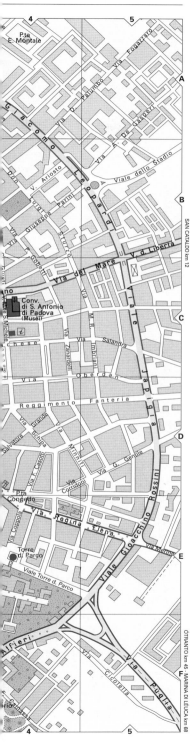

phitheater, dating from the 2nd c. A.D, one of the best preserved Roman monuments in Lecce. Overlooking the curve of the amphitheater is thè *Palazzo del Seggio*, or *Sedile* (1592), the ancient seat of communal government.

Castello (*D3*). The castle, with a trapezoid plan and corner lancet bastions, was built at the behest of Emperor Charles V (1539-48). This fortress is the only surviving part of the walls built by Charles V in 1539-49.

Museo Provinciale Sigismondo Castromediano* (*E2; open 9-1:30 and 2:30-7:30; Sat.-Sun. and holidays, 9-1*). This provincial museum is divided into three sections: the *Antiquarium*, with a notable collection of Messapic, Apulian, and Attic vases, terracottas and bronzes; the *topographic section*, with exhibits concerning towns of ancient Salento (note the sculptures from the local Roman theater); the *Pinacoteca*, with paintings from the Venetian, Roman, and Neapolitan schools and work by artists and sculptors from the Salento, evangelaries in copper and enamel, 17th-18th c. ceramics from manufactories in the Abruzzi and local plants, Murano glass, and ivory.

Arco di Trionfo (*B-C2*). The triumphal arch was built in 1548 for Charles V, whose armorial bearings are on the pediment. At the end of the square opening beyond the gate is the Obelisk dedicated to Ferdinand I of Bourbon in 1822.

Ss. Nicolò e Cataldo* (*A1*). In the enclosure of the cemetery, the church was founded by Tancredi (1180) in a style that shows a clear influence of Burgundian Romanesque architecture. It has a facade rebuilt by G. Cino (1719), with an earlier portal* and strips of floral arabesques, in a clearly Islamic style (12th c.); in the *interior*, note the cupola in the middle of the nave, frescoes dating from the 15th c. to the 17th c., the 16th-c. cloister with Baroque aedicula set on spiral columns.

Museo Missionario Cinese e di Storia Naturale (*C4; open Tue., Thu. and Sat. 9-12 and 5-7*). In Via Monte S. Michele 4, the museum is dedicated to missionary expeditions to China, with collections of Oriental art objects and shells and butterflies from Formosa.

Surrounding areas. At a distance of 3 km SW are the **excavations of Rudiae**, a Messapic town that later became Roman, and was then destroyed in the 12th c.; the birthplace of Ennius, the Latin poet. There are numerous buildings from Roman times, stretches of paved ancient road, Messapic tombs, the ruins of a small amphitheater, and remnants of the city walls.

At a distance of 13 km NE, facing the Rada di **San Cataldo**, is the beach of Lecce, with ruins of the *Roman port*, built by Hadrian.

Six km south is **San Cesario di Lecce**: in the *Palazzo Ducale*, there is a notable collection of contemporary art (*open 8-11 and 4-7*), with work by the sculptor Aldo Calò, born here.

Also worthy of note is the **Abbey of Santa Maria di Cerrate** and the Salentine peninsula.

Lucca**

Elev. 19 m, pop. 85,484; Toscana (Tuscany), provincial capital. The marble sleep of the lovely statue of Ilaria del Carretto, carved by J. della Quercia, in the church of S. Martino, seems a perfect symbol for this dignified city, enveloped in its proud past. Lucca is a thriving and modern town, but it jealously preserves the timeless image of the ancient city enclosed within its red walls. It stands on the left bank of the Serchio, in an exceedingly fertile alluvial plain, enclosed between the Apennine slopes of the Pizzorne and Monte Pisano, in a landscape of olive groves and rolling hills.

Historical note. The walls of Lucca, transformed two centuries ago into a pleasant tree-lined prome-

nade, were built between 1504 and 1645 and wer[e] never used in the city's defense. Earlier walls ha[d] withstood Florentine assaults, but in time Lucca an[d] Florence learned to live in peace and prosperit[y]. The clearest legacy of the Roman city is the ellip[ti]cal shape of the amphitheater in Piazza Anfiteatr[o]. Tall tower-houses and narrow winding lanes are m[e]mentoes of the Middle Ages, along with large R[o]manesque buildings, constructed as Lucca beg[an] to acquire wealth in the 12th c. The silk trade thrive[d] here, along with banking, though the 14th c. broug[ht] huge bank failures and widespread internecin[e] wars, followed by the rule of seigneurs. After the ru[le] of Uguccione della Faggiuola, Castruccio Castracan[i] and a few others, however, Lucca regained her fre[e]dom in 1369, virtually without interruption for fo[ur] centuries. Lucca never welcomed either the Inqu[i]sition or Jesuits, and during the Counter Reform[a]

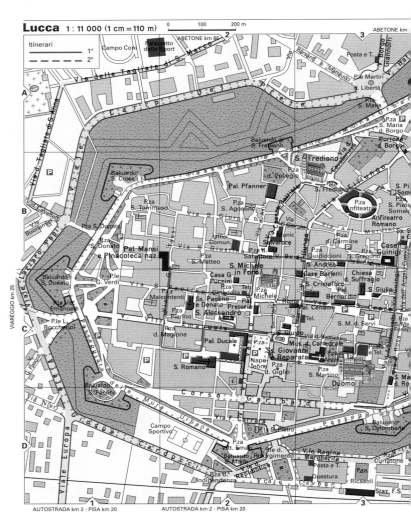

Lucca 1 : 11 000 (1 cm = 110 m)

on, Lucca, with Venice, was the site of printshops that violated the prohibitions of the Church. In 1805 Napoleon gave Lucca to his sister Elisa; in 1817, it fell to the Bourbons of Parma. Since becoming part of Tuscany in 1847, and part of Italy in 1860, Lucca has turned to trade in olive oil and fabrics.

Getting around. Much of the city within the walls is closed to traffic; tourists heading for hotels, however, are allowed through. The routes recommended are walking tours. You should leave your car outside the walls, or park it for a fee.

The monumental center

Piazza Napoleone, a square whose name reveals its date of foundation, was built at the same time as

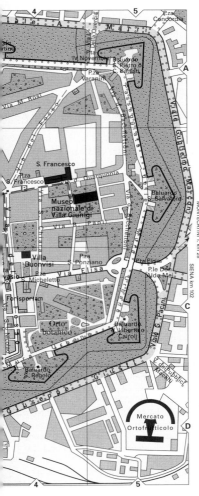

the tree-lined avenues along the walls; note the unrivalled monumental church of Ss. Giovanni e Reparata and the Duomo, as well as the narrow, attractive streets in the heart of Lucca.

Piazza Napoleone (*C2*). This vast square, lined with plane trees, is adorned by a Neo-Classic monument to the duchess Maria Luisa, by L. Bartolini (1843). It is flanked by the **Palazzo della Provincia**, formerly della Signoria or Ducale, begun in 1578 by B. Ammannati; interior by L. Nottolini, who also built the spectacular, stucco-adorned staircase* (19th c.).

Ss. Giovanni e Reparata* (*C3*). Built in the 12th c. and rebuilt in the 17th c., this church still has its original portal (1187). Recent archeological excavations (1969-90) have uncovered a series of fascinating structures, among which is the ancient Baptistery, a vast square room with a Gothic vault.

Piazza S. Martino (*C3*). With the adjacent *Piazza Antelminelli*, this square forms a handsome medieval setting dominated by the marble Duomo (see below) and bounded by low houses: left, *Palazzo Bernardi*, by B. Ammannati (1556); right, against the campanile, the typically medieval *Casa dell'Opera del Duomo* (13th c.).

Duomo** (*C3*). Dedicated to San Martino (St. Martin), this is Lucca's main church. It was built in Romanesque style in the 11th-13th c., but the interior was rebuilt in the 14th-15th c. The remarkable asymmetrical marble Romanesque facade* (1204), largely by G. da Como, comprises a portico supported by three broad arches and three rows of small light loggias, with polychrome casing and small varied columns; to the right is a stout 13th-c. campanile, adorned with parapets. Under the portico, note the reliefs*, begun in 1233, by a Lombard master; the reliefs on the left portal are attributed to N. Pisano; the doors of the central portal were carved by M. Civitali (1497). The sides of the cathedral date from the 14th c.; note the impressive apse*, which shows late Pisan influence. The elegant Gothic *interior* features sculptures and paintings by artists such as Civitali, Zuccari, Tintoretto, D. Ghirlandaio, P. di Noceto, D. Bertini da Gallicano, Giambologna, Juvarra, and Fra' Bartolomeo. In the center of the second chapel of the *left transept* is the justly renowned **funerary monument to Ilaria del Carretto****, a masterpiece by Jacopo della Quercia (1408) and one of the finest pieces of 15th-c. Italian sculpture.

Museo della Cattedrale (*C3*). *Open Apr.-Oct., Mon.-Sun., 10-6; Nov.-Mar., Mon.-Fri., 10-3; Sat.-Sun., 10-6.* In Piazza Antelminelli, this museum features religious treasures from the Duomo and the church of Ss. Giovanni e Reparata, including: a 14th-c. Flemish reliquary, a painting by F. Marti, and a handsome gilt cross, called the Croce dei Pisani*. Note the paintings and sculpture from the Duomo, by Jacopo della Quercia and Matteo Civitali.

S. Maria della Rosa (*C3*). Directly behind the *Palazzo Arcivescovile*, or archbishop's palace, this church was originally a Pisan-Gothic oratory (1309). The Renaissance portal is by Matteo Civitali; inside, fragments of the 2nd-c. B.C. Roman walls. From the nearby bastion known as *Baluardo S. Colombano* (*D3*), at the end of Via della Rosa, there is fine view of the Duomo.

Via Guinigi* (*B-C3*). Among the most attractive of Lucca's roads, this one still seems medieval. It features the **Case dei Guinigi***, a compact set of 14th-c. towers and brick houses, the palazzo at the corner of Via S. Andrea, and the *Torre Guinigi*, a tower topped by holm-oaks (*entrance to the top of the tower from Via S. Andrea; open Mar.-Sep., 9-7:30; Oct., 10-6; Nov.-Feb., 10-4:30; closed Mon.*).

Ss. Simone e Giuda (*B3*). This small 13th-c. church overlooks Via Guinigi; it has a simple grey stone facade, with three portals and an elegant window. In Via S. Andrea, after the entrance to the Torre Guinigi (see above), is the 13th-c. church of *S. Andrea* (*B3*); facing it is the late 14th-c. *Casa Gentili*.

Piazza del Salvatore (*B2*). In the square are a Neo-Classic fountain by L. Nottolini, the medieval *Torre del Veglio*, and the 13th-c. church of the *Misericordia*, with fine reliefs.

Piazza S. Michele* (*C2*). On the site of the Roman Forum, this square is a pulsing center of life in Lucca. Surrounded by 13th-c. buildings, its focal point is the marble church of S. Michele in Foro (see below); at the corner of Via V. Veneto is the *Palazzo Pretorio*, begun in 1492, possibly by M. Civitali, and enlarged in 1588 by V. Civitali. Around the corner, in Via di Poggio, is the *birthplace of Giacomo Puccini* (*open Jun.-Sep., 10-6; Oct.-May, Tue.-Sun., 10-1 and 3-6*).

S. Michele in Foro** (*C2*). This church was built between 1143 and the 14th c., and is an outstanding example of Pisan-Luccan architecture. The tall facade is surmounted by four rows of small loggias, with a lavish decoration* of marble inlay; note the colossal Romanesque statue of the Archangel Michael; low on the right corner is a statue of the Virgin with Child, by M. Civitali (1480). The left side, with its pronounced arches and 14th-c. loggia, is particularly handsome. Then there are the stout campanile, decorated with small arches and the Pisan-influenced apse*. The *interior* features frescoes, terracottas, paintings, and marble reliefs by such artists as G. di Simone, A. della Robbia, F. Lippi, A. Marti, and R. da Montelupo.

S. Paolino (*C2*). In a widened part of Via S. Paolino is this church, with a marble facade and handsome sides. Begun in 1522 by B. da Montelupo on the site of a huge Roman building, it was completed in 1536, and is Lucca's only example of a Renaissance church. *Inside*, two holy-water stoups by N. Civitali, a painted wooden sculpture by F. Valdambrino (1414), the choir stalls by N. and V. Civitali, a 14th-c. painted wooden Crucifix, a 15th-c. panel of the Coronation of the Virgin with a depiction of medieval Lucca, and a panel by A. Marti.

Palazzo Mansi* (*B-C2*). *Open 9-7; Sun., 9-2; closed Mon.* At n. 43 Via Galli Tassi, this 17th-c. building has a handsome porticoed courtyard. The interior is largely intact, with 18th-c furnishings. Note the *Salone della Musica*, frescoed in 1688 by G. G. Del Sole, and the *Camera dell'Alcova**, with silk embroideries, stuccowork and gilded inlaid wood; Flemish tapestries (1665). The palace houses the Pinacoteca Nazionale.

Pinacoteca Nazionale. *Open same hours as Palazzo Mansi.* This art gallery possesses paintings, from Italy and elsewhere, dating from the Renaissance to the early 18th c., arranged so as to imitate the collection of the Guardaroba Mediceo, a gift made to Lucca by Leopoldo II. Particularly noteworthy, among the *Tuscan paintings*, are works by: Beccafumi, Bronzino, V. Salimbeni, Pontormo, A. del Sarto; among the painters from other schools, mention should be made of Veronese, J. Bassano, Ligozzi, Tintoretto, S. Rosa, R. da Tivoli, J. Sustermans, Barocci, Zacchia the Elder, C. Dolci, Domenichino, Borgognone, Reni, P. Brill, J. Miel, G. Terborch, L. Carlevarijs, and D. Calvaert.

On the **second floor**, two more sections are dedicated to 19th-c. artists from Lucca, including P. Batoni, B. and P. Nocchi, A. Tofanelli, and M. Ridolfi, and *historic fabrics*, dating back to the 16th c., especially damasks, a local specialty. Note the *Tongiorgi Collection* of 6th-/10th-c. Coptic fabrics.

S. Romano (*C2*). This 13th-c. church has traces of its Gothic appearance (on the sides, especially) and a lively apse (1373). Inside, note the tomb* by M. Civitali (1490).

S. Alessandro (*C2*). This notable piece of early Luccan Romanesque architecture (11th c.) has a marble facade, a 13th-c. apse, and, inside, handsome Romanesque and re-used capitals (3rd-4th c.).

S. Frediano and the northern districts

Via Fillungo is medieval backbone of the historic center, with the handsome facade of the church of S. Frediano, the unique oval of Piazza del Mercato, the unrivalled treasures of Luccan art, displayed in the Museo di Villa Guinigi.

S. Giusto (*C2*). Overlooking Piazza S. Giusto, this late 12th-c. Romanesque church has a marble facade and a stuccoed interior.

Via del Battistero (*C3*). The handsome street runs from Piazza S. Giusto, passing by the 16th-c. *Palazzo Tegrimi Mansi*, at the corner of Via S. Donnino.

Via Fillungo* (*B-C3*). The main street of the historic center of Lucca is lined with fine shops but still has a medieval look, with old houses and towers. First, note the early 16th-c. *Palazzo Cenami* (*C2-3*), by N. Civitali, and, across from it, the 13th-c. Pisan-style church of **S. Cristoforo** (*C3*), with portal and rose window. At n. 43 is the 13th-c. *Casa Barletti Baroni*, with mullioned windows with terracotta casements also the 13th-c. *Torre delle Ore*.

Via C. Battisti (*B2-3*). This winding street is lined with fine 17th-/18th-c. palazzi, ending with the startling presence of the large crenelated campanile* of S. Frediano (see below). At n. 33, **Palazzo Controni-Pfanner** (*B2*), 1667, with an outside staircase* and 18h-c. statue-bedecked garden.

S. Frediano** (*B3*). Built in 112-47 and renovated

the 13th c., this church has a simple and noble façade, with a small loggia with architrave, surmounted by a Byzantine-style mosaic*. The lovely *interior*, with a nave with two aisles, ancient columns, and last apse, features works by A. Aspertini, A. Ciampanti, A. della Robbia, M. Civitali. Note the richly carved 12th-c. Romanesque font* at the foot of the *right aisle*. In the *left aisle* are the funerary slabs of L. Trenta and wife. In the *presbytery*, 12th-c. Cosmatesque mosaic floor, and the last chapel in the *left aisle* features **reliefs**** by J. della Quercia. Alongside the church are the relics of the 13th-c. *cemetery of S. Caterina*, in the form of a three-sided cloister.

Piazza Anfiteatro (*B3*), former Piazza del Mercato. This square, just off Via Fillungo, was opened in 1830 on the site of a 2nd-c. A.D. Roman amphitheater, hence the elliptical shape. Parts of the original walls of the theater can be seen; the houses that had been built in the arena were demolished. The houses now enclosing the piazza were built around the shape of the arena. Via Fillungo ends with the medieval *Portone dei Borghi* (*A-B3*), a city gate with two passages and round towers.

S. Pietro Somaldi (*B3*). This 12th-c. church has a Pisan facade with grey-and-white stripes, a handsome portal, and a solid terracotta campanile. Nearby, at the intersection with Via del Fosso (see below), is a tall column with ancient capital, crowned by a 17th-c. statue of the *Madonna dello Stellario* (*B4*); note also the Neo-Classic fountain by L. Nottolini.

S. Francesco (*B4*). This church was begun in 1228, rebuilt in the 14th and 17th c., and restored in the early 20th c. The white limestone facade has a portal and two aediculas, one dating from 1249. Inside, 15th-c. Florentine frescoes; choir with lectern by L. Marti (16th c.); on left wall, funerary plaques honoring the Luccan composers Boccherini and Giminiani.

Museo Nazionale di Villa Guinigi* (*B4-5*). *Open 9:30-7:30; Sun., 9-2; closed Mon.* This museum is set in the 15th-c. villa that once belonged to Paolo Guinigi (lord of Lucca from 1400 to 1430), a vast brickwork construction, with a ground-floor loggia and handsome mullioned windows restored to its original appearance following WWII. Recently, it was thoroughly restored and modernized. The museum contains almost exclusively art works produced for the city or surrounding territories, either by local artists or outsiders. The collections therefore give one an excellent idea of Lucca's artistic history through the centuries; the collections were established mainly following the Unification of Italy, through the confiscation of ecclesiastical holdings. **Ground floor.** *Archeological section*, with local finds dating from prehistoric to late Roman times: furnishings from Ligurian and Etruscan tombs, Roman inscriptions, architectural fragments, mosaics, a Greco-Hellenistic relief from Vallecchia, and a huge altar uncovered (1983) in Piazza S. Michele. Halls with collections of coins and ceramics are followed by rooms of *medieval art*: fragments of architectural decorations, church furnishings, and rare examples of Lombard jewelry and metalwork (note the shield

Lucca: Piazza Anfiteatro

found near the church of S. Romano), and 12th-/13th-c. sculpture and paintings. **First floor:** *Sculpture* from the *late 13th* to the *15th c.*, by artists including D. Orlandi, L. Marti, P. della Quercia, V. Frediani, M. and A. Ciampanti, M. da Lucca, M. Civitali, F. Marti, A. Aspertini, Fra' Bartolomeo, Zacchia the Elder, A. Marti, G. Vasari, P. Guidotti, G. Reni, P. da Cortona, Lombardi, Brugieri, and Luchi. Two rooms are devoted to the work of P. Paolini and G. Scaglia, interesting 17th-c. Luccan artists. The **gardens** contain archeological finds and medieval relics, including a 2nd-c. mosaic floor. Note the medieval lions from the city walls.

Via del Fosso (*A-C4*). One of Lucca's loveliest streets, it takes its name from the moat ("fosso"), that once lay east of the 13th-c. walls. Along Via del Fosso is the handsome *park* of the 16th-c. **Villa Buonvisi** (*C4*), with frescoes by V. Salimbeni; across from the villa is the little church of the *Santissima Trinità* (*B4*), built in 1589. Nearby, the 13th-c. *Porta dei Ss. Gervasio e Protasio* (*C4*), handsome city gate with two semicircular towers; also, against the walls, the **Orto Botanico** (*C4-5; opening time varies during the year, tel. 0583442160; closed Sun.*), the botanical gardens established in 1820.

S. Maria Forisportam (*C3-4*). This Romanesque, Pisan-style church (13th c.) has a marble facade with fine carved portals. In the square is a granite Roman column, once used as the finish line in town horse races (Palio). *Inside*, an early Christian sarcophagus and two paintings by Guercino. In the right transept, note the 17th-c. ciborium.

Via S. Croce (*C3-4*). This road runs straight, past medieval houses and aristocratic palazzi, from Porta dei Ss. Gervasio e Protasio to Via Fillungo. In the middle, note the 16th-c. Palazzo Bernardini (C3), by N. Civitali. Behind the palazzo is the 17th-c. church of the *Suffragio*, built in a plague-year burial ground (1630). To the left, the 13th-c. oratory of **S. Giulia**; inside is a 13th-c. painted Cross.

The walls. * Ancient and intact, these walls were one of the outstanding pieces of fortification in all Tuscany; they form a tree-lined ring around Lucca (4.2 km; built 1504-1645). With 11 bastions, these walls are about 21 m tall, offering charming views of the city. In summer, concerts and performances are held here; the *Baluardo S. Paolino* (*D1*) is the site of the Centro Internazionale per lo Studio delle Cerchie Urbane, with the summer *Museo Virtuale* (*tel. 0583419689*).

Lucera

Elev. 219 m, pop. 35,886; Puglia (Apulia), province of Foggia.

Historical note. Since the Arabs in Sicily were problematic guests, the remarkable Holy Roman Emperor Frederick II moved many of them here (in several migrations, from 1224 to 1246), and since these Saracens were among his most trusted soldiers, he cared for them quite well. Still some fifty years after his death the city was an Islamic enclave, until Charles II of Anjou slaughtered nearly all the Muslims, destroyed the settlement, and renamed the town Città di Santa Maria, or town of St. Mary, a name that was soon forgotten.

Places of interest. The Gothic **Duomo** * – built at the behest of Charles II of Anjou in the early 14th c., possibly as a form of expiation, over the ruins of the harem of Frederick II – is one of the best preserved pieces of architecture dating from the Angevin period in Southern Italy. It is made of square-hewn, yet lively, masses of wall; among the notable artworks *inside* is a wooden 14th-c. Crucifix*.
S. Francesco. This church, too, was built during the reign of Charles II; inside are frescoes from the 14th, 15th, and 17th c. Nearby is the Palazzo di Giustizia, one of Lucera's 18th-c. buildings.
The **Museo Civico Giuseppe Fiorelli** (*open summer, 9-1; Sat.-Sun., 8-1; winter, 9-1, Tue. and Fri. also 4-6:30; closed Mon.*) has a notable collection of archeological material, including a statue of Venus from the 1st c., coins, epigraphs and vases, and a Roman mosaic floor*.
Castello * (*open 9-1 and 4-6; summer until 7 p.m.; closed Mon.*). This castle occupies the terrace of Monte Albano to the west of town. Charles I of Anjou, in the 13th c., transformed the palace of Frederick II into a castle, as French and Italian master builders set up a massive pentagonal ring of walls, with square and pentagonal towers. You can tour the ruins of Frederick's palace, and the bare interior of the vast ring of walls, with cisterns, foundations of an Angevin church, and ruins of Roman buildings.
Anfiteatro Romano. To the east of the town, this Roman amphitheater, built during the reign of Augustus, is evidence of the shift from an ancient Daunian settlement to a Latin colony. Two entrance portals have been rebuilt, and it is possible to make out the elliptical cavea carved into the hillside.

Mantua / Mantova**

Elev. 19 m, pop. 48,288; Lombardia (Lombardy) provincial capital. The Mincio River flow around the city, spreading out into the thre lakes, crossed by two bridges, the Ponte de Molini and the Ponte di S. Giorgio. Thus, ur less you arrive from the south, you will ente Mantua across water, not unlike Venice, with view of the city reflected in the rippling su face. All around is the low-lying plain; the Po only 12 km away. This city is marked by quie streets, lovely colors, an overall Neo-Classi patina, with the sharply distinct monuments of the Middle Ages and the Renaissance. Mantu is, of course, an ancient "capital" (of the stat of the Gonzaga, which lasted nearly four ce turies), one of those Italian towns in which w can see the signs of a centuries-old conjunc tion of culture, power, wealth, high-minded pa tronage of the arts, splendor, and sickly deca The lakes warded off industrial developmen the city is tied to the land, in one of the mos prosperous agricultural areas in Europe.

Historical note. Roman Mantua was a small "o pidum," or armed camp; it is believed that it occ pied only the eastern corner of modern Mantua, th short space of the "civitas vetus" of the High Midd Ages, where the Gonzaga later built their palace. Th true creation of the city may date back to anoth time, however. At the beginning of the Age of th Communes, great hydraulic projects were underta en, under the supervision of Alberto Pitentino (1190 bringing the Mincio under control, directing its flo around the city, and creating lakes instead of mars es or "fens." The Rio was excavated, to link the Lag Superiore to the Lago Inferiore, and the Porto Cate na was dug. Thus, the city of the "second walle perimeter" extended as far as the Rio. The Commu nal government built new palazzi and establishe markets (Broletto, Palazzo della Ragione, Piazza dell Erbe). The Commune joined the two Lombar Leagues to fight imperial troops, and an age of pro perity and development ensued, as it had for the oth er cities of the Po Valley; like those cities, Mantu came under the rule of a seigneury, and formed large territorial state. The seigneury began in 127 with the Capitano del Popolo Pinamonte Bonacco si. After 55 years, there was a revolt, a famous "cac ciata," or expulsion, and the Bonaccolsi were replace by another Capitano del Popolo, Luigi Gonzag (1328). Under the Gonzagas the state lasted unt 1707, and the city of Mantua became its ambitiou ly crafted jewel, ornate, lovely, a renowned court du ing the finest centuries of Italian art, and then sadl declined into a far more provincial status. When th direct Gonzaga line died out in 1627, the successio passed to the cadet branch of the Gonzaga-Nevers Names of dynasties and of artists punctuated the changes and progressions of taste and style. Gian francesco Gonzaga (1407-1444) summoned Pisane lo to Mantua to paint frescoes for his court, frescoes of chivalrous grace, only recently rediscovered; around Ludovico II Gonzaga (1444-78) we find the artists of the early Renaissance: architects who studied under Brunelleschi, such as Luca Fancelli, the great Leon Battista Alberti, who designed the churches of S. Sebastiano and S. Andrea, and Andrea Mantegna, who worked for the family for most of his life. Isabella d'Este, the wife of Francesco II, played the role of high-minded patron of the arts with exquisite refinement, summoning to her court men of letters and artists, commissioning works by Leonardo da Vinci and Giovanni Bellini. In 1524 a student of Raphael arrived in Mantua – Giulio Romano, the great Mannerist artist from Rome. He was to leave his mark at court, in the city, and in the surrounding countryside (Palazzo Te lay outside the city walls, a pleasure house on an island). The height of splendor, though perhaps not of artistic excellence, came in the second half of the century. At the beginning of the 17th c. Monteverdi's "Orfeo" was first performed at court. To decide the succession of the duchy (it finally went to the House of Gonzaga-Nevers) war broke out, followed by the brutal sack and plunder by imperial troops, the plague (1630), and the beginning of decline, which brought Mantua under Austrian rule (1707), making it one of the strongholds of the "quadrilatero" (with Peschiera, Verona, and Legnago) and a barracks town (26 barracks at the end of the 18th c.). Mantua became part of Italy in 1866.

Getting around. The historic center is closed to traffic (except for access to hotels) everyday from 9:30 a.m. to midnight. Both recommended routes can be walked, though you may choose to use public transportation to return to the center from Palazzo Te, at the end of the second tour. Viale Mincio and the Lungolago dei Gonzaga, overlooking the Lago di Mezzo and Lago Inferiore, are pleasant promenades.

The ancient center and Palazzo Ducale

In the NE part of the city, the oldest section of Mantua, near the Ponte San Giorgio that divides the Lago di Mezzo from the Lago Inferiore, contains the most noted places and works. The walking tour that links them covers the masterpieces by L.B. Alberti, the architect of S. Andrea church, and Mantegna, who painted the Camera degli Sposi in the Castello di S. Giorgio.

Piazza Mantegna (*C4*). The basilica of S. Andrea looms over this little porticoed square at the end of Via Roma and at the beginning of Mantua's three monumental squares (Piazza delle Erbe, Piazza Broletto, and Piazza Sordello).

S. Andrea** (*B-C4*). This Renaissance masterpiece, designed by L.B. Alberti, was begun in 1472; work was continued in 1597-1600 and again in 1697-99; in 1732-65 the dome was added (F. Juvarra). The classical facade comprises a majestic arcade topped by a pediment; on the left side is a Gothic

campanile (1413), with large mullioned windows. Note the early 16th-c. portal, with reliefs.

The vast **interior***, grand and classical, has an aisleless nave and transept; six of the chapels are monumental, with 16th-c. frescoes and altarpieces. The first *chapel* on the left commemorates Andrea Mantegna: the tomb of the artist, with a bronze bust, paintings and decorations is by his own followers. In the left-hand transept is the Cappella Strozzi*, a chapel probably designed by G. Romano.

Piazza delle Erbe* (*C4*). The length of the square, dating from the low Middle Ages, is a balance between the enfilade of late Gothic and Renaissance porticoes of Via Broletto, flanking S. Andrea, and a remarkable series of monumental structures. At the corner of Piazza Mantegna, just past a 15th-c. *house* with terracotta decorations, is the slightly recessed Romanesque **Rotonda di S. Lorenzo*** (*open 15 Mar.-15 Nov., 10-12 and 3-5; 16 Nov.-14 Mar., 11-12*). The rotunda dates from the 11th c. but was later absorbed into the structure of the houses in the Jewish ghetto. It resurfaced in 1908 following a radical renovation; inside, ambulatory with arcades, with loggia and dome.

To the left of the rotunda, the **Torre dell'Orologio**, or clock tower, built by L. Fancelli in 1473; the astronomical-astrological clock, from that period, by B. Manfredi, was restored in 1989. Adjacent is the 13th-c. **Palazzo della Ragione** (restored), with battlements and mullioned windows, and 15th-c. portico. At the end of the square is the 12th-c. **Palazzo del Podestà**, rebuilt in the 15th c. The facade on the adjacent *Piazza Broletto* has a high tower and a 13th-c. statue of Virgil. The mullioned windows and loggia over the vault at the corner are remains of the Arengario (ca. 1300).

Museo Tazio Nuvolari e Learco Guerra (*C4*). *Open 10-1 and 3:30-6:30; Mar. and Nov.-Dec., Sat.-Sun.; Apr.-Oct., Tue.-Wed. and Fri.-Sun.; closed Jan.-Feb.* At. 9 in Piazza Broletto (entrance under the loggia), this museum features trophies and memorabilia of these great Formula 1 racers.

Piazza Sordello* (*B4-5*). This rectangular square, unusually large for the historic center, still preserves much of its medieval appearance. Follow the short stretch of Via Broletto, through the *passageway of S. Pietro*, by G.B. Bertani. On the left, crenelated 13th-c. palazzi, on the right, the facade of Palazzo Ducale; at the far end, the Duomo.

Palazzo Ducale** (*B5*). *Open 8:45-7:15; summer, Sat., also 9-11 p.m.; closed Mon; Mar.-Oct., compulsory reservation for groups, tel. 0376382150.* The two late 13th-c. porticoed buildings on Piazza Sordello to the right of the Duomo, along with many other buildings erected from the 13th to the 18th c., make up the Palazzo Ducale, or Ducal Palace of the Gonzagas, one of the most lavish creations of Italy under the seigneurs.

This "city within a city" extends toward the shores of the Lago Inferiore, or lower lake, enclosing palazzi, churches, inner squares, gardens, and porticoes, eloquent indications of the artistic and architectural fertility of the age of the Gonzagas. Extensive restoration is still under way, and may interfere with your tour; you should, however, be able to see paintings by D. Morone, V. Foppa, F. Bonsignori, G. Romano, G. Mazzola Bedoli, Tintoretto, Rubens, D. Fetti, G. Bazzani, and others, as well as Greek and Roman sculptures, sarcophagi, inscriptions, medieval and Renaissance sculptures (bust of F. Gonzaga*, attributed to Mantegna).

The most notable halls and apartments are: the *Sala delle Sinopie*, with an exhibit of the preparatory drawings found on the plaster beneath the frescoes by Pisanello, discovered in 1969-72; the adjacent *Sala di Pisanello*, with the unfinished **fresco cycle*** painted for G.F. Gonzaga; the *Appartamento degli Arazzi*, with copies of **nine tapestries** made in Flanders to cartoons by Raphael; the *Appartamento Ducale*, with inlaid decorated ceilings (late 16th-early 17th c.); the 17th-c. *Appartamento dei Nani* (dwarfs), actually a miniature reconstruction of the Scala Santa in Rome; the *Appartamento delle Metamorfosi*; the *Appartamento Estivale* (Summer Apartment), by G. Romano, renovated by G.B. Bertani (16th c.); the *Cortile della Cavallerizza* (16th c.); and a series of halls, frescoed and stuccoed by G. Romano and his school, by Primaticcio, and other 16th-c. artists, going from the *Galleria dei Mesi* (Hall of Months) to the majestic *Salone di Manto*. While touring the palace, you will also see the *Castello di S. Giorgio* (see below); in a corner tower is the famous **Camera degli Sposi**** (*tour limited to a few minutes, to preserve the works*), frescoed by A. Mantegna (1465-74) with scenes from the everyday life of the Gonzagas.

Museo del Risorgimento (*B5*). *Closed for restoration*. This museum of the Italian unification movement occupies four rooms at n. 42A in Piazza Sordello.

Duomo* (*B4-5*). Built in the Middle Ages, this cathedral still has an immense Romanesque bell tower and Gothic sections on the right side; most of the cathedral now standing dates from the 16th c. The 17th-c. facade reveals the influence of Roman Mannerism and Baroque; the *interior*, by G. Romano (1545), shows classical influence, with the aisles and the nave featuring flat, coffered ceilings. In the right aisle, 5th-c. sarcophagus, Gothic baptismal chapel with fragments of 14th-c. frescoes; in the left aisle, the 15th-c. *Cappella dell'Incoronata*, by L. Fancelli (1480).

Walk past the Duomo and the 15th-c. *Casa del Rigoletto*, and at the northern tip of Piazza Sordello you will see the large 19th-c. *Mercato dei Bozzoli* (*B5*), adjacent to Palazzo Ducale, which will become the site of the Museo Archeologico Nazionale di Mantova.

Castello di S. Giorgio (*B5*). This splendid urban castle, part of the Palazzo Ducale complex, dominates the waters between Lago di Mezzo and Lago Inferiore. Built in the late 14th c. by B. da Novara, it has four crenelated towers and a broad deep moat. Beyond the castle, along the Lungolago Gonzaga, is the outer facade of the "Rustica" by G. Romano; further along, off Piazza Arche, is the **Galleria Storica dei Vigili del Fuoco** (*C5; open Sat.-Sun. and holi-*

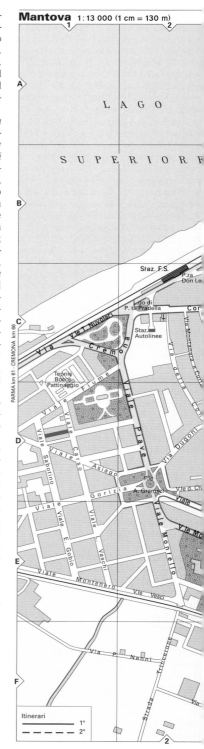

Mantova 1 : 13 000 (1 cm = 130 m)

Mantua: Palazzo Ducale

days, 9:30-12:30 and 2:30-7:30), a museum on the history of firefighting.

Teatro Scientifico* or *Accademia Virgiliana* (C5). Open Tue.-Sun., 9-12:30 and 3-8. The theater, at n. 47 Via Accademia, has a luminous facade designed by Piermarini (1771-75), which can be seen on the left from Piazza Arche. The interior, a jewel of Baroque theater architecture, was built by A. Galli Bibiena (1769) and has four tiers of boxes. Upstairs is the *Library*, with a collection of editions of Virgil's work and a collection of 18th-c. surgical instruments.

Leave Piazza Arche, turning right into Via Teatro Vecchio, along Via Scuderie Reali and Vicolo Ducale, among the secondary buildings of Palazzo Ducale, and take a passageway to the porticoed *Piazza di S. Barbara*, with the church of **S. Barbara** (B5; closed for restoration), built by G.B. Bertani in 1562-72. Another passageway, to the left, leads to the porticoed **Piazza Castello**, also by Bertani, and then to the Castello di S. Giorgio; a monumental 16th-c. frescoed corridor leads to Piazza Sordello.

The "Civitas Nova" and Renaissance Mantua

Setting off from the center, you will pass through the districts that belonged to the "city of the second walled perimeter," or the "Civitas Nova," the new district laid out at the end of the 12th c; after you cross the Rio, you will be in the later expansion of Mantua, until you reach Palazzo Te, at the time in open countryside, created by the remarkable genius of Giulio Romano for the pleasure of the court of Federico II Gonzaga.

Museo Diocesano Francesco Gonzaga (B4). Open 9:30-12 and 2:30-5; 18 Mar.-Jun and Sep.-Oct., Tue.-Sun.; Jul.-Aug., Thu. and Sat.-Sun.; Nov.-17 Mar., only Sun. At n. 55 in the huge Piazza Virgiliana, this museum of the diocese is set in a former monastery. It features paintings by 15th-/17th-c. painters, sacred goldwork* from the Duomo and from the basilica of S. Barbara, and 15th-/16th-c. armor.

Piazza Matilde di Canossa (B4). Set behind the large red *Palazzo Barbetta*, built on what is now V Cavour in 1784, this cozy little square is dominate by the impressive grotesque-work facade of **Pala zo Canossa**, built in the late 17th c., with one of th most interesting monumental staircases* of all Ita ian Baroque. Facing it is the little 18th-c. church the *Madonna del Terremoto*. In the square there is a so a typical 19th-c. **newspaper stall** of wrough iron, wood and glass, restored by FAI (Fondo pe l'Ambiente Italiano). Follow Via Fratelli Bandier and at n. 17 is a 15th-c. house with a carved port and frescoes on the facade; further along, at the co ner with Via Arrivabene, **Palazzo Arrivabene** (B3 in poor condition and much renovated, but with th original late 15th-c. porticoed courtyard.

S. Francesco (B3). This 14th-c. Gothic church wa heavily damaged in WWII and was restored to i original appearance; inside, 13th-/16th-c. frescoes b T. da Modena and others.

Palazzo d'Arco (B3). 1 Mar.-1 Nov., Tue.-Sun., 1 12:30 and 2:30-6; 5 Nov.-28 Feb., Sat., 10-12:30 an 2-5; Sun. 10-5. The long Neo-Classic facade, built i 1782-84, overlooks Piazza Carlo d'Arco. Donated t the city in 1973, this building is a fine intact exam ple of a noble residence; you can tour about 2 rooms. Note the 17th-/18th-c. furnishings, as well a paintings by F. Pourbus the Younger, F. Boselli, J. Deny N. da Verona, and L. Lotto. Pass through the hand some courtyard to reach a 15th-c. palazzo; the *Sal dello Zodiaco**, or Hall of the Zodiac, boasts fres coes by G.M. Falconetto (1520).

Piazza Martiri di Belfiore (C3-4). One of the fo cal points of Mantua's traffic, this square was built be tween 1925 and 1955 as part of the project that re sulted in the filling in of the central stretch of the Ri and the demolition of the convent of S. Domenico It extends toward Via Matteotti with an expanse o greenery that features the isolated Gothic *bell tow er* of S. Domenico; behind the tower is the double portico of the **Pescherie** (C4), built in 1535 b Giulio Romano, across the Rio.

Palazzo Sordi (C4-5). Standing near the eastern most end of the distinctive *Via Corridoni*, lined by 17th- and 18th-c. buildings, this palazzo extends it vast rusticated facade at n. 23 in Via Pomponazzo. is by the Flemish architect Frans Geffels (1680); not the courtyard and monumental staircase, with stat ues and stuccowork.

Palazzo Valenti (D4). This 17th-c. palazzo on the lef side of Via Frattini (n. 7) has a handsome porticoe courtyard. Also, at n. 9, the 15th-c. *Casa Andreasi* and at n. 5, a 15th-c. palazzo decorated with terracotta statues.

Via Chiassi (C-D3). Lined with palazzi from various periods, this street is notable for the 18th-c. Baroque facade of the church of **S. Maurizio** (C3), built in the early 17th c. by A.M. Viani. Just beyond, at the mouth of Via Poma, is the monumental church of **S Barnaba** (D3), with an 18th-c. facade by A. Galli Bi biena. At n. 18 Via Poma is the **Casa di Giulio Ro mano** (D3), designed by the artist (1544), in a Neo Classic style; facing it is the **Palazzo di Giustizia**

(Hall of Justice; *D3*), with its massive structure and caryatids on the front; it was built around 1620.

Casa di Andrea Mantegna (*D3*). *Open for exhibitions, Tue.-Sun., 10-12:30 and 3-6; other periods, Mon.-Fri., 10-12:30.* At n. 47 Via Acerbi, built in 1476, this house may have been designed and built by Mantegna himself, and has a circular courtyard.

S. Sebastiano* (*E3*). *Open 15 Mar.-15 Nov., 10:30-12:30 and 3-5; closed Mon.; tel. 037623640.* This beautiful classical church was built in 1460 to plans by L.B. Alberti; the facade was modified by restoration in 1925. Note the crypt, altar beneath a 16th-c. baldachin, and the monument to the Martyrs of Belfiore.

Palazzo Te** (*E-F3*). *Open 9-6; Mon., 1-6 p.m.* This spectacular suburban villa is one of the best preserved examples of 16th-c. architecture, built and decorated by G. Romano as a holiday home for Federico II Gonzaga. Made up of four low buildings around a courtyard, the building was recently restored. It is faced with imitation plaster ashlars: inside, the halls are lavishly decorated with frescoes and grotesque work, largely by G. Romano and followers: the *Sala di Psiche**, or Hall of Psyche, has noted Manneristic frescoes, and the *Sala dei Giganti**, or Hall of Giants, was praised by Vasari for its effect on the viewer. Also note the *Loggia di Davide*, linking the "cortile d'onore," or main courtyard, and the garden, which in turn is bounded by a monumental 17th-c. exedra and an *orchard*, used for temporary exhibits. Also suggestive is the *Appartamento della Grotta* which, beyond the *secret garden*, opens up in an artificial cave encrusted with shells and mosaics. The building also houses the **Museo Civico di Palazzo Te**, broken up into various sections: *Donazione Mondadori*, with paintings by A. Spadini and F. Zandomeneghi; *Donazione Giorgi*, with work by this 20th-c. painter; *Sezione d'Arte Moderna* (Mantuan artists, 1850-1950); *Sezione Gonzaghesca*, with medals, coins, et al., 1328-1707; *Collezione Egizia Acerbi*, with ancient Egyptian art and artifacts.

S. Maria del Gradaro (*E5*). This 13th-c. Gothic church, with pointed portal and rose window, was used as a barracks from 1775 till 1917, and was then restored to its original form in 1952-66. Inside, fragments of 13th-c. Byzantine-style frescoes.

Excursions. By motorboat (*Mar.-Oct.*), on the **Lago di Mezzo**, the **Lago Inferiore**, and along the course of the Mincio River, through the **Parco del Mincio** and the Chiusa, or lock, di Governolo, as far as the Po: all the way to *Sacchetta di Sustinente*, on the Po, from the embarcadero of Ponte S. Giorgio (*B5*); as far as *San Benedetto Po* from the embarcadero of Porto Catena (*D5; Motonavi Ades, tel. 0376322875; Navigazione Negrini, tel. 0376360870*).

Martina Franca

Elev. 431 m, pop. 46,905; Puglia (Apulia), province of Tàranto. The architectural setting, full of 18th-c. theatricality, with sudden surprising views through the narrow winding lanes of the dense historical center, is quite remarkable. At one end, after demolishing an Orsini fortress, the feudal lord, Duke Petracone V Caracciolo, began the construction (1669) of an enormous Ducal Palace, upon which he eventually spent 60,000 ducats. This was the beginning of a massive building campaign that continued well into the following century.

Places of interest. Four gates are what remain of the ancient walled perimeter, which once boasted 24 towers.

The **Palazzo Ducale** (town hall; *open by request, tel. 0804836111*) has a handsome iron balcony and 18th-c. frescoes in the interior.

The **Collegiata di S. Martino** (1774-75), with its theatrical facade, still features the Gothic bell tower of the earlier building, on the right facade; adjoining it is the *Palazzo della Corte, or Palazzo dell'Università* (1760) – *universitas* in Southern Italy meant the local community, as an administrative entity – with the Torre dell'Orologio (Clock Tower; 1734). Note the various little picturesque palazzi in Via Cavour. Of special note are the churches of *S. Domenico* (Rococo facade, Baroque interior) and the *Carmine* (at the edge of a panoramic terrace overlooking the green Valle d'Itria), dotted with "trulli."

Massa Marittima

Elev. 380 m, pop. 8823; Toscana (Tuscany), province of Grosseto. The ancient historic center, or *Città vecchia* (old town) clusters around the Duomo. This section has an intense medieval flavor and excellent artistic qualities; the *Città nuova* (new town) is more orderly in design, stands higher up the hill, and was an expansion planned in 1228. At that time, this Maremma community some 15 km from the sea was wealthy from its silver and copper mines, which played out in the late 14th c.; mining did not resume until 1830. Economic decline, due chiefly to malaria and ending only with the 19th-c. reclamation of the swamps, paradoxically served to preserve the remarkable townscape.

Getting around. Much of the historic center is closed to traffic; the itinerary that we suggest is predominantly a walking tour.

Places of interest. Piazza Garibaldi.* This monumental center of the "old town" is irregular in shape, and is closed off by the steps on which the Duomo is set at an angle. Downhill and to the left is the 13th-c. structure of the fountain known as the **Fonte dell'Abbondanza**. Opposite the Duomo, and to the right, is the stern *Palazzo Pretorio* (see below); further along are a 13th-c. house and tower known as *Casa dei Conti di Biserno* (n. 7), and *Torre di Biserno*. Adjacent is the **Palazzo Comunale***, a huge Romanesque structure made of travertine (13th-14th c.); inside are frescoes and the *Mostra della Resistenza* (*open by request, tel. 0566902289*), illustrating the Nazi massacre at La Niccioleta (June 1944). Facing the Palazzo Comunale is the *Loggia del Comune*, rebuilt in the 19th c.; behind it, on Via Parenti (n. 22), note the medieval *Palazzetto della Zecca*, or Mint, with handsome pointed arches on the facade.

Duomo.** Certainly one of the masterpieces of Pisan Gothic-Romanesque architecture, this cathedral was begun in the 11th c. and enlarged between 1287 and 1304. The facade is decorated with arcades and loggias; the portal is adorned with reliefs. The arcaded left side is dominated by the white-and-green covering of the nave; at the end, the massive bell tower, largely rebuilt around 1920. The luminous *interior* features handsome capitals on the assorted columns, frescoes, a pre-Romanesque relief, and 14th-c. stained glass in the rose window. Among the fine art, note the baptismal font*, with reliefs by G. da Como (1267); the Crucifix on panel by S. di Bonaventura (late 13th c.); another panel* by D. di Buoninsegna; a fragmentary panel by S. di Pietro, damaged by theft; on the main altar, a polychrome wooden Crucifix* by G. Pisano; wooden inlaid 15th-c. choir stalls; and the **Tomba di San Cerbone***, a funerary monument adorned with reliefs, a masterpiece by the Sienese artist G. di Gregorio (1324).

Palazzo Pretorio. This palace, which faces the Duomo, was built around 1230 and has an impressive facade. It now houses the **Museo Archeologico and Pinacoteca** (*open Apr.-Jul. and Sep.-Oct., 10-12:30 and 3:30-7; Aug., 10-1 and 4-10; Nov.-Mar., 10-12:30 and 3-5; closed Mon.*), which features, in the archeological section, remarkable local finds dating back to the 8th c. B.C. and, in the art gallery, works by S. di Pietro, Sassetta, A. Lorenzetti, and S. Folli.

Centro Espositivo di Arte Contemporanea. *Open Tue.-Fri., 3:30-5:30 (summer, 5-7); Sat.-Sun., 11-1 and 3:30-5:30 (summer, 4-7)*. At n. 5 Via Goldoni, it houses the *Collezione Angiolino Martini*, 750 works by Italian masters from the late 19th c. and 20th c.

Museo della Miniera. *Guided tours, Apr.-Oct., 10-12:30 and 3:30-6:30; Nov.-Mar, 10-12:30 and 3:30-5; closed Mon; tel. 0566902289*. Beneath the Città vecchia (*entrance in Via Corridoni*), this is a network of tunnels used as shelters during WWII, transformed in 1980 into a museum of mining and tunnelling.

Piazza Matteotti.* This square stands in the Città nuova; follow the steep Via Moncini, through *Porta alle Silici*. Note the dizzying arched walkway (1337) that links it with the 13th-c. *Torre del Candeliere*. All around are old houses and the curtain walls of the huge **Fortezza dei Senesi**, a fortress built after 1335.

Museo di Storia e Arte delle Miniere. *Open Apr.-Jun and Sep.-Oct., 10-11:30 and 3:30-5; Jul.-Aug., 10-11:30 and 4:30-7; closed Mon; Nov.-Mar., by request, tel. 0566902289*. At n. 4 in Piazza Matteotti, in the Renaissance *Palazzetto delle Armi*, this museum's four

halls document the history of mining in the area.

S. Agostino. Gothic church, dating from 1299-1313, with a handsome portal and polygonal apse (1348).

Matera

Elev. 399 m, pop. 56,924; Basilicata, provincial capital. The town is divided in two parts: a modern one, which developed in the plain, and an ancient one which "hugs" the steep slope of the "gravina", or gravel-lined gorge, with the rocky spur on which the Duomo stands in the middle. The houses are intertwined in an inextricable labyrinth, crisscrossed by narrow roads and stairways, sometimes placed one over the other. They are often cut out of the rock, with only a mansory facade. This type of dwelling is known as the "Sassi di Matera" (see below).

Places of interest. S. Giovanni Battista. This church was built in the early 13th c. and has remarkable architectural details; inside, note the influence of Burgundian Gothic.

S. Francesco di Assisi. In this church, rebuilt in the Baroque style in 1670, are eight panels of a polyptych* by Lazzaro Bastiani (15th c.).

The **Duomo*** was built in 1268-70 in the Apulian Romanesque style. The facade features a handsome portal and rose window, two carved portals and lavish windows along the sides; the campanile has twin-light mullioned windows.

The scenic route, or **Strada Panoramica dei Sassi***, allows you to enjoy a variety of views of the two valleys of Sasso Caveoso and Sasso Barisano; at a number of points it towers dizzyingly over the "gravina", or gravel-lined gorge where the Sassi lie. The **Sassi*** are ancient dwellings, cut out of caves, which are arranged according to a complex urban layout and reveal a variety of forms and solutions. In the 1950s and 1960s – when 15,000 people still lived in them – they were considered a symbol of misery and poverty and were progressively emptied. Today, this very ancient form of human settlement, largely spread in northern Africa and Anatolia, has been inscribed in UNESCO's World Heritage List.

Down along Via Buozzi, you reach the Sasso Caveoso and the square before the little church of *S. Pietro Caveoso*; high above on the right is the crag known as Monte Errone. High atop it stands the church of *S. Maria de Idris*, almost wholly carved out of rock; from it, you enter another small underground church with frescoes in the 11th-c. Byzantine style.

Merano / Meran*

Elev. 325 m, pop. 34,120; Trentino-Alto Adige; province of Bolzano. The Passìrio River crosses Merano, on its way to join the Adige; in the surrounding valley, hills teem with vineyards and orchards, with castles and mountains in the background. A gentle climate, fine strolls, eat parks and gardens, hotels where Hapsburg noble ladies once spent the summer, and afés where Danubian pastries and sweets empt one to laze away the day: the cosmopolitan mountain spa preserves some of ne Austro-Hungarian flavor of bygone eras. ake the waters which bubble from Monte S. igilio and S. Martino.

istorical note. Oddly enough, while the Gothic uomo and the medieval houses of Via dei Portici re Merano's historic center, and the residential outkirts of Maia/Mais constitute modern Merano, in ne 3rd c. the reverse was true – the Roman "Statio laiensis" stood among the gardens of what is now laia Alta/Obermais. We find mention of the town gain centuries later, in A.D. 857, as "Meirania." The ounts of Venosta took the name from the nearby astel Tirolo that in time spread to the entire Tylean region. With the decline of that house, the ukes of Carinthia took over for a while, then in 1363 ne Hapsburgs moved in, building near the old cen-er, between 1449 and 1480, the Castello Principesco Landesfürstliche Burg), as a residence of Sigisund, archduke of Austria. Floods and landslides ncroached in the 15th-16th c.; the capital was loved to Innsbruck; ravaged by the peasant wars, lerano declined in power and wealth. Under apoleon, the town was made part of Bavaria. From 814 until 1918 Austrian government gave the town ew pride, making it an international spa, which it emained under Italian rule after 1918. To the west nd south of the old center, on the left bank of the assirio, are boulevards, green gardens, hotels and llas, hot baths, the Lido, a race track, tennis courts nd skating rinks, as well as magnificent prome-ades. The new center is now in Piazza del Teatro, retching to the Casinò Municipale (Kursaal).

laces of interest. Piazza del Teatro. This square pens next to the Ponte del Teatro overlooking the assirio; it is the heart of Merano, where all the main reets in town meet.

orso Libertà. Running from the railway station to iazza della Rena, passing the *Kursaal* (1914) and ne *Pavillon des Fleurs* (1874), meeting places in own.

uomo.* This 14th-c. Gothic cathedral, dedicated) S. Nicolò, or St. Nicholas, is Merano's main monment, with its over 80-m bell tower, and buttresses. lote, along the sides, 14th-c. reliefs and frescoes. Inde is a 15th-c. carved altarpiece. Behind the cathe-ral is the little octagonal Gothic church of *S. Bar-ara*, with a fine fresco of St. Christopher.

ia dei Portici.* This is Merano's most distinctive treet, lined by porticoes and shops. At n. 68, note ne **Museo della Donna Evelyn Ortner** (*open aster-30 Nov., Mon.-Fri., 9:30-12:30 and 2:30-6:30; at. 9:30-1*), with collections of historical wom-nswear from 1870 to 1970, including hairpins, but-ons, and paper figurines. At n. 192 is the modern *alazzo Municipale*, or town hall (1929).

Museo Civico. *Open Tue.-Sat., 10-5; Sun., 10-1; Jul.-Aug., Sun. 4-7.* This museum has collections ranging from natural science and archeology to folklore and art, both medieval and modern.

Castello Principesco. *Open Tue.-Sat., 10-5; Sun., 10-1; Jul.-Aug., Sun. 4-7.* This princely castle stands in Via Galilei; built in 1480 by Archduke Sigismund of Austria, it boasts original furnishings and a collection of ancient musical instruments. Note the chair lift to Monte Benedetto (475 m, *in operation from Apr. to Oct.*).

Passeggiata Lungo Passìrio.* Running along the right bank of the Passìrio, in the shade of the poplars, this promenade runs downstream from the Ponte del Teatro to the *Lido di Merano*; upstream is the Casinò Municipale. At the *Ponte della Posta*, it changes its name to the **Passeggiata d'Inverno**, partly roofed, pushing through lush vegetation across the Ponte Romano, to the ruins of Castel S. Zeno.

Passeggiata d'Estate. Along the left bank of the Passìrio, this promenade runs from the *Ponte della Posta* (note 15th-c. Gothic church of *S. Spirito*), up the tree-shaded river to *Ponte Passìrio*. Note the marble statue of the empress Elizabeth, or "Sissi," as she is known here. You may continue to the villas, hotels, and parks of Maia Alta.

Passeggiata Tappeiner.* This promenade begins at Via Galilei, winding 4 km over the hills to Quarazze, just below Castel Tirolo; fine views of the Conca di Merano, a valley dotted with vineyards and orchards.

Ippodromo. From Piazza del Teatro, south along Via Piave, you will reach the race track, or Ippodromo di Maia Bassa, where horse races and steeplechases are held.

Messina

Elev. 3 m, pop. 259,156; Sicilia (Sicily), provincial capital. Only the name of Zancle, the 8th-c. B.C. Greek colony, survives; the same is true of Messana, which replaced Zancle in the 5th c. B.C. The Roman city was described by Cicero as "civitas maxima et locupletissima," high praise indeed for a town. The modern-day city of Messina has a very up-to-date appearance, extending along the shore of the straits; the roads are broad and parallel, and buildings are relatively low, out of fear of earthquakes (though the bell tower of the cathedral stands 60 m tall). In terms of communications, this is the gateway to Sicily, but the narrow strait that separates it from the "continent" may someday soon be spanned by a long-awaited suspension bridge.

Places of interest. Piazza del Duomo. This broad square opens out against a backdrop of hills, and is adorned with the **Fontana di Orione***, built by Montorsoli (1547-50).

Duomo.* This cathedral is a painstaking reconstruction of the church that developed over the centuries from its foundation, at the behest of the Norman king, Roger II (it was consecrated in 1197). The lower section of the facade, with bands of mosaics and reliefs, is as old as the three Gothic portals and the two 16th-c. portals on the sides. Among the works of art in the *interior*, note the statue of John the Baptist by Antonello Gagini (1525) and the tomb of the De Tabiatis* by the Sienese Goro di Gregorio (1333). **Santissima Annunziata dei Catalani.*** The little square in which this church stands is adorned with a statue by A. Calamecca (1572) of Don John of Austria, the victor of the Battle of Lépanto. The church was built in the second half of the 12th c., and altered in the 13th c.; the facade dates from the same period. The transept, dome, and apse with blind arcades and polychrome dressing date from the earlier building.

Via Garibaldi is the main road artery of the city, lined with the *Municipio*, or Town Hall, and the *Teatro Vittorio Emanuele*. In Piazza Unità d'Italia is the **Fontana del Nettuno**, a fountain by Montorsoli (1557) and, just beyond the palace of the Prefettura, the small church of **S. Giovanni di Malta**, of Renaissance origins.

Museo Regionale.* The most interesting tour in the city, however, is that of the regional museum (along the beach, past the lighthouse; *open summer, 9-1:30; Tue., Thu. and Sat. also 4-6:30; winter 9-1:30; Tue., Thu. and Sat. also 3-5:30*). The archeological section is being renovated; the sections on medieval and modern art offer a priceless documentation of the city's art history, with major masterpieces. Note especially: the Madonna degli Storpi*, a sculpture by Goro di Gregorio (1333); the **St. Gregory polyptych**** by Antonello da Messina (1473); Presentation in the Temple, Last Judgement, and Circumcision* by G. Aliprandi, 1519; Scylla*, originally part of the Fountain of Neptune; **Adoration of the Shepherds*** and **Resurrection of Lazarus***, paintings done by Caravaggio while traveling to Messina between 1608 and 1609. One interesting curiosity are the 9 gilt slabs with the Legend of the Sacred Letter (early 19th c.), which recurs in the clock of the Duomo as well.

Circonvallazione a Monte. Magnificent views can

Messina: Duomo

be enjoyed from many different points along these avenues that constitute the *"uphill ring road."*

Milan / Milano**

Elev. 122 m, pop. 1,300,977; Lombardy, regional and provincial capital. Thriving, open-handed, forward-looking: the Milanese pride themselves on their city's wealth, international ties, and metropolitan sophistication. Milan is Italy's second-largest city; the population swells each day by 20 percent as commuters and travellers flock into the city. Even so, the number of residents has declined in recent years. The city proper is relatively small (extending just 8 km from the golden spire of the Duomo, or cathedral); its influence extends over the surrounding plain, which is densely populated and heavily industrialized, especially to the north. Milan is a city of executives, marketers, and financiers. It is the capital of Italy's "service industry," and boasts more than 100,000 local businesses. It stands on the brink of the brave new "post-modern" world, as it quickly sheds the last remnants of its "blue-collar" past. Culturally, La Scala, the fabled opera house, is perhaps Milan's best-known landmark, but is only a small part of the city's rich artistic heritage. Milan is vast and hard-working; were business to disappear entirely from the landscape, however, a remarkable "art city" would still stand on the Lombard plains. On a clear, windy day from the roof of the Duomo, or any other vantage point, one can clearly see the Alps glittering with snow to the north (and, beyond them, all of Central Europe), to the south, east and west, the broad rolling expanse of the Po Valley, one of the wealthiest regions on earth.

Historical note. The terms "cerchia dei Navigli," or ring of Milan's canals, "Mura spagnole," or Spanish walls, and "bastioni", or ramparts, are still used every day in Milan to give directions or to indicate neighborhoods. Milan is arranged much like a giant cartwheel, with the Piazza del Duomo as its hub; concentric ring-roads intersect with the "spokes" that run out from the center. The Navigli, or canals, which once ringed the city, are now almost all covered over, and of the Spanish walls only the monumental gates still stand. Milan's beloved Duomo, or cathedral, is a relative newcomer, witness to only the last six centuries of Milan's 2400-year history. The Piazza del Duomo took on its modern appearance in the last few decades of the 19th c., following the unification of Italy in 1861. The city has always teetered between a love of tradition and a compelling drive to demolish and rebuild; nearly every venerable monument stands out of context, surrounded by newer structures. Thus, even in the medieval center of town, the overriding style is Neo-Classic, dating from the period described by Stendhal, one of Milan's illustrious "adoptive citizens."

The Insubri, a Celtic people, founded Milan around 388-386 B.C. The Romans conquered the town 150 years later, calling it "Mediolanum," or "central place," after the original Celtic name. In A.D. 286 it became the residence of the joint emperor, or "Augustus," appointed by Diocletian. Milan was roughly square in shape, with sides of 700 m. In A.D. 313, the Emperor Constantine decreed official tolerance of Christianity; the edict was published in Milan. Some six decades later, a former officer of the Empire, Ambrose, was elected bishop by the townsfolk. Honorius moved the imperial residence to Ravenna (402); when the Longobard chieftain Alboin marched into a vanquished Milan, in A.D. 569, bishop, clergy, and nobility collectively decamped to Genoa for seventy years. Milan's history during the first half of the second millennium of the Christian era strongly resembles that of Italy at large: governed by bishops, the Commune, or civic republic, Seignories, regional princes, and finally foreign occupation. The monument that best sums up the spirit of the civic republic is the innovative, Romanesque basilica of S. Ambrogio, an 11th-/12th-c. reconstruction of the ancient "basilica Martyrum." Shortly thereafter, in the mid-13th c., the Broletto Nuovo was built, marking the separation of civic government and the headquarters of the archbishop. Immediately thereafter, Milan came under a Seignory, that of the pro-Guelf Della Torre family; the pro-Ghibelline, aristocratic party overthrew the Della Torre party in 1277, led by the archbishop Ottone Visconti; Ottone's great grandson, Matteo Visconti, was named imperial vicar in 1294. In the 14th c., the Visconti seignory held growing sway over the towns and lands of Lombardy, Piedmont to the west, and Emilia to the south, economically subordinate to Milan. The epiphany of Visconti rule came when Gian Galeazzo (who in 1395 had purchased the title of duke, the only one among the lords of Italy) extended his rule over much of Northern Italy and beyond the Apennines. Court sages spoke of a royal crown to come, Venice and Florence strove mightily against him, in high alarm, and then, in 1402, the Black Death conveniently swept him from the stage of history. Gian Galeazzo's younger son, Filippo Maria, was barely able to pick up the few remaining pieces of his father's empire, and was the last Visconti duke. Marriage brought the son-in-law Francesco Sforza, a mighty condottiere, whose surname meant "Stormer," into the duchy; he become duke in 1450, following the nostalgic "Aurea Repubblica Ambrosiana," or Golden Ambrosian Republic. The Peace of Lodi of 1454 opened the few happy decades of a "balance of power" among the great regional states of Italy. Work went forward on the Duomo (which Gian Galeazzo Visconti had begun building in 1386). Antonio Filarete was introducing the concept of centrally planned buildings, as he built the vast Ospedale Maggiore, or central hospital, on land bestowed by the duke. Poetically, Filarete imagined an ideal city built to a symmetrical plan, naming it after his patron, "Sforzinda." The remarkable piece of hydraulic engineering known as the

Navigli was completed (originally a system of canals outside the city walls). The network of canals was dotted with "conche," or sets of locks, allowing boats to pass from one watercourse to another at a higher or lower water level. Of the various "darsene," or wetdocks, where the water is shut in and kept at a given level to facilitate the loading and unloading of ships, the Darsena del Laghetto di Santo Stefano, now Via Laghetto, was used by the bargemen and dock workers unloading huge blocks of Candoglia marble used in building the Duomo). At the turn of the 16th c., the city's population was approaching 100,000. In the words of one chronicler, "it appeared that all events heralded peace, and everyone waited only to gather great wealth, which seemed to lie at the end of every path." At the turn of the 15th c., in the Castello (Castello di Porta Giovia, as it was called then; Castello Sforzesco is the name used nowadays), Ludovico Sforza, the "Moor," and his wife Beatrice d'Este presided over what was widely called the most splendid court in Italy.

Here one could meet such luminaries as Bramante, who designed the epochal tambour of S. Maria delle Grazie, and Leonardo da Vinci, who was painting his Last Supper in the refectory of the convent next door to the church. The bountiful, well-irrigated, low-lying fields, manufacturing, and thriving trade with the rich lands over the Alps, all made the duchy of Milan Italy's wealthiest state. A tempting plum it was, and Louis XII of France was duly tempted; he cited a Visconti grandmother and laid claim to the duchy, sending an army to conquer Milan in 1499. His plan proved unsuccessful, but over the following three-and-a-half decades, as France battled the Hapsburgs for European preeminence, Lombardy – the key to Italy – was overrun variously, changing hands until it finally fell to the Spanish (1535), who ruled it thereafter for 170 years.

The years of Spanish rule witnessed the construction of the bastions that ringed Milan, the militant Counter-Reformation (Cardinal Carlo Borromeo was archbishop of Milan from 1560 to 1584), Mannerism and the Baroque (Alessi built Palazzo Marino, while Tibaldi started work on the church of S. Fedele dei Gesuiti). During the War of the Spanish Succession, the Austrians replaced Spanish rule (1706), reigning until 1859, with only a brief interlude in the Napoleonic years. The first century of Austrian rule, especially the reign of Maria Theresa, was a time of enlightened dictatorship. The aristocratic author Cesare Beccaria, the poet Giuseppe Parini, and the architect Piermarini – who built La Scala – all helped to give Milan the refined Neo-Classic style that Stendhal (1783-1842) so admired. Between 1796 and 1814, under the rule of Napoleonic France, Milan experienced unrest, ambitious reform, heavy taxes, and grandiose plans of urban renewal – some of which were actually implemented after the restoration. A second period of Austrian rule coincided with the years of Romanticism. (In Milan, Alessandro Manzoni wrote "I Promessi Sposi," while Francesco Hayez painted historic paintings and por-

Milano

1:20 000 (1 cm = 200 m)

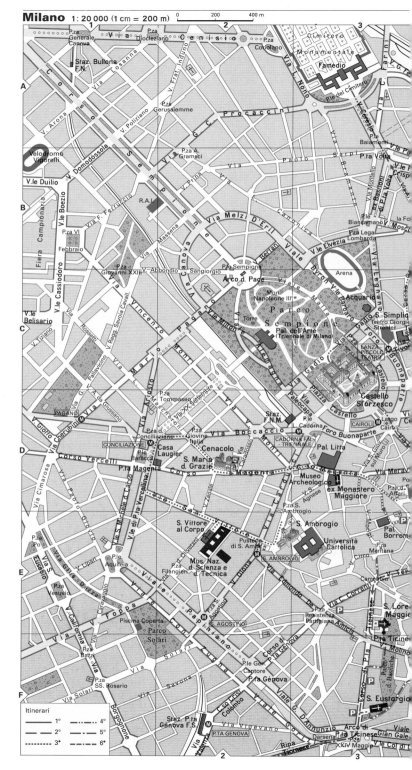

Itinerari

- 1° ..... 4°
- 2° -·-·- 5°
- 3° ..... 6°

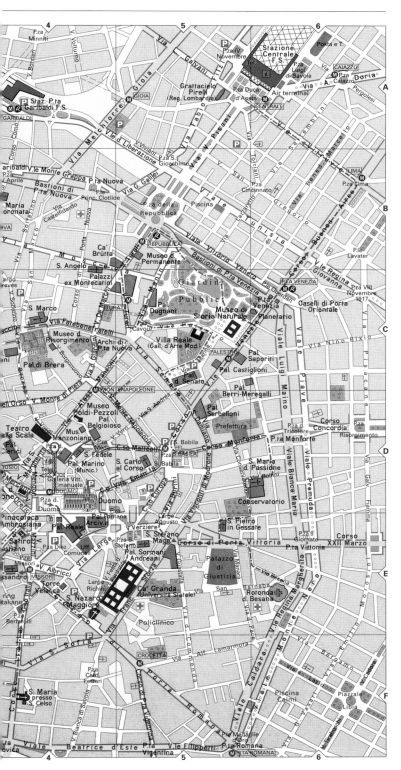

247

traits of society ladies and gala evenings at the La Scala opera house.) Milan grew rapidly from an agglomeration of winding medieval lanes to a modern, gas-lit city, within the ring of Navigli canals; between the Navigli and the outer ramparts, or Bastioni, houses and convents vied with orchards and gardens for space. As Milan grew, it gobbled up a dozen or more outlying towns and villages, attaining its current size in 1873. To commemorate the unification of Italy, Milan created the Piazza del Duomo and the Galleria, destroying a neighborhood to do so, and spending 43% of the city budget for twenty long years. The city grew rapidly – in 1861 the population was 196,000, roughly a tenth its current size – and construction boomed to keep pace, both within and without the Spanish walls. A similar boom followed the Allied bombings of 1943, as immigrants poured in from southern Italy in search of work in Milan's factories. The city's architecture reflects the dizzying pace of these various decades of growth: historicistic eclecticism, "Liberty" (Giuseppe Sommaruga; the term is the Italian version of Art Nouveau), the Novecento, Rationalism, and contemporary architecture (with relatively few skyscrapers, such as the Pirelli building and the Torre Velasca). During the same decades, noteworthy schools of art developed in Milan (Divisionism, Futurism, "Novecento," "Corrente," and abstract art), right up to the work of recent generations.

Getting around. Heavy traffic and a chronic lack of parking are good reasons not to plan on using your car. There are three subway lines and plenty of public transportation; count on using these.

The six routes suggested can all be considered walking tours, though you may choose to make use of public transportation for the longer sections (to reach the points indicated as outlying neighborhoods and surrounding areas, it is best to have your own means of transportation).

Piazza del Duomo and the "central core"

The Duomo, Corso Vittorio Emanuele, La Scala, Palazzo Marino, the Galleria, Palazzo della Ragione: famed and little-known city sights, in a stroll through memories and high society, never more than 400 m from the golden statue of the Madonnina (the small Virgin Mary) high atop the Duomo's central spire.

Piazza del Duomo (*D-E4*). This vast rectangle that fronts the Duomo is the city's geographic core, the hub of the great avenues that run outward like so many spokes, in line with the 19th c. urban plan.

Working just after Italy's Unification, Giuseppe Mengoni gave this piazza much of its modern-day appearance, designing the porticoes that run its length as well as the great portal that opens into the *Galleria Vittorio Emanuele II* (1878, see below), to the left of the facade of the Duomo. In the center of the square stands an equestrian statue to this sovereign, who was Italy's first king. Opposite the Galleria are the loggia-structures of the *Arengario* (1939-56), to

the left of which is the *Piazzetta Reale*, fronting Pala[zzo] zo Reale (see below), the site of some of the mo[st] important temporary exhibitions in town. Beyon[d] the palace lies **Piazza Diaz**.

Duomo** (*D4; open 7-7*). This cathedral, above a[ll] others, has come to symbolize Milan. Tradition state[s] that the church was founded in 1386, under the ru[le] of Gian Galeazzo Visconti, dedicated to "Santa Mar[ia] Nascente." It magnificently dominates the easter[n] side of the piazza, a vast and intricately fashione[d] marble structure, straw-yellow in color.

The seemingly interminable process of constructio[n] began under the direction of the "engineer genera[l]" S. da Orsenigo, assisted by other Lombard maste[rs;] he was succeeded by G. de' Grassi, and in the fir[st] half of the 15th c. – when plan and elevation too[k] final form – in turn by M. da Carona and F. degli O[r-] gani. Over the ensuing centuries, the supervision [of] construction fell to the leading "Visconti" architect[s,] among them Giovanni and Guiniforte Solari an[d] G.A. Amadeo (who designed the tambour) in th[e] second half of the 15th c., V. Seregni and P. Tibaldi i[n] the 16th c., L. Buzzi and F.M. Richini in the 17th c. I[n] 1765-69 F. Croce completed the tambour with th[e] main spire, on the top of which was placed in 177[4] the gilded statue of the "Madonnina." Napoleon o[r-] dered the completion of the facade (1805-13), fo[r] which one plan after another had been submitte[d] since the 17th c., and in 1811-12 the remarkable fo[r-] est of spires was finished.

As huge as the piazza itself may be, it does little [to] diminish the Duomo's vast size: 158 m long, 93 [m] wide at the transept, with an interior of 11,700 sq. [m;] the tallest spire rises 108 m. The church boasts mo[re] than 3400 statues, largely distributed over the 13[5] spires. The side view, from Piazzetta Reale, and th[e] rear view, from Corso Vittorio Emanuele, standar[d] fare of 19th-c. view painters, help us to appreciate [to] the full the sheer mass of Candoglia marble em[-] ployed, punctuated by buttresses and topped b[y] dizzying spires. In the rear, the massive transept an[d] polygonal apse are pierced by three enormou[s] stained glass windows.

The *interior*, with a four-aisle nave, is crossed by [a] short three-aisle transept with a deeply recesse[d] presbytery and ambulatory. In the shadowy coo[l-] ness, 52 colossal engaged piers line the nav[e,] transept, and apse, surmounted by huge capita[ls] adorned by statues of saints and prophets. Most [of] the spectacular stained-glass **windows*** date fro[m] the 15th and 16th c., though some date from th[e] 19th and 20th c.; especially noteworthy are the wi[n-] dows in the first, fifth, and sixth bays on the rig[ht,] and at the end of the right arm of the transept. A[l-] so, note the immense Gothic Trivulzio candelabru[m] at the end of the left arm of the transept.

Overlooking the ambulatory are the 14th-c. **portals** of the vestries; the portal on the left vestry is be[-] lieved to be the earliest piece of sculpture in th[e] Duomo, and is attributed to G. da Campione (1389[).] The stairway facing the south vestry leads down t[o] the *crypt*, which contains the remains of Sai[nt]

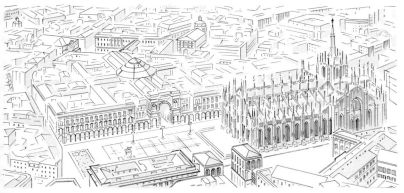

Milan: Piazza del Duomo and Galleria Vittorio Emanuele II

Charles Borromeo. Adjacent is the Duomo's **Tesoro***, or Treasury (*open 9-12 and 2:30-6*), which features remarkable goldwork, the earliest dating from the 4th and 5th c.

On the inner side of the facade a stairway leads down to the **Scavi paleocristiani** (*open Tue.-Sun., 9-5:30*), a series of Early Christian excavations where you can find the remains of the *Battistero di Giovanni alle Fonti*, a baptistery built around A.D. 378, to an octagonal plan. Here St. Ambrose, patron saint of the town, is said to have baptized St. Augustine. From the left side, outside the cathedral, you can climb up to the roof (*by foot or elevator, open 9-5:30*). Here you will see a second, "open-air" cathedral, over which looms the elaborate tambour; from here you can enjoy a splendid view of the city*. Near the elevator is the oldest spire on the Duomo, the **Guglia Carelli**, built in 1397-1404.

Palazzo Reale (*E4*). Although it was first built in the 14th c., its final, Neo-Classic form is the work of Piermarini (1778). It was the residence of Spanish and Austrian governors and was damaged by bombing in 1943. It now houses the Museo del Duomo and the Civico Museo d'Arte Contemporanea (museum of contemporary art), and various exhibition spaces.

Museo del Duomo.* *Open Mon.-Sun., 9:30-12:30 and 3-6.* This ground floor museum features 600 works, largely sculpture and architecture taken from the Duomo. There are also fragments of ancient stained glass pieces, tapestries, sketches, architectural models, and wooden carvings.

Civico Museo d'Arte Contemporanea (*E4*). *Closed for restoration.* This museum features 20th-c. Italian works of art, ranging from Futurism, the school of Pittura Metafisica (metaphysical painting), "Novecento," early abstract artists, the Roman school, "Corrente," and others. There are halls devoted to the work of Boccioni, De Chirico, Sironi, Morandi, De Pisis, Fontana, and others.

Piazza Fontana (*D-E4-5*). This piazza takes its name from the 18th-c. fountain; a commemorative plaque reminds us that the square was the site of a terrorist bombing that killed 16 people in 1969. The **Archbishop's Palace** (n. 2) dominates the square.

Corso Vittorio Emanuele II (*D4-5*). This pedestrian zone lined with porticoes and modern architecture, movie theaters and stores, was rebuilt after the heavy bombing of 1943.

At the beginning of the Corso, on the left, overlooking Piazza del Duomo, is *La Rinascente* (rebuilt in 1950), a famous Italian department store. Worth noting along the Corso is the Art Nouveau Piazza del Liberty (n. 8), and the Neo-Classic church of **S. Carlo al Corso**, built in 1839-47 (IV, *C6*).

Piazza S. Babila (*D5*). The result of extensive urban rebuilding in the 1930s and after WWII, this portico-lined piazza takes its name from the ancient church of **S. Babila**, with its 17th-c. column at the corner of Corso Monforte and Corso Venezia. The 11th-c. church was completely rebuilt between 1853 and 1906.

Corso Matteotti (*D4-5*). Carved out as a Fascist avenue in 1926-34, this is an outstanding example of state architecture of the era. It culminates in a large disk-shaped *statue* by A. Pomodoro (1980); to the right, note Piazza Belgioioso, with **Palazzo Belgioioso** (*D4*), by Piermarini (1772-81). At the corner of Via Morone is the *house* of the great 19th-c. writer Alessandro Manzoni (*D4*), now the **Museo Manzoniano** (*entrance from Via Morone n. 1; closed for restoration*). The brief Via Omenoni features the **Casa degli Omenoni*** (*D4*), with its mighty telamons underpinning the facade.

Piazza S. Fedele (*D4*). This pedestrian square features a monument to Alessandro Manzoni (1883) and the church of **S. Fedele**, built to plans by P. Tibaldi (1569) but completed only in 1835. It has remarkable paintings and, in the 17th-c. vestry, handsome carved cabinets. To the left of the church, is the rear facade* of **Palazzo Marino** (*D4; open by request, tel. 02878266*), built by Galeazzo Alessi (1553) in late Renaissance style and left unaltered by the 19th-c. reconstruction. From Via Marino (n. 2), one can view the inner courtyard*, with two orders of loggias, through the former main ceremonial portal. Nowadays Palazzo Marino, whose main facade is in Piazza della Scala, opposite the theater, is Milan's Town Hall.

Piazza della Scala (*D4*). A city block was torn

Milan: Piazza Mercanti

down in 1858 to make way for this square, designed by Luca Beltrami, who also rebuilt the facade of Palazzo Marino. In the center of the square stands a monument to Leonardo da Vinci (1872), overlooking La Scala.

Teatro alla Scala* (*D4; closed for restoration until 2004*). Italy's premier opera house, possibly the world's finest, La Scala was built in 1776-78 by Giuseppe Piermarini, in linear Neo-Classic style, on the former site of the church of S.Maria della Scala, hence the name. The hall seats 3000, has four tiers of boxes and two galleries, and is nicely finished in Neo-Classic style; partially destroyed by bombing in 1943, it was rebuilt and inaugurated with a legendary concert, directed by Arturo Toscanini.

Museo Teatrale alla Scala. (*Moved to Palazzo Busca-Collegio San Carlo, Corso Magenta 71; tel. 028053418*). It houses major collections of operatic and theatrical memorabilia; the Raccolta Verdiana is noteworthy.

Galleria Vittorio Emanuele II* (*D4*). Traditional meeting place of the Milanese, as well as one of the most remarkable pieces of the architecture of Milan after the Unification of Italy, the Galleria links Piazza del Duomo with Piazza della Scala. Built by G. Mengoni in 1865-78, it is crowned by a distinctive glass-and-steel roof that culminates in a central "octagon." There are four grand portals; the one facing the Duomo is connected to the porticoes of the piazza.

Palazzo della Ragione* (*D4*). Also called the *Broletto Nuovo*, it stands on what was once a large square, eliminated by the creation in 1867-78 of both *Via and Piazza Mercanti*. Built in 1233, this was the largest medieval town hall in Lombardy. The facade overlooking the piazza features a Romanesque relief* of Oldrado da Tresseno – its builder – on horseback (13th c.).

Facing the Palazzo della Ragione along Via Mercanti is *Palazzo dei Giureconsulti* (recently restored), with a portico and notable windows, almost entirely rebuilt since 1561, as have been many of the buildings along this street, dating from the 14th, 15th, and 17th c.

Brera and the "Quadrilatero della Moda"

In the northern part of town, enclosed within the Cerchia dei Navigli, this route takes you to the Pinacoteca di Brera, one of Italy's finest art galleries through streets studded with aristocratic mansions and smart boutiques. The understated elegance of this neighborhood has made it a capital of Italian fashion designers.

Piazza Cordusio (*D4*). Oval in shape, with a statue to the 18th-c. poet Parini, this piazza is Milan's "business center," and features the official turn-of-the-century architectural style.

Via Broletto (*D4*). This lovely old street, which continues as Via Ponte Vetero and then Via Mercato, is lined with 19th-c. office buildings, old working-class Milanese row houses, and small storefronts and business establishments.

S. Maria del Carmine (*C4*). Although the slightly fanciful "Lombard-Gothic" facade dates only from 1880, the church itself was founded in the 15th c. Running off to the left from the square is the narrow Via Madonnina, intersecting with *Via S. Carpoforo* and *Via Fiori Chiari*. Long-ago a neighborhood of ill repute, these narrow lanes now teem with expensive shops and elegant nightspots; there is a fine *Mercato dell'Antiquariato*, or antiques market (3rd Sat. of each month).

Palazzo di Brera* (*C4*). This impressive building at Via Brera n. 28 was headquarters of the Milanese Jesuits for two centuries (1572-1772); it then became home to many of the city's most important cultural institutions, including the Pinacoteca di Brera, the Biblioteca Nazionale Braidense, and the Accademia di Belle Arti.

Built in the 15th c., it was renovated by F.M. Richini (1651) and completed by Piermarini (1774). The elegant courtyard with two rows of arcades features a heroic bronze statue of Napoleon Bonaparte I, by A. Canova (1811).

Pinacoteca di Brera.** *Open Tue.-Sun., 8:30-7; 16 Jun.-15 Sep., Sat. open until 11 p.m.* Spread out through the forty or so halls of the first floor, this is one of the leading collections of paintings in Italy; it chiefly features works of the Lombard and Venetian schools of the 15th to 18th centuries.

Founded two centuries ago as a resource for the students of the Accademia, opened in 1803, the gallery grew rapidly throughout the 19th c. and the more recent acquisition of the Donazione Jesi (1976-84) gave Brera a 20th-c. dimension as well. Management problems and extensive restoration of the palazzo mean that some display rooms are closed, and many paintings are in storage.

More than 600 works are on display: *15th-/16th-c. Venetian, Lombard, and Emilian artists* (J. Bellini, his two sons, Gentile and Giovanni Bellini, Mantegna, Crivelli, Carpaccio, Lotto, Titian, Veronese, Tintoretto, and J. Bassano, B. Luini, Correggio); *central Italian painters from the 14th-16th c.* (A. Lorenzetti, G. da Fabriano, D. Bramante, P. della Francesca, Raphael, L. Signorelli); *non-Italian artists* (Van Dyck, Rubens, and

El Greco); *17th-c. Italians* (Ludovico, Agostino, and Annibale Carracci, Guercino, and Caravaggio); *18th-c. Italians* (Tiepolo, G.B Piazzetta, A. and P. Longhi, F. Guardi, Canaletto, Bellotto); and *19th-c. Italians* (A. Appiani, F. Hayez, S. Lega, G. Fattori, G. Pellizza da Volpedo). A major collection of 20th-c. work, the *Donazione Jesi*, includes paintings by Modigliani, Boccioni, Severini, Carrà, Campigli, Morandi, Sironi, De Pisis, Scipione, Picasso, and Braque; and sculpture by M. Rosso, A. Martini, and M. Marini.

Via Brera (*C-D4*). With *Via Solferino* and *Via S. Marco*, this street runs through the heart of one of Milan's most interesting neighborhoods; here art galleries vie with fine restaurants, bars, and cafés.

S. Marco (*C4*). Once overlooking the intersection of two canals, this church now faces out over the corner of Via S. Marco and Via Fatebenefratelli, just behind the Palazzo di Brera. It features the original portal, bell tower, and several statues upon the facade, dating from the 13th and 15th c.; in the interior are a number of paintings, frescoes, and other works.

Civico Museo del Risorgimento (*C4*). *Open Tue.-Sun., 9-1 and 2-5:30.* This museum of Italian history is housed in the Neo-Classic Palazzo Moriggia, at n. 23 in Via Borgonuovo. Along the way back to Via Manzoni, overlooking Via Verdi, is a particularly fine Baroque church, **S. Giuseppe** (*D4*), designed by F.M. Richini (1630).

Via Manzoni (*C-D4*). This venerable Milanese street is lined with handsome villas, many with large rear gardens. On your left, in *Largo Croce Rossa*, is a controversial monument to the late Italian president and Resistance leader Sandro Pertini (Aldo Rossi, 1990); beyond this is the tree-lined **Via dei Giardini** (*C4*), with the remains of a 15th-c. monastic cloister, in *Piazza S. Erasmo*. Past Via Monte Napoleone, Baroque and Neo-Classic *palazzi* and churches line the road. Via Manzoni ends with the **Arco di Porta Nuova**, a city gate dating from the 12th c.

Museo Poldi Pezzoli* (*D4*). *Open Tue.-Sun., 10-6.* This is an outstanding example of Milanese home-cum-museum, and its 23 halls give a sterling indication of the tastes of a private collector of the 19th c., in this case, Gian Giacomo Poldi Pezzoli. The collection includes 14th- to 19th-c. paintings and decorative arts: goldwork, enamels, Murano glass, Italian and European ceramics, furnishings, textiles (Persian carpet, signed and dated, 1542-43), lace and tapestries, mechanical clocks (Falck Collection) and sundials (Portaluppi Collection), weapons and armors. There are some masterpieces by artists such as Piero del Pollaiuolo, Botticelli, Piero della Francesca, Mantegna, Cosmè Tura, and F. Guardi; and a wide range of work by Lombard painters of the 15th and 16th c. (Bergognone, Boltraffio, Cesare da Sesto, Foppa, Luini) and 18th-c. Venetians (Tiepolo, Canaletto).

Via Monte Napoleone (*D4-5*). Almost entirely rebuilt in the Neo-Classic style, lined with aristocratic palazzi, this street – with the last section of Via Manzoni, Via della Spiga, and Via S. Andrea – encloses the "Quadrilatero della Moda," the fashion district featuring antique shops, jewelry stores, and leading fashion designers' retail outlets.

Museo Bagatti Valsecchi (*C-D5; open Tue.-Sun., 1-5:45; 1st Sun. of the month guided tours for children*). This late 19th-c. home in Via S. Spirito n. 10 offers a fine view of the home of a collector. The furnishings include 16th-c. Flemish tapestries, stained glass, hope chests, and a bed decorated with bas-reliefs of Bible scenes. There are also paintings and other works.

Museo di Storia Contemporanea (*D5*). Located in an 18th-c. palazzo, at n. 6 Via S. Andrea, this museum of contemporary history is the seat of temporary exhibitions; upstairs is the **Museo di Milano** (*open Tue.-Sun., 9-12 and 2-6*), with 600 18th-/19th-c. paintings and prints regarding Milan.

S. Ambrogio and the Quartiere Magenta

The centuries have left their mark in Milan, and this walk goes to the churches of S. Ambrogio, a Romanesque archetype, and Santa Maria delle Grazie, where Leonardo da Vinci painted his Last Supper, and then goes past the Biblioteca Ambrosiana and the Pinacoteca Ambrosiana.

Piazza S. Ambrogio (*D-E2-3*). This oddly shaped square was once a broad thoroughfare – Stradone di S. Ambrogio – running alongside the basilica. One end of the square is marked by the **Pusterla di S. Ambrogio**, built in 1939 in imitation of the medieval city gates (12th c.) and decorated by an authentic tabernacle with statues of patron saints (1360). Behind the basilica stands a military monument called the **Tempio della Vittoria** (*E2-3*), an octagonal tower (1927-30), and the **Università Cattolica del Sacro Cuore** (*E3*), one of the most important universities of the town, which features two cloisters by Bramante*.

S. Ambrogio** (*E2-3*). One of Milan's most distinctive landmarks, this basilica, dedicated to the city's patron saint, is a remarkable mixture of restoration and a founding monument of Lombard Romanesque. Built in A.D. 379 as the "Basilica Martyrum," it is the final resting place of St. Ambrose, who was buried here in A.D. 397. It was rebuilt extensively in the 9th and 10th c., and has undergone almost constant renovation since then. Standing before the basilica is a solemn rectangular **atrium***, with porticoes (1088-99) resting upon composite columns with carved capitals. On the far side of the atrium is the sloped-roof facade*, consisting of two storeys of loggias: the upper loggia features five arches of declining size. On either side is a bell tower, the one on the right dating from the 9th c., the one on the left, with pilaster strips and little arches, dating from 1128-44. On the left portal, note the pre-Romanesque relief of St. Ambrose*; the central portal is adorned with minute carvings of monstrous figures and a grapevine motif (8th and 9th c.).

The *interior* is laid out with a nave with two aisles, terminating in apses and separated by piers, roofed by broad cross vaults, with galleries along the aisles,

Milan: S. Ambrogio

tambour, and the deep central apse. In the third bay of the nave, on the left, above the sarcophagus of Stilicho (4th c.), is a **pulpit*** made of 11th-c. fragments. At the center of the presbytery, set on four porphyry columns from Roman times, is the *ciborium**, decorated with Lombard-Byzantine polychrome stuccoes (10th c.). Beneath the ciborium is the altar frontal known as **Altare d'Oro****, a precious work of goldsmithery from the Carolingian period in gold and silver sheet (Stories of Christ and St. Ambrose) with decorations in enamel and gems, by the Maestro Volvinio (835). In the apse, note the carved Gothic wooden choir (1469-71); in the vault is an enormous mosaic, with sections dating from the 4th and 8th c. and portions re-done in the 17th and 20th c.; in the crypt, silver urn (1897) with the bodies of St. Ambrose and two other saints. In the right aisle, fresco attributed to G. Ferrari; detached frescoes by Tiepolo; canvases and frescoes by Lanino. The seventh chapel leads into the **Sacello di S. Vittore in Ciel d'Oro*** (4th c.), a chapel whose cupola is decorated with 5th-c. mosaics with figures of saints. From the left aisle (first chapel, Christ and Angels* by Bergognone) you emerge under the *Portico della Canonica**, by Bramante (1492), rebuilt with original materials after heavy damage suffered in WWII.

Under the portico of the rectory is the entrance to the **Tesoro di S. Ambrogio** (Treasury, *open Tue.-Sun., 9:30-11:45 and 2:30-6*), which features goldwork, fabrics, tapestries, and other artwork from the basilica.

S. Vittore al Corpo *(E2)*. Set back on a small rectangular piazza, this Early Christian basilica was rebuilt in the late 16th c. The interior features 17th-c. paintings and a remarkable wooden choir.

To the left of the basilica is the former *Monastery of S. Vittore*, now the site of the Museo della Scienza della Tecnica (see below). Founded by Benedictine in the 11th c., the monastery was rebuilt in the 16th c. and repeatedly renovated; part of the cloisters and a few rooms survive from the original structure.

Museo Nazionale della Scienza e della Tecnica Leonardo da Vinci* *(E2)*. *Open Tue.-Fri., 9:30-5; Sat Sun. and holidays, 9:30-6:30; closed Mon; Sat.-Sun. guided workshops for children*. Opened in 1953 as museum documenting the development of science and industrial technology, the building extends over a vast area between Via Olona and Via S.Vittore (entrance from the Piazza, at n. 21). With more than 35,000 sq. m of exhibition space in three adjoining buildings, the museum has 28 sections. Temporary exhibits and conferences are held here; it also has notable specialized library (about 40,000 volumes). In the *monumental building* (once a monastery) is a great gallery devoted to Leonardo da Vinci, forming a considerable part of the museum, with extensive documentation concerning Leonardo, both as a scientist and as a technician and scholar of nature; other rooms given over to other areas of science and technology (computer science, timekeeping, acoustics, astronomy, telecommunications) and, in the basement, land-based transportation and metallurgy. There is a *rail transport building* with about twenty antique locomotives (steam and electric), railroad cars, signals, and other material documenting the technological development of trains in Italy. In the *air and sea transport building* there are sections concerning air transport (twenty antique airplanes, including a Blériot 11 from 1909) and maritime transport (the training ship "Ebe", the bridge of the trans-Atlantic liner "Conte Biancamano"); also, a section devoted to agriculture.

In this same complex is the **Civico Museo Navale Didattico** (*open 9:30-5; closed Mon.*), a museum on the history of ships, now being renovated.

Porta Magenta *(D1)*. The city gate was demolished in 1885, but the name persists, a name that describes the elegant neighborhood stretching along Corso Magenta, Via Ariosto, Via Pagano, and the Parco Sempione. Remarkable buildings date from the turn of the century.

Cenacolo Vinciano** *(D2)*. *Open Tue.-Sun., 8:15-7:30; 16 Jun.-15 Sep., Sat. until 9:45 p.m.; closed Mon.; compulsory reservation, tel. 0289421146*. On the far wall of the huge refectory of the former Dominican convent, to the left of the church of Santa Maria delle Grazie (see below), is Leonardo da Vinci's renowned fresco of **The Last Supper**** (1495-97), now completely restored after heavy damage during WWII.

S. Maria delle Grazie** *(D2)*. This church is one of the greatest monuments of the Milanese Renaissance. Built in Gothic style (1466-90), the church was given its apse in 1492, based on the design by Bramante, in the shape of a huge three-apse cube, topped by a polygonal tambour with a gallery. The elegant marble and terracotta decorations of the apse, and the 15th-c. marble portal in the facade are worthy of note.

The nave and two aisles are flanked by chapels, the bays divided by broad pointed arches resting on columns. The chapels and piers feature remarkable works by such artists as Gaudenzio Ferrari and Paris Bordone.

The Renaissance **tambour**** was meant to be a Sforza family mausoleum, and features a cupola set upon a drum held up by four spectacular arches. The dignified "graffito" decoration* (discovered in 1934-37 and restored in 1984-87) is attributed to Bramante; in the presbytery is a carved wooden choir (1470-1510). On the left is the lovely little **cloister****, again believed to be by Bramante. Then you enter the **Sagrestia Vecchia**, or Old Sacristy, with inlaid cabinets* and early 16th-c. paintings.

Corso Magenta (D2-3). This main thoroughfare runs through the heart of the Quartiere Magenta. In the first stretch only the facades survive from the 18th-c. buildings that once lined it; just past the Cerchia dei Navigli (ring of canals, many now covered over), or what is now Via Carducci, on the left (n.24) stands the **Palazzo Litta** by F.M. Richini (1648), now the offices of the State Railroads, with a Rococo facade (1763) and a splendid porticoed courtyard. Facing it is the former **Monastero Maggiore**, once an enormous Milanese nunnery, built in the 15th c., partly demolished in 1864-72 and badly damaged in WWII; the church of S. Maurizio and the entry cloister survive, part of the Museo Archeologico.

Civico Museo Archeologico (D3). Open Tue.-Sun., 9-5:30. At Corso Magenta n.15, it features remarkable *archeological and numismatic collections*. Of special interest are the sculptures (Aphrodite-Aura), portraits (Maximin the Thracian*), mosaics, ceramics, oil lamps, glass, bronzes, silver, barbarian funerary objects. There are also remarkable *collections of Attic and other ancient pottery* as well as a large *Etruscan collection*. From the garden, there is a fine view of two Roman towers.

S. Maurizio* (D3). Open Tue.-Sun., 9-12 and 2-5:30. This Renaissance church was begun in the 16th c. and completed in 1872-96. The interior features a remarkable fresco, attributed to B. Luini.

S. Maria alla Porta (D3). This church, built after 1652 by F.M. Richini, overlooks Via S. Maria alla Porta, which followed the Roman "decumanus maximus." Inside, note 17th-c. canvases and sculpture.

Heading back toward the beginning of Corso Magenta, you can follow the narrow Via Brisa (left) to the excavations of a large Roman building. Just behind the church is the "Quartiere degli Affari," or Financial District, the heart of which is the **Palazzo della Borsa**, the Stock Exchange building by P. Mezzanotte (1931), which stands on the site of the ancient Roman theater (relics in the basement). In nearby Piazza Borromeo (E3), at n.7, is the **Palazzo Borromeo**; in the inner courtyard (open by request) are frescoes* in the International Gothic style (first half of the 15th c.).

Piazza S. Sepolcro (E3-4). This is the site of the ancient Roman Forum, though no traces survive. Overlooking the piazza is the church of **S. Sepolcro**, founded in 1030, but rebuilt in 1894-97.

Pinacoteca Ambrosiana* (E4). Open Tue.-Sun., 10-5:30. This is one of the most important cultural institutions in Milan, dating from the early 17th c., with collections, chiefly Lombard and Venetian, of works by Botticelli, Bergognone, Luini, Bramantino, Leonardo, G.A. De Predis, Raphael, Tiepolo, Caravaggio, Moretto, Titian, and Bassano.

The Castello Sforzesco and Corso Garibaldi

The northwestern section of the historical center of Milan lies around the majestic structure of the Castello, its courtyards, great walls, and mighty towers redolent with the history of the Visconti and Sforza dukedom. Behind the castle lies the Parco Sempione (see below).

Via Dante (D3-4). One of the finest legacies of Milan under King Umberto (1890), this street provides a fitting link between Piazza Cordusio and the Castello Sforzesco. At n.2 is the *Palazzo Carmagnola*, all that survived of the wholesale demolition of the 19th c. Next to it, in Via Rovello, is the *Piccolo Teatro*, a prestigious Milanese theater founded in 1947. The *Nuovo Piccolo Teatro* by Marco Zanuso is in Piazzale Marengo.

At the end, Via Dante opens out into **Largo Cairoli**, with a monument to Garibaldi (1895). This is the spot marking the convergence of the two tree-lined semicircles of *Foro Buonaparte* and *Piazza Castello*, part of the unfinished Neo-Classic design by Antolini (1801) for a huge circular square around the Castello Sforzesco.

Castello Sforzesco** (C-D3). Open access to the courtyards, summer, 7-7; winter 7-6. This huge fortified complex – perhaps the most significant Renaissance monument still standing in Milan, despite its troubled history – has housed the city museums and other major cultural institutions since the end of the 19th c.

The castle was commissioned by Francesco Sforza (1450), and was built on an existing 14th-c. structure. It became the home of Galeazzo Maria Sforza, duke of Milan, in 1466. The new duke summoned artists to turn the castle into a stately home; among them were V. Foppa, C. Moretto, and B. Ferrini. Ludovico il Moro, in turn, summoned Leonardo da Vinci, Bramante, Filarete, Zenale, and Butinone. After the Spanish took Milan in 1535, the Castello became one of the largest and best-served citadels in Europe by the early 17th c. It was heavily damaged by a French siege under Louis XV (1733); Napoleon Bonaparte ordered the castle demolished in 1800, though his orders were only partly carried out. It was used as a barracks by the Austrian occupying army. In 1893 Luca Beltrami undertook a fairly rough-and-tumble restoration, demolishing and rebuilding freely to recreate the "original" appearance of the Castello.

The outer ramparts were demolished at the orders of Napoleon. The Castello is now a vast square building made of brick, with long curtain walls and huge windows framed in terracotta, massive corner towers, battlements, and a moat. In the center of the facade is the so-called *Torre del Filarete*, a reproduction (1905) of the 15th-c. tower. The arch at the foot of this tower opens out into a vast courtyard, the *Piazza d'Armi*, enclosed by three buildings (from the left): the Rocchetta, the Torre di Bona di Savoia (1477), and the Palazzo della Corte Ducale, with large terracotta Gothic windows. To the left of the entrance is the *Raccolta delle Stampe A. Bertarelli*, a collection of over 600,000 prints, ranging from the homeliest woodcuts to the most exquisite etchings. On the side of the Piazza d'Armi opposite the Torre del Filarete, you enter the *Corte Ducale*, or ducal courtyard, through a door surmounted by the Sforza crest, with a portico and Renaissance loggia on the left; to the right is the entrance to the Civici Musei (see below). A passageway on the left leads into the porticoed courtyard called *Cortile della Rocchetta*, with the entrance to the *Archivio Storico Civico* and to the *Biblioteca Trivulziana*, originally the private library of the Trivulzio family, purchased in 1935 by the City of Milan, with rare books and incunabula. Back in the Corte Ducale, the Porta del Barco is the gate which leads out into the Parco Sempione (see below); follow the moat off to the right, and you will reach the NE side of the Castello, with the *Ponticella di Ludovico il Moro*, a small bridge attributed to Bramante, but largely rebuilt during the 19th-c. reconstruction.

Musei del Castello. ** *Open Tue.-Sun., 9-5:30.* These museums comprise collections of sculpture, painting, and the applied arts; they are divided into three major sections, called Civiche Raccolte, respectively of ancient art (Arte Antica), applied arts (Arte Applicata), and archeology and numismatics (Archeologiche e Numismatiche), largely arranged in chronological order. Other important sections include the *Sala del Gonfalone*, with frescoes of heraldic devices of Spanish royalty and viceroys, and a gonfalon* of Milan, painted and embroidered (1566); the *Sala delle Asse**, with a frescoed vault, and heavily restored cartoons by Leonardo da Vinci, as well as the Belgioioso Collection of Dutch and Flemish 17th-/18th-c. paintings; the *Cappella Ducale*, a chapel with 15th-c. frescoes; the *Sala della Balla*, with **tapestries** depicting the months*, begun in 1503, designed by Bramantino and woven in Vigevano; and the *Sala del Tesoro*, the treasury hall with a fresco representing Argo.

Civiche Raccolte d'Arte Antica. *Collections of statuary*, largely from Milanese and Lombard monuments: sculpture from Early Christian, Longobard, Romanesque, and Gothic periods, as well as 15th-/16th-c. sculpture and architecture by A. di Duccio, A. Mantegazza, M. Michelozzi (Portal of the Banco Mediceo* in the hall of 16th-/17th-c. weapons), Bambaia, and Michelangelo (**Pietà Rondanini****). On the *first floor* are the 15th-/18th-c. *collection of furniture**, along with tapestries, paintings, statues, and wooden bas-reliefs; note the reconstruction of a hall from the Castello di Roccabianca (Parma) with a detached series of 15th-c. frescoes*.
Your next stop is the **art gallery** with paintings by:

Mantegna, Bembo, G. Bellini, Foppa, Bergognon Bramantino, C. da Sesto, Correggio, Lotto, Tintorett Fra' Galgario, Cerano, Magnasco, G.B. Tiepolo, and Guardi.

Civiche Raccolte d'Arte Applicata. This mus um of applied arts has a *ceramic section*, with por lain and majolica, enamels, Renaissance bronze fi urines, religious fabrics and clothing. It also include the *Museo degli Strumenti Musicali*, with a collectic of 640 musical instruments in five sections; als note the 18th-/19th-c. costumes.

Civiche Raccolte Archeologiche e Numism tiche. This is a branch of the Museo Archeologic in Corso Magenta (see), and features a *prehistoric se tion*, with much material on early Lombard culture an *Egyptian section*, with everyday objects and f nerary material; an *epigraph section*, with more tha 100 pieces. The *medal collection* includes rough 230,000 items, from the 6th c. B.C. to modern times

Parco Sempione (*C2-3*). Extending over an are of 47 hectares behind the Castello, this park wa arranged in the English style in 1893 by E. Alemagn with trees planted to offer a perspective on to th Arco della Pace.
To your left, as you leave the Castello through th Porta del Barco, you will find the **Palazzo dell'Art** (*C2*; 1932-33), housing the exhibition quarters of th Milan Triennale and of other events. Note the *Torn del Parco*, formerly Torre Littoria, built in 1932 by Gi Ponti, in steel tubing, 109 m tall, and the small bridg which was once on the Naviglio. At the end of th park, in the center, stands the **Arco della Pac** (Arch of Peace; *C2*), one of the most distinctive mo uments of the Neo-Classic period, by L. Cagnola, be gun in 1807 to honor Napoleon, and dedicated i 1838 to Francis I of Austria, and in 1859 rededica ed to the independence of Italy. It directs the gaz out over the *Corso Sempione*, the first stretch of th great Napoleonic road running toward the Lag Maggiore; note the old palazzi at n. 25, 27, 33, and 3(In the park to the right of the Castello is the **Aren Civica** (*B-C3*), a Neo-Classic construction fro Napoleonic times, built by L. Canonica (1807), wher sport events are held. Overlooking Via Gadio (n. 2 is the **Acquario Civico** (aquarium; *open Tue.-Sun 9:30-5:30*), with 48 tanks holding freshwater and sa water fish, reptiles, amphibians, and invertebrate The building is the only surviving construction fro the International Exhibition of 1906 and is a rar example of Art Nouveau in Milan.

Piccolo Teatro di Milano-Teatro Strehler (*C3*) Set back between Via Tivoli and Piazzale Marengo the theater is a work by Marco Zanuso (1984). Nea by, at n. 50 Foro Buonaparte, is the **Fondazione An tonio Mazzotta**, a private exhibition space with a interesting program of art shows.

Corso Garibaldi (*B-C3-4*). The central thorough fare of one of the oldest and most distinctive M lanese districts, this street runs along the ancien Roman "Way to Como," through a working-clas 19th-c. neighborhood, only partly changed by th arrival of the underground. On the left (n. 17), not the facade of the *Teatro Fossati* (1858-59), refurbished by M. Fossati.

S. Simpliciano* (*C3-4*). Set back on the Piazza S. Simpliciano, to the right of Corso Garibaldi, this Romanesque basilica was founded in the 4th c. but was drastically renovated in the 19th c. Some of the outside walls date back to 16 centuries ago, but in the facade only the central portal and some arches date back as early as the 12th c. Inside, note the large fresco* in the vault of the apse, by Bergognone (ca. 1515) and the carved wooden 16th-c. choir.

To the right of the basilica (Piazza delle Crociate n. 6) is the former **convent of S. Simpliciano**, now occupied by the Facoltà Teologica Interregionale, with a small 15th-c. cloister and a larger mid-16th-c. cloister*, possibly by V. Seregni.

S. Maria Incoronata (*B4*). Erected in the late 15th c., this church has a facade divided into two sections which correspond to its interior spatial organization. According to certain sources, the twin structure, with two identical aisles, was built at the behest of Francesco Sforza and his wife Bianca Maria as a symbolic seal of the happiness of their marriage. Inside, on the right, on the walls of the chapels, are 15th-c. funerary plaques and remains of frescoes in the apse (late 16th c.).

Cimitero Monumentale (*A3*). *Open Tue.-Sun., 8:30-5:15.* At the end of Viale Ceresio, this monumental cemetery was built in 1863-66 by C. Maciachini; in the middle of the long front facade is the *Famedio*, a sort of Milanese Pantheon, where leading citizens are buried. Chapels and monuments constitute an interesting gallery of Lombard architecture and sculpture of the late 19th and 20th c. (M. Rosso, E. Butti, L. Bistolfi, A. Wildt, and F. Messina).

Porta Ticinese and Porta Romana

Along the perimeter of the Spanish bastions, there once stood ten mighty town gates (late 16th c.); their names are still used for the districts into which they gave access, and five of them are still standing. In the southern part of Milan, between Porta Ticinese and Porta Romana, there are relics of early Christian times (S. Lorenzo), Renaissance monuments (S. Satiro, Cappella Portinari, Ca' Granda), and the surprising cityscape of the Navigli.

Piazza Missori (*E4*). A tangled welter of older and more recent architecture, this square marks the western extremity of the demolition done after WWII.

At the beginning of Via Albricci, in the middle, are the remains of the church of *S. Giovanni in Conca*, founded in early Christian times and rebuilt in the 11th c. To the right of the *Palazzo dell'INPS* (n. 8-10) by M. Piacentini (1929-31), is the brick facade of the 17th-c. *Collegio di S. Alessandro* (now part of the university); also note the church of **S. Alessandro**, behind Piazza Missori, begun in 1601 by L. Binago, continued by the Richini, father and son, and completed in 1710. Inside, late 17th-c. canvases and frescoes.

S. Maria presso S. Satiro* (*E4*). This church, an architectural gem of the early Renaissance, was built in 1476-86, with much work by Bramante, who worked on it after 1478. The facade, some distance from Via Torino, was rebuilt in 1871. In the rear, visible from Via Mazzini, is a late 10th-c. Romanesque campanile, behind which stands the older Cappella della Pietà*, a chapel with an elegant 15th-c. exterior.

The small *interior* has an aisleless nave and a transept covered with broad barrel vaults; note the cupola. The asymmetrical plan resulted in the famous false painted **presbytery***, behind the main altar, the work of Bramante. At the end of the left transept is the *Cappella della Pietà*, a chapel that was once a separate structure (Basilica di Ansperto, 9th c.), with a Greek-cross plan; on the altar, note the group of the Pietà, by A. de' Fondutis (1482-83). From the right side, you can enter the octagonal **Battistero*** (or baptistery), with two rows of pilaster strips and a dome, also by Bramante, decorated with a handsome frieze, also by de' Fondutis (1483).

Via Torino (*E3-4*). This major shopping thoroughfare follows the medieval road that led to the Duomo, or Cathedral. Set back at n. 3-5 in Via Spadari is the Art Nouveau facade of the **Casa Ferrario** (*E4*) by E. Pirovano (1904). Not far away, Via Torino is dominated on the right by the tall cylindrical structure of the church of **S. Sebastiano** (*E4*; 1577-95), built to fulfill a vow made in the hopes of halting an outbreak of the plague (1576). Designed by P. Tibaldi, but heavily modified since its construction, the interior has a circular plan and is crowned by an 18th-c. dome. Further along, and also on the right, is the church of **S. Giorgio al Palazzo** (*E3*), founded in A.D. 750, but rebuilt in Neo-Classic style by L. Cagnola (1800-21); inside, note the frescoes and panels by B. Luini (1516). At the end of Via Torino is the **Carrobbio** (*E3*), an ancient intersection of Roman origin (the name is believed to derive from the Latin word for "intersection"). Set back in Via S. Sisto (n. 10), in the former church of S. Sisto, is the **Museo-Studio Francesco Messina** (*E3*; *open Tue.-Sun., 9:30-12:30 and 1:30-5:30*) with numerous works by this artist (bronzes, polychrome statues, paintings, drawings, sketches).

S. Lorenzo Maggiore** (*E3*). This basilica is one of the most important and the oldest monuments in Milan, of considerable significance in the history of western architecture.

Before the church lies a broad square, with a bronze copy of a statue of the emperor Constantine, in commemoration of the Edict of Milan (A.D. 313), which gave civil rights and toleration to Christians throughout the Roman Empire. Note the 16 Roman **columns*** dating from the Imperial Age, once part of a temple (2nd-3rd c.), transported here in the 4th c., and inserted in the great quadriporticus (later destroyed) in front of the facade.

In its basic features, this is a late 16th-c. church, which incorporates the Early Christian church, built at the end of the 4th c. as a Palatine basilica and transformed into a Romanesque church in the 12th

c. The 16th-c. church still preserves the central plan of the original structure, with four corner towers and three chapels (best seen from behind).

The *interior*, with its central plan, can be compared to S. Vitale in Ravenna; the majestic circular hall, with exedrae, galleries, and an immense dome, is lined with a broad ambulatory. On the right, through an atrium with traces of 4th-c. mosaics and a Roman portal (late 1st c.), you enter the 4th-c. **Cappella di S. Aquilino****, an intact original chapel, octagonal in shape, with niches, a loggia, and dome: in two niches, more 4th-c. mosaics*; to the right of the entrance, 3rd-c. sarcophagus; on the altar, 16th-c. silver urn with the relics of S. Aquilino. A little stairway behind the altar leads down to the foundations, probably built with blocks of stone from the amphitheater. Behind the main altar of the church is the 4th-c. *Cappella di S. Ippolito*; on the left side of the church is the 6th-c. *Cappella di S. Sisto*.

Parco delle Basiliche (*E-F3*). Extending from Piazza della Vetra, behind S. Lorenzo, all the way to S. Eustorgio, this park offers a visual sweep encompassing both remarkable churches. To the right of the Basilica di S. Lorenzo stands the medieval **Porta Ticinese** gate, built in the 12th c., rebuilt in the 14th c., and further modified in 1861-65. On the outer facade, note the tabernacle with reliefs of saints, by the school of G. di Balduccio (14th c.). Beyond the gate, *Corso di Porta Ticinese* continues out of town through the heart of the working-class Quartiere Ticinese, with much of the flavor of the original medieval "borgo."

S. Eustorgio* (*F3*). One of the most notable monuments in Milan, this basilica has a complex and stratified structure, with fragments from the 7th c. and pieces of the Romanesque structure (12th c.), set in a building that was being modified and revamped until the late 15th c. Surrounded by a broad tree-lined area, the Neo-Romanesque facade dates from 1862-65; only the little loggia is intact (1597), in the left corner; at the end of the right flank, with its 15th-c. chapels, near the apse, stands the tall bell tower* (1297-1309), behind which you can see the

Milan: S. Lorenzo Maggiore

handsome exterior of the Cappella Portinari.

Inside, in the nave and aisles, divided by piers with 11th-/12th-c. capitals, note the deep apse. In the chapels on the right, 14th- and 15th-c. funerary monuments and frescoes (in the vaults; in the 1st chapel, triptych by Bergognone; in the 4th, funerary monuments to Stefano Visconti by G. di Balduccio). In the right transept, note the *Cappella dei Magi*, with a large Roman sarcophagus which held the supposed relics of the saint until 1164. On the main altar, note the unfinished marble frontal, possibly designed by G. de' Grassi (early 15th c.) and M. da Campione. Behind the apse (where you can see the foundations of the original 5th-c. basilica), from the pseudo-crypt you can enter the **Cappella Portinari**** (*open Tue.-Sun. 10-6; Thu. until 10 p.m.*), a gem of early Renaissance Tuscan-style architecture (1466). Long thought to be the work of Michelozzo, this chapel is square in plan, covered by a dome, with a sacellum in which stands the altar. It has elaborate and lavish decoration; especially fine is the polychrome Procession of Angels* holding festoons in the tambour beneath the dome, designed by a Tuscan master, and perhaps executed by V. Foppa. The **frescoes**** high on the walls are a masterpiece by V. Foppa (1468); in the middle is the marble Arca di S. Pietro Martire**, an urn carved by G. di Balduccio (1339). The little *Museo di S. Eustorgio* (*open by request*) features 17th-c. paintings and sacred furnishings from the 17th and 18th c.; it also has underground rooms, the remains of a *Roman and Early Christian cemetery*.

Porta Ticinese (*F3*). Do not confuse this gate with the medieval gate of the same name; this one stands isolated in the center of Piazzale XXIV Maggio. One of the most notable works of Milanese Neo-Classicism, it was built by L. Cagnola (1801-14) as an arch of triumph to commemorate Napoleon's victory at Marengo. Nearby is the **Darsena** (*F2-3*), an old town port and the only basin to survive from the complex system of canals that once ringed Milan; it now marks the convergence of the *Naviglio Grande*, running from Abbiategrasso and the *Naviglio di Pavia* which flows into the Ticino River.

Overlooking the water is a distinctive district of old Milan, once quite working-class, now as fashionable and expensive as can be, with restaurants, bars, and nightspots. In early June, the popular *Festa dei Navigli* is held here, and, on the last Sunday of each month, also the noted *Mercatone del Naviglio Grande*, with merchandise ranging from fine antiques to bric-a-brac. At n. 27 Ripa Ticinese is the **Museo del Giocattolo e del Bambino** (*F2; open 9:30-12:30 and 3-7:30; closed Mon. and Aug.*), a museum of toys, with a rotating exhibition of items from the 18th to the 20th c.

S. Maria presso S. Celso* (*F4*). Also known as *S. Maria dei Miracoli*, this church is a fine example of 16th-c. architecture; it was designed by Dolcebuono (1493) and completed in 1506. Before it stands a solemn quadriporticus*, a masterpiece by Cesariano from the early 16th c.; the four-register facade is by G. Alessi and M. Bassi (late 16th c.).

e *interior* has a nave with two aisles, 16th-c. dec-ations, fine dome, and presbytery surrounded by nbulatory. Beneath the dome, on either side of the oss-vault, statues by S. Lorenzi and A. Fontana, who so did the statue of the *Assunta* (Annunciate, 1586) the altar of the Madonna (to the left of the pres-tery), to which Milanese brides traditionally pay eir respects on their wedding day; in the pres-tery, note the handsome inlaid choir (1570). On e altar of the right transept and in the ambulato-are sculpture and paintings by P. Bordone, G. Fer-i, and Il Moretto; the altar in the left transept in-rporates a 4th-c. sarcophagus; in the 1st chapel the left, note the painting by Bergognone.

the right of the church of S. Maria dei Miracoli nds the Romanesque church of **S. Celso** (*open request, enquire in the sacristy*), built in the 10th c. t rebuilt by Canonica (1851-54), with a Lombard-manesque campanile and the original portal.

rso Italia (*E-F4*). This broad thoroughfare, run-g out from the center, was built at the turn of the ntury; in part it goes along the ancient "Corso di Celso"; roughly halfway along this broad street is e former church of **S. Paolo Converso**, now the adquarters of an auction house. Across the street a 17th-c. column. The church was built between 49 and 1580; the facade is by Cerano (1613); the ndsome interior is by the Cremonese architects tonio, Giulio, and Vincenzo Campi. Further along . 10) is the *Palazzo del Touring Club Italiano* (1914-), with the bookshop and offices.

rso di Porta Romana (*E-F4-5*). Linking Piazza ssori with *Porta Romana*, this street, built in 1598, ns along the course of what was originally the Ro-an "decumanus maximus," which was lined with onumental porticoes (2nd-3rd c.; you can see ces in the Missori station of the Metropolitana un-rground railway, line 3). In its first stretch, the Cor-alternates modern buildings with ancient palazzi t n. 6, the 17th-c. *Palazzo Annoni*) and is dominat-by the **Torre Velasca** (1958), a 26-storey office d apartment building, outstanding creation of stwar Milanese architecture.

Nazaro Maggiore* (*E4*). This basilica was found-by St. Ambrose (A.D. 386); much of the cross-ucture dates from the 4th c. It was rebuilt in the h c. (apse and tambour), and renovated exten-ely in later centuries.

notable work is the octagonal **Cappella ivulzio***, built by Bramantino (1512-50), con-ning the family tombs in a simple room, includ-g the Arca di G.G. Trivulzio, with the noteworthy tin inscription: "Qui numquam quievit quiescit; e" (He who never had rest is now resting; silence). om the chapel you can descend into the basili-proper. In the right arm of the transept is a Last pper by B. Lanino. To the right of the presbytery, te the 10th-c. *Basilichetta di S. Lino*; from the left m of the transept, you can enter the 16th-c. *Cap-lla di S. Caterina d'Alessandria*, with a fresco* by nino (1546).

' Granda* (*E4-5*). *Open 8:30-7; closed Sat. and Sun.* This is the former Ospedale Maggiore, or main hospital, used for health care until 1939 (now the campus of the Università Statale); it remains one of the most noteworthy monuments of 15th-c. Milan. It was founded in 1456 by Francesco Sforza and his wife Bianca Maria, and was enlarged between the 17th and 19th c. Devastated by bombing and subsequent fires in 1943, it has been radically re-stored.

The 15th-c. wing, on the right side of the long fa-cade, shows a style in transition from Gothic to Re-naissance; built by Filarete, it consists of an arched portico below and a floor of handsome terracotta mullioned windows. The central section is a lavish imitation of the 15th-c. wing; along with the vast in-ner courtyard* with portico and loggia, it was built in the 17th c. by F.M. Richini, F. Mangone, and G.B. Pessina. To the right of this courtyard, note the love-ly little late 17th-c. Cortiletto, a small courtyard with two rows of arcades. The notable *Quadreria dei Benefattori**, a portrait gallery, is being moved to the old stables of the abbey of Mirasole (*open by re-quest, contact the Amministrazione degli Istituti Ospe-dalieri, tel. 0255038278, 0255038276*).

Piazza S. Stefano (*E5*). This oddly shaped space is dominated by the Baroque facade and the tall bell tower (17th c.) of the church of **S. Stefano Mag-giore**, now headquarters of the *Archivio Storico Diocesano*, a religious archive; also note the 17th-c. former church of *S. Bernardino alle Ossa*, which takes its name ("Ossa," or bones) from a macabre chapel lined with human bones.

Porta Vittoria and the "Zona Venezia"

In the NE area of Milan, starting from the Verziere and continuing on beyond the walls, you will en-counter relics of the Baroque age, marks of 19th-c. opulence, streets and houses decorated with "floral" motifs and the scars of a metropolis undergoing constant rebuilding.

Largo Augusto (*E5*). Standing in this small square is the Colonna del Verziere, a column erected in the 17th c. as a votive offering after the end of the plague in 1577, by Ricchino, among others.

Running into this square is **Via Durini** (*D5*), lined with aristocratic palazzi, including, at n. 20, the *Casa Toscanini* (18th c.) and, at n. 24, the Baroque **Palaz-zo Durini**, also by F.M. Richini (1648). At the inter-section between *Corso di Porta Vittoria* and the Cer-chia dei Navigli (ring road along the course of the old canals) is the 18th-c. **Palazzo Sormani An-dreani** (*E5*), now housing the *Biblioteca Centrale Comunale*, or main library. Further along is the mas-sive *Palazzo di Giustizia* (Hall of Justice; *E5*) by Pia-centini and Rapisardi (1932-40). Set back on the Via Besana is the **Rotonda della Besana** (*E6*), a ro-tunda that was originally the cemetery of the Ospe-dale Maggiore (1713-25) and which is now used for exhibitions, with the former church enclosed by a circular portico.

S. Pietro in Gessate (*E5*). We are not sure who built this church (attributed either to P. Antonio or G. Solari), but we do know it was built from 1447 to 1475, in a transition style from Gothic to Renaissance. The facade was redone in 1912, and only the central portal survives. Inside, 15th-c. Lombard frescoes and paintings. The left transept is covered with frescoes by B. Butinone and B. Zenale (1490).

S. Maria della Passione* (*D6*). This large church, second only to the Duomo, was begun to a Greek cross plan in 1486, while the dome was completed by Cristoforo Lombardo in 1530. Transformed to a Latin-cross plan at the end of the 16th c., it was given a Baroque facade in 1692-1729. In the interior, on the piers of the nave and in the enormous octagon of the dome, are paintings* by D. Crespi, who also created the doors of the twin organs in the niches of the presbytery (the organ on the right is an Antegnati, 1558; the one on the left dates from 1610). In the right transept is a Deposition, attributed to Luini; in the left transept, Last Supper by Gaudenzio Ferrari. From the niche between the apse and the transept, you enter the **Sala Capitolare**, or Chapter House, with marvelous frescoes by Bergognone.

To the right of the church, in a former convent (early 16th-c. courtyard, attributed to C. Solari), is the **Conservatorio di Musica Giuseppe Verdi**, a conservatory with a remarkable *library* of musical scores (18th-19th c.). To the left of the church (Via Bellini n. 11) is the **Casa Campanini**, one of the most remarkable examples of Milanese Art Nouveau; 1909).

Corso Monforte (*D5-6*). This chief thoroughfare of what was once the "Borgo di Monforte" features (n. 35) the **Palazzo Isimbardi**, built in the 15th c. and repeatedly renovated; it is now headquarters of the Amministrazione Provinciale, or provincial government; the vault of the Sala della Giunta (*open by request, tel. 0277402416; guided tours, 1st, 3rd Fri. of each month, tel. 0272524301*) is decorated with a large painting by G. B. Tiepolo.

Corso Venezia (*C-D5-6*). This major thoroughfare has a series of aristocratic palazzi and parks, giving it the dignity of a major urban boulevard. It ends with the two massive structures of the **Caselli di Porta Orientale** (*C6*), custom houses which flank the gate, by R. Vantini (1827-28).

On the right in the first stretch of this street (n. 10), **Casa Silvestri** is a fine example of a small Renaissance palazzo (1475), with an elegant courtyard and 14th-c. fragments. Almost directly across the street (n. 11), note the portal (1652) of the **Seminario Arcivescovile**, done in 1565-77 by P. Tibaldi and V. Seregni, with a courtyard built in 1602-8 by A. Trezzi and F. Mangone. At the corner of Via S. Damiano (n. 16), note the enormous **Palazzo Serbelloni** with a Neo-Classic facade (1793).

Palazzo del Senato (*C5*). This noteworthy creation of the architecture of the Counter-Reformation (1608-30) has a facade by F. M. Richini and two majestic courtyards by F. Mangone. Restored after the bombing of 1943, it is now the headquarters of the Archivio di Stato, one of Italy's leading state archives.

Villa Reale* (*C5*). One of the finest creations of lanese Neo-Classicism, built in 1790 by L. Pollak the counts of Barbiano di Belgioioso. It was the idence of Napoleon and of Eugene de Beau nais, viceroy of Italy; the Austrian soldier Co Radetzky lived here (1857-58). Note the rear faca overlooking the garden; inside is the Galleria d'A Moderna, a gallery of modern art.

Galleria d'Arte Moderna* (*C5*). *Open Tue.-S. 9-5:30.* This gallery of modern art has a select lection of painting and sculpture, particularly L bard, from the Neo-Classic period (A. Canova, A. piani), the Romantic era (Piccio, F. Hayez) and late 19th c. (D. Ranzoni, T. Cremona, G. Segantini Rosso). Note the *Vismara Collection*, with work Tosi, Modigliani, De Pisis, and Morandi; **Il Qua Stato** (Fourth Estate) by G. Pellizza da Volpedo, chased with a public subscription in 1920; *Museo Marino Marini*, with a collection assemb by the sculptor himself, of his own work. The *colta Grassi* is a collection comprising objects art, fabrics, Oriental carpets, and especially 1 /20th-c. paintings of the French (Corot, Sisley, Ma Cézanne, Gauguin, Van Gogh, Vuillard, Bonna Toulouse-Lautrec, Utrillo) and Italian (Lega, R zoni, Boldini, De Nittis, Mancini, Spadini, Pelliz Segantini, Balla, Boccioni, Morandi) schools.

Annexed to Villa Reale is the **Padiglione d'A Contemporanea** (PAC) by Ignazio Gardella (19. where temporary exhibitions are held.

Piazza Cavour (*C5*). Situated between the arc of *Porta Nuova* and the *Giardini Pubblici* (pul park; see below) this square is dominated by *Palazzo dei Giornali*, or press building, built in 19 42 by G. Muzio, and by the tall building of the *C tro Svizzero* (1952). Set back on the right in Manin (n. 2) is the 18th-c. **Palazzo Dugnani**, v porticoes and loggias; inside, the central hall v frescoed* by G.B. Tiepolo. The building houses **Museo del Cinema della Cineteca Italia** (*open Fri.-Sun., 3-6*), with documents, memorabi and materials on the history of film-making.

Via Turati (*B-C5*). At the beginning of this str back on the left, at n. 5 Via Carlo Porta, are the he quarters of the Fondazione Corrente, with the *dio-Museo di Ernesto Treccani* (*open Wed.-Thu., other days, by request, tel. 0265722627*). On eitl side of Via Turati, on a line with Largo Donegan the sober complex of the former *Palazzi della M tecatini* (n. 2 dates from 1936-38 and n. 1 from 19 both by the architect Gio Ponti and associates; the far side of Via Moscova is the eclectic residen complex called *Ca' Brütta* (1919-22). In a furt stretch of Via Turati, at n. 34, is the **Museo della P manente** (1886; *open Tue., Wed., Fri., 10-1 and 2: 6:30; Thu. until 10 p.m.; Sat.-Sun. and holidays, 6:30*), where major art exhibits are held. At the e of the street, two twin tall buildings (1960s) mark transition to the huge, tree-lined *Piazza della pubblica*, built in the 1930s and rebuilt after WWI **S. Angelo** (*B-C4*). At the beginning of Via Mosco adjoining a Franciscan convent, this church is c

Milan: Grattacielo Pirelli

f the principal 16th-c. monuments in Milan, with a 7th-c. Mannerist facade. Inside, on the altars and in ne sacristy, 16th-/17th-c. canvases by A. Campi, the iammenghini, and by G.C. and C. Procaccini.

Giardini Pubblici (*C5*). Completely enclosed by long fence, this is the oldest public park in the ity; with an area of 17 hectares, it comprises a Neo-'lassic section (toward Corso Venezia), designed by 'iermarini (1783-86), with a later English-style gar-en (1857-81). In these gardens, aligned along Cor-o Venezia, are the **Planetario** (Planetarium; 1930-5; *open Tue. and Thu., 9 p.m.; Sat.-Sun. and holidays, and 4:30 p.m.*), where lectures and astronomical lide shows are held; and the Museo Civico di Sto-a Naturale (Natural History Museum).

Museo Civico di Storia Naturale* (*C5*). *Open Tue.-ri., 9:30-6; Sat-Sun. and holidays until 6:30; work-hops for children during holidays.* Founded in 1838 vith the donation to the city of the collections of the aturalists Jan and De Cristoforis, this museum is oused in an immense Neo-Romanesque building 1888-93). Despite heavy damage in 1943, it remains ne of the leading museums of natural history in Lurope, with a thriving research division (special-zed library, with over 30,000 volumes; huge research ollections). More than 20 halls on two floors feature ninerals, fossils, and stuffed animals, as well as mod-ls, dioramas*, and explanatory panels.

Df particular interest to the history of science, note he surviving material from the 17th-c. naturalistic *Museo Settala**; also, dinosaur skeletons and eggs; he skeleton of a 19-m whale; skeletons of extinct ertebrates (*Equus quagga, Alca impennis*); a single iant crystal of colorless topaz (40 kg.); and a large tuffed specimen of the *Tridacna gigantea*.

Corso Venezia (second stretch; *C5-6*). This monu-nental Neo-Classic boulevard is lined with solemn

facades overlooking the park of the Giardini Pub-blici; note, at n. 40, *Palazzo Saporiti* (1812) and, at n. 51, *Palazzo Bovara* (1787); at n. 47, **Palazzo Ca-stiglioni**, by G. Sommaruga (1900-1904), emblem of Italian Art Nouveau. Other interesting examples of the early 20th-c. Milanese style can be found in the area between Corso Venezia and Viale Majno: in par-ticular, at Via Cappuccini n. 8, **Palazzo Berri-Mere-galli** by G.U. Arata (1911-14); further along, on Via Malpighi (n. 3), is the *Casa Galimberti*, by G.B. Bossi (1903-4).

Corso Buenos Aires. (*B-C6*). This busy thorough-fare of the "zona Venezia," one of Milan's largest and most crowded neighborhoods, is also one of the city's main shopping streets. This is a continuation toward the outskirts of town of Corso Venezia, along what was in the 18th c. the "Strada Regia detta di Loreto," in a densely populated late 19th-c. neigh-borhood, now marked by episodes of urban blight.

Grattacielo Pirelli (*A5*). Since 1978 this skyscraper has been the headquarters of the regional govern-ment of Lombardy; it is safe to call this the most pres-tigious creation of postwar Milanese architecture. Built in 1955-60 by Gio' Ponti and associates, with the consultation of P.L. Nervi, it dominates Piazza Duca d'Aosta (127 m tall, the highest building in Mi-lan), facing the colossal building of the **Stazione Centrale** (*A6*), massively imposing, covered with decorations, designed by U. Stacchini and built in 1912-31; from the main gallery you can enter the *Museo delle Cere* (Wax Museum; *open 8-11 pm*).

Centro Direzionale (*A5*). Established by the regu-latory town plan drawn up after WWII, in the area between Via Fabio Filzi and Via Melchiorre Gioia, but left unfinished, this office district constitutes a hodge-podge of tall office buildings, mostly from the 1960s, and vacant lots; the easternmost point is the **Stazione Porta Garibaldi**, a railway station built in 1963 (*A4*), with adjacent twin *skyscrapers* of the rail-road corporation (F.S.; 1990-92).

The outlying neighborhoods

The originally walled perimeter of the Spanish bas-tions (Bastioni Spagnoli) encloses roughly 1/16th of the town area. The other 15/16ths have been built up heavily, largely within the past century and, in some areas, within the past 20 years. In the outlying terri-tory, note the infrastructure of the greater metropol-itan area (airport, sports stadium, race track), but al-so fragments of outlying towns and the medieval abbeys that reclaimed the low-lying plains: the sur-rounding areas begin in the city.

Villa Simonetta. At n. 36 Via Stilicone, this is a note-worthy example of a suburban aristocratic villa, built at the end of the 15th c. and rebuilt in 1547 by Domenico Giunti; restored, it is now the site of the Civica Scuola di Musica, a municipal music school.

Fiera Campionaria. This is Milan's trade fair (about 400,000 sq. m). It has another annex in Lacchiarel-la, to the west of the city. The main entrance is in

Piazzale Giulio Cesare; not far away (Piazza Buonarroti n. 29), is the *Casa di Riposo per Musicisti*, a retirement home for musicians, with the tomb of Giuseppe Verdi (*open by request at the front office, 10-12 and 2:30-5*), whose monument stands in the center of the square. Further along, toward the end of Viale Monte Rosa (Via Mosè Bianchi n. 94), inside the Pontificio Istituto Missioni Estere is the small *Museo Popoli e Culture*, featuring handicrafts from the Far East (*open Mon.-Sat., 9-12:30 and 2-6; closed holidays and Aug.*).

S. Siro. This residential neighborhood contains the most important sports facilities in Milan, including the Lido di Milano (with courses, gymnasiums, swimming pool and playgrounds for children), the Ippodromo (horse racing track), the Trottatoio (ditto), and the Stadio G. Meazza (soccer stadium). Inside the park of the Ippodromo is the huge statue of the **Cavallo di Leonardo**. This is a work by the sculptress Akamu based on the original drawings by Leonardo for a gigantic statue which was never executed. Further north is the **Q.T.8**, another residential district, designed in 1946 for the Eighth Esposizione Triennale of Milan, and built between 1950 and 1960, covering a surface area of 878,000 sq. m.

Certosa di Garegnano. At the far NW corner of Milan stands this former charterhouse, somewhat set back from Viale Certosa, in the shadow of the superhighway ramps. The church was rebuilt in the late 16th c. The interior, by V. Seregni, is lavishly decorated with frescoes* by D. Crespi (1629); in the presbytery, frescoes and paintings by S. Peterzano (1578).

Ospedale Maggiore. To the north of Milan, in the district of Niguarda, this hospital complex (300,000 sq. m) replaced the obsolete structure of the Ca' Granda in the 1930s. Built by Marcovigi and Arata, it is decorated, at the end of Viale Ca' Granda, by an impressive entrance, with reliefs and statues.

Palazzina Liberty. In the gardens of Largo Marinai d'Italia, is this handsome building by Migliorini (1908) with decorations in ceramics and floral reliefs, formerly part of a long-ago demolished central fruit-and-vegetable market; it has been restored, and is now the home of the Civica Orchestra di Fiati (City Woodwinds Orchestra).

Aeroporto di Linate. Originally named after the aviation pioneer Enrico Forlanini, this airport lies just outside the city limits, to the east of the center; the original Forlanini landing field dates from 1935-36, but it has been virtually eliminated by the various stages of rebuilding. Nearby is the large body of water (2.5 km long) of the **Idroscalo**, built in 1928 as a landing basin for seaplanes, and now used for water sports and swimming.

Abbazia di Chiaravalle.* This abbey, to the SE of Milan, stands in farmland that is part of the city; it was founded in 1135 by the Cistercians, who made it a stronghold in their agricultural colonization of the Milanese lowlands. The *church* was built in 1172-1221 in the French Gothic style; note the bell tower. *Inside*, there are large frescoes in the nave, above

the 17th-c. carved choir* and in the transepts (Fiam menghini; 17th c.), as well as a Virgin and Child b Luini in the right transept.

Mòdena

Elev. 34 m, pop. 176,022; Emilia-Romagna provincial capital. "The immense ocean of th horizon is broken, to the west, only by the tow ers of Mòdena": Stendhal described the land scape as he saw it from the hill above Bologna The towers he described still stand: the Torr dell'Orologio, atop Palazzo Comunale, but es pecially the 88-m-tall Ghirlandina, a militar structure more than a bell tower. In the ancier. center of town are the Duomo (Romanesqu masterpiece by Lanfranco and Wiligelmo), th curving porticoed streets of the Middle Age and the geometric grid of streets built by th d'Este family, who held Mòdena for 250 year after losing Ferrara (1598). The town is also fa mous for its wine (Lambrusco), food (tortelli ni and zampone), and tradition of fast car. (the Ferrari factory, at nearby Maranello).

Historical note. The Via Emilia still runs throug the heart of town. Here, in 183 B.C., between th rivers Secchia and Panaro, the Roman colony o Mutina was founded. In the late Roman Empire, Mò dena almost vanished, amidst extensive flooding o the undammed rivers; time passed, and in A.D. 89 new walls were built. In 1099, work began on th new Cathedral, still standing, and in 1135 Mòden. began to rule herself. In 1182, Mòdena founded he own university, in competition with that of her arch rival Bologna. Mòdena supported the imperia forces, and in the terrible defeat of Fossalta (1249) the Bolognese captured the son of Emperor Fred erick II. Forty years later, Mòdena was subjugated by the Este family of Ferrara (1288). The following yea work began on the Castello Estense, now home o the city art collections. Amid political turmoil, Mò dena continued to grow, trading by river and laced with canals whose names still indicate streets (Cor so Canal Chiaro, Via Canalino, Corso Canal Grande) In 1336, the Este returned to Mòdena, intertwining the history of the town with that of Ferrara for near ly three centuries. A new district was built, begin ning in 1546, along Via Ganaceto and Corso Cavour the canals were filled in, ducal gardens plantec (now public), and beginning in 1630, the enormous square structure of Palazzo Ducale arose. Mòdena became the capital of the Este dukes, who had los Ferrara to the popes; then Napoleon drove them off and in 1814 Mòdena came under the rule of an Aus trian Hapsburg. In 1859, Mòdena became part of the Kingdom of Italy, and between 1880 and 1920, the tree-lined city walls were demolished.

Places of interest. Piazza Grande. This piazza forms a monumental complex with the cathedra and its tower (see below). The 17th-c. building with porticoes, with a 13th-c. clock tower in the middle, is the *Palazzo Comunale*, or town hall; from the courtyard (*entrance in Via Scudari n. 20*), you can climb to the upper floor, with handsome rooms, decorated with frescoes and paintings by N. dell'Abate, E. dell'Abate, and B. Schedoni, and with coffered ceilings. In the small loggia, note the wooden bucket, subject of a local feud, immortalized in the mock-heroic poem, "La Secchia Rapita," by A. Tassoni.

Cattedrale.** Mòdena's most important monument, and a masterpiece of Romanesque architecture, this cathedral was begun in 1099 under the direction of the Lombard master Lanfranco with the help of the sculptor Wiligelmo, and was completed in the 13th c. by Campionese masters. It features a handsome tripartite facade, with three ornate portals (note the *central portal**), a handsome loggia, and a 13th-c. Gothic rose window. Of particular interest are the four bas-reliefs* by Wiligelmo (12th c.), among the earliest examples of Romanesque sculpture. Along the sides are *fine carved doors* and bas-reliefs by A. di Duccio. Adjacent to the three handsome apses is the massive bell tower, called **La Ghirlandina*** (86 m tall), with a Gothic crown, a symbol of Mòdena.

The austere *interior*, powerfully designed in brick, has a nave with two aisles and cross vaults. At the end of the nave is a fine *gallery** set on slender columns, with parapet decorated with reliefs by A. da Campione (ca. 1180); above it is a 14th-c. wooden Crucifix; to the left, a 13th-c. carved ambo. Midway on the left, a pulpit by Arrigo da Campione (1322). Huge crypt with 60 small columns (late 11th-c. capitals); on the right, a group of five polychrome statues, called the Madonna della Pappa*, by G. Mazzoni (1480). In the presbytery, a 13th-c. screen of slender columns bounds the main altar; note the inlaid choir by C. and L. Canozzi da Lendinara (1465). In the left apse, 15th-c. Tuscan bas-relief; marble statue attributed to A. di Duccio; intarsias* by C. da Lendinara (1477), and polyptych by S. Serafini (1384). In the *sacristy*, frescoes by F.B. Ferrari (1507). In the left aisle, works by M. da Firenze and D. Dossi. On the side of the Cathedral, at n. 6 in Via Lanfranco, is the **Museo Lapidario** (*open 9:30-12:30 and 3:30-6:30*) with Roman, medieval, and Romanesque stonework, including eight splendid 12th-c. metopes**.

S. Vincenzo. This 17th-c. church was made the Pantheon of the Este family. *Inside*, the once-rich decorations of the nave and cupola were damaged by Allied bombing in 1944; note the numerous family tombs.

S. Pietro.* A Renaissance church (1476-1518) with an elegant facade, and inside, fine paintings* by G. Romanino and F. Bianchi Ferrari, statues by A. Begarelli, and an inlaid choir (1543).

S. Francesco. This Gothic church, built in 1244, and since restored, has a group of terracotta sculptures by A. Begarelli (1523).

Palazzo dei Musei. A vast 18th-c. building (entrance at n. 5 Piazzale S. Agostino) that houses the many collections of the city of Mòdena; foremost

Mòdena: Cattedrale

among them, the Galleria Estense and the Biblioteca Estense (see below).

Museo Lapidario Estense. *Closed for restoration.* Located beneath the portico, and founded in 1828, this museum of plaques and inscriptions has a Greco-Roman and a medieval-to-modern section.

Biblioteca Estense* (*open 9-7:15; Fri.-Sat., 9-1:45; closed Sun.*). On the first floor, this is one of the richest libraries in Italy, with illuminated codices of great note, including the 15th-c. Bible* of Borso d'Este, illuminated by T. Crivelli.

Musei Civici. *Open Tue., 9-12 and 4-7; Wed.-Fri., 9-12; Sat., 9-1 and 4-7; Sun. and holidays, 10-1 and 4-7.* The municipal museums include various sections: the **Museo Civico di Storia e Arte Medievale e Moderna** has objects of sacred art and goldwork, weapons, musical and scientific instruments, fabrics and embroidery, and more; 17th-/18th-c. paintings in the **Galleria Campori**. The **Museo Civico Archeologico Etnologico** has collections that range from prehistoric artifacts and exhibits to Roman objects, as well as ethnographic material from New Guinea, Amazonia, Africa, and so on.

Galleria Estense.** *Open Tue.-Sun., 8:30-7:30.* Located on the top floor of the palazzo, this is one of the finest art galleries in Europe, particularly rich in works of the Emilian and Po Valley schools of the 14th to 18th c. As you enter, you will see various ancient Etruscan and Roman objects, as well as a marble bust of Francesco I d'Este* by Bernini. Among the paintings, at the beginning, are works by early Emilian artists, including paintings* by T. and B. da Modena, S. dei Crocifissi, and by Tuscans, including G. di Paolo. Among the 15th-/16th-c. Ferrarese and Modenese painters are C. Tura, A. and B. degli Erri, B. Bonascia, F.B. Ferrari, G. da Carpi, D. Dossi. Bronzes by B. di Giovanni; majolicas by S. da

Ravenna. Works by 16th-c. Florentines and Emilians include art by L. di Credi, Correggio, and L. Orsi. Non-Italian painters include: J. van Cleve, C. de Lyon, Velázquez, El Greco. Painters of the Venetian school include: Montagna, G. F. Caroto, J. and D. Tintoretto, J. Bassano, Veronese, and Palma the Younger. There are excellent medals, made for the d'Este family, by Pisanello and G. delle Corniole. Lastly, among the 17th-c. Emilian artists are Scarsellino, the Carracci, Guercino, G. Reni, L. Ferrari, and C. Cignani.
S. Agostino. This 17th-c. church features a terracotta group by A. Begarelli and a fresco by Tommaso da Modena. Take the Via Emilia, Mòdena's main strolling street, and on the left you will see the church of **S. Giovanni Battista**, built in 1730, with a handsome polychrome terracotta group by G. Mazzoni.
S. Maria Pomposa. This 18th-c. church was built with terracotta. Next door is the house of a renowned Italian writer, L.A. Muratori, of the same period; it now houses a research center and an archive of his work.
Palazzo Ducale.* *Open by request, tel. 059222145.* In Piazza Roma is the massive, lavish ducal palace of the d'Este family; note the courtyard and facade. Construction began around 1630, incorporating a castle built in 1288. Since 1862 it has housed the *Italian Accademia Militare*, or military academy.

Monreale*

Elev. 310 m, pop. 29,493; Sicilia (Sicily), province of Palermo. Located in a hilly area to the SW of Palermo, Monreale owes its renown primarily to its Duomo, or cathedral, a remarkable creation of the rich Norman culture in Sicily.

Places of interest. Duomo.** The facade of this cathedral stands between two towers (one of which is unfinished). Beneath the 18th-c. portico, note the portal, with its bronze *doors** by Bonanno Pisano (1186); along the left side, beneath the 16th-c. portico by the Gaginis is another portal with bronze *doors** by Barisano da Trani (1179). On the exterior of the *apses*, note the interplay* of the *entwined arches* and the polychrome inlays of limestone and lava. The interior has a relaxed rhythm, amidst the glittering golden mosaics. In the sanctuary, the ceiling is studded with Arabic stalactites; the floor made of porphyry and granite is original. Marble slabs dress the walls, where the **mosaics**** begin. These mosaics, completed between the end of the 12th c. and the mid-13th c., depict stories of the Old and New Testament, with legends in Latin and Greek. Particularly noteworthy are the *Stories from Genesis**, the *Christ Pantocrator** (in the vault of the apse, the visual and symbolic center of the church), and the two panels showing William II crowned by Christ and William II offering the church to the Virgin Mary. Also, note the sarcophagi of William I and William II, the 16th-c. chapel of S. Benedetto, and the 15th-c. chapel of the Crucifix; from there, you can enter the *Tesoro*, or treasury, (*open 9-12:30 and 3:30-6*). Fine view* from the *terraces*.

Chiostro** (*open 9-1 and 3-7*). This cloister, built at the same time as the church, was once part of a Benedictine monastery; it is surrounded by a portico with Gothic arches over slender twin columns; note the fountain in an enclosure.

Monte Sant'Angelo

Elev. 796 m, pop. 14,298; Puglia (Apulia), province of Foggia. It is believed that the sanctuary dates from the late 6th c., when the Longobards were organizing – politically and religiously – their dukedom of Benevento.

Places of interest. Santuario di S. Michele. Standing nearly at the end of the little oblong town, this sanctuary fronts a little square, at the top of the octagonal *campanile* (1274). Two arcades lead into the atrium, with a stairway leading down to the courtyard of the church, which has a Romanesque portal with bronze doors* (made in Constantinople, 1076). The *interior* has a single nave and Gothic arches. In the Grotta dell'Arcangelo, or Grotto of the Archangel, note the statue of St. Michael by A. Sansovino (16th c.), as well as a 12th-c. bishop's throne*, and a niche that collects the water dripping from the rock, believed to be miraculous. Numerous digs beneath the floor of this grotto have unearthed crypts dating back before A.D. 493, with frescoes from the time of the emperor Otto.
A stairway in front of the bell tower of the sanctuary leads to the ruined church of S. Pietro and the so-called **Tomba di Rotari***, probably a baptistery rebuilt around 1109. Alongside is the Romanesque church of **S. Maria Maggiore** (1170), with a carved portal (1198) and fragments of Byzantine-style frescoes (13th-16th c.) on the interior walls.
The **Museo di Arti e Tradizioni del Gargano Giovanni Tancredi** (*open winter, 8-2; closed Sat.-Sun; summer, 8-8; Sun. and holidays, 10:30-12:30 and 3-; closed Mon.*), installed in a former Franciscan convent, contains objects and pieces of folk art, along with costumes and documents of local tradition.
The **Castello**, a castle built on a Norman plan, was enlarged by the Aragonese (1494).
The *Rione Junno*, overlooking the cliff, with row houses – many dating from the 17th c. – occupies the SW area of town.

Excursion. At a distance of 9.2 km S is the ancient abbey church of **S. Maria di Pulsano**, rebuilt in the 12th c.

Montepulciano*

Elev. 605 m, pop. 13,890; Toscana (Tuscany), province of Siena. A statue of Pulcinella strikes the hours on the town bells, and the chimes echo through noble streets atop the ridge, in the town center, and in steep narrow lanes, below arches and vaults. Set high on a hilltop, Montepulciano overlooks the valley of the O cia and the Valdichiana. Among the architects who built this town are Michelozzo, A. da Sangallo the Elder, B. Peruzzi, and Vignola. The great scholar and poet Politian (Poliziano) was born here, as Agnolo Ambrogini; he took his pen name from his birthplace (in medieval Latin, "Mons Politianus").

Getting around. The area within the town walls is off limits to private cars: in summer (Jun.-Sep.) round the clock; the rest of the year from 7 a.m. until 8 p.m.; tourists can drive to their hotels, after receiving a permit at the Ufficio Turistico Comunale in Piazza Don Minzoni (near Porta al Prato; *tel. 05787121*). The route shown inside the walls is a walking tour; you may wish to drive to S. Biagio and S. Maria delle Grazie.

The city within the walls

Via di Gracciano nel Corso, Via di Voltaia nel Corso, Via dell'Opio nel Corso, Via Ricci, Via del Poggiolo, Piazza Grande: all these names are rich in history, in an urban setting that has maintained, virtually intact, its Renaissance flavor.

Porta al Prato. Spreading out before this gate is the 19th-c. *garden of Poggiofanti*. It is the main entrance to the historic center of Montepulciano and was originally part of the 13th-c. walls. It was rebuilt in the early 16th c. by A. da Sangallo the Elder; with two immense trapezoidal buttresses.

Via di Gracciano nel Corso.* Backbone of the "Borgo di Gracciano," this is the first leg of the Corso, which has been the central traffic artery of Montepulciano since the 16th c. Note the many aristocratic palazzi from that time.

On your right, at n. 91, is **Palazzo Avignonesi**, by the architect Vignola; across the road is a 19th-c. copy of the *Column of Marzocco* (the original is in the courtyard of the Museo Civico). Note the Florentine lion, which replaced the Sienese she-wolf in 1511. At n. 82 is the *Palazzo Tarugi*, also by Vignola, then **Palazzo Cocconi** (n. 68-72), believed to be by A. da Sangallo the Elder. At n. 73, *Palazzo Bucelli* (in poor condition); embedded in the base, Etruscan and Latin urns and inscriptions. Next is the church of S. Agostino (see below) and, facing it, the brick **Torre di Pulcinella** (1524), with a metal-and-wood figure of Pulcinella, or Punch, which strikes the hours. Further on, at n. 12, are *Palazzo Venturi's* fine windows; after the *Arco della Cavina*, the road enters *Piazza delle Erbe* near the three arches of the late 16th-c. **Loggia del Grano** (also by Vignola).

S. Agostino. This 15th-c. church, with a late Gothic/Renaissance facade* by Michelozzo, has a noteworthy portal with festoons and terracotta reliefs, also by Michelozzo, and a fine rose window. Inside, panel by G. di Paolo and painted wooden Crucifix attributed to Donatello. Note original choir chancel, by a follower of Pomarancio, the Crucifix attributed to A. Pollaiuolo, and Crucifixion by L. di Credi.

Via di Voltaia nel Corso. This second leg of the Corso runs through the southern part of the center, amid 16th-c. palazzi: on the left, at n. 21, is **Palazzo Cervini***, believed to be by A. da Sangallo the Younger; next to it is *Palazzo Bruschi* (n. 31), site of the popular 19th-c. *Caffè Poliziano*. At n. 55, *Palazzo Gagnoni-Grugni*, by Vignola. Also on the Corso are the 17th-c. *Collegio dei Gesuiti*, and the Baroque church of the **Gesù** (1689-1733), with an unfinished brick facade: the elegant, slightly elliptical interior is by A. Pozzo, while the false vault was added by S. Cipriani.

Via dell'Opio nel Corso. Last leg of the Corso, this road continues as *Via del Poliziano* toward the church of S. Maria dei Servi. At the intersection of Via delle Farine and Via del Teatro, at n. 1 Via del Poliziano, is the **birthplace of Poliziano**, Renaissance scholar and poet. Via del Teatro, running up to Piazza Grande and the center, is dominated by the 18th-c. **Teatro Poliziano**, with four rows of boxes, renovated in 1881.

Piazza Grande.* The monumental, hilltop center of town, sloping slightly, this square was given its modern-day appearance in the 15th c. by Michelozzo. On one side is the facade of the Duomo, on another side the Palazzo Comunale dominates (see below). Facing the Duomo is **Palazzo Nobili-Tarugi** (n. 3), attributed to A. da Sangallo the Elder; to its left, behind the late Renaissance well (**Pozzo de' Grifi e de' Leoni**, 1520), is the originally Gothic *Palazzo del Capitano del Popolo*. Also, at n. 13, note the Renaissance **Palazzo Contucci**, begun in 1519 by Antonio da Sangallo the Elder, and completed by B. Peruzzi.

Palazzo Comunale.* Built in several stages between the end of the 14th c. and the middle of the 15th c., the town hall has a stone facade by Michelozzo (1424), while its overall structure is reminiscent of the Palazzo della Signoria in Florence. Crowned by corbels and Guelph (or swallowtail) crenelations, the facade overlooking the square –

Montepulciano: S. Biagio

with a high rusticated base and a single austere portal – is in turn topped by a crenelated tower, offering a fine view* of the city, the Valdichiana, and the valley of the Orcia River. Note the 14th-c. courtyard, with cistern and loggias, recently restored.

Duomo.* This enormous late Renaissance church, by I. Scalza (1592-1630), has an unfinished facade and an unfinished 15th-c. bell tower, surviving from the previous church. The vast *interior* features a funerary statue* by Michelozzo (15th c.). Note two 15th-c. Sienese wooden statues, and, on the main altar, the large triptych* by T. di Bartolo (1401), as well as a painting by S. di Pietro, an early 14th-c. baptismal font, and a bas-relief by B. da Maiano.

Museo Civico Pinacoteca Crociani. *Open Tue.-Sun., 10-1 and 3-7 (16 Oct.-15 Apr., only until 6 p.m.).* Largely the creation of 19th-c. bequests, this museum is housed in the Gothic *Palazzo Neri-Orselli*, at n. 10 in Via Ricci. Among the artists are Margaritone d'Arezzo, the Maestro di Badia a Isola, B. di Lorenzo, J. Sustermans, J. di Mino del Pellicciaio, G. di Benvenuto, L. di Tommè, Sodoma, A. Puccinelli, Spagnoletto, P. Bordone, and A. della Robbia.

Via del Poggiolo. Lined, like Via Ricci, by lordly medieval and Renaissance homes, this road begins at *Piazza S. Francesco*, with a fine view* of the valley and S. Biagio; the church of *S. Francesco* has a handsome Gothic portal. Downhill is the church of **S. Lucia**, a mixture of early Baroque and Mannerist styles in the facade by F. del Turco (1633); inside, painting by L. Signorelli. Then you return to Piazza delle Erbe.

Churches and sanctuaries outside the walls

From the masterpiece of S. Biagio to the modest church of S. Agnese, four buildings offer evidence of the historic and economic standing of Montepulciano between the 14th and 17th c.

S. Biagio.* * Set in a lovely location SW of the historic center, on a natural terrace overlooking the surrounding hills, this church is a masterpiece by A. da Sangallo the Elder (1518-45), a solemn and harmonious travertine building with a Greek cross plan, topped by a high cupola and flanked by two bell towers. *Inside* is the majestic cupola again, with rose windows, and, on the main altar, a 14th-c. fresco of Virgin and Child and St. Francis. Overhead, a stained glass window by M. da Cortona (1568).

S. Maria dei Servi. Built in the 14th c., this church has a simple Gothic facade, with a solemn splayed portal; inside, a Virgin with Child* attributed to Duccio di Buoninsegna.

S. Agnese. On Piazza Don Minzoni, north of town, is an early 14th-c. church, rebuilt extensively. Inside, a stained glass rose window by M. da Cortona and fresco by Simone Martini.

S. Maria delle Grazie. Roughly 1 km north of town, along Viale Calamandrei, this late 16th-c. church is by I. Scalza. Inside, gilt stuccoes by A. da Cremona (1605), fine polychrome glazed terracotta by A. della Robbia, and a rare Renaissance organ.

Naples / Napoli**

Elev. 10 m, pop. 1,002,619; Campania, regional and provincial capital. This city, the third largest in Italy and the largest in the "Mezzogiorno," or Southern Italy, was for many centuries the capital of the largest Italian state, prior to the 19th-c. Risorgimento and unification. It served as a center of attraction in much the same way that Paris did for France or Madrid for Spain, a role that Rome has played – only recently – for the Italian peninsula. (Indeed, modern Naples' urbanistic and demographic problems are deeply routed in those distant times.) In one of the loveliest natural settings in all of Europe, celebrated throughout history for the variety of panoramic views, the mild weather, the luminous sea, and the gentle breezes, Naples is endowed with a superb heritage of monuments and artistic collections, at the center of an archeological zone that extends from Cumae to Pompeii, and is an attraction that draws visitors from all over the world. "Grand, luminous, and noble city," as one of its most illustrious sons, Giambattista Vico, once called it. Vico, the great historical philosopher, was an example of Naples' cultural and philosophical rigor that has always been the other face of unassuming Neapolitan humanism, immortalized by such actors as Salvatore Di Giacomo and Eduardo De Filippo.

Historical note. The origins of the earliest Greek settlement ("Palaeopolis," or "Parthenope") are linked to the expansionistic policies of Cumae, whose colonists settled on the slopes of Monte Echia. Neapolis (new city) remained an essentially Greek city, even when it was transformed from a Roman ally (326 B.C.) to a "municipium" (90 B.C.). In any case, the Romans of the ancient Republic and those of the newer Empire, captivated by the allure of ancient Greek culture, chose this as a place of study and leisure. In the villa of Lucullus, whose name has become a byword for rich living and fine cuisine, and whose home stood on the present-day site of the Castel dell'Ovo, Virgil composed his "Georgics"; an odd twist of fate brought the last emperor of Rome – Romulus Augustulus – to die in the same spot, in A.D. 476. Twenty years earlier, during the reign of Valentinian III, a new walled perimeter was built to enclose Naples within the bounds of the ancient city until the 10th c., when the ring of walls was enlarged to the SW to include the sites of the churches of Gesù Nuovo, S. Chiara, S. Maria la Nova, and S. Pietro Martire. Naples, in the meanwhile, after a short Gothic interlude, had become again, and definitively, Greek in A.D. 553. From that time on an influx of Byzantines restored the never entirely vanished Graeco-Latin bilingual tradition. The population had dropped to 20,000, but in the course of a few centuries it redoubled. In continual conflict with the bordering Longobard duchy of Benevento, the small

Neapolitan state – which included Cuma, Pozzuoli, Nola, and Sorrento – gradually became increasingly independent, until independence was complete in A.D. 763 with Duke Stefano II. This ruler assured hereditary ducal rule for his own descendants, while still maintaining nominal loyalty to Byzantium. The centuries that followed may well have been the most glorious years in the history of Naples: Neapolitan fleets, along with those of Amalfi and Gaeta, confronted the naval power of the Saracens, winning many great victories (among them, the famous triumph of Òstia, immortalized by Raphael in the Stanze Vaticane). Trade prospered too, as Naples exported the cloth it manufactured to the Arabs, between one battle and the next, in exchange for fine carpets. Still, in 1139, after prolonged resistance, even Naples was forced to yield before the steadily encroaching Normans under King Roger. With the end of the duchy, the political importance of Naples declined; it became part of a vast kingdom whose capital was at Palermo. Its commercial might remained, however, and was even augmented by a period of relative peace and by the decline of Amalfi. The city of Naples continued to develop, both inland, where the Castel Capuano was erected, and along the seashore, where an existing fortress was enlarged into the Castel dell'Ovo. The Normans in time were replaced by the Swabians. These new rulers encountered tacit but implacable Neapolitan hostility; the populace often sought the support of the pope against the Swabians. When Corradin was beheaded in 1268, the Swabians were replaced by the House of Anjou, who moved the capital from Palermo to Naples. Naples thus became the leading city in a kingdom that was called the Kingdom of Sicily by diplomats, but was commonly described as the Kingdom of Naples by one and all. The Angevins endowed their new capital with a new set of monuments. King Charles I erected the Castel Nuovo to serve as his palace, and the city spread to the area surrounding the new palace. The walled perimeter spread south from Castel Capuano to the area of the marketplace and west as far as Port'Alba. The port, which was brought within the ring of walls for the first time, was further protected by the great Molo Angioino. During this period, some of the loveliest churches in Naples were erected (S. Lorenzo Maggiore, S. Chiara, S. Domenico Maggiore, S. Pietro a Maiella, and S. Maria Donnaregina). The third Angevin king, Roberto, built the Castel S. Elmo. The capital grew even greater with the advent of the first king of the House of Aragon, in 1442, Alfonso the Magnanimous, who ruled until 1501. To the east stood tall and handsome walls; in part they can still be seen alongside the Via Rosaroll, and they included the entire Castel Capuano. To the west these walls extended as far as the present-day Via Toledo and, along the Via S. Brigida, the citadel of the Castel Nuovo. In the 14th c., Angevin Naples had attracted such painters as Pietro Cavallini from Rome, Simone Martini from Siena, Giotto from Florence, and such scholars and men of letters as St. Thomas Aquinas, Petrarch, and Boccaccio. The Renaissance court of Alfonso the Magnanimous witnessed the flowering of poetry with such names as Panormita, Pontano, and Sannazaro. This splendid season was quickly ended by the wars between France and Spain over the southern kingdom; finally in 1503 general Consalvo de Cordoba reduced Naples from its standing as the capital of a state to the humble rank of administrative center of a Spanish province. The authoritarian, repressive, and centralizing rule of the viceroys led to the immigration of barons into Naples, along with their clients and workers from the provinces, as well as Spanish nobles, officials, and soldiers. Here the foundations of the architectural and demographic problems of Naples were first laid; these problems were further aggravated by the remarkable birth-rate of the city. The viceroy Pedro de Toledo attempted, during his twenty-year reign, to solve this problem by undertaking one of the largest efforts at urban renewal in the history of Naples: the entire area between the Aragonian walls and the slopes of the Vómero as far as the present-day Corso Vittorio Emanuele was filled up with houses and tall buildings. The Via Toledo was built, running north to south, and for three centuries this was the main street of Naples and one of the best-known avenues in Europe. In a few decades, the population, which in Angevin times had been about 60,000, and by the turn of the 16th c. had risen above 100,000, at this point swelled to about 200,000. In the 17th c., despite rebellions which were put down with bloody violence (Masaniello led a famous revolt in 1647) and despite outbreaks of disease and plague (the famous pestilence in 1656 reduced the population – then well over 360,000 – by 200,000), the viceroys continued to finance monumental works, such as the new Palazzo Reale and the Palazzo degli Studi (now the site of the Museo Archeologico Nazionale), as well as a great many Baroque churches. The events of the European wars led an Austrian army to occupy Naples in 1707 without firing a shot. For 27 years Naples was the capital of a province, once Spanish and newly Austrian. In 1734 the great European powers assigned Naples to Charles of Bourbon, and once again the city became the capital of a kingdom. Naples was embellished with the Teatro S. Carlo, the Palazzo Reale di Capodimonte, the Albergo dei Poveri, and the Foro Carolino (the present-day Piazza Dante). The walls and many of the town gates were demolished, the outlying suburbs were incorporated into the city, and the Naples of early Bourbon rule came to resemble the Naples of the present day. The site of a royal court and seat of many foreign ambassadors, the city began to acquire a much higher tone, as is documented by the many accounts offered by foreign travellers making the Grand Tour. Under Napoleon, in 1799, the city was the capital of the short-lived Parthenopean Republic; after a very brief return of the Bourbon dynasty, it was again capital of the kingdom, ruled first by Napoleon's brother Joseph and later by his brother-in-law, Joaquin Murat (1806-1815). The decade under French rule produced a number

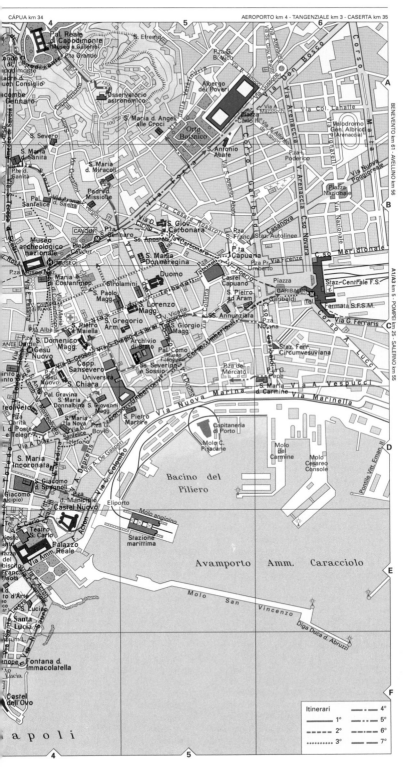

Pal. Reale
di Capodimonte
(Museo e Gallerie)
Pta Grande

S. Etremo

Pza G.
B. Mico

Osservatorio
astronomico

Albergo
dei Poveri

S. Maria d. Angeli
alle Croci

Orto
Botanico

Piazza
Carlo III

Via Col. Lahalle

Via Mazzocchi

Via Arenaccia

Corso Don Bosco

Velodromo
Gen. Albricci
(Arenaccia)

S. Severo

S. Antonio
Abate

Pza
Poderico

Via Arenaccia

Via Nuova
Poggioreale

S. Maria
d. Sanità

S. Maria
d. Miracoli

Pedro d.
Missione

Pte d.
Sanità

Pal.
Sanfelice

Via Arena
d. Sanità

Piazza
Nazionale

Via A. Arenaccia

CAVOUR

Museo
archeologico
nazionale

MUSEO

Pza.
Cavour

Pza
Museo N.

Via D.
Cirillo

P.ta
Gennaro

S. Giov.
a Carbonara

Ss. Apostoli

Via Carbonare

P.ta
Capuana

Via Foria

Via Cesare Rosaroll

Pza.
S. Franc. Staz. Autolinee

C.so Casanova

Via Firenze

Via Pr.

Umberto

C.so Maridionale

Cso Novara

Via Nazionale

S. Maria
Donnaregina

Duomo

Castel
Capuano

Piazza

Staz-Centrale F.S.

S. Maria
di Costantinop.

Girolamini

S. Paolo
Magg.

S. Lorenzo
Magg.

S. Pietro
a Aram

GARIBALDI

Fermata S.F.S.M.

S. Pietro
a Maiella

S. Gregorio
Arm.

V. Vicaria

S. Giorgio
Magg.

SS. Annunziata

Via Nolana

Via G. Ferraris

Corso A. Lucci

S. Domenico
Magg.

Gesù
Nuovo

Archivio
di Stato

Pal. Como
(Museo
Filangieri)

Corso Umberto I

Staz. Ferr.
Circumvesuviana

Capp.
Sansevero

Università

Ss. Severino
e Sossio

S. Chiara

Pal. Gravina

S. Maria
Donnalbina

S. Giovanni
Magg.

Pza del
Mercato

Pza G.
Pepe

Corso Garibaldi

S. Maria
d. Carmine

Via A. Vespucci

Via Marinella

S. Maria
la Nova

Pza G.
Bovio

S. Pietro
Martire

Via Nuova Marina

Via A. Diaz

Via Sanfelice

Via Depretis

S. Maria
Incoronata

Via A. De Gasperi

Via C. Colombo

Capitaneria
di Porto

Molo C.
Pisacane

Molo del
Carmine

Pontile Vitt. Eman. III

S. Giacomo
d. Spagnoli

Pza
d. Municipio

Bacino del
Piliero

Molo
Cesareo
Console

Castel Nuovo

Eliporto

Molo angioino

Teatro
S. Carlo

Palazzo
Reale

Stazione
marittima

Via Amm. Acton

Avamporto Amm. Caracciolo

S. Lucia

Molo San Vincenzo

Santa
Lucia

Fontana d.
Immacolatella

Diga Duca d. Abruzzi

Castel
dell'Ovo

a p o l i

Itinerari		
———————— 1°		—·—·—·— 4°
— — — — 2°		—··—··— 5°
············· 3°		—·—·—·— 6°
		———— 7°

Naples: Castel Nuovo

of new features: among them were the road that runs from the Palazzo degli Studi up to Capodimonte, the Via di Posìllipo, then known as Corso Napoleone, the Orto Botanico or botanical gardens, and the Osservatorio Astronomico, an observatory. During the second period of Bourbon rule (1815-1860) the Foro Ferdinandeo (now Piazza del Plebisicito) was opened, while along the Riviera di Chiaia the Villa Reale (now Villa Comunale) was built and Corso Maria Teresa (now Corso Vittorio Emanuele) was laid out. Gregorovius described that last-named avenue as one of the loveliest streets on earth. Between the end of the period of Bourbon rule and the earliest years of Italian unity (the population of Naples was already 450,000) Via del Duomo and Corso Garibaldi were built, cutting through the city from north to south, to provide air and a healthier setting in place of the dark and narrow alleys. But it was not until after the outbreak of cholera in 1884 that it was decided to demolish the lower area of the old city, with the creation of Via Depretis, Via Sanfelice, and the broad avenue of Corso Umberto I. Urban renovation continued for about 90 years, partly because of the massive destruction caused during WWII.

Between the two wars the city expanded into the new district known as the Rione Vasto near the central station, the Rione Vómero and the Rione Regina Elena to the west, the Rione Arenella and the Rione Materdei to the north, the Rione Luzzatti to the east, the Rione Speme on the slopes of Posìllipo, and Rione Fuorigrotta in the area of the Phlegraean Fields. The tunnels that ran under the hills of Posìllipo and Pizzo Falcone and the funiculars made communications among the various districts much easier. Urban renewal proceeded apace (Quartiere Carità), and along Via Diaz the new public buildings of the two decades of Fascism were erected. The chaotic reconstruction of the postwar period focused around the port, giving rise to the new Via Marina, and then developed an ultimately unsuccessful traffic center between Via Toledo, Via Medina, and Piazza del Plebiscito. In the meanwhile, the city continued to grow, on the hills of Posìllipo and in the Vómero-Arenella area, while economic trends and residential development pushed north (Secondigliano) and NE (Barra, Ponticelli). It was not until 1972 that the new urban zoning plan was approved, to replace the plan of 1939; there were no detailed plans for implementation, however, leading

to further delay and abuse. The recent classification of the historic center of Naples as a "world cultural heritage" status seems an official signal of a change in direction in the treatment of the "ancient heart" of the capital of Southern Italy.

Getting around. Traffic jams and regulations make driving in town problematic at best; part of the center of Naples is off limits to private vehicles. Of the five routes suggested, only the third and part of the first can be considered walking tours entirely; for the others, you may choose to use a taxi because public transport (the railway and the four cable railways for the Vòmero are an exception) is inadequate and unreliable.

From the harbor to the main museums

Besides maintaining their key role as the centers of political and administative power in the city, the Municipio (town hall), Castel Nuovo e Palazzo Reale bear interesting testimony to the history of Italy's southern capital. Via Toledo takes us back to the beginnings of Spanish rule; proceeding under another name, it then leads on to the Museo Archeologico Nazionale, commissioned by King Ferdinand IV to house the Farnese Collection and the archeological finds of the Herculaneum and Pompeii digs. The great Farnese Collection of art also led to the foundation of the city's second-largest museum, the Capodimonte Gallery, recently renovated and opened to the public.

Porto (*E4*). Naples' harbor is one of the most important in the Mediterranean; the Stazione Marittima (terminal; E5) is on the *Molo Angioino*; to the north is the Rococo *Immacolatella* building (D.A. Vaccaro, 18th c.), to the south is the Calata Beverello.

Piazza del Municipio (*D4*). At the far end of this lush green square is the 19th-c. *Palazzo del Municipio*, which incorporates the 16th-c. church of **S. Giacomo degli Spagnoli**, built at the behest of the viceroy Pedro da Toledo; inside, behind the main altar, is the *sepulcher** by G. da Nola (1539).

Castel Nuovo** (*E4; open 9-7, closed Sun.*) or Maschio Angioino (because it was built under Angevin rule; 1279-82) was entirely rebuilt at the behest of Alphonse I of Aragon (15th c.). It now has the massive 15th-c. appearance given it by Catalonian and

Tuscan architects, with a trapezoidal plan and round towers. The entrance, flanked by two towers, is the lovely **triumphal arch***, a celebrated 15th-c. creation by a number of sculptors, including F.Laurana; note in particular the relief of the triumph of Alphonse. Access to the courtyard, rebuilt in the 18th c., lies beyond the portal; on the far side, opposite the entrance, a 15th-c. outside staircase leads to the *Sala dei Baroni*, where local council sessions are held. *Interior*. The **Museo Civico** includes the **Cappella Palatina** (14th c.), the only surviving feature of the Angevin palace, with a Madonna by F. Laurana (1474). Sculptures from to the 14th and 15th c. and paintings from the 15th-18th c. are grouped in the two floors of the west wing of the castle; there are many notable works by 19th c. Neapolitan artists.

Palazzo Reale* (*E4*). It faces the church of S. Francesco di Paola, enclosing the NE side of the Piazza del Plebiscito. It was built by D. Fontana (1600-1602), restored and enlarged in 1743-48, and then subjected to further renovation and restoration. This was the palace of the Bourbons from 1734 to 1860. You can tour the Cortile del Fontana (the Fontana Courtyard, named after the architect) and the Scalone d'Onore (ceremonial stairway) in the atrium (at the base, note the bronze door* by the Parisian Guglielmo Monaco (1468) with reliefs, originally in the Castel Nuovo.) The **Museo dell'Appartamento Storico di Palazzo Reale**, or Historic Apartment (*open 9-7; closed Wed.*), has halls and rooms furnished with genuine 18th- and 19th-c. furniture and frescoes of the Neapolitan school (17th and 18th c.); it houses the Teatro di Corte (Court Theater; F.Fuga, 1768). The *Appartamento delle Feste* is occupied by the **Biblioteca Nazionale Vittorio Emanuele III**, a library where numerous manuscripts, including those of Tasso and Leopardi, and the burnt papyri* discovered in the Villa dei Papiri at Herculaneum, are preserved.

Piazza Plebiscito (*E4*). In this harmonious and monumental square, the elliptical curves of the colonnades join the pronaos of the sober Neo-Classic church of **S. Francesco di Paola** – built at the behest of King Ferdinand I to celebrate the return of the Bourbons (1815) – with its large cupola (P. Bianchi, 1817-46); of the two equestrian statues of Charles III and Ferdinand I, the former is by Canova.

Teatro S. Carlo (*E4*). This celebrated "temple of the opera" dates from 1737 but was rebuilt in Neo-Classic style during the 19th c. Directly opposite begins the *Galleria Umberto I*, dating from the end of the 19th c., a chief meeting spot for Neapolitans.

Via Toledo (*E-C4*). From Piazza Trieste e Trento (E4), extending up to the Museo Archeologico Nazionale, is the Via Toledo, the lively main thoroughfare of old Naples, the most popular strolling promenade. Note along this route the church of S. Nicola alla Carità (17th c.), the baroque *Palazzo Carafa di Maddaloni*, and the church of the *Spirito Santo* (C4), rebuilt in the 18th c.

Museo Archeologico Nazionale** (*C4; open 9-8; closed Tue.*). Installed in a building that was once a cavalry barracks and later the headquarters of the University, the Museo Archeologico is one of the world's leading archeological museums. Roman replicas of Greek sculpture, unearthed in the cities buried by the eruption of Mt. Vesuvius, were one of the great sources of knowledge of Greek art prior to the discovery of the few, rare originals; mosaics and paintings and minor collections complete the wonderful array of objects from Greco-Roman classical antiquity. The number of works is enormous, and they are arranged in over a hundred halls.

Among the **marble sculptures****, to mention only the most important: the Tyrannicides*, a funerary stele* from the 5th c. B.C.; an Athena* clearly derived from the work of Phidias; Eurydice and Hermes**, an Augustan-period copy of an original from the school of Phidias; the Aphrodite of the Gardens*; an excellent copy of the renowned **Doriforo****, or Offering bearer, by Polyclitus; a Diomedes from Cumae*; the Palestrita*; the Venus Callipige* from a Hellenistic original, a bronze statuette of Herakles; the colossal **Farnese Hercules***; torsos of Ares* and Aphrodite*; a Psyche* from Capua; a Venus from Capua*; the renowned **Farnese Bull****, the largest surviving group of marble statuary from antiquity; the Diana Ephesina*; a Seated Matron,* believed to depict Agrippina; a bust of Caracalla*; a bronze horse head, possibly dating from the 3rd c. B.C., once attributed to Donatello; the Augustus of Fondi*; a bust of Homer*; a statuette of a **Dancing Faun*** from Pompeii; the renowned sculptures of the Sleeping Satyr*, the Drunken Silene*, and Hermes Resting*; a portrait said to be of Seneca*; and, last but not least, the Farnese Atlas*, a Hellenistic sculpture.

Among the **paintings and mosaics***, aside from the world-renowned **Battle of Alexander versus Darius****, a mosaic based upon an Alexandrian painting, of unique historical and artistic worth, there are also the other major mosaics* from Pompeii, such as the Strolling Musicians*, Plato and His Disciples in the Gardens of Academe*, a bust of a woman* and a Cat Biting a Quail*; a collection of paintings*, including murals from Pompeii, Herculaneum, and Stabia, the most notable items of which are a group of women performing a funerary dance* from Ruvo, women playing astragalomacy* (divination with small bones or dice) in the Neo-Attic style, and Pasquius Proculus with his wife.

A special section contains works of art and other objects unearthed in the 18th c. at Herculaneum in the **Villa dei Papiri***.

Also note the collection of **valuables**, among which two gladiatorial helmets*, a vase in dark-blue glass*, a table of 115 pieces from the Casa del Menandro (House of Menander) in Pompeii, and the Tazza Farnese**, a cup in sardonyx from the Alexandrian school.

The exquisite collection of Campanian, Apulian, Lucanian, Etruscan, and Attic vases* can only be seen in part. The **Sale del Tempio di Iside** (Temple of Isis Halls) are rooms arranged to gather frescoes and archeological finds discovered in Pompeii in 1764-66.

Palazzo Reale di Capodimonte* (*A4*). On the site of what used to be a small village, King Charles of Bourbon decided to open the famous porcelain factory in 1739. A building to contain the art collections inherited from his mother, Elisabetta Farnese, was also established there. The manufactory was operative for just 20 years, while the palazzo, commissioned in 1734, has housed the Museo e Gallerie di Capodimonte since 1957. The park is also worth a visit.

Museo e Gallerie Nazionali di Capodimonte** (*A4; open 8:30-7; closed Mon.*). The Gallerie Nazionali (art galleries) are one of the most versatile and significant collections of paintings in Italy, formed mainly by the Farnese collection. Among the masterpieces to be seen here: St. Louis of Toulouse Crowns His Brother Robert of Anjou King of Naples** by Simone Martini; the **Crucifixion**** by Masaccio; the **Transfiguration**** by G. Bellini; the Zingarella**, or Gypsy Girl, by Correggio; Pope Paul III with His Nephews Ottavio and Alessandro Farnese** by Titian; the Parable of the Blind Men* by P. Bruegel; the **Flagellation**** by Caravaggio. Also worthy of note are the: Galleria dell'Ottocento, or Gallery of the 19th c., with numerous major works by Neapolitan painters; the Appartamento Storico e Museo – or Historic Apartment and Museum – with a collection of porcelain and majolica, the vast Collezione De Ciccio*, the David* by Pollaiuolo, and the Salottino di Porcellana** (1757-59), a masterpiece of porcelain produced by the factory of Capodimonte, from the palace of Portici.

In the handsome **park** stands the Fabbrica di Porcellane di Capodimonte (porcelain factory; active from 1743 to 1759).

Old Naples

This route covers the heart of the city and the straight district of "Spaccanapoli". Some of the city's most important monuments are located in this area. Apart from renowned churches like S. Chiara and S. Domenico Maggiore, veritable treasure troves of art, the area features some more typical characteristics of the city: jewelry shops, the Christmas crèche workshops in Via San Gregorio Armeno, and the picturesque neighbourhood of Forcella.

Incoronata (*D4*). This church stands along the Via Medina. In its two Gothic aisles, it features frescoes from the 14th-15th c.

S. Maria la Nova (*D4*). Along Via Monteoliveto, this 15th-c. church has two Renaissance cloisters; farther on, the **Palazzo Gravina*** (*D4*) is built in the Tuscan Renaissance style.

S. Anna dei Lombardi (*D4*). The nearby church of S. Anna dei Lombardi* can be considered a museum of Renaissance sculpture. Among other things are the marble altarpiece by B. da Maiano (1489); the Pietà in terracotta by G. Mazzoni (1492); a Manger and Saints* by A. Rossellino (1475); the Monument to Maria of Aragon* by A. Rossellino and B. da Maiano; frescoes by G. Vasari

Naples: Palazzo Reale di Capodimonte

and inlaid stalls* in the Old Sacristy.

Spaccanapoli (Via B. Croce and Via S. Biagio dei Librai) runs along an ancient "decumanus." Following this route, you will pass a number of renowned churches and old palazzi, including Palazzo Filomarino, where the philosopher Benedetto Croce lived and died.

Gesù Nuovo (*C4*). It is a fine example of Neapolitan Baroque, especially in the interior, with its rich colored marble decoration.

S. Chiara* (*C4*). It was rebuilt in the original style (1310-28), of clear Provençal Gothic inspiration and is one of the foremost monuments of medieval Naples. Inside, note the tomb of Marie de Valois* by Tino di Camaino and assistants (1333-38), and fragments of the funerary monument of Robert I Anjou by G. and P. Bertini from Florence (1343-45); the inscription "Cernite Robertum regem virtute refertum" is said to have been dictated by the poet Petrarch, it comments on the arts of the Trivium and Quadrivium, or pillars of Medieval Scholasticism, who are shown watching over the funerary statue of the dead king. Adjacent are the convent of the Minorites, with a handsome portal* leading into the choir and the **Chiostro maiolicato delle Clarisse**** (*open 9:30-1 and 2:30-5:30; Sun., 9:30-1*), a spacious cloister containing a splendid garden from 1742 at its center; the outside wall of the garden, the seats and the piers are covered with marvelous colored majolica*, hence the name.

S. Domenico Maggiore* (*C4*). In the convent adjacent to the church, Thomas Aquinas once taught and both Pontano and Giordano Bruno studied. Inside the church are frescoes attributed to Cavallini (circa 1308) and, in the Cappellone del Crocifisso a Crucifix* on panel from the 13th c., which supposedly spoke to St. Thomas, and a Deposition attributed to Colantonio.

Cappella Sansevero (*C4; open Jul.-Oct., 10-7; Nov.-Jun., 10-5; Sun. and holidays, 10-1:30; closed Tue.*). With 18th-c. decoration of colored marble, it is celebrated for the virtuoso statues of Disinganno (Disillusionment, by Queirolo), Pudicizia (Modesty, by A. Corradini) and **Christ Veiled*** (G. Sammartino, 1735).

S. Angelo a Nilo (*C4*). Known also as the "Cappella Brancaccio," it is a church in a little square with an ancient statue of the god of the River Nile. It contains the sepulcher of Rinaldo Cardinal Brancaccio*, by Donatello, Michelozzo, and Pagno di Lapo Portigiani (1426-28).

less interesting is the **Via dei Tribunali**, anoth-
of the ancient "decumani." S. Paolo Maggiore (C5)
583-1603) is a church set high atop a stairway in
e Piazzetta S. Gaetano, the site of the ancient Gre-
-Roman Forum; the interior is richly decorated
th marble inlay and frescoes.

Lorenzo Maggiore** (C5). One of the most im-
ortant medieval Neapolitan churches. The first
urch was built in the 6th c. on top of Roman struc-
res which have only recently been brought to light
ring excavations; this same church was then reilt at the express wish of Charles I and Charles II
1270-75. Of the Baroque renovation, only the fa-
de (1742) remains. The **interior** of this church is
Provençal Gothic inspiration; note the Gothic sep-
cher of Catherine of Austria* by Tino di Camaino
d assistants. From the 18th-c. cloister you can en-
r an area of Greek, Roman, and medieval archeo-
gical excavations (open 9-1).

erolamini (C5). The interior of the church of the
rolamini (16th-18th c.) is an interesting compos-
e example of Baroque decoration, though it is bad-
damaged; adjacent to the main cloister is a small
nacoteca (picture gallery; open 9:30-1; closed
n.).

o Monte della Misericordia (C5). Such were
e confraternity tasks (corporal works of mercy)
at, when the building was undergoing construc-
on (1658), the architect was asked to carve out a
ace for a portico in the lower part of the facade
here the needy could be welcomed. In the 17th-
church are sculptures by A. Falcone and paintgs by B. Caracciolo, L. Giordano, and the splendid
cts of Mercy** by Caravaggio; the adjacent *Pina-
oteca*, or art gallery (open by request, tel.
81446944), includes paintings from the Neapoli-
n school of the Pio Monte della Misericordia.

ia del Duomo follows an ancient "cardo" of the
reco-Roman city. The Renaissance **Palazzo Como***
C5; 1460-90), also called "Cuomo", possibly designed
y G. da Maiano, is the site of the **Museo Civico
aetano Filangieri** (soon to be reopened; tel.
81203175), with an estimable collection of
eapolitan paintings, Italian and Spanish arms and
rmor (16th-18th c.), European and Oriental ce-
mics and porcelain, and 16th-c. embroideries.

Giorgio Maggiore (C5). Rebuilt in the 17th c.
y C. Fanzago, the church still preserves, at the enance, the apse of the early Christian building, dat-
g from the 4th-5th c.

he Duomo** (C5) still maintains the soaring 13th-
, Gothic interior, with pointed arches and piers,
gainst which 110 ancient columns have been
laced. The third chapel in the right aisle is the 17th-
, **Cappella del Tesoro di S. Gennaro***, where the
reasury of St. Januarius is kept. It features a bronze
ate by Fanzago, and frescoes by Domenichino and
anfranco, a silver altar frontal dating from 1695, sil-
er statues of the Saint and the other patron saints
f Naples, little flagons of miracle-working blood, and
he saint's cranium, in a 14th-c. French reliquary. The
ssumption of the Virgin* by Perugino and assistants

is in the second chapel in the right transept; frescoes
dating from the late 13th-16th c., a mosaic floor from
the 13th c., a Sienese polyptych from the 14th c. and
the two tombs of the Minutolo family are in the **Cappella Minutolo**** (to the right of the presbytery);
a large 14th-c. fresco with a Tree of Jesse is in the
second chapel in the left transept. From the left aisle,
you can descend to the church of **S. Restituta**, the
first Christian basilica in Naples (4th c.); in the 5th-
c. **Baptistery,** fragments of original mosaics*; in the
sixth chapel in the left aisle, Virgin and Saints, in mosaic, by Lello da Orvieto (1322).

S. Maria di Donnaregina (B5). There are two
churches named S. Maria di Donnaregina*: the **Nuova** (or new) is Baroque (1649), and has an interior
frescoed and decorated with polychrome marble;
the **Vecchia** (or old) is an important medieval Franciscan Gothic monument, and contains the sepulcher of Mary, Queen of Hungary* by Tino di Camaino and G. Primario (1326) and, in the nuns'
choir, frescoes* from the first half of the 14th c., by
F. Rusuti and others.

Castel Capuano (C5). At the end of Via dei Tribunali, this castle is also known as the Vicaria (C5);
built by the Normans and enlarged by the Swabians,
it was the royal palace until the 15th c.

Porta Capuana* (B5), built in 1484 to a plan by
G. da Maiano, is one of the great masterpieces of the
Renaissance.

S. Giovanni a Carbonara* (B5), which stands
high atop an 18th-c. staircase, is a church that was
founded in 1343, rebuilt at the beginning of the 15th
c., and then modified and enlarged. Especially noteworthy are the sculptures, such as the Monumento
Miroballo* (16th c.), the monument to King Ladis-
laus* (1428) and the sepulcher of Sergianni Carac-
ciolo*. Note also the **Cappella Caracciolo di Vico**, a Renaissance masterpiece.

The Vòmero

This district may be considered a city within the
city; it is hard to believe that the hill slopes were
once dotted with farmhouses, patrician residences
and villas.

Piazza Vanvitelli (D2). The very center of a district which developed at the end of the 19th c. Once
characterized by handsome Art Nouveau architecture, its appearance is that of an anonymous middle-
class district, spoilt by real estate speculation.

Villa La Floridiana* (D2). King Ferdinand I gave
to his morganatic wife, Lucia Partanna, Duchess of
Floridia, the villa (1817-19) now known as La Floridiana. The magnificent park is famous for its abundance of splendid camelias; the Neo-Classic mansion houses the **Museo Nazionale della Ceramica Duca di Martina*** (open 9-2; closed Mon.), an
exquisite collection of porcelain and majolica from
the main factories of Europe and the East.

Castel S. Elmo (D3; open 8:30-7:30; closed Mon.).
A massive star-shaped fortress, rebuilt in the 16th c.

Naples: Certosa di S. Martino

It later became a prison (in 1799 revolutionaries were jailed here, as were many patriots of the Risorgimento). Splendid view** over the city and gulf from the terraces.

Certosa di S. Martino★★ (*D3; open 8:30-7:30; closed Mon.*). It is the genius of C. Fanzago which gave the Certosa di S. Martino, a charterhouse on a ridge of the Vòmero hill, its present-day aspect, in the most complete and exquisite 17th-c. Neapolitan Baroque. **The church**★, glittering with marble inlays, is itself a gallery of 17th-c. Neapolitan painting. You then pass through the interesting area of the convent; from the square in front of the Certosa, splendid panoramic view★.

Inside the Certosa is the **Museo Nazionale di S. Martino**★★ (*open same hours as the Certosa*). The museum includes: historical souvenirs and memorabilia of the Kingdom of Naples, the Neapolitan topography section, the section of feasts and costumes, the crèche section with the large Cuciniello Crèche★ and, across the main cloister★, the lavish Pinacoteca, or art gallery, the sculpture section, and the section of applied arts and memorabilia of the Certosa.

The Riviera

The legendary view of Naples was celebrated by painters in the 18th c., only to be followed by photographs and postcards in the 19th c. In touring this part of the Gulf of Naples – perhaps by car along the Posìllipo hill – one can understand why people used to say "Once you have seen Naples, you can die in peace."

S. Lucia (*E-F4*). Take Via N. Sauro, the first stretch of the magnificent beachfront promenade, or Lungomare, as far as Mergellina, and you will arrive at the

Porto di S. Lucia with its quay that leads to the Bo go Marinaro (fishing village); at the end of Via Sauro, note the *Fontana dell'Immacolatella* (*F4*) Baroque fountain.

Castel dell'Ovo (*F4?*). It was built in the 12th (though its current appearance dates from 1691) c the site of a villa that once belonged to Lucullus, great general of ancient Rome.

Riviera di Chiaia (*E2-3*). This elegant road use to be the site of the old Neapolitan promenade, f mous for its views and 17th-19th-c. houses, impo tant examples of which, especially in the openir stretch, still remain.

Villa Pignatelli (*E2; open 8:30-2; closed Mon.*). Su rounded by a beautiful garden, it houses the **Muse Principe Diego Aragona Pignatelli Cortes**, whic still preserves the flavor of the original patrician re idence; worthy of note are the large araucarias in th garden, as well as the *Museo delle Carrozze* (Mus um of Carriages).

Villa Comunale (*E 2-3*). The gardens of this m nicipal villa separate the Riviera di Chiaia from th beachfront promenade, or Lungomare of Via Cara ciolo, and enclose the **Stazione Zoologica** with th **Acquario**★ (Aquarium; *E2; open Mar.-Oct., 9-6, Sur 9:30-7:30; Nov.-Feb., 9-5; Sun., 9-2; closed Mon.*).

Piedigrotta (*E-F1*). The Piedigrotta district (s called because it extends from the tunnel – or "grota" – dug in the 1st c. B.C. underneath the hill of Pos lipo) features the church of S. Maria di Piedigrot (*F1*), originally built in the 13th c., with a Sienes wooden Madonna from the 14th c.

Parco Virgiliano (*F1*). Here you can visit the tom of Giacomo Leopardi and the so-called tomb of Vi gil, which was actually a Roman dovecote.

Mergellina (*F1*). Continuing along Via Caracciol you will reach one of the most enchanting sites i Naples: the inlet of Mergellina. In **S. Maria del Pa to** is the tomb of the Neapolitan Humanist poet Ja copo Sannazaro and the famous "Diavolo di Merge lina," a panel from the 16th c. showing St. Michae besting the Devil.

Posìllipo.★ A crossroads along the panoramic Vi di Posìllipo★ is the starting point for promenade and walks through the enchanting "region" of Posi lipo★, which takes its name from the Greek words fo "assuaging pain or grief." The Via di Posìllipo will tak you to Capo di Posìllipo, with a group of houses b the sea, and a little marina; to the little fishing villag of **Marechiaro**, high over the sea, where a plaqu on a house on a cliff indicates the "fenesta ca lu cive", the window in the famous song by Salvator Di Giacomo. Lastly, on the Pozzuoli shore, on the **is land of Nisida**, is the ancient volcanic crater, joine to the mainland by a breakwater bridge.

The remarkable vistas and views in this area are a of particular note, but perhaps the finest panora ma★★ of Naples is the one from the Belvedere c the **Eremo dei Camàldoli** (Hermitage of the Camaldolites, elev. 458 m, the highest point in th Campi Flegrei, or Phlegrean Fields, to the NW of th river; exit from A1).

Noto*

Elev. 152 m, pop. 21,663; Sicilia (Sicily), province of Siracusa. Set in a landscape of quarries and marshes, but also surrounded by citrus groves, almond orchards, and vineyards, Noto is a remarkable town, rebuilt in a lavish Baroque style following the ravages of the earthquake of 1693.

Places of interest. Corso Vittorio Emanuele.* The main street of Noto, which widens into three squares, from which monumental staircases ascend.
Piazza Immacolata. If you enter town from the Porta Nazionale, the first of these three squares is the Piazza Immacolata, with a stairway up to the church of **S. Francesco all'Immacolata** and the convent of the *Santissimo Salvatore.*
Museo Civico (*closed for restoration; tel. 0931836462*). In the above-mentioned convent is the town museum, which comprises an archeological section, with prehistoric and Greek finds, as well as a modern section.
Piazza del Municipio. In this square stands the elegant **Palazzo Ducezio*** (V. Sinatra, 18th c.) and the staircase that climbs up to the **Cattedrale**, with a spectacular 18th-c. facade; the interior is closed to the public because of the collapse of the dome in March 1996.
Piazza XVI Maggio. Continuing along the Corso, you will see this square, after the church of the *Collegio*; note the church of *S. Domenico.*
Santissimo Crocifisso. In the high part of Noto, this Baroque church contains a Virgin with Child* by F. Laurana (1471).

Orvieto*

Elev. 325 m, pop. 20,703; Umbria, province of Terni. The bluff of yellowish tufa on which Orvieto is built rises like a shoal, at the head of the green valley of the Paglia. An island in time, just as it may long ago have been an island in a gulf along the Tyrrhenian coast, Orvieto soars above the surrounding countryside. L. Maitani was summoned from Siena in 1290 when the walls of the Cathedral seemed about to collapse; he repaired them and began to design the remarkable facade, which was later completed by A. Pisano and A. Orcagna. The golden Gothic "triptych" of the facade should be seen from a distance, glittering in the sunset – words hardly suffice to describe it.

Historical note. With the Latin name of "Urbs Vetus," or old city, Orvieto is barely mentioned in the High Middle Ages in the writings of Paulus Diaconus and St. Gregory the Great. Whatever the ancient name of Orvieto, it certainly was a flourishing Etruscan town between the 7th-3rd c. B.C. In the 11th-12th c. the city developed a Communal government and was recognized in 1157 by the pope. Orvieto

tried to expand its rule over surrounding territory, but the civil factions of Guelphs and Ghibellines produced strife here, as they did in much of 13th-c. Italy. Romanesque architecture thrived: the churches of S. Andrea and S. Giovenale, the various towers, and the spectacular Palazzo del Popolo. A little later, the Gothic style pervaded Orvieto, in the churches of S. Francesco and S. Domenico, the Palazzo Papale, and above all, the Duomo, a masterpiece of Italian Gothic. Even then, Orvieto – which of course never required walls – occupied virtually all of the surface of the tufa plateau. Civil discord was quashed in 1354 by Cardinal Albornoz, who recognized Orvieto's government but built the fortress of the Rocca and reaffirmed the dedication of the town to the aims of the Church. As the quarrels raged between popes and anti-popes, between Rome and Avignon, Orvieto was tossed among outside rulers, but in 1448 it came under the rule of Pope Nicholas V, and its hectic medieval history subsided into order. The remarkable well, or Pozzo di S. Patrizio, was built, as were various 16th-c. palazzi. All modern expansion of the city has taken place at the foot of the plateau.

Getting around. We suggest leaving your car in one of the parking areas outside of town, and taking a bus into Orvieto. The cableway restored to service in 1990 links the railway station with Piazzale Cahen.

Places of interest. Piazzale Cahen. Across from the Rocca (see below), it can be reached from the railway station via the *cableway*, built in 1880 and recently restored to service. Near the square is the ancient gate known as *Porta Postierla.*
Rocca. This fortress was built at the orders of Cardinal Albornoz (1364), destroyed by the townspeople in 1390, and rebuilt in 1450. Used as a fort until the 18th c., it is now a park (fine view of the Paglia Valley). Visit the tufa ruins of the Etruscan **Tempio del Belvedere**, late 5th c. B.C.
Pozzo di S. Patrizio.* *Open: Oct.-Mar., 10-6; Apr.-Sep., 10-7.* This well, a unique and daring piece of architecture, was built, along with other cisterns and wells, at the order of Pope Clement VII after the Sack of Rome, to ensure that Orvieto would have an adequate water supply during a siege. Begun by A. da Sangallo the Younger in 1528, it was completed in 1537. It comprises a cylindrical chamber (diameter 13 m) that drops to a depth of 62 m; around it are two broad staircases, stacked in a double spiral, illuminated by 72 large windows along their length. In this way, men and mules could efficiently descend and climb with loads of water.
Corso Cavour. This main street winds its way through the center of Orvieto, lined with 16th-c. palazzi and medieval houses. At the beginning, a small lane on the right leads to the 13th-c. church of *S. Maria dei Servi*, entirely rebuilt in Neo-Classic style. On the left is the Romanesque church of **S. Stefano**, and on the left, the medieval church of *S. Angelo*, one of Orvieto's oldest, entirely rebuilt in

1828. A little further on, facing the *Teatro Mancinelli* (1864), is the 16th-c. facade of *Palazzo Petrucci*, begun, but not finished, by M. Sanmicheli.

Torre Civica. This medieval tower is 42 m high, and is topped by a bell, cast in 1316 for Palazzo del Popolo, with the 24 symbols of the Arts. At the base lies Via del Duomo. Next to it is **Palazzo dei Sette**, built around 1300, partly rebuilt in the 16th c., and now used as a cultural center.

Piazza del Duomo. This cozy square with its odd shape and proportions emphasizes the massive Duomo. The northern end of the square is bounded by *low medieval houses*; at the corner with Via del Duomo stands the *Torre del Maurizio* (1349), a tower whose name derives from the bronze figure that strikes the hours, originally designed to ensure steady work on the Duomo. Across the little square is Palazzo Faina, with the Museo Civico; to the right of the Duomo is Palazzo Soliano, site of the Museo dell'Opera del Duomo and the Museo Emilio Greco (see below).

Duomo.** Begun in 1290 and carried on (1308-30) by L. Maitani, who worked especially on the facade and the terminal section, this cathedral is certainly one of the finest creations of Italian Gothic architecture. The *facade*, which was completed in the 16th c., is shaped like an immense triptych, glowing and glittering with polychrome marble, statuary, and mosaics (it was redone in the 17th-18th c.). The central portal and the rose window* – by A. Orcagna – are particularly noteworthy. Also note the statues of prophets and apostles. The four pilasters that frame the portals are lined with **reliefs**** based on the Bible, by L. Maitani and assistants (early 14th c.); the same artists made the bronze symbols of the Evangelists above the pilasters and the group in the lunette over the central portal.

In the majestic **interior** (*open 7:30-12:45 and 2:30-7:15*) the *nave and aisles* are still Romanesque, while the transept and presbytery are Gothic in style. Note the baptismal font and holy-water stoups, wrought-iron, and reliefs by R. and F. da Montelupo. At the end of the right arm of the *transept* is the early 15th-c. *Cappella Nuova*, renowned for the **frescoes of the End of the World**** by Signorelli. Originally begun by Fra' Angelico (1477), with the help of B. Gozzoli, G. d'Antonio Fiorentino, and G. da Poli, the frescoes – outstanding masterpieces of Italian art history – were completed by Signorelli (1477-1504) with the theme of the Last Judgment. In the vault, the prophets shown with Christ the Judge are by Fra' Angelico and helpers, 1447; in the lunette, on the left, in the scene of the Antichrist preaching, the two figures in black are portraits of Signorelli and Fra' Angelico; also note the figures of poets from Homer to Dante. The raised *presbytery* is decorated with 2500 sq. m of frescoes by U. di Prete Ilario (1370-80), unusual in both size and subject (Glory of Mary). Note the majestic inlaid wooden choir* by G. Ammannati (1331-40). On the right wall of the left arm of the transept is a panel*, 1320, by L. Memmi. On the altar, a marble Gothic taber-

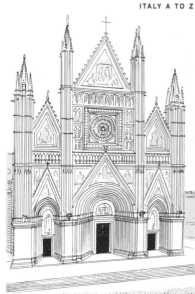

Orvieto: Duomo

nacle (1358) contains a famed reliquary** with a blood-stained cloth, supposedly from a host that bled to confound a Bohemian priest doubtful about the dogma of Transubstantiation (the Mass of Bolsena, 1263). The reliquary, by the Sienese U. di Vieri (1338), is a masterpiece of Italian goldwork. Nearby is a fresco* by G. da Fabriano (1425).

Palazzo Faina. *Open 31 Mar.-28 Sep., 10-1 and 2-6; 29 Sep.-30 Mar. (closed Mon.), 10-1 and 2:30-5.* This 19th-c. palazzo opposite the Duomo houses the *Raccolta Archeologica Civica* and the **Museo Claudio Faina**, comprising the city's collection and the archeological collections of Count Claudio Faina, a gift to Orvieto. Among the more notable items: 6th-/4th-c. B.C. Attic vases*, and a 4th-c. B.C. Etruscan sarcophagus* with traces of polychrome paint.

Palazzo Soliano.* This immense austere building made of tufa, with a large exterior staircase and three-light mullioned windows, was built at the behest of Pope Boniface VIII (1297-1304); the upper section was left unfinished, and was completed in the 16th c. The Guelph-style crenelations date from the late 19th-c. Upstairs, it will permanently house part of the Museo dell'Opera del Duomo* (see below). The ground floor houses the **Museo Emilio Greco** (*open Tue.-Sun., Apr.-Sep., 10-7; Oct.-Mar., 10-6*) opened in 1991; it features sculpture and paintings, donated by the artist himself (1947-present). Nearby, the Manneristi *Palazzo Buzi* (1580), by I. Scalza.

Museo dell'Opera del Duomo.* The museum has fine collections of sculpture, painting, liturgical objects, jewelry, largely from the Cathedral and other churches of the diocese. Palazzo Soliano will house the Renaissance section, while the medieval one is already in **Palazzo Papale**, a complex of three buildings from the 13th c., on the right-hand side of the Duomo. Among the artists whose work is present in this museum: C. di Marcovaldo, S. Martini, L. Signorelli, A. Pisano, L. Maitani; reliquary of S. Savino* by U. di Vieri and V. di Lando.

Museo Archeologico Nazionale. *Open 8:30-7:30; tel. 0763341039.* This archeological museum is also located in the Palazzo Papale, and comprises state collections and the collections of the Opera del Duomo, which document the process of its construction. Note the Etruscan funerary furnishings and the frescoes from the necropolis of Settecamini, with life-size figures; also, intact Etruscan suit of armor.

Parco delle Grotte. *Guided tours available by request at the Società Speleotecnica, tel. 0763344891.* The bluff of Orvieto is made largely of tufa, and over the centuries countless chambers have been carved into the soft stone; they are referred to as the "Grotte," or caves. They constitute a sort of underground city, now being studied systematically for the first time. An intricate network of passages and galleries links the many cavities, dating from different eras, and built for different purposes. The Etruscans built the narrow oval tunnels, storerooms for crops, and a number of very deep wells, along with more than 100 cisterns. In the Middle Ages, the "butti" were dug and used to toss rubbish in; the cisterns with grey plaster, the furnaces, and the ruins of Orvieto's first aqueduct also date from the Middle Ages. Many rooms date from the Renaissance as well. The tours are limited to the safest and most accessible areas.

S. Francesco. Founded in 1240 at the highest point in Orvieto, the walls and facade are original (note the rose windows and portal). Inside is a 14th-c. wooden Crucifix.

S. Lorenzo de' Arari. This little 13th-c. church has a lovely interior, with 14th-c. frescoes; the main altar features an Etruscan panel and a 12th-c. ciborium. Nearby is the *Porta Romana* (1822), built on the site of the ancient *Porta Pertusa* (ruins); from the park area, with the medieval *Palazzo Medici*, fine view of the valley of the Povero River, spanned by the medieval aqueduct. If you skirt the western edge of the bluff, you will reach the octagonal church of *S. Giovanni*; inside a 14th-c. fresco, and, in the adjacent convent, a fine Renaissance cloister.

S. Giovenale. This church was founded in 1004. It has a simple Romanesque facade and fortified bell tower. The interior, with tufa columns, was modified in the 13th c.; note fragments of 13th-c. frescoes, and the carved altarpiece from 1170. Nearby, charming medieval homes and the 13th-c. former church of *S. Agostino*, with a Baroque interior. The Museo della Ceramica, or Museum of Ceramics, will be installed here.

Via Malabranca. This handsome road runs along a slope on the surface of the bluff. At n. 14-18, notable old houses; at n. 22, the Renaissance *Palazzo Simoncelli* (by B. Rossellino); at n. 15, the 16th-c. *Palazzo Caravajal*. Turn onto **Via della Cava**, running downhill between rows of medieval houses to Porta Maggiore. Next to the church of *Madonna della Cava*, note the *well*, a deep cylinder drilled into the tufa, used from 1428 to 1546.

Piazza della Repubblica. The center of Orvieto ever since the Middle Ages, this square is dominated by the long facade of the 16th-c. *Palazzo Comunale*, by I. Scalza; on the same square is the simple facade of the 11th-c. church of **S. Andrea*,** with a **12-sided tower**. The portico on the left side was built during restoration (1926-30). The interior has fragments of 14th-c. frescoes; beneath the church, Villanovan and Etruscan remains and 6th-c. mosaic floors.

Palazzo del Popolo.** Begun around 1250, with a huge meeting hall over an open loggia, this building was enlarged at the end of the 13th c. with the addition of the residence of the Capitano del Popolo – equivalent to mayor – and a bell tower. As the politics of Orvieto changed, this building fell into neglect, and was used variously as a prison, workshop, warehouse, and silo. Restored in recent years (1987-90), it has recently been used for conferences and meetings; digs have uncovered Etruscan temples, a medieval aqueduct, and a large cistern. In the upper hall, note the 14th-c. frescoes. On the square is the little church of *S. Rocco*, built by M. Sanmicheli around 1525, as well as the 16th-c. *Palazzo Simoncelli*.

S. Domenico. This church, built in 1264, was drastically amputated in 1934; only the transept survived. Inside, note the monument to Cardinal Braye*, by A. di Cambio (1285); beneath the apse is a fine chapel by M. Sanmicheli.

Excursion. Necropoli del Crocifisso del Tufo (*open 8:30-7:30; winter, until 6:30*). At 1.5 km on the SS 71 road is this Etruscan necropolis dating from the 6th-c. B.C. and still quite orderly, with tombs lined up along two parallel roads.

Òstia Antica*

Elev. 2 m; Lazio (Latium), province and township of Rome. The Tiber flows past the medieval village, near the Castello – the castle, Renaissance in style, military in purpose – built by B. Pontelli, at the behest of Cardinal Giuliano della Rovere (later Pope Julius II). Nearby are the silent tombs, baths, temples, theaters, and forum of the port of ancient Rome, ruins as startling as those of Pompeii and Herculaneum.

Historical note. In 1575 flooding shifted the course of the Tiber, which once flowed past the Castello, moving it northward; for centuries, however, the deposits carried by the river had been pushing the seashore out, some 4 m per year. It is now 6 km away. Archeologists tell us that Òstia was founded in the early 4th c. B.C., a small camp 400 m from the ancient beach. By the 1st c. B.C., Òstia was given a new set of walls about 2.5 km in circumference. The Empire produced an even larger, thriving port city. Claudius built a new harbor, Trajan enlarged it, establishing a second city, Portus, that would in time supplant Òstia. The capital of the Empire moved

275

from Rome to Constantinople; the Goths ravaged Òstia, and of a once mighty city of 100,000, nothing remained but haunted ruins. Two industries now flourish here: an incessant series of archeological digs, and a steady flow of fascinated sightseers.

Places of interest. Castello di Giulio II. *Open Tue.-Sun., 9-1; Tue. and Thu. also 2:30-5 (summer) or 2:30-4:30 (winter).* Standing in the heart of the 15th-c. Rocca, or fortress, the castle was built in 1483-86 by B. Pontelli. Triangular in plan, it features two mighty circular towers and a pentagonal keep. In the adjacent Palazzo Episcopale, a series of frescoes* by B. Peruzzi (1508-1513) were found in 1977-79.

Via Ostiense. The ancient road from Rome to the port is the modern entrance to the **Scavi di Òstia Antica** (archeological site; *open summer, 9-6 or 7; winter 9-4; closed Mon.*).

Terme di Nettuno. These baths, built by Hadrian and adorned with fine mosaics, stand near the *barracks of the "Vigiles"*, or police, dating from the same period.

Teatro.* ** The original structure of the theater was built under Agrippa (1st c. B.C.), but a later, brick structure dates from A.D. 196. The tiers offer an excellent view* of the digs. Behind the proscenium extends the *Piazzale delle Corporazioni**, designed during Augustan times as a sort of lobby for intermissions: the double portico, rebuilt under Hadrian, contains the mosaics donated by various guilds. To the west the *Mitreo dei Sette Cieli*, or Mithreum of the Seven Heavens, one of 17 sanctuaries consecrated to Mithras in the 2nd-3rd c., and *four little temples* dedicated to the female deities that protected commerce in the early 1st c. B.C.

Via della Casa di Diana. A street lined with multi-storey apartment buildings; at the end is a 3rd-c. *"thermopolium"* (cafeteria), with counter, sinks, and a fresco advertising food and beverages.

Museo Ostiense* *(for information tel. 0656358099).* In the 11 halls of the 15th-c. *Casone del Sale*, this museum features the finest material found in 40 years of digs. Of particular note are the sarcophagi, Greek statuary, busts of emperors (especially Trajan), paintings, and mosaics.

Foro. Òstia's political center, this Forum was given the appearance we see today under Hadrian's rule. Overlooking it are: the *Capitolium*, Òstia's main temple (staircase and high podium survive); the houses of the Triclinia, with the *Terme del Foro*, the baths opened under Antoninus Pius and used till the 5th c.; the *Tempio di Roma e Augusto* (a temple of which only a statue of Roma and part of the pediment with a Winged Victory survive); the *Basilica Giudiziaria* built by Domitian or Trajan; to its right is a *round 3rd-c. temple*, for the emperor cult.

Via della Foce. Starting from the "Bivio del Castrum," this road runs past the "*Horrea Epagathiana*," a 2nd-c. warehouse, near the late Empire *Domus di Amore e Psiche*; nearby stand many popular apartment *houses* and baths (*Caseggiato di Serapide, Casette Tipo, Caseggiato degli Aurighi, Terme della*

Trinacria, and *Terme dei Sette Sapienti*). The road ends at the *Palazzo Imperiale*.

Insula delle Muse. One of the richest residential complexes to survive from the middle Empire, it lie in a part of Òstia that was rebuilt under Hadrian. Note the *Case a Giardino*, with 8 apartments sharing a "yard"; the *Porta Marina (C2)*, where the main street hit the ancient coastline; and the oldest **Synagogue*** in the West (1st c.).

Schola del Traiano. This was the headquarters of the guild of shipbuilders; it takes its name from a statue of Trajan found here.

Cardine Massimo. Running roughly north to south this was the main street of Òstia; nearby is the *Campo della Magna Mater*, a square dedicated to one of the oldest cults in the Roman world.

Domus della Fortuna Annonaria. Aristocratic home dating from the Late Empire; nearby is a Roman laundry, with original *dyeing vats*.

Padua / Padova*

Elev. 12 m, pop. 211,391; Veneto, provincial capital. Padua has an irregular urban layout, in which the thread of history is tangled and difficult to read, among the long low porticoes of the old town, the weeping willows that line the banks of the Bacchiglione and the area of Prato della Valle, and among the thriving modern sections devoted to business and manufacturing. The city has a seven-century-plus tradition of university studies. Among its art treasures are Giotto's frescoes in the famous Cappella degli Scrovegni, Donatello's work at the "Santo" (S. Antonio), and work by the young Titian, at the Scuola del Santo, masterpieces of Italian art history.

Historical note. Near the University, or Bo', you can still see the Tomb of Antenor, a Trojan hero who according to tradition, founded Padua in 1184 B.C. Certainly, Padua was founded later, not before the 8th or 7th c. B.C. The Paduan historian, Titus Livius, known as Livy, attests Padua's existence in 302 B.C. Livy also tells us that the Brenta River once ran through Padua and that it naturally changed its course, so that the Paduans were forced to divert the nearby Bacchiglione River into the old bed of the Brenta. The part of Padua enclosed by the two branches of the river, between the Specola, or Observatory, and the Porte Contarine, corresponds to the Roman city. In the 12th c., the first city walls were built along this watercourse; in this same period, Padua began to assert itself as a major political force in northern Italy. Following the wars against Frederick I Barbarossa, in the second half of the 12th c., Padua subjugated Vicenza, Bassano, and Feltre. In these years, the Palazzo della Ragione was built (1218-19), the University was founded by students and masters who left Bologna (1222); in these same years, amidst the turmoil of factional infighting, a Franciscan monk from Portugal preached

ounsels of peace – he was to become St. Antho-
y of Padua, and the people of the city began to
uild a vast and sumptuous basilica to his memo-
y, immediately after his death (1231). Ezzelino da
.omano took advantage of the continual intestine
ghting to rule Padua for several decades, but the
'ommunal government survived to enjoy free rule.
)uring that time Giotto was summoned to fresco
ıe Scrovegni Chapel and the University had Dante
.lighieri as an honored guest. It was in this same pe-
od that Padua built its porticoes, so rare among the
ities of Veneto; this development may possibly have
een due to the influence of the University, a direct
cion of the University of Bologna, city of porticoes
ar excellence. Over the next century or so, the Da
'arrara family ruled the city, beginning in 1318,
ielding to the Visconti (1389), who in turn ceded
adua to Venice (1405). During this period, Padua
as home for a while to the poet Petrarch. Although
ıe city had lost its political independence, it pre-
erved, in the 15th c., a certain artistic supremacy
ver Venice, with the work of Donatello and Man-
egna. A new, larger ring of walls was built. In the
9th c., when the walls were partly demolished, the
ity finally began to spread south (Bassanello) and
orth (Borgomagno). In that century, the historic
enter was gutted to make way for the Corso del
opolo; the same happened in the 20th c. for the
orso Milano, when many of Padua's canals were
lled in and paved over (Riviera is the name that
ow marks each of these former waterways).

;etting around. For your tour of Padua, we rec-
mmend two routes; you may walk the entire dis-
ance, or take public transportation for part of the
inerary.

he old historic center

 he Piazza delle Erbe, Piazza della Frutta, and Piaz-
a dei Signori, the romantic oxbow curve of the Bac-
highlione, the Bo', or University, the Neo-Classic Caf-
e Pedrocchi, Giotto's Scrovegni Chapel, the Eremi-
ıni, S. Sofia and its "Byzantine" apse, the historic cen-
er and the modern heart of Padua – all lie a short
istance from the great keel-roof of the Palazzo del-
ı Ragione, the "Salone," an ancient courthouse.

'iazza delle Erbe (*C3*). A lively fruit and veg-
table market is held here; it is lined by the Palaz-
o della Ragione, the Palazzo Comunale, and old
uildings with porticoes.

'alazzo Comunale, or *del Podestà*, now town hall
C3). This building dates from the 13th c. (note the
ıwer on the right side), was rebuilt by A. Moroni in
ıe mid-16th c. and enlarged in 1904.

'alazzo della Ragione* (*C2-3*). Also known as
ıe "Salone," this majestic building was founded in
218-19 and enlarged in 1306-1309; it was badly
amaged by a fire in 1420, which destroyed fine
'escoes by Giotto.

he *interior* (*open Apr.-Oct., 9-7; Nov.-Mar., 9-6; closed

Mon.) comprises a single huge room, 27 m wide, 78
m long, and 27 m tall; the walls are decorated with
frescoes, redone in 1430. Note the wooden reproduction of Donatello's equestrian statue of the Gattamelata (see below for original).
Duomo (*C2*). Founded in the High Middle Ages,
rebuilt in the 9th c. and again by 1124, today this
cathedral bears the marks of the renovation begun
in 1551, to plans by Michelangelo. The facade is unfinished, and the interior is starkly majestic. On the
transept walls are 14th-c. funerary monuments. In
the sacristy, 14th-c. panels and paintings by P. Bordone, J. da Montagnana, G. Tiepolo, and others. On
the right of the Duomo is the Baptistery (see below); behind it, in Via Dietro Duomo 15, is the *Museo
Diocesano* (*closed for restoration.*), the diocese museum with paintings, sculptures, and sacred objects.
Battistero* (*C2*). The 13th-c. Romanesque baptistery, with a square plan and a broad round cupola,
has an interior covered with *frescoes**, the masterpiece of G. de' Menabuoi (1374-76; also note his
polyptych on the altar) and a 13th-c. baptismal font.
The square is flanked by the *Palazzo del Monte di
Pietà*, the 14th-c. Palazzo Vescovile, and various medieval houses.
Piazza dei Signori (*C2*). Note in particular the elegant marble **Loggia del Consiglio*** (1496-1553);
also, the *Palazzo del Capitano* (1605), with a **triumphal arch** by G.M. Falconetto (1532), which
holds the first clock in Italy, built in 1344, but rebuilt
in 1437.
Past the arch is the *Corte Capitaniato*, with 16th-c.
buildings, and the **Liviano**, designed by Gio' Ponti
(1939), and now part of the University. In the atrium,
frescoes by M. Campigli and a statue of Livy by A.
Martini (1942). A spectacular *stairway** leads up to
the vast 16th-c. *Sala dei Giganti*, a hall decorated
with huge figures of kings and heroes (in a corner,
a 14th-c. portrait of Petrarch). Adjacent to the department of archeology is the *Museo di Scienze
Archeologiche e d'Arte* (*closed for restoration; tel.
0498203430*), devoted to archeology and Renaissance art (Donatello, B. Ammannati).
Piazza Insurrezione (*C2-3*). At the heart of modern Padua, this square is near the 18th-c. church of
S. Lucia, with noteworthy paintings (D. Campagnola, Sassoferrato, Padovanino) and, up high, mono-
chromatic canvases by G. Ceruti and G.B. Tiepolo.
Adjacent is the **Scuola di S. Rocco** (*C2-3; open
9:30-12:30 and 3:30-7:30*), built in the 15th-16th c.,
and frescoed by D. Campagnola, G. del Santo, and
others. At the mouth of Via Marsilio da Padova is
the so-called *Casa di Ezzelino**, a handsome 13th-
c. dwelling.
I Carmini (*B2-3*). This Romanesque church was
completed in 1494 and almost immediately rebuilt
to plans by L. da Bologna. Note the Renaissance
sacristy*. Adjacent is the **Scuola del Carmine***
(*open by request, contact sexton*), built in the 14th
c. and frescoed by D. and G. Campagnola, G. del Santo, and others.
Cappella degli Scrovegni** (*B3*). *Open 9-7; com-*

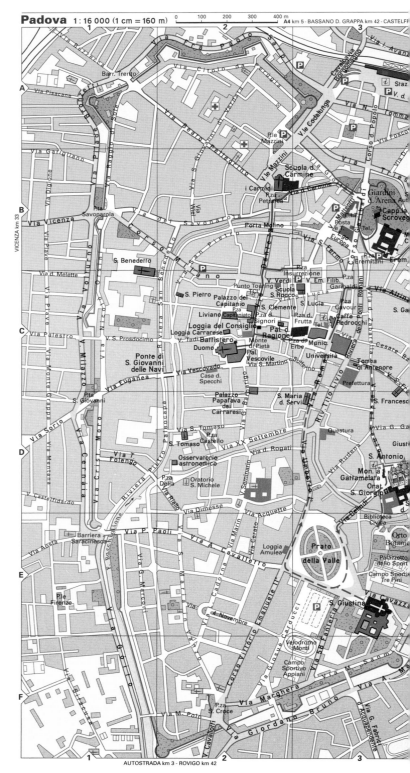

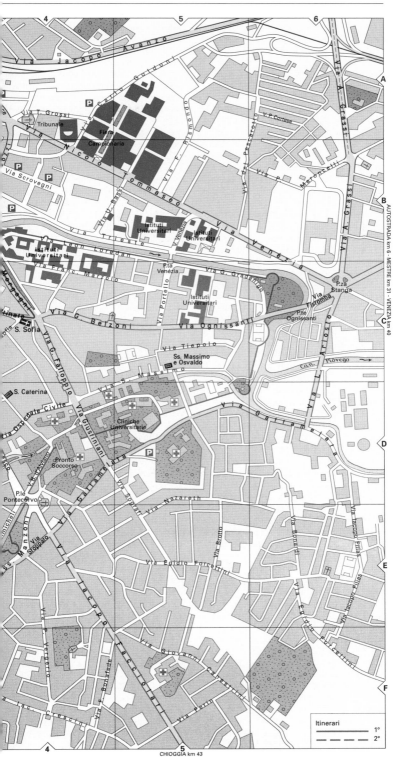

pulsory reservation, tel. 0492919929. This funerary chapel stands in the public gardens of the Arena, which take their name from the scattered ruins of the 1st c. A.D. *Roman amphitheater.* The little church, also known as *Madonna dell'Arena* or *S. Maria dell'Annunciata*, was built at the behest of Enrico Scrovegni, and consecrated in 1305.

Inside are the renowned **frescoes by Giotto****, executed before 1305 by the great master and his assistants, a towering masterpiece of Italian painting. Above the entrance, the Last Judgement; on the side walls, on the base, depictions of the *7 Virtues** (right) and the *7 Capital Sins** (left); above, in 38 panels, are *Stories of Mary and Christ*, showing Giotto's finest qualities: monumental composition, concise and expressive depiction, solid plasticism, emotional drama. In the presbytery, above the altar, statues by G. Pisano*; behind the altar, tomb of E. Scrovegni (d. 1336).

Musei Civici (*B3*). *Open Tue.-Sun., 9-7.* Set in the old Convento degli Eremitani (note remains of frescoes from various eras), to the left of the church, the municipal museums comprise an *archeological section*, with pre-Roman and Roman, Egyptian, Etruscan, and Early Christian material; the *Museo Bottacin*, with 19th-c. artwork and a valuable coin collection; the **Quadreria Emo Capodilista**, featuring more than 500 paintings by Venetian and Flemish artists, including Titian, Giorgione, and Giovanni Bellini; the **Pinacoteca**, with paintings by artists of the Venetian school, from the 14th to the 18th c., including Giotto, Guariento, B. Boccaccino, A. Vivarini, J. Bellini, P. Bordone, P. Veronese, J. and L. Bassano, J. Tintoretto, G. Romanino, G.B. Tiepolo, F. Guardi, M. and S. Ricci, and others; the *Raccolta dei Bronzetti e delle Placchette*, with creations by artists working in bronze, in the 14th-17th c. (A. Briosco, B. Ammannati, Sansovino, T. Aspetti); the *Raccolta di Ceramiche e Vetri* and the *Raccolta di Incisioni e Stampe*, with collections of, respectively, ceramics and glass, and prints and engravings.

Eremitani* or church of *Ss. Filippo e Giacomo* (*B3*). This Romanesque-Gothic church was built between 1276 and 1306; partially destroyed by bombing in 1944 (especially the apse), it was faithfully rebuilt. The lower section of the facade, in stone, has a large portal and other arcading that continue along the right side; note the Renaissance portal on that side with carvings of the Months, by the Florentine N. Baroncelli (ca. 1442).

Inside, along the walls of the single nave, with wooden ceiling, tombs and statues from the 14th-16th c.: tombs of J. da Carrara* (left) and U. da Carrara (right); two 15th-c. altar frontals; enormous tomb of M.M. Benavides by B. Ammannati (1546). Note the *Cappella Ovetari**, once famed for the frescoes by A. Mantegna, A. da Forlì, B. da Ferrara, and others, destroyed by bombs. What has survived are several religious paintings and a terracotta altarpiece by N. Pizzolo. In the presbytery and other chapels in the apse, 14th-c. frescoes and funerary monuments.

S. Sofia* (*C4*). This Romanesque church is the oldest in Padua and may have been founded in Car-

olingian times; it was rebuilt in the 11th c. and modeled in the 14th c. Note the facade, the apse and the remarkable ambulatory.

Piazza Cavour (*C3*). A lively hub of the city. In nearby square is the **Caffè Pedrocchi** (*C3*), a Ne Classic coffee shop dating from 1831, famous w tering spot of the city's students and intelligentsia **Via VIII Febbraio.** This street is flanked by the U versity on the left and the Palazzo del Municipio, town hall, on the right. The **University** (C3), co monly called the *Bo'*, is one of Europe's olde (1222). Galileo taught here, as did G.B. Morgagni is considered the cradle of modern medicine. T lovely *old courtyard**, studded with coats of arr and the stairs to the upper floors (*guided tours request, summer*). Don't miss the *anatomical theate* the first of its kind (1594), the *Sala dei Quarar* (where Galileo taught), and the *Aula Magna* (t great hall with coats of arms).

The Cittadella Antoniana

This route passes through the southern section central Padua, and begins at the square of the Tor of Antenor, near the University, where the previc tour ended. High point of this tour is the Basili del Santo, but of considerable interest are the O torio di S. Giorgio and the Scuola del Santo. Alo the route, other notable stops are the Orto Bota co (Europe's oldest botanical garden), the Prato d la Valle, and the church of S. Giustina. You return the center along Via Umberto and Via Roma.

Via S. Francesco. (*C-D 3-4*) On the Piazzale A tenore, which this road crosses, is the so-called **To ba di Antenore** (*C3*), an urn built in 1283 whi is said to contain the remains of Antenor, mythic founder of Padua, but actually holding the remai of a warrior of the 2nd-4th c. A.D. Along the roa note, at n. 9, the *Palazzo Romanin Jacur*, a Neo-Go ic reconstruction, and the church of **S. Frances** (*C-D3*), with notable frescoes.

Piazza del Santo (*D3*). Heart of the Cittadella A toniana, this square, featuring the monument to G tamelata, is surrounded by the Basilica del San the oratory of S. Giorgio, the Scuola di S. Anton and a series of porticoed houses.

Monument to Erasmo da Narni** (*D3*). It w built to commemorate this great condottiere of th Venetian Republic, known as the **Gattamela** (1370-1443). The statue is one of Donatello's m terpieces (1453).

S. Antonio** (*D3*). *Open 7-7.* This basilica, know locally simply as the **Santo**, is one of Italy's me renowned sanctuaries. It was built in a mixed R manesque and Gothic style between 1232 a about 1350, to house the tomb of St. Anthony of Pa ua (born in Lisbon in 1195, died in Padua, at L' cella, in 1231). The simple facade boasts handson portals, arches, and rose windows. The eight *cupol* of the roof show a mixture of Byzantine, Venetia and French Romanesque (Perigord) influence

adua: S. Antonio

hile the little towers and the two octagonal bell
wers give the church an eastern flavor.

side, the soaring nave and aisles with huge piers
ad to a deep presbytery surrounded by a lavish-
adorned ambulatory. In the right aisle is the tomb
the great Gattamelata (15th c.). In the *right
insept*, the 14th-c. **Cappella di S. Felice*** is
dorned with lovely frescoes* by Altichiero (1374-
). In the *presbytery*, the main altar is decorated
ith very fine **bronzes by Donatello**** (1443-50)
nd assistants. To the left of the altar, an astonishing
onze candelabrum* by A. Briosco (1515). Along
e walls, 12 bronze bas-reliefs by B. Bellano and A.
iosco. Around the presbytery runs the *ambulato-
*, with chapels opening out like rays; the 5th
apel, the Cappella delle Reliquie, by F. Parodi (as
e the statues; 1689), contains an impressive trea-
ry*: note the reliquaries (one supposedly holds
. Anthony's tongue, 13th c.), incense boats, and
ooden caskets that held the saint's remains. Fur-
er along are two other chapels; the Cappella del
eato Luca Belludi (1382) is decorated with freses* by G. de' Menabuoi.

the *left transept* is the **Cappella dell'Arca del
anto***, begun in 1500, with a stucco ceiling by
M. Falconetto (1533): on the walls, reliefs by T. and
Lombardo and J. Sansovino; other remarkable
onuments in this section by T. Aspetti, P. Lombar-
, and M. Sanmicheli. From the right aisle, you can
ter the **cloisters** (13th-15th c.). The first cloister,
illed the *Chiostro del Capitolo* or della Magnolia
240), leads into the Consiglio della Presidenza
ell'Arca, where you can admire a lovely fresco by
Mantegna. In the nearby *Chiostro del Noviziato*,
ith a well-curb dating from 1492, monument to C.
usso by A. Briosco; from the Chiostro del Generale
434), you can climb up to the *Biblioteca Antonia-
(open by request, tel. 0498242811)*, a library with
,000 volumes and many incunabula.

Giorgio* (*D3*). *Open Apr.-Sep., 9-12:30 and 2:30-
Oct.-Mar., until 5 p.m.* This 14th-c. oratory stands to
e right of the basilica; in the interior are **frescoes***
Altichiero and assistants (1379-84), one of the
most interesting pieces of 14th-c. Italian painting.

Scuola del Santo.* *Open same hours as the oratory of S. Giorgio.* Built beginning in 1427, and raised
in 1504, this building has its upper halls adorned
with a series of frescoes* by Venetian artists, including several by Titian; the finest set of early 16th-
c. paintings in Padua.

Palazzo Giustiniani (*D4*). This building, in Via Ce-
sarotti, n. 21, was a theatrical center for 16th-/17th-
c. Padua.

Orto Botanico (*E3*). *Open 9-1 and 3-6; for guided
and didactic tours, tel. 0498862173.* Founded in
1545, this botanical garden is the oldest in Europe,
and one of the finest in Italy.

Prato della Valle (*E3*). This is one of Europe's
largest squares (1775). Note the tree-covered islet in
the center, the *Isola Memmia*, adorned with 78 statues and surrounded by a canal.

S. Giustina* (*E3*). This enormous 16th-c. brick
church with a bare facade and eight cupolas has
a late 16th-c. bell tower, set on the base of the medieval one.

The *interior* is huge and solemn. From the right
transept, you can reach the *Sacello di S. Prosdoci-
mo*, part of the 6th-c. basilica, with the original
iconostasis. Note the *old choir* (*enquire in the front
office of the monastery*) dating from 1462, with fine
inlaid stalls. In the apse are a carved and inlaid walnut *choir** (1566) and large altarpiece by Veronese
(1575). Note, in the left transept, the Arca di S. Luca, or Tomb of St. Luke, with alabaster reliefs (1316).
In the 2nd chapel on the left, painting by S. Ricci.
To the right of the church is the Benedictine
monastery, now partly used as a barracks.

Via Umberto I (*D3*). The left side of this street has
porticoes and old buildings, especially at n. 8, *Casa
Olzignani*, a Renaissance-Gothic residence (15th c.)
rebuilt between 1900 and 1922.

Via Roma (*C-D3*). One of Padua's liveliest streets,
lined with porticoes and the church of **S. Maria
dei Servi** (*D3*), Gothic-Romanesque (1372-92); note
the frescoes (Pietà* by J. da Montagnana).

Paestum**

Elev. 18 m, Campania, province of Salerno,
township of Capaccio (pop. 20,597).

Historical note. This was a colony of Sybaris (late
7th c. B.C.) and was called Poseidonia, from the
name of the god of the sea; the town's prosperity, in
fact, came from maritime trade; the Lucanians conquered it (circa 400 B.C.), and it then became a Roman colony (273 B.C.) with the name of Paestum.

Places of interest. As you pass through the walls
of the **Porta Aurea**, the **area of monuments and
excavations** is on the right (*open 9-one hour before
sunset; closed 1 Jan., 1 May, 25 Dec.*).

There are three Greek temples: the **Basilica***, from
the mid-6th c. B.C., is the oldest of the temples of
Paestum; the **Tempio di Nettuno****, or Temple of

Paestum: Tempio di Nettuno

Neptune (450 B.C.), is considered by some to be the most beautiful Doric temple in the Greek world; set apart from the others is the smaller **Tempio di Cerere***, or Temple of Ceres, dating from the end of the 6th c.B.C.and probably dedicated to the goddess Athena.

The Roman **Forum** occupies the site of the Greek *agora*; there is still a building that may have been the *Curia*, ruins of *baths*, the **Tempio Italico** (273 B.C., modified in 80 B.C.), perhaps the *Comitium*, and the *amphitheater*.

The route of the **Via Sacra**, a street used for religious processions, skirts a residential section; the *decumanus maximus* runs past what may have been the *Gymnasium* and a sacred enclosure, with an *underground votive chapel** in the center (2nd half of the 6th c.).

A natural complement to this tour is a visit to the **museum****, of particular importance for the archaic **metopes**** of the "*thesauros*" and the six metopes** of the main temple (late 6th c. B.C.), which all come from the sanctuary of Hera at the mouth of the Sele River; a seated statue of Zeus** (mid-6th c.B.C.); the painted slabs from the Tomba del Tuffatore*, or Tomb of the Diver, an exceedingly rare example of Greek painting.

Palermo**

Elev. 14 m, pop. 683,794; Sicilia (Sicily), regional and provincial capital. On the north coast of Sicily, with the stern Monte Pellegrino as the constant point of reference throughout the landscape, dotted with the citrus groves of the Conca d'Oro, the city of Palermo preserves the memories, monuments, and atmosphere of Arab and Norman times as one of its two urban faces, the more remarkable and original of the two. The other face is that of the Baroque architecture that dates from the 17th-18th c., from the time of the Spanish viceroy and the Bourbon monarchs. The city can be considered as being split in two by the axis of Via Cavour and Via Volturno; to the north, near the port, is the modern section, with rectangular blocks and broad roads; to the south is the intricate and chaotic structure of the old section, once enclosed by medieval and Spanish walls. Two Spanish viceroys, the Duke of

Toledo (1565-66) and Maqueda, who governe Sicily from 1598 to 1601, built two straight a enues: the first is Corso Vittorio Emanuele, g ing from the Marina to the Palazzo dei N manni; the second avenue runs perpendicul to the first and parallel to the sea: Via Maqu da. These two avenues divide Palermo roug ly into four districts, of about the same siz and they meet in the little Piazza Vigliana, Quattro Canti, once the city center.

Historical note. Not much survives of Phoenicia Roman and Byzantine Palermo. Its economic a political power began with the Arabs, who held th town from 831 until 1072, making it the capital Arabian Sicily. The Arabs were succeded by the N mans, and Palermo enjoyed great prosperity and level of artistic and cultural achievement nev again equalled. This period created magnifice buildings, in which Arab, Latin and Byzantine fe tures mingle and merge, engendering a remarkab character and allure: the Cappella Palatina and th Martorana, with their splendid Byzantine mosai the churches of S. Giovanni degli Eremiti, S. Catalc the pavillions of La Zisa and La Cuba, with a d tinctive Muslim appearance; the exceedingly gra cathedral, whose interior was subsequently grea altered. Palermo declined under Anjou rule; the A jou were expelled from the city by the famous F volt of the Vespers in 1282; under the rule of th House of Aragon Palermo recovered somewhat. Th artistic tradition of the Normans can be clearly se in the great Palazzo Chiaramonte and Palaz Sclàafani, both from the 14th c. In the 15th c., th style and shapes of Catalonian Gothic came dominate, providing inspiration for M. Carneliva who designed Palazzo Abatellis and Palazzo A tamicristo and the lovely church of S. Maria de Catena. Under Spanish rule, in the 17th-18th c., th city took on the festive Baroque appearance that still preserves, in part. It was then that the church of S. Giuseppe dei Teatini, S. Caterina, and Gesù we built; they are decorated inside with spectacul marble inlays. Later, in the 18th c., the various o tories (S. Cita, Rosario, S. Lorenzo) acquired the spirited joyful arrays of stuccoes, by a great mast of the style, Giacomo Serpotta.

Getting around. The first three routes suggeste for a visit to the center of Palermo can be und taken on foot or with public transport. All thr start from Quattro Canti, an important piazza whe Corso Vittorio Emanuele and Via Maqueda co verge. To reach the monuments and resorts whi lie in the ouskirts of the town, described in the o er three routes, a car is useful.

The first fortified settlement

Starting from Quattro Canti, the common name the little Piazza Vigliena, going along the weste tretch of Corso Vittorio Emanuele, the first route akes in the oldest part of the city. This area is called Cassaro (from the Arabic "el Kasr", for castrum or castle) and lay in the heart of the city even in medieval times, when the construction of the Norman palace and the cathedral made it the center of political and religious power.

Corso Vittorio Emanuele. It runs from the Marina to the Palazzo dei Normanni. From the Quattro Canti, proceeding eastward, along this street or near it you will find many interesting monuments.

S. Giuseppe dei Teatini (*E4*). Immediately adjacent to the Quattro Canti stands this lavish Baroque church with its remarkable marble-studded interior, bedecked with stuccowork and frescoes.

Via Maqueda (*D4-F5*). Built in 1600 by the viceroy Maqueda, it runs from Porta Vicari (*F5*), also called Porta S.Antonino, to Piazza Verdi (*D4*). Note the 17th-c. church of *S. Nicolò da Tolentino* and the Palazzo S. Croce (18th c.).

Gesù* (*E4*). This was the first church of the Jesuits in Sicily. It was built in 1564 and later enlarged; the dome dates back to the mid-17th c. The interior is covered with wood inlays and marble carvings. It is a sterling example of Sicilian Baroque.

Palazzo Sclafani (*E3*). A fine example of Gothic civil architecture. Note the facade with its high interwined archwork, surrounding twin-light mullioned windows.

Cattedrale** (E3). This majestic Cathedral stands at the end of a verdant square; it is a monument of great interest. You should pay close attention to the details of its construction, as it is the result of a complex series of rebuildings, ranging from the first structure (by the Normans, in 1185) to renovation and addition of the dome by F. Fuga (1781-1801). The facade you see is from the 14th-15th c. It is linked to the bell tower by two pointed arches. On the right side, note the portico, in flamboyant Catalonian Gothic style; the *apsidal section** comprises three apses with intertwined arcades and polychrome encrustations. *Inside*. In the Neo-Classic interior, note, in the right aisle the renowned **imperial and royal tombs*** of Henry VI, Frederick II, Constance, and Roger II; in the chapel to the right of the presbitery, a silver urn (1631) containing the relics of Santa Rosalia, the patron saint of Palermo; in the left aisle, a Madonna* by F. Laurana (1469). Exquisite precious objects are preserved in the **Tesoro** (*open Sun., 4-8; summer, Mon.-Sat., 6:30 a.m.-7 p.m.; winter, 6:30-12 and 4-7*), or treasury, along with the golden tiara of Constance of Aragon, wife of Frederick II. In the sacristy is the Madonna by A. Gagini (1503), the leading member of a family of Palermitan sculptors (originally from Bissone, in the Canton Ticino, birthplace of Antonello's father, Domenico). The *crypt* dates from the 12th c.

In the **Palazzo Arcivescovile**, or archbishop's palace, the *Museo Diocesano* (*closed for restoration; tel. 091607111*), or diocese museum, has a notable array of sacred art from the 12th c.

Piazza della Vittoria (*E-F3*). Immense green space in front of the Norman Palace; its present appearance dates back to the 16th c., when an enormous open area was created for public ceremonies. Its current name commemorates the success of a local revolt against the Bourbon garrison in 1820. It is almost entirely taken up by the palm tree-lined park of *Villa Bonanno*.

Palazzo dei Normanni* (*F3*). On the other side of Villa Bonanno stands this vast and majestic building, one of Sicily's most significant monuments. Originally built by the Arabs, later a sumptuous royal palace under Norman rule, hence its name, and then used as the court of Frederick II. During this period, the building lay at the heart of great cultural changes, mingling the ancient classical heritage with Arab and Byzantine traditions (here, the "Scuola Siciliana" gave birth to Italian poetry).

Cappella Palatina** (*F3; open Mon.-Fri., 9-12 and 3-5; Sat., 9-12; Sun., 9-10 and 12-1*). Climbing the majestic staircase in the courtyard of the Norman Palace you reach the Palatine Chapel, one of the finest creations of the entire Norman monarchy (Roger II, 1132-40). The structure consists of a nave with two aisles separated by rows of Gothic arches set on ancient columns; note the mosaic floors and exquisite marble lining the lower half of the walls. There is an exceptional wooden ceiling, modeled with stalactite and honeycomb shapes, in distinctly Arab style (ca. 1143), over the nave. Near the sanctuary, the mosaic ambo* on columns, and a 13th-c. Paschal candelabrum*; above the marble lower panels, the walls are adorned with splendid 12th-c. **mosaics**** on a gold background, with Bible stories and stories of Saints Peter and Paul; there are Latin writings stretching the length of the aisles, as well as scenes from the Gospels, with phrases in Greek. Note the Christ Pantocrator, or Almighty Christ, surrounded by Archangels, Prophets, and Evangelists in the dome.

Appartamenti Reali. In the royal apartments (*closed to the public*) are the Sala di Ercole (or Sala del Parlamento), where the Assembly of Sicily now convenes, and the Sala di Re Ruggero, or King Roger, with mosaics* of hunting scenes (ca. 1170).

S. Giovanni degli Eremiti** (*F3; open 9-1; Sun. 9-12:30; Mon. and Thur., also 3-5*). This Norman church stands in a lovely garden and is one of the most enchanting sites in Palermo. In the garden, full of exotic plants, is an exquisite 13th-c. cloister*, with lovely little twin columns.

The southeastern section of the old town

Starting once again from Quattro Canti, it is possible to explore the sector of the city bounded by the southeastern stretch of Corso Vittorio Emanuele and the southern stretch of Via Maqueda. Following on from Palazzo Abatellis, which houses the important Galleria Regionale (art gallery), the route takes in the ancient Kalsa district, a fortified stronghold built by Muslims in 937.

Piazza Pretoria (*E4*). Adjacent to the Quattro Canti, it is almost entirely occupied by the fanciful

Palermo

1:15 000 (1 cm = 150 m)

0   100   200 m

Itinerari
1°
2°
3°

Banchina Quattroventi

Molo Nord

Molo Martello

Diga

foranea

P.za Giachery

Piazza

Alfanese
Ucciardone

P.za
Strazzeri

Banchina Puntone

Pontile S. Lucia

Pontile Piave

PORTO

A

B

Banchina Francesco Crispi

Approdo aliscafi per Ústica
Pontile Vitt. Véneto

A.A.
Staz. Marittima

Capitaneria
di Porto

Traghetti per Cagliari, Genova,
Napoli, Tunisi

Banchina Sammuzzo

Banchina trapezoidale

Molo Sud

MAR

TIRRENO

C

P.za
Ucciardone

Via E. Amari

Via Principe

Belmonte

Via Mariano Stabile

Via Roma

Via Cavour

P.ta
S. Giorgio

P.za XIII
Vittime

Via dei Cassari

P.za
S. Giorgio

Castello a Mare
(resti)

Prefettura

Museo archeologico

P.za
Olivella

Oratorio
d. Olivella

Via Bara

S. Giorgio
d. Genovesi

S. Cita

Oratorio
di S. Cita

Oratorio
d. Rosario

S. M.
Nuova

la Cala

Archivio
di Stato

Istituto
Nautico

Loggiato di
S. Bartolomeo

S. Maria
d. Catena

P.ta
Felice

S. Spirito

D

Villa

a Mare

S. Domenico

Via Meli

S. Eulalia
d. Catalani

S. Maria di
Porto Salvo

Museo d.
Marionette

Pal. Termini-
Pietratagliata

P.ze
Garraffello

P.za
Giudici

Piazza
Giulio
Marina

Pal.
Chiaramonte

Via Roma

S. Antonio

Oratorio
di S. Lorenzo

Palazzo
Mirto

S. Maria
d. Miracoli

La Pietà

S. Nicolò
d. Croctieri

S. Matteo

P.za
Cassa di
Risparmio

S. Francesco
d'Assisi

la Gancia

Pal.
Abatellis
(Galleria reg.)

P.za d.
Kalsa

S. Teresa

Fontana
Pretoria

Quattro Canti

S. Anna

S. Giuseppe
d. Teatini

S. Caterina

Munic.

Martorana

Croce
d. Vespri

Piazza

P.za
S. Euno

P.ta
Reale

Ingresso

Pal.
Bologni

S. Cataldo

P.za
d. Rivoluzione

S. Maria
d. Spásimo

Ingresso

Università

Palazzo
Speciale

S. Nicolò
da Tolentino

la Magione

P.za
Magione

Villa
Giulia

S. Chiara

Casa
Professa

Gesù

Pal.
Ajutamicristo

Biblioteca
comunale

Pal. Comitini
(ex Prefettura)

Castrofilippo

Orto

botanico

S. Nicolò
d'Albergheria

Pal.
S. Croce

P.za
Carmine

Via Milano

P.ta Garibaldi

Carmine

P.za
Giulio Cesare

P.ta
S. Antonino

S. Antonino

Corso Tukòry

Staz. Centrale
F.S.

Corso dei Mille

P.za
S. Agata

F

285

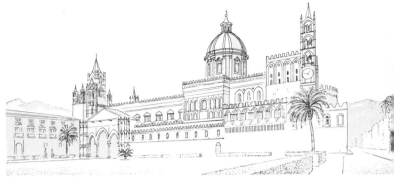

Palermo: Cattedrale

Fontana Pretoria*, a great fountain built by the Florentine F. Camilliani (1554-55).

S. Cataldo* (*E4*). This church, with blind arcades on the exterior walls, Arabic crenelation, three little cupolas, and a bare and lovely interior, is a perfect example of pure Norman style (ca. 1160).

Martorana.** Another gem of the Norman period, this church is also known as S. Maria dell'Ammiraglio (named after an admiral, George of Antioch, who had the church built). It dates from 1143, but it was partly rebuilt in the 16th-17th c.; note the addition of a Baroque facade along the side. The **bell tower**** is original, 4 storeys tall, with mullioned windows, corner columns, and polychrome intarsia. **Inside****, the original Greek cross plan, with the later addition of a series of bays, features two mosaics: Roger II being crowned by Jesus and George of Antioch at the feet of the Virgin Mary, on the pediment of what was a portico. Don't miss the splendid 12th-c. Byzantine **mosaics**** in the sanctuary, with Christ Pantocrator (ruler of the universe), the Archangels, the Prophets, and the Evangelists, in the dome. Note a Birth of Jesus and a Death of the Virgin Mary. Mosaic screens enclose the apses.

S. Lorenzo* (*E5; closed to the public*). The stucco decoration – with symbolic statues, stories from the lives of Ss. Lorenzo e Francesco (Saints Lawrence and Francis), and rejoicing cherubim – that adorns this oratory is considered to be Serpotta's masterpiece, in terms of expressivity and maturity.

S. Francesco d'Assisi* (*E5*). This Gothic church, one of the most important in Palermo, was built between 1255 and 1277, altered and enlarged several times; badly damaged during the bombardments of 1943. It features a series of Gothic and Renaissance chapels, flanking the smallest aisle.

Palazzo Chiaramonte* (*D6*). Set on the vast Piazza Marina, with the palm trees and rare plants of the Giardino Garibaldi at the square's center, is the Palazzo Chiaramonte, also known as the Steri (from the Latin "hosterium," in the sense of fortified palace). This stern and compact structure, with Gothic twin- and triple-light mullioned windows, and tufa-and-pumice intarsias, is a noble example of a medieval Sicilian palazzo. It was the headquarters of the ecclesiastical courts.

Museo Internazionale delle Marionette Antonio Pasqualino (*D6; Via Butera 1; open 9-1 and ⟨ 7; Sat. 9-1. closed Sun.*). This international museum of marionettes includes in its collections the "pup siciliani," puppets from the Neapolitan theater, an puppets and marionettes from many nations, as we as Asian shadow-theater puppets.

Palazzo Abatellis* (*E6*). In this palazzo, note th strong architecture, a blend of Catalonian Gothi and Renaissance style (1495).

Galleria Regionale della Sicilia* (*open 9-1:3(Sun. 9-12:30; Tue.-Thu. also 3-7*). Housed in Palazz Abatellis, this gallery has a major art collection. I particular: the marvelous **Annunciation**** by A tonello da Messina. Other fine masterpieces ar three saints*, also by Antonello, the lovely **bust c Eleanor of Aragon**** by F. Laurana, a famous fre co of the **Triumph of Death**** from the mid-15t c., originally in Palazzo Sclafani, the Madonna de Latte* by G. di Nicola, the **Malvagna Triptych**** b the Flemish painter Mabuse, and the exquisite Mala ga vase*, a piece of Hispanic-Moorish ceramics.

Foro Italico (*D-E6*). Opened in the 16th c., th beachfront promenade stretches from Monte Pelle grino to Monte Catafano with a superb view of th Gulf of Palermo. Nearby, the *Piazza della Kalsa* whose name comes from the Arabic "el Khalisa originally given to the surrounding district, a for fied stronghold. At the end of the piazza, the churc of **S. Teresa** (*E6*) is one of the most important e amples of Palermo Baroque architecture.

The northeastern section of the old town

The route leaves again from Quattro Canti, taking the area to the north of Corso Vittorio Emanuel running along Via Maqueda towards Piazza Verd and the lively Via Roma towards Piazza Olivella. Th Museo Archeologico Regionale, one of the most ir portant in Italy, is the highlight of the route.

S. Matteo (*E4*). A Baroque church built in 1633-4 the interior boasts marble works and four fine sta ues by G. Serpotta.

S. Antonio Abate (*D5*) Isolated on an emban ment, near the crossroads of Corso Vittor

Emanuele and Via Roma, this church was built in the 12th c. and rearranged in the 14th c.; the facade dates from the 19th c. Along the left side, you can walk down to Palermo's oldest market, the much loved Bocceria Vecchia, known as the **Vucciria**.

S. Maria di Porto Salvo (*D5*). Built in Renaissance style in 1526 and renovated in 1581, when the opening of Corso Vittorio Emanuele resulted in the destruction of the apsidal section, later replaced by a portal.

S. Maria della Catena* (*D5-6*). The name comes from the chain, or "catena," used to close off the harbor. In front of the church there is a flight of steps and a portico. The church dates from the late 15th c., stylistically a cross between Catalonian Gothic and the Renaissance.

Oratorio del Rosario di S. Domenico* (*D4-5; ring for the custodian, Via Bambinai 16*). The interior of this oratory is a masterpiece of grace and elegance, especially the **stucco decoration**** by G. Serpotta; canvases by L. Giordano and the Monreale painter, P. Novelli, considered the greatest Sicilian artist of the 17th c.; note also a canvas on the altar by Van Dyck.

S. Cita* (*D4; ring for the custodian*). The entrance to this oratory is beside the church of S. Cita, known also as S. Zita. Here there is other excellent stuccowork* by Serpotta.

S. Giorgio dei Genovesi (*C-D5*). This fine church dates from the late 16th c. and was built for the colony of Genoese people in Palermo.

Museo Regionale Archeologico** (*D4; open Mon., Thu. and Sat., 9-1:30; Tue., Wed. and Fri., 9-1 and 3-6:30; Sun., 9-1*). This major archeological museum occupies the 17th-c. building of a former convent. The entrance is through the lower cloister, with a fountain at its center. Some of the archeological finds discovered beneath the sea are housed here, including a vast and comprehensive collection of stone, lead and iron anchors*. In the hall dedicated to *classical sculpture*, particularly noteworthy among the enormous collections are the **sculptures from Selinunte****, especially the 3 metopes** from Temple C (mid-6th c. B.C.), two half metopes* from Temple T (5th c. B.C.), and 4 renowned metopes** from Temple E (460-450 B.C.). Other sections include prehistoric finds, Greek ceramics, Roman mosaics and frescoes.

The new city and Monte Pellegrino

This route takes in the modern areas of the city – whose development began in 1778 and continued into the 19th c. with the opening of Viale della Libertà – and areas lying outside the city too; it covers a visit to the Parco della Favorita and a suggested trip up panoramic Monte Pellegrino, where the celebrated sanctuary of S. Rosalia stands.

Piazza Verdi (*D4*). Laid out after the extensive demolition work in the late 19th c., this spacious tree-lined piazza is situated on the border of the new city and the old city. The imposing structure of the **Teatro Massimo** (*D3-4*), built between 1875 and 1897, one of the temples of Italian opera music and one of the largest theaters in Europe (7730 sq. m surface area), dominates the piazza.

Piazza Castelnuovo (*C3*). Together with the adjoining Piazza Ruggero Settimo, it forms a vast open space set off with monuments and palm trees. To the right, the vast bulk of the **Teatro Politeama** stands out. Built between 1867 and 1874 in classical style, the theater houses the Civica Galleria d'Arte Moderna.

Civica Galleria d'Arte Moderna Empedocle Restivo (*C3; open 8-8; Sun., 9-1; closed Mon.*). This modern art gallery has an interesting collection comprising works by 19th-century and contemporary artists.

Parco della Favorita* This magnificent park lies at the base of Monte Pellegrino and was built in 1799 at the behest of the Bourbon king of the Two Sicilies, Ferdinand, when he was forced to take refuge in Sicily after being rudely chased out of Naples by a French army.

Museo Etnografico Siciliano Giuseppe Pitrè (*open 8:30-1 and 3:30-6:30.*). Alongside the Palazzina Cinese, an early 19th-c. Chinese-style mansion built by a Bourbon king, is the Museo Etnografico Pitrè, one of the leading museums in the field of Sicilian traditions, costumes, and folkways. It comprises 31 halls.

Santuario di S. Rosalia.* Set high on the craggy limestone massif of Monte Pellegrino (606 m), this sanctuary of the patron saint of Palermo (13 km north) is made up of a convent and a cave-chapel (with a small natural spring said to flow with holy water that works miracles). In this cavern, the saint lived in penitence until her death (1166); a road leads further on to a broad square, with a colossal statue of S. Rosalia and a splendid view of sea and coastline.

In the outskirts

Villa Giulia* (*E6*) . Known also as Villa Flora, this is a lovely 18th-c. park with one side overlooking the sea. Adjacent is the **Orto Botanico** (*open winter, Mon.-Fri., 9-5; summer, Mon.-Fri., 9-6; Sat. and Sun. 9-1*), one of Europe's finest botanical gardens, founded in 1789, with plants from all over the world.

S. Giovanni dei Lebbrosi. In Corso dei Mille, in the southernmost section of Palermo, is this inter-

Palermo: S. Cataldo and Martorana

esting and fine church, which dates from 1070.

S. Spirito* (in the enclosure of the cemetery of S. Orsola). This squared-off church dates from the 12th c. In the plaza before the church, the anti-Anjou revolt of Palermo against its French garrison, known as the "Vespri Siciliani," was triggered on 31 March 1282. Inside is a 15th-c. painted wooden cross.

S. Maria di Gesù.* This 15th-c. church stands on the lower slopes of Monte Grifone in the southernmost section of Palermo.

Zisa** (*D1; open 9:30-1:30; Sun. 9:30-12:30; Tue. and Fri. also 3-5:30*). This building, which stands in the western part of Palermo, was erected in the 12th c. by the Norman kings of Sicily, William I and William II, and is a masterpiece of Muslim architecture. Its name derives from the Arabic word for splendid, "aziz," or ceramic tiles; it follows the Muslim architectural tradition of the pleasure house.

Cuba* (*F1; open 9-7; Sun. and holidays only in the morning*). This buildings was one of the pavillions in the park built by William II (1180); its appearance is exquisitely Islamic; there is even an inscription in Arabic in the frieze.

Surrounding areas. Eleven km NW (from A2) is the elegant beach resort of **Mondello**, next to a venerable old fishing village, north of Monte Pellegrino; near Punta Priola are a number of interesting caverns, inhabited in prehistoric times (paleolithic graffiti in the Grotta Addàura).

Fifteen km to the east is **Bagherìa** (80 m): Palermo's nobility built villas here from the 17th to the 19th c., in the countryside dotted with vineyards and citrus orchards. Architecturally, the finest one is Villa Valguarnera (1721), but the most famous is without a doubt Villa Palagonìa, renowned for its grotesque statues of dwarfs, beggars, Moors, Turks, musicians, chickadees and all sorts of cripples and freaks that line the high ground of the enclosure. The architect of the two villas was the Dominican monk Tommaso Maria Napoli.

Solunto.* Standing at an elevation of 235 m, this town on a ridge of Monte Catalfano (18 km east of Palermo) has a spectacular view of the sea. The Phoenicians founded an early trading town here, but the archeological site (*open 9-one hour before sunset*) has a Hellenistic-Roman city (4th c. B.C.-2nd c. A.D.): running off the from the main road at right angles are smaller roads, sometimes with steps, that follow the slope of the mountain; note the ruins of houses, the so-called Ginnasio (actually a home with a peristyle and atrium), a theater, and a "bouleuterion," or ancient Greek council chamber; the artifacts found in the digs are on display in an antiquarium.

Terrasini. This seaside village, about 15 km west of Carini, boasts a notable Museo Civico in three sections: the *section of natural history* (*tel. 0918682652, Via Calarossa 4*), the *archeological section* (*tel. 0918682652, Piazza Falcone e Borsellino 2*), and the Museo del Carretto Siciliano (*tel. 0918685636, Via Carlo Alberto Dalla Chiesa 38*), devoted to the history of the remarkable painted Sicilian carts.

Palestrina

Elev. 450 m, ab. 17,413; Lazio (Latium), province of Rome. When you go to the museum in Palazzo Barberini to see the mosaic depicting the flooding Nile, you will climb the same stairs up which people once climbed to consult the oracle. Medieval in appearance, this site is actually a combination of medieval architecture and the relics of the temple of Fortuna Primigenia, a venerated ancient Roman sanctuary. On the southern slope of Monte Ginestro, a ridge of the Monti Prenestini overlooking the Roman countryside, this complex stands on an ancient road running between the valleys of the Sacco and the Tiber.

Historical notes. Civitas Praenestina was its medieval name, hence Penestrina, and finally Palestrina; the medieval village gradually grew up on the site of the ancient, enormous, and long-abandoned sanctuary of Fortuna Primigenia, whose oracle had made the Roman city of Praeneste renowned throughout the Empire. From remains of the cyclopic walls, inscriptions, and funerary furnishings, we know that Praeneste existed in the 7th c. B.C. When the emperor Theodosius abolished all pagan worship, it spelled the end for the Temple of Fortuna Primigenia and for the city. The medieval village formed on the temple ruins; ruled by the powerful Colonna family, it suffered much destruction in periodic wars with the popes, until, in 1630, Francesco Colonna sold it to Carlo Barberini, brother of Pope Urban VIII. In 1525 the great composer Giovanni Pierluigi da Palestrina was born here. It was damaged by bombing in WWII, but the devastation was a blessing in disguise, allowing many of the structures of the ancient sanctuary to come to light, thus revealing one of the greatest monumental complexes in pre-Christian Italy.

Places of interest. Piazza Regina Margherita. This central square probably occupies the site of the Forum in Roman Praeneste. Overlooking it is a monumental, multistorey building, in which you can see remains of ancient walls and four Corinthian semicolumns; a 2nd-c. B.C. inscription identifies the *Aerarium*, in the basement. From the square, through the door to the left of the seminary, you enter the *Area Sacra*, a huge basilican space dug out of the side of the hill. On the right is the hall with apse, identified as the hall of the oracle. Once the great mosaic of the Nile stood here; it is now in the Museo Archeologico (see below). On the opposite side of the Area Sacra is the so-called *Antro delle Sorti*, or Cave of Destinies, a natural cavern that has been enlarged and built up, adorned with a mosaic floor depicting the bottom of the sea (1st c. B.C.) of which only fragments survive.

Duomo. This cathedral was built on the site of a Roman building made of tufa (possibly the "Iunonarium"), of which some relics survive. Only the facade

ilestrina: Palazzo Barberini

nd the bell tower remain of the original Roanesque structure. In the left aisle is a copy of
ichelangelo's Pietà di Palestrina.

intuario.* *Open 9-7.* You enter this monumental
omplex, dedicated to the goddess Fortuna Primi-
enia, dating from the mid-2nd c. B.C. and built on
an-made terracing, from Piazza della Cortina.
iree terraces rise, one above the other: the terrace
' the *Emicicli*, the terrace of the *Fornici*, and the
rrace of the *Cortina*. Overlooking the last terrace
the spare **Palazzo Barberini**, built in 1640 and
ow the site of the Museo Archeologico; at the base
' the building is a handsome staircase between
chitraved columns (15th c.).

iseo Nazionale Archeologico Prenestino.*
oen 9-7. Arranged in Palazzo Barberini, this mu-
·um comprises collections of artifacts found in
e sanctuary and the territory. Particularly inter-
ting pieces are a 4th-c. relief (Triumph of Con-
antine); a large 2nd-c. B.C. statue,* perhaps of For-
ne, badly damaged; bronze mirrors* and toiletries,
cluding cylindrical recipients. However, the best
ece is the renowned **mosaic*** of the flooding of
e Nile, probably dating from 80 B.C.

Rosalia. This church, next to Palazzo Barberini,
as built in 1656-60. In the rich Baroque interior,
ith four tombs by Barberini, a Pietà by Michelan-
:lo, known as the Pietà di Palestrina, once stood.
is now in Florence.

la degli Arcioni. This street takes its name from
e deep arches in the huge retaining wall that
olds up the terracing of the hill where the sanc-
ary was built. Recent excavations here have un-
arthed remains from the 1st c. B.C. The 17th-c. *Por-
del Sole* is a gate which leads into town.

illa Imperiale. Not far from the cemetery lie the
ins of a 2nd-c. building, now known as "Hadrian's
lla."

Parma**

Elev. 52 m, pop. 168,717; Emilia-Romagna,
provincial capital. The cities along the Via Emilia are united by their similar plains setting,
with nearby hill country, vigorous Po Valley architecture, cuisine with simple rich flavors, and
courtly manners. Each of these cities has a
distinctive personality due to its history. Parma
shows many aspects of its personality in the
medieval monuments upon which Antelami
worked, and in the delightful works created
by Correggio. The city is also a treasure trove
of opera and "bel canto," Stendhalian in the
refinement of its culture, and then, primarily,
ducal, if we may use the term (referring to the
three centuries, before Italian Unity, of Farnese
and Bourbon rule, with the interlude of the
ruler that the people of Parma still like to call,
with affectionate pretension, "la nostra Maria
Luigia," known to us as Marie Louise of Austria). Parma still maintains the atmosphere and
quality of life of a lesser European capital.

Historical note. The city is divided practically in
two by the river Parma, which runs through it from
south to north, but most of Parma's political and
artistic history has been concentrated on the right
bank of that stream; and the center of Parma is still
there, on the right bank. It expanded concentrical-
ly from there between the 11th-14th c., around the
plan of the old Roman colony, founded in 183 B.C.
The religious center of Parma developed to the
north of the Roman walls: the Duomo, or Cathedral,
which existed as early as 1046, was destroyed by
fire in 1055, was rebuilt and then damaged by earthquake in 1117, and was finally rebuilt shortly thereafter, this time to a rectangular plan, rather than a
square one, in the Romanesque style that we now
know. The Battistero, or Baptistery, on which
Benedetto Antelami worked, was begun in 1196.
These spectacular years of artistic creativity were
times of terrible conflict in political terms. Once the
conflict between the Guelphs and Ghibellines had
come to a halt, Parma enjoyed a period of peace in
the second half of the 13th c., during which the
Communal government gained in strength. The early decades of the 14th c., on the other hand, witnessed worsening conflict between the powerful
Corregeschi and Rossi families; as neither faction
managed to prevail, the city fell under foreign rule.
The House of the Della Scala was followed by the
Visconti in 1346. The Visconti held Parma for a century, until 1447; from 1449 until 1500 the city was
under Milanese rule, under the Sforza. The last major expansion of the walled perimeter to the south
and east took place under the Visconti, extending to
the Porta Nuova and Porta S. Michele and, to the
south, the Monastero delle Cappuccine. In the first
20 years of the 16th c., Parma repeatedly fell into
the hands of the French and the popes, until 1521,
when it definitively became part of the Papal States,

289

with Francesco Gucciardini as governor. In 1545 Pope Paul III Farnese gave Parma and Piacenza in fief to his son Pier Luigi; this was the origin of the duchy – which survived until 1860 – that had Parma as its capital (Piacenza was capital for a short period, until 1556). The architectural and cultural Renaissance brought about by the House of the Farnese resulted in the construction of the Palazzo della Pilotta with the adjacent Teatro Farnese, inaugurated in 1628 to the notes of music by Monteverdi; Palazzo Ducale with its grounds; the new Palazzo del Comune; and the great privileges and bequests given to the Università. In 1731 the Farnese dynasty died out, in a time of economic stagnation, and the Treaty of Aix-la-Chapelle in 1748 recognized the existence of the duchy (to which Guastalla was added, where a branch of the Gonzaga family had just died out), and awarded it to the Spanish prince Philip of Bourbon, born to a Farnese mother. Under him and under his son Ferdinand, both guided by the minister Du Tillot, Parma experienced a new period of economic and cultural activity. The Bourbon penchant for collecting lies at the origin of the Galleria Nazionale, the Biblioteca Palatina, and the Museo Archeologico Nazionale. The University grew considerably, and Bodoni established the ducal printing house. Following the turmoil of the Napoleonic period, the duchy did not fall back into the hands of the Bourbons, but was given as a lifelong holding to the second wife of Napoleon, and daughter of Francis I of Austria, Marie Louise (or Maria Luigia, as she is known here), who continued the works of generosity begun by her predecessors. She went down in popular myth as "l'amata sovrana," or "the beloved sovereign." During her reign, a new ducal theater was built, which we now know as the Teatro Regio, a symbol of Parma's musical life and one of Italy's most renowned opera houses. In 1847, after the death of Marie Louise, Parma once again fell under the rule of the Bourbon dynasty, who reigned here until 1860, when a plebiscite determined that it would be joined to the Kingdom of Sardinia, and then to the Kingdom of Italy. Between the end of the 19th c. and the early 20th c., Parma's walls were demolished; at that time, there had been few buildings outside these walls, and much farmland within them. At the turn of the 20th c., work began on the riverfront boulevards – the Lungoparma – and on the ring roads, or Viali di Circonvallazione, completed in 1932. Today, the city, chiefly due to the enormous development of the food industry, has expanded greatly in all directions, but especially to the north and along the Via Emilia: the 50,000 inhabitants of the early 20th c. have now become more than 150,000.

Places of interest. Piazza del Duomo* (*C4*). Intimate and silent, this square truly preserves its medieval character; surrounded by the Duomo, the Battistero, and the *Palazzo del Vescovado*.

Duomo** (*C4*). This cathedral is certainly one of the masterpieces of the 12th-c. Romanesque archi-

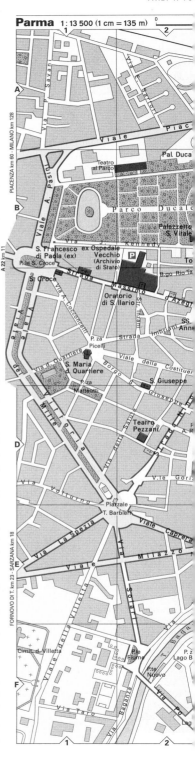

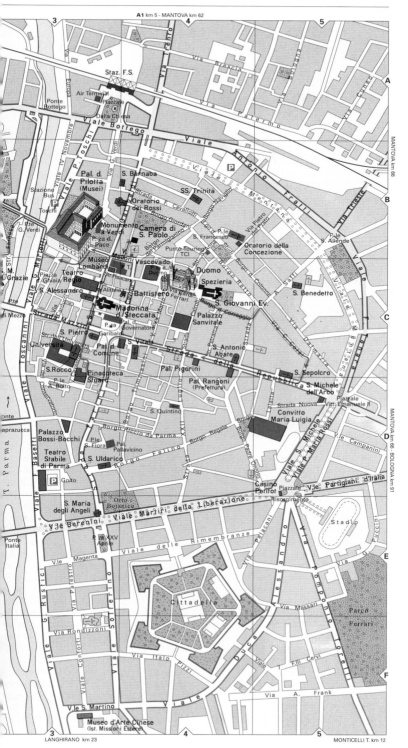

Parma: Duomo and Battistero

tecture of the Po Valley. Its austere facade is enlivened by three superposed rows of loggias; the central portal extends into a porch surmounted by an aedicula, by G. da Bissone (1281). The tall terracotta Gothic *bell tower* (1294) is noteworthy.

The *interior* features piers with lovely capitals. The walls of the high nave are frescoed (G. Mazzola-Bedoli, 16th c.); note the copper statue of the Archangel Raphael (1294). There are 15th-c. frescoes in various chapels, and an inlaid Baroque pulpit (1613). In the cupola is the majestic **Assumption of the Virgin** * * , by Correggio (1526-30). On the right wall of the right transept, the relief of the **Deposition** * by B. Antelami (1178). In the *apse*, note the 12th-c. episcopal throne*, with excellent high reliefs by Antelami, and the inlaid choir by C. da Lendinara (1473). In the huge *crypt* are the fragments of polychrome mosaics (especially the Early Christian depiction of fish).

Battistero * * (*C4*). *Open 9-12:30 and 3-6, 5 in winter.* This lively Romanesque-Gothic Baptistery (1196-1270) with an octagonal plan is combed with lovely architraved loggias. In the lower section, the reliefs* on the three portals and the decorative fillets and the statues* in the niches, by B. Antelami, are one of the masterpieces of Italian Romanesque sculpture.

The octagonal interior, with niches, two rows of small loggias, and high ribbed cupola, contains Antelami's high-reliefs of the **Months** *, the **Seasons** * (note Winter and Spring), and the **Signs of the Zodiac** *; the frescoes with a Byzantine flavor, in the lunettes and cupola, are largely from the late 13th c.; in the center of the Baptistery is a double baptismal font (13th c.).

Storica Spezieria di S. Giovanni Evangelista (*C4*). *Open 8:30-2; closed Mon.* At n. 1 in Borgo Pipa, behind the Benedictine monastery of S. Giovanni, is the old pharmacy of the Benedictines, founded in 1201. In operation until 1766, it was restored and reopened to the public in 1959. In the three rooms, adorned with 16th-c. frescoes, furniture, and shelves, there are 192 ceramic pharmacy jars dating from the 15th-17th c. Also, note the giant mortars; in a fourth room there are alembics, retorts, and ancient instruments.

S. Giovanni Evangelista * (*C4*). This Renaissance church (1510) has a facade and bell tower dating from the early 17th c. *Inside*, set in exceedingly elegant architecture, is a renowned cycle of **frescoes** * * by Correggio and Parmigianino. The vaults and candelabra were decorated by M. Anselmi (1520-21) under the guidance of Correggio; the painted lacunar ceiling and frieze are by F.M. Rondani, after drawings by Correggio (1522-23). In the *apse*, note the inlaid and carved choir* by M.A. Zucchi (1512-13), and paintings by G.M. Bedoli (ca 1556). In the transepts are four terracotta statues by A. Begarelli. Also worthy of note are the sacristy with inlaid early 16th-c. armoires, and three 16th-c. cloisters of the monastery (*open 6:30-12 and 3:30-8*). In the Sala Capitolare (enter from second cloister) there are two detached frescoes* by Correggio.

S. Sepolcro (*C5*). This 13th-c. church was renovated in the 15th c. (note carved candelabra, 1501, on the unfinished facade); various paintings and statues inside, worthy of note. In particular, however, in the first chapel on right, there are the late 15th-c. fresco* and the oil amphorae, unearthed below the church, evidence of human occupation of this site in Republican Roman times.

Piazza Garibaldi (*C3*). Called Piazza Grande in the 19th c., this square lies in the center of Parma with the monument to Garibaldi, *Palazzo del Governatore* with its *Torre* (1673), or tower, and the porticoed Palazzo del Comune (1627). Also, to right the former *Palazzo del Podestà* (13th c.).

Pinacoteca Giuseppe Stuard (*C-D3*). *Open Mon. Wed.-Sat., 9:30-6:30; Sun., 9-1:20.* This is the leading private collection of Parma (1834), owned by the church. The collection comprises over 270 paintings; works by early Tuscan painters (P. di Giovanni di Ambrogio, B. di Lorenzo, N. di Tommaso) and 17th-/18th-c. painters (B. Schedoni, S. Ricci, and Fontebasso).

Università (*C3*). Housed in a stern, majestic 16th c. building, once a Jesuit college, the University has the interesting **Raccolte di Storia Naturale** (*open Thu., 3-5; for groups and schools, by request, tel 0521234082*), or natural history collections, in such fields as paleontology, mineralogy, and zoology, as well as the Museo Zoologico Eritreo "Bottego," or Eritrean zoo, and the Raccolta "Piola," with ethnographic and zoological collections from the former Belgian Congo (present-day Zaire).

Strada Garibaldi (*B-C3-4*). This road runs past the Neo-Classic **Teatro Regio** (1829), one of Italy's most renowned opera houses (hall with four tiers of boxes). Almost directly across the road is the church of the Madonna della Steccata (see below). From Piazza Garibaldi the Strada Mazzini leads to the *Ponte di Mezzo*, a bridge over the Parma River; take the underpass along the right bank to see the remains of the *Roman bridge* on the Via Emilia, built during the reign of Augustus and used until the course of the river shifted in the 12th. c.

Madonna della Steccata * (*C3*). This church, designed by B. and G.F. Zaccagni (1521-25), is a Renaissance structure, with large semicircular apses and cupolas adorned with loggias. The majestic *interior* is decorated with frescoes by artists of the 16th-c. Parmesan school, among them B. Gatti, M. Anselmi, G. Mazzola-Bedoli, and Parmigianino. Also, note the funerary monument by L. Bartolini and, in the sacristy, the inlaid wooden armoires. Beneath the church are the tombs of the Farnese, dukes of Parma.

Piazza della Pace (*B3*). In this square, note the *Monumento al Partigiano* (1955), or monument to the WWII resistance fighter, and a *monument to G. Verdi* (1913). At the far side of the square, Palazzo della Pilotta (see below). Overlooking the square, in Strada Garibaldi at n. 15, in the Neo-Classic *Palazzetto di Riserva* (note stuccoes by E. Petitot), is the **Museo Glauco Lombardi** (*C3; open Tue.-Sat., 10-3; Sun. and holidays, 9-1*). This museum has a collection of memorabilia and documents from the entire period of Bourbon rule (18th-19th c.), and especially from the reign of Marie Louise, duchess of Parma (1816-1831), as well as the Napoleonic era. Note paintings, mostly by 18th-c. French artists.

Camera di S. Paolo★★ *or del Correggio* (*B4*). *Open 9-1:45; closed Mon.* A major center of Parmesan culture, adjacent to the former Benedictine nunnery of S. Paolo, it can be reached from the Strada Macedonio Melloni. Originally part of the private apartment of the abbess, it was renovated and decorated from 1514 on, at the behest of Giovanna da Piacenza. Correggio worked here in 1519, in his first major project, achieving one of the masterpieces of the mature Italian Renaissance. The hall is covered with an umbrella vault, divided into 16 gores, set on lunettes: Correggio painted a pergola with putti set in tondos, and in the lunettes★ he painted classical monochrome figures. In an adjacent room there are frescoes by A. Araldi (1514).

Palazzo della Pilotta (*B3*). Impressive building erected by the Farnese in 1583-1622, unfinished. Its name comes from the game of "pelota," played in a courtyard. It houses the Museo Archeologico Nazionale – the Galleria Nazionale – one of Italy's finest art galleries – and the Biblioteca Palatina.
Museo Archeologico Nazionale.★ *Open Tue.-Sun., 8:30-7:30.* Founded by Philip I of Bourbon in 1760, in conjunction with the dig at Veleia, this is one of Italy's earliest archeological collections, stocked largely with local finds. Note sculpture from the great Farnese and Gonzaga collections; an Egyptian collection; Greek, Italiot, and Etruscan ceramics; Greek and Roman coins; a fine 1st-c. B.C. bust of the head of a youth; the slab of the *Lex de Gallia Cisalpina*, and the **tabula alimentaria**, from Trajan's time. Moreover, there are local collections of prehistoric material, and Celtic artifacts as well. All sorts of Roman material (amphorae, bronzes, marble, mosaics) come last.
Galleria Nazionale.★★ *Open 8:30-2.* Of special importance in terms of Parmesan painting from the 15th to the 18th c., this gallery boasts a number of masterpieces by Correggio, among others. As a surprising and theatrical atrium to the Galleria you will pass through the magnificent **Teatro Farnese★**

(1617-18), one of the most attractive theaters on earth, rebuilt in the 1950s, following the damage from bombing in 1944. The collections are arranged in sections, by school and chronological order. In the medieval section you will find capitals and sculptural fragments, including three capitals by B. Antelami. Early painting of the 14th-15th c. includes works by A. Gaddi, P. Veneziano, Fra' Angelico, and B. Daddi. Then come frescoes and paintings by A. and B. degli Erri, F. Francia, and Leonardo da Vinci. In the section of 17th-c. Emilian painters are F. Mazzola, D. and B. Dossi, and Garofalo; among the 16th-c. Italian paintings are several Virgins and Child (by M. Anselmi, G. Gandini del Grano) and canvases by S. del Piombo and G. Romano. The section featuring the Parmesan school of the 16th-17th c. includes works by G.M. Bedoli, G.B. Tinti, and L. Spada; there are also works from the Flemish school (J. Sons, D. Calvaert), the Venetian (Tintoretto, Palma the Younger, El Greco), the Emilian (the Carracci) and the Lombard (G.C. Procaccini) schools. The 17th-c. section features works by painters of various schools: Bolognese (C. Aretusi, Guercino), Genoan (Genovesino, G.A. De Ferrari), Spanish (Murillo, Giobbe★), Flemish (A. van Dyck), and Lombard (C.F. Nuvolone). From 18th-c. Venice, works by G.B. Tiepolo, G.B. Piazzetta, Canaletto, and S. Ricci. The 19th-c. halls are noteworthy chiefly for some of the most important works by Correggio and Parmigianino.
In the same building is housed the *Biblioteca Palatina* (*open, reading room, Mon.-Thu., 8:30-6:45; Fri.-Sat., 9-1; manuscripts and rare books, Mon.-Sat., 8:30-12:30*), a library endowed with almost 700,000 volumes, 6620 manuscripts, 70,100 autograph manuscripts, 3041 incunabula, and 50,479 prints, engravings, and illuminated codices from the 9th-10th c.; part of the library is the *Museo Bodoniano* (*open by request, tel. 0521220411*), with a collection of editions by the great court printer.
Palazzo Ducale (*B2*). *Open only for groups, by request, tel. 0421230023.* The ducal palace is situated in a lovely park, created in 1561 on 20 hectares of land along the left bank of the Parma River. The palace was designed by Vignola, and enlarged by Petitot in 1767. Note the halls frescoed by Agostino Carracci, A. Tiarini, G. Mirola and with 18th-c. stuccowork.
Casa di Toscanini (*B2*). *Open Tue.-Sat., 10-1 and 3-6; Sun., 10-1.* N. 13 Borgo Tanzi, birthplace of the great conductor Toscanini; memorabilia.

The outlying districts

Cittadella (*E-F4*). This citadel was built by P.L. Farnese in the 16th c. to a pentagonal plan, with five bastions and a moat; handsome marble portal. Inside is a park.
Museo di Arte Cinese (*F3*). *Open Tue.-Sun., 9-12 and 3-7.* This museum of Chinese art is located in the *Istituto Saveriano per le Missioni Estere*, in Viale S. Martino n. 8; it has a collection of bronzes and porcelain, dating back to the 3rd millennium B.C.

Surrounding areas. The **Certosa di Parma** (*open Mon.-Fri., 8-12 and 2-5; Sat. and Sun. 9-12*), or Charterhouse of Parma, 4 km NE. Founded by Carthusian monks in 1285, this building figured in the novel by Stendhal; it is now a school for prison guards. In the church, frescoes by S. Galeotti and F. Bibiena. The **Castello di Torrechiara*** (*open Oct.-Mar., Tue.-Sun., 8:30-1:15; Apr.-Sep., Tue.-Fri., 9-1:45; Sat. and holidays, 9-6:15*), 17.5 km south, on the left bank of the Parma is one of the largest castles in the area. Built by P.M. Rossi (1448-60), it has three concentric sets of walls, with corner towers. Inside, note frescoes by C. Baglione and B. Bembo* (1463).

Pavìa*

Elev. 77 m, pop. 73,752; Lombardia (Lombardy), provincial capital. Lying along the Ticino river's left bank, just upstream from the confluence with the Po, Pavìa is surrounded by verdant riverine landscapes. "Centium turrium," a 14th-c. chronicler wrote, calling it the town of "100 towers." Ancient, brick-red towers, silent streets, snug little squares, and warm Lombard terracotta – this is the historic center, where 18th/19th-c. opulence is the facade to an underlying structure that dates back to the Middle Ages. Two famed Romanesque churches are benchmarks of Italian art. Pavìa's venerable university and its 16th-c. "collegi" are noteworthy presences here.

Historical note. The 48 "insulae" or blocks of Pavìa in Roman times stretch from Corso Carlo Alberto south to Corso Garibaldi; the checkerboard layout can still be seen, with the "cardo" and "decumanus," echoed by the center's chief streets (Strada Nuova, Corso Cavour and Corso Mazzini). Pavìa was capital of the Kingdom of Italy in the High Middle Ages. During the time of the communes (11th c. on), the thriving city had 40,000 inhabitants, one of the largest in northern Italy. Walls built then (13th. c.) enclosed the modern center (bounded by the Ticino-Viale della Libertà-N. Sauro-Gorizia-della Resistenza). At the same time, early medieval churches were rebuilt in brilliant Romanesque Pavian brickwork and masonry: first and foremost, S. Michele, as well as S. Pietro in Ciel d'Oro and the twin basilicas where the Duomo now stands. The tradition of study here dates back to A.D. 825, the University to 1361, when it was founded by a Visconti and by the emperor Charles IV. To help the school grow, the Visconti forbade their subjects to study elsewhere. A burst of activity after Milan subjugated Pavìa in 1359 resulted in the Castello Visconteo, the Piazza Grande (or Piazza della Vittoria), and the Strada Nuova, running to the bridge over the Ticino, built and covered during the 13th c. Construction began on the university campus in 1485. Artists working in Pavìa included Michelino da Besozzo, Pisanello, Foppa, Bramante, Leonardo da Vinci, and Solari. The construction of the Duomo

crowned an age of great artistic achievement. Bramante and Leonardo both worked on the design of the tambour that rose at the axis of the Greek cross plan, though it was not completed till centuries later. In a famed 1525 battle here, the Holy Roman Emperor's troops captured France's King Francis I. Spanish occupation was followed by Savoy rule (1743). Pavìa declined to a military border town, with a venerable university, that was enlarged under the rule of Austrian monarchs Maria Teresa and Joseph II. Great poets and scientists, such as A. Volta, L. Spallanzani, Vincenzo Monti, and Ugo Foscolo lectured here. During the 19th-20th c., the city prospered and became industrialized (the first synthetic silk mill in Italy opened here in 1905).

Getting around. A section of the historic center is closed to cars. The route shown is wholly a walking tour; you'll probably want to take public transportation back from Borgo Ticino.

Places of interest. S. Pietro in Ciel d'Oro.** This splendid Romanesque church was consecrated in 1132. The facade echoes the architecture of S. Michele, in a smaller version; the portal is adorned with fine carvings. Above the main altar is the Gothic marble **Arca di S. Agostino*** (tomb of St. Augustine, whose bones were moved to Pavìa in the 8th c.), executed by Lombard sculptors (1362). Behind the altar is a sarcophagus with the bones of Boethius, a late Roman philosopher executed by the Longobard king Theodoric as a traitor in A.D. 524.
Castello Visconteo.** Built by Galeazzo II Visconti in 1360, the castle is a great square brick building, with corner towers and two rows of Gothic mullioned windows and crenelations. Its north side was badly damaged during the Battle of Pavìa in 1525. The moat is temporarily the site of the stone remains of the Torre Civica, which collapsed in 1989. Note the huge *courtyard**, surrounded by a portico on three

Pavìa: S. Michele

sides, with terracotta decorations. Many halls of the castle are part of the yet unfinished **Musei Civici** (*open Dec.-Feb., Jul.-Aug., Tue.-Sat., 9-1:30; Sun., 9-1; Mar.-Jun., Sep.-Nov., Tue.-Fri., 9-1:30; Sat.-Sun., 10-7*). In these municipal museums you can see collections of *Roman and medieval archeology, sculpture*, mosaics, and the frescoes taken from S. Agata al Monte (15th c.). The **Pinacoteca Malaspina*** features works by Foppa, Boltraffio, Bergognone, Butinone, Giambono, G. Bellini, and Correggio. There is a Renaissance model of the Duomo.

Strada Nuova. Pavìa's main street runs north-south, from the Castello to the Ticino. Along it are the **Teatro Fraschini** (undergoing restoration), designed by A. Galli Bibiena and built in 1771, and the **University**, founded in 1485. Giuseppe Piermarini designed the Neo-Classic building that now stands here; inside are five handsome courtyards. Two of them lead to the adjacent former *hospital of S. Matteo* (now part of the university). The complex houses the **Museo per la Storia dell'Università di Pavìa** (*open by request, tel. 038229724*). In the nearby *Piazza L. da Vinci* stand three *Romanesque towers* and a medieval *crypt*.

Carmine. Built in 1390, the church has a monumental facade. Inside, works of art dating from the 15th-16th c.

Piazza della Vittoria or *Piazza Grande*. In the heart of Pavìa, edged with porticoes and 14th-/15th-c. houses. On one side is the ancient Town Hall, or **Broletto** (12th c.), with two rows of loggias (1563).

Piazza del Duomo. Adorned with statuary, the huge *Torre Civica* stood here till its collapse in 1989. Damage can still be seen on nearby houses.

Duomo.* A major monument of the Lombard Renaissance, the cathedral was partly designed by Bramante, Leonardo da Vinci, and Francesco di Giorgio Martini (1490), but construction continued almost to the end of the 16th c. The facade and cupola date from the late 19th c.

The *interior* is built to a Greek cross plan. Note the high, vast central cupola. Works by Bramante adorn the vaults of the crypt.

S. Michele.** Founded by the Longobards, this basilica was rebuilt in the mid-12th c. It is Pavìa's chief monument and a masterpiece of Romanesque architecture. Kings and emperors – Frederick Barbarossa, for one – were crowned here. Note the sandstone facade*, with loggia and pilaster strips. Carvings and reliefs (12th c.) adorn the sides and the three portals.

Inside, note the late 10th-c. Crucifix, carved main altar (1383), and late 15th-c. fresco.

S. Teodoro. This Romanesque church dates from the 12th c. Inside, a nave with two aisles and raised transept; 13th-/14th-c. frescoes and a view of Pavìa (1522), with its many medieval towers.

Ponte Coperto sul Ticino. Destroyed by bombing in 1944, this is a partly faithful reconstruction of the bridge built in 1354. Across the bridge lies the *Borgo Ticino*, with the 12th-c. Romanesque church of **S. Maria in Betlem**.

Perugia**

Elev. 493 m, pop. 156,673; Umbria, regional and provincial capital. Situated in the green valley of the Tiber and not far from Lake Trasimeno, Perugia is perched on a jagged hill, carpeting the ridges and slopes. N. and G. Pisano worked on the great fountain, or Fontana Maggiore, seven centuries ago; A. di Duccio planned and carved the facade of the church of S. Bernardino, the artist Perugino (from nearby Città della Pieve) frescoed the Sala dell'Udienza, and the local Renaissance architect G. Alessi constructed his first buildings here. The image is even older and more complex: Etruscan walls and arches, stern stone towers, the carved marble of palazzi and churches, the Guelph lion and the proud city griffon on the walls of Palazzo dei Priori. At sunset, you can see the lovely heart of Umbria, from a garden where the Rocca Paolina once stood, a fortress built by Pope Paul III and designed by A. da Sangallo the Younger. It was destroyed by the angry citizenry. Perugia is a perfect example of the Italian art of shaping cities into astonishing atmospheres.

Historical note. Perugia is an accretion of the original Etruscan and Roman settlements, with three extensions that crept over outlying ridges. The oldest inhabited section is of course on the hilltop, and is enclosed by the Etruscan walls that link Porta Marzia, Porta S. Ercolano, Porta Sole, the Arco Etrusco and the Arco della Mandorla. Here, from the 4th to the 1st c. B.C., was one of the capitals of Etruscan Italy, alternately allied with and fighting against the burgeoning power of Rome. During the great civil wars following the assassination of Julius Caesar, Perugia supported Mark Antony, and when Octavian triumphed, becoming the Emperor Augustus, Perugia paid the price, suffering siege and sack in 40 B.C. Byzantines ruled here, and Goths took the town in A.D. 547, followed by Longobards. Perugia ruled herself after the year 1000, though many popes resided here, and five conclaves were held here, away from the poisonous intrigues of Rome. Beginning in 1321, new and larger walls were built, and around the Palazzo dei Priori, streets were extended, while the Duomo and the churches of S. Francesco, S. Domenico, and S. Agostino rose. The 14th c. was a time of war, and Perugia held her own, until the popes cast their eyes on her. In time, Perugia had one seigneur after another, the best known being Braccio Fortebraccio da Montone, who began building Renaissance Perugia. Construction went on under the Baglioni, particularly Palazzo dei Capitani del Popolo and the Oratorio di S. Bernardino. Pope Paul III finally decided to bring Perugia into the papal fold, and on the ruins of the houses of the Baglioni he built the powerful Rocca Paolina (1540). The fortress was destroyed as Italy began to acquire its independence and unity, from 1848 to 1860. Perugia expanded onto the plains at the foot of the hill during the 20th c.

Getting around. We suggest three routes: the first winds entirely through the older, monumental heart of Perugia, within the Etruscan walls; the other two go through the northern and southern districts, within the 14th-c. walls. Because of Perugia's steep narrow streets and traffic regulations prohibiting cars in much of the center, we do not recommend that you drive. Elevators and escalators will take you from parking lots outside of the center up to the high part of town, and you can use buses to take you to the more distant monuments.

The city within the Etruscan walls

The first route runs almost completely through the high part of town, within the Etruscan walls. From Piazza IV Novembre it follows Corso Vannucci to Piazza Italia, goes down to Piazza Matteotti, and then follows Via dei Priori through a lovely medieval section of town, ending at the convent of S. Francesco al Prato.

Piazza IV Novembre* (*C3*). This square has been the heart of Perugia since Etruscan times, the center of religious and political power and of artistic achievement, with the Fontana Maggiore, Palazzo dei Priori, the Cattedrale, and the Loggia di Braccio Fortebraccio (see below).

Fontana Maggiore** (*C3*). Emblematic of the medieval "Commune" and symbol of Perugia, this fountain was built in 1275-78 to plans by G. and N. Pisano, as the outlet of the aqueduct from Monte Pacciano. It comprises two concentric marble basins, adorned with sculptures, and a bronze cup with a group of three Nymphs, or Theological Virtues. Note the beautiful reliefs depicting the **Months of the Year**** and the 24 statuettes on the upper basin.

Loggia di Braccio Fortebraccio (*C3*). This loggia was built in the 15th c., under the rule of Fortebraccio. Note the fragment of Roman wall as well as the *Palazzo Arcivescovile*, with the **Museo di Storia Naturale** (*temporarily closed*) with collections of natural history.

Via Maestà delle Volte* (*C3*). Leading down from Piazza IV Novembre to Piazza Felice Cavallotti, this street passes before 13th-c. houses and beneath dark passages, in what is one of the most evocative settings in medieval Perugia. The white-and-red striped Gothic arch is all that remains of the 14th-c. oratory of the *Maestà delle Volte*.

Cattedrale* (*C3*). Begun as a Gothic church in 1345 on the site of a Roman building, work on this cathedral went forward by fits and starts (1437-1587) but was never finished. The unfinished left side, partly covered in pink and white marble, overlooks the square. Dominating the steps on this side is a statue of Pope Julius III, by V. Danti (1555); to the right of the 16th-c. portal (G. Alessi) is a pulpit from which Bernardino da Siena once preached. *Inside* you will

RACCORDO AUTOSTRADALE A1 - AS

Perugia: Piazza IV Novembre, Palazzo dei Priori, and Fontana Maggiore

find a wide range of styles and decorative approaches. In the chapel of S. Bernardino is a Deposition by F. Barocci. Across from it is a chapel which holds the revered relic of the Virgin's supposed wedding ring (1498), which can be seen only on 30 July. In the apse, note the carved and inlaid choir* by G. da Maiano and D. del Tasso (1486-91).

Museo Capitolare di S. Lorenzo *(C3; open 11-1; Sun., also 4-7)*. Adjacent to the Cathedral, this museum features paintings and frescoes by Umbrian and Sienese artists of the 14th-16th c., including B. Caporali and M. di Guido da Siena, and a magnificent **Madonna in Trono** by L. Signorelli.

Palazzo dei Priori ** *(C3)*. Built in several stages (1293-1443) in a rigid Gothic style, this is one of the largest and most impressive "palazzi pubblici" in medieval Italy, a combination of courthouse and town hall. It is now Perugia's Town Hall. The oldest section comprises the three mullioned windows on the left, overlooking the piazza, and the first ten mullioned windows overlooking Corso Vannucci. Note the fine portal (ca. 1326) on the Corso, and the staircase and large Gothic portal, surmounted by bronze statues of the Guelph lion and the Perugian griffin (1281). This portal leads into the large **Sala dei Notari** * *(open 9-1 and 3-7; Oct.-May, closed Mon.)*.

Galleria Nazionale dell'Umbria ** *(C3)*. *Open 8:30-7:30; closed 1st Mon. of the month; tel. 0755720316.* On the third floor of Palazzo dei Priori, this gallery has one of the most important collections of 13th- to 18th-c. art of Central Italy, especially Umbria, Tuscany, and the Marche.

Founded in 1863, it was given to the Italian State in 1918 as the Regia Pinacoteca Vannucci and includes the art works from religious institutions closed after the Unification of Italy, and the works owned by Perugia's Accademia di Belle Arti. It has been located in the Palazzo dei Priori since 1879. Since 1918, the collection has grown constantly, through donations and acquisitions, and the museum now owns over 1500 works. For years, restoration and modernization have been underway. With time, more and more halls will be opened to the public.

Among the artists whose work is on display (in chronological order), the most important are: A. di

Cambio, M. da Perugia, M. da Siena, D. di Boninsegna, F. da Rimini, O. Nelli, L. Salimbeni, L. di Velletri, B. Gozzoli, and G. Boccati. Thoroughly represented here is Perugian painting of the late 15th c., including: B. Bonfigli, N. Alunno, F. di Lorenzo, Fra' Angelico, F. di Giorgio Martini, P. della Francesca, and Pinturicchio. There are many paintings by Perugino and his followers of the 15th-16th c., among them G. di Paolo, B. di Giovanni, D. Alfani. Then come works by painters of the Mannerist period, especially those of Central Italy. Among them are: V. Danti, G.B. Naldini, and M. Venusti. Up the spiral staircase, you can see works by artists of the 17th to 19th c., including P. da Cortona, O. Gentileschi, V. de Boulogne, S. Conca, P. Subleyras, C. Giaquinto, and F. Trevisani.

Collegio della Mercanzia * *(C3)*. *Open Mar.-Oct. and 20 Dec.-6 Jan., Mon.-Sat., 9-1 and 2:30-5:30; Sun. and holidays, 9-1; Nov.-19 Dec. and 7 Jan.-Feb., 8-2; Tue., Thu.-Fri., Wed. and Sat., 8-4:30; Sun. and holidays, 9-1; Nov.-Feb., closed Mon.* On the ground floor of Palazzo dei Priori, the entrance to the right of the main portal, it was the headquarters of the powerful guild of the merchants. Inside, the richly inlaid wood of the *Sala dell'Udienza* is particularly impressive.

Collegio del Cambio ** *(C3)*. *Open Mar.-Oct. and 20 Dec.-6 Jan., Mon.-Sat., 9-12:30 and 2:30-5:30; Sun. and holidays, 9-12:30; Nov.-19 Dec. and 7 Jan.-Feb., Mon.-Sat., 8-2; Sun. and holidays, 9-12:30; Nov.-Feb., closed Mon.* Headquarters of the powerful guild of the money-changers, this building was built in 1452-57 at the far end of the Palazzo dei Priori. From the vestibule (*Sala dei Legisti*) with its Baroque wooden benches, you enter the *Sala dell'Udienza* *, one of the great bequests of Renaissance culture. The magnificent wooden tribunal was carved and inlaid by D. del Tasso (1493); the walls and ceiling were frescoed by **Perugino** ** and workshop (possibly Raphael among them). In the adjacent *Cappella di S. Giovanni Battista*, note the frescoes by G. di Paolo (1513-28) and the altarpiece by M. di Ser Austerio (1512), a pupil of Perugino.

Corso Vannucci *(C-D3)*. Perugia's most elegant street, and the main one since Etruscan times; note the *Palazzetto dei Notari* (1438-46) and, at the other end, the 18th-c. *Palazzo Donini (D3)*.

Piazza Italia *(D3)*. This 19th-c. square was laid out

after the destruction of the 16th-c. papal fortress, the Rocca Paolina (1860); the far end is occupied by the porticoed *Palazzo del Governo* (*D3;* 1872), behind which are the *Giardini Carducci* (*D3*), gardens with a spectacular view** of the heart of Umbria.

Piazza Matteotti (*C3*). Built in the late 13th-c. on artificial terracing, it faces the long facade of the *Università Vecchia*, or Old University (1490-1514), and the elegant **Palazzo del Capitano del Popolo*** (*C4*) (1472-81), with fine portals, windows, and balcony. The arch at n. 18 leads to a covered market (1932) and a panoramic terrace. Note the 14th-c. porticoed *Via Volte della Pace*.

Chiesa del Gesù (*C4*). At the north end of Piazza Matteotti is this 16th-c. church, with a splendid Baroque altar, frescoes, and paintings by S. Amadei; see the *three oratories* below the church, with frescoes.

Via dei Priori (*C3*). This road passes under the Palazzo Comunale, through the *Arco dei Priori*, and descends through a district with a strong medieval flavor. On the left is the little 14th-c. church of *Ss. Severo e Agata*, with fine frescoes; facing it is the odd, twisting *Via Ritorta*. Further along, on the right, is the Baroque church of **S. Filippo Neri** (*C3;* 17th c.), with an altarpiece by P. da Cortona (1662); then, the church of *Ss. Stefano e Valentino*, built in the 12th c. Last, on the left, the high **tower of the Sciri*** (13th c.); then the road ends at the medieval *Porta Trasimena*. Note the 16th-c. church of the **Madonna della Luce*** (*C2*).

S. Bernardino* (*C2*). This church is a gem of Renaissance architecture and sculpture; it was built in honor of a saint who often preached in Perugia. The harmonious facade is by A. di Duccio (1457-61); note the statues and reliefs. Inside, the high altar is a 4th-c. Roman sarcophagus.

S. Francesco al Prato (*C2*). This immense Gothic church was built in the mid-13th c. and rebuilt often thereafter. Next door is the *Accademia di Belle Arti*, or Academy of Fine Arts, founded in the 16th c.; the *Museum* (*open 10-1; closed Sun.*) has a large collection of statues, paintings from the 19th-20th c., drawings, and prints.

The northern districts

This route covers the expansion of Perugia northward, beyond the Etruscan walls. From Piazza Danti, you follow Corso Garibaldi to Porta S. Angelo; then, from Piazza Fortebraccio, you continue to the church of S. Maria Nuova and Corso Bersaglieri, heart of the medieval Borgo di S. Antonio. You then return to the center along the Colle del Sole, enjoying a fine view from Piazza Rossi Scotti.

Piazza Danti (*C3*). Stretching along the right side of the Cathedral, this was Perugia's marketplace in the Middle Ages. At n. 18 is the entrance to the **Pozzo Etrusco** (*open Mar.-Oct., 10-1:30 and 2:30-6:30; Nov.-Feb., 10:30-1:30 and 2:30-4:30; Sat.-Sun., until 5:30*), or Etruscan Well, a 3rd-c. B.C. structure of no-

table size: 37 m deep, 5.6 m across. *Via Cesare Battisti* (*B-C3*), a terrace road built in 1901, runs past a long stretch of Etruscan walls (fine view to the north), and drops down to Piazza Fortebraccio. Next to the Arco Etrusco (see below) is the 17th-c. church of *S. Fortunato*.

Arco Etrusco* (*B3*). The Etruscan Arch was built in the 3rd c. B.C. and was the main gate of the Etruscan walls. Note the later Doric frieze, with the Roman inscriptions "Augusta Perusia" and "Colonia Vibia." The loggia and fountain on the left side date from the 16th c.

Piazza Fortebraccio (*B3-4*). This square is dominated by the Baroque *Palazzo Gallenga Stuart* (1748-58), now the Università Italiana per Stranieri. In nearby *Via S. Elisabetta*, note the large 2nd-c. Roman *mosaic* (*B3; open 8-7; closed Sat. and holidays*).

Corso Garibaldi (*A-B3*). This narrow street climbs through a medieval neighborhood lined with small, old buildings. On the right, the church of **S. Agostino** (*B4*) has several fine works of art: 14th/16th-c. frescoes, wooden choir by B. d'Agnolo (1502), and altarpiece by G. di Paolo. Along the Corso, at n. 179, is the **monastery of S. Caterina** (*A3*), built in 1574, perhaps by G. Alessi; at n. 191, the *monastery of the Beata Colomba* – note the paintings by G. Spagna; nearby, is the *monastery of S. Agnese* (*B3*), with a fresco* by Perugino.

S. Angelo* (*A3*). This remarkable Early Christian church (5th or 6th c.), with a central plan, has a 14th-c. Gothic portal. Inside, an ambulacrum, marked by 16 columns with Roman capitals, runs around a central space. On the walls are detached frescoes; in the baptistery there are frescoes by a 15th-c. Umbrian painter.

Porta S. Angelo (*A3*). The largest of Perugia's medieval gates, with parapets and loopholes, it marks the end of the long Corso Garibaldi; beyond it, in Via Monte Ripido, is the 13th-c. church of *S. Matteo degli Armeni* (*A2*).

Via Pinturicchio (*B-C4*). Return to Piazza Fortebraccio and follow this road to the 13th-c. church of **S. Maria Nuova** (*C4*). The portal on Via Pinturicchio and the bell tower date from the 16th c.; possibly by G. Alessi. *Inside*, banner painted by B. Bonfigli (1471); wooden choir* (1456); and 15th-c. frescoes by L. Vasari. Then take the 13th-c. *Arco dei Tei* to *Corso Bersaglieri* (*B4-5*) which leads through the Borgo di Porta *S. Antonio*, the last fragment of medieval Perugia, running past the church of S. Antonio, to the 14th-c. *Porta di S. Antonio* (*B5*).

S. Maria di Monteluce (*B5*). Founded in the 13th c., rebuilt in 1451, this church has a handsome twin portal and a marble facade in red-and-white panels. Inside, note the frescoes, including one by F. di Lorenzo. The adjacent monastery is now a hospital.

S. Severo (*C4*). In the small and isolated Piazza Raffaello, this ancient church, traditionally said to have once been a temple to the Sun, now has an 18th-c. appearance. The adjacent **chapel** (*open Mar.-Oct., 10-1:30 and 2:30-6:30; Nov.-Feb., 10:30-1:30 and 2:30-4:30; Sat.-Sun. until 5:30*) has a fine fresco* by

Raphael (1505-08), completed in the lower half by Perugino (1521).

Le Prome (*C4*). The highest *square* in Perugia, once the acropolis, set high atop a retaining wall with great arches (1374). Excellent view. Note the little church of *S. Angelo della Pace* (*C4;* 1545) and the 17th-c. *Palazzo Conestabile della Staffa*, now a library.

***

The southern districts

From Porta Marzia, in the eastern bastion of the long-destroyed Rocca Paolina, the route follows Corso Cavour, through the historic Borgo di Porta S. Pietro. The district first extended to the Porta S. Pietro, enclosed by 13th-c. walls and a few centuries later extended to Porta di S. Costanzo, just past the church of S. Pietro. One then returns, after various excursions, up the stairs of Paradiso and through the Arco della Mandorla.

Porta Marzia (*D3*). Set alongside the Via Porta Marzia, this Etruscan gate probably dates from the 2nd c. B.C.; it is now part of the *Rocca Paolina*, a fortress built by A. da Sangallo the Younger in 1540 and destroyed in 1860. The gate is one of the entrances to the subterranean **Via Bagliona**, which runs through the remains of the medieval district upon which the fortress was erected.

S. Ercolano (*D3-4*). Set against the ancient walls, this Gothic church (1297-1326) has a Roman sarcophagus as its main altar. To the right of the church, a stairway leads up to the Etruscan *arch of S. Ercolano* (*D3-4*), rebuilt in Gothic times.

S. Domenico* (*E4*). This impressive church was built during the 14th c., perhaps after a design by G. Pisano. Construction continued until 1482; note the truncated campanile. The *interior* shows clear marks of the 17th-c. renovation by C. Maderno. The altar-frontal* by A. di Duccio (1459) and the funerary monument to Pope Benedict XI* (early 14th c.), by a follower of A. di Cambio, are noteworthy.

Museo Archeologico Nazionale dell'Umbria* (*D-E4*). *Open 8:30-7:30; closed Mon.* Largely housed in an ancient Dominican convent, this museum comprises a Roman-Etruscan section and a prehistoric section. The collections originated with a gift in 1790, and include an impressive array of artifacts uncovered in Umbria and other parts of Italy. Apart from major finds from the Bronze and Iron ages, there is a substantial collection of documents concerning the history of Perugia under the Etruscans. Note the **Cippo di Perugia*** (3rd-2nd c. B.C.), the lengthy Etruscan text of a property agreement.

Porta S. Pietro* (*E4*). This gate has two faces: the interior is a simple 14th-c. construction; the exterior is an elegant monumental arch, built in the Renaissance by A. di Duccio and P. di Stefano (1475-80) but left unfinished.

Borgo XX Giugno (*E-F4-5*). This 15th-c. district is dominated by the church and monastery of S. Pietro; the street was widened in the 19th c.

S. Pietro** (*F5*). This basilica, located in a 10th-c. convent complex, preserves part of the original structure and, beneath it, a small Early Christian temple. Over it towers an elegant polygonal campanile; before it is a handsome 17th-c. cloister. *Inside*, the nave and aisles with ancient columns are splendidly decorated; the original basilica structure has been maintained. In the *nave*, a wooden 16th-c. ceiling and a series of large paintings by Aliense (1592). On the walls and altars of the *aisles* are paintings by E. da San Giorgio, Sassoferrato, Guercino, Perugino, G. Reni, and others; in the 15th-c. *sacristy* are four small paintings* by Perugino. In the *presbytery*, two carved chairs (1556) and a remarkable inlaid wooden choir*, considered to be among the finest in Italy (1525-26).

The former *Benedictine monastery* is now part of the university, and has two cloisters, the smaller one being a work by G. Alessi (1571). Inside is the interesting **Orto Botanico Medievale** (*open summer, 8-6:30; winter, 8-5*) a reconstruction of the medieval monastery garden of herbs.

Giardino del Frontone (*F4-5*). Once an Etruscan necropolis, this area was laid out as a garden in the 18th c. The handsome tree-lined avenues end in a small amphitheater, and there is a fine view of Assisi and Monte Subasio.

Porta S. Costanzo (*F5*). This 16th-c. gate marks the end of the Borgo XX Giugno. Just beyond it is the church of *S. Costanzo*, dating from the 11th c. but rebuilt in the 19th c.

S. Giuliana (*E3*). This church, built in 1253, has fragments of 13th-/14th-c. frescoes; in the adjacent former convent, a 14th-c. cloister.

Porta Eburnea (*D3*). This unadorned town gate dates from 1576; a stairway leads from the church of *S. Spirito* (1579-1689), not far from a Franciscan convent. Nearby is the ancient church of *S. Prospero* (*D2*), first built in the 7th c., with 13th-c. frescoes.

Arco della Mandorla (*D3*). This pointed arch, at the top of the *stairs of Paradiso* (*D3*), is a medieval version of an ancient Etruscan gate. The narrow but charming *Via Caporali* (*D3*) takes you back to the center of Perugia.

Surrounding areas. The **Ipogeo dei Volumni***, or Hypogeum (*open Sep.-Jun., 9-1 and 3:30-6:30; Jul.-Aug., 9-12:30 and 4:30-7*) lies 7 km SE, if you take Viale Roma and head down toward the Tiber (Tevere). It is an underground aristocratic Etruscan tomb complex, from the late 2nd c. B.C. It consists of a large chamber, or atrium, onto which many cells open. The furthest one contains 7 cinerary urns*.

Piazza Armerina

Elev. 697 m, pop. 22,382; Sicilia (Sicily), province of Enna.

Places of interest. The source of this site's great fame is the extraordinary archeological complex of the **Villa Romana del Casale**** (5.5 km SW; *open 9-1 and 3-one hour before sunset*), a huge Roman country villa (late 3rd-early 4th c.), now inscribed in

UNESCO's World Heritage List. It is an intriguing hypothesis, though not at all certain, that this villa belonged to a wealthy importer of wild African animals for the Roman games; the celebrated, brilliant **mosaic floors****, some of the largest and most impressive ones surviving from antiquity, are believed to be the work of African master craftsmen, based on certain similarities with mosaic floors found in Roman-occupied North Africa.

Numerous elaborate buildings, built in the late Roman architectural style, are arrayed around the *large peristyle**, which features a mosaic floor of the imperial family with handmaidens* in a square vestibule, and, on the north side, halls with mosaics of Eroti fishers* and a small game hunt*. The buildings include the baths, with the three classical sections of the *frigidarium*, the *tepidarium*, and the *calidarium*; the Corridoio della Caccia Grossa, or Corridor of the Hunt, with a long mosaic depicting hunting scenes*, the capture of wild beasts* and predatory animals attacking prey in the wild*, a composition that tells a story clearly related to the trade in animals for gladiatorial games in the amphitheaters of ancient Rome; the Sala delle Dieci Ragazze, or Hall of the Ten Girls*, which takes its name from the floor mosaic of ten young girls** intently engaging in athletic pursuits, covered in skimpy two-piece outfits that appear surprisingly modern to us.

On either side of the *basilica* are numerous rooms many with splendid mosaic floors, including one of Arione on a dolphin with an entourage of naiads and sea monsters*.

An *elliptical peristyle* lies before the *Sala del Triclinium**, with mosaics of the Labors of Hercules*, the Glorification of Hercules*, the Defeated Giants* and Lycurgus and Ambrosia*.

Pienza**

Elev. 491 m, pop. 2258; Toscana (Tuscany), province of Siena. This silent hilltop town with a spectacular view was built by a Renaissance architect for a Humanist pope: the ideal city of Renaissance philosophy.

Historical note. The ancient village of Corsignano belonged to the abbey of Monte Amiata as early as the 9th c.; it then fell to Siena, and finally to the Piccolomini family. In 1405 Enea Silvio Piccolomini was born here; in 1458 he became Pope Pius II. He renamed his native town after his papal name – Pienza – and hired a great Renaissance architect, B. Rossellino, to rebuild it. The new, very rigorous little city was built in three years, and the pope then ordered a number of cardinals to build houses there in the same style.

Places of interest. Piazza Pio II.** Set on the highest point of the hill, this masterpiece by Rossellino resulted from the remodelling of the town, between 1459 and 1462. The deaths of architect and pope, both in 1464, prevented completion of the project.

Rossellino demolished freely, reshaping the square and the buildings to trapezoidal plans, in agreement with the concepts of perspective set forth in "De re aedificatoria" by L.B. Alberti and other Renaissance treatises that called for reason, proportion, and symmetry in all architecture.

The "rear wall" of this ideal "open-air drawing room" is the facade of the Cathedral; on the right is Palazzo Piccolomini (see below), with a **well*** before it, also designed by Rossellino (1462). Opposite is the stern **Palazzo Vescovile** (once Palazzo Borgia) the home of the Museo Diocesano (*open 14 Mar.-Oct., Wed.-Mon., 10-1 and 3-6:30; Nov.-19 Dec. and 7 Jan.-13 Mar., Tue. and Sat.-Sun., 10-1 and 3-6; 20 Dec.-6 Jan., Wed.-Mon., 10-1 and 3-6; closed Tue.; tel. 0578749071*), the diocesan museum including the **cope of Pius II****, embroidered in gold and precious stones.

Cattedrale.** This cathedral, with its octagonal campanile, was inspired by the German "Hallenkirchen" which Pius II much admired; among the art works in the church, all specially commissioned by Pius II, are those by G. di Paolo, M. di Giovanni, Vecchietta, and S. di Pietro. Beneath the apse is the crypt (*open by request, contact the Museo della Cattedrale*), with a baptismal font* designed by Rossellino.

Palazzo Piccolomini.** *Open Tue.-Sun.; Jul.-Aug., 10-12:30 and 4:7; Jan.-Jun., Sep.-15 Nov. and 1 Dec.-15 Feb., 10-12:30 and 3-6; closed 15 Nov.-1 Dec. and 15 Feb.-1 Mar.; tel. 0578748503.* Larger than the cathedral beside it, its handsome perspectival arrangement is cunningly arrayed, and is clearly inspired by Palazzo Rucellai in Florence (likewise built by Rossellino to plans by L.B. Alberti). The fine inner courtyard leads to a hanging garden*, beneath the huge three-storey loggia* facing south. The rooms on the first floor are decorated in 15th-c. style, with fine antiques and priceless art; excellent view* of the garden and the Orcia valley.

Corso Rossellino. Main street of Pienza, lined with buildings and aristocratic houses designed by Rossellino. Toward Porta al Murello, beyond Palazzo Piccolomini and Palazzo Ammannati, the 13th-c. church of S. Francesco is the only medieval building left in town.

In the opposite direction, toward *Porta al Ciglio*, see the 15th-c. **Palazzo Jouffroy** (n. 30) and Palazzo Gonzaga (n. 38).

Pienza: Piazza Pio II

Pisa**

Elev. 4 m, pop. 92,379; Toscana (Tuscany), provincial capital. The columns of the Battistero, or Baptistery, were brought across the sea from Elba and Sardinia; the Camposanto, or Cemetery, encloses earth brought by galleon from Golgotha, in the Holy Land (1203). Even before the architect Buscheto began designing the Duomo, in the 11th c., he had been influenced by the Islamic architecture of the Levant, as well as by architecture from Armenia. The breezes from the sea are a fundamental component of this city – straddling the Arno River – which certainly holds a place of high honor in Italian art.

Historical note. Although its origins are distant and uncertain, the Romans certainly made Pisa a city, recognizing in its excellent harbor a base for expansion north and west across the Mediterranean. In those times, Pisa stood on the sea, where the Arno meets the Serchio, in the northern area of the modern town, between the Duomo, Porta a Lucca, and S. Zeno. The center soon shifted south, and the section of Pisa just described came to be known as "città vecchia," or old town. The first walls were built in the 10th c., when Pisa was already a mighty sea power; in the 11th c. her ships, with those of Genoa, chased the Arabs from Sardinia, and hunted them as far as Bône, in what is now Algeria, and in 1063 the Pisan fleet helped the Normans take Palermo. The Duomo was completed at the end of that century, and a larger ring of walls was built, the last walls the city built. The 12th c. was the golden age of the Pisan Maritime Republic. After supporting the First Crusade and founding colonies in the Near East, the Pisans led their own crusade against the Saracens in the Balearic Islands (1113-14); they stormed and sacked Amalfi, eliminating it as a seafaring power (1135-37); they controlled the entire Tyrrhenian coast, from Portovenere to Civitavecchia, as well as Sardinia (1162-5), received in fief from the emperor Frederick Barbarossa. These were also the years of artistic splendor: alongside the Duomo, or Cathedral, work began on the Battistero and the renowned Torre Pendente, or leaning tower, although the tower in question did not yet lean. Power and wealth bred new and revived old rivalries – with Lucca, over Apennine passes; with Genoa, over Eastern trade, and over Corsica and Sardinia; with Florence, over access to the sea. Still, Pisa defeated Genoa at Giglio (1241) and Acre (1258), and Florence at Montaperti (1260; Dante Alighieri fought in this battle). With the decline of imperial power, however, Pisa's might ebbed. Lucca and Florence grew bold, and in 1284 the Pisan fleet was destroyed by Genoa. In the 14th c., Pisa declined and more or less fell. Art and culture survived: the University thrived, the Camposanto was completed, in the Duomo G. Pisano carved the famous pulpit, and on the Lungarno S. Maria della Spina was built. Internal strife racked Pisa, however, and it was ruled, in succession, by Uguccione della Faggiuola, the Della Gherardesca family, the Gambacorta family (with Florentine patrons), the Visconti (1399), and, finally, by Florence (1406). Pisa languished in the late 15th c. As silting drove the seacoast west, the city lost its harbor, while malaria raged in the countryside; the population fell to about 8,000. As the Medici duchy became a grand-duchy, times improved; vast reclamations were undertaken, a canal linked Pisa to the new port of Livorno, the University built the first botanical garden in Europe. And in 1562 Cosimo I instituted the Order of the Knights of St. Stephen to fight piracy, in a last revival of maritime valor. Twelve galleys of the Order fought the Turks at Lepanto (1571). But that spark died out, and Livorno supplanted Pisa both in trade and war. Under the Medici Pisa built the Fortezza Nuova, the Ponte di Mezzo, the buildings in Piazza dei Cavalieri (G. Vasari), the Logge di Banchi, and many buildings on the Lungarni. After becoming part of Italy, Pisa expanded north and south. Manufacturing and one of Italy's finest universities now bring prosperity.

Getting around. Due to traffic and parking problems, both the routes recommended, shown on the map, are in pedestrian zones; public transportation may be useful for the longer stretches, as well as for returning to your starting point.

The Medici center and Piazza del Duomo

From the Ponte di Mezzo, the sight of the imposing ranks of venerable palazzi overlooking the Arno foreshadows – after you make your way through the 16th-c. Medici center of Pisa – the spectacular geometric perspective of the Campo dei Miracoli, a must for any visitor.

Ponte di Mezzo (*C4*). This oldest bridge in Pisa was rebuilt after WWII. It crosses the Arno in a single span, opening north onto Piazza Garibaldi. Note the bronze monument (1892).

Borgo Stretto (*C4*). One of the main streets of the old district, lined with handsome porticoes.

In a 17th-c. tabernacle at the head of the right portico, there is the copy of a wooden sculpture by Nino Pisano (the original is at the Museo di S. Matteo). A bit further on is the church of S. Michele (see below).

S. Michele in Borgo* (*C4-5*). Built in the 11th c., modified in the 14th c., this church has a Pisan-style facade (14th c.); note the portals and loggias. Inside, 13th-c. fresco and a 14th-c. marble Crucifix.

Piazza dei Cavalieri* (*B4*). Once the center of Pisa, during the Republic, this square was renovated under the Medici to accommodate the 16th-c. headquarters of the Order of the Knights of St. Stephen. Many of the buildings on the square are by G. Vasari, but one of them stands out: Vasari's **Palazzo dei Cavalieri*** (1562), which features a massive curving facade, a double stairway, a statue and a fountain by P. Francavilla (1596); on the right, the church of

Pisa: Duomo, Battistero, and Campanile

. Stefano dei Cavalieri (see below). Note also Vasari's **Palazzo dell'Orologio**, a building which is said to stand on the site of the captivity of Count Ugolino della Gherardesca, whose horrible death is recounted by Dante in his "Inferno".

. Stefano dei Cavalieri* (*B4*). The church and bell tower are by G.Vasari (1569); the marble facade dates from 1606. Inside: on the walls, three fragments of a 17th-c. processional ship; canvases and ceiling by Cigoli, Allori, Empoli, and Ligozzi. Note the painting by Bronzino (1564).

. Sisto (*B4*). This 11th-c. Romanesque church has an unassuming facade and sides decorated with hanging arches and ancient Pisan ceramic bowls, as decoration (copies; originals in the Museo di S. Matteo). Inside, note the late 13th-c. panel.

Via S. Maria (*B-C3*). Perhaps the most distinctive of Pisa's streets, lined with 17th-/18th-c. buildings, some of which belong to the university. Toward the Arno, at n.26, is the Domus Galilaeana (*C3; open by request, tel. 05023726*), with a major library of works by and about Galileo Galilei. Note, at the corner of Via Volta, a 13th-c. tower-house; also, the church of S. Giorgio dei Tedeschi (*B3*), and the 15th-c. Ospizio dei Trovatelli*.

Orto Botanico dell'Università (*B3*). *Open Mar.-Oct., Mon.-Fri., 8-5:30; Sat., 8-1; Nov.-Feb., Mon.-Fri., 8-; Sat., 8-1; entrance from Via Ghini n. 5*. This botanical garden was moved here from its previous site on the Arno in 1595 by Ferdinando I. It occupies over sq. km, with greenhouses and open plantings.

Piazza del Duomo** (*A3*). Also known as Campo dei Miracoli, this square holds the finest masterpieces of Pisan Romanesque art, and is one of the best known and most popular monuments in Italy. On the broad meadow, against the backdrop of crenelated medieval walls, stand the Duomo, Battistero, Campanile, and Camposanto (Cathedral, Baptistery, Tower, and Cemetery). Built in different periods, they are wonderfully homogeneous in color and style.

Campanile** (*A3*). Also known as the *Torre Pendente*, or Leaning Tower, it is the emblem of Pisa and one of the most famous towers in the world, both for its elegant white marble and for its decidedly odd tilt. Construction began in 1173, was halted as the ground began to sink, and was begun again in 1275, to be finished after 1350. Cylindrical, it has the same decorative motif as the apse of the Cathedral. Inside is a 294-step winding staircase, leading to the 54-m-high top of the tower. From here, Galileo is said to have performed his experiments concerning the pull of gravity on falling objects.

Duomo** (*A3*). *Open summer, 10-7:40; holidays, 1-7:40; spring and autumn, 10-5-40; holidays, 1-5:40; winter, 10-12:45 and 3-4:45; holidays, 3-4:45*. This impressive white building, with its elegant decoration, was built between 1064 and the 12th c. by Buscheto and Rainaldo, and is the crowning creation of Pisan Romanesque architecture. The facade is spectacularly adorned with four rows of small loggias, and decorated with marble statues and inlay. Followers of Giambologna made the bronze doors of the three portals. To the left of the apse is the Portal of S. Ranieri, with lovely bronze doors* by B. Pisano (1180).

The **interior**, solemn and beautifully lit, dressed in black-and-white marble, has a nave with four aisles divided by close-set columns, an elliptical dome, and a deep apse. In the nave, note the handsome bronze holy water stoups by F. Palma (1621); at the end of the nave is the marble **pulpit**** by G. Pisano (1302-11), a complex masterpiece of Italian Gothic sculpture. Almost directly across from it is the "lamp of Galileo," made of bronze, and designed by B. Lorenzi (1587); its swinging motion was long be-

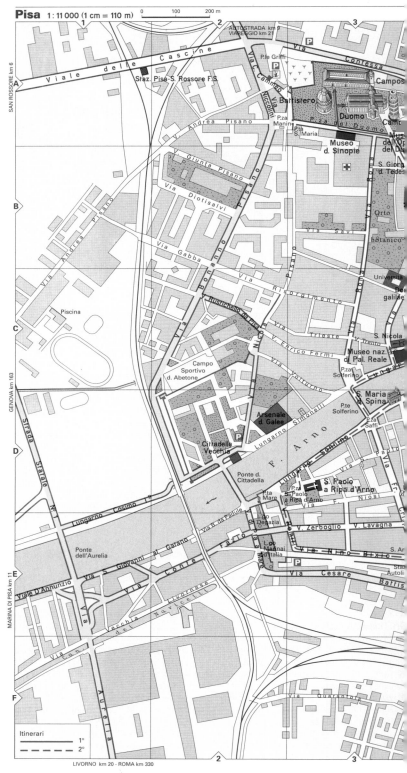

Pisa

1 : 11 000 (1 cm = 110 m)

0   100   200 m

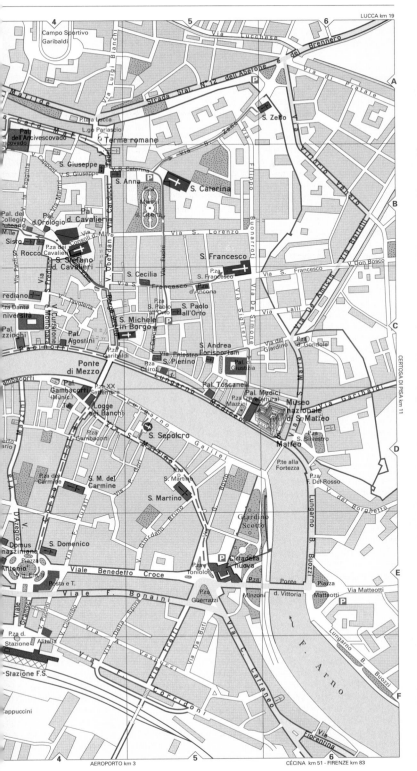

lieved to have inspired Galileo's discoveries concerning the pendulum (it is now known, however, that these discoveries were made six years before the lamp was installed). Right aisle: note the paintings by A. del Sarto and G.A. Sogliani. Right transept: 14th-c. mosaic, partly hidden by the chapel of S. Ranieri; also note the tomb of the Holy Roman Emperor Henry VII* by Tino di Camaino. Cross vault of the transept: remarkable 13th-c. Cosmatesque mosaic floor. Presbytery: two bronze angels by Giambologna (1602); 15th-c. inlaid stalls*; and paintings by A. del Sarto and Sogliani. On the altar, bronze Crucifix by Giambologna. In the vault of the apse, note the large 13th-c mosaic of the Savior between Mary and St. John the Evangelist* (the head of the latter is by Cimabue); below, paintings by Beccafumi, Sodoma, and Sogliani.

Battistero * * (A3). *Open summer, 8-7:40; spring and autumn, 9-5:40; winter, 9-4:40.* This majestic round Romanesque building, made of white marble, girded by arches and loggias with elegant Gothic crowning ornamentation, was begun in 1152 by Diotisalvi, continued in the next century by N. and G. Pisano, and completed around 1350, with a pyramidal eight-sided dome* by C. di Nese. The Baptistery has four exceedingly fine portals*: particular note should be given to the one facing the Cathedral.

Inside, note the octagonal baptismal font* by G. da Como (1246); on its left, supported by carved stone lions bearing columns on their backs, is the **pulpit** * * by N. Pisano (1260). Before the altar, 13th-c. Cosmatesque marble floor. Along the walls, large statues* by N. and G. Pisano and school, formerly set on the exterior of the Baptistery.

Camposanto * * (A3). *Open Nov.-Feb., 9-4:40; Mar and Oct., 9-5:40; Apr.-Sep., 9-7:40.* This perfect rectangular structure with blind arcades was begun in 1277 by G. di Simone. An inner gallery surrounds the meadow of the ancient cemetery. Of the two simple portals, the right one is surmounted by an elegant Gothic tabernacle (school of N. Pisano, 1350). Ravaged in July 1944 by a fire sparked by combat, its current appearance is the result of painstaking restoration. Intended for the burial of noble and illustrious citizens of Pisa, from the 15th c. on many funerary monuments were moved here (most are now restored to their original locations), along with a collection of mostly Roman sarcophagi*. The walls were decorated with frescoes, largely destroyed by time or the fire; many of the few that survive are protected in a room, which can be reached from the north arm. *West arm*: several remarkable Roman sarcophagi; a large marble Etruscan vase; the family tomb of the Conti della Gherardesca (1315-20), by a follower of G. Pisano; on the wall, chains from the ships of the Battle of Meloria. *North arm*: Greek and Roman funerary objects. In the Cappella Ammannati, monument to L. Ammannati (died in 1359), from the school of G. Pisano. To the left of the chapel is a hall of frescoes* by the so-called Maestro del Trionfo della Morte (1360-80; some identify this Master as Bonamico Buffalmacco): **Triumph of Death** * *, Last Judgement, Hell, and a Massàcre of Anchorites*; also a Landscape by T. Gaddi. In a huge hall next to the chapel, a series of large prints show the frescoes as they originally were. Also, note the 2nd-c. B.C. Greek marble vase*. In the Cappella Aulla, note the 2nd-c. A.D. "sarcophagus of Countess Beatrice"*, and the sarcophagus of the Sponsali*. *East arm*. Completely stripped of its original frescoes; note the tomb of G. Buoncompagni by B. Ammannati (1574); the tomb of O. Massotti, with a female figure by G. Duprè; and the renowned statue of the "Inconsolable Woman," by L. Bartolini (1842). *South arm*: tablets concerning the original Roman colony of Pisa, mosaics, two headless 2nd-c. statues, and Roman and medieval sarcophagi.

Museo delle Sinopie* (A3). *Open same hours as the Camposanto.* This museum in Piazza del Duomo has collections of preparatory drawings (usually ochre in color) of the frescoes that once decorated the Camposanto. It is the largest and most interesting collection of drawings by great 14th-c. artists. Note the work* by the Maestro del Trionfo della Morte, and the large Crucifixion*, for the first fresco done in the Camposanto (1320-30), by F. Traini; also, works by T. Gaddi, P. di Puccio, S. Aretino, B. Gozzoli, and A. Bonaiuti.

Museo dell'Opera del Duomo* (A3-4). *Open Nov.-Feb., 9-4:20; Mar and Oct., 9-5:20; Apr.-Sep., 9-7:20.* This large museum comprises collections of art from the monuments of the Campo dei Miracoli, and stands at the far eastern side of Piazza del Duomo. On the ground floor and in the cloister is the core of the collections: 11th-/14th-c. statuary. Note the Islamic bronze griffon; 12th-c. Burgundian wooden Christ; masterpieces by Nicola and G. Pisano, T. di Camaino, Nino Pisano, A. Guardi, and M. Civitali. Moreover, in the Duomo's Tesoro, or Treasury: ivory carvings by G. Pisano and fine religious metalwork. Upstairs, a vast array, from illuminated codices to Egyptian and Etruscan artifacts.

Piazza dell'Arcivescovado (A-B4). The 15th-c. *Palazzo Arcivescovile* stands here. Continuing along Via Maffi, with a fine view of the Duomo's apse and bell tower, and along the Largo del Parlascio, you will see ruins of 2nd-c. A.D. Roman baths; on the left is the Porta a Lucca (A4; 1544); from outside the gate, a fine view of the medieval walls* (1155).

S. Caterina* (B5). Built in the late 13th c., this church has a Pisan-style marble facade and a large rose window; the terracotta campanile is decorated with ceramic bowls. Inside are marble statues* by N. Pisano (1360); in the sacristy, paintings by Fra' Bartolomeo (1511) and F. Traini (ca. 1350).

S. Zeno (A5-6). Standing at the end of Via S. Zeno, alongside the 13th-c. Porta di S. Zeno, outside of which is a fine view of the medieval walls*, this church was founded before the year 1000, rebuilt in the 13th c., deconsecrated in 1809, and used as a warehouse until 1972. The interior is usually closed.

S. Francesco* (B-C5). Construction of this convent church, which first began in 1211, was undertaken again by G. di Simone in 1265-70 and completed in the 14th c.; the facade dates from 1603. Inside, Baroque altars and large canvases by Empoli, Passignano, and S. di Tito, frescoes by T. Gaddi (1342) and marble altarpiece by T. Pisano (14th c.). At the corner of the left transept, note the structures supporting the campanile. In the sacristy, frescoes by T. di Bartolo (1397).

S. Cecilia (*C5*). In Via S. Francesco, this small Romanesque church (1103) is made of stone and brick; not far off is the church of S. Paolo all'Orto, built in the 12th c. but later renovated.

S. Pierino (*C5*). This Romanesque church was built between 1072 and 1119; inside, fragments of frescoes, and a 13th-c. mosaic floor. Behind the main altar is a 13th-c. Crucifix.

Piazza Cairoli (*C5*). This cozy little square has a column with a 16th-c. statue of Abundance. Note the Via delle Belle Torri, one of Pisa's loveliest streets, despite damage done in WWII. Along it are 12th-13th-c. tower-houses.

S. Andrea Forisportam (*C5*). This simple 12th-c. Pisan-style church is decorated with hanging arches and terracotta bowls (copies). Handsome, original Romanesque interior.

Museo Nazionale di S. Matteo ** (*D5-6*). *Open 9-7; Sun. and holidays, 9-2; closed Mon*. Overlooking the Lungarno Mediceo, since 1949 this museum has occupied part of the convent of the Benedictine nuns of S. Matteo, a building adjacent to the 11th-c. bell tower, with a 13th-c. porticoed courtyard. Among the museum's vast collections, we should make special note of the collections of Pisan sculpture, Tuscan paintings of the 12th-15th c., and Pisan and Islamic medieval ceramics. A separate section in the former Palazzo Reale will house the works from private donations and from the collections of the Houses of the Medici, Lorraine, and Savoy.

Ground floor. Remarkable collection of *medieval ceramics*: series of ceramic basins*, some of 11th-c. Islamic origin, others from 13th-c. Pisa, used as ornaments on the exterior walls of Pisan churches; also, ceramic archeological finds from all over Pisa. Armor from the Gioco del Ponte, an example of rough sport begun in Pisa by the Medici in the 16th c.; also, one of the most important European collections of antique metal arms and armor (about 900 pieces).

First floor. *Sculpture from the 12th-14th c.*: eloquent examples of Pisan art with fragments of Romanesque buildings and statues; works by follower of G. Pisano, T. di Camaino, N. Pisano, F. Traino, A. and N. Pisano, F. di Valdambrino, A. di Giovanni; a rock-crystal cross from the late 13th-c. Venetian school. *Sculpture from the 15th c.*: works by Donatello**, a follower of Michelozzo*, workshop of Verrocchio*, della Robbia. *Painting from 12th-13th c.*: works by Berlinghiero, E. di Tedice, Giunta Pisano, Maestro di S. Martino. *Painting from the 14th c.*: works by D. Orlandi, S. Martini, G. di Nicola, L. di Tommè, B. Daddi, Maestro di S. Torpè, L. Memmi, C. di Pietro, B. da Modena, S. Aretino, M. di Bartolomeo, T. di Bartolo. *Painting from the 15th c.*: works by G. da Fabriano, Masaccio, Fra' Angelico, G. da Milano,

A. Veneziano, D. Ghirlandaio, B. Gozzoli, P. Schiavo, N. di Bicci, and L. di Bicci.

Lungarno Mediceo (*C-D5-6*). This riverfront quay runs from the Ponte alla Fortezza to Piazza Garibaldi: at the corner of Piazza Mazzini is the 13th-c. Palazzo dei Medici (D5), greatly modified by restoration effected in the early 20th c. Further along is the 16th-c. Palazzo Toscanelli.

S. Maria della Spina and the districts on the left bank

Here you can admire the miracle of the little church of S. Maria della Spina, seemingly floating upon the waters of the Arno, the simple facade of the church of S. Paolo, and the lively left bank, a district which sprang up in the 19th c.

Lungarno Pacinotti (*C3-4*). Stretching from Piazza Garibaldi to Ponte Solferino, this quay offers handsome views of the opposite bank. At n. 26, *Palazzo Agostini* (*C4*), and at n. 43, *Palazzo Upezzinghi*, designed by C. Pugliani (1594).

S. Frediano (*C4*). Not far from the university campus is this 11th-c. Pisan Romanesque church. Inside, note the 12th-c. Crucifix and a painting by A. Lomi (1604).

Museo Nazionale di Palazzo Reale (*C3*). *Open Mon.-Fri., 9-2:30; Sat., 9-1:30*. It is housed in the huge building at n. 56 on Lungarno Pacinotti, which was begun in 1559 by Cosimo I de' Medici, and later enlarged. The museum includes part of the collections of the Museo Nazionale di S. Matteo, especially items from the collections of the Houses of the Medici, Lorraine, and Savoy, becoming a museum of court life and art. Among the most important pieces are Flemish tapestries, a series of ivory miniatures, Medici portraits and the *Collezione Ceci*, with works by B. Strozzi, A. Magnasco, F. Francia, A. Canova.

S. Nicola (*C3*). Behind Palazzo Reale, part of this church's lower facade and the remarkable bell tower* date from the 13th c. Inside, note painting by F. Traino and statues by G. and Nino Pisano.

S. Maria della Spina ** (*D3*). This exquisite piece of Romanesque-Gothic architecture and art, originally a small church on the banks of the Arno, was enlarged in 1323. It was named after a thorn ("spina") believed to be from the true crown of thorns (now in S. Chiara). Disassembled and moved to higher ground to save it from the flooding of the river (1871), the church is girt by arcades enclosing mullioned windows and portals. Note the statues* on facade and spires by T. Pisano.

Lungarno Sonnino (*D2-3*). Across from this riverbank boulevard you can see the brick sheds, once boat yards (Arsenale delle Gallee, D2) of the Cavalieri di S. Stefano. At the end of Lungarno Simonelli, at the Ponte della Cittadella, is the Cittadella Vecchia (D2), the ruins of a Florentine fortress (1405).

S. Paolo a Ripa d'Arno* (*D3*). This handsome Pisan Romanesque church of the 11th c. has the same decorative pattern as the Duomo. Inside (much restored after damage of WWII), note the handsome columns,

supporting pointed Arab-style arches, and a painting by T. Vanni (1397). Behind the apse is the separate, octagonal **Cappella di S. Agata***, built in the 12th c.
S. Antonio (*E4*). Only the lower order of the facade survives from the original 14th-c. church. To the left, in Via Mazzini n. 71, is the Domus Mazziniana (*E4; open Mon.-Fri., 8:30-1:30; Sat., 8:30-12; Tue. and Thu. also 3-5:30*), commemorating Giuseppe Mazzini, a father of Italian Unity.
Corso Italia (*D-E4*). This lively pedestrian street links the railway station to the historic center of Pisa. Along the way are two churches: S. Domenico (*E4*), built in the 14th c., and badly damaged in WWII; and the 14th-c. S. Maria del Carmine (*D4*), with paintings by Allori, A. Lomi, and B. Lomi Gentileschi. When the Corso reaches the Arno, on the left, note the vast Loggia di Banchi, built in 1603-05 by C. Pugliani, for wool and silk traders. At the mouth of the Ponte di Mezzo, fine view of the north banks of the Arno.
Lungarno Galilei (*D4-5*). Between Ponte di Mezzo and Ponte alla Fortezza, this boulevard offers fine views of the Lungarno Mediceo. Note the octagonal church of **S. Sepolcro*** (D5), by Diotisalvi (1153). Inside, the tombstones of Pisan aristocrats, and painting by the school of B. Gozzoli.
Via S. Martino (*D4-5*). Main street of the old district of Chinzica, once inhabited by Arab and Turkish traders. In a square is the church of *S. Martino* (D5), built in 1332. Inside, frescoes and paintings by G. di Nicola, A. Veneziano, A. Lomi, and E. di Tedice.
Bastione Sangallo (*E5*). This bastion and the nearby walls are all that survive of the 15th-c. Cittadella Nuova, built by the Florentines, destroyed by the Pisans, and rebuilt by G. da Sangallo. Visit the lovely park known as Giardino Scotto.

Surrounding areas. The **Parco Naturale di Migliarino-S. Rossore-Massaciùccoli** (*for information, Ente Parco, tel. 050525500, or Consorzio per il Parco, tel. 050525211*), established in 1979, is a nature reserve which extends over 21,000 hectares along the coast between Viareggio and Livorno; it comprises the lake of Massaciùccoli, much maquis, beaches, forests, pine groves, and marshes.

Pistoia*

Elev. 67 m, pop. 85,866; Toscana (Tuscany), provincial capital. Situated within the diamond shape of the 14th-c. walls, the juxtaposition of light-and-dark striped marble, so typical of the medieval architecture of Pisa, Tuscany, and Liguria, here becomes more minute and subtle, setting a forest green against the pure white. Thus, the architecture here is perfectly matched with the surrounding landscape, and the stone blends with the plain of the Ombrone River and the nearby spurs of the Apennines. This harmony may seem surprising from a city that spawned so much art yet so much violence: the medieval chronicler, Giovanni Villani, recalls "the bad seed that came from Pistoia, en-

gendering black and white factions," the sourc of the raging factions that drove Dan Alighieri, a member of the "white" faction, in lifelong exile; another poet, Cino da Pistoi was of the "black" faction, and was also exile This "stilnovista" wrote that he liked to "see ot ers smitten in the face by blows of a swor and ships sent to the bottom of the sea."

Historical note. The walls, which still stand, we first built by local citizens in the early 14th c., and la er fortified by the Medici. Within them we can st see the plan of the Roman city of "Pistoria"; the Lo gobard city too, in the 8th c., lay within this area. Fo centuries all life at Pistoia remained within the bounds. Pistoia's true glory, however, began in th 11th c., and culminated in the 13th c., when loc bankers lent money to French princes and king Within the walls, the Pistoians were building the great Romanesque Cathedral and other churche and by the end of the 13th c., they began work c the Palazzo del Comune. The city's growth was soc thwarted, however, by Lucca in one direction, an Florence in the other. In 1306, the Pistoians surre dered to the joint forces of the two rival cities, wh sacked the town. Political decline ensued, and th great banking dynasties dwindled and died. In 132 the Pistoians made peace a second time with a be ligerent Florence, falling under its sway; in 1401, was incorporated into the Medici duchy. Centuries c silence and poverty followed, broken only in the la 18th c., with a reforming Jansenist bishop, Scipion de' Ricci. After 1850, the city grew timidly beyond i 14th-c. walls. More recently, the city has thrived, grow ing in all directions.

Places of interest. Piazza del Duomo.* The hi torical and artistic center of Pistoia, bounded by me dieval buildings, this square holds, of course, the Duo mo, with its tall bell tower, the Palazzo Vescovile, an the Battistero, with the Palazzo del Pretorio and Palaz zo del Comune facing each other. At the corner of Vi Tomba stands the medieval *Torre di Catilina*, whos name marks the fact that Catiline, a Roman con spirator denounced by Cicero, fled here and was de feated (62 B.C.), and then buried near Pistoia's walls **Duomo.**** *Open 9-12 and 4-7.* This Romanesqu cathedral was built in the Pisan style in the 12th 13th c., and has a stone facade with three rows c loggias, with a marble portico (late 14th c.). Th lunette over the central portal has an enameled te racotta bas-relief* by A. della Robbia (1505), wh also did the decorations of the barrel vaults. Note th enormous campanile.
The *interior* is majestic, and you should observe nu merous works of art. Among them: in the right aisle the early 14th-c. funerary monument of C. da Pistoia Crucifix on panel by C. di Marcovaldo (1275); mon umental silver **altar panel of S. Jacopo****, begu in 1287 and finished in the mid-15th c. At the end o the aisle is the entrance to the sacristy, mentioned b Dante in his "Inferno." Note the Cappella di S. Atte

th painting by M. Preti; also, a fine bronze candebrum by M. di Bartolomeo (1440). In the chapel to e left of the presbytery, canvas* by L. di Credi 485), and stele commemorating the bishop D. de' edici by A. Rossellino. At the foot of the left aisle, e monument to Cardinal Forteguerri (1419-73): the atues of Faith and Hope are by A. Verrocchio, those Christ and angels are by Verrocchio's pupils, nong them L. di Credi. Note the baptismal font by Ferrucci da Fiesole, designed by B. da Maiano.

attistero.** An admirable piece of Gothic archicture, octagonal in shape, this Baptistery was bean in 1338 by C. di Nese, to plans by A. Pisano, and ompleted in 1359. With white-and-green marble facg, it is surmounted by a blind gallery and has three ne portals, with reliefs and statues. Inside, 14th-c. ll baptismal font, restored in 1960.

alazzo dei Vescovi. *Guided tours, Tue., Thu. and i., 10, 11:30, 3.* This 14th-c. building with loggia and ullioned windows is a major piece of Pistoian civarchitecture of the Middle Ages, renovated in lat- centuries. It houses the **Museo Capitolare di an Zeno**, with exquisite artwork and sacred obcts from the Treasury of the Duomo, as well as fresdes and paintings. Also note the *archeological secon* documenting the origins of Pistoia.

alazzo del Podestà. This stern building dates from 367 and was enlarged in the mid-19th c. Note the ullioned windows and porticoed courtyard, studed with family crests in marble and terracotta; to ne left of the entrance is a stone "judge's bench," reored in 1507, where the accused were tried.

alazzo del Comune.* This austere and majestic wn hall, built with local Tuscan stone called "pietra erena" was begun in 1294 and enlarged in 1348-85. the left of the large central window, crowned by Medici crest, with papal keys honoring Leo X 513), is an odd head carved of black marble, probly depicting Musetto, the king of Majorca, defeatd by the Pistoian G. de' Ghisilieri (1113-14). This alazzo now houses the Museo Civico (see below); the courtyard, sculpture by M. Marini.

useo Civico. *Open 10-7; Sun. and holidays, 9-2:30; closed Mon.* Pistoia's town museum is housed n the two upper floors of the Palazzo del Comune,

where the handsome public halls feature frescoes and carved ceilings. Note especially, in the main hall, the wooden ceiling, the long 16th-c. bench, and the city crest, in marble, by the workshop of A. Verrocchio. In the museum proper, 13th- and 14th-c. paintings are on display. Note the rare panel with scenes from the life of St. Francis (1260-70), and a polyptych dated at 1310, and the wooden sculpture by F. di Valdambrino. From the 15th-16th c. are the altarpieces from local churches, by L. di Credi, G. Gerini, R. del Ghirlandaio, Fra' Paolino da Pistoia, G.B. Volponi, and B. del Signoraccio. A section features canvases from the 17th-18th c. by such artists as G. Gimignani, F. Vanni, M. Rosselli, P. Batoni, L. Cigoli, and others. Also note the *Collezione Puccini*, with works ranging from 17th-c. to 19th-c. furniture. A hall is also devoted to contemporary local painters.

Madonna dell'Umiltà.* This basilica, a major piece of Renaissance architecture, was built by V. Vitoni (1494-1522) and may have been designed by G. da Sangallo; it has an octagonal plan and is surmounted by a vast dome, by G. Vasari. On the main altar, fresco by P. Tacca; chapels decorated by B. Ammannati.

S. Francesco. Begun in 1289 and completed in the 15th c., this large church was greatly renovated over the centuries, especially in Baroque times; the whiteand-green striped marble facade dates from 1717. Inside, fragments of frescoes from the 14th-15th c.: work by P. Capanna, and others of the school of Giotto and of local schools; in the sacristy, frescoes in the manner of N. di Pietro Gerini, as well as fine work in the 14th-c. Sala Capitolare.

S. Andrea.** A 12th-c. church with a Romanesque facade in the Pisan style; over the architrave of the central portal, reliefs by Gruamonte and Adeodato (1166). Inside is one of the masterpieces of 12th-/13th-c. Italian sculpture: the **pulpit**** (1298-1301) by G. Pisano, who also carved the wooden Crucifix* in a 15th-c. tabernacle, midway up the right aisle. Also note the frescoes by G. da Pistoia, and the 14thc. baptismal font.

Ospedale del Ceppo.* This 13th- or 14th-c. hospital was named after a stump used to collect alms. Note the Florentine-style portico (1514), with medallions and a frieze* in polychrome terracotta, by G. della Robbia and S. Buglioni (1525-26).

S. Bartolomeo in Pantano. This Romanesque church was built in 1159; the portal is by Gruamonte (1167). Inside, note the pulpit* by G. da Como (1250), and fragments of 14th-c. frescoes.

Palazzo Rospigliosi. *Open 9-12 and 4-6.* This palazzo is a combination of several buildings from different eras, the oldest of which is adjacent to the cathedral. The entrance is from Ripa del Sale, up a double staircase. Upstairs is a handsome apartment, named after Clement IX, a Pistoian pope believed to have lived here. Note the 17th-c. furniture and paintings. Also, visit the Museo Diocesano, with sacred objects and artwork from local churches.

S. Pietro Maggiore. All that survives of the 13th-c. church is the right side and the lower section of the facade.

Pistoia: Piazza del Duomo

Fortezza di S. Barbara. This square fortress, in a park, stands on the site of a medieval fort; it was built in the 16th c. by G.B. Bellucci and B. Buontalenti.

S. Paolo. A Pisan-style church built in 1291-1302, with a handsome facade and a portal with carved lunette; note the Gothic tombs. Inside is a 14th-c. wooden Crucifix.

S. Domenico. Built in the late 13th c. and enlarged in 1380, this church holds a funerary monument-to Filippo Lazzari by B. and A. Rossellino (1462-68).

S. Antonio del Tau. Named after the "tau," or Greek "T," worn by its monks on their habits, this church was built in 1340 by Fra' Giovanni Guidotti; it has not been used for worship for two centuries. Inside there are the 14th-/15th-c. frescoes*.

In the former convent, restored in 1987, is the **Centro di Documentazione e Fondazione Marino Marini** (*open Tue.-Sat., 9-1 and 3-7; Sun. and holidays, 9-12:30*), with collections of the work of the Pistoian artist, including etchings, lithographs, and sculptures.

S. Giovanni Fuorcivitas.** Begun in the 12th c. and completed in the 14th c., this is one of Pistoia's largest Romanesque churches. Note the facing with bands of travertine and greenish marble; in the portal, architrave by Gruamonte (1162). Inside, note the marble pulpit* by Fra' Guglielmo da Pisa (1270); holy-water stoup* with reliefs by G. Pisano. In the presbytery, polyptych* by T. Gaddi (1353-55), fragments of frescoes from the early 14th c., and terracotta group* by the Della Robbia school.

Via Roma. At the beginning of this street, note the imitation-Renaissance Palazzo della Cassa di Risparmio (1905); nearby, on the opposite side of the street, is the Palazzo del Capitano del Popolo (late 13th c.), at the corner of Via della Stracceria, lined with medieval homes and workshops.

Pompeii** (excavations of) / Pompei** (scavi di)

Campania, province of Naples, township of Pompei (pop. 25,177). Situated on the last low buttress to the SW of Mt. Vesuvius not far from the Gulf of Naples, Pompeii is known throughout the world for its tragic destruction and for its miraculous discovery. This is a unique memento of the topography of a city of the ancient world, where life came to a sudden halt on 24 August 79.

Historical note. The site occupied by Pompeii was endowed perfectly by nature for trade and commerce. This city was exceedingly wealthy during Samnite times, when the area between the Via della Fortuna and the Via Stabiana was built up (this is where most of the public buildings were located), while the area to the north, between the Herculaneum gate and the gate of Nola remained largely residential. After taking part in the war of the Italic towns against Rome, in 80 B.C., Pompeii was forced to open its gates to Sulla, accepting a colony of veteran legionaries. Pompeii rapidly became a Roman

town, in language, customs, and architecture. D●ing this period, the theaters and the amphithea●were built, and many Samnite houses were reb●or at least redecorated. In A.D. 62 Pompeii was da●aged by an earthquake that was a prelude to ●catastrophe of A.D. 79, the terrifying eruption – vi●ly described in two letters from Pliny the Younge●Tacitus – that was announced by a giant bla●cloud. Scorching lapilli and a shower of ash rain●down, covering people and buildings under a bla●ket that was 4 to 5 meters high. In the 19th c. ca●were made of the bodies that came to light. T●corpses, which had the appearance of a pers●sleeping, much more than that of a dead pers●had been preserved by pumice and ashes; pum●tended to cover the dead body, preserving the ske●ton without flesh, while the ashes solidified up●the corpse, creating a sort of cast. All that was ●quired was to inject plaster into these "molds" in ●der to obtain a vivid image of the last seconds of ●of those who were unable to get away via the s●animals included. Over the centuries, an additio●2-m layer of earth and plants was added, and ev●the folk memory of where the city had once sto●was eventually lost. The first accidental discover●took place on the deserted hill, or Collina della C●ta, at the end of the 16th c. during the reclamati●of the Valle del Sarno; but it was not until 1748, ●der the rule of Charles III of Bourbon, that the f●subterranean explorations began, like those in H●culaneum. With the discovery in 1763 of an ●scription, the site was identified as that of Pompe●Excavations proceeded apace in 1806-1815 und●Joseph Bonaparte and Joaquin Murat, and again ●der the restored Bourbon dynasty (1815-1859). ●of this writing, 60 percent of the ancient city h●been uncovered; ancient Pompeii covered roug●66 hectares, and it is believed that the town had●population of 20,000 or 30,000.

The urban layout. In few other excavations in Ita●does one have as clear an idea as one has in Po●peii of just how the ancient Romans organized a c●The town that was destroyed by Mt. Vesuvius was, ●fact, much like Òstia, an especially complete exa●ple of a market town, with a clear distinction b●tween quarters serving a public function and re●dential areas. That is because the eruption basica●put a seal upon the Roman settlement, arresting ●development abruptly and definitively on 24 Augu●79. On that date, Pompeii was still almost entirely e●circled by walls, in which no fewer than eight gat●opened out to allow communications with the ch●settlements of the surrounding area (the names ●the gates often indicated the places toward whi●the roads led). The walls were punctuated at regu●intervals by towers. Only to the south – overlookin●the sea – did the walled perimeter serve, during th●Empire, to support the panoramic terraces of th●homes of particularly wealthy citizens. The urban la●out within the walls was structured in accordanc●with a traditional ancient city plan. There were tw●

in arteries running east-west ("decumani"); they
re intersected at right angles by the "cardines," run-
g north-south. The diagonal Via Consolare and the
ding Vicolo del Lupanare, as they are now called
talian, were characterized by an irregular layout.
th of the largest routes were paved with large
ving stones and were lined with sidewalks, while
"decumani" in particular were outfitted, at the
st important intersections, with raised walkways
owing pedestrians to cross the street easily. The
ding arteries of the town can be clearly recog-
ed by the deep ruts left by the passage of chari-
and carts (Via dell'Abbondanza and Via Conso-
e were in some areas actually carved with "tracks"
the heavy wheels). There were public fountains at
ssroads. Smaller streets, in turn, split up the urban
into "insulae," literally islands, blocks that were
uped into districts (the so-called "regiones").
se blocks were often occupied by one or more
idential buildings, but it was not uncommon for
eral "insulae" to be joined and used for the con-
ction of a large public facility (amphitheater, the-
r, baths). Another outcome of this geometric or-
ization were the signs ("regio VI, insula V," or "re-
V, insula XIV") which can be seen on nearly every
ner. They tell you what part of Pompeii you are in,
ile the "street address" of the structures lining the
et identify a progression of shops, vestibules of
mes, and factories, the same block after block.

e Pompeian house. Constructed around a
are courtyard (atrium), where the "impluvium"
the collection of rain water was located, the ar-
aic Pompeian house had, directly facing the en-
nce, the "tablinum" (dining room and living room)
d, on either side, the bedrooms ("cubicula") and
storerooms ("cellae"). This simple home was en-
ged by adding, in the back, a Hellenistic peristyle,
ich surrounded the garden ("viridarium") with its
onnade; around the peristyle stood the "triclinium"
ning hall, moved here from the "tablinum") and
er rooms for domestic use and for entertaining
eci}, exedrae). The rooms on the facade were
ed as shops; the upstairs area was used by tenants
slaves. The interior walls were decorated with the
ll-known Pompeian murals, in tempera or by en-
ustic process (pigments mixed with wax and ap-
ed while hot); these murals are generally divided
o four styles (usually numbered): the first style,
ploying encrustation (Samnite era), imitating a
rble facing in stucco; the second style, architec-
al (1st c. B.C.), in which false perspectives framed
ured compositions; the third style, which imitated
e Egyptian manner (Imperial Age, until A.D. 62), in
ich the architectural elements serve as ornamen-
ion; the fourth style, highly ornamental (A.D. 62-
), in which the figurative depictions are enclosed
complicated and capricious architectural ele-
ents. The archaic city, which occupied a small area
und the Forum and had an elliptical plan, grew
cording to a more comprehensive and rational-
d scheme, as is the case with modern cities.

The Pompeiian styles. One of the fundamental
points of reference for the study of the development
of Roman art is the heritage that has survived in Pompeii. The Pompeiian frescoes have been divided by
scholars into four successive chronological periods.
The "first style" (2nd c.-turn of the 1st c. B.C.) was actually Greek in origin and is characterized by imitation of architectural elements (socles, columns), in
colored stucco or jutting features; these features typ-
ified the buildings and tended to be brightly colored. The "second style" (1st c. B.C.) caught on in the
wake of Roman colonization; at first it echoed the interplay of light and shadow in the reliefs of the previous style, and then tended toward more developed
and fanciful elevations and solutions, making use of
jutting panels ("pinakes"), with plant motifs, masks,
and human figures. The "third style" (late 1st c. B.C.-
first half of the 1st c. A.D.) developed as a direct re-
action to the previous style. Here, spaces were no
longer constructed through illusionistic perspective,
but rather on a rigid horizontal and vertical grid-
work. The scenes depicted usually appeared at the
center of the panel, accompanied by Egyptian motifs, enclosed by candelabra featuring plant motifs
and small heads, while the landscapes developed
into veritable miniatures, with a few spare strokes.
The "fourth style" (mid-1st c. to A.D. 79) at first carried
on the refined design that characterized the latest
phase of the previous style – with a sharp prevalence
of panels embellished with textile-based decorative
techniques, interrupted by narrow views and airy architectural structures – with a greater emphasis on
colors (particularly prevalent was golden yellow and
shades that made sharp contrasts). Following the
earthquake of A.D. 62, there was a progressive rigid-
ity of shapes and the stereotypical repetition of decorative motifs, though the taste for illusionistic solutions returned, with architectural backdrops reminiscent of set design. There has been much debate,
ever since the first discoveries, concerning the pictorial techniques used by the ancients. We have more
reliable information on the colors, or paints, once
again thanks to Pliny the Elder, who listed a great
many colors in his "Naturalis Historia." Even then, dis-
tinctions were made between natural and artificial
colors, between dark and light shades, and there
were different costs as well. Usually, bright colors were

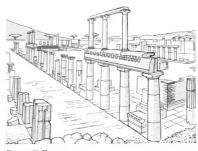

Pompeii: Forum

311

Pompei Scavi 1:8000 (1 cm = 80 m)

the most expensive (and the owner of the house himself would provide the painters with them), though they were also the colors that lasted longest, provided they were applied carefully and on walls that were not exposed to atmospheric agents (Vitruvius, for instance, recommends against using cinnabar red on surfaces exposed to the sun, as it tends to darken with light). As we observe Pompeiian walls with fragments of frescoes, we should keep in mind that dark colors, which certainly prevail over bright colors, are in many cases the result of the eruption and time, much more than of inexpert painters or poor-quality paints, although most Pompeiians did indeed use mid-to-low price paints. Almost wholly shrouded in mystery are the painters themselves. Only one signed his work – a certain Lucius – while all the other frescoes are anonymous.

Places of interest. The **excavations**** (*open 8 one hour before sunset*) have uncovered rough percent of the city's area, a combination of Osc Etruscan, and Greek cultures, later occupied by Samnites (late 5th c. B.C.) and by the Romans after 80 B.C. Pompeii was damaged by an ea quake in A.D. 62, before it was buried by the ash lava of the eruption (A.D. 79).

The entire city seems to leap alive from the s tered ruins. The paved streets are marked by the left by passing chariots, wagons, and carts; there sidewalks and large stones at the intersections, m ing pedestrian crossings; among the resider homes, painted and carved signs indicate the m hotels (*hospitia*), shops (*tabernae*), taverns (*car nae*), and bars (*thermopolia*) with tables on street; painted slogans or scratched-in graffiti

312

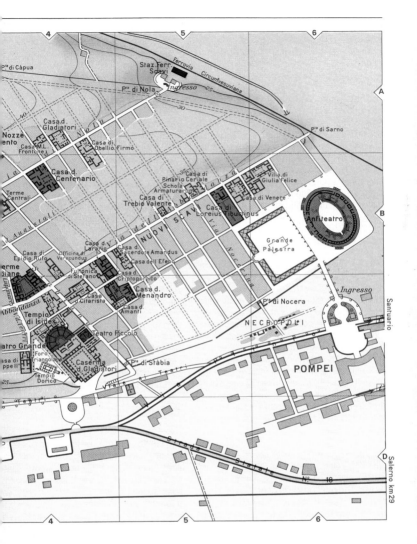

rt this or that candidate for elected public office, announce upcoming gladiatorial matches; huge allic symbols were used to ward off the evil eye. the entrance to the site is the **Antiquarium** (*C3*), museum which features material from excavations d the dramatic **casts*** of victims of the disaster. particular note: the rectangular plaza of the **Fo- um**** (*C3*) with the podium of the Temple of Jove, e Building of Eumachia, headquarters of the guild the "fullones" (cleaners, dyers, and manufacturers cloth) and the **Basilica***, the site of the admin- ration of justice and business; the Hellenistic *large eater*** (*C4*; 200-150 B.C.), which was later en- rged, on the hillside slope; the elegant *small the- er*** (*C4*); the **Anfiteatro*** (*B6*) dating from 80 C., the earliest surviving amphitheater known; and e *Terme Stabiane*** (Baths of Stabia; *B-C4*).

Among the best-known residential houses are the *Casa del Menandro** (House of Menander; *C5*), rich- ly decorated with frescoes; the *Casa di Loreius Tibur- tinus** (*B5*) with a triclinium decorated with scenes from the *Iliad* and the Labors of Hercules; the *Prae- dia di Giulia Felice** (*B6*), in which, alongside the house of the proprietress (Julia Felix), are a public bath and a rental block with shops; the exemplary **Casa dei Vettii**** (*B3*), in which the great *tricli- nium** is decorated with lovely ancient paintings; the *Casa degli Amorini Dorati** (House of the Gild- ed Cupids; *B3*); the **Casa del Fauno*** (House of the Faun; *B3*); the *Casa del Poeta Tragico* (House of the Tragic Poet; *B3*) offers a fine example of a mid- dle-class dwelling.

Outside the enclosure around the excavations is the **Villa dei Misteri**** (Villa of the Mysteries; *A1*): the huge painting dating from the 1st c. B.C. on the walls of one hall, depicting the Initiation of the Brides to the Dionysian Mysteries**, is a remarkable and exquisite piece of ancient art.

Portofino*

Pop. 565; Liguria, province of Genoa. This town lies on the southernmost extremity of the Monte di Portofino. Around a little seaside square and along the natural port is a fringe of Ligurian houses, tall, narrow, and brightly colored. In the water, during the high season, are luxury yachts flying every imaginable flag and elegant parties are the rule here. Inland, among the pines and holm-oaks, are the villas that were exclusive and elegant at the turn of the 20th c.

Places of interest. The port. As you stroll through the main square and then along the waterfront, you will enjoy remarkable scenes and landscapes of all sorts. The natural setting becomes even more spectular if you go to a corner of the square and take the Salita S. Giorgio up to the church of *S. Giorgio*, which grandly surveys two bodies of water (on one side the open sea, on the other the bay); the church was rebuilt after WWII. From the church courtyard you can enter the Castello di S. Giorgio (*open 10-5; summer, until 6; closed Tue.*), a 19th-c. adaptation of an existing building; beneath the church, a little lane runs out among the Mediterranean pine trees of the promontory, leading to the lighthouse at the *tip of the Cape*; from here you will enjoy a majestic view of the Golfo del Tigullio and the coast as far south as Sestri Levante.

Pozzuoli

Elev. 28 m, pop. 84,014; Campania, province of Naples. The phenomenon of bradyseism here can be detected through the holes dug by rock-boring sea mollusks in the columns of the Macellum, indicating that as the land rises and falls, the complex is alternately submerged and lifted out of the water.

Places of interest. The Macellum* – once known as Serapaeum – was the public market of the Roman town of Puteoli under the empire; the sixteen Corinthian columns, with the mollusk-burrowed holes mentioned above, supported a dome.
In the Anfiteatro**, or amphitheater (*open 9-one hour before sunset*), built in the 1st c. A.D., *naumachiae* (staged sea battles) were held, along with fights and hunts of wild beasts; a tour of the intriguing *cellars* * includes the shafts up which the cages of the wild beasts were hoisted into the arena.
The Terme di Nettuno, or Neptune's Baths, comprise the impressive remains of a bath structure; the nearby *Ninfeo di Diana* is actually the ruins of a nymphaeum.

The Mausolei di Via Celle are the best preser funerary complex on the Via Campana. They clude 14 buildings with a central hall and eleva funerary chambers, in some of which there are mains of painted or stucco decoration.

Ravello*

Elev. 350 m, pop. 2509; Campania, province Salerno. The center of town is the Piazza Ves vado.

Places of interest. High atop a stairway is the D mo*, founded in 1086, built in the 12th c., and d tically renovated in the 18th c.; note the bro door* (1179) and the 13th-c. campanile. *Inside:* pit* decorated with mosaics and reliefs by Nicc di Bartolomeo da Foggia (1272), and ambo* ing from about 1130.
Partly surrounding the Piazza Vescovado is park of the Villa Rufolo** (*open 9-one hour fore sunset; closed 1 Jan., 25 Dec.*): the comp of Moorish-Sicilian style buildings (13th c.), note particular the courtyard,* not unlike a small cl ter; in a building adjacent to the villa is the A *quarium*; also visit the *garden* * with exotic plan After you pass the church of *S. Francesco*, with its mantic Gothic cloister, you continue on to the V la Cimbrone*: the courtyard features superb cient fragments; at the end of the garden, note famous Belvedere Cimbrone**, a breathtak view on the gulf and Costiera Amalfitana.

Ravenna**

Elev. 4 m, pop. 138,418; Emilia-Romagna, prov cial capital. The unexcelled allure of this c springs from a chance twist of ancient his ry. In A.D. 402, the Emperor Honorius shift the capital of the Western Roman Empire fr Milan to this village on the Adriatic coast, w a strategic lagoon defending it inland. For t ensuing 150 years Ravenna was, variously, t heart of a moribund empire, the court of Gothic king educated in Constantinop named Theodoric, and the center of Byza tine Italy (lavishly adorned thanks to pro made in the wars against the Goths). Clas cal influence, Christian faith, and plenti funds made this a spectacular proving grou for the growing Byzantine artistic canon. Ar the centuries of quiet papal rule that followe left Ravenna magically intact. In the 15 ce turies since Ravenna's foundation, the Adri ic has receded to a distance of 12 km, b maritime trade still thrives here.

Historical note. The Emperor Augustus was t first to grasp Ravenna's potential as a port. This mo est Roman colony stood on a littoral strip, prote ed by the Adriatic on one side and by a vast lagoo landward. It became the second naval base of th

avenna: S. Vitale

oman Empire and, in A.D. 402, capital of the empire
Milan was threatened by the Goths). Despite the
mpire's decline, Ravenna began to accumulate its
tonishing trove of monuments. In 476, Odoacre
eposed the last Roman emperor; his successor,
heodoric, ruled here from 493 to 526. More monu-
ents were built: Theodoric's mausoleum, the basil-
a of S. Apollinare Nuovo, the church of S. Spirito,
d the Arian baptistery. Byzantium declared war
n the Goths, and in 540 the Byzantine general Belis-
rius took Ravenna. Three decades of peace fol-
wed, during which time such monuments as the
hurches of S. Vitale and S. Apollinare in Classe were
uilt. With the Longobard invasion of 568, Ravenna
as reduced to the capital of the Hexarchate (the
yzantine military district that held out for two cen-
ries). The Po River shifted its course northward,
rther isolating the city. In 751 Ravenna fell to the
ongobards. Its glory had ended. In the centuries
at followed, the city was ruled by archbishops and
n assortment of local nobility. The Da Polenta fam-
y, who ruled from 1302 to 1441, gained some degree
f immortality by offering hospitality to Dante
lighieri, who died and was buried here. Venice held
way here from 1441 to 1509, and new monuments
ere built for the first time in many centuries. Mod-
rn-day Piazza del Popolo became the center of
avenna. In front of the Palazzo del Comune, two
olumns were built, reminiscent of St. Mark's Square
Venice. The "Palazzetto Veneziano" was built, and
andsome Venetian-style houses were constructed
what is now Via Cairoli. After 1509, the Papal States
eld sway here; no noteworthy monuments date
om this period, nor from the 19th c. The industrial
oom of the 1950s and 1960s led to environmental
roblems, but also to the restoration and preserva-
on of Ravenna's historic center. The extraction of
ater and methane has exacerbated the centuries-
ng subsidence of Ravenna's monuments.

Getting around. We recommend two routes; both
egin from a centrally located piazza. The first route
a walking tour; the second one, at least partly
alkable, may require public transportation for the
econd half, which is on the outskirts of town.

S. Vitale, the Duomo, the Baptisteries

The Baptistery of the Arians; the complex of S. Vitale
with its remarkable windows and the tomb of Galla Placidia (sister of emperors, wife of a Visigoth
king, and in time herself empress); the Duomo with
the Baptistery of the Orthodox; and the ivory throne
of Maximian in the Museo Arcivescovile: these are
the highlights of the route through the western part
of Ravenna, beginning from Piazza del Popolo.

Piazza del Popolo. The heart of Ravenna, the
square features two Venetian columns (1483), the
15th-c. **Palazzo Comunale**, and the porticoed
Palazzetto Veneziano (1462; note the 6th-c. capitals,
with the signet of Theodoric).

Battistero degli Ariani. *Open 8:30-7.* Octagonal
building, probably from the early 6th c., with a mo-
saic-covered dome. Adjacent is the late 5th-c. church
of **Spirito Santo**, renovated in the 16th c.: Byzantine
capitals, 6th-c. ambo, ancient sarcophagus.

Via S. Vitale. At n. 28 is a 13th-c. house with mullioned
windows. At the end of the street, on the right, is the
basilica of *S. Vitale* and the tomb of Galla Placidia.

S. Vitale.** *Open winter, 9-7.* Construction began in
A.D. 526; consecrated in 547-48, this basilica is one
of the greatest Early Christian monuments. With an
octagonal plan, and a narthex at one face, even its
brick exterior reveals the Roman conception of
space reworked in Byzantine style. The **interior***
has a strikingly original structure; it is lavishly
adorned with marble and mosaic, and stunning effects are created by natural light. The dome is very
light, made with rings of hollow terracotta pipes;
painted in 1780. On one side is the *presbytery*, its
walls adorned with remarkable **mosaics*** that date
from the mid-6th c., still classical in style. Two panels in the lower section of the apse (the emperor
Justinian* and the empress Theodora*, with respective entourages) are more properly Byzantine
in their stylization. In the middle of the presbytery,
the 6th-c. altar, with a translucent slab of alabaster*.

Mausoleo di Galla Placidia.** *Open winter, 9:30-
4:30; summer, 9-7.* This chapel, built to a Greek cross
plan in the mid-5th c., boasts remarkable **mo-
saics****, prior to 450, perhaps the earliest in Ravenna. Note also the three ancient sarcophagi in the
apse and each transept.

Museo Nazionale.* *Open Tue.-Sat., 8:30-7:30.* An
eclectic array of collections, built around a nucleus dating from the early 18th c. Noteworthy collection of Roman and Early Christian artwork; arranged
around three cloisters of a Benedictine monastery,
the museum also has collections of ancient fabrics,
ivories, icons, paintings, and various works of art.

Piazza Kennedy, formerly Piazza del Mercato. Note
Palazzo Rasponi delle Teste (early 18th c.), and
facing it, *Palazzo Rasponi Murat* (15th c.).

Duomo. The Basilica Ursiana, built here in the early 5th c. and demolished in 1733, was replaced by
this Baroque structure; on the left side stands the
round, 10th-c. *campanile*; inside, at the end of the

central nave, the ambo* of Archbishop Agnellus (late 6th. c.).

Battistero Neoniano.** *Open 9-7.* Also called Baptistery of the Orthodox, this building with eight brick sides was probably built during the first half of the 5th c. The mosaics date from just after 450. Inside, two orders of arcades support the **mosaic-lined dome****, divided into three areas: the Baptism of Jesus in the Jordan, the river personified as an old man; the Apostles; and symbolic depictions of dominions and thrones.

Museo Arcivescovile.* *Open winter, 9-4:30; summer, 9-7.* Behind the Duomo, in the Arcivescovado, or archbishopric, this museum preserves collections of material from the ancient cathedral and other churches, including a headless porphyry statue*, early 6th-c. mosaics*, and the celebrated 6th-c. ivory **throne of Maximian****.

S. Apollinare Nuovo and the Mausoleo di Teodorico

The handsome marble statue of Guidarello, man of arms (Pinacoteca), the tomb of Dante Alighieri, who spent his last years in exile here, and the so-called Palace of Theodoric, king of the Goths, all mark this tour through the eastern portion of Ravenna. Although the barbarian king never lived in the palace that bears his name, he did build the church of S. Apollinare Nuovo, a curious mixture of barbarian style and classical inspiration.

Piazza S. Francesco. This is the heart of the "zone of Dante." Lord Byron once lived in Casa Oriani, which overlooks the piazza; it now contains the Biblioteca di Storia Contemporanea, a library of contemporary history.

S. Francesco.* This is a 5th-c. basilica rebuilt in the 10th c. and damaged in WWII. The main altar consists of the Urn of Liberius, adorned with reliefs; the crypt, now flooded, dates from the 9th-10th c.

Tomba di Dante.* *Open 9-7.* For the last five years of his life, Dante Alighieri was a guest in Ravenna of Guido Novello da Polenta; he died during the night of 13 September 1321, and was buried here. The modern-day tomb was built in 1780; the relief by P. Lombardo, depicting Dante reading, dates from 1483. Adjacent is the *Museo Dantesco* (*open Apr.-Sep., Mon.-Sun., 9-12 and 3-6; Oct.-Mar., Tue.-Sun., 9-12*).

S. Agata Maggiore. In Via Mazzini, this 5th-/6th-c. church was restored in the late 15th c. It features a round campanile and, inside, columns with Roman, Byzantine and Renaissance capitals.

S. Maria in Porto. A late 16th-c. church with noteworthy paintings (esp. by Palma the Younger), a Greek Madonna*, and a late Byzantine marble relief. Adjacent is a *former monastery*, with an admirable early 16th-c. **Loggetta Lombardesca***, a handsome Renaissance cloister*, and the **Pinacoteca Comunale**, or town art gallery* (*open Wed. and Sat., 9-1:30, Tue., Thu.-Fri., also 3-6; closed Mon., Sun. and holidays*). The collections include art works

by L. Monaco, Guercino, C. Bravo, N. Rondinelli, ar the famed sepulchral statue of Guidarello Guidar li*, a soldier of Ravenna, by T. Lombardo (1525).

Palazzo di Teodorico. Long said to be the sum tuous royal residence depicted in a mosaic still p served in S. Apollinare Nuovo, this is actually a la 7th-c. building, perhaps a barracks or a secretaria

S. Apollinare Nuovo.** *Open 9-7.* Built t Theodoric in 493-96, for the Arian sect, the chur has received various additions: the cylindrical ca panile* in the 9th or 10th c., the small portico in th 16th c., the gilt coffered ceiling in the 17th c. Th walls of the nave are lined with **mosaics**** in thr registers: the two upper ones date from the reig of Theodoric, and reveal the style of late classicisr the lower section dates from slightly later, and is e quisitely Byzantine in composition and style.

S. Giovanni Evangelista.* This 5th-c. basilica w restored and rebuilt after the heavy damage su tained during the war. In front is a Gothic porta adorned with bas-reliefs; to the right of the facac is a sturdy square 10th-c. bell tower. Inside are a cient columns, fragments of floor mosaics (di played on the walls), and, in the chapel to the le fragments of 14th-c. frescoes.

Rocca di Brancaleone. This square fort, with i four circular towers, built by Venice in the late 15 c., once commanded the city. It is now a playgroun also used for outdoor concerts and performance

Mausoleo di Teodorico.* *Open 8:30-7.* Standin alone against a backdrop of cypresses, about 2 k NE of the center. The king of the Goths ordered built around A.D. 520. An odd structure, with a mi ture of barbarian and classic styles, its dome is a si gle enormous block of limestone (1 m thick; 11 across) that was probably damaged during co struction. In the upper chamber, the porphyry sa cophagus must once have contained the king's bod

Surrounding areas. Basilica di S. Apollinar in Classe**, 5 km south, on the Adriatica road. A ter the intersection to Lido di Dante, you find th entrance to the *archeological site of Classe** (ope 9-7), with relics of the late Roman and Byzantin port facilities. Just past this, on the left of the road is the basilica, consecrated in 549 and an ou standing monument of Ravenna's Byzantine arti tic heritage. The round *campanile**, with its pro gression of one-, two-, and three-light mullioned wi dows, was built sometime after the 9th c. Inside, th nave and aisles are separated by columns made o Greek marble, topped by Byzantine capitals; in pa ticular, note the **mosaics*** (6th-7th c. and later).

Reggio di Calabria

Elev. 31 m, pop. 179,617; Calabria, provincia capital.

Historical note. The Chalcidians of Euboea foun their "promised land" in the Ionian "gulf" that th coastlines of Sicily and the Italian peninsula form

Reggio di Calabria
1:16 000 (1 cm = 160 m)

0   200   400 m

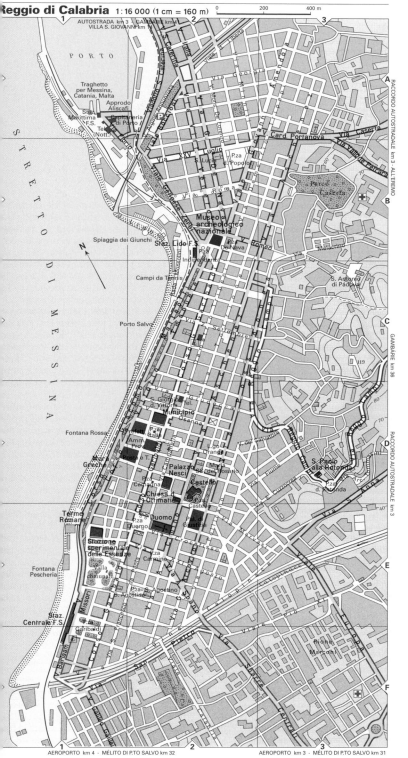

AUTOSTRADA km 3 - GAMBARIE km
VILLA S. GIOVANNI km 7

PORTO

Traghetto
per Messina,
Catania, Malta
Approdo
Aliscafi
Staz.
Marittima
F.S.
Capitaneria
di Porto
Tel.
(Nott.)

S T R E T T O

D I

M E S S I N A

Via Card. Portanova   Via Casaria

Via XXV Luglio
S. Lucia
P.za
del Popolo

Parco
Caserta

Museo
archeologico
nazionale

Spiaggia dei Giunchi   Staz. Lido F.S.

P.za
De Nava

V. Romeo

Malacrino

P.za
Indipendenza

S. Antonio
di Padova

Campi da Tennis

Porto Salvo

Settembre

Fontana Rossa

S. Giorgio
d. Vittoria   Tel.

Municipio

Osanna

P.za Italia

Amm.ne
Prov.
Pal.
Giustizia T.C.

V.le
d'Orange

Mura
Greche

Palazzo
Nesci

Maria
SS. del Rosario

S. Paolo
alla Rotonda

P.za
Calzagna

Chiesa d.
Ottimati

Castello

P.za
d. Rotonda

Castello

Terme
Romane

P.za
Duomo

Duomo

Pal. di
Giustizia

Stazione
sperimentale
delle Essenze

P.za
Carmine

Fontana
Pescheria

Villa
comunale

P.za S. Agostino
S. Agostino

Staz.
Centrale F.S.

Garibaldi

Riona
Marconi

before squeezing into the strait: in just a few years, toward the end of the 8th c. B.C., they founded Naxos and Zancle (Messina) on the Sicilian shore, and Rhegion on the opposite shore.

Places of interest. The **Museo Nazionale**** (*B2; open 9-7:30; closed 1st and 3rd Mon. of the month*) is the first and most interesting stop in any tour of the city. The immense archeological collections, with material unearthed at sites in Calabria and Basilicata, are fundamental for those who wish to understand the ancient culture of this section of Magna Graecia; a further attraction is constituted by the world-renowned **Bronzes of Riace****, two large statues of warriors, Greek originals from the mid-5th c. B.C., attributed to Phidias or his school. Of considerable interest are the artifacts found in ancient Locri with the *pinakes** (terracotta tablets) depicting in relief the myth of Persephone, a terracotta group with an Ephebus on Horseback (5th c. B.C.) and the marble group of the Dioscuri (early 5th c. B.C.). The section of medieval and modern art boasts two small panels by A. da Messina, with St. Jerome* and Abraham and the Angels* (1457), and the Return of the Prodigal Son* by M. Preti.

The **Lungomare*** (*C-D1-2*) is a magnificent promenade with a panoramic view of the Strait of Messina, the Monti Peloritani, and Monte Etna; at its southern extremity, you can see a stretch of **Greek walls** (*D1*), dating from the 4th c. B.C., and ruins of the *Terme Romane* (Roman Baths; *E1*).

The **Duomo** (*E2*) was rebuilt following the 1908 earthquake.

Of the **Castello** (*D2*), built during Aragonese rule (15th c.), only two circular towers and a stretch of the curtain walls still survive.

Rìmini

Pop. 131,062; Emilia-Romagna, provincial capital. Long sunny days on the beach, warm nights on the dance floor: Rìmini is the heart of Romagna's Riviera, the spectacular playground of Europe. This was just a fishing village when the first adventurous bathers ventured into the waves, in hats and ample suits. The 18th-/19th-c. breakwaters changed the shape of the beach, increasing the eastern shores with fine iridescent sand, and eroding the western ones. And overlooking the eastern beach is the luxurious Grand Hotel, so dear to the film director Fellini. Rìmini itself dates back to the 3rd c. B.C.; 17 centuries later, the local ruler, Sigismondo Malatesta (1429-1468), had Piero della Francesca paint his portrait, and asked Leon Battista Alberti to transform a little local church into the majestic Tempio Malatestiano, a major masterpiece of the early Renaissance.

Places of interest. Piazza Cavour. Historically the heart of Rìmini, this square has a statue of Pope

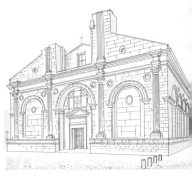

Rìmini: Tempio Malatestiano

Paul V (1613) and a 16th-c. fountain. On the N\ side are the 16th-c. *Palazzo Comunale* and the 13th c. *Palazzo dell'Arengo* (note loggia and mullione windows; upstairs are the large detached frescoes and, at the end, the 14th-c. Gothic *Palazzo d Podestà*. Also note the 19th-c. *Teatro Amintore Gall* **Castel Sismondo**. In the huge Piazza Malatesta, th castle was completed in 1446 and designed by Sig smondo Malatesta with the advice of Brunellesch Inside is the **Museo delle Culture Extraeurope** (*temporarily closed*), with African, Australian, an pre-Columbian ethnographic collections.

S. Agostino. This Romanesque-Gothic church date from 1247 and has a fine tall campanile*; insid 14th-c. frescoes, paintings by G. da Rimini, frescoe by the Maestro dell'Arengo, and a large 14th-c. Cr cifix*.

Piazza Tre Martiri. This square lies on the ancien Roman Forum, where Julius Caesar exhorted h troops in 49 B.C. after crossing the Rubicon. Als note the *Torre dell'Orologio*, or clock tower (1547 and the 17th-c. octagonal church of *S. Antonio*.

Arco d'Augusto.* Oldest of the surviving Roma arches, with medieval crenelations, it was built in 2 B.C. in honor of Augustus, who rebuilt the Vi Flaminia which joined the Via Æmilia at Rìmini.

Anfiteatro Romano. This Roman amphitheate dates from Hadrian's reign, and could originally se 10,000. Discovered in 1844 and unearthed in 192 35, it now comprises little more than parts of the are na and cavea and the exterior portico.

Tempio Malatestiano.** This church symbolize Rìmini, and is considered one of the masterpiece of the early Renaissance. A 13th-c. chapel stoo here, and was almost entirely rebuilt by L.B. Albe ti (1447-60), at the behest of Sigismondo Malatest Heavily damaged in WWII, the church was restore in the 1950s. The majestic facade (unfinished) take its style from Roman triumphal arches; along th side, solemn arches house the tombs of famou men and women.

The Gothic *interior* was renovated by the Verones architect M. de' Pasti. The handsome decoration by A. di Duccio. Note the tomb of S. Malatesta, t the right of the entrance. Note the **detached fre co**** by Piero della Francesca (1451), the tomb c sotta degli Atti*, perhaps by M. de' Pasti, and a **Crucifix**** on panel, painted by Giotto around 1312. Also, bas-reliefs* and tomb* by A. di Duccio (1454).

Museo della Città. *Open 14 Sep.-14 Jun., Tue.-Sat., 8:30-12:30 and 5-7; Sun., 8:30-12:30 and 4-7; 15 Jun.-13 Sep., Tue.-Sat., 10-12:30 and 4:30-7:30; Sun. and holidays, 4:30-7:30.* Set in a huge ex-convent still being restored (entrance at n. 1 in Via Tonini), this museum has Roman epigraphs, a Pinacoteca, or art gallery, and archeological and naturalistic sections. In the **Lapidario Romano**, of particular note: colossal Augustan milestone* from the "Via Æmilia," two altars* to Iuppiter Delichenus, mosaic floors. The **Pinacoteca** features works by 14th-c. Riminese artists such as: G. da Rimini, as well as Giovanni Bellini, D. Ghirlandaio, and G. Cagnacci.

Ponte di Tiberio*, or Tiberius's Bridge, originally spanned the Marecchia River (since shifted northward). Begun by Augustus and completed under Tiberius (A.D. 14-21), it has five arches. Nearby is the 16th-c. church of **S. Giuliano**, with paintings by Veronese and B. da Faenza (1409).

Surrounding areas. The **riviera of Rìmini**, made up of a series of tree-lined boulevards, with hotels, and seaside resort villages. To the NW, 4.5 km, is **Viserba**, with the villages of *Viserbella* and *Torre Pedrera*. To the SE, 7 km, is Miramare, after Rivazzurra, which has the Istituto Talassoterapico (saltwater and cures).

Rome / Roma**

Elev. 20 m, pop. 2,643,581; capital of the Italian Republic; Lazio (Latium), regional and provincial capital. "If," Stendhal once wrote, "as you go from one monument to the next in your Roman mornings, you should have the courage to become bored through lack of social interchange, no matter how indifferent you might be to the little conceits of the drawing room, in the end you will feel the joy of the arts..." This many-faceted city envelops and penetrates with its endless array of images, with its kaleidoscopic stimuli: the "walls and the arches," as one writer summed it up, the umbrella pines of Villa Borghese, the creations of Raphael and Michelangelo, Bernini and Borromini, the Spanish Steps at the Trinità dei Monti, seen through the eyes of Goethe or Keats, the old travertine from which you can hear echoing the biting wit and violent jibes of the "romanesque" poetry of Belli, where you can imagine the fanciful irony created by the late, great Federico Fellini, and the rushing, "blonde" Tiber. This city is incomparable, and part of its allure may lie in its history, which witnessed periods of great splendor followed by others of melancholy decadence. Rome, however, has always been reborn, hence its nickname: "The Eternal City." It has heaped up treasures and memories, and it boasts the fascination of a cityscape that still survives the assault of its suburbs.

Historical note. It all began here around the middle of the 8th c. B.C. – according to legend, on 21 April 754 B.C. – on the Palatine Hill, where settlements date back as far as the Bronze Age. This early Rome gradually spread out to cover, one by one, the other six hills – the Esquiline, Caelian, Viminal, Quirinale, Capitoline, and Aventine – and it was enclosed within the Servian walls (by the semi-legendary king, Servius Tullius). These walls of Rome were thoroughly rebuilt after the invasion of the Gauls in 378 B.C.; in comparison with the Aurelian walls of the 3rd c. A.D., they left out the Pincio, to the north, as well as the modern section of town to the east, bordered by the Rione Castro Pretorio, the Tiburtine, and the Lateran; excluded to the south was the entire area of the Baths of Caracalla, and to the west, Testaccio, Trastevere, and Campo Marzio. In the five centuries of the Roman Republic (509-31 B.C.), while Rome was becoming mistress of the entire Mediterranean basin, the city grew until, in the 1st c. B.C., it had attained a population of 400,000. For the first time, public works began to acquire a certain grandeur, as we can see from the Tabularium on the Campidoglio or the theater of Marcellus. Augustus (27 B.C.- A.D. 14) initiated the final development of the Imperial Forums, or Fori Imperiali, while Nero made the Palatine the site of a vast imperial palace. Rome attained its definitive appearance, however, only with the Flavian emperors (A.D. 69-96), who built the Colosseum and the Arch of Titus. In the 2nd c. Rome reached its greatest urban and demographic expansion, with a population of more than a million; by the beginning of the century, Trajan had built the largest of the Imperial Forums, known as Trajan's Forum. The 3rd c. began with the construction of the Baths of Caracalla, but the threat of barbarian invasions led the emperor Aurelian to build a new walled perimeter around Rome, between 271 and 275. The city continued to develop within those walls until 1870 and still enclose the historic center. Only a few major works (the Baths of Diocletian, the Basilica of Maxentius, the Arch of Constantine) were erected thereafter in Rome, and when the imperial court was transferred to Byzantium, or Constantinople (A.D. 330), Rome lost the title of capital of the empire.

Despite the restorations undertaken by Honorius at the turn of the 5th c., the Aurelian walls failed to protect Rome from the Goths in 410, nor from the Vandals in 455 and 472. In Christian and Byzantine Rome, afflicted with political turmoil and declining population (at the end of the Western Empire, there were only 100,000 people in the city), the neglected ancient monuments stood in the shadow of new churches, the latter often being built with architectural fragments and valuable material taken from the former. The formal prohibition of transforming temples into churches moved the center of town from the Forums and the Palatine to the Lateran, res-

Rome: Piazza S. Pietro

idence of the bishop of Rome. The first major city works of the Middle Ages were defensive in nature, and followed the sack by the Saracens (A.D. 846) of the basilicas of S. Pietro and S. Paolo (St. Peter and St. Paul). Pope Leo IV fortified part of the city, on the right bank of the Tiber, building new walls and linking them with the mausoleum of Hadrian, which was in turn transformed into a fortress (Castel S. Angelo): this was the birth of the "Leonine city." Though by this point the pope was the true lord of Rome, the 9th-11th c. were centuries of turmoil and bloody conflict among the local nobility, and between that nobility and the Holy Roman Emperors of Germany. In 1084, the Normans sacked the town; destruction was especially severe around the Caelian; the population shifted away from areas furthest from the river, and into the oxbow curve of the Tiber. The so-called Consular Commune formed in the mid-12th c., and from then to the end of the 13th c., many towers and palace-fortresses were built by the nobility, often incorporating ancient buildings. Rome in those years had shrunk to one-fourth of its ancient expanse; the popolation hovered between 17,000 and 50,000, and was clustered along the curving bank of the Tiber, between the bridges of Ponte S. Angelo and Ponte Rotto (the ancient Aemilian bridge). During the 13th-14th c., the autocratic power of the pope and his family grew, outweighing that of the Commune and the nobility. At the head of the nobility were the House of the Orsini (pro-pope) and the House of the Colonna (pro-emperor); the former controlled the strongholds along the Tiber, the latter controlled the area between the Mausoleum of Augustus and the Lateran. The celebration of the first Jubilee (1300) occurred in a thriving Rome, on its way to new glory, a Rome that attracted such great artists as Giotto, Pietro Cavallini, and Jacopo Torriti. The long "Avignonese captivity," also known as the "Babylonian captivity," the plague of 1341, the earthquake of 1349, and the failure of the attempt by Cola di Rienzo to establish a

supreme government that would encourage trad while keeping the local barons at bay, condemne Rome to long decades of poverty and misery. The return of the papal court from Avignon marke the beginning of a time of recovery. The popes hel temporal power as the princes of Rome and in 141? Pope Martin V Colonna was the first Roman pope i 40 years not opposed by an Avignonese antipope his reign also marks the dawn of the Renaissance His projects of reconstruction were carried on pr marily by the first Humanist pope, Nicholas V, wh commissioned work from L.B. Alberti and the a chitect B. Rossellino, who designed the new Basil ca of S. Pietro (St. Peter's). Sixtus IV (1471-1484) ur dertook the first real program of urban reconstruc tion, beginning with the Ponte Sisto. Julius II (150? 1513) brought the great architect Bramante t Rome, finally beginning work on the long-delaye Basilica di S. Pietro (St. Peter's); he also built the Vi Giulia, Rome's first great straight avenue; he com missioned Michelangelo to paint the ceiling of th Cappella Sistina (Sistine Chapel), and Raphael t paint the ceilings and walls of the new papal apar ments. The Medici popes Leo X and Clement V. brought a Florentine conception of city-planning t Rome, and built the Tridente, comprising the cen tral Via del Corso and the lateral Via di Ripetta an Via del Babuino. The Sack of Rome in 1527 brough work to a halt only temporarily. Pope Paul III Farnese commissioned Michelangelo to transform the Piaz za del Campidoglio, with the placement of the grea and ancient equestrian statue of Marcus Aurelius i the center of the piazza. Michelangelo also pro duced a new design for St. Peter's and laid out th Via dei Condotti, leading up to the church of Trinit dei Monti. The Protestant Reformation pushed th popes to reorganize their dominion and to wor even harder (and spend even more lavishly) t make their capital a luxurious and magnificent city In the second half of the 16th c., during the Counte

eformation, Pius IV built the arrow-straight Strada
a (now the Via del Quirinale and Via XX Settem-
e), Gregory XIII built the straight roads of Via Gre-
riana and Via Merulana and the Convents of the
gostiniani, the Teatini, the Filippini, and the Jesuits,
hose churches dominated the cityscape of late
th-c. Rome.

ue urban renewal came with Pope Sixtus V, how-
er, who in just five years (1585-90) gave Rome the
pearance that we know today. The plan called for
series of roads radiating out from the great Basi-
a of S. Maria Maggiore (Sixtus's favorite church)
the churches of S. Giovanni in Laterano (St. John
teran), S. Lorenzo Fuori le Mura, and Trinità dei
onti. As early as 1586 the Strada Felice was being
ilt – corresponding to the modern-day Via De-
etis, Via Quattro Fontane, and Via Sistina – followed
the boulevards that became modern-day Via
nisperna and Via S. Giovanni in Laterano. Sixtus V
as also a great lover of obelisks, installing them in
azza S. Pietro (St. Peter's Square), Piazza S. Giovanni
Laterano (St. John Lateran), Piazza del Popolo,
d Piazza dell'Esquilino. The Rome of Sixtus V was
en its crowning Baroque touches by Pope Alexan-
r VII (1655-67) with the work of Bernini on the
lonnade of Piazza S. Pietro (St. Peter's Square) and
e fountains of Piazza Navona. Between the late
th-early 18th c., Rome attained the height of its
rmal and theatrical splendor: the Spanish Steps of
e church of the Trinità dei Monti and the Trevi
untain are the most spectacular expressions of
at period. At the end of the 18th c., the waning po-
cal influence of the papacy and the growing eco-
mic crisis of the Papal States led to a slowing of
nstruction. French occupation and annexation
d to new political ideas, which found expression
Neo-Classic architecture and art. A series of truly
bitious reconstruction projects were intended to
ake Rome the second capital of Napoleon Bona-
rte's new empire, but in the five short years avail-
le (1809-1814) the French project was complet-
only in the Pincio and the rebuilding of Piazza
l Popolo and Piazza della Colonna Traiana (Tra-
's Column). With the return of Pius VII (1815),
me turned in upon itself, and for the rest of the
h c. declined in artistic and cultural importance.
er 1870, when Rome was established as the cap-
l of the Kingdom of Italy, it began to grow rapid-
by 1900 it had 400,000 inhabitants, twice the pop-
tion of 30 years before. Among the new boule-
rds built were the Via Nazionale, Via Cavour, and
rso Vittorio Emanuele II; also newly built were
e districts of the Esquilino (Esquiline Hill), the Ce-
(Caelian Hill), the Testaccio, and Prati. Among
e results of the Exposition of 1911 were the ur-
nization of the district of Vittoria and the recon-
uction of Valle Giulia; by the end of WWII, the dis-
ts of Flaminio, Salario, Nomentano, Ostiense, and
onteverde Vecchio had all been built. Major arche-
gical digs were undertaken in central Rome, and
ne buildings and sections were destroyed, some-
ng we can only regret; other major and laudable

projects were undertaken and completed, among
them the Città Universitaria (central university campus), the Foro Mussolini (now Foro Italico), Cinecit-
tà (the film studios), and the satellite city of EUR, designed to house the Universal Exhibition of 1942
(WWII of course prevented that). In the 1950s, EUR
was completed, becoming a major business and office center. Rome's population, which had reached
one million in the 1930s, was 1.5 million by the end
of WWII. Since then it has nearly doubled, and only recently has there been a decline. This led to
chaotic expansion and construction, with the usual real-estate speculation and illegal development.
In 1990 a new law was passed for Rome, the capital city: Rome's future depends on the projects in
the fields of archeology, the environment, traffic control, university expansion, and convention centers.

Getting around. Rome should be toured on foot,
if for no other reason than to enjoy the allure of a
city with a history dating back more than 25 centuries. This applies in particular to the historic center, enclosed within the bounds of the walls built
by Aurelian, where it is extremely difficult to park –
at times, impossible. Moreover, some areas of this
central section are off limits to traffic, or require
special permits. Public transportation is inevitably
crowded, even if it offers a good way of getting
around; especially useful are the two subway lines,
which were recently extended. For each of the 13
itineraries proposed, a detailed map shows the suggested route and the chief sights.

1   **Campidoglio, Fori Imperiali, Colosseum**
2   **Archeological Area of the Foro Romano
    and Palatino**
3   **Via del Corso, Via dei Condotti,
    and Piazza di Spagna**
4   **"Quartiere del Rinascimento"**
5   **From Piazza Barberini to Piazza
    del Popolo through the Pincio**
6   **Basilica di S. Pietro and the Musei
    Vaticani**
7   **"Quartiere delle Regioni", Villa
    Borghese museums, Foro Italico**
8   **Quirinale, Porta Pia, and Museo
    Nazionale Romano**
9   **On the Hills: Viminale, Esquilino,
    and Laterano**
10 **The "Passeggiata Archeologica"
    and the churches on the Celio**
11 **Foro Boario, Aventino, and S. Paolo
    fuori le Mura**
12 **Trastevere**
13 **Via Appia Antica and EUR**

1   **Campidoglio, Fori Imperiali, Colosseum**

A first sample of the splendor of classical times can
be had along this route, which runs from the high-

Roma/I 1:13 000 (1 cm = 130 m)

323

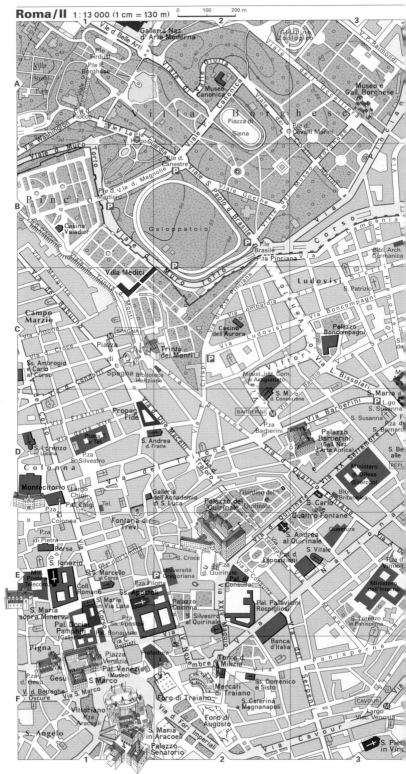

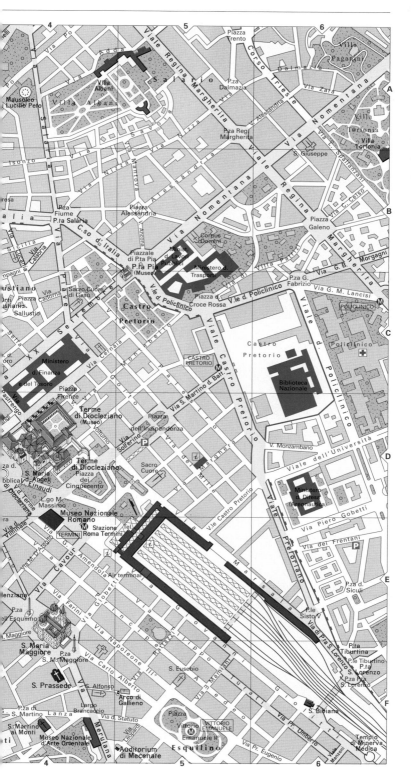

325

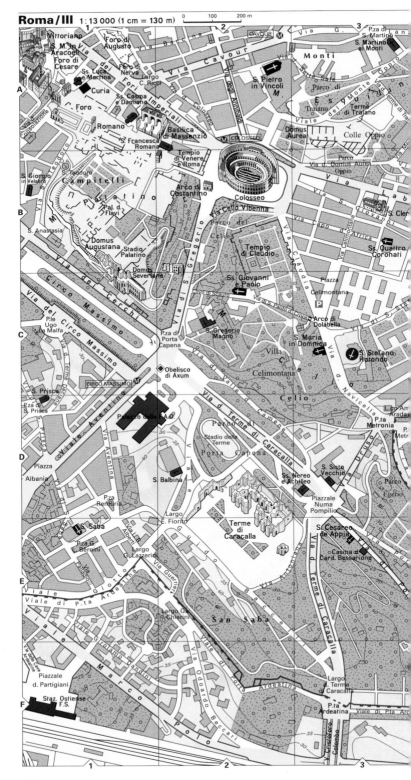

Roma/III

1:13 000 (1 cm = 130 m)

0   100   200 m

Vittoriano
S. M. in
Aracoeli
Ss. Luca
e Martina
Curia
Foro
Romano
S. Francesca
Romana
S. Giorgio
in Velabro
Campitelli
Pal. d.
Flavi
S. Anastasia
Domus
Augustana
Stadio
Palatino
Domus
Severiana
Foro di
Augusto
Foro di
Cesare
Ss. Cosma
e Damiano
Basilica
di Massenzio
Tempio di Venere
e Roma
Arco di
Costantino
Palatino
Foro di
Nerva
Largo
C. Ricci
Fori Imperiali
Via dei Fori Imperiali
Colosseo
Celio Vibenna
Parco del
Celio
Tempio
di Claudio
Ss. Giovanni
e Paolo

CAVOUR
Via G.
P.za di
S. Martino
S. Martino
ai Monti
Monti
S. Pietro
in Vincoli
Parco di
Esquilino
Traiano
Terme
di Traiano
Domus
Aurea
Colle Oppio
Parco
Via d. Domus Aurea
Oppio
Ss. Quattro
Coronati
Piazza
Celimontana

Via del Circo Massimo
Circo Massimo
Via del Cerchi
P.le del
Ugo
La Malfa
S. Prisca
P.za di
S. Prisca
Viale Aventino
Palazzo della F.A.O.
Piazza
Albania
P.za
Remuria
S. Saba
Pza G.
L. Bernini
Largo
G. Lazzerini
Obelisco
di Axum
CIRCO MASSIMO
P.za di
Porta
Capena
S. Gregorio
Magno
Villa
Celimontana
S. Maria
in Domnica
S. Stefano
Rotondo
Celio
Via di Terme di Caracalla
Parco di
Porta
Capena
Stadio delle
Terme
S. Balbina
Largo
C. Fiorito
Terme
di Caracalla
Ss. Nereo
e Achilleo
Piazzale
Numa
Pompilio
Arco di
Dolabella
Lgo An
Aradas
P.ta
Metronia
Parco
Egerio
S. Sisto
Vecchio
S. Cesareo
de Appia
Casina di
Card. Bessarione

Viale di P.ta Ardeatina
San Saba
Largo G.
d. Chierini
Piazzale
d. Partigiani
Staz. Ostiense
F.S.
Via Ardeatina
Largo
d. Terme
di Caracalla
P.ta
Ardeatina
Viale di P.ta Arc

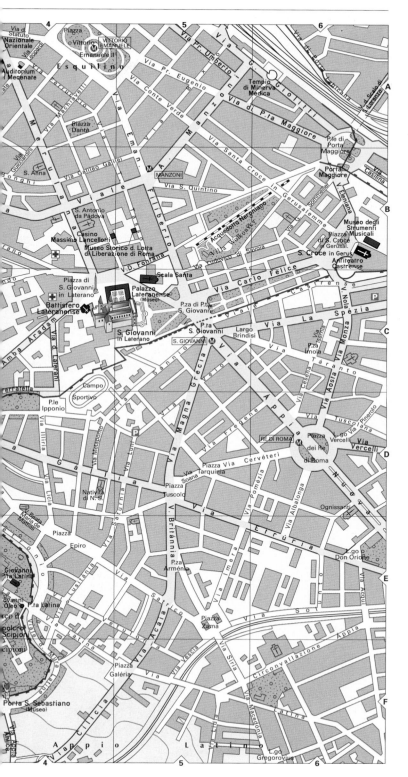

327

Roma/IV 1:13 000 (1 cm = 130 m)

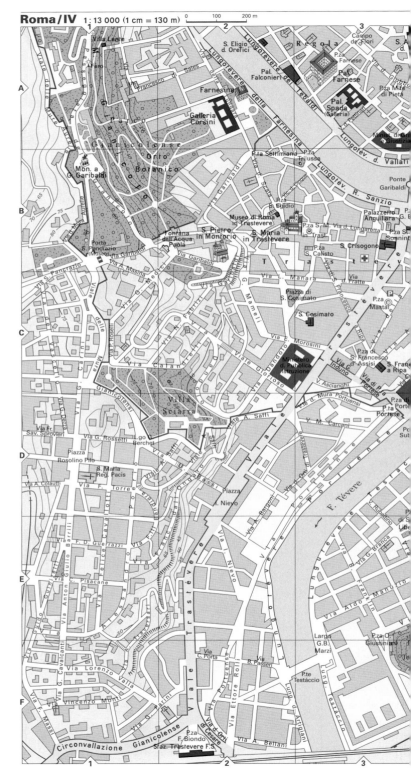

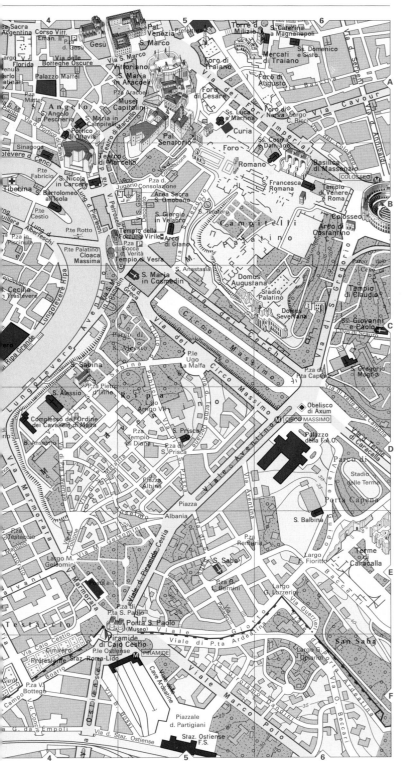

flown monument to Victor Emmanuel II, on Piazza Venezia, all the way to the magic of Michelangelo's Piazza del Campidoglio, or Capitol, and then to Via dei Fori Imperiali, alongside the expanse of ruins of the Fori Imperiali, or Imperial Forum, and within sight of the impressive mass of the Colosseo (Colosseum).

Piazza Venezia* (II, *F1*). The geometric center of Rome and the focal point of intense flows of traffic, it lies between Palazzo di Venezia and the Vittoriano (see below).

Palazzo di Venezia** (II, *F1*). This building, begun in 1455, was the first major civil construction of the Roman Renaissance, based on the design by L.B. Alberti. From 1564 to 1797 it was the residence of the Venetian ambassadors. In following years it was home to the ambassadors of France and, from 1814, Austria. It then became the Museo del Palazzo di Venezia (see below) and, in the 20th c., the headquarters of the Fascist Council. Note the 15th-c. portal and the fine porticoed courtyard.

Museo del Palazzo di Venezia.* *Open 8:30-7:30; closed Mon.* An extremely varied assortment of applied art works, this museum was established in 1922 in the former Cybo apartment and Palazzetto Venezia. The collections include early medieval ivories and goldwork (housed in the Sala Altoviti*, with stuccoes and frescoes by G. Vasari); French pastels; ceramic, majolica and porcelain items from the 14th-20th c., with special emphasis on the 18th-c. European manufactures; bronzes from the Barsanti and Auriti Collections; terracotta pieces; Russian, Italian and Northern European silverware.

Basilica di S. Marco** (II, *F1*). This is the palatine chapel of the Palazzo di Venezia, and overlooks Piazza S. Marco. Little survives of the original 4th-c. structure, though the bell tower dates from 1154 and a handsome mosaic in the apse dates from the 9th c. The largely Baroque *interior* features a 15th-c. carved ceiling; in the sacristy, reliefs by M. da Fiesole and G. Dalmata, and a St. Mark Evangelist by M. da Forlì. Excavation of the 9th-c. crypt is now underway.

Palazzetto Venezia** (II, *F1*). Built by Pope Paul II in 1464 as a porticoed open garden, it was moved to its present site in 1911-13, to make way for the Vittoriano (see below). In a corner of the facing piazza is a colossal female bust, from classical times, known to the people as Madama Lucrezia; like several other statues throughout Rome, this was used as a sort of bulletin board for satires and invectives against sovereigns and prelates.

Vittoriano** (II, *F1*; *open 10-4; closed Mon.*). This monument is dedicated to the first king of United Italy, Victor Emmanuel II. It was begun in 1885 by G. Sacconi and substantially completed in 1911. A notable feature of the Roman skyline, this vast white marble structure is topped by enormous bronze chariots (1927), and before them a grand stairway leads up to the *Altare della Patria* (or Altar to the Homeland). In the central niche stands a statue of Rome, by A. Zanelli. Beneath the statue is the tomb dedicated to all soldiers who died in war and

whose names remained unknown; on either side stairways lead up to a bronze equestrian statue Victor Emmanuel II, by E. Chiaradia and E. Gallo on the statue's base are depictions of the chief cit of Italy. Higher still is a portico (fine view*), wi statues of the Regions of Italy.

Museo Centrale del Risorgimento. *Open 10- closed Mon. and Aug.* Located in the Vittoriano, it dedicated to the Italian independence moveme and to WWI. You can also visit the *Sacrario de Bandiere delle Forze Armate (open 9:30-1; close Mon.; the army section closed for restoration)*, wi exhibits relating to the history of military flags.

Campidoglio* (II, *F1*; IV, *A5*). Of the seven hills ancient Rome, this, the Capitoline Hill, was the acro olis and the religious center (in 509 B.C. the temp of Capitoline Jove was inaugurated here, the mo important sanctuary in the Latin world, dedicated the triad of Jove, Juno, and Minerva). Ever since, has been the heart of Rome's government. It co sists of the "Capitolium" proper, to the right, and th "arx," on which stands the church of Aracoeli. B tween them is a saddle, with the Piazza del Camp doglio. Climbing up the west slope of the hill is th stairway of S. Maria di Aracoeli and the monume tal graded ramp*, designed by Michelangelo ar modified by G. della Porta; at the top is a balustrad decorated with late Empire statues of the Dioscu the so-called trophies of Marius (1st c.), statues Constantine and his son Constans I (4th c.), and tw milestone columns from the Appian Way.

Piazza del Campidoglio** (IV, *A5*). Michelang lo designed the monumental architecture of th square, surrounded by three buildings (in the mi dle, Palazzo Senatorio; on the right, Palazzo dei Co servatori; on the left, Palazzo Nuovo), the elega base that once held an ancient equestrian statu of Marcus Aurelius (a copy now stands here, whi

Rome: Piazza del Campidoglio

the original has since 1981 stood on the ground floor of the Museo Capitolino), and the pavement, actually installed in 1940.

Palazzo dei Conservatori** (IV, *A5*). This building, on the SW side of Piazza del Campidoglio, was designed and built by Michelangelo, with the help of G. della Porta (1568). The porticoed facade is crowned by a statue-lined balustrade; in the courtyard, note the fragments of a colossal statue of Constantine and trophies from a temple to Hadrian; Michelangelo also designed the facing **Palazzo Nuovo**, built by G. and C. Rainaldi (1655). These two buildings hold the collections of the Musei Capitolini.

Musei Capitolini.** *Open 9-7; summer, Sat., until 11 p.m.; closed Mon.* These museums comprise the Museo del Palazzo dei Conservatori, the Appartamento dei Conservatori, and the Pinacoteca Capitolina, housed at Palazzo dei Conservatori; the Tabularium, beneath Palazzo Senatorio; and the Museo Capitolino at Palazzo Nuovo. After the reopening of the museums in the year 2000, Palazzo Caffarelli has been included, where temporary exhibitions are held; from its terrace with café it is possible to admire one of the best views of Rome. In a few months, also Palazzo Clementino with the Capitoline Medal Collection will become part of the museums.

The museums originated from a donation by Pope Sixtus IV to the City of Rome, consisting of the bronzes formerly kept in the Lateran. To this donation was added, in 1733, the Albani Collection; under Benedict XIV, works from Hadrian's Villa at Tivoli were added, along with the "Forma Urbis Romae," dating from the reign of Severus. After Italy was unified, all material from excavations carried out there became part of these collections.

The *Museo del Palazzo dei Conservatori** has several remarkable collections of statuary. Many of the halls are now closed for restoration. The sculptures once placed outside under the portico are now on the first floor.

The *Appartamento dei Conservatori* – which is reached along a stairway lined with honorary reliefs of Marcus Aurelius and Hadrian and a late 13th-

c. statue of Charles of Anjou – comprises a series of richly decorated halls, with notable 16th-c. frescoes and friezes illustrating the history of Rome. These rooms are used as an official reception area by the city government. Among the works assembled here, ranging from the 5th c. B.C. to the 18th c., in particular mention should be made of the statues of Urban VIII* by Bernini (1635-39) and of Innocent X* by A. Algardi (1645-50) in the Sala degli Orazi e Curiazi; the Spinario* (boy removing a thorn from his foot), and a bronze statue from the 1st c. B.C., believed to be a portrait of Junius Brutus*, in the Sala dei Trionfi; and the renowned Capitoline Lupa, or She-Wolf*, an early 5th-c. B.C. bronze (Romulus and Remus were added in the 15th c. by Pollaiuolo), in the Sala della Lupa.

The *Pinacoteca Capitolina** is an art gallery with paintings from various schools, dating from the 14th-18th c. It was inaugurated by Benedict XIV in 1748. Among the *Emilian* and *Ferrarese painters of the 16th c.*, let us mention F. Francia, Garofalo, Ortolano, and D. Dossi. Among those from the *15th-/16th-c. Venetian school* are G.G. Savoldo, Palma the Elder, Titian, Lotto, and Tintoretto. From the rest of *17th-c. Europe* come works by Van Dyck, Rubens, and Velázquez. Among the *Umbrian, Tuscan, and Emilian painters of the 14th-15th c.*, of note are the works of M. d'Alba, C. dell'Amatrice, and N. di Bicci. *Italian 17th-c. painting* is exemplified by Caravaggio, Guercino, Domenichino, G. Reni, P. da Cortona, and G. Lanfranco. The Galleria Cini boasts a remarkable collection of fine 18th-c. porcelain*.

Downstairs, in the basement, is the Galleria di Congiunzione, an underground passage which links Palazzo dei Conservatori with Palazzo Nuovo. Here are the remains of the Tempio di Vèiove and, further on, the **Tabularium**. This Roman archives, built in 78 B.C., survives only in fragments; from here, you have a remarkable view of the Roman Forum*.

The **Museo Capitolino**, which occupies the entire Palazzo Nuovo, has collections largely made up of ancient Roman copies of Greek statuary; it is arranged according to Neo-Classic criteria. In a room next to the courtyard is the **equestrian statue of Marcus Aurelius**, brought here from Piazza del Campidoglio, after its time-consuming restoration (1981-90). This is an exceedingly rare example of ancient bronze statuary; only a case of mistaken identity saved it from being melted down in the Middle Ages – it was believed to depict the first Christian emperor, Constantine. It became a model for equestrian statuary in the Renaissance. The section devoted to *Eastern cults and monuments in Rome* (statues, reliefs, busts, and inscriptions dedicated to Mithras, Isis, and Serapis) and to sarcophagi in general (see the 2nd-c. sarcophagus of Amendola*) is followed by a thorough assortment of Hellenistic statuary and copies of originals. Among them are: the Capitoline Venus*, a Roman copy from a Hellenistic original influenced by the Cnidian Venus (3rd c. B.C.); Wounded Amazon*, copy of the masterpiece by Cresilas (5th c. B.C.); the Dying Gaul*, Roman copy of a 3rd-c. B.C. original from the school of Pergamon; Cupid and Psyche*, from a Hellenistic original (3rd-2nd c. B.C.); and Resting Satyr*, from an original by Praxiteles. Among the *mosaics* is a splendid depiction* of four doves drinking from a vase, from Hadrian's Villa. Among the *portraits*, there are 65 busts of emperors and 79 busts of philosophers (note Homer, Cicero, and Lysias), providing a vast sampling of Roman tastes from the 1st to the 3rd c. Among the *bronzes* is a tablet with the "lex de imperio Vespasiani," with which the Roman Senate conferred power on Vespasian.

Palazzo Senatorio* (IV, A5). Rome's city hall stands on the Tabularium (see below), and was designed by G. della Porta and G. Rainaldi (1605), based on a design by Michelangelo. Note the bell tower (1582) with the statue of Minerva-Goddess Roma; inside, statue of J. Caesar* (1st c. B.C.).

S. Maria in Aracoeli** (IV, A5). This church was built on the site of a temple to Juno, and takes its name from a supposed apparition of the Virgin Mary. to the emperor Augustus. Construction went on intermittently from the 13th to the 17th c., though it was first consecrated in 1291. The simple brick facade dates from the 13th c. It has basilican *interior* and offers a rich sampling of Roman art from the 13th-18th c. Note the rich carved ceiling (1575), and the 13th-c. Cosmatesque floors. Among the notable works of art are funerary monuments by A. Bregno and by Donatello; frescoes by Pinturicchio (1486); a tomb by A. di Cambio; two pulpits by L. and J. di Cosma (about 1200); frescoes by P. Cavallini, N. Martinelli, and B. Gozzoli (ca. 1454-58). The Cappella di S. Elena, in the left transept (1605), has a Cosmatesque altar depicting the emperor Augustus kneeling before the apparition of the Virgin Mary.

Via dei Fori Imperiali (IV, A-B5-6). This broad avenue, linking Piazza Venezia to the Colosseum, was built in 1931-33, and involved the destruction of dense and ancient neighborhoods.

Fori Imperiali. These were the Forums built outside the Roman Forum, first by J. Caesar, and by various later emperors.

Foro di Cesare (IV, A5). This Forum was dedicate in 46 B.C., during J. Caesar's lifetime, but was com pleted by Augustus. It was excavated in the 20th c.

Ss. Cosma e Damiano (IV, B6). The facade date from 1947 but the basilica is much older; ancien mosaics* in the triumphal arch and apse.

S. Francesca Romana (IV, B6). Built in the 9th c it boasts a shrine by G.L. Bernini (1649), 12th-c. mo saics*, and a 5th-c. icon*.

Colosseo** (III, A-B2; IV, B6). *Open 9-one hour be fore sunset*. The Colosseum's real name – *Flavia Amphitheatre* – indicates that Flavian emperors bui it, as a venue for public spectacles and combat be tween gladiators and wild beasts. Vespasian bega work on it, but Titus inaugurated it in A.D. 80, wit games said to have lasted for 100 days. Badly dam aged by earthquakes, the Colosseum was turned in to a fort during the Middle Ages, and a quarry du ing the Renaissance. Pope Benedict XIV put an en to the destruction of the monument in the 18th c but efforts at restoration began only in the 19th c (the most recent large-scale effort began in 1992) This enormous monument has an elliptical plan. It NE side is virtually intact and is 48.5 m tall; note th three rows of arcades and the attic above, with wir dows and square openings from which the "vela rium" – a huge cloth that shaded the spectators was hung. Four entrances led into the arena, whic held about 50,000 spectators and measured 86 x 5 m. The podium was reserved for the leading figure of the Empire; beneath the arena were galleries con taining the animals and the structures for the spec tacles, winched up into place.

Tempio di Venere a Roma (IV, B6). Built by Hadri an, from A.D. 121 on , it was completed by Antoni nus Pius. Very few ruins remain.

Arco di Costantino** (IV, B6). To commemorate Constantine's victory over Maxentius, Rome's Sen ate ordered the construction of this arch in A.D. 315 re-using statues, friezes, and medallions from mon uments dating from the reigns of Trajan, Hadrian and Marcus Aurelius (those created for this arch stand above and on either side of the archway). Re cent studies suggest the Arch of Constantine may be far older than was thought, by as much as three centuries. It has been restored several times and is consequently in very good conditions.

Domus Aurea (III, A-B23). *Open 9-7:45, until 11 p.m. closed Tue.; compulsory reservation, tel. 06 39967700* Enclosed by the park of the Colle Oppio (one of the summits of the Esquiline) is the great palace that Nero ordered built following the great fire of Rome in A.D. 64 (the structures that comprised the imper ial residence occupied all of what is now the Piaz za del Colosseo, where there was an artificial lake) it was later overshadowed by the *Bath of Trajan*, de signed by Apollodorus of Damascus, archetype of all later bath buildings (part of it was the nearby cis tern, know as the "Cisterna delle Sette Sale"). The ru ins of the imperial palace include a series of huge rooms, partly decorated with stuccoes and paint ings, in a style that came to be known as "grotesque.

Foro di Nerva (IV, A6). Begun by Domitian in the narrow space between the nearby *Forum of Peace* (on one exedra of this forum stands the Torre dei Conti; see route 9) and the Forum of Augustus (Foro di Augusto, see below). It was completed in A.D. 97 by Nerva. Note the surviving columns of the portico, topped by a frieze, and the core of the podium of the Temple of Minerva.

Foro di Augusto* (IV, A6). Decreed in 42 B.C. and inaugurated in 2 B.C., this forum mirrors the plan of the nearby Forum of Caesar. At the end is a rusticated enclosure wall, with the ruins of the Temple of Mars Ultor (note three surviving trabeated columns). To the left of this is a portico and an exedra, upon which stood in the 15th c. the **House of the Knights of Rhodes*** (*open by request; contact the Ufficio Mercati di Traiano-Fori Imperiali*). Dating from Augustan times is the splendid porticoed atrium.

Mercati di Traiano** (IV, A5-6). *Open 9-6:30; winter, until 5:30; closed Mon.; entrance at n. 94 Via IV Novembre.* The architect Apollodorus of Damascus planned this immense complex, known as Trajan's Market, adjacent to Trajan's Forum (see below); in the Middle Ages, other structures were added (for the Torre delle Milizie, see route 8). The front of the structure curves in a huge exedra; behind it runs the Via Biberatica, lined by shops, and to the left of this there is a huge roofed two-storey hall filled with shops (through which you enter from the Via IV Novembre); this was probably a trading room. An exhibit of architectural decorations from the Forums of Trajan and Augustus has been put on display in the ancient shops.

Foro di Traiano* (IV, A5). *Open same hours as the Mercati di Traiano.* Largest of the Fori Imperiali, Trajan's Forum was also built by Apollodorus of Damascus (A.D. 107). You can still see the "Basilica Ulpia" - columns at the center of the excavated area – and **Trajan's Column****, commemorating the emperor's victory over the Dacians (A.D. 101-103 and 107-08), nearly 40 m tall, with a spiral frieze depicting episodes from the Dacian Wars. A spiral staircase inside the column leads to the top, where a statue of St. Peter replaced the statue of Trajan in 1587.

Archeological Area of the Foro Romano and Palatino

This is the archeological route par excellence, running through the sites that gave birth to the Eternal City: the Roman Forum and the Palatine Hill. An unbroken succession of basilicas, arches, temples, and imperial residences, surrounded by verdant vegetation, with views straight out of a postcard. There is a great deal of restoration work being carried on here, as well as new digging, with surprising finds from time to time.

Foro Romano** (IV, A-B5-6). *Open 9-one hour before sunset; entrance from Largo Romolo e Remo, Via di Monte Tarpeo, and the Arch of Titus.* This is the Roman Forum, for centuries the heart of public life in ancient Rome. It was originally a marshy valley between the Capitoline, Palatine, Viminal, and Quirinal hills, and occupied by one of the oldest burial grounds in the city. Its history as a great forum began when construction of Rome's great sewer system, the Cloaca Maxima, permitted drainage of the marsh; by the late 7th c. B.C., it reached its standing as Rome's religious, political, commercial, and juridical center. Its final appearance was attained under Caesar and Augustus; earthquakes and barbarians reduced its splendor, and in the High Middle Ages its buildings were used first as churches and fortresses, and later as quarries, and even as pasture land (Campo Vaccino). Archeological excavation has virtually never ceased since the 19th c.

Basilica Emilia. Set at the bottom of the ramp leading into the archeological area, this basilica was founded in 179 B.C. and rebuilt a century later; it was destroyed by a fire when the Goths under Alaric sacked Rome. Trade was conducted and justice was administered here. The basilica consisted of a large hall divided by rows of columns, with a two-storey porch overlooking the Forum. The ruins now visible date from the restoration done by Augustus.

Curia.* According to tradition, Tullius Hostilius founded this building to house the Senate, although the brick building we now see was rebuilt under Diocletian following a fire in A.D. 283. Inside, the rectangular hall still preserves the low ledges on which the senators sat. Also seen here are the so-called Plutei di Traiano*, two balustrades which once decorated the tribune of the Rostri.

Tomba di Romolo. Standing before the Curia, beneath a modern shelter, is a square slab of black marble ("Lapis Niger"), a monument that the ancient Romans believed covered the tomb of Romulus, founder of the city; it is now thought to have been a sanctuary of the god Vulcan. A stele with a religious inscription dating from the 6th c. B.C. was found here, believed to be the earliest document in the Latin language.

Arco di Settimio Severo.** This arch dedicated to Septimius Severus was built in A.D. 203 to honor the emperor and his sons for their victories over the Parthians and Arabs; on the attic, the name Geta was cancelled after he was murdered by his brother, Caracalla.

Behind the arch – and outside the archeological area – are the churches of *Ss. Luca e Martina*, a domed building by P. da Cortona (1635-64), and S. Giuseppe dei Falegnami; beneath the latter is the entrance to the **Carcere Mamertino** (*open summer, 9:30-12:30 and 2:30-6:30; winter, 9-12 and 2-5*), the state prison in ancient Rome (2nd c. B.C.). It is said – with no historical foundation – that St. Peter was confined in the lower cell, and that he miraculously created a spring of fresh water, with which he baptized his jailers.

Rostri. The high platform to the left of the Arch of Septimius Severus was used as a speakers' podium; under Caesar it replaced the one that had been decorated in 338 B.C. with the beaks ("rostra") removed

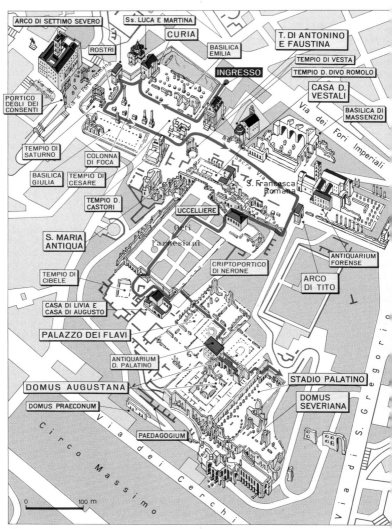

from the ships captured at Anzio.

Tempio di Saturno.** The Temple of Saturn is one of the oldest in the Forum (dedicated in 497 B.C.); the podium (42 B.C.) and eight Ionic columns still stand. Behind this temple, you will find the *Tempio della Concordia* (367 B.C.), the *Tempio di Vespasiano**, built by Domitian in A.D. 81 (three Corinthian columns), and the *Portico degli Dei Consenti*, the last monument in Rome devoted to a pagan cult.

Piazza del Foro. Extending before the Rostri, this almost rectangular square is paved with travertine; note the *Colonna di Foca*, the last monument erected in the Forum (A.D. 608), dedicated to a ruler of the Eastern Empire.

Basilica Giulia.** Separated from the Piazza del Foro by the *Via Sacra*, which ran east and west across the Forum (the paving remains; note the sev-

en bases of honorary columns from the reign Diocletian), this basilica was built by J. Caesar, com pleted by Augustus, and rebuilt by Diocletian. C the floor of this huge rectangular building there a still several gaming boards, etched into the marbl Along the east side of the complex runs the "*Vic Tuscus*," a road lined with Etruscan shops, whic linked the Roman Forum to the Foro Boario an the earliest port of Rome.

Tempio dei Càstori.** Dedicated in 484 B.C. the Dioscuri (Castor and Pollux), this temple w rebuilt more than once. Note the tall podium, wit three elegant trabeated Corinthian columns, fro the reign of Tiberius.

S. Maria Antiqua.* This church was built in th 6th c., incorporating part of the imperial palace behind the temple. It is the oldest Christian churc in the Forum. Abandoned in the 9th c., after terrib arthquakes, it was unearthed in 1900. Inside is an xceptional cycle of medieval frescoes.

empio di Cesare. Octavian dedicated this tem-le to Caesar in A.D. 29, on the site where his grand-ather's body had been cremated, marked by the emicycle with an altar in the center.

empio di Vesta. * Circular in plan, this temple is s it was when rebuilt, under Septimius Severus. In ie *Casa delle Vestali*, behind it, lived the Vestal Vir-ins, who guarded the sacred fire of Vesta, believed o have been burning since it was first lit by Numa ompilius, a legendary Sabine king of Rome of the th c. B.C. The complex lies around a huge court-ard, surrounded by a two-storey portico. Along the des of the courtyard were the living quarters of the rgins. Bases and statues commemorate the priest-sses that lived here between A.D. 291 and 364.

dicola di Giuturna. Near this small building, re-ored in 1954, a 2nd-c. B.C. basin marks the site of legendary freshwater spring.

egia. This was said to be the home of Numa Pom-ilius, second of Rome's seven kings, as well as the ome of the chief priest and a sacrarium dedicat-d to Mars, where sacrifices were also made to oth-r deities.

empio di Antonino e Faustina. * This temple as at first dedicated to Faustina alone; after the eath of Antoninus Pius (A.D. 161), it was also ded-cated to the emperor. In the 7th c., it was trans-ormed into the church of S. Lorenzo in Miranda. lote the Corinthian columns of the pronaos.

o the right of the temple, a patch of green marks the *ncient necropolis* (10th-8th c. B.C.), discovered in 902 (some material is now in the Antiquarium orense).

empio del Divo Romolo. This temple is said to ave been dedicated to Romulus, son of Maxentius, nough theories abound as to its real identity. It was ertainly undertaken by Maxentius (the portal, anked by two porphyry columns, frames the orig-nal bronze door*; note the lock, one of the oldest n existence) and completed by Constantine. In the th c. it was incorporated in the Basilica dei Ss. Co-ma e Damiano. Across the Via Sacra, walls and for-fications have been identified, dating from 730 to 40 B.C.

3asilica di Massenzio. ** Among the most im-ressive buildings of ancient Rome, it was begun by Iaxentius (308) and finished by Constantine. The riginal front overlooked the Colosseum, and a niche ield a statue of its builder, the emperor Maxentius. 'onstantine built a new facade, overlooking the Via 'acra, in which another niche held a statue of Con-tantine, which now stands in the Palazzo dei Con-ervatori. The original doors in gilded bronze were nelted to cover the first basilica of St. Peter.

Antiquarium Forense. Occupying what was once he monastery of S. Francesca Romana (see route), this museum contains the tomb furnishings of he archaic necropolis of the Palatine Hill.

Arco di Tito. ** This arch, dedicated to Titus, was uilt at the highest point along the Via Sacra to hon-

or the victories of Vespasian and Titus over the He-brews in A.D. 71. The Arch of Titus was restored by G. Valadier in 1821. In the archway are the reliefs* showing booty being brought back from Jerusalem and Victory crowning Titus.

Palatino ** (IV, *B-C5-6*). *Open same hours as the Foro Romano; entrance from the Arco di Tito and Via di San Gregorio.* It is on the Palatine Hill, high over the oxbow curve of the Tiber, overlooking the valley of the Forum and the first port of Rome, that the city's earliest memories reside. The earliest remains of huts date from the early Iron Age, precisely where tradition has it that Romulus's house was located; this home of the founder of Rome (754 B.C.) was continually restored until Imperial times. During the Republic, the Palatine was the residence of wealthy citizens, and from Augustus on it was the official res-idence of the emperor (hence the term, "palace"). In the Middle Ages it declined, as did the Forum; a period of renewed splendor came in the 16th c., when the Farnese built a magnificent villa here; that villa was dismantled by relentless archeologists, from the late 19th c. onward.

Uccelliere. These aviaries are all that survive of the Orti Farnesiani, a 16th-c. complex of gardens, by Vi-gnola. Note the fine view of the Forum. The garden behind it, from 1625 the earliest botanical garden in the world, extends over the "Domus Tiberiana," of which nothing can be seen from the surface.

Tempio di Cibele. Built in 204 B.C., this temple was rebuilt under Augustus. Nearby is a remarkable find from the earliest settlement of Rome: three *huts** from the early Iron Age, identified by holes left by the roof poles and drainage ditches.

Casa di Livia. * An inscription found on a water conduit has led scholars to identify this as the home of Livia, wife of Augustus. A typical mansion of the late Republic, this house is famous for the frescoes found in the rooms overlooking the square atrium. Recently unearthed to the south of this house is the **Casa di Augusto***, later incorporated into the Palaz-zo dei Flavi.

Palazzo dei Flavi. * This vast complex of buildings was the emperor's reception area (the "Domus Flavia"), with three halls for religious and political functions, a huge peristyle and triclinium, with two adjacent nymphaea with fountains, and part of the original marble floor. Beneath this palace, archeol-ogists have found the *Aula Isiaca*, consecrated by Caligula to the cult of Isis, the *Casa dei Grifi* (late 2nd c. B.C.), decorated with late Pompeiian-style paint-ings, and the *Domus Transitoria*, residence of Nero prior to the great fire of A.D. 64.

Antiquarium del Palatino. This gallery illustrates – through statues, fragments and other finds – the history of the Palatine Hill, and that of artistic deco-ration from the time of Augustus to late antiquity.

Domus Augustana. * Beginning with Domitian, and up until Byzantine times, the Roman emperors lived here; the palace was arranged on two or three storeys to accommodate the steep slope of the hill toward the Circus Maximus, which it overlooked.

Stadio Palatino. * Domitian ordered the construction of this immense building, surrounded by a portico which features, in the middle of the eastern side, the enormous niche of the imperial loggia. The oval enclosure of the race track was probably added by Theodoric.

Domus Severiana. * Equipped with its own bath system (there are traces near the curve of the Stadium), this building originated as an extension of the Domus Augustana, at the behest of Septimius Severus. From the terrace, you can enjoy a magnificent view* of the valley of the *Circus Maximus* below, and the Aventine Hill beyond it.

3 Via del Corso, Via dei Condotti, and Piazza di Spagna

This is a section of the historic center of Rome where the sea of automobiles has been replaced by a flood of tourists, flowing along through art galleries, churches built during the Counter Reformation, exclusive shops and, past the buildings of Italy's national government, resting by the soothing sounds of some of the loveliest fountains in Rome.

Via del Corso* (I, *C-F5-6*). At one end of this road is the Vittoriano (see route 1) and at the other, about 1.5 km away, is the Flaminian obelisk in Piazza del Popolo (see route 5). Running along the ancient Via Flaminia and lined with historic buildings, the Corso is Rome's traditional street for festivities and processions of illustrious visitors. In the 18th c. it became a magnet for cafés, bookstores, and newspaper offices. It is now partly a pedestrian mall, thronged especially on Saturdays with young people shopping for clothes.

Palazzo Doria Pamphilj* (I, *F6*). Chief among th' aristocratic buildings overlooking the Corso, and on of the very few that are still inhabited by the fami' that built it, it boasts a facade* by G. Valvassori (173 34), who in that same period closed off the courtya' to install the private art gallery (see below). Th' palace includes the church of *S. Maria in Via Lata*, stored by C. Fanzago. Across the Corso, in a sma' square further along, is the Baroque facade (' Fontana) of the church of *S. Marcello al Corso*, rebu' in 1519 by J. Sansovino, A. da Sangallo the Young' and A. Lippi on the site of a late 4th-c. church.

Galleria Doria Pamphilj. ** *Open 10-5; close' Thu.; entrance at n. 2 in Piazza del Collegio Roman'* This collection was began in 1651 by Pope Inn' cent X Pamphilj; marriages and purchases (esp' cially the dowry brought by Olimpia Aldobrandin' made it one of Rome's most notable private colle' tions. The gallery maintains its original layout, wi' over 400 paintings covering the period from the 16' to the 18th c. Among the more noteworthy artis' featured here, let us mention: Correggio, Tintorett' Raphael, Lotto, Bordone, Titian, Caravaggio, A. A' gardi, Guercino, M. Preti, F. Duquesnoy, L. Carracci, (di Paolo, A. Solario, J. Bassano, Parmigianino, Becc' fumi, J. van Schorel, J. Brueghel the Elder, P. Bruegh' the Elder, Velázquez, and Bernini.

S. Ignazio ** (I, *F6*). Enclosed in the structure ' the *Collegio Romano*, this church was built for th' Jesuits, beginning in 1582, at the behest of Ignati' of Loyola. It was completed in 1685, though th' cupola was added later. The travertine facade an' broad nave, adorned with gilt, frescoes, and marbl' are reminiscent of those of the Gesù church. Not' the renowned fresco of the vault, by A. Pozzo; th' remarkable perspective is best seen from the disk '

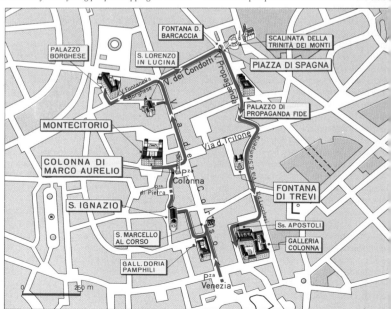

yellow marble in the center of the nave. Many other paintings and frescoes are by A. Pozzo, and A. Algardi. Facing the church are the so-called *Burrò* (I, *E6*), architectural oddities by F. Raguzzini (1728).

Palazzo della Borsa (I, *E6*). This Roman branch of the stock exchange is located in a building that includes the Temple of Hadrian, dedicated by the emperor to his son Antoninus Pius in A.D. 145. Note the 11 tall fluted columns, overlooking Piazza di Pietra.

Piazza Colonna (I, *E6*). This is the only monumental square along Via del Corso, with the column of Marcus Aurelius (see below). Surrounding it are: to the north, *Palazzo Chigi** (headquarters of the Italian government), begun in 1580-86; to the east, the *Galleria Colonna* (early 20th c.); to the west, the 19th-c. *Palazzo Wedekind*, with a portico incorporating 11 columns unearthed at Veio.

Colonna di Marco Aurelio** (I, *E6*). The continual frieze that winds along the 28 marble cylinders that make up this column narrate Marcus Aurelius' victories over the German tribes on the Danube. Built in A.D. 180-193, the column is 29.6 m tall, and is now topped by a bronze statue of St. Paul (1588-89).

Palazzo di Montecitorio* (I, *E5-6*). *Open 1st Sun. of the month (not every month), 10-6.* This palazzo overlooks the Piazza di Montecitorio, and the *obelisk of Psamtik II* (early 6th c. B.C.), which Augustus had shipped here from Heliopolis as part of a giant sundial. Pope Pius VI moved it here in 1792. The building was begun in 1653 by G.L. Bernini, who designed the slightly convex facade, and was completed by C. Fontana. Since 1871 it has been the *Chamber of Deputies of the Italian Parliament*. The chamber is decorated with an allegorical frieze by G.A. Sartorio (1908-12).

S. Lorenzo in Lucina (I, *D-E6*). This church was founded in the 4th c. and was extensively modified over the centuries; it was largely restored to its original form in the 19th-20th c. Note the 12th-c. bell tower and portico. Inside, the grate on which St. Lawrence supposedly was martyred; bust of G. Fonseca by Bernini; on the main altar, *Cruxifix** by Reni.

Palazzo Borghese* (I, *D5*). This building, which may have been designed by Vignola, and which was completed by F. Ponzio in 1605-14, belonged to another famous Roman family. Piazza Borghese is the site of a lively market of used books and old prints.

Via dei Condotti (I, *D6*). Built in the 16th c., this boutique- and gallery-lined street runs off from Via del Corso, with a view of the Spanish Steps (Scalinata della Trinità dei Monti, see below) and the church of the same name (see route 5) in the distance. It runs over the water conduits, or "condotti", of the ancient Aqua Virgo (hence the name) and has notable 17th-/18th-c. palazzi. N. 86 is the *Caffè Greco*, a centuries-old meeting place for writers and artists.

Piazza di Spagna* (I, *D6*). This is one of the most charming and theatrical settings of Baroque Rome, and a favorite with sightseers from around the world ever since the 16th c. Inns and taverns made way in the 19th c. for photographers and antiques dealers, who still hold sway in the nearby Via del Babuino

Rome: Scalinata della Trinità dei Monti

and Via Margutta. At the center of the square is the original **fountain of the Barcaccia** (1629), designed by P. and G.L. Bernini for Pope Urban VIII (note the image of the sun and the bees, symbol of Urban's family, the Barberini), set low in the street because of insufficient water pressure.

Scalinata della Trinità dei Monti** (I, *D6*). F. De Sanctis built this scenic stairway in 1723-26 to bridge the steep incline between the square and the Pincio; in springtime, the Spanish Steps, covered with blooming azaleas, frame the church of Trinità dei Monti (see route 5), and is used for fashion shows. The building to the right of the stairway is the *Keats-Shelley Memorial Foundation* (*open 9-1 and 3-6; Sat., 11-2 and 3-6; closed Sun.*), and on the other side is *Babington's*, the oldest tearoom in Rome.

Casa-Museo di G. De Chirico (II, *C1; Open Tue.-Sat. and 1st Sun. of the month, 10-1; compulsory reservation, tel. 066796546; entrance at n. 31 in Piazza di Spagna*). De Chirico's library, private collection and atelier with his working tools can now be seen in the house in which the most important Metaphysical painter of Italy lived for thirty years.

Palazzo di Propaganda Fide* (I, *D6*; II, *D1-2*). Built on the SE side of Piazza di Spagna, with a simple terracotta facade by G.L. Bernini (1644), it has a more elaborate facade on Via di Propaganda by F. Borromini. In front of the palazzo, note the column of the Immaculate Conception (Colonna dell'Immacolata Concezione); on 8 December a procession led by the pope terminates here.

S. Andrea delle Fratte (II, *D1-2*). Borromini built the bell tower and the drum of the cupola of this church, working on it from 1653 until his death; it was completed by M. De Rossi. Inside, note two angels carved by G.L. Bernini.

Galleria dell'Accademia di S. Luca (II, *D1*). *Closed for restoration; soon to be reopened.* Set in the 16th-c. *Palazzo Carpegna* (elliptical ramp and interior loggia by Borromini), it features works of the 17th-19th c. by artists from the academy, as well as by others. Among the artists whose work is found here are Baciccia, Raphael, J. Bassano, G.P. Pannini, J. Asselijn, Van Dyck, and Rubens.

Fontana di Trevi** (II, *D-E1*). The 18th-c. Trevi Fountain is a remarkably successful and theatrical fusion of architecture and sculpture. N. Salvi conceived it as a whirl of reefs, statues, and sprays of water (note, in the central niche, Ocean riding a chariot drawn by seahorses, by P. Bracci); according to popular belief, tossing a coin in the fountain assures that you will return to Rome.

Museo Nazionale delle Paste Alimentari (II, *E2; open Mon.-Sun., 9:30-5:30; entrance at n. 117 in Piazza Scanderberg*). This peculiar museum, the only one in the world devoted to pasta, was born from the collection of Vincenzo Agnesi, one of Italy's leading producer of this food.

Basilica dei Ss. Apostoli* (II, *E1*). Note the late 15th-c. portico. Although this church was built in the 4th c., it was almost entirely rebuilt in 1702-1708 by C. and F. Fontana. Among the sculptures arranged under the portico are a 2nd-c. relief with an imperial eagle, and the funerary stele by A. Canova (1807). The rich Baroque interior features a fresco by Baciccia. On the wall behind the third chapel to the right are 15th-c. frescoes*. To the left of the apse is a monument to Pope Clement XIV, Canova's first project in Rome (1789).

Galleria Colonna* (II, *E1-2*). *Open Sat., 9-1; closed Aug; entrance at n. 17 in Via della Pilotta*. This major patrician collection, begun by Girolamo Colonna in 1654-65, is housed in the 18th-c. *Palazzo Colonna*. We should mention works by Bronzino, Tintoretto, and Annibale Carracci, as well as 17th-c. paintings (F. Albani, Guercino, O. Borgianni) and a series of landscapes by G. Dughet and J. F. van Bloemen. Of interest is the nearby *Museo delle Cere* (wax museum), at the corner of Via IV Novembre (*open 9-8:30; Aug., until 11 p.m.*).

---

4 "Quartiere del Rinascimento"

This route runs through the so-called Renaissance district, a section of Rome around the great oxbow curve in the Tiber. Even in the dark centuries of the Middle Ages, this area was inhabited, and beginning in the Renaissance, a few of the most powerful Roman families chose to build their homes here (Palazzo Massimo, Palazzo Farnese, Palazzo Spada). The churches in this district are often linked to the "nations" that they represented (S. Giovanni dei Fiorentini, S. Maria dell'Anima, S. Luigi dei Francesi).

Il Gesù** (I, *F6*). This is the principal church of the Jesuits in Rome (built at the behest of Ignatius of Loyola, founder of the order, who is buried here) and the model for the churches of the Counter Reformation. It was begun in 1568 to a design by Vignola and completed by G. della Porta, who designed the facade in travertine (1571-77). The late Baroque *interior*, with a single nave, glitters with marble, bronze, gold, and frescoes. Note the frescoed

vault by Baciccia, and the chapel of St. Ignatius, by A. Pozzo (1696-1700). Adjacent to the church are the *rooms* where St. Ignatius once lived (*open 4-6; Sun., Jul.-Aug., 10-12; entrance at n. 45 in Piazza del Gesù*).

Corso Vittorio Emanuele II (I, *F3-6*). This extension of Via Nazionale toward St. Peter's (S. Pietro) was built from 1883 on through the district known as the "Quartiere del Rinascimento," destroying a dense section of Rome dating from the Middle Ages.

Area Sacra dell'Argentina* (I, *F5*). The ruins of temples that jut from the center of this chaotic Largo, or square, constitute the most extensive complex from Republican times still visible in Rome, unearthed in 1926-29. The circular structure is known as Temple B, possibly built in 101 B.C.; to the right of it is Temple A, built in the mid-3rd c. B.C.; to the left is Temple C, the oldest in the complex, possibly dedicated to the Italic deity Feronia; beyond it is Temple D, from the beginning of the 2nd c. B.C., mostly covered by the modern road surface.

Crypta Balbi (IV, *F5*). Not far from Largo Argentina, in Via delle Botteghe Oscure, is one of the four quarters of the **Museo Nazionale Romano** (*open 9-7:45; closed Mon.*; see also route 8). The different sections in the Crypta illustrate the evolution of this area of Rome from antiquity to the 20th c.

S. Andrea della Valle* (I, *F5*). This church – built from 1591 to 1650, mostly by C. Maderno – was also modeled after the Gesù; less, however, in the cupola* (the second tallest in Rome, after St. Peter's) or the facade (C. Rainaldi and C. Fontana, 1656-65), than in the interior, with a complex and impressive body of paintings by G. Lanfranco, Domenichino, and M. Preti.

Palazzo Massimo "alle Colonne"* (I, *F5; open only on 16 March*, for the anniversary of a miracle by St. Philip on Paolo Massimo, in 1538). The Massimo family still lives here, and documentation dates the family back to the 10th c., though they claim to trace their roots back to Quintus Fabius Maximus, "Cunctator." The family entrusted B. Peruzzi with rebuilding the entire block after the Sack of Rome in 1527; the Florentine architect built a convex facade with a six-column portico. Note the frescoes on the facade of the adjacent *Palazzo Massimo "Istoriato."*

Farnesina ai Baullari (I, *F4*). The building's real name is *Palazzetto Leroy*, after the Breton prelate who began it in 1522-23, and who had the French lilies on his coat of arms. These were also the symbol of the Farnese family, hence the new name. Wrongly said to be by Michelangelo, the Renaissance facade overlooks Via de' Baullari and Vicolo dell'Aquila. The building houses the **Museo Barracco.*** (*open weekdays, 9-7; closed Mon.*). This major collection of sculpture was the product of the efforts in the late 19th c. of Baron Giovanni Barracco, who emphasized his interest in ancient originals. Note in particular the sphinx of Queen Hatshepsut (1504-1450 B.C.), the head of an ephebe* (late 6th-c. B.C. original), head of the Kassel Apollo (copy of original by Phidias), mosaic from the Villa of Livia at Prima Porta, and others.

Palazzo della Cancelleria** (I, *F4*). This masterpiece of Renaissance architecture was built between 1485 and 1511-13. Once thought to be the work of Bramante, it is now thought that he worked only on the three-order courtyard*. The building includes the cardinal basilica of *S. Lorenzo in Damasco*.

Campo de' Fiori (I, *F4*; IV, *A3*). An ancient market that has maintained the popular flavor of past centuries. The monument to Giordano Bruno commemorates the Neapolitan philosopher and scientist, burnt at the stake here in 1600.

Palazzo Farnese** (IV, *A3*). Located in Piazza Farnese, this building's facade (note the magnificent cornice* adorned with the Farnese lilies) overlooks two fountains built with material from the Baths of Caracalla. Construction began in 1517, under the direction of A. da Sangallo the Younger; work continued under Michelangelo (cornice and balcony), Vignola and G. della Porta (facade overlooking the Tiber). The *interior* (*open 2nd Sun. of Sep.; on 14 July only for French citizens and Romans*) features a noteworthy atrium* and courtyard* and the first-floor gallery, frescoed by Annibale and Agostino Carracci, with the help of Domenichino and G. Lanfranco. This building now houses the French Embassy.

Palazzo Spada* (IV, *A3*). Governmental offices occupy part of this 16th-c. building; note the stucco and statuary of facade and courtyard. On the ground floor, the 9-m gallery* which F. Borromini succeeded in making appear quite large through a play of perspective. Inside is also the **Galleria Spada*** (*open Tue.-Sat., 8:30-7:30; Sun. and holidays until 6:30*), with paintings hung in rows according to the decorative tastes and the flavor of a 17th-c. aristocratic collection. Canvases are by 16th-/17th-c. artists, including: F. Muratori, Baciccia, Guercino, F. Trevisani, M. Cerquozzi, L. Baugin, and O. Borgianni.

Via Giulia* (I, *E-F3-4*; IV, *A2-3*). Now a pedestrian street, with the numbers running in opposite directions on either side as in Via del Corso, Via Giulia was designed by Bramante in the early 16th c. for Pope Julius II, as a location for the offices of the main institutions of the papal state. Note the palazzi (*Palazzo Falconieri*, n. 1, overlooking the Lungotevere with a loggia by F. Borromini; *Palazzo Sacchetti*, n. 66, 16th c.) and churches: **S. Eligio degli Orefici** (I, *F4*; IV, *A2*; *open by request; enquire at n. 9 in Via di S. Eligio*), designed by Raphael, and *S. Giovanni dei Fiorentini* (I, *E3*), begun under Leo X in 1519 by J. Sansovino, completed in 1602-20 by C. Maderno (18th-c. facade, however), who, with F. Borromini, was buried here. The *Museo Criminologico* (*open Tue.-Sat., 9-1; Tue. and Thu., also 2:30-6:30; closed Sun., Mon. and holidays; entrance at n. 29 Via del Gonfalone*) is located in the Prigioni, a former prison and is dedicated to criminology. The nearby **Oratorio del Gonfalone*** (I, *F3*; *open by request; enquire at n. 1B in the parallel Vicolo della Scimmia*) features a notable Mannerist fresco (1572-75).

Chiesa Nuova* (I, *F4*). This church is properly known as *S. Maria in Vallicella*; it was rebuilt at the behest of St. Philip Neri (1575) and consecrated in 1599; both facade and Baroque interior are reminiscent of the Gesù. Inside, artwork by P. da Cortona, Rubens (1606-08), O. Longhi, and F. Barocci. To the left of the church is the **Palazzo dei Filippini*** (1621-66), largely by F. Borromini.

Palazzo Braschi (I, *F4*). This is the last building of a Roman family that produced a number of popes; Pius VI commissioned C. Morelli to plan and build it in 1791. Note the magnificent interior staircase, with ancient columns. The rear facade features the famed Pasquino, best-known of Rome's "talking statues"; this damaged Roman statue was used by the

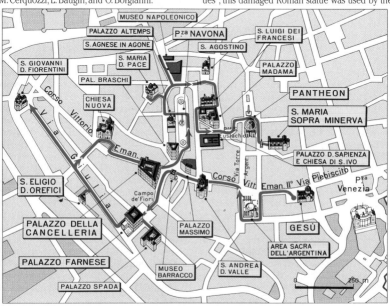

people of Rome as a sort of bulletin board for satires and tracts against the authorities. Inside is the **Museo di Roma*** (*recently restored and now open to the public*), dedicated to the history of Rome (note the watercolors by E. Roesler Franz).

Piazza Navona** (I, *E-F4-5*). This remarkable Baroque square takes its size and shape from the Stadium of Domitian, upon which it stands. Ruins of the stadium are found in some of the houses on the north side of the square; they can be seen from the Piazza di Tor Sanguigna. Also, note the crypt under S. Agnese in Agone (see below). This square was a traditional site of festivities and processions, especially during Carnival. At its center is the **Fontana dei Fiumi**** by G.L. Bernini (1651): a circular basin holds a reef supporting an obelisk from the reign of Domitian, as a lion and horse drink thirstily; allegorical statues of the rivers Nile, Ganges, Danube, and Rio de la Plata express, with their gestures, Bernini's contempt for his rival, Borromini, who built the nearby church of S. Agnese in Agone. On the two end sides of the piazza are the *Fontana del Moro* and *Fontana del Nettuno*, after Bernini's design.

S. Agnese in Agone* (I, *F4*). This church stands on the site where St. Agnes was said to have been pilloried nude, only to be miraculously covered by her hair; G. and C. Rainaldi began the rebuilding of the church in 1652, and it was completed by F. Borromini who gave it a concave facade, set between two bell towers. Beneath it are the ruins of the Stadium of Domitian.

S. Maria dell'Anima (I, *E4*). This church was built in the early 16th c. atop a chapel in a hospice for German, Dutch, and Flemish pilgrims. The *interior* (*entrance at n. 20 in Piazza di S. Maria della Pace*) is modelled on German churches. In the presbytery, note painting by G. Romano (1522); to the right, monument to Pope Adrian VI, architecture by B. Peruzzi.

S. Maria della Pace* (I, *E4*). Probably, B. Pontelli undertook the reconstruction of this church around 1480, but P. da Cortona designed the *facade*** during the restoration work of 1656. The facade is a theatrical backdrop, closing off the little Piazzetta di S. Maria della Pace. Inside, in the arch of the 1st chapel to the right, are the Sybils** painted by Raphael in 1514; on the altar of the facing chapel is a fresco by B. Peruzzi. Various chapels and altars were designed by A. da Sangallo the Younger and C. Maderno. The small adjacent *cloister*** (*open only for exhibitions; entrance at n. 5 of the Arco della Pace*), surrounded by a portico surmounted by a loggia, was Bramante's first project in Rome (1500-04). The nearby *Via dei Coronari* is now a street of antiques dealers.

Palazzo Altemps (I, *E4*). *Open 9-7:45: summer, Sat., until 11 p.m.; closed Mon.* This building (erected in 1471 on medieval foundations) has been under reconstruction since 1984. It houses some of the sculpture collections of the **Museo Nazionale Romano** (see route 8), among which is the famous and remarkable *Ludovisi Collection* of ancient art, assembled by Cardinal Ludovico in the 17th c. to decorate his own villa.

Museo Napoleonico (I, *E4*). *Open 9-7; closed Mon* Located in Palazzo Primoli, this museum documents – through paintings, statues, miniatures, prints, and manuscripts – the story of the Bonaparte family, related by marriage with the House of Primoli. On the upper floor of the palace, in the *Museo Mario Praz* (*open 9-1 and 2:30-6:30; Mon. 2:30-6:30*), the art collection of the famous critic is on exhibit. Beyond the Ponte Umberto I is the massive *Palazzo di Giustizia* (III, *D4*; 1888-1910), or hall of justice, known as "Palazzaccio" for its pompous architecture.

S. Agostino* (I, *E5*). A high stairway leads up to the white facade of this church, enlarged and renovated twice, once in 1479-83 and again in 1756-61 by L. Vanvitelli. Note statues by J. and A. Sansovino, the main altar by G.L. Bernini (1627), a fresco** by Raphael (1512), and an altarpiece** by Caravaggio (1605).

S. Luigi dei Francesi (I, *E5*). This is the church of the French in Rome, begun in 1518 and completed by D. Fontana in 1589. Inside, note paintings by Domenichino, and three **masterpieces**** by Caravaggio (1597-1602).

Palazzo Madama* (I, *F5*). The "madam" after whom this building is named was Margaret of Austria, a Medici widow. Built in 1503 and enlarged in the 17th c., this is the Italian Senate building (*open 1st Sat. of the month, but not every month, 10-6*). Its lavish facade overlooks *Corso del Rinascimento* (I, *E-F5*), which was built in 1936-38.

In the *Palazzo della Sapienza* (I, *F5*) next door, the University of Rome – known as "La Sapienza" – was located until 1935. Founded by Pope Boniface VIII in 1303, it is now in the Città Universitaria (see route 9). In the courtyard is a masterpiece by Borromini, the church of **S. Ivo*** (1642-50), with a remarkable spiral cupola*.

Pantheon** (I, *F5*). This is one of the most impressive monuments of antiquity as well as a fascinating example of Roman construction techniques. Built by Marcus Vipsanius Agrippa in 27 B.C., its was completely rebuilt by Hadrian in A.D. 118-125, though the original inscription remained on the pediment. It became a Christian church in A.D. 608, with the name of S. Maria ad Martyres, and a fortress in the Middle Ages. The bronze coating of the portico was removed in 1625 and used to cast the baldachin of St. Peter's and the cannons of Castel S. Angelo (hence the famous Pasquinade, lampooning Pope Urban VIII Barberini, "quod non fecerunt barbari, fecerunt barberini:" or "what the barbarians did not do, the Barberini did"). The gates of the pronaos, erected to prevent the marketplace from overflowing into the church, were removed after the Unification of Italy, when the Pantheon became the burial place and shrine of the kings of Italy.

The *pronaos* comprises 16 monolithic Corinthian columns, which support the triangular pediment. The brick *rotunda* is 43.3 m high, and is covered by a cupola of the same diameter. The *interior** is illuminated by only one light source, the 9-m-diameter oculus; the floor is largely original. Note the lacunar ceiling and the frescoes by M. da Forlì and Lorenzetto (commissioned by Raphael for his own tomb); buried here are kings Victor Emmanuel II and Humbert I and Queen Margherita.

S. Maria sopra Minerva** (I, *F5-6*). This church overlooks the square of the same name, with a marble elephant, designed by Bernini, supporting a 6th-c. B.C. Egyptian obelisk. It was built on the ruins of a temple, wrongly thought to be dedicated to Minerva Calchydica; in 1280, it was handsomely rebuilt by G. da Sangallo and C . Maderno, and then blighted architecturally in the 19th c. On the simple facade are lines marking (right corner) the level of the floods of the Tiber, from 1422 to 1870. *Inside* are handsome tombs and monuments by such great artists as A. Romano, M. da Fiesole, Verrocchio, G. da Maiano, G. di Cosma, A. da Sangallo the Younger, and Bernini. The most remarkable work is Michelangelo's statue of the **Resurrected Christ***, to the left of the presbytery. Note also the frescoes* by Filippino Lippi (1488-93). Buried here is Fra' Angelico (1455), with monument by I. da Pisa.

5   From Piazza Barberini to Piazza del Popolo through the Pincio

Among the views that Rome offers, the ones you can enjoy along this route are some of the best known and most photographed. Flashes also pop regularly inside the church of S. Maria del Popolo, an incredible concentration of masterpieces, near the green cupola of the Mausoleum of Augustus, and in the glassed-in pavillion of the Ara Pacis Augustae, up the hill of the Pincio.

Piazza Barberini (II, *D2*). This square received its name in 1625, when it was surrounded by aristocratic villas with vast grounds. Bernini built the *Fontana del Tritone**, the fountain that decorates the center of the square, in 1642-43, for Pope Urban VIII, a Barberini. Also by Bernini, at the corner of Via Veneto (see route 7), is the *Fontana delle Api* (1644), with its motif of bees, the emblem of the Barberini family.

Palazzo Barberini** (II, *D2-3*). Construction began in 1625, under the supervision of C. Maderno, who merged the lines of an urban patrician mansion with the broad green spaces of a villa. Following him, Bernini added the glassed-in loggia atop the portico and the stairway with a square well, leading up to the Galleria Nazionale d'Arte Antica (see below), while Borromini designed the spiral staircase* on the right of the facade.

Galleria Nazionale d'Arte Antica.** *Open weekdays, 9-7:30; closed Mon.* The art collection in this gallery includes works up to the 15th c., on exhibit on the first floor, and 16th-/18-c. paintings, on the second floor. Many of the rooms of the palace are frescoed with marvellous cycles, such as that by P. da Cortona**. Among the masterpieces now on display are those by B. Berlinghieri, the Maestro di Palazzo Venezia, Filippo Lippi, P. di Cosimo, F. di Giorgio Martini, A. Romano, Perugino, L. da Viterbo, A. del Sarto,

D. Beccafumi, Raphael, G. Romano, Bronzino, Tintoretto, Titian, El Greco, Caravaggio, M. Preti, G. Reni, Guercino, H. Holbein, Q. Metsys, G.L. Bernini, G. Bonito, and M. Benefial. In the *Appartamento Barberini* are lavish Rococo decorations and furnishings.

Via Sistina (II, *C-D2*). This street extends the first stretch of the Strada Felice, which Sixtus V (born Felice Peretti) built between the Trinità dei Monti and S. Maria Maggiore. At n. 24 Via Crispi, the *Galleria Comunale d'Arte Moderna e Contemporanea*, the museum of modern art of the city of Rome (*open weekdays, 9-7; holidays, 9-1:30; closed Mon.*), houses works by Italian artists of the 19th-20th c.

Chiesa della Trinità dei Monti* (II, *C1*). It was begun in 1502 at the behest of Louis XII of France, and consecrated in 1585. The interior has some traces of late Gothic style; note the frescoes by D. da Volterra and P. del Vaga. In front of the church is the *Sallustian obelisk*, placed here in the late 18th c. (the hieroglyphics are a Roman imitation of genuine Egyptian ones). There is a fine view*.

Villa Medici* (II, *C1*). Built by N. di Baccio Bigio and A. Lippi in 1564-75, this villa was purchased by the Medici and later taken over by the French in 1804 and used as the headquarters of the academy established in 1666 by Louis XIV to allow French artists to study in Rome. There are interesting bas-reliefs and statues on the facade overlooking the *gardens* (*open Apr.-Jun., Sun., 10-12*).

Pincio (II, *B1*). Along with the reconstruction of Piazza del Popolo (see below), at the turn of the 19th c. G. Valadier laid out, on the summit of the hill of the Pincio, the park of the same name, with its Neo-Classic lodge, or *Casina Valadier.* From the terrace, panoramic view** of Rome, from Monte Mario to the Vatican and the Janiculum.

Villa Borghese* (II, *A-B1-3*). This park, originally the garden of the 17th-c. estate of Cardinal Scipione Borghese (see route 7), is lined with busts of famous Italian and foreign personages. An early renovation of the estate came in the 18th c., when *Piazza di Siena** was opened (II, *A-B2*; the horse track is still

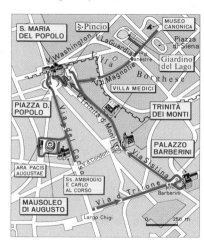

used) and the *Giardino del Lago* (II, *A1-2*) was laid out; from 1800-1830, many of the Neo-Classic structures were built, along with the "medieval" fortress, the Fortezzuola, which now houses the *Museo Canonica* (II, *A2; open weekdays, 9-7; holidays, 9-1:30; closed Mon.*), dedicated to the sculptor of that name.

S. Maria del Popolo** (I, *B5*). It was the people ("popolo," hence the name) of Rome who collected the money to build the first church on this site between the 11th and 12th c.; it was rebuilt in 1475-77, probably by A. Bregno. G.L. Bernini later modified both facade and **interior**, adapting the Baroque style to the original structure. Note the chapels by A. Bregno, C. Fontana, Raphael, Bernini, and A. Sansovino. Among the artwork, an early 13th-c. Byzantine panel*, remarkable stained glass windows, and frescoes by Pinturicchio; the choir was remodelled by Bramante between 1500 and 1509. The chapel to the left of the *presbytery* contains two **masterpieces**** **by Caravaggio** (1601-1602). In the *sacristy* are a marble altar** by A. Bregno and a 14th-c. Sienese Madonna.

Porta del Popolo* (I, *B5*). Replacing the Porta Flaminia in the Aurelian Walls, this famous gate was, for over a thousand years, the main entrance into Rome for those who arrived from the north. The outer facade was built in 1561-62 by N. di Baccio Bigio, while the inner one was added by G.L. Bernini in 1655, on the occasion of the arrival of Queen Christina of Sweden.

Piazza del Popolo* (I, *C5*). Rebuilt at the turn of the 19th c. by G. Valadier, who gave it the two hemicycles, statues, and fountains, this square is focused on the **Flaminian obelisk** (about 1200 B.C., placed here in 1589); also note the twin churches of *S. Maria dei Miracoli*, built in 1675-81 by C. Rainaldi and C. Fontana, and *S. Maria di Montesanto* (1662-79), upon which G.L. Bernini also worked.

Mausoleo di Augusto** (I, *D5*). *Open Sat.-Sun., 10-12.* Built in 27 B.C., during Augustus' lifetime, as a mausoleum for the first Roman emperor and his heirs, it fell into neglect in the Middle Ages, and was used as a quarry for marble and stone, and later as a theater. It was rediscovered in 1936-38; only the lower section is part of the ancient structure.

Ara Pacis Augustae** (I, *D5*). *Closed for restoration.* To celebrate the peace earned through his victories in Spain and Gaul, Augustus decided to build this Altar of Peace, and inaugurated it in 9 B.C. The reliefs (some originals and some molded copies) are important documents of late 1st-c. B.C. Roman art.

Ss. Ambrogio e Carlo al Corso (I, *D5-6*). This is the church of the Lombards in Rome, and was designed in 1610 by O. and M. Longhi the Younger, and completed by P. da Cortona in 1668-69. Inside there is an unusual ambulatory.

6 Basilica di S. Pietro and Musei Vaticani

The Vatican once ruled Rome, and has remained a true city within the city, a treasure trove of remark-

able sights. Devout pilgrims, the faithful, and the simply curious all consider it the eighth wonder of the world: they arrive in crowds from every corner of the world to pray before the altar of St. Peter's (S Pietro) and to tour the remarkable Vatican Museums, where the most popular attractions are th masterpieces of Michelangelo and Raphael.

Castel S. Angelo** (I, *D-E3-4*). This fortress provide an exceptional example of successive stratification and a wide array of utilizations through the ages (I is now the site of the Museo Nazionale di Castel S Angelo, see below). It was first built as a mausoleur for Hadrian and his heirs, around A.D. 123. The "Hadrianeum" was transformed into a fortifie bridgehead across the Tiber, and it became a papa fortress, linked to the Vatican by the little bridg known as the "passetto." Here pontiffs took refuge i cases of extreme danger (popular uprisings, inva sions, etc.). Much of the structure is ancient and orig inal; note the copy of the statue of the angel (afte which the castle is named) sheathing its sword.

Museo Nazionale di Castel S. Angelo.* *Open weekdays, 9-8; summer, until 11 p.m.; closed Mon.* The museum is particularly interesting both for the collections of ceramics, arms, and paintings, and for the history of the building itself. The *ambulatory* around the Roman walls features the surviving decoration from Hadrian's time. The *spiral ramp** leading to the room of imperial urns dates from the same period Note the five architectural models of the castle, ove time. The *Sale di Clemente VIII* feature frescoes by I del Vaga, as well as Renaissance sculptures, while the *Sale di Clemente VII* were decorated by N. di Liberatore, L. Signorelli, and C. Crivelli. Note stucco and frescoes by G. da Udine and G. Siciolante (1543 *Loggia di Paolo III*, attributed A. da Sangallo the Younger). The rooms that overlook the *"giretto" di Pi IV* (view*) were papal court residences, and late prison cells; the *Loggia di Giulio II*, overlooking Ponte S. Angelo (view*), is attributed to G. da Sangallo. The *Appartamento di Paolo III** (1542-49), former residence of the pope, is a fine example of Roman Mannerism. The *Camera dell'Adrianeo*, or Chamber o the Hadrianeum, features a frieze with mythologica scenes and ancient Roman monuments. The *Caglios tra*, with art by L. Luzi, was once a prison cell for

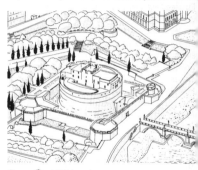

Rome: Castel S. Angelo

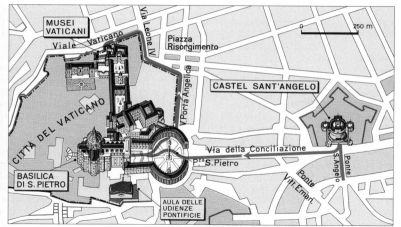

Cagliostro, famous 18th-c. Italian adventurer and impostor. The *terrace*, at the foot of the statue of the angel (1752), affords an excellent view**.

Via della Conciliazione (I, *E2-3*). The first plan for this boulevard – designed as a monumental accessway to St. Peter's – dates from 1936 (M. Piacentini and A. Spaccarelli); it was completed in 1950. It resulted in the destruction of a lovely Renaissance and medieval neighborhood (you can sense from the nearby Borgo Pio and Borgo Vittorio what it looked like). Also note the church of *S. Maria in Traspontina* (I, *D-E3*; begun in 1566, completed in 1668), whose dome was built lower than planned so as not to interfere with cannon fire from Castel S. Angelo. Also note *Palazzo Torlonia* (I, *E2*; 1500-20).

Città del Vaticano (I, *C-E1-2*). The Vatican City is located on the Colle Vaticano in the western part of Rome; it is an independent state, established formally in 1929. The pope comprises all three branches of government (legislative, executive, and judiciary). The state has its own currency and stamps, a daily newspaper ("L'Osservatore Romano"), and its own police force (including the Swiss Guards). The election of a new pope is usually held in the Sistine Chapel, by cardinals who are "locked in" (hence the term "conclave", with key). The election is announced by a puff of white smoke; deadlocks are announced by puffs of black smoke.

Enclosed within the Vatican walls, but with enclaves in Rome proper (in fact, the four basilicas, the Palazzo del Laterano, the Palazzo della Cancelleria, and the Palazzo di Propaganda Fide, as well as the Pope's summer residence at Castel Gandolfo, all enjoy the privilege of extraterritoriality), Vatican City, which covers 0.44 sq. km, dates from the 9th c. You can visit the famed Musei Vaticani, but also have a tour of the Vatican state itself (*open by request; contact the Ufficio Informazioni Pellegrini e Turisti, in Piazza San Pietro*) as well as the Vatican Gardens.

Piazza S. Pietro** (I, *D-E2*). In 1656-67, G.L. Bernini designed a four-fold colonnade, in two great hemicycles, surmounted by 140 statues, so as to embrace the square (St. Peter's Square) standing before the

basilica, and to create a solemn vestibule (when seen from the circular stone set between the obelisk and the fountains, the colonnade appears to have only a single row of columns). In the middle stands the **Vatican obelisk** (25.5 m tall), brought from Alexandria under Caligula and set in the Circus where St. Peter met his martyrdom; it was then moved here by D. Fontana. An anecdote relates that as the obelisk was being raised, it seemed the ropes were about to give; one Ligurian sailor had the presence of mind to cry out, "Throw water on the ropes!" The obelisk was thus saved; a grateful pope gave the sailor a monopoly to sell palm leaves in Rome on the occasion of the Sunday preceding Easter, or Palm Sunday. The fountains are by C. Maderno (right; 1613) and C. Fontana (left; 1677).

Basilica di S. Pietro** (I, *E1*). St. Peter's Cathedral is the heart of the Catholic religion throughout the world, and is certainly the largest and most impressive church in Christendom (it covers a total surface area of 22,067 sq. m, is 218 m in length, and from the ground to the cross atop the dome is 136 m tall). It is said to stand on the tomb of St. Peter.

In 1452 Pope Nicholas V decided to rebuild the original basilica, founded by the Emperor Constantine around A.D. 320. Work did not begin until 1506, under Pope Julius II, with designs by Bramante, and later, by Raphael, B. Peruzzi, and Antonio da Sangallo the Younger. The shape of the floor plans wavered between a Greek and Latin cross. Michelangelo, put in charge in 1546, envisioned a Greek cross topped by a cupola, set in the center of a square; this plan was followed by others by Vignola, P. Ligorio, G. della Porta, and D. Fontana. At the behest of Pope Paul V, C. Maderno returned to the Latin cross plan, extending the nave of the church with three additional chapels on each aisle; he also built the facade. On 18 November 1626, Pope Urban VIII consecrated the church.

Facade. The three-level stairway leads up to the facade, with eight great columns, topped by a trabeation and balustrade; atop this are statues of Christ, John the Baptist, and the Apostles (except St. Peter), and two clocks. The *central balcony* over the portico is where the pope gives Rome his benediction. The **cupola****, designed by Michelangelo, was built by G. della Porta and D. Fontana. Five arches lead into the *portico*; five bronze doors lead into the church.

Interior. The best idea of this vast interior can be had from the papal altar. *Nave.* Along the floor, markers show the sizes of other churches. Note the statue of St. Peter, by A. di Cambio (13th c.). The luminous **cupola**** stands upon four pillars (in the niches, 17th-c. statues of saints). Beneath the cupola is the papal altar, covered by the great **baldachin*** (1633) cast by Bernini with bronze pried from the Pantheon; the bees on the columns, symbols of the Barberini family, are reminders of Pope Urban VIII. In the Confessione, 99 perpetual lamps mark the "tomb of St. Peter." *Right aisle.* In the first chapel is the **Pietà****, the masterpiece by a young Michelangelo (1498-99). Note the wooden Crucifix by P. Cavallini, the wrought-iron gates by Borromini, and the gilded ciborium by Bernini (1674). *Right transept.* Monument to Clement XIII*, by A. Canova (1784-92). *Apse.* Remarkable bronze work of the throne of St. Peter, by Bernini (1656-65), with a gilt stucco "Gloria." In the niches on either side, monuments to Urban VIII* by Bernini (right; 1627-47) and Paul III* by G. della Porta (left; 1551-75). *Left aisle.* The tomb of Pius VII by B. Thorvaldsen (1823) is the only work by a Protestant artist in St. Peter's. Tomb of Innocent VIII* by Pollaiolo (1498). Note the monument to the Stuarts by A. Canova. The *baptistery* features a porphyry basin that may have been taken from the tomb of Hadrian.

Museo Storico Artistico-Tesoro di S. Pietro. *Open 9-7; entrance from the corridor of the sacristy.* This museum is all that remains of the papal treasury, plundered repeatedly but still rich in masterpieces. Note the column upon which Christ supposedly rested in the temple of Jerusalem; a Byzantine dalmatic*, long (and wrongly) said to belong to Charlemagne; a 6th-c. cross*; a ciborium by Donatello; the monument to Pope Sixtus IV* by Pollaiolo; candelabra by B. Cellini; the sarcophagus of Junius Bassus* (4th c.).

Sacre Grotte Vaticane. *Open winter, 7-5; summer, 7-6; entrance from the right transept.* These grottoes lie beneath the nave, and contain the tombs of popes (note the tomb of Boniface VIII*, in part by A. di Cambio); there are also chapels, mosaics, and reliefs. You may also tour the *Necropoli Precostantiniana* (open by request; contact the Ufficio Scavi della Fabbrica di S. Pietro)*, a pagan cemetery with later Christian tombs.

Climb up to the **Cupola di S. Pietro**, or Dome of St. Peter's*. *Open winter, 8-5; summer, 8-6; entrance from the portico of the basilica.* An elevator will take you up to the terrace (view* of the main dome and the two side domes, added by Vignola for decorative effect); two stairways lead up to the circular corridor (view of the mosaics inside the cupola) and to the lantern, where a spiral staircase leads to the outer gallery with a panoramic view**.

Palazzi Vaticani (I, *D1*). Since 1378 they have bee the residence of the popes, who previously lived i the Lateran. These buildings were erected unde Nicholas V, and continued under Sixtus IV (Sistin Chapel), Julius II (Cortile del Belvedere), Leo (Logge di S. Damaso), Paul III (Cappella Paolina an Sala Regia), Sixtus V (buildings on Piazza S. Pietro and Urban VIII (Scala Regia). As the art collection grew, sections were turned into museums (Palazze to di Innocenzo VIII), and various additions and rer ovations were made.

Musei Vaticani** (I, *D1*). *Open summer, Mon.-Fri. 8:45-3:30; Sat., 8:45-12:30; winter, 8:45-12:30; close Sun., except the last Sun. of the month, when entranc is free.* The transfer of the Museo Storico Vaticano in to the Palazzo Lateranense in 1987 was the most re cent of the various transitions that have affected th collections assembled by different popes since th Renaissance. The opening of the Museo Pio Clementino was the first instance of a museum housed in the Palazzi Vaticani; Gregory XVI found ed the Museo Gregoriano Egizio and the Museo Gre goriano Etrusco; Leo XIII opened the Appartamen ti Borgia to the public, while Pius XI, John XXIII, an Paul VI helped to set up the picture gallery and co lections which were once displayed in the Palazzo Laterano.

Pinacoteca Vaticana** (15). It was Pope Pius V who founded this remarkable collection, which i now housed in the palazzo that Pius XI built in 1932 It was formed by gathering the paintings from th pontifical palaces which could be spared after th Treaty of Tolentino, by which France claimed th best of them (of the many which the Vatican wa forced to give to France, only 77 were recovere through the efforts of A. Canova). Among the mas terpieces of Italian art here, note works by M. d'Arez zo, B. Daddi, **Giotto** and helpers (Stefaneschi Polyp tych), P. Lorenzetti, S. Martini, G. di Paolo, Sassetta, G da Fabriano, Fra' Angelico, Filippo Lippi, **M. da For lì** (fragment of the fresco of the Ss. Apostoli), E. de Roberti, C. Crivelli, Perugino, **Raphael** (the ten ta pestries** woven in Brussels after his cartoons; the Transfiguration**, his last work), Leonardo da Vinci, Giovanni Bellini, Titian, P. Bordone, Domenichino, **Caravaggio** (Deposition**), G. Reni, G. M. Crespi, and F. Mancini. Also, examples of Byzantine, Slavic, Greek, and Russian sacred art.

Museo Gregoriano Profano* (16). This museum was first housed in the Palazzo Lateranense, where Pope Gregory XVI displayed, in 1844, Greek and Roman material, found mainly in digs conducted in the Papal State; in the late 19th c., a collection of pagan epigraphs was added. The *section of original Greek statuary* includes the stele of Palestrita* (an Attic relief from the mid-5th c. B.C.), numerous fragments of sculptures* from the Parthenon in Athens, and a head of Athena similar to works from Magna Grecia (mid-5th c. B.C.). In the *section of Roman copies of Greek originals*, note the statue of Marsyas*, a statue of Sophocles, and a relief showing Menander and the Comedy. The *section of 1st-/early 2nd-c.*

Roman sculpture includes a relief with personifications of the Etruscan cities of Tarquinia, Vulci, and Vetulonia, and the Altar of Vicomagistri* (about A.D. 30-40). The *section of sarcophagi* includes items from the 2nd-4th c. In the *section of 2nd-/3rd-c. Roman sculpture*, a torso of a statue, possibly depicting Trajan or Hadrian, stands out.

Museo Pio Cristiano (16). This museum, too, founded by Pius IX in 1854, was originally located in the Palazzo Lateranense, and was transferred here by John XXIII. Remarkable architectural and sculptural exhibits, along with mosaics (note an inscription, on the stele of Abercius, dating from the reign of Marcus Aurelius, the earliest Christian reference to Mass).

Museo Missionario-Etnologico (16) This museum offers a description of religious, social, and economic life in countries outside Europe, and exhibits of Christian art in the missionary context.

Museo Gregoriano Egizio* (1). This Egyptian museum was opened in 1839 by Gregory XVI; it features steles and statues dating from ancient Egypt to the 6th c. A.D. The collections comprise mummies, sarcophagi, jewelry, vases, and reliefs (including Assyrian reliefs, with possible traces of the great fire that destroyed Nineveh).

Cortile della Pigna. The great statue of a pine cone (pigna) that gives the name to this courtyard stands on a stairway beneath the great niche designed by Bramante, along with the larger courtyard (1587-88).

Museo Chiaramonti (2). The museum still follows the arrangement by A. Canova, who laid out the collections of ancient statuary and inscriptions for Pope Pius VII. The museum proper comprises numerous Roman copies of Greek works, and a few originals. Following the museum, in the short side opening on to the Cortile del Belvedere, is the *Braccio Nuovo*, a Neo-Classic gallery housing the noteworthy **statue of Augustus***, a Wounded Amazon (5th c. B.C.), the Nile*, and other works.

Museo Pio-Clementino* (3). The Greek and Roman sculptures in this museum came from the collections of Clement XIV, with additions made by Pius VI. Among them are outstanding masterpieces of ancient art: the sarcophagus of Lucius Cornelius Scipio Barbatus, consul in 298 B.C.; the **Apoxyomenos***, sole surviving copy of a renowned bronze by Lysippus (340-320 a.C.); the **Belvedere Apollo***, from a 4th-c. B.C. Greek original; the renowned **Laocoön***, copy attributed to the sculptors Hagesandros, Athenodoros, and Polydoros of Rhodes, found in the Domus Aurea in 1506 – this statue served as an inspiration to Michelangelo and the Mannerists; a **Hermes**; the Meleager*, a Roman copy of a 4th-c. B.C. Greek statue; a remarkable Apollo Saurochthonos*, based on a bronze original by Praxiteles; the Barberini candelabra* (2nd c.); the **Cnidian Venus***, a Roman copy of a renowned statue by Praxiteles (4th c. B.C.); the **Belvedere torso***, the Jove of Otrìcoli*; the 4th-c. sarcophagi of St. Helena** (mother of Constantine) and Constantina** (daughter of that emperor). By A. Cano-

va are the statues of Perseus* (1800) and of two wrestlers. Behind the Apoxyomenos is the *stairway by Bramante*, built around the turn of the 16th c.

Museo Gregoriano Etrusco* (4). Founded by Pope Gregory XVI in 1837, this museum of Etruscology is one of the earliest. The halls, arranged as they were in the 19th c., are in some cases still decorated with 16th-c. art. Tomb furnishings and ceramics document the earliest Etruscan and Latium Iron Age (9th-8th c. B.C.). The Calabresi urn dates from the mid-7th c. B.C. The Mars of Todi* (late 5th-c. B.C.) was donated to a public figure of Celtic descent, as the inscription in Umbrian language along the edge of the armor indicates. The remarkable Attic vases come from tombs of southern Etruria. The Guglielmi Collection includes more than 800 pieces of Etruscan and Greek ceramics and bronzes. The pieces of the Falcioni Collection come from the territory of Viterbo.

Biblioteca Apostolica Vaticana (6). Following the *Sala della Biga* (5) – a room lined with Carrara marble, named after the biga, or ancient two-wheeled chariot,* reassembled in the late 18th c. – this library was founded by Sixtus IV in 1475, and moved to its present location by Sixtus V; note the Salone Sistino*, decorated with fine frescoes. Next to the library is the *Museo Profano,* which was founded to hold the Etruscan, Roman, and medieval collections assembled by popes Clement XIII and Pius VI.

Galleria degli Arazzi (7). The gallery features the tapestries* with scenes from the life of Christ, woven in the 16th c. in Brussels by P. van Aelst, based on cartoons by students of Raphael.

Stanze di Raffaello** (8). Pope Julius II, in 1508, decided to decorate several of the rooms in the apartments of Nicholas V. At the suggestion of Bramante, he contacted Perugino, Sodoma, B. Peruzzi, and Lotto, but finally settled on Raphael, who worked here until 1517. The *Sala di Costantino* was then completed in 1525 by G. Romano and by G.F. Penni. Among the three rooms, or "stanze," particular note should be given, in the *Stanza di Eliodoro* *, to the **Mass at Bolsena****, depicting a miracle of 1263, and the **Liberation of St. Peter,**** renowned for its light effects, with reference to the imprisonment of Pope Leo X during the battle of Ravenna. In the *Stanza della Segnatura* ** *, note the **Disputation over the Sacrament****, and, on the facing wall, the **School of Athens**** with Plato and Aristotle and the great minds of Antiquity, as well as **Parnassus***. In the *Stanza dell'Incendio*, note the *Fire of Borgo**, executed by G. Romano and G.F. Penni, to cartoons by Raphael.

Loggia di Raffaello.* (9). This is part of the loggia of S. Damaso, commissioned by Julius II in 1512, started by Bramante and continued by Raphael; and then finished under Leo X in 1518. Designed by Raphael but completed by his pupils, the frescoes depict scenes from the Old and New Testaments. The stuccoes and grotesques are by G. da Udine.

Appartamento Borgia* (10). These rooms were named after Pope Alexander VI Borgia, who lived

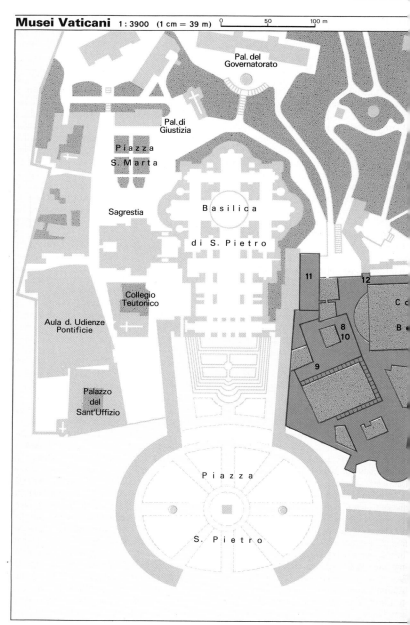

Musei Vaticani 1 : 3900 (1 cm = 39 m)

here and had it painted by Pinturicchio and students (1492-95). Of the six rooms – occupied by part of the Collezione d'Arte Religiosa Moderna (see below) – three are in the Torre Borgia and three in the Palazzo di Niccolò V. Note the Sala dei Santi**, masterpiece by Pinturicchio, and the Sala dei Misteri della Fede*, painted with his students (in one lunette, a portrait of Alexander VI).
Cappella di Niccolò V.* You enter this chapel from the Sala di Costantino through the Sala dei

Chiaroscuri. It is entirely decorated with frescoes** by Beato Angelico (1448-50).
Collezione d'Arte Religiosa Moderna.* This collection of modern religious art was inaugurated in 1973 by Pope Paul VI; it occupies 55 halls and offers a vast overview of all major world schools.
Cappella Sistina** (11). The Sistine Chapel is the official private chapel of the pope. Here, the conclaves in which the popes are elected are held. It may fairly be called the most famous part of the

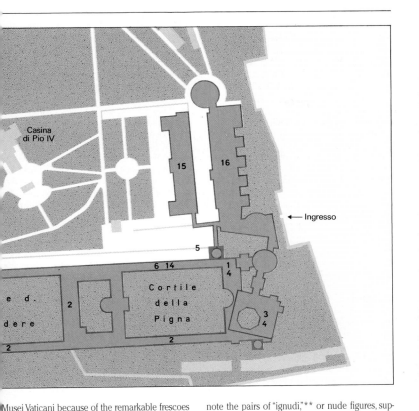

Casina
di Pio IV

15   16

← Ingresso

5

6 14   1
4

e   d.   2   C o r t i l e
d e l l a
d e r e   P i g n a   3
4

2   2

Musei Vaticani because of the remarkable frescoes that adorn it. It was built in 1475-81 under Sixtus IV; it was during that initial phase of construction that the marble roodscreen* dividing the rectangular chapel into two areas was built, as was as the railing around the choir; both are by M. da Fiesole, G. Dalmata, and A. Bregno. The frescoes were executed in three different periods: those on the side walls and facing the altar were done in 1481-83, those on the ceiling and in the lunettes above the windows date from 1508-12, and those on the far wall date from 1536-41. *Side walls and those facing the altar.* This decorative complex was executed by the leading Tuscan artists of the late 15th c. for Pope Sixtus IV, and includes Stories from the Life of Moses (note work by Botticelli and Signorelli) and Stories from the Life of Jesus (again, work by Botticelli, as well as by D. Ghirlandaio and Perugino); between the windows, portraits of popes by Ghirlandaio, Botticelli, C. Rosselli, and Fra' Diamante. *Ceiling.* It is decorated with the celebrated **fresco cycle**** (restored 1981-90) that Michelangelo began for Julius II on 10 May 1508 and completed on 31 October 1512, creating, upon a surface of some 800 sq. m, a mixture of architectural, plastic, and pictorial elements that – at that time – was unprecedented. The work is organized on three levels: in the central zone, Stories from Genesis (note the Creation of Adam**) and Stories from the Old Testament; between the panel,

note the pairs of "ignudi,"** or nude figures, supporting medallions; beneath them, monumental figures of Prophets and Sibyls; in the lunettes over the windows and in the gores of the ceiling, Ancestors of Christ. *Wall over the altar.* Here, Michelangelo frescoed for Pope Paul III the **Last Judgement**** (1536-41), the painter's interpretation of the apocalyptic "Dies Irae," or Day of Wrath. The restoration carried out in 1990-93 to recreate the ancient splendor of color eliminated the work done by D. da Volterra, who – at the behest of Pope Pius IV – had covered the nudity of many figures, earning the scornful nickname of "braghettone," or "britches."

The Vatican palaces also house a series of other galleries, rooms and museums which complete the magnificence of the papal collections. They include: the *Galleria Lapidaria* (11), a collection of epigraphs instituted by Clement XIV; the *Sala delle Nozze Aldobrandine* (12), named after a splendid fresco (Wedding, or "nozze", of Alexander the Great and Roxanne), possibly from the age of Augustus, and unearthed in 1605; the 120-m-long *Galleria delle Carte Geografiche* (13), decorated with wall paintings of maps by A. Danti, showing how the world was thought to be in 1580-83; note the accuracy, as well as the central location of Rome in each map. In the same wing is the little *Museo Sacro* (13), established by Pope Benedict XIV in 1756 to exhibit early Christian finds; the *Galleria dei Candelabri* (14) named after the candle holders under each arch.

Museo Storico Vaticano. This is a separate section of the same museum, located in the Palazzo Lateranense (see route 9); it illustrates the history of the popes and papal cerimonial, as well as the Vatican armed forces and means of transport through carriages, litters, and old automobiles.

7 "Quartiere delle Regioni", Villa Borghese museums, Foro Italico

This route runs through a district of Rome that should really be considered part of the city center, even though it does lie outside the walls; it offers a very pleasant stroll through a world of art, ranging from ancient, pre-Christian times (Museo Etrusco di Villa Giulia), to the collections of the 17th c. (Museo Borghese and Galleria Borghese), and on to the most recent trends in contemporary art (the Galleria Nazionale d'Arte Moderna). The Foro Italico offers an interesting view of the architecture that developed during the Fascist period.

Via Veneto (II, *B-D2-3*). This is, by definition, the street of luxury hotels in Rome, as well as of cafés and the sites of the famous "Dolce Vita." At the beginning of the sloping street, a double-staircase marks the church of *S. Maria della Concezione* (II, *D2*), also known as the church of the Cappuccini, or Capuchins, built in 1626-30; you will find paintings by G. Reni, G. van Honthorst, and Caravaggio here. Beneath the church is the *cemetery of the Capuchins* (Cimitero dei Cappuccini), comprising five chapels lined with skeletons and bones. In the second curve of Via Veneto stands *Palazzo Boncompagni* (II, *C3*; 1886-90), also known as *Palazzo Margherita*, now the site of the U.S. Embassy.

Casino dell'Aurora (II, *C2*). *Open by request; enquire at n. 44 Via Ludovisi.* This is all that survives of the 17th-c. Villa Ludovisi, devoured by the growing city in the late 19th c. Note frescoes by Guercino in the Sala dell'Aurora, by A. Circignani in the Sala del Camino and, perhaps, by Caravaggio in a room on the ground floor. This villa once held the famous Ludovisi Collection of ancient marble statues, now in Palazzo Altemps.

Porta Pinciana (II, *B2*). This simple arch of travertine, flanked by two cylindrical towers, was built by the Byzantine general Belisarius during a siege by the Goths; it runs through the Aurelian Walls (see route 10). Beyond this gate is an entrance to Villa Borghese (see route 5).

Museo e Galleria Borghese★★ (II, *A3*). *Compulsory reservation, tel. 0632810; entrance every two hours; open weekdays, 9-7:30; summer, Sat., until 11 p.m.; Sun. 9-1; closed Mon.* Set in the Casino Borghese that was built at the orders of Cardinal Scipione in 1608-17 (designed by F. Ponzio), this has been described as the "queen of all private collections on earth." It is divided into a remarkable collection of material from classical times, and a gallery of paintings, along with

major pieces of Baroque and Neo-Classic sculpture. The *Museo Borghese* was founded in 1608, when works from old St. Peter's were added to the collection of the cardinal. What we see today is only part of a once far vaster collection; a great deal was given by Camillo Borghese to France under Napoleon, and now constitutes the core of the Louvre's classical collection. Among the works from Roman times, still arranged according to 19th-c. tastes, one should note: a colossal head of Hadrian; a mosaic with scenes of hunting in the Circus and gladiatorial fights (310-320), the Athena Parthenos copied from the original, by Phidias, and others. Also, note the masterpieces by A. Canova (**Venus Victrix**★★ or Portrait of Pauline Borghese, sister of Napoleon) and G.L. Bernini (David★, in which the face is a self-portrait of the sculptor; and **Apollo and Daphne**★★, 1624).

The *Galleria Borghese* also originated from a collection belonging to Cardinal Scipione, to which were added other collections, chief among them that of Olimpia Aldobrandini. Among the paintings, note those by: S. Botticelli, Fra' Bartolomeo, Raphael (**Deposition of Christ**★★), Pinturicchio, A. del Sarto, L. Cranach the Elder, Correggio (**Danae**★★), Bronzino, G. G. Savoldo, L. Lotto, Palma the Elder, Domenichino, P. da Cortona, Caravaggio, G.L. Bernini, P.P. Rubens, A. Sacchi, J. Bassano, Ortolano, F. Francia, Correggio, D. Dossi, Titian, Giovanni Bellini, A. da Messina, V. Carpaccio, and P. Veronese.

Bioparco (II, *A2-3*). *Open winter, 9:30-5; summer, 9:30-6.* This zoo was founded in 1911 in the park of Villa Borghese; inside is the *Museo Civico di Zoologia* (*open 9-5; closed Mon.*), or Zoological Museum.

Galleria Nazionale d'Arte Moderna★ (I, *A6*). *Open 9:30-7:30; summer, Sat., until 11 p.m.; closed Mon.* This national gallery of modern art is housed in the *Palazzo delle Belle Arti* built in Valle Giulia by C. Bazzani for the International Exposition of 1911. Originally (1883) intended for Italian artists only, the gallery opened its doors to non-Italian artists in 1909; at the same time, the collection was installed in this Palazzo, which was later enlarged. This is one of the largest collections of Italian painting, sculpture, and graphics of the 19th-20th c.

The last arrangement has divided the works in four sectors. The *south-west wing* includes works from Napoleon's time to the Unification of Italy, with Neo-Classic and Romantic painting and sculpture. The *south-east wing* is devoted to late 19th-c. art, celebrating also the Italian Risorgimento; it is organized by schools of painting. In the *north-east wing* are international works which were exhibited in the 1911 show and the first Biennials in Venice; it includes donations from Balla, Guttuso and Schwartz. The *north-west wing* includes works of 20th-c. avant-gardes, like American Abstract Expressionism or post-informal art.

Villa Giulia★ (I, *A5-6*). Built for Julius III by B. Ammannati, G. Vasari, and Vignola in 1551-55, this villa presents a series of three courtyards, with a loggia★ by Ammannati (note the signature on the right pil-

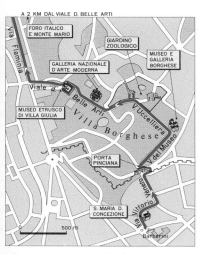

lar) and a nymphaeum, with a fountain.

Museo Etrusco di Villa Giulia. ** *Open 8:30-7; closed Mon.; workshops for young children, by reservation, tel. 068412312.* The material of this remarkable Etruscan museum is arranged by place of discovery, including Latium, Umbria, and southern Etruria. The museum was founded in 1889. The Etruscan and Faliscan civilizations are documented, both through locally produced items and items imported, especially from Greece. From the digs done at Pyrgi come three gold laminae** with Etruscan and Punic inscriptions. Dating from 1916 and 1939, the finds, at Vejo, of clay statues (Goddess with Child*; **Herakles***) from the temple of Portonaccio, masterpieces of 6th-c. B.C. Etruscan sculpture, while from the tombs of Cervèteri come the famous sarcophagus of the Married Couple (Sposi)* (ca. 530 B.C.) and the 7th-/6th-c. B.C. Greek vases. From the area around Vejo comes the Chigi oenochoe* (640-625 B.C.), and from Castro are bronze chariot handles* (530-520 B.C.). The Castellani collection, acquired in 1919, contains a vast and complete array of Greek and Etrusco-Italic ceramics from the 8th-1st c. B.C., as well as glasswork and goldwork; the Pesciotti collection comprises bronze cineraria, bucchero pottery*, and amphorae. Note the decorations* from the Etrusco-Italic temple of "Falerii Veteres" (now Civita Castellana), dating from the 6th-1st c. B.C. From Palestrina come the furnishings** of the Barberini and Bernardini tombs, including ivory, gold, silver, and bronze objects of Syrian and Cypriot production (mid-7th-c. B.C.). Lastly, the Ficoroni cist* dates from the end of the 4th c. B.C..

Via Flaminia (1, *A-B5*). This road runs along the route of the old Via Flaminia, inaugurated in 223-219 B.C. by the censor Caius Flaminius; it went to Ariminum (modern-day Rimini). At the center of the green strip that separates it from the parallel Viale Tiziano is the church of **S. Andrea**, built by Vignola. The *Stadio Flaminio* (1957-59) and the *Palazzetto dello Sport* (1956-58) are sports facilities built for the 1960 Olympic Games, held in Rome. Under con-

struction is the Auditorium by R. Piano, while at n. 80 is the recently opened Explora-Museo dei Bambini, an area conceived to teach children how to live in a city and exploit its facilities. The Via Flaminia crosses the Tiber on the *Ponte Milvio*, or Milvian Bridge, built in wood in the 3rd c. B.C., rebuilt in tufa stone in 109 B.C., and again by G. Valadier in 1805.

Villa "ad Gallinas Albas." *Open Sun., 9-1 and 3-one hour before sunset.* When this villa belonged to Livia, the wife of Augustus, it was in the open countryside. It is now on the edge of the Roman suburb, or Borgata di Prima Porta, along the Via Flaminia. The villa, where the famous statue of Augustus of Prima Porta was found in 1863-64 (now in the Musei Vaticani), featured remarkable frescoes and a bath facility. Some detached frescoes have been reassembled in the Museo Nazionale Romano.

Foro Italico. Situated at the foot of Monte Mario, this is a sports complex built at the behest of Mussolini to celebrate the fusion of sports and Fascist ideology; work began in 1928, but it was not finished until after WWII. An obelisk that was originally built in honor of Mussolini, and named after him, marks the entrance; behind it is the Viale del Foro Italico, a broad avenue decorated by mosaic pavement and punctuated by blocks commemorating important dates in the history of the Italian Empire and Republic, leading to the *Stadio dei Marmi* (1932), with its low tiers decorated with statues of athletes, and to the *Stadio Olimpico*, built in 1950-53 and roofed over in 1990.

Monte Mario. On its slopes is *Villa Madama** (*not open to the public*), designed by Raphael in 1518, and once the home of Madama Margherita di Parma (hence the name); here is also the Osservatorio Astronomico e Meteorologico, the astronomical observatory with the adjoining *Museo Astronomico e Copernicano* (*open Wed. and Sat., 9:30-12*). Devoted to military life and values is the *Istituto Storico e di Cultura dell'Arma del Genio*, founded in 1906 at the behest of Victor Emmanuel III, which includes the Museo Sotrico dell'Arma del Genio and the Museo Storico dell'Architettura Militare (*both open Tue. and Thu., 9:30-12:30*).

---

8 Quirinale, Porta Pia, and Museo Nazionale Romano

This route runs through the NE section of Rome, within the walled perimeter, past the Quirinal area, center of the Italian government and two churches central to the famed rivalry between two great architects, Bernini and Borromini (S. Andrea and S. Carlino). The route then leads to a trove of Roman antiquities, namely the Baths of Diocletian and the vast collections of the Museo Nazionale Romano. At this point you will make a short detour out through the gate of Porta Pia, where an Italian army of unification once stormed the walls of Rome (1870); here you will see the ancient complex of S.

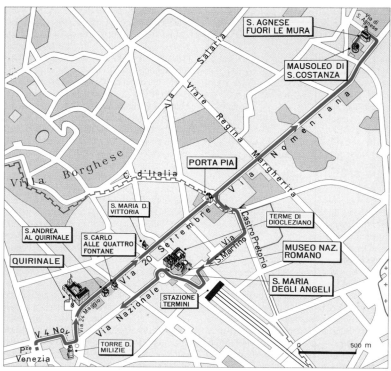

Agnese Fuori le Mura, which contains the famous Mausoleum of S. Costanza.

Torre delle Milizie. This is the largest surviving baronial tower in Rome, built on the site of the Mercati di Traiano (see route 1).

Palazzo Pallavicini Rospigliosi (II, *E2*). Begun by F. Ponzio in 1605 and completed by C. Maderno in 1616, the palazzo now belongs to the Pallavicini family. The *Casino Pallavicini* (*open 1st day of the month, 10-12 and 3-5*) was frescoed by Reni in 1614, with his famous Aurora* (Dawn). The *Galleria Pallavicini* (*not open to the public*) is one of the leading galleries in Rome, and contains work by Italian and foreign artists.

Piazza del Quirinale * (II, *E2*). Overlooking one of the finest views of Rome, this square was given its current appearance in the 18th c., when the **fountain of Montecavallo** was laid out in the center of the square, with the ancient Roman replica of a 5th-c. B.C. statue of the Dioscuri*. Another noteworthy work is the obelisk, from the Mausoleum of Augustus. The *Palazzo della Consulta* (designed by F. Fuga, 1732-34) now houses Italy's Supreme Court.

Palazzo del Quirinale * (II, *D-E2*). This building complex has always been linked to power: it was a summer residence of the popes, then the Savoy royal family, and, since 1946, of the president of Italy. Begun in 1573, a remarkable series of architects worked on it: M. Longhi the Elder, O. Mascherino, D. Fontana, F. Ponzio, C. Maderno, and G.L. Bernini. The

interior (*open Sun., 8:30-12:30*) is noteworthy, especially the great stairway by Ponzio, and the Cappella Paolina, built by Maderno to rival the Sistine Chapel in size. Fine art abounds; the gardens still maintain their 16th-c. design.

S. Andrea al Quirinale * (II, *E2*). Overlooking Via del Quirinale with a curving pronaos, this church is one of the masterpieces of Bernini (1658). Inside, note the lavish Baroque style.

S. Carlo alle Quattro Fontane * (II, *D3*). Borromini worked all his life on this church, especially on the facade, which he left unfinished at his death in 1667. He built the interior to the size of a pier of the cupola of St. Peter's. Note the odd adjacent little cloister*, with an octagonal plan (1635-36). The *intersection of the Quattro Fontane*, with four fountains, is the crossroads of two main papal roads.

S. Maria della Vittoria * (II, *D3*). Built by C. Maderno (1608-1620), the interior of this church is a sumptuous example of Baroque decoration. Among artwork by Domenichino, of particular note, in the left transept, is the famous marble statue of **St. Theresa in Ecstasy** ** by G.L. Bernini (1646). Across the road is the *Fontana del Mosè* (D. Fontana, 1587), and nearby is the late 16th-c. church of *S. Bernardo alle Terme*.

Museo Numismatico della Zecca Italiana (II, *C-D4*). *Open Tue.-Sat., 9-12:30*. This numismatic museum of the Italian Mint is located in the building of the Ministry of the Treasury and features medals from as far back as the 15th c., as well as a collection of coins from the Kingdom of Italy, the Italian

Republic, and the various sovereign states of the Italian peninsula.

Orti Sallustiani (II, *C4*). These gardens lie in the middle of Piazza Sallustio, 14 m below street level due to the gradual rise of the level of the surrounding ground. The ruins are those of a circular hall, once part of a larger building, originally owned by Julius Caesar, later by Tiberius, and thereafter part of the imperial estates. It was heavily damaged by the Goths under Alaric.

Porta Pia** (II, *B-C5*). Built in 1561-64, at the end of the Strada Pia, to a design by Michelangelo, this is the only Roman gate to face inward toward the city (the outer facade was added in 1853-69). Its prominent place in Italian history dates from 1870, when the Aurelian walls were "breached" on 20 September and Papal Rome fell to the army of the Risorgimento; there is a commemorative column topped by a statue of Victory. In the courtyard is the *Museo Storico dei Bersaglieri* (*closed for restoration*) dedicated to the sharpshooters of the Italian army.

Via Nomentana (II, *A-B5-6*). This broad tree-lined boulevard follows the route of an ancient Roman road that ran toward Nomentum, modern-day Mentana. An Ionic porch on the right marks the entrance to the grounds of the 19th-c. *Villa Torlonia* (II, *A6*), once the private residence of Benito Mussolini. The grounds were made a public park in 1978, and feature a number of interesting buildings erected in the last two centuries; among them is the **Casina delle Civette** (Owls Lodge), whose original Art Nouveau window glasses are part of the *museum* of the same name (*open summer, 9-7; winter, 9-5; closed Mon*).

S. Agnese Fuori le Mura.* From the Via Nomentana you can see the 15th-c. campanile of this church, first built in the 4th c. From the courtyard of n. 349, a staircase takes you inside: note the handsome columns, the wooden ceiling, and the statue of the saint by N. Cordier. The 7th-c. mosaic in the apse is a particularly fine piece of Byzantine art. You can also tour the *catacombs of S. Agnese* (*open 9-12 and 4-6; closed holidays, Mon.-Tue. aft.*), which are well preserved.

Mausoleo di S. Costanza.** After touring the complex of S. Agnese, you may turn to this major Early Christian monument, built in the early 4th c. as a mausoleum for the daughters of Constantine, Constance and Helena. It was soon turned into a baptistery and, later (13th c.), a church. The round ambulatory is decorated with exceedingly fine 4th-c. mosaics**.

Piazza dei Cinquecento (II, *D4*). This square, named in honor of those who died in the battle of Dògali, was rebuilt in 1950 after the completion of the *Stazione Centrale di Termini*, the railway station which was begun in 1937 in view of the Universal Exposition. To the left of the entrance to the station are notable ruins of the so-called *Servian walls*, supposedly built by Servius Tullius, one of the legendary seven kings of Rome.

Museo Nazionale Romano** (II, *D-E4*). This museum's collections – taken from digs effected after 1870 and from the former Museo Kircheriano – are shown in four different locations: the Terme di Diocleziano (or Baths of Diocletian; see below), Palazzo Altemps (see route 4), Palazzo Massimo alle Terme (see below), and the Crypta Balbi, in Via delle Botteghe Oscure (see route 4).

Palazzo Massimo alle Terme. *Open 9-7:45; closed Mon.* The five sections open to the public illustrate five aspects of Roman artistic culture between the 1st c. B.C. and the late Empire. A series of *portraits* (note the **statue of Augustus from the Via Labicana**) are used to show the shifts in style from the late Republic to the Augustan age. Among the *statuary* are copies of Greek works used to decorate imperial residences and public buildings, as well as official busts and portraits. Also noteworthy are the so-called ships of Nemi*, bronze decorations from floating platforms once anchored before the villa of Caligula. *Painting and mosaics* between the 1st c. B.C. and the end of the Empire are documented with the frescoes from the Villa **"ad Gallinas Albas,"**** (see route 7), along with the **frescoes from the Villa della Farnesina***, an Augustan complex overlooking the Tiber. The *numismatic section* analyzes coins in economic terms, ranging from trade routes to depressions and slumps; the *jewelry section* features some items found with the mummy of Grottarossa.

Terme di Diocleziano** (II, *D4*). *Open 9-7:45; closed Mon.* The Baths of Diocletian offer an important example of structures put to continual use; built as a public facility between 298 and 306, they were then used as a church in the 16th c., and finally, in 1889, they were adopted as the site of the Museo Nazionale Romano. The recent renovation allows visitors to admire Michelangelo's cloister, the protohistoric section, and the *Epigraphic Department*, with 10,000 inscriptions, which illustrates the political, social, and religious development of Rome from the 1st c. B.C. to the late Empire. The Baths are also used for temporary exhibitions.

S. Maria degli Angeli** (II, *D4*). You enter from *Piazza della Repubblica*. This church was built by Michelangelo, who adapted the ancient "tepidarium" and adjacent rooms. In the mid-18th c., L. Vanvitelli shifted the church's orientation considerably, re-

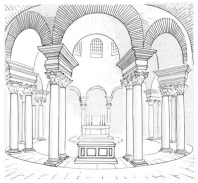

Rome: Mausoleo di S. Costanza

structuring the main interior nave to accommodate the altarpieces* taken from St. Peter's, which still adorn the walls (note the ones by P. Batoni and P. Subleyras). In the right arm, note the funerary monuments to V. E. Orlando, Admiral P. Thaon di Revel (both by P. Canonica), and Marshall A. Diaz, all Italian leaders in WWI.

Aula Ottagona (II, *D4*). *Open same hours as the Terme di Diocleziano.* The former Sala della Minerva is another room of the enormous complex of the Baths; it was converted into a planetarium in 1928, and in 1991 the statues that once adorned the Baths of ancient Rome were placed on display here.

Via Nazionale (II, *D-E2-4*). When this street was built in the 19th c., it was meant to be the monumental entrance to Rome, along with Piazza dell'Esedra, for those who arrived in the new capital of Italy by train. It is now a major artery linking the Stazione Termini with Piazza Venezia. Midway along it, a stairway runs down to the church of *S. Vitale* (II, *E3*), consecrated in 412, and rebuilt more than once. Note the nearby *Palazzo delle Esposizioni* (P. Piacentini, 1877-83). The *Palazzo della Banca d'Italia* (II, *E-F2*) is a noteworthy work of late 19th-c. Roman eclecticism.

9 On the Hills: Viminale, Esquilino, and Laterano

You can tour one Early Christian basilica after another here; though often restored and even rebuilt, the churches that you will see along this route in the SE section of Rome (within the walls) are often of exceedingly ancient origin. Surrounding them is a section of Rome built in the late 19th c., to accommodate the civil servants of Italy's new capital, on ground previously occupied by villas and verdant countryside.

Via Cavour (II, *E-F2-4*). This avenue was built in the late 19th c. to ease traffic between the Forums and the Stazione Termini over the Quirinal and Esquiline hills. The *Torre dei Conti* was built in the early 13th c. (II, *F2*).

S. Pietro in Vincoli* (II, *F3*). First built in the 5th c., and still standing amidst an ancient residential neighborhood, this church was restored in the late 15th c., and again in the early 18th c. by F. Fontana. It was named for the chains ("vincula") of St. Peter, subject of a miracle involving St. Leo I the Great, in the 5th c. In the transept is the mausoleum of Pope Julius II*, only partly completed by Michelangelo; of the statues that he planned and partly executed, only the famous **Moses**** is still here (1514-16?; the Prigioni, or Captives, are now in Paris and Florence), though he worked on the statues of Lia and Rachel. In the confession, or shrine, note two bronze doors, attributed to Caradosso, behind which are the supposed chains of the saint; also, in the second altar on the left, is a 7th-c. mosaic.

S. Martino ai Monti (II, *F4*). The *towers of the Capocci and the Graziani* which stand in Piazza di S. Martino ai Monti are medieval, while the basilica of S. Martino ai Monti dates from the 5th c., although it was rebuilt to some extent after 1636. Surviving from the original structure are a set of columns and a hall that dates back to the 3rd c.; note the Roman and medieval architectural fragments, bits of 9th-c. frescoes, and a 6th-c. mosaic.

S. Prassede* (II, *F4*). This basilica was founded in A.D. 489 and features two of the finest pieces of Byzantine art in Rome. In the 9th-c. *Cappella di S. Zenone***, note the portal, floor, and mosaics; the triumphal arch bears fine 9th-c. mosaics*, as does the apse (less certain).

S. Maria Maggiore** (II, *E-F4*). This is one of the five patriarchal basilicas, and the most important of those dedicated to the Virgin Mary. Legend has it that the church was first built on the site of a miraculous snowfall in August 356. Various renovations were effected throughout the centuries, and in the 18th c. F. Fuga gave the church a new facade; note the 14th-c. bell tower. In the loggia over the portico are late 13th-c. mosaics by F. Rusuti.

The **interior*** still appears much as the ancient basilica must have been. The *nave* still has part of the 12th-c. floor and a magnificent 16th-c. wooden ceiling; tradition has it that the gold used to gild it was the first to arrive from the New World. Above the trabeation are 5th-c. mosaic panels*, extensively restored in 1593; in the triumphal arch, exquisite mosaics* from the same century. Before the papal altar, with baldachin by Fuga, is the confession, with relics, supposedly of the Nativity of Bethlehem. The huge *apse* is covered with an equally vast mosaic* by J. Torriti (1295). Note the paintings, frescoes, and sculptures by P. Cavallini, G. Guerra and C. Nebbia, A. di Cambio, G. di Cosma, the Cavalier d'Arpino, and G. Reni. Various chapels were designed by D. Fontana, F. Ponzio, and Michelangelo.

Piazza dell'Esquilino (II, *E4*). This is the terminus of the long avenue of the Strada Felice (see route 5); in 1587, Sixtus V erected here one of the obelisks that were originally located at the entrance of the Mausoleum of Augustus. The nearby church of *S. Pudenziana* dates from the 4th c., as you can see from the mosaic* in the apse.

Via Merulana (II, *F4*; III, *A-B4*). Pope Gregory XIII built this road, in part along an ancient route, linking the basilicas of S. Maria Maggiore and S. Giovanni in Laterano; it was completed by Sixtus V. At the beginning of this chaotic thoroughfare (one of the main arteries in the late 19th-c. district of the Esquiline), slightly to one side, is the *Arco di Gallieno* (II, *F5*), originally the Porta Esquilina in the Servian walls, but rebuilt in Augustan times, and dedicated to the Emperor Gallienus in A.D. 262.

Museo Nazionale d'Arte Orientale (II, *F4*). *Open 8:30-2; Tue., Thu. and holidays, 8:30-7:30; closed 1st, 3rd Mon. of the month.* Located in *Palazzo Brancaccio* (1886-1912), this museum of Oriental art was established in 1957, and comprises collections of material from digs conducted by the Istituto Italiano per L'Africa e l'Oriente (IsIAO), in Iran, Pakistan, and

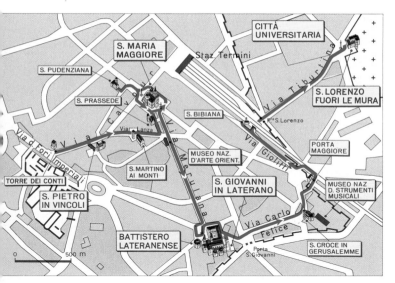

ghanistan. The museum is divided into sections at document the history and culture of the enormous territory stretching from Iran to Japan. The nian section ranges from the 4th millennium B.C. the 8th c. A.D.; note the finds from Afghanistan hazni, 11th-12th c.). There is much material from cient Gandhara, scrolls and statues from Southst Asia, Chinese bronzes (14th c. B.C.-1st c. A.D.), d Japanese and Korean bronzes and pottery.

azza di S. Giovanni in Laterano (III, *B-C4-5*). e *Obelisco Lateranense***, or Lateran obelisk, ich stands in the center of this square, is the tallest 1 m) and oldest (it stood before the Temple of non in Thebes as early as 1500 B.C., and it was ected in the Circus Maximus in A.D. 357) obelisk ll standing in Rome; it was placed here as the wning touch to the renovation of this area in the e 16th c. by Sixtus V.

lazzo Lateranense (III, *C4-5*). Built by D. Fontana 1586-89, this building was later used as a hospital d to house the museums that were subsequently ved into the Vatican; it enjoys the privilege of exterritoriality, and is not subject to Italian law. It w houses the *Museo Storico Vaticano* (*open Sat., 9, 10:30, 12; 1st Sun. of the month, 9-12*), comising the Papal Apartment (note frescoes by Man-rist painters) and the historical museum proper e route 6).

ttistero Lateranense* (III, *C4*). The Emperor Con-antine had this baptistery built on the site of a 1st-villa and 2nd-c. baths; in the Cappella di S. Rufina te the 5th-c. mosaics; in that of S. Venanzio, the 7th-mosaic decorations of the apse and triumphal ch; finally the Cappella di S. Giovanni Evangelista atures noteworthy late 12th-c. bronze doors.

Giovanni in Laterano** (III, *C4-5*). St. John Lat-an is the Cathedral of Rome, built between 313 d 318 by order of Constantine; it was renovated peatedly, especially by D. Fontana and by F. Borro-

mini. The facade, surmounted by 15 statues, is by A. Galilei (1732-35); in the portico, the central doorway has bronze doors* taken from the Roman Curia. The **interior*** has a nave with four aisles and a vast transept; stretching over the nave is a 16th-c. wooden ceiling.* Statues of apostles date from the 18th c. An ogival tabernacle dates from 1367, decorated with frescoes from the same period, later retouched by A. Romano and F. di Lorenzo; it houses the relics of the supposed heads of Saints Peter and Paul. Note the sculptures, frescoes, and mosaics by A. Bregno, I. da Pisa, Giotto, A. di Cambio, J. Torriti, J. da Camerino, and the Cavalier d'Arpino. From the transept, you can enter the *museum* of the basilica. The adjacent *cloister*** is by Vassalletto (1215-32); along the walls are fragments of architecture and sculpture from the ancient basilica, and Roman and Early Christian archeological finds.

Scala Santa (III, *C5*). Sixtus V asked D. Fontana to build this structure to cover what is said to have been a set of steps that Jesus climbed prior to his trial. Even now, the faithful climb it on their knees, to peer through grates at the Sancta Sanctorum* (*open winter, 6:15-12 and 3-6:15; summer, 6:15-12 and 3:30-6:45*), the private papal chapel decorated with 13th-c. mosaics and frescoes. At n. 145 Via Tasso is the *Museo Storico della Liberazione di Roma* (*open Tue., Thu., Fri., 4-7; Sat.-Sun., 9:30-12:30; closed Aug.*), or Museum of the Liberation of Rome, the headquarters of the SS in WWII; in Via Aleardi, note the *Casino Massimo Lancellotti* (*open Tue., Thu, 9-12 and 4-7; Sun., 10-12*) with frescoes by the Nazareni, German painters of the early 19th c.

S. Croce in Gerusalemme* (III, *B6*). The earliest documentation of a place of Christian worship here dates from the early 4th c., when Helena, mother of Constantine, consecrated a room in her own home to Christian worship. The church, however, was rebuilt in the form of a basilica in 1144-45 and again in 1743 by Pope Benedict XIV. The church is now largely 18th c. in style, though the floors are Cosmatesque; the apse has a fresco attributed to A. Romano (1492 ca.); the tomb of Cardinal Quiñones* is by J. Sansovino (1536). In the Cappella di S. Elena, at the foot of the right aisle, is a ceiling mosaic* by M. da Forlì or B. Peruzzi (1510 ca.).

Museo Nazionale degli Strumenti Musicali (III, *B6*). *Open 8:30-7:30; closed Mon.* This museum of musical instruments has collections dating from antiquity to the 20th c., largely from the collection of Evan Gorga; note the famous Barberini harp* and a piano* built by Bartolomeo Cristofori in 1722.

Porta Maggiore* (III, *B6*). This gate is the beginning of the Via Prenestina and the Via Labicana; it made use of arches of aqueducts built by Caligula in A.D. 38 and completed by Claudius in A.D. 52. On Piazzale Labicano, near the central archway, is the *tomb of Eurisax* (1st c. B.C.), a baker, as one can see from the frieze showing the production and sale of bread. Nearby, next to the earthen bank of the railroad, is the entrance to the **Basilica di Porta Maggiore** (*open by request; contact the Soprintendenza Archeologica di Roma*), a 1st-c. subterranean sanctuary decorated with fine stuccowork*, discovered in 1917.

Tempio di Minerva Medica (III, *A6*). Scholars still debate the function of this ten-sided hall, built in the 4th c.; it is named after a statue of the goddess Minerva, with a serpent, found here. Further along is the church of *S. Bibiana* (II, *F6*), founded in early Christian times and rebuilt in 1624-26 by G.L. Bernini (note his statue of the saint* on the main altar).

S. Lorenzo Fuori le Mura.** This basilica is one of the five patriarchal churches, and is the result of a fusion of two churches. The first one was built in 330 by order of Constantine, as a shrine for the burial of the relics of Christian martyrs. In the 6th c. a parallel church was built, which was covered in the 13th c. by another building. Bombed and damaged on 19 July 1943, it was restored to the 13th-c. forms. In particular, note the portico*, which supports a trabeation adorned with a frieze, and the Romanesque campanile.

Inside, you can readily perceive the sections of the two different churches. The ambos and paschal candelabra in the nave are by the Cosmati (13th c.). The presbytery is older: the trabeation* dates from the 4th c., the mosaic on the triumphal arch from the 6th c., and the ciborium from 1148. The adjacent Romanesque *cloister* dates from the late 12th c.

Città Universitaria (II, *C-D6*). This giant campus, designed by M. Piacentini, was built in the 1930s and enlarged in the 1960s.

---

10 The "Passeggiata Archeologica" and the churches on the Celio

Little known to the majority of tourists, who venture no further than the immense Baths of Caracalla, this southern section of Rome is full of astonishing sights, the ideal place for an "archeological promenade".

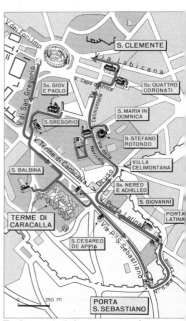

The first surprise is the vast expanse of greenery, a ic of the gr,ounds of the numerous villas that sto here until 1870, when the new capital of Italy beg to grow rapidly; you will also note a seemingly er less succession of churches, largely of ancient origi made more appealing by the bucolic setting.

Via di S. Gregorio (III, *B-C2*). This street passes the Palatine, where the ruins of *Nero's aqueduc* can be seen; note the *obelisk of Axum*, brought fr Ethiopia in 1937, and the *offices of the FAO.*

S. Gregorio Magno (III, *C2*). Largely Baroque, t church features a miraculous fresco, which supp edly once spoke to the saint; in the nearby *orate of S. Andrea (open 9-1 and 4-7)*, frescoes by G. Re Domenichino, Pomarancio, and G. Lanfranco.

Ss. Giovanni e Paolo* (III, *C2*). In the late 4th the first nucleus of this church was built on the s of the house of the two martyrs. Later destroyed the Goths under Alaric and by Norman invaders was rebuilt by Pope Paschal II in the late 12th From that period date the Romanesque apse, t buttresses along the side, and the architraved po co on the face, with adjacent campanile* – no the ceramic basins. The rest of the church is later style. Underneath the church (*open by request; c tact the offices of FEC*) are rooms dating from cl sical antiquity, used in the 2nd c. by one of the e liest Christian communities in Rome (t nymphaeum features a 3rd-c. fresco).

Terme di Caracalla** (III, *D-E2*). *Open 9-one ho before sunset; Mon., 9-1.* The impressive ruins of t Baths of Caracalla, inaugurated by that emperor 217, which continued to operate until the 6th c., a the most notable monument in the Passeggia Archeologica, or Archeological Promenade, esta shed between 1887 and 1914 to protect the Roman ruins thus far excavated; this praiseworthy project was undermined under Fascism, as the walkways were transformed into arteries for automobile traffic toward the EUR section. The baths, which occupied a total area of 330 sq. m, presented the traditional succession of frigidarium-tepidarium-calidarium, and had not only gymnasiums, but also libraries.

S. Balbina (III, *D2*). This church, first consecrated in A.D.595, was restored in 1927-30; inside, note the Crucifixion, possibly by M. da Fiesole and G. Dalmata.

Ss. Nereo e Achilleo (III, *D3*). Founded by Pope Leo III on the site of a 4th-c. church; note the mosaics in the triumphal arch. Other sections of the church, including the main altar and the bishop's throne, date from the 12th c.

Via di Porta S. Sebastiano* (III, *E-F3-4*). This street, lined by low walls, runs through one of the last green areas to survive the burst of construction of the past 20 years; unfortunately it has become a fast-traffic artery linking the Colosseum with Via Appia Antica. The church of *S. Cesareo de Appia** (III, *E3; open by request, tel. 0657285738*) features a late 16th-c. ceiling and a 2nd-c. mosaic. Near the end of the road is the entrance to the **tomb of the Scipioni** (*closed for restoration*), a powerful Roman family buried here from the beginning of the 3rd c. to 139 B.C.

Porta S. Sebastiano** (III, *F4*). Before this gate stands the *Arco di Druso* (211-216), an arch which supported the aqueduct that conveyed water to the Baths of Caracalla; it is surely one of the most monumental gates in the Aurelian walls (built against the barbarian onslaughts, 3rd c. A.D., rebuilt in the 5th c. by Honorius, and restored in the 6th c. by the Byzantine eunuch general Belisarius). It takes its name from the basilica toward which the Roman Appian Way, or Via Appia, led. Inside the gate is the *Museo delle Mura di Roma* (*open 9:30-2; Tue., Thu. and Sat. also 4-7; Sun. 9-1, closed Mon.*), which illustrates the history of the Roman walls. This museum is the beginning of

the walking tour of the **Aurelian walls**, which are particularly well preserved between this gate and the Nuova Porta Ardeatina, 400 m to the west. Six m tall, with a square tower every 100 feet, they were built on existing walls, and have been repeatedly restored and reinforced, especially after the Sack of Rome in 1527.

Porta Latina (III, *E4*). This gate has Roman features; note the travertine arch, the molding of the cornice, and the battlements. Just inside is the *Oratorio di S. Giovanni in Oleo*, an oratory rebuilt in the early 16th c. and restored by F. Borromini. The adjacent church of *S. Giovanni a Porta Latina* is a medieval building with a Romanesque bell tower and a fine fresco cycle in the nave.

S. Maria in Domnica* (III, *C3*). Set atop the Celio, or Caelian Hill, with a portico by A. Sansovino, this church was first rebuilt in the 9th c. and again in the 16th c. by Pope Leo X. Inside, beneath the wooden lacunar ceiling (1566) is a frieze with heraldic devices by G. Romano; on the triumphal arch and in the apse, mosaics* from the reign of Pope Paschal I (early 9th c.). To the left of the church is the entrance to the *Villa Celimontana* (III, *C-D2-3*), a public park. On the right, note the 13th-c. portal* by J. and C. dei Cosmati, beyond which is the *Arco di Dolabella* (III, *C3*), possibly a gate in the Servian Walls. Across the Via della Navicella, a wall conceals the 5th-c. church of **S. Stefano Rotondo*** (*entrance at n. 7 of the Via S. Stefano Rotondo*), the oldest church with a round plan in Rome; note the original colonnade in the outer wall.

Ss. Quattro Coronati* (III, *B3*). In one version, this church is dedicated to four soldiers who became martyrs because they refused to worship a statue of Aesculapius; in another, it was four Dalmatian sculptors who refused to carve such a statue. In any case, it was built before the end of the 6th c., rebuilt in 1111, and given its cloister and oratory in the late 12th c. Note the frescoes, in the church and in the *oratory of S. Silvestro** (*open by request; equire at the Ruota delle Monache*), as well as the star-and-cross decoration, with five majolicas, unique in Rome. Also, note the rare 13th-c. liturgical calendar.

S. Clemente** (III, *B3*). The first church was built here in the 3rd c. over a house built in the 2nd c.; burnt by Norman invaders in 1084, it was replaced with the present church by Pope Paschal II. Renovations were carried out in 1713-19. The lovely interior of the *upper basilica*, with Roman columns and Cosmatesque floor, looks much as it did in the 12th c. (despite the 18th-c. frescoes in the nave); the schola cantorum*, the ciborium, and the bishop's throne all date from the 12th c. The apse is decorated with a magnificent 12th-c. mosaic**; the fresco beneath it is from the 14th c. The Cappella di S. Caterina, in the left aisle, is adorned with frescoes** executed between 1428 and 1431 by Masolino da Panicale and, perhaps, Masaccio. The *lower basilica* (*open 9-12:30 and 3:30-6; Sun. 10-12 and 3:30-6; entrance from the sacristy*) preserves, in the fresco of the nave, one of the earliest documents in vernacular Italian. Beneath the basilica are ancient Roman ruins, as well as a 3rd-c. *mithreum* and a 6th-c. Christian *baptistery*.

Rome: S. Clemente

11 Foro Boario, Aventino, and S. Paolo Fuori le Mura

From the noisy confusion of ancient marketplaces to the silence of Early Christian churches, this route explores the heart of ancient Rome, tucked away in the oxbow curve of the Tiber, near the Isola Tiberina, and Rome's earliest river port; it then goes up into the quiet of the Aventine Hill, a haven of silence just a short walk from the city center, where little villas surrounded by greenery stand beside churches founded in ancient times. A pleasant side trip is the Basilica di S. Paolo Fuori le Mura, or St. Paul without the Walls; inside the 19th-c. exterior, it conceals masterpieces from the 13th c.

Via del Teatro di Marcello (IV, A-B4-5). This is another avenue built under Fascism (1926-41), as part of the route linking Rome and the Lido di Òstia, wiping away a section of the city dating from the Middle Ages.

S. Maria in Campitelli (IV, A4). C. Rainaldi built this remarkable example of late Roman Baroque in 1662-67. The main altar contains the enamelled image (said to work miracles) of S. Maria in Portico Campitelli, dating from the 11th c. The nearby block (between Via de' Funari, Via Caetani, Via delle Botteghe Oscure, and Via Paganica) once belonged to the Mattei family. Worth noting are: at n. 32 in Via Caetani, *Palazzo Mattei di Giove*, begun by C. Maderno in 1598; *Palazzo Mattei di Paganica*, built in 1541, perhaps by Nanni di Baccio Bigio, on the ruins of the theater of Balbus (13 B.C.). In the middle of Piazza Mattei is the *Fontana delle Tartarughe** (Fountain of Turtles), designed by G. della Porta (1581-84; the turtles were added in 1658, probably by G.L. Bernini).

Teatro di Marcello** (IV, A-B4). Begun by Julius Caesar and dedicated in 13 or 11 B.C. by Augustus to his nephew Marcellus, this theater had been abandoned by the 5th c.; it was reused in 1523-27 by B. Peruzzi for the construction of *Palazzo Orsini*, which is centered on the auditorium of the former theater.

Portico di Ottavia (IV, A4). The five Corinthian columns with trabeation once formed part of a building erected in 146 B.C. and rebuilt by Augustus in 27-23 B.C. for his sister Octavia; it was again rebuilt by Septimius Severus and Caracalla (A.D. 203). The propylaeum was, from the Middle Ages to the 19th c., the site of a lively market, dealing especially in fish (hence the name of the church of *S. Angelo in Pescheria*, which is preceded by the *Casa dei Vallati*, dating from the 14th c. and restored in 1927). On the left side of Via del Portico d'Ottavia are unremarkable buildings where the Jewish ghetto once stood (from 1555 to 1848). In the Sinagoga Nuova, or New Synagogue, there is a historical exhibit relating to the Jewish community in Rome (*Mostra della Comunità Ebraica di Roma; open Mon.-Thu., 9-5; Fri., 9-2; Sun., 9-12:30; closed Sat.*). Further along the same street is the *Casa dei Manili**; on the facade is the date of construction: 2221 after the foundation of Rome, i.e., A.D. 1468.

S. Nicola in Carcere (IV, B4). The facade, by G. della Porta, is made from the remains of two columns from an ancient temple of Juno (197 B.C.). The right side features two others from the Temple of Hope (built after the First Punic War); the left side, columns from the Temple of Janus (260 B.C.). This medieval church makes much use of ancient material. Across the street, note the *Area Sacra di S. Omobono**, dating from the 6th c. B.C.

Isola Tiberina* (IV, B4). Linked to the Tiber's left bank by the 2000-year-old *Ponte Fabricio** and to the right bank by the *Ponte Cestio* (the central arch is ancient, the rest was rebuilt in the 19th c.), this ship-shaped island was sacred to Aesculapius. Pope Otto III built the church of *S. Bartolomeo all'Isola*, rebuilt in the late 16th c. From the island's southern tip you can see the remains of Rome's first stone bridge (181-179 B.C.), known as Ponte Rotto, or broken bridge.

Piazza della Bocca della Verità (IV, B-C4-5). This square stands on the site of the Foro Boario (the livestock market in classical times), and is lined by two Republican Age temples: the square-plan *Tempio della Fortuna Virile** (IV, B5), and the round-plan *Tempio di Vesta** (IV, B4-5), the oldest surviving marble temple. The *Casa dei Crescenzi** dates from 1040-65, and includes classical decorative motifs. Dating from Roman times are the monuments in the nearby Via del Velabro: the 4th-c. *Arco di Giano** (IV, B5), or Arch of Janus; the *Arco degli Argentari*; and the *Cloaca Maxima* (open by request), which, according to legend, was built by Tarquinius Priscus to drain the Valle del Foro. To the left of the Arco degli Argentari is the medieval church of *S. Giorgio in Ve-*

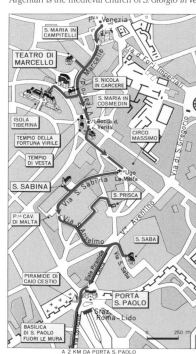

A 2 KM DA PORTA S. PAOLO

bro (the Romanesque portico and campanile were almost entirely destroyed by a terrorist bombing in July 1993, and have almost been rebuilt), dedicated by the moneychangers in A.D. 204 to Septimius Severus and his family.

Maria in Cosmedin* (IV, C5). Built in the 6th c., was given to the Greek community, who so embellished it that it was called "Kosmidion," or lovely [ence], Cosmedin). The bell tower* to the right of [l]e portico dates from the 12th c. Inside the porti[c]o is the famous Bocca della Verità**, or Mouth of [T]ruth, a sewer cover, carved with a mascaron, which [p]opular tradition said would bite the hand of a liar. [In]*side* is an 8th-c. mosaic floor, a Gothic baldachin [by] D. di Cosma il Giovane (1294), and 8th-c. fres[c]oes; the fragment of mosaic* in the sacristy came [fr]om the original St. Peter's.

[Ci]rco Massimo (IV, C-D5-6). The Circus Maximus, [cl]early visible from Piazzale Ugo La Malfa, was be[gu]n, according to tradition, by Tarquinius Priscus, [o]ne of the seven kings of Rome, in the valley be[tw]een the Palatine and the Aventine hills, and it re[m]ained in use until A.D. 549. It seated 300,000, and [is] now a park. From the square, view* of the ruins [of] the imperial palaces on the Palatine Hill; also a [fi]ne view of the nearby *Parco Savello* (IV, C4-5).

Sabina* (IV, C-D4). The intervention in the first [h]alf of the 20th c. restored this basilica to its origi[n]al appearance; this may be the most complete ex[a]mple of a 5th-c. Christian church. The cloister and [be]ll tower date from the 13th c. In the atrium, the [po]rtal preserves the original 5th-c. carved wooden [do]ors**. The *interior* features a fragment of mosaic [o]ver the doorway with an inscription* in golden let[te]rs commemorating the foundation of the church; [a] 5th-c. frieze with red and green panels over the ar[c]ades, and the schola cantorum, or choir, made of [re]assembled ancient fragments (5th-9th c.).

[C]omplesso dell'Ordine dei Cavalieri di Malta [(I]V, D4). *Open Sat., 10 and 11.* The headquarters of [th]e Order of the Knights of Malta are enclosed with[in] a massive wall (if you peek through the keyhole, [y]ou can see the dome of St. Peter's), and was given [it]s present appearance in the 18th c. by G.B. Piranesi, [w]ho rebuilt the church of S. Maria del Priorato, as [w]ell as the villa and the grounds.

Prisca (IV, D5). An archeological complex worth [a] tour lies under the church, which is dedicated to [a] 1st-c. martyr. The complex in question is a [M]*ithraeum* (open 2nd, 4th Sun. of the month, 3-4) [w]ith partial ruins of a 1st-c. home, a nymphaeum [bu]ilt during the reign of Trajan, and a number of [ro]oms dedicated to the ancient Persian god Mithras, [d]ecorated with frescoes depicting initiatory rites of [th]is cult.

Saba* (IV, E5). Legend has it that this church was [bu]ilt on the site of the house of the mother of Pope [G]regory I the Great; certainly an old monastery [st]ood here, at one point Cistercian. Note the portal [b]y J. di Lorenzo di Cosma, dated 1205; the floor in[si]de is also Cosmatesque, and there are handsome [la]te 13th-c. frescoes.

Porta S. Paolo** (IV, E4-5). This gate was the ancient "Porta Ostiensis" in the Aurelian walls (the inner front, with two passages, dates from the 3rd c.; the outer front, set between two semicylindrical crenelated towers, dates from the reign of Honorius); it marked the beginning of the Via Ostiensis, which led to the seaport of ancient Rome. The adjacent **Piramide di Caio Cestio*** (IV, E-F4) is a pyramid standing 36 m tall, which was built in just 330 days in the late 1st c. B.C.

Centrale Termoelettrica Montemartini (*off map*). The original electric plant was open in 1911-13. It has recently been turned into a cultural site (*open Tue.-Sun., 9-30-7*) where, next to the old machinery, more then 400 pieces from the Musei Capitolini (see route 1) and the former Antiquarium comunale are on display. Among them, of note are the group with the presentation of Hercules at Olympus, the pediment of the temple of Apollo Sosianus, and a huge mosaic with hunting scenes.

S. Paolo Fuori le Mura.* The largest of the patriarchal basilicas after St. Peter's, St. Paul without the Walls was built in the time of Constantine over the grave of St. Paul, and consecrated in 324; it was enlarged and embellished over the centuries, until it was entirely razed by a fire on 15-16 July 1823. It was rebuilt to the plan and size of the original, and consecrated in 1854. On the Via Ostiense stands the campanile, known as the "faro," or "lighthouse," for its unusual shape. The *interior*, 131.65 m long, 65 m wide, and 29.7 m tall, glitters with marble, mostly from the 19th c. To the right of the main entrance are the bronze doors* of the ancient basilica (1070). The frieze over the arcades features medallions with portraits of the popes from St. Peter to John Paul II. The triumphal arch bears 5th-c. mosaics. Over the main altar, note the Gothic ciborium** by A. di Cambio (1285), with bas-reliefs and statues; on the right, a paschal candelabrum* by N. di Angelo and P. Vassalletto (12th c.). In the apse is a mosaic* from the time of Honorius III. The adjacent *cloister*, completed by 1214, is in part by the Vassalletto. Note the *paintings* by Bramantino and Cigoli.

12 Trastevere

This was a section of Rome originally frequented by merchants and pilgrims, who arrived in town near the Isola Tiberina and received care and assistance in the many hospitals and hospices in the area. Trastevere is now a district which bears a quintessentially Roman atmosphere; the Viale di Trastevere follows a maze of narrow lanes and small squares where you can often find open-air restaurants. There are also numerous churches and art collections, as well as breathtaking views, such as the one you can enjoy from the top of the Janiculum.

S. Carlo ai Catinari (IV, A4). Barnabite monks had this church built by R. Rosati, who designed and erected it (1612-20; note the cupola), and G.B. Soria, who did the facade (1636-38). The frescoes on the interior of the facade are by M. and G. Preti, those in the spandrels of the cupola are by Domenichino; the Cappella di S. Cecilia* features decorations by A. Gherardi (1692-1700); the panel on the main altar is by P. da Cortona.

S. Crisogono (IV, *B3*). Standing just behind the 13th-c. *Palazzetto Anguillara*, with a tower, on Piazza Sonnino, is the church of S. Crisogono, first built as a basilica in the 5th c., rebuilt in its present form in 1123-29, then restored in 1620-26. Inside, note the 17th-c. stucco decorations and the wooden coffered ceiling, the 13th-c. Cosmatesque floor, and the mosaic from the school of Pietro Cavallini in the vault of the apse. In the nearby church of *S. Agata* is the image of the Madonna de' Noantri, patron saint of the "rione," or neighborhood.

S. Cecilia in Trastevere* (IV, *C4*). This 9th-c. church was built on the site of the house of the saint's husband; she was martyred under the reign of Marcus Aurelius. Much of the interior and the facade were rebuilt in the 18th c., though the mosaic frieze in the portico and the campanile date from the 12th c. In the vestibule, funerary monuments by P. Taccone (right; late 14th c.) and M. da Fiesole (left; ca. 1473). At the foot of the right aisle, a corridor, with frescoes by P. Brill, leads to the calidarium (note the ancient steam pipes), where the saint was steamed over three days before her martyrdom. In the presbytery, the Gothic ciborium* by A. di Cambio (1293); beneath the main altar, a statue of S. Cecilia* by S. Maderno (1600), who depicted the body as it was found in its tomb, in 1599; over the apse is a great mosaic* dating from ca. 820. The *nun's choir* (*open Tue. and Thu., 10-11:30*) is decorated with a Last Judgment* by P. Cavallini (ca. 1289-93, and rediscovered in 1900; the finest piece of pre-Giotto painting in Rome).

Ospizio di S. Michele a Ripa Grande (IV, *C-D3-4*). Originally a school for boys in the 17th c., and later the chief center for education and charity in Rome, it was turned over to the state in 1969.

The nearby **Porta Portese** is worth a mention not for its artistic value, but because it is the site of one of the liveliest markets of second-hand clothes and objects, held every Sunday morning.

S. Francesco a Ripa (IV, *C3*). The original church was founded in the 10th c. but was completely rebuilt in 1681-85 by M. De Rossi; when St. Francis came to Rome he stayed in the adjacent convent. In the left transept, note the statue of the Blessed Ludovica Albertoni* by Bernini (1671-75).

S. Maria in Trastevere* (IV, *B2-3*). In the heart of Trastevere, this church dates from the 4th c. but was rebuilt in its modern form in 1138-48. The facade preserves a 13th-c. mosaic; before it is a portico, to the side a Romanesque bell tower. You enter under three doorways with re-used cornices from the imperial period. *Inside*, a nave with two aisles with large ancient trabeated columns run beneath a rich wooden coffered ceiling designed by Domenichino (1617). The mosaics** near the windows are by P. Cavallini (1291). In the chapel to the left of the apse, note the 6th-c. encaustic painting**.

Museo di Roma in Trastevere (IV, *B2*). *Open 1 7:30; closed Mon.* This museum documents Roma popular traditions and the city's urban, econom and social development, from the 18th c. onwar note the watercolors by E. Roesler Franz.

Piazza Trilussa (IV, *B2-3*). This square stands on th riverfront boulevard, or Lungotevere, at the *Ponte S sto* (IV, *A-B3*), a bridge rebuilt under Pope Sixtus I in 1473-75 (the only bridge built over the Tiber fro classical times until 1870) on the site of an olde span; it is adorned with the 17th-c. *Fontana dell'Acqu Paola* and a monument to the Roman poet Triluss

Via della Lungara (IV, *A-B2*). This marks the b ginning of a boulevard built by Julius II, to plans b Bramante, along with the parallel Via Giulia (se route 4), and the *Porta Settimiana* (IV, *B2*), a reco struction of a passage through the Aurelian wal built by Alexander VI. At the end of the first road o to the left from Via della Lungara is the *Orto Bota ico*, or botanical garden (*open summer, Tue.-Sat., 6:30; winter, 9-4:30*).

Palazzo Corsini (IV, *A2*). This building takes name from the last family to own it; the Corsini pu chased it in 1736. In the 17th c. it was the residenc of Queen Christina of Sweden, and the Accadem dell'Arcadia was founded here. F. Fuga designed th facade overlooking Via della Lungara. The "cultu al" tradition of the palazzo continues even now, it houses both the *Accademia dei Lincei*, founded 1603, and the Galleria Corsini.

Galleria Corsini.* *Open Tue.-Sun., 9-7.* The rece restoration of the rooms which house it, has give new splendor to the only private Roman art colle tion still intact, begun in the mid-18th c. by Cardin Neri Corsini. Among the 16th-/17th-c. artists, Italia and not, whose work is featured here, we shou mention: G. da Milano, F. Francia, Fra' Angelico, Fr Bartolomeo, J. Bassano, Rubens, Van Dyck, Murillo, van Cleve, A. Algardi, G.B. Foggini, Caravaggio, O. Ge tileschi, Maestro del Giudizio di Salomone, Tournier, P. Wouwerman, G. Dughet, A. Brueghel, Berentz, C. Maratta, N. Poussin, G.B. Piazzetta, G. Rer G. Lanfranco, D. Creti, M. de Caro, Spagnoletto,

Gargiulo, and L. Giordano. The Corsini goblet and throne are Roman works dating from the 1st c. B.C. **Farnesina**** (IV, A2). *Open 9-1; closed Sun.* This villa, a masterpiece of Renaissance architecture, was built by B. Peruzzi (1506-1520) for the Sienese banker A. Chigi. In 1580 it became property of the Farnese family; it lost its gardens and the loggia (attributed to Raphael) when the Lungotevere, or boulevards running along the Tiber, were built. Inside, where the Gabinetto Nazionale delle Stampe is located, you can visit the Loggia di Psiche, frescoed** to cartoons by Raphael, 1517; the Sala del Fregio, with a frieze with mythological scenes painted partly by Peruzzi; the Sala di Galatea, with **frescoes**** by Raphael (1513-14), S. del Piombo, Peruzzi, and D. Beccafumi; the Salone delle Prospettive, painted by Peruzzi with perspectival subjects (1518-19); and the bedroom, with a fresco by Sodoma (1517).

S. Pietro in Montorio** (IV, B2). This church was heavily rebuilt in the late 15th-c.; its name comes from the ancient name of the Janiculum ("Mons Aureus"). Inside are a Flagellation* by S. del Piombo and a chapel designed by G.L. Bernini. In the cloister, to the right of the church, is the little **Tempietto del Bramante****, 1508-1512, a small building in the form of a classical temple, supposedly built on the site of St. Peter's crucifixion. Fine view* from the square in front of the church.

Passeggiata di Gianicolo* (IV, A-B1). Beginning from the **fountain of the Acqua Paola** (IV, B2), built by F. Ponzio and G. Fontana for Paul V (1608-1612), the promenade offers one of the loveliest strolls in Rome, overlooking the city. The finest view can be had from the *equestrian monument to G. Garibaldi* (IV, B1; 1895), though another fine panorama** can be enjoyed from the *Faro* (IV, A1; III, F2), a lighthouse given to Rome by the Italians in Argentina.

S. Onofrio al Gianicolo (I, F2). This church was begun in 1439 and completed in the 16th c. (the frescoes in the portico are by Domenichino, those in the apse are by B. Peruzzi, or perhaps by J. Ripanda). The great poet Torquato Tasso lived in the nearby convent, where he died in 1595.

Villa Doria Pamphilj. This is the largest public park in Rome, once a hunting preserve and pleasure park in the 18th c. (note the *Casino d'Allegrezze*). The avenues are named after major events in the history of the Roman Republic.

---

13 Via Appia Antica and EUR

In the southern section of Rome you find two attractions. The first one is the best known, and comprises a succession of ancient tombs from the dawn of Christianity, and Roman ruins, lining the ancient Appian Way. The second attraction is unique: the EUR, with buildings that hark back to the classical style, and glorify Roman Fascism in the 1920s-40s.

Via Appia Antica.** The "queen of the roads" of ancient Rome was opened in 312 B.C. by the censor Appius Claudius Caecus. The Appian Way followed an older route toward the Alban Hills, and eventually extended all the way to Brindisi, becoming the main route to the East; it fell into disrepair in the Middle Ages, and was replaced in the 16th c. by the Via Appia Nuova. It was rediscovered in the late 18th c. Not until 1988 did the Region of Latium establish an archeological park along the road. This park is noteworthy both for the ancient artifacts displayed and for the lovely natural setting, as yet undeveloped.

Domine Quo Vadis? Here, it is said, Jesus appeared to St. Peter as he fled Rome. When the apostle asked Christ, "Domine quo vadis?" (Lord, where are you going?), Christ supposedly replied, "Eo Romam iterum crucifigi," (I am going to Rome, to be crucified once again). Peter then returned to the city, where he was martyred. The church was given its modern appearance in the 16th c.

Catacombe di S. Callisto.* *Open 8:30-12 and 2:30-5:30; closed Wed.* The catacombs were the official cemetery of the popes in the 3rd c., discovered in 1849. Note the Crypt of the Popes, the tomb of St. Cecilia, with 9th-c. frescoes, and the Cubicles of the Sacraments, adorned with early 3rd-c. paintings.

S. Sebastiano.* This basilica, founded in the 4th c. near the cemetery where the apostles Peter and Paul were briefly interred and where St. Sebastian was buried, was rebuilt in the 17th c. by F. Ponzio and G. Vasanzio. In the first chapel on the right is a stone with a footprint imbedded in it, supposedly left by Jesus during the famous "Domine quo vadis?" episode (see above). Also, note statue of St. Sebastian by A. Giorgetti (1671-72). Beneath the church are the ancient **Catacombe di S. Sebastiano** (*open 8:30-12 and 2:30-5:30; winter, until 5; closed Wed.*), unfortunately in poor shape, because they were the only usable Christian cemetery for centuries. Note a bust of the saint by G.L. Bernini and a chapel dedicated to Pope Honorius III, with 13th-c. frescoes.

Complesso di Massenzio. This archeological complex (3rd-4th c.) comprises the Circus of Maxentius (it seated 10,000), and the mausoleum of Romulus, built by Maxentius for his son; still to be excavated is the imperial palace, located between the circus and the tomb.

Tomba di Cecilia Metella.* *Open 9-one hour before sunset.* As an inscription on a plaque notes, a monument in this road commemorates the daughter of Metellus Creticus – and wife of Crassus – and was erected around 50 B.C. Set on a square base is a cylindrical structure, crowned by a frieze with relief carvings; the crenelation dates from the Middle Ages, when this tomb was used as the donjon of a fortified castle.

Tomba dei Curiazi. Situated in the heart of the ancient section of the Via Appia, and amidst the lovely landscape of the Roman Campagna, dotted with ruins and umbrella pines, this small hillock, supposedly the Tomb of the Curiatii, actually covers ruins from the late Roman Republic. According to tradition, this is where the combat was fought between

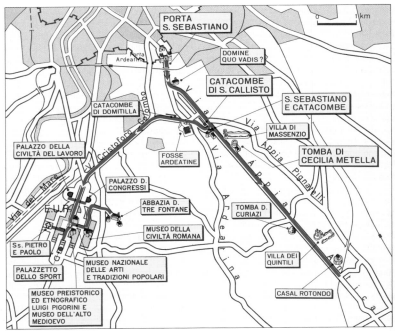

the three Horatii brothers, champions of Rome, and the three Curiatii brothers, champions of Alba Longa, to determine which city should rule the other. Note the nearby tombs of the Horatii, also dating from the late Republic.

Villa dei Quintili. *Open 9-one hour before sunset; closed Mon.* This villa, originally the property of the Quintili family and later of the Emperor Commodus, was so large that the area is still known as "Old Rome." From the Via Appia you can see the majestic arches of the aqueduct that supplied water to the villa. Note the *Casal Rotondo*, a cylindrical tomb.

Fosse Ardeatine. *Open Mon.-Fri., 8:15-6:45; Sat.-Sun., 8-15-3:30.* The atrocious massacre that made these Ardeatine Caves sadly famous occurred on 24 March 1944, when, as a reprisal for a partisan attack in Via Rasella, the Germans slaughtered 335 civilians in these pozzolana quarries. The adjacent *museum (open same hours as above)* contains documents on the Nazi occupation of Rome, following Italy's attempted separate peace.

Catacombe di Domitilla. *Open 8:30-12 and 2:30-5; closed Wed.* These catacombs developed between the 3rd and 5th c., and extend underground through nearly 15 km of tunnels. The church of *Ss. Nereo e Achilleo* above them was built in the late 4th c. to house the relics of martyrs who were killed under Diocletian; one of the little columns of the ciborium bears a rare depiction of the Beheading of a Martyr.

Via Cristoforo Colombo (III, *F3*). This was originally part of the Via Imperiale, which linked Piazza Venezia to the Lido di Roma; its name changes as soon as it exits the Aurelian walls.

EUR. The planned Universal Exposition of 1942 offered Italy's Fascist regime an excuse to build a new district to the south of Rome, planned in monumental style, in the wake of the victorious war in Ethiopia, by M. Piacentini. Work was halted in 1943. Following WWII, the project was altered, making it more of a business center, but the original architectural design was maintained; the sports facilities were built for the Rome Olympics of 1960. Since the 1970s, most of the monumental buildings have been turned into museums, all of which propose workshops for children and young people (*tel. 0684123127*).

Palazzo della Civiltà del Lavoro.* The "Square Colosseum," as this building is also called, was based on the Flavian amphitheater and was built (1938-43) with a distinctive array of 216 arches on its four faces. Facing it is the *Palazzo dei Congressi* (VII, *B2-3*) designed by A. Libera and built from 1938 to 1954.

Museo Nazionale delle Arti e Tradizioni Popolari. *Open 9-8; closed Mon.* Housed in a building erected from 1939 to 1942, surrounding *Piazza Marconi*, this museum is devoted to Italian customs and traditions, from the earliest times until the 20th c. There are 750 costumes and 3000 pieces of jewelry in the collection.

Museo Nazionale Preistorico-Etnografico Luigi Pigorini.* *Open Mon.-Sun., 9-8.* This is one of the leading European museums in the field of ethnography, and since 1962 its collections have been housed in the Palazzo delle Scienze (1939-43). They originated in the 17th c. from the "scientific research" of Athanasius Kircher, who wished to "document the lives of modern-day savages in order to understand those of prehistoric savages." The collection grew greatly through the tireless efforts, in the late 19th c. and early 20th c., of Luigi Pigorini.

The *prehistoric section* contains material from Lazio (Latium), the region of Rome, dating from the late Paleolithic to the early Bronze Age, and much material concerning the transition from the late Bronze Age to the early Iron Age (10th c. B.C.); also, material on the Villanovian culture of Etruria, Africa, Asia, America and Oceania.

Ss. Pietro e Paolo. This "neighborhood church" has a distinctive cupola; built in white marble, it was designed in 1938 and consecrated in 1955.

Palazzo dello Sport. Perched high atop a hill, overlooking a man-made lake around which Via Cristoforo Colombo runs, splitting into two, is what may fairly be called the finest athletic facility built for the 1960 Olympics, held in Rome. Designed by M. Piacentini and P.L. Nervi (1958-60), this sports arena holds 16,000 spectators. The modern building on the eastern shore of the lake houses the *Museo delle Poste e delle Telecomunicazioni* (*open 9-1; closed Sat.-Sun.*), a museum devoted to the history of the mail and telecommunications, with collections ranging from the earliest known letter slot (1633) to the automatic electronic calculator "ELEA 9003," designed by E. Fermi.

Museo dell'Alto Medioevo. *Open 9-2; Sun. and holidays, 9-1; closed Mon.* This museum of the High Middle Ages has collections that include tomb furnishings, goldwork, reliefs, and Coptic fabrics.

Museo della Civiltà Romana.* *Open 9-7; Sun., 9-1:30; closed Mon. (rooms 1-15; the room of the Trajan Column is closed for restoration).* This museum occupies a building in the Fascist style, constructed in 1939-52 for the CEO of Fiat. The materials displayed here, all casts and models designed to illustrate Roman civilization and its spread through the ancient world, come from two major exhibitions: the "Mostra Archeologica" held at the Baths of Diocletian in 1911, and the "Mostra Augustea della Romanità" of 1937; they were placed in this museum in 1955. Of special note are the **model of Rome** in the time of Constantine, in 1:250 scale, and the casts of Trajan's Column (Colonna Traiana), made at the behest of Napoleon III in 1860.

Abbazia delle Tre Fontane. According to legend, the three fountains mentioned in the name of this abbey originated when the head of St. Paul, who was decapitated here, bounced three times; archeologists tell us only that there was a Christian cemetery here in the 3rd c., a church in the 4th c., and a new church and abbey built in 1140 by the followers of St. Benedict. The complex comprises the church of *Ss. Vincenzo e Anastasio* *, founded by Honorius I in 625 and completed by Honorius III in 1221, the church of *S. Maria Scala Coeli*, built by G. della Porta (1581-84), and, at the end of the avenue, the church of *S. Paolo*, rebuilt in 1599-1601 by G. della Porta and containing the three fountains (the mosaic floor is from Òstia).

Sabbioneta*

Elev. 18 m, pop. 4490; Lombardia (Lombardy), province of Mantova. It is said that the duke Vespasiano Gonzaga, a valiant soldier wounded time and time again in battle, carried Vitruvius's renowned architectural treatise with him at all times, even during hard campaigning. When the 16th-c. duke drew up the plans for his little capital city, he imagined it as perfectly finished in every detail, within the star-shaped perimeter of the walls. Sabbioneta – honored as a 'small latter-day Athens' for the enlightened and very learned court that was held there – is an exemplary model of an 'ideal city', conceived and built to suit its prince, in perfect accordance with the canons of Renaissance urban planning.

Opening hours. *Guided tours for groups through the main buildings, starting from the "Pro Loco" (Piazza d'Armi); Apr.-Sep., Tue.-Sun., 9:30-12:30 and 2:30-6; holidays until 7; Oct.-Mar., Tue.-Sun., 9:30-12:30 and 2:30-5; holidays until 6; for reservation, tel. 0375221044.*

Piazza Ducale* (or *Garibaldi*). This is the center of Sabbioneta. Partly bounded by small portico-fronted palazzetti, this square preserves its ancient appearance. Note the Palazzo Ducale and the **Parrocchiale** (parish church, 1581), which contains the 18th-c. Cappella del Sacro Cuore, a chapel by Antonio Bibiena.

Palazzo Ducale.* This ducal palace was built in 1568 and features a ground-level portico. The "piano nobile" has marble windows, and there is a turret in the center of the facade. In the interior are halls with carved wooden ceilings and frescoes by Bernardino Campi, Alberto Cavalli, and others. In particular, note the four wooden equestrian statues of the Gonzagas, and the Galleria degli Antenati, with busts in stucco of the dynasty.

Behind the palazzo is the church of the **Incoronata** (1588), with an octagonal plan, with the mausoleum of Vespasiano Gonzaga by G.B. Della Porta (1592) and the bronze statue* of the duke, by L. Leoni (1588).

Museo d'Arte Sacra. *Open holidays, 10:30-12:30 and 2:30-6:30; weekdays, by reservation, tel. 0375 220299; guided tour included in the one organized by the APT.* Not far away, the parrocchiale, or parish church, in Via Pesenti 6, contains the treasure of the Gonzaga dynasty: ancient silver, fabrics, and clothing, manuscripts, charters, and a portable organ from the 16th c.

Teatro Olimpico.* A masterpiece by Vincenzo Scamozzi, who built it in 1588. The interior has a rectangular plan, with tiered steps and loggia. On the walls, excellent frescoes of the Venetian school.

Piazza d'Armi or *Castello*. This is the ancient parade ground, with a Roman column in the center. It is surrounded on one side by the long buildings of the Galleria degli Antichi (1584).

Palazzo del Giardino.* Built between 1577 and 1588 as a pleasure palace for the prince, this holiday home is filled with halls and antechambers, decorated with frescoes, stuccoes, and grotesques by the Campi brothers and the school of Giulio Romano; from here you pass into the *Galleria degli Antichi*, 97 m long, with a wooden ceiling and walls decorated with frescoes.

Salerno

Elev. 4 m, pop. 147,010; Campania, provincial capital. The old town lies on a slope, with all its Norman landmarks and monuments, overlooking the sea.

Places of interest. Piazza Amendola. The square is the political heart of the city, lined with the Town Hall (Palazzo di Città) to the east, and the Prefettura to the west. A large green expanse separates it from the late 19th-c. *Teatro Verdi*, where a tree-lined avenue starts, known as *Lungomare Trieste.*
Via dei Mercanti. Narrow, twisting, rich in atmosphere, the street starts from the Arco di Arechi and is the central thoroughfare of the old town. Follow it and you will reach the Baroque church of *S. Giorgio* (in a side street), which has frescoes by Solimena (1675). Of interest are two museums: the **Collezione di Ceramiche Alfonso Tafuri** (*open Mon.-Sat., 9-1; Thu. also 4-7; by request, tel. 089227782*), with ceramic works from Campania; and the *Pinacoteca Provinciale*, in Palazzo Pinto, (*open 9-1 and 4-7; closed Mon.*), with works by A. da Salerno, M. Pino, F. Guarino e painters active in the territory of the city.
Duomo.** A remarkable monument, with a long and complex architectural history; it was built (1076-85) at the behest of Robert Guiscard, when Salerno was the capital of the Norman realm. It stands at the top of a stairway with, alongside, a campanile* (12th c.), surmounted by intertwined arches; with ancient columns; raised Islamic arch-

es; the intarsiate mullioned loggia of the great atrium – all indicate the composite culture of the Norman era. The Romanesque portal has celebrated bronze doors* from Constantinople (1099). In the *interior*, with a nave with two aisles, note the exquisite works of art: the two mosaic-encrusted **ambos**** (13th c., on the right; 12th c., on the left) adjacent to the iconostasis* (1175); mosaics in the right apse, where Pope Gregory VII is buried, in the vault of the left apse, and on the marble screen of the main altar; the monument to Queen Margherita di Durazzo* (15th c.), and a Baroque *crypt* with the supposed relics of the Evangelist Matthew.
The **Museo Diocesano** (*temporarily closed*) contains, among other items, an illuminated Exultet* from the 13th c. and an ivory **altar frontal**** from the 12th c.
Castello di Arechi (elev. 263 m; *open 9-one hour before sunset; closed Mon.*). High overhead stands the impressive castle built by successive waves of Byzantines, Longobards, and Normans. It boasts a fine view and an exquisite collection of ceramics, ranging from the 8th to the 19th c.
Museo Archeologico Provinciale (*open 9-7*). The Archeological Museum of the Province of Salerno is located inside the S. Benedetto complex. On exhibit are prehistoric stone artifacts, found in the nearby area of Palinuro, funerary furnishings dating from the Iron Age, and several finds of Etruscan origin and of the same period from Campania.

San Clemente a Casàuria* (Abbazia di / Abbey of)

Elev. 194 m, pop. 902; Abruzzo, province of Pescara, township of Castiglione a Casàuria. This Benedictine abbey lies in the valley of the Pescara River, not far from the Rome-Pescara highway. It was founded by Louis II, emperor of the West and king of Italy, in A.D. 871; in so doing, the emperor was fulfilling a vow he had taken while imprisoned in the duchy of Benevento. In the following year, he had the relics of the pope and martyr St. Clement brought there, through the concession of Pope Adrian II. The abbey suffered devastation and looting but was rebuilt in the 12th c., and remained a powerful institution until the 14th c. The remarkable architecture of the church can be glimpsed at the end of a short drive; only the ground floor of the monastery survives. The name Casàuria comes from "Casa Aurea" or "Casa Urii," Latin names that hark back to a temple of Jove Urios, bringer of winds.

Places of interest. Abbey church.* The modern building dates substantially from the 12th-c. reconstruction. The facade, with a handsome portico*, has a lovely central portal with bronze doors* (1192). In the nave, note the pulpit* set on four columns, with lavish decorative friezes and rosettes in the classical style and the 12th-c. candelabra for

Salerno: Duomo

S. Clemente a Casàuria: interior

the Paschal candles; in the apse, an Early Christian sarcophagus serves as an altar, beneath a 15th-c. ciborium*. In the *crypt* part of the 11th-c. apse survives, set within its 12th-c. successor. In the surrounding park, note Roman and medieval architectural fragments. The monastery is the new home of the *Museo dell'Abbazia* (*tel. 0858885828*), which has on display plaques and other finds from the Roman site of *Interpromium*.

San Gimignano*

Elev. 324 m, pop. 6956; Toscana (Tuscany), province of Siena. In the 13th c. there were nine "hospitatores," or hotels, for the merchants who flocked here; the pride of the newly rich families were 72 tall towers (by law, none could overtop the *Rognosa*, the tower of the town government). Saffron, too, was worked here, and sold throughout Europe. Nowadays, of the original towers, only 15 survive; a sudden economic decline preserved this skyline, so typical of a medieval hill town.

Getting around. The area inside the walls is closed to private traffic; with prior authorization, tourists may drive to their hotels. Large parking areas are located near the walls, but in high season these may be full. The routes shown are walking tours.

Places of interest. Porta S. Giovanni. This 13th-c. gate has a distinctive Sienese flathead arch, and is part of the **medieval walls*** that surround the center (rebuilt in 1262) and open onto the Via Francigena, the main axis of the little town.

Via S. Giovanni. This road runs slightly uphill past many 12th/13th-c. buildings: to the right, the remains of the Pisan Romanesque facade of **S. Francesco**, then tower-houses and, at left, at n. 40, the elegant **Palazzo Pratellesi**, now the *town library*, which boasts a collection of over 10,000 manuscripts. Be-

coming even more medieval, on the left is the tall *Torre Cugnanesi*, and just beyond, the **Arco dei Becci**, an arch through which you enter Piazza della Cisterna; on the right, the *Torre dei Becci*.

Via Quercecchio. Along this road, note the Oratorio di S. Francesco, now a small **Museo Ornitologico** (*open Apr.-Sep., 11-6*), or museum of ornithology. A series of stairways leads up to the **Rocca di Montestaffoli**, a fortress built in 1353 and dismantled in 1558. Note the pentagonal plan and surviving walls; the sole surviving tower affords a fine view** of the town's central group of towers.

Piazza della Cisterna.* Triangular in shape, this square is linked to Piazza del Duomo by an open passageway, forming a harmonious set of spaces that have been the center of San Gimignano since the 13th c. The cistern, in the middle of the huge space paved with herringbone brickwork, dates from 1237 and was enlarged in 1346. To the right of the Arco dei Becci, entering the square, are Casa Razzi, Casa Salvestrini (now a hotel), and the 13th-c. **Palazzo Tortoli-Treccani** (n. 22). Across the square, *Palazzo dei Cortesi* (n.5), with the tall Torre del Diavolo; also note the twin towers of the *Ardinghelli*, built in the 13th c. and diverging slightly.

Piazza del Duomo.* Linked to Piazza della Cisterna, and paved with the same herringbone brickwork, this square is lined with medieval houses and towers. Overlooking it is the Collegiata, or collegiate church, to the left of which is the facade of Palazzo del Popolo (see below). Across the square is the ancient **Palazzo del Podestà*** (1239), with its handsome loggia and massive tower called the *Torre Rognosa* (51 m tall); nearby, at the mouth of Via S. Matteo, are the *Torre Chigi* (1280) and the twin towers known as *Salvucci*.

Collegiata.* *Open 21 Jan.-28 Feb., 9:45-12 and 3:15-4:30; Tue., 9:30-5; Sun. and holidays, 1-7; Apr.-Oct., 9:30-7:30, Sat., 9:30-5; Sun. and holidays, 1-5; Nov.-20 Jan., 9:30-5; Sun. and holidays, 1-5.* This 12th-c. Romanesque building, with a simple 13th-c. facade, has been renovated and restored many times. Inside are paintings and sculpture by great artists: G and B. da Maiano, T. di Bartolo, B. Gozzoli, J. della Quercia, B. da Siena and G. da Asciano, B. di Fredi, D. Ghirlandaio, and A. da Colle. Of particular interest is the **Cappella di S. Fina*** (*closed during mass*), a chapel which is one of the most significant works of the Tuscan Renaissance. From the left aisle, you enter the small 14th-c. cloister of S. Giovanni, open on Piazza Pecori.

Museo d'Arte Sacra. *Open Apr.-Oct., 9:30-7:30; Nov.-Mar., 9-5.* In the tiny Piazza Pecori, the museum comprises five halls inside *Palazzo della Propositura*, with mullioned windows. Note 16th-c. an Egyptian floral-pattern carpet*, a marble bust by B. da Maiano (1493), the 15th-c. altar frontal of the "golden doves;"* the panel of the Madonna della Rosa by B. di Fredi, a painted wooden Crucifix* by G. da Maiano.

Palazzo del Popolo.* Built in 1288 and enlarged in 1323, this building has lost its crenelation but preserves its mayoral crests and three rows of windows; note, at left, two large arcades* and, at right, the *Torre*

San Gimignano: Piazza della Cisterna

Grossa* (54 m; 1311; *open Mar.-Oct., 9:30-7:20; Nov.-Feb., 10:30-4:20*). Fine view from top*. In the courtyard is a cistern (1361), and under the portico a fresco by Sodoma (1507). An exterior stairway leads up to the Museo Civico.

Museo Civico.* *Open Mar.-Oct., 9:30-7:20; Nov.-Feb. (closed Fri.), 10:30-4:20*. On the *first floor* of Palazzo del Popolo is the enormous *Sala di Dante*, adorned by the Maestà*, a fresco by L. Memmi (1317); an inlaid door leads to the Sala delle Adunanze Segrete (Hall of Secret Assemblies); note the chairs, from 1475) and another adjacent room, with pharmacist's vases from Faenza (16th-17th c.), Florence, and Siena. *Second floor*: Camera del Podestà, frescoed by M. di Filippuccio, and three halls used as a gallery, with Tuscan school paintings (13th-15th c.): C. di Marcovaldo, B. Gozzoli, Filippino Lippi, Pinturicchio, N. di Ser Sozzo, T. di Bartolo, and M. di Filippuccio.

Via del Castello. Lined with 14th-c. buildings, this street runs off the Piazza della Cisterna, and ends at the 13th-c. church of *S. Lorenzo in Ponte*; note the 15th-c. marble portal of the former convent of S. Domenico, now a prison. A plaque says that the monk, reformer, and martyr G. Savonarola stayed here.

Via S. Matteo.* Northernmost stretch of the Via Francigena that went through San Gimignano, it is lined with medieval houses and palazzi. First, note the twin towers, the Torri Salvucci, *Palazzo Pettini* and *Torre Pettini* (n. 2); pass through the *Arco della Cancelleria*, once a city gate. The 13th-c. Palazzo della Cancelleria and the Romanesque church of **S. Bartolo** are interesting. At n. 12-14 is a late 13th-c. towerhouse, the **Casa Pesciolini**, and at n. 52, the slightly rusticated 15th-c. *Casa Francardelli*. At n. 60-62, Palazzo Tinacci, and, facing it, at n. 97, *Palazzo Bonaccorsi*. Last comes Porta S. Matteo (A1; 1262).

Piazza S. Agostino. Irregular in shape, it is dominated by the church of S. Agostino; on one side is the little 11th-c. church of **S. Pietro**, with a simple facade adorned with a rose window.

S. Agostino.* *Open 7-12 and 3-6 (summer, until 7)*. This imposing Romanesque-Gothic church, built in 1280-98, has a stark brick facade with four Gothic windows on the right side. Inside, note artwork by S. Mainardi, B. da Maiano (1494), P. F. Fiorentino, B. di Fredi, P. del Pollaiolo (1483), and frescoes by B. Gozzoli and G. d'Andrea (1465), L. Memmi (1320). From the left transept, you can enter the cloister of the adjacent convent.

Spedale di S. Fina. Built in the 13th c. and still used as a hospital, this building overlooks *Via Folgore da S. Gimignano*: inside, frescoes by S. Mainardi and busts of saints by P. Torrigiani. Further on, to the left, is the 13th-c. church of S. Jacopo, and from there, you can turn right to follow the city walls, reaching Porta alle Fonti, and from there climb down to the Fonti, which are springs covered with Gothic arches (12th-14th c., restored in 1852).

Museo Archeologico and **Spezieria di S. Fina.** *Open 11-6; Nov.-15 Jan., closed Fri*. Both in Via Folgore da S. Gimignano; the archeological museum includes Roman and Etruscan finds, while the Spezieria has a collections of vases and ceramics from the nearby hospital.

San Marino

Elev. 739 m, pop. 4428; capital of the Republic of San Marino. Two stonecarvers fleeing persecution as Christians took refuge on Elba, and became lies. One was St. Leo, the other was St. Marinus, or "Marino," after whom San Marino is named. Monte Titano, a jagged limestone ridge with a handsome silhouette, visible from the beaches, stands between the valleys of Marecchia and the Conca, between Romagna and Montefeltro. On it lies the medieval village that constitutes the capital, overlooking the countryside of the rest of the republic at its base (61,19 sq. km; pop. 26,128). For anyone who is vacationing on the Riviera di Romagna, the thrill of this venture out of Italian territory is exciting and enjoyable. A must.

Places of interest. S. Francesco (*B2*). Adjacent to the *Porta di S. Francesco* (1451), the main entrance to the town, is this church, which dates from 1361 but was greatly transformed in the 17th-18th c. The facade, the apse, and the adjoining portico still bear traces of the original 14th-c. structure. The adjoining *Pinacoteca e Museo di S. Francesco* (*open Apr.-Sep. 8-8; Oct.-Mar., 8:50-5*) contains a small gallery of paintings, featuring the Adoration of the Magi, a fresco by A. Alberti.

Piazzetta del Titano (*B2*). This teeming square was originally the site of one of the town gates of the second walled perimeter. Overlooking it is the *Palazzo Pergami Belluzzi*, which is the new site of the **Museo di Stato** (*open same hours as S. Francesco*) The collection comprises two main parts: historical and archeological, on the one hand, and artistic on the other. In the first section are excavated materials and tools from the Neolithic, Bronze, and Iron ages, along with pottery and other objects. Much of the artwork was donated in the 19th c., and there are can-

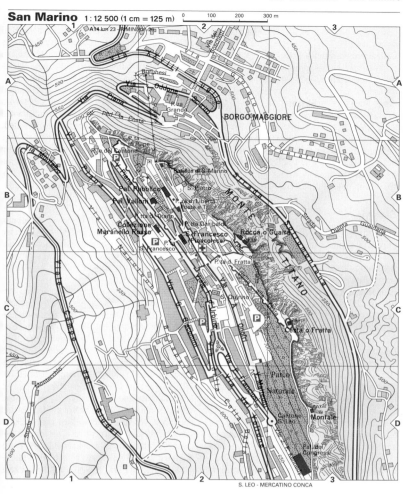

San Marino 1:12 500 (1 cm = 125 m)

S. LEO - MERCATINO CONCA

vases by Michele Giambono and Bernardo Strozzi, as well as paintings from the Tuscan school of the 15th c. and the Bolognese school of the 17th c.

Via Carducci (*B1-2*). This street goes from the lively Piazzetta del Titano to the 15th-c. *Porta della Rupe*, lined with aristocratic buildings from the 16th-17th c. (numbers 145, 146, 151, and 152). Among them, note *Palazzo Valloni*, at n. 141, once the site of the Museo di Stato, or state museum.

Piazza della Libertà (*B2*). This square is the heart of town, with a fine panoramic view and the **Palazzo del Governo**, or *Palazzo Pubblico* (*open Nov.-Feb., 8:45-4; Mar. and 15 Sep.-Oct., 8:30-12:30 and 2-6; Apr.-14 Sep., 8-8; closed 1 Jan., 2 Nov. aft., 25 Dec.*), built in the late 19th c. in 14th-c. style, with a spectacular interior. Slightly uphill is the Neo-Classic Basilica of *S. Marino*, built in 1836, on the site of the ancient "pieve," or parish church. In the surrounding area, note the *Museo delle Cere*, or Wax Museum (*open Oct.-Mar., 8:30-12:30 and 2:5:30; Apr.-Jun. and Sep., 8:30-6:30; Jul.-Aug., 8:30-8*), with effigies of lo-

cal celebrities and great opera singers.

Rocche.* *Open same hours as the Palazzo del Governo.* Set on the three knobs of the ridge of Monte Titano, almost sheer above the plains, stand three fortresses, called either the Rocche or the *Penne*. The first of the three, known as either the **Rocca** or *Guaita* (*A2*), at an elevation of 738 m, may date from the 11th c., but was rebuilt in the 15th c. and again later. It now houses temporary exhibitions. The second one, known as the **Cesta** (*B2*), at an elevation of 749 m, dates from the 13th c. but was rebuilt; it now houses the **Museo delle Armi Antiche**, or Museum of Ancient Weapons, (*open same hours as S. Francesco and Museo di Stato*) with cutting arms and firearms from all over. The third, called the **Montale** (*off map*), was built in the 13th c. and was almost entirely rebuilt in 1935. There is a vast panoramic view* of the Romagna plains below, the sea, and the distant Apennines.

At n. 26 of the sloping street to the Rocca is the *Museo delle Curiosità* (*open Mar.-Jun. and 16 Sep.-*

Oct., 9-6:30; Jul.-15 Sep., 9-midnight; Nov.-Feb., 10-5:30), an incredible collection of unusual objects, figures and facts.

Collezione Maranello Rosso (*B2*). *Temporarily closed*. Located by the ancient town walls, in Via Tonnini n. 10, is a display of 27 legendary Ferrari cars, dating from as early as 1951 to recent times.

Borgo Maggiore. In this little village at the base of the mountain – an obligatory route for all those entering S. Marino – is the very modern church of the *Beata Vergine della Consolazione* (1966); note, in Via Boschetti, the **Museo delle Auto d'Epoca** (*open 9:30-12:30 and 2-7:30; tel. 0549906290*), with over 160 vintage automobiles dating from as early as 1908, manufactured in Italy and elsewhere.

Sàssari

Elev. 225 m, pop. 120,803; Sardegna (Sardinia), provincial capital. Sardinia's second largest city lies along the slopes of a limestone tableland stretching down to the Gulf of Asinara, only about 10 km away. Sàssari in the north rivals Cagliari in the south, and prides itself on its culture and music. In 1899 the king of Italy, Umberto I, came here on an official visit; proud horsemen in traditional costume paraded before him, originating the tradition – still very much alive – of the "Cavalcata Sarda."

Historical note. Originally a haven for those in flight from Saracens, Pisans, and Genoans, Sàssari fell under the rule of the latter through the end of the 13th c. As the city grew, it built walls (early 14th c.; still visible in Corso Trinità) which entirely contained the city until the early 18th c. After four centuries of Spanish rule, Sàssari became Piedmontese in the 18th c. Beginning in the mid-19th c., Sàssari destroyed its walls, its Pisan towers, and its Aragonese castle, building a new, more modern city alongside the old one, with straight roads and broad squares, on the Piedmontese model. This development continued in this century, pushing up the Hill of the Cappuccini and toward the plain of Baddi Mannu. Though life, perhaps, improved, much of Sàssari's historic heritage was thus lost.

Places of interest. **Piazza Castello**. The fortress that gave this square its name was razed in the late 19th c. to make room for the modern settlement. The center of the new town is **Piazza d'Italia**, a square arranged in the 1970s and flanked by the majestic *Palazzo della Provincia*, in late Neo-Classic style.

Museo Nazionale Sanna. * *Open 9-8; closed Mon.* Since 1932 this museum has occupied the palazzo built by the Sanna family for their own collections and for the archeological material of the University. The *archeological section* begins with the prehistoric period. A major section is devoted to the Sardinian civilization of the "Nuraghe," with the so-called "tombs of the giants" and remarkable 10th-c. B.C. bronzes. The Phoenician period features pottery,

bronzes, and statuettes; the Punic, a series of funerary stelae, as well as scarabs and amulets; the Roman, glass, gold, mosaics, and a bronze tablet. Coins date from Roman and Carthaginian times. The *art gallery* – which will be moved to the new *Museo Arte Sàssari* in the restored Casa Professa della Compagnia di Gesù – features paintings by Sardinian masters of the past, as well as contemporary works by the Cavaro, B. Vivarini, Mabuse, and G. Marghinotti. Local folklore and customs are also documented in the *ethnographic section*.

Corso Vittorio Emanuele II. This avenue passes through the old part of town, with buildings in the 15th-c. Catalan Gothic style (note *Casa Farris*, n. 23, and the *Casa di Re Enzo*, n. 42) standing alongside 19th-c. buildings. The church of *S. Antonio* features an 18th-c. retable, by B. Augusto.

Mura Medievali. Fragments of the city walls, built by Pisans and Genoans in the 13th-14th c. and demolished in the 19th c., still stand along Corso Trinità. Near the church of the Trinità, you can see the *Fonte Rosello*, a foutain built in 1605-06 by Genoan stone-workers.

Duomo. * In the heart of the medieval section, the Cathedral was rebuilt in the late 15th c., on the site of a 12th-c. parish church. The *interior*, like the exterior, is Gothic in style; note the 14th-c. Sienese tempera on the main altar and the wooden choir. The adjacent *Museo del Tesoro del Duomo* (*open 9-12 and 4-7; closed Sun.*) features a late 15th-c. processional standard*. Nearby, the *Palazzo Ducale* (1775-1805) is a breath of Piedmontese style.

S. Maria di Betlem. All that remains of the original 12th-c. church is the lower half of the facade; the upper half, with rose window, dates from 1465. *Inside*, note the early 15th-c. wooden statues, and the *cloister* with the 16th-c. Fontana del Brigliadore.

S. Pietro in Silki. Although a church of this name stood here in the 12th c., the oldest portion still standing is the base of the bell tower (13th c.). Inside, note the Sardinian version of Catalan Gothic in the 1st chapel on the left; the 4th houses a venerated 14th-c. simulacrum.

Segesta*

Elev. 304 m; Sicilia (Sicily), province of Trapani, township of Calatafimi-Segesta (pop. 7328).

Historical note. This was once a city of the Elimi, a western Sicilian people that blended Greek customs with Phoenician and Carthaginian influences. The city vanished in the High Middle Ages, but the magnificent temple remains, standing on a rise.

Places of interest. **Tempio** ** (*open 9-one hour before sunset*). Standing out in the green landscape, the temple has a peristyle of 36 unfluted Doric columns, supporting a trabeation with flat metopes and two pediments. This construction dates from the 5th c. B.C., comprising the single circuit of columns still standing, enclosing the open-air altar of an indigenous cult. Segesta was a rival of Selinunte, and may have had a seaside market town and harbor near what is now Castellammare del Golfo.

Città Antica. The road that reaches Monte Barbaro (431 m) in less than one kilometer passes thorugh the site where the ancient town lay. The few remains include an imposing square tower, ruins of the old walls, a fortified gate.

Teatro*. Datable around the mid-3rd c. B.C. , the theater faces north, perhaps not to distract the spectators with the extraordinary view* which extends all the way to distant Monte Èrice. Still visible are the huge hemycycle stalls, while beyond the stage are the remains of pre-existing dwellings.

Selinunte*

Elev. 32 m, Sicilia (Sicily), province of Trapani, township of Castelvetrano (pop. 30,045).

Historical note. Westernmost of the ancient Greek colonies in Sicily, this town was settled in 628 B.C. by the colonists of Megara Hyblaea, rose to its peak of glory in the 5th c. B.C., and was destroyed by Carthage in 409 B.C. It is notable for its temples.

Getting around. The archeological site is officially included in the *Parco Archeologico* (*open 9-two hours before sunset*). It was impossible to establish which divinity the temples were dedicated to, and they are consequently referred to as Temple A, B, etc.

Places of interest. Eastern temples*. This is a group of three temples. A single column emerges from the mass of ruins of *temple G*, probably dedicated to Zeus, one of the largest of Greek antiquity, Doric, with an eight-column peripteros, and a cella; it seems to have been begun in 550 B.C. and left unfinished, possibly because of the Punic invasion in 409 B.C. *Temple F* is in the middle and is the smallest. It has a six-column peripteros (560-540 B.C.). Majestically standing out from the landscape, on the other hand, is **Temple E****, all of whose columns were raised in the mid-1950s, with part of the trabeation and of the walls of the cella. This magnificent Doric construction dates from the first two decades of the 5th c. B.C., and has a six-column peripteros; four handsome metopes of its sculptural decoration

Selinunte: Temple E

are now in the Museo Archeologico in Palermo.

Acropolis.* Walking for a stretch along the *walls* made of enormous square blocks of stone, you climb up to the broad, high acropolis*. It was crossed by two intersecting roads, and there are ruins of a number of temples: base of *temple O*; base and drums of fluted columns of *Temple A*; fourteen raised columns (1925-27) and part of the trabeation of **Temple C**, the oldest one in the acropolis (three remarkable metopes from this temple are now in Palermo); pronaos and cella of *Temple B*; the remains of *Temple D*; ruins of Punic houses (4th-3rd c. B.C.), and the base of a small archaic temple, possibly the source of six other, small metopes, now in Palermo. At the northern tip of the acropolis is the main gate, or *Porta Nord*, defended on the outside by magnificent **fortifications***.

Città Antica. On the hill to the north of the acropolis are the ruins of ancient houses and of a site which was probably used as a necropolis after the destruction in 409 B.C.

Santuario della Malophoros. This sacred precinct, called a sanctuary, lies on the hill beyond the river. Still visible are the ruins of a very ancient small altar, of the altar of sacrifices and of the temple, dedicated to Malophoros, or bearer of pomegranates, probably Demeter.

Siena**

Elev. 322 m, pop. 54,256; Toscana (Tuscany), provincial capital. Certainly the most distinct and homogeneous of all Tuscany's cities, Siena lies in a hilly landscape similar to that seen in the famous 14th-c. fresco in the Palazzo Pubblico, "Assedio del Castello di Montemassi da parte di Guidoriccio da Fogliano". Located in the heart of the Tuscan highland, on the rises that separate the valley of the Arbia River, tributary of the Ombrone, from the valley of the Elsa River, tributary of the Arno. Compact and clearly 14th-c. in style, Siena is a city of a single era, with a single past, a city that never ventured down from the three hills along which its steep streets slope, safely girded by the perimeter of its walls. From Duccio di Buoninsegna to Sassetta, the Sienese artistic tradition has always been separate from, and in some sense counterpoised to the art of Florence. It is said that the finest Italian spoken is the version found here.

Historical note. Within Siena's walled perimeter you can clearly see three hills, which lay at the origin of the three "terzieri" (instead of quarters) into which the town is divided: the "terziere di Città" corresponds to the original core of the city. The earliest historical documents known date from Longobard times, when Siena was the headquarters of a "gastaldo," an officer of the royal court. During the barbarian invasions, the city's strategic hilltop position made it an easily defended site; its population grew accordingly. Little is known of the long dark centuries before this. An-

Siena: Piazza del Campo

cient "Sena," apparently founded by the Senoni tribe of Gauls, was called Sena Etruriae to distinguish it from another city, Sena Gallica (modern Senigallia). It became an Etruscan town and later a Roman military colony, and was called Sena Julia. With the Frankish conquest, the Longobard "gastaldi" were replaced by Carolingian counts who were in turn faced with the encroachments of increasingly powerful bishops; under the patronage of those bishops, Communal government developed, taking power largely for itself. "Consoli," or consuls, were named for the first time in 1147, and under their rule Siena began to extend its dominion outside the city walls, which by now enclosed all three hills in a single fortified perimeter. Siena's expansion toward Poggibonsi and the Val d'Elsa may have had imperial approval, but it necessarily led to conflict with the Guelph city of Florence. An endless series of wars, prompted by trade issues, thus broke out, as Siena became one of the main Ghibelline strongholds in Tuscany. The government of Siena had meanwhile shifted from rule by the "Consoli" to rule by a "Podestà," but real power remained firmly in the hands of the rich merchant families of the town, who traded throughout Europe and who were threatened by competing towns, especially Florence. Fighting continued from 1141 until 1235, when a crushing military defeat led to political reform. The power of the Podestà was now moderated, with the establishment of the Consiglio dei Ventiquattro (Council of 24), with equal representation of nobles and commoners. The Italian activities of the Swabian emperors bolstered the ambitions of Ghibelline Siena; in 1260 Siena defeated Florence at Montaperti, regaining Montepulciano and Montalcino. The attack of Charles of Anjou, however, proved fatal: the defeat at Colle marked the end of Ghibelline Siena's ascendancy.

A papal excommunication had already hurt the merchants and bankers of the city, making it difficult for them to obtain repayments of their loans and bills; this led to a shift of allegiance for many mer-

chants, from Ghibelline to Guelph. As a result, Guelph government was formed in 1270. This gov ernment remained in power until 1355. It was the best government Siena had ever had. Peace wa made with Florence, and Siena was able to tend to the prosperity of its possessions. These were year of triumphant Gothic architecture and art, when Siena became what we see today. Between the turn of the 14th c. and about 1350, the Sienese built Palaz zo Pubblico, with the Torre del Mangia, the Palazz del Capitano del Popolo, and Palazzo Tolomei, the first privately owned palazzo. Work continued on the Duomo, only to be interrupted in 1339 to begin work on the colossally ambitious Duomo Nuovo, o New Cathedral, a church so large that the existing Duomo was meant to serve merely as its transept Among the projects actually completed were the Cappella di Piazza, the Battistero, or Baptistery, and the churches of S. Domenico and S. Francesco, lat er renovated. In this same period, Sienese Gothic art began its stunning development: in 1308 Duc cio di Buoninsegna was commissioned to paint a major altarpiece for the Duomo; in 1315 Simone Martini frescoed his "Maestà" in the Palazzo Pubbli co; a decade later, the fresco of the "Assedio del Castello di Montemassi" (Siege of the Castle of Mon temassi) was painted; between 1338 and 1340 Am brogio Lorenzetti depicted in his frescoes the con cept of good government. In Siena, Gothic became synonymous with art, and Gothic buildings were erected throughout the first half of the 15th c. (Log gia della Mercanzia, Palazzo Buonsignori). It was not until the years between 1460 and 1480 that the Florentine Renaissance, with Palazzo Piccolomini and Palazzo Spannocchi, began to appear in Siena. This new influence, however, went beyond art: Siena was politically subjugated by Florence and by Angevin politics; war with Pisa, the famine of 1326, and the Black Death of 1348 had all provoked discontent and uprisings. In 1399 Siena offered itself to the duke of Milan, Gian Galeazzo Visconti; when he died, however, civil unrest broke out again, in spite of the sermons on peace preached by St. Catherina (S. Caterina) and St. Bernardino.

In 1487 power was seized by Pandolfo Petrucci, who governed Siena until his death (1512). His successors were unable to cement their power, and Siena fell into an imperial wardship. An insurrection took place, the emperor's Spanish garrison was driven out, and war followed, with a terrible siege. In 1555 a broken, starving Siena surrendered to an imperial army led by Cosimo I de' Medici. A small band of diehards retreated to Montalcino and kept the banner of the Sienese republic flying until 1559. The peace of Cateau-Cambrésis put an end to Republic freedom in Siena, and a new overlord took over, in the person of Cosimo I. The unification of Tuscany brought little if any benefit to Siena over the next two centuries: during that entire period, the Grand Duchy of Tuscany maintained a customs barrier between the former state of Siena and the state of Florence, with serious economic repercussions for Siena. It was not until a Hapsburg-Lorraine ruler, Pietro Leopoldo, took over in the late 18th c., that agriculture and trade began to revive. Construction and expansion practically ceased, and the only notable monument from that period is the Baroque church of S. Maria di Provenzano. In 1779 the ancient fortress of Lizza was transformed into a public park, and was enlarged further after Italy was unified. And it was not until the 20th c. that Siena expanded beyond its walls: the fortress of S. Barbara was converted into a public park, and new districts were built, among them, S. Prospero. Nowadays, Siena is home to a number of prestigious cultural institutions, such as the Università (one of Italy's oldest universities), and the Accademia Musicale Chigiana.

The Palio. This remarkable, centuries-old horse race takes place in the heart of Siena, twice a year. Held in the Piazza del Campo, the race is run to commemorate the holidays of the Madonna di Provenzano (2 July) and the Assumption (16 August). This is the deepest-rooted, and, in a sense, the most authentic of Italy's folk events. Competing, by turn, are ten of the city's seventeen historic "contrade," or neighborhoods. The names of these "contrade" are: Aquila, Bruco, Chiocciola, Civetta, Drago, Giraffa, Istrice, Leocorno, Lupa, Nicchio, Oca, Onda, Pantera, Selva, Tartuca, Torre, Valdimontone (literally, Eagle, Caterpillar, Snail, Owl, Dragon, Giraffe, Porcupine, Unicorn, She-Wolf, Shell, Goose, Wave, Panther, Forest, Tortoise, Tower, and Valley of the Ram). Each has a banner with an image corresponding to its name. Before the race, as the excitement builds among the townspeople (understandable excitement; the horses are raced bareback, ridden by jockeys who will do nearly anything to eliminate their rivals), a spectacular historical procession takes place, in costume, in which each "contrada" marches, with banners, followed by the Carro del Trionfo, or Carroccio, literally the Carriage of Triumph, with the "palio," a splendid silk drape awarded to the winning "contrada."

Getting around. Almost all of the area inside Siena's walls is closed to traffic; tourists heading for hotels can enter if they have written reservations or special permits for loading and unloading luggage, but they cannot park, even in the evening and at night. There is plenty of parking outside town, served by shuttle buses; in the summer, and on holidays, it is tough to find parking near the gates of town and on the ring roads.

The Campo and the Terzo di S. Martino

Siena branches out into three hilltop ridges, or "terzi," urban districts each of which is then split up into "contrade." From the Campo, in the shadow of the Palazzo Pubblico, the Terzo di S. Martino extends east to Porta Romana.

Piazza del Campo** (*D3*). This outstanding testimony to the city's medieval harmony of layout and composition, the Piazza – called **Campo** by the Sienese – with its remarkable shell shape, has always lain at the heart of life in the city. First paved with elaborate brickwork in 1347, the square is dominated by the facade of the Palazzo Pubblico and the elegant silhouette of the Torre del Mangia, the tower which marks the perspectival vanishing point. Along the other sides of the square extends a line of ancient palazzi, some of them crenelated and turreted, interrupted by narrow lanes and "chiassi" leading to the broader streets behind. The square was first laid out in 1169. As early as 1297, a decree of the Republic, one of the first zoning regulations known to history, established standards for buildings facing the Campo. These palazzi were continually improved and beautified over the centuries; some were radically rebuilt in the 18th c., and then restored to their original Gothic style in the 19th c. **Fonte Gaia**, a rectangular basin in the center of the Campo, was created in 1419 by J. della Quercia; the original exquisite marble panels are now in the Museo Civico. Note, to the right of the fountain, the curving facade of **Palazzo Sansedoni** and, to the left, the crenelated **Palazzo d'Elci.**

Palazzo Pubblico** (*D3*). Symbolic of the independence and wealth of Siena's oligarchic ruling class, this town hall is certainly one of the finest achievements of Gothic civil architecture in Tuscany. As if to underscore the shift from a fortress to a residential palazzo, the popular government "of the Nine" had the central, taller wing of this building erected between 1284 and 1305; the two side wings were completed in 1310, with another storey added in 1680. The lower stone section of the facade, once lightened by great doors, balanced the upper brick section, still punctuated by two rows of elegant, three-light, mullioned windows. It is crowned by parapets and the vast disk known as "monogramma di Bernardino" (1425). As work continued on the exterior, the greatest painters of Sienese art were summoned to decorate the interior, in celebration of the wisdom and taste of the leaders of the Republic. The

Siena 1 : 11 000 (1 cm = 110 m)

0   100   200 m

Staz. F.S.
P.za
C. Rosselli

Viale

Viale

Giuseppe

Mazzini

Viale Sardegna

300

325

A

300

Antiporto di Camollia

Viale Vitt. Emanuele

Viale Vittorio

Porta
Camollia

Piazza
G. Amendola

Via Fiume

Via Don Giovanni Minzoni

B. Bixio

B

Monluc

Fontegiusta

V.le N. Sauro

Campansi

Barriera
S. Lorenzo

Via Garibaldi

Viale C. Battisti

Viale A. Diaz

S. Stefano

P.za
d. Sale

S. Sebastiano

Fonte
d'Ovile

S. Andrea

Fonte
Nuova

Via d'Ovile

P.za
d'Ovile

300

S. Francesco

C

Viale R. Franci

Giardini
della Lizza

Viale C. Maccari

P.za
A. Gramsci

Via Montanini

Via B. Peruzzi

S. Michele al Monte
di S. Donato

Piazza
S. Francesco

Oratorio di
S. Bernardino

Viale Vitt. Veneto

Fortezza di

Campo
Sportivo

Piazza
d. Libertà

Via XXV Aprile

Via di Stadio Comunale

Stadio
Comunale

P.za
Matteotti

Poste e T.

S.M. d. Nevi

Via dei Rossi

S. Pietro
a Ovile

S. Maria di
Provenzano

S. Barbara
(o Medicea)

P.za
Salimbeni

Pal.
Salimbeni

P.za
Provenzano
Salvani

D

Viale Vitt. Veneto

V.le dei Mille

Via Curtatone

Via di Paradiso

Via d. Sapienza

Via T. Pendola

P.za
S. Domenico

Biblioteca
d. Intronati

Pza
S. Caterina

Pal.
Tolomei

Via Banchi di sopra

S. Cristoforo

Casellare
d. Ugurgieri

Università

S. Giovanni
d. Staffa

S. Domenico

Sant. della
Casa di S. Caterina

Via di Fontebranda

Croce d.
Travaglio

Banchi di sotto

Via

Pal.
Piccolomini

Loggia
d. Papa

Fonte
Branda

P.ta
Fontebranda

P.za
Fontebranda

Logg. d.
Mercanzia

Il Campo

Via Cecco Angiolieri

Misericordia

S. Martino

Via Roma

E

Via Esterna di Fontebranda

Duomo

Pal.
arcivescovile

P.za
d. Selva

Museo
d. Opera

Via del Pellegrini

Pal. d.
Magnifico

Pal.
Pubblico
(Museo
civico)

P.za d.
Mercato

S.
Sebastiano

P.za d.
Duomo

Prefettura

Pal.
Piccolomini

Pal. Chigi-
Saracini

Via di Città

Spedale
di S. M. d. Scala

P.za
Postierla

Pinacoteca
nazionale

Via P. Mascagni

S. Pietro
alle Scale

Via Stalloreggi

Via di Casato

Prato
d. Agostino

Via di

275

300

325

300

Pal.
Pollini

Via T. Pendola

Via Sarrocchi

Via di Cerchia

S. Agostino

Via Pier Andrea Mattioli

F

Via d. Laterino P.ta
Laterino

Via E. S. Bastianini

S. Niccolò
al Carmine

Via di Diana

Via di Monteliscai

Accademia
d. Fisiocritici

Orto
botanico

275

Via di S. Marco

Via dalla Sapienza

300

300

P.ta S. Marco

Via di

P.ta Tufi

Itinerari

1° ————
2° — — —
3° ···········

2

GROSSETO km 73

3

370

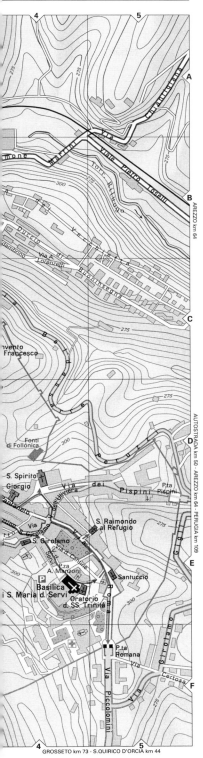

works they created now form the collections of the Museo Civico (see below); a number of halls, used by the city government, are generally closed to the public. Above the left wing rises the soaring profile of the **Torre del Mangia*** (102 m), built in 1325-48. The sober brick shaft is crowned by a stone corbel structure, probably designed by L. Memmi; it in turn works as the base for a stone structure which serves as the belfry. At the base of the tower, the so-called **Cappella di Piazza** is a marble loggia joined to the facade of the Palazzo Pubblico; built from 1352 to 1376 to fulfill a vow taken during the Black Death of 1348, its upper section was completed in 1461-68. The sadly deteriorated fresco over the altar was by Sodoma (1537-39).

The portal to the right of the Piazza Chapel leads to the porticoed *courtyard of the Podestà* (1325). At the far side, on the right, is the *Teatro dei Rinnovati*, once the hall of the Gran Consiglio della Repubblica, rebuilt as a theater in 1560, and once again rebuilt, after two fires, by A. Galli Bibiena in 1753. On the left, entrance to the 503-step stairway to the top of the Torre del Mangia *(open 15 summer, 10-6; winter, 10:30-4:30)* with its fabulous view* of Siena. Further to the right, the entrance to the *Magazzini del Sale*, partly subterranean rooms with brick vaults, used for temporary shows, and for the exhibitions organized by the **Museo per Bambini** *(tel. 0577292209)*.

Museo Civico** *Open 10-7; Nov.-15 Mar., until 6:30.* This museum comprises an impressive gallery of paintings as well as the monumental halls of the Palazzo Pubblico. From the courtyard of the Podestà, you climb first of all to the 19th-c. *Sala del Risorgimento* (late 19th-c. frescoes by Tuscan artists, including C. Maccari). A steep staircase leads up to the loggia (see below), followed by the *Sala di Balìa*, with 15th-c. frescoes; the *Sala dei Cardinali*, with sculptures by a student of J. della Quercia and detached frescoes; the *Sala del Concistoro*, featuring a carved portal* by B. Rossellino (1446) and frescoes by D. Beccafumi in the vault. The *anticappella* (room before the chapel), with frescoes by T. di Bartolo (1414), contains ancient gold jewelry, including the mid-15th-c. gold rose of Pope Pius II; the *cappella** (or chapel), features a wrought-iron gate (1437), an inlaid wood **choir**** (1415-28) by D. di Niccolò, fine frescoes by T. di Bartolo (1407), and an altarpiece* by Sodoma. In the *Sala del Mappamondo*, a great hall where the Council of the Republic met, is the renowned fresco of the **Maestà**** by S. Martini (1315). Facing it is the **Siege of the Castle of Montemassi by Guidoriccio da Fogliano**** (1328-29), a fresco whose long-standing attribution to Martini is being debated. The hall contains other fine works by S. di Pietro, Sodoma, and Duccio di Buoninsegna. In the *Sala della Pace* is the remarkable **Allegory of Good and Bad Government****, frescoes painted for the Government of the Nine by A. Lorenzetti in 1338-40. Next comes the *Sala dei Pilastri*, with 13th-/15th-c. Sienese paintings, including works by G. da Siena, A. Lorenzetti, N. di Bartolomeo, and M. di Giovanni.

371

The *gallery* features Italian and especially Sienese paintings from the 16th-18th c., notable among them works by J. Roos and B. di David. Upstairs, the *Loggia dei Nove*, overlooking the Piazza del Mercato and the Sienese countryside, displays the fragments of the Fonte Gaia*, by J. della Quercia, reassembled in 1904 (*undergoing restoration, to be moved*).

Università degli Studi (*D3*). At the corner of Via S. Vigilio, overlooking Via Banchi di Sotto (n. 55-57), this *former convent* was founded in the 11th c. and repeatedly renovated until the Neo-Renaissance version of 1891. Now the office of the Rector of the University of Siena, this building has, since 1816, been the headquarters of the ancient Sienese Studio, which dates back to the 13th c. Note the Gothic *funerary monument* in the courtyard. If you follow *Via S. Vigilio*, a covered entrance (on the left, after Via Angiolieri) leads into the courtyard of the **Castellare degli Ugurgieri**, a medieval fortress-home. On Via Bandini are the Renaissance palazzi of the *Bandini Piccolomini* family (n. 25-29).

Palazzo Piccolomini* (*D3*). This impressive piece of architecture from the later Florentine Renaissance was built from 1469 on by P.P. del Porrina, probably to a plan by B. Rossellino, and enlarged in the 17th c. The light rustication of the facade overlooking Via Banchi di Sotto (n. 52) is crowned by a broad cornice: note the two large marble crests over the main doorway, with the heraldic device of the Piccolomini family. This building contains the *State Archives*, with vast collections of historical documents, and, especially, the records of the Sienese Republic. Four halls on the second floor contain the *Museo dell'Archivio di Stato** (*closed for restoration*), featuring the **collection of the Biccherne**, 103 painted wooden tablets which served as covers for books of public records, commissioned from 1258 to 1659, and painted by such great artists as A. and P. Lorenzetti, G. di Paolo, Vecchietta, S. di Pietro, F. di Giorgio Martini, and D. Beccafumi. The Archives also contain documents concerning episodes or persons mentioned in Dante's Divine Comedy, the will of Boccaccio, and writings of St. Catherine of Siena.

Logge del Papa (*D3*). This elegant Renaissance loggia with three arcades marks the eastern end of Via Banchi di Sopra; it was built by A. Federighi (1462) at the behest of Pope Pius II Piccolomini.

S. Martino (*D3*). Nearby is one of Siena's oldest churches, which gave its name to the Terzo di S. Martino. Built in 1537, with a solemn facade dating from 1613, the church has nothing of the original, much-older structure. Inside, note the Baroque ciborium by G. Mazzuoli (1649) and the marble altars, with paintings by G. Reni and D. Beccafumi.

Salicotto (*E3-4*). Linked to Via del Porrione and Via S. Martino by many steep cross-lines, this old district of Siena was largely "sanitized" in the 1930s; where it comes closest to Via S. Martino, the buildings on the right of Vicolo delle Scotte, once part of the Ghetto, include the classical Sephardic *Synagogue* built by G. del Rosso (1756).

S. Girolamo (*E4*). This convent was founded in 1354; inside is a painting by S. di Pietro.

Basilica dei Servi* (*E4*). This immense church whose full name is S. Clemente in S. Maria dei Servi, was begun in the 13th c. and was not completed and consecrated until 1533, with the 15th-c. facade still unfinished. Alongside it stands a 14th-c. campanile (completely restored in 1926). From the broad stairway before it, you have a fine view* of the walled city.

The luminous *interior*, with a nave with two aisles and slender marble columns, preserves the original Renaissance plan, though it is sadly marred by 19th-c. "restorations." Of special interest, among the many artworks by the Sienese school between the 13th-16th c., are the **Madonna del Bordone** by C. di Marcovaldo, and works by M. di Giovanni, N. di Segna, S. di Bonaventura, P. Lorenzetti, B. Fungai, T. di Bartolo, and G. di Paolo.

Oratorio della Santissima Trinità (*E4-5*). *Open by request; enquire in the Contrada di Valdimontone, tel. 0577222590.* Just behind the Basilica dei Servi overlooking Via Valdimontone, this oratory was built around 1380 and was renovated at the end of the 16th c.; inside, stuccoes and frescoes by V. Salimbeni, A. Casolani, and L. and C. Rustici.

Via Roma (*E4-5*). This twisting road links Via di Pantaneto with Porta Romana. Set back at the end of Via del Refugio is the church of *S. Raimondo al Refugio* with a Baroque travertine facade and works by F. Vanni, S. Folli and R. Manetti. Further along is the little church of the **Santuccio**, founded in the 14th c. and rebuilt in the 16th c. Note the 17th-c. frescoes by V. Salimbeni. In the sacristy is the *Museo della Società di Esecutori di Pie Disposizioni* (*entrance at n. 71; open Mon., Wed., Fri. 9-1; Tue. and Thu., 3-5*), with work by 14th-/16th-c. Sienese painters.

Porta Romana* (*F5*). Built after 1328, this is the largest of the gates in the 14th-c. walls. Going down beyond the gate, along Via Piccolomini, is the church of **S. Maria degli Angeli in Valli**, a 15th-c. building with an elegant marble Renaissance portal.

S. Spirito (*D4*). Overlooking the oddly shaped Piazza S. Spirito, with its handsome 16th-c. *fountain* known as "de Pispini," this solemn brick Renaissance church features a portal believed to be by B. Peruzzi (1519). Inside, paintings by Sodoma and D. Beccafumi, and a terracotta crèche by A. della Robbia.

Via di Pantaneto (*D-E3-4*). Lined by 16th-/17th-c. buildings, this road runs out to the *Porta di S. Maurizio*; to the left of the gate, note the *Fonte di S. Maurizio*, a 14th-c. fountain.

S. Giorgio (*D4*). This church dates from the Middle Ages and overlooks Via di Pantaneto with a vast Roman Baroque facade, by G.P. Cremona (1730-38) inside, painting by F. Vanni.

The Duomo, Pinacoteca Nazionale, and Terzo di Città

Its skyline marked by the 13th-c. dome of the Cathedral and by its white- and black-striped bell tower the Terzo di Città is the oldest district of Siena. With the paintings of the Pinacoteca, the pulpit by Nicola Pisano in the Cathedral, and the Maestà by Duccio di Boninsegna in the Museo dell'Opera, this route becomes a short course in some of the finest art that Italian history has to offer.

Loggia della Mercanzia* (*D3*). This elegant Gothic-Renaissance structure (1417-44) is made of three broad arcades, with statues in niches and 16th-c. frescoes and stuccoes beneath its vaults; note the two 15th-c. marble benches, with carved reliefs. The loggia stands near Siena's central crossroads, where Via Banchi di Sotto and Via Banchi di Sopra, once part of the medieval Via Francigena, meet Via di Città, which leads to the Spedale and the Duomo.

Via di Città* (*D-E2-3*). The refined main avenue of the section of ancient Siena where the Longobard Gastaldo once lived, is still distinctly medieval in flavor; it climbs in a gentle curve, lined with elegant stores and 14th-/15th-c. aristocratic palazzi. Just past *Chiasso del Bargello*, with a charming view of the Palazzo Pubblico, the 14th-c. *Palazzo Patrizi* (n. 75-77) is the headquarters of the Accademia degli Intronati, a celebrated Sienese cultural institution founded in the 16th c. Further on is the vast curving facade of the 13th-c. **Palazzo Chigi-Saracini*** (*open by request, tel. 057722091*), featuring archeological artifacts, sculptures, furniture, ceramics, and Tuscan paintings from the 14th-17th c., including works by Sodoma, Sassetta, and Beccafumi. Practically facing it is **Palazzo Piccolomini o delle Papesse*** (n. 126), almost certainly built by B. Rossellino (1460). Since 1998 it has housed the *Centro di Arte Contemporanea "Le Papesse"* (*open 12-7 by request, tel. 057747920*) a cultural center for the promotion of the arts. On the other side, also note the 14th-c. *Palazzo Marsili* (n. 132), heavily restored in the 19th c.

Piazza Postierla (*E2*). Dominated by the medieval *tower-house of the Forteguerri*, this square has a 15th-c. *column* and is lined by the 16th-c. *Palazzo Chigi alla Postierla*, designed by Riccio (in Via del Capitano, n. 1); also, the 13th-c. *Palazzo del Capitano del Popolo* (n. 15), drastically renovated in 1854, restored to early Gothic.

Piazza del Duomo* (*E2*). Dominated by the black-and-white marble mass of the Duomo, high atop its stepped platform, the asymmetrical piazza features some of Siena's oldest and most important buildings. To the left of the cathedral is the *Palazzo Arcivescovile*, built in 1718-24 in 14th-c. Gothic style; facing it is the long facade of the *Spedale di S. Maria della Scala* (see below) and, to the right of the cathedral, the 16th-c. **Palazzo del Governatore dei Medici**, now the seat of police administration and provincial government. Further on is *Piazza Jacopo della Quercia* originally planned as the site of the enormous, but unbuilt, Duomo Nuovo; relics of this project can seen in the colonnade and the surrounding buildings, as well as in the "facciatone," the unfinished facade of the "new cathedral."

Duomo** (*D-E2*). *Open summer, 9-7:30; winter, 7:30-1 and 2:30-5; Sun. and holidays, only in the aft.* The

Siena: Duomo

pride of Siena, intended to be the "the greatest monument in Christendom," this is one of the most successful creations of Italian Romanesque-Gothic.

An earlier cathedral was built here around the 9th c.; a larger one was built in its place and consecrated in 1179, but beginning in 1215-20 the building was rebuilt and enlarged; only the crypt remained intact. All scholars now agree that the architect was Nicola Pisano. Work began on the facade in 1284. In 1339 work began on the ambitious – even overweening – project to make the Cathedral merely a transept of another, immense cathedral, the Duomo Nuovo; the Sienese gave up this folly in 1357. Between 1377 and 1382 the facade and apse were completed.

The majestic *facade*, largely the Romanesque-Gothic creation of G. Pisano, stands out for its exquisite decoration and many sculptures, largely by Pisano and his school. Many of the originals are now in the Museo dell'Opera Metropolitana. Note, on the right side of the Cathedral, the large Gothic windows and the Porta del Perdono: in the lunette, a copy of a bas-relief by Donatello; the original is in the Museo dell'Opera. The tall Romanesque *bell tower** was built in the late 13th c. White- and black-striped, it has a progression of mullioned windows, ranging from one-light to six-light, at the top.

The **interior**, built to a Latin cross plan, has a huge nave and aisles; the grandiose proportions are underscored by the black-and-white stripes of the walls and by the **marble floor**** with color decoration and etched depictions. This immense artwork, with its 56 panels depicting sacred and profane scenes, unique in art history, is covered for protection, and can only be seen during solemn occasions. Among the artists who worked on it, from 1373 to 1547, were G. di Stefano, N. di Bartolomeo, A. Federighi, Pinturicchio, Beccafumi, and F. di Giorgio Martini. Worn down by the shoes of the faithful, part of the floor was completely redone in the 19th c. by A. Maccari. A noteworthy counter-facade, with *central portal* and columns attributed to G. di Stefano. Above it, over the arcades, along the nave and the presbytery runs a 15th-/16th-c. cornice with terracotta busts of the popes.

The **transept**, with its double aisle, has hexagonal cross vaults and a great dome, with a twelve-sided base. Six large gilded statues of saints (G. di Stefano, 1488) stand beneath a blind gallery, adorned with depictions of patriarchs and prophets. At the opening of the *right transept* is the circular Baroque *Cappella del Voto*, attributed to G.L. Bernini (1662), who also did the two marble statues. Inside the chapel, the 13th-c. Madonna del Voto, and a masterpiece by M. Preti (1670). In the middle of the *presbytery* is the high altar by B. Peruzzi (1532), topped by a bronze ciborium* by Vecchietta, which replaced Duccio's Maestà in the early 16th c.; on the nearby pillars, the various angels are by G. di Stefano (1489), F. di Giorgio Martini (1490) and Beccafumi (1548-51). In the *apse*, note the 14th-c. wooden choir,* partly inlaid by Fra' Giovanni da Verona (1503), assembled here in the 19th c. but originally from Monte Oliveto Maggiore; on high is the exquisite circular stained glass* of 1288 (one of the earliest made in Italy) to cartoons by D. di Buoninsegna. To the left of the presbytery, note the fine holy-water stoup* by G. di Turino (1434) at the entrance to the *sacristy*, with frescoes by B. di Bindo (1412). From here, you can reach the Chapter House, with portraits of Sienese popes and bishops, and two paintings by S. di Pietro.

In the *left transept*, the octagonal marble **pulpit**** by N. Pisano (1266-68), a masterpiece of Italian Gothic sculpture (also by his son Giovanni, and others, including A. di Cambio); the stairs are by B. Neroni, Il Riccio (1543). At the beginning of the left transept is an elegant portal by Marrina, through which you enter the Renaissance *Cappella di S. Giovanni Battista** (1492), with paintings by Pinturicchio (1504-06), partly redone by Rustichino (1615-16); throughout, sculpture by Donatello (1457), A. Federighi (ca. 1460), G. di Stefano, N. di Bartolomeo (1487), T. di Camaino (1317), and F. Vanni (1596).

At the end of the left aisle is the entrance to the **Libreria Piccolomini**** (*open 16 Mar.-Oct., 9-7:30; Nov.-15 Nov., 10-1 and 2:30-5*), a Renaissance library built beginning in 1492 by the future pope Pius III, to hold the books of his uncle, Pope Pius II. The marble facade was decorated in classical style by Marrina (1497), and bears a fresco by Pinturicchio; note the polychrome wooden group of sculptures by A. di Betto (1421). The walls of the library are frescoed with the **Scenes from the Life of Pius II**** by Pinturicchio (1502-1509): in the middle is the group of the Three Graces*, a 3rd-c. Roman copy from a Hellenistic original; on display are exquisite illuminated 15th-c. choir books*. Next to the entrance, in the aisle of the cathedral, note the huge Piccolomini altar*, begun by A. Bregno in 1481: four of the statues of saints are by Michelangelo (1503-04), while the Virgin with Child (center, top) is attributed to J. della Quercia.

Spedale di S. Maria della Scala (*E2*). This huge medieval hospital complex was built to serve pilgrims and the poor, between the 9th and 11th c.; the facade was renovated repeatedly through the 13th-15th c., and features large mullioned windows. Of particular note, inside (*open May-Sep., 10-6; Oct.-Apr. 10:30-5:30*) is the vast *infirmary*, or "Pellegrinaio," with a series of **frescoes*** depicting the hospital's history and everyday operation, by D. di Bartolo, P. della Quercia, and Vecchietta (1440-44). Part of the facade is the flank of the 13th-c. church of the **Santissima Annunziata**, rebuilt in 1466; inside, note the Crucifix (ca. 1330) and impressive 15th-c. organ; also, a statue* by Vecchietta (1476) and a fresco by S. Conca (1732). As Siena's new polyclinic is completed, the Spedale is being retired as a working hospital; there are plans to convert it into a "cultural citadel."

Museo Archeologico Nazionale (*E2*). *Open 9-2; Sun. and holidays, 9-1; closed 1st, 3rd Sun. of the month.* With a separate entrance at the beginning of the Via del Capitano, this archeological museum was recently (1993) renovated and reinstalled in two huge halls in the Spedale di S. Maria della Scala. Its collections comprise material (vases, urns, kraters, coins, and jewelry) from prehistoric, Etruscan, and Roman periods, largely drawn from the 19th-c. private collections that constitute the museum's historical core; these are found in the *antiquarium*. In the *topographic section* are archeological finds, mostly tomb furnishings, found in Siena and its territory (Murlo, Chianti, and the Upper Val d'Elsa).

Museo dell'Opera Metropolitana* (*E2*). *Open 16 Mar.-Oct., 9-7:30; Nov.-15 Mar., 9-1:30.* Housed in a building in Piazza Jacopo della Quercia, built as early as the 15th c. in what had been intended as the right aisle of the planned Duomo Nuovo, or New Cathedral, this museum comprises works of art from the decoration and furnishing of the Cathedral. On the *first floor*, the *Sala di Duccio* features, on the facing wall, the front of the **Maestà**** by Duccio di Buoninsegna (1308-11), a masterpiece of Sienese art, commissioned for the main altar of the Cathedral; on the other side of the room, the back of the altarpiece. On the right wall, a notable **triptych**** by P. Lorenzetti (1342), and a Madonna* by the young Duccio (ca. 1283). In the three other rooms on this floor, wooden statues, golden reliquaries, ivory crosiers, and illuminated choir books outdo one another in splendor. Note the small wooden Crucifix* by G. Pisano; also, three wooden busts of saints*, by F. di Valdambrino (1409).

Second floor. In the middle of the first hall, an early 13th-c. Madonna dagli Occhi Grossi* (named for her outsized eyes); four saints by A. Lorenzetti; and various works by such artists as G. di Paolo, S. di Pietro, a follower of Sassetta, G. di Cecco. In the other rooms are works by M. di Giovanni, D. Beccafumi (**St. Paul Enthroned***), Pomarancio; also altarpieces, liturgical garb, and other objects. From the last room, you can climb up to the top of the unfinished facade of the Duomo Nuovo, known in Siena as the "facciatone," or "great facade" (fine view*).

Ground floor. At the center, a **relief**** by J. della Quercia and a bas-relief **tondo**** by Donatello; along the walls, ten **statues**** by G. Pisano (1284-

96), once on the facade of the Cathedral, masterpieces of Gothic sculpture.

S. Giovanni Battista* (*D2*). This is Siena's *baptistery*, and is located beneath the apse of the Duomo, on Piazza S. Giovanni. You take a 15th-c. staircase down to it, through the **portal*** by G. di Agostino, intended to be part of the right side of the giant Duomo Nuovo (1345); midway down is the *Crypt of Statues*, used for exhibitions.

The church, built amid the arches that support the extended apse of the Duomo over Valle Piatta, has a Gothic facade, with three large splayed portals. Inside, amid frescoes by many mid-15th-c. artists, including Vecchietta, note the great hexagonal **baptismal font**** (1416-34), a masterpiece of the early Tuscan Renaissance, believed to have been built under the overall direction of J. della Quercia. This sculptor also did the marble ciborium with the statue of John the Baptist and bas-reliefs; the bronze angels are by Donatello and G. di Turino, who also did the bas-reliefs, along with G. di Neroccio, J. della Quercia, T. di Sano, and L. Ghiberti.

Palazzo del Magnifico (*D2*). Overlooking Piazza S. Giovanni and Via dei Pellegrini, to the left of the baptistery, this palazzo was named after P. Petrucci, lord of Siena from 1487 to 1512. It was built in 1504-09, by G. Cozzarelli; the facade is in poor condition. Facing the church of S. Giovanni Battista, in the facade of n. 12/13, a bust marks the birthplace of the architect F. di Giorgio Martini.

Pinacoteca Nazionale** (*E3*). *Open Mon. 8:30-1:30; Tue.-Sat., 8:15-7:15; Sun., 8:15-1:15.* On the left side of Via S. Pietro, this art gallery is located in the early 15th-c. *Palazzo Buonsignori* (n. 29), and the adjacent Gothic *Palazzo Brigidi*, both of which have been restored in the Romantic style of the 19th c.

This gallery dates from the 18th c., when a great scholar named G. Ciaccheri began to collect the work of Sienese "primitive" artists, and it has been in the present location since 1930, filling some thirty rooms. This is certainly one of the most important collections for an understanding of Sienese painting as it developed from the late 12th c. to the early 17th c. From the elegant courtyard of Palazzo Buonsignori, a stairway (right) leads to the **second floor**. *Sienese painters* featured include, from *the 13th c.*: G. da Siena, Maestro del S. Pietro, Maestro del S. Giovanni; from *the 14th c.*: D. di Buoninsegna (**Virgin of the Franciscans****), N. di Segna, U. di Nerio, B. di Fredi , L. di Tommè, S. Martini (**Virgin and Child****), L. Memmi, A. Lorenzetti (**Annunciation****), P. Lorenzetti, P. di Giovanni Fei, B. Bulgarini, D. di Bartolo, M. da Besozzo, L. Monaco, S. Aretino, and T. di Bartolo; from the *15th c.*: G. di Paolo (**Our Lady of Humility****), Sassetta, Maestro dell'Osservanza, M. di Giovanni, N. di Bartolomeo, F. di Giorgio Martini, P. di Domenico, G. di Benvenuto, S. di Pietro, and Vecchietta.

You descend to the **first floor**, where there are other works by *Sienese painters of the 15th c.*: G. da Cremona, P. degli Orioli, G. Genga, Pinturicchio, and B. Fungai; and of the *16th c.*: D. Beccafumi, Sodoma (**Christ at the Column****), and Brescianino.

On the **third floor** is the *Collezione Spannocchi*, featuring works by northern Italian and central European artists of the 15th-16th c., among them: A. Dürer, L. Lotto, Sofonisba Anguissola, Q. Massys, P. Bordone, and Palma the Younger.

S. Pietro alle Scale (*E3*). Founded in the 13th c. and rebuilt in the 18th c., this church has fragments of frescoes by L. da Verona and segments of a polyptych by A. Lorenzetti; on the main altar, note the canvas by R. Manetti.

S. Agostino (*E3*). Built in the 13th c. and renovated in 1747-55 by L. Vanvitelli, this church overlooks the *Prato S. Agostino*; before it extends a 19th-c. portico by A. Fantastici. The luminous, Neo-Classic interior has works by Perugino, A. Lorenzetti (Cappella Piccolomini), F. di Giorgio Martini, L. Signorelli, R. Manetti, and Sodoma. Also note the marble altar by F. del Turco (1608), majolica floors, and 15th-c. wooden Virgin.

Accademia dei Fisiocritici (*F3*). This respected academy for the study of science was founded in 1691 by P.M. Gabrielli, and still does extensive research, Located at n. 5 in Prato S. Agostino, across from the church, the academy has many collections of the life sciences, with part of the **Museo dell'Accademia dei Fisiocritici** (*open Mon.-Wed. and Fri., 9-1 and 3-6; Thu., 9-1*) installed in the cloister, and on the ground and first floor; outside is a *botanical garden* (*open Mon.-Fri., 8:30-12:30 and 2:30-5:30; Sat., 8:30-12:30*).

S. Niccolò al Carmine (*F2*). This church overlooks the vast semicircular expanse of Piano dei Mantellini, and can be reached from Prato S. Agostino along the distinctive *Via T. Pendola*, with its venerable homes, and then down along Via di S. Quirico, past the 16th-c. *Palazzo Pollini* (n. 39-41). The church was founded in the 14th c. and renovated often in the 15th-16th c.; note the campanile attributed to B. Peruzzi (1517). Inside are paintings by Beccafumi, Sodoma, A. Casolani (1604), and G. del Pacchia; the high altar is by T. Redi. To the right of the church (n. 40), note the Neo-Classic facade of *Palazzo Incontri*, designed by S. Belli (1799-1804).

Via Stalloreggi (*E2*). This road twists and turns past craftsmen's workshops with a medieval flavor, extending Via di Città along the hill of Castelvecchio; at the far end, near Piano dei Mantellini, is the *Arco delle Due Porte*, an old city gate incorporated in the surrounding buildings; on the inner side, a 14th-c. fresco by B. di David. Returning toward Piazza Postierla, on the right, *Via di Castelvecchio* passes by a series of houses and lanes that make up a medieval district; at the intersection of Via Stalloreggi and Via di S. Quirico, note the *tabernacle*, with a Pietà by Sodoma.

The Terzo di Camollìa and S. Domenico

In the northern part of town, extensively modified in the 19th-20th c., you can still find the memories of two great, eloquent Sienese saints: St. Bernardino would preach in the oratory near S. Francesco; the son of a washerman, Caterina Benincasa, or St.

Catherine of Siena, lived near the Fonte Branda, in a house that had been turned into a sanctuary as early as the 15th c.

Banchi di Sopra (*D3*). The backbone of the Terzo di Camollìa, this road climbs with a slight curve from the Croce del Travaglio, breaking off at *Piazza Tolomei*, with its column crowned by the she-wolf of Siena (1610). On the left, the 13th-c. **Palazzo Tolomei*** (n. 11). On the right side of the palazzo, in Vicolo della Torre, a plaque bears the verses from Dante's Divine Comedy concerning Pia dei Tolomei, believed to have lived in this house.

S. Cristoforo (*D3*). Facing Palazzo Tolomei, still in the "terzo" of S. Martino, this Romanesque church has a Neo-Classic brick facade; inside, a canvas by G. del Pacchia (1508); outside, a handsome little 12th-c. cloister (rebuilt in 1921) with a view of the intact original apse.

S. Maria di Provenzano (*C-D 3*). This majestic basilica, with a fine view of the surrounding walls and hillsides, was built immediately after the Medici conquest, in 1595-1604; inside, marble floor (1685) and immense main altar by F. del Turco (1617-31), with the 15th-c. terracotta image of the Madonna di Provenzano.

S. Pietro a Ovile (*C3*). This former church overlooks Via del Giglio and is now used as a university lecture hall: note paintings by G. di Pietro and G. di Paolo (ca. 1440).

S. Francesco (*C3*). This huge 14th-c. Franciscan basilica, flanked by the oratory of S. Bernardino (see below) stands on a large square overlooking a panoramic landscape stretching to the hills of Chianti, in the distance. It was completed in 1482, partly destroyed by fire in 1655, and restored to the original Gothic form by G. Partini in 1885-92; the Neo-Gothic facade dates from 1894-1913. Inside, note the fragments of frescoes that once adorned Porta Romana, by Sassetta and S. di Pietro (1447-50), and other 14th-c. **frescoes**** by P. Lorenzetti, A. Lorenzetti, and L. Vanni. Also note the portal, by F. di Giorgio Martini.

Convento di S. Francesco (*C3*). To the right of the church (n. 7), this former convent is now largely used by the university: it encloses a large Renaissance cloister, with a handsome Gothic portal by D. di Agostino, leading to the large 15th-c. *crypt*, now a university library.

Oratorio di S. Bernardino* (*C3*). *Open 15 Mar.-Oct., 10:30-1:30 and 3-5:30.* Built in the 15th c. on the site where St. Bernardino da Siena once preached, this two-level oratory has a fine Renaissance portal (1574). In the rooms adjacent to the oratory is the **Museo Diocesano di Arte Sacra** (*open same hours as the oratory*) with precious collections from the churches and convents of the diocese. A vestibule with an exquisite relief* by G. di Agostino (ca. 1336) precedes the *upper oratory**, which today is the heart of the museum and one of the most interesting examples of Renaissance architecture; there are 15th-c. inlays and stuccoes as well as frescoes* and panels by Sodoma, G. del Pacchia, and Beccafumi (1518-37).

Porta Ovile (*C3*). Built in the 13th c., this gate w incorporated in the 14th-c. walls; from S. Frances take the steep *Via del Comune*. In the small aedi ula, is the fresco by S. di Pietro. Then, outside th walls, note the 13th-c. *Fonte d'Ovile* (fountain). Clim back up *Via di Vallerozzi* toward the center, and yc will pass, on the right, the **Oratorio di S. Rocc** (*C3; open by request; enquire at the Contrada del Lupa, tel. 0577286038*), with paintings by R. Van: and V. Salimbeni and frescoes by Rutilio Manetti, l Mei, and S. Salimbeni. Behind the Oratorio, in V. *del Pian d'Ovile*, is the **Fonte Nuova d'Ovile** (*C 3*), a fountain built in 1295-1303, a fine mediev: blend of monumental form and practical functio: As you walk from Via di Vallerozzi to Via dell'Abb dia, you will see the church of **S. Michele al Mont di S. Donato** (*C3*), built in 1147, and extensive renovated since; inside, a wooden group by Ve chietta. Facing the church is the enormous *Rocc dei Salimbeni*, a 13th-c. fortress rebuilt in Gothic sty in 1883-87 (see below).

Piazza Salimbeni (*C2-3*). "Invented" at the end the 19th c. by the architect G. Partini as part of greater Sienese "Gothic revival," at its center is a *mo ument to Sallustio Bandini* (1880); on the left is th mid-16th-c. *Palazzo Tantucci*, by Riccio.
On the right side is the Neo-Renaissance facade, b G. Partini (1877-82), of *Palazzo Spannocchi*, an im tation of the original, by G. da Maiano (1473), in Vi Banchi di Sopra. At the far end stands **Palazz Salimbeni**, once part of a fortress; the 14th-c. Got ic facade is largely the fruit of 19th-c. restoration by Partini (1871-79). The entire complex serves a the offices of *Monte dei Paschi*, an important Sienes bank dating from the Middle Ages: noted historica archive and fine art collections.

S. Maria delle Nevi (*C2*). This small oratory wa built in 1471 by F. di Giorgio Martini; the sober Re naissance facade overlooks Via dei Montanini; ir side, altarpiece by M. di Giovanni (1477).

Biblioteca Comunale degli Intronati (*D2*). Ope: *by request, tel. 0577280704; closed Sat. aft. and Sur* At n. 5 in Via della Sapienza, in the building wher Siena's Studio, or university, was founded, is this ma jor city institution, based on an 18th-c. donation. Th library now has more than half-a-million volumes including codices illuminated by 12th-/15th-c Sienese artists (L. Vanni, Sassetta, S. di Pietro) and : major collection of drawings and prints. A bit furthe along, the steep *Costa di S. Antonio* offers a fine view of the Duomo and its area; continue down, alon; the Vicolo del Tiratoio, to the Santuario della Cas: di S. Caterina (see below) and the Fonte Branda then return to the center of town along the **Via del la Galluzza**, renowned for the succession of me dieval arches through which it passes.

Santuario della Casa di S. Caterina (*D2*). Ope: *summer, 8:30-12:30 and 2:30-6; winter, 9-12:30 anc 3-5:30.* The sanctuary includes a complex of build ings that have grown up around the birthplace o Caterina Benincasa – Sienese mystic and saint (St Catherine of Siena, 1347-1380), patron saint of Italy with St. Francis) – along the *Portico dei Comuni 'Italia* (1941), where there is a fine 15th-c. well. An trium with loggia, attributed to B. Peruzzi, leads to ne right to the church of the *Crocifisso*, with a 13th-. Crucifix, before which the saint supposedly re-eived her stigmata; facing it is the *Oratorio Supe-ore*, with a gilt lacunar ceiling and majolica floors 16th c.), adorned with 16th-/17th-c. paintings by A. asolani, A. Salimbeni, F. Vanni, R. Manetti, and B. ungai. Continue down to the *Oratorio della Ca-era*, with frescoes by A. Franchi (1896); on the al-r, a 16th-c. masterpiece by G. di Benvenuto; adja-ent is the cell of the saint. Further down is the *Ora-rio di S. Caterina in Fontebranda* (1465-74), still in se; in the interior are frescoes by Sodoma, G. del acchia, and others; on the altar, a wooden statue* f the saint by N. di Bartolomeo (1475).

onte Branda (*D2*). At the end of Via S. Caterina, nis is the best-known of Siena's fountains, standing n the shadow of S. Domenico. Mentioned by Boc-accio, and documented as early as 1081, it was re-uilt in 1246, entirely in brick; the merlons and cor-ice of small arches are modern. Nearby is the anoramic *Vicolo di Camporegio*, with steps leading p to S. Domenico.

. Domenico* (*D2*). The nucleus of the huge brick othic basilica, still standing, was built between 1226 nd 1262-65. Enlarged around 1350, the church had difficult existence: badly damaged by fire (1443 nd 1531), war (1548-52), and earthquake (1798), it vas extensively restored and modified in 1941-62. Devoid of its *facade*, the basilica has a 15th-c. cam-anile, lopped short in 1793, and still has much of s Cistercian apse. *Inside*, note the high mullioned vindows; the huge transept has six apsidal chapels from the apsidal terrace, fine view* of central iena, the Duomo, and the Fonte Branda, below).

iena: S. Domenico and Fonte Branda

On the right as you enter, is the *Cappella delle Volte*, with a fresco of St. Catherine by A. Vanni, believed to be the only accurate portrait of her. Along the right wall of the church, a 14th-c. wooden Crucifix and marble portal to the **Cappella di S. Cateri-na**, with frescoes* by Sodoma and paintings by F. Vanni; the marble tabernacle (G. di Stefano; 1466) contains a reliquary with the saint's head. In the sacristy, standard by Sodoma; at the end of the nave, painting by F. di Giorgio Martini and fresco by P. Lorenzetti.

On the modern main *altar*, note the elegant marble ciborium* and the candle-bearing angels* by B. da Maiano (1475). Note the paintings by M. di Gio-vanni, B. di Giovanni, F. di Vannuccio, Sodoma, R. Manetti, S. di Pietro, and B. Salimbeni.

Fortezza di S. Barbara or *Medicea* (*C1*). This huge square fort with corner bastions was built for Cosi-mo I de' Medici and designed by B. Lanci (1561). Now a public park, it offers a fine view of the hills and city. Inside is the *Enoteca Italiana* (*open midday-1 a.m.; Mon., until 2 p.m.; closed Sun.*), a wine shop featuring local wines and delicacies. Nearby is the *garden of La Lizza* (*C1-2*), established as a park in 1779 and enlarged at the turn of the 20th c.

Chiesa di Fontegiusta (*B2*). Set back on the left side of Via di Camollìa, near the customs office of the *Porta di Pescaia* (closed in 1368), this church was built in 1482-84 with a brick facade (1489). In-side, note the marble main altar*, by Marrina (1517), with a late 14th-c. fresco and, on the far wall, a painting by F. Vanni (1590).

Porta Camollìa (*B1*). This 17th-c. reconstruction of a 14th-c. gate still bears an inscription honoring Ferdinando I de' Medici, a symbol of Sienese hos-pitality: "Cor magis tibi Sena pandit" (Siena opens its heart to you, wider than this gate). Outside the gate, along Viale Cavour, is the tall crenelated *Antiporto di Camollìa* (*A1*; 1270); at the end of the road, near where it meets the Via Cassia, is the medieval Palaz-zo dei Diavoli, restored in 1859.

Sorrento

Elev. 50 m, pop. 17,532; Campania, province of Naples.

Places of interest. The center of the little town is **Piazza Tasso** (named after the poet Torquato Tas-so, who was born here in 1544); a terrace overlooks the gorge that runs down to the Marina Piccola. The *Basilica di S. Antonino* has an 11th-c. portal on the side. A bell tower, set on an arch atop four columns, stands before the **Duomo**, rebuilt in the 15th c. *In-side*, note the choir, a fine piece of intarsia of the Sorrento school. There are ruins of a *Roman arch* in the 16th-c. walls on the side uphill of the town.

Near the entrance to the **Villa Comunale**, note the handsome public park, dotted with palm trees overlooking the sea, and the church of *S. Francesco*, with a little *cloister* of Arab-style intertwined arch-es (14th c.).

Surrounding areas. The coastline stretching from Sorrento is known as the **Costiera Sorrentina**, and offers lovely sights evoked by the poets of the past. At **Punta del Capo***, note the ruins of the *Villa di Pollio Felice.*

Spoleto*

Elev. 396 m, pop. 37,647; Umbria, province of Perugia. "When you draw near Spoleto," wrote Montesquieu, who was on his way from Rome, "the landscape changes entirely: fertile, well-tended, populous lands; lush hills and mountains; and many olive groves." This is in fact the landscape of the Valle Umbra. Rocky, compact, and austere, grey in the intense green, the Rocca, or fortress, surveys the medieval town below. This is the setting of the "Festival dei Due Mondi," or "Festival of Two Worlds." Everywhere, the art, history, and culture of many centuries intertwine: a handsome 19th-c. theater alongside a creation of Alexander Calder.

Historical note. Nearly every period of history has left its mark in Spoleto. The large polygonal stones of the walls date from the pre-Roman Umbrian settlement; the square blocks are from the Roman "colonia," while those shaped like parallelepipeds date from the age of Sulla. Dating from Augustus's reign are the Ponte Sanguinario, the Arco di Druso, and the ruins of a Roman house. A few centuries later a temple, the theater, and the amphitheater were built. Though the Early Christian churches of S. Salvatore and S. Pietro still stand, nothing survives from the High Middle Ages, when Spoleto was the powerful capital of a flourishing duchy, Longobard and later Frankish and Carolingian. The duchy reached its height in 889, when Guido II was crowned king of Italy and, two years later, Holy Roman Emperor. The duchy declined politically, while Romanesque art flourished: the churches of S. Eufemia, S. Gregorio Maggiore, and Ss. Giovanni e Paolo. In 1155 Frederick I destroyed the defiant city, with its ancient cathedral; the modern Duomo was built on the site, and consecrated in 1198. By 1231, the "ducatus spoletinus" had been incorporated into the papal state. Loss of independence did not mean loss of artistic excellence: the 14th-/15th-c. Gothic church of S. Domenico, the Rocca, the Renassiance frescoes of Filippo Lippi, and the Baroque church of S. Filippo. In the late 18th c. G. Valadier worked here, on the Duomo and outside of town (Villa Pianciani). In the late 19th c., the Teatro Nuovo and the Teatro Caio Melisso were built, and later made famous by the Spoleto "Festival dei Due Mondi."

Getting around. For a visit to the historic center, we recommend a walking tour; while a second route includes the monuments outside the walls, for which we recommend driving or taking public transportation.

The historic center

This route runs past Spoleto's chief monuments with the most notable Roman ruins, S. Eufemia, the Duomo, the Rocca, and the Palazzo Comunale. From the dense medieval center of Spoleto, this route goes all the way to the Ponte Sanguinario, near Porta Garibaldi, at the northern end of the old city.

Piazza della Libertà. Right in the middle of Spoleto, this square is bounded to the south by the Neo-Classic Palazzo Ancaiani. Look down on the ruins of the **Teatro Romano**, dating from the early Imperial Age (partly rebuilt in 1954), in the shadow of the medieval church and monastery of S. Agata (now the Museo Archeologico).

Via Brignone. This road runs up from Piazza della Libertà to the monuments in the center of Spoleto. On the right, Palazzo Mauri; not far off, the Arco di Monterone, one of the mighty gates in the Roman walls, possibly dating from the 3rd c. B.C.

Arco di Druso.* This travertine arch was built in the 1st c. B.C. as a monumental entrance to the Roman Forum; it stands next to the 11th-c. church of S. Ansano. Next to the arch and in part beneath the church are the ruins of a Roman temple, with a pronaos with six marble columns.

S. Ansano. Completely rebuilt in the late 18th c., this church has a fragment of a fresco by Spagna. In the 11th-c. crypt*, with 8th-c. columns, note fragments of Byzantine-style frescoes.

Piazza del Mercato. This square lies at the end of Via Arco di Druso; note 17th-c. Palazzo Leti. It occupies a small part of the vast Roman Forum. Note the lovely Fonte di Piazza (1746-48), a fountain in the Roman style.

Palazzo Comunale. Completely rebuilt in the late 18th c., the town hall preserves only the massive 13th-c. tower and some fragments of the 15th-c. frescoes in the great Salone delle Udienze. Upstairs is the **Pinacoteca Comunale** (*open 10-1 and 3-6, closed Mon.*), with two detached frescoes by Spagna originally in the Rocca. Among the painters whose work is in this gallery, mention should be made of the Maestro di Cesi, A. de Saliba, N. Alunno, Maestro di S. Alò, Guercino, S. Conca, and S. Parrocel.

The western wing of Palazzo Comunale, added in 1913, stands on the ruins of a Roman mansion (*entrance from Via Visiale; open same hours as the Pinacoteca*), believed to have belonged to the mother of the Emperor Vespasian.

Piazza Campello. Take the short Via del Municipio to this square, which affords views between old buildings on your right. This park-like square overlooks all Spoleto, and is bounded by *Palazzo Campello* (1597-1600), the 13th-c. former church of *Ss. Simone e Giuda*, with the 17th-c. Fontana del Mascherone. Towering overhead is the **Rocca** (*open for groups with entrance every hour, tel. 074343707 0743223055*), a fortress built in 1359-70 by Gattapone for Cardinal Albornoz.

Via del Palazzo dei Duchi. With its old shops with

stone counters, set in the arches of the church of S. Donato, this road takes its name from an enormous Roman building, partly buried, which was believed to be the palace of Theodoric, the Longobard king. At the corner of Via Fontesecca, note the *Casa dei Maestri Comacini*, home of master builders of the Romanesque period.

Palazzo Arcivescovile. Last rebuilt in the 15th c., this bishop's palace overlooks the 16th-c. facade of *Palazzo Martorelli-Orsini*. Upstairs is the Museo Diocesano (*open summer, 10-12:30 and 4-7; winter, 10:12:30 and 3-6; closed Tue.*), with a collection of religious art and objects from the diocese: note paintings by D. Beccafumi and F. Ragusa. On the palazzo grounds are ruins of a major 1st-c. B.C. Roman building, and the little church of S. Eufemia.

S. Eufemia.* Located in the courtyard of Palazzo Arcivescovile, this ancient church was rebuilt in the early 12th c. and again rebuilt often in the centuries that followed. Note the 13th-c. frontal and the fresco in the apse.

Piazza del Duomo. This spectacular square is bounded by the elegant facade of the Duomo; to the right is the 16th-c. *Palazzo Rancani*. On the far side of the square stands the **Palazzo della Signoria**, a complex of buildings supported by massive piers. At one end is the *Casa dell'Opera del Duomo* (1419); at the far end, near the Duomo, is the octagonal church of *S. Maria della Manna* (1528). In the middle is the little *Teatro Caio Melisso* (1877-80); note the 3rd-c. A.D. sarcophagus, now a fountain.

Duomo.** *Open Mar.-Oct., 7:30-12:30 and 3-6; Nov.-Feb., until 5.* Built in Romanesque style in the 12th c. over the older church of S. Maria in Vescovado, this cathedral has a majestic facade and a mighty campanile. The most outstanding elements are the elaborate rose window, with four smaller rose windows and symbols of the four Evangelists, the enormous

Byzantine-style mosaic (1207), and the fine Romanesque portal (prior to 1198). The **interior** was radically transformed in the early 17th c., but the 12th-c. mosaic floor in the nave is largely original. Note the bronze bust of Pope Urban VIII, by G.L. Bernini (1640) and the fresco* by Pinturicchio. In the right transept, a canvas by Annibale Carracci and the tomb of the painter Filippo Lippi (who died in Spoleto in 1469), designed by his son Filippino. To the right of the presbytery is the Cappella della Santissima Icona, a chapel with a 12th-c. Byzantine icon, donated to Spoleto by the emperor Frederick I Barbarossa. In the apse, **frescoes**** by Filippo Lippi (with Fra' Diamante and M. d'Amelia; 1467-69); main and lateral altars by G. Valadier (1792). Also, the Crucifix by A. Sozio (1187), painted on parchment and applied to a shaped panel.

S. Filippo Neri. In Piazza Mentana, this church was built around 1650. It houses a painting by S. Conca.

Ss. Giovanni e Paolo. This small Romanesque church, consecrated in 1178, stands near Via Filittèria. Inside, note the 12th-c. frescoes, and a depiction of the murder of St. Thomas a Becket in the Cathedral of Canterbury.

Galleria d'Arte Moderna e Contemporanea. *Open 15 Mar.-15 Oct., 10:30-1 and 3-6:30; 16 Oct.-14 Mar. (closed Tue.), 10:30-1 and 2:30-5.* Located in the *Palazzo Rosari-Spada*, at the end of a downhill lane running off Corso Mazzini, this gallery of modern art came into existence when the town of Spoleto acquired the award-winning artworks of the "Premio Nazionale Spoleto" (1953-66); more art was donated over time. Among the artists are C. Accardi, A. Burri, M. Ceroli, G. Capogrossi, P. Consagra, and P. Pascali. A hall is devoted to L. Leonardi, a Spoleto-based painter and sculptor. Also, the original version of the Teodolapio, a large bronze by A. Calder, which has stood in front of the train station since 1962.

Convento di S. Agata. Built upon the houses of the Corvi family (1395) and later modified, this Benedictine monastery has the stern appearance of a fortified residence; inside, a lovely 16th-c. cloister with terracotta columns. The church stands on buttresses sunk in the Roman theater; inside, fragments of 13th-c. frescoes. The former monastery is the home of the **Museo Archeologico Nazionale** (*open 9-7; tel. 0743223277*), with artifacts, mostly Roman, found during digs in the Spoleto area.

S. Domenico. Built in the late 13th c., with white-and-red bands, this church boasts notable 14th-/15th-c. frescoes. Also, inside, a 14th-c. panel, a 15th-c. fresco, an altarpiece with gold leaf background (Maestro di Fossa, early 14th c.), and a carved 14th-c. Crucifix. Nearby, the Teatro Nuovo (1854-64) is the headquarters of the *Museo del Teatro* (*open by request, tel. 0743223419*) with a collection of posters, photographs and other documents related to the theater.

Via Cecili. Bounded by a well-preserved stretch of tall **city walls** (6th and 3rd c. B.C.), with Roman and medieval strata, this road runs from Piazza Torre dell'Olio; on the left, the medieval Porta Fuga com-

Spoleto: Duomo

memorates the defeat of the besieging Carthaginians; alongside the medieval *Palazzo Vigili* stands the tall Torre dell'Olio, from which it is said that boiling oil ("olio") was poured onto Hannibal's troops.
S. Nicolò. This former church was built in the early 14th c. and is now used for conferences and cultural events. Beneath it, the little 14th-c. *S. Maria della Misericordia* church still has traces of old frescoes.
S. Gregorio Maggiore.* This 12th-c. church has much of the original Romanesque building, and stands beside a huge 12th-c. bell tower; note the 16th-c. portico, with the baptistery on the left (14th-c. frescoes). Inside are 12th-/15th-c. frescoes.
Piazza Garibaldi. Next to Porta Garibaldi, a city gate last rebuilt in the 15th c., this square is also strategically close to the Roman bridge known as **Ponte Sanguinario.** The three-arch bridge was built during the reign of Augustus, and was left behind when the course of the river shifted (access by a partly hidden stairway). Nearby are ruins of an enormous 2nd-c. A.D. Roman amphitheater; visible in the courtyard of the military Caserma Minervio, in Via Anfiteatro.

The monuments outside the walls

This tour takes in religious buildings of remarkable architectural and artistic quality, including the churches of S. Pietro and S. Salvatore, built outside Spoleto's walls; also, the ancient church of S. Paolo inter Vineas, SW of the town center, and the spectacular Ponte delle Torri.
S. Paolo inter Vineas. Built in early Christian times, this church was refounded in the 10th c. as a Benedictine convent and was rebuilt in 1234. Inside, note the 13th-c. frescoes*.
S. Pietro* (*D2*). Built upon Roman ruins, enlarged in the 13th c., and later enlarged, this church stands on the lowest slopes of Monteluco. Note in particular the 12th-c. facade* of finely carved stone, and in particular the carved branch motifs around the central portal; also, the emblems and the bas reliefs depicting scenes from the New Testament. *Inside*, note the 15th-c. baptismal font and the stoup.
Ponte delle Torri.* This majestic bridge stands 76 m tall and stretches 230 m in length; its ten arches now support foot traffic but once brought water to the Rocca. It spans the Tessino, linking Colle S. Elia with Monteluco. It was first built in the 12th c. and was then restructured by Gattapone in the 14th c. You can reach it from the road for Monteluco (left at the first hairpin turns), or walk up from Piazza Campello.
S. Ponziano. Believed to have been built on the grave of a martyr, this 12th-c. Romanesque church stands just beyond the Tessino, next to the Flaminia road. Note the cornices and hanging arches, simple portal, and rose window with symbols of the Evangelists. Also noteworthy are the peculiar crypt and fine reused columns.
S. Salvatore.* This early Christian basilica (4th-5th c.) stands on the slopes of the Colle Luciano, just over 1 km from Piazza della Vittoria. Rebuilt over the centuries, the front and apse are original; the facade has three marble portals. Inside, note the fragments of 14th-c. frescoes, and in a niche in the center of the apse, a 9th-c. painted gem-encrusted cross.

Syracuse / Siracusa**

Elev. 17 m, pop. 126,282; Sicilia (Sicily), provincial capital. Until Roman times, this was the most powerful and magnificent city in all of Sicily. Today, it is an impressive and intriguing sight, with a mixture of late Baroque architecture – vivid yet damaged by the passage of time, from the reconstruction of the city following the terrible earthquake of 1693 – and ancient classical architecture. It is situated in an exquisite landscape of sea, rocks, Mediterranean vegetation, under a clear blue sky. Recent expansion of the city has largely followed the road leading to Catania.

Historical note. Siracusa was founded, according to tradition, in 734 B.C. by Greek settlers from Corinth; it had soon attained such wealth that in turn it founded a number of colonies in Sicily. Internal dissension caused the city to fall under the rule of the tyrant Gelon in 485 B.C. Siracusa enjoyed remarkable prosperity under him and under his successor, Hiero. In 466 B.C., the city returned to democratic government, extended its influence over nearly all of Sicily, and eventually entered into harsh conflict with Athens, trouncing the city soundly (414 B.C.). Over the course of the centuries, the city had grown considerably and become quite lovely; of all its monuments, however, only the ruins of the Temple of Apollo have survived, along with the spectacular remains of the Temple of Athena, incorporated into the Duomo. With the elimination of the Athenian menace, Siracusa was threatened by the even more dangerous threat of Carthage. The city managed to withstand the new danger under the rule of Dionysius (406-367 B.C.), who built the Castello Eurialo, one of the most perfect works of fortification of the ancient world; later, in 343 with the generous assistance of Timoleon, who sailed from Corinth to the rescue of Siracusa with a thousand soldiers; and finally under Agathocles (316-289 B.C.). The government of the two tyrants may have brought Siracusa to its greatest splendor. The growing threat of Carthage remained on the horizon, however, and it was only under the rule of Hiero II (265-215 B.C.) that the city enjoyed a period of relative peace. This ruler was responsible for the almost total reconstruction of the theater and the great sacrificial altar that stood before it. Finally, caught up in the great war between Carthage and Rome, Siracusa was laid waste in 212 B.C.; under the Romans, it became the capital of Sicily, but this was the start of a slow decline. It still built a few monuments, such as the complex of the Ginnasio

nd the amphitheater. Enormous catacombs be-
peak the presence of a large Christian comunity.

Getting around. We propose two routes. One ex-
lores the modern city, built from the 19th c. on the
mainland around the classical pentapolis, with the
rcheological museum as the fulcrum. The other
inerary explores the little island of Ortigia, where
he different phases of Syracuse's history are still
resent in the archeological styles.

he mainland

his route takes in the districts of the pentapolis
which were abandoned after the classical age and
uilt again from the 19th century on. It is advisable
o use your car to tour this area.
Parco Archeologico della Neàpoli** (*A1-2; B1-
; open 9-one hour before sunset*). The heart of any
rcheological tour of Syracuse is the archeological
ark of the Neàpolis (Greek for "new city"), which
ncludes most of the classical monuments of Greek
nd Roman Syracuse. Access is allowed only to the
Greek theater and the Latomia del Paradiso (see
elow). The other ruins are visible from the gates
f the park. Nonetheless, the area has retained the
ascinating atmosphere of the past.
an Nicolò dei Cordari (*B2*). The church, near
he entrance of the park, dates back to the 11th c.
nd still has its original apse. Below it is an Imper-
al Age pool which served as a cistern for the am-
hitheater.
ara di Ierone II (*B1*). The base cut into the rock
ndicates the altar of Hieron II, which was built for
ublic sacrifices (3rd c. B.C.); during the Roman
mpire, an immense porticoed plaza stood before
, with a large pool in the middle.
eatro Greco** (*A-B1*). This marvelous Greek the-
ter, cut almost entirely out of living rock, appears
s it was following the renovation in 230 B.C., dur-
ng the reign of Hieron II. However, the theater ex-
sted as early as the 5th c. B.C., when tragedies by
eschylus were performed there, and it was further
dapted in Roman times. The semicircular cavea is
till intact; it was enormous (with a seating capaci-
y of 15,000), and it still has 46 of the original 61
ers of seats; it encloses the orchestra, behind which
vas the platform of the skene, little of which remains
ntact (Charles V used it as a quarry for material
vith which to fortify Ortigia). *Fine view** of the city
rom the terrace at the top of the tiers of seats.
atomia del Paradiso** (*A2*). This the the largest
f the many Latomie, or quarries, where the white
mestone was extracted to build the town and its
valls. The Latomia del Paradiso is interesting for
he Orecchio di Dionisio, or Ear of Dionysius, and
he Grotta dei Cordari.
Orecchio di Dionisio* (*A2*). It is an artificial cave,
5 m long, 5 to 11 m wide, and 23 m tall, that tapers
lmost like a Gothic arch at the top. It was given its
ame by the painter Caravaggio (1608), who be-

Syracuse: Piazza del Duomo

lieved the legend that Dionysius, the ruthless "tyrant"
of 4th-c. B.C. Syracuse, used this as a prison because
of its remarkable acoustic properties of amplifica-
tion, which allowed the tyrant to hear every word
the unwary prisoners uttered.
Grotta dei Cordari* (*A2; not open to the public*).
For centuries, and until just a few decades ago, rope
and cable makers (or "cordari") practiced their
trade in this long cave supported by narrow pillars,
with odd lighting effects and walls decked with
moss and maidenhair ferns.
Anfiteatro Romano* (*B2*). After passing by the
small 11th-c. church of *San Nicolò dei Cordari*, an avenue leads to the belvedere from which the amphitheater can be seen. The ellyptical structure was
largely carved from the living rock in the 3rd c. A.D.,
and was only slightly smaller than the Arena of
Verona. In the marble balustrades, the names of the
owners of the places of honor are still visible.
S. Giovanni Evangelista* (*A3*). Once you have left
the archeological area, the route takes you to the ruins of this little church, razed by the earthquake of
1693. From here you can descend to the **Cripta di
S. Marciano** (the first bishop of Syracuse; (*open 9-
1 and 2:30-6; closed Mon*)), a Greek cross plan crypt
with fragments of frescoes from various periods on
the walls. Also underground is the **Catacomba di
S. Giovanni*** (*same opening hours as the crypt*), a
4th-/5th-c. underground necropolis, with thousands of
burial niches, rotundas and crypts in the main gallery.
Museo Archeologico Regionale Paolo Orsi**
(*A3-4*). *Open 9-2; Tue.-Wed. and Fri., also 4-7:30;
closed Mon.* Housed in the Villa Landolina, this is
one of the leading archeological museums in all
of Italy. It is divided into three sections, covering a
period of time of more than a millennium.
Section A. It is dedicated to prehistory and also includes a geological section. The evolutionary phases of Sicilian civilizations are explored during the different ages, including the Bronze and Copper Ages.
Section B. This part of the museum documents the
centers of Greek colonization, dividing them into

Ionic and Doric. Worthy of note are the sculptures found at *Megara Hyblaea*, and the celebrated **Venere Anadiomene****, a statue of Venus found in 1804. Of the same high artistic value is a statue of a **Winged Victory****.

Section C. This part features the inland sub-colonies of Sicily, among which are *Eloro*, Akrai, Kasmenai e Kamrina.

Bassa Acradina (*A4-5*). This road is flanked by a rocky slope with many caves, some of which were used for the cult of heroes. It leads to the **Latomia dei Cappuccini** (*A5; not open to the public*), near the convent of the same name. The huge cave has fascinating areas with vaults and pillars.

S. Lucia (*B4*). This church, rebuilt in the 17th c. with a great tree-lined square before it, was built on the site indicated by tradition as that of the martyrdom of St. Lucy, a virgin of 3rd-/4th-c. Syracuse. Among the remarkable artworks once here, especially the Burial of St. Lucy* by Caravaggio, most are now in Palazzo Bellomo.

Ginnasio Romano (*C3*; 1st c. A.D.). Of the *quadri-porticus* that surrounded the ancient Roman gymnasium, only the perimeter is still visible.

Foro Siracusano (*C-D3*). A shaft and several bases of columns are all that remain of the ancient agora in this large modern square.

Isola di Ortigia

This is a walking route which explores the little island transformed into a city-fortress over the centuries. Here traces of Greek, Byzantine, Norman, Swabian, Aragonese, Italian Renaissance and Baroque civilization can be seen.

Piazza Archimede (*E5*). The square is the heart of the island and is decorated with the *Fontana di Artemide*. Of the many buildings which surround it, to the south is *Palazzo Lanza*, to the west *Palazzo dell'Orologio*.

Piazza del Duomo (*E5*). Located in the highest part of the island, this is a handsome Baroque architectural complex.

Duomo.** The cathedral features an 18th-c. Baroque facade by A. Palma (1728-54; note the chiaroscuro), but it was built by incorporating the intact outer colonnade of a Doric temple of Athena (5th c. B.C.; the capitals and shafts of the columns can be seen protruding from the side wall in Via Minerva). The nave of the church was once the cella of the temple; among the furnishings in the church, note the baptismal font, made of a Hellenistic krater, supported by little bronze 13th-c. lions. Also note the painting of St. Zosimo*, attributed to Antonello da Messina (removed as a precautionary measure), as well as 16th-c. paintings* by A. Gagini.

Fonte Aretusa* (*F5*). This spring, partly covered by the papyrus plants which grow in abundance, has been bubbling forth into a basin overlooking the sea for millennia. Pindar and Virgil celebrated it in their poems, a fact which lent it a romantic renown linked

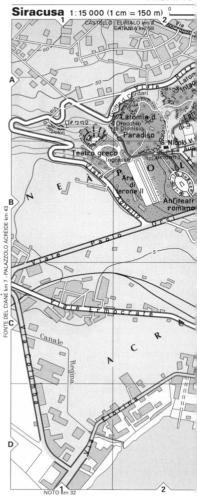

Siracusa 1:15 000 (1 cm = 150 m)

to the myth of the nymph Arethusa, who threw her self into the sea to elude the pursuit of Alphaeu According to the myth, she reappeared as a sprin while Alphaeus transformed himself into an unde water river to follow her, till they finally merged the waters; the freshwater spring of the "*Occhio della Z lica*," feeding into the harbor, is said to be Alphaeus

Galleria Regionale* (*E5*). *Open 9-1:30; Sun., 9-* The gallery housed in *Palazzo Bellomo* (*E5*) boas fine architecture, a collection of *statues*, and a goo *art gallery*, with an **Annunciation**** by A. da Mess na (1474) and the **Burial of St. Lucy*** by Cara vaggio, plus an enormous 18th-c. model of the city

Castello Maniace* (*F5; closed to the public*). Th tip of the island is occupied by this castle, built b Frederick II in 1239; it is square, with round corne towers, a Gothic portal*, and, overlooking the sea, large three-light mullioned window*.

Via Vittorio Veneto (*D-E5*). This is the main stree

ANIA km 58

Cittadella d. Sport

Latomia Casale

Latomia d. Cappuccini

Chiesa dei Cappuccini

Tomba di Archimede

Lgo Cappuccini

Necropoli tropicelli

Via Politti

A

Catacombe di S. Giovanni

S. Giovanni Evangelista

Museo archeologico

Catacombe di Vigna Cassia

Museo d. Papiro

S. Maria di Gesù

Viale Teocrito

Villa Landolina

Madonna delle Lacrime

Stadio comunale

Via Gorizia

S. Lucia

S. LUCIA

B

Via Testaferrata

Via Giovanni

Cappella d. Sepolcro

Pza d. Vittoria

Via Di Natale

Via Ragusa

Pza S. Lucia

Via Trapani

Via Statele

Via Moscu

Arsenale Antico

Pza d. Repubblica

Tel.

Pza Euripide

MAR IONIO

C

Stazione F.S.

Pza Arsenale

Imbarcadero di S. Lucia

Sacrario ai Caduti

Via A. Diaz

Via Dante

Porto Piccolo

nasta mano

Elorina

Ple Marconi

Pza Lepanto

Borgo S. Lorenzo

Viale Montedoro

Via Umberto

Posta e T.

Darsena

Pza d. Posta

P

Tempio di Apollo

D

Via Bengasi

Via Rodi

Pte Nuovo

P.ta Umbria

Via Resalibera

S. Pietro

Ch. d. Carmine

Ple IV Novembre

Staz. Marittima F.S.

Mura greche

Via XX Settembre

Via Minerva

S. Tommaso

Pontile S. Antonio

Darsena

S. Maria d. Miracoli

S. Filippo Neri

Pal. Mergulese Montalto

Pta Marina

Via Maestranza

S. Francesco

Porto Grande

Traghetto per Malta, Catania, Napoli

P

Ch. del Collegio

Foro Italico

Pza Archimede

Prefettura

Belvedere S. Giacomo

Pal. Beneventano

Munic.

ORTIGIA

S. Lucia alla Badia

Duomo

Duomo

Pza

S. Giov. Battista

S. Lucia alla Badia

Pal. Arcivescovile

S. Giuseppe

Capitaneria di Porto

Ch. d. Montevergine

Acquario Tropicale

Pal. Bellomo

Regione

Fonte Aretusa

S. Martino

Pal. Blanco

MAR IONIO

Spirito Santo

F

nerari

1°

2°

Castello Maniace

4

of Spanish Syracuse. Along it are narrow lanes, notable churches, and Baroque palazzi.

Surrounding areas. At a distance of 8 km to the west, note the **Castello Eurìalo**** (*open 9-one hour before sunset*), the finest and most intact military structure to survive from Greek times, built (402-397 B.C.) by Dionysius the Elder atop the Epipolis to provide security against the Carthaginians; it was partly rebuilt in Byzantine times. The site is interesting in terms both of archeology and landscape.

Taormina**

Elev. 204 m, pop. 10,669; Sicilia (Sicily), province of Messina.

Places of interest. Palazzo Corvaia.* *Open 9-1.* It stands at the entrance into town, not far from the gate of *Porta Messina,* and *Piazza Vittorio Emanuele,* which lies on the former site of the Forum. This 15th-c. building features a crenelated facade, mullioned windows with slender columns, and a Catalonian Gothic portal. On the left side of the palace is the little church of *S. Caterina d'Alessandria,* built in the second half of the 17th c. Behind the church, note the **Odeon**, a building from Imperial times, with five wedge-shaped arrays of steps; the front of the skene was constituted by the side of a Hellenistic temple; you can still see some of the steps of the temple base.
Teatro Greco.** *Open summer, 9-6:30; winter 9-4.* This theater probably dates from the Hellenistic period (3rd c. B.C.), and was entirely rebuilt in Roman times (perhaps the 2nd c. A.D.): the cavea was built in a natural hollow on the side of a hill; of the skene, which had a facade of columns and niches, major ruins survive (something quite rare for an ancient theater), and slender cypresses peek out from among them. The **view**** from the cavea and the terraces above the skene is as breathtaking as it was described by Goethe. In the house of the custodian a small *antiquarium* (*soon to be reopened*) houses architectural marble and stone fragments from the city building, as well as financial documents, and statuary.
Corso Umberto I. Pleasant cafés and elegant shops line this main street which runs from one end of the city to the other. Downhill from the first section of this thoroughfare, are the **Naumachie*** one of the most important Roman monuments in Sicily, an imposing stretch of walls built in imperial times to terrace the hillside where a huge cistern for collecting water lay. Interrupting Corso Umberto is the panoramic terrace of **Piazza IX Aprile**, with the former Gothic church of *S. Agostino* (1448).
Through *Porta di Mezzo* and under the *Torre dell'Orologio*, or clock tower, you enter the medieval district; portals and mullioned windows, in Romanesque and Gothic style, embellish the houses.
Cattedrale. Originally built in the 13th c., the cathedral has a long history of construction. The two side portals date from the 15th c. and the 16th c.; in the interior are 15th-/16th-c. polyptychs of the

school of Messina (Visitation by A. Giuffrè and Virgin and Saints, by A. De Saliba).
Corso Umberto I ends at *Porta Catania* . On the left note the vast mullioned windows of the **Palazzo dei Duchi di Santo Stefano*** (14th-15th c.; *open 8:30-12:30 and 3-5; summer, until 7; closed Sun.*).

Surrounding areas. Above the city stands the medieval structure of the **Castello di Taormina** (398 m; *open 9-one hour before sunset*), with a magnificent panoramic view* of the ancient acropolis.
At a distance of 5 km note the picturesque little town of **Castelmola***, built high atop a crag (529 m); the setting is archaic yet refined, and there is another celebrated *view** from the terrace of the Caffè S. Giorgio.

Tàranto

Elev. 15 m, pop. 208,214; Puglia (Apulia), provincial capital. An islet set between two peninsulas almost completely separates the Mar Grande (inlet of the Gulf of Tàranto, bounded by the Chéradi islands and by harbor breakwaters) from the inner Mar Piccolo. The city mostly occupies the islet (the Città Vecchia, or old town) and the peninsula to the SE.

Historical note. Archita di Tàranto is a name of some renown in the history of science: he delved into the fields of mathematics, astronomy, music, and cosmogony, as well as ethics and politics. Between 367 and 361 B.C. he ruled the city of Tàranto, and for the town, an ancient Spartan colony said to have been founded in 706 B.C., this may have been its finest moment: it was the most important city in all Magna Graecia (the ancient colonial cities and settlements of Greece in southern Italy) and it had introduced the Apulian tribes of the inland cities to Greek culture. There was a pact with Rome of mutual non-interference, so that Roman ships were, under no conditions, to sail past the Lacinian promontory (now Capo Colonna). But the Roman ships did indeed venture past the promontory, and war broke out (280 B.C.). It did the Tarentines little good to appeal to Pyrrhus, the greatest general of his age; with 25,000 troops and the first elephants used in battle in Italy, he defeated the Romans, but so suffered in doing so that he achieved what was henceforth known as a Pyrrhic victory. Eventually, the Romans took Tàranto (then known as Tarentum). Among the slaves taken to Rome was a boy called Livius Andronicus: the father of Roman dramatic and epic poetry. Although it had been subjugated, Tàranto remained a Greek city until the time of the Roman Empire. Thus, the museum of Tàranto is an absolute must for anyone who wishes to understand the history of Magna Graecia.

Places of interest. Museo Archeologico Nazionale** (*closed for restoration; temporary exhibition of the collections at Palazzo Pantaleo, in Corso Vittorio Emanuele II*). The museum exhaustively illus-rates the history of Magna Graecia from prehistoric times, with finds from most of the territories of southern Italy.

The *prehistoric section* goes from the Paleolithic to the Iron and Bronze Ages, with finds from Torre Castelluccia and Torre Saturo.

The **history of Taras and Tarentum** is told through many finds discovered in the hundreds of necropolises found in the territory.

The *statuary* comprises pieces dating from the 6th c. B.C. to Roman times, with famous works such as the **Ugento Zeus****, a bronze by a local artist. Many local marble statues were inspired by the art of Lysippus, who was active in Tàranto. The busts and heads of Roman personages, and the tomb furnishings, are also noteworthy.

Among the other *sculptures*, the most interesting pieces are the **reliefs** in local stone which decorated the funerary temples, and the marble sarcophagus of an athlete.

Ceramic production is represented by thousands of vases which testify to the evolution in style and techniques over the centuries. A notable example of this is the **Coppa con pesci****, or goblet with fish.

Many works of *goldsmithery and jewelry* come from the Apulian necropolises, and were probably produced in Tàranto, where this craft was active as early as the 4th-3rd c. B.C. The most outstanding of these are the **funerary furnishings**** from Canosa, including two caskets in embossed silver, a glass box, a gold-plated tubular sceptre, and many fascinating jewels. Finally, more than 50,000 *terracotta figurines* complete this extraordinary itinerary inside the second largest archeological museum in southern Italy.

Castel S. Angelo. The castle was built in 1480 by Ferdinand of Aragorn on the southwest end of the canal. It features the traditional cylindrical corner towers. From the square behind it starts the **Via del Duomo** the main street of the Città Vecchia, which runs almost exactly as it was during the Middle Ages, with, on either side, a labyrinth of alleys and lanes. At the beginning of the road, note three columns, surviving from a *Greek temple* dating from the 6th c. B.C. Further along (in Via Paisiello, *plaque*), note the birthplace of the composer Giovanni Paisiello.

Duomo. The cathedral dates from the 10th-11th c., but was modified and renovated on more than an occasion. The facade (1713) is Baroque, while the columns dividing nave and aisles are from pagan temples, with Roman and Byzantine capitals. The coffered ceiling is a 17th-c. addition, while on the floor are remains of the ancient mosaics.

S. Domenico Maggiore. In this church, set high atop a long staircase, note the Baroque altars in the Leccese style; facade and presbytery both belong to the original early 14th-c. construction.

Tarquinia*

Elev. 133 m, pop. 15,079; Lazio (Latium), province of Viterbo. The great Etruscan city of "Tarxuna" stood on a strategic highland, now the plain of Cìvita; its port later became the Roman colony of Gravisca. The city now appears predominantly medieval, dense with towers and buildings dotted with dark volcanic tufa. It is set on a hill not far from the original settlement; close by is a renowned Etruscan necropolis, unrivalled for its tomb paintings.

Places of interest. Palazzo Vitelleschi.** This palazzo, built by the lords of Corneto in 1436-39, now houses the Museo Nazionale Tarquiniense (see below). A mixture of Gothic and Renaissance styles, the palazzo boasts a handsome loggia and an elegant inner *courtyard** adorned with sarcophagi and carved slabs. Little of the original interior decoration has survived.

Museo Nazionale Tarquiniense.** *Open 9-7; closed Mon.* This museum, founded in 1916, comprises the Bruschi-Falgari Collection and various materials belonging to the town of Tarquinia. It was subsequently enriched with material from the excavations of the necropolis and the ancient settlement on the plain of Cìvita. Most of the material dates from the 6th-3rd c. B.C. The collections include funerary slabs and sarcophagi, both Etruscan and Roman (note the Magnate, the Obeso, and the Sacerdote), the so-called **Cavalli Alati** (Winged Horses, a relief from the temple known as the Ara della Regina); Villanovian tomb furnishings and early ceramics; the **Vase of Bochoris***, from the tomb of an Egyptian pharaoh, proof of trade between Etruria and the eastern Mediterranean as early as the 7th c. B.C.; Greek vases* of Corinthian and Attic production; and bronze mirrors. Yet to be displayed are frescoes* removed from the tombs of the Olimpiadi, the Letto Funebre, and the Triclinio.

Not far from here, in a former quarry, Omero Bordo recently opened the *Etruscopolis (open summer, 10-7; winter, 10-6; closed Wed.)*, a life-size reconstruction of tombs and Etruscan dwellings.

Palazzo Comunale. Originally Romanesque, rebuilt in Baroque style, this building stands in the hilltop Piazza Matteotti.

S. Francesco. Consecrated in the 12th c., this church is a combination of Gothic and Romanesque.

Palazzo dei Priori. Situated near the 13th-c. former church of *S. Pancrazio*, it comprises four 12th-c. towers, in the heart of the intricate **medieval district** – note the church of **S. Martino*** and the 17th-c. *Duomo*, which worth a visit for the frescoes by Pastura. The Palazzo dei Priori houses the *Museo della Ceramica (open Mon.-Fri., 10-12 and 4-6; Sat., 10-12)* which exhibits medieval ceramic pieces found in two wells in the center of town.

S. Maria di Castello.** *Open by request; enquire in the house to the left of the church.* A church in the oldest part of Tarquinia, *Castello*, overlooking the Marta River Valley and still enclosed by medieval walls with towers. Note the central portal. *Inside*, note the lovely capitals on the pillars, the mosaic floors**, the octagonal baptismal font**, the pergamon by G. di Guittone (1209), and the ciborium. On the southern slopes of Castello is the Romanesque church of *S. Maria di Valverde* (*closed for restoration*).

Excursion. To the **Etruscan necropolis of Mon-terozzi** ** (*open 9-5*), in the countryside to the east of town. The area of underground tombs, some marked by mounds, dates from the 7th c. B.C. to Roman times. The tombs are decorated with wall paintings. Among the most interesting tombs are those of the *Tori*, with a depiction of Achilles's ambush of Troilus; *Auguri**, with scenes of combat (both late 6th c. B.C.); *Barone** (6th-5th c. B.C.), with ritual scenes (note flutist and horsemen); *Caccia e Pesca* (about 530 B.C.); *Cardarelli* (about 500 B.C.) with dancing scenes; *Giocolieri* (about 530-520 B.C.); *Leonesse* (about 530 B.C.) with dancers; *Leopardi* (5th c. B.C.) with musicians; *Orco*, with Greek-style deities (4th-3rd c. B.C.).

Tivoli

Elev. 235 m, pop. 52,809; Lazio, province of Rome. Overlooking the Roman countryside from a ridge of the Monti Tiburtini, Tivoli stands among centuries-old olive groves; the river Aniene runs around it in an oxbow curve, plunging from rocky heights in astonishingly romantic waterfalls. In Roman times this was a famed vacation spot, with fine climate and natural scenery (among those who spent their summers here were Sallust, Catullus, Horace, and Maecenas); after the 16th c., aristocratic villas gilded the lily, with fountains, grottoes, overlooks, terraces, statues, and brooding rows of cypress trees. Hadrian's Villa lies beneath it.

Places of interest. Villa d'Este. ** *Open 8:30-6:45; closed Mon*. Built by P. Ligorio in the 16th c. for Cardinal Ippolito II d'Este, this building was originally a Benedictine convent; Ligorio also designed the park and many fountains. The fairly rigorous palazzo features halls frescoed by such 16th-c. Roman painters as L. Agresti, F. Zuccari, and G. Muziano. From the superb loggia you enjoy a fine view of the **garden****, which drops away in symmetrical terraces, clad in rich vegetation and enlivened by numerous fountains and sprays. From the stairway, you climb down past the *Fontana del Bicchierone*, a fountain perhaps by Bernini (on left, the stuccoed *Grotta di Diana*), to the entrancing *Viale delle 100 Fontane*, with fountains and statues. Everywhere are fountains: among them the *Fontana di Tivoli*, probably by P. Ligorio; *Fontana di Roma*, with miniature reproductions of Roman buildings; *Fontana dei Draghi*, also by Ligorio; and the great *Fontana dell'Organo*. The central avenue ends at the *Rotonda dei Cipressi*, with its centuries-old cypresses.

S. Maria Maggiore. Founded in the 13th c. and rebuilt in the 16th c., this church has a late Gothic portal and rose window; inside, artworks by B. da Montelupo, J. Torriti, and B. da Siena.

S. Pietro alla Carità. Founded in the 5th c., this

church boasts handsome columns, possibly take from Hadrian's Villa, and a Romanesque facade an bell tower. The district in which it is located is de ted with late medieval houses.

S. Silvestro. Situated in the small oblong *Piaz del Colonnato*, named after its portico of Roma columns, this Romanesque church has an apse de orated with 13th-c. frescoes. Not far off, facing th 16th-c. church of *S. Nicola*, is a group of two-store medieval houses.

Duomo. With a portico dating from 1650 and a m dieval Romanesque bell tower, this church possess some fine artwork, including a large 13th-c. group wooden statues of the Deposition* and an exqu ite 12th-c. triptych (*covered, visible only on soler occasions*).

Next to the Duomo is an 18th-c. washing tank an the **Mensa Ponderaria** (*temporarily closed*), an a cient Roman public scale, with weights and marb slabs with measures of capacity. Along the steps the *Via del Duomo*, lined with medieval houses, yo will reach the *Palazzo Comunale*, rebuilt at the er of the 19th c.

Tempio di Vesta.* On the site of the ancient acro olis, on a rocky ridge overlooking the valley with waterfalls, is a small, round, well-preserved 2nd temple, dedicated either to Vesta or to Hercule Near it is the **Tempio di Tiburno**, the myth founder of Tivoli.

Villa Gregoriana.* *Open 10-one hour before su set; access from Largo S. Angelo*. This immense pa is laid out around the **waterfall**** of the Anie River (vertical drop of 160 meters). First you c scend to the overlook of the *Grande Cascata*, th great waterfall, where the water plunges from a ma made channel, inaugurated in 1835 by Pope G gory XVI. Next you tour the *Grotta delle Sibille* an two other *waterfalls* – the *Cascatelle Piccole* and t *Cascata Bernini* – before reaching the astonishi and deafening *main overlook** of the Grande C scata. Then you continue on to two more grotto the *Grotta della Sirena*, where the water rush straight down, and the *Grotta di Nettuno*, heavily e crusted with mineral deposits.

Rocca Pia (*closed for restoration*). This power fortress, built by Pius II (1461), dominates Viale Tr ste. Near it are the ruins of a huge Roman Imper Age *amphitheater* (2d c. A.D.). Further east is t 15th-c. church of **S. Giovanni**, with frescoes attr uted to A. Romano (1475).

Todi*

Elev. 400 m, pop. 16,722; Umbria, province of P rugia. If you head south along the Tiber from P rugia, high on a bluff over the valley appears patch of medieval Umbria, ancient bell towe and colorful roofs amid the green and yello

Historical note. In Todi, the strongest influence still the 13th c., when the last and largest circle walls was built, along with many of the buildings e central square, and the enormous church of S. ortunato. In ancient times, Todi belonged to the Umrians, and marked the boundary with the Etruscans he name "Tuder" means border), and eventually beame an Etruscan town. The Roman period has left ome noteworthy relics, among them the great nichs of the Mercato Vecchio. Of the monuments produced in later centuries, when Todi was under paal rule, the most notable is the 16th-c. church of S. aria della Consolazione, just outside the city walls.

laces of interest. **Piazza del Popolo.*** This quare stands atop the hill, in the center of town. verlooking it are the Gothic **Palazzo dei Priori**, n the south, and the Palazzo del Popolo and the alazzo del Capitano, to the west. To the north is the athedral, or Duomo. Near the Duomo is Palazzo esi, attributed by some to A. da Sangallo the ounger.

alazzo del Popolo* or *del Podestà*. Stern Gothic chitecture, from 1214-28, marks this building, linked y an exterior stairway to the **Palazzo del Capi- no del Popolo*** (1290). On the third floor are the **useo-Pinacoteca** (*open Mar. and Sep., 10:30-1 and 5; Apr.-Aug., 10:30-1 and 2:30-6; Oct.-Feb., 10:30-1 d 2-4:30; closed Mon. except in Apr.; tel. 758944148*). The new layout has divided the colctions in several sections: *Museo della Città*, of a storic character; the *archeological, numismatic and brics sections*; and the *Pinacoteca*, with interesting intings, among which a fine panel by Spagna.

uomo.* This cathedral was begun in the 12th c., d renovated in the 13th-14th c. Note the Gothic ortals and rose window in the facade. Inside, note e fresco by F. da Faenza (16th c.), fresco by Spagna 525), and altarpieces. A ramp to the left of the uomo leads, through a portal by Vignola, to the lazzo Vescovile, built in 1593.

Fortunato.* This church was begun in 1292, aced dramatically atop a stairway, with two little omanesque lions before it. In the 15th-c. facade,

note the Gothic central portal*. A fine work in the interior is the Virgin and Angels* by M. da Panicale (1432); also, fragments of paintings by the school of Giotto. In the apse, a fine carved wooden choir (1590). In the 16th-c. crypt Jacopone da Todi (1230-1306), a religious poet, is buried.

Piazzale IV Novembre. To the right of S. Fortunato; note the ruins of the 14th-c. fort, and the view*.

Piazza del Mercato Vecchio. This square is lined with the ruins of a huge Roman building from the 1st-c. B.C. Also note the medieval fountain.

S. Maria in Camuccia. Small 13th-c. Romanesque church, in a setting of medieval buildings.

S. Maria della Consolazione.* Standing in isolation, outside the medieval walls, in a lovely hilly setting, this church is one of the masterpieces of the Umbrian Renaissance. Begun in 1508, among its architects were Bramante, B. Peruzzi, Vignola, and M. Sanmicheli.

Mura Medievali, or Medieval Walls. Built in the 13th c. A well preserved section, with square towers, can be seen along the outer ring road that runs from the Tempio della Consolazione to Porta Romana.

Convento di Montesanto. This convent was built in the early 13th c. in a site holy to the Etruscans, and came, with later additions, to resemble a fortress. Marvelous view from the entrance square.

Torcello* (Isola di / Island of)

Veneto, province and township of Venice. The stern cathedral; the nearly millennium-old campanile that rears up over this little village, marking it from afar; the few scattered buildings and ruins, clustered around a grassy clearing, commemorating the main square of a long-vanished town. Torcello was the heir to the Roman town of Altino and had a population of 20,000, a bishop, a port, and salt marshes. All this when the site of Rialtine Venice was still swept by wind and waves. Now Torcello is an island of gardens, where outt-of-season fruit and vegetables are cultivated, or where artichokes are grown. Surrounded by silent waters and other islands, it lies in the NE section of the lagoon 10 kilometers from Piazza S. Marco.

Places of interest. S. Maria Assunta.** Dating from the 7th c., but rebuilt in the 11th c., along with its campanile, the cathedral of the first major lagoon settlement stands by the remains of the baptistery and by a narthex which was enlarged in the 14th-15th c. The *interior* has a nave with two aisles with columns topped by classical and Byzantine capitals; the floor is decorated with 11th-c. marble inlay and mosaics. In the counter-facade, note the remarkable Giudizio Universale, or Last Judgement*, a large 12th-/13th-c. mosaic; in the nave, iconostasis with marble plutei (or dwarf walls between pillars) with bas-reliefs (10h c.) and 15th-c. paintings in the architrave. To the left of the altar, note the original inscription commemorating the foundation of the

di: Duomo

Torcello: S. Fosca

church (A.D. 639), believed to be the earliest document of Venetian history.

S. Fosca.* This Romanesque construction with a central plan (11th c.) is surrounded on the outside by a pentagonal portico and with apses with two rows of arcades; the interior has a Greek cross plan.

Museo di Torcello. *Open Apr.-Oct., 10:30-5:30; Nov.-Mar., 10-5; closed Mon. and holidays.* This museum is housed in the 14th-c. *Palazzo dell'Archivio* and *Palazzo del Consiglio*: it features archeological material from Altino and the lagoon (reliefs, bronzes, ceramics) and various objects from the 11th-16th c. (sculpture, paintings), including the remains of the ancient silver altarpiece of the cathedral (13th c.).

Trani

Pop. 53,732; Puglia (Apulia), province of Bari. From the Piazza del Duomo the view is unforgettable. The sea crashes with foaming spray at the foot of this pink cathedral, with its towering campanile, jutting so much over the water that it seems as if it is about to set sail.

Places of interest. Cattedrale.** Begun in the 12th c. and completed midway through the 13th c., this cathedral is one of the most complete and refined examples of Pugliese Romanesque. The central portal features exquisite bronze doors* by Barisano da Trani (1180 ca.). The campanile was rebuilt after WWII with original materials. *Inside*, beneath the transept, is the *crypt of S. Nicola**, dense with slender columns; from here you can enter the church of *S. Maria*, and a crypt, which extends the length of the church underground. Still lower is the *Hypogaeum of S. Leucio*, pre-Romanesque.

Nearby is the **Museo Diocesano** (*open winter, 9:30-12:30; summer, also 4-7; Sun., by request, tel. 0883584632*), the museum of the diocese with medieval paintings and architectural and sculptural fragments.

Castello. The castle was built by Frederick II (1233-49) and rebuilt several times before the final restoration. It has a quadrangular plan with a imposing tower.

Ognissanti. This church formed part of the Ospedale dei Templari, or Hospital of the Knights Templar, in the 12th c.

In the historic center, with its virtually intact medieval structure, are the synagogue and various interesting churches, including *S. Giacomo*, *S. Andre* (Byzantine style, with a Greek-cross plan), an *S. Francesco*, consecrated in 1184.

The **Museo delle Carrozze** (Carriage Museum *open by request, tel. 0883482641; 9:30-12 and 4-6* is located in the 18th-c. Palazzo Antonacci.

Trent / Trento*

Elev. 194 m, pop. 104,906; Trentino-Alto Adige regional and provincial capital. The town stands at the convergence of the valleys tha run through Trentino amidst the Alps (Al Giudicarie, Valle Anaunia, Valli dell'Avisio, Va sugana). It has always been the focal point c its region, and is surrounded by mountair drained by the Adige, a river linking the P Valley to the Alps and all that lies beyone Trent is a town of stern medieval and R naissance architecture, where mountains gre the gaze on every hand.

Historical note. In the Stone Age, primitive peoples lived on the Doss Trento, which towers over 1 m above the banks of the Adige. This was a fortre in Roman times, though the town of Tridentu stood on the other bank of the Adige, near the h toric center. Abandoned in the High Middle Ag for the Doss (Early Christian ruins), Trent was slo ly repopulated, with a surge in the 13th c., when th Adige ran along the modern locations of the V Torre Vanga and Via Torre Verde. Back then, Tre had been detached, along with the entire Marc Veronese, from the Kingdom of Italy, and incorp rated into Bavaria by the Emperor Otto I in 952. Th marked the beginning of Trent's German identi Shortly after the year 1000 the German Holy Roma emperors gave the bishops of Trent temporal po er, in a bid to keep the strategic mountain pass open. And the prince-bishops immediately four themselves caught up in the rivalry between th pro-pope Guelphs and the pro-emperor Ghibelline In 1273 the bishops were stripped of their power the counts of the Tyrol, who thus incorporated t town. Trent then fell to Rudoph of Hapsburg, with popular uprising in 1407, supported by Venice, th ended in a bloody Tridentine defeat, and, a cen ry later, a treaty with Maximilian I. From 1516 to 15 Trent was ruled by a bishop, Bernardo Cardinal Cles, who gave the city its Renaissance appearan and built the Castello del Buonconsiglio and t church of S. Maria Maggiore. He also laid t groundwork for the Council of Trent, which m from 1545 and 1563, largely in the Duomo and Maria Maggiore, and which started the Counter R formation. The following century, under the Madru zo family bishops, was Trent's golden age; succe sive ages are largely occupied with military histo with a siege in 1703, French occupation in 1796 a 1801, a brief annexation to Bavaria (1806-1809) a to Napoleon's Kingdom of Italy (1810-1813). The Austro-Hungarian Empire ruled until 1918, a time of growing prosperity. The course of the Adige was shifted, and the city grew, northward and southward.

Getting around. Part of the historic center of Trent is closed to traffic, especially Via Manci, Via Belenzani, and Piazza del Duomo. The route we recommend is a walking tour, except for the visit to the Museo d'Arte Moderna e Contemporanea in Palazzo delle Albere, which can be reached by car or by public transport.

Places of interest. Piazza di Fiera. This square is lined with about 100 m of *crenelated walls*, built in 1230; to the west, at the end of Via Mazzini, is the *Torrione*, ruins of a 16th-c. round tower, now used as living quarters. Ample underground parking.

Museo Tridentino di Scienze Naturali. *Open 9-12:30 and 2:30-6; closed Mon*. Housed in the 16th-c. *Palazzo Sardagna*, in Via Calepina at n. 14, with walls frescoed by Fogolino, this museum of natural science has collections of geology, prehistory, zoology, and botany. Note the prehistoric art from the Tridentine region.

Piazza del Duomo.* The monumental center of Trent, adorned by the 18th-c. *Fontana del Nettuno*, this square is surrounded by noble residences and buildings. On the south is the long side of the Duomo. To the east is the 13th-c. *Palazzo Pretorio*, with mullioned windows, site of the Museo Diocesano (see below), and the *Torre Civica*. To the NE, the two 16th-c. *Case Cazuffi*, with facade frescoes by Focolino; note the small *Fontana dell'Aquila*.

Duomo.** This cathedral, a stern mixture of Romanesque and Gothic (12th-13th c.), with a powerful 16th-c. bell tower, is flanked by charming little loggias, with large rose windows in facade and transept, lavish portals, and a handsome apse (adjacent to which is the so-called Castelletto, a battlemented 13th-c. building, with mullioned windows). *Inside*, a high nave with aisles, polystyle piers and cross vaults. Note the flying staircases cutting diagonally across the walls at the foot of each aisle. Along the walls, various 16th-c. funerary monuments. Note the Altar of S. Anna with the altarpiece by Fogolino; nearby, the *Cappella del Crocifisso* contains a historic wooden crucifix (16th c.) by the German sculptor S. Frey. Here, the decrees of the Council of Trent were promulgated. At the head of the left aisle, 13th-c. stone statue of the Madonna degli Annegati (named after the fact that those drowned in the river Adige were brought before the statue to be identified, when it still stood in a niche outside the church).

Beneath the church, remains of the 6th-c. *Early Christian basilica* (*open Mon.-Sat., 10-12 and 3-6*), unearthed in 1977, with mosaic walls and fragments of sculpture.

Palazzo Pretorio. This building lines the east side of Piazza del Duomo and houses the Museo Diocesano (see below). Next to it is the 13th-c. *Torre Civica* (the civic tower, 41 m tall).

Museo Diocesano Tridentino.* This religious museum features the most precious treasures of the Cathedral: seven Flemish *tapestries**, executed in Brussels by P. van Aelst at the turn of the 16th c.; carved altars and statues, panels and paintings, all from the 14th-18th c. are also on exhibit.

Via Belenzani.* This broad, elegant road is one of the loveliest in Trent; it is lined by Renaissance Venetian-style palazzi, some with frescoed facades. In particular, note at n. 20 the 16th-c. *Palazzo Geremia*; at n. 32, the *Casa Alberti Colico*, with frescoes by Fogolino. Across the street, *Palazzo Thun*, now the town hall. At the end of the street is the church of *S. Francesco Saverio*, the finest Baroque church in Trent.

Via Manci. This street is lined with remarkable palazzi, among them n. 63, the Baroque *Palazzo Galasso*, 1602; n. 57, the 16th-c. *Palazzo Pedrotti*, headquarters of the Società degli Alpinisti Tridentini (SAT, an association of mountaineers), with the small *Museo della SAT* (*open Tue. and Thu., 4-7; Sat., 3-7*), dedicated to the mountains; just beyond, the 16th-c. *Palazzo Salvadori*, once a synagogue. At the end of the road is the early 16th-c. *Palazzo del Monte* – note the frescoes of the Labors of Hercules, executed around 1540.

Castello del Buonconsiglio.** Ancient residence of the bishop-princes, this castle stands within an enclosure wall studded with low keeps.

The castle comprises several wings: to the north, topped by the round *Torre Grande*, the battlemented 13th-c. *Castelvecchio*, modified in 1475, with a lovely central courtyard with stacked loggias; note the frescoes by Fogolino and others. In the center, the so-called *Giunta Albertiana*, a wing built to join the north and south wings in the 17th c.; to the south, the *Magno Palazzo*, Renaissance in style, with a broad loggia overlooking the Cortile dei Leoni. Note the splendid frescoes by G. Romanino (1531-32).

Inside is the **Museo del Castello del Buonconsiglio-Monumenti e Collezioni Provinciali*** (*open Oct.-Mar., 9-12 and 2-5; Apr.-Sep., until 5:30; closed Mon.*), with sections also in Castel Beseno, Castel Stenico, and Castel Thun. It features ancient, medieval, and modern art. From the entrance, you cross

Trent: Duomo

the garden, and on the right you can see the cells of Italian heroes D. Chiesa, C. Battisti, and F. Filzi, executed here in 1916. The Museum, with artifacts, coins, codices, sacred objects, and paintings, occupies many rooms in the Magno Palazzo and the Castelvecchio; note the carved wooden ceilings and frescoes by D. Dossi, Romanino, and Fogolino and the frescoes of the *12 Months** (*March* has been lost) by anonymous 15th-c. artists.

In one restored building in the complex, you will find the **Museo Civico del Risorgimento e della Lotta per la Libertà** (*open same hours as the Museo del Castello*), with memorabilia and documentation of WWI and the Italian Resistance movement of WWII.

Piazza Raffaello Sanzio. Note the yellow-and-green tiled *Torre Verde*, dating from the 13th c., with fragments of the ring of walls of which it was a part.

Piazza Dante. Located elsewhere the modern *Palazzo della Regione* (A. Libera, 1954-62) to the east, the train station to the NW, and the Palazzo della Provincia to the north, this square boasts a large public garden with a famed *monument to Dante*, by C. Zocchi (1896), a symbol of Italian resistance under Austrian domination. To the west, note the 12th-c. Romanesque church of *S. Lorenzo*, rebuilt in 1955 after heavy damage from bombing in WWII.

S. Apollinare. Across the river Adige, this 14th-c. Romanesque-Gothic church has a portal and rose window in red Veronese porphyry.

Palazzo delle Albere . *Open 15 Sep.-15 Jun., 9-12:30 and 2:30-6:15; 16 Jun.-14 Sep., 10-12:30 and 2:30-7*. This square "suburban" villa with corner towers and moat was built around 1535 by the bishop-prince C. Madruzzo. It is the site of the Tridentine section of the **Museo d'Arte Moderna e Contemporanea di Trento e Rovereto** (MART; *open Tue.-Sun., 10-6*) with documentation of fundamental phases of Italian art, from Romanticism and Divisionism, and the Ca' Pesaro period to the Novecento movement, and from Spatialism to the Informal. Among the Trent-born artists are E. Prati, U. Moggioli, L. Bonazza, T. Garbari, and F. Depero.

Torre Vanga. Square and crenelated, this tower was built in the 13th c. to protect a bridge over the river Adige.

S. Maria Maggiore. Renaissance church (1520-1524), with noteworthy portal and campanile, the site of many of the meetings of the Council of Trent; inside, artwork by P. Ricchi (1664) and G.B. Moroni (1551), and a marble chancel choir by V. and G. G. Grandi (1534). Continuing along Via Rosmini, near n. 18, in a garden-courtyard, note the mosaic floor of a 2nd-c. A.D. *Roman villa*.

Treviso*

Elev. 15 m, pop. 81,771; Veneto, provincial capital. Narrow porticoed streets, lovely vignettes, and astonishing monuments rearing high, a welter of medieval lanes set within the old walls, Gothic and Renaissance paintings – Treviso, set at the confluence of the Botteniga River (once

called the Cagnan) and the Sile, is also "entwined with the restless filigree of water, studded everywhere with emerald patches of trees and gardens" (G. Comisso). Small and mid-sized businesses drive the economy, though its many gardens and orchards make Trevisan cuisine to say it again with Comisso, "human and complete, based on a thorough understanding of the health and tastes of living creatures."

Historical note. Etchings of the 16th-18th c. show us a fortified Treviso, the work of a newly alert Venice immediately following the great defeat of Agnadello (1509). The walls of this stronghold can still be seen in part, with only three gates: Porta Altinia, Santi Quaranta, and P.S. Tomaso. Within the haven of those walls stood, for many centuries, medieval Treviso; bombardments of WWI and bombing in WWII destroyed that town only partially, happily enough. Treviso was born in the Middle Ages. Even though under Augustus an ancient settlement was elevated to Roman outpost, with the name of Tarvisium, the city – off the main roads but with a river port – grew especially during the High Middle Ages. It prospered under Goth and Longobard rule, and became a capital in Carolingian times. The center grew in an "island" between the two branches of the river Cagnan, where the Romans had lived, building on the site of a pagan temple the Duomo, Battistero, and Episcopio, or bishop's palace. Treviso fought against the emperor in league with the Po Valley towns, and from 1207 ruled itself. In 1210, Treviso built the Palazzo dei Trecento, named after the 300 members of the city council. It was a major center for troubadors, such as Sordello, attracted by the city's love of poetry and song. Even when self-rule gave way to seigneurs, Treviso kept its reputation as a prosperous town of book lovers and connoisseurs of poetry. Venice took Treviso in 1339, lost her in 1381, and took her back in 1388. The town slumbered for centuries in an agrarian backwater; and under Austrian rule (1813-1866) the railroad link to Venice shifted the center of the town south, to the station; from here to Porta S. Tomaso, along the walls, at the turn of the 20th c., was built a promenade that still sets Treviso apart.

Places of interest. S. Nicolò.* This Gothic church dates from the 13th c., and is made entirely of brickwork, with tall windows and apses. The interior has a nave with two aisles, transept, and five chapels. Note the colossal round piers. Among the artists whose work adorns the church, we should mention: T. da Modena, L. Bregno, A. da Treviso, M. Pensaben, G. Savoldo, and Andrea da Murano. Note the remarkable organ, built by A. Palma, with doors painted by G. Lauro. In the chapel to the right of the *presbytery*, 14th-c. frescoes (also note frescoes in sacristy); on the altar is a canvas by the Anonymous Venetian. Also note the *Monument to the Senator Agostino Onigo**, by the sculptor Giovanni Buora and the painter Lorenzo Lotto.

Seminario Vescovile. Adjacent to the church, in

ormer convent, is the *Sala del Capitolo dei Domeniani* (*open summer, 8-6; winter, 8-5:30*), decorated with oteworthy frescoes by Tommaso da Modena (1352), nd three small museums (*open Sun., 9-12; for groups y request, tel. 04223247*): the *Museo Etnografico degli ndios del Venezuela*, with tribal objects from Amaonia; the *Museo Zoologico Giuseppe Scarpa*, with alian vertebrates and exotic reptiles; the *Museo di rcheologia e Paleontografia Precolombiana del Suamerica* featuring pre-Columbian culture.

Museo Civico Luigi Bailo.* *Open 9-12:30 and :30-5; Sat.-Sun., 9-12 and 3-7; closed Mon., Christas and 1 Jan*. Located at n. 22 in Borgo Cavour, his museum houses the archeological and art colections of the town of Treviso. In the *archeological ection* are objects from the Copper, Bronze, and Iron ges (axes, buckles, swords*), Roman artifacts (urns, laques, sculptures, portraits, bronzes), as well as culptures from early Christian times and the High liddle Ages. In the *gallery* are paintings and states: in particular, by Venetian and local artists: G. da reviso the Elder, G. da Treviso the Younger, P.M. Penacchi, and L. Pozzoserrato. Special note should be ven to the works by G. da Fabriano, Giovanni Belli, C. da Conegliano, L. Lotto, Titian, Pordenone, P. Borone, J. Bassano, R. Carriera, F. Guardi , P. and A. onghi. Also, works by 19th-c. painters (F. Hayez, I. affi) and a sculpture by A. Canova.

the *Galleria Comunale d'Arte Moderna* are works the Trevisan sculptor Arturo Martini: note the bust Lilian Gish.

useo della Casa Trevigiana. *Open Tue.-Sat., 9-:30 and 2:30-5; Sun., 9-12; closed Mon*. Located in e *Casa da Noal*, at n. 38 Via Canova, this late Goth building houses a collection of medieval and Reaissance marble sculptures, terracotta, wooden states, ancient weapons, and musical instruments. Next or, at n. 40, is the Renaissance *Casa Robegan*; in the arby Via Riccati, which leads to Piazza del Duomo: n. 52-56 note the mid-15th-c. house, and, across the eet, a series of 15th- and 16th-c. houses, frescoed.

uomo.** Originally built in the Middle Ages (Roanesque sections on the left side, column-bearing ons on either side of the pronaos): the apse of this thedral was rebuilt in the 15th-16th c., and the rest as rebuilt in the 18th c. Before it stands a Neo-Clas six-pillar pronaos, built in 1836. The *interior*, dided into three spaces, with seven cupolas, includes works by noteworthy painters and sculptors. nong them are A. Vittoria, A. Lombardo, P. Bordone, da Treviso the Elder, Titian, G. A. Pordenone, P. and Lombardo, and L. Bregno. Note the 11th-c. *crypt*, th a forest of little columns and re-used capitals ossibly 8th c.).

attistero. To the left of the Duomo, this Roanesque baptistery (11th c.) has a 14th-c. bas-ref on the pediment, Roman friezes on either side the portal, and, inside, fragments of 12th-c. freses in the apses. Note the large 11th-c. bell tower.

useo Diocesano di Arte Sacra. *Open Mon.-Thu., 2; Sat. 9-12 and 3-6; closed Fri. and Sun*. Entrance this museum of sacred art is at n. 9 Via Canoniche.

Treviso: Piazza dei Signori

Note the various marble reliefs*, the fresco by T. da Modena, the tapestries and other objects from the Treasury of the Cathedral.

Calmaggiore. This lovely and busy main street of the old town is lined by 15th- and 16th-c. porticoes and homes.

Piazza dei Signori.* In the middle of Treviso, the medieval flavor of this square is due to the complex of Communal buildings (many of them rebuilt) on three sides. To the east, **Palazzo dei Trecento***, from about 1210 (wholly rebuilt, 1946-52), then *Palazzo del Podestà* with the *Torre Civica*, and, on the west side, the ancient *Palazzo Pretorio*.

Loggia dei Cavalieri. Romanesque arcaded structure (1276-77), once a meeting place for Treviso's nobility.

Piazza del Monte di Pietà. Behind Piazza dei Signori is the ancient *Palazzo del Monte di Pietà*, with the **Cappella dei Rettori*** (*open Mon.-Fri., 9-1 and 3-5; only for groups, by request 10 days before the visit; tel. 0422654320*), a small 16th-c. room, richly adorned with paintings and decorated leather walls (17th c.).

S. Lucia and S. Vito. In Piazza S. Vito, these two medieval churches have been joined into one. Of the two, **S. Lucia**, with frescoes by T. da Modena, is the more interesting, though both are worth a visit.

Pescheria. This islet on the Bottenga River is the site of the fish market; note the welter of canals and little lanes that converge here.

S. Francesco.* This Gothic church, built in 1230, was rebuilt in 1928; note the frescoes by Tommaso da Modena, the tombs of Francesca, daughter of Petrarch (d. 1384), and Pietro, son of Dante Alighieri (d. 1364).

Porta S. Tomaso. The most monumental of the three gates in Treviso's Venetian-built walls, it dates from 1518 (G. Bergamasco); note the lion of St. Mark's, emblem of Venice.

S. Caterina dei Servi di Maria. *Closed for restora*

tion. This 14th-c. church was devastated by Allied bombing in 1944, restored, and made into an art gallery. Note the paintings, by Tommaso da Modena and others.

S. Maria Maggiore. This Gothic church was built in 1473 and has a handsomde 15th-c. *cloister*.

Villa Manfrin. As you head toward Conegliano, note this huge estate, dating from 1783, with vast gardens open to the public.

Surrounding areas. The Parco Naturale Regionale del Fiume Sile is a natural park running the length of the Sile River (about 95 km); flora and fauna are one attraction; noble villas and industrial archeology are two more (boat trips are available on the lower course of the Sile; *for information, tel. 0422788663*).

Trieste*

Pop. 216,459; Friùli-Venezia Giulia, regional and provincial capital. If you first see Trieste from the Adriatic, or from a train, or if you arrive by car, dropping down along the road that descends from the Karstic highlands, it appears set as on a stage, between the lighthouse to the north and the modern harbor to the south. In the words of Italian poet Umberto Saba, "young city, with its masculine adolescence, formless and unrestrained, growing between the sea and the harsh hills behind." Some consider the finest architecture and urban settings of Trieste to be found in the courtly order of the Borgo Teresiano (the district named after the empress Maria Theresa; her father, Emperor Charles VI, laid the foundations for the growth of modern Trieste by establishing the free port here). Unquestionably, the 19th-c. buildings that line the shore speak eloquently of the city's past as the great maritime outlet of the Austro-Hungarian Empire (the name Trieste comes from an ancient word meaning "market"). The cultural tradition here is intensely Italian, yet cosmopolitan and receptive to Europe. The view of the Gulf of Trieste and the Adriatic beyond is alluring; these is a sense of the sea, in the light of summer and even winter, when the impetuous "bora" wind brings good weather.

Historical note. Trieste became what it is today in the 18th-19th c.; before, it was a tiny village. A Roman colony named Tergeste in the late 1st c., it was triangular in plan, with the seashore as the base, and the hill of S. Giusto as the tip. The medieval walls ran down from the Castello to the sea like two long arms, enclosing the same triangle. What survives from Roman times are the ruins of the basilica of the Forum, on the hill, the Roman theater, and the so-called arch of Riccardo, probably a gate in the walls. From medieval times, only the cathedral of S. Giusto is worthy of any note. Trieste, which was for many years under

Byzantine rule, and was only briefly ruled by Goth and Longobards, became part of the Carolingian Em pire around 788. In 948 the king of Italy, Lothar gave the bishop John and his successors tempor power over Trieste. This date marks the beginning Trieste's growth as an independent town. In 1236 a other bishop named John, in financial straits, sol his rights to govern the city; pressed by the patriarc of Aquileia and the counts of Gorizia and Venice, T este surrendered itself in 1382 to the duke of Austr Leopold II. Trieste thus survived, leading a mode existence within the realm of the Hapsburgs, in re ative independence. The structure of the city r mained that of the medieval town it had once bee right up until the 17th c., when it had a populatio of just 3,000. Everything changed in the 18th c. Th Hapsburgs, following their victories over the Turk penetrated into the Balkans and Charles VI, follo ing the War of Spanish Succession, ruled as the Ki of Naples for 20 years. Having proclaimed, in de ance of Venice, freedom of navigation in the Adri ic Sea, in 1719 the emperor gave Trieste the status free port. That was only the beginning. The empre queen, and archduchess Maria Theresa did ev more to encourage maritime trade, promoting t creation of a large market, attracting merchants a bankers, small businessmen and craftsmen, labore and porters. By the end of the century Trieste had population of 30,000. In the area that was once c cupied by ancient salt flats – which offered a me ger income, enough to allow the city's waning a tocracy to eke out its existence – rose a new city, a checkerboard layout. The "borgo teresiano," or "d trict of Theresa," followed, in an area reclaimed fr the sea at the foot of the Colle di S. Vito or the "b go giuseppino," or "district of Joseph." Following t crisis of three occupations by Napoleonic troo development continued in a frenzy. During this p riod the most renowned Neo-Classic edifices we built: Palazzo Carciotti, Palazzo della Borsa, church of S. Antonio Nuovo, the Teatro (now Tea Verdi); and between 1831 and 1838 the most portant companies were established: Assicurazi Generali, Lloyd Austriaco (now Lloyd Triestino), Arsenale del Lloyd, and the Riunione Adriatica Sicurtà. By 1819 Trieste had established Italy's fi steamship line. The last decades of the 19th c. a the early years of the 20th c. witnessed further velopment of Trieste, which grew from a populati of 176,000 in 1900 to a population of 247,000 in 19 the fourth largest city in the Austro-Hungarian E pire. The city continued to grow to the east of w is now Via Carducci, in the "borgo franceschino" a in the so-called "rioni industriali" which gobbled farm villages in the surrounding area. The city gan to grow once again, expanding into the outsk and developing residential districts, when it was nexed by Italy (1918), after the political shifts in hinterland drastically reduced its importance a port, pushing Trieste toward greater industrializati In the period following WWII as well, Trieste hove in a limbo as a potential Free Territory for alm en years, and then became part of Italy again only in 1954. In this period the industrial zone of Zaule was created, along with the satellite town of Borgo san Sergio; low-cost housing was also built for tens of thousands of refugees from Istria. Despite this massive immigration, Trieste, after a long period of demographic stagnation, is declining sharply in population, and is now the 15th largest city in Italy (in 1921 it was the 7th largest). The city's current economic situation – it lost nearly all of its regional and provincial territory after 1945, and has a national boundary only a few kilometers from its city center - is not an easy one, nor does a promising future appear from the bloody reports of war and death from the neighboring lands that were once Yugoslavia.

Getting around. The three routes recommended here can be considered walking tours, though you may wish to take public trasportation for some of the longer stretches, or to return to your point of departure. It should in any case be kept in mind that traffic regulations discourage the use of private cars in the historic center, and that cars are less than practical in other parts of town, where space is limited.

Piazza dell'Unità d'Italia and the "Città Vecchia"

On the Colle di S. Giusto the walls went down from the Castello to the sea like two long arms, enclosing the "Città Vecchia," or "old city." Trieste lived within this narrow space until the 18th c. From the heart of Trieste, the sunny "stage" of Piazza dell'Unità d'Italia, the route runs up to the hill, discovering both the view and the past.

Piazza dell'Unità d'Italia (*C2-3*). The heart of old Trieste, built on landfill of the ancient Roman port, this square was opened to the sea in the 19th c., to become a sort of stage, with the eclectic backdrop of the **Palazzo Comunale** (1875), by G. Bruni. Two monumental *flagpoles* (1933) mark the edge of the square overlooking the Bacino di S. Giusto; before the Palazzo Comunale, on the right, is a Baroque *column* with a *statue of Charles VI*, who made Trieste a free port, and the reassembled *fountain of the Quattro Continenti* (or Four Continents, 1751). Along the left side of the square is the *Palazzo del Governo* (1904-5), a bulky revue of Italian architectural styles, by E. Artmann, and the 19th-c. *Casa Stratti*, with the historical mirror-lined *Caffè degli Specchi*. On the right side, the immense **Palazzo del Lloyd Triestino**, by H. Ferstel (1880-83), with two allegorical fountains; alongside, a building styled after the French Renaissance (1875), now a hotel, and the elegant **Palazzo Pitteri** (1785), a blend of Baroque and Neo-Classic.

S. Maria Maggiore (*C3*). Behind the Palazzo Comunale, this church on the slopes of the hill of S. Giusto overlooks an area that was ravaged in the 1930s by urban renewal. Built in 1627-82 and enlarged by A. Pozzo, it has a handsome Baroque facade; to the right of the main altar, note the venerated Virgin painted by Sassoferrato. To the right, downhill, the little 11th-c. basilica of **S. Silvestro**, restored in the 1920s; the simple facade has a handsome Gothic rose window, while inside you can see fragments of ancient frescoes.

Arco di Riccardo (*C3*). Behind S. Maria Maggiore, at the beginning of Via del Trionfo, this arch is one of the gates of ancient Roman Trieste, built by Octavian in 33 B.C. Recently restored, the arch has a single passageway, and is decorated with pilaster strips. Continue downhill along Via del Trionfo, past the notable early 19th-c. Neo-Classic facade of **Casa Pancera**, by M. Pertsch (1818). Climb up Via S. Michele and, on the right (n. 13), you will see Trieste's *Anglican church* (1830-31), now an art gallery for temporary exhibitions. Set back on Via Madonna del Mare, at the heart of one of the old town's most distinctive and neglected districts, is the Istituto Magistrale Carducci (n. 11), a secondary school built atop the remains of an Early Christian **basilica**, with 5th-c. mosaic floors (*open by request; contact the school*).

Civico Museo di Storia e Arte (*C3*). *Open Tue. and Thu.-Sun., 9-1; Wed., 9-7; closed Mon.* At n. 15 in Via Cattedrale, this is the main part of Trieste's museums of art and history, with eight rooms of a collection that is largely archeological. Note the prehistoric artifacts (from the Paleolithic to the Iron Age, especially from the necropolis* of S. Lucia di Tolmino; 8th-5th c. B.C.). Also, fine collections* of Greek and Italic vases and terracottas, silverwork, bronzes, glass, ceramics, ivory, amber, and classical sculptures and reliefs.

The museum also includes the *Gabinetto Numismatico*, with collections of Greek, Roman, and medieval coins (mints of Aquileia, Trieste, and Venice), and the *Gabinetto delle Stampe e dei Disegni*, with prints and drawings, featuring also 274 drawings* by G.B. Tiepolo (Sartorio Collection).

Next to the museum is the **Orto Lapidario** (*open same hours as the museum*), or epigraphic garden, with inscriptions and architectural fragments from ancient to modern Trieste, Aquileia, and Istria; opened in 1843. A small classical building, commemorating the great German archeologist J.J. Winckelmann (murdered in a Triestine tavern in 1768), houses a collection of Roman sculpture.

Piazza della Cattedrale (*C3*). This large tree-lined square, on the hill of S. Giusto, is bounded by the bastions of the Castello. The Cattedrale di S. Giusto, with the little 14th-c. Gothic church of *S. Michele al Carnale* next to it, stands atop the stairway that concludes Via della Cattedrale.

On the left, facing the campanile of S. Giusto, is the *Colonna dell'Aquila* (1560), a column originally crowned by an imperial eagle, which was removed under Napoleon and replaced by the symbols of Trieste; to the left of the stairway, overlooking the gulf is an *altar* (1929) commemorating the end of WWI. At the base of the Castello extends the *Roman "platea,"* or plaza, with ruins of the 2nd-c. A.D. *basi-*

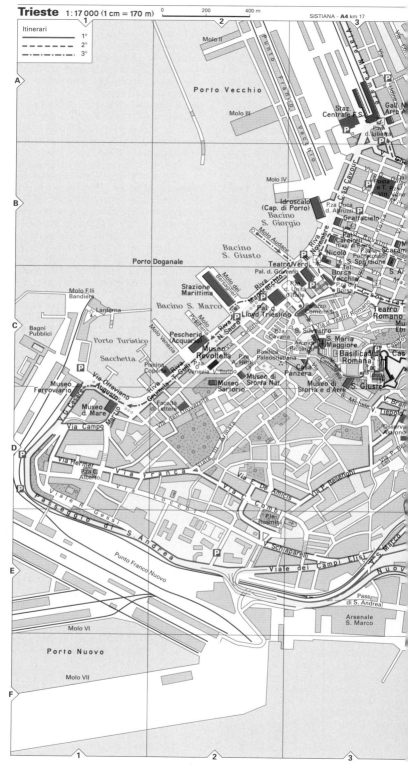

Trieste 1:17 000 (1 cm = 170 m)

0   200   400 m

SISTIANA - **A4** km 17

Itinerari
1°
2°
3°

Porto Vecchio

Molo II

Molo III

Molo IV

Idroscalo
(Cap. di Porto)

Bacino
S. Giorgio

Bacino
S. Giusto

Porto Doganale

Molo Audace

Stazione
Marittima

Molo dei
Bersaglieri

Bacino S. Marco

Molo F.lli
Bandiera

Lanterna

Bagni
Pubblici

Porto Turistico

Sacchetta

Molo Venezia

Molo
Pescheria

Pescheria
(Acquario)

Museo
Revoltella

Piscina
Coperta

Museo
Ferroviario

Via Chiaviano

Via G. Cesare

Via Augusto

Museo
d. Mare

Via Campo

Museo di
Storia Nat.

Museo
Sartorio

Facoltà
di Lettere

Via dell'Università

Via Hermet

P.za C.
Alberto

Via F r a n c a

Viale R. Gessi

Passeggio di S. Andrea

Punto Franco Nuovo

Molo VI

Porto Nuovo

Molo VII

Viale E. De Amicis

Via P. Besenghi

P.le
Resmini

Comb

Via Schiaparelli

Viale dei Campi Elisi

Via S. Marco

Nuov

Pass.
di S. Andrea

Arsenale
S. Marco

Teatro Verdi

Pal. d. Governo

Riva
Novembre

Riva d.
Unità d'Italia

Pal. d.
Lloyd Triestino

Palazzo
Comunale

P.za
Cavana

Basilica
Paleocristiana

P.za
A. Hortis

Arco di
Riccardo

Casa
Panzera

Museo di
Storia e d'Arte

S. Silvestro

S. Maria
Maggiore

Basilica
Romana

Cas

S. Giusto

Via S. Michele

V. Bran

Tiepolo

Osserva
Astrono

Via P. Besenghi

Staz.
Centrale F.S.

Gall. N
Arte A

P.za
d. Libertà

Posta
e T. P.za
Vitt. Vene

Cso Cavour

P.za Duca
d. Abruzzi

Grattacielo

Pal.
Carciotti
(Cap. di Porto)

Ponterosso

S. Spiridione

S. Nicolo

Borsa
Vecchia

P.za d.
Borsa

Scaram

Teatro
Romano

Mu
Ebr

Via del Teatro Romano

Via di Teatro Romano

394

Trieste: S. Giusto

lica and the so-called *Capitoline temple* (1st c.A.D.); note the *Monumento ai Caduti*, a somber monument by A. Selva (1934) which commemorates the soldiers who died in war (fine view* of city and port).

S. Giusto★★ (*C3*). This is Trieste's greatest monument and symbol, built in the 14th c. by joining two 5th-c. Romanesque basilicas: S. Giusto (right) and Assunta (left). The simple *facade* features a large 14th-c. Gothic rose window; the central portal contains fragments of a Roman stele. The 14th-c. campanile, with its fortified appearance, stands on the ruins of a Roman temple; note the Byzantine-Romanesque statue of S. Giusto.

The *interior* has a nave with four asymmetrical aisles; the nave, straddling the two ancient buildings, has a 16th-c. painted vault, rebuilt in 1905. The central apse is also modern (1843), with a mosaic by G. Cadorin (1932) based on fragments of an original. In the right apse, blind arch with 13th-c. frescoes and a notable mosaic; note also fragments of the 5th-c. mosaic floor. In the left apse, 12th-c. Venetian mosaics*; in the left aisle, panel by B. Carpaccio (1540). Also note the Baptistery, with a 9th-c. baptismal font.

Castello★ (*C3*). *Open 9-sunset*. The castle we now see was built between 1470 and 1630, on the site of an older Venetian fortress, which in turn stands on what was probably once a prehistoric fortification. Restored in the 1930s and converted to a museum and open-air theater (Cortile delle Milizie), its bastions offer fine views of Trieste and its gulf. In the square is a 15th-c. tower, and in the building next to it the **Civico Museo del Castello** (*open 9-1, closed Mon.*), laid out in a series of rooms with the original furnishings of the castle. In the chapel is a 17th-c. wooden statue of Christ, a statue of John the Baptist, works of 15th-c. Friulan art and paintings of sacred subjects; the Venetian room has furniture from the home of the Triestine historian G. Caprin (16th-c. chests, 17th-c. Flemish tapestries); the two huge rooms of the watch feature a collection* of antique

weapons (in particular, 17th-c. inlaid ivory powder flask). In the Cortile delle Milizie, or courtyard, note the newly restructured "bottega del vino," or wine shop; the so-called "flowering bastion" is used for temporary exhibits, while the Lalio tower houses the Lapidario Tergestino.

The "Borgo Teresiano" and the modern city

Along this route, running north of the hill, or Colle di S. Giusto, you will see the 19th-c. center of business, trade, and international commerce, as well as the relaxed, Neo-Classic atmosphere of the urban expansion brought about by Maria Theresa.

Piazza della Borsa (*C3*). This broad, triangular square in front of the Borsa, or stock exchange, is linked by Via Capo di Piazza to Piazza dell'Unità d'Italia, and is one of the centers of life in Trieste. In the middle of the square is a *column* with a bronze *statue* of Emperor Leopold I of Hapsburg (1673); to the left, coming from Piazza dell'Unità d'Italia, the *Tergesteo* (1842), once a critical link in international commerce at Trieste. Also, note the **Palazzo della Borsa Vecchia**, by A. Molari (1806-09), and facing it, *Casa Bartoli* (n. 7B), an Art Nouveau home by M. Fabiani (1905). To the left at the corner of Corso Italia (n. 9), *Palazzo Romano* (1760-70), renovated in 1919, a significant example of Triestine Baroque.

Teatro Comunale Giuseppe Verdi (*C3*). Behind the Tergesteo, this Neo-Classic theater (1801) had among its architects G.A. Selva, M. Pertsch, and G. Piermarini; the *Museo Teatrale Carlo Schmidl* (presently housed at the Museo Morpurgo, see below) is being moved to the historic Palazzo Gopcevich.

S. Nicolò dei Greci (*B3*). Overlooking the Riva III Novembre, on the left side of Piazza Tommaseo, near a famous café, this Greek Orthodox church was built in 1784-87 and has a sober Neo-Classic facade with twin bell towers, by M. Pertsch (1819-21).

Canal Grande (*B3*). Dredged in 1750-56, this canal offered safe anchorage and a more convenient way to unload ships directly into warehouses in the new "Borgo Tteresiano," reclaimed with landfill from the surrounding salt marshes. At the canal's mouth, on the right, are **Palazzo Carciotti** by M. Pertsch (1802-5), and the old *Hôtel de la Ville* (1839, rebuilt more than once), now offices of a bank. On the opposite bank, at the head of Via Rossini, is **Palazzo Aedes**, by A. Berlam (1926-28). At the end of the canal is the spectacular Neo-Classic facade of the church of **S. Antonio Nuovo**, by P. Nobile (1827-42).

Piazza Ponterosso (*B3*). The oldest square in the "Borgo Teresiano," it takes its name from a wooden drawbridge that once linked the two banks of the Canal Grande, replaced in 1840. Adorning the square, which is surrounded by buildings in the eclectic "official" style of the Empire, stands an 18th-c. fountain, surmounted by the popular figure of the so-called *"Giovannin."* Dominating the space between Piazza Ponterosso and the neighboring Piazza S. Antonio Nuovo is the glittering mass of the church of the **Santissima Trinità and S. Spiridione Taumaturgo**, built by the Serbian Orthodox community to plans by C. Maciachini (1869): inside, note the lavish 19th-c. iconostasis and the remarkable silver accessories and furnishings.

Museo Scaramangà di Altomonte (*B3; open Tue.-Fri., 10-12*). At n. 1 in Via F. Filzi, across the Canal Grande, is this small but important collection concerning the history and art of Trieste, with rotating shows. As you approach Corso Italia, this section of the "Borgo Teresiano" blends the sort of eclectic architecture seen in the office buildings on Piazza della Repubblica, with interesting examples of a transition from Italian Art Nouveau (Liberty) to Rationalism, as in the former *Casa Smolars*, by R. De-paoli (1906-07), at the corner of Piazza della Repubblica and Via Dante (n. 6), *Casa Fontana* (Via Mazzini 5, at the corner of Via Roma), and the bank offices at n. 9 in Via Roma.

Corso Italia (*C3-4*). This busy avenue linking Piazza della Borsa to the eastern districts of Trieste, is the site of the traditional "liston" (or stroll).

Along it are large buildings by major architects of Fascism, such as the *Casa delle Assicurazioni Generali* (n. 1-3) and the *offices of the Banco di Napoli* (n. 5), both by M. Piacentini (1935-39), or the so-called "*grattacielo*" (skyscraper) by U. Nordio (1936) in Largo Riborgo, as well as surviving bits of the old Austro-Hungarian boulevard. Among them, note the Neo-Classic *Casa Steiner* (n. 4), by M. Pertsch (1824); *Casa Hierschel* (n. 9), by A. Buttazzoni (1833), the Neo-Tuscan *Casa Ananian* (n. 12), by G. Polli (1905), and the building at the corner of Piazza Goldoni (n. 22), with Art Nouveau pediment, by R. Depaoli (1908).

Teatro Romano* (*C3*). This Roman theater, on the slopes of the hill of S. Giusto, was partly unearthed in 1938; it seated 6000 and dates from the early 2nd c. A.D. Behind it, in Via di Donota, is a small **Antiquarium** (*open Thu., 10-12; by request, tel. 04043631*) with artifacts from the digs, from a 1st-c. A.D. home and a slightly later cemetery that was used until the 6th c.

Museo della Comunità Ebraica (*C3*). *Open Mon. and Thu., 10-1; Tue.-Wed., 4-7; Sun. 10-1 and 5-8; by request, tel. 040633819*. Located in Via del Monte n. 7, parallel to Corso Italia, where a Polish Ashkenazi synagogue stood in the 1920s, the museum was founded in 1993 to house collections of Jewish art and culture in Trieste, especially religious furnishings.

Civico Museo Mario Morpurgo de Nilma (*C4*). *Open Tue., Thu. and Fri.-Sun., 9-1; Wed., 9-7*. Set back from Corso Italia, at n. 5 in Via Imbriani, this eclectic palazzo by G. Berlam (1875), built for a family of Triestine bankers and merchants, now houses several sections of the Civici Musei. On the *first floor* is the *Museo Teatrale "C. Schmidl,"* (*open same hours as the Museo Morpurgo*) featuring old instruments, theater memorabilia, portraits, and posters; on the *second floor* is the former home of Mario Morpurgo de Nilma, furnished in the late 19th-c. middle-class Triestine style: paintings by Delacroix and Daubigny, sculpture (wooden polychrome statues by Veit Stoss;

15th-16th c.), prints, Bohemian crystal, ceramics.

Via Carducci (*B-C4*). This major boulevard was built in 1850 upon a covered-over drainage canal. Follow it from Piazza Goldoni until you reach Viale XX Settembre and Via Battisti on the right. Via Battisti leads to the 19th-c. *Giardino Pubblico*, or public garden; the tree-lined Viale XX Settembre, a popular promenade, is lined with cafés, theaters, and cinemas: at n. 35, the **Teatro Eden** (*B4*), is a fine piece of Italian Art Nouveau, by G. Sommaruga (1906), while n. 45 is the *Politeama Rossetti* (*B5; 1878*), a landmark in the history of Italian theater and of the city of Trieste. Continue along until you reach the western extremity of the "Boschetto," the city's **botanical gardens** (*B5; temporarily closed*). Take a left turn from Via Battisti into Via Donizetti and, at n. 4, at the corner of Piazza Giotti, you will see the monumental **Synagogue** (*B4*), by R. and A. Berlam (1906-12).

Piazza Oberdan (*B4*). Built as an impressive entrance to Trieste in the 1920s-30s, it stands on the site where, in 1882, the Italian patriot G. Oberdan was hanged by the Austrians. In the square is the terminus of the popular "*Tram Opicina*" (cable tramway built in 1902), and, on the right, three monumental buildings set on large arcades, by U. Nordio (1929-39). At n. 4 in Via XXIV Maggio is the *Casa del Combattente*, a military monument which, on the ground floor, houses the **Sacrario Oberdan** (*open 9-1; closed Mon.*), with the room where the Italian national hero spent his last night, and a monument commemorating him by A. Selva. On the first floor, the **Civico Museo del Risorgimento** (*open same hours as the Sacrario*) features memorabilia and documentation of the history of Trieste and its struggle for independence.

Piazza della Libertà (*A3*). This monumental square built at the end of the 19th c. is surrounded by stern buildings; among them note *Palazzo Economo* (n. 7; see below); it is dominated by the huge Neo-Renaissance facade of the *Stazione Centrale* (1878), or main railway station. Nearby, note the bus station, built in 1986-89 from a former *grain silo* (1890).

Galleria Nazionale d'Arte Antica (*A3*). *Open 9-1:30; closed Sun.* Located on the second floor of Palazzo Economo, at n. 7 Piazza della Libertà, this museum comprises the Mentasti collection of 15th-/19th-c. Italian paintings. The seven rooms of the gallery contain drawings by Canaletto (10 sketches); detached frescoes by Romanino; paintings by L. Cranach the Elder, G. Assereto, G.A. and F. Guardi, F. Solimena, Fra' Galgario, G.M. Crespi, G. Tominz; and a "salone piemontese," 18th-c. room with mirrors and boiseries from Palazzo S. Tommaso in Turin.

As you climb up into the early 20th-c. district above the station, first *Via Ùdine*, and then the *Salita di Gretta*, lead to the panoramic *Via del Friùli*, and on to the **Faro della Vittoria** (*A3, off map; Apr-Set, 9-11 and 4-6; closed Wed.; Oct.-Mar., holidays only, 10-3*), a monumental lighthouse by A. Berlam (1927) commemorating those who died at sea; fine view* of the Gulf of Trieste. Overlooking *Via Commerciale* (*A4*) are several notable Art Nouveau *houses* (n. 21, 23, 25).

The Harbor and the Rive

Facing east, the Rive (the banks) are Trieste's majestic face, overlooking the water of the port, and gleaming in the light of the gulf. Extending into the waves are the huge jetties, from which ocean liners once set sail. Along the "passeggiata," or sea-front promenade, lie the aquarium and five museums.

Molo Audace (B2). This pier is a panoramic "promenade on the sea" which divides the Bacino di S. Giusto from the Bacino di S. Giorgio; from the head, where there is a bronze wind rose, you can enjoy a fine view* of Trieste's waterfront. The Bacino di S. Giorgio, to the right of the pier, was used between the wars for seaplanes (first civilian flight in 1926); note the old terminal, or *Idroscalo*, by R. Pollack (1930). Behind it is the **Porto Vecchio** (A-B 2-3), which extends up to Bàrcola, with four basins protected by a breakwater (1868-90). Over Bàrcola, on the Colle di Gretta, stands the *Faro della Vittoria*, a lighthouse; in the distance, the *Castello di Miramare* (see below). To the left of the pier is the Bacino di S. Giusto, with **customs offices** (B-C 2), further along the marina, or Porto Turistico.

Rive (A-C 2-3). These broad sea-side avenues, lined with handsome Neo-Classic buildings, form a unique promenade with the grand piers between the *Porto Vecchio* and the *Lanterna* (C1), the lighthouse at the tip of the pier known as Molo Fratelli Bandiera. *Molo dei Bersaglieri*. This pier, with its *monument to Nazzario Sauro*, holds the 1930s building of the **Stazione Marittima** (C2), by U. Nordio, now a conference and exhibition center. Further along is the sadly deteriorating Art Nouveau building of the **Pescheria** (C2), by G. Polli (1913), with the adjacent **Civico Acquario Marino** (open 10-8; closed Mon.), with tanks of Adriatic fish and marine invertebrates, and some tropical fish, as well as freshwater fish, amphibians, and reptiles from Friùli-Venezia Giulia.

Museo Revoltella* (C2). Open 10-7; closed Tue. The entrance is at n. 27 in Via Diaz; this Neo-Renaissance building by F. Hitzig (1852-58) was donated, with 19th-c. furnishings, to the city of Trieste in 1866-69 by a businessman and patron of the arts, Pasquale Revoltella. Enlarged from the 1960s on by C. Scarpa (the so-called *ala scarpiana*, or Scarpa wing, was completed in 1992), it has become the **Galleria d'Arte Moderna** of Trieste, with a major collection of 19th-/20th-c. sculpture and painting, from Italy and Central Europe (some 40 rooms). Of note: statues by A. Canova and J.A. Houdon; paintings by G. Tominz, F. Hayez, D. Induno, F. De Nittis, L. Nono, L. Balestrieri, G. Previati, I. Zuloaga, F. Casorati, A. Nathan; decorative panels by V. Timmel; and contemporary art by G. Manzù, L. Minguzzi, R. Guttuso, L. Fontana, and Afro. From the terrace in the Scarpa wing, fine view* of Trieste.

Civico Museo di Storia Naturale (C2). Open 8:30-1:30; closed Mon. This museum of natural history occupies some 20 rooms on the first and third floors of the *Palazzo della Biblioteca Civica*, or Library, at n. 4 in Piazza Hortis. Founded in 1846, it features collections of paleontology, marine zoology, comparative anatomy, botany, and entomology, as well as collections of amphibians, reptiles, and birds. It also has a set of late 19th-c. herbaria and a specialized library, with nearly 10,000 volumes.

Civico Museo Sartorio (C2). Open 9-1; closed Mon.; undergoing restoration; visits only by reservation, tel. 040310500). This fine example of a late 19th-c. home is set in an 18th-c. city villa, rebuilt in Neo-Classic style in 1820-38 by N. Pertsch, at n. 1 in Largo Papa Giovanni XXIII. Ground floor: collection of antique European ceramics* and temporary exhibitions. First floor: rooms furnished in Neo-Gothic and Biedermeier styles; 17th-/19th-c. paintings (note work by Tiepolo and followers). On the second floor are rotating exhibitions of Triestine collections, especially from the 18th c. Recently installed is the *Stavropulos Collection** of Italian, German, and Hungarian painting and sculpture (paintings by A. Martini, P. Brill, G. Tominz, and Mihály Munkácsy; sculpture by Veit Stoss, P. Breuer, and V. Mukina).

Civico Museo del Mare* (D1). Open 8:30-1:30, closed Mon. Located in a modern building at n. 5 in Via di Campo Marzio, this museum of the sea was founded at the turn of the 20th century. It now occupies about 30 rooms on three floors, providing a general history of shipbuilding up to the 19th c. and a section on the history of fishing, featuring the systems, equipment, and boats of the Adriatic; note models showing how various types of nets are deployed.

Museo Ferroviario (C-D1). Open 9-1; closed Mon. Located in the handsome, Art Nouveau former station of Campo Marzio, by R. Seelig (1907; closed in 1960), this railroad museum was founded in 1984. It features documents, models, and memorabilia; outside, about 15 locomotives, mostly steam engines, stand on rails, alongside early 20th-c. cars from the Italian, Austrian, Hungarian, and German railways.

Surroundings. Risiera di S. Sabba (F4, off map). Open 16 May-Oct. and 6 Nov.-Mar., Tue.-Sun., 9-1; Apr. 15 May and 1-5 Nov., Tue.-Sat., 9-6; Sun. and holidays, 9-1. In the industrial section south of Trieste, in Ratto Pileria n. 1 (take the Valmaura exit from the ring road), stands a former rice-husking plant, now a national monument, notorious for its use, under Nazi occupation, first as a marshalling yard for Jews bound for concentration camps, and later as a death camp. Note the **Museo della Risiera di S. Sabba**, with documents and photographs concerning the Italian Resistance movement.

Foiba di Basovizza (A6, off map). As you leave town, on the right of the SS 14 road to Basovizza, a plaque commemorates the karstic sinkhole, now a national monument, where hundreds, possibly thousands, of victims of military and political reprisals were tossed between 1943 and 1945, during the occupation, first by the Nazis, and later by Tito.

Castello di Miramare. Open Apr.-Sep., 9-6:30; Mar. and Oct., 9-5; Nov.-Feb., 9-4. At 8 km to the north-west, along coastal road 14, Miramare is the most famous castle of Trieste, built according to Neo-Renaissance canons by C. Junker (1856-60) for Archduke Maximilian of Hapsburg, who lived here until his departure to Mexico. The building stands on the tip of a scenic promontory and is renowned not only for the sights (hence the name Miramare), but also for its furnishings, paintings, ivories, porcelains and objects which testify to the princely life of those who lived here. The castle is surrounded by a huge garden "à l'italienne" (*open, 9-one hour before the closing time of the castle*) featuring rare trees and plants.

Troia

Elev. 439 m, pop. 7689; Puglia (Apulia), province of Foggia.

Places of interest. Cattedrale.** This cathedral is the monument for which this little town, perched along a ridge of a hill overlooking the Tavoliere plain, is widely known. Founded in 1093 on the structure of an existing Byzantine building, it is considered a masterpiece of Romanesque Apulian architecture. The rose window* in the facade is framed by a large arcade and is closed off with fretwork screens. The bronze door* is by O. da Benevento (1119). In the *interior*, decorated with elaborate marble carvings of Muslim origin (1169), the first two piers in the presbytery incorporate Byzantine porphyry columns.
The *Tesoro*, or Treasury (*open by request, tel. 0881970064*), includes three celebrated illuminated scrolls of the "Exultet", from the 12th-13th c., silverware, Arab ivory caskets, and enamels.
In front of the cathedral, in the old Benedictine convent, is the *Museo Diocesano* (*open by request, tel. 0881970870*), a museum of religious furnishings, paintings and Baroque fragments.
S. Basilio. This is the oldest church (11th c.) in Troia, the only trace of the Greek Orthodox religion, which ended with the Norman invasions. Blind arches and the portal are reminiscent of Romanesque art; in the interior, one of the columns, formerly an altar, is decorated with crowned ox heads.
Museo Civico (*open by request, tel. 0881970870; 8-1 and 4-6; closed Sun. and holidays*). Located in Palazzo d'Avalos, at n. 80 in Via Regina Margherita, this museum includes two archeological sections, a ceramics section, and a plaster section.

Turin / Torino*

Elev. 239 m, pop. 991,870; Piemonte (Piedmont), regional and provincial capital. Founded in ancient times at the confluence of the Dora Riparia with the Po, Turin now extends along the left bank of the Po, from the confluence with the Stura di Lanzo, downstream, to that of the Sangone, upstream. On the opposite bank rise the Prealpine hills, which loom over the city and make up a very pleasant part of the lives of the Turinese. In the distance, one can make out the silhouette of the Alps. Turin is a major city, the fourth largest in Italy; it is thoroughly up-to-date, busy, and courteous. In the heart of the city, both architecturally and historically, is the ancient capital of the dynasty of the Savoia, or Savoy. Dramatic, Baroque, and abounding in fine buildings, this central area has extended its restrained regularity to outlying neighborhoods of varied and dignified nineteenth-century construction, with ample piazzas, broad straight boulevards, and long lines of shade trees. Turin is known best as an industrial metropolis and as Italy's car-manufacturing capital; socially, it has a reputation of formal "drawing-room" entertaining, in the neighborhoods of Piazza San Carlo, Via Roma, and surrounding areas. The city, however, also boasts a surprisingly rich artistic and cultural life, and a wealth of monuments.

Historical note. It is customary to attribute Turin's checkerboard layout to the grid of the Roman colony, but that is only a partial explanation: this is a city that grew in carefully planned expansions, becoming a regional, then ducal, and finally royal capital. The location was first chosen by the Ligurian tribe of the Taurini; the Roman colony, which must have existed under Caesar, was refounded by Augustus around 29 B.C.; the "Julia Augusta Taurinorum" occupied the rectangular area, less than 800 m long, with 72 "insulae," or blocks, between what is now Palazzo Madama and Via della Consolata, between Porta Palatina, Porta Romana, and Via S. Teresa. The medieval history of Turin is intricate and relatively marginal: the Savoy enter into the city's history when the town was already a thousand years old: in 1046 Adelaide, daughter of Olderico Manfredi II, marquis of Turin and its territory, married Oddone di Savoia, son of Umberto Biancamano. The House of Savoy only established permanent possession of the city in 1280, under Tommaso III. The city remained within the Roman perimeter until the 17th c. In the 13th c. Guglielmo di Monferrato built a fortress-home against the Porta Decumana, the first structure of what would one day be Palazzo Madama; in 1404 the university was founded, at the behest of Ludovico di Savoia, approved by Benedict XIII, the pope in Avignon, and by the emperor Sigismund. Meo del Caprina designed and decorated (1491-98) for the bishop Domenico della Rovere the Duomo, or cathedral, almost the only Renaissance monument in Turin. The House of Savoy had possessions on both sides of the Alps, in parts of what are now Switzerland and France, as well as Italy, and they rarely lived on the Italian side of the Alps; the capital of the Savoy duchy was Chambery, and the Italian possessions seemed of marginal interest. In the European wars of the early 16th c., the duchy came close to catastrophe. Emanuele Filiberto led the Spanish army in a decisive battle against the French in northern France; he regained the duchy through the Peace of Cateau-Cambrésis, 1559, with a solemn entry into Turin, finally freed of French occupation, on 7 February 1563. Thus began the history of Turin as a capital city, more than two centuries of transformations that turned it into the Turin we know today. Emanuele Filiberto immediately built a mighty fortified stronghold, the Cittadella, a five-pointed star at the SE corner of the Roman rectangular camp (1564-1568; only the keep survives, at the corner of Via Cernaia and Corso Galileo Ferraris). There were three major enlargements of the city, one under Carlo Emanuele I, a second beginning in 1673 (Amedeo di Castellamonte), and a third after 1714 (under Vittorio Amedeo II, with Filippo Juvarra as architect). Then, beginning in 1736, under Carlo Emanuele II, the Via Dora Grossa (now Via Garibaldi, originally the Roman "decumanus") was rebuilt; in Gothic times, it had been a porticoed market street. Among the epochal constructions were the church of S. Maria del Monte on the Monte dei Cappuccini (Vittozzi, late 16th c.); the Castello del Valentino, on the banks of the Po, transformed by Carlo and Amedeo di Castellamonte (1630-1660); and the Basilica di Superga, by Juvarra (1716), supposedly erected to fulfill a vow made by Vittorio Amedeo II during the siege of 1706. The city now truly looked like a Baroque capital, but as De Brosses observed, "there was none of the usual unpleasantness of seeing huts next to palaces." In effect, the original aspect of the Turinese Baroque palazzo (four, six, or eight to an "isola," or block) was a sort of social integration: the owner lived on the piano nobile, middle class families above them, and the poor on the upper floors. In the Napoleonic era, all of the city's fortifications were dismantled. Turin became a haven for those working to unite Italy, the beacon of a united nation, and began to grow and modernize. In 1853 it had a population of 160,000; tree-lined boulevards called "corsi" were laid out (a total of 130). On 14 March 1861, in a wooden pavilion in the courtyard of Palazzo Carignano, the Italian Parliament voted unanimously to make Victor Emmanuel II king of Italy. Turin was the first capital of a united Italy (1861-65); there were two days of riots when it was learned that Florence was to become capital in its place. Then came a period of industrialization, with Turin's new status as the peak of the "industrial triangle" (with Genoa and Milan); now it was the "automobile capital." A remarkable piece of engineering, the Mole Antonelliana began to lift its spire above the surrounding town (it was begun as a Jewish synagogue in 1863 and was completed by the city in 1897). In 1899 FIAT was founded, although automobiles were already being built in Turin. In 1923 the factory of the Lingotto began operations; on the roof was a test track, where models such as the Balilla and the Topolino made their first runs. In the census of 1939 Turin had a population of 700,000; the modern population is about a million, a result of massive immigration from the south of Italy and the incorporation of surrounding villages into the city.

Getting around. Turin has no large pedestrian zone (save for a stretch of Via Garibaldi), but its famed porticoes, distinctive features of the historic

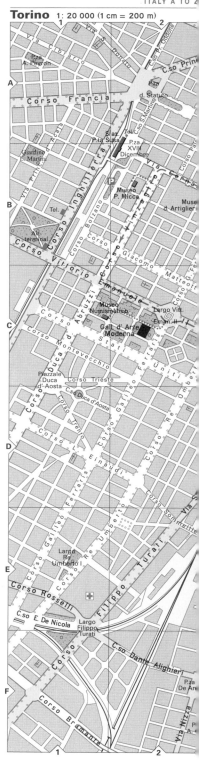

Torino 1: 20 000 (1 cm = 200 m)

100   200   300 m

401

center, offer a long and pleasant covered walkway, extending for a good 18 kilometers. Of the four routes proposed, three can be walked, while the fourth requires a car or public transport.

Palazzo Madama and "Turin the Capital"

The oldest buildings along this square-shaped route through the heart of the city date primarily from the 17th c. Some of the most illustrious sites in this capital city – first of a Savoy duchy and later of a Savoy kingdom – are found here, many of them by the hands of the "court architects" Guarino Guarini and Filippo Juvarra. This was also a Roman colony many centuries ago, and traces of that period can be seen in the regular checkerboard pattern of streets, as well as in other details. The Roman walled perimeter, within the bounds of which Turin remained until the 17th c., also enclosed the medieval city.

Piazza Castello (*B4*). This immense square is surrounded by regular porticoed palazzi (the 90-m skyscraper that stands on the western side dates from 1934), and was designed in 1584 by A. Vittozzi. This is the heart of Turin.

Isolated at the center of the square stands Palazzo Madama. A 19th-c. wrought-iron gate separates it from Piazza Reale, beyond which you can see the dome of the Cappella della Sacra Sindone and the bell tower of the Duomo; opposite Palazzo Madama rises the dome of the church of S. Lorenzo. On the eastern side of the square is the facade of the **Teatro Regio**, the only surviving 18th-c. part of a building which has been recently rebuilt and reopened (1973, adjoining it is a small *Museo Teatrale*, or museum of the theater, temporarily closed); further off is the Mole Antonelliana (see below). On the western side of this square, opposite Palazzo Madama, are the offices of the regional government of Piedmont.

Palazzo Madama** (*B4*). This great palazzo in the center of the square sums up in its long process of construction the history of Turin itself. It incorporates the remains of an ancient Roman gate (front towers), which was transformed in the Middle Ages into a castle; this castle, enlarged in the 15th c. by the House of Savoy, with corner towers and mullioned windows, became the home of Madama Reale (hence its current name) Maria Cristina, the widow of Vittorio Amedeo I and the regent of Carlo Emanuele II, in the 17th c.; in 1721 F. Juvarra designed and built the monumental Baroque facade. The palazzo now holds the **Museo Civico di Arte Antica*** (*open, Tue.-Sun., 10-8*), featuring artwork largely from Piedmont, including sculpture (T. di Camaino*), wooden carvings, paintings (A. da Messina, Pontormo, M. Spanzotti, M. d'Alba, D. Ferrari, and G. Jaquerio), illuminated manuscripts (**Les très belles Heures du Duc de Berry****, illustrated by J. van Eyck and his school), furniture*, tapestries, glass, ceramics, ivory, and embroidery.

S. Lorenzo* (*B4*). This small church, of great ar-

chitectual interest, is one of the loveliest in Turin. Devoid of the facade – it has the elevation of a palazzo instead – it was built between 1668 and 1680 is one of the major works by G. Guarini. Note the complex structure of the central plan interior, decorated with polychrome marble, stuccoes, and gilding; especially, note the cupola.

Armeria Reale* (*B4*). *Open Tue.-Sun., 8:30-7:30.* Beneath the portico to the right of the fence around Palazzo Reale, at n. 191, is the entrance to one of the most notable collections of arms and armor in Europe. Of special note: the weapons of Emanuele Filiberto (1561); parade arms and armor, from Milanese, French, and Flemish manufactories (16th c.); firearms from the finest German smiths (17th c.); firearms from Brescia and the other leading European armsmakers; weapons from different places in Asia, and other remarkable specimens.

Palazzo Reale* (*B4*). *Open only for guided tours; 9-6; closed Mon.* Built in 1660, this enormous royal palace with its stern facade was, until 1865, the residence of the House of Savoy. The interior features spectacular examples of furnishing and decoration from the 17th-19th c. Note especially the painted and carved coffered ceilings and the wooden floors, and the interesting collection of large vases from the Far East. The **Scala delle Forbici***, a stairway that runs from the entry hall to the upstairs apartments, is a remarkable creation of F. Juvarra, who also designed the decorations in the remarkable little *Chinese room*. Behind the palace (accessible from the courtyard) extend the **royal gardens** (*open 9-one hour before sunset*), created in the French style in the late 17th c.

Palazzo Chiablese (*B4*). To the left of the Piazzetta Reale, this 17th-c. palace, rearranged in the 18th c., once housed the Museo Nazionale del Cinema, a museum of cinematography which was moved to the Mole Antonelliana.

Duomo* (*B4*). This cathedral was built in 1491-98, and has a Renaissance facade, the only one in Turin, made of white marble, with three portals in the Tuscan style; standing alone to the left of cathedral is the mighty *bell tower*, built in Romanesque style around 1470, and made even taller in 1720. The interior contains the columned nave and aisles, simple and austere; on the wall, near the entrance, note the tomb of Anna de Créquy. To the side of the presbytery, you can go up to the **Cappella della Sacra Sindone*** (*restored after the fire of 1997*), a remarkable chapel designed by G. Guarini (1668-94), entirely faced with black marble and with a conical cupola comprising six stacked rows of arches. On the walls, note four monuments to members of the House of Savoy; above the sumptuous altar is a silver urn containing the *Sindone*, the shroud that is believed to have been used to wrap the body of Jesus after it was taken down from the Cross; it supposedly bears the miraculous impressions of His face and hands. This precious relic, which became a possession of the House of Savoy in 1430 and was first placed here in 1694, is displayed to the public only on rare occasions; in the left aisle of the Duomo you can see a life-size photograph.

Piazza Cesare Augusto (*A4*). In this square there are a number of items of archeological interest: remains of walls, a stretch of Roman road (between the two statues of Caesar and Augustus), and the **Porta Palatina***, 1st c. A.D., a gate with four vaults topped by two rows of windows and flanked by two polygonal towers, forming part of the city walls. To the left of the Duomo, beyond a fence that runs along the NW wing of the Palazzo Reale, are the remains of the **Roman theater** (1st-3rd c.).

Museo di Antichità (*A4*). *Open Tue.-Sun., 8:30-7:30; entrance also from the royal gardens.* At n. 105 Corso Regina Margherita is the entrance to this museum of antiquities. It occupies what were once the greenhouses of Palazzo Reale, and contains archeological material, ranging from prehistoric times to late Roman and barbarian times. Of particular importance: Cypriot and Greek ceramics; the Etruscan collection; silver from the treasure of Marengo, with a portrait of Lucius Verus; collection of Roman glass.

S. Domenico (*A3*). This Gothic 14th-c. church, restored in 1906-08, has only one portal. In the chapel at the end of the left aisle, note the 14th-c. frescoes.

Corso Regina Margherita. On the right side of this avenue, in Via Cottolengo, is the **Cottolengo** (*A3*), or Piccola Casa della Provvidenza, a hospital founded by S. Giuseppe Cottolengo in 1828, a celebrated institution of Christian charity, and the headquarters of the *Opere Salesiane*, the organization founded by S. Giovanni Bosco (1846); note the adjoining church of **Maria Santissima Ausiliatrice** (1868), where the body of the saint is kept.

Santuario della Consolata* (*A3*). Formed by the union of two churches, this sanctuary was built in 1678 by G. Guarini, who transformed the existing church of S. Andrea into a vestibule of the new sanctuary. To the right of the Neo-Classic facade (1860) is the 11th-c. Romanesque bell tower, part of the original structure. The *interior* is built to a hexagonal plan, and is surrounded by elliptical chapels and decorated with lavish marble and gilt stucco; in the chapel to the left of the presbytery, note the kneeling statues of the queens Maria Teresa and Maria Adelaide, by V. Vela (1861).

As you continue along Via della Consolata you will see, at the corner of Piazza Savoia, the *Palazzo Martini di Cigala* (1716), attributed to Juvarra, with a handsome atrium opening out onto the courtyard.

Carmine (*A3*). Designed by Filippo Juvarra, with an austere 19th-c. facade, this church has a luminous interior, with a barrel vault ceiling. Not far off, at n. 1 in Via della Consolata, stands the 18th-c. **Palazzo Paesana di Saluzzo**, with a loggia-lined courtyard, once one of the most luxurious homes in Turin. Also of note is **Palazzo Faletti di Barolo**, in Via delle Orfane 7 (*open Mon. and Wed., 10-12 and 3-5; Fri., 10-12*).

Via Garibaldi (*B3-4*). This is a shopping street, off-limits to automobiles, and lined with 18th-c. houses and palazzi. Continuing along it toward Piazza Castello you will see, on the right, the church of the

Ss. Martiri (*B3*), built to plans by P. Tibaldi after 1577, with decorations inside of marble, stucco, and bronze. Next to the church is the **Cappella della Pia Congregazione dei Banchieri e Mercanti** (chapel of bankers and merchants), a fine example of Baroque architecture of the late 17th c., with many canvases by A. dal Pozzo. Further along, on the left, is the *Palazzo di Città*, 1659-63, whose main facade overlooks the Piazza di Città, with a monument to the Conte Verde (1853).

Corpus Domini (*B3*). A short detour to the left, along the narrow Via Porta Palatina, leads to the church of Corpus Domini, built to plans by A. Vittozzi (1609-71) on the site of a miracle that supposedly occurred 150 years previous (the miracle involved a mule and a stolen monstrance, or ostensory).

Santissima Trinità (*B4*). Continuing further along the Via Garibaldi, just before you reach Piazza Castello, note (on the left) the Neo-Classic facade of the church of the Santissima Trinità, designed by Ascanio Vittozzi (1606), with an interior built to a circular plan and dome, lavishly faced with marble by F. Juvarra (1718).

The 19th-c. avenues and the modern heart of Turin

The late 16th-c. citadel and the fortifications with which Turin defended itself against a French siege in 1706 were demolished under Napoleon. In the spaces thus left free (this route runs along them in part), these 19th-c. avenues, or Corsi, and the broad tree-lined boulevards, laid out before the invention of the automobile, interpreted in a new architectural language the old and aristocratic image of Turin. This route ends along Via Roma, the best-known road in Turin: central thoroughfare of a Baroque addition, renovated in questionable style in the early 20th c., it remains, with the Baroque square that lies across its middle, the "drawing-room" of Turin.

Via Pietro Micca (*B3-4*). Lined by buildings in eclectic architectural style, it starts from the western corner of Piazza Castello and is one of the most elegant streets in Turin, with porticoes along the right side; it was built with a diagonal line of demolition in 1894 through an old neighborhood.

S. Maria di Piazza (*B3*). Set back along a cross street of Via Pietro Micca, this small church was rebuilt in 1751 to plans by A. Vittone, but the facade dates from 1830. The interior is interesting; note the cupola and the theatrical altar.

Cittadella (*B2*). At the beginning of the long porticoed Corso Galileo Ferraris, in a garden, stands the keep of the Cittadella, all that remains of the enormous fortress built by Emanuele Filiberto of Savoy in 1564-68. It houses the **Museo Storico Nazionale dell'Artiglieria** (*open only for exhibitions*), which features a collection of firearms and memorabilia of the Piedmontese corps of artillery and engineers.

Museo Pietro Micca (*B2*). *Open 9-7; closed Mon.* Not far off, to the west, at n. 7 in Via Guicciardini, in

Turin: Piazza S. Carlo

the area once occupied by the fortress, stands this museum with models, maps, and memorabilia of the Cittadella di Torino (Turin Citadel) during the time of the French siege, in 1706. A custodian will take you into the underground chambers beneath the building (they once extended 14 km under the city). Here, Pietro Micca, an Italian national hero, sacrificed his life to save the town. Follow the porticoes of *Corso Vinzaglio* and you will reach the broad and tree-lined **Corso Vittorio Emanuele II**, a central thoroughfare in the modern section of Turin; once you reach *Largo Vittorio Emanuele II* (*C2*), in which looms a monument dating from 1899, you will take a right into Corso Galileo Ferraris, and will soon reach the Galleria d'Arte Moderna.

Galleria d'Arte Moderna e Contemporanea* (*C2*). *Open 9-7; closed Mon*. At n. 31 Via Magenta, this is one of the leading collections of modern art in Italy, occupying a modern building with 19th-c. art on the first floor. The works are predominantly by Piedmontese painters (M. d'Azeglio, Fontanesi, Avondo, Delleani, Grosso, Quadrone, Reycend, and G. Pellizza), although the Lombards (Hayez, Cremona, Induno), Tuscans (Fattori, Lega, Signorini), Venetians, and painters from other parts of Italy are also well represented. The second floor is devoted to the Futurists, early 20th-c. painters (Spadini, Modigliani, De Chirico, Carrà, Tosi, Casorati, Morandi, Scipione, Rosai, and De Pisis) and painters of later generations (Mafai, Menzio, Paulucci, Spazzapan, Birolli, Guttuso, Cassinari, Morlotti, and Santomaso) all the way up to the modern avant-gardes. Among the sculptors, we should mention Canova, Marocchetti, Vela, Gemito, Medardo Rosso, Andreotti, Martini, Marini, Manzù, Fazzini, and Mastroianni. European art is present with works by Courbet, Renoir, Léger, Utrillo, Pascin, Klee, Ernst, and Chagall, as well as the contemporary artists Tobey, Hartung, Le Moal, Manessier, Gischia, Tal Coat, and Tamayo.

Civiche Raccolte di Numismatica, Etnografia e Arti Orientali (*C1*). *Open 9-7; closed Mon*. Not far from the Galleria d'Arte Moderna, at n. 8 Via Bricherasio, is this collection of Greek, Roman, Byzantine, and Italian coins, from the Middle Ages to modern times, along with plates, seals, and medals;

there are also collections of material from Africa, the Americas, and Oceania, archeological finds from Gandhāra, in India, and items of Chinese art.

Stazione di Porta Nuova (*C-D3*). Return to Largo Vittorio Emanuele II and then take Corso Vittorio Emanuele II to the railway station of Porta Nuova (1860-68), with a broad portico on the facade.

Piazza S. Carlo* (*C3*). This square is linked with Piazza Carlo Felice, on one side, and Piazza Castello, on the other, by *Via Roma*, Turin's main thoroughfare, lined with porticoes and elegant shops. This square was given its current appearance – with symmetrical porticoed palazzi along the main sides – in the 17th c. The southern end features the two churches of *S. Cristina* (Baroque, by F. Juvarra) and *S. Carlo*, whose 19th-c. facade reproduces many of the architectural motifs found in S. Cristina; in the center of the square is an equestrian monument to Emanuele Filiberto, by C. Marocchetti (1838).

S. Teresa (*B3*). This Baroque church (1642-74) may have been built to plans by A. Costaguta; the facade dates from 1764. Inside, note the rich marble decoration and the spectacular altar of S. Giuseppe* by Juvarra (1735). Alongside the church, at n. 5 Via S. Teresa, is the *Museo della Marionetta* (*open by request, tel. 011530238*), with puppets, marionettes, backdrops, and costumes created by the Lupi brothers for the traditional Teatro Gianduia.

The Galleria Sabauda, the Museo Egizio, and the Baroque quarter

When the city was still enclosed within its fortified walled perimeter, expansion took place through well-planned projects, beginning with the shift outward of bastions and ramparts. The district to the SE of Piazza Castello, explored by this route, was added from 1673 on, and still shows the stern style of the Piedmontese Baroque, illuminated by the brilliant flashes of architectural genius of Guarino Guarini. Marks of cultural continuity can be seen in the two most prestigious collections of art in Turin, the Galleria Sabauda and the Museo Egizio.

Palazzo Carignano (*B4*). The palace overlooks

Piazza Carignano, with a statue of the Turin-born Italian philosopher and politician Vincenzo Gioberti (1859). Among the stern buildings that surround it is the *Teatro Carignano*, where, in 1775, Vittorio Alfieri's first tragedy, Cleopatra, was performed. Built by G. Guarini (1679-85), the palazzo belonged to the Carignano branch of the House of Savoy; Carlo Alberto (1798) and Vittorio Emanuele II (1829; later king of Italy) were born here. The kingdom of Italy was proclaimed in the courtyard, on 14 March 1861; Italy's first parliament met here, until the capital was moved to Florence (1865). A new wing that closes off the courtyard and the monumental facade overlooking Piazza Carlo Alberto were built in the 19th c. The palazzo contains the **Museo Nazionale del Risorgimento Italiano** (*open 9-7; closed Mon.*), with a major collection of documents, memorabilia, and other material concerning the period of the struggle for Italian unification, with manuscripts by Garibaldi, Cavour, Mazzini, and Vittorio Emanuele II; a section is devoted to the Italian Resistance movement in WWII.

Palazzo dell'Accademia delle Scienze (*B4*). This imposing brick Baroque building, by G. Guarini (1678), houses two of the most important collections in Turin: the Museo Egizio and the Galleria Sabauda. **Galleria Sabauda**** *Open 8:30-7:30; closed Mon.* Housed on the second and third floors of the Palazzo dell'Accademia delle Scienze, this is a first-rank collection of paintings, boasting, among other things, remarkable paintings of the Flemish and Dutch schools. There are works by Piedmontese painters of the 15th-16th c.: M. d'Alba, Spanzotti, G. and D. Ferrari, Sodoma, and Giovenone. There is a notable group of works by Tuscan painters: B. Daddi, Fra' Angelico, Pollaiolo, L. di Credi, and Bronzino. Among the Venetians we should mention Mantegna, B. Montagna, Veronese, Tintoretto, Bassano, Schiavone, and Savoldo. There are many works by 17th-/18th-c. Italian painters: Carracci, Reni, Guercino, B. Strozzi, O. Gentileschi, G.B. Tiepolo, Magnasco, Bellotto, Piazzetta, Ricci, and Guardi. Particularly noteworthy is a group of Flemish and Dutch paintings by J. van Eyck, R. van der Weyden, Memling, Petrus Christus, Van Dyck, G. Dou, Rembrandt, J. van Ruisdael, P. Potter, and others. The collection of the princes of Savoy includes portraits by F. Clouet and Van Dyck. Also worthy of note is the *Gualino Collection*, comprising a major group of paintings by early Italian masters, including a painter active prior to Giotto, Botticelli, E. de' Roberti, and Veronese, as well as Chinese sculpture and medieval furniture.

Museo Egizio** (*B4*). *Open 8:30-7:30; closed Mon.* In the Palazzo dell'Accademia delle Scienze, this is one of the most notable collections of Egyptian antiquities in all Europe. On the ground floor is the statuary section, with remarkable material: 10 seated statues and 11 standing statues of the lion-headed goddess, Sachmis; the pharaohs Tuthmosis I (1505-1493 B.C.), Tuthmosis III (1490-1436 B.C.), Amenophis II (1438-1412 B.C.), Haremhab (1333-1306 B.C.), and Ramesses II* (1290-1224 B.C.). Of

special note is the reassembled "speos"* (little cliff temple) of El-Lesiya, with bas-reliefs dating from 1450 B.C., a gift (1966) from Egypt to Italy. On the first floor are collections of various material: sarcophagi, mummies, canopic vases, statuettes, weapons, tools, papyrus (Book of the Dead), and paintings, illustrating various aspects of Egyptian civilization (daily life, culture, religion, the funerary cult, etc.). Especially noteworthy is a small room with material from the tomb of a married couple, Kha and Merit (1430-1375 B.C.), uncovered intact.

S. Filippo Neri (*B-C4*). Begun in 1675, this church was completed in 1772 by F. Juvarra. Before it is a classical pronaos (1835); note the vast interior, with stuccoed relief, marble, and paintings. Alongside the church is the *Oratorio di S. Filippo* (*C4*), an oratory also designed by Juvarra; facing it is the *Palazzo Carpano*, built in 1686 to a design by M. Garove, pupil of Guarini. Note the spiralling columns.

Piazza Carlo Emanuele II (*C4*). Built at the end of the 17th c., this square has, at its center, a *monument to Cavour* (1873). Not far off are the *Museo di Antropologia e di Etnografia* (Museum of Anthropology and Ethnography, at n. 17 Via Accademia Albertina; *open Tue., Thu., and Sat., 3-5; guided tours by request, tel. 0115621284*), and the *Museo di Scienze Naturali* (Museum of Natural Sciences; , at n. 36 Via Giolitti; *open 10-7; closed Tue.*).

Piazza Cavour (*C4*). The square, with little hillocked flowerbeds, dotted with trees and 19th-c. homes, is adjacent to the so-called *Aiuola Balbo*, a large garden created in 1835 on the site of ancient fortifications. From Piazza Cavour, continuing further along the Via Giolitti, you will soon reach *Piazza Maria Teresa*, a quiet tree-lined square in a residential neighborhood, which has retained the appearance of early 19th-c. Turin.

Piazza Vittorio Veneto (*C5*). This large rectangular square, surrounded on three sides by porticoes, was designed and built between 1825 and 1830 in the area in which the 17th-c. Porta di Po once stood. Overlooking the river Po, it has as a backdrop in the large church of the Gran Madre di Dio (see below) and the hills behind it.

Via Po (*B-C4-5*). This broad thoroughfare is lined with uniform rows of buildings and porticoes; built in 1675, it links the enormous Piazza Vittorio Veneto with Piazza Castello. In a cross street on the right, Via Montebello, stands the **Mole Antonelliana*** (*B5*), a remarkable construction by A. Antonelli, now an emblem of the city. Begun in 1863 and completed toward the end of the century, it was originally built entirely in masonry and stone. It stands 167.5 m tall; the spire, torn down by a hurricane on 23 May 1953, has since been rebuilt. Originally built as a synagogue, it has a huge single hall some 85 m tall; the original structure has been fortified by a skeleton in reinforced cement. Take an elevator up (*open Jan.-Feb., Tue.-Sun., 11-5; Sat., 11-11; Mar.-Dec., Tue.-Sun., 10-8; Sat., 10 a.m.-11 p.m.*) to a broad terrace above the cupola for a remarkable view of Turin and the surrounding area.

Museo Nazionale del Cinema (*B5*). *Open Tue.-Sun., 10-8; Sat., 10 a.m.-11 p.m.* Situated in the Mole Antonelliana, the museum illustrates the technical and artistic development of the cinema industry and of photography. The first rooms are devoted to forms of entertainment which preceded cinema, based on the vision of moving images.

Galleria dell'Accademia Albertina (*C4*). *Open Tue.-Sun., 9-12 and 3-7.* Located in the Palazzo dell'Accademia Albertina di Belle Arti, at n. 6 Via dell'Accademia Albertina, this museum contains paintings and drawings by G. and D. Ferrari, Spanzotti, Filippo Lippi, and 17th-c. artists from Italy (O. Gentileschi; Cavarozzi) and elsewhere in Europe (P.Brill; S.Vouet). On the Via Po, just before Piazza Castello, on the right you will see the stern facade of the **University** (*B4*), built in 1713 to plans by M.Garove, with a porticoed courtyard and a loggia decorated with statues and busts of illustrious historical figures.

The banks of the Po River

The Po River, and the surrounding hills, which rise verdant over the opposite bank, are some of the most distinctive features of Turin, deeply rooted in the mindset and customs of its population. All the same, the city discovered the delights of the banks of the Po fairly late; aside from the Castello del Valentino, a princely outlying villa, Turin did not turn to the riverbanks until the 19th c. It then made the riverbanks into a public park, as well as a showcase: the medieval "Borgo," Torino Esposizioni, and the buildings of the Centennial Celebrations of the Unification of Italy (1961) are three approaches to the concept of "showing the city's best face," in three different times and three different cultural contexts.

Gran Madre di Dio (*C5*). From Piazza Vittorio Veneto (see above) the *Ponte Vittorio Emanuele I* (1810-15), the oldest masonry bridge in Turin, leads up to this large church, built to commemorate the return of the House of Savoy in 1814, following the Napoleonic period. Built between 1818 and 1831 by F. Bonsignore in Neo-Classic style (modelled after the Pantheon), the church houses, in the crypt, the *Ossario ai Caduti* (a sanctuary to the Italian dead of WWI). To the side of the bridge are the Neo-Classic 19th-c. **Murazzi**, built to contain the river (*C-D5; embarcadero for boat rides on the river*).

Monte dei Cappuccini (*D5*). This isolated wooded hill served as a fortified position protecting the city. On the hilltop (284 m) stands the church of *S. Maria del Monte*; this church, with a luminous interior richly decorated with marble, was built by A. Vittozzi (1583-96), who also designed the adjoining convent. Alongside it is the **Museo Nazionale della Montagna Duca degli Abruzzi*** (*open 9-7*), with a vast array of documentary material concerning mountains, the history and techniques of climbing, geology, landscapes, culture and peoples of the mountains, and expeditions outside of Europe. From the square in front of the building, remarkable view* of the city

and the Alps, from Monviso to Monte Rosa.

Parco del Valentino* (*D-F4; open 9-7*). Public park on the left bank of the Po, built in 1830. On the grounds, lined with boulevards and paths, is the large **Castello del Valentino** (*E4*), built in 1630-6(by C. di Castellamonte on the model of French cas tles of the 16th-17th c., with a broad rectangula courtyard opening out to the city, and a majestic ter racotta facade overlooking the river Po. To the left o the castle is the entrance to the University's *Ort Botanico* (*open Apr.-Sep., Sat.-Sun. and holidays, 9- and 3-7; by request and for schools, Mon.-Fri., tel 0116707446*), one of the leading botanical garden in Italy, and one of the first (1729). Further along near the banks of the Po, is the **Borgo Medieval** (*F4; open 9-7; closed Mon.*), a remarkable array o faithful reproductions of medieval houses and cas tles from the Valle d'Aosta, built for the Internation al Exposition of 1884. The *Palazzo Torino Esposizion* (*F4; 1948*), at the southern edge of the park, on Cor so D'Azeglio, is a complex of exhibition pavilions some designed by P. Nervi and R. Morandi.

Museo dell'Automobile Carlo Biscaretti di Ruf fia.* *Open 10-6:30, closed Mon.* At n. 40 Corso Unità d'Italia, this car museum offers a remarkable assort ment of material on the history and development o the automobile in Italy, and a survey of world pro duction. Among the many cars on exhibit, note the "Itala" that won the race from Peking to Paris in 1907 the earliest steam-driven cars, the first Fiat (1899) the cars that raced in the first Giro d'Italia (1901), rac ers, and limousines; there is also a section devote to the early years of the Touring Club Italiano.

Not far from the museum, in a park area overlook ing both Po and hills, stand various buildings, in cluding the *Palazzo del Lavoro*, by P.L. Nervi, nov the headquarters of the Organizzazione Inter

Turin: Gran Madre di Dio

nazionale del Lavoro and other professional institutions, and the *Palazzo delle Mostre*, an exhibition
hall with a remarkable "sail" roof; both buildings
were erected to commemorate the Centennial of
Italian Unity, for the "Italia 61" Expo.

Corso Agnelli. This road is lined by the *FIAT Mi-
rafiori factories*, built in 1938 and later enlarged; to
one side of the complex is the auto test track. In Via
Nizza stands the old **FIAT Lingotto factory**, built after WWI, and now used for art exhibits. Note the
multi-storey construction; cars can drive on any
storey and from one storey to another, through the
helical ramps, culminating in the remarkable test
track on the roof of the factory.

Surrounding areas. Basilica di Superga*, elev.
670 m, 10 km east of Turin, along the road flanking
the Parco Regionale Naturale Collina di Superga.
This remarkable hillside church was built at the behest of Vittorio Amedeo II to fulfill a vow taken during the French seige of 1706, designed by F. Juvarra
(1731) in "regal" classical style. The *crypt* (*open 9:30-
7:30; Sat.-Sun., 9:30-6:30*) contains the tombs of the
Savoy kings up to Carlo Alberto, as well as numerous princes of the House; behind the basilica is a
plaque that commemorates the tragic plane crash
that occurred here in 1949, killing the entire "Torino"
soccer team.

Palazzina di Caccia di Stupinigi* (*open summer,
9-11:50 and 2-5:20; winter, until 4:20; closed Mon.*),
10.5 km SW of town; the celebrated Rococo work
by F. Juvarra was built in 1730 as a hunting lodge
for Vittorio Amedeo II (Victor Amadeus II). It is surrounded by vast grounds and it now houses the interesting *Museo di Storia, Arte e Ammobiliamento*
(*open 10-6:45; closed Mon.*), with furniture and decorations dating from the 17th-18th c., from the royal
residences of Piedmont.

Ùdine*

Elev. 113 m, pop. 94,932; Friùli-Venezia Giulia,
provincial capital. From the high hill of the
Castello, you can see quite a bit of the "Patria
del Friùli," the great plain stretching to the Alps.
When the patriarchs moved here in the 13th
c. from Cividale, Ùdine became capital of
Friùli, a great marketplace, a cultural center,
and crossroads of the Alps. At the foot of the
hill, beneath the Castello, is a piazza in which
Venetian, Gothic, and Renaissance architecture all blend and mingle. The young artist
Tiepolo, at the time just 30, came to paint Bible
stories in the palace of the bishop.

Historical note. In all likelihood, the castle was
built as an outpost during the raids of the Huns; it
is documented as early as 983 as the castle of
Udene." In the 13th c., Ùdine became the residence
of the patriarch, the capital of Friùli (the Pieve di S.
Maria in Castello dates from this period, almost
alone). During the 14th c., Ùdine was torn by fac-

tions, and in 1420 the town – and all of Friùli – became possessions of the Venetian Republic, largely
left to administer themselves amid new artistic and
economic growth. The 15th-16th c. witnessed the
construction of Piazza della Libertà, the Palazzo del
Comune, the Porticato di S. Giovanni, and even the
modern structure of the Castello. In the 18th c. Tiepolo decorated the Duomo, the Palazzo Arcivescovile,
and the Oratorio della Purità. Venice fell, Napoleon
fell, and even the Austrians were firmly ejected, and
in 1866 Ùdine and Friùli became part of united Italy.
Only after WWI did the city grow beyond the walls,
and it continues to expand to this day.

Getting around. Part of the historic center of Ùdine
is closed to traffic, and the entire area within the ring
roads is heavily regulated. The routes we recommend
are walking tours, though you may choose to take
public transportation to the Galleria d'Arte Moderna.

Piazza della Libertà, the Castello, and the Duomo

The "Venetian" square and the monuments of "patriarchal" and Venetian rule stand at the foot of the hill
of the Castello, historical cradle of Ùdine, set high
enough to enjoy quite a panoramic view.

Piazza della Libertà. Elegant focal point of all
Ùdine, this plaza stands at the base of the hill of the
castle, surrounded by a harmonious complex of
Venetian-style buildings. Once Piazza Nuova, then
Piazza Contarena, its modern appearance has
changed little from how it looked in the 16th c. Of
particular interest are the Loggia del Lionello and
the portico of S. Giovanni (see below), to the left of
which an arch leads into the castle.

Loggia del Lionello.* This is the *Palazzo del Comune*, or town hall, built in 1448-56 by B. delle Cisterne to plans by the goldsmith N. Lionello from
Ùdine, in elegant Venetian Gothic style. Faced with
alternating bands of white and pink stone, it is dominated by the large ground-floor loggia, with
balustrade. Note the statue of the Virgin, by B. Bon
(1448).

Porticato di S. Giovanni.* This spectacular piece
of Renaissance architecture by B. da Morcote (1533)
comprises a long portico on slender columns,
crowned by the elegant *Torre dell'Orologio* (1527),
or clock tower, with the Venetian lion of St. Mark's
and two Moors, who strike the hours. In the middle,
a broad arch leads to the *Cappella di S. Giovanni*,
now Pantheon dei Caduti, a chapel dedicated to soldiers killed in war.

Note the *statues of Peace, Justice, Hercules, and Cacus*; on the right, a 15th-c. column with the *lion of St.
Mark's*, and a handsome *fountain* by G. da Carrara
(1542).

Castello. This sober 16th-c. castle was built from 1517
on by G. Fontana and G. da Udine upon the site of
the earlier castle of the patriarchs of Aquileia. It was

Ùdine: Piazza della Libertà

badly damaged by an earthquake in 1976, and reopened in 1990. To reach it, take the *Salita al Castello* (1563) from Piazza della Libertà, pass through the *Bollani arch*, by Palladio (1556), and stroll through the lovely portico known as *Lippomano* (1487). The castle is dominated by the observatory ("*specola*"), with a spectacular view*.

Civici Musei e Galleria di Storia e Arte.* *Open 9:30-12:30 and 3-6; Sun. and holidays, 9:30-12:30; closed Mon.* These museums and galleries have been located in the Castello since 1906. The complex comprises four main sections: the Galleria d'Arte Antica; the Museo Archeologico; the Gabinetto dei Disegni e delle Stampe; and the *Biblioteca d'Arte, Storia ed Etnografia* with over 20,000 volumes and the Fototeca, or photographic archives. On the piano nobile, the *Salone del Parlamento della Patria del Friùli** features frescoes by P. Amalteo, G.B. Grassi, and G.B. Tiepolo.

The **Galleria d'Arte Antica**, organized chronologically, has a collection comprising paintings from the late Middle Ages to the 19th c., including Friulian and Italian artists. Of particular note, works by G.B. Tiepolo, early Friulan artists, the "school of Tolmezzo" (14-15th c.), and Renaissance and 18th-c. artists such as D. da Tolmezzo, V. Carpaccio, A. Bellunello, P. da San Daniele, P. Amalteo, G.A. da Pordenone, Palma the Younger, Caravaggio, A. Carneo, S. Bombelli, B. Strozzi, L. Carlevarijs, M. and S. Ricci, N. Grassi. Also, works by 19th-c. artists, including: O. Politi, B. Bison, and F. Giuseppini.

The **Museo Archeologico** has collections – including glass, arms and armor, ceramics – that range from the Mesolithic to the Iron Age, to ancient Roman times, and on up through the Middle Ages to the Renaissance. It also includes the *Raccolte Numismatiche*, or numismatic collections with the *Colloredo Mels Collection** (about 50,000 Roman, Byzantine, barbarian, and medieval coins); the *Toppo Collection** (amber, semiprecious stones, glass, and Roman perfume jars and jewelry from Aquileia); and the *Torrelazzi Collection** (Roman and 18th-/19th-c. carved gems).

The **Gabinetto dei Disegni e delle Stampe** exhibits a rotating selection of the rich array of prints and drawings (some 10,000 items) in the museum, including work by A. Dürer, G.B. Tiepolo, G.A. Pordenone, and F. Chiarottini.

S. Maria di Castello.* *Open by request; enquire at the Museo del Castello.* Documented from the 6th c.

A.D., this church was enlarged in the 12th c. and modified frequently; damaged by earthquake in 1976 and restored, it boasts an elegant facade and massive bell tower, by G. Negro. Note the fragments of 13th-c. frescoes* in the arches and apses.

The church is joined to the Castello by the *Griman* arch (1522); next to it is the entrance to the *Gothic Casa della Confraternita di S. Maria di Castello*, with frescoes; the **Casa della Contadinanza**, built after 1511, was reassembled in 1931.

S. Maria delle Grazie. Overlooking the great tree-lined oval of Piazza 1 Maggio, this 18th-c. basilica by G. Massari was given a Neo-Classic pronaos by V. Presani (1838-51). Inside, behind the main altar, Virgin with Child by L. Monteverde (1522).

Palazzo Arcivescovile. This imposing 16th-c. palazzo overlooks Piazza Patriarcato; on the second floor is a **gallery*** with a fresco by the young Tiepolo (1726-28), and rooms frescoed by Tiepolo and G. da Udine.

The building houses the **Museo Diocesano e Galleria del Tiepolo** (*open Wed.-Sun., 10-12 and 3:30-6:30*), featuring objects of sacred art from early Christian times to the 19th c., from Ùdine and Aquileia. Note the 15th-c. wooden altars of the "school of Tolmezzo." To the right, at n. 3, stands the 17th-c. *Palazzo Antonini Belgrado*, with frescoes by G. Quaglio (1698).

Duomo.* Despite extensive remodelling over the centuries, this cathedral preserves its impressive 14th-c. Gothic form, especially in the handsome sharply splayed central portal (with carved lunette) and in the German-school 14th-c. portal* on the left side (near the campanile); on the right side, Renaissance portal by C. da Carona. The unfinished campanile was built in the 15th c. atop the octagonal base of the 14th-c. Baptistery.

Inside, note paintings by G.B. Tiepolo, organ doors painted by P. Amalteo, and a carved wooden pulpit (1737). The entrance to the theatrical Baroque complex of the presbytery and the cross vault, with spectacular stucco decorations, is flanked by two organs with decoration by Pordenone, L. Floreani, and G.B. Grassi; note the statues and marble carvings on the main altar (1717) and the two colossal *tombs of the Manin*, by M. Calderoni and F. Picchi (18th c.).

To the left of the presbytery is the entrance to the *Museo del Duomo* (*closed for restoration*), which includes the 14th-c. *Cappella S. Nicolò*, a chapel with frescoes* by V. da Bologna (1348-49) and panels by his pupil the Maestro dei Padiglioni; also in the museum is the ancient *Baptistery*, beneath the campanile, with fine architecture and monuments.

Oratorio della Purità. *Open by request; enquire in the sacristy of the Duomo.* Directly across from the right side of the Duomo, this 18th-c. oratory by L. Andreoli has paintings and frescoes by G.B. Tiepolo and his son, G.D. Tiepolo.

Madonna del Carmine. On the outskirts toward the railroad station, in Via Aquileia, this 16th-c. church has a fine 14th-c. funerary monument executed by F. De Sanctis.

S. Francesco. *Open only for temporary exhibitions.* Of the original Romanesque convent church (12th c.), heavily damaged in the fighting in 1945, all that survives are the left side and the apse and campanile overlooking the modern Piazza Venerio. Inside, where concerts and exhibitions are held, note the fragments of 14th-/15th-c. frescoes of the School of Rimini.

Museo Friulano di Storia Naturale . *Closed for restoration.* Located in 18th-c. Palazzo Giacomelli, at n. 1 Via Grazzano, this museum of natural science has a broad array of exhibits documenting various aspects of Friùli-Venezia Giulia.

Piazza Matteotti and the Galleria di Arte Moderna

The different aspects of Ùdine and the life of its streets can be seen in the western section, amid venerable churches (the 18th-c. Baroque Cappella Manin), palazzi of the 1500s, and museums – if last, not least, the Galleria di Arte Moderna, abounding in masterpieces of the Italian Novecento.

Via Rialto. Among the most attractive streets of the historical center, this was the main street in medieval "Villa Udin," as the town was called. Cars prohibited. Behind the *Loggia del Lionello*, it begins with the monumental *municipal office building*, by R. D'Aronco (1911-30). Beneath the portico, but on the parallel *Via Cavour* side, is the historic *Caffè Contarena* (1925).

Piazza Matteotti. "Piazza S. Giacomo" to the Udinese, this may be the town's oldest square, documented back in 1248 with the name of "Forum Novum." Its modern layout – square, surrounded by houses with low porticoes – was the brainchild of T. Lippomano (1486); note the *fountain*, by G. da Udine (1542).

S. Giacomo. Built in the late 14th c., this church has a lively Lombardesque facade, by B. da Morcote; note paintings inside.

Monumento alla Resistenza. At the center of Piazzale XXVI Luglio, this huge monument to Italy's Resistance movement in WWII was designed by G. Valle and F. Marconi (1959-69); the sculptural group is by D. Basaldella. On the north side of the square is the *Tempio-Ossario dei Caduti d'Italia*, a funerary shrine to Italy's dead in WWI, built in 1931; it holds the remains of 20,000 soldiers.

Via Zanon. Lined by one of the few surviving stretches of Ùdine's distinctive non-covered "rogge," or irrigation ditches, this street has several handsome palazzi, mostly from the 18th c. At the corner of Via dei Torriani is the 13th-c. *Torre di S. Maria*, a surviving tower of the old walls. Behind it, beyond the sober front of *Palazzo Torriani* (n. 4), is the 18th-c. **Cappella Manin** (*B1; closed to the public*), a jewel of Baroque architecture.

Via Mercatovecchio. One of the most popular strolling streets in Ùdine, this was also the town's first marketplace, a distinction that dates from 1223. Broad and slightly curving, this handsome street is lined with porticoes; note the building of the **Monte di Pietà** (1690). Beneath the portico, in the middle, is a *chapel* with fine wrought-iron and frescoes* by G. Quaglio (1694).

Palazzo Antonini. Now a bank, at n. 3 in Via Gemona, this palazzo was built, beginning in 1570, to a plan by A. Palladio. Unfinished though it may be, its facade is quite distinguished and original. Practically facing it, on the right of Via Antonini, is the 17th-c. *Palazzo Antonini-Cernazai*, now part of the university.

Galleria d'Arte Moderna.* *Open 9:30-12:30 and 3-6; Sun. and holidays, 9:30-12:30; closed Mon.* This separate section of the *Musei Civici* is set in the *Palamostre* (1968) in Piazzale Paolo Diacono (n.22) and occupies two storeys in a succession of "open space" areas.

The museum's collections include works by Italian and especially Friulian and Venetian artists. It offers a broad and thorough survey of 20th-c. schools of art. Of special note, the Astaldi Collection (about 200 works) with masterpieces by Italian artists from the 1920s to the 1960s.

On the *upper floor*, along with a section on modern and contemporary architecture (original drawings by R. D'Aronco), there are exhibits of works by artists from Friùli-Venezia Giulia, including Pellis, Crali, Pittino, Pizzinato, Zigaina, and Alviani, as well as works by A. Martini, M. Mafai, C. Cagli, and F. Casorati, and a collection of 1970s American art (W. De Kooning). The *ground floor* is primarily taken up with the *Astaldi Collection***, which includes, in particular, works by G. Severini, G. De Chirico, Savinio, M. Sironi, G. Morandi, M. Campigli, O. Rosai, F. Pirandello, and C. Carrà; in a separate space are works by the Udinese artists Dino, Mirko, and A. Basaldella.

Urbino**

Elev. 485 m, pop. 15,114; Marche, province of Pesaro e Urbino. Montaigne wrote: "It is said that the duke's palace has as many rooms as there are days in the year." The writer visited the city and palace when the last Montefeltro duke was still alive; he expressed disappointment. The result of peevishness? Or an indication that there are fashions in everything? The location, a hilly spur on the reliefs dividing the Metauro and Foglia valleys, midway between the Adriatic and the ridge of the Apennines, was inhabited in prehistoric times. Today, Urbino, with its "astonishing palace" (Vasari), "so expensive and daunting to build," as Raphael's father once wrote, is a university town rich with memories of an illustrious court (among the artists and architects who worked here, let us mention L. Laurana, F. di Giorgio Martini, P. della Francesca, and perhaps S. Botticelli). It seems that every detail of this town was carved, painted, or planned by a superior mind. Raphael and Bramante both came from here (the latter from Fermignano, 5 km south).

Historical note. This town still lies within the walls built in 1507, on two hills separated by the hollow of Piazza della Repubblica; one hill lies SE, with the Duomo and Palazzo Ducale; the other lies NW, with Piazza Roma. Time seems to have stopped in the Renaissance here; most of Urbino's buildings date from the 15th-16th c. The Baroque barely grazed this town, and little if anything seems to have survived from earlier times. No monuments remain from the major Roman municipium of "Urbinum Metaurense," only inscriptions. The age of the Goths, the sack by the Byzantine general Belisarius, Longobard rule, the Carolingians, and the Church – none left a trace. Little remains of Romanesque Urbino, though the Gothic age survives in the churches of S. Agostino, S. Domenico, S. Francesco, all renovated since. The counts of Montefeltro became the dukes of Urbino in 1443; the second duke was Federico II, the most famous member of the dynasty, renowned for the portrait by Piero della Francesca, now in the Uffizi. A skillful condottiere, Federico served popes, Florence, and Naples, and tripled his realm in doing so. He was more illustrious in peace than war, as his court attracted the great minds of the Humanist Renaissance, among them L. B. Alberti, Pisanello, P. della Francesca, M. da Forlì, P. Uccello, D. da Settignano, D. Rosselli, and others still. From Flanders and Spain came painters and weavers of tapestries; for 14 years, 30-40 scribes worked to make Federico's library the richest in Europe. The architect L. Laurana rebuilt the Palazzo Ducale, one of the masterpieces of Renaissance architecture. This was Urbino's golden age. Federico's son married a Gonzaga and held high the splendor of a court immortalized by B. Castiglione ("The Courtier"). As if a spell had been cast, Raphael was born in Urbino in 1483, and Bramante, in 1444, not far away. The Della Rovere family took over in 1508, and Urbino flourished one last time; in 1626 it was ceded to the pope. Stripped of its treasures, the town declined sharply, and the Napoleonic occupation did the rest. After Italian unification, the university began to restore the city to health and prosperity.

Getting around. The area contained within the walls is off limits to private cars; the route we recommend, shown on the map, is a walking tour.

Places of interest. Piazza del Mercatale. This enormous square, at the foot of the town walls, is now a parking lot. With the 17th-c. sandstone gate of the *Porta Valbona*, this is the main entrance to Urbino. Note, inside the semicircular 15th-c. bastion, the **spiral ramp of steps**, designed by F. di Giorgio Martini (restored in 1976), which leads directly into the center, to the porticoes of Corso Garibaldi.

Corso Garibaldi. Flanked by a long portico and overshadowed with the three tall apses of the Duomo and the west side of Palazzo Ducale – with two slender towers and three stacked loggias – this road runs past the brick **Teatro Sanzio** (C2; 1853), on the left. Designed by Ghinelli, this fine opera house

Urbino: Palazzo Ducale

stands on the semicircular 15th-c. bastion overlooking Piazza del Mercatale.

Piazza della Repubblica. At the center of Urbino, situated between the two hills, this square is the hub of all roads. On the north side, note the stern *Collegio Raffaello* (1705).

Duomo. Designed by F. di Giorgio Martini and built at the behest and expense of Federico da Montefeltro, this cathedral was almost entirely rebuilt in Neo-Classic style by G. Valadier, following the earthquake of 1789; the facade is by C. Morigia (1802). Inside, note paintings by C. Maratta, C. Cignani, and C. Unterpergher; in the left aisle, painting by F. Barocci.

From the right aisle, you can enter the **Museo Diocesano Albani** (*open 9-12 and 2-6; closed Mon. aft.*), featuring paintings of the 14th-16th c. (Barocci, A. da Bologna), an English 13th-c. bronze lectern*, a Paschal candelabrum* by F. di Giorgio Martini, and illuminated parchments and music.

Piazza Rinascimento. Bounded on one side by the mullioned windows of the long facade of Palazzo Ducale, this square boasts an Egyptian obelisk, brought here from Rome in 1737; opposite is the Gothic former church of **S. Domenico**, now a gallery, with elegant portal (1451; in the lunette, copy of terracotta by L. della Robbia, original in Palazzo Ducale). Note also the **Palazzo dell'Università**, once the residence of the Montefeltro family (armorial bearings on portal).

Palazzo Ducale.** *Open by reservation, 9-7; Mon., 9-2; tel. 0722322625.* The most important monument in Urbino, the ducal palace constituted the model for the unfortified princely residence of the Renaissance. The palazzo houses both the Galleria Nazionale delle Marche and the Museo Archeologico Urbinate (see below).

The building was the creation of the Dalmatian architect L. Laurana, who was summoned in 1465 by Duke Federico da Montefeltro to enlarge the original structure, the part with elegant twin-light mullioned windows, overlooking Piazza Rinascimento (ca. 1444). Laurana concentrated the building around the handsome courtyard*, and gave it the famed facade overlooking the valley to the west, with small stacked balconies, flanked by slender towers*. The two wings facing Piazza Duca Federico were completed by F. di Giorgio Martini, while the elegant decoration of portals and windows was done by A. Barocci.

Galleria Nazionale delle Marche.** *Open same hours as Palazzo Ducale*. Housed in the Palazzo Ducale since its foundation in 1912, this is the region's leading museum. On the ground floor, adjacent to the Museo Archeologico, are displayed 71 panels depicting the machinery of war and peace built by A. Barocci in the late 15th c., to plans by F. di Giorgio Martini. The monumental stairway, known as the Scalone d'Onore* leads up to the loggias, where handsome inlaid doors lead into the various rooms of the Galleria Nazionale.

Appartamento di Jole. In the older eastern wing of the palazzo, this suite comprises seven rooms, foremost among them the Sala della Jole. Note the carved fireplace, by M. di Giovanni da Fiesole; also worthy of note are the lunette in glazed terracotta by L. della Robbia, and works by A. di Duccio, and F. di Giorgio Martini. In the other rooms, there are badly damaged frescoes attributed to G. Boccati; in the bedroom* of Federico da Montefeltro are rare examples of 15th-c. furnishings, with painted decorations by G. da Camerino, and paintings by G. Boccati and G. di Giovanni. *Appartamento dei Melaranci.* In these three rooms you will find an array of 14th-c. artworks, as well as frescoes* by the Maestro di Campodonico; a polyptych* by G. Baronzio (1345); a Crucifix by the Maestro di Verucchio; a triptych by the Maestro dell'Incoronazione di Urbino; a Virgin with Child by A. Nuzi. *Appartamento degli Ospiti.* Here we have 15th-c. wooden sculptures, ceiling stuccoes by F. Brandani, a trove of 103 15th-c. gold coins, and works by C. and V. Crivelli, A. Vivarini, and Giovanni Bellini.

Appartamento del Duca Federico.* This apartment includes the most exquisite rooms in the palazzo: the Sala delle Udienze, a reception hall with handsome stone decorations, as well as the **Flagellation**** and the **Madonna di Senigallia****, by Piero della Francesca; the **Studiolo*** of Duke Federico, with inlays by B. Pontelli, executed to drawings by Botticelli, F. di Giorgio Martini, and Bramante, and **14 small panels**** by J. van Gand and P. Berruguete, with Portraits of Illustrious Men (there were originally 28 portraits, but 14 are now in Paris, in the Louvre); the Cappellina del Perdono* (spiral staircase), a chapel with marble decorations; the Camera da Letto del Duca, the duke's bedroom, with carved fireplace, attributed to D. Rosselli and F. di Simone Ferrucci, portrait of Federico da Montefeltro and his son Guidobaldo* by P. Berruguete, and a Virgin with Child, school of Verrocchio. The duke's apartment is completed by the spectacular Sala degli Angeli, overlooking the hanging garden, with its immense fireplace with a frieze of putti* by D. Rosselli, fine inlaid doors* with design attributed to S. Botticelli, and the artworks: Communion of the Apostles* by J. van Gand, Miracle of the Profaned Host*

by P. Uccello, **View of an Ideal City***, attributed to L. Laurana; a bas-relief by T. Fiamberti and a 15th-c. carved inlaid chest with a view of a city. In the Sala delle Veglie are works by L. Signorelli and G. Santi. *Appartamento della Duchessa.* Here are a number of rooms, decorated later than the rooms toured so far, with 16th-c. works. In the vestibule, see the stained glass by T. Viti, and a fine Florentine bas-relief. In the Salotto della Duchessa (note the stucco ceiling* by F. di Simone Ferrucci) are works by Raphael (**La Muta****), Bramantino, and T. Viti; in the bedroom are works by various 16th-c. artists, Titian (**Last Supper***), Raffaellino del Colle, and V. Pagani, and notable Flemish tapestries. In the wardrobe and adjacent room there are works by Tibaldi, Zuccari, and Brandani (ceiling). In the immense Sala del Trono, or Throne Room (35 x 15 m), seven handsome tapestries based on cartoons by Raphael.

Appartamento Roveresco. The second floor, completed during the reign of Guidobaldo II della Rovere, to the design of B. Genga, is devoted to the paintings of F. Barocci, early 17th-c. artists, and ceramics. In particular, note the work of Barocci and his pupils (Vitali, Marini) and works by O. Gentileschi, G. F. Guerrieri, A. Lilli, Mastelletta, S. Cantarini, and C. Ridolfi. In the last rooms, 15th-c. terraces that were enclosed in the 16th c., you can see, variously, work by F. Barocci, A. De Carolis, and ceramics from Faenza, Deruta, Siena, and other local centers. Last comes the long Galleria del Pasquino (note the 15th-c. battlements, built into the enclosure walls) with the furnishings for the wedding of Federico Ubaldo della Rovere and Claudia de' Medici (1621), the work of C. Ridolfi and G. Cialdieri.

Cellars. These huge, recently restored rooms can be reached from the courtyard down a ramp. First you see the stables, then, on the left, the kitchens, baths, and storerooms, and on the right the laundry rooms, ice room, and other facilities.

Museo Archeologico Urbinate. *Open same hours as the Galleria Nazionale.* This archeological museum is accessible directly from the courtyard of Palazzo Ducale. In five rooms, it shows a collection of funerary epigraphs. Note the Lastra del Marmorarius Eutropus* (early 4th c. A.D.) and a relief of Ulysses and the Sirens (1st c. A.D.).

Oratorio di S. Giuseppe. *Open summer, weekdays, 10-12:30 and 3-5:30; holidays, 10-12:30; winter, 10-12:30.* In Via Barocci, this church has a fine old crèche* by F. Brandani (1522); fine paintings.

S. Giovanni Battista* (*open same hours as the Oratorio di S. Giuseppe*). This oratory, just beyond the one of S. Giuseppe, dates from the late 14th c. (the facade is modern). The single-nave interior with a handsome wooden ceiling, is decorated with a series of frescoes* by the brothers I. and L. Salimbeni (1416). From the stairs on the left of the building, a fine view of Palazzo Ducale and its towers.

Via Raffaello. This distinctive road runs steeply up from Piazza della Repubblica to Piazzale Roma; fine views. It begins at the 14th-c. church of **S. Francesco**; inside, note 16th-c. reliefs in the Cappella

del Sacramento, and a canvas by F. Barocci in the apse. Uphill is the **Casa di Raffaello**, birthplace of Raphael *(open summer, 9-1 and 3-7; Sun. and holidays, 10-1; winter, 9-2; Sun. and holidays, 10-1)*, with copies of work by the great artist, and a few paintings (by Raphael's father, G. Santi, G. Romano, and T. Viti); note a fresco executed by the young Raphael.
Piazzale Roma. Atop one of Urbino's hills, this square offers a vast panorama* of the surrounding mountains. Note the monument to Raphael (1897). From here, along Viale Buozzi, you have a fine view of the 16th-c. walls, with the *Fortezza Albornoz*.
Colle dei Cappuccini. At about 1 km from Piazza del Mercatale, this hill is the campus of the university, built in 1966 to a plan by G. De Carlo.

Venice / Venezia**

Elev. 2 m, pop. 308,717; Veneto, regional and provincial capital. This town has exhausted every adjective, and outstripped all astonishment. In the earliest times, the pilgrims who came here to set sail for the Holy Land noted this city "set in the middle of the sea, built neither on mountain slope nor in bounteous plain, but only upon wooden poles, something that may seem unbelievable," and where "you go by boat, from house to house, through every street" (Dietrich von Schachten). The mainland is only 4 km away, and the sea is just 2 km away; the city has more than 100 islands, as many canals, over 400 bridges, and just one "piazza" (every other square, circle, and triangle is either a "campo" or a "campiello"). Venice is at once unreal and exceedingly real – many have pointed this out. It seems to emerge from the void at the meeting ground of two infinities, the water and the sky, the ground here being so understated and hidden that it hardly counts. This city-republic's long and glorious political history extends over a millennium (tradition lists 120 Doges of Venice). A good portion of its history cannot be described as a chapter of Italy's history, but rather as part of something much larger; for more than a century, Venice was the capital of the entire Mediterranean Sea, and hence, the center of world trade. In its golden and sensuous autumn, Venice knew that it was still the European capital of theater, of celebration, of the joy of living, the desire of every educated mind. "Those days are long gone, but the beauty is still here" (Lord Byron): Venice survived the end of the Venetian Republic, trailing a great series of unsolved problems. The city now represents for all humanity (a humanity that loves Venice with so suffocating a love that it may yet prove fatal) the unattainable dream of a place where time stands still, the alluring Fata Morgana of a completely different way of life.

Historical note. Of course, in reality Venice did not spring out of a void, nor was it miraculously born of the sea, as the city's chroniclers long maintained, anxious to nullify any historical claims that either the Papacy or the Holy Roman Empire might choose to enforce. The Venetians, these "strange animals who neither plow, nor sow, nor harvest" (Cassiodorus, 6th-c. Roman historian), amazed even the earliest visitors who were ready and willing to believe the local mythology. Recent archeological research, on the other hand, has clearly shown that there was a continuous settlement of the lagoon area that dates back to Roman times. And it is widely accepted that the Longobard invasion of the 6th c. forced various tribes of "Venetia," which formed part of the Augustan X Region to seek refuge among the islets of the lagoon. The center of these new settlements was first known as "Civitas Nova," and later Heraclea, in the long-vanished lagoon of Oderzo, later Malamocco, and finally, at the beginning of the 9th c., the island of Rialto called the "Civitas Rivoalti." These lands were invariably dependent upon Byzantium, and neither Longobards nor Franks ever managed to set foot upon them. They were governed first by maritime tribunes, and later by a single officer, the duke, or Doge, at first named by the Byzantine rulers, but as early as the 8th c., elected by the people's assembly. It was the anomalous environmental setting in which Venice rose that saved the city from those harsh wars that tattered and bloodied the cities of the mainland throughout the Middle Ages. In the 8th c., Venice was already substantially the city that we know, with its "calli," "campi," churches, palazzi, and "fonteghi." And yet it is a radically different city because, having no other territory into which it could expand, Venice was forced to do all its new building on the same area, rebuilding and raising its buildings, covering over the shoals and sandbanks of the lagoon, extending the walkways (bridges and "fondamenta") as canals and "rii" became narrower. In the 14th c., the population of Venice was already more than 130,000, roughly the same as the population at the end of the Republic, at the turn of the 19th c. During those five centuries, Venice took to the seas, acting at first in the name of the Eastern Roman Empire, or Byzantium, to which it formally belonged, but in reality looking only to its own self-interest, ignoring everything that was happening on the mainland behind it. The first goal was to establish free rein over the Adriatic Sea. The major steps involved treaties with the Istrian cities, an expedition into Dalmatia in the year 1000 against the pirates that operated from there, and a campaign – at the behest of Byzantium – against the Normans, who were trying to control both shores of the channel of Otranto further south. The Venetians thus attained their first objective. Venice had unimpaired access to the routes of the Levant, and thus became a competitor of Pisa and Genoa. While the conflict with Pisa over the trading ports of Syria was soon dampened by the instability of those outposts, constantly under attack by the Saracens, the parallel conflict with Genoa over the possession of the trading ports of the Aegean Sea in time led to a fight to the death. The astute Venetian masterpiece of politics and mil-

Venice: Piazza S. Marco

itary strategy – the conquest of Constantinople in 1204 by Crusaders transported by Venetian ships – allowed the Venetian Republic to take control of "a quarter and an eighth of the Empire."

Early in the 13th c., then, Venetian power in the Levant had reached its peak. The profits that came from the Venetian trade fleet were so enormous that they allowed the construction of the astonishing city of marble and stone that we see today, already the wonder of the 13th-14th c. So mighty a sea power could hardly help but come into conflict with Genoa, on the Tyrrhenian coast, working to cultivate the same trade routes with the Levant. Just as Venice had played the card of the Crusaders in 1204, Genoa in 1261 played the card of the Greek rulers of Byzantium, lending its great fleet to the restoration of the Paleologus dynasty of emperors in Constantinople, in exchange for immense commercial concessions. For over a century the two maritime republics fought sea battles, neither one ever quite eliminating their rival; then Genoa tried to deliver a final blow by taking the war to Chioggia, in the Venetian lagoon. It brought Genoa a defeat from which the city never quite recovered. For Venice, the Peace of Turin of 1381 that ended the "War of Chioggia" reconfirmed its almost total control of trade with the Levant, which was, as Fernand Braudel later wrote, tantamount to dominion over all international trade of that time. For nearly a century, from that fateful 1381 until 1498, the year in which Vasco da Gama made his triumphant return to Lisbon after his circumnavigation of Africa, Venice held the status that in later centuries fell to Antwerp, London, and New York. Everything passed through her hands: gold from Africa, silver from Central Europe, and the pepper, spices, cotton, and silk carried from the Far East by caravan and then loaded onto ships in the ports of Egypt and Syria. Despite the Turkish threat, increasingly menacing following the fall of Constantinople in 1453, this was the Golden Age of the Venetian Republic. On the Piazza di Rialto, near the little church of S. Giacometto, merchants and bankers held their "borsa," or exchange, while manufactories produced woolen cloth and silk fab-

rics and exquisite glass objects, exported around the world. In the Arsenale, anywhere from 2000 to 3000 master craftsmen stood ready to produce a hundred galleys in just two months' work. In order to safeguard its back, Venice expanded during the 15th c. from its stronghold of Treviso, in the hinterland, taking control of Padua, Vicenza, Verona, Belluno, Feltre, Udine, Brescia, Bèrgamo, Ravenna, and later, Cremona and Ferrara. The 16th c., on the other hand, marked the end of this centuries-long triumph: on the mainland, by the leagues that the states of Europe and Italy formed against Venice (Venice's defeat at Agnadello in 1509 marked an end to all further expansion on land); at sea, by the exhausting wars Venice fought against the Turks, wars that – despite the great victory at Lepanto in 1571 – were to end with the loss of Cyprus and most of the trading ports in the Aegean and in the Peloponnesus; in the field of trade, because the great currents of sea traffic were slowly but inexorably shifting westward, out of the Mediterranean Sea and into the great oceans; likewise because of the development of mighty nation-states. Fully aware that its prosperity was coming to an end, Venice spent part of its enormous wealth in the 16th c. on a thorough revamping of its urban image. In the 16th c., the aristocracy of Venice accentuated the ongoing competition to build palazzi on the Grand Canal, a competition that was to continue throughout the following centuries, culminating in the great monumental waterway that it is today. In the 17th c., Venice still had the strength to take positions against the pope, the Hapsburgs, and Spain, in the controversy over the interdiction, in the wars of Uscocchi and Gradisca, and in the so-called conspiracy of Bedmar, from the name of the Spanish ambassador who was behind it. In later years, the remaining energy of the Venetian Republic ebbed away in further wars against the Turks, finally culminating in 1669 in the loss of the island of Candia (Crete), inadequately counterbalanced by Venetian conquests in Dalmatia and the temporary reconquest of the Peloponnesus (Morea). After the peace of Passarowitz (1718), which obliged Venice to cede Morea, out of all its far-flung maritime

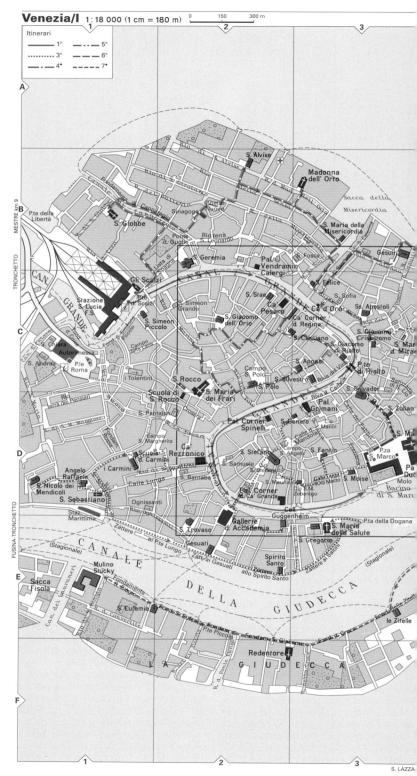

Venezia/I 1:18 000 (1 cm = 180 m)

414

S. LAZZA

S. ERASMO

A

Murano

S. Michele
in Isola

Isola
di S. Michele

B

Cimitero

Vedere
VENEZIA/II

ndamente Nova

C

Ss. Giovanni
e Paolo

S. Francesco
d. Vigna

lleoni

S. Lorenzo

Formosa

Sc. di S. Giorgio
d. Schiavoni

Darsena
Grande

Can. di
Rio Nuovo

D

S. Zaccaria

C. d.
Bandiera

B. M.
d. Pietà

S. Giovanni
in Bragora

Torri d. Arsenale

S. Pietro
di Castello

Isola
di S. Pietro

Rive degli
Schiavoni

Museo
Navale

Corderie

C. di Ruga

Pal. d. Sport

S.
Biagio

Canal Dio S. Biagio

Riva dei Sette Martiri

Via Garibaldi

Fondam. di
S. Anna

Via Garibaldi

Secco Marina

CANALE

DI

S.

MARCO

Via Trieste

Riva dei Partigiani

Esposizione
Internazionale
d'Arte Moderna

Giardini
Pubblici

Via 24 Maggio

Isola

E

Bacino

S. Giorgio
Maggiore

Isola
di S. Giorgio
Maggiore

della Grazia

Teatro
Verde

Via Indipendenza

4 Novembre

Parco Rimembranze

di

S. Elena

Via Viale Plava

Campo
Sportivo

S. Elena

Via Vittorio Veneto

F

0 50 100 150 m

A

Pal. Labia (RAI)
Campo S. Geremia
S. Geremia
Cannaregio
Canal di Cannaregio
STAZ. S.LUCIA FS – P.LE ROMA
Riva di Biasio
Lista Vecchia dei Bari
Pal. Correr Contarini
S. Marcuola
S. Marcuola
Pal. Vendramin Calergi
la Maddalena
Pal. Correr
S. Fosca
Rio Nuova Str. Nova
S. Fosca
Pal. Giovannelli
Rio di Noale
Strada
Pal. Erizzo
Pal. Gussoni
P.to Pasqualigo
S. Felice
C A N A L
Fondaco dei Turchi (Museo di Storia Naturale)
S. Giovanni Decollato
Dep. del Megio
Salizzada d. Stae
Pal. Belloni Battagia
S. Stae
Ca' Pesaro (Galleria d'Arte Moderna)
Ca' Corner d. Regina (Archivio Biennale)
Pal. Fontana Rezzonico
Ca' d (Gall. Fra
Pal. Sa

B

Campo N. Sauro
S. Giacomo dell'Orio
Campo S. Giacomo dell'Orio
Campiello d. Sbcoe
Rio Marin
Calle d. Tintor
S. Maria Mater Domini
Rio
S. Cassiano
S. Cassiano
Pal. Brandolin-Morosini
Calle dei Botteri
Ruga
Beccarie
Pesche
C° d
Spezia

C

Scuola di S. Giovanni Evangelista
Calle del Caffetieri
Campo S. Stin
Calle d. S. Agostin
R. di S. Polo
Rio Terra
Pal. Corner Mocenigo
Campo S. Polo
Calle dei Nomboli
S. Aponal
Campo S. Aponal
S. Silvestro
C° da Paradiso
Elem
S.
Riv

S. Rocco
S. Maria d. Frari
Pal. Michiel
C° di Frari
S. Polo
P.ta S. Polo
Rio delli
Rio di S. Polo
Riva del Ca
C A N A L

D

C° S. Rocco
Scuola di S. Rocco
Rio della Frescada
S. Pantalon
Campo S. Tomà
S. Tomà
Calle dei Saoneri
Pal. Pisani Moretta
Pal. Grimani-Marcello
Pal. Bernardo
Pal. Papadopoli
S. Silvestro
Pal. Grimani
Ca' Farsetti
Pal. Marcello dei Leoni
Pal. Giustinian Persico
S. Beneto
S. Lure
Croseta
Calle Larga
R. Ca' Foscari
STAZ. S.LUCIA FS.
Pal. Balbi (Regione Veneto)
Pal. Contarini d. Figure
Palazzi Mocenigo
Pal. Corner Spinelli
Corte dell'Albero
C° S. Beneto
Pal. Fortuny
Camp Manir

E

Ca' Foscari (Università)
Ca' Rezzonico (Museo del '700)
Pal. Giustinian
Pal. Grassi
Pal. Moro Lin
Calle delle Carrozze
Salizzada S. Samuele
S. Samuele
Ca' d. Duca
S. Barnaba
Calle d. Traghetto
Rio Malpaga
Pal. Loredan dell'Ambasciatore
Pal. Contarini d. Scrigni
Rio di S. Vidal
S. Vidal
ex-Chiesa di S. Vidal
Pal. Pisani (Conservatorio)
Pal. Cavalli Franchetti (Ca' Granda)
P.ta dell'Accademia
Oratorio Annunziata
Campo S. Angelo
Calle degli Avvocati
Calle de la Mandola
Calle dei Frati
Pal. Loredan
S. Stefano
Campo S. Stefano
S. Maurizio
Campo S. Maurizio
S. Maria Zobenigo
C°
S. M. Zobenigo
Pal. Conta Fasar
Pal. Giustinian Lolin
Teatro la Fenice
Calle d. Fenice
S. Fanin
Rio di Fenice
Rio
Calle

F

S. Trovaso
Campo S. Trovaso
Rio di S. Trovaso
Riva A. Foscarini
Gallerie d. Accademia
Rio della Toletta
Pal. Cini
C°
S. Vio
Pal. Contarini Dal Zaffo
Collezione Guggenheim
Pal. Darjo
Pal. Da Mula
S. Maria Zobenigo
C A N A L   G R A N D
S. Gregorio
S. d. S

holdings ("da mar"), all that remained were the Ionian isles. Venice's long and glorious history was coming to an end. The decline in manufacturing, trade, and military might almost seemed to prompt Venice to attempt to establish itself as a new European capital of festivities and theater, and of an "avant-garde" tourism. And after so many carnival celebrations, in 1797 a Corsican general named Bonaparte put an end to this aristocratic Republic that had outlived itself. For Venice, no longer capital, this was to be the beginning of a new, more modest life. For many years it was occupied by Austria, save for a brief rebellion in 1848-49, until it was unified with Italy in 1866. These various political events left marks in the city itself. After the unification of Italy, between 1868 and 1871, a new road was built, running parallel to the Grand Canal, linking Rialto with the train station; it was called the Strada Nuova. Beginning in 1880 construction began on the new port, known as the Marittima. Between 1880 and 1882 the Calle Larga XXII Marzo was built, and, slightly further out on the Grand Canal, along the Riva degli Schiavoni and at the Lido, the major hotels were built. Beginning in 1922, the pavilions of the Biennale were built; between 1930 and 1933, the automobile bridge was built, followed by the construction of the huge parking area in Piazzale Roma; and during the same years, the opening of the Rio Nuovo provided an alternative to the Grand Canal. With the creation of the great industrial zone on the mainland, Mestre and Marghera were joined with Venice in 1926. The great decline in population in the historic center in the last 40 years has brought the population of Venice proper from 184,000 in 1950 to the current low level of fewer than 90,000 (140,000 with all of the islands and the littoral strip), as against more than 200,000 on the mainland. This has only worsened the city's problems, which include the ravages of flooding ("acqua alta"), the challenge of restoring the city's architectural heritage, and the dangers posed by the invasions of tourists that pour constantly through Venice.

Getting around. In Piazzale Roma, the terminus of automobile access to Venice, there certainly are paid parking areas, but, particularly on weekends and at the height of the tourist season, there is considerable danger of long lines, traffic jams, and endless delays; it is therefore advisable to leave your car at the Tronchetto parking area, with connections to the historic center by "vaporetto" or by private water taxis. As an alternative, you may choose to park your car in Mestre or Marghera and continue by bus or train to Venice, across the Ponte della Libertà. More than any other city, Venice is a place for walking, and you should plan to walk extensively, through "calli" and "campielli," over bridges, discovering the always astonishing charm of lesser-known districts and areas that have escaped the crush of mass tourism. The handiest way to move from place to place in Venice and to reach the various areas of town is by the "vaporetti", or waterbuses, run by the public transportation system, ACTV, which provides

an extensive and reliable network of connections and destinations. A useful and not particularly expensive way to get across the Grand Canal, from bank to bank, is the "traghetto in gondola," or "ferry gondola"; the "gondola di rappresentanza," or luxury gondola, while one of the symbols of this lagoon city, is used only for sightseeing, and can be found in specific "gondola stands," so to speak, scattered throughout Venice, at rates established by the city government.

The Grand Canal

The great aristocratic families of Venice competed in building lovely palazzi on the Grand Canal, "the loveliest thoroughfare, I believe, in the whole world" (Philippe de Commynes). But before that time, the ground floor areas were stocked with merchandise, the mezzanines were used for keeping count of everything that was loaded into or unloaded from the galleys that docked directly at the front doors, and the Ponte di Rialto, a wooden bridge back then, could be drawn up to let ships pass through. The wealth of Venice derived from trade, and its beauty certainly sank its roots in that activity. This route runs the length of the Grand Canal, from Piazzale Roma to the Bacino di S. Marco, or Basin of St. Mark's, with descriptions of the most notable buildings along that body of water. Many of these palazzi will be featured in subsequent routes, with more detailed descriptions, of the interior as well, when the buildings house museums or art collections.

Grand Canal.** This is Venice's main interior waterway, and it runs through the city from NW to SE, linking the various districts. The canal is 3800 m in length, and ranges from 30 to 70 m in breadth; it winds in a broad, backward S. Ever since the 14th c., work has been going on to straighten and reinforce the banks of the Grand Canal, giving it its present-day appearance. It originally served as part of the harbor of Venice, and was used to transport merchandise to the market of Rialto; from the 16th c. on, it became the place where the Venetian nobility built its lavish homes and palazzi. It is lined with unbroken successions of sumptuous residences (the distinctive mooring poles that stand before each palazzo are often emblazoned with painted heraldic devices) which range in age from the 13th c. (the Byzantine "case-fondaco," or homes-cum-warehouses) to the 18th c. The stunning array of facades along the Grand Canal expresses the full range of styles, but translated into the distinctive architectural language of Venice, with airy fretwork, mullioned windows with pointed arches, and impressive loggias.

The area around St. Mark's

This was the heart of the Venetian state: from high atop the campanile the government was summoned to council; the Doge would walk majestically

LEFT BANK

ailway Station of Venezia-Santa Lucia (I, *C1*), built
the late 19th c. on the site of the convent of S. Lu-
ia, and rebuilt in 1954.
ontile degli Scalzi (the term "pontile," used through-
ut this listing, means pier, and indicates the landing
harf of waterbuses).
li Scalzi* (I, *B1*), Baroque church built by B.
onghena for a community of Carmelites, who
oved here from Rome around 1650.

---

onte degli Scalzi (I, *B1*), built in stone in 1934, is one of the three bridges crossing the Grand Canal.

---

anale di Cannaregio (I, *B1-2*), the second-largest
anal in Venice, after the Grand Canal, crossed by the
andsome *Ponte delle Guglie*. To the left, *S. Geremia*
I, *A1*), 18th-c. church with broad facade (1871) and
omanesque bell tower in terracotta. Adjacent to it
the 17th-c. **Palazzo Labia** (II, *A1*), regional head-
uarters of RAI television; the spectacular Salone
elle Feste is frescoed by G.B. Tiepolo (1745-56).
alazzo Correr Contarini (II, *A1*), sumptuous 17th-c.
uilding, called "Ca' dei Cuori" after the hearts feared in the family crests.
ontile di S. Marcuola.

alazzo Vendramin Calergi* (II, *A2*), an elegant
enaissance building, designed by M. Codussi and
ompleted by the Lombardo brothers (1509). R. Wag-
er died here, 13 February 1883; it is the winter lo-
ation of the Casinò Municipale.
alazzo Erizzo alla Maddalena (II, *A2*), 15th-c. Goth-
, subsequently heavily renovated.

alazzo Gussoni (II, *A3*), elegant 16th-c. building at-
ibuted to Sanmicheli; its facade was once deco-
ted with frescoes by Tintoretto.

alazzo Fontana-Rezzonico (II, *A-B3*), built in the
th-17th c., in the late style of Sansovino.
a' d'Oro** (II, *B3*), sumptuous 15th-c. Gothic ar-
itecture, rebuilt in the 19th c.; it houses the *Galle-
a G. Franchetti*.
ontile Ca' d'Oro.
alazzo Sagredo (II, *B3*), Byzantine in origin, rebuilt
Gothic style.

RIGHT BANK

Pontile S. Chiara: this pier leads to **Piazzale Roma**
(I, *C1*), where the Ponte della Libertà (1933) con-
nects Venice to Mestre, on the mainland.
Giardino Papadopoli (I, *C1*), a garden on the area
where the convent of S. Croce once stood.
S. Simeon Piccolo (I, *B1*), Neo-Classic church (1738),
with a green cupola.

Fondaco dei Turchi (II, *A2*), Venetian-Byzantine in
style, but heavily restored in 1858-69; it houses the
Museo di Storia Naturale.
Depositi del Megio (D. del Miglio; II, *A2*), ancient granary of the Venetian Republic, an austere crenelated terracotta building, dating from the 15th c.
Palazzo Belloni Battagia (II, *A2*), 17th-c. architecture
by B. Longhena, with an ample loggia on the piano
nobile.
Pontile S. Stae.
S. Stae (S. Eustachio; II, *A-B2*), 17th-c. church with a
lively Baroque facade, by D. Rossi (1709).

Ca' Pesaro* (II, *B2-3*), a spectacular example of
Venetian Baroque, begun by B. Longhena (1628) and
completed by A. Gaspari (1710); it houses the *Galleria d'Arte Moderna* and the *Museo d'Arte Orientale*.

Ca' Corner della Regina (II, *B3*), this impressive
classical work by D. Rossi (1724) has two storeys of
loggias; it is the headquarters of the *Archivio Storico
della Biennale di Venezia* (Biennial Archives).

Palazzo Brandolin-Morosini (II, *B3*), 15th-c. Gothic
building, with a Byzantine plan and two elegant loggias; rebuilt in the 14th c.

Pescheria (II, *B3*), this Neo-Gothic porticoed building was built in 1907, as the center of Venice's fish
market.

LEFT BANK

Palazzo Michiel dalle Colonne (II, *B4*), renovated in the late 17th c., with a ground-floor portico and elegant loggias.

Ca' da Mosto (II, *B4*), typical 13th-c. "casa-fondaco," or "house-warehouse," heavily renovated, with two storeys added; in the lower section, it still has Byzantine features. From the 16th to the 18th c., this was the famous Albergo Leon Bianco.

Fondaco dei Tedeschi (II, *C4*), rebuilt in 1505-1508 by Scarpagnino to a plan by G. Tedesco, with ground-floor portico; its facade was once decorated with frescoes by Giorgione and Titian.

RIGHT BANK

Fabbriche Nuove (II, *B4*), building designed by Sansวino (1554-56), with long ground-floor portico; houses the Tribunale (Law Courts).

Fabbriche Vecchie (II, *B-C4*), extensive porticoe building, part of the complex of structures built ▐ Scarpagnino (1522); it is now used as a fruit ar vegetable market.

Palazzo dei Camerlenghi (II, *C4*), elegant Renaสance building, possibly by G. Bergamasco (1528 with two floors of arched loggias.

Ponte di Rialto* (II, *C4*). This is the best-known bridge in Venice, rebuilt in 1591 by A. da Ponte. It is 48 ⏐ long and 22 m wide, and has a single arch, with a chord of 28 m and a height of 7.5 m. Above it are a s ries of arcades.

Pontile di Rialto.

Palazzo Dolfin Manin (II, *C-D4*), Renaissance building by J. Sansovino (1536-75), with ground-floor portico; now holds offices of the Banca d'Italia.

Palazzo Bembo (II, *C-D4*), late Gothic building, built upon Venetian-Byzantine structures that can be faintly detected.

Palazzo Loredan and Ca' Farsetti (II, *D3*; Municipio), Venetian-Byzantine buildings from the 12th-13th c., with one floor of unbroken loggias.

Palazzo Grimani* (II, *D3*), impressive three-storey Renaissance building, with broad arcades set on pilasters and columns; masterpiece of M. Sanmicheli (1556-75), it now houses offices of the judiciary.

Palazzo dei Dieci Savi (II, *C4*), porticoed Renaissan๑ building constructed by Scarpagnino in 1521.
Riva del Vin.

Pontile S. Silvestro.

Palazzo Papadopoli (II, *C-D3*), sumptuous mid-1€ c. mansion, with two rows of spacious loggias.

Palazzo Bernardo (II, *D2*), 15th-c. Gothic, rich adorned.

Palazzo Grimani-Marcello (II, *D2*), elegant Loๆ bardesque style (early 16th c.), with three-arch lc gias on the upper floors.

Palazzo Pisani-Moretta (II, *D2*), Gothic (first half the 15th c.), with two handsome loggias with int๑ laced arches.

Palazzo Giustinian-Persico (II, *D2*), Renaissance ๑ chitecture (16th c.).

Palazzo Marcello dei Leoni (II, *D1*), named after t two Romanesque lions on either side of the door
Pontile S. Tomà.

Palazzo Corner Spinelli* (II, *D2*), a fine piece of early Renaissance architecture, with two storeys of large twin-light mullioned windows, designed by M. Codussi (late 15th c.).
Pontile S. Angelo.

Palazzi Mocenigo (II, *D1-2*), a complex of four buildings of the 16th-18th c. Residents have included Giordano Bruno (1592) and Lord Byron (1818).

Palazzo Contarini delle Figure (II, *D-E1*), Renaissance building dating from the first half of the 16th c.; its name comes from the caryatids over the portal.

Palazzo Balbi (II, *D1*), called "in volta di Canal," t large classical building was constructed to a desiๆ by A. Vittoria in 1590; it holds the offices of the F gion of Veneto.

Ca' Foscari* (II, *E1*), begun in 1452, with two lo ly eight-arched loggias, this was certainly one of t most sumptuous homes in Gothic Venice; it is n๐ part of the university.

LEFT BANK

Palazzo Moro-Lin (II,*E1*), 17th c., known as the "house of the 13 windows."
Palazzo Grassi (II,*E1*), Baroque, with imposing classical style, by G. Massari (18th c.): headquarters of the Fondazione Grassi, it is used for major events and art exhibitions. On the stairway, note the lively frescoes by M. Morlaiter (18th c.).
S. Samuele (II, *E1-2*), church originally built in the 11th c., with a charming little Venetian-Romanesque bell tower (12th c.); temporary exhibitions are held here.
Ca' del Duca (II,*E1-2*), dates from the 19th c., but includes 15th-c. sections; it houses collections of 18th-c. Venetian porcelain and Oriental art *(closed for restoration and reorganization)*.

Palazzo Giustinian Lolin (II,*E-F2*), Baroque building, by B. Longhena (1630 ca.), with two storeys of tall loggias.

RIGHT BANK

Palazzi Giustinian (II, *E1*), elegant Gothic buildings from the late 15th c., with long facades punctuated by mullioned windows. In one of these buildings, R. Wagner composed "Tristan und Isolde."
Ca' Rezzonico* (II, *E1*), a spectacular Baroque building begun by B. Longhena (1649) and completed by G. Massari (ca. 1750); it houses the *Museo del Settecento Veneziano*.
Pontile di Ca' Rezzonico.

Palazzo Loredan dell'Ambasciatore (II,*E1*), late Gothic, dating from the 15th c.; in two niches on the facade, two Lombardesque putti bearing shields.

Palazzo Contarini degli Scrigni (II, *F1*), comprising two sections: one is late Gothic, the other was designed by V. Scamozzi (1609).

Gallerie dell'Accademia (II,*F1-2*), housed in the former convent of *S. Maria della Carità*.
Pontile dell'Accademia.

Ponte dell'Accademia (II,*F2*), wooden, built in 1934 to replace a 19th-c. iron bridge.

Palazzo Cavalli Franchetti (II,*F2*), dates from the 15th c., enlarged and renovated at the end of the 19th c.

Palazzo Cornèr della Ca' Granda* (II,*F2-3*), magnificent building by J. Sansovino (1533-36 ca.), with a three-register classical facade; it is now the headquarters of the Prefecture.
Pontile S. Maria Zobenigo.

Palazzo Contarini Fasan (II,*F3*), a fine example of flamboyant Gothic style (1475); it is commonly called the "House of Desdemona."

Palazzo Treves de' Bonfili (I,*F4*) dates from the 17th c., with a classical facade; the interior is exemplary in terms of Neo-Classic furnishings and decorations (turn of the 19th c.).
Ca' Giustinian (II,*E-F4*), late Gothic (1474), with three rows of windows and loggias; this is the headquarters of the administration of the Venice Biennale.
Pontile S. Marco.

Palazzo Contarini Dal Zaffo (II,*F2*), a fine example of early Renaissance Venetian architecture, possibly by G. Buora.
Palazzo Cini (II,*F2*), the Renaissance facade is reflected in the little Rio S.Vio; this building houses the *Collezione V. Cini (open in the summer months, and for temporary exhibits)*, with 13th-/14th-c. Tuscan paintings.
Palazzo Da Mula (II,*F2*), late Gothic, from the end of the 15th c., with three rows of four-light loggias.
Palazzo Venier dei Leoni (II,*F2-3*), designed in 1749, it houses the *Peggy Guggenheim Collection of Contemporary Art*.
Palazzo Dario (II,*F3*), Renaissance building, attributed to P. Lombardo (1487), with a facade marked by triple four-light loggias.
Former Abbey of S. Gregorio (II,*F3*), founded in 1160, extensively rebuilt, with a 14th-c. Gothic portal.
Pontile della Salute.

S. Maria della Salute* (II, *F3*), Baroque masterpiece by B. Longhena.

Punta della Salute, or *Punta della Dogana* (II, *F4*), this handsome landmark frames the entrance to the Bacino di S. Marco, with the long low building of the *Dogana da Mar,* which existed in the 15th c. as a customs dock, repeatedly rebuilt since.

around the square in procession; St. Mark's was the Doge's chapel; in the Doge's Palace, government councils would convene, the Doge had his apartments, and judgement was passed by the Venetian Inquisition. Often those judged unfavorably would be executed at one of the columns in the Piazzetta; beneath the portico, crews were recruited while galleys lay at dock on the Molo, or wharf. This elite architectural image was meant to reflect the power of the Venetian Republic and the culture of the aristocracy that ran it. The route recommended here is limited to St. Mark's Square (Piazza S. Marco) and the smaller Piazzetta S. Marco.

Piazza S. Marco** (II, *E4-5*). This magnificent space, St. Mark's Square, has long been both a symbol and the drawing room of the Venetian community. Rectangular in shape, surrounded by porticoes, with cafés and shops, the square culminates in St. Mark's Cathedral, with its slender, solitary bell tower. Bounding it on the north are the **Procuratie Vecchie**, a long 12th-c. building, with two rows of loggias, rebuilt in the 16th c., in part by J. Sansovino. This building was once the headquarters of the highest magistrates of the Venetian Republic. To the east is the **Torre dell'Orologio** (1496-99, M. Codussi), the clock tower topped by bronze statues of two Moors, which strike the hour on a great bell. Facing this building, on the south side of the square, stretch the **Procuratie Nuove**, built from 1582 (V. Scamozzi) to 1640 (B. Longhena), and continuing the motif of the adjacent Libreria Sansoviniana. Under the porticoes are various fine cafés; chief among them, the 18th-c. *Caffè Florian*. The narrow west end of the square is closed off by the *Ala Napoleonica* (Napoleon's wing, 1810); inside, note the monumental staircase.

Basilica di S. Marco** (II, *E5*). At the heart of the religious and public life of Venice, this church was the place where the doge was invested, and one of the prime symbols of Venice and its history. Founded in the 9th c. to house the body of the Evangelist St. Mark, patron saint of Venice (the body was stolen from Alexandria in Egypt in A.D. 828), the building clearly shows, in its complex and articulated structure, the different phases of construction, early Romanesque-Byzantine sections being juxtaposed with Gothic and 16th-c. architecture. Rebuilt in many different sections and at many different times, this church acquired the distinctive outline of a Byzantine church, with a large central dome and hemispheric cupolas, topped by smaller onion domes. The *facade* comprises two storeys and five arcades, with a cuspidate Gothic crown (14th-15th c.), with aediculas and statues. The lower register, with its five portals with bronze doors, presents a complex interweaving of arches, columns, and marble decoration; particularly noteworthy are the 13th-c. reliefs in the central arch (Months, Virtues, Prophets), and those in the intrados of the largest arch (the Trades and Vocations; 15th c.). The mosaics in the facade, except for those in the vault of the first arch, were redone in the 17th-18th c. On the upper terrace, copies of the four horses brought in 1204 from Constan-

tinople (the originals are in the Museo di S. Marco). On the *northern side* is a portal decorated with a 13th-c. relief, Byzantine bas-reliefs from the 12th c., and the tomb of Daniele Manin (1868). On the *southern side* is one of the two side entrances, before which stand two pillars adorned with reliefs, brought here from the town of Acre after 1256; some consider these Syrian art dating from the 5th c., others believe them to be Byzantine-Islamic work of the 12th c. At the corner with the Porta della Carta (see Palazzo Ducale), note the porphyry group of the Tetrarchs (or Four Kings), possibly a Syrian creation of the 4th c.; near the corner of the square is the "pietra del bando," or the "stone of proclamations," a fragment of a Syrian column from which the decrees of the Republic were once read aloud; it was shattered by the collapse of the bell tower in 1902. In the *atrium*, or narthex, before the entrance to the church proper, the marble mosaic floor dates from the 11th-12th c. The walls have a facing of marble and columns; vaults and little cupolas glitter with Venetian-Byzantine mosaics* (Stories from the Old Testament) of the 12th-13th c. Three portals, with bronze 11th-c. doors, afford access into the church. In the arcade of the central door, you can look up into the 16th-c. mosaic vault of the Arcone del Paradiso. The **interior**** (*open summer, 9:30-5; Sun., 2-5; winter, 9:45-4:30; Sun., 2-4:30*) is a typical Byzantine structure, built to a Greek cross, with a nave and two aisles in each arm, divided by colonnades above which are galleries; massive arches support the five mosaic-lined cupolas. The floor, which has dips and humps due to the settling of the building on the dense forest of wooden poles that constitute the foundation, is in mosaic, with geometric patterns (12th c.; partly redone).

The **mosaics****, with their golden background, decorating the upper walls and the cupolas, are one of the Basilica's greatest adornments and riches. Created by Byzantine and Venetian craftsmen in the 12th-14th c., they were partly redone during the 16th-17th c., to cartoons by Titian, Tintoretto, Veronese and others. Among the earliest mosaics, easily recognized by the stylized forms and the hieratic poses of the figures, note those that run along the walls of the side aisles (Christ, Mary, Prophets, and Apostles), those in the cupolas, and especially the scene of the Ascension in the main cupola.

The *Battistero*, or Baptistery, built in the 14th c. by closing off part of the atrium, is located in the right aisle of the base of the Greek cross. It contains the tombs of various doges and a baptismal font by J. Sansovino (1545); in the little cupolas of the ceiling, note the 14th-c. mosaics. Adjoining is the *Cappella Zen*, a chapel decorated with 13th-c. mosaics with a 16th-c. bronze altar and the great sepulcher of Cardinal G.B. Zen (1501), by P. Savin.

The **presbytery** is set above the crypt and enclosed by a marble screen (iconostasis), surmounted by statues of the Dalle Masegne (1394). The main altar, which contained the body of St. Mark (S. Marco), is supported by four columns* made of alabaster arved with reliefs, and with 12th-c. capitals, surmounted by a ciborium decorated with six statues from the 13th c. Behind the main altar is the renowned **Pala d'Oro****, a notable altarpiece of Byzantine and Venetian goldwork (10th-14th c.), studded with enamels and gems. In the niche to the left of the apse, note the bronze door* of the sacristy, the last creation of J. Sansovino (1546-69). In the left transept is the *Cappella della Madonna Nicopeia*, with 12th-c. image of the Virgin, taken from Constantinople, and considered the protectress of the city.

You can enter the **Tesoro di S. Marco** (Treasury; open summer, 9:45-5; winter, 9:45-4:30; Sun., 2-4:30) from the end of the right transept. The Treasury collection, certainly one of the richest arrays of sacred art in all Italy, contains liturgical objects of Byzantine goldsmithery, much of it plundered from Constantinople (1204). Installed in three halls, this collection comprises vases, goblets, chalices, reliquaries, Gospels, and altar frontals, largely from the 12th-13th c.

Galleria di S. Marco. *Open summer, 9-7; winter, 9-* This museum is located on the same level as the Gallerie; you can reach them from the atrium of the basilica. The museum collection includes illuminated choir books, fragments of mosaics from the basilica, a polyptych by P.Veneziano (1345) and 15th-paintings, 16th-c. tapestries, and ancient Persian carpets. In one hall are the **four horses*** in gilded bronze, a Greek creation from the 4th or 3rd c. B.C., or possibly Roman art dating from the 4th c. A.D., transported to Venice from the hippodrome of Constantinople in 1204 as booty for the Doge Dandolo during the Fourth Crusade.

Piazzetta dei Leoni (II, D5). To the left of the Basilica, this little square takes its name from two lions made of red Verona marble (1722). At the end of the piazza, note the Neo-Classic *Palazzo Patriarcale* (1837-70).

Campanile di S. Marco (II, E5). *Open summer, 9-7; winter, 9:30-3:30.* This bell tower of St. Mark's cathedral stands alone, rising 96.8 m over Venice. Built in the 9th c., probably atop a watch tower, and rebuilt in the 16th c., it was entirely rebuilt once again in 1912, following the sudden early morning collapse of the old tower (happily, no one was hurt and damage to surrounding buildings was limited) on 14 July 1902. From the top of the tower, panoramic view* of Venice and of the lagoon. At the base, note the marble **loggia***, an elegant piece of architecture by J. Sansovino (1537-49), who also did the bronze statues.

Civico Museo Correr* (II, E4). *Open Apr.-Oct., 9-7; Nov.-Mar., 9-5; workshops for children, tel. 041 5236830.* Housed in the Ala Napoleonica and in the Procuratie Nuove, this museum has exhibits of all sorts, concerning life and art in the Serenissima from the 14th to the 18th c. Note A. Canova's Dedalus and Icarus. Major art gallery **(Pinacoteca*)**, with Venetian paintings from the 14th-16th c., as well as Ferrarese, Flemish, and German art. The gallery possesses masterpieces by J. Bellini, and by his two sons Gentile and Giovanni, A. Vivarini, V. Carpaccio, C. Tura. A. da Messina, L. Lotto, as well as by German (L.

Cranach) and Flemish painters (Van der Goes, D. Bouts). In the same building is the **Museo del Risorgimento e dell'800 Veneziano** (*open Apr.-Oct., 10-6; Nov.-Mar., 10-5; closed Tue.*), with documents and memorabilia of Venetian history, from the late 18th c. until it became part of Italy (1866).

Piazzetta S. Marco* (II, E5). Between Palazzo Ducale and the Libreria Sansoviniana, overlooking the Molo di S. Marco, with the island of S. Giorgio in the distance. At the bank are two 12th-c. *columns*, once the site of executions.

Palazzo Ducale** (II, E5). Residence of the doge and headquarters of the highest magistracies of the Republic, this building is the symbol of the power and glory that was Venice. Founded as a castle in the 9th c., the Doge's Palace attained its current size in the 14th-15th c., a masterpiece of Venetian Gothic architecture. Above the ground-floor portico (note the capitals of the columns and the corner reliefs) is a very elegant loggia. Two magnificent balconies (15th-16th c.) interrupt the series of large Gothic windows that stretch along the facades overlooking both wharf and square. The Gothic *Porta della Carta*, by G. and B. Bon (mid-15th c.), adjacent to the wall of St. Mark's basilica, leads into a beautiful **courtyard****, with two bronze 16th-c. well heads in the center. The courtyard is a combination of Gothic (W and S sides) and Renaissance (E side) styles. Near the entrance are the Baroque facade of the clock (1615) and the *Foscari Arch*, a Gothic monument (1470) by A. Rizzo. Facing this is the *Scala dei Giganti**, designed by Rizzo, with statues of Mars and Neptune by J. Sansovino (1554); here, the newly elected doge swore to uphold the laws of Venice.

Interior. *Open Apr.-Oct., 9-7; Nov.-Mar., 9-5; Sun., workshops for children, tel. 0415236830.* Along a stairway beneath the SE side of the portico, you climb up to the Gothic loggia; from here, the *Scala d'Oro** (1558; note gilt stuccoes by A. Vittoria in the ceiling) leads to the first piano nobile, where you cross the great *Sala delle Mappe* (note the maps on the walls) to the rooms that were once the *residence of the Doge*, amidst spectacular Renaissance ceilings and fireplaces, paintings and frescoes by Giovanni Bellini, Titian, and V. Carpaccio. Cross back through the Sala delle Mappe, and then enter the *Sala degli Scudieri* (two paintings by D. Tintoretto). You then climb to the second piano nobile, where you can tour the council rooms of the highest magistracies of the Serenissima. The tour begins from the *square atrium*: in the 16th-c. wooden ceiling, note the canvases by J. Tintoretto; on the walls are paintings by Veronese and F. Bassano. *Sala delle Quattro Porte*, named for the four monumental doorways, decorated with statues and columns: ceilings frescoed by Tintoretto; on the wall is a famed painting* by Titian (1556). In the *Anticollegio*, fine paintings adorn the walls (Tintoretto, Veronese, J. Bassano) and ceiling. *Sala del Collegio*: on the walls are canvases by Tintoretto and Veronese; the carved ceiling boasts panels by Veronese. *Sala del Senato*: at the center of the spectacular ceiling is a painting by J. and D. Tintoretto; on the walls, canvases by Palma the Younger. *Sala del Consiglio dei Dieci*: in the carved gilt ceiling, panels* by Veronese. *Sala della Bussola*: near the door, a little slot, from which secret accusations were pushed in through the "mouth of the lion" outside. *Sala dei Tre Capi del Consiglio dei Dieci*: on the ceiling, panels* by Veronese and Zelotti; on the walls, paintings by H. Bosch. *Sala d'Armi del Consiglio dei Dieci*: armor, weapons, and trophies of war. You then descend to the *passage of the Maggior Consiglio*, with canvases by Tintoretto and Palma the Younger, and from there, you enter the *Sala della Quarantia Civil Vecchia* and the *Sala dell'Armamento*, where you can see what remains of the great fresco of Heaven, by Guariento (1365-67), irreparably damaged by a terrible fire in 1577. In the next loggia are statues of Adam and Eve* by A. Rizzo (1464). *Sala del Maggior Consiglio* (53 x 24 m): like the subsequent Sala dello Scrutinio, the decorations of this room date from after the fire of 1577. The walls feature paintings by Tintoretto (in particular, note the painting of Heaven*, 7.45 x 24.65 m, executed on several canvases by J. and D. Tintoretto, with the help of Palma the Younger, and others), L. Bassano, Aliense, Palma the Younger, and others; also note the frieze with 76 portraits of doges (the portrait of Marin Faliero, beheaded in 1355 for conspiracy, is covered with black paint), by J. and D. Tintoretto; in the middle of the spectacular ceiling, the Apotheosis of Venice* by Veronese; in the ovals on either side, canvases by Palma the Younger and Tintoretto. *Sala della Quarantia Civil Nuova* and *Sala dello Scrutinio*: on the walls and ceilings, paintings by Tintoretto, Aliense, Palma the Younger, A. Vicentino, and others. After you descend to the Loggia, you can see some of the Prigioni Vecchie (Old Prison), known as the *Pozzi* (Wells), consisting of dark, narrow cells. After crossing the **Ponte dei Sospiri** (Bridge of Sighs), comprising two corridors, one above the other, you can tour the *Prigioni Nuove* (New Prison, 16th c.).

Libreria Sansoviniana * (II, *E5*). This masterpiece of 16th-c. Venetian architecture by J. Sansovino was completed, after the architect's death (1570), by V. Scamozzi. The luminous classical building is the old site of the Biblioteca Marciana, but can now be toured only during temporary exhibitions; a monumental stairway leads to the vestibule, with the ceiling* frescoed by Titian, and to the great hall, with paintings by Veronese, Tintoretto, and Schiavone.

Museo Archeologico. *Open Apr.-Oct., 10-9; Sab., 10-midnight; Sun., 10-8; Nov.-Mar., 10-2; entrance at n. 17 in the portico of the Libreria.* This archeological museum occupies a number of rooms in the Procuratie Nuove, with a major collection of Greek and Roman sculpture, including a series of Greek statues of goddesses* dating from the 5th-4th c. B.C. (Demeter; Hera; Athena); three wounded Gauls (3rd c. B.C.); the Hellenistic Grimani altar*; busts of Trajan and Vitellius; the Hellenistic Zulian cameo*. Also, marble fragments, epigraphs, and Roman coins.

Palazzo della Zecca (II, *E5*). Extending from the Libreria Sansoviniana, on the Molo, is a stern palazzo built by J. Sansovino (1537-66) and used as a mint.

It now houses the *Biblioteca Nazionale Marcia* based on a bequest by the Cardinal Bessaric (1468). Among the most important works in this pendous library is the Grimani breviary dating fr the late 15th c., with exquisite miniatures.

Ponte della Paglia (II, *E5*). This bridge is called erally, the Bridge of Straw, because this was the do ing point where that material was unloaded for c veyance to the prison and stables of the Pala Ducale (Doge's Palace); the bridge spans the Ric Palazzo. From atop the bridge you can see the e side (Renaissance) of the Palazzo Ducale with 17th-c. Ponte dei Sospiri (Bridge of Sighs; see abo through which prisoners were led from their cell face the State Inquisitors. Beyond the bridge is Riva degli Schiavoni, with the vaporetto stops of Linee Interlagunari (inter-lagoon lines).

The Accademia, Ca' Rezzonico, and the Zattere, as far as S. Maria della Salute

Venetian art, perhaps the finest in the world, is s tered everywhere: you will find it in churches, pala and, of course, in art galleries. It is found in the o routes, as well, but this route, extending in a ring to west of St. Mark's Square, on the far side of the Gr Canal, covers perhaps the most celebrated treasu of Venetian art: the Accademia, with masterpiece Bellini, Giorgione, Carpaccio, Tiziano, Tintoretto, an rivalled collection; Ca' Rezzonico, with its 18th-c. pa ings and frescoes; S. Sebastiano, where Veronese pa ed. The art of the Venetian masters should certa be counted as one of the foremost attractions of city; nor can you really sense the meaning, style, substance of that art anywhere else on earth. A running the length of the Fondamenta delle Zatt this route ends at the church of S. Maria della Sal

Campo S. Moisè (II, *E4*). The regular shape of Campo is bounded by the facade of the churcl **S. Moisè** (1668), a refined example of the spec ular Venetian Baroque (inside, note the fine sc ture and paintings, including a later work by toretto). Another excellent example of exuber Baroque decoration can be seen in the facad the church of **S. Maria del Giglio** (or *Zobenige E3*; 1683), located a little further along, in Camp Maria Zobenigo. Rebuilt after 1750, it contains table paintings: in particular, works by P.P. Rubens, ma the Younger, S. Ricci, and J. Tintoretto.

Campo S. Fantin (II, *E3*). This charming squar bounded by elegant, white facades; the wellhe date from the 15th c. The famed **Teatro La Fen** stands here; almost entirely destroyed by a se fire on January 29, 1996, it is now being restored; ing it is the Renaissance church of **S. Fantin**, be by Scarpagnino (1507-49), and completed b Sansovino (1564), whose work can be seen in apse and in the marble chancel inside. On the is the former *Scuola di S. Fantin* (late 16th c.), wh since 1812 has been the headquarters of a liter and scientific academy founded by Napoleon.

ampo S. Stefano, or *Campo Morosini* (II, *E2*). At
e center of this square is a statue of N. Tommaseo
1882). The square lies at the intersection of major
enetian thoroughfares. It is lined by notable build-
gs, including, at n. 2945, *Palazzo Loredan*, a long
uilding dating from 1536, now housing the Istituto
eneto di Scienze, Lettere ed Arti, founded in 1810.
verlooking the square is the church of S. Stefano.

Stefano* (II, *E2; open Mon.-Sat., 10-5; Sun., 1-5*).
hurch built in the 14th c. with a Gothic portal
442). Vast interior, with fine Renaissance monu-
ents and Gothic choir (1488). In the sacristy,
aintings by P. Veneziano, B. Vivarini, Palma the El-
er, and Tintoretto. From left aisle, you reach the
5th-c. cloister.

alazzo Fortuny (II, *D3*) This 15th-c. palazzo, once
nown as Palazzo Pesaro degli Orfei, dominates the
ampo S. Beneto with its Gothic facade. Inside is the
luseo Fortuny (*closed for restoration*), with a col-
ction of work by the Spanish painter and deco-
tor Mariano Fortuny y Madrazo (1861-1949), in
alls that he himself decorated and furnished. On
e upper floors are the *Centro di Documentazione
otografica* (a photographic institute) and the *Don-
zione Virgilio Guidi* (*closed for restoration*), with 80
aintings by the Roman artist Guidi, who lived in
enice for many years. Nearby is the 17th-c. church
f *S. Beneto*; note the altarpiece by B. Strozzi and a
ainting by G.D. Tiepolo.

alazzo Pisani (II, *E-F2*). This majestic 16th-/18th-
palazzo, headquarters of the Conservatorio di Mu-
ca "Benedetto Marcello," stands in the Campiello
sani. To the right of Campo S. Stefano is the 18th-
church of *S. Vidal*, deconsecrated and now used
or art exhibitions; note the handsome altarpiece*
y V. Carpaccio (1514) and the canvas by G.B. Piaz-
etta (1730).

onte dell'Accademia (II, *F2*). This bridge was built
1934 to replace a 19th-c. iron bridge. It offers a fine
ew of the Grand Canal: in one direction as far as
e mouth of the Bacino di S. Marco, with the church
f S. Maria della Salute; on the other, as far as the
urve in the canal known as the "Volta del Canal."

allerie dell'Accademia** (II, *F1-2*). *Open Mon.,
15-2; Tue.-Sun., 8:15-7:15*. This is the greatest col-
ction of works by painters of Venice and Venetia,
om the 14th-18th c. Originally a collection of
orks by the students of the Accademia, the gal-
ries were enriched by Napoleon's suppression of

religious institutes, and then by private bequests.
Beginning with a hall devoted to artists active from
the *late 14th c. to the mid-15th c.* (P. and L. Veneziano,
J. del Fiore), you then pass through a series of halls
with *works of the 15th c.*, by artists such as: Giovanni
Bellini, Carpaccio, C. da Conegliano, M. Basaiti, Montagna, and G. Buonconsiglio, as well as C. Tura, Mantegna, and P. della Francesca. The Gallery also features masterpieces of *15th-c. Venetian art*, by such
masters as Giorgione, Lotto, Veronese, Titian, Tintoretto, Tiepolo, Palma the Elder, and J. Bassano. *Artists
of the 17th-18th c.* include: Ricci, Guardi, Canaletto,
Solimena, Strozzi, Piazzetta, P. and A. Longhi, and Zuccarelli. In Hall XX are eight *huge canvases* painted
in the late 15th c. by Gentile Bellini, V. Carpaccio, G.
Mansueti, and L. Bastiani, while Hall XXI features the
Ciclo di S. Orsola, the St. Ursula legend by V. Carpaccio (1490-96). The tour ends with paintings by A. Vivarini, G. d'Alemagna, and Titian.

Collezione Peggy Guggenheim (II, *F2-3*). *Open
10-6; Sat., 10-10; closed Tue.* This major collection of
European and American avant-garde art is installed
in the 18th-c. *Palazzo Venier dei Leoni*, on the Grand
Canal. This was the Venetian home of the American
collector and patron of the arts, Peggy Guggenheim.
The works are arranged according to school; note
works by Mondrian, Klee, Balla, Severini, Ernst, Miró,
De Chirico, and Picasso. Among the works from the
period after WWII, note the ten paintings by J. Pol-
lock, done between 1942 and 1947.

Ca' Rezzonico* (II, *E1*). Impressive Baroque residence, built on the Grand Canal from 1649 (B.
Longhena) to 1750 (G. Massari). It houses the **Museo
del Settecento Veneziano*** (*open 10-6; closed
Tue.*), which displays, in luxurious rooms (note frescoed ceilings by G.B. Tiepolo), documentation on
18th-c. Venetian life and culture. The art gallery includes works by G.B. Piazzetta, F. Zuccarelli, G. Zais,
P. Longhi, Rosalba Carriera, Canaletto, Guardi. Note
the frescoes* by G.A. Guardi and G.D. Tiepolo.

Campo S. Margherita (I, *D2*). This distinctive center of local neighborhood life serves as a marketplace, and is lined by old homes. At the northern
corner, you can see the lopped-off bell tower of the
former church of *S. Margherita* (17th c.), partly enclosed by the surrounding houses; in the center of
the "campo," two wellheads that date back to 1529.

Scuola Grande dei Carmini (I, *D1*). *Open 9-6; Sun.,
9-4*. This 17th-c. building, once the headquarters of a
very powerful confraternity, is believed to be by Bal-
dassarre Longhena. The halls are decorated with stuccoes, wooden frontals, and paintings from the 17th-
18th c.; in the upstairs hall, note the exquisite ceiling,
with nine canvases* by G.B. Tiepolo (1739-44), masterpiece of the artist's late period; also note the painting of Judith and Holofernes, by G.B. Piazzetta.

I Carmini (I, *D1*). Convent church from the 14th
c., with a Renaissance facade with a curving crown
(early 16th c.) and a 14th-c. portal on the left side.
Inside, note the nave and aisles lined with monolithic columns, and the lavish 17th-c. decorations in
the nave. Among the many paintings and sculp-

enice: Ponte di Rialto

tures, note work by C. da Conegliano (ca. 1509), F. di Giorgio Martini (ca. 1474), and L. Lotto (1529). Alongside the church is the entrance to a one-time *monastery*, with a handsome 16th-c. cloister.

S. Sebastiano* (I, *D1*). This elegant Renaissance church is noteworthy primarily for the paintings and frescoes** done here by P. Veronese (1555-65). Veronese was buried here in 1588. Also note statues and monuments by T. Lombardo and Sansovino; in the vestibule is a work by Titian.

Angelo Raffaele (I, *D1*). Said to have been founded in the 7th c., and certainly rebuilt in 1639, this church has a largely 17th-c. interior. In particular, note the paintings by G.A. Guardi, which adorn the parapet of the organ. Not far off is the church of **S. Nicolò dei Mendìcoli**, one of the oldest in Venice, rebuilt between the 12th and 16th c., with a porch; the campanile is Romanesque. Inside, note the ancient columns and rich array of canvases, statues, and ornaments of all sorts, as well as the fine gilt and carved wooden frames (late 16th c.).

Zattere (I, *E1-3*). This pleasant promenade extends along the broad Canale della Giudecca, which runs between Venice proper and the large island of Giudecca. The exceedingly long "fondamenta," or quay (nearly 2 km) is split up into four stretches, named after an outstanding building or landmark: Zattere al Ponte Lungo, Zattere ai Gesuati, Zattere allo Spirito Santo, Zattere ai Saloni. As you walk along the first stretch, you pass the 16th-c. church of **S. Trovaso** (II, *F1*), with two virtually identical facades (inside: note the 18th-c. organ by G. Callido; 15th-c. painting by M. Giambono; Renaissance relief with Angels and Symbols of the Passion, in the chapel in the right transept). In the presbytery, the chapel to its left, and the Cappella del Sacramento, there are canvases by J. and D. Tintoretto, including a remarkable Last Supper*. Continue along toward the Punta della Dogana and you will find the 18th-c. church of the **Gesuati** (I, *E2*); the elegant interior features artwork by Tiepolo, Piazzetta, and Tintoretto; also note the statues and reliefs by G.M. Morlaiter (18th c.) on the walls. The church of the *Spirito Santo*, which gives its name to the next stretch of the Zattere, has a simple Renaissance facade (1506).

Punta della Dogana (II, *F4*). This "customs point" extends from the mouth of the Grand Canal to the Canale della Giudecca, extending out into the Bacino di S. Marco, facing the island of S. Giorgio. Note the long low building of the **Dogana da Mar** (Maritime Customs; 1677), built as early as the 15th c. to process merchandise arriving by sea. The spectacular point, designed as a ship's prow with loggia, has a corner tower with a group of 17th-c. bronzes, depicting two Atlases supporting the terrestrial orb, with a revolving figure of Fortune (by B. Falcone).

S. Maria della Salute* (II, *F3*). This masterpiece of Baroque architecture was built by B. Longhena (1631-87) after the Venetian Senate decided to have it built in gratitude for surviving an outbreak of plague. This majestic marble structure, with an octagonal plan, is studded with statues and topped by a great dome;

one of the outstanding features of the Venetian sky line. The majestic *interior* culminates in the high cup la and the main altar. To the left is the *great sacrist* on the altar and in the ceiling, paintings by Titian; the right of the altar, a large canvas by Tintoretto.

Campo della Salute (II, *F3-4*). One of the few "campi," or squares, that overlook the Grand Canal this one offers a spectacular view of the basin of S Mark's (Bacino di S. Marco). To the left of the church of the Salute, set high on its stepped base, is the *Se minario Patriarcale* (III, *F4*), an austere building de signed and built by B. Longhena (1671), organized around a cloister and a monumental staircase. A joining it is the remarkable **Pinacoteca Manfre diniana** (*open by request, enquire at the Seminario tel. 041911131*), with noteworthy works by 15th /18th-c. artists, including Giorgione, C. da Conegliano Filippino Lippi, and Beccafumi. Among the sculp ture, there are two Renaissance reliefs by T. Lon bardo and a terracotta bust by A. Canova.

The Mercerie, Rialto, the Frari, and the Scuola di S. Rocco

The nobles of Venice would return from the mee ings of the state council along the Mercerie, wher even now fine goods are offered invitingly for sal along the most popular promenade in the city. A ter their government work, the aristocrats woul head back to their ledgers, accounts, and corre spondence, across the Grand Canal, in the Rialto which back then was the commercial and financia heart of Venice, and is nowadays the main food ma ket. This route crosses the Grand Canal via the Pont di Rialto, and on through the two Sestieri of S. Pol and S. Croce, wrapping around the first curve in th canal, to the church of the Frari (Franciscan friars and the Scuola di S. Rocco, remarkable treasures c exquisite painting. You then return to the Ponte c Rialto, via Campo S. Polo and Campo S. Aponal.

Mercerie* (II, *D4-5*). Broken up into several se tions, with constantly changing names, running from St. Mark's Square to the Rialto, this is one of Venice liveliest streets, dotted with shops (hence the name At the end of the first segment (Merceria de l'Orologio) is the church of **S. Zulian** (II, *D5*), re built by J. Sansovino (1553-55); inside are painting by Veronese and Palma the Younger.

S. Salvador (II, *D4*). Nearly at the end of the Me cerie is the 16th-c. church of S. Salvador, with i white Baroque facade (1663), overlooking Camp S. Salvador. Inside, in a setting of stern elegance, is a abundance of fine art: note the monument to th Procuratore Andrea Dolfin by G. del Moro, and th monument to the Doge Francesco Venier* by Sanso vino (1561); also works by Titian (1560 and 1566 and P. Bordone. To the right of the church is the fo mer *convent of S. Salvador*, built in the 16th c., whic features two cloisters.

Campo S. Bartolomio (II, *C4*). In the past a livel marketplace, this square is now one of the busies and most exciting meeting spots in Venice, at the convergence of routes from Piazza S. Marco, from Rialto, and from the train station. In the center of the square is a *monument to Carlo Goldoni* (1883); also note the 18th-c. church of *S. Bartolomio*, long the place of worship of the German community that lived in the nearby Fondaco.

Ponte di Rialto* (II, *C4*). Until the 19th c., this renowned bridge was the only solid link between the two banks of the Grand Canal. It is lined by double arcades, packed with shops; the sides bear 16th-c. reliefs. Lovely view of the Grand Canal. On the right bank, to the right, the *Palazzo dei Camerlenghi*; to the left, *Palazzo dei Dieci Savi*.

Campo S. Giacomo di Rialto (II, *C4*). Formerly the center of Venice's financial activity, this square spreads out to the right of the *Ruga degli Orefici*. Bounded by the porticoes of the *Fabbriche Vecchie*, it features the 16th-c. statue of the "Gobbo di Rialto," a hunchback supporting the stairway; decrees and condemnations were once proclaimed here. Note the facade, with 15th-c. portico, of the church of **S. Giacomo di Rialto** (S. Giacometto), said to be the oldest church in Venice, but actually built in the 12th c. and rebuilt in 1601. Inside, note the handsome medieval columns and the artworks by Marco Vecellio, V. Scamozzi, and G. Campagna (1604).

S. Cassiano (II, *B3*). This 17th-c. church turns its right side to the Campo S. Cassiano, a busy thoroughfare. Founded many centuries ago, but repeatedly rebuilt, this church still has a 13th-c. terracotta bell tower; inside, in the presbytery, three canvases by Tintoretto, including a Crucifixion* (1568).

Ca' Corner della Regina (II, *B3*). This classical-style building by D. Rossi (1724) with a double loggia belonged to the family of Caterina, queen of Cyprus, who was born here in 1454. It now contains the *Archivio Storico della Biennale di Venezia* (archives of the Venice Biennale; *open Mon.-Sat., 9-1*), an international center for the study of contemporary art.

Ca' Pesaro* (II, *B2-3*). One of the largest palazzi on the Grand Canal, it features a broad courtyard with a large well, by J. Sansovino, and a majestic entrance hall. On the first and second floors is the **Galleria Internazionale d'Arte Moderna** (*closed for restoration*), with work from the Venice Biennale. It boasts work by great names of the 20th c.: Morandi, Boccioni, Savinio, Carrà, Sironi, Rosai, Miró, De Pisis, Chagal, Kandinsky, Klimt (painting); Moore, Messina, Martini, Arp, Pomodoro, Calder (sculpture). Also, major artists of the 19th c., including: G. Pellizza, Hayez, Fattori, De Nittis, Corot, Bonnard. On the third floor is the **Museo d'Arte Orientale*** (*open with entrance at every hour, 8:15-2; closed Mon.*), with one of the largest collections of Japanese art from the Edo period (1614-1868), as well as Chinese (porcelain and jade) and Indonesian art (fabrics, shadow puppets).

Campo S. Maria Mater Domini (II, *B2*). Regular in shape, this square has a 14th-c. well head in the center and, all around, late Byzantine and Gothic buildings. It takes its name from the adjoining Renaissance church of **S. Maria Mater Domini** (1502-40), with

a facade attributed to J. Sansovino and a harmonious interior built to a Greek cross. Inside, paintings by V. Catena (1520) and a very young Tintoretto.

S. Giacomo dell'Orio (II, *B1*). In one of the few tree-lined squares of central Venice, this church, one of Venice's oldest, still preserves its 12th-c. structure in the apsidal area; note the 13th-c. terracotta campanile. Inside, there are a 14th-c. wooden ceiling and many exquisite works of art: a 13th-c. stoup and a Lombardesque pulpit; a wooden 14th-c. Crucifix by P. Veneziano; Virgin and Saints* by Lotto (1546); and paintings by Veronese (1572 and 1577) and Palma the Younger (1575).

Fondaco dei Turchi (II, *A2*). This exemplary 13th-c. "casa-fondaco," or "warehouse-home," was used from 1621 until 1838 as a warehouse and hotel for Turkish traders. Transformed by restoration in the 19th c., it now houses the **Museo Civico di Storia Naturale** (*closed for restoration; to be reopened in 2003*), with collections of fossils, mammals, minerals, marine fauna, herbaria, and entomological and ethnographic collections.

Scuola Grande di S. Giovanni Evangelista* (II, *C1; open by request, tel. 041718234*). From an elegant Renaissance courtyard by P. Lombardo (1481) you enter to find, facing each other, the Gothic church of *S. Giovanni Evangelista*, and the Scuola Grande, whose blends of style testify to the long period of construction (14th-18th c.). Inside, note the spectacular staircase* (M. Codussi, 1498), a hint of things to come, both in the huge Gothic hall on the ground floor and in the lavish 18th-c. room upstairs. Note paintings by J. Guarana, G.D. Tiepolo, D. Tintoretto, P. Longhi, Palma the Younger, and others.

S. Maria Gloriosa dei Frari** (II, *C-D1; open Mon.-Sat., 10-5; Sun., 1-5*). With its massive 14th-c. campanile (the second tallest in Venice, after St. Mark's), this church was built by the Franciscans from 1340 to 1443. Gothic in style, it has a stern facade, marble portals (along the the sides as well), and a handsome apse. The portal on the facade has statues by B. Bon, P. Lamberti, and A. Vittoria.

The **interior** is vast and majestic and features monuments and fine art. In the center of the *nave*, note the Gothic-Renaissance choir* of the monks, with marble screen and carved inlaid wooden stalls. *Right aisle*: the monument to Titian and statue by A. Vittoria. *Right transept*: monuments by P. Lombardo and L. Bregno. *Sacristy*: triptych** by Giovanni Bellini (1488), in the original frame; certainly one of his masterpieces. The *apsidal chapels on the right* houses various Gothic tombs, with a polyptych by B. Vivarini (1482), and a wooden sculpture by Donatello (ca. 1450). *Presbytery*: altarpiece** by Titian; monument to the Doge F. Foscari* by A. and P. Bregno; funerary urn of the Doge Niccolò Tron*, by A. Rizzo, a masterpiece of the Venetian Renaissance. *Apsidal chapels on the left*: paintings and statues by B. Licinio, A. Vivarini, M. Basaiti, B. Vivarini, and J. Sansovino. *Left aisle*: altarpiece** by Titian; note the colossal "funerary machine" conceived by B. Longhena for Doge Giovanni Pesaro (1669), and the pyramidal monument to A. Canova, designed by Canova himself.

Scuola Grande di S. Rocco** (II, *D1*). *Open 28 Mar.-2 Nov., 9-5:30; 3 Nov.-27 Mar., 10-4*. This building was erected between 1516 and 1560, at first to plans by Bartolomeo Bon, and later under the supervision of Sante Lombardo and Scarpagnino. On the facade, elements of the early Renaissance (ground floor) mix with Baroque bellwethers (upper floor). *Inside*, the vast halls are decorated with the complete series of large **canvases** by Jacopo Tintoretto**, executed between 1564 and 1587, at the peak of his creative prowess. The tour begins on the upper floor, which you reach by taking the immense stairway* by Scarpagnino (1544-46); on the wall, The Plague of 1630, masterpiece by Antonio Zanchi (1666). In the *Sala dell'Albergo*, decorated by Tintoretto, the monumental Crucifixion* (1565) and dramatic scenes of the Passion; on the ceiling, S. Rocco in Glory, the first canvases done here by the master. On easels: Christ Carrying the Cross*, attributed variously to Giorgione and Titian; Ecce Homo, youthful work by Titian. In the ceiling of the impressive *Sala Maggiore*, 21 canvases with stories from the Old Testament; on the walls, 12 stories from the New Testament; on the altar, Glory of S. Rocco, also by Tintoretto. On either side of the altar, on easels: Annunciation, by Titian; Visitation and Self-Portrait, by Tintoretto; Abraham Visited by Angels and Hagar Succoured by Angels, by G.B. Tiepolo. In the *hall* on the ground floor, note the eight large canvases that Tintoretto painted in 1583-87; note in particular, Annunciation, Flight into Egypt, St. Mary Magdalene and S. Maria Aegyptica; on the altar, S. Rocco, statue by Girolamo Campagna (1587).

S. Rocco* (II, *C1*). This church, rebuilt in the 18th c., features paintings* by Tintoretto as well as by S. Ricci and G.A. Pordenone.

Campo S. Polo (II, *C2*). This is one of the largest and most distinctive "campi," or squares, in Venice. It was once used as a setting for popular festivals. It is lined by palazzi (14th-18th c.), as well as the apse of the ancient church of **S. Polo**, Byzantine in origin, but repeatedly modified, and largely rebuilt at the turn of the 19th c. On its side are a large 15th-c. Gothic portal and a 14th-c. campanile; inside, note the wooden keel ceiling, and the paintings by J. Tintoretto, G.B. Tiepolo, and Palma the Younger; the organ was built by G. Callido, 1763.

Campo S. Aponal (II, *C3*). This small but lively square features the former church of **S. Aponal** (S. Apollinare), rebuilt in the Gothic style in the 15th c., with a brick facade and a handsome Romanesque-Gothic campanile with mullioned windows.

S. Silvestro (II, *C3*). This ancient church was rebuilt around 1850, with a Neo-Classic facade from the early 20th c. It features a few notable paintings by J. Tintoretto and Carl Loth. Between the two altars is the entrance to the *Ex Scuola dei Mercanti di Vino* (16th c.); note canvases by G. Diziani.

S. Giovanni Elemosinario (II, *C3-4*). This ancient church breaks up the dense line of buildings along *Ruga Vecchia S. Giovanni*, the main thoroughfare linking Rialto and S. Polo. Destroyed by fire in the early

16th c., and rebuilt by Scarpagnino in 1538, it still has the late 14th-c. bell tower. The interior is simple and elegant, built to a Greek cross: on the main altar is a painting by Titian (1533); also, paintings by G.A. Pordenone (1530).

Ss. Giovanni e Paolo, S. Maria dei Miracoli, and Ca' d'Oro

The great churches of the two medieval orders of preaching monks seem to preside spiritually over Venice from their adjacent sites: the Frari, to the west, and Ss. Giovanni e Paolo (S. Zanipolo) of the Dominicans, to the north of the square. In this route "behind" St. Mark's, and through part of the Sestiere di Castello, Ss. Giovanni e Paolo and its "campo," with the renowned monument to Colleoni by Verrocchio, lies midway after the Pinacoteca Querini Stampalia, a valuable introduction to life in Venice in bygone eras, and before the delicate Lombard-style church of S. Maria dei Miracoli and the final luminous view of the Grand Canal, at the Ca' d'Oro.

Campo S. Maria Formosa (II, *C5*). You reach this Campo from the church of S. Zulian (see preceding route) by following the Calle delle Bande. One of the liveliest and most interesting "campi," or squares, in Venice, once used as an open-air theater.

S. Maria Formosa* (II, *C-D5; open Mon.-Sat., 10-5; Sun., 1-5*). This church was first built in the 7th c., and rebuilt in 1492 by M. Codussi; the facades date from the 16th c. and the bell tower from the 17th c. Inside, artworks by B. Vivarini and Palma the Elder.

Palazzo Querini Stampalia* (II, *D5*). Built around 1528, this building overlooks a handsome little "campiello" along the Rio di S. Maria Formosa. Headquarters since 1869 of the *Fondazione Querini Stampalia*, it houses a major library, and, on the second floor, the impressive *Galleria della Fondazione Querini Stampalia* (*open Tue.-Thu. and Sun., 10-6; Fri.-Sat., 10-10; closed Mon.*). In the 20 halls, decorated with 18th-c. stuccoes and furnishings, are works by Venetian painters from the 14th-18th c., including: D. and C. Veneziano, Giovanni Bellini, L. di Credi, V. Catena, Palma the Elder, L. Giordano, P. Vecchia, G.B. Tiepolo, P. Longhi, F. Zugno, and G. Bella.

Campo dei Ss. Giovanni e Paolo* (II, *B-C5*). After St. Mark's Square, this is the most monumental in Venice; distinguished by the facades of the church of Ss. Giovanni e Paolo (in terracotta) and the adjacent Scuola di S. Marco; at its center is a 16th-c. well head. The fulcrum of the "campo" is the **equestrian monument to Bartolomeo Colleoni*** (II, *B-C5*), a masterpiece of Renaissance statuary by A. Verrocchio (1481-88).

Ss. Giovanni e Paolo, or S. Zanipolo** (II, *B-C6*). This grand Gothic church was built by the Dominicans from 1246 to 1430, and it was established from about 1450 on as the site of the solemn funerals of the doges. In the impressive terracotta facade, which was left unfinished, note the marble portal by Bartolomeo Bon (1461); pay special atention to the right side and the polygonal apses*. The **interior**, with its solemn soaring Gothic structure, is similar to that of the church of the Frari, and like the Frari it contains monuments to doges, commanders, and other illustrious personages of the ancient Venetian Republic, from the 14th-17th c. *Counterfacade*: three monuments to the Mocenigo, among them the monument of the Doge Pietro Mocenigo* by Pietro Lombardo (1481). *Right aisle*: 1st altar, Virgin and Saints, attributed to Francesco Bissolo: on the next wall, monument to Marcantonio Bragadin, attributed to Vincenzo Scamozzi; 2nd altar, polyptych by a young Giovanni Bellini (ca. 1465). At the end of the aisle is the *Cappella di S. Domenico* (1716), in the carved and gilded ceiling of which is the Glory of t. Domenick* by G.B. Piazzetta (1727). *Right transept*: altarpiece by Lorenzo Lotto (1542); large Gothic window with painted glass (15th c.). On the walls of the *presbytery*, note the tombs of the doges: on the left, monument of the Doge Andrea Vendramin* by Pietro and Tullio Lombardo (15th c.); on the same wall, the Gothic monument of the Doge Marco Corner*, with statues of the Virgin and Saints by Giovanni Pisano. At the end of the left transept, under the monument of the Doge A. Venier by P.P. Dalle Masegne, is the entrance to the 16th-c. *Cappella del Rosario*, devastated by fire in 1867; on the rebuilt ceiling, canvases* by Paolo Veronese; in the presbytery, statues and two bronze candelabra by Alessandro Vittoria. *Left aisle*: beneath the 18th-c. organ by Gaetano Callido, triptych by Bartolomeo Vivarini; among other things, note the monument of the Doge Tomaso Mocenigo, by Tuscan artists in 1423, and the monument of the Doge Nicolò Marcello, by Pietro Lombardo (after 1474).

Scuola Grande di S. Marco* (II, B5-6). This building is now a hospital; its long elegant marble facade was built in the early Venetian Renaissance by P. and T. Lombardo and G. Buora (1487-90); the curved coping is by M. Codussi (1495) and the lunette over the portal by B. Bon. Inside, note the handsome blue-and-gold coffer ceiling, and paintings by Palma the Younger, Tintoretto, and G. Mansueti. Also, note the former *Dominican convent of Ss. Giovanni e Paolo*, rebuilt by B. Longhena in 1660-75.

S. Maria dei Miracoli* (II, B5; open Mon.-Sat., 10-5; Sun., 1-5). This small, isolated church in the narrow Campo dei Miracoli is one of the most exquisite creations of the early Venetian Renaissance. Built by Pietro Lombardo with the help of his sons Antonio and Tullio (1489), this church has a facing of polychrome marble which enlivens the elegant architecture of the sides and the front; it is crowned with a semicircular pediment. The interior is equally elegant, with marble facing, a lacunar vault, and busts of saints painted by P.M. Pennacchi (1528); note the fine sculptural decorations by T. Lombardo. The hanging choir over the entrance is adorned with a Virgin and Child by Palma the Younger.

S. Giovanni Crisostomo (II, B-C4). This Renaissance church was built by Mauro Codussi (1497-1504). In the interior are paintings by Giovanni Bellini (1513) and Sebastiano del Piombo, and a marble altarpiece by Tullio Lombardo.

Ss. Apostoli. (II, B4). Renovated in 1575, possibly to a design by A. Vittoria, this church features the Renaissance Cappella Corner, attributed to M. Codussi (1499), with sculpture believed to be by T. Lombardo (16th c.) and a painting by G.B. Tiepolo (1748) on the altar.

Strada Nuova (II, A-B3-4). This broad thoroughfare was built in 1871 to link Rialto with the train station, laying waste to a great deal of old Venetian architecture. Its southern side is lined by the secondary facades of the palazzi overlooking the Grand Canal; in the *Calle della Ca' d'Oro* stands the entrance to the Ca' d'Oro (see below). At the end of the street, at Campo S. Felice, you will see the left side of the church of *S. Felice* (II, A3; 1531-46), with clear-cut, elegant Renaissance lines.

Ca' d'Oro* (II, B3). Built in the Gothic style by B. Bon and M. Raverti (1422-40), this palazzo takes its name from the gold that once adorned the facade; this facade still presents polychrome marble, a lower portico and two upper loggias with lovely balconies and remarkable crenelation. Inside is a fine courtyard, with well head by B. Bon (1427).

With the adjacent *Palazzo Giusti*, it houses the **Galleria Giorgio Franchetti*** (open Mar.-Sun., 8:15-7:15; Mon., 8:15-2), created from the private collection of the Turinese musician Giorgio Franchetti, who donated it to the Italian state in 1916, along with the Ca' d'Oro. The remarkable collection includes European and Italian paintings, marbles, bronzes, and Venetian ceramics. In the halls near the broad Porteghi overlooking the Grand Canal are works by: (first floor) A. Vivarini, A. Mantegna, V. Carpaccio, G. da Rimini, B. Diana, M. Giambono, G. Ferrari, L. Signorelli, C. Braccesco, A. di Bartolo, and J. del Sellaio. Among the sculptures: Apollo (1498), by P.J. Alari; bronzes and marbles by T. Lombardo, V. Gambello, and G.M. Mosca; and medals by Pisanello, Gentile Bellini, and S. Savelli. A 15th-c. carved staircase leads up to the second floor, were 16th-c. Flemish tapestries and busts by A. Vittoria are displayed; among the paintings are works by Titian, Tintoretto, F. Guardi, Van Eyck, and other Flemish and Dutch artists.

Cannaregio: from the Scalzi to the Gesuiti and the Island of S. Michele

The route suggested here remains in the Sestiere di Cannaregio, in NW Venice, bounded by the Grand Canal and the lagoon. From the church of the Scalzi, near the train station of S. Lucia, the route runs past major churches, along lively city thoroughfares, and through evocative little squares. You will walk along the broad canal of Cannaregio for a stretch, and then, after you tour the church of S. Giobbe, you will head east and enter the Ghetto, one of the most picturesque sections of Venice, with its tall distinctive tower-houses and exquisite old synagogues. This route ends in the NW section of the Sestiere, in secluded areas of remarkable beauty.

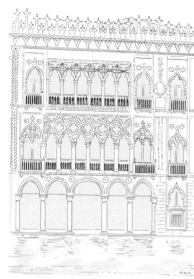

Venice: Ca'd'Oro

Gli Scalzi* (I, *C1*). Built by B. Longhena beginning in 1654, this building's lavish interior is reminiscent of the Roman Baroque. Note frescoes by G.B. Tiepolo.

S. Giobbe* (I, *B1*). Built from 1450 on Gothic style, and completed by P. and T. Lombardo in the Renaissance, it boasts a carved portal, a marble altarpiece by A. Rossellino (15th c.), and, in the sacristy, a 16th-c. ceiling. Cross over the *Ponte dei Tre Archi* (I, *B1*) to reach the Fondamenta di Cannaregio.

Ghetto Nuovo (I, *B2*). This, the New Ghetto, was built in one of the three sectors that make up the Venetian Ghetto, where the Jews were forced to live from 1516 until 1797; this is a small block, or island, surrounded by a ring of water and tall buildings. Note the **Museo Ebraico** (*open for guided tours, Oct.-May, 10-5:30; Jun.-Sep., 10-7; closed Sat.*), which features collections of objects, sacred furnishings, tapestries, codices, and other interesting examples of Jewish art in Venice in the 17th-19th c. In the dense architectural structure of the Ghetto, small cupolas mark the presence of synagogues, also known as Scuole (or Schools) for the variety of functions they served. The most spectacular is the *Scuola Levantina* (I, *B2*) in the Ghetto Vecchio (or Old Ghetto), founded in 1538 and renovated in the 17th c., possibly by B. Longhena.

S. Alvise (I, *B2; open Mon.-Sat., 10-5; Sun., 1-5*). This church, built in the 14th c., overlooks a solitary square; inside are paintings by G.B. Tiepolo. In the nave, note an early "barco" (hanging choir chancel, for nuns), supported by columns.

Madonna dell'Orto* (I, *B3; open Mon.-Sat., 10-5; Sun., 1-5*). This 15th-c. church with a terracotta facade overlooks a lovely little Campo; note the portal and bell tower, with cupola by B. Bon. Inside, paintings by J. Tintoretto, who was buried here in 1594, and a painting by C. da Conegliano (ca. 1493).

S. Maria della Misericordia (I, *B3*). Founded, with the adjoining abbey, in the 10th c., this church was rebuilt in the 13th c. and modified repeatedly in th following centuries. At an angle with the Baroqu facade (1651-59) is the 15th-c. elevation of the *Scu la Vecchia di S. Maria della Misericordia*, built in 131 and enlarged several times thereafter. The two a gels on the architrave of the portal are all that su vives of a relief by Bartolomeo Bon, now in the Vi toria and Albert Museum, London. Not far off is th *Scuola Nuova di S. Maria della Misericordia*, designe by J. Sansovino and built between 1534 and 1583

I Gesuiti (II, *A5*). The original church of the Cr ciferi was rebuilt between 1715 and 1730 for the J suits, with a Baroque facade, based on Roma church architecture. The interior is spectacular, de orated with marble inlay and white and gold stu cowork. Note the paintings by Titian (1558) and b a young J. Tintoretto. A major series of paintings, e ecuted by Palma the Younger between 1583 an 1591, is in the nearby *Oratorio dei Crociferi*, found ed in the 13th c. and rebuilt at the end of the 16 c. From this church, you can easily reach the *Fo damenta Nuove*, with a notable view of the broa expanse of water and the first islands of the nort ern lagoon (S. Michele and Murano).

Isola di S. Michele (I, *A-B4-5; waterbus from th Fondamenta Nuove*). This remarkable Venetian i land cemetery is filled with white crosses and ra monuments; the church of *S. Michele in Isola* (I, *A4* with its elegant Renaissance facade, is by Mau Codussi (1469-78).

S. Zaccaria, the Arsenale, and the Rive. The Islands of S. Giorgio and Giudecca

The "Rive," or shores, from the Zecca east, are the "f cade of Venice," a city that shows its best face t those who arrive from the sea; the square in from of the church of S. Giorgio Maggiore on the islan of S. Giorgio offers a remarkable view of that facad This route will take you there, after a walk throug the Sestiere di Castello, with tours of the church S. Zaccaria and the canvases by Carpaccio in th Scuola di S. Giorgio degli Schiavoni, as well as an e amination of the Venetian maritime tradition (th entrance to the Arsenale, the Museo Navale). S. Gio gio is a brilliant, luminous church, designed by Pa ladio. The tour concludes with the church of th Redentore on the island of Giudecca, another Vene ian masterpiece by the same great architect.

Palazzo Trevisan-Cappello (II, *D5*). The Renai sance facade, attributed to Bartolomeo Bon (earl 16th c.), can be seen particularly well from the nea by *Ponte della Canonica*. On the right, view of th Rio di Palazzo, with the rear facade of the Palazz Ducale (Doge's Palace) and the Ponte dei Sospi (Bridge of Sighs). At the end of the Fondamenta the entrance to the former Benedictine convent S. Apollonia (12th-13th c.), now housing the **Muse Diocesano d'Arte Sacra** (*open Mon.-Fri., 10:3 12:30*). In the restored Romanesque cloister is th *Lapidario Marciano*, with a collection of Roman an

Byzantine fragments, largely from the Basilica di S. Marco (St. Mark's); upstairs are paintings and sacred accessories from Venetian churches.

Campo S. Zaccaria (II, *D-E6*). You enter through a portal, in the flamboyant Gothic style, surmounted by a relief dating from around 1430, possibly by a Tuscan artist. This "campo" is small and charming; it is dominated by the facade of the church of S. Zaccaria, to the right of which is a distinctive terracotta campanile (13th c.), while to the left stand the arcades (occupied by shops) of the 16th-c. cloister of the ancient monastery. The "campo" is bounded to the north by late 15th-c. arches, which once surrounded the monastery's cemetery; a 16th-c. portal (n. 4693) marks the entrance to the one-time *Benedictine nunnery*, once the wealthiest and most prestigious in Venice (now a Carabinieri barracks).

S. Zaccaria * (II, D-*E6*). Built in Gothic style in the 15th c., completed by M. Codussi (1480-1515), who built the multi-register facade, a fine creation of the Venetian Renaissance. The church boasts paintings and frescoes by G. Bellini, Tintoretto, G.B. Tiepolo, A. del Castagno and F. da Faenza, A. Vivarini, and G. d'Alemagna. Note the inlaid choir (1455-64).

S. Giorgio dei Greci (II, *D6*). This 16th-c. church (1561) of the Greek Orthodox community was the most important foreign church in Renaissance Venice; the interior of the rectangular hall is solemn and majestic, lavishly decorated (stalls, marble icon stalls with late Byzantine paintings with gold background). On the left, near the Istituto Ellenico (Greek Institute), is the *Museo delle Icone Bizantine e Postbizantine* (open 9-12:30 and 1:30-4:30; Sun., 10-5), with a collection of about 80 Byzantine icons.

Scuola di S. Giorgio degli Schiavoni * (I, *D4*). Open weekdays, 9:30-12:30 and 3:30-6:30; holidays, 9:30-12:30; closed Mon. This church was built in the early 16th c. It is particularly renowned for the **paintings by V. Carpaccio** ** in the ground floor hall (1501-11), considered masterpieces.

S. Francesco della Vigna (I, *C4*). This large 16th-c. church, designed by Jacopo Sansovino, has a classical-style facade, by A. Palladio (1564-70). The vast interior abounds in fine artworks, with paintings by Fra' Antonio da Negroponte (1450) and sculptures by Pietro Lombardo and students (1495-1510). In the presbytery, funerary monuments to the doge Andrea Gritti, possibly by Sansovino; also, note paintings by G. Bellini (1507) and P. Veronese (1551).

Campo Bandiera e Moro (I, *D4*). At the edge of the more popular walking routes, this square is bounded to the north by the Gothic facade of the *Palazzo Gritti* (late 14th c.); note the five-light mullioned window, adorned with polychrome marble. In this square stands the Gothic church of **S. Giovanni in Bragora**, rebuilt in 1475, with a distinctive brick facade. Inside are notable paintings, by C. da Conegliano (1502), A. Vivarini, and F. Bissolo. In the presbytery, the vault was decorated with stuccoes by A. Vittoria (1596) and there are paintings by C. da Conegliano (1494) and P. Bordone. In the left aisle, two paintings by A. Vivarini (1490-93).

Arsenale (I, *C-D5*). *Closed the public*; part of this area, however, can be seen by taking the n. 5 vaporetto line through the inner canal. A tall, crenelated walled perimeter, surrounded by canals, marks off the impressive complex of boatyards that dates back to the 12th or early 13th c. and was enlarged repeatedly over the centuries. This is where the fleets of Venice were built, fleets that constituted the foundation of centuries of wealth and power for the ancient maritime republic. The entrance on the land side is marked by a *portal* * (1460), believed to date from the early Venetian Renaissance; it is surmounted by a great lion (symbol of St. Mark), attributed to Bartolomeo Bon. In 1692-94 a terrace was built in front of the portal, adorned with Baroque allegorical statues; on either side of this terrace are two stone lions, originally from Greece (the one on the left was located in the harbor of the Piraeus). To the right are two other, smaller lions, one of which comes from the island of Delos. The area of the Arsenale contains buildings of considerable architectural and historical interest. Among them are the *building of the Bucintoro* (in the Arsenale Vecchio), where the Doge's vessel was docked; the *Gaggiandre* (Darsena Arsenale Nuovissimo), two enormous wet docks built in 1568-73, supposedly to plans by J. Sansovino; the *Corderie della Tana* (south side of the Arsenale), 300 m in length, where hemp was stored and the great cables were made for the ships (now a site for temporary exhibitions). The *Officina Remi* (or Oar Workshop) now houses a detached section of the Museo Storico Navale (see below).

Isola di S. Pietro (I, *D6*). Just behind the Arsenale, this island is a secluded and lovely enclave at the easternmost tip of Venice; from the 8th to the early 19th c. it was the center of religious power in the city. Note the church of *S. Pietro di Castello*, which was, until 1807, the cathedral of Venice. Founded over a thousand years ago (9th c.), rebuilt and renovated repeatedly in the 16th-17th c., this church has a monumental facade from 1594-96 and an isolated campanile, by M. Codussi (1482-90).

Museo Storico Navale (I, *D5*). Open 8:45-1:30; Sat., 8:45-1; closed Sun. In Campo S. Biagio, at the end of the Riva degli Schiavoni, this museum is located in an austere, late 16th-c. building that was formerly a granary of the Republic. The museum offers documentation of the history of the Venetian navy (16th-18th c.) and the Italian Marina Militare (Italian Navy) from 1860 to modern times, with memorabilia, models, etchings, and other material. Of particular interest: a model of the Bucintoro, a splendid galley that was once used by the Doge in the ceremony of the wedding between Venice and the Sea; a large model of a 16th-c. Venetian galleass; models of frigates and sailing ships of the 18th c. A separate section of the Museo Navale, with actual historical vessels, is in the Officina Remi in the Arsenale.

Giardini Pubblici (I, *E-F5-6*). This great park was built in the Napoleonic era, and modified around 1850 to suit the Romantic tastes of the time. In it are the various pavillions of the *Biennale d'Arte* (Venice

Biennial), a major international exposition of painting, sculpture, graphics, and decorative arts established in 1895. The pavilions of the individual nations reflect the architectural trends of more than half a century (1907-64), and some are quite excellent.

Riva degli Schiavoni* (II, *E6*; I, *D-E4*). This broad walkway along the Bacino di S. Marco takes its name from the sailors of Schiavonia (or Slavonia, the Dalmatian coast), who moored here. Following the Riva toward St. Mark's, you will see the 18th-c. church of **S. Maria della Visitazione** (I, D4), particularly silent inside (built in part as a concert hall); note the ceiling, frescoed by G.B. Tiepolo. Further on is an equestrian monument to Victor Emmanuel (E. Ferrari, 1887). After the *Ponte del Vin* (II, *E6*), the Riva tends to be crowded with sightseers; note the Gothic *Palazzo Dandolo*, now the *Hotel Danieli*, and the massive *Prigioni Nuove* (1589-1614).

S. Giorgio Maggiore* (I, *E4*). *Waterbus from Riva degli Schiavoni, lines 82.* This church (*open 9:30-12:30 and 2:30-6:30*) stands on the island of the same name; it was designed and partly built by A. Palladio (1565-83, completed in 1611). Majestic interior, with paintings by S. Ricci, G. Campagna, Tintoretto, and V. Carpaccio (1516; *canvas to be seen by request*). From the 18th-c. campanile (*open same hours as the church*), a fine view* of Venice and the Lagoon.

Monastero di S. Giorgio Maggiore (I, *E4*). *Open Mon.-Sat., 9:30-1 and 2:30-6:30; Sun., 9:30-12 and 2:6:30.* Headquarters of the Fondazione "Giorgio Cini," this is a complex of rooms arranged around two *cloisters**; some of the finest architects from ca. 1500 to ca. 1700 worked on it, including A. Palladio, G. and A. Buora, and B. Longhena. On the ground floor, on the far wall of the *Refettorio* (Refectory), by A. Palladio, is the Wedding of the Virgin, by J. Tintoretto. A monumental double staircase by B. Longhena (1643-44) goes up to the first floor, where the *Biblioteca Longheniana*, furnished with carved 17th-c. bookshelves, contains over 100,000 volumes of art history. In the large grounds, you can admire the *Teatro Verde* (I, *E4*; 1951) in which open-air performances are staged.

Giudecca (I, *E-F1-4*). *Waterbuses from Riva degli Schiavoni or from the Zattere ai Gesuati, lines 52 and 82.* Narrow and elongated, set between the Canale della Giudecca and the south lagoon, this strip of land may take its name from the settlement of Jews ("Giudei") here during the Middle Ages. Because of its location, secluded but still on the Bacino di S. Marco, from the 16th c. on it became a favored site for pleasure gardens and villas, where the homes of the nobles alternated with gardens, orchards, and monasteries. In the 19th c., with the decline of the Venetian aristocracy and the suppression of convents, the island slowly became the domain of barracks, prisons, factories, and large working class districts. A long stroll on the "fondamenta," or quay, which has different names in the various stretches, runs around the whole island, offering excellent views of the Canale della Giudecca. From the *Zitelle* (I, *E3*), a large complex comprising a church and a hospice for poor young women, built in 1579-86 (perhaps designed by A. Palladio), you will reach the church of the Redentore (see below). To the west, past the 11th-c. church of *S. Eufemia* (I, *E1-2*), with sumptuous 18th-c. decorations inside, you will continue along the *Fondamenta di S. Biagio* (I, *E1*), the westernmost stretch of the island, marked by industrial buildings. At the end of the Fondamenta, across a metal bridge, stands the impressive Neo-Gothic structure of the *Mulino Stucky* (1896), now abandoned.

Redentore* (I, *F2-3*). This votive temple was built by the Venetian Senate during a terrible pestilence; set on the island of Giudecca, it was conceived as the final destination for the solemn procession of the Redentore (3rd Sun. in July), which crossed the canal on a bridge of boats. Considered one of A. Palladio's masterpieces, it was begun in 1577, and completed by A. da Ponte in 1592, after Palladio's death. Classical and majestic, it has an aisleless nave and a fine cupola. On the altars and in the sacristy, paintings by F. Bassano, Palma the Younger, J. Tintoretto, G. Campagna, A. Vivarini, F. Bissolo, and P. Veronese.

Verona**

Elev. 59 m, pop. 252,689; Veneto, provincial capital. The river Adige lingers lovingly as it passes through this city on the last foothills of the Monti Lessini, overlooking the boundless plains spreading out before it. Here the timeless past meets the city's everyday life, as well: the Veronese still attend the ancient Roman Arena; they pray in the Romanesque church of S. Zeno before Andrea Mantegna's altarpiece; they stroll over the red Scaliger bridge; and they shop in the ancient Piazza delle Erbe. A city of farmers, manufacturers, and merchants, it has always been the crossroads for Italy's trade with Germany and Europe to the north. "There is no world without Verona walls," says Romeo upon being banished, with Juliet in his heart; the same phrase can describe the completeness of the universe that is Verona.

Historical note. When Theodoric, the great 6th-c. king of the Goths, built a castle on the hill of S. Pietro (a 19th-c. Austrian castle now stands on that site), the left bank of the Adige had been set aside solely for worship and sport. Verona's founders, however, had first settled here, where the hill overlooks the narrowest turn in the serpentine oxbow curve of the river. By the first century B.C., when Verona became a Roman city, the urban area occupied the entire peninsula described by the river's right bank; its southern face was bounded by a wall in which two gates opened (they still exist; Porta dei Borsari and Porta dei Leoni). Piazza delle Erbe was the Forum. Three centuries later, the emperor Gallienus built new walls far enough south to include the great 1st-c. amphitheater. Two bridges spanned the river (one, the Ponte della Pietra, still stands). It was only in the 12th c. that Verona's Communal government expanded the city, building walls that can still be seen in Via del Pallone, and digging a moat – the Adigetto – from the Castelvecchio to the Aleardi bridge. Later, the Della Scala family came to rule Verona, and Cangrande I attempted to form a vast northern Italian state, only to be thwarted by an alliance among the alarmed leaders of Venice, Florence, and Milan. Some indication of the breadth of his ambitions can be had from the vast new walls he built, which stood until the turn of the 20th c. Cangrande's successors were less warlike, and were content to embellish Verona with marble bridges, the Arche Scaligere, and the fountain of Madonna Verona, or to build the spectacular Castelvecchio and the Scaliger bridge. None of this saved them from Visconti domination in 1387, or from Venetian rule shortly thereafter, in 1405. The Venetians brought great art but economic decline; Verona suffered more atrophy after the great plague of 1630. The treaty of Lunéville in 1801 established the boundary between French and Austrian Empires along the Adige. The city was made part of the Republic of Italy, while the left bank became Austrian, and took the name of Veronetta. From 1815 on, Verona fell under Austrian rule, until Italy's unification 50 years later. Since WWII, the city has expanded greatly.

Getting around. The historic center of Verona is partly a pedestrian zone and partly reserved to limited traffic according to certain schedules. Tourists are in any case always allowed to drive to their hotels. The first route suggested is a walking tour, since the monuments are all relatively close; the second route, on the other hand, is far longer, and may require the use of public transportation.

Roman Verona and Veronetta

The Roman city of Verona lay within the oxbow curve of the river Adige, around present-day Piazza delle Erbe, then the Forum: this is Verona's ancient nucleus, though the prevailing flavor is medieval, with the influence of the Della Scala rule and Venetian domination. On the left bank of the river, between Ponte Nuovo and S. Giorgio in Braida, you are in Veronetta.

Piazza delle Erbe* (*C5*). On the site of the Roman Forum, this rectangular square is lined with venerable houses and towers. At its center, amidst the stands of the daily market, you can see the column known as *Colonna del Mercato* (1401); the *Berlina* or *Capitello* (16th c.), a building where town leaders took office; and the *fountain of Madonna Verona** (1368). On the SW side of the square is the 14th-c. *Casa dei Mercanti*, with mullioned windows and parapets; on the far end is the *Torre del Gardello* (1370) and the late Baroque *Palazzo Maffei*; on the NE side are the 15th-c. *Case Mazzanti*, the Palazzo del Comune with the tall Torre dei Lamberti (see below) and the *Arco della Costa* (1470), an arch named after the whale rib, or "costa," that hangs from it, leading to Piazza dei Signori.

Verona: Piazza delle Erbe

Piazza dei Signori* (*C5*). Once the administrative heart of Verona, it stands as a courtyard enclosed by monumental buildings linked by arcades. At its center stands a 19th-c. *monument to Dante*.

Palazzo del Comune or *Palazzo della Ragione*. Dating from the late 11th c., the town hall was heavily reworked in the 16th c.; the *courtyard**, or Mercato Vecchio, is Romanesque, with a round-arched portico and mullioned windows; note the 15th-c. exterior staircase made of pink marble.

The building includes the 84-m *Torre dei Lamberti* (*open 9-6:30; closed Mon.*), a tower built between 1172 and ca. 1450; superb view from the top.

Palazzo del Capitanio, formerly *Tribunal*, is a 14th-c. building, renovated in the 19th c. Note portal by M. Sanmicheli.

Palazzo della Prefettura. Once the Della Scala residence (both Dante and Giotto were guests here), it was built in the 14th c. and restored in 1929-30. The portal is by Sanmicheli (1533).

Loggia del Consiglio*. Built in the late 15th c. for the city council, this is a splendid piece of Veronese Renaissance architecture, with purity of line and artistic composition. Note the elegant portico and twin mullioned windows set between small columns; lively color and handsome sculptures enliven the facade. An arch with a statue on it links the 16th-c. loggia to the adjacent *Casa della Pietà*, rebuilt in 1490. On its left is the *Domus Nova*, a 17th-c. reconstruction of the Della Scala home of the Podestà, or mayor.

Arche Scaligere* (*B-C5*). To the right of the Palazzo del Governo, you enter the Piazzaletto delle Arche, one of the loveliest spots in Verona. Here is the little Romanesque church of *S. Maria Antica* (12th c.), with its handsome interior, and the Arche Scaligere, monumental tombs of the lords of Verona. Enclosed by a 14th-c. iron gate with the heraldic "ladder" ("Scala"), the tombs are crowned by Gothic baldachins and adorned with 14th-c. statues. They are the **Tomb of Mastino II** (to the left), the precious **Tomb of Cansignorio**, the rich **Tomb of Alberto I**, and the *Tomb of Giovanni* della Scala. Above the portal of the church – one of the earliest pieces of Veronese Romanesque – is the **Tomb of Cangrande I**, who died in 1329, and a copy of an equestrian statue of this condottiere.

S. Tommaso Cantuariense (*C6*). Across the *Ponte Nuovo*, this 15th-c. church has an unfinished terra-

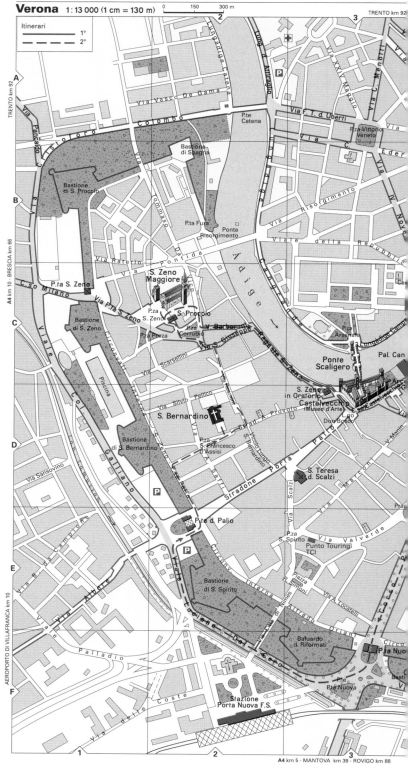

Verona 1:13 000 (1 cm = 130 m)

Itinerari
1°
2°

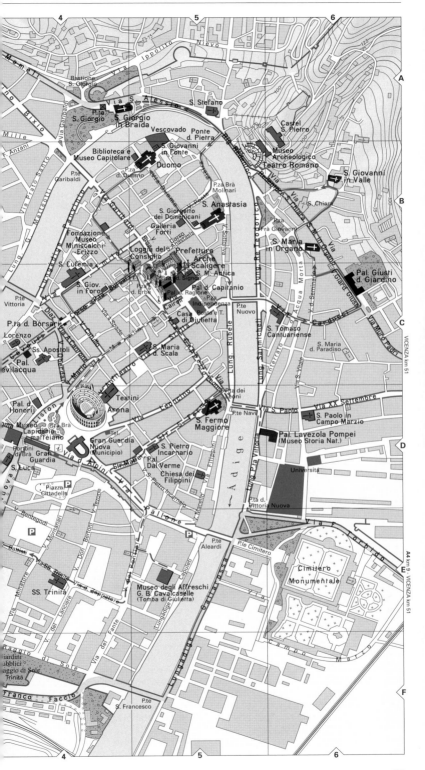

VICENZA km 51

A4 km 9. VICENZA km 51

435

cotta facade with a marble portal. Nearby, in Via Muro Padri, the late 15th-c. church of **Ss. Nazaro e Celso** (*C6; off map*) features a Gothic facade and, inside, works by Venetian Renaissance painters. Note the *chapel of S. Biagio*.

Palazzo Giusti del Giardino (*C6*). Late 16th c., this mansion has a lovely garden (*open summer, 9-8; winter, 9-one hour before sunset*), with cypress-lined avenues, a maze, and a terrace with view.

S. Maria in Organo (*B6*). This fine piece of architecture dates from 1481; the facade is a mixture of Gothic and Renaissance styles. The interior features handsome frescoes and altarpieces. The magnificent *choir* and sacristy boast excellent intarsias (late 15th-early 16th c.). Note the crypt, with fragments of the 7th-c. church and of the Roman walls.

S. Giovanni in Valle (*B6*). Founded in the High Middle Ages, and rebuilt in Romanesque style in the late 12th c., this church boasts fine apses, cloister, and campanile. Inside, 14th-c. frescoes. In the crypt, the *Arca dei Ss. Simone e Giuda*, a tomb carved in the 4th c.

Area Archeologica del Teatro Romano (*B5-6*). *Open 9-6:30; closed Mon.* This remarkable archeological complex on the hill of S. Pietro, comprises chiefly the ancient Roman *theater* (built early 1st c. A.D.). Above it stands the little church of *Ss. Siro e Libera* (rebuilt in the 14th c.). The theater is used for theater and dance in the summer.

Museo Archeologico. *Open Tue.-Sun., 10-6:30.* Housed in a 15th-c. convent, with the entrance located atop the steps of the theater (elevator; handsome view), this archeological musem features relics of Roman Verona. From the 15th-c. cloister, you enter the *church*; note the frescoes and fine triptych altarpiece. From terraces, excellent views of Verona.

S. Stefano (*A5*). Founded in the 5th c., partly rebuilt in the 12th c., this church preserves some of its original structure. Note the handsome facade and octagonal terracotta tambour, as well as the 10th-c. crypt.

S. Giorgio in Braida (*A4-5*). With its massive dome, by Sanmicheli, this church overlooks the river Adige's oxbow curve. Built between 1477 and 1536, its white marble facade dates from the 17th c. The interior, solemn and harmonious, with an aisleless nave, is decked with paintings by J. Tintoretto, P. Veronese, Moretto da Brescia, Girolamo dai Libri, and G.F. Caroto. Before the church is the early 16th-c. **Porta S. Giorgio**.

Ponte della Pietra (*A-B5*). Roman in origin, this bridge was destroyed in WWII and rebuilt with original materials in 1957-59. Excellent view of the banks of the Adige.

S. Anastasia (*B5*). This Gothic church is made entirely of brick and was built by the Dominicans (1290-1481), when the bell tower was finished. The unfinished facade has a splendid 14th-c. *portal*. The majestic *interior* boasts fine works of art. In particular, note the holy water stoups, with the odd "hunchbacked" statues supporting them (16th c.); the Fregoso altar (1st on the right) by Sanmicheli (1565); frescoes by Liberale da Verona; a handsome

Renaissance altar (1502), with a painting by Girolamo dai Libri; a fresco by Altichiero (1370 ca.); two Gothic tombs and terracotta reliefs by Michele da Firenze (1435); a large fresco of the Last Judgement, by the 14th-c. Maestro del Giudizio Universale; and a tomb by Nanni di Bartolo (1429). From the left transept (note painting by F. Morone) a door leads to the Cappella Giusti, which a fresco of St. George and the Dragon* by Pisanello. To the left of the church, note the Gothic *tomb of Guglielmo Castelbarco* and the small Gothic church of *S. Giorgetto*.

Via Duomo. At the beginning of this street, on the left, in Via A. Forti n. 1, is the 18th-c. *Palazzo Forti-Emilei* (in the courtyard, note the Romanesque wing), which houses temporary exhibits. Next to it is the **Galleria Comunale d'Arte Moderna e Contemporanea Achille Forti** (*open 9-7; closed Mon.*). In the halls of this museum, various works by 19th-/20th-c. artists, including paintings by F. Hayez, G. Fattori, M. Bianchi, F. De Pisis, and U. Boccioni and sculptures by M. Rosso, G. Manzù, and G. Duprè.

Duomo (*B5*). Dominating the Piazza del Duomo, this 12th-c. Romanesque cathedral was renovated in the Gothic style (15th c.) and has Renaissance additions. On the front, note the monumental two-storey *porch*, adorned with reliefs by Maestro Nicolò (1139); another porch from the same period stands on the right side; the 16th-c. campanile, Romanesque at the base, was designed by Sanmicheli, and was left unfinished. The 12th-c. *apse*, in tufa stone, is one of the most exquisite creations of Veronese Romanesque architecture; it is studded with pilaster strips and a very fine frieze in the cornice. The Gothic *interior* has broad arches set on tall piers. In the chapels and the presbytery, enclosed by a semicircular columned *choir* by Sanmicheli (1534), are various paintings and statues from the 14th-16th c.

To the left of the Duomo is a Romanesque *cloister* with twin columns (ca. 1140), and fragments of mosaic floors from the Early Christian basilica; you can enter the little church of *S. Elena* (Romanesque, on Early Christian foundations and structures) and the ancient baptistery of *S. Giovanni in Fonte* (13th-c. octagonal baptismal font*), both 12th-c. Behind the Duomo, the *Palazzo del Vescovado* has a Renaissance facade decorated with Venetian merlons (1502) and a portal adorned with statues.

Biblioteca Capitolare (*B5*). *Open 9:30-12:30; Tue. and Fri., 10-12 and 4-6; closed Thu. and Sun.* Housed in the *Palazzo del Canonicato* (rebuilt in 1948), to the left of the Duomo, this is one of the leading ecclesiastic libraries in Europe. Among its most precious items, note 4th-c. Virgil's manuscripts, the 6th-c. Codex of Justinian, illuminated manuscripts, and the Canonical Archives, with 11,000 parchments. Also located in this building is the *Museo Pinacoteca Canonicale* (open Sat., 10-1 and 1:30-5; Sun., 1:30-5) with paintings and sculpture from the 14th-19th c.

Museo Miniscalchi-Erizzo (*B4*). *Open Tue.-Sat., 4-7; Sun., 10:30-12:30 and 4-7.* In the newly restored 15th-c. Palazzo Miniscalchi-Erizzo, in Via S. Mammaso 2/A, this museum has 16 halls with collections of archeological material, bronzes, scultures, majolicas, weapons, armors, drawings, and paintings by Venetian masters of the 16th-18th c.

Corso di Porta Bórsari. This typical road of old Verona runs along the course of the Roman "decumanus maximus." Note the little Romanesque church of *S. Giovanni in Foro* (C4).

Porta dei Bórsari* (*C4*). This gate was the main entrance to Verona in Roman times. It was built in the middle of the 1st c.

S. Eufemia (*C4*). This long narrow Gothic church was completed in the 14th c.; note the handsome portal from 1476. Transformed in 1739, it has frescoes from the 14th c. and Venetian paintings from the 14th-16th c.

The Addizione Scaligera

The southward expansion, or "addizione", marked by the walls built under Cangrande I Della Scala was sufficient for Verona's growth through the 19th c.: the Arena, Castelvecchio and the Ponte Scaligero, S. Zeno Maggiore (with Andrea Mantegna's altarpiece) are the three high points of the area contained between the southern and western ramparts.

Piazza Bra' (*D4*). Once a country field ("braida"), this garden-like square is now the center of Verona, a meeting place for the Veronese. To the NE is the Arena (see below); to the SE is the Neo-Classic **Gran Guardia Nuova**, or *Palazzo Municipale* (town hall; 1838); to the south is the Baroque building of the *Gran Guardia* (begun in 1610, completed in 1836, housing temporary exhibitions) and the two arcades and the pentagonal tower of the *Portoni della Bra'*, built ca. 1480. Nearby is the complex of the *Accademia Filarmonica* (with Library-Museum, for scholars only) and the **Museo Lapidario Maffeiano** (*open 9-2:30; closed Mon.*), founded in the 18th c. by Scipione Maffei, containing plaques and marble epigraphs from Greek, Etruscan, and Roman times (mithraic relief* from the 2nd c.), as well as from the early Christian and medieval periods. To the NW, various palazzi (at n. 16, the *Palazzo degli Honorij*, later Palazzo *Guastaverza*, by M. Sanmicheli, 1554) with porticoes, along which runs the "Listón," an elegant and lively marble-paved promenade.

Arena** (*D4*). Open (*entrance from the fifth arch*), *9-6:30; Jul.-Aug., 8-3:30; closed Mon.* One of the largest surviving Roman amphitheaters (after the Colosseum and that of Capua), the Arena was built in the 1st c. in limestone from the Valpolicella. All that survives of the outer ring are three rows of arcades, while the second ring maintains intact two rows of 72 arches. In the oval-shaped interior (44.43 x 73.58 m), a tribune (cavea) with 44 tiers of seats (restored), with a seating capacity of 22,000, surrounds the stage, or "platea." Operas are performed here in the months of July and August.

Via Mazzini (*C4-5*). This road links Piazza Bra' and Piazza delle Erbe; it is a pedestrian mall, lined with elegant shops.

Casa di Giulietta (*C5*). *Open 9-6:30, closed Mon.* In Via Cappello, at n. 21-23, is what is believed to be the *house of Juliet Capulet*, Shakespeare's tragic heroine. The 13th-c. Gothic building features the renowned balcony (rebuilt) from which she is supposed to have spoken to Romeo. Continuing along Via Leoni, note the remains of the Roman gate, or **Porta dei Leoni***, dating from the 1st c B.C.

S. Fermo Maggiore* (*D5*). This church comprises two buildings, superimposed; the lower one dates from the 11th-12th c., while the upper one is Gothic, and dates from the 13th-14th c. It has a handsome facade with a large, deeply splayed Romanesque portal (on the left, Arca di Fracastoro, tomb of a physician of the House of Della Scala in the 14th c.) and a twin portal (1363) with a porch on the left side. Note the complex of apses (the smaller *apses* are Romanesque, the largest one is Gothic).

The *interior* of the **upper church**, with an aisleless nave and a keel roof (1314), abounds in 14th-/15th-c. frescoes and 15th-/16th-c. sculpture; in the lunette of the portal, Crucifixion attributed to Turone; on the right, near the ambo, Angels with Scrolls*, fragment of a detached fresco by S. da Verona; midway up the left side is the Baroque Cappella della Madonna, with 16th-c. paintings, and altarpiece by G.F. Caroto (1528). At the 1st altar on the left, altarpiece by Battista dal Moro; in the corner, the *Monument to Brenzoni**, by the Florentine N. di Bartolo (1439), framed by the renowned fresco of the Annunciation* by Pisanello. From the right transept, you can enter the remains of the ancient Romanesque *cloister* and then descend to the **lower church**, with a nave with two aisles (the nave is divided midway by slender pillars), and fragments of frescoes from the 11th-13th c.; behind the main altar is a 14th-c. wooden Crucifix.

Palazzo Lavezola Pompei* (*D6*). Standing on the left bank of the river Adige, beyond the Ponte delle Navi, at n. 9 in Lungadige Porta Vittoria, this mid-16th-c. palazzo is one of the finest creations of Sanmicheli; it is the home of the **Museo Civico di Storia Naturale*** (*open 9-7; Sun., 2-7; closed Fri.*), one of Italy's finest museums of natural history, with an especially notable collection of fossil fauna and flora* from Bolca. The museum also includes a specialized library, a photographic archive, and research laboratories.

Stradone S. Fermo (*D5*). This road is lined with notable houses and palazzi, from the 16th-19th c., partly rebuilt; in particular, at n. 13 is the *Palazzo Della Torre*, by the school of Sanmicheli (16th c.), with a fine courtyard and garden. At the end of the street is the church of *S. Pietro Incarnario*, built on Roman foundations, with its 14th-c. bell tower and, inside, detached 12th-c. fresco (Crucifixion). After the dogleg, the name changes to Stradone Maffei, and here you will find *Palazzo Dal Verme*, where the great dramatist, scholar, and soldier Scipione Maffei was born and died. At the end of the road is a stretch of crenelated *walls*, built by the Della Scala family.

Museo degli Affreschi (*E5*). *Open 9-6:30; closed Mon.* Take a left off Via del Pontiere, and, in a complex formed by the cloister and church of *S. Francesco al Corso*, this museum contains the most important series of Veronese frescoes, detached from their original sites since the 19th c. In particular, note the 16th-c. frescoes, including the lovely allegorical scenes by D. Brusasorci. From the cloister, a stairway leads down to the so-called *Tomba di Giulietta* (Tomb of Juliet), where the star-crossed lover of Romeo was supposedly buried.

Corso di Porta Nuova. Designed by Sanmicheli, this broad thoroughfare runs from the Portoni della Bra' in the center to the train station. At the end of the Corso stands the massive, isolated **Porta Nuova** (*F3*), a gate also built by Sanmicheli (1546).

Viale Dal Cero. This road runs just outside the *Baluardo dei Riformati* and the *Bastione di S. Spirito*, fortifications constructed by the Austrians in place of earlier walls built by the Della Scala, which still encircle the city, extending over a circumference of about 10 km.

Porta del Palio* (*E2*). So-called because the horse race of the Palio once ran along it (mentioned by Dante Alighieri), this is the loveliest of the gates designed by Sanmicheli for Verona's walled perimeter.

S. Bernardino* (*D2*). Built in the mid-15th-c., in a transitional style between Gothic and Renaissance, this church features a large cloister in front of the facade. The interior contains many fine 15th-/16th-c. Veronese paintings and frescoes. Domenico Morone painted the organ doors (1481) and the walls of the library, now called the **Sala Morone*** (1503).

S. Zeno Maggiore** (*C1-2*). This masterpiece of Italian Romanesque architecture is, with the Arena, one of Verona's two most celebrated monuments. It stands in a broad, quiet square, set between a 13th-c. tower of the ancient abbey (on the left) and a solitary bell tower (11th c.). Built in the 9th c. upon the tomb of Verona's first bishop, who died in 380, it was so badly damaged in an earthquake in 1117 that it was entirely rebuilt in the 12th-13th c. The elegant tufa facade, adorned in the center with the wheel of fortune, a great 13th-c. rose window, has a *portal** with reliefs by Maestro Nicolò (1138), and an exquisite *door* with 24 12th-c. bronze **panels*** depicting Bible stories and lives of the saints.

The *interior* is simple and majestic, and features a Crucifix by Lorenzo Veneziano (1360 ca.); at the head of the right aisle is an octagonal 12th-c. baptistery. Noteworthy frescoes and statues dating from the 13th c. On the main altar, a **triptych**** by Mantegna (1459). Noteworthy wooden Gothic choir. From the left aisle, you can step out to the handsome Romanesque *cloister*.

S. Procolo (*C2-*). Founded in the 5th-6th c., the church has a crypt with wall decoration from the 12th-14th c. The little 13th-c. Romanesque church of *S. Zeno in Oratorio*, with a Gothic facade, houses a stone on which, according to legend, the saint used to sit while fishing in the river Adige.

Castelvecchio** (*C-D3*). The principal monument of civil architecture of medieval Verona, it was built by Cangrande II della Scala as a residence and

fortress in 1354-57; the keep was added in 1375. Th▮ massive brick structure, with towers and battlement▮ comprises two wings divided by the battlement▮ bridge: the eastern, rectangular building surrounds ▮ great courtyard; the western one was the palace, an▮ has a double set of walls, two courtyards, and dra▮ bridges. This castle houses the Civico Museo d'Art▮

Civico Museo d'Arte.* *Open 9-6:30; closed Mo▮* This museum houses fine collections of art, chief▮ of the Veneto school (14th-18th c.): extensive work b▮ Veronese artists, including the early painters Turon▮ Altichiero, Stefano da Verona, Pisanello; the 15th-▮ artists F. Morone, P. Cavazzola, G.F. Caroto; and the 16t▮ c. artists P. Veronese and P. Farinati. Among the othe▮ Veneto artists: A. Mantegna, J. Bellini, Giovanni Bel▮ ni, C. Crivelli, B. Montagna, A. Vivarini, B. Strozzi, J. Ti▮ toretto, G.B. Tiepolo, and F. Guardi. Works by variou▮ Flemish artists are also on show. Note the many a▮ cient artifacts, including fragments of Early Christia▮ glass, 7th-c. goldwork, the Tesoretto di Isola Rizza, wit▮ 4th-c. silver; cloth and silk from the Arca, or tomb, ▮ Cangrande I; miniatures. Arms from Longobard time▮ to the 17th c. Excellent 14th-c. Veronese statuary, i▮ cluding the **equestrian statue of Cangrande I***

Ponte Scaligero* (*C3*). This bridge links th▮ Castelvecchio with the other bank of the river Ad▮ ge; it is a massive structure, with three arches on pi▮ lars with towers, entirely made of brick. It was rebu▮ after destruction in WWII.

Corso Cavour* (*C3-4*). This is one of the lovelie▮ streets in Verona; it runs from the Piazzetta d▮ Castelvecchio, where the reassembled 1st-c. **Arc▮ dei Gavi** stands, a rare example of a four-pier R▮ man arch, all the way to the Porta dei Bórsari. It ▮ lined with aristocratic palazzi: at n. 44, *Palazzo Cano▮ sa*, by Sanmicheli (1537); at n. 19, the spectacula▮ **Palazzo Bevilacqua*** (*C4*), a masterpiece, also b▮ Sanmicheli (ca. 1534). Facing this palazzo is th▮ Gothic entrance arcade of the 12th-c. Romanesqu▮ church of **S. Lorenzo**; note the two round tower▮ and remarkable interior. A little further along, on th▮ right, note the small bell tower and the side of th▮ Romanesque church of the *Ss. Apostoli*; from th▮ sacristy, you can enter the partly subterranean littl▮ 8th-c. church of *Ss. Tosca e Teuteria*.

Vicenza*

Elev. 39 m, pop. 109,738; Veneto, provincial cap▮ ital. This town stands in the gentle green Venet▮ ian plain, now an industrialized area, at the foo▮ of the Monti Bèrici; other mountains loom o▮ the horizon. Vicenza is linked to the name o▮ Andrea Palladio. The 16th-c. Paduan architec▮ was certainly thinking of his Vicentine clients▮ when he rejoiced at having "found gentlemer▮ of so noble and generous a spirit and such ex▮ cellent discrimination, that they believed in m▮ reasoning and abandoned that old-fangle▮ manner of building without a line of decora▮ tion or a single thing of beauty..." This "new" beauty – classicizing and Palladian – pervade▮

the city, harmonizing with the fragments of Venetian Gothic, and with another face of Vicenza, with bridges, canals, haunting vignettes, and sudden views of hills and alpine foothills.

Historical note. All of Vicenza's history can be recounted in the growth of the urban grid. Vicetia (from "vicus," Latin for village) became Roman with Padua, in 49 B.C. The Roman municipium was small, but its layout can still be seen. Modern Vicenza traces its origin back to the 12th c., when the Commune joined the league against the emperor Frederick I Barbarossa. Vicenza finally became a Venetian holding in 1404, but those two centuries marked the layout of the town. As Vicenza stagnated and even shrank in later years, the city's outline remained fixed. Later, under Venice, the city expanded south, to Porta Lupia and P.Monte, and NW, to Porta Pusterla. Within its walls, Vicenza remained stable: its population was 30,000 at the end of the 16th c. and the same at the turn of the 20th c. Still, from 1450 to 1600, the town so changed its architecture that it was never the same. The great culmination was the work of Palladio. The Basilica, Palazzo Chiericati, the Teatro Olimpico, and the Rotonda are all prototypes of a classicizing architecture that developed, with Scamozzi, until 1800.

Getting around. Much of the historic center – inscribed in UNESCO's World Heritage List – is closed to traffic; visitors going to hotels are allowed through, however. The route recommended can be covered entirely on foot.

Places of interest. Piazza dei Signori.* This is the monumental center of Vicenza including, on the south side, the Basilica, with the adjacent slender 82-m *Torre di Piazza* (12th c.); at the far end, the two *columns of the Piazza*, one topped by the Lion of St. Mark's (1520), the other by a statue of the Savior (1640); on the NE side, the **Loggia del Capitaniato***, also known as *Loggia Bernarda*, an unfinished work by Palladio (1571), and the long facade of the 16th-c. *Palazzo del Monte di Pietà*, with the Baroque facade of the church of *S. Vincenzo* in the center (1614; inside, marble Deposition* by O. Marinali).

Basilica.** *Open Tue.-Sat., 9-5.* The most important monument in Vicenza, one of the outstanding buildings of the Venetian Renaissance, built between 1549 and 1617, the basilica is a masterpiece by A. Palladio, who enclosed the existing 15th-c. Gothic *Palazzo della Ragione* in a sumptuous marble sheath, featuring a classical portico and loggia. The term "Basilica," first used by Palladio himself, here means a building in which justice was administered. On the right side, a stairway leads up to the loggia, and from here you enter the Gothic hall, which occupies the entire upper floor of the building. Nearby, in the Piazza delle Erbe, stands the medieval *Torre del Girone*, or *Torre del Tormento*.

S. Maria in Foro. This 15th-c. church overlooks Piazza delle Biade; inside, altarpiece by B. Montagna.

Vicenza: Basilica

Casa Pigafetta. Located at n. 9 in Via Pigafetta, this house was built in a flamboyant Venetian Gothic style in the 15th c. It was the birthplace of A. Pigafetta, who sailed with Magellan on the first circumnavigation of the earth (1519-22), and wrote a detailed account of the journey.

S. Nicola da Tolentino. *Open 22 Mar.-25 Oct., Tue., 9-12.* This 16th-c. oratory is decorated with stuccoes that frame numerous paintings by F. Maffei, G. Carpioni, A. Zanchi, and others. From the nearby *bridge of S. Michele* (1623), you have a fine view of the center of Vicenza; in the Contrà Piancoli, note the buildings at n. 4, 6, and 8.

Piazza del Duomo. The square is overlooked by the Duomo, and, at n. 11, the *Palazzo Vescovile*, or bishop's palace, rebuilt in Neo-Classic style in 1819 and partly after being damaged in WWII; in the courtyard of the palace is the splendid **Loggia Zeno*** (*open Mon.-Fri., 9-12*), a Renaissance creation by B. da Milano and T. da Lugano. On the south side of the square, next to the Palazzetto Roma (now offices of the APT), you can enter the **Roman cryptoporticus** (*open Sat., 10-11:30*), part of a 1st-c. A.D. Roman house.

Duomo.* Still in its original 13th-/16th-c. forms, the Vicenza Cathedral has a Gothic facade (1467) in polychrome marble, attributed to D. da Venezia, and an elegant Renaissance apse (1482-1508). The 11th-c. Romanesque bell tower, built on Roman foundations, stands across the street.

The Gothic interior, with a vast aisleless nave and cross vaults, features paintings by F. Maffei, L. Veneziano, and B. Montagna.

Piazza Castello. This square features *Palazzo Piovini* (1656-58), now a warehouse, and the unfinished *Palazzo Porto*, built by V. Scamozzi to plans by Palladio (late 16th c.). At the end of Corso Palladio (see below) stands a mighty *tower*, the only relic of the medieval castle of the Della Scala family. Outside the *Porta Castello* are the *public gardens*, once belonging to Villa Salvi, with the *Loggetta Valmarana*, a small loggia in Palladian style (1592), set alongside a stream of running water.

Ss. Felice e Fortunato.* This basilica is a mainstay in the religious history of Vicenza. It was built in the late 10th c., and restored to its Romanesque forms in the early 20th c. Worthy of note are the 4th-/5th-c. mosaic floors, from an earlier building on the same site; also, the distinctive little 12th-c. bell tower with 14th-c. additions.

439

Corso Andrea Palladio* *(first stretch)*. This main street runs through Vicenza, east to west, amidst a series of monumental homes and churches, dating from the 14th-18th c. At n. 13, the enormous *Palazzo Thiene*, later *Bonin-Longare*, attributed to Palladio and completed by V. Scamozzi; at n. 45, the Renaissance *Palazzo Capra-Clementi* (late 15th-c.); at n. 47, the Venetian Gothic *Palazzo Thiene*, with handsome five-light mullioned window; at n. 67, the elegant Venetian Gothic *Palazzo Braschi-Brunello*, with a portico.

Corso Fogazzaro. One of Vicenza's liveliest streets, it is lined with fine Baroque and Renaissance residences. On the right, at n. 16, the solemn *Palazzo Valmarana-Braga* (1566) by Palladio; further along, the *Palazzo Repeta*, by F. Muttoni (1711).

S. Lorenzo.* Impressive Franciscan church, in brickwork and Gothic style (13th c.). On the facade, note the *portal** decorated with statues (1344). Inside, amidst round piers, various funerary monuments dating from the 14th-16th c, an altar relief by Pojana, and a fresco by B. Montagna. The cloister (1492) features a round-arch portico.

Carmine. In Corso Fogazzaro, this Neo-Gothic construction preserves portals and other elements from the long-demolished 14th-c. church of S. Bartolomeo (14th-15th c.). *Inside*, paintings by Veronese, Bassano, and B. Montagna.

Galleria d'Arte Municipale. *Open only for exhibitions*. Set in a 16th-c. former church, in a nook in Corso Palladio, this city art gallery features paintings by local artists such as S. Prunato, and G.A. Fumiani.

Palazzo Trissino-Baston.* At n. 98 in Corso Palladio, the palace, which now houses the city hall, is lined with a tall portico with Ionic columns. A masterpiece by V. Scamozzi (1592), it has a handsome courtyard and, on the second floor *(open by request, contact the custodian)*, are the Sala della Giunta, or Council Hall, adorned with a frieze by G. Carpioni, and the Sala degli Stucchi, with 17th-c. decoration.

Contrà Porti.* This road runs past a number of splendid palazzi: at n. 6-10, the 15th-c. Venetian Gothic *Palazzo Cavalloni-Thiene*; at n. 11, the vast **Palazzo Barbaran-Porto**, by Palladio (1571), soon to become the Museo Palladiano; at n. 12, the Renaissance *Palazzo Thiene* (head office of the Banca Popolare), designed by Palladio, with facade by L. da Bologna (1489); at n. 14, the Gothic *Palazzo Trissino-Sperotti* (1450-60), with an elegant balcony; n. 17, the Venetian Gothic *Palazzo Porto-Breganze* (1481), with a handsome Renaissance portal and a porticoed courtyard; at n. 16, the Renaissance *Palazzo Porto-Fontana*; n. 19, the magnificent Venetian Gothic *Palazzo Porto-Colleoni* (late 14th c.); at n. 21, the unfinished **Palazzo Iseppo da Porto**, later *Palazzo Festa*, by Palladio (1552).

S. Marco. This 18th-c. church, with a lavish facade, is worth a visit for the painting of the Ecstasy of St. Theresa by S. Ricci.

Contrà Zanella. This street is lined with notable buildings: at n. 2, **Palazzo Sesso-Zen**, a rare piece of Vicentine Gothic; at n. 1, on the Piazzetta S. Stefano, the crenelated Renaissance *Palazzo Negri De Salvi*; to the left, the Baroque church of *S. Stefano* (painting* by Palma the Elder); further along, the Palladian rear facade of Palazzo Thiene (see above).

Corso Palladio* *(second stretch)*. At n. 147, **Palazzo Dal Toso-Franceschini-Da Schio***, known as *Ca'd'Oro*, a gem of Venetian Gothic architecture of the 14th-15th c.; to the left, the garden of the 13th-c. church of S. Corona (see below); at n. 165-67, the *Casa Cogollo*, inaccurately but frequently called *Casa di Palladio*, with a late Renaissance facade (1559-62), possibly by G.A. Fasolo.

S. Corona.* This Dominican church, built from 1261 on, has an imposing marble central portal and an elegant campanile. The *interior* has Gothic nave with aisles, with a deep, raised Renaissance presbytery (1489), built by L. da Bologna. On various altars throughout the church are paintings by P. Veronese (1573), Giovanni Bellini, L. Bassano, and B. Montagna. Also, note the high altar (1669), the 15th-c. inlaid wooden choir, and the handsome 14th-c. reliquary, which contains a Thorn from the Crown of Christ, displayed only on Good Friday.

In the adjacent convent are the *Museo Naturalistico*, *(open Tue.-Sun., 9-5; Jul.-Aug., Sun. and holidays, 9-7; 1 Nov., 8 Dec., 6 Jan., 9-12:30; tel. 0444320440)* with exhibits of natural history, and the **Museo Archeologico** *(open same hours as the Museo Naturalistico)*, with collections ranging from the Stone Age to the High Middle Ages.

N. 25 of Contrà S. Corona is the Baroque *Palazzo Leoni Montanari*, the seat of a private museum featuring an interesting **art collection** *(open Fri.-Sun., 10-6)*. The paintings, of the 18th-c. Venetian school, are by outstanding artists such as P. Longhi, Canaletto, L. Carlevarijs, F. Guardi.

Piazza Matteotti. This broad green space is flanked by Palazzo Chiericati, site of the Museo Civico (see below), and, to the left, in a garden scattered with carved marble pieces, by the Teatro Olimpico (see below); behind the theater rises a medieval tower.

Museo Civico-Pinacoteca.* *Open same hours as the museums of S. Corona*. Located in **Palazzo Chiericati***, a work by Palladio (1550; the ceilings of three halls on the ground floor were frescoed by D. Brusasorci, G.B. Zelotti, and E. Forbicini), this museum opened in 1855. It includes a section of medieval art, and one with works from the Venetian school (16th-18th c.). In the first section, 13th-c. Venetian painting is represented by P. Veneziano, B. da Vicenza, G. Buonconsiglio, and others. In the second section are works by 15th-/16th-c. artists such as C. da Conegliano, B. Montagna, P. Veronese, J. Tintoretto, J. Bassano, and 17th-/18th-c. artists such as G. Carpioni, F. Maffei, S. and M. Ricci, P. della Vecchia, G. Zais, G.B. Tiepolo; there are also noteworthy still-lifes and landscapes from the 17th-18th c. Also works by B. Boccaccino, F. del Cairo, L. Giordano, and especially the Flemish artists H. Memling and Van Dyck; note the Virgin and Child*, a terracotta by J. Sansovino. The museum also has a precious collection of drawings by A. Palladio.

Teatro Olimpico.** *Open Tue.-Sun., 9:30-5; Jul.-Aug., until 7*. The theater is the last creation of Pal-

ladio (1580), completed by his son Silla in 1582-83. The largest of the reception halls is the so-called "Odeo", or Odeon, a meeting place for the Accademia degli Olimpici, built by V. Scamozzi in 1608, with frescoes by F. Maffei. Then comes the Antiodeo; from here, along stairways that lead to the upper loggias, you enter the theater proper. Built in wood and stucco, it imitates the forms of classical theaters with a semielliptical auditorium made up of thirteen rows and crowned by columns and a balustrade with statues. The lavish stage features an imposing permanent set on two registers, adorned with 95 statues; its three arches open up towards the architectural perspectives of the seven roads of the ancient city of Thebes, designed by V. Scamozzi.
S. Maria in Aracoeli. The church is one of Vicenza's few Baroque monuments, designed by G. Guarini and built by C. Borella (17th c.) to an elliptical plan.
S. Pietro. This Gothic church has a late 16th-c. facade and fine paintings inside. The nearby hospice (note the monument to its founder, in theatrium, by A. Canova) includes a 15th-c. cloister*.

Surrounding areas. Villa Valmarana ai Nani* and **La Rotonda***, about 3 km SW. Villa Valmarana (open 15 Mar.-5 Nov., Wed.-Sun., 10-12; in the aft., except Mon., 15 Mar.-Apr., 2:30-5:30; May-Sep., 3-6; Oct.-5 Nov., 2-5) was built in 1665-70, with later work in 1736 by F. Muttoni; it is renowned for the frescoes** by G.B. Tiepolo and his son Gian Domenico (1757). The famed **Villa La Rotonda***, to which you can easily walk from Villa Valmarana (open 15 Mar.-4 Nov., 10-12 and 3-6; Tue.-Sun., garden only; Wed. also inside), is Palladio's best known creation (1550); the upper section was completed by V. Scamozzi (1606). Note the dome frescoes by L. Dorigny.

Villa Adriana (Hadrian's Villa)*

Elev. 76 m; Lazio (Latium), province of Rome, township of Tivoli. This was the largest of the ancient Roman imperial villas. Hadrian oversaw the project for over 20 years, lavishing his thorough knowledge of late Hellenistic culture on it, building theaters and libraries as well as tributes to places he had seen in his extensive travel through the eastern provinces. Work ended only four years before Hadrian's death. This vast field of ruins, devastated, plundered, forgotten, and then rediscovered (1450), mingles the allure of history and archeology with a lovely landscape, near the Aniene River, at the base of the Monti Tiburtini.

Tour. Open 9-one hour before sunset. The archeological area can be toured following one of the itineraries available at the Museo Didattico, where the 18th-c. iconography relating to the villa is on exhibit.
Pecile. This huge rectangular quadriporticus (232 x 97 m) was used as a gymnasium; it also contained a garden and had a large pool in the center. Its western side stands atop a tall buttressing, containing the so-called Cento Camerelle, small rooms distributed over four storeys, used either as warehouses or slave quarters.
Teatro Marittimo. You enter from the NE corner of the Pecile through a large rectangular hall, the Sala dei Filosofi (it is believed that the seven niches in the apse contained statues of the Seven Greek Wise Men). The building takes its name from its shape (theater-like) and the decoration with marine subjects. It consists of two concentric structures: an Ionic-columned portico and a little round house, separated by a ring-shaped canal spanned with movable bridges. The house, placed on a little island, was a miniature Roman "domus," with rooms laid out around a peristyle. This was the emperor's personal retreat. South of the Teatro Marittimo are the ruins of a bath house; note the "heliocaminus," a round pool used for sunbathing, and a "frigidarium," or pool of cold water. A building with three exedrae, possibly a banquet hall, opens at the SE corner of the Pecile; in the middle is a rectangular hall with a basin, surrounded by four courtyards. You then continue through a long nymphaeum with peristyles decorated with polychrome marble floors.
Terme.* This huge bath house is divided into two sections: the Grandi Terme and Piccole Terme, or Large and Small Baths. The **Piccole Terme** may have been for women, and were surrounded by courtyards with exedrae and gardens; they comprised a large oblong room, an octagonal hall surrounded by smaller roooms, and a "frigidarium," or cold bath, with two curving basins.
In the **Grandi Terme**, for men, are the rests of the "frigidarium," with a large open-air rectangular pool and a semicircular basin; the adjacent hall has fine stuccoes in the vault. Grouped around a circular hall in the same complex are various rooms, one of them, the "calidarium," with a pool and three furnaces to heat it.
Canopo. Set in a little man-made valley girt by a wall to the east and by a two-storey row of rooms to the west, this is an architectural tribute to the Egyptian town of Canopus, famed for its huge Temple of Serapis. Along the edge of the long pool (119 x 18 m) are column fragments and casts of statues, among which are four caryatids and two Sileni. At the northern extremity, two sculptural groups, the Tiber and the Nile. The Serapeo, or Serapeum, was possibly used as a banquet hall.
Antiquarium. Closed for restoration. Located just to the right of the Canopo, this small museum contains statues, portraits, and mosaics; note the originals of the caryatids in the Canopo.
Pretorio. Just behind the Grandi Terme is this three-storey building, once believed to be barracks for Pretorian Guards, but actually warehouses. Note the series of rooms, still with plaster, possibly dwellings of the staff. From here, if you climb up to the olive grove to the east of the Piccole Terme you will note a large quadriporticus with a large fish-basin; below is an underground portico, reserved for the emperor's summertime strolls (on

the plaster, note signatures of 17th-c. visitors).

Palazzo Imperiale. The ruins of the imperial palace, believed to be the emperor's winter residence because of the discovery of a sophisticated heating system, covers a total area of 50,000 sq. m, comprising three complexes of residential and official rooms, distributed around three peristyles. To the SE is the *Piazza d'Oro*, or Golden Square, named for the lavish artifacts found here. On the central line of the square is the monumental semicircular *Ninfeo di Palazzo*, or Palace Nymphaeum, which may have been used as a summertime dining area. Adjacent to it is the *Sala dei Pilastri Dorici*, or Hall of the Doric Pillars, with a courtyard and fluted pillars.

Cortile delle Biblioteche. The Courtyard of the Libraries, which architecturally links the older parts of the villa with the later additions, takes its name from two multi-storey buildings, known respectively as the *Greek Library* and the *Latin Library*, with tower-shaped triclinia. On the southern side of the courtyard, under the terrace of the Palazzo Imperiale, is a *cryptoporticus* dating from the Republican age, with four galleries cut out of the tufa. On the NE side is a huge room with find ten guest rooms (*hospitalia*), with black-and-white mosaic floors; in each room there are three rectangular sleeping niches.

Terrazza di Tempe. At the SE corner of this terrace is the tree-shaded *Padiglione di Tempe*, a lofty three-storey belvedere overlooking the *Valle di Tempe*, a valley named after the Vale of Tempe, in Thessaly, sacred to Apollo.

Teatro Greco. This Greek Theater – near the *Ninfeo*, the little *Tempietto di Venere*, and the 18th-c. lodge called the *Casino Fede* – still possesses a few features of the original theater.

Viterbo*

Elev. 326 m, pop. 58,380; Lazio (Latium), provincial capital. This town has two noteworthy features: an abundance of cheerful fountains, and an intense, exquisite medieval atmosphere. Set on an irregular plain at the foot of the Cimini mountains, along the Via Cassia, this was the historical capital of Upper Latium, the ancient Tuscia of the Romans. It still has turreted city walls, with seven gates. The Palazzo dei Papi is a reminder of the looming papal presence in Viterbo's history. One memorable conclave resulted in the election of Gregory X, but only after 33 months of attempts, when the Capitano del Popolo Raniero Gatti, on the advice of St. Bonaventure, locked the quarrelsome cardinals in the Palazzo, tore the roof off the council hall, and stopped sending in food...

Historical note. The eight rows of great stone blocks on the Ponte del Duomo and a few fragments of city walls are all that remain of what was probably an Etruscan town. The name Viterbo is often said to have derived from the Latin "vetus urbs," or "old city." Certainly, the city's triangular plan is me-

dieval, based on the original village at the confluence of two rivers, where Piazza S. Lorenzo now stands. The nearby medieval district of S. Pellegrino, with 13th-c. architecture, reminds the visitor that the 1200s were Viterbo's most flourishing century. After long wars with Otto IV and Frederick II, and even the city of Rome, Viterbo became the capital of the papacy in 1257, when Pope Alexander IV fled here from the Eternal City. Many popes reigned here, until the people finally rebelled, and were excommunicated en masse. After two centuries, the papal state conquered Viterbo with an army. After surviving intact for ages, 20 years of Fascist rule, the Allied bombings of 1944, and the unbridled construction of the past 50 years have done more damage than the previous seven centuries.

Places of interest. Piazza del Plebiscito. The square is the political heart of the city since it is flanked by the medieval *Palazzo del Podestà* and the 18th-c. *Palazzo della Prefettura*, both adorned by columns with the lion symbolizing Viterbo. The adjacent *Palazzo dei Priori*, now city hall, was built in the 15th c. under Pope Sixtus IV and later renovated. The 15th-c. facade conceals a courtyard with a fine view of the river valley below. Also overlooking the square is the church of *S. Angelo in Spatha*, Romanesque but rebuilt; on the facade is a copy of the sarcophagus of the "Bella Galiana" (the original is in the Museo Civico) and, inside, a fragment of a 14th-c. triptych. In Via Ascenzi, note the handsome 14th-c. portal* of the Gothic church of *S. Maria della Salute*.

Via S. Lorenzo. Linking the political heart of Viterbo with the religious heart, this street runs through a dense medieval district. The 15th-c. *Palazzo Chigi* and the medieval *Torre di Borgognone* are noteworthy. Just beyond is the Piazza del Gesù, with the 11th-c. Romanesque *church* of the same name; note the 17th-c. fountain.

S. Maria Nuova.* This Romanesque church, one of Viterbo's oldest (1080), features – at the left corner of the facade – the pulpit from which St. Thomas Aquinas once preached. The *interior* is basilican; note the 15th-c. ceiling with tempera panels. Also worthy of note are a 13th-c. Crucifix; from the same period, a triptych* on leather; and artwork by Balletta, M. Giovannetti, and Pastura. On the left side of the church, you can enter the adjacent Longobard *cloister* (*open 10-1 and 4-7:30*).

Palazzo Farnese. Beyond the Ponte del Duomo, a bridge that includes a number of Etruscan blocks (visible on the right), you can recognize the palazzo by the twin-light mullioned windows on its right side, 14th-c. features which were employed in this Renaissance residence.

Cattedrale.* The Cathedral was built in the 12th c., and the campanile*, revealing Tuscan influences, a century later, while the facade was completed in 1570. *Inside*, note the columns on the capitals and the Cosmatesque floors; the late 15th-c. baptismal font by F. da Ancona; 14th-c. fragments of frescoes; and the late 13th-c. Madonna della Carbonara*.

oused in some recently restored rooms adjacent
o the Cathedral is the **Museo del Colle del Duomo** (*open 9-12:30 and 3-5:30; winter, until 4:30*); on
xhibit are church furnishings, reliquaries, paintings
nd sculptures.

alazzo dei Papi.** Built in 1255-67 as a papal
esidence, this is Viterbo's best known monument
nd the most important example of Viterbese Goth-
c architecture. Some exceedingly lively conclaves
ook place here. A staircase leads up to the battle-
ented facade; to the right runs the elegant log-
ia** (view*); the fountain dates from the 15th c.
ote the *Museo d'Arte Sacra*, with 17th-c. paintings
nd sculptures in wood and stone.

ia S. Pellegrino.* This is the main street of the
edieval district**, dotted with towers, mullioned
vindows, and elevated walkways. In the handsome
tle Piazza S. Pellegrino* note the **Palazzo degli
lessandri**, a 13th-c. home with balcony, next to
vo medieval towers. At n. 60 is the *Museo della
Macchina di S. Rosa* (*open summer, Wed.-Sun., 10-1
nd 4-8; winter, Fri.-Sun., 10-1 and 4-7*) in which doc-
ments, photographs and traditional objects tell the
ory of the festivity dedicated to the local saint.

ontana Grande. Beyond the 15th-c. *Case dei Gat-
** is the most famous fountain in Viterbo, func-
oning since 1279.

. Sisto.* Built in the 9th c. on the site of a pagan
emple, enlarged in the 12th-13th c., and rebuilt after
VWII, the church boasts an ancient apse and two
ell towers, one based on the transept, the other ris-
ng from the city walls. Note the unusual columns
ear the triumphal arch and the main altar.

asa Poscia. Another typical example of an early
4th-c. Viterbese home; note the "profferlo," distinctive
xterior staircase supported by a hanging arch.

. Maria della Verità. Built in the 12th c. just out-
ide the *city walls*, this church was badly damaged
n WWII; inside, note the Mazzatosta Chapel, with
escoes* by L. da Viterbo (1469).

luseo Civico.* *Open summer, 9-7; winter, 9-6; closed
Mon*. It is located in a former convent; note the Goth-
c cloister*. Among the *archeological finds* displayed
ere are sarcophagi, in particular the Roman one,
nown as the Sarcophagus of the Bella Galiana*,
vith hunting scenes. Among the *painters*, we should
mention S. del Piombo, Pastura, and G. F. Romanelli.
Noteworthy collection of pharmacy vases.

. Giovanni in Zoccoli. This 11th-c. church, rebuilt
fter the war, features a rose window surrounded
y the symbols of the four Evangelists. Inside, a
olyptych by Balletta.

. Rosa. This church and the 13th-c. saint's nearby
ome (*open Thu. and Sun., 9:30-12 and 4-5:30; sum-
ner, until 6*) form the saint's sanctuary; inside, an-
ther polyptych by Balletta.

. Marco. Founded by Cistercian monks and con-
ecrated by Innocent III in 1198, this church fea-
ures an apse frescoed by G. F. d'Avanzarano.

Rocca Albornoz. Cardinal Albornoz began work
n this fortress in the mid-14th c. Numerous popes
arried on construction, at one point summoning
Bramante (he designed the courtyard). Restored in
the 1960s, the Rocca now houses the Museo Archeologico Nazionale.

Museo Archeologico Nazionale.* *Open 9-7;
closed Mon*. The section that can now be viewed in
the Rocca Albornoz provides documentation of the
archaic Etruscan architecture of Viterbo and surrounding areas, through material excavated at San
Giovenale (1956-65) and Acquarossa (1966-78). Providing, respectively, material ranging from the Stone
Age to the Middle Ages, and the structure of an entire Etruscan city of the 7th c. B.C., the finds offer
such fascinating details as painted tiles from pitch
roofs, an entire portico, and primitive siding as well
as terracotta fixtures.

S. Francesco. The reconstruction done after WWII
retained the church's Gothic style (13th c.). Inside,
note the tomb of Pope Adrian V* (d. 1276), believed
to be the first monument by A. di Cambio.

Volterra*

Elev. 531 m, pop. 11,686; Toscana (Tuscany),
province of Pisa. "At the summit of a high hill,"
recalls Stendhal, Volterra surveys the surrounding heights between the valleys of the
Era and the Cècina. The landscape mingles
lush greenery with hard white lines of ridges
and erosion. This city is stern and medieval
in its skyline. All around are workshops where
craftsmen shape the alabaster taken from the
ground here. The Museo Guarnacci features
fine alabaster work from Etruscan times.

Historical note. Etruscan civilization reached this
town, originally called Velathri, relatively late,
around the end of the 7th c. B.C., probably from
Populonia along the course of the river Cècina. The
town flourished immediately, prospering on trade
in metals (it controlled Elba and Corsica) and lum-
ber, grain, and alabaster. The Etruscan walls extended for 7 km and enclose 102 hectares; this is

Viterbo: the medieval district

three times the length and area of the medieval walls, which encompass the modern town. Roman "Volaterrae" declined when the Pisa-Tortona road across the Apennines cut it out of the mainstream of commerce (109 B.C.). For more than a thousand years, Volterra slumbered quietly. The 13th-14th c. saw a prosperous town, fighting against local lords and the towns of San Gimignano, Pisa, Siena, and Florence; it was Florence that finally subjugated Volterra, and Lorenzo the Magnificent built the Fortress of the Rocca Nuova as an emblem of that subjugation.

Getting around. The area inside the town walls is closed to traffic from 10 to 1 and from 5 to 8 p.m. (from 10 to 8 on holidays); visitors heading for hotels are allowed in to drop off or pick up luggage. The route is a walking tour; you may choose to drive to the Balze (see below).

Places of interest. Piazza dei Priori.* This square has been the site of markets since A.D. 851. One of Italy's loveliest medieval squares, it is lined with handsome buildings, some of which are original.

Palazzo dei Priori.* Built in 1208-54, this massive crenelated building is punctuated by three rows of mullioned windows, and a lovely tower. Still serving as the town hall, on the first floor are the Sala del Consiglio, with frescoes and paintings, and the Sala della Giunta, with an inlaid 15th-c. desk.

Duomo.* Behind Palazzo dei Priori, overlooking Piazza S. Giovanni, this Romanesque cathedral dates from the 12th c.; the facade is simple and understated, while the interior is rich and lavishly covered with marble. Among the artists who worked on the cathedral: R. Cioli, M. da Fiesole, F. di Valdambrino, M. Albertinelli, and B. Gozzoli. Worthy of note are the finely wrought pulpit* on four columns, assembled in the 16th c. with 13th-c. sculptures; the 13th-c. gild and silver-plated polychrome wooden group; and the handsome Gothic wooden choir (1404). Facing the Duomo is the **Battistero**, or Baptistery, a fine octagonal 13th-c. building with a Romanesque portal and green-and-white striped front; inside, baptismal font* by A. Sansovino (1502).

Museo del Duomo di Arte Sacra. Open 16 Mar.-4 Nov., 9-1 and 3-6; 5 Nov.-15 Mar., Tue., 9-1; all-inclusive ticket with the Pinacoteca and Museo Guarnacci. Entrance at n. 1 in Via Roma, from the portico behind the bell tower of the Duomo. This museum has collections of sculpture, architectural fragments, metalwork, and paintings of a religious nature. Note the works by A. della Robbia, A. Pollaiolo, Giambologna, and R. Fiorentino.

Quadrivio dei Buomparenti.* This fascinating crossroads in the historic center features the very tall **Casa-Torre Buomparenti***, a 13th-c. tower-house, connected by a catwalk to the Torre Buonaguidi.

Via Ricciarelli. This road is lined with medieval and Renaissance churches and houses.

Pinacoteca* and **Museo Civico**. Open 16 Mar.-Nov., 9-7; 5 Nov.-15 Mar., 9-2; all-inclusive ticket with the Museo dell'Opera and Museo Guarnacci. At n. in Via dei Sarti, the art gallery and town museum are located in the Palazzo Solaini, attributed to A. d Sangallo the Elder. The fifteen halls feature Floren tine, Sienese, and Volterran artists, from the 14th-17t c.; among them are T. di Bartolo, B. di Giovanni, F. Valdambrino, D. Ghirlandaio, L. Signorelli, Ross Fiorentino, P. de Witte, B. Franceschini, D. da Volterra also medals and coins.

Palazzo Incontri-Viti. Open 16 Mar.-30 Sep., 9-Sat.-Sun. and holidays also 3-5:30; closed Tue.; te 058884047. This 16th-c. palazzo, with the entranc at n. 41 in Via dei Sarti, has a facade attributed to Ammannati. The interior is worth touring; note th Volterran alabasters*.

S. Michele Arcangelo. Overlooking the "piazzetta of the same name, this church has a handsome Ro manesque facade and, inside, a Della Robbia terra cotta and a painting by Il Pomarancio. Note the 13th c. Tuscan tower-house.

Teatro Romano. Open 16 Mar.-Nov., 11-5; closed i bad weather. This Roman theater, built under Au gustus, can be clearly seen from Via Lungo le Mur del Mandorlo, at the outer end of Via Guarnacci.

Fortezza. Not open to the public. Still used as prison, this is one of the most formidable fortresse built during the Italian Renaissance. From Piazza X. Settembre, you can enter the public gardens; not the interesting **Parco Archeologico Enrico Fiu mi** (open 11-5; closed in bad weather).

Museo Etrusco Guarnacci.* Open 16 Mar.-4 Nov. 9-7; 5 Nov.-15 Mar., 9-2; all-inclusive ticket with th Pinacoteca and Museo dell'Opera. Entrance at n. 1 in Via Don Minzoni; the museum features notewor thy **collections**** of Etruscan cinerary urns mad of tufa, alabaster, and terracotta, Etruscan sculp ture* (among which the famous **Ombra della Sera***, a very slender human figure in bronze), an a collection* of more than 3000 Etruscan, Greek and Roman coins.

Via Matteotti.* A charming road through the mos truly medieval section of Volterra. It is lined with 13th-c. tower-houses; at the end, on the left (n. 25 the stern Palazzo Maffei, 1527.

Porta all'Arco.* This gate is the center of the al abaster workshops; the gate itself is a mixture of Ro man and Etruscan features; note the three heads o Etruscan deities.

Viale dei Ponti. Beginning in Piazza Martiri della Libertà, this road offers a fine stroll with excellen views* of the Cècina valley.

Surrounding areas. At the **Balze***, 2 km NW, leav ing through Porta S. Francesco. The Balze are a vas and spectacular sink of gullies and ravines. Remains of Etruscan walls can be seen, though many othe buildings have been swallowed up by the slow pro gressive collapse of the soil. Note the 11th-c. abbey (being restored and reinforced).

Hotels, Restaurants, and Tourist Services

Hotels, Restaurants, and Tourist Services

The places indicated in this section correspond either to towns described in the A to Z section, or to towns mentioned in the routes or elsewhere, provided that they have comfortable hotels of some note. For every town, the province (abbreviation) and the postal code ⊠ are indicated. The telephone numbers include both area code and subscriber's number. Those calling Italy from abroad must dial the international code for Italy (0039), followed by the area code (including the 0) and the subscriber's number. All information has been carefully checked before going to print. Changes in the following data may occur at any time, and it is consequently advisable to check them before departure. Readers' observations and suggestions are gratefully accepted.

Public offices of interest to tourists. The symbol ⓘ refers to offices providing information and assistance to travellers and tourists (*APT, IAT, AIAT, EPT, ATL, Pro Loco*, and so on, according to various regional organizations), of which the address, telephone and fax numbers, and e-mail and/or web site (where available) are provided.

The symbol ⊿ precedes the address and telephone number of the *railway stations*. Free information service for FS – the State Railroad Company – is available by phoning 892021.

The symbol ⊹ indicates the closest (within 20 km) *highway exit* or exits, followed by the official number of the highway.

Airports are preceded by the symbol ✈. Other information includes the address and telephone number of the airport; the telephone/fax numbers of the main airlines; the bus or train links with the town.

Shipping companies are indicated with the symbol ⚓ , together with their address and telephone/fax numbers.

For the main *winter sports resorts*, a brief description of the facilities is provided following the symbol ⚐.

Hotels. The list contains a selection of hotels, arranged by categories according to the official classification established by the Italian Tourism Law (from ✿✿✿ to ✦). For every hotel listed, the following information is provided: the name, the address, the telephone and/or fax numbers, the e-mail and/or web site (where available), the total number of rooms, the periods in which the hotel is open (if it is seasonal), the closing periods. The available hotel facilities are indicated through symbols, namely: ☒ for air conditioning, ✿ for a garden or grounds, ⊿ for an outdoor pool, ⊿ for an indoor pool, ✗ for a tennis court, 🅿 for a private parking garage, 🅿 for special parking arrangements, Ⓟ for a parking lot, and ♿ for facilities for the disabled.

Restaurants. The list offered here includes restaurants chosen by TCI and arranged in five different categories (from ⫸ to ⫯). This is not an official classification, only an indicative ranking from the luxury restaurant to the most unpretentious according to some criteria: the level of quality, comfort, setting, and price. For each restaurant, information provided is: the name, address, telephone and/or fax numbers, e-mail and/or web site (where available), number of seats, days and periods of the year when the restaurant is closed. The number of seats available outdoors and indoors is indicated as follows: 35/60 capacity. The symbols are: ☒ advisable reservation, Ⓟ private parking, ✿ a garden, ☒ air conditioning. The symbol ⫸ specifies the type of cooking (either classic Italian, regional, or distinctly local, international, or sophisticated ["fine"] cuisine), while ⌂⚲ refers to an available list of quality wines.

For both hotels and restaurants a list of accepted *credit cards* is given. The relating symbols are ☒ for American Express, ☒ for Diner's, ☒ for Visa, and ☒ for Master Card.

References to maps. Public offices, items of interest to sightseers, hotels, and restaurants in the towns for which maps are provided are followed by a letter and number which refer to its location on the map itself (when there is more than one map, the references are preceded by a Roman numeral for the map).

Aeolian Islands / Isole Eolie (ME) ✉ 98055

🛈 *AA*, at Lipari, Corso Vittorio Emanuele 202, tel. 0909880095; www.netnet.it/aasteolie.

⛴ *NGI*, tel. 0909284091 (transportation to Milazzo).
Siremar, tel. 0909811312 (Transportation to Milazzo and Naples).
SNAV, tel. 0909812448 (transportation to Messina, Milazzo, Reggio di Calabria and, seasonal, to Naples and Palermo).

at Lipari ✉ 98055

Hotels and restaurants

*** **Villa Meligunis** Via Marte 7, tel. 0909812426, fax 0909880149; villameligunis@netnet.it; 37 rms.; ♨ ♿ 🅰🅴 ⊙ 🚃 ᴍᴄ.

*** **Carasco** township of Porto delle Genti, tel. 090 9811605, fax 0909811828; www.carasco.it; mid-April-mid-October; 89 rms.; ♨ ♒ 🅿 🅰🅴 ⊙ 🚃 ᴍᴄ.

*** **Giardino sul Mare** Via Maddalena 65, tel. 090 9811004, fax 0909880150; open April-October; 40 rms.; 🏠 ♨ ♒ 🅰🅴 ⊙ 🚃.

ᵀᵀ **Filippino** Piazza Municipio, tel. 0909811002 ⊠; fax 0909812878; www.filippino.it; filippino@net net.it; ℳ Aeolian (seafood) ◑ local and national; 100/100 capacity; closed Monday in the off season, for a certain period of time between November and December; 🏠 ❀ 🅰🅴 ⊙ 🚃 ᴍᴄ.

ᵀ **E Pulera** Via Diana, tel. 0909811158 ⊠; www.filip pino.it; ℳ Aeolian ◑ local and national; 80 capacity; open June-October only evening; ❀ 🅰🅴 🚃 ᴍᴄ.

at Panarea ✉ 98050

Hotels

*** **Cincotta** (no restaurant), Contrada S. Pietro, tel. 090983014, fax 090983211; open Easter-September; 29 rms.; 🏠 ♨ ♒ 🅰🅴 🚃.

*** **La Piazza** (no restaurant), Via S. Pietro, tel. 090 983154, fax 090983003; open April-October; 31 rms.; ♨ 🅰🅴 🚃.

at Malfa, on the Isola Salina ✉ 98050

Hotels

*** **Signum** Via Scalo 15, tel. 0909844222, fax 090 9844102; www.netnet.it/salina/signum; signun.sa lina@netnet.it; 24 rms.; ♨♿ ⊙ 🚃 ᴍᴄ.

at Santa Marina Salina, on the Isola Salina ✉ 98050

Restaurants

ᵀ **Porto Bello** Via Bianchi 1, tel. 0909843125 ⊠; ℳ Aeolian (seafood) ◑ local and national; 25/135 capacity; closed Wednesday in winter, November; 🅰🅴 ⊙ 🚃 ᴍᴄ.

at Strómboli ✉ 98050

Hotels

*** **La Sirenetta** township of Ficogrande, Via Marina 33, tel. 090986025, fax 090986124; www.netnet. it/hotel/lasirenetta; open April-October; 55 rms.; 🏠 ♨ ♒ ♿ ♨ 🅰🅴 ⊙ 🚃 ᴍᴄ.

at Vulcano ✉ 98050

Hotels

** **Eolian** at Porto Ponente, tel. 0909852151, fax 0909852153; open April-September; 88 rms.; ♨ ♒ ✕ 🅿 🅰🅴 ⊙ 🚃 ᴍᴄ.

Agrigento ✉ 92100

🛈 *AAPIT*, Viale della Vittoria 255, tel. 0922401352 (*B3*); aapit-agrigento@libero.it; *AA*, Via C.Battisti 15, tel. 20454 (*A2*); aastagrigento@oasi.net.

⛟ *Stazione F.S. (railway station)*, Piazza Marconi 3, tel. 892021.

🛤 *Imera* (A19 Palermo-Catania).

⛴ *Siremar*, at Porto Empedocle, tel. 0922636683 (transportation to Lampedusa).

Hotels and restaurants

*** **Kaos** Villaggio Pirandello, tel. 0922598622, fax 0922598770; www.athenahotels.com; 105 rms.; 🏠 ♨ ♒ ✕ 🅿 🅰🅴 ⊙ 🚃 ᴍᴄ; (*C1*).

*** **Villa Athena** Via Panoramica dei Templi 33, tel. 0922596288, fax 0922402180; www.athenahote ls.com; 40 rms.; 🏠 ♨ ♒ 🅿 🅰🅴 ⊙ 🚃 ᴍᴄ; (*B-C2*).

ᵀ **Ruga Reali** Cortile Scribani 8, tel. 092220370 ⊠; ℳ Sicilian (seafood) ◑ local and national; 66/44 capacity; closed Wednesday and Saturday at midday except July and August; 🅰🅴 ⊙ 🚃 ᴍᴄ; (*A2*).

at Villaggio Mosè, 8 km

Hotels

*** **G.H. dei Templi** Viale Leonardo Sciascia, tel. 0922610175, fax 0922606685; www.italiaabc.it/ az/ghdeitempli; 146 rms.; 🏠 ♨ ♒ 🅿 🅰🅴 ⊙ 🚃 ᴍᴄ.

*** **Tre Torri**, tel. 0922606733, fax 0922607839; www.mediatel.it/public/tre-torri; hotel3t@media tel.it; 118 rms.; 🏠 ♒ 🅿 🅰🅴 ⊙ 🚃 ᴍᴄ.

Alberobello (BA) ✉ 70011

🛈 *AA*, at Bari, *Ufficio turistico comunale*, Piazza Ferdinando IV 4, tel. 0804325171.

⛟ *Stazione Ferrovie del Sud-Est (railway station)*, Viale Margherita, tel. 0804323308.

🛤 *Gioia del Colle* (A14 Bologna-Taranto).

Hotels and restaurants

*** **Dei Trulli** Via Cadore 32, tel. 0804323555, fax 0804323560; www.inmedia.it/hoteldeitrulli; htrulli @inmedia.it; 28 rms.; 🏠 ♨ ♒ 🅿 🅰🅴 ⊙ 🚃 ᴍᴄ.

*** **Astoria** Viale Bari 11, tel. 0804323320, fax 080 4321290; 59 rms.; 🏠 ♨ 🅰 🅿 ♿ 🅰🅴 ⊙ 🚃 ᴍᴄ.

ᵀᵀᵀ **Il Poeta Contadino** Via Indipendenza 21, tel. 080 4321917 ⊠; ℳ Pugliese and fine cuisine ◑ Italian and international; 70 capacity; closed Sunday evening and Monday except in summer, for a period of time in January; 🏠 🅿 🅰🅴 ⊙ 🚃 ᴍᴄ.

ᵀᵀ **Chiusa di Chietri** SS 172 road at km 29.800, tel. 0804325481; www.lachiusadichietri.it; ℳ Pugliese and classic ◑ local and national; 600 capacity; closed Tuesday, November; 🏠 ❀ 🅿 🅰🅴 ⊙ 🚃 ᴍᴄ; also hotel.

ᵀᵀ **Trullo d'Oro** Via Cavallotti 27, tel. 0804321820; ℳ Pugliese and classic ◑ Italian and international; 150 capacity; closed Monday, January; 🏠 ❀ 🅿 🅰🅴 ⊙ 🚃.

Alghero (SS) ✉ 07041

🛈 *AA*, Piazza Portaterra 9, tel. 079979054; *EPT, Information Office*, Aeroporto Fertilia, tel. 935124; infotourism@infoalghero.it.

⛟ *Stazione Ferrovie della Sardegna (railway station)*, Via don Minzoni, tel. 079950785.

✈ *Airport* at Fertilia, tel. 079935282. Transportation from Piazza della Mercede.
Alitalia, information tel. 079935037.

Hotels and restaurants

*** **Calabona** township of Calabona, tel. 079975728, fax 079981046; www.hotelcalabona.it; open April-October; 110 rms.; 🏠 ♨ ♒ 🅰🅴 ⊙ 🚃 ᴍᴄ.

*** **Villa Las Tronas** Lungomare Valencia 1, tel. 079981818, fax 079981044; 29 rms.; 🏠 ♨ ♒ 🅿 🅰🅴 🚃 ᴍᴄ.

*** **Continental** (no restaurant), Via F.lli Kennedy 66, tel.

079975250, fax 079981046; hotel-calabona@tiscali.it; seasonal; 32 rms.; ♿ P AE ⑩ 🎫.

★★★ **Florida**, Via Lido 15, tel. 079950500, fax 079985424; hotelflorida@ssnet.it; 76 rms.; 🏄 ♿ ⚓ P AE ⑩ 🎫 MC.

★★★ **Riviera**, township of Lido San Giovanni, Via F.lli Cervi 6, tel. 079951230, fax 079984119; open March-October; 55 rms.; 🏄 ♿ ⚓ ☐ AE ⑩ 🎫 MC.

🍴 **La Lepanto** Via Carlo Alberto 135, tel. 079979116; ⅀ Sardinian 🍷 local; 160 capacity; closed Monday in winter; 🏄 AE ⑩ 🎫 MC.

🍴 **Al Tuguri** Via Maiorca 113, tel. 079976772 ☒; www.altuguri.it; ⅀ Sardinian (seafood) and Catalonian 🍷 local; 35 capacity; closed Sunday, mid-December-mid-January; 🏄 🎫.

Amalfi (SA) ✉ 84011

ℹ️ *AA*, Corso Repubbliche Marinare 19, tel. 089871107; aziendasoggiornoturismo@catamail.com.

🚉 *Stazione F.S. (railway station)*, at Salerno, bus service.

⛽ *Vietri sul Mare* (A3 Napoli-Reggio di Calabria).

⚓ *Alicost*, tel. 089873301 (ferryboat and hydrofoil, seasonal, to Capri, Ischia, Positano and Salerno). *Cooperativa Sant'Andrea*, tel. 089873190 (ferryboat seasonal to Positano and Salerno) *Navigazione Libera del Golfo*, tel. 0895520763 (ferryboat and hydrofoil to Positano, hydrofoil to Salerno and Sorrento).

Hotels and restaurants

★★★★ **Il Saraceno** Via Augustariccio 25, tel. 089831148, fax 831595; www.saraceno.it; open April-October; 56 rms.; 🏄 ♿ ⚓ P AE ⑩ 🎫.

★★★★ **Miramalfi** Via Quasimodo 3, tel. 089871588, fax 089871287; www.miramalfi.it; closed November-mid-December; 49 rms.; 🏄 ⚓ AE ⑩ 🎫 MC.

★★★ **Aurora** (no restaurant), Piazzale dei Protontini 7, tel. 089871209, fax 089872980; www.amalfinet.it/hotelaurora; open April-October and Christmas-Epiphany (6 January); 29 rms.; ♿ AE ⑩ 🎫 MC.

★★★ **Bellevue** (no restaurant) Via Nazionale 163, t. 089831349, fax 089831568; 13 rms.; 🏄 P AE ⑩ 🎫 MC.

★★★ **La Bussola** Lungomare dei Cavalieri 16, tel. 089871533, fax 089871369; www.labussolahotel.it; 63 rms.; 🏄 � P AE ⑩ 🎫 MC.

🍴 **La Caravella** Via M. Camera 12, tel. 089871029 ☒; www.ristorantelacaravella.it; ⅀ Amalfi (seafood) 🍷 local and national; 40 capacity; closed Tuesday, and for a certain period of time in November and December; 🏄 AE ⑩ 🎫 MC.

🍴 **Da Gemma** Via Fra' Gerardo Sasso 10, tel. 089871345 ☒; ⅀ classic (seafood) 🍷 local and national; 40/50 capacity; closed Wednesday except in summer, mid-January-mid-February; 🏄 AE ⑩ 🎫 MC.

🍴 **Smeraldino** Piazzale dei Protontini 1, tel. 089871070; ⅀ Amalfi (seafood) 🍷 local and national; 120 capacity; closed Wednesday, and for a certain period of time between January and February; P AE ⑩ 🎫.

Anagni (FR) ✉ 03012

ℹ️ *Pro Loco*, at Frosinone Piazza Innocenzo III, tel. 0775727852.

🚉 *Stazione F.S. (railway station)*, Anagni Scalo, bus service, tel. 0775767077.

⛽ *Anagni-Fiuggi T.* (A1 Milano-Roma-Napoli).

Hotel and restaurants

★★★★ **Villa La Floridiana**, Via Casilina at km 63.700 tel. 0775769960, fax 0775769961; www.vlf.cjt.net; closed for a certain period of time between August and September; 9 rms.; 🏄 ♿ P AE ⑩ 🎫

🍴 **Della Fontana** at Osteria della Fontana, Via Casilina 23, tel. 0775768577; www.paginegialle.it ⅀ Ciociaria and classic (seafood) 🍷 local and national; 188 capacity; closed Sunday and Monday evening, and for a certain period of time in August; 🏄 ❁ P AE ⑩ 🎫 MC.

Ancona ✉ 60100

ℹ️ *APTR*, Via Thaon de Revel 4, tel. 071358991; www.regione.marche.it; *IAT*, Stazione Marittima (ship passenger terminal), seasonal, tel. 071201183.

🚉 *Stazione F.S. (railway station)*, Piazza Rosselli, tel. 892021.

⛽ *Ancona Nord, Ancona Sud*, (A14 Bologna-Taranto).

✈ *Aeroporto Raffaello Sanzio*, Falconara Marittima, tel. 07128271. Bus service from the railway station and other stops in town. *Alitalia*, Airport, tel. 0712827234. *Air Dolomiti*, information tel. 07128271.

⚓ *Stazione Marittima (ship passenger terminal)*, molo S. Maria: information c/o *IAT*, tel. 071201183. *Adriatica*, tel. 071204915 (ferryboat to Croazia and Greece). *Superfast*, tel. 071200817 (ferryboat to Albania and Montenegro).

Hotels and restaurants

★★★★ **G.H. Palace** (no restaurant), Lungomare Vanvitelli 24, ✉ 60121, tel. 071201813, fax 0712074832 closed Christmas-Epiphany (6 January); 40 rms. 🏄 ☐ P AE ⑩ 🎫 MC.

★★★★ **Jolly Miramare** Rupi di Via XXIX Settembre 14 ✉ 60122, tel. 071201171, fax 071206823; www.jollyhotels.it; 89 rms.; 🏄 ♿ P AE ⑩ ♿ 🎫 MC.

★★★ **City** (no restaurant), Via Matteotti 112/114, ✉ 60121, tel. 0712070949, fax 0712070372; closed Christmas-Epiphany (6 January); 39 rms.; 🏄 ♿ ♿ AE ⑩ 🎫 MC.

🍴 **Passetto** Piazza IV Novembre 1, ✉ 60124, tel. 07133214 ☒; ⅀ Marche and classic 🍷 Italian and international; 80 capacity; closed Monday and Sunday evening, and for a certain period of time in August; 🏄 P AE ⑩ 🎫 MC.

🍴 **Moretta** Piazza Plebiscito 52, ✉ 60121, tel. 07202317 ☒; www.trattoriamoretta.com; ⅀ Marche (seafood) 🍷 local and national; 80/50 capacity closed Sunday, and for a certain period of time in January; ❁ 🏄 P AE ⑩ 🎫 MC.

at Portonovo, 12 km ✉ 60020

Hotels

★★★★ **Fortino Napoleonico** Via Poggio 166, tel. 071801450, fax 071801454; www.fastnet.it/market/fortino; 30 rms.; 🏄 ♿ P ⚓ ✕ ♿ AE ⑩ 🎫 MC.

★★★★ **Emilia** Via Poggio 149, tel. 071801145, fax 071801330; www.hotelemilia.com; period when closed may vary; 29 rms.; 🏄 ♿ ⚓ ✕ P ♿ AE ⑩ 🎫 MC.

Aosta/Aoste ✉ 11100

ℹ️ *Ufficio Informazioni Turistiche*: Piazza E. Chanoux 8, tel. 0165236627; www.regione.vda.it/turismo.

🚉 *Stazione F.S. (railway station)*, Piazza Manzetti 1, tel. 892021.

🏛 *Aosta Est, Aosta Ovest* (A5 Torino-Traforo Monte Bianco).

✈ *Aeroporto C. Gex*, Saint-Christophe, tel. 0165 303301. Bus service of town transport system. *Air Vallée*, information tel. 0165303304.

Hotels and restaurants

**** **Europe** Piazza Narbonne 8, tel. 0165236363, fax 016540566; hoteleurope@tiscali.it; 71 rms.; 🖾 🗐 🗐 🚾 🗁.

**** **Classhotel Aosta** Corso Ivrea 146, tel. 0165 541845, fax 0165236660; www.classhotel.com; info.aosta@classhotel.com; 105 rms.; 🖾 🗐 🗐 ♿ 🖾 ⓌⒹ 🚾 **MC**.

* **Mignon (no restaurant), Viale Gran S. Bernardo 7, tel. 016540980, fax 016543227; 26 rms.; 🗐 🗐.

¶¶ **Le Foyer** Corso Ivrea 146, tel. 016532136, fax 0165239474 ✉; 🕽 fine cuisine ⒬ Italian and international; 50 capacity; closed Monday evening and Tuesday, and for a certain period of time in January and July; 🗐 🖾 ⓌⒹ 🚾 **MC**.

¶¶ **Vecchia Aosta** Piazza Porte Pretoriane 4, tel. 0165 361186 ✉; 🕽 Val d'Aostan ⒬ Italian and international; 120/30 capacity; closed Wednesday (except in July and August), and for a certain period of time in February and November; 🖾 ⓌⒹ 🚾 **MC**.

¶¶ **Vecchio Ristoro** Via Tourneuve 4, tel. 0165 33238 ✉; 🕽 Fine cuisine from Val d'Aosta and Valtellina ⒬ Italian and international; 30 capacity; closed Sunday and Monday at midday (except holidays), June and for a certain period of time in November; 🖾 ⓌⒹ 🚾 **MC**.

at Porossan, 2 km ✉ 11100

Hotels

**** **Milleluci** (no restaurant), tel. 0165235278, fax 0165235284; www.milleluci.com; hotelmilleluci@hotelmilleluci.com; 33 rms.; ♨ ✕ 🗐 ♿ 🖾 ⓌⒹ 🚾 **MC**.

Aquileia (UD) ✉ 33051

ℹ *APT*, at Grado; *Pro Loco*, Piazza Capitolo, tel. 043191087.

🚉 *Stazione F.S. (railway station)*, at Cervignano del Friuli, tel. 892021; bus service.

🏛 *Palmanova* (A4 Torino-Milano-Trieste and A23 Palmanova-Tarvisio).

Hotels and restaurants

**** **Patriarchi** Via Giulia Augusta 12, tel. 0431 919595, fax 0431919596; www.hotelpatriarchi.it; patriarc@wavenet.it; 23 rms.; 🖾 ♨ 🗐 🖾 ⓌⒹ 🚾 **MC**.

¶ **Colombara** at La Colombara, Via S. Zilli 42, tel. 043191513 ✉; www.lacolombara.it; 🕽 Friulian (seafood) and classic ⒬ local and national; 100 capacity; closed Monday; 🗐 🖾 ⓌⒹ 🚾 **MC**.

Arezzo ✉ 52100

ℹ *APT*, Piazza della Repubblica 28, tel. 0575 377678; info@arezzo.turismo.toscana.it.

🚉 *Stazione F.S. (railway station)*, Piazza della Repubblica 1, tel. 892021; *Stazione La Ferroviaria Italiana*, Via G. Monaco 37, tel. 057539881.

🏛 *Arezzo* (A1 Milano-Roma-Napoli).

Hotels and restaurants

**** **Etrusco Palace Hotel** Via Fleming 39, tel. 0575 984067, fax 0575382131; www.etruscohotel.it; etrusco@etruscohotel.it; 80 rms.; 🖾 🗐 🗐 🗐 🖾 ⓌⒹ 🚾.

**** **Continentale** (no restaurant), Piazza Guido Monaco 7, tel. 057520251, fax 0575380485; www.hotelcontinentale.it; 73 rms.; 🖾 🗐 ♿ 🖾 ⓌⒹ 🚾.

**** **Minerva** Via Fiorentina 4, tel. 0575370390, fax

0575302415; www.hotel-minerva.it; 132 rms.; 🖾 ♨ 🗐 🗐 ♿ 🖾 ⓌⒹ 🚾.

**** **Piero della Francesca** Via Adigrat 1 ang. Via Romana, tel. 0575901333, fax 0575940436; www.hotelpierodellafrancesca.it; info@hotelpierodella francesca.it; 40 rms.; 🖾 🗐 ♿ 🖾 ⓌⒹ 🚾 **MC**.

¶¶ **Buca di San Francesco** Via S. Francesco 1, tel. 057523271 ✉; www.bucadisanfrancesco.3000.it; inbuca@tin.it; 🕽 Arezzo ⒬ local and national; 40 capacity; closed Monday evening and Tuesday and for a certain period of time in July; 🖾 🖾 ⓌⒹ 🚾.

¶ **Cantuccio** Via Madonna del Prato 76, tel. 0575 26830; www.il-cantuccio.it; 🕽 Tuscan ⒬ local and national; 60 capacity; closed Wednesday and for a certain period of time in July; 🖾 🖾 ⓌⒹ 🚾.

Arona (NO) ✉ 28041

ℹ *IAT*, Piazzale Duca d'Aosta, tel. 0322243601.

🚉 *Stazione F.S. (railway station)*, Piazzale Duca d'Aosta, tel. 892021.

🏛 *Arona* (A26 Voltri-Gravellona Toce).

⚓ *NLM-Navigazione Lago Maggiore*, tel. 800-551801 (boat to Angera, Luino, Stresa and Borromee Islands, Verbania and other places; seasonal service to Locarno and Swiss part of the lake).

Hotels and restaurants

**** **Atlantic** Corso della Repubblica 124, tel. 0322 46521, fax 032248358; www.atlanticarona.com; hotel@atlanticarona.com; 79 rms.; 🖾 🖾 ⓌⒹ 🚾 **MC**.

**** **Concorde** Via Verbano 1, tel. 0322249321, fax 0322249372; www.concordearona.com; hotel@concordearona.com; 82 rms.; 🖾 🗐 ♨ ♿ 🖾 ⓌⒹ 🚾 **MC**.

**** **Giardino** Corso della Repubblica 1, tel. 0322 45994, fax 0322249401; www.wel.it/hrgiardino; hgiardino@mythos.it; 56 rms.; 🖾 ♨ 🖾 ⓌⒹ 🚾 **MC**.

¶¶¶ **Taverna del Pittore** Piazza del Popolo 39, tel. 0322243366, fax 032248016 ✉; 🕽 fine cuisine ⒬ Italian and international; 50 capacity; closed Monday and for a certain period of time between December and January; 🖾 🖾 ⓌⒹ 🚾.

¶¶ **Pescatori** Lungolago Marconi 27, tel. 032248312 ✉; www.ristorantepescatori.it; 🕽 classic ⒬ national; 40 capacity; closed Tuesday, and for a certain period of time in January; 🖾 🖾 ⓌⒹ 🚾.

Àscoli Piceno ✉ 63100

ℹ *IAT*, Palazzo dei Capitani, Piazza del Popolo 1, tel. 0736253045; www.turismo.marche.it.

🚉 *Stazione F.S. (railway station)*, Piazzale Stazione 3, tel. 0736341004.

🏛 *Ascoli Piceno* (highway intersection S. Benedetto del Tronto-Ascoli Piceno).

⛷ at Monte Piselli, ski resorts.

Hotels and restaurants

**** **Gioli** (no restaurant), Viale De Gasperi 14, tel. 0736255550, fax 0736255550; closed Christmas-Epiphany (6 January); 56 rms.; 🗐 🖾 ⓌⒹ 🚾 **MC**.

**** **Pennile** (no restaurant), Via Spalvieri, tel. 0736 41645, fax 0736342755; 28 rms.; ♨ 🗐 🖾 ⓌⒹ 🚾.

¶¶ **Gallo d'Oro** Corso Vittorio Emanuele 13, tel. 0736 253520 ✉; 🕽 fine and Marche cuisine ⒬ local and national; 150 capacity; closed Sunday, Christmas-New Years's Day, and for a certain period of time between June and July; 🖾 🖾 ⓌⒹ 🚾 **MC**.

Asolo (TV) ✉ 31011

ℹ *IAT*, Piazza D'Annunzio 2, tel. 0423529046; apt.asolo@libero.it.

🚉 *Stazione F.S. (State railway station)*, at Montebelluna or Castelfranco Veneto; bus service.

🛣 *Treviso Nord* (A27 Mestre-Belluno).

Restaurants

🍴 **Ai Due Archi** Via Roma 55, tel. 0423952201 ☒; ᛙ classic ◠ local and national; 40 capacity; closed Wednesday evening and Thursday, and for a certain period of time in January; ᙀ ᙀ ᙀ ᙀ.

🍴 **Villa Razzolini Loredan** at Casella, 2 km, tel. 0423951088; ᛙ Venetian regional and classic ◠ Italian and international; 200 capacity; closed Monday evening and Tuesday, and for a certain period of time in January; ᙀ ✿ ᙀ ᙀ ᙀ ᙀ.

Assisi (PG)   ☒ 06081

ℹ *APT*, Piazza del Comune, tel. 075812534, www.umbria2000.it (*B3-4*).

🚉 *Stazione F.S. (railway station)*, Santa Maria degli Angeli, tel. 0758040272; bus service.

🛣 *Orte* (A1 Milano-Roma-Napoli), *Perugia* (Val di Chiana-Perugia highway intersection).

Hotels and restaurants

★★★ **Subasio** Via Frate Elia 2, tel. 075812206, fax 075816691; 61 rms.; ᙀ; ᙀ ᙀ ᙀ (*A1*).

★★★ **Dei Priori** Corso Mazzini 15, tel. 075812237, fax 075816804; www.assisihotel.net; closed mid-January-February; 34 rms.; ᙀ ᙀ ᙀ ᙀ ᙀ ᙀ (*B4*).

★★★ **Umbra** Via degli Archi 6, tel. 075812240, fax 075 813653; closed mid-January-mid-March; 25 rms.; ᙀ ᙀ ᙀ ᙀ ᙀ ᙀ (*B3*).

★★★ **Windsor Savoia** Viale Marconi 1, ☒ 06082, tel. 075812210, fax 075813659; hotelwindsor@edisons.it; 34 rms.; ᙀ ᙀ ᙀ ᙀ ᙀ ᙀ ᙀ (*B1-2*).

🍴 **Frantoio** Vicolo Illuminati, tel. 075812883; www.fontebella.com; fontebel@krenet.it; ᛙ Umbrian (truffles) ◠ Italian and international; 600 capacity; closed Monday from November to February; ✿ ᙀ ᙀ ᙀ ᙀ ᙀ; also hotel; (*A-B2*).

🍴 **Medio Evo** Via Arco dei Priori 4/B, tel. 075 813068 ☒; ᛙ Umbrian and classic ◠ local and national; 120 capacity; closed Wednesday and Sunday evening, and for a certain period of time in January and August; ᙀ ᙀ ᙀ ᙀ ᙀ (*B3*).

🍴 **La Fortezza** Vicolo della Fortezza 2/B, tel. 075 812418 ☒; www.lafortezzahotel.com; ᛙ Umbrian ◠ Italian and international; 55 capacity; closed Thursday, February, and for a certain period in July; ᙀ ᙀ ᙀ ᙀ (*B4*).

Bari   ☒ 70100

ℹ *ARET*, Piazza Moro 33/a, tel. 0805242361; www.pugliaturismo.com; (*D5*).

TCI, Via Melo 233, tel. 0805242448; negozio.bari@touringclub.it; (*D5*).

🚉 *Stazione F.S. (railway station)*, Piazza Moro, tel. 892021; *Stazione Ferrovia Bari-Nord*, Piazza Moro 50/b, tel. 0805789511; *Station Ferrovie Appulo-Lucane*, Piazza Aldo Moro 51, tel. 080 5725227; *Station Ferrovie del Sud-Est*, Via Oberdan, tel. 0805462446.

🛣 *Bari Nord, Bari Sud* (A14 Bologna-Taranto).

✈ *Aeroporto Civile (city airport)* at Palese, tel. 0805835230.

Air One, reservations tel. 8488-48880.

Alitalia, reservations tel. 8488-65641.

⚓ *Stazione Marittima (ship passenger terminal)*, Molo San Vito, information tel. 0805216860.

Adriatica di navigazione, tel. 0805530360 (ferryboat to Albania and Croazia).

Morfimare, tel. 0805210022 (ferryboat to Monte negro).

Portrans, tel. 0805211416 (ferryboat to Greec hydrofoils to Albania).

Ventouris Ferries, tel. 0805212840 (ferryboat Greece).

Hotels and restaurants

★★★ **G.H. Ambasciatori** Via Omodeo 51, ☒ 7012 tel. 0805010077, fax 0805021678; www.hotel-an basciatori.it; prenota@hotel-ambasciatori.it; 17 rms.; ᙀ ᙀ ᙀ ᙀ ᙀ ᙀ ᙀ ᙀ; (*off map*).

★★★ **Mercure Villa Romanazzi Carducci** Via Capruz 326, ☒ 70124, tel. 0805427400, fax 08 5560297; www.villaromanazzi.com; 117 rms.; ᙀ ᙀ ᙀ ᙀ ᙀ; (*D4*).

★★★ **Palace Hotel** Via Lombardi 13, ☒ 70122, tel. 08 5216551, fax 0805211499; www.palacehotelba it; 196 rms.; ᙀ ᙀ ᙀ ᙀ ᙀ ᙀ; (*C4*).

★★★ **Victor Clarine** (no restaurant), Via Nicolai 69/7 ☒ 70122, tel. 0805216600, fax 080521260 www.victorservice.com; 77 rms.; ᙀ ᙀ ᙀ ᙀ ᙀ ᙀ; (*D4*).

★★★ **Boston** (no restaurant), Via Piccinni 155, ☒ 70122, tel. 0805216633, fax 0805246802; www. media.it/boston; 70 rms.; ᙀ ᙀ ᙀ ᙀ ᙀ; (*C4*)

★★★ **7 Mari**, Via Verdi 60, ☒ 70123, tel. 080534150 fax 0805344482; 56 rms.; ᙀ ᙀ ᙀ ᙀ ᙀ; (*o. map*).

🍴 **Ai 2 Ghiottoni** Via Putignani 11, ☒ 70121, te 0805232240; ᛙ Pugliese and classic ◠ Italia and international; 180 capacity; closed Sunda and for a certain period in August; ᙀ ᙀ ᙀ ᙀ; (*C5*).

🍴 **Nuova Vecchia Bari** Via Dante 47, ☒ 70121, te 0805216496 ☒; ᛙ Bari ◠ local and national; 10 capacity; closed Friday and Sunday evening, ar for a certain period of time in August; ᙀ ᙀ (*C5*

🍴 **Piccinni** Via Piccinni 28, ☒ 70122, tel. 08 5211227 ☒; ᛙ Pugliese and classic ◠ Italia and international; 140/100 capacity; closed Su day and for a certain period of time in August; ᙀ ✿ ᙀ ᙀ; (*C5*).

Bellagio (CO)   ☒ 2202

ℹ *IAT*, Piazza Mazzini, tel. 031950204; www.bella ᴳ olakecomo.com.

🚉 *Stazione F.S. (railway station)*, at Lecco, Como ᴳ Varenna; bus and boat services.

🛣 *Como Sud* (A9 Lainate-Como-Chiasso).

⚓ *NLC-Navigazione Lago di Como*, tel. 0319501 03195980 (boat to Mandello del Lario, hydrofoil Colico, Como and other places; ferryboat to Ca denabbia, Menaggio and Varenna).

🎿 at Parco San Primo, ski resorts.

Hotels and restaurants

★★★ **G.H. Villa Serbelloni** Via Roma 1, tel. 03 950216, fax 031951529; www.villaserbelloni. inforequest@villaserbelloni.it; open April/mic November; 83 rms.; ᙀ ᙀ ᙀ ᙀ ᙀ ᙀ ᙀ ᙀ ᙀ.

★★★ **Belvedere** Via Valassina 31, tel. 031950410, fa 031950102; www.belvederebellagio.com; ope April-October; 70 rms.; ᙀ ᙀ ᙀ ᙀ ᙀ ᙀ ᙀ; ope

★★★ **Florence** Piazza Mazzini 46, tel. 031950342, fa 031951722; open April-October; 32 rms.; ᙀ ᙀ

★★ **Fioroni** Viale D. Vitali 2, tel. 031950392, fa 031951970; 14 rms.; ᙀ ᙀ ᙀ ᙀ ᙀ.

🍴 **Silvio** Via Carcano 12, tel. 031950322 ☒; www bellagiosilvio.com; belsilv@tin.it; ᛙ Lake Com ◠ national; 200/100 capacity; closed Epiphany January)-February; ✿ ᙀ ᙀ; also hotel.

Bergamo ✉ 24100

🛈 *APT*, Viale V. Emanuele 20, tel. 035210204; www.apt.bergamo.it (*C2-3*); *IAT*, Vicolo Aquila Nera 2, tel. 035242226; iat.bergamo@apt.bergamo.it (*A2*).

🚉 *Stazione F.S. (railway station)*, Piazzale Marconi 7, tel. 892021.

🚆 *Bergamo* (A4 Torino-Milano-Trieste).

✈ *Airport* at Orio al Serio, tel. 035326111. Bus service from the coach station of Autolinee di Bergamo and the central railway station in Milan.
Air Dolomiti, reservations tel. 800-13366.
Air One, reservations tel. 8488-48880.
Azzurra Air, Via Paleocapa 3/D, tel. 035 4120511 (*E4*).
Gandalf, airport, tel. 0354595011.
Volare Airlines, reservations tel. 800-454000.

Hotels and restaurants

★★ **Cappello d'Oro** Viale Giovanni XXIII 12, ✉ 24121, tel. 035232503, fax 035242946; www.hotelcappellodoro.it; 92 rms.; 🅿 🆓 🅿 🆑 🌐 🍽 🆎 (*D3*).

★★ **Starhotel Cristallo Palace** Via B. Ambiveri 35, ✉ 24126, tel. 035311211, fax 035342031; 90 rms.; 🅿 🛁 🆓 🆑 🌐 🍽 🆎 (*off map*).

★★ **Arli** (no restaurant), Largo Porta Nuova 12, ✉ 24122, tel. 035222014, fax 035239732; arli@spm.it; 56 rms.; 🅿 🆓 🆑 🌐 🍽 🆎 (*D3*).

★★ **Piemontese** (no restaurant), Piazza G. Marconi 11, ✉ 24122, tel. 035242629, fax 035230400; 57 rms.; 🅿 🆓 🆑 🌐 🍽 🆎 (*E4*).

🍴 **Da Vittorio** Viale Giovanni XXIII 21, ✉ 24121, tel. 035218060 ✉, fax 035210805; www.davittorio.com; 🍽 classic 🍷 Italian and international; 130 capacity; closed Wednesday, and for a certain period of time in August; 🅿 🆓 🆑 (*D4*).

🍴 **Lio Pellegrini** Via S. Tomaso 47, ✉ 24121, tel. 035247813 ✉; www.liopellegrini.it; 🍽 Tuscan and fine cuisine 🍷 Italian and international; 50 capacity; closed Monday and Tuesday at midday, and for a certain period of time in January and in August; 🌐 🆓 🍽 🆎 (*B4*).

Giopì e la Margì Via Borgo Palazzo 27, ✉ 24125, tel. 035242366 ✉; www.giopimargi.com; 🍽 Lombard 🍷 local; 80 capacity; closed Sunday evening and Monday and for a certain period of time in January and August; 🅿 🆓 🍽 🆎 (*C5*).

Bergamo Alta

Hotels and restaurants

★ **Agnello d'Oro** Via Gombito 22, ✉ 24129, tel. 035 249883, fax 035235612; 20 rms.; 🆑 🌐 🆎 (*A2*).

Trattoria del Teatro Piazza Mascheroni 3, ✉ 24129, tel. 035238862; 🍽 Bergamasque 🍷 local and national; 80 capacity; closed Monday and for a certain period of time in July and August; 🅿; (*A1*).

Bologna ✉ 40100

🛈 *IAT*, Piazza Maggiore 6, tel. 051246541; www.comune.bologna.it/bolognaturismo (*D3*); *Information Office,* Stazione F.S., Piazza Medaglie d'Oro 4, tel. 051246541 (*A3*); *Information Office* c/o airport, arrivals terminal, tel. 051246541.
TCI, Strada Maggiore 29, tel. 0512961476; shop.bologna@touringclub.it (*D5*).

🚉 *Stazione F.S. (railway station)*, Piazza Medaglie d'Oro 1, tel. 892021.

🚆 *Bologna-Arcoveggio* (A13 Bologna-Padova); *Bologna-Borgo Panigale* (A14 Bologna-Taranto); *Bologna-Casalecchio* (A1 Milano-Roma-Napoli); *Bologna-S. Lazzaro* (A14 Bologna-Taranto).

✈ *Aeroporto G. Marconi*, at Borgo Panigale, tel. 0516479615. Service with "aerobus" from railway station (*A3*).
Air Littoral, c/o airport, tel. 0516472064.
Air Sicilia, c/o airport, tel. 0516472339.
Air Vallée, reservations tel. 0165303303.
Alitalia, Via Riva di Reno 65, tel. 0516300111 (*C3*).
Alitalia, information tel. 8488-65643
Italy First, reservations tel. 800-739855.
Meridiana, c/o airport, tel. 0516479271.
Volare, reservations tel. 800-222166.

Hotels

★★★L **G.H. Baglioni** Via Indipendenza 8, ✉ 40121, tel. 051225445, fax 051234840; www.baglionihotels.com; 125 rms.; 🅿 🆓 🆑 🌐 🍽 🆎 (*C3*).

★★★ **Al Cappello Rosso** (no restaurant), Via de' Fusari 9, ✉ 40123, tel. 051261891, fax 051227179; cappellorosso@tin.it; 33 rms.; 🅿 🆓 🆑 🌐 🍽 🆎 (*D3*).

★★★ **Boscolo Hotels Tower** Viale Lenin 43, ✉ 40138, tel. 0516010909, fax 0516010700; www.boscolohotels.com; htower@boscolo.com; 150 rms.; 🅿 🆓 🅿 🆑 🌐 🍽 🆎 (*D-E6, off map*).

★★★ **Internazionale** (no restaurant), Via dell'Indipendenza 60, ✉ 40121, tel. 051245544, fax 051 249544; www.monrifhotels.it; 116 rms.; 🅿 🆓 🔥 🆑 🌐 🍽 🆎 (*B4*).

★★★ **Royal Hotel Carlton** Via Montebello 8, ✉ 40121, tel. 051249361, fax 051249724; www.monrifhotels.it; 240 rms.; 🅿 🛁 🆓 🔥 🆑 🌐 🍽 🆎 (*B3*).

★★★ **Starhotel Excelsior** Via Pietramellara 51, ✉ 40121, tel. 051246178, fax 051249448; www.starhotels.it; 193 rms.; 🅿 🆓 🔥 🆑 🌐 🍽 🆎 (*A3*).

★★★ **Astoria** (no restaurant), Via F.lli Rosselli 14, ✉ 40121, tel. 051521410, fax 051524739; www.astoria.bo.it; 38 rms.; 🅿 🛁 🆓 🅿 🆑 🌐 🍽 🆎 (*A2*).

★★★ **Dei Commercianti** (no restaurant), Via de' Pignattari 11, ✉ 40124, tel. 051233052, fax 051 224733; www.cnc.it/bologna; hotcom@tin.it; 34 rms.; 🅿 🆓 🆑 🌐 🍽 🆎 (*D3-4*).

★★★ **Il Guercino** (no restaurant), Via Luigi Serra 7, ✉ 40129, tel. 051369893, fax 051369893; www.guercino.it; guercino@guercino.it; 41 rms.; 🅿 🆓 🅿 🔥 🆑 🌐 🍽 🆎 (*A4, off map*).

★★★ **Orologio** (no restaurant), Via IV Novembre 10, ✉ 40123, tel. 051231253, fax 051260552; www.cnc.it/ bologna; 34 rms.; 🅿 🆓 🆑 🌐 🍽 🆎 (*D3*).

★★★ **Paradise** (no restaurant), Vicolo Cattani 7, ✉ 40126, tel. 051231792, fax 051234591; www.informatutto.it/hotelparadise; closed Christmas-Ephiphany (6 January) and August; 8 rms.; 🅿 🛁 🆑 🌐 🍽 🆎 (*C4*).

★★★ **Re Enzo** (no restaurant), Via Santa Croce 26, ✉ 40122, tel. 051523322, fax 051554035; 51 rms.; 🅿 🆓 🆑 🌐 🍽 🆎 (*C1*).

★★★ **Touring** (no restaurant), Via de' Mattuiani 1/2, ✉ 40124, tel. 051584305, fax 051334763; www.hoteltouring.it; 36 rms.; 🅿 🆓 🔥 🆑 🌐 🍽 🆎 (*E4*).

Restaurants

🍽🍴 **Pappagallo** Piazza Mercanzia 3, ✉ 40125, tel. 051231200, fax 051232807 ✉; 🍽 Emilian and classic 🍷 Italian; 80 capacity; closed Sunday and for a certain period of time in August; 🅿 🆓 🌐 🍽 🆎 (*D4*).

🍴🍴 **Battibecco** Via Battibecco 4, ✉ 40123, tel. 051223298, fax 051263579 ✉; 🍽 Emilian and classical 🍷 Italian and international; 50/10 capacity; closed Saturday at midday and Sunday; 🅿 🆓 🌐 🍽 🆎 (*D3*).

🍴🍴 **Bitone** Via Emilia Levante 111, ✉ 40139, tel. 051546110 ✉; 🍽 Emilian 🍷 Italian; 90 capacity; closed Monday and Tuesday, August; 🅿 🆓 🌐 🍽 🆎 (*off map*).

🍴🍴 **Rodrigo** Via della Zecca 2/H, ✉ 40121, tel. 051 235536, fax 051220445 ✉; 🍽 Bolognese and

¶¶ classic ◊☖ Italian and international; closed Sunday, and for a certain period of time in August; 🅿 ⒶⒺ ⓓ 🚋 ᴍᴄ; (D3).

¶¶ **Al Cambio** Via Stalingrado 150, ✉ 40128, tel. 051328118 ✉; ᴗ fine and Emilian cuisine ◊☖ local and national; 44 capacity; closed Sunday, August and Christmas-Epiphany (6 January); 🅿 🅿 ⒶⒺ ⓓ 🚋 ᴍᴄ; (A5, off map).

¶¶ **Diana** Via dell'Indipendenza 24, ✉ 40121, tel. 051231302 ✉; ᴗ Emilian ◊☖ national; 160 capacity; closed Monday, and for a certain period of time in January and August; 🅿 ❀ ⒶⒺ ⓓ 🚋 ᴍᴄ; (C3-4).

¶¶ **Panoramica** Via San Mamolo 31, ✉ 40136, tel. 051580337 ✉; ᴗ Emilian and classic ◊☖ Italian and international; 40 capacity; closed Sunday and for a certain period of time in August; ❀ 🅿 ⒶⒺ ⓓ 🚋 ᴍᴄ; (F3).

¶¶ **Biagi alla Grada** Via della Grada 6, ✉ 40122, tel. 051553025; ristorantebiagiallagrada@hot mail.com; ᴗ Bolognese ◊☖ local and national; 100 capacity; closed Tuesday and Christmas-Epiphany (6 January); 🅿 ⒶⒺ ⓓ 🚋 ᴍᴄ; (C1).

¶¶ **Grassilli** Via del Luzzo 3, ✉ 40125, tel. 051 222961 ✉; ᴗ Bolognese ◊☖ Italian; 35 capacity; closed Wednesday evening and holidays evening, mid-July-mid August and Christmas-Epiphany (6 January); ⒶⒺ ⓓ 🚋; (D4).

¶ **La Terrazza** Via del Parco 20, ✉ 40138, tel. 051 531330 ✉; ᴗ Mediterranean ◊☖ local and national; 35 capacity; closed Sunday and for a certain period of time in August; ⒶⒺ ⓓ 🚋; (D6, off map).

Bolzano/Bozen   ✉ 39100

🆔 *AA*, Piazza Walther 8, tel. 0471307001; www. bolzano-bozen.it; *Alto Adige Marketing*, Piazza Parrocchia 11, tel. 0471413809; www.hallo.com.

🚆 *Stazione F.S. (railway station)*, Via Garibaldi, tel. 892021.

🕂 *Bolzano Sud or Bolzano Nord* (A22 Brennero-Modena).

✈ *Aeroporto Dolomiti*, tel. 0471255255. Taxi service from town.
Austrian Airlines, reservations tel. 0642014579.

Hotels and restaurants

★★★ **Greif** (no restaurant), tel. 0471318000, fax 0471 318148; www.greif.it; 33 rms.; 🅿 ⒶⒺ ⓓ 🚋 ᴍᴄ.

★★★ **Parkhotel Laurin** Via Laurin 4, tel. 0471311000, fax 0471311148; www.laurin.it; info@laurin.it; 96 rms.; 🅿 ♨ ♒ ⓓ ⒶⒺ ⓓ 🚋.

★★★ **Scala-Stiegl** Via Brennero 11, tel. 0471976222, fax 0471981141; www.scalahot.com; info@scala hot.com; 65 rms.; ♨ ♒ 🗐 🅿 ⓓ 🚋.

★★★ **Magdalenerhof** Via Rencio 48/A, tel. 0471 978267, fax 0471981076; www.tophotels.com/ magdalenerhof; 39 rms.; 🅿 ♨ ♒ 🗐 🅿 ⓓ ⒶⒺ ⓓ 🚋 ᴍᴄ.

★★★ **Pirker** Via Merano 52, tel. 0471250103, fax 0471251514; hotel.pircher@dnet.it; 22 rms.; 🅿 ♨ ♒ 🗐 🅿 ⓓ 🚋 ᴍᴄ.

¶¶¶ **Laurin** Via Laurin 4, tel. 0471311000, fax 0471 311148 ✉; www.laurin.it; ᴗ Mediterranean (seafood) ◊☖ italian and international; 128 capacity; 🅿 ❀ ⒶⒺ ⓓ 🚋 ᴍᴄ; Park Hotel Laurin chain.

¶¶ **Rastbichler** Via Cadorna 1, tel. 0471261131 ✉; ᴗ classic ◊☖ Italian and international; 60 capacity; closed Saturday at midday and Sunday, and for a certain period of time between January and February, and in August; ❀ 🅿 ⒶⒺ ⓓ 🚋 ᴍᴄ.

¶ **Vögele** Via Goethe 3, tel. 0471973938 ✉; wirtshaus.voegele@tin.it; ᴗ Alto-Adige ◊☖ Italian and international; 38 capacity; closed Sunday and Saturday evening; 🚋 ᴍᴄ.

Bordighera (IM)   ✉ 18012

🆔 *IAT*, Via Vittorio Emanuele 172, tel. 0184262322.

🚆 *Stazione F.S. (railway station)*, Piazza Eroi della Libertà, tel. 892021.

🕂 *Bordighera* (A10 Ponte S. Luigi-Genova).

Hotels and restaurants

★★★ **G.H. del Mare** Via Portico della Punta 34, te 0184262201, fax 0184262394; www.grandhote delmare.it; closed mid-October-Christmas; 9⁞ rms.; 🅿 ♨ ♒ ✕ 🅿 🗐 ⓓ ⒶⒺ ⓓ 🚋 ᴍᴄ.

★★★ **Parigi** Lungomare Argentina 16/18, tel. 018⁞ 261405, fax 0184260421; info@hotelparigi.com 55 rms.; ♒ ⒶⒺ ⓓ ⒶⒺ 🚋 ᴍᴄ.

★★★ **Astoria** Via T. Tasso 2, tel. 0184262906, fax 018 2621612; www.bordighera.it/astoria; closed a ce⁞ tain period of time between November and De⁞ cember; 24 rms.; ⒶⒺ ⓓ 🚋 ᴍᴄ.

★★★ **Mirelia** Via C. Balbo 7/Via Roseto 10, tel. 018⁞ 254891, fax 0184261377; 15 rms.; ♨ 🅿 ⒶⒺ ⓓ 🚋 ᴍᴄ.

★★★ **Villa Elisa** Via Romana 70, tel. 0184261313, fa⁞ 0184261942; www.villaelisa.com; villaelisa@m⁞ sterweb.it; closed November-mid-December; 3⁞ rms.; 🅿 ♨ ♒ 🅿 ⓓ ⒶⒺ ⓓ 🚋 ᴍᴄ.

¶¶¶ **La Via Romana** Via Romana 57, tel. 018⁞ 266681, fax 0184267549 ✉; www.laviaromana.i⁞ viaromana@masterweb.it; ᴗ Ligurian and Sici⁞ ian (seafood) ◊☖ Italian and international; 45 ca⁞ pacity; closed Wednesday and Thuesday at mi⁞ day, and a certain period of time in October; 🅿 ⒶⒺ ⓓ 🚋 ᴍᴄ.

¶¶¶ **Carletto** Via Vittorio Emanuele 339, tel. 018⁞ 261725 ✉; ᴗ fine and Ligurian cuisine ◊☖ Italia⁞ and international; 35 capacity; closed Wednesda⁞ for a certain period of time in July, and betwee⁞ November and December; 🅿 ⒶⒺ ⓓ 🚋 ᴍᴄ.

Brescia   ✉ 25100

🆔 *APT*, Corso Zanardelli 38, tel. 0304341⁞ www.bresciaholiday.com; (C4).
TCI corso Cavour 35, tel. 03046458; tci.bresci⁞ @numerica.it. (C4)

🚆 *Stazione F.S. (railway station)*, Piazzale Stazione tel. 892021; *Stazione FNM*, Piazzale Stazione, te⁞ 03046027.

🕂 *Brescia Centro* (A21 Torino-Brescia), *Bresci⁞ Ovest* (A4 Torino-Milano-Trieste).

✈ *Aeroporto Gabriele D'Annunzio* at Montichiar⁞ tel. 0309656511. Shuttle service from the rai⁞ way station.
Ryan Air, reservations tel. 199-114114 (pay call)⁞

Hotels and restaurants

★★★ **Vittoria** Via X Giornate 20, ✉ 25121, tel. 03⁞ 280061, fax 030280065; www.hotelvittoria.com info@hotelvittoria.com; 66 rms.; 🅿 🗐 🅿 ⒶⒺ ⓓ 🚋 ᴍᴄ; (B-C3).

★★★ **Ambasciatori** Via S. Crocefissa di Rosa 92, ✉ 25128, tel. 030399114, fax 030381883; www.bre⁞ ciaholiday.com/ambasciatori; ambascia@tin. it; 6⁞ rms.; 🅿 🗐 🅿 ⓓ ⒶⒺ ⓓ 🚋 ᴍᴄ; (off map).

★★★ **Park Hotel Ca' Nöa** Via Triumplina 66, ✉ 2512⁞ tel. 030398762, fax 030398764; canoa@protos.⁞ 80 rms.; 🅿 🗐 🅿 🗐 ⒶⒺ ⓓ 🚋 ᴍᴄ; (A3, off map).

★★★ **UNA Hotel Brescia** Viale Europa 45, ✉ 2513⁞ tel. 0302018011, fax 0302009741; unabresci⁞ @unahotel.com; 145 rms.; 🅿 ♒ 🅿 🗐 ⒶⒺ ⓓ 🚋 ᴍᴄ (A5, off map).

¶¶¶ **La Sosta** Via S. Martino della Battaglia 20, ✉ 25121, tel. 030295603, fax 030292589 ✉

www.lasosta.it; lasosta@tin.it; ⅀⅀ Brescian and classic ⓓ⅄ Italian and international; 120 capacity; closed Monday evening and Sunday and for a certain period of time in January and August; 🏢 ✱ 🅿 🄰🄴 ⓓ 🚾 🅼🄲; (C4).

¶ **Canton del Vescovo** Via A. Callegari 2/C, ✉ 25121, tel. 0303759801 ✕; luca.guerrin@tiscali.it; ⅀⅀ classic ⓓ⅄ Italian and international; 50 capacity; closed Monday; 🏢 ✱ 🄰🄴 ⓓ 🚾 🅼🄲 (C5).

Bressanone/Brixen (BZ)   ✉ 39042

ℹ *Associazione Turistica*, Viale Stazione 9, tel. 0472836401; info@brixen.org.

🚉 *Stazione F.S. (railway station)*, Piazza della Stazione 21, tel. 0472833368.

⛪ *Bressanone* (A22 Brennero-Modena).

⛷ at Plose, ski resorts; included in the area of *Dolomiti Superski*.

Hotels and restaurants

★★★ **Elephant** Via Rio Bianco 4, tel. 0472832750, fax 0472836579; www.acs.it/elephant; elephant.brix en@acs.it; open mid-March-October and December/ Christmas-Epiphany (6 January); 44 rms.; 🏢 ♨ ≋ ✕ 🔲 🅿 🄰🄴 ⓓ 🚾 🅼🄲 .

★★★ **Grüner Baum** Via Stufles 11, tel. 0472274100, fax 0472274101; www.gruenerbaum.it; closed for a certain period of time between November and December; 80 rms.; ♨ ≋ ≋ 🔲 🅿 🄰🄴 ⓓ 🚾 🅼🄲

★★★ **Bel Riposo** (no restaurant) Via Dei Vigneti 1, tel. and fax 0472836548; 15 rms.; ♨ 🅿 🄰🄴 🅼🄲

★★★ **Senoner-Undterdrittel** Lungo Rienza 22, tel. 0472832525, fax 0472832436; hotelsenoner@dnet.it; closed November; 21 rms.; ♨ 🔲 🅿 🄰🄴 ⓓ 🚾 🅼🄲

¶ **Fink** Via Portici Minori 4, tel. 0472834883; ⅀⅀ Alto-Adige ⓓ⅄ Italian and international; 90 capacity; closed Tuesday evening and Wednesday, and for a certain period of time in February and July; 🏢 🚾.

¶ **Oste Scuro-Finsterwirt** Vicolo del Duomo 3, tel. 0472835343 ✕; www.finsterwirt.com; ⅀⅀ Alto-Adige and classic ⓓ⅄ local and national; 70 capacity; closed Sunday evening and Monday, and for a certain period of time between January and February and between June and July; ✱ 🄰🄴 ⓓ 🚾.

Breuil-Cervinia (AO)   ✉ 11021

ℹ *AIAT*, Via Carrel 29, tel. 0166949136; www.monte cervino.it.

🚉 *Stazione F.S. (railway station)* at *Châtillon;* bus service.

⛪ *Saint-Vincent-Châtillon* (A5 Torino-Traforo Monte Bianco).

⛷ ski and cross-country sky; included in the area of *Cervinia-Valtournenche-Zermatt*, tel. 0166944311.

Hotels and restaurants

★★★ **G.H. Cristallo** Via Piolet 6, tel. 0166943411, fax 0166948377; open December-April and July-August; 107 rms.; ♨ ≋ ✕ 🔲 🅿 ♿ 🄰🄴 ⓓ 🚾 🅼🄲

★★★ **Hermitage** Via Piolet, tel. 0166948998, fax 0166949032; www.hotelhermitage.com; info@ hotelhermitage.com; seasonal; 36 rms.; ♨ ≋ 🔲 🅿 🄰🄴 ⓓ 🚾 🅼🄲

★★★ **Astoria** Piazzale Funivie, tel. and fax 0166 949062; open November-April and August-mid-September; 30 rms.; 🔲 🄰🄴

★★★ **Excelsior-Planet** Piazzale Planet 1, tel. 0166 949426, fax 0166948827; www.excelsiorplanet. com; open November-April and July-August; 46 rms.; ≋ 🔲 🅿 🚾 🅼🄲.

★★★ **Sertorelli Sporthotel** Via Rey 28, tel. 0166 949797, fax 0166948155; www.emmeti/welcome/ valdaosta; sertorelli@libero.it; 65 rms.; open November-April and mid-June-mid-September; 🏢 🔲 🅿 ♿ 🄰🄴 ⓓ 🚾 🅼🄲.

¶ **Cime Bianche** Località La Vieille, tel. 0166949046 ✕; www.breuilcervinia.com; ⅀⅀ Val d'Aostan ⓓ⅄ local and national; 70 capacity; closed Monday, period when closed may vary; 🅿; also hotel.

Burano (VE)   ✉ 30012

ℹ *IAT* at Venice.

⛴ *ACTV*, tel. 899-909090 (pay call); steamboat to Venice.

Restaurants

¶ **Gatto Nero-da Ruggero** Fondamenta della Giudecca 88, tel. 041730120 ✕; ⅀⅀ Venetian (seafood) and fine cuisine ⓓ⅄ Italian and international; 100/50 capacity; closed Monday, and for a certain period of time in January and November; 🄰🄴 ⓓ 🚾 🅼🄲.

Busseto (PR)   ✉ 43011

ℹ *IAT*, Piazza Verdi 10, tel. 052492487; info@bus setolive.com.

🚉 *Stazione F.S. (railway station)*, Viale Pallavicino, tel. 892021.

⛪ *Cortemaggiore* (A21 Dir. Torino-Brescia to Fiorenzuola); *Fidenza-Salsomaggiore Terme* (A1 Milano-Roma-Napoli).

Hotels

★★★ **I Due Foscari** Piazza Rossi 15, tel. 0524930039, fax 052491625; 20 rms.; 🏢 ♨ 🅿 🄰🄴 ⓓ 🚾 🅼🄲.

Cagliari   ✉ 09100

ℹ *EPT*, Piazza Deffenu 9, tel. 070604241; enturis moca@tiscali.it; (E3); *Information Office*, Via Roma, Stazione Marittima *(ship passenger terminal)*, tel. 070668352; (E2); *AA*, Piazza Matteotti 9, tel. 070669255; aastinfo@tiscali.it; (D2); *ESIT*, Via Mameli 95, tel. 800-013153, 0706023341 (C2).
TCI, Via Dante 72/A, tel. 070650312; tci.cagliari @tisca lin.it (C5)

🚉 *Stazione F.S. (railway station)*, Piazza Matteotti, tel. 070662573; *Stazione Ferrovie della Sardegna*, Piazza Repubblica, tel. 070491304.

✈ *Airport* at Elmas, tel. 070211211. Bus service from Piazza Matteotti.
Air Dolomiti, Alpi Eagles, Volare, c/o airport, tel. 0702128263.
Alitalia, information tel. 8488-65643.
Meridiana, c/o airport, tel. 070240111.

⛴ *Stazione Marittima (ship passenger terminal)*, Via Roma, Molo Sanità, information: Autorità Portuale, tel. 070679531.
Linea dei Golfi, Via Sonnino Sidney, tel. 070 658413 (ferryboat to Livorno only on Sundays).
Sardinia Ferries, tel. 078925200 (ferryboat to Civitavecchia).
Tirrenia, Via Roma, tel. 070666065 (ferryboat to Genova, Civitavecchia, Naples, Palermo, Trapani).

Hotels

★★★ **Mediterraneo** Lungomare Colombo 46, ✉ 09125, tel. 070301271, fax 070301274; 124 rms.; 🏢 ♨ 🅿 🄰🄴 ⓓ 🚾; (F4).

★★★★ **Panorama** Viale Diaz 231, ✉ 09126, tel. 070307691, fax 070305413; www.hotelpanorama.it; 90 rms.; AE VISA MC; (*F6*).

★★★★ **Regina Margherita** (no restaurant), Viale Regina Margherita 44, ✉ 09124, tel. 070670342, fax 070668325; www.hotelreginamargherita.com; 99 rms.; AE VISA MC; (*D3*).

★★★ **Jolly Cagliari** Circonvallazione Nuova 626, ✉ 09134, tel. 070521373, fax 070502222; 129 rms.; AE VISA MC; (*A5, off map*).

★★★ **Italia** (no restaurant), Via Sardegna 31, ✉ 09124, tel. 070660410, fax 070650240; 108 rms.; AE VISA; (*D2*).

★★★ **Ulivi e Palme** Via P. Bembo 25, ✉ 09131, tel. 070485861, fax 070486970; www.sardegnasud.com; sardegnasud@iol.it; 23 rms.; AE VISA MC; (*A5, off map*).

Restaurants

Dal Corsaro township of Poetto, ✉ 09126, tel. 070370295, fax 070653439; Sardinian (seafood); local and national; 70 capacity; closed Monday at midday, open mid-June-mid-September; AE VISA MC; (*D3*).

Flora Via Sassari 47, ✉ 09123, tel. 070664735; Sardinian and classic; Italian and international; 80 capacity; closed Sunday, and for a certain period of time in August; AE VISA MC; (*C2*).

Antica Hostaria Via Cavour 60, ✉ 09124, tel. 070665870; Sardinian and classic (seafood); local and national; 80 capacity; closed Sunday and for a certain period of time in August, and Christmas-Epiphany (6 January); AE VISA MC; (*D3*).

Camogli (GE) ✉ 16032

IAT, Via XX Settembre 33, tel. 0185771066.

Stazione F.S. (railway station), Via XX Settembre, tel. 892021.

Recco (A12 Genova-Rosignano).

Hotels and restaurants

★★★★ **Cenobio dei Dogi** Via Cuneo 34, tel. 01857241, fax 0185772796; www.cenobio.it; cenobio@cenobio.it; 107 rms.; AE VISA.

★★ **La Camogliese** (no restaurant), Via Garibaldi 55, tel. 0185771402, fax 0185774024; camogliese@libero.it; 16 rms.; AE VISA MC.

Vento Ariel Calata Porto 1, tel. 0185771080; Ligurian and classic; Italian and international; 18/12 capacity; closed Wednesday, and for a certain period of time in January; AE VISA MC.

Capri (Island of) (NA)

at Capri: *AA*, Piazza Umberto I, tel. 0818370686; www.capritourism.com; *Information Office*, embankment of the port, Marina Grande, tel. 0818370634; touristoffice@capri.it.

at Anacapri (seasonal): *AA*, Via G. Orlandi 59, tel. 0818371524.

Alicost, tel. 089873301 (seasonal ferryboats and hydrofoils to Amalfi).

Caremar, tel. 0818370700 (ferryboat and hydrofoil to Naples, hydrofoil to Sorrento).

Linee Marittime Partenopee, tel. 0818376995 (seasonal hydrofoil to Castellammare di Stabia, Naples, Ischia, Sorrento and Torre Annunziata).

Navigazione Libera del Golfo, tel. 0818370819 (hydrofoil to Naples and Sorrento, seasonal sailboat to Positano).

SNAV, tel. 0818377577 (hydrofoil to Naples).

at Capri ✉ 80073

Hotels

★★★★★L **G.H. Quisisana** Via Camerelle 2, tel. 081 8370788, fax 0818376080; www.quisi.com; info@quisi.com; open mid-March/mid-November; 150 rms.; AE VISA MC.

★★★★ **Casa Morgano** (no restaurant), Via Tragara 6, tel. 0818370158, fax 0818370681; www.caprionline.com/morgano; casamorgano@capri.it; open April-October; 28 rms.; AE VISA MC.

★★★★ **La Pazziella** (no restaurant), Via P. Reginaldo Giuliani 4, tel. 0818370044, fax 0818370085; 20 rms.; AE VISA.

★★★★ **Punta Tragara** Via Tragara 57, tel. 0818370844, fax 0818377790; www.hoteltragara.com; open April-October; 47 rms.; AE VISA.

★★★★ **Syrene** Via Camerelle 51, tel. 0818370522, fax 0818370957; syrene@capri.it; open April- October; 34 rms.; AE VISA.

★★★ **Villa Sarah** (no restaurant), Via Tiberio 3/A, tel. 0818377817, fax 0818377215; www.villasarah.it; open Easter-October; 20 rms.; AE VISA MC.

★★ **Florida** (no restaurant), Via Fuorlovado 34, tel. 0818370710, fax 0818370042; closed January-February; 19 rms.; AE VISA.

Restaurants

Capannina Via delle Botteghe 12 bis, tel. 081 8370732, fax 0818376990; www.capannina.capri.it; Campanian (seafood); Italian and international; 120 capacity; open mid-March-mid-November and Christmas-Epiphany (6 January), closed Wednesday; AE VISA MC.

Aurora Via Fuorlovado 18, tel. 0818370181; Neapolitan; Italian and international; 90/40 capacity; closed Ephypany (6 January)-Easter; AE VISA MC.

Da Paolino at Marina Grande, Via Palazzo a Mare 11, ✉ 80070, tel. 0818376102; www.capri.it/it/paolino; Campanian (grilled fish and meat); local and national; 120 capacity; open Easter-October; summer in evening; closed Wednesday in the off season; AE VISA MC.

Gemma Via Madre Serafina 6, tel. 0818377113; www.dagemma.com; Campanian (seafood); local and national; 60 capacity; closed Monday and January; AE VISA MC.

La Pigna Via Lo Palazzo 30, tel. 0818370280; Campanian (seafood); Italian and international; 200 capacity; closed February; AE VISA MC.

at Anacapri ✉ 80071

Hotels and restaurants

★★★★ **Capri Palace** Via Capodimonte 2/B, tel. 081 9780111, fax 0818373191; www.capri-palace.com; open March-November; 83 rms.; AE VISA MC.

★★ **Bellavista** Via Orlandi 10, tel. 0818371463, fax 0818370957; syrene@capri.it; open April-October; 15 rms.; AE VISA MC.

Cucciolo at Damecuta, Via La Fabbrica 52, tel. 0818371917; Campanian; Italian and international; 40/80 capacity; open mid-March-mid-November (solo la sera in estate); closed Tuesday in the off season; AE VISA MC.

Caserta ✉ 81100

EPT, Piazza Dante 43, tel. 0823321137; www.casertaturismo.com.

Stazione F.S. (railway station), Piazza Carlo III, tel. 892021.

Caserta Nord, *Caserta Sud* (A1 Milano-Roma-Napoli).

Hotels and restaurants

*** **Europa** Via Roma 19, tel. and fax 0823325400; www.hoteleuropa.cjb.net; hotel.europa@tin.it; 60 rms.; 🕭 🗐 🅿 🖭 ⑩ 💳 ᴍᴄ.

*** **Jolly** Viale Vittorio Veneto 9, tel. 0823325222, fax 0823354522; www.jollyhotels.it; caserta@jollyho tels.it; 107 rms.; 🕭 🗐 🅿 🖭 ⑩ 💳 ᴍᴄ.

👖 **Le Colonne** Via Nazionale Appia 13, tel. 0823 467494 ☒; 〗〖 Campanian (seafood) ◗ᵣ local and national; 500 capacity; closed Tuesday and every evening; for a certain period of time in August; 🕭 🅿 🖭 ⑩ 💳 ᴍᴄ.

at San Léucio, 4 km   ☒ 81020

Restaurants

👖 **Antica Locanda** Piazza della Seta, tel. 0823305444 ☒; anticalocanda@libero.it; 〗〖 Campanian ◗ᵣ local and national; 60 capacity; closed Sunday evening and Monday, and for a certain period of time in August; 🕭 🖭 ⑩ 💳 ᴍᴄ.

Castelfranco Veneto (TV)   ☒ 31033

🄘 *IAT*, Via F. Maria Preti 66, tel. 0423491416.

� *Stazione F.S. (railway station)*, Via Melchiorri, tel. 892021.

🕂 *Padova Est* (A4 Torino-Milano-Trieste); *Treviso Sud* (A27 Mestre-Belluno).

Hotels and restaurants

*** **Al Moretto** (no restaurant), Via S. Pio X 10, tel. 0423721313, fax 0423721066; www.albergoalmor etto.it; albergo.al.moretto@apl.it; closed Christmas-Epiphany (6 January) and August; 36 rms.; 🕭 🛦🅿 🖭 ⑩ 💳 ᴍᴄ.

*** **Fior** township of Salvarosa, Via dei Carpani 18, tel. 0423721212, fax 0423498771; 44 rms.; 🕭 🛦 🏊 ✕ 🗐 🅿 🖭 ⑩ 💳 ᴍᴄ.

*** **Roma** (no restaurant), Via F. Filzi 39, tel. 0423 721616, fax 0423721515; www.sevenonline.it/al bergoroma; 82 rms.; 🕭 🅿 🚳 🖭 ⑩ 💳 ᴍᴄ.

👖 **Alle Mura** Via Preti 69, tel. 0423498098 ☒; 〗〖 classic (seafood) ◗ᵣ Italian and international; 80 capacity; closed Thursday and August; 🕏 🕭 🖭 ⑩ 💳 ᴍᴄ.

👖 **Barbesin** township of Salvarosa, eastern belt road, tel. 0423490446 ☒; www.barbesin.it; info@ barbesin.it; 〗〖 Venetian (seafood) ◗ᵣ Italian and international; 200 capacity; closed Wednesday evening and Thursday, for a certain period of time in January and August; 🕏 🕭 🅿 🖭 ⑩ 💳 ᴍᴄ.

Catania   ☒ 95100

🄘 *AAPIT*, Via Cimarosa 10, tel. 0957306279-0957306222; www.apt.catania.it; (*C3*); *Information Offices*: Stazione Centrale F.S., tel. 095 7306255 (*C5*); c/o Airport, tel. 0957306266; at the port (seasonal), tel. 0957306209.

� *Stazione F.S. (railway station)*: Piazza Giovanni XXIII, tel. 892021; *Stazione Ferrovia Circumetnea*, Via Caronda 352/A (al Borgo), tel. 095541111.

🕂 *Catania Nord* (A18 Messina-Catania); *Catania Sud* (A19 Palermo-Catania).

✈ *Aeroporto Fontanarossa*, tel. 095340505. Shuttle service from the city by *Alibus*; bus service by AMT from the railway station.
Air Sicilia, c/o Airport, tel. 09572322153.
Alitalia, reservations tel. 8488-65641.
Alpi Eagles, Corso Sicilia 29, tel. 0957151483 (*C3-4*)
Meridiana, reservations tel 199-111333.
Volare, reservations tel. 8488-24425.

Hotels and restaurants

*** **Excelsior Grand Hotel** Piazza Verga 39, ☒ 95129, tel. 0957476111, fax 095537015; www. thi.it; 173 rms.; 🕭 🛦 🚳 🖭 ⑩ 💳 ᴍᴄ; (*B4*).

*** **Jolly Bellini** Piazza Trento 13, ☒ 95129, tel. 095 316933, fax 095316832; 159 rms.; 🕭 🅿 🖭 ⑩ 💳 ᴍᴄ; (*B3*).

*** **Jolly Hotel Ognina** (no restaurant), Via Messina 628, ☒ 95126, tel. 0957528111, fax 0957121856; 56 rms.; 🕭 🅿 🖭 ⑩ 💳 ᴍᴄ; (*A6, off map*).

👖 **I Tre Bicchieri** Via S. Giuseppe al Duomo 31, ☒ 95124, tel. 0957153540, fax 0952500712 ☒; www.osteriaitrebicchieri.it; 〗〖 fine and Mediter-ranean cuisine ◗ᵣ Italian and international; 60 capacity; closed Sunday and Monday at midday, August; 🅿 🖭 ⑩ 💳 ᴍᴄ; (*D3*).

👖 **Siciliana** Viale Marco Polo 52/A, ☒ 95126, tel. 095376400, fax 0957221300 ☒; www.lasicilia na.it; 〗〖 Sicilian ◗ᵣ Italian and international; 90/100 capacity; closed Monday, Sunday evening and holidays, and for a certain period of time in August; 🕏 🕭 🖭 ⑩ 💳 ᴍᴄ; (*A3, off map*).

👖 **Poggio Ducale - Da Nino** of the Hotel Poggio Ducale, Via Paolo Gaifami 5, ☒ 95126, tel. 095 330016; www.poggioducale.it; poggioducale@ poggioducale.it; 〗〖 fine and Sicilian cuisine (sea-food) ◗ᵣ Italian and international; 60 capacity; closed Sunday evening and Monday at midday, and for a certain period of time in August; 🕭 🅿 🖭 ⑩ 💳.

Certosa di Pavìa (PV)   ☒ 27012

🄘 *APT* at Pavia.

� *Stazione F.S. (railway station)*, Certosa di Pavia, tel. 892021.

🕂 *Pavia Nord* (highway intersection: Pavia-Bere-guardo/A7 Milano-Genova).

Restaurants

👖 **Locanda Vecchia Pavia al Mulino** Via al Monu-mento 5, tel. 0382925894, fax 0382933300 ☒; 〗〖 Lombard and classic ◗ᵣ Italian and international; 60 capacity; closed Monday and Wednesday at midday, and for a certain period of time in January and in August; 🕏 🕭 🅿 🖭 ⑩ 💳 ᴍᴄ.

👖 **Chalet della Certosa** Piazzale Monumento 1, tel. 0382925615; nuovochaletdellacertosa@tin.it; 〗〖 Lombard and classic ◗ᵣ Italian; 250/150 capacity; closed Monday, except holidays, period when closed may vary; 🕭 🕏 🖭 ⑩ 💳 ᴍᴄ.

Chioggia (VE)   ☒ 30015

🄘 *IAT* at Sottomarina, Lungomare Adriatico 101, tel. 0415540466; www.chioggiaturismo.it.

� *Stazione F.S. (railway station)*, Via Granatieri di Sardegna, tel. 892021.

🕂 *Padova Est* (A4 Torino-Milano-Trieste).

⛴ *ACTV*, tel. 899-909090 (pay call); steam boat to Pellestrina and to Lido di Venezia, the second stretch by bus.

Restaurants

👖 **El Gato** Campo S. Andrea 653, tel. 041401806, fax 041405224 ☒; 〗〖 Venetian (seafood) ◗ᵣ Italian and international; 40 capacity; closed Monday and at midday from Tuesday to Friday, January-mid-February; 🕭 🖭 ⑩ 💳 ᴍᴄ.

👖 **Al Bersagliere** Via C. Battisti 293, tel. 041401044 ☒; 〗〖 Venetian (seafood) ◗ᵣ Italian and interna-tional; 80 capacity; closed Tuesday and for a cer-tain period of time in November; 🕭 🖭 ⑩ 💳 ᴍᴄ.

at Sottomarina, 1 km   ☒ 30019

Hotels

*** **Bristol** Lungomare Adriatico 46, tel. 0415540389, fax 0415541813; www.hotelbristol.net; reservations@hotelbristol.net; closed January; 65 rms.; 🏨 ♿ ⚐ P 🅿 🚽 MC.

*** **Airone** Lungomare Adriatico 50, tel. 041492266, fax 0415541325; www.boscolo.com/hotels; hotels@boscolo.com; closed mid-December-mid-January; 96 rms.; 🏨 ♿ ⚐ 🅿 P 🚽 ⓦ 🚽 MC.

Cividale del Friùli (UD)   ☒ 33043

ℹ️ **ARPT**, Corso Paolino d'Aquileia 10, tel. 0432 731461; www.regione.fvg.it/benvenuti/cividale/welcome.htm.

🚉 **Stazione Ferrovia Udine-Cividale** (railway station), Viale Libertà 23, tel. 0432731032.

🛣️ **Palmanova, Udine Nord** or **Udine Sud** (A23 Palmanova-Tarvisio).

Hotels and restaurants

*** **Roma** (no restaurant), Piazza Picco, tel. 0432 731871, fax 0432701033; www.hotelroma-cividale.it; info@hotelroma-cividale.it; 50 rms.; ♿ P 🚽 ⓦ 🚽 MC.

🍴 **Trattoria alla Frasca** Via de Rubeis 8/A, tel. 0432 731270 ☒; 🍽️ Friulan and classic (mushrooms) 🍷 local and national; 60/20 capacity; closed Monday, for a certain period of time in January; 🌐 🚽 ⓦ 🚽.

Como   ☒ 22100

ℹ️ **APT**, Piazza Cavour 16, tel. 031269712; www.lakecomo.it; (A2).

🚉 **Stazione F.S.** (railway station), Piazzale San Gottardo 1, tel. 892021; **Stazione FNM**, Largo Leopardi 3, tel. 031304800.

🛣️ **Como M. Olimpino, Como Sud** (A9 Lainate-Como-Chiasso).

⚓ **NLC-Navigazione Lago di Como**, Via Cernobbio 18, tel. 031579211, 800-551801 (boat and hydrofoil to Bellagio, Colico and other places).

Hotels and restaurants

*** **Como** Via Mentana 28, tel. 031266173, fax 031 266020; www.hcomo.it; closed mid-December-mid-January; 76 rms.; 🏨 ⚐ 🅿 P ♿ 🚽 ⓦ 🚽 MC; (C3).

*** **Le Due Corti** Piazza Vittoria 15, tel. 031328111, fax 031328800; 60 rms.; 🏨 ♿ ⚐ 🅿 P ♿ 🚽 ⓦ 🚽 MC.

*** **Villa Flori** road to Cernobbio 12, tel. 03133820, fax 031570379; www.hotelvillaflori.com; lariovillaflori@galactica.it; closed December-February; 45 rms.; 🏨 ♿ 🅿 P 🚽 ⓦ 🚽 MC; (A1, off map).

*** **Continental** Viale Innocenzo XI 15, tel. 031 260485, fax 031273343; 65 rms.; 🅿 P ♿ 🚽 ⓦ 🚽 MC; (B2).

*** **Park Hotel** (no restaurant), Viale F.lli Rosselli 20, tel. 031572615, fax 031574302; parkhotelmeuble@tiscali.it; open March-November; 41 rms.; 🏨 🅿 🚽 ⓦ 🚽 MC; (A1).

🍴🍴 **Raimondi** Road to Cernobbio 12, tel. 031338233, fax 031570379 ☒; 🍽️ Lombard and classic 🍷 local and national; 60 capacity; closed Monday, Christmas-mid-February; 🏨 🌐 🚽 ⓦ 🚽; (A1, off map).

🍴 **Trattoria delle Catene** Via Borsieri 18, tel. 031263775 ☒; www.lecatene.it; 🍽️ Lake Como 🍷 Italian and international; 48/20 capacity; closed Sunday and August; 🏨 🌐 🚽 ⓦ 🚽; (B2).

Cortina d'Ampezzo (BL)   ☒ 32043

ℹ️ **APT**, Piazzetta San Francesco 8, tel. 04363231; www.apt-dolomiti-cortina.it; Piazza Roma 1, tel. 04362711.

🚉 **Stazione F.S.** (railway station) at Calalzo di Cadore or Dobbiaco; bus service.

🛣️ **Pian di Vedoia** (A27 Mestre-Belluno).

🎿 downhill and cross-country skiing; included in the area of Dolomiti Superski.

Hotels

*** **Miramonti Majestic G.H.** township of Pezziè 103, tel. 04364201, fax 0436867019; www.geturhotels.com; miramontimajestic@geturhotels.com; open Christmas-March and July-August; 105 rms.; ♿ ⚐ 🍴 🅿 P 🚽 ⓦ 🚽 MC.

*** **Ancora** Corso Italia 62, tel. 04363261, fax 0436 3265; seasonal; www.hotelancoracortina.com; open December-March and July-mid-September; 50 rms.; 🅿 P ♿ 🚽 ⓦ 🚽 MC.

*** **Bellevue** Corso Italia 197, tel. 0436883400, fax 0436867510; www.cortinanet.it/bellevue; h.bellevue@cortinanet.it; open mid-December-mid-April and July-mid-September; 65 rms.; ♿ 🅿 🚽 MC.

*** **De la Poste** Piazza Roma 14, tel. 04364271, fax 0436868435; www.hotels.cortina.it/delaposte; open Christmas-mid-April and mid-June-September; 80 rms.; 🅿 P 🚽 ⓦ 🚽 MC.

*** **Columbia** (no restaurant), Via Ronco 75, tel. 04363607, fax 04363001; www.sunrise.it/cortina/alberghi/columbia; open December-mid-April and mid-June-mid-October; 19 rms.; ♿ 🅿 🚽 ⓦ 🚽.

*** **Franceschi Park Hotel** VIa C. Battisti 28, tel. 0436867041, fax 04362909; www.cortinanet.it/franceschi; open Christmas-Easter and mid-June-mid-September; 49 rms.; ♿🍴 🅿 🚽 ⓦ 🚽 MC.

*** **Pontechiesa** Via Marangoni 3, tel. 04362523, fax 0436867343; www.dolomiti.it/hotelpontechiesa; hotelpontechiesa@dolomiti.it; open mid-December-March and mid-June-September; 31 rms.; ♿🅿 🚽 ⓦ 🚽.

*** **Menardi** Via Majon 110, tel. 04362400, fax 0436 862183; www.sunrise.it/hmenardi; info@hotelmenardi.it; open Christmas-March and mid-June-mid-September; 49 rms.; ♿ 🅿 P 🚽 MC.

Restaurants

🍴🍴 **El Toulà** Via Ronco 123, tel. 04363339, fax 0436 2738 ☒; 🍽️ local and classic 🍷 Italian and international; 70 capacity; open Christmas-Easter closed Monday; 🅿 🚽 ⓦ 🚽.

🍴 **Tivoli** Via Lacedel 34, tel. 0436866400, fax 0436 3413 ☒; dona51@libero.it; 🍽️ fine cuisine 🍷 Italian and international; 50/30 capacity; open December-mid-April and mid-July-midSeptember closed Monday in the off season; 🅿 🚽 ⓦ 🚽.

🍴 **Beppe Sello** Via Ronco 68, tel. 04363236, fax 04363237 ☒; www.beppesello.it; 🍽️ local and classical 🍷 Italian and international; 70 capacity; open December-Easter and mid-May-mid-September closed Tuesday; 🅿 🚽 ⓦ 🚽 MC; also hotel.

🍴 **Baita Fraina** Via Fraina 1, tel. 04363634 ☒; www.italiaabc.com/a/baitafraina; 🍽️ local 🍷 Italian and international; 50 capacity; open December-mid-April and July-September; closed Monday in the off season; 🅿 🚽 MC.

at Pocol, 6 km

Hotels

** **Pocol** tel. 04362602, fax 04362707; hpocol@tin.it; open Christmas-March and mid-June-September; 17 rms.; ♿ 🅿 P 🚽 MC.

Cortona (AR)   ☒ 52044

ℹ️ **IAT**, Via Nazionale 42, tel. 0575630352; info@cortona ntiquaria.com; (B2).

�82 *Stazione F.S. (railway station)* at Camucia, tel. 892021; bus service.

🕇 *Cortona* (Val di Chiana-Perugia highway junction).

Hotels and restaurants

★★★ **Il Falconiere** at San Martino a Bocena, tel. 0575612679, fax 0575612927; www.ilfalconiere. com; 12 rms.; 🏠 ♨ ♒ 🏊 📶 🅿️ & 🅰🅴 ⓦ 🚇 ᴍᴄ

🍴🅟 **Il Falconiere** at San Martino a Bocena, tel. 0575612679, fax 0575612927 ✉; www.ilfalco niere.com; ilfalcon@ilfalconiere.com; � Tuscan and fine cuisine ₲ᵥ Italian and international; 20 capacity; closed Wednesday in winter, period when closed may vary; 🍷 🅿️ 🅰🅴 ⓦ 🚇 ᴍᴄ

🍴 **Preludio** Via Guelfa 11, tel. 0575630104 ✉; www. cortona.net/preludio; � Tuscan ₲ᵥ local and national; 50 capacity; closed Monday and for a certain period of time in November; 🅿️ 🅰🅴 ⓦ 🚇 ᴍᴄ; (*B1*).

at Pòrtole, 9 km

Hotels

★★★ **Portole** Via Umbro Cortonese 39, tel. 0575 691008, fax 0575691035; www.emmeti.it/HRpor tole.html; open April-November; 20 rms.; ♨ ✗ 🅿️ 🅰🅴 ⓦ 🚇 ᴍᴄ

Cosenza   ✉ 87100

ℹ️ *APT*, Corso Mazzini 92, tel. 098427485-0984 27271.

TCI, Via Macallè 21/B, lateral to Corso Mazzini, tel. 0984795099; tci.cosenza@centroviaggi.com.

�82 *Stazione F.S. (railway station)*, Contrada Vaglio Lise, tel. 892021.

🕇 *Cosenza* (A3 Napoli-Reggio Calabria).

Hotels and restaurants

★★★ **Royal** Via Molinella 24/E, tel. 0984412165, fax 0984411777; www.web.tiscalinet.it/royal; royalhot @tin.it; 44 rms.; 🏠 🅿️ 🅰🅴 ⓦ 🚇 ᴍᴄ

🍴 **Giocondo** Via Piave 53, tel. 098429810 ✉; � Calabrian ₲ᵥ local and national; 80 capacity; closed Sunday evening, August; 🏠 🅰🅴 ⓦ 🚇 ᴍᴄ

🍴 **L'Arco Vecchio** Via Archi di Ciaccio 21, tel. 098472564; � Calabrian ₲ᵥ local and national; 50 capacity; closed Sunday; 🏠 🅿️ 🅰🅴 ⓦ 🚇 ᴍᴄ

Courmayeur (AO)   ✉ 11013

ℹ️ *AIAT*, Piazzale Monte Bianco 13, tel. 0165 842060; www.courmayeur.net.

�82 *Stazione F.S. (railway station)* at Pré-Saint-Didier; bus service.

🕇 *Morgex* (A5 Torino-Traforo Monte Bianco).

🎿 downhill and cross-country skiing.

Hotels and restaurants

★★★ **Pavillon** Strada Regionale 62, tel. 0165846120, fax 0165846122; www.valdigne.com/courmayeur/ pavillon; open December-April and mid-June-mid-October; 50 rms.; ♨ ♒ 🏊 🅿️ & 🅰🅴 ⓦ 🚇 ᴍᴄ

★★★ **Royal e Golf** Via Roma 87, tel. 0165831611, fax 0165842093; www.hotelroyalgolf.com; open December-mid-April and mid-June-mid-September; 86 rms.; ♨ ♒ 🏊 🅿️ & 🅰🅴 ⓦ 🚇 ᴍᴄ

★★★ **Courmayeur** Via Roma 158, tel. 0165846732, fax 0165845125; www.courmayeurhotel.com; info@ hotelcourmayeur.com; open June-September and December-April; 26 rms.; 🅿️ 🅰🅴 ⓦ 🚇 ᴍᴄ

★★★ **Croux** (no restaurant), Via Circonvallazione 94, tel. 0165846735, fax 0165845180; www.hotelcroux.it; info@hotelcroux.it; open December-mid-April and mid-June-September; 33 rms.; ♨ 🅿️ 🅰🅴 ⓦ 🚇 ᴍᴄ

★★ **Chalet Val Ferret** township of Planpincieux, tel. and fax 0165844959; www.courmanet.com/ chalet.html; chalet@netvallee.it; open mid-June-mid-September; 7 rms.; ♨ 🅿️ 🅰🅴 ⓦ 🚇 ᴍᴄ

🍴 **Cadran Solaire** Via Roma 122, tel. 0165844609 ✉; � Val d'Aostan and classic ₲ᵥ local and national; 70 capacity; open November-April and June-September; closed Tuesday; 🅰🅴 ⓦ 🚇

🍴 **Pierre Alexis 1877** Via Marconi 54, tel. 0165 843517 ✉; � Val d'Aostan ₲ᵥ local and national; 80 capacity; closed Monday, October-November; 🅿️ 🅰🅴 🚇

at Entrèves, 3 km

Hotels and restaurants

★★★ **La Brenva** Strada La Palud 12, tel. 0165869780, fax 0165869726; www.labrenva.com; labrenva@tin.it; closed May and October; 12 rms.; ♨ 🅿️ 🅰🅴 ⓦ 🚇 ᴍᴄ

★★★ **Pilier d'Angle** tel. 0165869760, fax 0165869770; www.pilierdangle.it; info@pilierdangle.it; open December-April and mid-June-September; 19 rms.; ♨ 🅿️ 🅰🅴 ⓦ 🚇 ᴍᴄ

🍴 **La Maison de Filippo** tel. 0165869797 ✉; www. lamaison.com; � Val d'Aostan ₲ᵥ local and national; 140/80 capacity; closed Tuesday, June-mid-July and November-mid-December; 🅿️ 🚇 ᴍᴄ

Cremona   ✉ 26100

ℹ️ *APT*, Piazza del Comune 5, tel. 037223233; www.aptcremona.it.

�82 *Stazione F.S. (railway station)*, Via Dante 68, tel. 892021.

🕇 *Cremona* (A21 Torino-Brescia).

Hotels and restaurants

★★★ **Continental** Piazza Libertà 26, tel. 0372 434141, fax 0372454873; 62 rms.; 🏠 🅴 🅿️ 🅰🅴 ⓦ 🚇 ᴍᴄ

★★★ **Ibis Cremona** (no restaurant), Via Mantova, tel. 0372452222, fax 0372452700; ibis.cremona@ accor-hotels.it; closed Christmas-Epiphany (6 January) and August; 100 rms.; 🏠 🅴 🅿️ & 🅰🅴 ⓦ 🚇 ᴍᴄ

★★★ **Duomo** Via Gonfalonieri 13, tel. 037235242, fax 0372458392; 23 rms.; 🅰🅴 ⓦ 🚇

🍴 **La Sosta** Via Sicardo 9, tel. 0372456656 ✉; ristla sosta@libero.it; � local ₲ᵥ local and national; 60 capacity; closed Sunday evening and Monday, August; 🏠 🅰🅴 ⓦ 🚇

Desenzano del Garda (BS)   ✉ 25015

ℹ️ *IAT*, Via Porto Vecchio 34, tel. 0309141510.

�82 *Stazione F.S. (railway station)*, Piazzale della Stazione, tel. 892021.

🕇 *Desenzano* (A4 Torino-Milano-Trieste).

⚓ *NLG-Navigazione Lago di Garda*, tel. 0309149511 (seasonal boat and hydrofoil to Malcesine, Riva del Garda, Sirmione and other places).

Hotels and restaurants

★★★ **Desenzano** (no restaurant), Viale Cavour 40, tel. 0309141414, fax 0309140294; hoteldesenzano@ gardalake.it; 40 rms.; 🏠 ♨ 🅴 🅿️ & 🅰🅴 ⓦ 🚇 ᴍᴄ

★★★ **Park Hotel** Lungolago C. Battisti 17, tel. 030 9143494, fax 0309142280; www.cerinihotels.it; park.hotel@gardalake.it; 57 rms.; 🏠 ♨ 🅴 🅿️ & 🅰🅴 ⓦ

★★★ **Piccola Vela** Via Dal Molin 36, tel. and fax 030 9914666; piccola-vela@gardalake.it; 43 rms.; 🏠 ♨ ♒ 🏊 🅴 🅿️ 🅰🅴 ⓦ

★★★ **City** (no restaurant), Via Sauro 29, tel. 030 9911704, fax 0309912837; www.hotelcity.it; info@

457

hotelcity.it; closed mid-December-mid-January; 39 rms.; ⌗ ▤ ⊞ Ⓐ ⓓ ☲ ᴹᴄ.

★★★ **Enrichetta** township of Rivoltella, Via F. Agello 12, tel. 0309119231, fax 0309901132; 24 rms.; ⌗ ▤ 🄿 🕭 Ⓐ ⓓ ☲ ᴹᴄ.

★★★ **Piroscafo** Via Porto Vecchio 11, tel. 0309141128, fax 0309912586; www.hotelspromotion.com/piroscafo; closed January/February; 32 rms.; ⌗ 🄿 Ⓐ ⓓ ☲ ᴹᴄ.

¶¶¶ **Cavallino** Via Gherla 30 corner of Muracchette, tel. 0309120217, fax 0309912751 ✉; ⑃ particular ⚲ Italian and international; 50 capacity; closed Monday and Tuesday at midday, and for a certain period of time in November; ✿ Ⓐ ⓓ ☲.

¶¶¶ **Esplanade** Via Lario 10, tel. 0309143361, fax 030 9143361 ✉; ⑃ fine cuisine ⚲ Italian and international; 40 capacity; closed Wednesday; ✿ 🄿 Ⓐ ⓓ ☲ ᴹᴄ.

Elba (Island of) (LI)

ℹ️ *APT* at Portoferraio, Calata Italia 26, tel. 0565 914671; www.arcipelago.turismo.toscana.it.

🚉 *Stazione F.S. (railway station)* at Piombino Marittima; bus service from Portoferraio to the main ports of the island.

⛴ *Moby Lines*, tel. 0565918101 (ferryboat to Piombino).
Toremar, tel. 0565918080 (ferryboat to Piombino).

at Capolìveri ✉ 57031

Hotels

★★★ **Antares** at Lido di Capoliveri, tel. 0565940131, fax 0565940084; open May-mid-October; 49 rms.; ⛛ ♨ ✕ 🄿.

★★★ **Capo Sud** at Lacona, Via del Campo Marinaro 311, ✉ 57037, tel. 0565964021, fax 0565964263; www.hotelcaposud.it; info@hotelcaposud.it; open May-September; 42 rms.; ⌗ ⛛ ♨ ✕ 🄿.

★★ **Dino** at Pareti, tel. 0565939103, fax 0565968172; www.hoteldino.com; hoteldino@elbalink.it; open April-October; 30 rms.; ⛛ 🄿.

at Marciana ✉ 57030

Hotels and restaurants

★★★ **Del Golfo** at Pròcchio, tel. 0565907565, fax 0565907898; open mid-May/September; 102 rms.; ⌗ ⛛ ♨ ✕ 🄿 Ⓐ ⓓ ☲.

★★★ **Bel Tramonto** (no restaurant), at Patresi, tel. 0565908027, fax 0565908280; open April-October; 20 rms.; ⛛ ♨ 🄿 Ⓐ ⓓ ☲ ᴹᴄ.

★★★ **Valle Verde** at Pròcchio-Spartàia, tel. 0565 907287, fax 0565907965; www.elbalink.it/hotel/valleverde; open May-mid-October; 42 rms.; ⌗ 🄿.

¶¶ **Lo Zodiaco** at Pròcchio, Via del Mare 19, tel. 0565907630 ✉; lozodiaco@tiscali.it; ⑃ Leghorn; ⚲ Italian and international; 70 capacity; open April-mid-October, closed Monday; ✿ Ⓐ ⓓ ☲ ᴹᴄ.

at Marciana Marina ✉ 57033

Hotels

★★★ **Gabbiano Azzurro Due** (no restaurant), Viale Amedeo 94, tel. 0565997035, fax 0565997034; www.hotelgabbianoazzurrodue.it; open Easter-mid-October; 20 rms.; ⌗ ⛛ ♨ ♨ ▤ 🄿 Ⓐ ⓓ ☲.

★★★ **Tamerici** Viale Aldo Moro 10, tel. 056599445, fax 056599573; tamerici@elbalink.it; closed mid-November-December; 44 rms.; ⌗ ⛛ ♨ ✕ 🕭 ☲.

at Marina di Campo ✉ 57034

Hotels and restaurants

★★★ **Riva del Sole** Viale degli Eroi 11, tel. 0565 976316, fax 0565976778; www.elbalink.it; open April-mid-October; 57 rms.; ⌗ 🄿 🕭 Ⓐ ⓓ ☲ ᴹᴄ.

★★★ **Dei Coralli** Via degli Etruschi 81, tel. 0565976336, fax 0565977748; hcoralli@tin.it; open Easter-mid-October; 62 rms.; ⌗ ⛛ ♨ ✕ 🄿 Ⓐ ⓓ ☲.

¶¶ **Bologna** Via Firenze 27, tel. 0565976105; ⑃ Livornese and classic ⚲ local and national; 300 capacity; open mid-March-October; ✿ Ⓐ ⓓ ☲ ᴹᴄ.

at Porto Azzurro ✉ 57036

Hotels

★★★ **Belmare** (no restaurant), Banchina IV Novembre 21, tel. 056595012, fax 0565921077; closed mid-November-mid-December; 25 rms.

at Portoferràio ✉ 57037

Hotels and restaurants

★★★ **Airone del Parco e delle Terme** at San Giovanni, tel. 0565929111, fax 0565917484; closed Christmas- Epiphany (6 January); 85 rms.; ⌗ ⛛ ♨ ✕ 🄿 Ⓐ ⓓ ☲ ᴹᴄ.

★★★ **Hermitage** at La Biòdola, tel. 0565974811, fax 0565969984; open May-mid-October; 130 rms.; ⌗ ⛛ ♨ ✕ 🄿 Ⓐ ⓓ ☲.

★★★ **Acquaviva Park Hotel** at Acquaviva, tel. 0565915392, fax 0565916903; open mid-May-September; 39 rms.; ⛛ ♨ 🄿.

★★★ **Paradiso** at Viticcio, tel. 939034, fax 939041; www.elbaturistica.it; open Easter-mid-October; 46 rms.; ⌗ ⛛ ♨ ✕ 🄿.

¶ **Da Vittorio** Via dell'Amore 54, tel. 0565917446 ✉; ⑃ local ⚲ Italian; 40/20 capacity; closed Tuesday and for a certain period of time in January and February; ⌗ Ⓐ ⓓ ☲ ᴹᴄ.

at Rio Marina ✉ 57038

Hotels

★★★ **Marelba** at Cavo, Via Pietri, ✉ 57030, tel. 0565 949920, fax 0565949776; open May-September; 52 rms.; ⛛ 🄿.

★★★ **Rio** Via Palestro 31, tel. 0565924225, fax 0565 924162; www.elbahotel.it; 35 rms.; Ⓐ ☲.

Èrice (TP) ✉ 91016

ℹ️ *AA*, Viale Conte Pepoli 11, tel. 0923869388.

🚉 *Stazione F.S. (railway station)* at Trapani; bus service.

🕇 *Erice* (A29 Dir. Alcamo-Trapani).

Hotels and restaurants

★★★ **Moderno** Via Vittorio Emanuele 63, tel. 0923869300, fax 0923869139; www.pippocatalano.it; modernoh@tin.it; 40 rms.; ⌗ ▤ Ⓐ ⓓ ☲ ᴹᴄ.

★★★ **Elimo** Via Vittorio Emanuele 73, tel. 0923869377, fax 0923869252; elimoh@comeg.it; 21 rms.; ♨ 🄿 ▤ ▤ Ⓐ ⓓ ☲ ᴹᴄ.

¶¶ **Monte San Giuliano** Vicolo S. Rocco 7, tel. 0923 869595 ✉; www.montesangiuliano.it; ⑃ Sicilian ⚲ local and national; 70/100 capacity; closed Monday (except in summer); ⌗ Ⓐ ⓓ ☲ ᴹᴄ.

Faenza (RA) ✉ 48018

ℹ️ *IAT*, Piazza del Popolo 1, tel. 054625231; proloco faenza@racine.ra.it.

🚉 *Stazione F.S. (railway station)*, Piazza Battisti 7, tel. 892021.

🕇 *Faenza* (A14 Bologna-Taranto).

Restaurants

¶ **Enoteca Astorre** Piazza della Libertà 16/A, tel. 0546681407; ⑃ Romagnola and classic ⚲ local and national; 80/60 capacity; closed Sunday, August; ⌗ ✿ Ⓐ ⓓ ☲ ᴹᴄ.

Fano (PU)   ✉ 61032

📋 *IAT*, Viale Battisti 10, tel. 0721803534; iat.fano@ regione.marche.it.

🚆 *Stazione F.S. (railway station)*, Piazza della Stazione 2, tel. 0721803627.

⛨ *Fano* (A14 Bologna-Taranto).

Hotels and restaurants

★★★ **Elisabeth** Viale Carducci 12, tel. 0721804241, fax 0721804242; www.mobilia.it/elisabeth; closed Christmas-January; 37 rms.; 🅿 ♨ 🆑 🆏 ⊙ 🎫 **MC**.

★★★ **Angela** Viale Adriatico 13, tel. 0721801239, fax 0721803102; 37 rms.; ♨ 🅿 🆑 ⊙ 🎫 **MC**.

★★★ **Corallo** Via L. da Vinci 3, tel. 0721804200, fax 0721803637; www.mobilia.it/corallo; closed Christmas-Epiphany (6 January); 37 rms.; 🅿 🆑 🆏 ⊙ 🎫.

🍴 **Casa Nolfi** Via Gasparoli 59, tel. 0721827066 ☒; ⑴ Marche (seafood) Ⓘ Italian; 35 capacity; closed Sunday evening and Monday; 🅿 🆏 ⊙ 🎫 **MC**.

Ferrara   ✉ 44100

📋 *IAT*, Castello Estense, tel. 0532209370-0532 299303; www.ferraterraeacqua.it; *(C4)*; *Informacittà*, Piazza Municipale 23, tel. 0532419374-0532240623; *(C-D4)*

🚆 *Stazione F.S. (railway station)*, Piazzale della Stazione, tel. 892021.

⛨ *Ferrara* (Porto Garibaldi-Ferrara highway junction), *Ferrara Nord* or *Ferrara Sud* (A13 Bologna-Padova).

Hotels and restaurants

★★★ **Duchessa Isabella** Via Palestro 70, tel. 0532 202121, fax 0532202638; closed August; 27 rms.; 🅿 ♨ 🅿 🆑 ⊙ 🎫 **MC**; *(B-C5)*.

★★★ **Annunziata** (no restaurant), Piazza Repubblica 5, tel. 0532201111, fax 0532203233; www.annun zi-ata.it; closed 15 August and Christmas-Epiphany (6 January); 24 rms.; 🅿 🆑 🅿; *(C4)*.

★★★ **Ripagrande** Via Ripagrande 21, tel. 0532765250, fax 0532764377; 40 rms.; 🅿 🆑 🅿; *(D3)*.

★★★ **De Prati** (no restaurant), Via Padiglioni 5, tel. 0532 241905, fax 0532241966; www.hoteldeprati.com; info@hoteldeprati.com; 13 rms; 🅿 🆑 🎫 **MC**; *(C4)*.

🍴 **La Provvidenza** Corso Ercole I d'Este 92, tel. 0532205187 ☒; ⑴ Ferrarese and classic (fish and mushrooms) Ⓘ Italian and international; 80/40 capacity; closed Monday, and for a certain period of time in August; 🅿 ✳ 🅿 🆑 ⊙ 🎫 **MC**; *(A4)*.

🍴 **Max** Piazza della Repubblica 16, tel. 0532209309 ☒; ⑴ "marinara" Ⓘ Italian; 35/10 capacity; closed Monday and Sunday at midday, and for a certain period of time in July; 🅿 🆑 ⊙ 🎫 **MC**; *(C4)*.

🍴 **Antica Trattoria Volano** Viale Volano 20, tel. 0532761421; ⑴ Ferrarese Ⓘ local and national; 80 capacity; closed Friday, and for a certain period of time in July and August; 🅿 🅿; *(F4)*.

Fièsole (FI)   ✉ 50014

📋 *IAT*, Via Portigiani 3, tel. 055 598720; www.comu ne.fiesole.fi.it.

🚆 *Stazione F.S. (railway station)* at Florence; bus service.

⛨ *Firenze Sud* (A1 Milano-Roma-Napoli).

Hotels and restaurants

★★★ **Villa Aurora** Piazza Mino 39, tel. 05559100, fax 05559587; 27 rms.; 🅿 ♨ 🅿 🆏 ⊙ 🎫.

★★★ **Villa San Michele** Via Doccia 4, tel. 0555678200,

fax 0555678250; reservations@villasanmichele. net; open April-December; 38 rms.; 🅿 ♨ 🅿 🅿 🆏 **MC**.

★★★ **Villa Fiesole** (no restaurant), Fra' Angelico 35, tel. 055597252, fax 055599133; www.villafiesole.it; in fo@villafiesole.it; 28 rms.; 🅿 ♨ 🅿 🅿 🆑 🆏 ⊙ 🎫 **MC**.

🍴 **Carpe Diem** Via Giuseppe Mantellini 2/B, tel. 055599595 ☒; www.paginegialle.it/carpediem; ⑴ Tuscan Ⓘ Italian and international; 100/50 capacity; closed Monday at midday, and for a certain period of time in January and August; 🅿 ✳ 🅿 🆏 ⊙ 🎫 **MC**.

Florence   ✉ 50100

📋 *APT*, Via Manzoni 16, tel. 05523320; www.firenze. turismo.toscana.it; *(D6, off map)*; *Information Office*, Via Cavour 1r, tel. 055290832; *(E4)*; *Uffici Informazioni del Comune (City Information Offices)*, Borgo S. Croce 29/r, tel. 0552340444; infotur.scro ce@comune.fi.it; *(E5-6)*; Piazza Stazione S.M.N. 4, tel. 0552381226; turismo3@comune.fi.it; *(B2)*; c/o Airport, tel. 055315874; infoaeroporto@safnet.it.

🚆 *Stazione F.S. (railway station)* Centrale-S. Maria Novella, Piazza della Stazione, tel. 892021.

⛨ *Firenze Certosa, Firenze Nord, Firenze Signa, Firenze Sud* (A1 Milano-Roma-Napoli); *Sesto Fiorentino* (A11 Firenze-Mare).

✈ *Aeroporto Vespucci* at Peretola, tel. 055373498; bus service (Vola in bus) from the railway station of Santa Maria Novella (*B2*), tel. 800424500-800373760 .

Alitalia, Lungarno Acciaiuoli 10/r, tel. 0552788232-8488-65641 (*E4*).

Hotels

★★★ **G.H. Villa Cora** Viale Machiavelli 18, ✉ 50125, tel. 0552298451, fax 055229086; www.villacora.it; 48 rms.; 🅿 ♨ 🅿 🆑 🅿; 🆏 ⊙ 🎫 **MC**; *(off map)*.

★★★ **Grand Hotel** Piazza Ognissanti 1, ✉ 50123, tel. 055288781, fax 055217400, www.theluxurycol lection.firenze.net; 107 rms.; 🅿 🅿 🅿 🅿 ⊙ 🎫 **MC**; *(C1)*.

★★★ **Helvetia e Bristol** Via dei Pescioni 2, ✉ 50123, tel. 055287814, fax 055288353; www.thecharmin gthotels.com; 67 rms.; 🅿 🅿 🆑 🆏 ⊙ 🎫 **MC**; *(C-D3)*.

★★★ **Regency** Piazza D'Azeglio 3, ✉ 50121, tel. 055 245247, fax 0552346735, www.regency-hotel. com; 35 rms.; 🅿 ♨ 🅿 🅿 🆏 ⊙ 🎫 **MC**; *(off map)*.

★★★ **Savoy** Piazza della Repubblica 7, ✉ 50123, tel. 0552735555, fax 0552735888; www.rfhotels.com; 107 rms.; 🅿 🅿 🆑 🆏 ⊙ 🎫 **MC**; *(C-D4)*.

★★★ **Westin Excelsior Hotel** Piazza Ognissanti 3, ✉ 50123, tel. 055264201, fax 055210278; www.west in.com; 168 rms.; 🅿 🅿 🅿 🆑; 🆏 ⊙ 🎫; *(C-D1-2)*.

★★★ **Anglo American Hotel Regina** Via del Giglio 9, ✉ 50123, tel. 0552398095, fax 055214632; www. boscolo.com; 92 rms.; 🅿 ♨ 🅿 🆏 ⊙ 🎫 **MC**; *(off map)*.

★★★ **Astoria Palazzo Gaddi** Via Garibaldi 9, ✉ 50123, tel. 055282114, fax 055268513, www.framon-ho tels.com; 113 rms.; 🅿 ♨ 🅿 🅿 🆏 ⊙ 🎫 **MC**; *(B-C3)*.

★★★ **Brunelleschi** Piazza S. Elisabetta 3, ✉ 50122, tel. 05527370, fax 055219653, www.hotelbrunelle schi.it; 96 rms.; 🅿 🅿 🆏 ⊙ 🎫; *(C-D4)*.

★★★ **Continental** (no restaurant), Lungarno Accia-iuoli 2, ✉ 50123, tel. 05527262, fax 055 283139, www.lungarnohotels.com; 48 rms.; 🅿 🅿 🆑 🆏 ⊙ 🎫 🎫; *(E3-4)*.

★★★ **Croce di Malta** Via della Scala 7, ✉ 50123, tel. 055 218351, fax 055287121, croce.malta@crocedimalta. it; 98 rms.; 🅿 🅿 🆑 🆏 ⊙ 🎫 **MC**; *(C2)*.

★★★ **Executive** (no restaurant), Via Curtatone 5, ✉ 50123, tel. 055217451, fax 055268346; www.ho telexecutive.it; info@hotelexecutive.it, 38 rms.; 🅿 🅿 🆑 🆏 ⊙ 🎫 **MC**; *(B-C1)*.

★★★ **G.H. Baglioni** Piazza Unità Italiana 6, ✉ 50123,

459

tel. 05523580, fax 0552358895, hotel.baglioni@firenzealbergo.it; 195 rms.; 🄿 🄴 🄰🄴 🄰🄳 🄰 🄼🄲; (*B3*).

★★★ **Gallery Hotel Art** (no restaurant), Vicolo dell'Oro 5, ✉ 50123, tel. 05527263, fax 055268557; www.lungarnohotels.com; gallery@lungarnohotels.com, 65 rms.; 🄿 🄴 🄖 🄰🄴 🄰🄳 🄰 🄼🄲; (*E3-4*).

★★★ **Jolly Carlton** Piazza Vittorio Veneto 4/A, ✉ 50123, tel. 0552770, fax 055294794; 157 rms.; 🄿 🄰🄴 🄰🄳 🄰 🄼🄲; (*off map*).

★★★ **Londra** Via Jacopo da Diacceto 18, ✉ 50123, tel. 05527390, fax 055210682, info@hoellondra.com; 158 rms.; 🄿 🄴 🄿 🄰🄴 🄰🄳 🄰 🄼🄲; (*off map*).

★★★ **Lungarno** Borgo S. Jacopo 14, ✉ 50125, tel. 05527261, fax 055268437, www.lungarnohotels.com; 69 rms.; 🄿 🄴 🄖 🄰🄴 🄰🄳 🄰 🄼🄲; (*E3*).

★★★ **Montebello Splendid** Via Montebello 60, ✉ 50123, tel. 0552398051, fax 055211867; www.milanflorencehotel.it; hms@tin.it; 54 rms.; 🄿 🄰🄴 🄖 🄰🄴 🄰🄳 🄰 🄼🄲; (*off map*).

★★★ **Plaza Hotel Lucchesi** Lungarno della Zecca Vecchia 38, ✉ 50122, tel. 05526236, fax 055 2480921, www.plazalucchesi.it; phl@plazalucchesi.it; 39 rms.; 🄿 🄴 🄖 🄰🄴 🄰🄳 🄰 🄼🄲; (*F6*).

★★★ **Raffaello** Viale Morgagni 19, ✉ 50134, tel. 055 4224141, fax 055434374; www.raffaellohotel.it; raffael@texnet.it; 141 rms.; 🄿 🄰🄴 🄿 🄰🄴 🄰🄳 🄰 🄼🄲; (*off map*).

★★★ **Rivoli** (no restaurant), Via della Scala 33, ✉ 50123, tel. 055282853, fax 055294041; www.hotelrivoli.it; hotel.rivoli@firenzealbergo.it; 65 rms.; 🄿 🄰🄴 🄰🄴 🄰🄳 🄰 🄼🄲; (*B-C2*).

★★★ **Starhotel Michelangelo** Viale F.lli Rosselli 2, ✉ 50123, tel. 0552784, fax 0552382232, www.starhotels.it; michelangelo.fi@starhotels.it; 119 rms.; 🄿 🄴 🄖 🄰🄴 🄰🄳 🄰 🄼🄲;

★★★ **Torre di Bellosguardo** (no restaurant), Via Roti Michelozzi 2, ✉ 50124, tel. 0552298145, fax 055 229008, torredibellosguardo@dada.it; 16 rms.; 🄰🄴 🄰🄴 🄿 🄰🄴 🄰🄳 🄼🄲; (*off map*).

★★★ **Villa Carlotta** Via Michele di Lando 3, ✉ 50125, tel. 0552336134, fax 0552336147; www.venere.it/firenze/villacarlotta; villa.carlotta@italyhotel.com; 32 rms.; 🄿 🄰🄴 🄿 🄰🄴 🄰🄳 🄰 🄼🄲; (*off map*).

★★★ **Ville sull'Arno** LungarnoC. Colombo 5, ✉ 50136, tel. 055670971, fax 055678244, hotel@villesullarno.it; 47 rms.; 🄿 🄰🄴 🄰🄴 🄿 🄰🄴 🄰🄳 🄰🄴; (*off map*).

★★★ **Albion** Via il Prato 22/r, ✉ 50123, tel. 055214171, fax 055283391; www.hotelalbion.it; info@hotelalbion.it; 21 rms.; 🄿 🄴 🄰🄴 🄰🄳 🄰 🄼🄲; (*off map*).

★★★ **Balestri** (no restaurant), Piazza Mentana 7, ✉ 50122, tel. 055214743, fax 0552398042, www.hotel-balestri.it; 46 rms.; 🄿 🄴 🄰🄴 🄰🄳 🄰 🄼🄲; (*E5*).

★★★ **Capitol** Viale Amendola 34, ✉ 50121, tel. 0552343201, fax 0552345925; www.vivahotels.com; 92 rms.; 🄿 🄴 🄰🄴 🄰🄳 🄰 🄼🄲; (*off map*).

★★★ **David** (no restaurant), Viale Michelangiolo 1, ✉ 50125, tel. 0556811695, fax 055680602; www.davidhotel.com; 24 rms.; 🄿 🄰🄴 🄿 🄰🄴 🄰🄳 🄰 🄼🄲; (*off map*).

★★★ **Della Signoria** (no restaurant), Via delle terme 1, ✉ 50123, tel. 055214530, fax 055216101; www.hoteldellasignoria.com; 27 rms.; 🄿 🄰🄴 🄰🄳 🄰 🄼🄲; (*D-E4*).

★★★ **Grifone** Via Pilati 20-22, ✉ 50136, tel. 055 623300, fax 055677628, www.hgrifo.com; 70 rms.; 🄿 🄿 🄖 🄰🄴 🄰🄳 🄰 🄼🄲; (*off map*).

★★★ **Hermitage** (no restaurant), Vicolo Marzio 1/Piazza del Pesce, ✉ 50122, tel. 055287216, fax 055212208; www.hermitagehotel.com; 27 rms.; 🄿 🄰🄴 🄴 🄰🄴 🄼🄲; (*E4*).

★★★ **Il Guelfo Bianco** (no restaurant), Via Cavour 29, ✉ 50129, tel. 055288330, fax 055295203; www.ilguelfobianco.it; 29 rms.; 🄿 🄴 🄖 🄰🄴 🄰🄳 🄰 🄼🄲; (*B4-5*).

★★★ **Le Cascine** (no restaurant), Largo F.lli Alinari 15, ✉ 50123, tel. 055211066, fax 055210769; www.hotellecascine.it; 20 rms.; 🄿 🄴 🄖 🄰🄴 🄰🄳 🄰 🄼🄲; (*B3*).

★★★ **Loggiato dei Serviti** (no restaurant), Piazza SS. Annunziata 3, ✉ 50122, tel. 055289592, fax 055 289595; www.venere.it/ firenze/loggiato-serviti; 29 rms.; 🄿 🄰🄴 🄰🄴 🄰🄳 🄰 🄼🄲; (*A-B5-6*).

★★★ **Morandi alla Crocetta** (no restaurant), Via Laura 50, ✉ 50121, tel. 0552344747, fax 0552480954; www.hotelmorandi.it; 10 rms.; 🄿 🄴 🄰🄴 🄰🄳 🄰 🄼🄲; (*B6*).

★★★ **Orto de' Medici** (no restaurant), Via S. Gallo 30, ✉ 50129, tel. 055483427, fax 055461276; www. ortodeimedici.it; 31 rms.; 🄿 🄴 🄰🄴 🄰🄳 🄰 🄼🄲; (*A5*).

★★★ **Villa Azalee** (no restaurant), Viale F.lli Rosselli 44, ✉ 50123, tel. 055214242, fax 055268264; www.villa-azalee.it; 26 rms.; 🄿 🄰🄴 🄴 🄖 🄰🄴 🄰🄳 🄰 🄼🄲; (*off map*).

★★★ **Villa Liberty** (no restaurant), Viale Michelangiolo 40, ✉ 50125, tel. 0556810581, fax 0556812595; www.hotelvillaliberty.com; 18 rms.; 🄿 🄴 🄿 🄰🄴 🄰🄳 🄰 🄼🄲; (*off map*).

★★ **Annabella** (no restaurant), Via Fiume 17, ✉ 50123, tel. 055281877, fax 055264206; www.zip.to/annabella; 8 rms.; 🄴 🄰🄳 🄰; (*A1-2*).

★★ **Casci** (no restaurant), Via Cavour 13, ✉ 50129, tel. 055211686, fax 0552396461; www.hotelcasci.com; closed for a certain period of time in January; 25 rms.; 🄴 🄖 🄰🄴 🄰🄳 🄰 🄼🄲; (*B4*).

★★ **Cimabue** (no restaurant), Via B. Lupi 7, ✉ 50129, tel. 055475601, fax 0554630906; www.hotelcimabue.it; closed for a certain period of time in December; 16 rms.; 🄿 🄴 🄰🄴 🄰🄳 🄰 🄼🄲; (*off map*).

★★ **Lombardi** (no restaurant), Via Fiume 8, ✉ 50123, tel. 055283151, fax 055284808; www.hotellombardi.com; 15 rms.; 🄿 🄴 🄰🄴 🄰🄳 🄰 🄼🄲; (*B3*).

Restaurants

🍴🍴🍴 **Enoteca Pinchiorri** Via Ghibellina 87, ✉ 50122, tel. 055242777, fax 0552244983 ⌧; www.pinchiorri.it; 🍴 Tuscan and original 🍷 Italian and international; 50 capacity; closed Sunday and Monday at midday and Wednesday, Christmas and August; ❀ 🄿 🄰🄴 🄰🄳 🄰 🄼🄲; (*D6*).

🍴🍴 **Sabatini** Via de' Panzani 9/A, ✉ 50123, tel. 055 211559, fax 055210293 ⌧; 🍴 Tuscan and classic 🍷 Italian and international; 180 capacity; closed Monday; ❀ 🄿 🄰🄴 🄰🄳 🄰 🄼🄲; (*C3*).

🍴🍴 **Alle Murate** Via Ghibellina 52/r, ✉ 50122, tel. 055 240618; 🍴 fine cuisine Tuscan 🍷 Italian and international; 65 capacity; closed Monday, Christmas; 🄿 🄰🄴 🄰🄳 🄰 🄼🄲; (*D5-6*).

🍴🍴 **Beccofino** Piazza degli Scarlatti 1/r (lungarno Guicciardini), ✉ 50125, tel. 055290076 ⌧; 🍴 Tuscan and original 🍷 Italian and international; 100 capacity; closed Monday (midday on Monday in summer); 🄿 🄰🄴 🄰🄳; (*E2*).

🍴🍴 **Cantinetta Antinori** Piazza Antinori 3, ✉ 50123, tel. 055292234, fax 0552359877 ⌧; 🍴 Tuscan 🍷 Italian; 45 capacity; closed Saturday, Sunday, Christmas and for a certain period of time in August; 🄿 🄰🄴 🄰🄳 🄰 🄼🄲; (*C3*).

🍴🍴 **Cibreo** Via del Verrocchio 8/r, ✉ 50122, tel. 0552341100, fax 055244966 ⌧; cibreo.fi@tin.it; 🍴 Tuscan and classic 🍷 Italian and international; 70 capacity; closed Sunday and Monday, Christmas and August; 🄿; (*off map*).

🍴🍴 **La Baraonda** Via Ghibellina 67/r, ✉ 50122, tel. 0552341171 ⌧; labaraonda@tin.it; 🍴 Tuscan 🍷 Italian and international; 70 capacity; closed Sunday, midday on Monday and Christmas; ❀ 🄰🄴 🄰🄳 🄰 🄼🄲; (*off map*).

🍴🍴 **Osteria n. 1** Via del Moro 18/20, ✉ 50123, tel. 055 284897 ⌧, fax 055294318; 🍴 Tuscan and innovative 🍷 Italian and international; 100 capacity; closed Sunday, midday on Monday and for a certain period of time in August; 🄿 🄰🄴 🄰🄳 🄰 🄼🄲; (*D2*).

🍴🍴 **Taverna del Bronzino** Via delle Ruote 25-27/r, ✉ 50129, tel. 055495220 ⌧; 🍴 classic 🍷 local and national; 70 capacity; closed Sunday, August; 🄿 🄰🄴 🄰🄳 🄰 🄼🄲; (*off map*).

🍴 **Buca Mario** Piazza Ottaviani 16/r, ✉ 50123, tel. 055214179 ⌧; 🍴 Tuscan 🍷 local; 100 capacity; closed Wednesday, and Thursday at midday, August; 🅿 🅰🅴 ⓐ 🈷 🆛; (C2).

🍴 **Cavallino** Piazza della Signoria/via delle Farine 6/r, ✉ 50122, tel. 055215818 🆛; 🍽 Tuscan and classic 🍷 local and national; 100 capacity; closed Wednesday (except in summer); 🅿 ♦ 🅰🅴 ⚶ 🈷 🆛; (D4).

🍴 **Coco Lezzone** Via Parioncino 26/r, ✉ 50123, tel. 055287178 🆛; 🍽 Tuscan 🍷 local and national; 80 capacity; closed Sunday, Christmas, July-August; (D3).

🍴 **Dino** Via Ghibellina 51/r, ✉ 50122, tel. 055 241452 🆛; ristorante.dino@dada.it; 🍽 Tuscan 🍷 local and national; 80 capacity; closed Sunday evening, Monday; 🅿 🅰🅴 ⓐ 🈷 🆛; (off map).

🍴 **I Quattro Amici** Via degli Orti Oricellari 29, ✉ 50123, tel. 055215413 🆛; www.accademiadel gusto.it; 🍽 Tuscan and classic 🍷 Italian and inter-national; 90 capacity; 🅿 🅰🅴 ⓐ 🈷 🆛; (B1-2).

🍴 **Mamma Gina** Borgo S. Jacopo 37/r, ✉ 50125, tel. 0552396009 🆛; www.mammagina.it; 🍽 Tuscan 🍷 Italian and international; 130 capacity; closed Sunday, August; 🅿 🅰🅴 ⓐ 🈷 🆛; (D2-3).

🍴 **I' Toscano** Via Guelfa 70/r, ✉ 50129, tel. 055 215475 🆛; www.itoscano.it; 🍽 Tuscan 🍷 local; 80 capacity; closed Tuesday, August; 🅰🅴 ⓐ 🈷 🆛; (A4).

Forte dei Marmi (LU)   ✉ 55042

ℹ️ *APT*, Viale A. Franceschi 8, tel. 058480091; www.versilia.turismo.toscana.it.

🚆 *Stazione F.S. (railway station)* at Querceta; bus service.

🛣️ *Versilia* (A12 Genova-Rosignano e Civitavecchia-Roma).

Hotels and restaurants

⭐⭐⭐ **Augustus** Viale Morin 169, tel. 0584787200, fax 0584787102; www.versilia.toscana.it/augustus; open mid-April-mid-October; 68 rms.; 🅿 🅰 ⚶ 🅿 ♿ 🅰🅴 ⓐ 🈷.

⭐⭐⭐ **Byron** Viale Morin 46, tel. 0584787052, fax 0584 787152; www.hotelbyron.net; info@hotelbyron. net; 28 rms.; 🅿 🅰 ⚶ 🅿 🅰🅴 ⓐ 🈷 🆛.

⭐⭐⭐ **Raffaelli Park** Via M. Mazzini 37, tel. 0584787294, fax 0584787418; www.raffaelli.com; closed for a certain period of time in December; 28 rms.; 🅿 🅰 ⚶ ✕ 🅿 🅰🅴 ⓐ 🈷 🆛.

⭐⭐⭐ **Ritz Forte dei Marmi** Via F. Gioia 2, tel. 0584 787531, fax 0584787522; www.versilia.net/upga/ritz/index.html; 32 rms.; 🅰 ⚶ 🅿 🅰🅴 ⓐ 🈷 🆛.

⭐⭐⭐ **Franceschi** Via XX Settembre 19, tel. 0584 787114, fax 0584787471; open mid-March-October; 55 rms.; 🅿 🅰 🅿 🅰🅴 ⓐ 🈷.

⭐⭐⭐ **Le Pleiadi** Via M. Civitali 51, tel. 0584881188, fax 0584881653; www.hotellepleiadi.it; open April-mid-October; 30 rms.; 🅿 🅰 🅰🅴 ⓐ 🈷.

⭐⭐⭐ **Mignon** Via Carducci 58, tel. 0584787495, fax 0584787494; www.hotelmignon.it; open mid-March-October; 34 rms.; 🅿 🅰 ⚶ 🅿 ♿ 🈷.

🍴 **Barca** Viale Italico 3, tel. 058489323, fax 0584 83141 🆛; 🍽 classic 🍷 Italian and international; 130 capacity; closed Monday or Tuesday and for a certain period of time between November and December; 🅿 ♦ 🅿 🅰🅴 ⓐ 🈷 🆛.

🍴 **La Magnolia del Byron** Viale Morin 46, tel. 0584 787052, fax 0584787152 🆛; www.hotelbyron.it; 🍽 Tuscan and classic (seafood) 🍷 Italian and inter-national; 90 capacity; closed November; 🅿 ♦ 🅿 🅰🅴 ⓐ 🈷 🆛; part of the Albergo Byron.

Frascati (RM)   ✉ 00044

ℹ️ *IAT*, Piazza Marconi 1, tel. 069420331; iatfrascati@virgilio.it.

🚆 *Stazione F.S. (railway station)*, piazzale della Stazione, tel. 892021.

🛣️ *Monte Porzio Catone* (A1 Dir. Roma Nord, Sud).

Hotels and restaurants

⭐⭐⭐ **Flora** (no restaurant), Viale Vittorio Veneto 8, tel. 069416110, fax 069416546; www.hotel-flora.it; 37 rms.; 🅿 🅰 ⚶ 🅰🅴 ⓐ 🈷 🆛.

⭐⭐ **Eden Tuscolano** Via Tuscolana 15, tel. 06 9408589, fax 069408591; www.edentuscolano.it; 36 rms.; 🅿 ♿ 🅰🅴 ⓐ 🈷 🆛.

🍴 **Cacciani** Via A. Diaz 13, tel. 069420378 🆛; www.cacciani.it; 🍽 Roman and classic 🍷 Italian and international; 120 capacity; closed Monday (from October to May also evenings, on holidays), for a certain period of time in January and August; 🅿 also hotel.

Gardone Riviera (BS)   ✉ 25083

ℹ️ *IAT* (seasonal), Corso della Repubblica 8, tel. 036520347.

🚆 *Stazione F.S. (railway station)* at Desenzano del Garda; bus service.

🛣️ *Desenzano* (A4 Torino-Milano-Trieste).

Hotels and restaurants

⭐⭐⭐ **G.H. Gardone** Corso Zanardelli 84, tel. 0365 20261, fax 036522695; www.grangardone.it; open April-mid-October; 180 rms.; 🅿 🅰 ⚶ 🅿 🅿 ♿ 🅰🅴 ⓐ 🈷 🆛.

⭐⭐⭐ **Savoy Palace** Corso Zanardelli 2/4, ✉ 25080, tel. 0365290588, fax 0365290556; www.savoypalace.it; open March-October; 60 rms.; 🅿 🅰 ⚶. 🗒 🅰 🅰🅴 ⓐ 🈷 🆛.

⭐⭐⭐ **Bellevue** Corso Zanardelli 40, tel. 0365290080, fax 0365290088; www.tin.it/tebaide/bellevue; open April-mid-October; 32 rms.; 🅰 ⚶ 🗒 🅿 🈷.

⭐⭐⭐ **Monte Baldo** Corso Zanardelli 110, tel. 0365 20951, fax 036520952; www.relaxongarda.com; open mid-April-mid-October; 40; 🅰 ⚶ 🅿 🅰🅴 ⓐ 🈷.

🍴🍴 **Villa Fiordaliso** Corso Zanardelli 150, tel. 0365 20158, fax 0365290011 🆛; www.relaischateaux.fr/fiordaliso; info@villafiordaliso.it; 🍽 Lombard-Venetian 🍷 Italian and international; 80/180 ca-pacity; open February-November, closed Monday and Tuesday at midday; 🅿 ♦ 🅿 🅰🅴 ⓐ 🈷 🆛; also hotel.

🍴 **La Stalla** Via dei Colli 14, tel. 036521038 🆛; 🍽 local and classic 🍷 Italian and international; 100 capacity; closed Tuesday except holidays, for a certain period of time in January; ♦ 🅿 🅰🅴 ⓐ 🈷 🆛.

at Fasano del Garda, 3 km   ✉ 25080

Hotels and restaurants

⭐⭐⭐ **G.H. Fasano** Corso Zanardelli 190, tel. 0365 290220, fax 0365290221; www.grand-hotel-fasano.it; open April-October; 68 rms.; 🅰 ⚶ ✕ 🗒 🅿.

Genoa   ✉ 16100

ℹ️ *IAT*, Stazione Porta Principe, tel. 0102462633; www.genovatouristboard.net; (B2); Area Porto An-tico, tel. 010248711; iat.portoantico@apt.genova.it (B-C1); Aeroporto Cristoforo Colombo, tel. 0106015247; aeroporto@apt.genova.it.

🚆 *Stazione F.S. (railway station)*, Porta Principe, Pi-azza Acquaverde, tel. 892021; *Stazione Brignole*, tel. 892021.

🛣️ *Genova Est* (A12 Genova-Rosignano), *Genova Ovest* (A7 Milano-Genova), *Genova Pegli* (A10 Ponte S. Luigi-Genova).

461

✈ *Cristoforo Colombo Airport* at Sestri Ponente, tel. 01060151. Bus service by "Volabus" from the railway station of Brignole; bus no. 151 from the railway station of Cornigliano, and from Sestri Ponente, with main stop at Villa Gavotti.
Air Dolomiti, information, tel. 800-013366.
Air Italy, information, tel. 800-634538.
Air Sicilia, information, tel. 800-634538.
Alitalia, Via XII Aprile 12, tel. 01054931 (*C4-5*).

⚓ *Stazione Marittima (ship passenger terminal)*, ferry terminal, tel. 010256682.
Grandi Navi Veloci, Via Fieschi 17, tel. 010 589331 (ferryboat to Palermo and, seasonal, to Olbia, Porto Torres and Barcellona).
Moby Lines, Calata della Chiappella, tel. 010 2541513 (seasonal ferryboat to Bastia).
Tirrenia, Ponte Cristoforo Colombo, tel. 01026981 (ferryboat to Olbia and, seasonal, to Cagliari and Arbatax; express service to Olbia and, seasonal, to Porto Torres).
Tris, Piazza della Vittoria 12/24, tel. 0105762411 (seasonal ferry to Palau and Corsica).

Hotels

★★★ **Bristol Palace** (no restaurant), Via XX Settembre 35, ☒ 16121, tel. 010592541, fax 010561756 www.hotelbristolpalace.com; 133 rms.; 🅿 🄴 ♿ 🄰🄴 ⓓ 🆚 ᴍᴄ; (*D4*).

★★★ **City** Via S. Sebastiano 6, ☒ 16123, tel. 01055451, fax 010586301; www.bestwestern.it/city-ge; city.ge @best western.it; 66 rms.; 🅿 🄴 🄰🄴 ⓓ 🆚 ᴍᴄ; (*C4*).

★★★ **Jolly Hotel Plaza** Via M. Piaggio 11, ☒ 16122, tel. 01083161, fax 0108391850; www.jollyhotels. it; 143 rms.; 🅿 🄴 ♿ 🄰🄴 ⓓ 🆚 ᴍᴄ; (*C4-5*).

★★★ **Sheraton Genova Hotel** Via Pionieri e Aviatori d'Italia, ☒ 16154, tel. 01065491, fax 0106549055; www.sheratongenova.com; 283 rms.; 🅿 🄴 🅿 ♿ 🄰🄴 ⓓ 🆚 ᴍᴄ; (*off map*).

★★★ **Starhotel President** Corte Lambruschini 4, ☒ 16129, tel. 0105727, fax 0105531820; www.star hotels.it; 193 rms.; 🅿 🄴 🄰🄴 ⓓ 🆚 ᴍᴄ; (*D6*).

★★★ **Agnello d'Oro** (no restaurant), Via delle Monachette 6, ☒ 16126, tel. 0102462084, fax 010 2462327; www.hotelagnellodoro.it; hotelagnello doro@libero.it; 35 rms.; 🄴 🅿 🄰🄴 ⓓ 🆚 ᴍᴄ; (*B2*).

★★★ **Alexander** (no restaurant), Via Bersaglieri d'Italia 19/r, ☒ 16126, tel. 010261371, fax 010265257; 35 rms.; 🅿 🄴 🄰🄴 ⓓ 🆚; (*B2*).

★★★ **Europa** (no restaurant), Vico delle Monachette 8, ☒ 16126, tel. 010256955, fax 010261047; 38 rms.; 🅿 🅿 🄰🄴 ⓓ 🆚; (*B2*).

★★★ **Galles** (no restaurant), Via Bersaglieri d'Italia 13, ☒ 16126, tel. 0102462820, fax 0102462822; 20 rms.; 🅿 🄴 🄰🄴 ⓓ 🆚 ᴍᴄ; (*B2*).

★★★ **Viale Sauli** (no restaurant), Viale Sauli 5, ☒ 16121, tel. 010561397, fax 010590092; htl.sauli@mclink.it; 56 rms.; 🅿 🄴 🄰🄴 ⓓ 🆚 ᴍᴄ; (*D5*).

Restaurants

🍴 **Antica Osteria del Bai** at Quarto dei Mille, Via Quarto 12, ☒ 16148, tel. 010387478, fax 010 392684 ☒; bai@publinet.it; 🍴 Ligurian and classic ⌂⍾ local, Italian and international; 80 capacity; closed Monday, and for a certain period of time in January and August; 🅿 🄴 ⓓ 🆚 ᴍᴄ; (*off map*).

🍴 **Edilio** Corso De Stefanis 104, ☒ 16139, tel. 010880501, fax 010811260 ☒; 🍴 Ligurian and Piedmontese ⌂⍾ Italian and international; 80 capacity; closed Sunday evening and Monday, and a certain period of time in August; 🅿 🅿 🄰🄴 ⓓ 🆚 ᴍᴄ; (*A4*).

🍴 **Gran Gotto** Viale Brigata Bisagno 69/R, ☒ 16121, tel. 010564344 ☒; grangotto@libero.it; 🍴 Ligurian and fine cuisine ⌂⍾ Italian and international; 60 capacity; closed Saturday at midday and Sunday, and for a certain period of time in August; 🅿 🄰🄴 ⓓ 🆚 ᴍᴄ; (*E-6*).

🍴 **La Bitta nella Pergola** Via Casaregis 52, ☒ 16129, tel. 010588543 ☒; 🍴 fine and Liguria cuisine ⌂⍾ Italian and international; 40 capacity; closed Sunday evening, Monday, and for a certain period of time in January and August; 🅿 🄴 🄰🄴 ⓓ 🆚 ᴍᴄ; (*F6*).

🍴 **Zeffirino** Via XX Settembre 20, ☒ 16121, tel. 010591990, fax 010586464 ☒; www.ristorante zeffirino.com; zeffirino@ghgnet.com; 🍴 Liguria and classic ⌂⍾ Italian and international; 180 capacity; 🅿 🅿 🄰🄴 ⓓ 🆚 ᴍᴄ; (*D5*).

🍴 **Baldin** Piazza Tazzoli 20/r, Sestri Ponente, ☒ 16154, tel. 0106531400 ☒; 🍴 Ligurian (fish, mushrooms) ⌂⍾ Italian and international; 60 capacity; closed Sunday and Monday evening, a certain period of time in January and August; 🅿 🄰🄴 ⓓ 🆚 ᴍᴄ; (*off map*).

🍴 **Bruxaboschi** at San Desiderio, Via Mignone 8, ☒ 16133, tel. 0103450302 ☒; bruxaboschi@libe ro.it; 🍴 Ligurian (mushrooms) ⌂⍾ Italian and international; 150 capacity; closed Monday, Sunday evening, Christmas-Epiphany (6 January), and August; 🏕 🄰🄴 ⓓ 🆚 ᴍᴄ; (*off map*).

🍴 **Genio** Salita S. Leonardo 61/r, ☒ 16128, tel. 010588463 ☒; riffi@libero.it; 🍴 Genoese ⌂⍾ local and national; 55 capacity; closed Sunday, August; 🄰🄴 ⓓ 🆚 ᴍᴄ; (*D4*).

🍴 **Le Rune** Vico Domoculta 14/r, ☒ 16121, tel. 010594951; 🍴 Ligurian ⌂⍾ local and national; 70 capacity; 🄰🄴 🆚 ᴍᴄ; (*C4*).

Gubbio (PG) ☒ 06024

🅸 *IAT*, Piazza Oderisi 6, tel. 0759220693; info@iat gubbio.pg.it.

⚏ *Stazione F.S. (railway station)* at Fossato di Vico o Perugia, bus service.

✈ *Perugia* (Raccordo Val di Chiana-Perugia).

Hotels and restaurants

★★★ **Park Hotel ai Cappuccini** Via Tifernate, tel. 0759234, fax 0759220323; www.parkhotelaicapp uccini.it; 95 rms.; 🅿 ♨ ⚘ 🍴 🅿 🅿 ♿ 🄰🄴 ⓓ 🆚 ᴍᴄ.

★★★ **Bosone Palace** (no restaurant), Via XX Settembre 22, tel. 0759220688, fax 0759220552; closed February; 30 rms.; 🄰🄴 ⓓ 🆚 ᴍᴄ.

★★ **Oderisi-Balestrieri** (no restaurant), Via Mazzatinti 2-12, tel. 0759220662, fax 0759220663; closed February; 40 rms.; 🄴 ♿ 🄰🄴 ⓓ 🆚 ᴍᴄ.

🍴 **Taverna del Lupo** Via Ansidei 6, tel. 075 9274368, fax 0759271269 ☒; www.mencarelli group.com; 🍴 Umbrian (mushrooms and truffles) ⌂⍾ Italian and international; 150 capacity; closed Monday; 🅿 🄰🄴 ⓓ 🆚 ᴍᴄ; also hotel.

🍴 **La Fornace di Mastro Giorgio** Via Mastro Giorgio 2, tel. 0759221836 ☒; 🍴 Umbrian (mushrooms and truffles, fish) ⌂⍾ local and national; 120 capacity; closed Tuesday and Wednesday at midday and for a certain period of time in January; 🄰🄴 ⓓ 🆚 ᴍᴄ.

Herculaneum (NA) ☒ 80056

⚏ *Stazione Ferrovia Circumvesuviana*, Piazza Ferrovia, tel. 800-053939.

✈ *Ercolano* (A3 Napoli-Reggio Calabria).

Hotels

★★★ **Punta Quattroventi** Via Marittima 59, tel. 0817773041, fax 0817773757; 37 rms.; 🅿 ♨ ♨ 🅿 🄰🄴 ⓓ 🆚.

Ischia (Island of) (NA) ☎ 081

🅸 at Ischia: *AA*, Via Iasolino, tel. 0815074231; www.ischiaonline.it/tourism.

⛴ *Alicost*, tel. 081991888 (hydrofoil and ferryboat to Naples, seasonal hydrofoil to Capri and Sorrento). *Caremar*, tel. 081991953 (hydrofoil and ferryboat to Naples, Pozzuoli and Procida). *Linee Marittime Partenopee*, tel. 0818376995 (hydrofoil to Capri). *Snav*, tel. 081996403 (hydrofoil to Naples and island of Procida). *Traghetti Pozzuoli*, tel. 081992803 (ferryboat to Pozzuoli).

at Ischia   ✉ 80077

Hotels and restaurants

***✰ G.H. Punta Molino Terme** Lungomare C. Colombo 23, tel. 081991544, fax 081991562; www.puntamolino.it; open mid-April/October; 82 rms.; 🅿 ♨ 🏊 🌊 ✕ 🅿 🆔 ⑳ 🚇.

✰✰ Continental Terme Via M. Mazzella 74, tel. 081991588, fax 081982929; www.ischia.it/conti terme; leohotel@pointel.it; open April-October; 244 rms.; 🅿 ♨ 🏊 🌊 ✕ 🅿 🆔 ⑳ 🚇 MC.

✰✰ G.H. Excelsior Via E. Gianturco 19, tel. 081 991522, fax 081984100; excelsior@pointel.it; open May-October; 85 rms.; 🅿 ♨ 🏊 🌊 ✕ 🅿 ♿ 🆔 ⑳ 🚇.

✰✰ Jolly delle Terme Via De Luca 42, tel. 081 991744, fax 081993156; www.jollyhotels.it; ischia @jollyhotels.it; closed Epiphany (6 January)-mid-March; 194 rms.; 🅿 ♨ 🏊 🌊 🅿 ♿ 🆔 ⑳ 🚇 MC.

✰✰ Bristol Hotel Terme Via Marone 10, tel. 081 992181, fax 081993201; bristol@pointel.it; open April-October; 61 rms.; ♨ 🏊 🆔 🆔 🚇 MC.

🍴 **Damiano** Nuova Circonvallazione, tel. 081 983032 ⊠; 🍴 Ischian and classic 🍷 local and national; 50 capacity; open April-October only evening; 🆔 🚇 MC.

🍴 **Gennaro** Via Porto 66, tel. 081992917, fax 081 983636 ⊠; 🍴 Ischian and classic 🍷 local and national; 100 capacity; open mid-March-October, closed Tuesday in the off season; 🅿 🆔 🚇 MC.

at Barano d'Ischia   ✉ 80070

Hotels

✰✰ Parco Smeraldo Terme at Lido dei Maronti, Via Maronti 21, tel. 081990127, fax 081905022; www.hotelparcosmeraldo.com; open April-October; 72 rms.; 🅿 ♨ 🌊 ✕ 🆔 🚇.

✰✰ St. Raphael Terme at Testaccio, Via Maronti 5, tel. 081990508, fax 081990922; www.saintrapha el.it; open April-November; 40 rms.; ♨ 🏊 🅿 🆔 ⑳ 🚇 MC.

at Casamìcciola Terme   ✉ 80074

Hotels

✰✰ Elma Park Hotel Terme Corso Vittorio Emanuele 57, tel. 081994122, fax 081994253; www.hotelel ma.it; 73 rms.; 🅿 ♨ 🏊 🌊 ✕ 🅿 🆔 ⑳ 🚇 MC.

✰✰ Stefania Terme Piazzetta Nizzola 16, tel. 0819941302, fax 081994295; www.ischiahotels.it/ hotels/stefania; hotelstefania@flashnet.it; open April-October; 30 rms.; 🅿 🅿 🆔 ⑳ 🚇 MC.

✰✰ Monti Calata S. Antonio 7, tel. 081994074, fax 081900630; open April-mid-November; 26 rms.; ♨ 🏊 🌊 🅿 🆔 ⑳ 🚇 MC.

at Forio   ✉ 80075

Hotels

✰✰ La Bagattella at San Francesco, Via T. Cigliano 8, tel. 081986072, fax 081989637; www.labagattel la.it; labagattella@flashnet.it; open April-October; 53 rms.; 🅿 ♨ 🏊 🌊 🌊 🅿.

✰✰ Parco Maria at Cuotto, Via Provinciale Panza 212, tel. 081909040, fax 081909100; closed for a certain period of time between November and December and Epiphany (6 January) and mid-February; 98 rms.; ♨ 🌊 🌊 🅿.

at Lacco Ameno   ✉ 80076

Hotels

***✰ Regina Isabella e Royal Sporting** Piazza S. Restituta, tel. 081994322, fax 081900190; www. reginaisabella.it; closed for a certain period of time between November and Christmas; 134 rms.; 🅿 ♨ 🏊 🌊 ✕ 🅿 🆔 ⑳ 🚇 MC.

✰✰ San Montano Via Montevico, tel. 081994033, fax 081980242; info@sanmontano.com; open April-October; 67 rms.; 🅿 ♨ 🏊 🌊 ✕ 🅿 🆔 ⑳ 🚇 MC.

✰✰ Grazia Terme Via Borbonica 2, tel. 081994333, fax 081994153; www.hotelgrazia.it; info@hotel grazia.it; open April-October; 58 rms.; 🅿 ♨ 🏊 🌊 ✕ 🅿 🆔 🚇.

✰✰ La Reginella Piazza S. Restituta 1, tel. 081 994300, fax 081980481; open Easter-mid-October and Christmas period; 90 rms.; 🅿 ♨ 🏊 🌊 ✕ 🅿 🆔 ⑳ 🚇.

✰✰ Don Pepe Terme Via Circumvallazione 39, tel. 081994397, fax 081996696; www.hoteldonpepe. it; info@hoteldonpepe.it; open mid-February-October; 70 rms.; 🅿 ♨ 🏊 🌊 🅿 🆔 🚇 MC.

✰✰ Villa Angelica Via IV Novembre 28, tel. 081994524, fax 081980184; www.villaangelica.it/ ita/centrale.htm; angelica@pointel.it; open April-mid-November; 20 rms.; ♨ 🏊 🌊 🆔 🚇 MC.

at Sant'Angelo   ✉ 80070

Hotels and restaurants

✰✰ Park Hotel Miramare Via C. Maddalena 29, tel. 081999219, fax 081999325; open April-October; 54 rms.; ♨ 🏊 🌊 ✕ ⑳ 🚇.

✰✰ Casa Celestino S.P. Succhivo-Sant'Angelo n. 159, tel. 081999213, fax 081999805; open April-October; 20 rms.; 🆔.

🍴 **Lo Scoglio** Via Cava Ruffano 58, tel. 081999529; 🍴 Campanian (seafood) 🍷 local and national; 100 capacity; open April-November and Christmas holidays; 🆔 ⑳ 🚇 MC.

L'Àquila   ✉ 67100

ℹ️ *IAT*, Piazza S. Maria di Paganica 5, tel. 0862 410808; presidio.aquila@abruzzoturismo.it; (*B4*); *Information Office*, Via XX Settembre 8, tel. 086222306; (*C3*).

🚉 *Stazione F.S. (railway station)*, Piazza della Stazione, tel. 892021.

🛣 *L'Aquila Est* or *L'Aquila Ovest* (A24 Roma-Teramo).

Hotels and restaurants

✰✰ G.H. del Parco Corso Federico II 74, tel. 0862 413249, fax 086265938; 36 rms.; 🆔 🅿 🆔 ⑳ 🚇 MC; (*C4*).

✰✰ Amiternum Bivio S. Antonio, tel. 0862315757, fax 0862315987; www.hotelamiternum.it; 60 rms.; 🅿 🆔 🅿 ♿ 🆔 ⑳ 🚇; (*off map*).

✰✰ Duca degli Abruzzi Viale Giovanni XXIII 10, tel. 086228341, fax 086261588; www.hda.it; mail@ hda.it; 120 rms.; 🅿 ♨ 🆔 🅿 ♿ 🆔 ⑳ 🚇; (*B3*).

✰✰ Duomo (no restaurant), Via Dragonetti 6/10, tel. 0862410893, fax 0862413058; 30 rms.; 🆔 🚇 MC; (*C4*).

🍴 **Osteria Antiche Mura** Via XXV Aprile 2, tel. 086262422 ⊠; 🍴 local 🍷 local and national; 60 capacity; closed Sunday and for a certain period of time in August and December; ⚘ 🅿 🚇 MC; (*A2*).

Lecce   ✉ 73100

ℹ️ *ARET*, Via Vittorio Emanuele 24, tel. 0832 248092; www.pugliaturismo.com; (*D2*).

🚉 *Stazione F.S. (railway station)*, Viale Quarta 4, tel. 892021; *Stazione Ferrovie del SudEst*, Viale Quarta, tel. 0832668111.

Hotels and restaurants

★★★ **Cristal** (no restaurant), Via Marinosci 16, tel. 0832372314, fax 0832315109; www.hotelcristal.it; 68 rms.; 🖼 ✕ 🗚 🕭 🍽 🚾 MC; (*off map*).

★★★ **President** Via Salandra 6, tel. 0832311881, fax 0832372283; www.roundhotels.it; 154 rms.; 🖼 🗐 🖻 ♿ 🗚 🕭 🚾 MC; (*C5*).

🍽🍽🍽 **Picton** Via Idomeneo 14, tel. 0832332383 ✉; www.acena.it/picton; ✕ Apulian (seafood, herbs) 🍷 Italian and international; 110 capacity; closed Monday, for a certain period of time in June and November; 🖼 🗚 🕭 🍽 🚾 MC; (*C2*).

🍽 **Villa della Monica** Via Ss. Giacomo e Filippo 40, tel. 0832458432 ✉; ✕ Salento and classic 🍷 local and national; 500 capacity; closed Tuesday, and for a certain period of time in January and between July and August; 🖼 ✤ 🅿 🗚 🕭 🚾 MC; (*B-C4*).

Lèrici (SP) ✉ 19032

ℹ️ *IAT*, Via Biagini 6, tel. 0187967346.

🚆 *Stazione F.S. (railway station)* at Sarzana; bus service.

🕇 *Sarzana* (A12 Genova-Rosignano).

⛴ *Navigazione Golfo dei Poeti*, tel. 0187732987 (ferryboat, seasonal, to Monterosso al Mare, Portofino, Portovenere, Vernazza, Isola Palmaria).

Hotels and restaurants

★★★ **Europa** Via Carpanini 1, tel. 0187967800, fax 0187965957; www.europahotel.it; europa@europahotel.it; 35 rms.; 🖼 🗚 🅿 🕭 🍽 🚾 MC.

★★★ **Shelley & delle Palme** Lungomare Biaggini 5, tel. 0187968204, fax 0187964271; shelleyspa@libero.it; 49 rms.; 🖼 🗐 🗚 🕭 🍽 🚾 MC.

🍽 **Calata** Via Mazzini 4, tel. 0187967143 ✉; ✕ classic (seafood) 🍷 local and national; 80/100 capacity; closed Tuesday and for a certain period of time between December and January; ✤ 🗚 🕭 🍽 MC.

at Fiascherino, 4 km ✉ 19030

Hotels

★★★ **Cristallo** (no restaurant), Via Fiascherino 158, tel. 0187967291, fax 0187964269; www.space.tin.it/viaggi/pifabian; albero.cristallo@libero.it; open mid-March-October; 35 rms.; 🖼 🗚 🅿 🗚 🕭 🚾 MC.

★★★ **Il Nido** Via Fiascherino 75, tel. 0187967286, fax 0187964225; www.space.tin.it/viaggi/pifabian; open April-mid-November; 36 rms.; 🗚 🗐 🅿 🗚 🕭 🚾 MC.

Lèvanto (SP) ✉ 19015

ℹ️ *IAT*, Piazza Cavour, tel. 0187808125.

🚆 *Stazione F.S. (railway station)*, Piazza della Stazione, tel. 892021.

🕇 *Carrodano* (A12 Genova-Rosignano).

Hotels and restaurants

★★★ **Nazionale** Via J. da Levanto 20, tel. 0187808102, fax 0187800901; www.nazionale.it; closed November-mid-March; 38 rms.; 🗚 🅿 🗚 🕭 🍽.

🍽 **Loggia** Piazza del Popolo 7, tel. 0187808107 ✉; www.locandalaloggia.com; locandalaloggia@hotmail.com; ✕ Ligurian 🍷 Italian and international; 60 capacity; closed Wednesday except in summer, February; 🗚 🕭 🚾 MC.

464

Lido di Òstia (RM) ✉ 00121

ℹ️ *APT* at Rome; *Pro Loco*, Piazzale Stazione Lido Centro 34, tel. 065627892.

🚆 *Stazione Ferrovie Cotral*, Piazzale Stazione Lido Centro, tel. 800-431784.

🕇 *S.S. 8 Via del Mare* and *8/bis Ostiense* (Grande Raccordo Anulare di Roma).

Hotels and restaurants

★★★ **Airport Palace Hotel** Viale dei Romagnoli 165, tel. 065692341, fax 065698908; airportpalace@tiscali.it; 275 rms.; 🖼 🗐 🅿 🗚 🕭 🚾.

★★★ **Satellite Palace Hotel** Via delle Antille 49, tel. 0656183, fax 065698908; satellitepalace@tiscali.it; 262 rms.; 🖼 🚴 🗐 🗚 🕭 🚾.

★★★ **Sirenetta** Lungomare Toscanelli 46, tel. 06 5623963, fax 065622310; martinim@mbox.tin.it; 60 rms.; 🚴 🅿 🗚 🕭 🚾.

★★★ **Tirrenia** (no restaurant), Lungomare Toscanelli 74, tel. 0656304192, fax 0656324850; hotel.tirrenia@flashnet.it; 11 rms.; 🚴 🅿 🗚 🕭 🚾.

🍽 **Le Bizze de il Tino** Via dei Lucilii 17-19, tel. 065622778 ✉; msalvatori@tiscali.it; ✕ fine cuisine 🍷 Italian; 35 capacity; closed Monday and Sunday; for a certain period of time in January and August; 🖼 🗚 🕭 🍽 🚾 MC.

🍽 **Sbarco d'Enea** at Òstia Antica, Via dei Romagnoli 675, 00119, tel. 065650253 ✉; ✕ classic (seafood) 🍷 Italian; 410 capacity; closed Monday, February; ✤ 🗚 🕭 🚾 MC.

Lucca ✉ 55100

ℹ️ *APT*, Piazza S. Maria 35, tel. 0583419689; www.lucca.turismo.toscana.it; (*A3*).

🚆 *Stazione F.S. (railway station)*, Piazza Ricasoli, tel. 892021.

🕇 *Lucca* (A11 Firenze-Mare).

Hotels and restaurants

★★★ **G.H. Guinigi** Via Romana 1247, tel. 05834991, fax 0583499800; www.grandhotelguinigi.it; 158 rms.; 🖼 🅿 ♿ 🗚 🕭 🚾; (*C5, off map*).

★★★ **Celide** (no restaurant), Viale Giusti 25, tel. 0583954106, fax 0583954304; Hotelcelide@arcadiatel.it; 62 rms.; 🖼 🅿 🗚 🕭 🚾; (*C-D5*).

★★★ **La Luna** (no restaurant), Via Fillungo corner of Corte Compagni 12, tel. 0583493634, fax 0583 490021; closed for a certain period of time in January; 30 rms.; 🗐 🗚 🕭 🍽 🚾; (*B3*).

★★★ **Rex** (no restaurant), Piazza Ricasoli 19, tel. 0583 955443, fax 0583954348; www.hotelrexlucca.com; 25 rms.; 🖼 ♿ 🗚 🕭 🚾; (*D3*).

★★ **Stipino** (no restaurant), Via Romana 95, tel. 0583 495077, fax 0583490309; 21 rms.; 🖼 🗚 🅿 🗚 🕭 🚾; (*B5, off map*).

🍽🍽🍽 **Buca di Sant'Antonio** Via della Cervia 3, tel. 0583 55881, fax 0583312199 ✉; www.lunet.it/aziende/bucadisantonio; la.buca@lunet.it; ✕ Lucchesia 🍷 local and national; 90 capacity; closed Sunday evening and Monday, and for a certain period of time in January and July; 🖼 🗚 🕭 🚾; (*C2*).

🍽 **Del Teatro** Piazza Napoleone 25, tel. 0583 493740 ✉; ✕ Tuscan and classic (seafood) 🍷 local and national; 110 capacity; closed Tuesday; ✤ 🗚 🕭 🚾; (*C2*).

at Massa Pisana, 4 km ✉ 55050

Hotels and restaurants

★★★ **Locanda L'Elisa** Via Nuova per Pisa 1952, tel. 0583379737, fax 0583379019; www.lunet.it/aziende/locandaelisa; locanda.elisa@lunet.it; closed January and November; 10 rms.; 🖼 🗚 🚴 🅿 🗚 🕭 🚾 MC.

at Ponte a Moriano, 9 km   ✉ 55029

Restaurants

¶¶¶ **Mora** Via Sesto di Moriano 1748, tel. 0583 406402, fax 0583406135 ⊠; ⅜⅝ Lucchesia and Garfagnana ◖◗ Italian and international; 60 capacity; closed Wednesday, and for a certain period of time in January; ✿ ⊼⊟ ⓐ ⊞ Ⓜ⨍.

at San Michele in Escheto, 4 km   ✉ 55050

Hotels

✩✩✩ **Villa San Michele** (no restaurant), Via della Chiesa 462, tel. 0583370276, fax 0583370277; www.hotelvillasanmichele.it; htlvillasmichele@tin.it; open April-October; 22 rms.; ⊠ ⊼ ℙ ⊼⊟ ⓐ Ⓜ⨍.

Madonna di Campìglio (TN)   ✉ 38084

ℹ *APT*, Via Pradalago 4, tel. 0465442000; www.campiglio.net.

⊠ *Stazione F.S. (railway station)* at Trento; bus service.

⊼ *S. Michele all'Adige-Mezzocorona* or *Trento Centro* (A22 Brennero-Modena).

⅄ downhill and cross-country skiing; included in the area of *Superskirama Dolomiti Adamello-Brenta*.

Hotels and restaurants

✩✩✩ **Chalet Hermitage** Via Castelletto 65, tel. 0465441558, fax 0465441618; www.chalethermitage.com; hothermitage@campiglio.net; open January-April and July-September; 29 rms.; ⊼ ⊼ ⊟ ℙ ⓖ Ⓜ⨍.

✩✩✩ **Spinale Club Hotel** Via Monte Spinale 39, tel. 0465441116, fax 0465442189; www.editeltn.it/ hotelspinale; open December-mid-April and July-mid-September; 59 rms.; ⊼ ⊼ ⊠ ⊼⊟ ⓐ ⊞ Ⓜ⨍.

✩✩✩ **Alpina** Via Sfulmini 5, tel. 0465441075, fax 0465 443464; www.alpina.it; hotel@alpina.it; open December-mid-April and mid-June-mid-September; 27 rms.; ⊼ ⊠ ℙ ⓖ ⊼⊟ ⓐ ⊞ Ⓜ⨍.

✩✩✩ **Chalet dei Pini** (no restaurant), Via Campanile Basso 24, tel. 0465441489, fax 0465441658; www.chaletdeipini.com; open December-mid-April and mid-June-mid-September; 11 rms.; ⊼ ⊟ ℙ ⊼⊟ Ⓜ⨍.

✩✩✩ **Dolomiti Hotel Cozzio** Via Cima Tosa 31, tel. 0465441083, fax 0465440003; web.tiscali.it/hotel dolomiti; dolomitihotel@cr-surfing.net; open December-April and July-September; 29 rms.; ⊟ ℙ ⓖ ⊞.

✩✩✩ **Oberosler** Via Monte Spinale 27, tel. 0465 441136, fax 0465443220; www.hoteloberosler.com; open December-April and July-mid-September; 42 rms.; ⊼ ⊟ ℙ ⊼⊟ ⓐ ⊞ Ⓜ⨍.

¶¶ **Alfiero** Via Vallesinella 5, tel. 04655440117 ⊠; alf bono@tin.it; ⅜⅝ of Trento and classical ◖◗ local and national; 95 capacity; open December-April and mid-Juny-mid-July; ℙ ⊼⊟ ⓐ ⊞.

¶ **Artini** Via Cima Tosa 47, tel. 0465440122 ⊠; ⅜⅝ of Trento and classic (mushrooms) ◖◗ local and national; 160 capacity; open December-April and July-September; ⊠ ⊼⊟ ⓐ ⊞ Ⓜ⨍.

at Campo Carlo Magno, 3 km

Hotels

✩✩✩ **Golf Hotel** Via Cima Tosa 3, tel. 0465441003, fax 0465440294; www.golfhotelcampiglio.it; open mid-December-March and mid-June-mid-September; 114 rms.; ⊼ ⊟ ℙ ⊼⊟ ⓐ ⊞ Ⓜ⨍.

Mantua   ✉ 46100

ℹ *APT*, Piazza Mantegna 6, tel. 0376328253; www.aptmantova.it; (*C4*).

⊠ *Stazione F.S. (railway station)*, Piazza Don Leoni, tel. 892021.

⊼ *Mantova Nord, Mantova Sud* (A22 Brennero-Modena).

Hotels and restaurants

✩✩✩ **San Lorenzo** (no restaurant), Piazza Concordia 14, tel. 0376220500, fax 0376327194; www.hotel sanlorenzo.it; 32 rms.; ⊠ ⊟ ⓖ ⊼⊟ ⓐ ⊞ Ⓜ⨍; (*C4*).

✩✩✩ **Bianchi Stazione** (no restaurant), Piazza Don Leoni 24, tel. 0376326465, fax 0376321504; 53 rms.; ⊠ ⊼ ⊟ ℙ ⊼⊟ ⓐ ⊞.

✩✩✩ **Mantegna** (no restaurant), Via Filzi 10, tel. 0376 328019, fax 0376368564; hotel.mantegna@alta vista.it; closed Christmas-Epiphany (6 January); 39 rms.; ⊠ ⊟ ℙ ⊼⊟ ⓐ Ⓜ⨍; (*C4*).

¶¶¶ **Aquila Nigra** Vicolo Bonacolsi 4, tel. 0376 327180, fax 0376226490 ⊠; www.aquilanigra.it; aquilanigra@aruba.it; ⅜⅝ Lombard ◖◗ Italian and international; 60 capacity; closed Sunday (Sunday evening in April/May and September/ October) and Monday, and for a certain period of time in January and August; ⊠ ⊼⊟ ⓐ ⊞ Ⓜ⨍; (*B4*).

¶¶ **Cigno-Trattoria dei Martini** Piazza d'Arco 1, tel. 0376327101 ⊠; ⅜⅝ Mantuan and classic ◖◗ Italian and international; 80 capacity; closed Monday and Tuesday, and for a certain period of time in January and in August; ⊠ ✿ ⓐ ⊞ Ⓜ⨍; (*B3*).

¶¶ **Ochina Bianca** Via Finzi 2, tel. 0376323700 ⊠; www.operaghiotta.com; info@operaghiotta.com; ⅜⅝ Mantuan and classic ◖◗ Italian and international; 80 capacity; closed Monday and Tuesday at midday, and for a certain period of time in January and July; ⊠ ✿ ⊼⊟ ⊞ Ⓜ⨍; (*B3-4*).

Marina di Ravenna (RA)   ✉ 48023

ℹ *IAT*, seasonal, Viale delle Nazioni 159, tel. 0544530117.

⊠ *Stazione F.S. (railway station)* at Ravenna; bus service.

⊼ *Ravenna* (A14 Dir. Bologna-Taranto).

Hotels and restaurants

✩✩✩ **Park Hotel Ravenna** Viale delle Nazioni 181, tel. 0544531743, fax 0544530430; www.getur hotels.com; open March-November; 144 rms.; ⊠ ⊼ ⊼ ⊠ ℙ ⊼⊟ ⓐ ⊞ Ⓜ⨍.

✩✩✩ **Bermuda** Viale della Pace 363, tel. 0544 530560, fax 0544531643; hotelbermuda@libe ro.it; closed mid-December-mid-January; 23 rms.; ⊠ ⊼ ⊼⊟ ⓐ ⊞ Ⓜ⨍.

¶¶¶ **Gloria** Viale delle Nazioni 420, tel. 0544530274, fax 0544530377 ⊠; www.ristorantegloria.com; info@ristorantegloria.com; ⅜⅝ Romagna (seafood) ◖◗ local and national; 160 capacity; closed Wednesday, September; ⊠ ✿ ℙ ⊼⊟ ⓐ ⊞ Ⓜ⨍.

at Marina Romèa, 3 km beyond the harbor channel

Hotels

✩✩✩ **Columbia** Viale Italia 70, tel. 0544446038, fax 0544441070; www.hotelcolumbia.tsx.org; closed for a certain period of time between December and January; 44 rms.; ⊠ ⊼ ⊼ ⊼⊟ ⓐ ⊞ Ⓜ⨍.

Martina Franca (TA)   ✉ 74015

ℹ *IAT*, Piazza Roma 37, tel. 0804805702.

⊠ *Stazione Ferrovie del Sud Est*, Viale della Stazione, tel. 0804808151.

⊼ *Gioia del Colle* (A14 Bologna-Taranto).

Hotels and restaurants

✩✩✩ **Dell'Erba** Viale dei Cedri 1, tel. 0804301055, fax

0804301639; 49 rms.; 🏊 ♨ ⚱ 🛏 P 👤 🅰️ ⓦ 🚇 MC.

▐▌ **Villaggio In** Via Arco Grassi 8, tel. 0804805911 ⌧; 🍴 Murge; 180 capacity; closed Monday, and for a certain period of time in November; 🏊 🚇 MC.

Massa Maríttima (GR)   ✉ 58024

🔲 *APT at Grosseto; AMATOUR Tourist Office*, Via Parenti 22, tel. 0566902756.

🚉 *Stazione F.S. (railway station) at Follonica; bus service.*

🚏 *Rosignano (A12 Genova-Rosignano and Civi-tavecchia-Roma).*

Hotels and restaurants

★★★ **Il Sole** (no restaurant), Via della Libertà 43, tel. 0566901971, fax 0566901959; 51 rms.; 🖥 🅰️ 🚇.

★★ **Duca del Mare** Piazza Alighieri 1, tel. 0566 902284, fax 901905; www.cometanet.it/ducadel mare; closed mid-November-mid-December and mid-January-mid-February; 28 rms.; 🏊 🏊 ⚱ 🛏 👤 🅰️ 🚇 MC.

▐▌ **Bracali** at Ghirlanda, Via di Perolla 2, ✉ 58020, tel. 0566902318; fax 0566940302 ⌧; ristorante bracali@libero.it; 🍴 fine cuisine 🍷 Italian and international; 30 capacity; closed Monday and Tuesday, for a certain period of time between January and February, and November; 🏊 ❀ P 🅰️ ⓦ 🚇 MC.

Matera   ✉ 75100

🔲 *APT*, Via De Viti De Marco 9, tel. 0835333541; presidiomatera@aptbasilicata.it.

🚉 *Stazione Ferrovie Appulo-Lucane*, Stazione Centrale, Piazza Matteotti, tel. 0835332861.

🚏 *Mottola-Castellaneta (A14 Bologna-Taranto).*

Hotels and restaurants

★★★ **Italia** Via Ridola 5, tel. 0835333561, fax 0835 330087; 47 rms.; 🏊 🅰️ ⓦ 🚇 MC.

★★★ **Sassi Hotel** (no restaurant), Via S. Giovanni Vecchio 89, tel. 0835331009, fax 0835333733; www. paginegialle.it/hotelsassi-01; hotelsassi@virgi lio.it; 16 rms.; 🖥 🅰️ ⓦ 🚇 MC.

▐▌ **Casino del Diavolo** Via La Martella 48, tel. 0835261986 ⌧; www.casinodeldiavolo.com; 🍴 Lucanian 🍷 local and national; 100/60 capacity; closed Monday; 🏊 ❀ P ⓦ.

at Venùsio, 7 km

Restaurants

▐▌ **Venusio** Via Lussemburgo 2, tel. 0835259081, fax 0835259082 ⌧; 🍴 Lucanian and Apulian (seafood) 🍷 Italian and international; 60/80 capacity; closed Sunday evening and Monday, for a certain period of time in January and August; 🏊 ❀ P 🅰️ ⓦ 🚇 MC.

Merano / Meran (BZ)   ✉ 39012

🔲 *AA*, Corso Libertà 35, tel. 0473272000; info@ meranin fo.it.

🚉 *Stazione F.S. (railway station)*, Via IV Novembre, tel. 892021.

🚏 *Bolzano Sud (A22 Brennero-Modena).*

🎿 at Merano 2000, downhill and cross-country skiing; included in the area of *Ortler Skiarena*.

Hotels and restaurants

★★★★ **G.H. Palace - Schloss Maur** Via Cavour 2/4, tel. 0473271000, fax 0473271100; www.palace. it; info@palace.it; 137 rms.; 🏊 🏊 ⚱ 🛏 🖥 P 👤 🅰️ ⓦ 🚇 MC.

★★★ **Castel Rundegg** Via Scena 2, tel. 0473234100, fax 0473237200; www.rundegg.com; info@runde gg.com; 30 rms.; 🏊 🏊 ⚱ 🛏 P 🅰️ ⓦ 🚇.

★★★ **Villa Tivoli** Via Verdi 72, tel. 0473446282, fax 0473446849; www.villativoli.it; open April-mid-November and for a certain period of time between November and December; 25 rms.; 🏊 ⚱ 🖥 🛏 P 🅰️ ⓦ 🚇 MC.

★★★ **Schloss Labers** Via Labers 25, tel. 0473234484, fax 0473234146; open mid-March-November; 30 rms.; 🏊 ⚱ 🍴 🖥 🛏 P 🅰️ ⓦ 🚇 MC.

★★★ **Westend** Via Speckbacher 9, tel. 0473447654, fax 0473222726; www.westend.it; period when closed may vary; 21 rms.; 🏊 P 👤 🅰️ ⓦ 🚇 MC.

★★★ **Zima** (no restaurant), Via Winkel 83, tel. 0473 230408, fax 0473236469; www.hotelzima.com; open March-October and December; 23 rms.; 🏊 🏊 P.

▐▌ **Sissi** Via Galilei 44, tel. 0473231062, fax 0473 237400 ⌧; 🍴 fine cuisine 🍷 Italian and international; 50 capacity; closed Monday, period when closed may vary; 🏊.

▐ **Weinstube Schloss Rametz** Via Labers 4, tel. 0473212227; 🍴 Alto Adige; 80 capacity; closed Wednesday and for a certain period of time in June; 🏊 ❀ P.

at Fragsburg, 7 km

Hotels

★★★★ **Castel Fragsburg** Via Fragsburg 3, tel. 0473244071, fax 0473244493; www.fragsburg. com; open April-October; 18 rms.; 🏊 ⚱ 🛏 👤 MC.

Messina   ✉ 98100

🔲 *AAPIT*, Via Calabria is. 301 bis, tel. 090674236-090674271; *AA*, Piazza Cairoli 45, tel. 090 2935292.

🚉 *Stazioni F.S. (railway stations)*, Piazza Repubblica, tel. 892021.

🚏 *Messina Boccetta (A20 Messina-Buonfornello), Messina Centro (A18 Messina-Catania).*

⚓ *Stazione Marittima (ship passenger terminal)*, Wharf L. Rizzo, information: *AA*, tel. 0902935292. *Ferrovie dello Stato*, tel. 090679795 (ferryboat to Villa San Giovanni with link to Reggio di Calabria). *Meridiano Lines*, tel. 0965712208 (ferryboat to Reggio di Calabria). *NGI*, tel. 3358427785 (ferryboat to Reggio di Calabria). *SNAV*, tel. 090364044 (hydrofoil to Isole Eolie). *Tourist Ferry Boat*, tel. 0903718510 (ferryboat to Villa San Giovanni).

Hotels and restaurants

★★★ **Jolly dello Stretto** Via Garibaldi 126, ✉ 98126, tel. 090363860, fax 0905902526; 96 rms.; 🏊 P 🅰️ ⓦ 🚇.

★★★ **Royal Palace Hotel** Via T. Cannizzaro 224, ✉ 98122, tel. 0906503, fax 0902921075; royalpalace @framon-hotels.com; 106 rms.; 🖥 🅰️ 🅰️ ⓦ 🚇 MC.

▐▌ **Alberto** Via Ghibellina 95, ✉ 98123, tel. 090 710711 ⌧; sporting3@tiscali.it; 🍴 Sicilian (seafood) 🍷 Italian; 80 capacity; closed Sunday evening and Monday, August; 🏊 🅰️ ⓦ 🚇 MC.

▐ **Le Due Sorelle** Piazza Municipio 4, ✉ 98122, tel. 09044720; 🍴 Sicilian (seafood) 🍷 local and national; 30 capacity; closed Monday, August; P.

Mestre (VE)   ✉ 30170

🔲 *IAT*, at Venice. *TCI*, Piazzale Candiani 7, tel. 0415060228; nego zio.venezia@touringclub.it.

🚉 *Stazione F.S. (railway station)*, Piazzale Favretti, tel. 892021.

✠ *Mestre Est* or *Mestre Marghera* (A4 Torino-Milano-Trieste).

Hotels and restaurants

★★★ **Bologna & Stazione** Via Piave 214, ✉ 30171, tel. 041931000, fax 041931095; www.hotelbologna.com; 120 rms.; 🅿 📺 🆔 ⚋ 🍷 ᴍᴄ.

★★★ **Michelangelo** (no restaurant), Via Forte Marghera 69, ✉ 30173, tel. 041986600, fax 041986052; 51 rms.; 🅿 ♨ 📺 🅿 🆔 ⚋ 🍷 ᴍᴄ.

★★★ **President** (no restaurant), Via Forte Marghera 99/A, ✉ 30173, tel. and fax 041985655; info@ hp-president.com; 51 rms.; 🅿 📺 🅿 🆔 ⚋ 🍷.

❢❢❢ **Dall'Amelia** Via Miranese 113, ✉ 30171, tel. 041 913955, fax 0415441111 🖂; ᴊ❘ Venetian regional, fine cuisine (seafood) 🍷 Italian and international; 200 capacity; closed Wednesday 🍽 ❀ 🆔 ⚋ 🍷 ᴍᴄ; also hotel.

❢❢ **Caffè Concerto** at Favaro Veneto, Via Passo S. Boldo 21, ✉ 30030, tel. 041634100 🖂; caffeconcerto@inwind.it; ᴊ❘ Venetian 🍷 Italian and international; 60 capacity; closed Sunday and for a certain period of time in August; 🆔 🆔 ⚋ 🍷 ᴍᴄ.

Milan
✉ 20100

ℹ️ *APT*, Via Marconi 1, corner of Piazza Duomo, tel. 0272524301; www.milanoinfotourist.com; (*D-E4*); *IAT*, Stazione Centrale (Galleria di Testa; i.e., main atrium), tel. 0272524360; (*A6*).

TCI, Corso Italia 10, tel. 028526304; negozio. milano@touringclub.it; (*E4*).

🚉 *Stazione F.S. (railway station)* Centrale, Piazza Duca d'Aosta, tel. 892021; *Stazione FNM*, Piazzale Cadorna, tel. 0220222-028511236.

✠ *Corso Lodi* (A1 to Bologna-Roma), *Piazza Kennedy* (A4 to Turin, A8 to Varese, A9 to Como-Chiasso), *Sistema tangenziale* (by-pass highway), *Via La Spezia* (A7 to Genova); *Viale Certosa* (A4 to Turin, A9 to Varese, A9 to Como-Chiasso), *Viale Palmanova* (A4 to Bergamo-Venezia).

✈ *Airports: Forlanini* at Linate, tel. 0274852200. Service by ATM bus no. 73 from Piazza S. Babila or by coach from the terminal in Piazza Luigi di Savoia. *Malpensa*, near Gallarate, tel. 02 74852200. Railway service via State Railways and Ferrovie Nord Milano "Malpensa Express"; coach service via "Malpensa Bus Express"; "Shuttle" from the central railway station, or via "Caronte" from Linate airport and Sesto S. Giovanni.

Air Dolomiti, reservations tel. 800-013366.
Air Europe, reservations tel. 8488-24425.
Air One, reservations tel. 8488-488880.
Air Sicilia, reservations tel. 800-412411.
Alitalia, Piazzale Cadorna 14, tel. 0224992500 (*D2*); Via Albricci 5, tel. 0224992700 (*E4*).
Alpi Eagles, information tel. 0415997788.
Azzurra, reservations tel. 8488-25725.
Blue Panorama Airlines, information tel. 02 58587106.
Eurofly, information tel. 0258583452.
Federico II, reservations tel. 0881760030.
Gandalf, reservations tel. 8488-00858.
Meridiana, Via Albricci 7, tel. 0258417333 (*E4*).
Volare Airlines, reservations tel. 8488-24425.

Hotels

★★★★ **Excelsior Gallia** Piazza Duca d'Aosta 9, ✉ 20124, tel. 0267851, fax 0266716239; www.excelsiorgallia.it; 237 rms.; 🅿 📺 🆔 ⚋ 🍷 ᴍᴄ; (*A5*).

★★★★ **Four Seasons** Via Gesù 8, ✉ 20121, tel. 02 77088, fax 0277085000; www.fourseasons.com; 118 rms.; 🅿 ♨ 📺 🆔 ⚋ 🍷 ᴍᴄ; (*D4*) .

★★★★ **G.H. et de Milan** Via Manzoni 29, ✉ 20121, tel.

02723141, fax 0286460861; www.grandhoteletdemilan.it; 95 rms.; 🅿 📺 🆔 ⚋ 🍷; (*D4*).

★★★★ **Principe di Savoia** Piazza della Repubblica 17, ✉ 20124, tel. 0262301, fax 026595838; www.luxurycollection.com; 399 rms.; 🅿 ♨ 📺 🆔 ⚋ 🍷; (*B5*).

★★★★ **The Westin Palace** Piazza della Repubblica 20, ✉ 20124, tel. 0263361, fax 02654485; www.westin.com; 244 rms.; 🅿 📺 🆔 ⚋ 🍷 ᴍᴄ; (*B5*).

★★★ **Carlton Baglioni** Via Senato 5, ✉ 20121, tel. 02 77077, fax 02783300; carlton.milano@baglioni-palacehotels.it; 92 rms.; 🅿 📺 🆔 ⚋ 🍷; (*C-D5*).

★★★ **Antares Hotel Rubens** Via Rubens 21, ✉ 20148, tel. 0240302, fax 0248193114; www.antareshotels.com; 87 rms.; 🅿 📺 🅿 🆔 ⚋ 🍷; (*off map*).

★★★ **Bristol** (no restaurant), Via Scarlatti 32, ✉ 20124, tel. 026694141, fax 026702942; closed for a certain period of time in August; 68 rms.; 🅿 📺 🆔 ⚋ 🍷; (*A-B6*).

★★★ **Brunelleschi** Via Baracchini 12, ✉ 20123, tel. 02 88431, fax 02804924; 128 rms.; 🅿 📺 🆔 ⚋ 🍷; (*E4*).

★★★ **Carlyle Brera Hotel** Corso Garibaldi 84, ✉ 20121, tel. 0229003888, fax 0229003993; www.brerahotels.com; 96 rms.; 🅿 📺 🅿 🆔 ⚋ 🍷; (*C3*).

★★★ **De La Ville** Via Hoepli 6, ✉ 20121, tel. 02867651, fax 02866609; www.delavillemilano.com; delaville@tin.it; 109 rms.; 🅿 ♨ ♨ 📺 🆔 ⚋ 🍷 ᴍᴄ; (*D4*).

★★★ **D'Este** (no restaurant), Viale Bligny 23, ✉ 20136, tel. 0258321001, fax 0258321136; 79 rms.; 🅿 ♨ 📺 🆔 ⚋ 🍷 ᴍᴄ; (*F4*).

★★★ **Hermitage** Via Messina 10, ✉ 20154, tel. 02 33107700, fax 0233107399; www.monrifhotels.it; closed for a certain period of time in August; 131 rms.; 🅿 ♨ 📺 🆔 ⚋ 🍷; (*A2-3*).

★★★ **Hilton Milan** Via Galvani 12, ✉ 20124, tel. 02 69831, fax 0266710810; www.hilton.com. 319 rms.; 🅿 ♨ 📺 🆔 ⚋ 🍷 ᴍᴄ; (*A5*).

★★★ **Jolly Hotel President** Largo Augusto 10, ✉ 20122, tel. 0277461, fax 02783449; www.jollyhotels.it; 242 rms.; 🅿 📺 🅿 🆔 ⚋ 🍷 ᴍᴄ; (*D-E5*).

★★★ **Jolly Hotel Touring** Via Tarchetti 2, ✉ 20121, tel. 026335, fax 026592209; www.jollyhotels.it; 289 rms.; 🅿 📺 🅿 🆔 ⚋ 🍷 ᴍᴄ; (*B5*).

★★★ **Lloyd** (no restaurant), Corso di Porta Romana 48, ✉ 20122, tel. 0258303332, fax 0258303365; www.ttsnetwork.com/lloyd; closed Christmas holidays and August; 57 rms.; 🅿 📺 🆔 ⚋ 🍷 ᴍᴄ; (*F5*).

★★★ **Michelangelo** Via Scarlatti 33 corner of Piazza L. di Savoia, ✉ 20124, tel. 0267551, fax 026694232; www.milanhotel.it; michelangelo@milanhoel.it; 300 rms.; 🅿 📺 🅿 🆔 ⚋ 🍷; (*A6*).

★★★ **Regency** (no restaurant), Via Arimondi 12, ✉ 20155, tel. 0239216021, fax 0239217734; www.regency-milano.com; closed for a certain period of time in August, and Christmas holidays; 59 rms.; 🅿 📺 🅿 🆔 ⚋ 🍷; (*off map*).

★★★ **Starhotel Ritz** Via Spallanzani 40, ✉ 20129, tel. 022055, fax 0229518679; www.starhotels.it; 195 rms.; 🅿 📺 🆔 ⚋ 🍷 ᴍᴄ; (*B6*).

★★★ **Starhotel Rosa** Via Pattari 5, ✉ 20122, tel. 02 8831, fax 028057964; www.starhotels.it; 260 rms.; 🅿 📺 🆔 ⚋ 🍷 ᴍᴄ; (*D4*).

★★★ **UNA Hotel Century** Via F. Filzi 25/B, ✉ 20124, tel. 0267504, fax 0266980602; www.unahotel.com; 144 rms.; 🅿 ♨ 📺 🆔 ⚋ 🍷 ᴍᴄ; (*A5*).

★★★ **Windsor** Via Galileo Galilei 2, ✉ 20124, tel. 026346, fax 026590663; www.hotelwindsor.it; 118 rms.; 🅿 📺 🆔 ⚋ 🍷; (*A6*).

★★★ **Augustus** (no restaurant), Via Napo Torriani 29, ✉ 20124, tel. 0266988271, fax 026703096; www.augustushotel.it; info@augustushotel.it; closed Christmas holidays and for a certain period of time in August; 56 rms.; 🅿 📺 🆔 ⚋ 🍷 ᴍᴄ; (*B6*).

★★★ **Canada** (no restaurant), Via S. Sofia 16, ✉ 20122, tel. 0258304844, fax 0258300282; www.canadahotel.it; 35 rms.; 🅿 📺 🆔 ⚋ 🍷; (*F4*).

★★★ **Ibis Milano Centro** Via Finocchiaro Aprile 2, ✉

20124, tel. 0263151, fax 026598026; 425 rms.; 🆙 📶 ♿ 🅰🅴 ⓓ 🚇 Ⓜ🅲; (B5).

★★★ **Mennini** (no restaurant), Via Napo Torriani 14, ✉ 20124, tel. 026690951, fax 026693437; www.hotel mennini.com; closed August; 65 rms.; 📶 🆙 🅰🅴 ⓓ 🚇; (A6).

★★★ **Sant'Ambroeus** (no restaurant), Viale Papiniano 14, ✉ 20123, tel. 0248008989, fax 0248008687; htlstamb@tin.it; 52 rms.; 📶 🆙 🅰🅴 ⓓ 🚇 Ⓜ🅲; (F2).

Restaurants

🍴🍴🍴🍴 **Savini** Galleria Vittorio Emanuele II, ✉ 20121, tel. 0272003433, fax 0272022888 🖂; www.thi.it; savini@thi.it; 🍴 Lombard, Piedmontese and Venetian Ⓟ Italian and international; 350 capacity; closed Sunday, August and Christmas holidays; 📶 🅰🅴 ⓓ 🚇 Ⓜ🅲; (D4).

🍴🍴🍴 **Boeucc** Piazza Belgioioso 2, ✉ 20121, tel. 02 76020224, fax 02796173 🖂; 🍴 Lombard and classic Ⓟ local and national; 140/160 capacity; closed Saturday and at midday on Sunday, Easter, August and Christmas holidays; 📶 🅰🅴 ⓓ 🚇; (D4).

🍴🍴🍴 **Casanova Grill** Piazza della Repubblica 20, ✉ 20124, tel. 02633364001, fax 02654485 🖂; www.westin.com; 🍴 classic Ⓟ Italian and international; 50 capacity; 📶 🅿 🅰🅴 ⓓ 🚇 Ⓜ🅲; (B5).

🍴🍴🍴 **Hong Kong** Via Schiapparelli 5, ✉ 20125, tel. 02 67071790; 🍴 Chinese Ⓟ Italian and international; 70/12 capacity; closed Monday; 📶 🅰🅴 ⓓ 🚇; (off map).

🍴🍴🍴 **Il Luogo di Aimo e Nadia** Via Montecuccoli 6, ✉ 20147, tel. 02416886, fax 0248302005 🖂; www.aimoenadia.com; 🍴 fine and classic cuisine Ⓟ Italian and international; 40 capacity; closed Saturday at midday and Sunday, August and Christmas holidays; 📶 🅰🅴 ⓓ 🚇 Ⓜ🅲; (off map).

🍴🍴🍴 **L'Ulmet** Via Olmetto 21, ✉ 20123, tel. 02 86452718, fax 0272002486 🖂; 🍴 fine cuisine Ⓟ Italian and international; 60 capacity; closed Sunday and at midday on Monday, August and Christmas-Epiphany (6 January); 📶 🅰🅴 Ⓜ🅲; (E3-4).

🍴🍴🍴 **Sadler** Via Conchetta corner of Via Troilo 14, ✉ 20143, tel. 0258104451, fax 0258112343 🖂; www.sadler.it; sadler@sadler.it; 🍴 fine cuisine Ⓟ Italian and international; 45 capacity; closed Sunday, and for a certain period of time in January and August; 📶 ♨ 🅰🅴 Ⓜ🅲; (off map).

🍴🍴🍴 **Al Porto** Piazza Cantore, ✉ 20123, tel. 02 89407425, fax 028321481 🖂; 🍴 "marinara" (seafood) Ⓟ Italian and international; 90 capacity; closed Sunday and at midday on Monday, August and Christmas holidays; 📶 🅿 🅰🅴 ⓓ 🚇 Ⓜ🅲; (F2).

🍴🍴🍴 **Bistrot Duomo** Via S. Raffaele 2, ✉ 20121, tel. 02877120, fax 02877035 🖂; bistrot.duomo@tiscali.it; 🍴 Lombard and classic Ⓟ Italian and international; 100/50 capacity; closed Sunday and at midday on Monday, and for a certain period of time in August; 📶 🅰🅴 ⓓ 🚇 Ⓜ🅲; (D5).

🍴🍴🍴 **Conte Camillo** Galleria di Piazza Cavour 3, ✉ 20121, tel. 026570516, fax 026592263 🖂; www.hotelcavour.it; hotelcavour@traveleurope.it; 🍴 Lombard and classic Ⓟ Italian and international; 60 capacity; closed August and Christmas-Epiphany (6 January); 📶 🅰🅴 ⓓ 🚇 Ⓜ🅲; (C5).

🍴🍴🍴 **Il Sambuco** Via Messina 10, ✉ 20154, tel. 02 33610333, fax 0233611850 🖂; 🍴 classic (seafood) Ⓟ Italian and international; 80 capacity; closed Saturday at midday and Sunday, and for a certain period of time in August and Christmas-New Year's; 📶 ♨ 🅿 🅰🅴 ⓓ 🚇 Ⓜ🅲; (A2-3).

🍴🍴🍴 **Le Cinque Terre** Via Appiani 9, ✉ 20121, tel. 02 6575177, fax 02653034 🖂; 🍴 Ligurian (seafood) Ⓟ Italian and international; 80 capacity; closed Saturday at midday and Sunday, and for a certain period of time in August; 📶 🅰🅴 ⓓ 🚇 Ⓜ🅲; (B4).

🍴🍴🍴 **Tre Pini** Via T. Morgagni 19 corner of Via Arbe, ✉ 20125, tel. 0266805413, fax 0266801346 🖂; 🍴

classic Ⓟ Italian; 100 capacity; closed Saturday, August and Christmas holidays; ♨ 🅰🅴 ⓓ 🚇 Ⓜ🅲; (off map).

🍴🍴🍴 **Valtellina** Via Taverna 34, ✉ 20134, tel. 027561139, fax 027560436 🖂; 🍴 Valtelline (pizzoccheri, mushrooms) Ⓟ local and national; 50 capacity; closed Monday, New Year's-Epiphany (6 January) and for a certain period of time in August; ♨ 🅿 🅰🅴 ⓓ 🚇 Ⓜ🅲; (off map).

🍴🍴 **Albric** Via Albricci 3, ✉ 20122, tel. 02 72004766 🖂; 🍴 Apulian Ⓟ Italian; 150 capacity; closed Saturday at midday and Sunday, and for a certain period of time in August and Christmas holidays; 📶 🅰🅴 ⓓ 🚇 Ⓜ🅲; (E4).

🍴🍴 **Alfredo-Gran San Bernardo** Via Borgese 14, ✉ 20154, tel. 023319000, fax 0229006859 🖂; 🍴 Milanese Ⓟ Italian and international; 60 capacity; closed Sunday (in June-July also Saturday), August and Christmas holidays; 📶 🅰🅴 ⓓ 🚇 Ⓜ🅲; (off map).

🍴🍴 **Capanna** Via Donatello 9, ✉ 20131, tel. 02 29400884 🖂; 🍴 Tuscan and classic Ⓟ Italian and international; 110 capacity; closed Saturday and for a certain period of time in August; 📶 ⓓ 🚇 Ⓜ🅲; (C5).

🍴🍴 **Cavallini** Via M. Macchi 2, ✉ 20124, tel. 02 6693771; 🍴 classic Ⓟ Italian; 150 capacity; closed Saturday and Sunday, August and Christmas-Epiphany (6 January); 📶 ♨; (B6).

🍴🍴 **Da Berti** Via Algarotti 20, ✉ 20124, tel. 02 6694627, fax 026884158 🖂; 🍴 Lombard Ⓟ Italian and international; 150 capacity; closed Sunday, and for a certain period of time in August and Christmas-Epiphany (6 January); ♨ 🅰🅴 ⓓ 🚇 Ⓜ🅲; (off map).

🍴🍴 **Il Verdi** Piazza Mirabello 5, ✉ 20121, tel. 02 6590797; 🍴 classic Ⓟ Italian and international; 60 capacity; closed Sunday, a certain period of time in August, and Christmas-New Year's; 📶 🅿; (C4).

🍴🍴 **Masuelli San Marco** Viale Umbria 80, ✉ 20135, tel. 0255184138 🖂; www.masuelli-trattoria.com; 🍴 Lombard and Piedmontese Ⓟ Italian and international; 65 capacity; closed Sunday and at midday on Monday, mid-August-mid-September and Christmas-Epiphany (6 January); 📶 🅰🅴 ⓓ 🚇 Ⓜ🅲; (off map).

🍴🍴 **Sushi-Kòboo** Viale Col di Lana 1, ✉ 20136, tel. 028372608; www.sushi-koboo.com; 🍴 Japanese Ⓟ Italian and international; 65 capacity; closed Monday and for a certain period of time in August; 🖂; (F3).

🍴 **Osteria Via Prè** Via Casale 4, ✉ 20144, tel. 02 8373869 🖂; 🍴 Ligurian Ⓟ local and national; 60 capacity; closed Monday at midday, and for a certain period of time in August; 📶 🅰🅴 ⓓ 🚇 Ⓜ🅲; (F2).

Mòdena   ✉ 41100

🄸 *IAT*, Piazza Grande 17, tel. 059206660; www.comune.modena.it.

🚆 *Stazione F.S. (railway station)*, Piazza Dante, tel. 892021.

🛣 *Modena Nord* or *Modena Sud* (A1 Milano-Roma-Napoli).

Hotels

★★★ **Canalgrande** Corso Canalgrande 6, tel. 059 217160, fax 059221674; www.canalgrandehotel.it; info@canalgrandehotel.it; 74 rms.; 📶 ♨ 🆙 🅰🅴 ⓓ 🚇 Ⓜ🅲.

★★★ **Central Park Hotel** (no restaurant), Viale Vittorio Veneto 10, tel. 059225858, fax 059225141; www.italyhotels.it; closed Christmas-Epiphany (6 January), and August; 48 rms.; 📶 ♨ 🅰🅴 ⓓ 🚇 Ⓜ🅲.

★★★ **Real Fini** (no restaurant), Via Emilia Est 441, tel.

0592051511, fax 059364804; www.hrf.it; hotel.re al.fini@ hrf.it; closed for a certain period of time in August, and Christmas-Epiphany (6 January); 87 rms.; 🏠🖥️📖♿🅰️⬆️🚋 MC.

★★★ **Lux** (no restaurant), Via Galilei 218/A, tel. 059 353308, fax 059341400; closed August, and Christmas-Epiphany (6 January); 43 rms.; 🏠 🅿️ 🅰️ ⬆️ 🚋 MC.

★★★ **Ritz** (no restaurant), Via Rainusso 108, tel. 059 820101, fax 059828515; www.ritzhotel.it; ritzho tel@ tiscali.it; 144 rms.; 🏠🖥️🅿️🅰️⬆️🚋 MC.

Restaurants

🍴🍴 **Fini** Rua Frati Minori 54, tel. 059223314, fax 059 220247 ✉️; info@hrf.it; 🍴 Modenese and classic 🅾️♀️ Italian and international; 120 capacity; closed Monday and Tuesday, Christmas-New Year's, and for a certain period of time between July and August; 🏠 🅿️ 🅰️ ⬆️ 🚋.

🍴🍴 **Borso d'Este** Piazza Roma 5, tel. 059214114 ✉️; 🍴 fine and Emilian cuisine 🅾️♀️ Italian and international; 40 capacity; closed Saturday at midday and Sunday, August; 🏠 🅰️ ⬆️ 🚋.

🍴🍴 **Le Temps Perdu** Via Sadoleto 3, tel. 059220353, fax 059210420 ✉️; 🍴 classic (seafood) 🅾️♀️ Italian and international; 35 capacity; closed Monday, and for a certain period of time in August; ✿ 🅿️ 🅰️ ⬆️ 🚋.

🍴 **Oreste** Piazza Roma 31, tel. 059243324; 🍴 Emilian and classic 🅾️♀️ local and national; 80 capacity; closed Sunday evening and Wednesday, Christmas holidays and for a certain period of time in July; 🏠 🅰️ ⬆️ 🚋 MC.

🍴 **Strada Facendo** Via Emilia Ovest 622, tel. 059334478 ✉️; stradafacendo@libero.it; 🍴 local 🅾️♀️ Italian and international; 40/80 capacity; closed Saturday at midday and Sunday, Christmas holidays and August; 🏠 🅰️ ⬆️ 🚋 MC.

Monreale (PA)   ✉️ 90046

ℹ️ **AA**, Piazza Vittorio Veneto 1, tel. 0916564501.

🚉 Stazione F.S. (railway station) at Palermo; bus service.

✈️ Palermo (A19 Palermo-Catania).

Restaurants

🍴 **Taverna del Pavone** Vicolo Pensato 18, tel. 0916406209 ✉️; 🍴 Sicilian 🅾️♀️ local; 35 capacity; closed Monday, for a certain period of time between September and October; 🏠 ⬆️ 🚋 MC.

Montepulciano (SI)   ✉️ 53045

ℹ️ **APT** at Chianciano Terme; Tourist Office Comunale, Via di Gracciano nel Corso 59/A, tel. 0578757341.

🚉 Stazione F.S. (railway station) at Chiusi; bus service.

✈️ Chiusi-Chianciano T., Val di Chiana (A1 Milano-Roma-Napoli).

Hotels and restaurants

★★★ **Granducato** (no restaurant), Via delle Lettere 62, tel. 0578758610, fax 0578758597; www.lenni.it; granducato@lenni.it; 54 rms.; 🏠 ✖️ 🖥️ 🅿️ ♿ 🅰️ ⬆️ 🚋 MC.

★★★ **Il Marzocco** Piazza Savonarola 18, tel. 0578 757262, fax 0578757530; closed for a certain period of time between November and December; 16 rms.; 🖥️ 🅿️ 🅰️ ⬆️ 🚋.

🍴 **La Grotta** township of San Biagio, tel. 0578 757607 ✉️; 🍴 Tuscan 🅾️♀️ Italian and international; 50 capacity; closed Wednesday, Epiphany (6 January)-end February; ✿ 🅰️ ⬆️ 🚋.

Monterosso al Mare (SP)   ✉️ 19016

ℹ️ **IAT**, Via Fegina, tel. 0187817506.

🚉 Stazione F.S. (railway station), Via Fegina, tel. 892021.

✈️ Brugnato-Borghetto di Vara (A12 Genova-Rosignano).

⛴️ Navigazione Golfo dei Poeti, tel. 0187732987 (seasonal ferryboat to Lerici, Portofino, Portovenere, Vernazza, Isola Palmaria).

Hotels and restaurants

★★★ **Porto Roca** Via Corone 1, tel. 0187817502, fax 0187817692; www.portoroca.it; open mid-March-October; 43 rms.; ⬆️ 🏠 🅰️ ⬆️.

★★★ **La Colonnina** (no restaurant), Via Zuecca 6, tel. 0187817439, fax 0187817788; open April-October; 20 rms.; ⬆️.

🍴 **Miky** Via Fegina 104, tel. 0187817608; www.risto rantemiky.it; 🍴 Ligurian 🅾️♀️ local and national; 60 capacity; closed Tuesday (except summer); ✿ 🏠 ⬆️ 🚋 MC.

Monte Sant'Angelo (FG)   ✉️ 71037

ℹ️ **APT** at Foggia; Tourist Office comunale, Piazza Municipio, tel. 0884 564567.

🚉 Stazione F.S. (railway station) at Foggia; bus service.

✈️ Foggia, S. Severo (A14 Bologna-Taranto).

Hotels and restaurants

★★★ **Michael** (no restaurant), Via R. Basilica 86, tel. 0884565519, fax 0884563079; www.gargano.it/ alberghi/michael; 10 rms.; 🏠 ⬆️ 🚋.

🍴 **Li Jalantuùmene** Piazza De Galganis, tel. 0884 565484 ✉️; www.li-jalantuumene.it; 🍴 Apulian rivisitata; 45/65 capacity; closed Tuesday in winter and for a certain period of time in January; 🏠 ⬆️ 🚋 MC.

Murano (VE)   ✉️ 30121

ℹ️ **IAT** at Venice.

⛴️ **ACTV**, tel. 899-909090 (pay call); steam boat to Venice.

Restaurants

🍴 **Busa alla Torre** Campo S. Stefano 3, tel. 041 739662; 🍴 Venetian 🅾️♀️ Italian; 80 capacity; closed for a certain period of time in January; 🏠 ⬆️ 🚋 MC.

Naples   ✉️ 80100

ℹ️ **EPT Information Office**, Stazione Centrale, tel. 081206666-081268779; www.ept.napoli.it; (B-C6); EPT Information Office, Stazione Mergellina, tel. 0817612102; (E-F1); AA, Piazza del Gesù Nuovo, tel. 0815523328; info@aziendaturismona poli.com; (C4); Information Office, Via S. Carlo, tel. 081402394; (E4).

🚉 Stazione F.S. (railway station) Centrale, (Naples Main Station), Piazza Garibaldi, tel. 892021; Stazione Ferrovia Circumvesuviana, Corso Garibaldi 387, tel. 0817722444; Stazione Ferrovia Cumana, Piazza Montesanto, tel. 0815513328.

✈️ S. Giorgio a Cremano (A3 to Reggio di Calabria), S. Giovanni a Teduccio (A1 to Rome), Sistema Tangenziale Est-Ovest (by-pass highway from A1 near Casoria to Pozzuoli, with frequent exits to the northern districts of the city).

✈️ Airport Capodichino, tel. 081789380-081789259.

Service via bus no. 3/S by ANM, leaving from the Beverello wharf and the railway station or from Piazza Municipio by CLP bus.

Air One, reservations tel. 8488-48880.

Alitalia, reservations tel. 8488-65641.

Alpi Eagles, reservations tel. 0815992351.

Meridiana, Via De Pretis 78, tel. 0815526661.

Volare, reservations tel. 8488-24425.

🚢 *Stazione Marittima (ship passenger terminal)*, Molo Beverello, information EPT tel. 0817612102; at Mergellina (hydrofoils), information tel. 081 7612102.

Alicost, tel. 0815522838 (hydrofoil and ferryboat to Ischia, Sorrento).

Caremar, tel. 0815513882 (hydrofoil or ferryboat to Capri, Ischia and Procida).

Navigazione Libera del Golfo, tel. 0815520763 (hydrofoil to Capri and Positano).

SNAV, tel. 0817612348 (temporarily from the Beverello wharf: hydrofoil to Capri, Procida, Casamicciola Terme and ferryboat to Palermo).

Tirrenia, tel. 0817201111 (ferryboat to Cagliari and Palermo).

Ustica Lines, tel. 092322200 (seasonal hydrofoil to Isole Egadi, Trapani and Ustica).

Hotels

★★★ **G.H. Parker's** Corso Vittorio Emanuele 135, ✉ 80121, tel. 0817612474, fax 081663527; www.bcedit.it/parkershotel.com; ghparker@tin.it; 83 rms.; 🅿 🗗 🅿 🖭 🛗 ; (E2).

★★★ **Excelsior** Via Partenope 48, ✉ 80121, tel. 0817640111, fax 0817649743; www.excelsior.it; 123 rms.; 🅿 🗗 ♿ 🖭 🛗 ; (F4).

★★★ **G.H. Vesuvio** Via Partenope 45, ✉ 80121, tel. 0817640044, fax 0817644483; www.prestigehotels.it; 165 rms.; 🅿 🗗 ♿ 🖭 🛗 🛗 ; (F4).

★★★ **Jolly Ambassador's** Via Medina 70, ✉ 80133, tel. 081416000, fax 0815518010; 250 rms.; 🅿 🗗 🖭 🖭 🛗 🛗 ; (D2).

★★★ **Majestic** Largo Vasto a Chiaia 68, ✉ 80121, tel. 081416500, fax 081410145; www.prestigehotels.it; 116 rms.; 🅿 🗗 ♿ 🖭 🖭 🛗 ; (E3).

★★★ **Miramare** (no restaurant), Via N. Sauro 24, ✉ 80132, tel. 0817647589, fax 0817640775; www.hotelmiramare.com; 31 rms.; 🅿 🗗 🖭 🖭 🛗 🛗 ; (E4).

★★★ **Paradiso** Via Catullo 11, ✉ 80122, tel. 081 7614161, fax 0817613449; 74 rms.; 🅿 🗗 🖭 🖭 🛗 ; (F1).

★★★ **Rex** (no restaurant), Via Palepoli 12, ✉ 80132, tel. 0817649389, fax 0817649227; www.hotelrex.it; 40 rms.; 🅿 🗗 🖭 🖭 🛗 ; (F4).

★★★ **Splendid** Via A. Manzoni 96, ✉ 80123, tel. 0817141955, fax 0817146431; 44 rms.; 🅿 ♨ 🅿 🖭 🛗 ; (off map).

★★★ **Starhotel Terminus** Piazza Garibaldi 91, ✉ 80142, tel. 0817793111, fax 081206689; www.starhotels.it; 168 rms.; 🅿 🗗 🖭 🖭 🛗 🛗 ; (B-C5-6).

Restaurants

🍴 **Cantinella** Via Cuma 42, ✉ 80132, tel. 0817648684, fax 0817648769 ✉; 🍽 regional and classic 🍷 Italian and international; 80 capacity; closed Sunday (from June to September), and for a certain period of time in August; 🅿 🅿 🖭 🖭 🛗 ; (E4).

🍴 **'A Fenestella** Calata Ponticello a Marechiaro 25, ✉ 80123, tel. 0817690020, fax 0815750686 ✉; 🍽 Neapolitan (seafood) 🍷 local and national; 180 capacity; closed Wednesday at midday and Sunday evening; Sunday in July and August, 15 August; 🅿 🅿 🖭 🛗 🛗 ; (off map).

🍴 **Ciro a Santa Brigida** Via S. Brigida 71/73, ✉ 80132, tel. 0815524072, fax 0815528992 ✉; 🍽 regional and classic 🍷 local and national; 130 ca-

pacity; closed Sunday (except December), and for a certain period of time in August; 🅿 🖭 🖭 🖭 🛗 ; (D-E4).

🍴 **Megaris** Via S. Lucia 175, ✉ 80121, tel. 081 7640511, fax 0817648580 ✉; administration @santalucia.it; 🍽 regional and classic 🍷 Italian and international; 70 capacity; closed Sunday; 🅿 🖭 🖭 🛗 ; (F4).

🍴 **Sacrestia** Via Orazio 116, ✉ 80122, tel. 081 664186, fax 0817611051 ✉; 🍽 Neapolitan 🍷 Italian and international; 130 capacity; closed Sunday evening and Monday at midday, and for a certain period of time in August; 🅿 ⚜ 🅿 🖭 🖭 🛗 ; (F1).

🍴 **San Carlo** Via Cesario Console 18/19, ✉ 80132, tel. 0817649757 ✉; 🍽 regional and classic (seafood) 🍷 local and national; 60 capacity; closed Sunday; 🅿 🅿 🖭 🖭 🛗 ; (E4).

🍴 **Cavour** Piazza Garibaldi 34, ✉ 80142, tel. 081 283122; www.hotelcavournapoli.it; 🍽 Neapolitan and classic 🍷 local and national; 250 capacity; also hotel; 🅿 🅿 ; (B-C5-6).

🍴 **Don Salvatore** Via Mergellina 5, ✉ 80122, tel. 081 681817 ✉; www.donsalvatore.it; 🍽 regional and classic (seafood) 🍷 Italian and international; 125 capacity; closed Wednesday; 🅿 🅿 🖭 🖭 🛗 ; (F1).

🍴 **La Bersagliera** Borgo Marinari 10/11, ✉ 80132, tel. 0817646016 ✉; www.labersagliera.it; 🍽 Neapolitan (seafood) 🍷 local and national; 250 capacity; closed Tuesday and for a certain period of time in January; 🅿 🖭 🖭 🛗 ; (F4).

🍴 **La Cantina di Masaniello** Via Donnalbina 28, ✉ 80134, tel. 0815528863 ✉; 🍽 regional 🍷 Italian; 60 capacity; closed Sunday; 🅿 🖭 🖭 🖭 🛗 ; (D4).

🍴 **Mimì alla Ferrovia** Via Alfonso d'Aragona 21, ✉ 80139, tel. 0815538525; www.mimiallaferrovia.it; 🍽 regional 🍷 Italian and international; 180 capacity; closed Sunday, and for a certain period of time in August; 🅿 🅿 🖭 🖭 🛗 ; (B-C6).

🍴 **Umberto** Via Alabardieri 30, ✉ 80121, tel. 081 418555 ✉; www.umberto.it; 🍽 regional and classical 🍷 Italian and international; 160 capacity; closed Monday and for a certain period of time in August; 🅿 🅿 🖭 🖭 🛗 🛗 .

at Agnano Terme, 11 km ✉ 80125

Hotels

★★★ **American Park** Via E. Scarfoglio 15, tel. 081 5706529, fax 0815708180; american.hotel@mclink.it; 100 rms.; 🅿 ♨ ♨ 🅿 🅿 ♿ 🖭 🖭 🛗 .

Noto (SR) ✉ 96017

ℹ️ *AAPIT Information Office*, Piazzale XVI Maggio, tel. 081573779; noto.apt@tin.it.

🚉 *Stazione F.S. (railway station)*, Piazzale Stazione, tel. 892021.

🛣 *Catania Est* (A18 Messina-Catania), *Catania Sud* (A19 Palermo-Catania).

at Lido di Noto, 8 km

Hotels

★★★ **Eloro Hotel Club** tel. 081812244, fax 081 812200; open March-September; 222 rms.; 🅿 ♨ ♨ 🗙 🅿 🖭 🖭 🛗 .

★★★ **Vilal Mediterranea** (no restaurant), Viale Lido, tel. and fax 081812330; 15 rms.; ♨ ♨ 🅿 ♿ .

Nùoro ✉ 08100

ℹ️ *EPT*, Piazza Italia 19, tel. 078430083; www.enteturismo.nuoro.it.

♻ *Stazione Ferrovie della Sardegna*, Via Lamarmora 10, tel. 078430115.

Hotels and restaurants

★★★ **Grazia Deledda** Via Lamarmora 175, tel. 0784 31257, fax 078431258; angesann@tin.it; 72 rms.; 🏠 🖭 🕰 ⏸ 🈂

★★★ **Grillo** Via Mons. Melas 14, tel. 078438678, fax 078432005; 46 rms.; 🖃 🕰 ⏸ 🚻 MC.

★★★ **Paradiso** Via Aosta 44, tel. 078435585, fax 0784 232782; 42 rms.; 🏠 🖃 🅿 ♿ 🕰 🚻.

❙❙ **Canne al Vento** Viale Repubblica 66, tel. 0784 201762 ⊠; ※ "Barbaricina" ◖◗ local; 130 capacity; closed Sunday, Christmas holidays and for a certain period of time in August; 🏠 🕰 ⏸ 🚻 MC.

Olbia (SS) ✉ 07026

🛈 *AA*, Via Catello Piro 1, tel. 078921453; aastol@tiscali.it.

♻ *Stazione F.S. (railway station)*, tel. 078922477.

✈ *Aeroporto Costa Smeralda*, tel. 0789563444. Bus service (no. 2 of Azienda Municipale Trasporti Urbani) from Via D'Annunzio.

Meridiana, reservations tel. 078969300.

⚓ Stazione Marittima *(ship passenger terminal)*, Viale Isola Bianca; information AA, tel. 0789 21453.

Grimaldi, c/o Unimare, tel. 078923524 (seasonal ferryboat to Genoa).

Lloyd Sardegna, Viale Isola Bianca, tel. 0789 21411 (ferryboat to Livorno and, seasonal, to Civitavecchia, Genoa).

Hotels and restaurants

★★★ **Colonna Palace Hotel** (no restaurant), Via Montello 9, tel. 078924173, fax 078924162; www.itihotels.it; itihotels@tiscali.it; 74 rms.; 🏠 🅿 🕰 🚻 MC.

★★★ **Centrale** (no restaurant), Corso Umberto I 85, tel. 078923017, fax 078926464; www.hotelcentraleolbia.it; patriziopo@tiscali.it; 23 rms.; 🏠 🕰 🚻.

❙❙❙ **Gallura** Corso Umberto 145, tel. 078924648, fax 078924629 ⊠; ※ "marinara" ◖◗ local and national; 80 capacity; closed Monday and Christmas holidays; 🏠 🕰 ⏸ 🚻; also hotel.

❙ **Gambero** Via Lamarmora 6, tel. 078923874 ⊠; ※ "marinara" ◖◗ local; 60 capacity; closed Sunday (except summer), Christmas holidays; 🏠 🕰 🚻 MC.

at Lido di Pittulongu, 7 km

Hotels

★★★ **Stefania** Strada Panoramica at km 4.8, tel. 0789 39027, fax 078939186; hotelstefania@tiscali.it; closed November; 28 rms.; 🏠 ♨ ♨ ✕ 🅿 🖃 🕰 ⏸ 🚻 MC.

Orbetello (GR) ✉ 58015

🛈 *APT* at Grosseto; *Pro Loco Lagunare*, Piazza della Repubblica, tel. 0564860447.

♻ *Stazione F.S. (railway station)* at Orbetello Scalo, tel. 892021; bus service from Ancona.

✙ *Civitavecchia Nord, Rosignano* (A12 Genova-Rosignano and Civitavecchia Roma).

Hotels

★★★ **Vecchia Maremma** (no restaurant), township of Quattrostrade, Via Aurelia at km 146, ⊠ 58016, tel. 0564862147, fax 0564862347; www.vecchiamaremma.it; 50 rms.; 🏠 ♨ ♨ 🅿 ♿ 🕰 ⏸ 🚻 MC.

Orvieto (TR) ✉ 05018

🛈 *IAT*, Piazza del Duomo 24, tel. 076341772; info@iat.orvieto.tr.it.

♻ *Stazione F.S. (railway station)* at Orvieto Scalo, tel. 0763304177, 892021; cable railway service.

✙ *Orvieto* (A1 Milano-Roma-Napoli).

Hotels and restaurants

★★★ **Maitani** (no restaurant), Via Maitani 5, tel. and fax 0763342011; closed for a certain period of time in January; 40 rms.; 🏠 ♨ ✕ 🖃 🕰 ⏸ 🚻 MC.

★★★ **Valentino** (no restaurant), Via Angelo da Orvieto 32, tel. and fax 0763342464; closed for a certain period of time between January and February; 17 rms.; 🏠 🖃 ♿ 🕰 ⏸ 🚻 MC.

❙❙❙ **Giglio d'Oro** Piazza Duomo 8, tel. 0763341903; ※ fine and Umbrian cuisine and classic ◖◗ local and national; 50 capacity; closed Wednesday, period when closed may vary; 🏠 🕰 🚻 MC.

❙❙❙ **Osteria dell'Angelo** Piazza XXIX Marzo 8/A, tel. 0763341805 ⊠; ※ fine cuisine ◖◗ Italian and international; 20 capacity; closed Monday and for a certain period of time in July; 🏠 🚻 MC.

❙❙ **I Sette Consoli** Piazza S. Angelo 1/A, tel. 0763 343911 ⊠; mstopp@tin.it; ※ fine and Umbrian cuisine ◖◗ Italian and international; 25 capacity; closed Wednesday (November-March also Sunday evening) and for a certain period of time in February; ※ 🕰 ⏸ 🚻 MC.

❙ **Trattoria La Grotta** Via Luca Signorelli 5, tel. 0763341348 ⊠; ※ Umbrian ◖◗ Italian and international; 60 capacity; closed Tuesday, and for a certain period of time in January; 🏠 🕰 ⏸ 🚻 MC.

at Orvieto Scalo, 5 km ✉ 05019

Hotels

★★★ **Villa Ciconia** township of Ciconia, SS 71 road to Arezzo at km 35.2, tel. 0763305582, fax 0763 9302077; www.bellaumbria.net/hotel villaciconia; closed for a certain period of time in January or February; 12 rms.; 🏠 ♨ 🅿 🕰 ⏸ 🚻 MC.

★★★ **Gialletti** (no restaurant), Via A. Costanzi 71, tel. 0763301981, fax 0763305064; www.hotelgialletti.it; hgialletti@libero.it; 51 rms.; 🏠 🖃 🅿 ♿ 🕰 ⏸ 🚻 MC.

Padua ✉ 35100

🛈 *IAT*, Galleria Pedrocchi 9, tel. 0498767927; www.apt.padova.it; *(C3)*; *IAT*, Atrio Stazione F.S., tel. 049875207; *(A3)*; *IAT*, seasonal, Piazza del Santo, tel. 0498753087; *(D3)*.

TCI, Via Verdi 7 corner of Via Belle Parti, tel. 049 8754227; negozio.padova@touringclub.it; *(C2)*.

♻ *Stazione F.S. (railway station)*, Piazzale Stazione, tel. 892021.

✙ *Padova Est* (A4 Torino-Milano-Trieste); *Padova Zona Industriale* (A13 Bologna-Padova); *Padova Ovest* (A4 Torino-Milano-Trieste).

Hotels

★★★ **Grand'Italia** (no restaurant), Corso del Popolo 81, ⊠ 35131, tel. 0498761111, fax 0498750850; www.hotelgranditalia.it; 61 rms.; 🏠 🖃 ♿ 🕰 ⏸ 🚻 MC; *(A3)*.

★★★ **Milano** Via P. Bronzetti 62, ⊠ 35138, tel. 0498712555, fax 0498713923; www.hotelmilanopadova.it; 80 rms.; 🏠 🅿 ♿ 🕰 ⏸ 🚻 MC; *(B1)*.

★★★ **Plaza** Corso Milano 40, ⊠ 35139, tel. 049656822, fax 049661117; www.plazapadova.it; 142 rms.; 🏠 🖃 ♿ 🕰 ⏸ 🚻 MC; *(B-C2)*.

★★★ **Al Cason** Via Frà Paolo Sarpi 40, ⊠ 35138, tel. 049662636, fax 0498754217; www.hotelalcason.com; 48 rms.; 🏠 🖃 🕰 ⏸ 🚻 MC; *(A2-3)*.

★★★ **Europa** Largo Europa 9, ✉ 35137, tel. 049 661200, fax 049661508; www.paginegialle.it/htl europa; hotele@libero.it; 64 rms.; 🏢 ᴀᴇ ⊚ 🚇 ᴍᴄ; (B3).

★★ **Al Fagiano** (no restaurant), Via Locatelli 45, ✉ 35123, tel. and fax 0498753396; www.alfagiano.it; info@alfagiano.it; 29 rms.; ℗ ᴀᴇ ⊚ 🚇 ᴍᴄ; (D3).

Restaurants

🍴🍴🍴 **Antico Brolo** Corso Milano 22, ✉ 35139, tel. 049664555; fax 049656088 ✉; 🍽 fine cuisine ◊♀ Italian and international; 55 capacity; closed Monday; 🏢 ❀ ᴀᴇ ⊚ 🚇 ᴍᴄ; (B-C2).

🍴 **Belle Parti** Via Belle Parti 11, ✉ 35139, tel. 0498751822 ✉; 🍽 Venetia regional and classic (seafood) ◊♀ Italian and international; 90 capacity; closed Sunday, and for a certain period of time in August; 🏢 ᴀᴇ ⊚ 🚇 ᴍᴄ; (C2).

🍴 **Trattoria ai Porteghi** Via Cesare Battisti 105, ✉ 35121, tel. 049660746; 🍽 classic ◊♀ Italian; 40 capacity; closed Sunday and Monday at midday, August; 🏢 ᴀᴇ ⊚ 🚇 ᴍᴄ.

at Ponte di Brenta, 5 km ✉ 35020

Hotels

★★★ **Le Padovanelle** Via Chilesotti 2, tel. 049625622, fax 049625320; www.padovanelle.it; lepadova nelle.hotel@libero.it; 40 rms.; 🏢 ⚓ ⏦ 🌊 ✕ ℗ ᴀᴇ ⊚ 🚇.

Paestum (SA) ✉ 84063

ℹ️ **AA**, Via Magna Grecia 151, tel. 0828811016; www.paestumtourism.it.

🚃 *Stazione F.S. (railway station)*, Via Porta Giustizia, tel. 892021.

🚏 *Battipaglia* (A3 Napoli-Reggio di Calabria).

Hotels and restaurants

★★★ **Le Palme** at Laura, Via Sterpinia 33, tel. 0828 851025, fax 0828851507; www.lepalme.it; lepa lme@paestum. it; open mid-March-October; 84 rms.; 🏢 ⚓ ⏦ ✕ 🏢 ℗ ᴀᴇ ⊚ 🚇 ᴍᴄ.

★★★ **Cristallo** at Laura, Via P. della Madonna 39, tel. 0828851077, fax 0828851468; 36 rms.; 🏢 ⚓ ℗.

★★★ **Esplanade** Via Poseidonia, tel. 0828851043, fax 0828851600; www.hotelesplanade.com; es planade@paestum.it; 28 rms.; 🏢 ⚓ ⏦ ✕ ℗ ᴀᴇ ⊚ 🚇 ᴍᴄ.

★★★ **Park Hotel** Linora coast road, tel. 0828811134, fax 0828722310; parkhotelpaestum@tin.it; 28 rms.; ⚓✕ 🏢 ℗ ᴀᴇ ⊚ 🚇 ᴍᴄ.

🍴 **La Pergola** at Capaccio Scalo, Via Nazionale 1, tel. 0828723377 ✉; 🍽 local (seafood, mushrooms) ◊♀ local and national; 50 capacity; closed Monday (except in summer), period of closing may vary; ❀ ℗ ᴀᴇ ⊚ 🚇 ᴍᴄ.

🍴 **Nettuno** Via Principe di Piemonte 2, tel. 0828 811028 ✉; www.ristorantenettuno.com; 🍽 regional and classic (seafood) ◊♀ Italian; 100 capacity; closed Monday in the off season, period when closed may vary; 🏢 ❀ ℗ ᴀᴇ ⊚ 🚇 ᴍᴄ.

Palermo ✉ 90100

ℹ️ **AAPIT**, Piazza Castelnuovo 34, tel. 091583847-0916058351; www.palermotourism.com; (C3); *Information Office*, Stazione F.S. Centrale, tel. 6165914; (F5); *Information Office* at the airport, tel. 591698; *AA*, Salita Belmonte 43 (Villa Igea), tel. 0916398011; www.aziendautonomaturismopa lermomonreale.it; (A4).

🚃 *Stazione F.S. (railway stations)* Centrale, Piazza G. Cesare, tel. 892021.

🚏 *Palermo* (A19 to Catania, A20 to Messina), *Paler*

mo-V. Belgio (A29 and A29 Dir. to Mazara del Vallo and Trapani).

✈️ *Aeroporto Falcone-Borsellino*, tel. 0917020111. Service from the main railway station via the Pristia e Comandè Co. bus or via the *Trinacria Express* train.
Air Europe, information tel. 0917020294.
Air Sicilia, Via Pasubio 9, tel. 0916261222.
Air Vallée, reservations tel. 0165230982.
Alitalia, Via Mazzini 59, tel. 0916019111; (B3).
Alpi Eagles, reservations tel. 0415997788.
Federico II Air, reservations tel. 0881760030.
Meridiana, reservations tel. 199-111333.

🚢 *Stazione Marittima (ship passenger terminal)*, embankment Francesco Crispi quay; information: AAPIT, tel. 091583847-0916165914.
Grimaldi, tel. 091587832 (ferryboat to Genoa, Livorno and Salerno).
Siremar, tel. 091582403 (hydrofoil and ferryboat to Ustica).
SNAV, tel. 091333333 (seasonal hydrofoil to Aeolian Islands and ferryboat to Naples).
Tirrenia, tel. 0916021111 (ferryboat to Cagliari and Naples).

Hotels and restaurants

★★★ **Villa Igiea Grand Hotel** Salita Belmonte 43, ✉ 90142, tel. 0916312111, fax 091547654; www.vil laigiea.thi.it; 115 rms.; 🏢 ⚓ ⏦ ✕ ℗ ♿ ᴀᴇ ⊚ 🚇; (off map).

★★★ **Holiday Inn Palermo** Viale Regione Siciliana 2620, ✉ 90145, tel. 0916983111, fax 091408198; www.holiday-inn.com/palermoitaly; 95 rms.; 🏢 🖥 ♿ ᴀᴇ ⊚ 🚇 ᴍᴄ; (off map).

★★★ **Jolly del Foro Italico** Foro Italico 22, ✉ 90133, tel. 0916165090, fax 0916161441; www.jollyho tels.it; 277 rms.; 🏢 ⚓ ⏦ ℗ ᴀᴇ ⊚ 🚇 ᴍᴄ; (E6).

★★★ **Europa** Via Agrigento 3, ✉ 90141, tel. and fax 0916256323; www.abeuropa.com; europahotel @tiscali.it; 73 rms.; 🏢 ᴀᴇ ⊚ 🚇 ᴍᴄ; (B3).

🍴🍴🍴 **Cedro** Via Monte Pellegrino 62, ✉ 90142, tel. 091 6281111, fax 0916372178; www.astoriapalace. com; 🍽 Sicilian and classic (seafood) ◊♀ local and national; 250 capacity; 🏢 ℗ ᴀᴇ ⊚ 🚇 ᴍᴄ; (D4).

🍴🍴🍴 **Il Ristorantino** Piazzale De Gasperi 19, ✉ 90146, tel. 091512861, fax 0916702999 ✉; 🍽 Sicilian ◊♀ local and national; 60 capacity; closed Monday, and for a certain period of time in August; 🏢 ❀ ᴀᴇ ⊚ 🚇 ᴍᴄ; (off map).

🍴🍴🍴 **Scuderia** Viale del Fante 9, ✉ 90146, tel. 091 520323, fax 091520467 ✉; 🍽 Sicilian and classic (seafood) ◊♀ Italian and international; 80/60 capacity; closed Sunday, and for a certain period of time in August; 🏢 ❀ ᴀᴇ ⊚ 🚇 ᴍᴄ; (off map).

🍴 **Regine** Via Trapani 4/A, ✉ 90141, tel. 091586566 ✉; www.cd-net.it/ristoranteregine; 🍽 Sicilian and classic ◊♀ local and national; 50 capacity; closed Sunday, August; 🏢 ᴀᴇ ⊚ 🚇 ᴍᴄ; (B3).

🍴 **Santandrea** Piazza S. Andrea 4, ✉ 90133, tel. 091334999 ✉; 🍽 Sicilian ◊♀ Italian and international; 80 capacity; closed Tuesday (Sunday from July to September), and for a certain period of time in January; 🏢 ❀ ⊚ 🚇 ᴍᴄ; (D4-5).

at Mondello, 10 km ✉ 90151

Hotels and restaurants

★★★ **Mondello Palace** Viale Principe di Scalea 2, tel. 091450001, fax 091450657; 83 rms.; 🏢 ⚓ ⏦ ℗ ᴀᴇ ⊚ 🚇 ᴍᴄ.

★★★ **Splendid Hotel la Torre** Via Piano Gallo 11, ✉ 90151, tel. 091450222, fax 091450033; www.lato rre.com; 179 rms.; 🏢 ⚓ ⏦ ✕ ℗ ᴀᴇ ⊚ 🚇.

🍴 **Bye Bye Blues** Via del Garofalo 23, tel. 091 6841415 ✉; www.byebyeblues.it; 🍽 fine and Sicilian cuisine ◊♀ Italian and international; 40 capacity; closed Tuesday, November; 🏢 ❀ ᴀᴇ ⊚ 🚇 ᴍᴄ.

Palestrina (RM)   ✉ 00036

i *APT* at Rome; *Pro Loco*, Piazza della Cortina, tel. 069534019.

⊞ *Stazione F.S. (railway station)* at Zagarolo, tel. 892021; bus service.

⊪ *Valmontone* (A1 Milano-Roma-Napoli).

Hotels

★★★ **Stella** Piazzale della Liberazione 3, tel. 06 9538172, fax 069573360; www.hotelstella.it; ᴀᴇ ⱺ 🚻 ᴍᴄ.

Parma   ✉ 43100

i *IAT*, Via Melloni 1/A, tel. 0521218889; www.turismo.comune.parma.it/turismo; (*B4*).
TCI, Strada S. Anna 19/A, tel. 0521504257; tci.parma @tin.it; (*B4*).

⊞ *Stazione F.S. (railway station)*, Piazzale Dalla Chiesa 11, tel. 892021.

⊪ *Parma* (A1 Milano-Roma-Napoli); *Parma Ovest* (A15 Parma-La Spezia).

✈ *Airport G. Verdi*, tel. 0521982626. Bus service via "Aerobus" from the historic center and the railway station (A3).
Alitalia, information tel. 8488-65643.
Gandalf, reservations tel. 8488-00858.

Hotels

★★★ **Palace Hotel Maria Luigia** Viale Mentana 140, tel. 0521281032, fax 0521231126; www.sinahotels.com; 101 rms.; 🅿 🔊 ⱷ ᴀᴇ ⱺ 🚻 ᴍᴄ; (*B4*).

★★★ **Park Hotel Stendhal** Via Bodoni 3, tel. 0521 208057, fax 0521285655; stendhal.htl@rsadvnet.it; 62 rms.; 🅿 🔊 🅿 ᴀᴇ ⱺ 🚻 ᴍᴄ; (*B4*).

★★★ **Daniel** Via Gramsci 16, tel. 0521995147, fax 0521 292606; www.ascom.pr.it; closed August and Christmas; 32 rms.; 🅿 🔊 🅿 ᴀᴇ ⱺ 🚻 ᴍᴄ; (*B1, off map*).

★★★ **Farnese International Hotel** Via Reggio 51/A, tel. 0521994247, fax 0521992317; www.farneseho tel.it; 76 rms.; 🅿 ⱷ 🅿 ᴀᴇ ⱺ 🚻 ᴍᴄ; (*A3, off map*).

★★★ **Torino** (no restaurant), Via Mazza 7, tel. 0521 281046, fax 0521230725; www.hotel-torino.it; closed for a certain period of time in August; 33 rms.; 🅿 ⱷ 🔊 ⱷ ᴀᴇ ⱺ 🚻 ᴍᴄ; (*C3-4*).

Restaurants

††† **Al Tramezzo** at San Lazzaro Parmense, Via Del Bono 5/B, ✉ 43026, tel. 0521487906, fax 0521 484196 🖂; www.ascom.pr.it/promoparma; ᴊ Emilian and fine cuisine ᴊᴋ Italian and international; 65 capacity; closed Monday, and for a certain period of time in July; 🅿 🅿 ᴀᴇ ⱺ 🚻 ᴍᴄ.

††† **La Greppia** Strada Garibaldi 39/A, tel. 0521 233686, fax 0521221315 🖂; ᴊᴋ fine and Parmesan cuisine ᴊᴋ Italian and international; 50 capacity; closed Monday and Tuesday, July and Christmas holidays; 🅿 ᴀᴇ ⱺ 🚻 ᴍᴄ.

††† **Parizzi** Via Repubblica 71, tel. 0521285952, fax 0521285027 🖂; parizzi.rist@libero.it; ᴊᴋ Parmesan and fine cuisine ᴊᴋ Italian and international; 60 capacity; closed Monday, period when closed may vary; 🅿; (*C-D5*).

†† **Parma Rotta** Via Langhirano 158, tel. 0521 966738, fax 0521968167; www.parmarot ta.com; parmarotta@tiscali.it; ᴊᴋ Parmesan (pasta dishes) ᴊᴋ Italian and international; 100 capacity; closed Monday and, in summer, Sunday; ❀ 🅿 ᴀᴇ ⱺ 🚻; (*off map*).

Pavia   ✉ 27100

i *APT*, Via Fabio Filzi 2, tel. 038222156; www.apt.pavia.it.

⊞ *Stazione F.S. (railway station)*, Piazzale Stazione, tel. 892021.

⊪ *Pavia Nord* (Pavia-Bereguardo/A7 Milano-Genova highway junction).

Hotels and restaurants

★★★ **Moderno** Via Vittorio Emanuele II 41, tel. 0382 303401, fax 038225225; www.hotelmoderno.it; 54 rms.; 🅿 🔊 🅿 ⱷ ᴀᴇ ⱺ 🚻 ᴍᴄ.

★★★ **Ariston** Via A. Scopoli 10/D, tel. 038234334, fax 038225667; hotel.ariston@aritonparty.com; closed Christmas-Epiphany (6 January); 60 rms.; 🅿 🔊 🅿 ᴀᴇ ⱺ 🚻 ᴍᴄ.

★★★ **Excelsior** (no restaurant), Piazza Stazione 25, tel. 038228596, fax 038226030; 27 rms.; 🅿 🔊 ⱷ ᴀᴇ ⱺ 🚻 ᴍᴄ.

†† **Il Cigno** Via P. Massacra 2, tel. 0382301093 🖂; risto ranteilcigno@interfree.it; ᴊᴋ creativa ᴊᴋ Italian and international; 26 capacity; closed Monday, and for a certain period of time in January and August; 🅿 ᴀᴇ ⱺ 🚻 ᴍᴄ.

† **Osteria del Naviglio** Via Alzaia 39/B, tel. 0382 460392 🖂; ᴊᴋ classic ᴊᴋ Italian and international; 40 capacity; closed Saturday and Sunday at midday, August; 🅿 ᴀᴇ 🚻 ᴍᴄ.

Perugia   ✉ 06100

i *IAT*, Piazza IV Novembre 3, tel. 0755736458; www.umbria2000.it; (*C3*).

⊞ *Stazione F.S. (railway station)*, Piazza Vittorio Veneto, tel. 892021; *Stazione Ferrovia Centrale Umbra*, Piazzale Bellucci, tel. 07554038.

⊪ *Perugia* (Val di Chiana-Perugia highway junction).

✈ *Aeroporto Regionale Umbro* at Sant'Egidio, tel. 075592141. Bus service from Piazza Italia (*D3*) and from the railway station (*E1*).
Alitalia, c/o Aeroporto, tel. 0755921432.

Hotels

★★★★ **Brufani** Piazza Italia 12, ✉ 06121, tel. 075 5732541, fax 0755720210; www.brufanipalace.com; 🅿 🔊 🅿 ⱷ ᴀᴇ ⱺ 🚻 ᴍᴄ; (*D3*).

★★★ **Giò Arte e Vini** Via R. D'Andreotto 19, ✉ 06124, tel. and fax 0755731100; www.hotelgio.it; 130 rms.; 🅿 🅿 ⱷ ᴀᴇ ⱺ 🚻 ᴍᴄ; (*C1*).

★★★ **La Rosetta** Piazza Italia 19, ✉ 06121, tel. and fax 0755720841; larosetta@perugiaonline.com; 94 rms.; ⱷ ᴀᴇ ⱺ 🚻 ᴍᴄ; (*D3*).

★★★ **Perugia Plaza Hotel** Via Palermo 88, ✉ 06129, tel. 07534643, fax 07530863; www.umbriahotels.com; 108 rms.; 🅿 ⱷ 🔊 🅿 ᴀᴇ ⱺ 🚻 ᴍᴄ; (*off map*).

★★★ **Grifone** Via Pellico 1, ✉ 06126, tel. 075 5837616, fax 0755837619; www.grifonehotel.com; info@grifoneho tel.com; 50 rms.; 🅿 ⱷ ᴀᴇ ⱺ 🚻 ᴍᴄ; (*off map*).

★★ **Signa** (no restaurant), Via del Grillo 9 corner of Corso Cavour, ✉ 06121, tel. and fax 075 5724180; 23 rms.; ⱷ ᴀᴇ 🚻 ᴍᴄ; (*E4*).

Restaurants

†† **Aladino** Via delle Prome 11, ✉ 06122, tel. 075 5720938 🖂; ᴊᴋ fine and Sardinian cuisine; 55/30 capacity ᴊᴋ Italian and international; open only evening; closed Monday, and for a certain period of time in August; 🅿 ᴀᴇ ⱺ 🚻 ᴍᴄ; (*B-C4*).

†† **Enoteca Giò** Via R. D'Andreotto 19, ✉ 06124, tel. 0755731100 🖂; www.hotelgio.it; ᴊᴋ Umbrian ᴊᴋ Italian and international; 250 capacity; closed Sunday evening and Monday at midday; 🅿 🅿 ᴀᴇ ⱺ 🚻 ᴍᴄ; (*C1*).

†† **Osteria del Gambero** Via Baldeschi 17, ✉ 06123, tel. 0755735461 🖂; ᴊᴋ fine cuisine ᴊᴋ Italian; 45 capacity; closed Monday, and for a period of time in January and June; 🅿 🚻 ᴍᴄ; (*C3*).

† **Locanda degli Artisti** Via Campo Battaglia 10, ✉ 06122, tel. 0755735851 🖂; www.perugiaonline.

com/locandadegliartisti; ✸✸ Umbrian and Lucanian 🍴 local and national; 80 capacity; closed Tuesday, and for a certain period of time in January; 🄿 🄰🄴 🄿 🅅🅸🅂🄰 🄼🄲; (D4).

at Bosco, 10 km ✉ 06080

Hotels

✱ **Relais San Clemente** tel. 0755915100, fax 075 5915001; www.relais.it; 64 rms.; 🄿 ♠ ☇ ✕ 🄿 🄰🄴 🄰🄳 🅅🅸🅂🄰 🄼🄲.

at Ponte Valleceppi, 7 km ✉ 06087

Hotels

*** **Vega** Strada Montalcino 2/A, tel. 0756929534, fax 0756929507; vegahot@tin.it; closed Christmas holidays; 42 rms.; ♠ ☇ 🄿 ♿ 🄰🄴 🄰🄳 🅅🅸🅂🄰 🄼🄲.

Pescara ✉ 65100

🛈 *APTR*, Via Fabrizi 171, tel. 08542900212; www. regione.abruzzo.it; *IAT*, Via Paolucci, tel. 085 4219981; presidio.pescara@abruzzoturismo. it; *IAT* c/o aeroporto, tel. 0854322120.

� *Stazione F.S. (railway station)*, Via Ferrari, tel. 892021.

�∥ *Pescara Nord-Città S. Angelo, Pescara-Chieti* (A14 Bologna-Taranto); *Pescara-Villanova* (A25 Torano-Pescara).

✈ *Aeroporto Pasquale Liberi*, tel. 0854324200. Urban bus service from the main railway station.
Air One, c/o Cagidemetrio, Via Ravenna 3, tel. 0854213022.

🚢 *Pentatour*, Viale G. Bovio 106, tel. 0854213208 (hydrofoil or pleasure boat to Croatia).

Hotels and restaurants

✱ **Carlton** Viale della Riviera 35, ✉ 65123, tel. 085373125, fax 0854213922; www.italiaabc.it/az/carlton; 71 rms.; 🄿 🄱🄿 🄰🄴 🄰🄳 🅅🅸🅂🄰.

✱ **Esplanade** Piazza I Maggio 46, ✉ 65122, tel. 085292141, fax 0854217540; www.esplanade.net; 150 rms.; 🄿 🄴 🄰🄴 🄰🄳 🅅🅸🅂🄰.

✱ **Plaza** Piazza Sacro Cuore 55, ✉ 65122, tel. 0854214625, fax 0854213267; plazahotel@tin.it; 68 rms.; 🄿 🄴 🄰🄴 🄰🄳 🅅🅸🅂🄰.

*** **Alba** (no restaurant), Via M. Forti 14, ✉ 65122, tel. 085389145, fax 085292163; 50 rms.; 🄿 🄴 ♿ 🄰🄴 🄰🄳 🅅🅸🅂🄰.

*** **Ambra** (no restaurant), Via M. Forti 38 corner of Quarto dei Mille, ✉ 65122, tel. 085378247, fax 378183; 61 rms.; 🄿 🄴 🄰🄴 🄰🄳 🅅🅸🅂🄰 🄼🄲.

🍴🍴🍴 **Guerino** Viale della Riviera 4, ✉ 65123, tel. and fax 0854212065; ✸✸ seafood 🍴 Italian and international; 80 capacity; closed Thursday (except July and August), Christmas-Epiphany (6 January); 🄰🄴 🄰🄳 🅅🅸🅂🄰 🄼🄲.

🍴 **Cantina di Jozz** Via delle Caserme 61, ✉ 65127, tel. 085690383; ✸✸ regional 🍴 local and national; 120 capacity; closed Sunday evening and Monday, and for a certain period of time in January; 🄿 🄰🄴 🄰🄳 🅅🅸🅂🄰 🄼🄲.

🍴 **Regina del Porto** Via Paolucci 65, ✉ 65121, tel. 08534151 ✉; ✸✸ fine cuisine 🍴 local and national; 100 capacity; closed Monday, August; 🄿 🄰🄴 🄰🄳 🅅🅸🅂🄰.

Piazza Armerina (EN) ✉ 94015

🛈 *AA*, Via Cavour 1, tel. 0935680201.

Hotels and restaurants

*** **Park Hotel Paradiso** Contrada Ramaldo, tel. 0935680841, fax 0935683391; 65 rms.; 🄿 ♠♠ ✕ 🄿 🄰🄴 🄰🄳 🅅🅸🅂🄰 🄼🄲.

🍴 **Al Fogher** Contrada Bellia 1, tel. 0935684123 ✉; ✸✸ Sicilian and fine cuisine 🍴 Italian and international; 70 capacity; closed Sunday evening

and Monday, Christmas and for a certain period of time in January and between June and July; ✾ 🄿 🄰🄴 🅅🅸🅂🄰.

Pienza (SI) ✉ 53026

🛈 *APT* at Chianciano Terme; *Tourist Office*, Corso Rossellino 55, 0578749071.

🚂 *Stazione F.S. (railway station)* at Chiusi; bus service on week days.

�∥ *Chiusi-Chianciano Terme* (A1 Milano-Roma-Napoli).

Hotels and restaurants

*** **Relais il Chiostro di Pienza** Corso Rosellino 26, tel. 0578748400, fax 0578748440; closed January-mid-March; 37 rms.; ♠ ☇ 🄿 ♿ 🄰🄴 🄰🄳 🅅🅸🅂🄰 🄼🄲.

🍴 **Buca delle Fate** Corso Rossellino 38/A, tel. 0578748272 ✉; www.labucadellefate.it; ✸✸ Tuscan 🍴 local; 120 capacity; closed Monday, and for a certain period of time in January and June; 🄰🄴 🄰🄳 🅅🅸🅂🄰 🄼🄲.

Piombino (LI) ✉ 57025

🛈 *AVT*, Via Ferruccio 4, tel. 0565220852; www.turismopiombino.it; *Information Office*, seasonal, Via Ferruccio 2, tel. 0565225639; *Tourist Office comunale*, Via Ferruccio, tel. 056563269.

🚂 *Stazione F.S. (railway station)*, Piazza Niccolini, tel. 892021.

�∥ *Rosignano* (A12 Genova-Rosignano and Civitavecchia-Roma).

🚢 *Lloyd Sardegna*, tel. 0565222300 (ferryboat to Sardinia)
Moby Lines, tel. 0565276077 (ferryboat to the isle of Elba).
Toremar, tel. 056531100 (ferryboat to the isle of Elba and, weekly, to Pianosa)

Hotels and restaurants

✱ **Centrale** Piazza Verdi 2, tel. 0565220188, fax 0565220220; 41 rms.; 🄿 🄰🄴 🄰🄳 🅅🅸🅂🄰 🄼🄲.

*** **Collodi** (no restaurant), Via Collodi 7, tel. 0565 224272, fax 0565224382; 27 rms.; 🄿 🄴 🄰🄴 🅅🅸🅂🄰 🄼🄲.

🍴 **Calamoresca** at Calamoresca, tel. 056542029 ✉; ✸✸ seafood 🍴 local and national; 50 capacity; closed Wednesday in the off season; 🄿 🄰🄴 🄰🄳 🅅🅸🅂🄰 🄼🄲.

Pisa ✉ 56100

🛈 *IAT*, Via Cammeo 2, tel. 050560464; www.pisa.turismo.toscana.it; (A2); Piazza Stazione F.S. Centrale, tel. 050560464; iat.stazione@tiscali.it; (F3-4); aeroporto Galilei, tel. 050503700.

🚂 *Stazione F.S. (railway stations)* Centrale, Piazza della Stazione, tel. 892021.

�∥ *Pisa Centro* (A12 Genova-Rosignano e Civitavecchia-Roma), *Pisa Nord* (A11 Firenze-Mare).

✈ *Aeroporto G. Galilei* at San Giusto, tel. 050500707.
Air Dolomiti, information tel. 050500707.
Alitalia, at the airport, tel. 05020221.
Meridiana, reservations tel. 05005532961.

Hotels and restaurants

✱ **Jolly Hotel Cavalieri** Piazza Stazione 2, ✉ 56125, tel. 05043290, fax 050502242; pisa@jollyhotels.it; 100 rms.; 🄿 🄴 ♿ 🄰🄴 🄰🄳 🅅🅸🅂🄰 🄼🄲; (E-F4).

*** **Leonardo** Via Tavoleria 17, ✉ 56126, tel. 050 579946, fax 050598969; www.pisaonline.it/hotelleonardo; 27 rms.; 🄿 🄿 ♿ 🄰🄴 🅅🅸🅂🄰 🄼🄲; (C4).

*** **Roma** (no restaurant), Via Bonanno Pisano 111, ✉ 56126, tel. 050554488, fax 050550164; www.

pisaonline.it/hotelroma; 27 rms.; 🏩 ♿ Ⓟ 🅰🅴 🚇 Ⓜ️Ⓒ; (A-B2).

*** **Verdi** (no restaurant), Piazza Repubblica 5, ✉ 56127, tel. 050598947, fax 050598944; 32 rms.; 🅰🅴 🆑 🚇 Ⓜ️Ⓒ.

††† **Ristoro dei Vecchi Macelli** Via Volturno 49, ✉ 56126, tel. 05020424, fax 050506008 ✉; ♨ Tuscan ⬡ Italian and international; 45 capacity; closed Wednesday and at midday on Sunday; 🏩 🅰🅴 🆑 🚇; (C2).

†† **Antica Trattoria da Bruno** Via Bianchi 12, ✉ 56123, tel. 050560818 ✉; www.pisaonline.it; ♨ Tuscan ⬡ Italian and international; 150 capacity; closed Monday evening and Tuesday; 🏩 🅰🅴 🚇; (A4).

† **Artilafo** Via Volturno 38, tel. 05027010 ✉; ♨ fine and Tuscan cuisine ⬡ local and national; 29/40 capacity; closed Sunday, August; 🏩 ✳ 🆑 🚇 Ⓜ️Ⓒ; (C2-3).

Pistoia ✉ 51100

ℹ️ *IAT*, Piazza Duomo 4, tel. 057321622; www.turismo.toscana.it.

🚉 *Stazione F.S. (railway station)*, Piazza Dante Alighieri, tel. 21119, 892021.

🛣️ *Pistoia* (A11 Firenze-Mare).

Hotels and restaurants

*** **Arcobaleno** township of Sammommè, Via Valdi e Sammommè 37, ✉ 51020, tel. 0573470030, fax 0573470147; www.wel.it; arcoble@tin.it; closed for a certain period of time in November and between January and February; 33 rms.; ♿ ♨ ✖ 🖥 Ⓟ ♿ 🅰🅴 🆑 🚇 Ⓜ️Ⓒ.

*** **Leon Bianco** (no restaurant), Via Panciatichi 2, tel. 057326676, fax 057326704; www.promonet.it/leonbianco; mariaric@tin.it; 27 rms; 🅰🅴 🆑 🚇 Ⓜ️Ⓒ.

*** **Milano** (no restaurant), Viale Pacinotti 10/12, tel. 0573975700, fax 057332657; 55 rms.; Ⓟ 🅰🅴 🆑 🚇 Ⓜ️Ⓒ.

† **Lo Storno** Via del Lastrone 8, tel. 057326193 ✉; ♨ Tuscan ⬡ local; 50 capacity; closed Sunday, August; ✳ 🚇 Ⓜ️Ⓒ.

at Castagneto di Pitèccio, 12 km ✉ 51030

Restaurants

††† **Castagno di Pier Angelo** Via del Castagno 46/B, tel. 057342214 ✉; ♨ Tuscan (seafood, mushrooms) ⬡ Italian and international; 80/20 capacity; closed Monday, for a certain period of time in January and between October and November; ✳ Ⓟ 🅰🅴 🚇 Ⓜ️Ⓒ.

Pompei (NA) ✉ 80045

ℹ️ *AA*, Via Sacra 1, tel. 0818507255; www.uniplan.it/pompei/azienda; *Information Office*, Porta Marina Inferiore 12, tel. 800-013350.

🚉 *Stazione F.S. (railway station)*, Piazza XXIII Marzo 1, tel. 892021; *Stazione Ferrovia Circumvesuviana Villa dei Misteri*, Porta Marina Superiore, tel. 0817722444; *Stazione Ferrovia Circumvesuviana*, Piazza Vittorio Veneto, tel. 0817722444.

🛣️ *Pompei, Scafati* (A3 Napoli-Reggio di Calabria).

Hotels and restaurants

*** **Amleto** (no restaurant), Via Bartolo Longo 10, tel. 0818631004, 0818635585; www.hotelamleto.it; info@hotelamleto.it; 26 rms.; 🏩 🖥 ♿ 🅰🅴 🚇 Ⓜ️Ⓒ.

*** **Forum** (no restaurant), Via Roma 99, tel. 081 8501170, fax 0818506132; www.hotelforum.it; pompei@hotelforum.it; 24 rms.; 🏩 ♿ 🖥 🅰🅴 🆑 🚇 Ⓜ️Ⓒ.

*** **Giovanna** (no restaurant), Via Acquasalsa 18, tel. 0810818506161, fax 0818507323; www.hotelgiovanna.it; 24 rms.; 🏩 ♿ Ⓟ 🅰🅴 🚇 Ⓜ️Ⓒ.

††† **Il Principe** Piazza B. Longo 8, tel. 0818505566, fax 0818633342 ✉; www.ilprincipe.com; info@ilprincipe.com; ♨ regional and classic, fine cuisine ⬡ Italian and international; 70 capacity; closed Sunday evening and Monday, Christmas holidays and August; 🏩 🅰🅴 🆑 🚇 Ⓜ️Ⓒ.

† **Da Andrea** at Pompei Scavi, Via Plinio 52, tel. 0815363498; www.mariusetcaesar.it; ♨ Neapolitan ⬡ local; 300 capacity; closed Monday evening in the off season; 🏩 Ⓟ 🅰🅴 🆑 🚇 Ⓜ️Ⓒ.

Porto Cervo (SS) ✉ 07020

Hotels and restaurants

★★★ **Balocco** (no restaurant), tel. 078991555, fax 078991510; open April-October; 30 rms.; 🏩 ♿ ⛵ Ⓟ 🅰🅴 🆑 🚇.

††† **Gianni Pedrinelli** at junction for Perero, tel. 0789 92436, fax 078992616 ✉; www.giannipedrinelli.it; ♨ Sardinian ⬡ Italian; 130 capacity; open March/October; ✳ Ⓟ 🅰🅴 🚇 Ⓜ️Ⓒ.

at Cala di Volpe, 8 km

Hotels and restaurants

★★★ **Cala di Volpe** tel. 0789976111, fax 0789976617; open March-October; 123 rms.; 🏩 ♿ ⛵ ✖ Ⓟ 🅰🅴 🆑 🚇.

*** **Valdiola** tel. 078996215, fax 078996652; 33 rms.; 🏩 ♿ ⛵ Ⓟ 🅰🅴 🆑 🚇.

††† **Pevero Golf Club**, tel. 0789958000, fax 0789 96572 ✉; ♨ classic (seafood) ⬡ Italian and international; 80 capacity; open April-November; 🅰🅴 🆑 🚇 Ⓜ️Ⓒ.

at Liscia di Vacca, 2 km

Hotels

★★★ **Pitrizza** tel. 0789930111, fax 0789930611; www.luxurycollection.com; open May-October; 51 rms.; 🏩 ♿ ⛵ 🖥 Ⓟ 🅰🅴 🆑 🚇.

at Romazzino, 9 km

★★★ **Romazzino** tel. 0789977111, fax 078996258; www.luxurycollection.com/romazzino; open April-October; 94 rms.; 🏩 ♿ ⛵ ✖ Ⓟ 🅰🅴 🆑 🚇 Ⓜ️Ⓒ.

Portofino (GE) ✉ 16034

ℹ️ *IAT*, Via Roma 35, tel. 0185269024.

🚉 *Stazione F.S. (railway station)* at Santa Magherita Ligure; bus service.

🛣️ *Rapallo* (A12 Genova-Rosignano).

Hotels and restaurants

★★★ **Nazionale** (no restaurant), Via Roma 8, tel. 0185 269575, fax 0185269578; info@nazionaleportofino.com; open mid-March-November; 12 rms.; 🚇 Ⓜ️Ⓒ.

★★★ **Piccolo Hotel** Via Duca degli Abruzzi 31, tel. 0185269015, fax 0185269621; www.domina.it; dopiccol@tin.it; closed for a certain period of time between November and December; 23 rms.; ♿ 🖥 Ⓟ 🅰🅴 🚇.

★★★ **Splendido** Viale Baratta 16, tel. 0185267801, fax 0185267806; reservations@splendido.net; open April/mid-November; 68 rms.; 🏩 ♿ ⛵ ✖ 🖥 Ⓟ 🅰🅴 🆑 🚇 Ⓜ️Ⓒ.

★★ **Eden** (no restaurant), Vico Dritto 18, tel. 0185 269091, fax 0185269047; www.italyhotels.it; eden@ifree.it; 12 rms.; 🏩 ♿ 🅰🅴 🆑 🚇.

††† **Chuflay Bar** Via Roma 2, tel. 0185267802, fax 0185267807 ✉; www.splendido.orient-express.com; ♨ Ligurian ⬡ Italian and international; 50 capacity; open only evening; closed November/December; 🏩 🅰🅴 🆑 🚇 Ⓜ️Ⓒ; also hotel.

††† **Puny** Piazza Martiri dell'Olivetta 5, tel. 0185 269037 ✉; ♨ regional and classic ⬡ local and

national; 40 capacity; closed Thursday (also Monday at midday and Friday in summer), mid-December-mid-February.

🍴 **Da ü Batti** Vico Nuovo 17, tel. 0185269379 ☒; regional 🍷 Italian and international; 70 capacity; closed Monday, December-mid-January; ✿ 🆎 ⓪ 🚾 **MC**.

🍴 **Delfino** Piazza Martiri dell'Olivetta 40, tel. 0185 269081; 🍴 regional and classic 🍷 Italian and international; 80 capacity; closed Monday in the off season, November; 🆎 ⓪ 🚾.

Portovènere (SP) ☒ 19025

📋 *IAT*, Piazza Bastreri 1, tel. 0187790691; www.portovenere.it.

🚂 *Stazione F.S. (railway station)* at La Spezia; bus service.

🛣 *Stagnoni* (A15 Parma-La Spezia).

⚓ *Navigazione Golfo dei Poeti*, tel. 0187732987 (ferryboat, seasonal, to Lerici, Monterosso al Mare, Vernazza, isola Palmaria).

Hotels and restaurants

★★★ **Royal Sporting** Via dell'Ulivo 345, tel. 0187 790326, fax 0187777707; www.royalsporting.com; open mid-March-October and mid-December-mid-January; 62 rms.; 🅿 ♨ ♒ ✕ 🗐 🆎 ⓪ 🚾 **MC**.

★★★ **Paradiso** Via Garibaldi 34, tel. 0187790612, fax 0187792582; www.hotelportovenere.it; info@hotelportovenere.it; 22 rms.; 🗐 🆎 ⓪ 🚾 **MC**.

🍴🍴 **Taverna del Corsaro** Calata Doria 102, tel. 0187790622, fax 0187766056 ☒; p.bercini@tin.it; 🍴 regional (seafood) 🍷 Italian and international; 130 capacity; closed Monday, November/ December; 🆎 ⓪ 🚾 **MC**.

at Le Grazie, 3 km ☒ 19022

Hotels and restaurants

★★★ **Della Baia** Via Lungomare 111, tel. 0187790797, fax 0187790034; www.baiahotel.com; hbaia@cdh.it; 34 rms.; 🅿 ♒ 🅿 ⚄ 🆎 ⓪ 🚾 **MC**.

Positano (SA) ☒ 84017

📋 *AA*, Via del Saracino 4, tel. 089875067.

🚂 *Stazione Ferrovia Circumvesuviana* at Sorrento; bus service.

🛣 *Castellammare di S.* (A13 Napoli-Reggio di Calabria).

⚓ Alicost, tel. 0898781430 (seasonal hydrofoil to Amalfi, Capri and Naples).
Cooperativa Sant'Andrea, tel. 089873190 (seasonal ferryboat to Amalfi and Salerno).
Navigazione Libera del Golfo, tel. 0895520763 (ferryboat and hydrofoil to Amalfi, hydrofoil to Salerno and Sorrento, seasonal pleasure boat to Capri).

Hotels and restaurants

★★★ **Le Agavi** Via G. Marconi 127, tel. 089875733, fax 089875965; www.agavi.com; open April-October; 70 rms.; 🅿 ♨ ♒ 🅿 🆎 ⓪ 🚾 **MC**.

★★★ **Le Sirenuse** Via C. Colombo 30, tel. 089875066, fax 089811798; sirenuse@macronet.it; 60 rms.; 🅿 ♨ 🅿 🆎 ⓪ 🚾 **MC**.

★★★ **Buca di Bacco** Via Rampa Teglia 4, tel. 089 875699, fax 089875731; www.bucadibacco.it; bacco@starnet.it; open April-October; 47 rms.; 🅿 🆎 ⓪ 🚾 **MC**.

★★★ **Romantik Hotel Poseidon** Via Pasitea 148, tel. 089811111, fax 089875833; poseidon@starnet.it; closed January-March; 48 rms.; 🅿 ♨ ♒ 🗐 🅿 🆎 ⓪ 🚾 **MC**.

★★★ **Casa Albertina** Via della Tavolozza 3, tel. 089875143, fax 089811540; www.casalbertina.it; info@casalbertina; 21 rms.; 🅿 🗐 🆎 ⓪ 🚾 **MC**.

★★★ **Savoia** (no restaurant), Via C. Colombo 73, tel. 089875003, fax 089811844; www.savoiapositano.com; closed for a certain period of time between November and December; 39 rms.; 🅿 🆎 ⓪ 🚾.

🍴 **Donna Rosa** Via Montepertuso 97/99, tel. 089811806 ☒; donnarosaristorante@libero.it; 🍴 regional and fine cuisine 🍷 Italian and international; closed Tuesday in winter, Monday and Tuesday at midday in summer, 6 January-February; 50 capacity; 🅿 🅿 🆎 ⓪ 🚾 **MC**.

🍴 **Le Tre Sorelle** Via del Brigantino 23/25, tel. 089875452; 🍴 local (seafood) 🍷 local and national; 70 capacity; closed Thursday (from November to April), for a certain period of time in January; 🆎 ⓪ 🚾 **MC**.

Pozzuoli (NA) ☒ 80078

📋 *AA*, Piazza Matteotti 1/A, tel. 0815266639-0815265068; aziendaturismopozzuoli@libero.it.

🚂 *Stazione F.S. (railway station)*, Via Oriani 2, tel. 892021; *Stazione Ferrovia Cumana*, Via Sacchini, tel. 0815513328.

🛣 *Pozzuoli-Cuma* (Naples eastern and western by-pass highway).

⚓ *Caremar*, tel. 0815262711 (ferryboat to Ischia). *Traghetti Pozzuoli*, tel. 0815267736 (ferryboat to Casamicciola Terme and Ischia).

Hotels and restaurants

★★★ **Santa Marta** at Arco Felice, Via Licola Patria 28, ☒ 80072, tel. 0818042404, fax 0818042406; 34 rms. 🅿 🅿 ⓪ 🚾 **MC**.

★★★ **Solfatara** Via Solfatara 163, tel. 0815262666, fax 0815263365; www.hotelsolfatara.it; info@hotelsolfatara.it; 31 rms.; 🅿 ♨ 🅿 🆎 ⓪ 🚾 **MC**.

🍴 **Ninfea** Via Italia 1, tel. 0818661326, fax 0818665308; 🍴 regional 🍷 local and national; 700 capacity; closed Tuesday in the off season; 🅿 🅿 🆎 ⓪ 🚾 **MC**.

Rapallo (GE) ☒ 16035

📋 *IAT*, Via Vittorio Veneto 7, tel. 0185230346; info apt@apttigullio.liguria.it.

🚂 *Stazione F.S. (railway station)*, Piazza Molfino, tel. 892021.

🛣 *Rapallo* (A12 Genova-Rosignano).

⚓ *Servizi Marittimi del Tigullio*, tel. 0185284670 (ferryboat to Portofino).

Hotels and restaurants

★★★ **Astoria** (no restaurant), Via Gramsci 4, tel. 0185 273533, fax 018562793; astoria@rapallo.omninet.it; closed December-mid-January; 22 rms.; 🅿 🅿 🆎 ⓪ 🚾 **MC**.

★★★ **Eurotel** Via Aurelia Occidentale 22, tel. 0185 60981, fax 018550635; www.tigullio.net/eurotel; 63 rms.; 🅿 ♨ ♒ 🗐 🅿 🆎 ⓪ 🚾 **MC**.

★★★ **Giulio Cesare** Corso Colombo 52, tel. 0185 50685, fax 018560896; www.hotel-giulio-cesare.it; closed November-mid-December; 33 rms.; 🅿 🆎 🚾 **MC**.

★★★ **Riviera** Piazza IV Novembre 2, tel. 018550248, fax 018565668; www.hotel-riviera.it; closed November-mid-December; 20 rms.; 🅿 ♨ 🆎 ⓪ 🚾 **MC**.

★★★ **Stella** (no restaurant), Via Aurelia Ponente 6, tel. 018550367, fax 0185272837; www.hotelstella-riviera.com; info@hotelstella-riviera.com; closed mid-January-mid-February; 27 rms.; 🅿 🗐 🆎 ⓪ 🚾 **MC**.

¶¶ **Roccabruna** township of Savagna, Via Sotto la Croce 6, tel. 0185261400 ✉; webtiscali.it/rocca bruna.indice.html; mauro.niki@tiscali.it; ❯❮ fine cuisine 🍴 Italian and international; 30 capacity; closed Monday, and for a certain period of time in November; 🅿 ✤ Ⓟ 🄰🄴 ⑳ 🌃 ᴍᴄ.

Ravello (SA) ✉ 84010

ℹ *AA*, Piazza Duomo 1, tel. 089857096; www.ravel lo.it/aziendaturismo.

Hotels and restaurants

★★★ **Palumbo** Via Toro 16, tel. 089857244, fax 089858133; www.hotelpalumbo.it; reception@ho telpalumbo.it; 21 rms.; 🅿 ♨ Ⓔ Ⓟ 🄰🄴 ⑳ 🌃 ᴍᴄ.

★★★ **Rufolo** Via S. Francesco 1, tel. 089857133, fax 089857935; www.hotel-rufolo.it; closed February; 30 rms.; 🅿 ♨ ♨ Ⓔ 🄰🄴 ⑳ 🌃 ᴍᴄ.

★★★ **Graal** Via della Repubblica 8, tel. 089857222, fax 089857551; www.hotelgraal.it; info@hotelgraal.it; 36 rms.; 🅿 ♨ ♨ Ⓔ 🄰🄴 ⑳ 🌃 ᴍᴄ.

¶¶¶ **Rossellinis** Via S. Giovanni del Toro 28, tel. 089 818181, fax 089858900 ✉; ❯❮ fine cuisine 🍴 Italian and international; 50 capacity; open March-October and Christmas holidays, only evening; 🅿 Ⓟ 🄰🄴 ⑳ 🌃 ᴍᴄ.

¶¶ **Salvatore** Via Boccaccio 2, tel. 089857227 ✉; ❯❮ of Amalfi 🍴 local; 180 capacity; closed Monday from November to March; 🄰🄴 🌃.

Ravenna ✉ 48100

ℹ *IAT*, Via Salara 8/12, tel. 054435404; www.turis mo.ravenna.it; *IAT* (seasonal), Via Maggiore 122, tel. 0544482961; *IAT* (seasonal), Via delle Industrie 14, tel. 0544451539.

🚂 *Stazione F.S. (railway station)*, Piazza Farini, tel. 892021.

🛣 *Ravenna* (A14 Bologna-Taranto dir. di Ravenna).

Hotels and restaurants

★★★ **Jolly Hotel** Piazza Mameli 1, tel. 054435762, fax 0544216055; www.jollyhotels.it; ravenna@jollyho tels. it; 84 rms.; 🅿 🅿 Ⓟ ♿ 🄰🄴 ⑳ 🌃 ᴍᴄ.

★★★ **Class Hotel Ravenna** Via della Lirica 141, tel. 0544270290, fax 0544270170; www.classhotel. com; 69 rms.; 🅿 Ⓟ ♿ 🄰🄴 ⑳ 🌃 ᴍᴄ.

★★★ **Diana** (no restaurant), Via Rossi 47, tel. 0544 39164, fax 054430001; www.ravennabedandbre akfast.it; hoteldiana@netgate.it; 33 rms.; 🅿 ♨ Ⓔ ♿ 🄰🄴 ⑳ 🌃 ᴍᴄ.

¶¶¶ **Antica Trattoria al Gallo 1909** Via Maggiore 87, tel. 0544213775 ✉; algallo1909@libero.it; ❯❮ regional 🍴 local and national; 50 capacity; closed Sunday evening, Monday, Tuesday, Easter and Christmas holidays; 🅿 ✤ 🄰🄴 ⑳ 🌃 ᴍᴄ.

¶¶ **Chilò** Via Maggiore 62, tel. 054436206 ✉; ❯❮ regional (pasta dishes) 🍴 local and national; 60/50 capacity; closed Thursday; ✤ 🄰🄴 ⑳ 🌃 ᴍᴄ.

Reggio di Calabria ✉ 89100

ℹ *IAT*, Corso Garibaldi 329, tel. 0965892012 (*D2*); Stazione Centrale F.S., tel. 096527120 (*E-F1*); *IAT*, aeroporto, tel. 0965643291.

🚂 *Stazione F.S. (railway station) Centrale* , Piazza Garibaldi 1, tel. 892021.

🛣 *Reggio di Calabria* (Via Italia) and other exits into town (A3 to Naples).

✈ *Aeroporto Tito Minniti*, at Ravagnese, tel. 0965 640517. Bus service via AMA, from the port (no. 125) and from Corso Garibaldi and the railway station (no. 114); coach service via Cavalieri and hydrofoils to and from Messina.

Air One, at the airport, tel. 0965644394.
Air Vallée, reservations tel. 0165230982.
Alitalia, at the airport, tel. 09655643095.

🚢 *Stazione Marittima (ship passenger terminal)*, Via Florio, information: *IAT*, tel. 0965892012.
Ferrovie dello Stato, tel. 090679795 (train service to Messina).
Meridiano Lines, tel. 0965712208 (ferryboat to Messina).
NGI, tel. 3358427784 (ferryboat to Messina).
SNAV, tel. 0909812448 (hydrofoil to Isole Eolie).

Hotels and restaurants

★★★ **G.H. Excelsior** Via Vittorio Veneto 66, ✉ 89121, tel. 0965812211, fax 0965893084; 84 rms.; 🅿 🅿 ♿ 🄰🄴 ⑳ 🌃; (*B2*).

¶¶ **Baylik** Vico Leone 3, ✉ 89121, tel. 096548624 ✉; ❯❮ fine cuisine 🍴 local and national; 80 capacity; closed Thursday, and for a certain period of time in August; 🅿 🄰🄴 ⑳ 🌃 ᴍᴄ; (*off map*).

Rimini ✉ 47900

ℹ *IAT*, Piazzale Federico Fellini 3, tel. 054156902; www.riminiturismo.it; *IAT*, Stazione F.S., Via Dante, tel. 054151331; infostazione@comune. rimini. it; *IAT* (seasonal), Viale Martinelli 11/A, Miramare, tel. 0541372112; infomiramare@co mune.rimini.it; *IAT* (seasonal), Viale S. Salvador 65/A, Torre Pedrera, tel. 0541720182; in fotorrepedrera@comune.rimini.it; *IAT* (seasonal), Viale G. Dati 180/A, Viserba, tel. 0541 738115; infoviserba@comune.rimini.it; *Centro d'informazione comunale*, Corso d'Augusto 156/158, tel. 0541704112, urp@comune.rimini.it.

🚂 *Stazione F.S. (railway station)*, Piazzale Battisti, tel. 892021.

🛣 *Rimini Sud* or *Rimini Sud* (A14 Bologna-Taranto).

✈ *Airport* at Miramare, tel. 0541715711. Bus service from the railway station.
Minerva Airlines, at the airport, tel. 0541715711.

Hotels

★★★ **Ambasciatori** Viale Vespucci 22, tel. 054155561, fax 054123790; www.hotelambasciatori.it; info@ hotelambasciatori.it; 66 rms.; 🅿 ♨ ♨ Ⓔ Ⓟ 🄰🄴 🌃 ᴍᴄ.

★★★ **Diplomat Palace** Viale Regina Elena 70, tel. 0541380011, fax 0541380414; www.diplomat palace.it; 75 rms.; 🅿 ♨ Ⓟ 🄰🄴 ⑳ 🌃 ᴍᴄ.

★★★ **Waldorf** Viale Vespucci 28, tel. 054154725, fax 054153153; www.waldorf.it; 60 rms.; 🅿 ♨ ♨ ✕ Ⓟ 🄰🄴 ⑳ 🌃 ᴍᴄ.

★★★ **Acasamia** Viale Parisano 34, tel. 0541391370, fax 054191816; acasamia@iper.net; closed November; 40 rms.; 🅿 ♨ Ⓔ 🄰🄴 ⑳ 🌃 ᴍᴄ.

★★★ **Ariminum** Viale Regina Elena 159, tel. 0541 380472, fax 054189301; www.ariminumhotels. it; info@ariminumhotels.it; 50 rms.; 🅿 Ⓟ 🄰🄴 ⑳ 🌃 ᴍᴄ.

★★★ **Luxor** Viale Tripoli 203, tel. 0541390990, fax 0541 392490; www.hoteluxor.com; closed mid-December-Christmas; 34 rms.; 🅿 Ⓔ Ⓟ ♿ 🄰🄴 ⑳ 🌃 ᴍᴄ.

★★★ **Marittima** (no restaurant), Viale Parisano 24, tel. and fax 0541392525; marittima@tiscali.it; 40 rms.; 🅿 Ⓟ 🄰🄴 ⑳ 🌃 ᴍᴄ.

★★★ **Relais Mercure Tiberius** Viale Cormons 6, tel. 054154226, fax 054127631; www.accor-hotels.it; tiberius@iper.net; 81 rms.; 🅿 Ⓔ Ⓟ 🄰🄴 ⑳ 🌃 ᴍᴄ.

★★★ **Villa Lalla** Viale Vittorio Veneto 22, tel. 0541 55155, fax 054123570; www.villalalla.com; info@ villalalla.com; 40 rms.; 🅿 ♨ Ⓔ Ⓟ 🄰🄴 ⑳ 🌃 ᴍᴄ.

Restaurants

¶¶¶ **Acero Rosso** Viale Tiberio 11, tel. 054153577,

fax 054155461 ⊠; ⅓ⁱ fine cuisine ⌂ Italian and international; 45/15 capacity; closed Monday (in winter also Sunday evening), 15 August and Christmas holidays; ⌂ ❀ Æ ⍟ ☲ ᴹᶜ.

⅋⅋ **Squero** Lungomare Tintori 7, tel. 054127676 ⊠; ⅓ⁱ seafood ⌂ Italian; 100 capacity; closed Tuesday in winter, November-mid-January; Æ ⍟ ☲ ᴹᶜ.

at Marebello, 5 km

Hotels

★★★ **Carlton** Viale Regina Margherita 6, tel. 0541 372361, fax 0541374540; 67 rms.; ⌂ ♨ ℙ.

at Miramare, 7 km   ⊠ 47831

Hotels

★★★★ **Due Mari** Viale Principe di Piemonte 53, tel. 0541 370660, fax 0541375610; www.italiaabc.it/hotel duemari; 60 rms.; ⌂ ♨ ℙ Æ ⍟ ☲.

★★★ **Giannini** Viale Principe di Piemonte 10, tel. and fax 0541370736; www.hotelgiannini.it; open June- mid-September; 56 rms.; ⌂ ♨ ▤ ℙ ☲ ᴹᶜ.

at Rivazzurra, 6 km

Hotels

★★★ **De France** Viale Regina Margherita 48, tel. 0541 379711, fax 0541379700; open mid-March-October; 65 rms.; ⌂ ♨ ℙ ♿ Æ ⍟ ☲ ᴹᶜ.

Riva del Garda (TN)   ⊠ 38066

ℹ **APT**, Giardini di Porta Orientale 8, tel. 0464 554444; www.gardatrentino.it.

▦ **Stazione F.S. (railway station)** at Rovereto; bus service.

⅋ **Rovereto Sud-Lago di Garda Nord** (A22 Brennero-Modena).

⛴ **NLG-Navigazione Lago di Garda**, tel. 0457 550433 (ferryboat and hydrofoil to Desenzano del G., Malcesine, Peschiera del G., Sirmione and other towns).

Hotels and restaurants

★★★★ **Du Lac et Du Parc** Viale Rovereto 44, tel. 0464 551500, fax 0464555200; www.hoteldulac-riva.it; info@hoteldulac-riva.it; open March-October; 170 rms.; ⌂ ♨ ☇ ⎅ ✗ ▤ ℙ Æ ⍟ ☲ ᴹᶜ.

★★★★ **G.H. Liberty** Viale Carducci 3/5, tel. 0464553581, fax 0464551144; 84 rms.; ♨ ☇ ℙ ♿ Æ ⍟ ☲ ᴹᶜ.

★★★ **Centrale** Piazza 3 Novembre 27, tel. 0464 552344, fax 0464552138; www.welcometogarda lake.com; hotelcentrale@trentino.com; closed mid-November-mid-December; 70 rms.; ⌂ Æ ⍟ ☲ ᴹᶜ.

★★★ **Luise** Viale Rovereto 9, tel. 0464552796, fax 0464554250; www.rivadelgarda.com/louise; luise@riva delgarda.com; 69 rms.; ⌂ ♨ ☇ ✗ℙ ♿ Æ ⍟ ☲ ᴹᶜ.

⅋⅋ **Al Volt** Via Fiume 73, tel. 0464552570; ⅓ⁱ Tridentine and local ⌂ Italian and international; 50 capacity; closed Monday, mid-February-mid-March; Æ ⍟ ☲ ᴹᶜ.

Rome   ⊠ 00100

ℹ **APT**, Via Parigi 5/11, tel. 06488991; www.romaturismo.com; (II, D4); **Information Office** at airport, tel. 0665954471; **APT/Prov.**, Via XX Settembre 26, tel. 06421381; azienturismoprovroma@tiscali.it; (II, C4); **Comune di Roma**, call-center, tel. 06 36004399; **Information booth**, Termini Station, in front of platform no. 4, tel. 0648906300 (II, E4-5). **TCI**, Via del Babuino 20, tel. 0636005281; negozio.roma@touringclub.it; (I, C5) .

▦ **Stazioni F.S. (railway stations)**, tel. 892021; **Ferrovie Cotral**, tel. 800-431784.

⅋ **Circonvallazione Tiburtina** (access to A24 to L'Aquila, Teramo and Pescara); **Grande Raccordo Anulare** (by-pass highway linking the different parts of town to the highways without entering the city); **S.S. 215 Tuscolana** (to A1 towards Naples); **S.S. 4 Salaria** (to A1 towards Milan); **S.S. 6 Casilina** or **S.S. 215 Tuscolana** (to A1 towards Naples); **Via della Magliana** (to the Roma-Fiumicino intersection and to A12 Civitavecchia-Roma).

✈ **Airports: Leonardo Da Vinci** at Fiumicino, tel. 0665951. Railway service to Termini and Ostiense stations; night bus service by Cotral from Stazione Tiburtina; **G.B. Pastine** at Ciampino, tel. 794941. Bus service by Cotral from the Anagnina stop, underground line A.
Air Dolomiti, information tel. 0665953640.
Air Europe, information tel. 800-454000.
Air One, information and reservations tel. 06 488800.
Air Sicilia, information tel. 0642012653.
Air Vallée, reservations tel. 0165303303.
Alitalia, Via Bissolati 11 (II, C3), tel. 0665628222; Stazione Termini, booth at platform 24 (II, E5); Via Marchetti 111 (off map), information tel. 0665641.

Hotels

★★★L **Aldrovandi Palace** Via U. Aldrovandi 15, ⊠ 00197, tel. 063223993, fax 063221435; www.aldrovandi.com; hotel@aldrovandi.com; 135 rms.; ⌂ ♨ ☇ ℙ Æ ⍟ ☲ ᴹᶜ; (off map).

★★★L **Bernini Bristol** Piazza Barberini 23, ⊠ 00187, tel. 064883051, fax 064824266; www.berninibristol.com; 125 rms.; ⌂ ▤ Æ ⍟ ☲ ᴹᶜ; (II, D2).

★★★L **Cavalieri Hilton** Via Cadlolo 101, ⊠ 00136, tel. 0635091, fax 0635092241; www.cavalieri hilton.it; 371 rms.; ⌂ ♨ ☇ ⎅ ✗ ▤ ℙ Æ ⍟ ☲ ᴹᶜ; (off map).

★★★L **Eden** Via Ludovisi 49, ⊠ 00187, tel. 06478121, fax 064821584; www.hotel-eden.it; reservations@hotel-eden.it; 121 rms.; ⌂ ▤ Æ ⍟ ☲ ᴹᶜ; (II, C2).

★★★L **Hassler-Villa Medici** Piazza Trinità dei Monti 6, ⊠ 00187, tel. 06699340, fax 066789991; www.hotelhasslerroma.com; hasslerroma@mclink.it; 100 rms.; ⌂ ♨ Æ ♿ Æ ⍟ ☲ ᴹᶜ; (II, C1-2).

★★★L **Lord Byron** Via G. de Notaris 5, ⊠ 00197, tel. 06 3224541, fax 063220405; info@lordbyronhotel.com; 37 rms.; ⌂ ♨ Æ Æ ⍟ ☲ ᴹᶜ; (off map).

★★★L **St. Regis Grand** Via Vittorio Emanuele Orlando 3, ⊠ 00185, tel. 0647091, fax 064747307; www.stregis.com; 161 rms.; ⌂ ▤ ♿ Æ ⍟ ☲ ᴹᶜ; (II, D3-4).

★★★ **Artdeco** Via Palestro 19, ⊠ 00185, tel. 06 4457588, fax 064441483; 49 rms.; ⌂ ▤ Æ ⍟ ☲; (II, C5).

★★★ **Atlante Garden** (no restaurant), Via Crescenzio 78/A, ⊠ 00193, tel. 066872361, fax 066872315; www.atlantehotels.com; atlante.garden@atlante hotels.com; 60 rms.; ⌂ ▤ Æ ⍟ ☲ ᴹᶜ; (I, D2).

★★★ **Atlante Star** Via Vitelleschi 34, ⊠ 00193, tel. 06 6873233, fax 066872300; atlante.star@atlanteho tels.com; 61 rms.; ⌂ ♨ ▤ ℙ Æ ⍟ ☲ ᴹᶜ; (I, D3).

★★★ **D'Inghilterra** Via Bocca di Leone 14, ⊠ 00187, tel. 0669981, fax 0669922243; 105 rms.; ⌂ Æ ⍟ ☲; (I, D6).

★★★ **Farnese** (no restaurant), Via A. Farnese 30, ⊠ 00192, tel. 063212553, fax 063215129; 23 rms.; ⌂ ▤ ℙ Æ ⍟ ☲ ᴹᶜ; (I, B4).

★★★ **Jolly Leonardo da Vinci** Via dei Gracchi 324, ⊠ 00192, tel. 06328481, fax 063610138; www.jolly hotels.it; 256 rms.; ⌂ ▤ Æ ⍟ ☲; (I, C4).

★★★ **Jolly Midas** Via Aurelia 800, ⊠ 00165, tel. 06 66396, fax 0666418457; www.jollyhotels.it; 347 rms.; ⌂ ♨ ▤ ℙ Æ ⍟ ☲ ᴹᶜ; (off map).

★★★ **Jolly Vittorio Veneto** Corso d'Italia 1, ⊠ 00198, tel. 068495, fax 068841104; www.jollyhotel.it; 201 rms.; ⌂ ▤ ♿ Æ ⍟ ☲ ᴹᶜ; (II, B3).

★★★ **Massimo D'Azeglio** Via Cavour 18, ⊠ 00184, tel. 064870270, fax 064827386; www.bettojaho tels.it; 198 rms.; ⌂ ▤ Æ ⍟ ☲ ᴹᶜ; (II, E4).

★★★ **Mediterraneo** Via Cavour 15, ⊠ 00184, tel. 06

4884051, fax 064744105; www.bettojahotels.it; 262 rms.; 🏠 🅿 🆚 🆎 🅿 🆚 🅼🅲; (II, *E4*).

★★★ Mondial (no restaurant), Via Torino 127, ✉ 00184, tel. 06472861, fax 064824822; md3058@mclink.it; 84 rms.; 🏠 🅿 🅿 🆎 🅿 🆚 🅼🅲; (II, *D-E4*).

★★★ Napoleon Piazza Vittorio Emanuele 105, ✉ 00185, tel. 064467264, fax 064467282; www.napoleon.it; 80 rms.; 🏠 🅿 🆎 🅿 🅼🅲; (III, *A4*).

★★★ President Via Emanuele Filiberto 173, ✉ 00185, tel. 06770121, fax 067008740; www.hotelpresident.com; 192 rms.; 🏠 🅿 🅿 👶 🆎 🅿 🆚 🅼🅲; (III, *B5*).

★★★ Rivoli Via Taramelli 7, ✉ 00197, tel. 063224042, fax 063227373; 54 rms.; 🏠 🅿 🆎 🅿 🅼🅲; (*off map*).

★★★ Arcangelo (no restaurant), Via Boezio 15, ✉ 00192, tel. 066874143, fax 066893050; hotel.arcangelo@travel.it; 33 rms.; 🏠 🅿 🅿 🆎 🅿 🆚; (I, *D3*).

★★★ Canada (no restaurant), Via Vicenza 58, ✉ 00185, tel. 064457770, fax 064450749; www.hotelcanadaroma.com; 70 rms.; 🏠 🅿 🆎 🅿 🆚 🅼🅲; (II, *D5*).

★★★ Corot (no restaurant), Via Marghera 15/17, ✉ 00185, tel. 0644700900, fax 0644700905; www.hotelcorot.it; 28 rms.; 🏠 🅿 👶 🆎 🅿 🆚; (II, *D5*).

★★★ Domus Aventina (no restaurant), Via di S. Prisca 11/B, ✉ 00153, tel. 065746135, fax 0657300044; www.domus-aventina.com; 26 rms.; 🏠 🅿 🆎 🅿 🆚 🅼🅲; (IV, *D5*).

★★★ Fontanella Borghese (no restaurant), Via Largo Fontanella Borghese, ✉ 00186, tel. 0668809504, fax 066861295; www.fontanellaborghese.com; 24 rms.; 🏠 🆎 🅿 🆚 🅼🅲; (I, *D-E5*).

★★★ Igea (no restaurant), Via Principe Amedeo 97, ✉ 00185, tel. 064466913, fax 064466911; www.igearoma.com; 42 rms.; 🏠 🆎 🅿 🆚 🅼🅲; (II, *E5*).

★★★ Mozart (no restaurant), Via dei Greci 23/B, ✉ 00187, tel. 0636001915, fax 0636001735; www.hotelmozart.com; 56 rms.; 🏠 🆎 🅿 🆚; (I, *C5-6*).

★★★ Piccadilly (no restaurant), Via Magna Grecia 122, ✉ 00183, tel. 0670474858, fax 0670476686; www.bestwestern.com; 55 rms.; 🏠 🅿 🅿 🆎 🅿 🆚 🅼🅲; (III, *D5*).

★★★ Villa del Parco (no restaurant), Via Nomentana 110, ✉ 00161, tel. 0644237773, fax 0644237572; www.venere.it/roma/villaparco; villaparco@mclink.it; 29 rms.; 🏠 🛎 🅿 🅿; (*off map*).

★★★ Villa Florence (no restaurant), Via Nomentana 28, ✉ 00161, tel. 064403036, fax 4402709; www.venere.it/roma/villa-florence; 34 rms.; 🏠 🛎 🅿 🅿 🆎 🅿 🆚 🅼🅲; (II, *B5*).

Restaurants

🍴🍴 La Terrazza Via Ludovisi 49, ✉ 00187, tel. 06 478121, fax 064821584 ⊠; 🍴 Mediterranean 🍷 Italian and international; 65 capacity; 🏠 🅿 🆎 🅿 🆚 🅼🅲; (II, *C2*).

🍴🍴 Relais le Jardin Via G. de Notaris 5, ✉ 00197, tel. 063220404, fax 063220405 ⊠; www.lordbyronhotel.com; 🍴 classic 🍷 Italian and international; 60 capacity; closed Sunday; 🏠 🅿 🆎 🅿 🆚 🅼🅲; part of the Lord Byron hotel; (*off map*).

🍴🍴 Sans Souci Via Sicilia 20, ✉ 00187, tel. 06 42014510, fax 064821771 ⊠; www.sanssouci.com; sanssouci@mclink.it; 🍴 fine cuisine 🍷 Italian and international; 100 capacity; open only evening; closed Monday, and for a certain period of time in August; 🏠 🆎 🅿 🆚 🅼🅲; (II, *C2-3*).

🍴 Alberto Ciarla Piazza S. Cosimato 40, ✉ 00153, tel. 065818668, fax 065884377 ⊠; 🍴 regional (seafood) 🍷 Italian and international; 70 capacity; closed Sunday; 🏠 🆎 🅿 🆚 🅼🅲; (IV, *C2*).

🍴 La Rosetta Via della Rosetta 8, ✉ 00187, tel. 066861002, fax 0668215116 ⊠; www.larosetta.com; larosetta@tin.it; 🍴 "marinara" 🍷 Italian and international; 60 capacity; closed Saturday at midday and Sunday, and for a certain period of time in August; 🏠 🆎 🅿 🆚 🅼🅲; (I, *E5*).

🍴🍴🍴 Agata e Romeo Via Carlo Alberto 45, ✉ 00185, tel. 064466115, fax 064465842 ⊠; agataeromeo@tiscali.it; 🍴 Latium and Sannio 🍷 Italian and international; 42 capacity; closed Saturday and Sunday, period when closed may vary; 🏠 🆎 🅿 🆚 🅼🅲; (II, *F4-5*).

🍴🍴🍴 Ciro Via Vittoria 22, ✉ 00186, tel. 063614148, fax 0636092654 ⊠; cirofisch@jumpy.it; 🍴 "marinara" 🍷 Italian and international; 50 capacity; closed Sunday, August; 🏠 🆎; (I, *D6*).

🍴🍴🍴 Giovanni Via Marche 64, ✉ 00187, tel. 06 4821834, fax 064817366 ⊠; 🍴 classic 🍷 Italian and international; 100 capacity; closed Friday evening and Saturday, August; 🏠 🆎 🅿 🆚 🅼🅲; (II, *C3*).

🍴🍴🍴 San Luigi Via Mocenigo 10, ✉ 00192, tel. 06 39720704, fax 0639722421 ⊠; 🍴 fine cuisine 🍷 Italian and international; 60 capacity; closed Sunday at midday, and for a certain period of time in August; 🏠 🆎 🅿 🆚 🅼🅲; (I, *C1*).

🍴🍴🍴 Taberna de' Gracchi Via dei Gracchi 266, ✉ 00192, tel. 063213126 ⊠; 🍴 classic (grilled meat and fish) 🍷 local and national; 160 capacity; closed Sunday, Monday at midday, and for a certain period of time in August; 🏠 🅿 🆎 🅿 🆚 🅼🅲; (I, *C3*).

🍴 Al Ceppo Via Panama 2, ✉ 00198, tel. 06 8419696 ⊠; alceppo@tiscali.it; 🍴 Marche and classic 🍷 Italian and international; 100 capacity; closed Monday, and for a certain period of time in August; 🏠 🆎 🅿 🆚 🅼🅲; (*off map*).

🍴 Aurora 10 da Pino il Sommelier Via Aurora 10, ✉ 00187, tel. 064742779 ⊠; www.paginegialle.it/aurora10; 🍴 Roman, Sicilian and classic 🍷 local and national; 50 capacity; closed Monday; 🏠 🅿 🆚 🅼🅲; (II, *C2*).

🍴 Charly's Saucière Via di S. Giovanni in Laterano 270, ✉ 00184, tel. 0670495666; 🍴 French-Swiss 🍷 Italian and international; 48 capacity; closed Saturday and Monday at midday, Sunday, and for a certain period of time in August; 🏠 🆎 🅿 🆚 🅼🅲; (III, *B-C4*).

🍴 Checco er Carettiere Via Benedetta 10, ✉ 00153, tel. 065800985 ⊠; 🍴 Roman and "marinara" 🍷 Italian; 110/70 capacity; closed Sunday evening; 🏠 ❄ 🆎 🅿 🆚 🅼🅲; (IV, *B2-3*).

🍴 Felice Via Mastro Giorgio 29, ✉ 00153, tel. 06 5746800 ⊠; 🍴 Roman 🍷 local; 50 capacity; closed Sunday, and for a certain period of time in August; (IV, *E4*).

🍴 Girarrosto Toscano Via Campania 29, ✉ 00187, tel. 064821899 ⊠; www.travel.it/roma/toscano; 🍴 Tuscan 🍷 Italian; 115 capacity; closed Wednesday; 🏠 🆎 🅿 🆚 🅼🅲; (II, *B-C2-3*).

🍴 L'Ortica Via Flaminia Vecchia 573, ✉ 00191, tel. 063338709 ⊠; 🍴 Neapolitan 🍷 Italian and international; 50 capacity; closed Sunday, and for a certain period of time in August; 🆎 🅿 🆚 🅼🅲; (*off map*).

🍴 Paris Piazza S. Calisto 7/A, ✉ 00153, tel. 06 5815378 ⊠; 🍴 of Lazio 🍷 Italian and international; 100/70 capacity; closed Sunday evening, Monday, August; 🏠 ❄ 🆎 🅿 🆚 🅼🅲; (IV, *B3*).

🍴 Peppone Via Emilia 60, ✉ 00187, tel. 06483976 ⊠; 🍴 Roman and classic 🍷 local and national; 60 capacity; closed Sunday, holidays and before holidays in August, Easter and Christmas holidays; 🏠 🆎 🅿 🆚 🅼🅲; (II, *C2*).

🍴 Taverna Giulia Vicolo dell'Oro 23 corner of Via Giulia, ✉ 00186, tel. 066869768 ⊠; tavgiu@tiscali.it; 🍴 Ligurian 🍷 Italian; 70 capacity; closed Sunday, August; 🏠 🆎 🅿 🆚; (I, *E3*).

🍴 Agustarello a Testaccio Via G. Branca 98, ✉ 00153, tel. 065746585 ⊠; 🍴 Roman 🍷 local and national; 40/30 capacity; closed Sunday, for a certain period of time between August and September; ❄; (IV, *E3*).

🍴 Scoglio di Frisio Via Merulana 256, ✉ 00185, tel. 064872765 ⊠; 🍴 Neapolitan 🍷 Italian; 200

capacity; closed only evening; ⊠ ⒶⒺ ⓌⒹ ⚏ ᴹᶜ; (II, F4).

Ÿ Alfredo a Via Gabi Via Gabi 36, ⊠ 00183, tel. 0677206792 ⊠; www.alfredoaviagabi.it; ⅀ Roman (seafood and mushrooms) ◊ᵧ Italian; 70 capacity; closed Tuesday, for a certain period of time in August; ⊠ ⒶⒺ ⓌⒹ ⚏ ᴹᶜ; (III, D5).

EUR

Hotels and restaurants

⋆ Aris Garden Via Aristofane 101, ⊠ 00125, tel. 0652362443, fax 0652352968; www.rosciolihotels.com; 110 rms.; ⊠ ⌖ ⌖ ⌖ ✕ Ⓟ ⌖ ⒶⒺ ⓌⒹ ⚏.

⋆ Shangri Là Corsetti Viale Algeria 141, ⊠ 00144, tel. 065916441, fax 065413813; shangrila@tiscali.it; 52 rms.; ⊠ ⌖ ⚏ ⅀ Ⓟ ⌖ ⒶⒺ ⓌⒹ ᴹᶜ.

⋆ Sheraton Roma Viale del Pattinaggio, ⊠ 00144, tel. 0654531, fax 065940689; www.sheraton.com/Roma; res497sheratonroma@sheraton.com; 647 rms.; ⊠ ⌖ ⚏ ✕ Ⓟ ⌖ ⒶⒺ ⓌⒹ ⚏ ᴹᶜ.

ŸŸ Vecchia America-Corsetti Piazza Marconi 32, ⊠ 00144, tel. 065911458; ⅀ regional and classic (seafood) ◊ᵧ Italian and international; 200 capacity, closed Monday evening; ⊠ ❀ ⒶⒺ ⓌⒹ ⚏ ᴹᶜ.

Sabbioneta (MN) ⊠ 46018

ⓘ APT at Mantova; Pro Loco, Via V. Gonzaga 27, tel. 037552039.

Restaurants

*** Duca Via della Stamperia 18, tel. 037552474, fax 0375220021; closed for a certain period of time between January and February; 10 rms.; ⊠ ⌖ ⚏ ᴹᶜ.

ŸŸ Parco Cappuccini Via Santuario 30, tel. 0375 52005; ⅀ Mantuan and classic ◊ᵧ Italian; 250 capacity; closed Monday, Wednesday evening and Christmas holidays; ❀ Ⓟ ⒶⒺ ⚏.

Saint-Vincent (AO) ⊠ 11027

ⓘ AIAT, Via Roma 62, tel. 0166512239; aiatsaintvincent@libero.it.

⊿ Stazione F.S. (railway station) at Châtillon; bus service.

ⵜ Saint-Vincent-Châtillon (A5 Torino-Traforo Monte Bianco).

Hotels and restaurants

⋆ G.H. Billia Viale Piemonte 72, tel. 01665231, fax 0166523799; www.aostavalley.com/billia; 246 rms.; ⊠ ⌖ ⌖ ⌖ ✕ Ⓟ ⌖ ⒶⒺ ⓌⒹ ⚏ ᴹᶜ.

*** Elena Piazza Zerbion 2, tel. 0166512140, fax 0166537459; www.saint-vincent-hotels.com/elena/; hotel.elena@libero.it; closed mid-November-mid-December; from May to October restaurant I Due Nani; 48 rms.; ⊡ Ⓟ ⒶⒺ ⓌⒹ ⚏ ᴹᶜ.

** Leon d'Oro Via E. Chanoux 26, tel. 0166512202, fax 0166537345; www.adava.vao.it; adava.servizi@galactica.it; 50 rms.; ⌖ ⊡. Ⓟ ⒶⒺ ⓌⒹ ⚏ ᴹᶜ.

Ÿℍ Batezar Via G. Marconi 1, tel. 0166513164, fax 0166512378 ⊠; ⅀ Val d'Aostan and Piedmontese ◊ᵧ Italian and international; 30 capacity; closed Wednesday, and for a certain period of time in November and June; ⒶⒺ ⓌⒹ ⚏ ᴹᶜ.

ŸŸ Le Grenier Piazza Zerbion 1, tel. 0166512224 ⊠; ⅀ Val d'Aostan and classic ◊ᵧ Italian and international; 60 capacity; closed Tuesday and at midday on Saturday and Sunday, for a certain period of time in June and in January; Ⓟ ⓌⒹ ⚏ ᴹᶜ.

Sala Comacina (CO) ⊠ 22010

Restaurants

Ÿ Taverna Blu Via Puricelli 4, tel. 0344555107 ⊠; ⅀

Lake Como ◊ᵧ Italian and international; 70 capacity; closed Tuesday, November; ❀ Ⓟ ⒶⒺ ⓌⒹ ⚏ ᴹᶜ; also hotel.

Salerno ⊠ 84100

ⓘ EPT, Piazza Vittorio Veneto 1, tel. 800-213289, 089231432; www.crmpa.it/ept/; AA, Via Roma 258, tel. 089224744.

⊿ Stazione F.S. (railway station), Piazza Vittorio Veneto 30, tel. 892021.

ⵜ Salerno Centro (A3 to Naples), Salerno-Fratte (A30 to Nola and Caserta, highway intersection to Avellino).

⛴ Alicost, tel. 089873301 (seasonal hydrofoil and ferryboat to Amalfi)
Cooperativa Sant'Andrea, tel. 089873190 (seasonal ferryboat to Amalfi and Positano).
Grimaldi, tel. 0815517716 (ferryboat to Palermo).
Linee Marittime Partenopee, tel. 0818376995 (seasonal hydrofoil to Capri and Ischia).
Navigazione Libera del Golfo, tel. 0815520763 (hydrofoil to Amalfi and Positano).

Hotels and restaurants

⋆ Jolly delle Palme Lungomare Trieste 1, ⊠ 84121, tel. 089225222, fax 089237571; www.jollyhotels.it; salerno@jollyhotels.it; 104 rms.; ⊠ ⊡ Ⓟ ⒶⒺ ⓌⒹ ⚏.

*** Fiorenza (no restaurant), Via Trento 145, ⊠ 84131, tel. and fax 089338800; www.hotelfiorenza. it; fiorealb@tin.it; 30 rms.; ⊠ ⊡ Ⓟ ⒶⒺ ⓌⒹ ⚏ ᴹᶜ.

*** Plaza (no restaurant), Piazza Vittorio Veneto 42, ⊠ 84123, tel. 089224477, fax 089237311; www. speednet.org /plaza; 42 rms.; ⊠ ⊡ Ⓟ ⒶⒺ ⓌⒹ ⚏ ᴹᶜ.

ŸŸ Al Cenacolo Piazza Alfano I 4, ⊠ 84125, tel. 089 238818 ⊠; ⅀ regional (seafood) ◊ᵧ Italian and international; 60 capacity; closed Sunday evening and Monday, Christmas holidays and for a certain period of time in August; ⊠ ⒶⒺ ⓌⒹ ⚏ ᴹᶜ.

Salò (BS) ⊠ 25087

ⓘ IAT, Lungolago Zanardelli, tel. 21423; iat@comune.salo.bs.it.

⊿ Stazione F.S. (railway station) at Desenzano del Garda or Brescia; bus service.

ⵜ Brescia Est, Desenzano (A4 Torino-Milano-Trieste).

⛴ NLG-Navigazione Lago di Garda, tel. 0309149511 (boat and hydrofoil, seasonal, to Desenzano del G., Peschiera del G., Riva del G., Sirmione and other places).

Hotels and restaurants

⋆ Laurin Viale Landi 9, tel. 036522022, fax 0365 22382; closed January; 37 rms.; ⌖ ⊡ Ⓟ ⒶⒺ ⓌⒹ ⚏.

*** Bellerive (no restaurant), Via P. da Salò 11, tel. 0365520410, fax 0365521969; 20 rms.; ⌖ Ⓟ ⒶⒺ ⓌⒹ ⚏ ᴹᶜ.

*** Benaco Lungolago Zanardelli 44, tel. 036520308, fax 036521049; www.benacohotel.it; 20 rms.; ⓌⒹ ⚏ ᴹᶜ.

ŸŸ Lepanto Lungolago Zanardelli 67, tel. 0365 20428 ⊠; ⅀ classic (lake and sea fish, mushrooms) ◊ᵧ Italian and international; 40/55 capacity; closed Thursday, mid-January-February; ❀ ⓌⒹ ⚏; also hotel.

San Gimignano (SI) ⊠ 53037

ⓘ APT at Siena; Pro Loco, Piazza Duomo 1, tel. 0577940008.

⊿ Stazione F.S. (railway station) at Poggibonsi; bus service.

†↑ *Poggibonsi* (Firenze-Siena highway intersection).

Hotels and restaurants

↑ **Villa San Paolo** (no restaurant), road to Certaldo, km 4, tel. 0577550100, fax 0577955113; www.ho telvillasanpaolo.com; sanpaolo@iol.it; closed mid-January/mid-February; 18 rms.; 🏨 ♨ ≋ ✕ 🅿 ♿ 🅰🅴 ⬜ MC.

*** **Da Graziano** Via Matteotti 39/A, tel. 0577940101, fax 0577940655; www.sangimignano.com/dagra ziano; hotelgraziano@cybermarket.it; closed Epiphany (6 January)-February; 11 rms.; 🏨 🅰🅴 ⬜ ⬜ MC.

*** **La Cisterna** Piazza della Cisterna 24, tel. 0577 940328, fax 0577942080; www.sangimignano. com/lacisterna; lacisterna@iol.it; closed Epiphany (6 January)-mid-March; 49 rms.; 🏨 🅰🅴 ⬜ ⬜ MC.

†↑ **Dorandò** Vicolo dell'Oro 2, tel. 0577941862 🖂; web.tin.it/dorando; ✕ fine cuisine ♨ local; 35 capacity; closed Monday in the off season, mid-January-February; 🏨 🅰🅴 ⬜ ⬜ MC.

† **Osteria delle Catene** Via Mainardi 18, tel. 0577 941966 🖂; ✕ Tuscan ♨ local; 40 capacity; 🏨 🅰🅴 ⬜ ⬜ MC.

San Marino (Republic of) 🖂 47890

🛈 *Ufficio di Stato per il Turismo*, Contrada Omagnano 20, tel. 0549882998; www.omniway.sm; (B2).

🚃 *Stazione F.S. (railway station)* at Rimini; bus service.

†↑ *Rimini Sud* (A14 Bologna-Taranto).

Hotels and restaurants

↑ **G.H. San Marino** Viale Onofri 31, tel. 0549 992400, fax 0549992951; www.omniway.sm/fiera/ grandhotel; 63 rms.; 🏨 🅿 🅰🅴 ⬜ MC; (C2).

↑ **Titano** Contrada del Collegio 31, tel. 0549 991006, fax 0549991375; www.sanmarinosite. com/titano/index.html; open mid-March-mid-December; 48 rms.; 🅿 🅿 🅰🅴 ⬜ MC; (off map).

*** **Quercia Antica** Via Capannaccia 7, tel. 0549 991257, fax 0549990044; www.querciantica.com; 26 rms.; 🏨 ♨ 🅿 🅿 🅰🅴 ⬜ MC; (C2).

*** **Villa Giardi** (no restaurant), via P. Ferri 22, tel. 0549991074, fax 0549992285; www.wel.it/villagi ardi; giardi@omniway.sm; 8 rms.; ♨ 🅿 🅰🅴 ⬜ ⬜ MC.

†↑↑ **Righi-la Taverna** Piazza Libertà 10, tel. 0549 991196, fax 0549990597 🖂; ✕ Emilian and fine cuisine ♨ Italian and international; 80 capacity; closed Wednesday in winter, for a certain period of time in January; 🏨 🅰🅴 ⬜ MC; (B2).

† **Buca San Francesco** Piazzetta Feretrano 3, tel. 0549991462; ✕ Romagna ♨ local; 60 capacity; closed Friday in winter, mid-November-mid-December; 🏨 🅰🅴 ⬜ MC; (B2).

San Remo (IM) 🖂 18038

🛈 *APT*, Largo Nuvoloni 1, tel. 018459059; www.apt. rivieradeifiori.it.

🚃 *Stazione F.S. (railway station)*, Corso Cavallotti, tel. 892021.

†↑ *San Remo* (A10 Ponte S. Luigi-Genova).

Hotels

↑↑ **Royal Hotel** Corso Imperatrice 80, tel. 0184 5391, fax 0184661445; www.royalhotelsanremo. com; royal@royalhotelsanremo.com; closed October-mid-December; 138 rms.; 🏨 ♨ ≋ ✕ 🅿 🅰🅴 ⬜ MC.

↑ **Eveline Portosole** (no restaurant), Corso Cavallotti 111, tel. 0184503430, fax 0184503431; www. evelineportosole.com; 22 rms.; 🏨 ♨ ♿ 🅿 🅰🅴 ⬜ ⬜ MC.

↑ **Nazionale** Corso Matteotti 3, tel. 0184577577, fax 0184541535; nazionale.im@bestwestern.it; 78 rms.; 🏨 🅰🅴 ♿ 🅰🅴 ⬜ MC.

↑ **Nike** (no restaurant), Via F.lli Asquasciati 37, tel. and fax 0184531428; www.hotelnike.com; closed for a certain period of time between November and December; 41 rms.; 🅿 🅰🅴 ⬜ MC.

*** **Lolli Palace** Corso Imperatrice 70, tel. 0184 531496, fax 0184541574; www.tourism.it; lolli_ palace@tin.it; 48 rms.; 🏨 🅿 🅿 🅰🅴 ⬜ ⬜ MC.

*** **Paradiso** Via Roccasterone 12, tel. 0184571211, fax 0184578176; www.paradisohotel.it; paradiso hotel@sistel.it; 41 rms.; 🏨 ♨ 🅿 🅿 🅰🅴 ⬜ MC.

*** **Villa Sylva** Via Garbarino 2, tel. 0184509801, fax 0184509231; h.villasylva@rosenet.it; 30 rms.; ♨ 🅿 🅰🅴 ⬜ ⬜ MC.

** **Corso** Corso Cavallotti 194, tel. 0184509911, fax 0184509231; corso@tourism.it; closed November; 18 rms.; 🅿 🅿 🅰🅴 ⬜ MC.

Restaurants

†↑↑ **Paolo e Barbara** Via Roma 47, tel. 0184531653, fax 0184545266 🖂; ✕ Ligurian ♨ Italian and international; 30 capacity; closed Wednesday and at midday on Thursday, for a certain period of time in December, January and July; 🏨 🅰🅴 ⬜ ⬜ MC.

†↑ **La Pignese** Piazza Sardi 7, tel. 0184501929 🖂; ✕ Ligurian ♨ Italian and international; 100 capacity; closed Monday, for a certain period of time in June; 🏨 🅰🅴 ⬜ ⬜ MC.

Sansepolcro (AR) 🖂 52037

🛈 *APT* at Arezzo; *Promo Tours & Services*, Piazza Garibaldi 2, tel. 0575740536.

🚃 *Stazione Ferroviaria Centrale Umbra (railway station)* Piazza Battisti 1, tel. 0575742094.

†↑ *Arezzo* (A1 Milano-Roma-Napoli).

Hotels and restaurants

↑ **La Balestra** Via dei Montefeltro 29, tel. 0575 735151, fax 0575740282; labalestra@leone.it; 52 rms.; 🏨 🅿 🅿 🅰🅴 ⬜ MC.

*** **Fiorentino** (no restaurant), Via Pacioli 60, tel. 0575740350, fax 0575740370; albergofiorenti no@technet.it; 26 rms.; 🅿 🅰🅴 ⬜ MC.

†↑↑ **Oroscopo di Paola e Marco** at Pieve Vecchia, Via Togliatti 68, tel. 0575734875 🖂; marco.mercati @tin.it; ✕ Tuscan ♨ Italian and international; 30 capacity; closed Sunday, for a certain period of time in January and between June and July; 🌐 🅿 ⬜ ⬜ MC; also hotel.

Santa Margherita Ligure (GE) 🖂 16038

🛈 *IAT*, Via XXV Aprile 2/B, tel. 0185287485; apt tigul lio.liguria.it.

🚃 *Stazione F.S. (railway station)*, Piazzale Nobili, tel. 892021.

†↑ *Chiavari*, *Rapallo* (A12 Genova-Rosignano).

⛴ *Servizio Marittimo del Tigullio*, Via Palestro 8/1B, tel. 0185284670 (ferryboat to Chiavari, Lavagna, Portofino and Rapallo).

Hotels and restaurants

↑ **Imperiale Palace Hotel** Via Pagana 19, tel. 0185 288991, fax 0185284223; www.hotelimperiale. com; info@hotelimperiale.com; open Easter-October; 93 rms.; 🏨 ♨ ≋ 🅿 🅰🅴 ⬜ MC.

↑ **Continental** Via Pagana 8, tel. 0185286512, fax 0185284463; closed November-mid-December; 76 rms.; 🏨 ♨ 🅿 🅿 🅰🅴 ⬜ MC.

↑ **G.H. Miramare** Promenade Milite Ignoto 30, tel. 0185287013, fax 0185284651; www.grandhotelmi ramare.it; 84 rms.; 🏨 ♨ ≋ 🅿 ♿ 🅰🅴 ⬜ ⬜ MC.

*** **Laurin** (no restaurant), Lungomare Marconi 3, tel. 0185289971, fax 0185285709; www.laurin hotel.it; info@laurinhotel.it; 43 rms.; 🅿 ⚐ 🆎 ⏣ 🏧 **MC**.

*** **Minerva** Via Maragliano 34/D, tel. 0185286073, fax 0185281697; www.hminerva.it; hminerva@tiscali.it; 35 rms.; ♨ 🅿 🖫 ♿ 🆎 ⏣ 🏧 **MC**.

*** **Tigullio et de Milan** Corso Rainusso 3, tel. 0185 287455, fax 0185281860; hotel_tigullio_et_de_milan@newnetworks.it; closed November-Christmas; 42 rms.; 🅿 ♨ 🅿 🖫 🆎 ⏣ 🏧 **MC**.

🍴 **Cambusa** Via Bottaro 1, tel. 0185287410 🖂; office@artedivivere.it; 🍽 Ligurian 🍷 local and national; 30 capacity; closed Thursday in winter and for a certain period of time in November; 🅿 🆎 ⏣ 🏧 **MC**.

🍴 **Oca Bianca** Via XXV Aprile 21, tel. 0185288411 🖂; 🍽 classic 🍷 local and national; 28 capacity; closed Monday, and for a certain period of time between January and February; 🅿 🆎 ⏣ 🏧 **MC**.

🍴 **Trattoria Cesarina** Via Mameli 2/C, tel. 0185 286059; 🍽 Ligurian (fish, mushrooms) 🍷 local and national; 50 capacity; closed Tuesday, mid-December-January; 🆎 ⏣ 🏧.

Santa Teresa Gallura (SS)   ⊠ 07028

ℹ️ *AA*, Piazza Vittorio Emanuele 24, tel. 0789 754127; www.regione.sardegna.it/aaststg.

🚆 *Stazione F.S. (railway station)* at Olbia; bus service.

⚓ *Moby Lines*, Via del Porto, tel. 0789751449 (summer ferryboat to Bonifacio in Corsica).
Saremar, Piazza del Porto 51, tel. 0789754156 (ferryboat to Bonifacio in Corsica).

Hotels and restaurants

*** **G.H. Corallaro** township of Rena Bianca, tel. 0789755475, fax 0789755431; www.hotelcoral laro.it; info@hotelcorallaro.it; open mid-April-October; 81 rms.; 🅿 ♨ ⚐ 🅿 ♿ 🆎 ⏣ 🏧 **MC**.

*** **Miramare** (no restaurant), Piazza della Libertà 6, tel. 0789754103, fax 0789754672; open mid-May-mid-October; 14 rms.; 🆎 ⏣ 🏧 **MC**.

*** **Sole e Mare** Via Carducci 1/3, tel. 0789754224, fax 0789755676; open April-September; 20 rms.; ♨ 🆎 🏧 **MC**.

🍴🍴 **S'Andira** township of Santa Reparata, Via Orsa Minore 1, tel. 0789754273 🖂; sandira@tiscali.it; 🍽 classic (seafood) 🍷 local; 60/20 capacity; open May-September; ⚘ 🅿 🆎 ⏣ 🏧 **MC**.

Sàssari   ⊠ 07100

ℹ️ *EPT*, Viale Caprera 36, tel. 079299546; www.en turismosassari.it; *AA*, Viale Umberto I 72, tel. 079 233534-079231331; aastss@tiscali.it.

🚆 *Stazione F.S. (railway station)*, Corso Vico 10, tel. 079260362; *Stazione Ferrovie della Sardegna*, Viale Sicilia 20, tel. 079241301.

Hotels and restaurants

*** **Grazia Deledda** Viale Dante 47, tel. 079271235, fax 079280884; 127 rms.; 🅿 🖫 🅿 🆎 ⏣ 🏧 **MC**.

*** **Carlo Felice** Via Carlo Felice 43, tel. 079 271440, fax 079271442; carlofelice@tiscali.it; 60 rms.; 🅿 ♨ 🅿 ♿ 🆎 ⏣ 🏧.

*** **Leonardo da Vinci** (no restaurant), Via Roma 79, tel. 079280744, fax 0792857233; www.leo nardodavincihotel.it; info@leonardodavinciho tel.it; 118 rms.; 🅿 🖫 🆎 ⏣ 🏧 **MC**.

🍴 **Castello** Piazza Castello 7, tel. 079232041 🖂; 🍽 Sardinian 🍷 local and national; 120 capacity; closed Wednesday except June-August; 🅿 ⚘ 🆎 ⏣ 🏧 **MC**.

Selinunte (TP)   ⊠ 91020

ℹ️ *Information Office AAPIT*, Parco Archeologico, tel. 092446251.

🚆 *Stazione F.S. (railway station)* at Castelvetrano; bus service.

🛉 *Castelvetrano* (A29 dir. Alcamo-Trapani).

at Marinella, 1 km

Hotels

*** **Alceste** Via Alceste 21, tel. 092446184, fax 092446143; www.hotelalceste.it; closed mid-January- mid-February and mid-November-mid-December; 26 rms.; 🅿 ♨ 🅿 🆎 ⏣ 🏧 **MC**.

Siena   ⊠ 53100

ℹ️ *APT*, Piazza del Campo 56, tel. 0577280551; www.siena.turismo.toscana.it; (*D3*).

🚆 *Stazione F.S. (railway station)*, Piazza Rosselli 7, tel. 0577204228, 892021.

🛉 *Siena* (Siena-Florence highway intersection).

Hotels

*** **Garden** Via Custoza 2, tel. 057747056, fax 0577 46050; www.gardenhotel.it; info@gardenhotel.it; 125 rms.; 🅿 ♨ 🆎 ⏣ 🏧 **MC**; (*off map*).

*** **Jolly Excelsior** Piazza La Lizza, tel. 0577 288448, fax 057741272; 126 rms.; 🅿 🆎 ⏣ 🏧 **MC**; (*C2*).

*** **Villa Scacciapensieri** Via di Scacciapensieri 10, tel. 0577441441, fax 0577270854; www.villascac ciapensieri.it; closed Epiphany (6 January)-mid-March; 30 rms.; 🅿 ♨ ⚐ ✖ 🖫 🅿 ♿ 🆎 ⏣ 🏧 **MC**; (*off map*).

*** **Italia** (no restaurant), Via Cavour 67, tel. 0577 41177, fax 057744554; www.gardenhotel.it; italiah @iol.it; 67 rms.; 🅿 🆎 ⏣ 🏧 **MC**; (*off map*).

*** **Piccolo Hotel Oliveta** (no restaurant), Via E.S. Piccolomini 35, tel. 0577283930, fax 0577 270009; www.oliveta.com; 15 rms.; closed for a certain period of time between January and February; 🅿 ♨ 🅿 🆎 ⏣ 🏧; (*F5*).

*** **Sangallo Park Hotel** (no restaurant), Strada di Vico Alto 2, tel. 0577334149, fax 0577333306; www.sangalloparkhotel.it; info@sangalloparkho tel.it; 50 rms.; 🅿 ♨ ⚐ 🅿 ♿ 🆎 ⏣ 🏧 **MC**; (*off map*).

*** **Santa Caterina** (no restaurant), Via Piccolomini 7, tel. 0577221105, fax 0577271087; www.siena net.it/hsc; 22 rms.; 🅿 ♨ 🅿 🆎 ⏣ 🏧 **MC**; (*F5*).

Restaurants

🍴🍴 **Antica Trattoria Botteganova** Via Chiantigiana 29, tel. 0577284230 🖂; 🍽 Tuscan and fine cuisine 🍷 Italian and international; 50 capacity; closed Monday, and for a certain period of time between July and August; 🅿 🅿 🆎 ⏣ 🏧; (*A-B5*).

🍴 **Al Mangia** Piazza del Campo 42, tel. 0577 281121 🖂; 🍽 Tuscan 🍷 local and national; 60 capacity; closed Wednesday in the off season; 🅿 🆎 ⏣ 🏧 **MC**; (*D3*).

🍴 **Marsili** Via del Castoro 3, tel. 057747154 🖂; 🍽 Tuscan 🍷 local and national; 140 capacity; closed Monday; 🅿 🆎 ⏣ 🏧 **MC**; (*E2-3*).

🍴 **Medio Evo** Via dei Rossi 40, tel. 0577280315 🖂; 🍽 Tuscan 🍷 local; 200 capacity; closed Thursday, and for a certain period of time in July and between January and February; 🆎 ⏣ 🏧; (*C3*).

Sirmione (BS)   ⊠ 25019

ℹ️ *IAT*, Viale Marconi 8, tel. 030916114-030916245.

🚆 *Stazione F.S. (railway station)* at Desenzano del Garda; bus service.

🛉 *Sirmione* (A4 Torino-Milano-Trieste).

🚢 *NLG-Navigazione Lago di Garda*, tel. 030 9904880 (boat and hydrofoil, seasonal, to Desenzano, Malcesine, Riva and other towns).

Hotels and restaurants

⁣⁣* **Continental** Via Punta Staffalo 7/9, tel. 030 9905711, fax 030916278; www.continetalsirmione.com; hotelcontinental@yahoo.it; open April-October; 59 rms.; 🏨 ♣ ♨ 🗐 🅿 🖭 ⓓ 🚾 ᴍᴄ

⁣⁣* **Flaminia** (no restaurant), Piazza Flaminia 8, tel. 030916078, fax 030916193; www.hotelflaminia.com; flaminia.hotel@libero.it; 43 rms.; 🏨 🅿 🖭 ⓓ 🚾 ᴍᴄ

*** **Golf & Suisse** (no restaurant), Via Condominio 2, tel. 0309904590, fax 030916304; www.gardalake.it/rossi-aparthotel; open April-October; 30 rms.; ♣ ♨ 🖭 ⓓ 🚾 ᴍᴄ

🍴 **La Rucola** Via Strentelle 3, tel. 030916326 ✉; ⅋ fine cuisine 🍷 Italian and international; 25 capacity; closed Thursday, Friday at midday, January-mid-February; 🏨 🖭 ⓓ 🚾 ᴍᴄ

at Lugana, 4 km   ✉ 25010

Hotels

*** **Derby** Via Verona 122, tel. 030919482, fax 030 9906631; closed mid-December-January; 14 rms.; 🏨 ♣ 🗐 🅿 ⓓ 🚾 ᴍᴄ

Sorrento (NA)   ✉ 80067

ℹ️ *AA*, Via De Maio 35, tel. 0818074033; aastsorrento@libero.it.

🚋 *Stazione Ferrovia Circumvesuviana (railway station)*, Piazza G.B. De Curtis, tel. 0817722444.

🕇 *Castellammare di S.* (A3 Napoli-Reggio di Calabria).

🚢 *Alicost*, tel. 0818781430 (hydrofoil to Capri, Naples and, seasonal, to Ischia).
Caremar, tel. 0818370700 (hydrofoil to Capri).
Navigazione Libera del Golfo, tel. 0818071812 (ferryboat and hydrofoil to Capri, Positano; hydrofoil to Amalfi).

Hotels

⁣⁣* **G.A. Excelsior Vittoria** Piazza T. Tasso 34, tel. 0818071044, fax 0818771206; www.exvitt.it; exvitt@exvitt.it; 107 rms.; ♣ ♨ 🖭 ⓓ 🚾 ᴍᴄ

⁣⁣* **Bellevue Syrene** Piazza della Vittoria 5, tel. 081 8781024, fax 0818783963; www.bellevue.it; info@bellevue.it; 73 rms.; 🏨 ♣ ♨ 🖭 ⓓ 🚾 ᴍᴄ

⁣⁣* **Bristol** Via del Capo 22, tel. 0818784522, fax 081 8071910; www.acampora.it/bristol; bristol@acampora.it; 165 rms.; 🏨 ♣ ♨ 🅿 🖭 ⓓ 🚾 ᴍᴄ

⁣⁣* **Carlton International** Via Correale 15, tel. 081 8072669, fax 0818071073; open March-November; 76 rms.; 🏨 ♣ ♨ 🗐 🅿 🖭 ⓓ 🚾 ᴍᴄ

⁣⁣* **G.H. Ambasciatori** Via Califano 18, tel. 081 8782025, fax 0818071021; www.manniellohotels.it; 103 rms.; 🏨 ♣ ♨ 🅿 🖭 ⓓ 🚾 ᴍᴄ

⁣⁣* **G.H. Royal** Via Correale 42, tel. 0818073434, fax 0818772905; www.manniellohotels.it; open April-October; 96 rms.; 🏨 ♣ ♨ 🅿 🖭 ⓓ 🚾 ᴍᴄ

⁣⁣* **Imperial Tramontano** Via Vittorio Veneto 1, tel. 0818782588, fax 0818072344; www.tramontano.com; imperial@tramontano.com; closed for a certain period of time between January and February; 116 rms.; 🏨 ♣ ♨ 🅿 🖭 ⓓ 🚾 ᴍᴄ

⁣⁣* **La Solara** Via del Capo 118, tel. 0815338000, fax 0818071501; www.lasolara.com; info@lasolara.com; 38 rms.; 🏨 ♣ ♨ 🅿 🖭 ⓓ 🚾 ᴍᴄ

*** **Rivage** Via Capo 11, tel. 0818781873, fax 081 8071253; www.hotelrivage.com; info@hotelrivage.com; 48 rms.; closed for a certain period of time between January and February; 🏨 🅿 ♿ 🖭 ⓓ 🚾 ᴍᴄ

*** **Villa di Sorrento** (no restaurant), Viale Enrico

Caruso 6, tel. 0818781068, fax 0818072679; belmare@belmare-travel.com; 20 rms.; 🏨 🖭 ⓓ 🚾 ᴍᴄ

** **La Minervetta** Via del Capo 25, tel. 0818073069, fax 0818773033; 12 rms.; 🅿 🖭 ⓓ 🚾 ᴍᴄ

Restaurants

🍴 **Caruso** Via Sant'Antonino 12, tel. 0818073156, fax 0818072899 ✉; ⅋ regional and classic (seafood) 🍷 Italian and international; 90 capacity; 🏨 🖭 ⓓ 🚾 ᴍᴄ

🍴 **L'Antica Trattoria** Via Padre R. Giuliani 33, tel. 0818071082 ✉; ⅋ regional 🍷 Italian; 120 capacity; closed Monday, February; 🏨 ❀ 🖭 ⓓ 🚾 ᴍᴄ

🍴 **Vela Bianca** Marina Piccola 11/13, tel. 081 8781144 ✉; www.hotelilfaro.com; ⅋ Neapolitan 🍷 Italian and international; 100 capacity; closed Tuesday, and for a certain period of time between January and February; 🏨 🖭 ⓓ 🚾 ᴍᴄ

Spoleto (PG)   ✉ 06049

ℹ️ *IAT*, Piazza della Libertà 7, tel. 0743220311; www.umbria2000.it.

🚋 *Stazione F.S. (railway station)*, Piazzale Polvani, tel. 892021.

🕇 *Orte* (A1 Milano-Roma-Napoli), *Ponte San Giovanni* (intersection to Val di Chiana-Perugia).

Hotels and restaurants

⁣⁣* **Dei Duchi** Viale G. Matteotti 4, tel. 074344541, fax 074344543; www.hoteldeiduchi.com; hotel@hoteldeiduchi.com; 49 rms.; 🏨 ♣ 🖭 ⓓ 🚾 ᴍᴄ

⁣⁣* **Gattapone** (no restaurant), Via del Ponte 6, tel. 0743223447, fax 0743223448; gattapone@mail.caribusiness.it; 15 rms.; 🏨 ♣ 🖭 ⓓ 🚾 ᴍᴄ

*** **Clitunno** Piazza Sordini 6, tel. 0743223340, fax 0743222663; www.hotelclitunno.com; info@hotelclitunno.com; 45 rms.; 🏨 🅿 🖭 ⓓ 🚾 ᴍᴄ

** **San Carlo Borromeo** Via S. Carlo 13, tel. 0743 225320, fax 0743207146; www.itwg.com/itw 12670.asp; 38 rms.; ♣ ♨ ♿ 🖭 ⓓ 🚾 ᴍᴄ

🍴 **Apollinare** Via S. Agata 14, tel. 0743223256, fax 0743221885 ✉; hotelaurora@virgilio.it; ⅋ Umbrian and fine cuisine 🍷 Italian and international; 55/45 capacity; closed Tuesday except summer and Festival period; 🏨 🅿 🖭 ⓓ 🚾 ᴍᴄ

🍴 **Tartufo** Piazza Garibaldi 24, tel. 074340236 ✉; truffles@libero.it; ⅋ Umbrian and fine cuisine (mushrooms and truffles) 🍷 local and national; 70/40 capacity; closed Sunday evening and Monday, for a certain period of time in July; 🏨 🖭 ᴍᴄ

🍴 **Sabatini** Corso Mazzini 52/54, tel. 0743221831; ⅋ Umbrian and classic 🍷 local and national; 100 capacity; closed Monday, and for a certain period of time in January and between July and August; ❀ 🖭 ⓓ 🚾

Stresa (VB)   ✉ 28838

ℹ️ *ATL*, Via Principe Tommaso 70/72, tel. 0323 30416; www.lagomaggiore.it; *IAT*, Piazza Marconi 16, tel. 032330150; proloco.stresa@libero.it.

🚋 *Stazione F.S. (railway station)*, Via Carducci 1, tel. 892021.

🕇 *Carpugnino* (A26 Voltri-Gravellona Toce).

🚢 *NLM-Navigazione Lago Maggiore*, tel. 800-551801 (boat to Baveno, Isole Borromee, Verbania and other towns; seasonal service to Locarno and the Swiss part of the lake).

Hotels and restaurants

⁣⁣*⁣* **G.H. des Iles Borromées** Corso Umberto I 67, tel. 0323938938, fax 032332405; www.borromees.it; 175 rms.; 🏨 ♣ ♨ 🌊 ✕ 🗐 🅿 ♿ 🖭 ⓓ 🚾 ᴍᴄ

★☆★ **G.H. Bristol** Corso Umberto I 73, tel. 032332601, fax 032333622; www.grandhotelbristol.com; open March-November; 260 rms.; 🏠 ♨ ⚓ 🛋 🏊 👤 🅰️ 🅰️ 🚇 MC.

★☆★ **La Palma** Corso Umberto I 33, tel. 032332401, fax 0323933930; www.hlapalma.it; open March-November; 124 rms.; 🏠 ♨ ⚓ 🅿️ 🅿️ 👤 🅰️ 🚇 🚇 MC.

★★★ **Du Parc** Via Gignous 1, tel. 032330335, fax 0323 33596; www.stresa.net/hotel/duparc; open April-mid-October; 21 rms.; ♨ 🅿️ 🅰️ 🚇 MC.

★★★ **Flora** Via Sempione Nord 26, tel. 032330524, fax 032333372; florastresa@libero.it; open mid-March-mid-November; 23 rms.; 🏠 ♨ 🅰️ 🚇 🚇.

★★★ **Primavera** (no restaurant), Via Cavour 39, tel. 032331286, fax 032333458; www.stresa.it; hotel primavera@stresa.it; open March-mid-November and Christmas holidays; 31 rms.; 🅿️ 👤 🅰️ 🚇 🚇.

🍴 **Il Triangolo** Via Roma 61, tel. 0323332736; 🍽️ classic 〽️ local and national; 70 capacity; closed Tuesday except summer, and for a certain period of time between November and December; 🅰️ 🚇.

🍴 **Piemontese** Via Mazzini 25, tel. 032330235 ✉️; 🍽️ Piedmontese and fine cuisine 〽️ Italian and international; 60/50 capacity; closed Monday, December-January; ✻ 🅰️ 🚇.

at the Mottarone, 20 km, or by cableway ✉️ 28836

Restaurants

🍴 **Eden** tel. 0323924873; 🍽️ Piedmontese (mushrooms) 〽️ local and national; 150 capacity; closed Tuesday in the off season, and for a certain period of time in November; ✻ 🅿️ 🅰️ 🚇 MC; also hotel.

Syracuse ✉️ 96100

ℹ️ *AAPIT*, Via S. Sebastiano 43, tel. 0931481200; www.apt-siracusa.it; (A3); *AA*, Via Maestranza 33, tel. 0931464255; www.flashcom.it/aatsr; (E5).

🚃 *Stazione F.S. (railway station)*, Piazza Stazione, tel. 892021.

✈️ *Catania Est* (A18 to Messina); *Catania Sud* (A19 to Palermo).

Hotels and restaurants

★☆★ **Holiday Inn Siracusa** Viale Teracati 30, tel. 0931463232, fax 093167115; 83 rms.; 🏠 🅿️ 🅰️ 🚇 🚇 MC; (A3).

★☆★ **Jolly** Corso Gelone 43/45, tel. 0931461111, fax 0931461126; www.jollyhotels.it; 100 rms.; 🏠 🅿️ 🅰️ 🚇 🚇 MC; (C3).

★★★ **Relax** Viale Epipoli 159, tel. 0931740122, fax 0931740933; www.sistemia.it/relax; relax@sistemia.it; 42 rms.; 🏠 ♨ 🅿️ 🅰️ 🚇 🚇 MC; (off map).

🍴 **Don Camillo** Via Maestranza 92/100, tel. 0931 67133 ✉️; doncamillo@estranet.it; 🍽️ Sicilian 〽️ Italian; 120 capacity; closed Sunday, November and Christmas holidays; 🏠; (D5).

🍴 **Jonico-'a Rutta 'e Ciauli** Riviera Dionisio il Grande 194, tel. 093165540 ✉️; 🍽️ Sicilian (seafood) 〽️ local; 150/160 capacity; closed Tuesday, Christmas; ✻ 🅰️ 🚇 MC; (A-B5).

Taormina (ME) ✉️ 98039

ℹ️ *AA*, Piazza S. Caterina, tel. 094223243; www.taormina-ol.it.

🚃 *Stazione F.S. (railway station)* at Giardini Naxos; bus service.

✈️ *Taormina* (A18 Messina-Catania).

Hotels and restaurants

★☆★ **San Domenico Palace** Piazza S. Domenico 5, tel. 0942613111, fax 0942625506; www.thi.it; 108

rms.; 🏠 ♨ ⚓ 🅿️ 🅿️ 👤 🅰️ 🚇 🚇 MC.

★☆★ **Excelsior Palace** Via Toselli 6, tel. 094223975, fax 094223978; 88 rms.; 🏠 ♨ ⚓ 🅿️ 🅰️ 🚇 🚇 MC.

★☆★ **Villa Diodoro** Via Bagnoli Croce 75, tel. 0942 23312, fax 094223391; www.gaishotels.com; 102 rms.; 🏠 ♨ ⚓ 🅿️ 🅰️ 🚇 🚇 MC.

★★★ **Bel Soggiorno** (no restaurant), Via Pirandello 60, tel. 094223342, fax 0942626298; 18 rms.; ♨ 🅿️ 🅰️ 🚇 MC.

★★★ **Vello d'Oro** Via Fazzello 2, tel. 094223788, fax 0942626117; www.hotelvellodoro.com; open March-October; 50 rms.; 🏠 🅿️ 🅰️ 🚇 MC.

★★★ **Villa Belvedere** Via Bagnoli Croce 79, tel. 0942 23791, fax 0942625830; www.villabelvedere.it; open mid-March-mid-November and Christmas-Epiphany (6 January); 47 rms.; ♨ ⚓ 🅰️ 🚇 MC.

🍴 **La Giara** Vico La Floresta 1, tel. 094223360, fax 094223233 ✉️; 🍽️ fine cuisine (seafood) 〽️ local and national; 200 capacity; closed midday and Monday except summer, January/February and November; 🏠 🅰️ 🚇.

🍴 **Al Duomo** Vico Ebrei 11, tel. 0942625656 ✉️; 🍽️ Sicilian 〽️ local; 40 capacity; closed Sunday in the off season, February; 🏠 🅰️ 🚇 MC.

🍴 **Griglia** Corso Umberto 54, tel. 094223980 ✉️; www.tao.it/intelisano; 🍽️ Messina (seafood) 〽️ local and national; 80 capacity; closed Tuesday, mid-November-mid-December; 🏠 🅰️ 🚇 🚇.

at Capo Taormina, 3 km ✉️ 98030

Hotels

★☆★ **G.A. Capotaormina** Via Nazionale 105, tel. 0942 572111, fax 0942625467; www.capotaorminahotel.com; open March-November; 202 rms.; 🏠 ♨ 🅿️ 🅰️ 🚇 🚇 MC.

Tàranto ✉️ 74100

ℹ️ *ARET*, Corso Umberto I 113, tel. 0994532392; www.pugliaturismo.com.

🚃 *Stazione F.S. (railway station)*, Piazza Libertà, tel. 892021; *Stazione Ferrovie del SudEst*, Via Galeso, tel. 0994704463.

✈️ *End of highway* (A14 to Ancona and Bologna).

Hotels and restaurants

★☆★ **G.H. Delfino** Viale Virgilio 66, tel. 0997323232, fax 0997304654; www.grandhoteldelfino.it; 200 rms.; 🏠 ♨ ⚓ 🅿️ 🅰️ 🚇 🚇 MC.

★★★ **Park Hotel Mar Grande** (no restaurant), Viale Virgilio 90, tel. 0997351713, fax 0997369494; www.hphotel.it; 93 rms.; 🏠 ♨ 🅿️ 🅰️ 🚇 🚇 MC.

🍴 **Il Caffè** Via D'Aquino 8, tel. 0994525097; 🍽️ Taranto 〽️ local and national; 105 capacity; closed Tuesday, and for a certain period of time in November; 🅰️ 🚇 MC.

🍴 **Assassino** Lungomare Vittorio Emanuele III 29, tel. 0994593447; 🍽️ local and classic 〽️ Italian and international; 130 capacity; closed Sunday in summer and Friday in winter, and for a certain period of time in August; 🏠 🅰️ 🚇 🚇 MC.

Tarquinia (VT) ✉️ 01016

ℹ️ *IAT*, Piazza Cavour 1, tel. 0766856384; turistica@tiscali.it.

🚃 *Stazione F.S. (railway station)* at Tarquinia Stazione, tel. 892021; bus service.

✈️ *End of highway* (A12 Civitavecchia-Roma).

Hotels and restaurants

★★★ **Tarconte** Via della Tuscia 19, tel. 0766856141, fax 0766856585; hoteltarconte@libero.it; 53 rms.; 🅿️ 🅿️ 🅰️ 🚇 🚇 MC.

🍴 **Bersagliere** Via B. Croce 2, tel. 0766856047; 🍽️ seafood 〽️ Italian; 300 capacity; closed Monday and Sunday evening, Christmas-Epiphany (6 January), July; 🏨 ❄ 🅿 🆎 ⑩ 🚳 MC.

at Tarquinia Lido, 7 km ✉ 01010

Hotels

★★★ **La Torraccia** (no restaurant), Viale Mediterraneo 45, tel. 0766864375, fax 0766864296; www.italiaab c/az/latorraccia; torraccia@tin.it; closed Christmas-Epiphany (6 January); 18 rms.; 🏨 ♨ 🆎 ⑩ 🚳 MC.

Tivoli (RM) ✉ 00019

ℹ️ *IAT*, Piazza Garibaldi, tel. 0774311249; iat.tivoli @tiscali.it.

🚊 *Stazione F.S. (railway station)*, Viale Mazzini, tel. 892021.

🛤️ *Tivoli* (A24 Roma-Teramo).

Restaurants

🍴 **Adriano** township of Villa Adriana, Via Villa Adriana 194, ✉ 00010, tel. 0774382235 ✖; www. hoteladriano.it; 𝄞 Roman and fine cuisine 🍷 Italian and international; 90/150 capacity; closed Sunday evening in winter; 🏨 🆎 🚳; also hotel.

at Bagni di Tivoli, 9 km ✉ 00011

Hotels

★★★ **G.H. Duca d'Este** Via Tiburtina Valeria 330, tel. 07743883, fax 0774388101; www.ducadeste. com; 184 rms.; 🏨 ♨ ♒ ♒ ✕ 🖥 🅿 ♿ 🆎 ⑩ 🚳 MC.

Todi (PG) ✉ 06059

ℹ️ *IAT*, Piazza Umberto I 6, tel. 0758943395; info@ iat.to di.pg.it.

🚊 *Stazione Ferrovia Centrale Umbra (railway station)* at Ponte Rio, tel. 0758942092; bus service.

Hotels and restaurants

★★★ **Villa Luisa** Via Cortesi 147, tel. 0758948571, fax 0758948472; www.villaluisa.it; villaluisa@villa luisa.it; 40 rms.; 🏨 ♨ ♒ 🅿 ♿ 🆎 ⑩ 🚳.

🍴 **Umbria** Via S. Bonaventura 13, tel. 0758942737 ✖; 𝄞 Umbrian (truffles) 🍷 local and national; 150 capacity; closed Tuesday; 🏨 🆎 ⑩.

Torcello (VE) ✉ 30012

ℹ️ *IAT* at Venice.

⛴️ ACTV, tel. 899-909090 (pay call); steam boat from Venice.

Restaurants

🍴 **Locanda Cipriani** Piazza S. Fosca 29, tel. 041 730150, fax 041735433 ✖; www.locandacipriani. com; 𝄞 classic (seafood) 🍷 Italian; 100/150 capacity; closed Tuesday, Epiphany (6 January)-mid-February; 🏨 🆎 ⑩ 🚳.

Torre del Greco (NA) ✉ 80059

ℹ️ *EPT* at Naples; *Pro Loco*, Via Sepolcri 16, tel. 081 8623163.

🚊 *Stazione F.S. (railway station)*, Via S. Maria La Bruna, tel. 892021.

🛤️ *Torre del Greco* (A3 Napoli-Reggio di Calabria).

Hotels

★★★ **Sakura** Via E. De Nicola 26, tel. 0818493144, fax 0818491122; www.pregiohotel.com; sakura hotel@libero.it; 77 rms.; 🏨 ♨ ♒ ✕ 🖥 🅿 ♿ 🆎 ⑩ 🚳 MC.

★★★ **Marad** Via S. Sebastiano 24, tel. 0818492168, fax 0818828716; www.marad.it; marad@marad. it; 74 rms.; 🏨 ♨ ♒ 🖥 🅿 ⑩ 🚳 MC.

Trani (BA) ✉ 70059

ℹ️ *IAT*, Piazza Trieste 10, tel. 0883588830.

🚊 *Stazione F.S. (railway station)*, Piazza XX Settembre, tel. 892021.

🛤️ *Trani* (A14 Bologna-Taranto).

Hotels and restaurants

★★★ **Royal** Via De Robertis 29, tel. 0883588777, fax 0883582224; 45 rms.; 🏨 🖥 🅿 🆎 ⑩ 🚳 MC.

🍴🍴🍴 **Torrente Antico** Via Fusco 3, tel. 0883487911 ✖; 𝄞 fine cuisine 🍷 Italian and international; 30 capacity; closed Sunday evening and Monday, and for a certain period of time in January and in July; 🏨 🆎 ⑩ 🚳.

Trent ✉ 38100

ℹ️ *APT del Trentino*, Via Romagnosi 11, tel. 0461 839000; www.trentino.to; *APT di Trento*, Via Manci 2, tel. 0461983880; www.apt.trento.it.
TCI, Via Garibaldi 27, tel. 0461221161; negozio. trento@touringclub.it.

🚊 *Stazione F.S. (railway station)*, Piazza Dante, tel. 892021; *Stazione Ferrovia Trento-Malè*, Via Dogana 2, tel. 0461238350.

🛤️ *Trento Centro* (A22 Brennero-Modena).

Hotels and restaurants

★★★ **Boscolo Grand Hotel** Via V. Alfieri 1, tel. 0461 271000, fax 0461271001; www.boscolo.com; 136 rms.; 🏨 🖥 🅿 ♿ 🆎 ⑩ 🚳.

★★★ **Buonconsiglio** (no restaurant), Via Romagnosi 16/18, tel. 0461272888, fax 0461272889; www.ho telbuonconsiglio.it; hotelhb@tin.it; closed 15 August and Christmas holidays; 46 rms.; 🏨 🖥 ♿ 🆎 ⑩ 🚳.

★★★ **America** Via Torre Verde 50, tel. 0461983010, fax 0461230603; www.hotelamerica.it; info@hotela merica.it; 67 rms.; 🏨 🖥 🅿 🆎 ⑩ 🚳 MC.

🍴🍴🍴 **Osteria a le Due Spade** Via Don Rizzi 11 corner of Via Verdi, tel. 0461234343 ✖; 𝄞 Tridentine and fine cuisine 🍷 Italian and international; 40 capacity; closed Sunday and at midday on Monday; 🏨 ❄ 🆎 ⑩ 🚳 MC.

🍴 **Chiesa** Parco S. Marco, tel. 0461238766 ✖; al chies@tin.it; 𝄞 Tridentine 🍷 Italian and international; 100 capacity; closed Sunday, period when closed may vary; ❄ 🆎 ⑩ 🚳 MC.

Treviso ✉ 31100

ℹ️ *IAT*, Piazzetta Monte di Pietà 8, tel. 0422547632; www.seveonline.it/tvapt.

🚊 *Stazione F.S. (railway station)*, Piazza Duca d'Aosta, tel. 892021.

🛤️ *Treviso Nord* or *Treviso Sud* (A27 Mestre-Belluno).

✈️ *Airport*, Via Noalese 63, tel. 0422315131. Bus service from the railway station.
Ryan Air, reservations tel. 199-114114 (pay call).

Hotels

★★★ **Ca' del Galletto** (no restaurant), Via S. Bona Vecchia 30, tel. 0422432550, fax 0422432510; www. sevenonline.it/cadelgalletto; cadelgalletto@seven online.it; 73 rms.; 🏨 ♒ ✕ 🅿 🆎 ⑩ 🚳 MC.

★★★ **Carlton** Largo Porta Altinia 15, tel. 0422411661, fax 0422411620; www.hotelcarlton.it; info@hotel carlton.it; 93 rms.; 🏨 ♨ 🖥 🅿 🆎 ⑩ 🚳 MC.

★★★ **Al Foghèr** Viale della Repubblica 10, tel. 0422 432950, fax 0422430391; www.alfogher.com; fogh er@alfogher.com; 55 rms.; 🏨 🖥 🅿 ♿ 🆎 ⑩ 🚳 MC.

★★★ **Scala** Viale Felissent 1, tel. 0422307600, fax 0422 305048; www.hotelscala.com; 🏨 ♨ 🅿 🆎 ⑩ 🚳 MC.

★★ **Campeol** (no restaurant), Piazza Ancillotto 11, tel.

042256601, fax 0422540871; 14 rms.; ⒶⒺ ⓄⒹ ⓋⓈⒶ ⓂⒸ.

🍴🍴🍴 **Alfredo** Via Collalto 26, tel. 0422540275, fax 0422542105 ✉; catering@iol.it; 🍴 regional ⓁⒼ local and national; 100 capacity; closed Sunday evening and Monday, for a certain period of time in August; 🏧 ⒶⒺ ⓄⒹ ⓋⓈⒶ.

🍴🍴 **Al Bersagliere** Via Barberia 21, tel. 0422579902 ✉; 🍴 local (seafood); 50/70 capacity; closed Sunday and at midday on Saturday, and for a certain period of time in August; 🏧.

🍴🍴 **Beccherie** Piazza Ancillotto 10, tel. 0422540871 ✉; 🍴 local ⓁⒼ local and national; 80 capacity; closed Sunday evening and Monday, and for a certain period of time in July; 🏧 ⒶⒺ ⓄⒹ ⓋⓈⒶ ⓂⒸ.

🍴🍴 **L'Incontro** Largo di Porta Altinia 13, tel. 0422 547717 ✉; 🍴 regional and classic ⓁⒼ local; 75 capacity; closed Wednesday and at midday on Thursday, and for a certain period of time in August; 🏧 ⒶⒺ ⓄⒹ ⓋⓈⒶ.

🍴 **Trattoria all'Antico Portico** Piazza S. Maria Maggiore 18, tel. 0422545259 ✉; www.anticoporti co.it; anticoportico@libero.it; 🍴 local ⓁⒼ Italian; 35/25 capacity; closed Tuesday; 🏧 ⒶⒺ ⓄⒹ ⓋⓈⒶ ⓂⒸ.

Trieste ✉ 34100

ARPT, Via Rossini 6, tel. 040365152; www.regio ne.fvg.it; (*B3*); **APT**, Via San Nicolò 20, tel. 040 6796111; www.triestetourism.it; (*C3*); **IAT**, Stazione F.S., tel. 04044114; (*A3*); **IAT**, Riva III Novembre 9, tel. 0403478312; aptour@libero.it; (*B3*).

🚉 *Stazione F.S. (railway station)*, Piazza della Libertà 8, 892021.

🚌 *Trieste Miramare-Sistiana* (A4 Torino-Milano-Trieste).

✈ *Airport Friuli-Venezia Giulia* at Ronchi dei Legionari, tel. 04817731. Bus service by "APT" from the coach station in Piazza Libertà (*A3*).
Air Dolomiti, reservations tel. 800-013366.
Alitalia, information tel. 8488-65643.
Minerva Airlines, at Alitalia, reservations tel. 8488-65641.

🚢 *Stazione Marittima (ship passenger terminal)*, Molo dei Bersaglieri 3, information: *Promotrieste*, tel. 040304888.
Adriatica Navigazione, Piazza Unità d'Italia 6, tel. 040367529 (hydrofoil, seasonal, to Grado, Lignano Sabbiadoro and Slovenia).
Trieste Trasporti, tel. 04077951 (boat to Muggia).

★★★ **Greif Maria Theresia** Viale Miramare 109, ✉ 34136, tel. 040410115, fax 040413053; www.greif group.net; 36 rms.; 🏧 🏊 Ⓟ ♿ ⒶⒺ ⓄⒹ ⓋⓈⒶ; (*off map*).

★★★ **G.H. Duchi d'Aosta** Piazza Unità d'Italia 2, ✉ 34121, tel. 0407600011, fax 040366092; www.ma gesta.com; 55 rms.; 🏧 🖥 ⒶⒺ ⓄⒹ ⓋⓈⒶ ⓂⒸ; (*C2*).

★★★ **Riviera & Maximilian's** township of Grignano, strada Costiera 22, ✉ 34014, tel. 040224551, fax 040224300; www.magesta.com; 69 rms.; 🏧 🏊 🏊 Ⓟ ♿ ⒶⒺ ⓄⒹ ⓋⓈⒶ ⓂⒸ.

★★★ **San Giusto** (no restaurant), Via C. Belli 3, ✉ 34137, tel. 040764824, fax 040763826; 62 rms.; 🏧 🖥 Ⓟ ⒶⒺ ⓄⒹ ⓋⓈⒶ ⓂⒸ; (*D4*).

🍴🍴 **Ai Fiori** Piazza Hortis 7, ✉ 34124, tel. 040300633 ✉; www.aifiori.com; info@aifiori.com; 🍴 local (seafood) ⓁⒼ Italian and international; 40 capacity; closed Sunday and Monday, Christmas-New Year's, and July; 🏧 ⒶⒺ ⓄⒹ ⓋⓈⒶ ⓂⒸ; (*C2*).

🍴🍴 **Scabar** Erta di S. Anna 63, ✉ 34149, tel. 040810368 ✉; 🍴 local ⓁⒼ local and national; 50 capacity; closed Monday, February and August; 🍴 Ⓟ ⒶⒺ ⓄⒹ ⓋⓈⒶ ⓂⒸ; (*off map*).

Turin ✉ 10100

ATL, Piazza Castello 161, tel. 011535181-011 535901; www.turismotorino.org; (*B4*); **IAT**, Stazione Porta Nuova, tel. 011531327; (*C-D3*); **IAT**, c/o airport, tel. 0115678124.
TCI Via S. Francesco d'Assisi 3, tel. 5627207; negozio.torino@touringclub.it; (*B3*).

🚉 *Stazioni F.S. (railway stations)* Porta Nuova, Piazza Carlo Felice, tel. 892021; *Stazione F.S.* Porta Susa, Piazza XVIII Dicembre, tel. 892021; *Stazione Ferrovie SATTI*, Via Giachino 10, tel. 800-990097.

🚌 *Corso Francia* (A32 to Bardonecchia), *Corso Grosseto* (Torino-Caselle junction and A5 to Aosta and Monte Bianco Tunnel), *Corso Orbassano* (Torino-Pinerolo junction), *Corso Romania* (A4 to Milan), *Corso Trieste* (A6 to Savona), *Sistema tangenziale* (by-pass highway to all the highways without entering the city).

✈ *Airport* at Caselle Torinese, tel. 0115676361. Bus service from the railway stations of Porta Nuova and Porta Susa, and from Via Stradella 242; the SATTI railway line links Stazione Dora with the new station at the airport.
Air Dolomiti, reservations tel. 800-013366.
Air One, reservations tel. 892021.
Air Vallée, reservations tel. 0165303303.
Alitalia, c/o airport, tel. 0115678338.
Meridiana, reservation tel. 199-111333.

★★★★ **G.H. Sitea** Via Carlo Alberto 35, ✉ 10123, tel. 011 5170171, fax 011548090; www.thi.it; 117 rms.; 🏧 🍴 ⒶⒺ ⓄⒹ ⓋⓈⒶ ⓂⒸ; (*C4*).

★★★ **Jolly Hotel Ambasciatori** Corso Vittorio Emanuele II 104, ✉ 10121, tel. 0115752, fax 011 544978; 199 rms.; 🏧 🖥 ⒶⒺ ⓄⒹ ⓋⓈⒶ ⓂⒸ; (*C1*).

★★★ **Jolly Hotel Ligure** Piazza Carlo Felice 85, ✉ 10123, tel. 0115641, fax 011535438; www.jolly hotels.it; 169 rms.; 🏧 🖥 ⒶⒺ ⓄⒹ ⓋⓈⒶ; (*C3*).

★★★ **Jolly Hotel Principi di Piemonte** Via Gobetti 15, ✉ 10123, tel. 0115629693, fax 0115620270; www. jollyhotels.it; 107 rms.; 🏧 🖥 ⒶⒺ ⓄⒹ ⓋⓈⒶ ⓂⒸ; (*C3*).

★★★ **Starhotel Majestic** Corso Vittorio Emanuele II 54, ✉ 10123, tel. 011539153, fax 011534963; www. starhotels.it; 162 rms.; 🏧 🖥 ⒶⒺ ⓄⒹ ⓋⓈⒶ; (*C3*).

★★★ **Turin Palace Hotel** Via Sacchi 8, ✉ 10128, tel. 0115625511, fax 0115612187; www.thi.it; 123 rms.; 🏧 🖥 ♿ ⒶⒺ ⓄⒹ ⓋⓈⒶ ⓂⒸ; (*C3*).

★★★ **Villa Sassi** Strada Traforo del Pino 47, ✉ 10132, tel. 0118980556, fax 0118980095; www.villasassi. com; info@villasassi.com; closed August; 16 rms.; 🏧 🏊 Ⓟ ⒶⒺ ⓄⒹ ⓋⓈⒶ; (*off map*).

★★★ **Boston** (no restaurant), Via Massena 70, ✉ 10128, tel. 011500359, fax 011599358; hotel.bos ton@hotelres.it; 90 rms.; 🏧 🏊 Ⓟ ♿ ⒶⒺ ⓄⒹ ⓋⓈⒶ; (*D2*).

★★★ **Crimea** (no restaurant), Via Mentana 3, ✉ 10133, tel. 0116604700, fax 0116604912; www.torino.as; 49 rms.; 🏧 🖥 ⒶⒺ ⓄⒹ ⓋⓈⒶ ⓂⒸ; (*D5*).

★★★ **Genio** (no restaurant), Corso Vittorio Emanuele II 47, ✉ 10125, tel. 0116505771, fax 0116508264 www.hotelres.it; 120 rms.; 🏧 🖥 ♿ ⒶⒺ ⓄⒹ ⓋⓈⒶ ⓂⒸ; (*C-D3*).

★★★ **Genova e Stazione** (no restaurant), Via Sacchi 14/B, ✉ 10128, tel. 0115629400, fax 0115629896; www.hotelres.it/html/hotgnr.htm; hotelgenova@ hotelres.it; closed for a certain period of time in August; 59 rms.; 🏧 🖥 Ⓟ ♿ ⒶⒺ ⓄⒹ ⓋⓈⒶ ⓂⒸ; (*D3*).

★★★ **Giotto** (no restaurant), Via Giotto 27, ✉ 10126 tel. 0116637172, fax 0116637173; 50 rms.; 🏧 🖥 Ⓟ ⒶⒺ ⓄⒹ ⓋⓈⒶ ⓂⒸ; (*F3*).

★★★ **Gran Mogol** (no restaurant), Via Guarini 2, ✉ 10123, tel. 0115612120, fax 0115623160; hotel gmogol@hotelres.it; closed August; 45 rms.; 🏧 🖥 ⒶⒺ ⓄⒹ ⓋⓈⒶ; (*C3*).

★★★ **Piemontese** (no restaurant), Via Berthollet 21, ⊠ 10125, tel. 0116698101, fax 0116690571; hotel. piemontese@hotelres.it; 35 rms.; 🅿 🔲 🆎 ⊛ 📟 ᴍᴄ; (*D3*).

★★★ **Plaza** (no restaurant), Via Petitti 18, ⊠ 10126, tel. 0116632424, fax 011678351; www.hotelpresi dent-to.it; 65 rms.; 🅿 🔲 🆎 ⊛ 📟 ᴍᴄ; (*F2*).

Restaurants

🍽 **Del Cambio** Piazza Carignano 2, ⊠ 10123, tel. 011546690, fax 011535282 ⊠; www.thi.it; 🍴 Piedmontese and classic 🍷 Italian and international; 150 capacity; closed Sunday, New Year's-Epiphany (6 January) and August; 🅿 🆎 ⊛ 📟; (*B4*).

🍽 **Neuv Caval 'd Bròns** Piazza S. Carlo 151, ⊠ 10123, tel. 0115627483, fax 011543610 ⊠; www. cavalbrons.it; ross@cavalbrons.it; 🍴 Piedmontese and fine cuisine 🍷 Italian and international; 65 capacity; closed Sunday, Saturday at midday and for a certain period of time in January and August; 🅿 🆎 ⊛ 📟 ᴍᴄ; (*B-C4*).

🍽 **Villa Sassi-El Toulà** Strada Traforo del Pino 47, ⊠ 10132, tel. 0118980556, fax 0118980095 ⊠; www.villasassi.com; 🍴 Piedmontese and classic 🍷 Italian and international; 40 capacity; closed Sunday, August; 🅿 ❀ 🅿 🆎 ⊛ 📟; part of the Villa Sassi hotel; (*off map*).

🍽 **Balbo** Via A. Doria 11, ⊠ 10123, tel. 0118395775, fax 0118151042 ⊠; 🍴 Piedmontese and fine cuisine (seafood) 🍷 Italian and international; 60 capacity; closed Monday, and for a certain period of time between July and August; 🅿 🆎 ⊛ 📟 ᴍᴄ; (*C4*).

🍽 **La Prima Smarrita** Corso Unione Sovietica 244, ⊠ 10134, tel. 0113179657, fax 0113179191 ⊠; www.laprimasmarrita.it; primasmarrita@libero.it; 🍴 fine cuisine 🍷 Italian and international; 70 capacity; closed for a certain period of time in August; 🅿 ❀ 🆎 ⊛ 📟 ᴍᴄ; (*off map*).

🍽 **Villa Somis** Strada Val Pattonera 138, ⊠ 10133, tel. 0116614266, fax 0116613086 ⊠; 🍴 fine cuisine 🍷 local and national; 150 capacity; closed Monday, and for a certain period of time in January; ❀ 🅿 🆎 ⊛ 📟 ᴍᴄ; (*off map*).

🍽 **Al Bue Rosso** Corso Casale 10, ⊠ 10131, tel. 0118191393; 🍴 Piedmontese and classic 🍷 Italian and international; 60 capacity; closed Monday and at midday on Saturday, and for a certain period of time in August; 🅿 🆎 ⊛ 📟 ᴍᴄ; (*C5*).

🍽 **Mina** Via Ellero 36 bis, ⊠ 10126, tel. 0116963608 ⊠; 🍴 Piedmontese 🍷 Italian and international; 140/240 capacity; closed Monday (also Sunday evening from mid-June to mid-September), August; 🅿 🆎 ⊛ 📟; (*off map*).

🍽 **Porta Rossa** Via Passalacqua 3/B, ⊠ 10122, tel. 011530816 ⊠; 🍴 classic 🍷 Italian and international; 50 capacity; closed Saturday at midday and Sunday, August; 🅿 🆎 ⊛ 📟 ᴍᴄ; (*A2*).

🍽 **Spada Reale** Via Principe Amedeo 53, ⊠ 10123, tel. 0118171363 ⊠; 🍴 fine cuisine 🍷 Italian and international; 120 capacity; closed Saturday at midday, Sunday and for a certain period of time in August; 🅿 🆎 ⊛ 📟 ᴍᴄ; (*C5*).

Taverna delle Rose Via Massena 24, ⊠ 10128, tel. 011538345 ⊠; 🍴 Piedmontese and Venetian regional 🍷 Italian; 80 capacity; closed Saturday at midday, Sunday and August; 🅿 🆎 ⊛ 📟 ᴍᴄ; (*C3*).

Udine ⊠ 33100

ℹ *ARPT (Regional Chamber of Tourism)*, Piazza I Maggio 7, tel. 0432295972; www.regione.fvg.it.

🚉 *Stazione F.S. (railway station)*, Viale Europa Unita 40, tel. 892021.

🛣 *Udine Nord* or *Udine Sud* (A23 Palmanova-Tarvisio).

✈ *Airport Friuli-Venezia Giulia* at Ronchi dei Legionari, tel. 04817731. Bus service via "APT" from the coach station in Via Leopardi.
Air Dolomiti, reservations tel. 800-013366.
Alitalia, information tel. 8488-65643.
Minerva Airlines, at Alitalia, reservations tel. 8488-65641.

Hotels and restaurants

★★★ **Astoria Hotel Italia** Piazza XX Settembre 24, tel. 0432505091, fax 0432509070; www.hotelastoria. udine.it; 75 rms.; 🅿 🔲 🆎 ⊛ 📟 ᴍᴄ.

★★★ **Executive** township of Cussignacco, Via A. Masieri 4 corner of Viale Palmanova, tel. 0432 602880, fax 0432602858; www.hotelexecutive. net; info@hotelexecutive.net; 77 rms.; 🅿 🔲 🔥 🆎 ⊛ 📟 ᴍᴄ.

★★★ **La' di Moret** Viale Tricesimo 276, tel. and fax 0432545096; www.ladimoret.it; hotel-ladimoret@ xnet.it; 82 rms.; 🅿 🏊 🎾 🍴 🆎 ⊛ 📟 ᴍᴄ.

★★★ **President** (no restaurant), Via Duino 8, tel. 0432 509905, fax 0432507287; www.hotelpresident-ud. com; 67 rms.; 🅿 🔲 🆎 ⊛ 📟 ᴍᴄ.

🍽 **Alla Vedova** Via Tavagnacco 9, tel. 0432470291 ⊠; 🍴 Friulian 🍷 local; 140 capacity; closed Sunday evening, Monday and for a certain period of time in August; 🅿 ❀ 🅿 📟 ᴍᴄ.

🍽 **Lepre** Via Poscolle 27, tel. 0432295798; 🍴 Friulian 🍷 local; 70 capacity; closed Tuesday, and for a certain period of time in August; 🅿 🆎 ⊛ 📟.

Urbino (PU) ⊠ 61029

ℹ *IAT*, Piazza Rinascimento 1, tel. 07222613; iat. urbino@regione.marche.it.

🚉 *Stazione F.S. (railway station)* at Fano or Pesaro; bus service.

🛣 *Pesaro-Urbino* (A14 Bologna-Taranto).

Hotels and restaurants

★★★ **Bonconte** Via delle Mura 28, tel. 07222463, fax 07224782; www.viphotels.it; 23 rms.; 🏊 🅿 🆎 ⊛ 📟 ᴍᴄ.

★★★ **Mamiani** Via Bernini 6, tel. 0722322309, fax 0722327742; www.info-net.it/hotelmamiani; info@ hotelmamiani.it; closed Christmas-Epiphany (6 January); 72 rms.; 🅿 🔥 🅿 🆎 ⊛ 📟 ᴍᴄ.

★★★ **Raffaello** (no restaurant), Via S. Margherita 40, tel. 07224896, fax 0722328540; 14 rms; 🆎 ⊛ 📟 ᴍᴄ.

🍽 **Il Cortegiano** Via Puccinotti 13, tel. 0722320307 ⊠; 🍴 regional (truffles) 🍷 local and national; 100 capacity; closed for a certain period of time in January; 🅿 ❀ ⊛ 📟 ᴍᴄ.

Venice ⊠ 30100

ℹ *IAT*, San Marco 71/F, tel. 0415298711; www.turis movenezia.it; (II, *E4*); *IAT*, San Marco, Venice Pavillon; (II, *F4*); *IAT*, Stazione F.S. Santa Lucia; (I, *C1*); *IAT*, Piazzale Roma; (I, *C1*); *IAT*, Isola del Tronchetto (*off map*); at Lido, Gran Viale S. Maria Elisabeta 6/A (*off map*); *IAT*, at the airport, arrival area.

🚉 *Stazione F.S. (railway station) Santa Lucia*, Fondamenta Santa Lucia, tel. 892021.

🛣 *Mestre Est* or *Mestre Marghera* (A4 Torino-Milano-Trieste).

✈ *Aeroporto Marco Polo* at Tessera, tel. 041 2609260. Bus service from Piazzale Roma (I, *C1*) and links by "Flybus" from the railway station of Mestre.
Air One, reservations tel. 8488-48880.
Alitalia, information tel. 8488-65643
Alpi Eagles, reservations tel. 0415997788.
Volare Airlines, reservations tel. 800-454000.

⏠ *ACTV*, tel. 899-909090 (pay call); steam boat to the Lagoon islands, Punta Sabbioni, Chioggia.

★★★ **Danieli** Castello 4196, Riva degli Schiavoni, ✉ 30122, tel. 0415226480, fax 0415200208; reso72 danieli@luxurycollection.com; 233 rms.; 🏢 🗐 🏢 ⏰ 🏢 MC; (I, E6).

★★★ **Gritti Palace** S. Marco 2467, Campo S. Maria del Giglio, ✉ 30124, tel. 041794611, fax 0415200942; www.luxurycollection.com/grittipalace; 91 rms.; 🏢 🗐 🗚 ⏰ 🏢 MC; (II, F3).

★★★ **Bellini** Cannaregio 116, Lista di Spagna, ✉ 30121, tel. 0415242488, fax 041715193; www.bo scolohotels.com; 97 rms.; 🏢 🕭 🗐 🗚 ⏰ 🏢; (I, B2).

★★★ **Cavalletto & Doge Orseolo** S. Marco 1107, Calle del Cavalletto, ✉ 30124, tel. 0415200955, fax 041 5238184; www.sanmarcohotels.com; 107 rms.; 🗚 ⏰ 🏢 MC; (II, E4).

★★★ **Gabrielli Sandwirth** Castello 4110, Riva degli Schiavoni, ✉ 30122, tel. 0415231580, fax 041 5209455; hotelgabrielli@libero.it; closed December-January; 100 rms.; 🏢 🕭 🗐 🗚 ⏰ 🏢 MC; (I, D4).

★★★ **Luna Hotel Baglioni** S. Marco 1243, Calle Larga de l'Ascension, ✉ 30124, tel. 0415289840, fax 0415287160; www.baglionihotels.com; 115 rms.; 🏢 🗚 ⏰ 🏢 MC; (II, E4).

★★★ **Starhotel Splendid Suisse** S. Marco Mercerie 760, ✉ 30124, tel. and fax 0415286498; www. starhotels.it; 160 rms.; 🏢 🗚 ⏰ 🏢 MC; (II, D4).

★★★ **Abbazia** (no restaurant), Cannaregio, Calle Priuli 68, ✉ 30121, tel. 041717333, fax 041717949; www.venezialberghi.com; 39 rms.; 🏢 🕭 🗚 ⏰ 🏢 MC; (I, B1).

★★★ **Ala** (no restaurant), S. Marco 2494, Campo S. Maria del Giglio, ✉ 30124, tel. 0415208333, fax 0415206390; www.hotelala.it; info@hotelala.it; 85 rms.; 🏢 🗚 ⏰ 🏢 MC; (II, F3).

★★★ **American** (no restaurant), Dorsoduro 628, Fondam. Bragadin (S. Vio), ✉ 30123, tel. 041 5204733, fax 0415204048; www.hotelamerican. com; hotameri@tin.it; 29 rms.; 🏢 🗐 🗚 🏢 MC; (I, E2).

★★★ **Ateneo** (no restaurant), S. Marco 1876, Calle Minelli, ✉ 30124, tel. 0415200777, fax 041 5228550; www.ateneo.it; 20 rms.; 🏢 🗚 ⏰ 🏢 MC; (II, E3).

★★★ **Bisanzio** (no restaurant), Castello 3651, Calle della Pietà, ✉ 30122, tel. 0415203100, fax 041 5204114; www.bisanzio.com; email@bisanzio. com; 42 rms.; 🏢 🗚 ⏰ 🏢 MC; (I, D4).

★★★ **Ca' d'Oro** (no restaurant), Cannaregio 4604, Corte Barbaro, ✉ 30131, tel. 0412411212, fax 0412414385; www.hotelcadoro.it; info@hotelca doro.it; 17 rms.; 🏢 🗚 ⏰ 🏢 MC; (II, B3).

★★★ **Do Pozzi** (no restaurant), S. Marco 2373, Calle Larga XXII Marzo, ✉ 30124, tel. 0415207855, fax 0415229413; hotel.dopozzi@flashnet.it; closed for a certain period of time in January; 29 rms.; 🏢 🗚 🗐 🗚 ⏰ 🏢 MC; (II, E3-4).

★★★ **La Fenice et Des Artistes** (no restaurant), S. Marco 1936, Campiello della Fenice, ✉ 30124, tel. 0415232333, fax 0415203721; fenice@feni cehotels.it; 69 rms.; 🏢 🗚 🗐 🗚 ⏰ 🏢 MC; (II, E3).

★★★ **Olimpia** (no restaurant), S. Croce 395, Fondamenta delle Burchielle, ✉ 30135, tel. 041 711041, fax 0415246777; www.hotel-olimpia.com; 35 rms.; 🏢 🗚 🗐 🗚 ⏰ 🏢 MC; (I, C1).

★★★ **Pausania** (no restaurant), Dorsoduro 2824, Fondamenta Gherardini, ✉ 30123, tel. 0415222083, fax 0415222989; 26 rms.; 🏢 🗚 🗚 ⏰ 🏢 MC; (I, D1).

★★★ **Spagna** (no restaurant), Cannaregio 184, Lista di Spagna, ✉ 30121, tel. 0415115011, fax 041 2750256; www.cash.it/hotel.spagna; hotel.spa gna@cash.it; 19 rms.; 🏢 🗐 🗚 ⏰ 🏢 MC; (I, B2).

★★ **Agli Alboretti** Accademia 884, Rio Terrà A. Foscarini, ✉ 30123, tel. 0415230058, fax 041 5210158; www.cash.it/alboretti; closed for a cer-

tain period in January; 19 rms.; 🗚 🗐 🗚 ⏰ 🏢 MC; (II, F2).

🍴 **Antico Martini** S. Marco 1983, Campo S. Fantin, ✉ 30124, tel. 0415224121, fax 0415289857 🗚; www.anticomartini.com; info@anticomartini.com; ☕ classic (seafood) 🍷 Italian and international; 40 capacity; closed Tuesday and at midday on Wednesday; 🏢 🗚 ⏰ 🏢 MC; (II, E3).

🍴 **Antico Pignolo** San Marco 451, Calle dei Specchieri, ✉ 30124, tel. 0415228123, fax 041 52090007 🗚; anticopignolo@libero.it; ☕ Venetian and classic (seafood) 🍷 Italian and international; 140/110 capacity; closed Tuesday in the off season; 🏢 ✳ 🗚 ⏰ 🏢 MC; (II, D5).

🍴 **Harry's Bar** S. Marco 1323, Calle Vallaresso, ✉ 30124, tel. 0415285777, fax 0415208822; ☕ Venetian and classic 🍷 Italian and international; 80 capacity; 🏢 🗚 ⏰ 🏢 MC; (II, E-F4).

🍴 **Il Sole sulla Vecia Cavana** Cannaregio 4624, rio Terà SS. Apostoli, ✉ 30131, tel. 0415287106, fax 0415238644; ☕ Venetian and fine cuisine; 70/120 capacity; closed Monday, period when closed may vary; 🗚; (II, B4).

🍴 **Osteria da Fiore** S. Polo 2202, Calle del Scaleter ✉ 30125, tel. 041721308, fax 041721343 🗚; www.dafiore.com; ☕ Venetian and fine cuisine 🍷 Italian and international; 48 capacity; closed Sunday and Monday, Christmas-mid-January and August; 🏢 🗚 ⏰ 🏢 MC; (II, C2).

🍴 **Ai Gondolieri** Dorsoduro 366, S. Vio, ✉ 30123, tel 0415286396 🗚; www.aigondolieri.com; ☕ Venetian regional 🍷 Italian; 50 capacity; closed Tuesday Christmas holidays; 🏢 🗚 ⏰ 🏢 MC; (II, F3).

🍴 **Ai Mercanti** S. Marco 4346/A, Calle dei Fuseri, ✉ 30124, tel. 0415238269 🗚; ☕ Venetian regional (seafood) 🍷 Italian and international; 50/95 capacity; closed Sunday and Monday at midday, period when closed may vary; 🏢 🗚 ⏰ 🏢 MC; (II, D4)

🍴 **Al Conte Pescaor** S. Marco 544, piscina S. Zulian, ✉ 30124, tel. 0415221483 🗚; ☕ Venetian (seafood) 🍷 Italian and international; 100 capacity; closed Sunday, and for a certain period of time between January and February; 🏢 🗚 ⏰ 🏢 MC; (II, D5).

🍴 **Antica Besseta** S. Croce 1395, Salizzada de Ca Zusto, ✉ 30121, tel. 041721687 🗚; www.yeaah com/anticabesseta; ☕ Venetian (seafood) 🍷 Italian and international; 46 capacity; closed Tuesday and at midday on Wednesday (except April-October), and for a certain period of time between January and February; 🏢 🗚 ⏰ 🏢 MC; (II, B1).

🍴 **Covo** Castello 3968, Campiello della Pescaria, ✉ 30122, tel. 0415223812 🗚; ☕ Venetian (seafood) 🍷 Italian and international; 50 capacity; closed Wednesday and Thursday, for a certain period of time in August, and mid-December-mid-January 🗚; (I, C-D4).

🍴 **Giardinetto-da Severino** Castello 4928, Ruga Giuffa, ✉ 30122, tel. 0415285332 🗚; ritaparm@ tin.it; ☕ Venetian (seafood) 🍷 local and national 100 capacity; closed Thursday, and for a certain period of time between January and February; ✳ 🗚 ⏰ 🏢 MC; (II, D6).

🍴 **Osteria Alle Testiere** Castello 5801, Calle del Mondo Novo, ✉ 30122, tel. 0415227220 🗚; ☕ Venetian 🍷 Italian; 25 capacity; closed Sunday Monday, August and Christmas holidays; 🏢 ⏰ 🏢 MC; (II, C5).

🍴 **Al Graspo de Ua** S. Marco 5094, Calle dei Bombaseri, ✉ 30124, tel. 0415200150, fax 041 5209389 🗚; graspo.deua@flashnet.it; ☕ Venetian regional and classic 🍷 Italian and international; 120 capacity; closed Monday and Tuesday and for a certain period of time in January; 🏢 🗚 ⏰ 🏢 MC; (II, C4).

⛏ **Tre Spiedi** Cannaregio 5906, salizzada San Canzian, ✉ 30131, tel. 0415208035; ⅷ Venetian 🍴 local; 48 capacity; closed Monday, Sunday at midday, for a certain period of time between July and August; 🎫 💳 📺 **MC**; (II, *C5*).

Lido di Venezia

Hotels and restaurants

⭐⭐⭐ **Westin Excelsior** Lungomare Marconi 41, ✉ 30126, tel. 0415260201, fax 0415267276; www. westin.com; open mid-March-mid-November; 196 rms.; 🏨 ♨ ♒ ✕ 🅿 🖥 🖕 🎫 💳 📺 **MC**.

⭐⭐⭐ **Biasutti (Adria-Urania-Villa Nora)** Via E. Dandolo 27/29, ✉ 30126, tel. 0415260120, fax 0415261259; www.bestwestern.it; closed December-January; 69 rms.; 🏨 ♨ 🅿 🎫 💳 📺 **MC**.

⭐⭐⭐ **Belvedere** Piazzale S.M. Elisabetta 4, ✉ 30126, tel. 0415260115, fax 0415261486; 30 rms.; 🏨 🅿 🎫 💳 📺.

⭐⭐⭐ **Biasutti (Villa Ada)** Via Dandolo 24, ✉ 30126, tel. 0415260120, fax 0415261259; biasuttihotels @tin.it; closed December-January; 17 rms.; 🏨 ♨ 🅿 🎫 💳 📺 **MC**.

⭐⭐⭐ **Villa Pannonia** Via Doge Michiel 48, ✉ 30126, tel. 0415260162, fax 0415265277; www.italiaabc. com/a/pannonia; closed for a certain period of time in December; 32 rms.; ♨ 🅿 🎫 💳 📺 **MC**.

Verona ✉ 37100

ℹ️ *IAT*, Piazza delle Erbe 42, tel. 0458000065; www. tourism.verona.it; (*C5*); *IAT*, Via degli Alpini 9, 045 8068680; (*D4*); *IAT*, Stazione F.S., tel. 045 8000861; (*F2*); *IAT* at the airport, tel. 0458619163. *TCI*, Via della Valverde 75, tel. 045595697; negozio.verona@touringclub.it; (*E3*).

🚆 *Stazione F.S. (railway station)*, Piazzale XXV Aprile, tel. 892021.

⛟ *Verona Est* (A4 Torino-Milano-Trieste); *Verona Nord* (A22 Brennero-Modena); *Verona Sud* (A4 Torino-Milano-Trieste).

✈ *Aeroporto Valerio Catullo* at Caselle di Sommacampagna, tel. 0458095666. Bus service from the railway station. (*F2*).
Air Dolomiti, reservations tel. 800-013366.
Alitalia, information tel. 8488-65643.
Meridiana, Corso Porta Palio 46, tel. 0458089711; (*D2-3*).
Volare Airlines, reservations tel. 800-454000.

Hotels

⭐⭐⭐ **Due Torri Baglioni** Piazza S. Anastasia 4, ✉ 37121, tel. 045595044, fax 0458004130; www.baglionihotels.com; 90 rms.; 🏨 🅿 🎫 💳 📺 **MC**; (*B5*).

⭐⭐⭐ **Firenze** (no restaurant), Corso Porta Nuova 88, ✉ 37122, tel. 0458011510, fax 0458030374; www. hotelfirenze.it; 47 rms.; 🏨 🖥 🅿 🎫 💳 📺 **MC**; (*E3*).

⭐⭐⭐ **San Marco** (no restaurant), Via Longhena 42, ✉ 37138, tel. 0455569011, fax 045572299; www. sanmarco.vr.it; sanmarco@sanmarco.vr.it; 62 rms.; 🏨 ♨ ♒ 🅿 🖕 🎫 💳 📺 **MC**; (*C1*).

⭐⭐⭐ **Giulietta e Romeo** (no restaurant), Via Tre Marchetti 3, ✉ 37121, tel. 0458003554, fax 045 8010862; www.giuliettaeromeo.com; 30 rms.; 🏨 🖥 🎫 💳 📺 **MC**; (*C4*).

⭐⭐⭐ **Italia** (no restaurant), Via Mameli 58/64, ✉ 37126, tel. 045918088, fax 0458348028; www.hotelitalia. tv; 58 rms.; 🏨 🖥 🎫 💳 📺 **MC**; (*A4*).

⭐⭐⭐ **Piccolo Hotel** (no restaurant), Via Camuzzoni 3/B, ✉ 37138, tel. 045569400, fax 045577620; marti nipiccolo@sis.it; 42 rms.; 🏨 🖥 🎫 💳 📺 **MC**; (*E1-2*).

⭐⭐ **Torcolo** (no restaurant), Vicolo Listone 3, ✉ 37121, tel. 0458007512, fax 0458004058; closed for a certain period of time between January and February; 19 rms.; 🏨 🖥 🎫 💳 📺 **MC**; (*D4*).

Restaurants

⛏⛏ **Arche** Via Arche Scaligere 6, ✉ 37121, tel. and fax 0458007415 🖃; ⅷ regional 🍴 Italian and international; 60 capacity; closed Sunday and at midday on Monday, mid-January-mid-February; 🖥 🎫 💳 📺 **MC**; (*B-C5*).

⛏ **Re Teodorico** Piazzale Castel S. Pietro, ✉ 37129, tel. 0458349990; ⅷ classic 🍴 Italian and international; 120 capacity; closed Wednesday, January; ❈ 🎫 💳 📺 **MC**; (*A6*).

⛏ **Tre Corone** Piazza Brà 16, ✉ 37121, tel. 045 8002462, fax 0458011810 🖃; ⅷ regional and classic 🍴 local and national; 160 capacity; closed Thursday, January; 🖥 🎫 💳 📺 **MC**; (*D4*).

⛏ **Greppia** Vicolo Samaritana 3, ✉ 37121, tel. 045 8004577; www.ristorantegreppia.com; ⅷ local 🍴 local and national; 150 capacity; closed Monday, for a certain period of time in June; 🖥 ❈ 🎫 💳 📺 **MC**; (*C5*).

Viareggio (LU) ✉ 55049

ℹ️ *APT*, Viale Carducci 10, tel. 0584962233; www. versilia.turismo.toscana.it; *Information Office*, seasonal, at the railway station, tel. 46382.

🚆 *Stazione F.S. (railway station)*, Piazza Dante, tel. 892021.

⛟ *Viareggio-Camaiore* (A12 Genova-Rosignano and Civitavecchia-Roma).

Hotels

⭐⭐⭐ **Astor Hotel** Lungomare Carducci 54, tel. 0584 50301, fax 058455181; www.astorviareggio.com; astorpr@tin.it; 68 rms.; 🖥 🎫 💳 📺 **MC**.

⭐⭐⭐ **Excelsior** Viale Carducci 88, tel. 058450726, fax 058450729; www.paginegialle.it/excelsior-13; via reggio.excelsior@flashnet.it; open April/October; 83 rms.; 🏨 🖥 🅿 🎫 💳 📺 **MC**.

⭐⭐⭐ **Palace Hotel** Via Gioia 2, tel. 058446134, fax 058447351; 75 rms.; 🏨 🖥 🖕 🎫 💳 📺 **MC**.

⭐⭐⭐ **Garden** Via Foscolo 70, tel. 058444025, fax 0584 45445; 40 rms.; 🏨 🖥 🎫 💳 📺 **MC**.

⭐⭐⭐ **Kursaal** Via Mentana 19, tel. 058449713, fax 0584 30813; open April-October; 36 rms.; 🎫 💳 📺 **MC**.

⭐⭐⭐ **Villa Tina** Via Saffi 2, tel. and fax 058444450; hotelvillatina@tin.it; 14 rms.; 📺 **MC**.

Restaurants

⛏⛏ **Il Patriarca** Viale Carducci 79, tel. 058453126, fax 058454240 🖃; ⅷ Tuscan 🍴 Italian and international; 70 capacity; closed Wednesday and for a certain period of time in January; 🖥 🅿 🎫 💳 📺 **MC**.

⛏ **Il Porto** Via M. Coppino 319, tel. 0584383878 🖃; ⅷ Tuscan 🍴 local and national; 90 capacity; closed Sunday, Monday at midday and for a certain period of time between December and January; 🖥 🅿 🎫 💳 📺 **MC**.

⛏ **Il Punto Divino** Via Mazzini 229, tel. 058431046 🖃; ⅷ Tuscan and classic 🍴 Italian and international; 60 capacity; closed Monday (at midday from mid-July to mid-August); January; 🖥 🎫 💳 📺.

Vicenza ✉ 36100

ℹ️ *IAT*, Piazza Matteotti 12, tel. 0444320854; www. ascom.vi.it/aptvicenza.

🚆 *Stazione F.S. (railway station)*, Viale Roma, tel. 892021.

⛟ *Vicenza Est* (A4 Torino-Milano-Trieste); *Vicenza Nord* (A31 Vicenza-Piovene Rocchette); *Vicenza Ovest* (A4 Torino-Milano-Trieste).

Hotels and restaurants

⭐⭐⭐ **Alfa Fiera** Via dell'Oreficeria 50, tel. 0444565455, fax 0444566027; www.alfafierahotel.it; info@alfa fierahotel.it; 90 rms.; 🖥 ♨ 🅿 🎫 💳 📺.

*★★ **Campo Marzio** Viale Roma 21, tel. 0444545700, fax 0444320495; www.hotelcampomarzio.com; hcm@ tradenet.it; 35 rms.; 🏨 P 🏧 ⊙ ▦ MC.

*★★ **Jolly Hotel Europa** S.S.Padana road to Verona 11, tel. 0444564111, fax 0444564382; www.jolly hotels.it; vicenza_europa@jollyhotels.it; 127 rms.; 🏨 🛗 P 👟 🏧 ⊙ ▦ MC.

*★★ **Quality Inn Viest** (no restaurant), Strada Pelosa 241, tel. 0444582677, fax 0444582434; www.as com.vi.it/viest; 61 rms.; 🏨 ♨ 🛗 P 🏧 ⊙ ▦ MC.

*★★ **Continental** Viale G.G. Trissino 89, tel. 0444 505476, fax 0444513319; www.continental-hotel. it; hotel.continental.vi@iol.it; 55 rms.; 🏨 🛗 P 🏧 ⊙ ▦ MC.

††† **Nuova Cinzia e Valerio** Piazzetta Porta Padova 65/67, tel. 0444505213, fax 0444512796 ⊠; 〉¶ Venetian regional (seafood) ◊🍷 Italian; 80 capaci-ty; closed Sunday evening and Monday, August and 1 January; 🏨 🏧 ⊙ ▦ MC.

†† **Antico Ristorante Agli Schioppi** Contrà del Castello 26/28, tel. 0444543701; www.italiaabc. it/az/aglischioppi; 〉¶ Venetian regional ◊🍷 local and national; 50/25 capacity; closed Saturday evening and Sunday, and mid-July-mid-August and Christmas holidays; 🏨 🏧 ⊙ ▦ MC.

†† **Da Remo** Via Caimpenta 14, tel. 0444911007 ⊠; daremo@tin.it; 〉¶ local ◊🍷 local and national; 100 capacity; closed Sunday evening and Monday, Christmas-Epiphany (6 January) and August; ✤ P 🏧 ⊙ ▦ MC.

Vieste (FG)   ⊠ 71019

✓ *IAT*, Corso Fazzini 8, tel. 0884707495; aptiatvie ste@tin.it; *IAT*, Piazza Kennedy, tel. 0884708806.

�" *Stazione F.S. (railway station)* at Foggia; bus ser-vice.

✝ *Poggio Imperiale* (A14 Bologna-Taranto).

🚢 Adriatica di Navigazione, tel. 0884708501 (hydro-foil, seasonal, to the Tremiti Islands).

Hotels and restaurants

*★★ **Pizzomunno Vieste Palace** Lungomare di Piz-zomunno (beachfront), tel. 0884708741, fax 0884707325; www.pizzomunno.it; pizzomunno@ viesteonline.it; open April-September (annual for meeting); 205 rms.; 🏨 ♨ ♒ ❌ 🛗 P 🏧 ⊙ ▦ MC.

★★★ **I Melograni** Lungomare Europa 48, tel. and fax 0884701088; www.imelograni.it; open mid-April-mid-September; 102 rms.; 🏨 ♨ ♒ P 👟 ▦ MC.

†† **Locanda Dragone** Via Duomo 8, tel. 0884 701212 ⊠; 〉¶ Apulian ◊🍷 local and national; 85 capacity; open April-October; closed Tuesday; 🏨 🏧 ⊙ ▦ MC.

Viterbo   ⊠ 01100

✓ *APT*, Piazza S. Carluccio, tel. 0761304795; apt viterbo@libero.it.

�" *Stazioni F.S. (railway stations)*, Porta Fiorentina and Porta Romana, tel. 892021; *Stazione Fer-rovie Cotral*, Viale Trieste, tel. 0761 342902.

✝ *Orte* (A1 Milano-Roma-Napoli).

Hotels and restaurants

*★★ **Mini Palace Hotel** (no restaurant), Via S. Maria della Grotticella 2/B, tel. 0761309744, fax 0761 344715; www.minipalacehotel.com; info@minipa lacehotel.com; 40 rms.; 🏨 🛗 P 👟 🏧 ⊙ ▦ MC.

★★★ **Balletti Palace Hotel** Via F. Molini 8, tel. 0761 344777, fax 0761345060; 105 rms.; 🏨 ♨ P 🏧 ⊙ ▦ MC.

†† **Villa Gambara** township of Bagnaia, Via Jacopo Barozzi 36, tel. 0761289182 ⊠; gambara@free domland.it; 〉¶ regional ◊🍷 Italian; 80 capacity; closed Monday, period when closed may vary; 🏨 ✤ ⊙ ▦ MC.

at San Martino al Cimino, 7 km   ⊠ 01030

Hotels

*★★ **Balletti Park Hotel** Via Umbria 2/A, tel. 0761 3771, fax 0761379496; www.balletti.com; info@ balletti.it; 40 rms.; 🏨 ♨ ♒ ❌ P 🏧 ⊙ ▦ MC.

Volterra (PI)   ⊠ 54048

✓ *IAT*, Via G. Turazza 2, tel. 058886150; provolterra @libero.it.

�" *Stazione F.S. (railway station)* at Saline di Volterra, tel. 892021; bus service.

✝ *Firenze Signa* (A1 Milano-Roma-Napoli).

Hotels and restaurants

*★★ **San Lino** Via S. Lino 26, tel. 058885250, fax 0588 80620; www.hotelsanlino.com; closed mid-Novem-ber-mid-December; 43 rms.; ♒ 🛗 👟 🏧 ⊙ ▦ MC.

★★★ **Sole** (no restaurant), Via dei Cappuccini 10, tel. and fax 058884000; 10 rms.; P 🏧 ⊙ ▦ MC.

†† **Del Duca** Via di Castello 2, tel. 058881510 ⊠; 〉¶ Tuscan and fine cuisine ◊🍷 local and national; 35 capacity; closed Tuesday (except from July to September); period when closed may vary; ✤ 🏧 ⊙ ▦ MC.

†† **Vecchia Osteria dei Poeti** Via Matteotti 55, tel. 058886029 ⊠; 〉¶ Tuscan ◊🍷 local; 50 capacity; closed Thursday, mid-January-mid-February; 🏧 ⊙ ▦ MC.

The words in Roman type refer to places quoted in the "Excursions" chapter; those in bold refer to the main entries in the chapter "Italy A to Z". The numbers in Roman type refer to the "Excursions" or "Italy A to Z" chapters; those in Italics refer to the "Hotels, Restaurants, and Tourist Services" chapter.

Staying in Bologna

Hotels in the historical town centre
www.bolognaitaly.it
ospitalita@bolognaitaly.it

emilia romagna

Conference rooms for 50 to 1,500 people. Palazzo Albergati and Palazzo Isolani.
Shopping in 400 prestigious shops in Via D'Azeglio, Galleria Cavour, Corte Isolani

★★★★

AL CAPPELLO ROSSO
Albergo in Bologna dal 1375

40123 BOLOGNA
Via de' Fusari, 9
Tel. 051 261891
Fax 051 227179
info@alcappellorosso.it

★★★★

HOTEL COMMERCIANTI

40124 BOLOGNA
Via dè Pignattari, 11
Tel. 051 233052
Fax 051 224733
hotcom@tin.it

★★★★

HOTEL CORONA D'ORO 1890

40126 BOLOGNA
Via Oberdan, 12
Tel. 051 236456
Fax 051 262679
hotcoro@tin.it

★★★★

HOTEL SAN DONATO

40126 BOLOGNA
Via Zamboni, 16
Tel. 051 235395
Fax 051 230547
info@hotelsandonato.it

★★★

HOTEL PALACE

40121 BOLOGNA
Via Montegrappa, 9/2
Tel. 051 237442
Fax 051 220689

★★★[S]

HOTEL OROLOGIO

40123 BOLOGNA
Via IV Novembre, 10
Tel. 051 231253
Fax 051 260552
hotoro@tin.it

★★★

HOTEL ROMA

40123 BOLOGNA
Via D'Azeglio, 9
Tel. 051 226.322
Fax 051 239.909
N. Verde 800-219868
prenotazioni@mailbox.dsnet.it

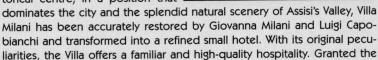

Civic Museums
Bassano del Grappa

Civic Museum

archeological museum and gallery put up in the convent of the medieval church of Saint Francis. In the rooms and halls, archeological materials (ceramics, bronzes and juwels) and masterpieces (panels, canvases, statues - clay, gypsum, marble) by Guariento, Bambono, Francesco il Vecchio, Jacopo, Francesco, Leandro dal Ponte, Magnasco, Crespi, Marinali, Tiepolo, Canova, Hayez, Molmenti are kept.

Engravings and Design Cabinet

An important heritage of designs came to the Museum by legacy (Riva, Stecchini, Sartori Canova) and by purchase (Marinoni). The sheet by Romanino, Zelotti, Bassano, Fetti, Maffei, Giambattista e Giandomenico Tiepolo, Guardi, Quarenghi, Canova (2000 designs) e the albums by Orazio Marinali are here preserved. The collection of engravings, consisting of 30.000 sheet, includs the huge group of the Remondini Engraving Shop. The Cabinet can be consulted by appointment.

Ceramic Museum. Sturm Palace

The Museum, staged in 1992 in the XVIIIth century palace of the Ferrari family, inherited by the Town Council in 1943 by Sturm's legacy, preserves graffito ceramiche, majolicas, porcelains, potteries, that offer a wide screen of the production in Bassano and Nove between the XIII and the XX century. Particularly relevant the XVIII century section by Antonibon. Also a choice of contemporary artistic production is shown.

MUSEO CIVICO
Bassano del Grappa, Piazza Garibaldi
Telephone +39 0424 522235 / 523336
Fax +39 0424 523914
www.museobassano.it - info@museobassano.it

Opening Hours
From Tuesday to Saturday: 9.00-18.30
Sunday: 15.30-18.30

MUSEO DELLA CERAMICA - PALAZZO STURM
Bassano del Grappa, Via Schiavonetti
Telephone +39 0424 524933 / 522235
Fax +39 0424 523914

Opening Hours
From April 1st to October 31st: 9.00-12.30 and 15.30
Sunday morning and Monday, closed
From November 1st to March 31st: Friday, 9.00-12.30
Saturday and Sunday: 15.30-18.30

★ ★ ★ ★ Hotel Galles

Best Western

Galles Hotel is located in corso Buenos Aires, one of the most beautiful commercial streets of the Milan's downtown area, close to the exit of Lima underground station. The hotel's position allows rapid access to the biggest railway station, the airports and to all the major motorway junctions. The hotel has been refurbished in accordance to the latest rules concerning hotel accomodation. The hotel is modern and rational and also very functional for the total satisfaction of its guests. Galles Hotel offers you 150 rooms with self adjustable air conditioning, minibar, Tv and pay-tv, radio and safety-box. The hotel also has an American bar, five conference rooms seating up to 120 people and La Terrazza Restaurant. This is a roof garden situated on the sixth floor of the hotel where you can taste fine italian cusine and its specialities. The really new proposal of the Galles Hotel is the fitness center with sauna, turkish bath and gym.

Via Ozanam, 1 (c.so Buenos Aires) - Italia - 20129 MILANO
Tel. +39 02 20 48 41 - Fax: +39 02 20 48 422
e-mail: reception@galles.it - http://www.galles.it

Farm Holidays

Hoping to see you soon in Italy!

Farm Holidays, Agriturist's Booking Center,
is formed by a group of experts who visit
and choose Agriturists Farms, Countryside
residences and charming homes all around
Italy. They aim to ensure the best
quality-price choices.
To receive information for a perfect solution
to your needs,
please call us or send us an e-mail.

Farm Holidays

Via Manin 20, C.P. 84
58100 Grosseto - ITALIA
Tel. (+39) 0564 417418 – 418051
Fax (+39) 0564 421828
www.travelandtravel.com

Distance

Kilometres/Miles

km to mi	mi to km
1 = 0.62	1 = 1.6
2 = 1.2	2 = 3.2
3 = 1.9	3 = 4.8
4 = 2.5	4 = 6.4
5 = 3.1	5 = 8.1
6 = 3.7	6 = 9.7
7 = 4.3	7 = 11.3
8 = 5.0	8 = 12.9

Meters/Feet

m to ft	ft to m
1 = 3.3	1 = 0.30
2 = 6.6	2 = 0.61
3 = 9.8	3 = 0.91
4 = 13.1	4 = 1.2
5 = 16.4	5 = 1.5
6 = 19.7	6 = 1.8
7 = 23.0	7 = 2.1
8 = 26.2	8 = 2.4

Weight

Kilograms/Pounds

kg to lb	lb to kg
1 = 2.2	1 = 0.45
2 = 4.4	2 = 0.91
3 = 6.6	3 = 1.4
4 = 8.8	4 = 1.8
5 = 11.0	5 = 2.3
6 = 13.2	6 = 2.7
7 = 15.4	7 = 3.2
8 = 17.6	8 = 3.6

Grams/Ounces

g to oz	oz to g
1 = 0.04	1 = 28
2 = 0.07	2 = 57
3 = 0.11	3 = 85
4 = 0.14	4 = 114
5 = 0.18	5 = 142
6 = 0.21	6 = 170
7 = 0.25	7 = 199
8 = 0.28	8 = 227

Liquid Volume

Liters/U.S. Gallons

L to gal	gal to L
1 = 0.26	1 = 3.8
2 = 0.53	2 = 7.6
3 = 0.79	3 = 11.4
4 = 1.1	4 = 15.1

Liters/U.S. Gallons

L to gal	gal to L
5 = 1.3	5 = 18.9
6 = 1.6	6 = 22.7
7 = 1.8	7 = 26.5
8 = 2.1	8 = 30.3

Temperature

Fahrenheit/Celsius

F	C
0	-17.8
5	-15.0
10	-12.2
15	-9.4
20	-6.7
25	-3.9
30	-1.1
32	0
35	1.7
40	4.4
45	7.2

Fahrenheit/Celsius

F	C
50	10.0
55	12.8
60	15.5
65	18.3
70	21.1
75	23.9
80	26.7
85	29.4
90	32.2
95	35.0
100	37.8

• The Heritage Guide •

This definitive cultural guide to monuments, museums, and architectural and archeological sites is produced by the Touring Club of Italy, the country's foremost publisher of authoritative maps and guidebooks for over a century.

Special features in The Heritage Guide to Italy:

- large pullout map of the entire country
- 120 maps and plans of cities and historical sites
- 80 driving tours with detailed maps
- nearly 1,000 descriptions of cities, towns, villages, and landmarks

Each book in The Heritage Guide series provides:

- Dozens of full-color maps: an overview of each city plus detailed neighborhood plans
- Color photographs and line drawings accompanying detailed and up-to-date text
- Travelers' information with selected addresses of museums, galleries, theaters, cultural institutions, stores for fine shopping, cafes, and pastry shops
- Listings of accommodations and restaurants with quality ratings, price range, addresses, and telephone and fax numbers

"Even the smallest towns in this thorough guidebook are limned with care, their history, architecture, and art described lovingly. These are books to please the soul."

—U.S. News & World Report

The complete Heritage Guide collection from the Touring Club of Italy:

Italy	ISBN	88-365-2746-9
Florence	ISBN	88-365-1518-5
Milan and Turin	ISBN	88-365-1519-3
Naples	ISBN	88-365-1520-7
Parma	ISBN	88-365-2259-9
Rome	ISBN	88-365-1523-1
Sicily	ISBN	88-365-2747-7
The Italian Riviera	ISBN	88-365-2114-2
The Marches	ISBN	88-365-1467-7
Umbria	ISBN	88-365-1458-8
Venice	ISBN	88-365-1517-7

Distributed in Usa / Canada by Publishers Group West

Book + Map US $ 24.95

ISBN 88-365-2746-9

52495>

9 788836 527465